Charles W. Kegley, Jr. / Eugene R. Wittkopf

University of South Carolina   Louisiana State University

AMERICAN

FOREIGN POLICY

PATTERN AND PROCESS

Fifth Edition

St. Martin's Press
New York

Editor: Beth A. Gillett
Manager, publishing services: Emily Berleth
Senior editor, publishing services: Doug Bell
Project management and illustrations: York Production Services
Production supervisor: Dennis Para
Cover design: Rod Hernandez
Cover image: Masterfile Corporation

Library of Congress Catalog Card Number: 94-74776

Manufactured in the United States of America.

0 9 8   7   6
f   e   d   c   b

For information, write:
St. Martin's Press, Inc.
175 Fifth Avenue
New York, NY 10010

ISBN: 0-312-07536-7

Published and distributed outside North America by
MACMILLAN PRESS LTD
Houndmills, Basingstoke, Hampshire RG21 6XS and London
Companies and representatives throughout the world.

ISBN 0-333-65875-2

A catalogue record for this book is available from the British Library.

Acknowledgments

Acknowledgments and copyrights appear at the back of the book on pages 629–635, which constitute an extension of the copyright page.

For Linda and Barbara

SUMMARY TABLE OF CONTENTS

• • •

CONTENTS

• • •

• • •

FOCUS BOXES, MAPS, AND ILLUSTRATIONS

• • •

Focus Boxes

• • •

Maps

Illustrations

PREFACE

• • •

The world has experienced dramatic changes during the half decade since the last edition of *American Foreign Policy: Pattern and Process* was published. Already the winds of change were stirring when we went to press with the fourth edition in late 1990: The Berlin Wall had fallen, hundreds of thousands of American troops were poised to defend Saudi Arabia against further Iraqi aggression following its invasion of Kuwait, and the Soviet Union had joined the United States in the United Nations Security Council to support the collective use of force against Iraq. But even more dramatic changes would follow, as first the Soviet external empire crumbled and then the Soviet Union itself imploded. The United States suddenly found itself "victorious" in its long Cold War struggle with Soviet communism, emerging as the world's sole remaining superpower. It also was among the victors in the Persian Gulf War, leading President George Bush to speak wistfully of a new world order in which the rule of law would reign supreme, but a surge of ethnic nationalism—often accompanied by violent conflict—quickly dissipated hopes that the post-Cold War world would be a more orderly and peaceful one.

For nearly half a century, the Cold War contest with the Soviet Union was the keystone of American foreign policy. Inevitably, then, its end affects American foreign policy, raising profound questions about the nation's role in world affairs as it faces the new millennium:

- Does the Cold War legacy—captured in the themes of anticommunism, containment, global activism, reliance on military might, and a preference for interventionist means—continue to inform the thinking of American policymakers?
- What challenges and opportunities do changes in the post-Cold War political and economic systems' structures pose for the United States?
- Have the American people tired of the burdens of leadership, preferring to return to the nation's historic pattern of isolation from world affairs, not global activism?
- Will the president remain the preeminent player in the foreign affairs government, defining the nation's role in war and peace and setting priorities that other nations should follow?

• • •

- Or will Congress now assert its prerogatives, constraining the president's foreign policy flexibility in the absence of clear threats to the national security, altering the mix of foreign and domestic priorities, and shifting resources away from long-standing policy instruments?

- What impact will the down-sizing of the defense establishment exert on the Pentagon's ability to project power and protect the nation's interests and those of its allies?

- Will the generation of policymakers on the horizon, who are unschooled in the thinking of the 1930s and 1940s that informed the nation's response to the Soviet challenge, opt for radically new approaches to the challenges the nation will face in the new millennium?

These are among the questions we address in this new edition of *American Foreign Policy: Pattern and Process*.

Anticommunism and containment of the Soviet Union served as guideposts of American foreign policy for nearly half a century, ordering priorities at home as well as abroad. With globalism, military might, and interventionism, they became the enduring themes of American foreign policy, proving resistant to fundamental change through nine consecutive presidencies from Truman to Bush. Thus persistence and continuity were the hallmarks of American foreign policy throughout the Cold War, as both the ends of foreign policy and the means policymakers used to pursue them became firmly entrenched. Anticommunism and containment no longer serve as guideposts, but American foreign policy is still resistant to fundamental change. The legacy of Cold War thinking itself militates against radical departures from the past, but policy persistence and continuity also derive from the nation's enduring principles, values, and interests: peace and prosperity, stability and security, democracy and defense. These in turn are reinforced by the process of policy making—the "system" at home and abroad and the individuals who make decisions and the roles they occupy as described and explained by the sources of American foreign policy. These forces comprise the analytical framework used in this as in previous editions of the book, which maintains that five sources—international, societal, governmental, role, and individual—collectively influence decisions about foreign policy goals and the means chosen to realize them.

Although we have retained the overall structure and thematic thrust of previous editions of *American Foreign Policy: Pattern and Process*, this edition of the book departs from its predecessors in fundamental ways. Those familiar with previous editions will first note that the book's design has been changed to make it more accessible to students, and that a glossary has been added as a learning aid. Key terms appearing in the glossary are identified in the chapters with italicized ***boldface*** type.

The book's temporal frame and the corresponding conceptual content have been reoriented. These changes are especially evident in Chapter 3, where the enduring themes in American foreign policy whose origins lie in the early days of the Republic are used to illuminate the nation's interests and values and to show the heritage that informs contemporary debates about American foreign policy. We cast the debates as contests between internationalists and isolationists and between realists and idealists—the latter a contest between power and principle. These changes place the Cold War into a broad historical and theoretical context that portray it as part of the ongoing pattern of conflict and cooperation that makes up world politics, not a historical aberration. We revisit the contest between power and principle repeatedly in later chapters, as we now draw on a longer historical frame of reference than previously. Chapter 6, for example, begins with historical materials on the multipolar system in which the United States was born includes a neorealist perspective on the impact of incipient multipolarity on the future of American foreign policy.

Countless other changes have been made as we confronted the task of updating the book's scholarship and substantive content to reflect both the end of the Cold War and the changes facing the United States at the dawn of the new millennium. Chapters 8 and 9 have been reorganized to give them a sharper conceptual orientation. Chapter 8 now examines societal characteristics, and Chapter 9 addresses how these characteristics are translated into the policy process. Chapters 4 and 5 on the instruments of American foreign policy now include consideration of the widespread tendency to employ sanctions rather than force, to emphasize multilateral rather than unilateral approaches to conflict management and resolution, and to intervene abroad for humanitarian purposes in addition to more narrowly defined national interests. The utility of both the new and old instruments of policy inform contests between Congress and the president and concerns about the post-Cold War role of bureaucratic agencies in making and executing policy—topics examined in Chapters 11, 12, and 13.

The conceptual orientation of Chapter 7 has been changed. Drawing on hegemonic stability theory, we now ask how the changing position of the United States in the world political economy affects both the system and the willingness and ability of the United States to exercise leadership. The change comports well with recent scholarship and the post-Cold War shift from geostrategic issues to geoeconomics. It also provides a compelling theoretical prism through which to examine the Clinton administration's foreign economic policies, practices, and management strategies—the latter explored in Chapter 10, where we also draw on historical models to address recent challenges to the president's preeminent foreign and domestic policy roles. We inquire further into the Clinton's administration's foreign policy management in Chapter 14, which also includes a case study of Clinton's presidential character.

These are but a few examples of the many changes, large and small, in this edition of *American Foreign Policy: Pattern and Process.* Changes in the world and changes in the United States dictated that they be made, but we were guided in our interpretation of them by the countless people who have contributed to this book since the first edition was published in 1979. The contributions have come in many forms: detailed critiques, evaluations on "comment cards" sent to our publisher, ideas shared with St. Martin's highly professional sales representatives, student evaluations, and other means. All have shaped our efforts to provide superior scholarship and an effective teaching and learning instrument. Our intellectual debt is also evident in the book's list of references, which continues to grow as scholars from a number of disciplines add to the breadth and depth of our understanding of American foreign policy and processes.

We remember with gratitude the many people named in the prefaces of previous editions of the book. Still others have made special contributions of time and insight to this edition, and we are pleased to acknowledge them: Leann Brown (University of Florida), Dan Caldwell (Pepperdine University), Ellen C. Collier (Library of Congress), Vincent Davis (University of Kentucky), Muhammad Islam (Louisiana State University), Christopher Kautz (Louisiana State University), Dave Layman (WBRZ Television, Baton Rouge, Louisiana), and William Watts (Potomac Associates). Don Reisman, former executive editor at St. Martin's, proved invaluable; without his support and encouragement, this edition would not have happened. The patient professionalism of Doug Bell at St. Martin's Press and Dolores Wolfe at York Production Services helped to bring the book to fruition.

Charles W. Kegley, Jr.
Eugene R. Wittkopf

ABOUT THE AUTHORS

• • •

CHARLES W. KEGLEY JR. received his doctorate from Syracuse University. Currently, he is Pearce Professor of International Relations at the University of South Carolina. President of the International Studies Association (1993–1994), Kegley has held appointments at Georgetown University, the University of Texas, Rutgers University, and the People's University of China. He is the editor of *Controversies in International Relations Theory: Realism and the Neoliberal Challenge* (St. Martin's Press, 1995) and *The Long Postwar Peace* (HarperCollins, 1991). With Gregory A. Raymond, Kegley is the coauthor of *A Multipolar Peace? Great-Power Politics in the Twenty-First Century* (St. Martin's Press, 1994) and *When Trust Breaks Down: Alliance Norms and World Politics* (University of South Carolina Press, 1990).

EUGENE R. WITTKOPF received his doctorate from Syracuse University. Currently R. Downs Poindexter Professor of Political Science at Louisiana State University, Wittkopf is a past president of the Florida Political Science Association and of the International Studies Association/South. He has also held appointments at the University of Florida and the University of North Carolina at Chapel Hill. Wittkopf is the author of *Faces of Internationalism: Public Opinion and American Foreign Policy* (Duke University Press, 1990) and the editor of the second editions of *The Future of American Foreign Policy* (St. Martin's Press, 1994) and *The Domestic Sources of American Foreign Policy* (St. Martin's Press, 1994).

Together, Kegley and Wittkopf have coauthored and edited several texts and readers for St. Martin's Press, including *World Politics: Trend and Transformation*, fifth edition (1995); *The Future of American Foreign Policy* (1992); *The Nuclear Reader: Strategy, Weapons, War*, second edition (1989); and *The Domestic Sources of American Foreign Policy* (1988). They are also the coeditors of *The Global Agenda: Issues and Perspectives*, fourth edition (McGraw-Hill, 1995).

• • •

CHAPTER 1

CONTINUITY AND CHANGE IN AMERICAN FOREIGN POLICY: A THEMATIC INTRODUCTION

• • •

A long-term consistency of behavior is bound to burden American democracy when the country rises to the stature of a great power.

Alexis de Tocqueville, 1835

We must challenge the changes now engulfing our world toward America's enduring objectives of peace and prosperity, of democracy and human dignity.

President William Jefferson Clinton, 1993

Throughout history, major wars have led to transformations of the international political system and to changes in the position of states within it. The twentieth century is no exception. Three times in the past eighty years—in World War I, World War II, and the Cold War—the world experienced international contests for power and position of global proportions and with global consequences. Each conflict also forced the United States to confront its destiny as its political, economic, and military importance in the world grew.

The American presidents who occupied the White House during the waning days of each of the contests shared a common vision of the nation's future, grounded in liberalism and idealism. Woodrow Wilson, under whose leadership the United States entered the war against Germany in 1917 and fought to create "a world safe for democracy," called for an association of nations whose purpose in the new world order would be to guarantee the "political independence and territorial integrity [of] great and small states alike." Franklin D. Roosevelt, president during World War II until his death in April 1945, portrayed the moral basis for American involvement in World War II as an effort to secure "four freedoms"—freedom of speech and expression, freedom of worship, freedom from want, and freedom from fear. He, too, supported creation of a new association of the United Nations, as the allies were called, to secure and maintain the structure of peace once the war against Germany and Japan was ended. And like Wilson, Roosevelt's vision of the postwar world embraced the principles of self-determination and an open international marketplace. Harry S Truman, Roosevelt's successor, carried forward much of Roosevelt's vision, eventually adapting its principles to his own definition of the post-World War II world order.

In November 1989 the Berlin Wall came tumbling down. It had stood as perhaps the most emotional symbol of the division between East and West and of the Cold War that had raged between the United States and the Soviet Union for more than forty years. Less than a year later Iraq invaded the tiny desert kingdom of Kuwait. The United States, now with the unprecedented support of the Soviet Union in the United Nations Security Council, took the lead in organizing a military response to Iraq's aggression based on the same principle of collective security that Wilson, Roosevelt, and Truman had embraced. On the heels of the initiation of war against Iraq and within a month of the disintegration of the Soviet Union into a loosely knit commonwealth of independent states, President George Bush delivered a State of the Union Address in which he spoke repeatedly of the "next American century," in which the "rule of law" would reign supreme in the "new world order." He extolled America's leadership role, urging that "only the United States of America has the moral leadership and the means to back it up." "As Americans, we know there are times when we must step forward and accept our responsibility to lead the world again from the dark chaos of dictators, toward the brighter promise of a better day."

Once before, however, the United States had rejected the call for leadership and responsibility. Woodrow Wilson failed in his bid to have the United States join the League of Nations, of which he had been the principal architect. In this and other ways the United States turned away from the challenge of international involvement that World War I had posed, opting instead to return to its historic pattern of isolation from the machinations it associated with Europe's power politics, which Wilson had characterized as an "old and evil order," one marked by "an arrangement of power and suspicion and dread." The strategy contributed to the breakdown of order and stability in the decades following World War I, thus setting the stage for the twentieth century's second global contest for international power and position.

World War II was geographically far broader and militarily more destructive than World War I. And it transformed world politics irrevocably. The position of the United States in the structure of world politics also was altered dramatically as it emerged from the war with unparalleled capabilities. In 1947 British author Harold J. Laski described the new world political circumstances:

> America bestrides the world like a colossus; neither Rome at the height of its power nor Great Britain in the period of its economic supremacy enjoyed an influence so direct, so profound, or so pervasive. It has half the wealth of the world today in its hands, it has rather more than half of the world's productive capacity, and it exports more than twice as much as it imports. Today literally hundreds of millions of Europeans and Asiatics know that both the quality and the rhythm of their lives depend upon decisions made in Washington. On the wisdom of those decisions hangs the fate of the next generation. (Laski 1947, 641)

World War II not only propelled the United States into the status of an emergent superpower but also transformed the way the nation responded to the challenges of the postwar world. Isolationism was now the victim, as American leaders and eventually the American people embraced internationalism and global activism—a new vision predicated on assumptions about international politics derived from their experience in world war and the turmoil that preceded it. Wilsonian idealism gave way to the doctrine of political "realism," which focused on power, not ideals. Containment became the preferred strategy for dealing with the Soviet Union in the latest contest for power and position, demanding resources and commitment beyond anything the nation had previously experienced. Some forty years later the United States would emerge "victorious" in this contest, as first the Soviet external empire and then the Soviet Union itself disintegrated. Meanwhile, the ideology of communism also fell into widespread disrepute.

Ironically, the end of the Cold War has removed the very things that gave structure and purpose to post-World War II American foreign policy: fear of communism, fear of the Soviet Union, and a determination to contain both. These convictions were also important in stimulating the internationalist ethos embraced by the American people and especially their leaders since World War II. Now these guideposts, which had imposed a rough sense of order and discipline on the world, are gone. Few bemoan the end of the Cold War, but widespread debate about the ends and means of American foreign policy—not unlike that which occurred after World Wars I and II—reflects the absence of an overarching foreign policy paradigm. At issue is whether the United States will continue its global activism or whether it will turn inward, reverting to some form of isolationism as in the past. Anthony Lake, President Bill Clinton's adviser for national security affairs, put it this way in a 1993 speech at the Johns Hopkins University: "There is a . . . fundamental foreign policy challenge brewing for the United States. It is a challenge over whether we will be significantly engaged abroad at all. . . . On one side is protectionism and limited foreign engagement; on the other is active American engagement abroad on behalf of democracy and expanded trade."

Clinton himself made it clear that he, like his predecessor, George Bush, believed "American leadership in the face of global change" was "imperative." He also drew parallels between the challenges the United States now faces in shaping the post-Cold War era and those that Truman and others faced in shaping the post-World War II world. Noting that "we stand at the third great moment of decision in the twentieth century," he asked, almost rhetorically, "Will we repeat the mistakes of the 1920s or the 1930s by turning inward, or will we repeat the successes of the 1940s and 1950s by reaching outward and improving ourselves as well?"

On America's Purposes and Role in Postwar Worlds . . . .

The ideals, principles, and values Bush and Clinton activated to rationalize American engagement in the post-Cold War world are strikingly similar to those Truman used to energize the American people for the Cold War contest. Thus anticommunism, anti-Sovietism, and containment have dissipated, but the reasons underlying them persist. "Not since the late 1940s has our nation faced the challenge of shaping an entirely new foreign policy for a world that has fundamentally changed," Clinton observed in his inaugural address. "Like our counterparts then," he continued, "we need to design a new strategy for protecting American interests by laying the foundations for a more just and stable world."

H 6

H 7

What are those interests and foundations? Now, just as in the late 1940s, they are peace and prosperity, stability and security, democracy and defense. And, now as then, all of these qualities rest on American leadership and global activism, as indicated by the presidential themes summarized in Focus 1.1. It is not surprising, therefore, that despite the end of the Cold War, the basic parameters of American foreign policy are resistant to change, even as the world undergoes dramatic political reconfiguration. As former Secretary of State Dean Rusk observed, "the central themes of American foreign policy are more or less constant. They derive from the kind of people we are . . . and from the shape of the world situation." That viewpoint perhaps explains why American foreign policy remained unchanged for so long and why even today, in the face of dramatic global changes, new definitions of new purposes and principles are so elusive.

Critics and supporters alike of post-Cold War American foreign policy, as portrayed first by Bush's administration and then by Clinton's, found cause for concern about its direction and underlying rationale. Some see it as exceedingly bound to the principles of the past—a "sole-remaining superpower syndrome." From this viewpoint American policymakers continue to believe that "the United States must remain 'activist' in foreign policy and be prepared to intervene in any of the world's problems" even at a time when "foreign policy is no longer where the action is" (Clarke 1993). Others see it as so determined to find new purposes that it has forgotten the lessons of the past. Thus while some criticized the Clinton administration as too willing to intervene in world trouble spots, others chided it for its "self-containment," arguing that the foreign policy support accorded the nation's first president whose formative years spanned the Vietnam War, not World War II, "has been sapped by the philosophy of retrenchment, the ideology of abdication, [and] the professions of weakness that seem to be [its] underlying premises" (Rodman 1993). Meanwhile, the liberal vision of a new world order that George Bush so proudly promised has fallen by the wayside as nuclear and conventional weapons proliferation, ethnic conflict, and the rise of regional trade blocs, among other persistent concerns, lead some to ask "What New World Order?" (Nye 1992). The theme is central to Clinton's view of the post-Cold War world: "The world clearly remains a dangerous place," he often said. "Ethnic hatreds, religious strife, the proliferation of weapons of mass destruction, the violation of human rights flagrantly in altogether too many places around the world still call on us to have a sense of national security in which our national defense is an integral part." Thus the United States finds itself bound by history even as many of the fears and strategies that shaped it have dissipated.

The veracity of the particular criticisms directed at recent American foreign policy behavior is open to dispute. More troublesome is the persistent charge, which comes from both sides of the political spectrum, that American foreign policy in the post-Cold War era has failed to respond innovatively to a world undergoing rapid and sometimes radical change. Rusk is undeniably correct in characterizing the "the kind of people we are" and "the shape of the world situation" as the wellsprings of American foreign policy, but the particular goals and the means chosen to sustain them cannot be explained by these powerful if simple ideas. We must understand much more—about the world, about America and its system of government, about the behavior of political leaders and others responsible for the nation's foreign policy, and about ide-

Focus 1.1

POSTWAR THEMES IN AMERICAN FOREIGN POLICY: TRUMAN, BUSH, AND CLINTON ON AMERICA'S INTERESTS AND VALUES

• • •

ON GLOBAL ACTIVISM AND AMERICAN LEADERSHIP

"After every war we have solemnly resolved to prevent future wars. We have learned, however, that we must devote the best efforts . . . to make those resolutions come true. . . . This time we have . . . assumed the responsibility which I believe God Almighty intended this great Republic to assume after the first World War."

—*Harry S Truman, June 1949*

"We can never safely assume that our future will be an improvement over the past. Our choice as a people is simple. We can either shape our times, or we can let the times shape us. And shape us they will, at a price frightening to contemplate—morally, economically, and strategically."

—*George Bush, December 1992*

"We can't be strong abroad unless we're strong at home. And we cannot be strong at home unless we are actively engaged in the world which is shaping events for every American."

—*Bill Clinton, April 1993*

ON PEACE AND PROSPERITY

"We seek to lay the groundwork of a world trading system which will strengthen and safeguard the peace. We want no return to the kind of narrow economic nationalism which poisoned international relations and undermined living standards between the two World Wars."

—*Harry S Truman, April 1946*

"For much of this century, it's been America's destiny to stand for liberty and against intolerance and to fight for freedom against oppression. Now, at long last, the moment has come for the lovers of freedom around the world to reap the rewards of our vigilance."

"The opportunity we face is historic: the first chance in more than half a century to build democratic peace and prosperity for America and for the world."

—*George Bush, July 1992*

"It falls to us to avoid the complacency that followed World War I without the spur of the imminent threat to our security that followed World War II. . . . Our sacred mission is to build a new world for our children—more democratic, more prosperous, and more free of ancient hatreds and modern means of destruction."

—*Bill Clinton, September 1994*

Focus 1.1 *(continued)*

ON STABILITY AND SECURITY

"We shall not realize our objectives . . . unless we are willing to help free peoples to maintain their free institutions and their national integrity against aggressive movements that seek to impose upon them totalitarian regimes. . . . that . . . , by direct or indirect aggression, undermine the foundations of international peace and hence the security of the United States."

—*Harry S Truman, March 1947*

"We will continue to lead in support of freedom everywhere—not out of arrogance, and not out of altruism, but for the safety and security of our children. This is a fact: Strength in the pursuit of peace is no vice; isolationism in the pursuit of security is no virtue."

—*George Bush, February 1992*

"When our vital interests are challenged or the will and conscience of the international community is defied, we will act— with peaceful diplomacy whenever possible, with force when necessary."

—*Bill Clinton, January 1993*

ON DEMOCRACY AND DEFENSE

"The task of Americans today is fundamentally the same as it was in Washington's time. We, too, must make democracy work and we must defend it against its enemies. Our task today is . . . with the right of other peoples to choose their form of government, to improve their standards of living, and to decide what kind of life they want to lead."

—*Harry S Truman, February 1950*

"As the world's most powerful democracy, we are inescapably the leader, the connecting link in a global alliance of democracies. The pivotal responsibility for ensuring the stability of the international balance remains ours."

—*George Bush, March 1990*

"The spread of democracy is one of the best guarantees of regional peace and prosperity and stability that we could ever have. . . . Democracies . . . don't wage war on each other, engage in terrorism, or generate refugees. Democracy makes it possible for allies to continue their close relations despite changes in leadership."

—*Bill Clinton, July 1993*

alism and realism as competing world views—if we are to understand what explains American foreign policy and its fundamental and persistent qualities and characteristics. That is our purpose in this book.

We begin by defining *foreign policy* as the goals that the nation's officials seek to attain abroad, the values that give rise to those objectives, and the means or instruments used to pursue them. Our purpose, then, is to understand how and why the interaction of values, ends, and means shapes American foreign policy—sometimes stimulating change and promoting innovation, more commonly constraining the nation's ability to respond innovatively to new challenges, even when circumstances demand it. We direct particular attention to the period since World War II, when the United States emerged as the dominant power in world politics and the American people rejected isolationism in favor of global activism. We will argue, first, that the adaptations in American foreign policy that occurred during the Cold War (roughly 1947 to 1989) were confined largely to the means used to achieve persistent ends sustained by immutable values. Thus we propose that although tactics changed during the Cold War, the goals of American foreign policy and the values that sustained them did not.

We will also argue that the confluence of values and political forces that sustained American foreign policy during the Cold War persists to the present. The purpose of foreign policy is to cope with the environment external to the nation. Clearly this environment has changed in recent years—and dramatically so—but the combination of external (international) and internal (domestic) forces continues to shape how the United States responds to the world beyond its borders. These forces are powerful. Therefore, they constrain the ability of the United States to respond innovatively to a new world order. Change is possible, but for the reasons we examine in the chapters that follow, it does not come easily.

Consider, by way of illustration, how the past informs the present. As noted, anticommunism, anti-Sovietism, and containment were defining elements of American foreign policy during the Cold War. All are now history. Still, the rhetoric of that era persists: Fear of alien ideas—once communism, now Islamic fundamentalism—permeates policy thinking; the perceived need to combat threatening forces—once the Soviet Union, now Iran and Iraq and perhaps a revanchist Russia—remains pervasive; and a preference for military intervention to realize policy objectives—once anticommunist in nature, now a broader menu—continues. Furthermore, the United States remains, at least for now, committed to global activism in shaping a world order consonant with its interests and values: peace and prosperity, stability and security, democracy and defense. Thus strains of continuity with the Cold War past—sustained by persistent ideals, principles, and values—continue to characterize American foreign policy in the post-Cold War present.

Patterns in American Foreign Policy   . . . .

The determination of American policymakers during the Cold War era to contain the expansion of Soviet influence is a clear illustration of the interactions among enduring values, persistent goals, and more variable tactics. Believing that Soviet communism was an alien ideology threatening to the American way of life, President Truman, who initiated the strategy of **containment**, sought to inhibit the Soviet Union's participation and power in world affairs. Under Dwight Eisenhower, "brinkmanship"—the threat of escalation to the brink of nuclear war—was emphasized as the United States sought not to constrain Soviet behavior but to compel it in particular ways. "Competitive coexistence" was practiced under John Kennedy and Lyndon Johnson, who, as Soviet military capabilities increased, shifted from Eisenhower's brinkmanship and threat of massive nuclear retaliation to reliance on a form of deterrence known as "assured destruction." Under Richard Nixon, Gerald Ford, and Jimmy Carter, "détente" became the watchword, with containment now pursued by a linkage strategy that sought to reward cooperative Soviet behavior rather than intimidate Soviet leaders through coercive diplomacy. That Soviet leaders, like their American counterparts, could be "trusted" was a novel breakthrough.

Ronald Reagan, during his first term in office, returned to a militant, confrontational approach toward the goal of containing Soviet expansionism when he described the Soviet Union as an "evil empire." During his second term, however, Reagan, too, became more accommodating toward the nation's historic adversary. As dramatic changes in the Soviet Union itself and in its foreign policy continued apace, George Bush professed a desire to "move beyond containment." Nevertheless, he proceeded cautiously and with restraint, never fully abandoning the goal of containing Soviet influence in world affairs. Thus, while the tactics of the containment policy evolved over time, its basic tenets and the centrality of its purpose endured. Indeed, the containment of the Soviet Union remained the primary objective of American foreign policy through nine successive administrations and until the very end of the Cold War, despite extraordinary changes in the nation's foreign and domestic environment. "There were tactical disagreements" about containment during the four decades in which it defined America's Cold War foreign policy, observes former Secretary of State Henry Kissinger (1994b), "but no challenge to the overriding concept."

If we are to understand, on the one hand, the interaction between foreign policy ends, means, and the values that sustain them, and on the other, how and why the United States responds to unfolding global developments in the manner it does, we must adopt an analytical perspective focusing on recurrent behavior rather than transient events. Thus, we seek to understand characteristic *patterns* of American foreign policy evident in the nation's behavior toward others. A **policy pattern** is a way of generalizing about and describing the overall thrust and direction of foreign policy. Such generalizations do not describe completely or accurately every foreign policy decision and the reasons behind it. Thus, when we make generalizations, we risk distorting history and committing occasional errors of interpretation. Still, by generalization we gain the ability to differentiate the common and perpetual from the infrequent and ephemeral.

Our contention that contemporary American foreign policy is marked by recurring patterns neither denies the possibility of policy change nor sees policy as inevitably paralyzed by the fetters of the past. Nor do we contend that freedom, democracy, prosperity, and related enduring values in American foreign policy result in similar goals and tactics regardless of circumstances. Instead, we maintain that if we look only at the events that make up the day-to-day conduct of the nation's foreign relations or the political rhetoric called on to explain them, we risk failing to see the overall pattern and thus confusing temporary fluctuations with enduring change.

An infatuation with current events diminishes our ability to see long-term, and ultimately more significant, developments and to identify turning points instituting new trends. Former Under Secretary of State George W. Ball lucidly cautioned against the danger:

> Unhappily, the way we live, including dependence on television and visual impressions, reinforces the short attention span of most Americans. Our current foreign policy practices focus public concern on only one problem at a time, . . . *yet in the episodic and visual comprehension of our foreign policy, there is serious danger that the larger significance of developments will be lost in a kaleidoscope of unrelated events. Continuities will be obscured, causal factors unidentified.* . . . Because we do not have a sense of where things started or why they are leading where they are, we are surprised by events that should have been predictable. We are so often impressed by the symbols of policy—two political leaders shaking hands or drinking toasts together—that we fail to recognize those symbols as mere reflections that have meaning only as part of a process within a larger context. (Ball 1976, 323–24; emphasis added)

An analogy with the stock market might clarify this idea. On any day the stock market—as indexed, for example, by the Dow Jones Industrial Average—may go up or down, with exactly the opposite happening the next day. What is the meaning of such day-to-day fluctuations? The significance is difficult to determine unless we view the changes over a week, a month, or even a year. Then we might begin to see characteristics of an emerging bull market (advancing stock values and prices) or a new bear market (declining values and prices). In fact, we might even be able to go back to the daily stock market quotations and identify the point at which the previous market trend was broken and a new pattern set into motion. In and of themselves, however, the daily quotations often are quite meaningless. Only through a retrospective analysis is one able to discern major shifts in direction and perhaps determine the point at which a new trend was set in motion. Much the same holds true in politics as in markets: Without knowing where we have been, it is difficult to know where we are going. And in both politics and markets accurate predictions are extremely difficult.

The stock market analogy also helps to clarify how change may occur in American foreign policy even as underlying values like peace, freedom, and democracy endure. Just as the trends in the stock market may shift because of the daily activities of large numbers of investors, so, too, new patterns in American foreign policy may emerge as the nation's policymakers set new priorities and devise new means to deal with changing global conditions. Although we suspect that such adaptations more often will be marginal deviations from past patterns than comprehensive adjustments to new circumstances, over the long run gradual adaptations can culminate in basic reorientations. It bears emphasizing, however, that we can only reach conclusions about change and continuity in American foreign policy if we view it as a dynamic historical process—a phenomenon that proceeds through the continued interaction of long-term and short-term forces. Thus we must adopt an analytical perspective that seeks to uncover general patterns often obscured by day-to-day variations and by the discordant details of current events. Viewed in this way, contemporary American foreign policy reveals an overriding pattern of persistence and continuity.

American Foreign Policy Processes

The proposition that American foreign policy has been governed by persistence and continuity may be disquieting to some, including those who may subscribe to its underlying values. In the eyes of the casual observer of international affairs, change in American foreign policy may appear endemic. Headlines routinely proclaim bold initiatives in American foreign policy, asserting that new approaches to world problems are being pursued and that the current administration (whichever it might be) has rejected the tired policies of its predecessor in favor of imaginative programs designed to solve both old and new problems. The practice of attaching presidents' names to the policies they promote—Kennedy's "New Frontier," for example, or the "Reagan Doctrine"—reinforces the image of imminent change. The presidential campaign messages transmitted by the media also tend to obscure policy continuities, as each contender for the Oval Office is motivated to capture headlines by striking a pose emphasizing the need for policy change and his or her ability to produce it. Incumbents, too, are encouraged to emphasize that because they have so improved on the policies of the past, the promise of further accomplishments invites their reelection. The resulting political rhetoric gives the public the impression that change is nearly automatic. Thus democratic processes linked to the electoral cycle typically focus on change, not continuity, and on the initiatives and new policy pronouncements of both presidents and presidential aspirants.

The record, however, suggests how mistaken exaggerated attention to high-sounding political rhetoric and transient departures in action can be. Viewed from a long-term perspective, what initially looks like a turning point more often than not becomes another point at which American foreign policy has failed to turn. Instead, existing policies remain, as each administration fails (deliberately perhaps?) to recognize the echo of previous policy rhetoric and action in its own words and deeds. The historically minded observer experiences *déjà vu* when comparing current policies with the past; what is sold as an innovation turns out to be at most a shift in emphasis.

The hypothesis that the basic underlying values and goals of American foreign policy are resistant to change prompts consideration of the reasons why. Besides campaign rhetoric, each new occupant of the Oval Office has perceived himself, at least initially, to be devising an innovative policy leading to a new era in American foreign relations. Bill Clinton thus fits a long tradition, as he promised during his first campaign to infuse his administration's foreign policy with "bold new thinking." However, measurable departures from the established direction of policy are rare—and Clinton proved to be no exception. Indeed, when policy departures have occurred, they seldom have been permanent: Prevailing assumptions that deviate only modestly from ongoing courses of action are the more characteristic pattern, as a combination of external factors and the American foreign policy process militates against sharp departures from the past and instead encourages "staying the course."

Joseph A. Califano, a former member of Jimmy Carter's cabinet, provides insight into the phenomenon:

> Presidents since Roosevelt have pursued essentially similar foreign policy objectives on the major issues that face this nation abroad. Where change has come . . . it has often been dramatically expressed. But it has invariably evolved through broad, bipartisan consensus. . . . The . . . international policies of most administrations are founded in a more substantial and nonpartisan ideological consensus than the rhetorical idiosyncrasies and disparate styles and means most presidents tend to reveal. . . . To some extent, a president is a prisoner of historical forces that will demand his attention whatever his preference in policy objectives . . . . Every president is a victim as well as molder of events. (Califano 1975, 238, 245)

In addition to the constraints of domestic and historical forces, presidents value consistency for its own sake, for there is both logic and reward in the stable pursuit of a continuous set of policy preferences. "A consistent and dependable national course must have a base broader than the particular beliefs of those who from time to time hold office," President Eisenhower's secretary of state, John Foster Dulles, argued. Not surprisingly, therefore, President-Elect Bill Clinton's first foreign policy words emphasized not "change"—a prominent theme of his campaign—but persistence: "I want to reaffirm the essential continuity of American foreign policy and my desire to seek bipartisan support for our role in the world." The inclination to retain, not revise, existing national objectives follows a time-honored tradition well illustrated by Harry Truman's advice to Eisenhower, who succeeded him: "What I've always had in mind was and is a continuing foreign policy."

As these viewpoints suggest, policy continuity may be in the national interest because, through time, all nations become enmeshed in friendships, enmities, and obligations that cannot be overturned at a moment's notice without jeopardizing their security and prosperity. "Serious nations do not redefine their national interests every few years. . . . Foreign accomplishments generally come about because a nation has been able to sustain a course of action over a long period of time" (Destler, Gelb, and Lake 1984).

Even in those instances when policy modifications occur as the result of the interaction of enduring values, persistent goals, and the need to adjust tactics to changing circumstances, forward movement typically occurs *incrementally*—by piecemeal accommodation to emergent realities. Roger Hilsman (1967), a foreign policy adviser in the Kennedy and Johnson administrations, describes incrementalism as a means of policy modification in this way: "Rather than through grand decisions on grand alternatives, policy changes seem to come through a series of slight modifications of existing policy, with the new policy emerging slowly and haltingly by small and usually tentative steps, a process of trial and error in which policy zigs and zags, reverses itself, and then moves forward in a series of incremental steps." Because leaders must continually respond to new demands, changes in policy may occur. However, because these modifications typically are not so much reorientations as piecemeal readjustments, basic policy directions remain intact. Thus the historical pattern of foreign policy behavior is marked by a preference for gradual adaptation rather than fundamental reorientation. In this sense the end of the Cold War—radical as its challenge is—has stimulated comparatively little change in how the United States seeks to cope with the external environment.

Pattern and Process in American Foreign Policy:
From Description to Analysis and Evaluation . . . .

The end of the Cold War is a radical departure from the past. It changes profoundly the nature of the world the United States now faces. The critical question for the United States in the twilight of the twentieth century is whether it will constructively adapt its policies to the end of the Cold War and the related dramatic changes now sweeping the world. How can the United States best promote domestic political change in eastern Europe, Russia, and the other post-Soviet states to protect its own interests and values? How might the emergence of a united Europe or an integrated Pacific Rim as powerful independent political or economic actors on the world stage influence the definition and pursuit of U.S. interests and objectives? What strategies can the United States follow to deter the proliferation of nuclear and other weapons of mass destruction? What consequences do changes in the global environment portend for the relations between the United States and the developing economies of the Global South as they seek to realize living standards like those of U.S. residents? Our ability to answer these questions depends importantly on our understanding of both the pattern and process of American foreign policy.

The thesis that American foreign policy is marked by patterns of continuity more than change requires documentation and clarification. This is the purpose of Part II, in which we identify and examine the major assumptions that have guided American foreign policy throughout its history and the means used to achieve them. The issue addressed in these chapters is how a nation can best reconcile the need for both stability and adaptive change, even as its basic values remain unchallenged.

We also must understand the international and domestic sources of American foreign policy and how they both stimulate and constrain foreign policy action. This is the purpose of Parts III through VII, in which we examine the external environment, the domestic political setting, the structure and operation of the government, the roles that policymakers occupy, and the characteristics of policymakers themselves. The *process* of foreign policy making occurs within this social, political, and institutional milieu. Here we consider how the confluence of international and domestic political forces both stimulates and constrains the ability of the United State to respond to the multitude of issues it now faces: aiding Russia, coping with Japan, stopping nuclear proliferation, redefining the North-South agenda. As we will see, the persistence of basic underlying values cannot alone explain the nation's halting responses to the challenges it now faces and the search for innovative policies that distance the United States from its Cold War past. The policy process itself also plays an important role in shaping American foreign policy. Precedent, habitual ways of thinking, and bureaucratic inertia play an important role in a process that often stifles reconsideration of long-range goals and radical departures from existing patterns—to the point that Americans sometimes appear to be "our own worst enemy" (Destler, Gelb, and Lake 1984). Still, if adaptive changes in post-Cold War American foreign policy are to occur, they can come about only through the creative response to new challenges by those involved in the policy process itself.

We begin our inquiry into the sources of American foreign policy in Chapter 2, in which we provide an analytic framework useful in exploring the interaction of pattern and process in American foreign policy.

SUGGESTIONS FOR FURTHER READING

Brown, Seyom. *The Faces of Power: Constancy and Change in United States Foreign Policy from Truman to Clinton*, 2nd ed. New York: Columbia University Press, 1994.

Brzezinski, Zbigniew. *Out of Control: Global Turmoil on the Eve of the 21st Century*. New York: Scribner's Sons, 1993.

Destler, I. M., Leslie H. Gelb, and Anthony Lake. *Our Own Worst Enemy: The Unmaking of American Foreign Policy*. New York: Simon and Schuster, 1984.

Mueller, John. *Quiet Cataclysm: Reflections on the Recent Transformation of World Politics*. New York: HarperCollins, 1995.

Nacht, Alexander. "U.S. Foreign Policy Strategies," *Washington Quarterly* 18 (Summer 1995): 195–210.

Naylor, Thomas H. *The Cold War Legacy*. Lexington, Mass.: Lexington Books, 1991.

Oye, Kenneth A., Robert O. Lieber, and Donald Rothchild, eds. *Eagle in a New World: American Grand Strategy in the Post-Cold War Era*. New York: HarperCollins, 1992.

Rosecrance, Richard, and Arthur A. Stein, eds. *The Domestic Bases of Grand Strategy*. Ithaca, N.Y.: Cornell University Press, 1993.

Szulc, Tad. *Then and Now: How the World Has Changed since World War II*. New York: Morrow, 1990.

Yankelovich, Daniel, and I. M. Destler, eds. *Beyond the Beltway: Engaging the Public in U.S. Foreign Policy*. New York: Norton, 1994.

CHAPTER 2

. . .

THE ANALYSIS OF AMERICAN FOREIGN
POLICY: THE MANY FACES OF CAUSATION

. . .

*Unlike the last forty years, the task before us is . . . more complex, and it is
more nuanced. It has become less susceptible to the giant gesture, the single
solution, or the overarching doctrine.*

Secretary of State James Baker, 1989

*If you do anything significant, it's always going to be hard, because the
reason things don't change is . . . there are interests or habits that are
adverse to things that people know at one level ought to be done.*

President Bill Clinton, 1994

How can we organize our thinking and collect evidence to explain continuity and
change in the United States' response to the world around it? We must think systematically to answer such seemingly simple questions as "What drives American foreign policy?" and "What forces promote or inhibit changes in it?" To facilitate that thinking
process we use a framework first proposed by political scientist James N. Rosenau (1966,
1980) which groups all the potential forces influencing a nation's foreign policy into five
source categories: the *external* (global) environment, the *societal* environment of the nation, the *governmental* setting in which policy making occurs, the *roles* occupied by policymakers, and the *individual* characteristics of foreign policy-making elites. Each of
these source categories encompasses a large cluster of variables that, together with clusters comprising other source categories, shape the course of American conduct abroad.
Thus, to understand why American foreign policy has or has not changed over time, we
must first identify and isolate the multiple factors that affect U.S. behavior toward others. The framework enables us to perform this task admirably. Furthermore, it suggests
guidelines for assessing the relative importance of the multiple factors that account for
the United States' performance in world politics and for determining the conditions under which continuity or change will predominate in the post-Cold War era.

The Sources of American Foreign Policy   . . . .

The premise underlying the analytical framework is that each source category can be
treated as a causal agent which acts in conjunction with the others to determine how

the United States behaves in international politics. Thus the framework stipulates a theoretical "funnel of causality" (Campbell et al. 1960), as illustrated in Figure 2.1.

The figure depicts the *inputs* to the foreign policy-making process as the external, societal, governmental, role, and individual source categories of the analytical framework. The inputs give shape and direction to the actions the United States pursues abroad, which can be thought of as the *outputs* of the foreign policy-making process. That is, the foreign policy behavior of the United States is the **dependent variable**—which we wish to explain—and the source categories and the clusters of variables contained within them are the **independent variables**—those that explain its behavior. Thus the terms "independent variables", "inputs", and "source categories" all refer to the forces that exert a causal impact on the course of American foreign policy. That policy, in turn, is described in the terms "output(s)" and "dependent variable". The outputs (dependent variable) will be multifaceted in most instances, but we will focus primary attention on the recurring *patterns* of behavior that define the key elements comprising American leaders' responses to external challenges the United States faces in an often dangerous international environment.

Note, however, that whether we are attempting to explain a single foreign policy

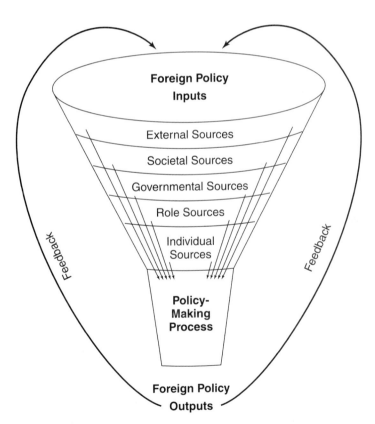

Figure 2.1 The Sources of American Foreign Policy as a Funnel of Causality

event or a sequence of related behaviors, no source category by itself fully determines outputs. Instead, the categories are interrelated and *collectively* determine foreign policy decisions, and hence foreign policy outputs. They do so in two ways: (1) by generating the necessity for foreign policy decisions that result in foreign policy action; and (2) by influencing the decision-making process that converts inputs into outputs.

The policy-making process is what converts inputs into outputs. Here is where those responsible for the nation's foreign policy make the actual choices that affect its destiny. The process is complex because of its many participants and because policy-making procedures cannot be divorced from all of the interdependent sources that shape decision makers' responses to situations demanding action. Conceptually, then, we can think of the foreign policy-making process as the **intervening variable** that links foreign policy inputs to outputs.

In practice, it is frequently difficult to separate the inputs (sources) themselves from the policy-making process which converts them into outputs. Once that conversion has been made, however, as those in positions of authority make their choices, external action commences—in the form of policy pronouncements and declarations, for example, or in the sending of troops abroad and the granting of foreign aid. By monitoring these outcomes of the policy-making process we can describe and explain the pattern of American foreign policy.

It should now be clear why Figure 2.1 depicts a causal or explanatory model. It views each policy decision as the result of the multiple prior events taking place in the funnel. Thus the model stipulates the conditions that precede and promote policy decisions (bearing in mind that it is frequently difficult to distinguish decision making itself from its prior conditions—that is, the source categories). Policy outcomes depend on the prior occurrences in the funnel and are explained by the combined impact of the source categories on the decisions reached in the policy-making process.

Figure 2.1 also tells us something about the constraints under which policymakers must operate, as each of the interrelated sources of American foreign policy is "nested" within an ever-larger set of variables. The framework views individual decision makers as constrained by their policy-making roles, roles defined by their positions within America's foreign policy-making institutions. Those governmental variables are cast within its more encompassing societal setting, which in turn operates within an even larger international environment, comprising other nations, nonstate actors, and global trends and issues to which the United States as a global actor responds.

Just as policymakers are constrained by the combination of forces that impact policy outcomes, the processes that translate inputs into outputs follow a temporal sequence. Changes in the sources of American foreign policy occurring at time t influence decisions at a later time $(t + 1)$, which lead to policy outcomes at a still later time $(t + 2)$. Furthermore, these policy outcomes have consequences for the source categories themselves at a later $(t + 3)$ time (because they exert "feedback" on the independent variables), so that foreign policy actions alter the source conditions that influence subsequent $(t + 4)$ policy making.

The series of decisions the Bush administration made in 1990 and 1991 that led the United States to defend Saudi Arabia from Iraqi attack and to use force to oust Iraq from Kuwait illustrates the multiple considerations that go into the policy-making process and how choices made at one time affect those made later.

The background to those decisions began more than a decade earlier. In late 1979 Iranian radicals captured the American embassy in Teheran, where they held over fifty American diplomats hostage for more than a year. Within a month of this event the Soviet Union invaded Afghanistan. In response to these developments the Department of Defense (popularly referred to as the Pentagon) began to plan for a massive air and sea lift of U.S. military personnel and equipment and ground deployment of heavy armor and antitank weapons against a potential aggressor in the Middle East, assumed at the time to be either Iran or the Soviet Union. It became Operations Plan 90-1002 (Woodward and Atkinson 1990). Thus changes in the external environment stimulated preparations in the United States for what later became the U.S. response to Iraq's aggression against Kuwait. We can think of these preparations as taking place at time t.

Iraq invaded Kuwait in August 1990—time $t + 1$. The Bush administration decided to respond, drawing a "line in the sand" and declaring that this aggression "will not stand." The administration's move to deter an Iraqi attack on Saudi Arabia built on Operations Plan 90-1002. Thus Operation Desert Shield was initiated—time $t + 2$. Three months later, in November 1990, Bush announced that the United States would significantly increase the number of U.S. troops in Saudi Arabia beyond the 200,000-plus already there to provide it with "offensive capability"—time $t + 3$. This set the stage for military action against Iraq, which commenced with a massive air attack on the evening of January 16, 1991—time $t + 4$. The wisdom of military action rather than continued application of pressure through sanctions (which had been imposed by the United Nations early in the crisis) was debated in Congress and elsewhere in the United States almost until the hour that the missiles were fired and the bombs began to fall. Thus domestic political considerations and the role of the different branches of government in the policy process were among the considerations Bush faced as he contemplated the use of force. In retrospect, however, it is clear that the temporal sequence of events affected the final choice significantly. Most important was the decision to move from a defensive to an offensive capability. Because this limited the ability of the United States to rotate fresh troops in and out the Persian Gulf region, the administration's decision at $t + 3$ profoundly shaped its decision to launch Operation Desert Storm at $t + 4$.

As this example shows, the model depicted in Figure 2.1 is dynamic as well as causal. It accounts for past policy pronouncements and behaviors and for their effects on later policy choices. Because the model is not tied analytically to a single slice of time, the entire historical record of American foreign policy is amenable to analysis and explanation based on the insights it suggests. Furthermore, because policy outcomes affect the relative importance of policy determinants at a later point in time, some policy choices are better explained by one or more source categories at one time and by another combination later.

Explaining Policy Patterns

The discussion to this point implies something about the meaning of "explanation" and "cause" as they are used in this book. These terms require elaboration because their meaning is intimately linked to the book's analytical approach and its level of abstraction.

There are different types of explanations and competing notions of what it means "to explain" phenomena. The ***nomological mode of explanation*** is appropriate for our purposes. Nomological explanations use lawlike statements (*nomos* is Greek for "law") to explain a particular event or a class of events. Usually such statements explain events by reference to generalizations or covering laws, which attach cause to effect. "Democracies settle their disputes peacefully, not through war" is an example of a generalized, lawlike statement relating cause to effect. Peaceful conflict resolution is the effect, and type of political system the cause. The relationship between cause and effect in this particular lawlike statement also implies a temporal sequence. Because the mode of conflict resolution depends on the type of political systems in dispute, "cause" implies a sequence in time between event A and event B. Thus mode of governance is an antecedent to the choice between war and peace, much as the source categories of American foreign policy depicted in Figure 2.1 are antecedents to foreign policy decisions.

Most lawlike statements in social science are hypotheses linking independent variables (causes) to dependent variables (effects) at some level of probability.[1] Thus we cannot say with certainty that democracy leads to nonviolent forms of conflict resolution, only that there is a tendency or comparatively higher probability for this outcome over others. The following is a pertinent illustration of this mode of explanatory logic:

> An example of a general explanatory sentence, confirmed to some degree . . . might be that, of the national states that have a differentiated foreign affairs establishment [where decision-making power and authority are dispersed among several centers, not concentrated in any one], 90 percent also manifest continuity in their foreign policy behavior. This is a statistical law in the form, if A, the probability of B is [90 percent]. If someone asks why changes in administration from the Democratic to Republican parties and back again in the United States have not greatly affected the nature of American foreign policy, we could refer to our "law" for an explanation. Our generalization states that 90 percent of the states that belong to the class of states that have differentiated foreign policy bureaucracies also are members of the class of states that show continuity in foreign policy. Thus, because the United States has a differentiated foreign policy establishment, it is a member of the first class and very likely, but not certainly, a member of the second class; it is for this reason that changes in political leadership seem to have no effect. (McGowan 1975, 64)

In this example the lack of dramatic changes in the pattern of American foreign policy, at least during the Cold War and arguably beyond, is explained by reference to a general law positing that bureaucratic differentiation in foreign affairs establishments (in terms of the number of independent units that share responsibility for policy formulation and execution) is directly related to foreign policy continuity. The more differentiated the foreign affairs machinery, the stabler the foreign policy. The explanatory logic in the example thus suggests how observable patterns of American foreign policy behavior can be explained by institutional features of the governmental machinery responsible for making and implementing foreign policy decisions.

The example also illustrates the interdependence of description (what) and explanation (why), and why explanation requires thinking in causal terms about classes of phenomena rather than about discrete events. In this book, the class of phenomena we seek to describe is the pattern of American foreign policy (our dependent variable), and we seek to explain it using the explanatory classes (the independent variables) labeled external, societal, governmental, role, and individual sources. Reference to these multiple sources implicitly rejects the widespread impulse to search for a single cause of American foreign policy.

By rejecting out of hand single-factor explanations of American foreign policy, we reject what most of us intuitively find most satisfying—simplicity. To understand complex social phenomena and deal with an inherently ambiguous reality, most of us resort to concepts that artificially bring order out of chaos. Similarly, efforts to understand the sources of American foreign policy are often reduced to simple and therefore psychologically satisfying single-factor explanations. Some analysts, for example, base their explanations of American foreign policy almost exclusively on what they see as the predatory characteristics of its capitalist economic system. Others attribute nearly dictatorial powers to the activities of private interest groups who put their personal gain ahead of the national interest. Both "explanations" of American foreign policy may contain kernels of truth, and under some circumstances they may account for certain aspects of policy more accurately than competing explanations. However, because each relies so completely on a single-factor explanation in the face of an array of equally plausible alternatives whose explanatory power in most instances cannot be dismissed, neither can be taken seriously as the sole explanation.

Political pundits who seek to seek to shape policy opinion often use the rhetoric of particular explanations to promote their political causes. Because foreign policy actions almost invariably result from multiple sources, however, we are well advised to think in multicausal terms if our goal is to move beyond rhetoric toward an understanding and explanation of the complexity of reality.

Our rejection of single-factor explanations of American foreign policy is based in part on empirical observation and in part on the logic underlying the analytical framework we employ. Let us turn, therefore, to a fuller explication of the source categories that organize the subsequent explanatory analysis.

An Overview of the Source Categories

Our analytical framework groups the factors that collectively influence American foreign policy into five source categories: the external (global) environment, the societal setting in the United States, the governmental setting, the roles occupied by policy makers, and the individual characteristics of foreign policy-making elites. As noted, the five source categories are assumed to be exhaustive (i.e., they embrace every potential source of American foreign policy) and mutually exclusive (nonoverlapping). Let us examine each in more detail.

External Sources

The *external source category* refers to the attributes of the international system and to the characteristics and behaviors of the state and nonstate actors comprising it. It includes all "aspects of America's external environment or any actions occurring abroad that condition or otherwise influence the choices made by its officials." "Geographical 'realities' and ideological challenges from potential aggressors" that shape the decisions of foreign policy officials are obvious examples (Rosenau 1980). Thus the external source category draws attention to the attributes of other nations, the kinds of behavior they display toward the United States, and how these attributes and actions influence American foreign policy behavior. Broadly speaking, then, the external category refers to the impact of the state of the world on the United States.

Because this category consists of so many variables (entailing *all* the characteristics common to the global arena and changes in it[2]), the questions it prompts are innumerable: What types of governments populate the global system? Are they allies or antagonists? How many formal alliances and other military coalitions exist in the system? Do they have sufficient military might and internal cohesion to deter attack from outsiders? What kinds of issues populate the global agenda, and which of the many other states hold similar positions to those of the United States? Do the many international organizations that now exist enjoy authority and legitimacy independent of their national members? Does the international legal system effectively prohibit certain kinds of behavior while encouraging others? The answers to these questions and many others are assumed to influence significantly the foreign policy behavior of the United States (or, for that matter, of any nation). Thus the external environment is a theoretically potent and multifaceted source of American foreign policy, and changes in it may be hypothesized to stimulate changes in American external conduct. In the same way, of course, changes in the behavior of the United States may affect the external environment.

Examples abound to support the hypothesis that changes in the international environment stimulate changes in American foreign policy, especially in the wake of the Cold War. The collapse of communism and the disintegration of the Soviet Union have caused the United States to grant aid to Russia in hopes of ensuring the success of its experiment in democratic governance. Iraq's invasion of Kuwait, noted earlier, stimulated the decision to deploy U.S. combat troops to the Middle East for the first time. The determination of the Clinton administration to secure the agreement binding the United States, Canada, and Mexico in a single North American free trade zone (NAFTA) was motivated in part by a determination to enhance U.S. economic competitiveness vis-à-vis Japan and the nations in Europe who are building their own free trade area, the European Union.

There is nothing new about the idea that a nation's foreign policy is conditioned by factors external to it. Indeed, the theoretical perspective that emphasizes a causal connection between the international system and American foreign policy making enjoys a long tradition and wide following. Political *realists* in particular argue that the distribution of power in the international system, more than anything else, influences how its nation-members act. Nations in turn are motivated to acquire power to their own advantage. Because all states are assumed to be motivated by the same drives, the principal way to understand international politics and foreign policy, according to this perspective, is to follow the interactions of states in the international arena or, in other words, to focus on the external source category (see Waltz 1979 and the discussion of political realism in Chapter 3).

The argument that external forces help to shape American foreign policy requires us to recognize that a nation's actions abroad are necessarily affected by what others do and by changes in what the international environment renders practicable. External variables help define the limits of the possible. They preclude certain choices and reduce the utility of some while making others more attractive. In this way the international system imposes constraints on American decision makers and limits their freedom to take policy initiatives. Thus it promotes policy continuity by narrowing the range of viable options. But the external environment can also stimulate policy change. Nowhere is this more evident than in Europe, where the end of the Cold War has stimulated the search for a new role for NATO (North Atlantic Treaty Organization), whose historic mission of deterring a Soviet and Warsaw Pact military attack on Western Europe has been rendered obsolete.

As important as the external environment is, it would be wrong to think that it alone can dictate foreign policy. It is more accurate to argue that "factors external to the actor can become determinants only as they affect the mind, the heart, and the will of the decision-maker. A human decision to act in a specific way . . . necessarily represents the last link in the chain of antecedents of any act of policy. A geographical set of conditions, for instance, can affect the behavior of a nation only as specific persons perceive and interpret these conditions" (Wolfers 1962). Thus external factors alone do not determine how the United States behaves in world politics, but they do influence how decision makers may choose to act. Clearly, then, they are a source of American foreign policy. We will focus attention on external factors in Chapters 6 and 7.

Societal Sources

The *societal source category* comprises "those nongovernmental aspects of a political system that influence its external behavior. Its major value orientations, its degree of national unity, and the extent of its industrialization are but a few of the societal variables that can contribute to the contents of a nation's external aspirations and policies" (Rosenau 1980). The source category thus draws attention to the characteristics of American society that shape its relations with other nations.

Forces within the societal category traditionally have been stressed by those who see the domestic climate shaping American foreign policy more strongly than external conditions. Robert Dallek's *The American Style of Foreign Policy: Cultural Politics and Foreign Affairs* (1983) and Loren Baritz's *Backfire: A History of How American Culture Led Us into Vietnam and Made Us Fight the Way We Did* (1985) are illustrative interpretations of American foreign policy that rest on societal explanations. Neo-Marxist critics of American foreign policy, who identify as its driving forces the capitalist economic system and the need to safeguard foreign markets for American economic exploitation, also rely on societal variables. Similarly, if we recall how American territorial expansion and imperialism in the nineteenth century were often rationalized by references to "manifest destiny" and the belief that Americans were a "chosen people" with a divine right to expand, we find many accounts that argue that American ideological preferences influenced American policies toward peoples outside the nation's territorial jurisdiction.

Other explanations of postwar American diplomatic conduct also rely heavily on societal characteristics. Some analysts maintain that the vast natural resources and territorial size of the United States made its globalist aspirations inevitable. Others interpret American foreign policy as a product of the pressures exerted by special interest groups. Ethnic interest groups in particular are sometimes credited with an ability to "control" the content and conduct of American policy toward particular countries, such as Israel and the Arab states. Similarly, the often overtly military orientation of American foreign policy during the Cold War is sometimes attributed to various "ruling elite" theories, such as the one associated with President Eisenhower's warning in 1961 that a "military-industrial complex" could acquire unwarranted influence over policy making.

Because American foreign policy clearly is rooted in domestic sources, the impact of societal forces is potentially strong. As one analyst pointedly argued, "To change [America's] foreign policy, its internal structure must change" (Isaak 1977). The impact of societal variables will be explored fully in Chapters 8 and 9.

Governmental Sources

Richard Nixon once noted "If we were to establish a new foreign policy for the era to come, we had to begin with a basic restructuring of the process by which policy is made." Jimmy Carter echoed this theme repeatedly in his 1976 presidential campaign by maintaining that to change policy one must first change the machinery that produces it. Ronald Reagan offered a variant on that theme in 1980, arguing that the greatest policy failures in the past could be attributed to the "excessive growth and unnecessary size of government." Bill Clinton's "reinventing government" program continued in that tradition, seeking to implement more-successful foreign and domestic policies by making government work more efficiently.

Underlying these viewpoints is the assumption of a relationship between the way the U.S. government is organized for making foreign policy decisions, on the one hand, and the substance of American policy, on the other. This is the core notion of a governmental influence on foreign policy. The **governmental source category** in turn refers "to those aspects of a government's structure that limit or enhance the foreign policy choices made by decision-makers" (Rosenau 1980).

Facets of the American system of governance undeniably influence what the United States does—and does not do—abroad. American foreign policy is shaped by (1) the Constitution, which divides institutional responsibility for making and implementing foreign policy among the three branches of government; (2) the rise of presidential dominance in foreign policy making, resulting in what has been termed the "imperial presidencies" of Lyndon B. Johnson and Richard M. Nixon; (3) the bureaucratization of policy making, which finds a broad array of executive branch departments and agencies competing for a role in the policy-making process; and (4) growth in the sheer size of governmental institutions, which may contribute to a fractionalized and inefficient decision-making structure.

Governmental variables are more likely to constrain what the United States can do abroad and the speed with which it can do it than to enhance its ability to act with innovation and dispatch. Size and bureaucratization, for example, militate against policy reversals. (According to one of Parkinson's famous laws, "The useful results of diplomacy are usually in reverse proportion to the number of diplomatists" [Parkinson 1972–1973].) Those factors combine with the constitutional division of power between the executive and legislative branches of government to promote policy compromise and incrementalism over policy innovation and revision. Thus governmental factors in general and democratic institutions in particular inhibit the nation's ability to change rapidly its course in world affairs. As the French political sociologist Alexis de Tocqueville (1969 [1835]) observed, "Foreign politics demand scarcely any of those qualities which a democracy possesses; and they require, on the contrary, the perfect use of almost all those faculties in which it is deficient."

Although the nature of the American government is an intrinsically important influence on the nation's foreign policy, we must be wary not to rely too heavily on it as an explanation of American foreign policy. The governmental source category does more to direct attention to the *means* the nation's leaders adopt to realize particular ends than it does about the *goals* themselves. Thus it tells us more about how decisions are reached and implemented in policy-making institutions than it does about why particular objectives are selected in the first place. Still, means and ends are inextricably intertwined, as means often become important reflections of ends. The interaction of the two will be evident in our treatment of the governmental source category in Chapters 10, 11, and 12.

Role Sources

The structure of government and the roles that people occupy within it are closely associated influences on and explanations of American foreign policy. The ***role source category*** refers to the impact of the office on the behavior of its occupant. Roles are important because decision makers indisputably are influenced by the socially prescribed behaviors and legally sanctioned norms attached to the positions they occupy. Because the positions policymakers hold affect their behavior, policy outcomes can be influenced by the kinds of roles existing in the policy-making arena more than by the particular individuals who happen to be in authority at any given moment.

Role theory goes far in explaining why, for example, American presidents act, once in office, so much like their predecessors and why each has come to view American interests and goals in terms so similar to the images maintained by previous occupants of the Oval Office. The view that the office makes the person has been expressed thus:

> If we accept the proposition . . . that certain fundamentals stand at the core of American foreign policy, we could argue that any president is bound, even dictated to, by those basic beliefs and needs. In other words, he has little freedom to make choices wherein his distinctive style, personality, experience, and intellect shape America's role and position in international relations in a way that is uniquely his. It might be suggested that a person's behavior is a function not of his individual traits but rather of the office that he holds and that the office is circumscribed by the larger demands of the national interest, rendering individuality inconsequential. (Paterson 1979, 93)

Correspondingly, this reasoning suggests that merely changing the person sitting behind the desk in the Oval Office will not bring about fundamental change in the nation's policies. Roles, it seems, determine behavior more than do the qualities of individuals. Perhaps this explains why Jimmy Carter proved to be a less liberal president than many Democrats had expected, why Ronald Reagan was not as conservative a president as many Republicans had hoped, and why Bill Clinton seemed to vacillate from one side of the political spectrum to the other.

The role concept is also useful in explaining the kinds of policy decisions habitually made by and within the large bureaucratic organizations that bear responsibility for the implementation of foreign policy—that is, for explaining not individual behavior but group behavior. Role pressures may lead, for instance, to attitudinal conformity within bureaucracies and to deference to the orthodox views within an agency. As John Kenneth Galbraith (1970–1971) argues, there is a "tendency for any bureaucracy, military or civilian, in the absence of the strongest leadership, to continue to do whatever it is doing. This is a matter of the highest importance, one that explains the most basic tendencies of our foreign policy." Such tendencies are clearly more conducive to continuity than to innovation in policy. The "system" places a premium on behavioral consistency and constrains the capacity of individuals to make a policy impact. It is therefore difficult for individuals at every level of government to escape their roles by rocking the boat and challenging conventional thinking.

In addition, role factors help account for the inability of presidents to get policies implemented by established bureaucratic agencies which typically view the national interest not as the president does but instead (as role theory suggests they will) from the perspective of their own parochial needs and institutional preferences. Furthermore, because bureaucratic agencies compete with one another for influence over policy outcomes, decision making is highly politicized and choices emerge from a bargaining process. Accordingly, the ability of a president to engineer policy change is severely compromised, just as the capacity of a nation managed by fragmented bureaucracies to change policy directions is limited. Thus role restraints on policy innovation go a long way in explaining the resistance of American foreign policy to change even as the world changes.

Conversely, of course, adaptations in American policy also can be explained in part by changes in role definitions. Occupants of the same policy-making roles may interpret them differently, and their variant interpretations may influence the positions they take on issues and ultimately policy outcomes. Some are aggressive in expanding the definition of their policy domain, others deferential to the initiatives of their colleagues (competitors?). Some see the role of government in private life as intrusive, others as restrained. Often these differing orientations reflect partisan and philosophical differences, but they are not easily separated from conceptions that particular individuals hold of the policy-making positions to which they have been recruited. Thus, because part of the definition or expectation of some roles in the U.S. government is the product of leadership and the occupant's choice, changes in role definitions may be sources of policy discontinuity, just as the maintenance of established definitions is a source of policy continuity. Hence role and individual sources interact: What cannot be explained by role sources might be explained by individual sources, and vice versa.

We examine the impact roles exert on foreign policy-making processes in Chapter 13.

Individual Sources

Finally, our explanatory framework identifies as a fifth policy source the individual characteristics of decision makers—the skills, personalities, beliefs, and psychological predispositions that define the kind of people they are and the types of behavior they exhibit. The ***individual source category*** includes "all those aspects of a decision-maker—. . . values, talents, and prior experiences—that distinguish his [or her] foreign policy choices or behavior from those of every other decision maker" (Rosenau 1980). Former Secretary of State John Foster Dulles's pious diplomacy, stemming from his strict Presbyterian upbringing, illustrates how personal traits may influence the conduct of American diplomacy (see Holsti 1962).

H2S   The premise that an individual decision maker's attributes are a source of American foreign policy rests on the assumption that decision makers possess unique personal qualities resistant to molding and modification by role variables. The thesis that every individual is unique is not difficult to accept, and the assumption that idiosyncratic qualities can make a difference in the kinds of decisions reached is plausible. Consider the following:

- Why did the United States persist in bombing North Vietnam for so long in the face of clear evidence that the policy of "bombing the North Vietnamese into submission" was failing and, if anything, was hardening their resolve to continue fighting? Could the answer be that President Johnson was unable to admit failure, that he had a psychological need to preserve his positive self-image by "being right"?

- Why did the United States act so boldly in forcing the Soviet Union to remove its missiles from Cuban soil during the 1962 Cuban missile crisis? (President Kennedy estimated the odds of nuclear annihilation were "between one in three and even.") Kennedy had been, by his own confession, outbargained and humiliated by Soviet Premier Khrushchev at their 1961 summit meeting in Vienna. Could it be that Kennedy's pride prompted him to teach Khrushchev a lesson, to show him his composure under pressure and his toughness? ("We stood eyeball to eyeball, and *he* was the first to blink.")

- Why did Secretary of State Dulles publicly insult Chou En-Lai of the People's Republic of China by refusing at the 1954 Geneva Conference to shake Chou's extended hand? Could it be that he viewed the Chinese leader as a symbol of an atheistic doctrine so abhorrent to his own values that he chose to scorn the symbol?

- Would the United States have embarked on a moralistic campaign for human rights in the late 1970s had the country not been led by a president, Jimmy Carter, who was inspired by the moral tenets of his evangelical faith?

- Would the Bush administration have been as timid toward Chinese political repression following the Tiananmen Square crackdown in June 1989 if President Bush had not previously been the U.S. representative to China, leaving him with numerous personal relationships with Chinese leaders?

Theories emphasizing the personal characteristics of political leaders enjoy considerable popularity. This is partly because democratic theory leads us to expect that individuals elected to high public office will be able either to sustain or to change public policy to accord with popular preferences, and because the electoral system compels aspirants for office to emphasize how their administration will be different from that of their opponents. The habit of naming American policies after their presidential proponents (the Monroe, Truman, and Nixon Doctrines are examples) contributes to the image that individuals do, in fact, matter. It is an image further reinforced by the widespread tendency in American politics to attribute "greatness" to presidents, sometimes even to think of them as heroic.

However, in the same way that other single-factor explanations of American foreign policy are suspect, we must be wary of ascribing too much importance to the impact of individuals. Individuals may matter, and in some instances they clearly do, but the mechanisms through which individuals influence foreign policy outcomes are likely to be much subtler than popular impressions would have us believe.

As suggested above, one way individual variables become important is through the interpretations different persons attach to the roles they occupy. Roles are constraining forces that mold people's behavior regardless of their personal preferences or predispositions. The boundaries of those constraints are not immutable, however. Instead, most roles—particularly those associated with the highest levels of the governmental structure—permit a range of interpretation often based on idiosyncratic choice. One person may see his or her role as permitting considerable latitude in choosing among policy options; another occupant of the same role may see little room for maneuver.

Then, too, the type of person holding office may affect the style if not the content of policy. This is especially obvious in the presidency. Truman and Eisenhower espoused very similar policies, but how the two men pursued those policies bears the imprint of their respective backgrounds and personalities. The same contrast might be drawn between the policy-making styles of Ronald Reagan and George Bush, even though the latter served the former as vice president unobtrusively for eight years. Hence, no explanation of American foreign policy would be complete without a consideration of the characteristics unique to those who make that policy. This is the subject of Chapter 14.

The Multiple Sources of American Foreign Policy   . . . .

The explicitly multicausal perspective of our analytical framework begins with the premise that we must look in different places if we want to find the origins of American foreign policy. And it tells us where to look, thus providing a helpful guide to understand policy and how it is made.

Rosenau clearly illustrates the utility—and necessity—of explaining U.S. foreign policy decisions by reference to multiple factors by asking us to consider the influences underlying the U.S. invasion of Cuba at the Bay of Pigs in 1961. This was a plan devised to "liberate" the island from its nascent communist regime, conceived under Eisenhower but not carried out until the early months of Kennedy's administration.

The plan was a product of the Central Intelligence Agency (CIA), which recruited and trained the "army" of Cuban exiles who invaded their homeland and which also gathered the intelligence information on which the invasion was based—information that predicted an uprising of the Cuban people against the Castro regime. Against this background, Rosenau wonders what might have led to a different foreign policy choice.

> To what extent was [the decision to proceed with the plan] a function of the individual characteristics of John F. Kennedy . . . ? Were his youth, his commitments to action, his affiliations with the Democratic Party, his self-confidence, his close election victory—and so on through an endless list—relevant to the launching of the invasion and, if so, to what extent? Would any President have undertaken to oust the Castro regime upon assuming office in 1961? If so, how much potency should be attributed to such role-derived variables? Suppose everything else about the circumstances of April 1961 were unchanged except that Warren Harding or Richard Nixon occupied the White House; would the invasion have occurred? Or hold everything constant but the form of government. Stretch the imagination and conceive of the U.S. as having a cabinet system of government with Kennedy as prime minister; would the action toward Cuba have been any different? Did legislative pressure derived from a decentralized policy-making system generate an impulse to "do something" about Castro, and, if so, to what extent did these governmental variables contribute to the external behavior? . . . Assume once more a presidential form of government. Place Kennedy in office a few months after a narrow election victory, and imagine the Cuban situation as arising in 1921, 1931, or 1951; would the America of the roaring twenties, the depression, or the McCarthy era have "permitted," "encouraged," or otherwise become involved in a refugee-mounted invasion? . . . Lastly, hold the individual, role, governmental, and societal variables constant in the imagination, and posit Cuba as 9,000 rather than 90 miles off the Florida coast; would the invasion have nevertheless been launched? (Rosenau 1980, 130–131)

Regardless of the responses to these questions, the simple act of posing them facilitates appreciation of the numerous forces shaping foreign policy. Furthermore, it also helps to define the factors that presumably have contributed to the persistence of the view held by decision makers that Cuba is a "problem" and to explain variations in the way different administrations have responded to that problem. In the particular case of the Bay of Pigs episode, widely regarded as a preeminent foreign policy "fiasco," American behavior clearly stemmed from more than one factor and can be explained only by reference to several variables. No single-factor explanation is adequate.

The questions posed about the Bay of Pigs invite similar questions about the forces that explain long-term patterns in American foreign policy goals and instruments and the forces that might make them amenable to change. Take, for instance, the dominant theme of American foreign policy since World War II: the containment of the Soviet Union. As we noted in Chapter 1, every administration from Truman to Bush voiced opposition to Soviet communism and pronounced a determination to contain its expansion. Why did this basic orientation of post–World War II American foreign policy remain so constant? Why was change, when it did occur, so gradual, so incremental?

To answer these questions, we must look in a variety of places. At the level of the international system, for instance, the advent of nuclear weapons and the subsequent fear of destruction from a Soviet nuclear attack promoted a status quo American policy designed primarily to deal with this paramount fear. Would the United States have acted differently over the past fifty years had international circumstances been different? What if the Soviet Union had not achieved superpower status? Would that have removed the restraining fear that a war between the United States and the Soviet Union would devastate both? Or what if the retreat of Soviet power and rejection of communism had occurred much sooner? Perhaps it was the persistence of the Soviet threat that so colored international politics for decades that stimulated and perpetuated the anti-Soviet goal dominating post–World War II American foreign policy.

Or consider whether the entrenched preoccupation with Soviet communism would have endured for so long had nationalistic sentiments within American society eroded—or if a mobilized American public without fear of external enemies had revolted against high levels of peacetime military expenditures. And ask as well whether American foreign policy might have shifted in the 1950s were it not for the anticommunist, witch-hunting tactics Senator Joseph McCarthy initiated shortly after communist forces came to power in China in 1949, in what many Americans viewed as a Soviet gain at America's expense.

Or turn instead to the governmental sector: Would American foreign policy have changed more rapidly had foreign policy making not become dominated by the office of the presidency—if instead the balance between the executive and legislative branches (fostered by the Constitution) had been preserved throughout the 1960s? Indeed, would American foreign policy have been different and more flexible if "Cold Warriors" had not populated the innermost circle of presidential advisers in the 1950s and 1960s and if career professionals within the foreign affairs bureaucracy had challenged their singular outlook?

And then consider whether American foreign policy might not have escaped the rigidity of its prolonged anticommunist posture if ideological orthodoxy had been reduced by fewer role pressures for conformity. Would the decisions reached after 1947 have been different had decision-making roles been less institutionalized and more flexible and encouraged advocacy of more diverse opinions? Might American policymakers have sought more energetically to move "beyond containment" prior to the late 1980s had policy-making roles been defined so as to allow more long-range planning and less timidity in responding to new opportunities?

Finally, consider the hypothetical prospects for change in American policy had other individuals risen to positions of power during this period. Would the cornerstone of American postwar policy have been so virulently anticommunist if Franklin Roosevelt had lived out his fourth term in office; if Adlai Stevenson and his choice of a secretary of state, and not Eisenhower and Dulles, had been responsible for American policy throughout the 1950s; if Kennedy's attempt to improve relations with the Soviets had not been terminated by an assassin's bullet; if Hubert Humphrey had managed to obtain the 400,000 extra votes in 1968 necessary to make him, and not Nixon, president; if George McGovern's call for America to "come home" had gained him the presidency; if Henry "Scoop" Jackson, and not Jimmy Carter, had replaced Gerald Ford in 1976; or if Ronald Reagan's bid to turn Jimmy Carter out of office in 1980 had failed? What coloration would American foreign policy have assumed had the 1988 election placed the responsibilities of the presidency in the hands of Michael Dukakis instead of George Bush?

To pose these hypothetical situations is to question whether the presence of different officials with different personalities, psychological needs, and political preferences might have made a difference in the ability of the United States to frame new policies toward the Soviet Union. Would other individuals have produced a different outcome? Might the Cold War have ended earlier if a different occupant of the Oval Office had eschewed the militantly confrontational policy embraced by Ronald Reagan during his first term in office? Or was this posture—a product of Reagan's personal antipathy toward communism—a critical step in bringing about the end of the global confrontation?

Moving beyond the Cold War, would the United States' response to Iraq's invasion of Kuwait have been the same if Bill Clinton—the first American president born after World War II and whose formative years included the war in Vietnam—had been in the White House instead of George Bush, who had been a World War II Navy combat pilot? Or would Clinton, too, have found that the responsibilities of the presidency moved him inexorably in the direction of a military challenge to Iraq's aggression?

"What-if" questions are rarely answerable. Asking them, however, creates awareness of the problem of tracing causation, as it forces us to consider different influences and possibilities. Thus, to answer even partially the question "Why has the United States acted the way it has in its foreign policy?" we need to examine each of its major sources. Collectively, these identify the many constraints and stimuli facing American decision makers, thus providing insight into the factors that promote continuity and change in America's relations with others.

Recognizing that each source category places some constraint on decision makers' latitude, we will conduct our exploration in descending order of the "spatial magnitude" of each explanatory category. Following a description and interpretation of American foreign policy patterns in Chapters 3, 4, and 5, we will turn first to the external environment (Part III), the most comprehensive of the categories influencing decision makers. Next we will examine societal sources (Part IV) and then proceed to the way in which the American political system is organized for foreign policy making (Part V). From there we will shift focus again to role sources (Part VI), which partly flow from and are closely associated with the governmental setting. Finally, we will consider the importance of individual personalities, preferences, and predispositions in explaining foreign policy outcomes (Part VII).

By looking at external, societal, governmental, role, and individual sources of American policy independently, we can examine the causal impact that each exerts on America's behavior toward the rest of the world. Our survey will show that certain factors are more important in some instances than in others. Individuals are likely to be especially important in crisis situations, for example, and Congress is likely to be heavily involved in "structural policy," where both interest groups and elements of the permanent foreign policy bureaucracy exert considerable influence (Ripley and Franklin 1991). Thus it is impossible to determine conclusively which source of American foreign policy is most potent in explaining that policy, just as single-factor explanations of American foreign policy are inherently suspect. In Chapter 15, where we probe the future of American foreign policy, we will nonetheless speculate about how interrelationships among the sources of American foreign policy might affect its course in the new millennium.

NOTES

1. Since hypotheses are, in effect, only expectations, they must be confirmed through empirical testing before confidence can be placed in their validity as generalizations.

2. In practice, it useful to distinguish between "systemic" and "external" sources of foreign policy. The former are aggregate or general attributes of the international environment (for example, the amount of alliance or war) which are shared by all nations—not just the United States. The latter are relationships between particular countries (for example, interactions between the United States and Russia). Given this distinction, the elaboration of the external source category in Chapters 6 and 7 will emphasize primarily external rather than systemic explanations of American foreign policy.

SUGGESTIONS FOR FURTHER READING

Evangelista, Matthew. "Issue-Area and Foreign Policy Revisited," *International Organization* 43 (Winter, 1989): 147–71.

Hermann, Charles F. "Changing Course: When Governments Choose to Redirect Foreign Policy," *International Studies Quarterly* 34 (March 1990): 3–21.

Hermann, Charles F., Charles W. Kegley, Jr., and James N. Rosenau, eds. *New Directions in the Study of Foreign Policy*. Boston: Allen and Unwin, 1987.

Hogan, Michael J., and Thomas G. Paterson, eds. *Explaining the History of American Foreign Relations*. New York: Cambridge, 1991.

Mastanduno, Michael, David A. Lake, and G. John Ikenberry. "Toward a Realist Theory of State Action," *International Studies Quarterly* 33 (December 1989): 457–74.

Neack, Laura, Jeanne A. K. Hey, and Patrick J. Haney, eds. *Foreign Policy Analysis: Continuity and Change in Its Second Generation*. Englewood Cliffs, N.J.: Prentice Hall, 1995.

Pierson, Paul, "When Effect Becomes Cause: Policy Feedback and Political Change," *World Politics* 45 (July 1992): 595–628.

Rosenau, James N. "Pre-theories and Theories of Foreign Policy," pp. 115–69 in *The Scientific Study of Foreign Policy*, rev. ed. New York: Nichols, 1980.

Smith, Steven M. *Foreign Policy Adaptation*. New York: Nichols, 1981.

Zelikow, Philip. "Foreign Policy Engineering: From Theory to Practice and Back Again," *International Security* 18 (Spring 1994): 143–71.

CHAPTER 3

• • •

POWER AND PRINCIPLE: THE GOALS OF AMERICAN FOREIGN POLICY IN HISTORICAL PERSPECTIVE

• • •

I know of no change in policy, only of circumstances.

Secretary of State John Quincy Adams, 1823

The aspirations that many feel today for a new global order may prove as misplaced as the 1920s belief that war had been abolished.

James B. Steinberg, Director, U.S. Department of State
Policy Planning Staff, 1994

Peace and prosperity, stability and security, democracy and defense—these are the enduring values and interests of American foreign policy. Freedom from the dictates of others, commercial advantage, and promotion of American ideas and ideals are among the persistent foreign policy goals tied to these values and interests. Isolationism and internationalism are competing strategies the nation has tried during its two-century history as means to its policy ends. Historically these strategies have also been closely intertwined with idealism and realism, competing visions of the nature of humankind, of international politics and states' foreign policy motivations, and of the problems and prospects for achieving a peaceful and just world order.

During World War I Woodrow Wilson articulated the premises of **idealism**, summarizing them in a famous speech before Congress in January 1918 which contained fourteen points. They included a call for open diplomacy, freedom of the seas, removal of barriers to trade, self-determination, general disarmament, and, most importantly, abandonment of the balance-of-power system of international politics—an "arrangement of power and of suspicion and of dread"—in favor of a new, **collective security** system grounded in an international organization, the League of Nations. Under the system envisioned by Wilson, states would pledge themselves to join together to oppose aggression by any state whenever and wherever it occurs. Together, Wilson's revolutionary ideas called for a new world order completely alien to the experiences of the European powers which now lay exhausted from four years of bitter war.

Europe's bloody history led its leaders to embrace not idealism as an approach to foreign policy and the problem of war but, instead, **political realism**. For them *realpolitik*, as realism is sometimes called, translated into a foreign policy based on rational calculations of power and the national interest. The approach built on the political

• • •

31

philosophy of the sixteenth-century Italian theorist Niccolò Machiavelli, who emphasized in his treatise *The Prince* a political calculus based on interest, prudence, and expediency above all else, notably morality. Moral crusades, like "making the world safe for democracy," as Wilson had sought with U.S. entry into World War I, are anathema to realist thinking. Similarly, "realists view conflict as a natural state of affairs rather than a consequence that can be attributed to historical circumstances, evil leaders, flawed sociopolitical systems, or inadequate international understanding and education" (Holsti 1995).[1] In contrast, "Wilson's idea of world order derived from Americans' faith in the essentially peaceful nature of man and an underlying harmony of the world. It followed that democratic nations were, by definition, peaceful; people granted self-determination would no longer have reason to go to war or to oppress others. Once all the peoples of the world had tasted of the blessings of peace and democracy, they would surely rise as one to defend their gains" (Kissinger 1994a).

American history and American foreign policy have never been free of the debate between idealists and realists or from contentions about the role of ideals and self-interest in the nation's foreign policy. As one former policymaker recently wrote, "we and the British . . . are still divided about whether the foreign policy of a democracy should be concerned primarily with the structure and dynamics of world politics, the balance of power, and the causes of war, or whether we should leave such cold and dangerous issues to less virtuous and more cynical peoples, and concentrate only on the vindication of liberty and democracy" (Rostow 1993).

The end of the Cold War has added new fuel to this continuing controversy. The breakdown of international peace in the 1930s and the onset of the Cold War between democratic capitalism and Soviet communism seemed to vindicate realism's precepts and to discredit idealism's. With its focus on power and national interests, realism quite simply accorded better with the "realities" of a world divided. American foreign policy in turn often looked like that of other great powers, as the nation found military might and intervention useful instruments of statecraft in a war with an adversary that challenged the very foundations on which the nation rested. Wilsonian idealism was never entirely extinguished, however, and it now vies prominently with the logic of *realpolitik* as the nation again struggles to come to terms with the role of power and principle in a world where liberalism and democracy have emerged "victorious" over Marxism-Leninism and Soviet communism. Also at issue is whether the nation should continue to pursue an activist posture in the world or revert to isolationism.

In Part II of *American Foreign Policy: Pattern and Process* we examine the goals of American foreign policy over the course of the nation's history and the strategies and tactics used to realize them. We begin in this chapter with a brief look at the nation's philosophy and behavior as it first sought to ensure its independence and then expanded to become a continental nation and eventually an imperial power. Isolationism dominated thinking (if not always action) during this period, and it reasserted itself in the period between the two world wars of this century, interludes when the United States, contrary to isolationist warnings, participated actively in European balance-of-power politics. We then turn to the Cold War as history. This was a time of internationalism, indeed, global activism, as the United States, unlike in the decades following World War I, now actively sought to shape the structure of world peace and security. We conclude with a consideration of the principles and goals of American foreign policy that vie for prominence in the post-Cold War era and ask once more how the contest between realism and idealism, between power and principle, informs the contemporary debate about the wisdom of global involvement or withdrawal.

We continue our inquiry into the goals and instruments of American foreign policy in Chapters 4 and 5. There we direct primary attention to America's rise to globalism in the decades following World War II and examine how military might and interventionism were brought into the service of America's foreign policy goals.

Ideals and Self-Interest, 1776–1941: Expansionism, Imperialism, and Isolationism

Two motivations stimulated the colonists who came to America two centuries ago: "material advantages and utopian hopes" (Gilbert 1961). Freedom from England and, more broadly, from the machinations of Europe's great powers became necessary for their realization. Thomas Paine, a revolutionary pamphleteer famed for his *Common Sense*, expressed shock that "America, without the right of asking why, must be brought into all the wars of another, whether the measure be right or wrong, or whether she will or not." The seeds of nonentanglement and isolationism were sown in this environment. Paine again: "It is the true interest of America to steer clear of European contentions, which she never can do, while, by her dependence on Britain, she is made the make-weight in the scale of British politics."

Paine also worried that freedom was at stake. "The New World had become 'the asylum for the persecuted lovers of civil and religious liberty,' while in England 'a corrupt and faithless court' abused liberty, and elsewhere in the Old World liberty was simply denied. Americans were thus marked out as the keepers of the flickering flame of liberty" (Hunt 1987). Born of the view that the new nation was somehow different from all others—a "city on a hill," Ronald Reagan would say two centuries later—the protection of liberty is a task no American leader has ever refused to embrace.

John Adams, another revolutionary patriot, later wrote that "we should separate ourselves, as far as possible and as long as possible, from all European politics and wars." George Washington had enshrined that reasoning in the nation's enduring political mythology when he warned the nation in his farewell address to "steer clear of permanent alliances with any portion of the foreign world." "Why," he asked, "by interweaving our destiny with that of any part of Europe, entangle our peace and prosperity in the toils of European ambition, rivalship, interest, humor or caprice?" He worried that participation in balance-of-power politics with untrustworthy and despotic European governments would lead to danger abroad and the loss of democratic freedoms at home. If the country interacted with corrupt governments it would become like them: Lie down with dogs, get up with fleas. Ironically, however, an alliance with France was the critical ingredient in ensuring the success of the American revolutionaries as they fought for the opportunity to pursue material advantages and utopian hopes.

Hamilton, Jefferson, and American Continentalism

With freedom won, the new Americans now had to preserve it. Thomas Jefferson and Alexander Hamilton posed alternative postures to meet the challenge and to move the nation beyond it—toward greatness.[2] Jefferson, Washington's secretary of state and the nation's third president, saw the preservation of liberty as the new nation's quintessential goal. For him, a policy of aloofness—*isolationism*—was the best way to preserve and develop the nation as a free people. He echoed Washington's concern as the United States faced a second war with Britain: "We especially ought to pray that the powers of Europe may be so poised and counterpoised among themselves that their own security may require the presence of all their forces at home leaving the other parts of the world in undisturbed tranquility."

Jefferson recognized that foreign trade was necessary to secure markets for American agricultural exports and essential imports. Thus he was prepared to negotiate commercial treaties with others and to protect the nation's ability to trade. "For that, however, the country needed no more than a few diplomats and a small navy. 'To aim at such a navy as the greater nations of Europe possess, would be a foolish and wicked waste of the energies of our countrymen'" (Hunt 1987).

Hamilton, the first secretary of the Treasury, offered quite different prescriptions. Beginning with assumptions about human nature central to the perspective of classical realism—that, in his words, "men are ambitious, vindictive, and rapacious"—Hamilton concluded pessimistically that "conflict was the law of life. States no less than men were bound to collide over those ancient objects of ambition: wealth and glory" (Hunt 1987). Thus, because power and self-interest dominate world politics, the goals of American foreign policy were clear: develop the capabilities necessary to enable the United States to be (again in Hamilton's own words) "ascendant in the system of American affairs . . . and able to dictate the terms of the connection between the old and the new world!"

Hamilton's immediate impact on American political life ended when he was fatally wounded in a duel with Aaron Burr in 1804, but the influence of his ideas on foreign and domestic policy and the perceived need for strong executive leadership continued. As president, for example, Jefferson himself acted in Hamiltonian ways: He threatened an alliance with Britain to counter France's reacquisition of the Louisiana territory ceded to Spain in the 1763 Treaty of Paris and, having acquired it, threatened to take the Floridas from Spain. The power of the presidency grew accordingly.

Jefferson was more interested in the port of New Orleans as a vehicle to promote commercialism abroad than in all of the Louisiana territory, but the territorial expansion of the United States continued in the half-century following his purchase of the vast territory drained by the Mississippi River named after the king of France. The Floridas and portions of Canada were annexed next, followed by Texas, the Pacific Northwest, and California and portions of several other states in the present-day southwestern United States. The war with Mexico precipitated by President James K. Polk led to Mexico's cession of the vast California territory. His threatened military action over the Oregon Country also helped to add the Northwest to the new nation. The expansionist spirit that animated these episodes is reflected in the policy rhetoric of their proponents. In 1846, for example, William H. Seward, who later became secretary of state, pledged, "I will engage to give you the possession of the American continent and the control of the world."

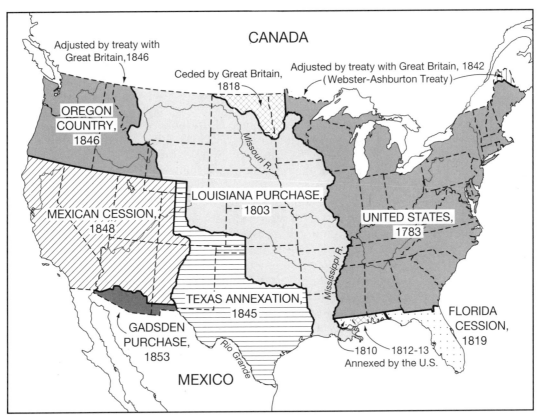

Map 3.1 Birth of a Continental Nation: U.S. Territorial Expansion by the Mid-Nineteenth Century
Source: Walter LaFeber, *The American Age: United States Foreign Policy at Home and Abroad,* 2nd ed. (New York: Norton, 1994), p. 132.

By mid-century the United States had expanded from sea to shining sea (see Map 3.1). In the process, however, conflict over how to treat the issue of slavery in the newly acquired territories rended American society and politics. Four years of civil war suspended the progress of America's "***Manifest Destiny***" (the widespread belief that it was the destiny of the United States to spread across the continent). It also resulted in more American casualties than any other conflict in the nation's history.

A Nation Apart

Beginning in 1796, the Napoleonic Wars raged in Europe intermittently for nearly two decades. Although the War of 1812, the North American theater of this conflict, involved the United States in the Europeans' competition for "wealth and glory," the years following the European settlement at the Congress of Vienna saw U.S. isolationism taking on the trappings of "a divine privilege, the perceived outcome of American national wisdom and superior virtue" (Serfaty 1972).

In 1823, President James Monroe sought to remove the United States from

Europe's intrigues by distancing himself from its ongoing quarrels. In a message to Congress he declared the Western Hemisphere "hands off" from European encroachment: "We owe it . . . to candor and to the amicable relations existing between the United States and [European] powers to declare that we should consider any attempt on their part to extend their system to any portion of this hemisphere as dangerous to our peace and safety." What would later be known as the **Monroe Doctrine** in effect said that the New World would not be subject to the same forces of colonization perpetrated by the Europeans on others. Little noticed at the time, Monroe's declaration later would play an important role in shaping America's interventions throughout the hemisphere. Well into the twentieth century it continued to shape thinking significantly about the role and responsibilities of the United States toward its hemispheric neighbors.

Intrigue with foreign powers punctuated the contest between North and South during the Civil War, but in its aftermath the nation turned inward—a pattern repeated in the twentieth century. Even as it focused on reconstruction, however, the nation's expansionist drive continued. Alaska was bought from Russia in the 1860s, and Native Americans in the West were systematically subdued as the United States consolidated its continental domain. Here Manifest Destiny was little more than a crude euphemism for, and rationalization of, a policy of expulsion and extermination of Native Americans who were, in contemporary terminology, "nonstate nations." Thereafter, the advocates of expansionism increasingly coveted Cuba, Latin America, Hawaii, and various Asian lands. Not until the end of the nineteenth century, however, would the United States assert its Manifest Destiny beyond the North American continent—this time in pursuit of empire. By then, moralism had become closely intertwined with the Americans' perception that they were a nation apart, one with a special role and mission in world politics.

Manifest Destiny embodied the conviction that Americans had a higher purpose to serve in the world than others. Theirs was not only a special privilege but also a special charge: to protect liberty, to promote freedom. That purpose was served best by isolating the American republic from the rest of the world, not becoming involved in it.

Democratic promotion—to "make the world safe for democracy"—would dominate much of American foreign policy in the twentieth century, but in the nineteenth it sought liberty. Equality and democracy were not typically within its purview. **Democracy** refers to political processes—"free elections contested by freely organized parties under universal suffrage for control of the effective centers of government" (T. Smith 1994a). **Liberty** (individual freedom) and *liberalism* (the advocacy of liberty) focus on individual freedom (see also Chapter 8). The differences are important, as liberty may exist even when democracy does not (although the reverse is unlikely). Thus European liberals at the time of America's founding were not necessarily democrats. "Their claims were for liberty not equality. Their opposition to democracy was based on fear of the mob—an aroused, uneducated public that knew not how to govern and so would deliver the state into the hands of a tyrant promising equality by dispossessing the holders of property" (T. Smith 1994a). It is not surprising, therefore, that property rights dictated who could and could not vote in the early American republic. Not until the 1830s, with the election of Andrew Jackson, could the United States begin to be properly called a democracy. At that time Alexis de Toqueville, a French political sociologist, published his famous treatise *Democracy in America*, in which he described America's uniqueness within the community of nations, focusing on the role that ordinary people played in its political processes. "Had Tocqueville arrived a decade earlier, his account might not have been so perspicacious" (T. Smith, 1994a). Indeed, the issue of property rights would plague the nation for another quarter-century.

Although the American republic was the champion of liberty in its first century, its approach was passive, not active. It chose to act as an example, "a beacon of light on liberty," demonstrating to the world how a free society could run its affairs and holding itself as a model for others to emulate if they chose. But the United States would *not* assume responsibility for the world, even in the name of freedom; it would *not* be an agent of international reform, seeking to impose on others its way of life. Secretary of State John Quincy Adams prescribed the nation's appropriate world role in an often-quoted speech, delivered on July 4, 1821:

> Wherever the standard of freedom and independence has been or shall be unfurled, there will [America's] heart, her benedictions, and her prayers be. But she goes not abroad in search of monsters to destroy. She is the well-wisher to the freedom and independence of all. She is the champion and vindicator of her own. She will recommend the general cause by the countenance of her voice, and by the benignant sympathy of her example. . . . [Otherwise] she might become the dictatress of the world. She would no longer be the ruler of her own spirit. (see also Kennan, 1995)

The nation was not unengaged, however. Even as its ideals colored its self-perceptions, self-interest dictated the exercise of power. Crises and military engagements with European powers and Native Americans were recurrent as the nation expanded across the continent. Elsewhere the rule was **unilateralism**, not acting in concert with others. Thus the United States alone fostered the creation of Liberia in the 1820s, opened Japan to commercial relations in the 1850s, and scrambled to control Samoa in the 1880s. Then, in 1895, it asserted its self-proclaimed Monroe Doctrine prerogatives against the British in a dispute involving Venezuela. The United States now effectively claimed that it alone enjoyed supremacy in the Western Hemisphere, and it was evident that the United States had the capability to back its claim. In the decades following the Civil War the United States emerged as the world's major industrial power. By 1900 it had surpassed Great Britain as the world's leading producer of coal, iron, steel, and textiles. "Moreover, the great merger movement of 1897 onward had made American industry the most large-scale in the world" (McCormick 1989). The stage was being set for the United States to assume Britain's mantle as the world's leading economic power and rule maker—a global hegemon.

Isolationism under Siege: Imperialism and Interventionism

Diplomatic historians credit jingoistic "yellow journalism" (press sensationalism) with a role in provoking the United States to declare war against Spain in 1898.[3] In fact, multiple motives—all centered on Cuba, which for several years had engaged in insurrection against Spain—caused President William McKinley to seek congressional authorization for the use of force to end the Cuban war. They ranged from humanitarian concerns to commercial interests and growing expansionist sentiments. Senator Albert Beveridge, speaking in 1898, for example, referred to Americans as "a conquering race." "We must obey our blood," he urged, "and occupy new markets and if necessary new lands."

With victory in the "splendid little war" with Spain, the United States gained a primary goal: suzerainty over Cuba. It also became an imperial power. The Philippines now became a Pacific territory, joining Hawaii, which had become a U.S. territory in 1898. Puerto Rico and Guam also joined the new imperium. The United States was suddenly transformed into a great power. Thus the Spanish-American War is properly regarded as a watershed in American foreign policy, as it opened a new era in America's relations with the rest of the world.

McKinley eschewed outright annexation of Cuba, but the Philippines posed a more vexing choice. McKinley was interested principally in the port at Manila, and he worried about the problem of governing the Filipinos. The popular story of how McKinley decided to colonize the Philippines came from his revelation before church leaders in 1899:

> I walked the floor of the White House night after night until midnight; and I am not ashamed to tell you . . . that I went down on my knees and prayed Almighty God for light and guidance more than one night. And one night it came to me. . . . [T]here was nothing left to do but take them all, and educate the Filipinos, and uplift and civilize them as our fellow-men. . . . And then I went to bed, and . . . slept soundly." (cited in LaFeber 1994, 213)

Although historians are skeptical of this story, they do not deny that the United States then embarked on a project that persists until the present—to sponsor democracy elsewhere. First, however, it was necessary to put down a Filipino rebellion, which proved to be a bloody, four-year battle, "the first of many antirevolutionary wars fought by the United States in the twentieth century" (LaFeber 1994). Only then could the United States concern itself with the Philippines' internal political processes. Attention to Philippine political development meant that democratic promotion—not just the abstraction of liberty—was now America's concern (T. Smith 1994a).

The McKinley administration is also credited with advancing American interests in China. In 1899 John Hay, McKinley's secretary of state, sought to enlist European support for the traditional nineteenth-century (unilateral) American policy of free competition for trade with China—that is, an **Open Door** policy toward China. In 1900 he advised European powers in the second of his "open-door notes" that the United States would not tolerate the division of China into "spheres of influence," insisting instead that its territorial integrity be respected. Regarded by some as an expression of the United States' growing foreign commercial interests and by others as an expression of American moralism and naiveté about balance-of-power politics, the Open Door was also based on a realistic appraisal of the limits of American power. Hays himself advised McKinley in terms Alexander Hamilton would surely have approved: "The inherent weakness of our position is this: we do not want to rob China ourselves, and our public opinion will not permit us to interfere, with an army, to prevent others from robbing her. Besides, we have no army. The talk of the papers about 'our preeminent moral position giving the authority to dictate to the world' is mere flap-doodle" (cited in LaFeber 1994).

Foreign policy issues figured prominently in the election of 1900. William Jennings Bryan, the Democratic Party candidate and later Woodrow Wilson's secretary of state, carried the anti-imperialist banner. Theodore (Teddy) Roosevelt, McKinley's vice presidential running mate, was the champion of imperialism. Roosevelt had served in the Navy Department early in the McKinley administration and, with Captain Alfred Mahan, an early geopolitical strategic thinker, had promoted the development of sea power as a route to American greatness. Roosevelt succeeded to the presidency when an assassin's bullet felled McKinley. The shooting occurred only one day after McKinley claimed, in a speech on America's new world role, that "isolation is no longer possible or desirable."

Roosevelt is remembered for speaking softly while carrying a big stick. A leader of the "Rough Riders" during the Spanish-American War as well as an advocate of strong naval power, Roosevelt's presidency (1901–1909) was marked by a series of power assertions and interventions, primarily in Latin America. The United States forced Haiti to clear its debts with European powers, fomented insurrection in Panama to win its independence from Colombia and secure American rights for an isthmian canal, established a financial protectorate over the Dominican Republic, and occupied Cuba. Roosevelt also mediated the end of the Russo-Japanese War (1904–1905), from which Japan emerged as a dominant and increasingly aggressive Far Eastern power even as it agreed to maintain the open door in China, a key American interest.

Many of Roosevelt's specific actions were later rationalized in his corollary to the Monroe Doctrine. In 1904, in response to economic chaos in the Dominican Republic which threatened foreign involvement, Roosevelt announced to Congress that "the adherence of the United States to the Monroe Doctrine may force the United States, however reluctantly, . . . to the exercise of international police power." In fact, however, the **Roosevelt Corollary** went well beyond Monroe's initial intentions (LaFeber 1994). The United States would now oppose Latin American revolutions, not support them. It would not only oppose European intervention into hemispheric affairs but support its own. It would use American power to bring hemispheric economic affairs under its tutelage. And it would now use military force to set hemispheric affairs straight, unlike Monroe who saw no need to flex military muscle. Thus the Roosevelt Corollary to the Monroe Doctrine set the stage for a new era in U.S. relations with its southern neighbors—most of whom came to resent the colossus to the North.

Roosevelt's rhetoric and behavior accorded well with the tenets of political realism as an imperial America faced the new millennium. Indeed, Roosevelt was the first U.S. president to embrace unambiguously the principles of power politics central to the realist view of international politics. Henry Kissinger, himself a prominent realist, describes Roosevelt's foreign policy approach approvingly:

Like his predecessors, Roosevelt was convinced of America's beneficent role in the world. But unlike them, Roosevelt held that America had real foreign policy interests that went far beyond its interest in remaining unentangled. Roosevelt started from the premise that the United States was a power like any other, not a singular incarnation of virtue. If its interests collided with those of other countries, America had the obligation to draw on its strengths to prevail.

. . . No other president defined America's world role so completely in terms of national interest, or identified the national interest so comprehensively with the balance of power. (Kissinger 1994a, 38–39)

Roosevelt's policies and the assumptions underlying them contrast sharply with the precepts of Wilsonian liberalism. "Universal law and not equilibrium, national trustworthiness and not national self-assertion were, in Wilson's view, the foundations of international order. . . . Nothing annoyed Roosevelt as much as high-sounding principles backed by neither the power nor the will to implement them (Kissinger 1994a). Roosevelt also accused Wilson, as Kissinger puts it, "of pandering to isolationist sentiment to help his re-election in 1916." But, he continues, "Wilson's policy was quite the opposite of isolationism. What Wilson was proclaiming was not America's withdrawal from the world but the universal applicability of its values and, in time, America's commitment to spreading them." Thus Wilson "restated what had become the conventional American wisdom since Jefferson, but put it in the service of a crusading ideology. . . . America's special mission transcends day-to-day diplomacy and obliges it to serve as a beacon of liberty for the rest of mankind" (Kissinger 1994a).[4]

Dollar diplomacy describes the period from 1900 to 1913. As American business interests in the Caribbean and Central America mushroomed, the United States flexed its muscles to protect them. Roosevelt's interventionist tactics were continued by his successor, William Howard Taft, who at one point described his administration's policies as "substituting dollars for bullets." Hence the term "dollar diplomacy."

Little changed with Wilson's election, as the data in Focus 3.1 make clear (see also Fromkin 1994b). Until the outbreak of war in Europe Wilson was consumed by foreign policy challenges in China, Mexico, and the Caribbean, often resorting to military intervention to achieve his ends. "Determined to help other peoples become democratic and orderly, Wilson himself became the greatest military interventionist in U.S. history. By the time he left office in 1921, he had ordered troops into Russia and half a dozen Latin American upheavals" (LaFeber 1994). Intervention arguably was not inconsistent with Wilsonian idealism, but in some sense it reflected its failure. "Wilson wanted elections, real change, order, and no foreign interventions—all at once," observes historian Walter LaFeber (1994). "He never discovered how to pull off such a miracle."

In May 1915 a German submarine torpedoed the *Lusitania*, pride of the British merchant marine. Nearly 1,200 lives were lost, including 128 Americans. The attack precipitated a crisis with the United States on the issue of neutrals' rights on the high seas. Wilson's attention now shifted from Asia and the Western Hemisphere to Europe, leading finally to his call for a new collective security system to replace the war-prone balance of power and for other fundamental reforms in international relations. Wilson's efforts to implement his vision failed during his lifetime. The refusal of the United States Senate to approve the Versailles peace settlement and U.S. membership in the League of Nations was a particularly devastating personal defeat for Wilson. Without American participation, the League itself was doomed to failure.

Focus 3.1
DAWN OF A NEW MILLENNIUM: THE USE OF AMERICAN ARMED FORCES ABROAD INITIATED DURING THE ROOSEVELT, TAFT, AND WILSON ADMINISTRATIONS, 1901–1921

• • •

THEODORE ROOSEVELT

1901 Colombia (State of Panama). U.S. troops protect American property and keep transit lines open on the isthmus during revolutionary disturbances.

1902 Colombia. U.S. forces protect American lives and property at Bocas del Toro during civil war.

1902 Colombia (State of Panama). U.S. troops are used to keep railroads running and to prevent the landing of Colombian troops in Panama.

1903 Honduras. U.S. forces protect the American consulate at Puerto Cortez.

1903 Dominican Republic. Marines land at Santo Domingo to protect American interests.

1903 Syria. U.S. forces protect the consulate in Beirut.

1903–1904 Abyssinia. Marines protect the U.S. Consul General during treaty negotiations.

1903–1914 Panama. U.S. forces protect American interests and lives following the revolution for independence for construction of the Panama canal.

1904 Dominican Republic. American and British forces establish a no-fighting zone and protect American lives and interests during revolutionary fighting.

1904 Tangier, Morocco. A marine guard lands to protect the consul general.

1904 Panama. U.S. troops protect American interests and lives at Ancon during a threatened insurrection.

1904–1905 Korea. A marine guard is sent to protect the American legation at Seoul during the Russo-Japanese War.

1906–1909 Cuba. U.S. forces seek to restore order, protect foreigners, and establish a stable government.

1907 Honduras U.S. troops protect American interests in Trujillo, Ceiba, Puerto Cortez, San Pedro, Laguna, and Choloma during war between Honduras and Nicaragua.

WILLIAM HOWARD TAFT

1910 Nicaragua. U.S. forces protect American interests at Bluefields.

1911 Honduras. American troops protect American lives and interests during civil war.

1911 China. U.S. troops dispatched at various sites as the nationalist revolution approaches.

1912 Honduras. A small U.S. force temporarily lands at Puerto Cortez.

1912 Panama. U.S. troops supervise Panamanian elections outside the canal zone.

Focus 3.1 *(continued)*

WILLIAM HOWARD TAFT *(continued)*

1912 Cuba. U.S. forces protect American interests in the province of Oriente and Havana.

1912 China. U.S. troops protect American lives and interests during revolutionary activities.

1912 Turkey. U.S. forces guard the American legation at Constantinople during the Balkan War.

1912–1925 Nicaragua. U.S. forces dispatched to protect American interests remain to promote peace and stability.

1912–1941 China. U.S. troops engage in continuing protective action following disorders that began with the Kuomintang rebellion.

WOODROW WILSON

1913 Mexico. U.S. marines evacuate American citizens and others.

1914 Haiti. U.S. forces protect American nationals.

1914 Dominican Republic. U.S. forces protect Puerto Plata and Santo Domingo City.

1914–1917 Mexico. Undeclared Mexican-American hostilities.

1915–1934 Haiti. U.S. forces maintain order during chronic threatened insurrection.

1916 China. U.S. forces land to quell rioting on American property in Nanking.

1916–1924 Dominican Republic. U.S. forces maintain order during chronic threatened insurrection.

1917 China. U.S. troops land to protect American lives at Chungking.

1917–1918 Germany and Austria-Hungary. World War I.

1917–1922 Cuba. U.S. forces protect American interests during and following insurrection.

1918–1919 Mexico. U.S. troops enter Mexico pursuing bandits and fight Mexican troops at Nogales.

1918–1920 Panama. U.S. troops act as police during election disturbances and later.

1918–1920 Soviet Russia. U.S. troops protect the American consulate at Vladivostok and remain as part of an allied occupation force; later American troops intervene at Archangel in response to the Bolshevik revolution.

1919 Dalmatia. U.S. forces act as police in feud between Italians and Serbs.

1919 Turkey. U.S. marines protect the American consulate during the Greek occupation of Constantinople.

1919 Honduras. U.S. troops maintain order during attempted revolution.

1920 China. U.S. troops protect lives during a disturbance at Kiukiang.

1920 Guatemala. U.S. troops protect the American legation and interests.

1920–1922 Russia (Siberia). U.S. marines sent to protect U.S. radio station and property on Russian Island, Bay of Vladivostok.

Source: Adapted from Ellen C. Collier, "Instances of Use of United States Armed Forces Abroad, 1778–1993," CRS Report for Congress, October 7, 1993.

Still, the principles of Wilsonian idealism, as we have noted, have never been extinguished. Indeed, the distinguished historian Walter LaFeber (1994) writes that Wilson was the first American president "to face the full blast of twentieth-century revolutions," and that his "responses made his policies the most influential in twentieth-century American foreign policy. 'Wilsonianism' became a term to describe later policies that emphasized internationalism and moralism and that were dedicated to extending democracy." We will return to that insight toward the end of this chapter.

Isolationism Resurgent: Interwar Idealism and Withdrawal

The League of Nations as an American foreign policy program died in the presidential election of 1920. Warren G. Harding defeated Wilson, who was stricken with a debilitating stroke while campaigning at home for the League. Harding's foreign policy program called for a "return to normalcy," effectively one that sought "relief from the burdens that international engagement brings" (Mandelbaum 1994).

Disillusionment with American involvement in World War I would eventually set in, undermining Americans' "confidence in the old symbols of internationalism and altruistic diplomacy" and their "assurance that America's mission should be one of magnanimous service to the rest of the world" (Osgood 1953). Disillusionment became especially prevalent in the 1930s, as isolationism again emerged as the dominant American foreign policy strategy. Initially, however, idealism remained an accepted approach to international politics, perhaps out of popular indifference. Military intervention in Latin America and China also perpetuated the unilateralist thrust of American foreign policy evident even before the turn of the century. Nicaragua in particular was the target of a prolonged intervention, lasting from 1926 to 1933. While there, U.S. troops confronted Augusto Sandino, an anti-American guerrilla leader with strong mass support and whose name a later generation of Nicaraguan revolutionaries would adopt. American troops did not kill Sandino, but they left in place an American trained national guard commanded by Anastasio Somoza, who was eventually overthrown by the new Sandinistas.

Even as the United States practiced interventionism during the 1920s, thus perpetuating a now firmly established policy pattern, American policymakers also enthusiastically pursued key elements of the idealist paradigm. With the Washington Naval Conference of 1921 the United States sought through arms limitations to curb a triangular naval arms race involving the United States, Japan, and Britain. A series of treaties followed whose general purpose was to maintain the status quo in the Far East. The program conformed to idealist precepts, but no enforcement provisions were included. Thus realists argue that "the transient thrill afforded by the Washington Conference was miserable preparation for the test of political leadership provided by the ominous events that undermined the Far Eastern settlement a decade later" (Osgood 1953).

Realists also criticize the 1928 Pact of Paris, popularly known as the ***Kellogg-Briand Pact*** (after the U.S. secretary of state, Frank B. Kellogg, and the French foreign minister, Aristide Briand, who negotiated it). The agreement sought to deal with the problem of war by making it illegal. Realists thus regard it as "the perfect expression of the utopian idealism which dominated America's attempts to compose international conflicts and banish the threat of war in the interwar period. . . . The Pact of Paris simply declared that its signatories renounced war as an instrument of national policy. . . . It contained absolutely no obligation for any nation to do anything under any circumstances" (Osgood 1953).[5]

The German reparations issue involved the United States intimately, but even here the United States sought detachment, not involvement in world affairs. During World War I the United States emerged as a creditor nation—that is, it sold more abroad than it bought (which remained true until the early 1970s). To finance sales to Britain and France during the war, it granted credits to the allied powers. After the war it insisted that the debts be repaid. Eventually the issue of debts became linked to the payment of reparations by Germany, which under the punitive elements of the Treaty of Versailles was held responsible for starting World War I. Various schemes were devised to settle the debt-reparations issue, but none proved satisfactory. The issue helped to estrange the United States from the European democracies as the economic depression of the 1930s set in and war clouds again overshadowed Europe.

As fascism rose during the 1930s and the world political economy fell into deep depression, neither the outlawry of war nor the principle of collective security stemmed the onslaught of renewed militarism. Germany, Italy, and Japan repeatedly challenged the post–World War I order, Britain and France seemed powerless to stop them, and the United States retreated into an isolationist shell. In the U.S. Senate a special committee chaired by the extreme isolationist Gerald P. Nye held hearings that attributed American entry into World War I to war profiteers—"merchants of death" they were called. Congress passed a series of neutrality acts between 1935 and 1937 whose purpose was to steer America clear of the emerging European conflict. The immediate application came in Spain, where General Francisco Franco, with the help of Hitler, sought to overthrow the Spanish republic and replace it with a fascist regime. The neutrality acts effectively barred the United States from assisting the anti-fascist forces.

The Great Depression reinforced isolationist sentiments in the United States. As noted earlier, Britain was the world's preeminent economic power in the nineteenth century. As the preponderant power in politics as well as economics—a global hegemon—it promoted an open international economic system based on free trade. Its power began to wane in the late nineteenth century, however. Following World War I Britain's ability to exercise the leadership role necessary to maintain the open world political economy was severely strained. The United States was the logical candidate to assume this role, but it refused (see also Chapter 7).[6] Britain's inability to exercise leadership and the United States' unwillingness to do so were primary causes of the Great Depression (Kindleberger 1973). Economic nationalism now became the norm. Tariffs erected by one nation to protect its economy from foreign inroads led to retaliation by others. The volume of international trade contracted dramatically, causing reduced living standards and rising economic hardship. Policymakers who sought to create a new world order following World War II would conclude that economic nationalism was a major cause of the breakdown of international peace. Indeed, the perceived connectedness of peace and prosperity is one of the major "lessons of the 1930s" that continues to inform American foreign policy even today.

Another lesson was learned when Britain's policy of trying to appease Hitler failed.

In September 1938—meeting in Munich, Germany—Britain and France made an agreement with Hitler that permitted Nazi Germany to annex a large part of Czechoslovakia in return for what British Prime Minister Nevill Chamberlain called "peace in our time." Instead, on September 1, 1939, Hitler's Germany attacked Poland. Britain and France, honoring their pledge to defend the Poles, declared war on Germany two days later. World War II had begun. The lesson drawn from the **Munich Conference**—that *aggressors cannot be appeased*—would also inform policymakers' thinking for decades to come.

In the two years that followed Hitler's initial onslaught against Poland—years that saw German attacks on France, Britain, and the Soviet Union—Franklin Roosevelt deftly nudged the United States away from its isolationist policies in support of the Western democracies (see Langer and Gleason 1952). Germany's blatant exercise of *machtpolitik* (power politics) challenged the precepts of idealism that had buttressed the isolationism of the 1930s. Still, Roosevelt was careful not to jettison idealism as he prepared the nation for the coming conflict.

> Roosevelt understood that only a threat to their security could motivate [the American people] to support military preparedness. But to take them into a war, he knew he needed to appeal to their idealism in much the same way that Wilson had. . . . Thus "balance of power" was not a term ever found in Roosevelt's pronouncements, except when he used it disparagingly. What he sought was to bring about a world community compatible with America's democratic and social ideals as the best guarantee of peace. (Kissinger 1994a, 390)

In the spring of 1941 Congress passed and Roosevelt signed the **Lend-Lease Act**. It permitted the United States to assist others deemed vital to the United States, thus committing the United States to the Allied cause against the Axis powers, Germany and Italy. The proposal provoked a bitter controversy in the United States. Senator Arthur Vandenberg, then a staunch isolationist (converted to internationalism after the war), remarked that Lend-Lease was the death-knell of isolationism: "We have tossed Washington's Farewell Address into the discard," he wrote in his diary. "We have thrown ourselves squarely into the power politics and the power wars of Europe, Asia, and Africa. We have taken a first step upon a course from which we can never hereafter retreat" (cited in Serfaty 1972). The next step occurred when Japan attacked Pearl Harbor on December 7, 1941. No longer could America's geographic isolation from the world, reinforced by the vast oceans separating it from Europe and Asia, support its political isolation.

Technological change—the ability of Japan to strike at vital American interests thousands of miles from its own homeland—destroyed the rationale of isolationism. The diplomatic record of America's first century and a half does not, however, support the view that isolationism was an inappropriate policy. Isolationism is given a bad name, perhaps, because its practice during the 1930s removed the United States as an effective player in the European balance of power. Had it been involved—had it followed the prescriptions of realism, at least as viewed by realists themselves—it might have helped avert the catastrophe of World War II. Still, it is important to emphasize that isolationism "never meant total isolation from the world," only "political detachment" (Deibel 1992; see also Crabb 1986). That it successfully nurtured the United

States to the status of a great power is not easily dismissed—which is why even today (neo)isolationism continues its appeal as an American foreign policy strategy.

Recapitulation: The Oscillations of Isolationism and Internationalism

Although by the 1940s Americans had become firmly wedded to isolationism as a foreign policy strategy, the history of the republic indicates that a penchant for internationalism had also been evident. The internationalist tradition entailed diverse practices, including not only the exercise of power but also intervention in the political affairs of others, the economic penetration of foreign markets through investment and trade, maintenance of a high diplomatic profile, sensitivity to threats to the nation's honor, and a determined effort to transplant American values and institutions abroad. At the extreme, the internationalist tradition made the United States an imperial republic—a "nascent empire" in George Washington's words.

In practice those sentiments reflected less an American desire to acquire others' territory and resources than an underlying attitude about the nation's unique place in the world. From that ethnocentric view it was but a short step to messianic crusading. Self-righteously presuming its innate virtue and innocence, the United States based its behavior on the premise that the nation had a special *mission* in the world. "American foreign policy makers," it has been said, "appear to share a naive belief that American ideals and ideas can and should solve all the problems of the world and that it is their mission to actively apply these ideals abroad" (van den Haag 1985; see also Stoler, 1987). "The assumption is that we are the anointed custodians of the rules of international behavior," historian Arthur Schlesinger (1984) has written, "and that the function of United States policy is to mark other states up or down, according to their obedience to our rules."

Because American policymakers historically have been unable to reconcile the advantages of withdrawing from the world with the benefits of reforming it, the nation's global posture has alternated between periods of "introversion" and "extroversion"—that is, between periods of isolationist withdrawal and global involvement. Debates among policymakers as to which role best serves the national interest have never been resolved conclusively. America's vacillation between isolationism (introversion) and internationalism (extroversion) appears to fluctuate in rhythmic *cycles*, with each taking twenty-five to thirty years (a political generation) to run its course.

Focus 3.2 records this cyclical pattern, as described by Frank Klingberg (1983, 1990; see also Schlesinger 1986). The cycles comport well with the preceding discussion. The first isolationist phase ends with Washington's farewell address, giving way to the early expansionism of the new republic. It ends at roughly the time of the Monroe Doctrine. The next extrovert phase begins shortly before the Mexican-American War, which extended the nation to the Pacific, and ends shortly after the acquisition of Alaska as the nation turned inward, now focused on Civil War reconstruction and a series of domestic economic downturns. The Spanish-American War and World War I dominate the next internationalist phase, when the United States emerges as a world power, not simply a regional one. It ends with the American rejection of the Versailles settlement. A period of intense isolationism followed, as the

Focus 3.2
CYCLES OF INTROVERSION (ISOLATIONISM) AND EXTROVERSION
(INTERNATIONALISM) IN AMERICA'S FOREIGN POLICY
• • •

Introversion	Extroversion
1776–1798	1798–1824
1824–1844	1844–1871
1871–1891	1891–1919
1919–1940	1940–1966
1967–1986	1986–

United States, after several years of prosperity, sought to cope with economic depression while rejecting the burdens of international leadership.

What is noteworthy is that idealism punctuated much of the isolationism of the 1920s and 1930s, just as it had stimulated internationalism earlier in the century. "An absolute national morality," contends historian Louis Hartz (1955), "is inspired either to withdraw from 'alien' things or to transform them: it cannot live in comfort constantly by their side." Thus moral idealism prescribes either isolationism or internationalism, as such thinking invites either withdrawal from an immoral world or a quest to reform it. Consequently, idealism may contribute to the cyclical swings between introversion and extroversion evident in America's diplomatic history.

With the onset of World War II, the United States stood poised to embark on a new extrovert phase. The ethos of *liberal internationalism*—"the intellectual and political tradition that believes in the necessity of leadership by liberal democracies in the construction of a peaceful world order through multilateral cooperation and effective international organizations" (Gardner 1990)—now animated the American people and their leaders as they embarked on a period of global activism not previously witnessed.

Internationalism Resurgent: Global Activism in the Post-World War II World Order

"Every war in American history," writes historian Arthur Schlesinger (1986), "has been followed in due course by skeptical reassessments of supposedly sacred assumptions." World War II, more than any other, served such a purpose for America. It both crystallized a mood and acted as a catalyst for it, resolved contradictions and helped clarify values, and produced a consensus about the nation's world role. Most of its leaders were now convinced that the United States should not, and could not, retreat from world affairs as it had after World War I. The isolationist heritage was pushed aside as they enthusiastically plunged into the task of shaping the world to American preferences. Thus a new epoch in American diplomacy unfolded as, with missionary zeal, the

United States once more sought to build a new world order on the ashes of Dresden and Berlin, Hiroshima and Nagasaki.

In 1947 President Truman set the tone of postwar American policy in the doctrine that bears his name: "The free peoples of the world look to us for support in maintaining their freedoms. . . . If we falter in our leadership, we may endanger the peace of the world—and we shall surely endanger the welfare of our own nation." Later policy pronouncements prescribed America's missionary role. "Our nation," John F. Kennedy asserted in 1962, was "commissioned by history to be either an observer of freedom's failure or the cause of its success." Ronald Reagan echoed that sentiment nearly two decades later: "We in this country, in this generation, are, by destiny rather than choice, the watchmen on the walls of world freedom." "Other nations have interests," declared Secretary of State Dean Rusk in 1967. "The United States has responsibilities."

Consistent with its new sense of global responsibility, the United States actively sought to orchestrate nearly every significant global initiative. It was a primary sponsor and supporter of the United Nations. It engineered creation of regional institutions, such as the Organization of American States, and promoted American hegemony in areas regarded as American spheres of influence. It pushed hard for the expansion of foreign trade and the development of new markets for American business abroad.[7] It launched an ambitious foreign aid program. And it built a complex network of military alliances, both formal and informal. Its pursuit of these ambitious foreign policy objectives created a vast American "empire" circling the globe. Focus 3.3 summarizes the scope of America's commitments and involvements abroad in 1991, when the United States emerged as the world's sole remaining superpower—and exactly a half-century after the Japanese attack on Pearl Harbor cemented the nation's entry into World War II.

Against this background, "the first global society," a phrase used by Zbigniew Brzezinski, President Carter's national security assistant, appropriately describes the United States. Indeed, for half a century few aspirants to the White House would risk challenging the appropriateness of an active leadership role for the nation. To have done so would have been to attack a widely accepted and deeply ingrained national self-image that both led to and was sustained by extensive global interests and involvements.

However relentlessly pursued, America's postwar globalist vision did not go unchallenged. Consistent with the hypothesized quarter-century cycle between extroversion and introversion, by the mid-1960s enthusiasm for globalism began to wane. The Vietnam War tragedy coincided with—indeed, caused—popular pleas for a U.S. retreat from world affairs. President Nixon's declaration in 1970—later known as the *Nixon Doctrine*—that "America cannot—and will not—conceive all the plans, design all the programs, execute all the decisions, and undertake all the defense of the free nations of the world" took cognizance of a resurgent isolationist mood.

The Carter administration also acknowledged limits to American power but sought to minimize them. The Reagan and Bush administrations, on the other hand, vigorously rejected the rhetoric of restraint. Thus the lack of enthusiasm for active global involvement in the 1970s was a temporary pause in the internationalist thrust of American foreign policy characteristic since World War II. "We hear it said that we

Focus 3.3
AMERICA'S HALF CENTURY: NONMILITARY AND MILITARY DIMENSIONS OF GLOBAL ACTIVISM AT THE END OF THE COLD WAR

• • •

NONMILITARY INVOLVEMENTS

- The United States maintained diplomatic offices in 160 nations and participated in over fifty major international organizations and eight hundred international conferences.
- U.S. broadcasting services promoted America's message and world view in forty-eight languages beamed throughout the world.
- The value of U.S. exports reached $421.7 billion, while its imports from abroad stood at $487.1 billion. In 1941 total U.S. trade with the rest of the world—exports plus imports—totaled $8.8 billion.
- U.S. economic aid to ninety countries exceeded $11.0 billion, bringing to $246.1 billion the total amount of foreign economic assistance granted to other countries since World War II. From June 1941 through June 1945 the United States spent $49 billion on foreign aid, all for military objectives.
- U.S. direct investment abroad stood at $361.5 billion.

MILITARY INVOLVEMENTS

- Bilateral and multilateral treaties, executive agreements, and policy declarations committed the United States to the defense of over forty nations.
- In 1990, prior to the Persian Gulf buildup, 435,000 U.S. troops were stationed at 395 major military bases and hundreds of minor bases in thirty-five foreign countries. In 1940, one year before the Lend-Lease Act was passed, the entire U.S. Army consisted of 269,000 officers and enlisted personnel.
- 47,000 Navy and Marine Corps personnel were aboard ships outside U.S. territorial waters. Another 10,000 were stationed at military bases on American territories in the Pacific. In 1940, one year before Pearl Harbor was attacked, the entire U.S. Navy consisted of 54,000 officers and enlisted personnel.
- 12,000 strategic nuclear warheads were deployed on 1,600 intercontinental and sea-based missiles and 260 intercontinental bombers.
- Nonstrategic forces levels included more than 8,000 tactical nuclear weapons, 16,000 battle tanks, 7,000 combat aircraft, 2,000 attack helicopters, and 300 aircraft carriers and major ships.

Focus 3.3 *(continued)*

- The United States agreed to sell $20.9 billion of military equipment to other nations, bringing the total value of sales since the Korean War to $210 billion. Another $81.6 billion was spent in other forms of military aid and training.

- The nation's budget for military preparedness stood at $320,900,000,000—a figure that exceeded the gross national product (GNP) of all but a handful of the world's other nations. In 1940—the same year that Nazi Germany attacked and occupied Belgium, the Netherlands, and France—the combined budgets of the Army and Navy departments was $1,798,645,000—1.8 percent of the nation's GNP.

live in an era of limits to our powers. Well, there are [also] limits to our patience," President Reagan proclaimed. Secretary of State Shultz intoned in 1985 that we are not "just observers; we are participants, and we are engaged. America is again in a position to have a major influence over the trend of events." American policymakers emphatically denied a proposition popular in the late 1980s—that the United States was "overcommitted," with obligations abroad exceeding its resources, a classic symptom of "imperial overstretch" (Kennedy 1987). Instead, they proclaimed that the United States was a rising power, not a declining one. The role of world policeman was reaffirmed and extended, along with its burdens. "We're going to affect the future substantially," asserted Secretary of State James Baker. "We can . . . be a force for freedom and peaceful change unlike any country in the world." He added later that "there is no substitute for American leadership."

The Cold War as History: Idealism and Realism, Anticommunism and Containment

Three tenets were uppermost in the minds of American policymakers following World War II. The first, as noted, centered on global activism. The others focused on the challenge of Soviet communism. Together the three tenets—summarized in Focus 3.4—defined a new orthodoxy that not only replaced the isolationist mood of the 1930s but also shaped a half century of American foreign policy.

Anticommunism: Challenge to American Ideas and Ideals

Fear of communism—and an unequivocal rejection of it—played a major part in shaping the way the United States perceived the world throughout the Cold War. Communism was widely seen as a doctrinaire belief system diametrically opposed to "the American way of life," one intent on converting the entire world to its own vision. Because communism was perceived as inherently totalitarian, antidemocratic, and anticapitalist, it also was perceived as a real threat to freedom, liberty, and prosperity throughout the world. Combating this threatening, adversarial ideology became an

Focus 3.4
THE NEW ORTHODOXY: GLOBALISM, ANTICOMMUNISM, AND CONTAINMENT

• • •

1. The United States must reject isolationism permanently and substitute for it an active responsibility for the direction of international affairs.
2. Communism represents a dangerous ideological force in the world, and the United States should combat its spread.
3. Because the Soviet Union is the spearhead of the communist challenge, American foreign policy must contain Soviet expansionism and influence.

obsession—to the point, some argued, that American foreign policy itself became ideological (Commager 1983; Parenti 1969). The United States now often defined its mission as much in terms of the beliefs it opposed as those it supported. In words and deeds, America seemingly stood less *for* something, as in the nineteenth century, than *against* something: the communist ideology of Marxism-Leninism. So pervasive and strident was this posture that it appeared (Secretary of State Adams' warning from the 1820s notwithstanding) that the United States had now gone abroad in search of monsters to destroy.

Official pronouncements about America's global objectives as they developed in the formative decade following World War II routinely stressed the menace posed by Marxist-Leninist (communist) doctrine. "The actions resulting from the Communist philosophy," charged Harry Truman in 1949, "are a threat." "We face a hostile ideology—global in scope, atheistic in character, ruthless in purpose, and insidious in method," warned President Eisenhower. "Unhappily," he continued, "the danger it poses promises to be of indefinite duration."

One popular view of "the beast" that helped sustain the anticommunist impulse was the belief that communism was a cohesive monolith to which all adherents were bound in united solidarity. The passage of time steadily reduced the cogency of that viewpoint, as communism revealed itself to be more polycentric than monolithic. Communist Party leaders became increasingly vocal about their own divisions and disagreements concerning communism's fundamental beliefs, and the greatest fear that some felt were the motives of other communist states. Moreover, even if communism was in spirit an expansionist movement, it proved to be more flexible than initially assumed, with no timetable for the conversion of nonbelievers. By the late 1980s, however, communist leaders everywhere were themselves experimenting with free enterprise, capitalist incentives, and democratic reforms. All were motivated by the conviction that communism was not a viable program with which to organize the politics and economics of their societies. Later, their countries' abrupt rejection of Communist Party rule in favor of democratic capitalism proved unambiguously the inaccuracy of the stereotypic image of a unified communist bloc cemented by ideological consensus. Nonetheless, the vision of communism as a monolith helped to shape and sustain a half-century of anticommunism.

A related conviction that also contributed to the anticommunist impulse was the belief that communism was endowed with powers and appeals that would encourage its continued spread. The view of communism as an expansionist, crusading force intent on converting the entire world to its beliefs, whose doctrines, however evil, might command widespread appeal was a potent argument (see Almond 1954). The *domino theory*, a popular metaphor in the 1960s, asserted that one country's fall to communism would stimulate the fall of those adjacent to it. Thus, like a row of falling dominoes, an unstoppable chain reaction would unfold, bringing increasing portions of the world's population under the domination of totalitarian, communist governments. "Communism is on the move. It is out to win. It is playing an offensive game," warned Richard Nixon in 1963, who earlier in his political career had chastised Truman's secretary of state as the "dean of the cowardly college of Communist containment" and recommended "dealing with this great Communist offensive" by pushing back the Iron Curtain with force. The lesson implied by the domino metaphor is that only American resistance could abate the seemingly inevitable communist onslaught. It was especially potent in explaining America's resolve to fight in Vietnam.

The anticommunist goal became institutionalized following World War II. From then until the United States became mired in the Vietnam War, few in the American foreign policy establishment challenged the assumption that communism was a cohesive and powerful conspiratorial movement which had to be opposed. And few challenged the belief that the Cold War was rooted in ideological causes. Policy debates centered largely on how to implement the anticommunist drive, not on whether communism posed a threat. Some of the ideological fervor of American foreign policy rhetoric receded during the 1970s with the Nixon-Kissinger effort to limit communist influence through a strategy of détente. References in policy statements to communism itself as a force in world politics also declined. President Carter went so far as to declare that "we are now free of that inordinate fear of communism which once led us to embrace any dictator who joined us in our fear." But the anticommunist underpinnings of American foreign policy did not vanish.

The theme of "communism as the principal danger" gained renewed emphasis under Ronald Reagan, whose Manichean world view depicted the world as a place where the noncommunist "free world," led by the United States, engaged in continuous battle with the communist world led by the Soviet Union, which he described as an "evil empire." Later, as domestic change in Eastern Europe and the Soviet Union itself accelerated, the more virulent forms of anticommunism waned. Richard Schifter, an assistant secretary of state in the Bush administration, declared that "communism has proven itself to be a false god." Rejected gods do not need to be condemned. The Bush administration nonetheless chose to emphasize a worldwide transition to democracy inspired by the desire to extirpate the curse of communist ideology from the world. Secretary of State Baker: "Our idea is to replace the dangerous period of the Cold War with a democratic peace—a peace built on the twin pillars of political and economic freedom."

The historical import of anticommunism should be neither minimized nor forgotten, as the impact of the beliefs about communism in the American policy-making community was enormous. Successful opposition to communism became one of America's most important interests, coloring not only what happened abroad but also much of what took place at home by requiring the expenditure of enormous psychological and material treasure—and sometimes threatening cherished values.

The Containment of Soviet Influence

As the physically strongest and the most vocal Marxist-Leninist state, the Soviet Union stood at the vanguard of the communist challenge. Hence the third tenet of the new orthodoxy emergent after World War II: The United States must contain Soviet expansionism and influence.

Several corollary beliefs buttressed the determination to contain Soviet communism:

- The Soviet Union is an expansionist power, intent on maximizing communist power through military conquest and "exported" revolutions.
- The Soviet goal of world domination is permanent and will succeed unless blocked by vigorous counteraction.
- As the leader of the "free world," the United States is the only nation able to repel Soviet aggression and restore the balance of power.
- The United States must increase its military power relative to the Soviet Union to enable it better to contain Soviet expansion.
- Appeasement will not work—force must be met with force if Soviet expansionism is to be stopped.

A Soviet-centric foreign policy flowed from this interrelated set of beliefs whose durability persisted for decades. Furthermore, the precepts of political realism now came to dominate American foreign policy as the purpose of the containment strategy was the preservation of the security of the United States "through the maintenance of a balance of power in the world" (Gaddis 1992; see also Gaddis 1982; Kissinger 1994b). As one scholar put it, "realists sought to reorient United States policy so that American policymakers could cope with Soviet attempts at domination without either lapsing into passive unwillingness to use force or engaging in destructive and quixotic crusades to 'make the world safe for democracy.' Their ideas were greeted warmly by policymakers, who sought . . . to 'exorcise isolationism, justify a permanent and global involvement in world affairs, [and] rationalize the accumulation of power'" (Keohane 1986b).[8]

To understand what brought about these durable assumptions, the containment strategy derived from them, and the doctrine of political realism that sustained them, it is useful to trace briefly alternative interpretations of the origins of the Cold War and, following that, the strategies of containment that America's Cold War presidents pursued.

The Origins of the Cold War: Competing Hypotheses

In 1835 Alexis de Tocqueville predicted that the United States and Russia were destined by fate and historical circumstance to become rivals. He argued that "there are today two great peoples which, starting out from different points of departure, advance toward the same goal—the Americans and the Russians. . . . Each of them will one day hold in its hands the destinies of half of mankind." Tocqueville could not foresee the advent of Marxism-Leninism or the possibility that ideological differences would contribute to the dispute he regarded as inevitable. Instead, his prediction was based on the logic of *realpolitik*.

A Conflict of Interests From this perspective, rivalry between the emergent superpowers following World War II was inescapable. The preeminent status of the United States and the Soviet Union at the top of the international hierarchy made each suspicious of the other. And each had reasons to counter the other's potential global hegemony.

> The principal cause of the Cold War was the essential duopoly of power left by World War II, a duopoly that quite naturally resulted in the filling of a vacuum (Europe) that had once been the center of the international system and the control of which would have conferred great, and perhaps decisive, power advantage to its possessor. . . . The root cause of the conflict was to be found in the structural circumstances that characterized the international system at the close of World War II. (Tucker 1990, 94)

But was the competition necessary? During World War II the United States and the Soviet Union had both demonstrated an ability to subordinate their ideological differences and competition for power to larger purposes, namely—the destruction of Hitler's Germany. Neither relentlessly sought unilateral advantage. Instead, both practiced accommodation to protect their mutual interest. Their success in remaining alliance partners suggests that Cold War rivalry was not predetermined, that continued collaboration was possible.

After the war, American and Soviet leaders both expressed in official discourse their hope that wartime collaboration would continue (Gaddis 1972). Harry Hopkins, for example, a close adviser to President Roosevelt, reported that "The Russians had proved that they could be reasonable and farseeing and there wasn't any doubt in the minds of the President or any of us that we could live with them and get along with them peacefully for as far into the future as any of us could imagine."

Roosevelt argued that it would be possible to preserve the accommodative atmosphere the great powers achieved during the war if the United States and the Soviet Union each respected the other's national interests. He predicated his belief on an informal agreement that suggested that each great power would enjoy dominant influence in its own *sphere of influence* and not oppose the others in their areas of influence (Morgenthau 1969; Schlesinger 1967). As presidential policy adviser John Foster Dulles noted in January 1945, "The three great powers which at Moscow agreed upon the 'closest cooperation' about European questions have shifted to a practice of separate, regional responsibility." Agreements about the role of the Security Council in the new United Nations (in which each great power would enjoy a veto) obligated the

United States and the Soviet Union to share responsibility for preserving world peace, further symbolizing the expectation of continued cooperation.

If these were the superpowers' hopes and aspirations when World War II ended, why did they fail? To answer that question, we must go beyond the logic of *realpolitik* and probe other explanations of the origins of the Cold War.

Ideological Incompatibilities   Another interpretation holds that the Cold War was simply an extension of the superpowers' mutual disdain for each other's political system and way of life. Secretary of State James F. Byrnes embraced this thesis following World War II, arguing that "there is too much difference in the ideologies of the U.S. and Russia to work out a long term program of cooperation." Thus the Cold War was a conflict "not only between two powerful states, but also between two different social systems" (Jervis 1991).

The interpretation of the Cold War as a battle between diametrically opposed systems of belief contrasts sharply with the view that the emergent superpowers' differences stemmed from discordant interests. Although the adversaries may have viewed "ideology more as a justification for action than as a guide to action," once the interests they shared disappeared, "ideology did become the chief means which differentiated friend from foe" (Gaddis 1983). From this perspective, the Cold War between the United States and the Soviet Union centered less on a conflict of interests between rivals for global power and prestige than on a contest between opposing belief systems about alternative ways of life. Such contests allow no room for compromise, as they pit right against wrong, good against evil; diametrically opposed belief systems require victory. Adherents animated by the righteousness of their cause view the world as an arena for religious war—a battle for the allegiance of people's minds. Thus American policy rhetoric—like that employed to justify religious wars and religious persecutions in the past—advocated "sleepless hostility to Communism—even preventive war" (Commager 1965). Such an outlook virtually guarantees pure conflict: Intolerance of competing belief systems is rife, and cooperation or conciliation with the ideological foe entails no virtue. Instead, adversaries view the world in **zero-sum** terms: When one side wins converts, the other side necessarily loses them.

Lenin thus described the predicament—prophetically, it happened: "As long as capitalism and socialism exist, we cannot live in peace; in the end, either one or the other will triumph—a funeral dirge will be sung either over the Soviet Republic or over world capitalism."

Misperceptions   A third explanation sees the Cold War rooted in psychological factors, particularly the superpowers' *misperceptions* of each other's motives, which their conflicting interests and ideologies reinforced. Mistrustful parties see in their own actions only virtue and in those of their adversaries only malice. Hostility is inevitable when such "we-they," "we're OK, you're not" mirror images exist (Bronfenbrenner 1961). Moreover, as a nation's perceptions of its adversary's evil intentions become accepted as dogma, its prophecies also become self-fulfilling (see White 1984).

A month before Roosevelt died, he expressed to Stalin his desire, above all, to prevent "mutual distrust." Yet, as noted, mistrust soon developed. Indeed, its genesis could be traced to pre-war years, particularly in the minds of Soviet leaders, who recalled American participation in the 1918–1919 Allied military intervention in Russia, which turned from its initial mission of keeping weapons out of German hands into an anti-Bolshevik undertaking. They also were sensitive to United States' failure to recognize the Soviet Union diplomatically until 1933 in the midst of a depression (perceived as a sign of capitalism's weakness and its ultimate collapse).

The wartime experience did little to assuage Soviet leaders; rather, their anxieties were fueled by such memories as:

- U.S. procrastination before entering the war against the fascists
- America's refusal to inform the Soviets of the Manhattan atomic bomb project or to apprise them of wartime strategy to the same extent as the British
- the delay in sending promised Lend Lease supplies
- the failure to open up the second front (leading Stalin to suspect that American policy was to let the Russians and Germans destroy each other)
- the use of the atomic bomb against Japan, perhaps perceived as a maneuver to prevent Soviet involvement in the Pacific peace settlement.

Those suspicions were later reinforced by the willingness of the United States to support previous Nazi collaborators in American-occupied countries, notably Italy, and by its pressure on the Soviet Union to abide by its promise to allow free elections in areas vital to Soviet national security, notably Poland. Soviet leaders also were resentful of America's abrupt cancellation of promised Lend Lease assistance, which Stalin had counted on to facilitate the postwar recovery. Thus Soviet distrust of American intentions stemmed in part from fears of American encirclement that were exacerbated by America's past hostility.

To the United States, on the other hand, numerous indications of growing Soviet belligerence warranted distrust. These included:

- Stalin's announcement in February 1946 that the Soviet Union was not going to demilitarize its armed forces, at the very time that the United States was engaged in the largest demobilization by a victorious power in world history
- the Soviet Union's unwillingness to permit democratic elections in the territories it had liberated from the Nazis
- its refusal to assist in postwar reconstruction in regions outside of Soviet control
- its removal of supplies and infrastructure from Soviet-occupied areas
- its selfish and often obstructive behavior in the fledgling new international organizations
- its occasional opportunistic disregard for international law and violation of agreements and treaties
- its infiltration of Western labor movements.

Harry Truman typified the environment of distrust. Upon assuming the presidency after Roosevelt's death he declared: "If the Russians did not wish to join us they could go to hell" (Tugwell 1971). In this climate of suspicion and distrust—of mirror images and self-fulfilling prophecies—the Cold War grew (see Focus 3.5). "Each side thought that it was compelled by the very existence of the other to engage in zero-sum competition, and each saw the unfolding history of the Cold War as confirming its view" (Garthoff 1994; see also Kennan 1976).

If the Cold War originated in divergent images and each power's insensitivity to the impact of its actions on the other's fears, it is difficult to assign blame for the deterioration of Soviet-American relations. Both parties were responsible because both were victims of their misperceptions. The Cold War was not simply an American response to communist aggression, once the orthodox American view. Nor was it simply a product of America's postwar assertiveness, as revisionist historians later argued (see Schlesinger 1986). Both victors in the war against Nazi Germany felt threatened. And each had legitimate reasons to regard the other with suspicion. Thus, we can view the Cold War as a conflict over reciprocal anxieties bred by the way policymakers on both sides interpreted each other's actions.

In addition to divergent interests, ideologies, and images, a complete accounting of the origins of the Cold War would include such factors as the pressures exerted by interest groups and changes in the climate of opinion within each society, innovations in weapons technology and the shifts in strategic balances they introduced, and the role that military planners played in fomenting the conflict. Regardless of the reasons for its eruption, however, the Cold War became *the* central issue in world affairs. Its shadow stretched across the entire landscape of world politics from 1945 until its ultimate demise in 1991.

To understand the role that power and principle played in shaping American foreign policy during this prolonged global conflict, we must go beyond the origins of the Cold War and chart the course of superpower relations across the Cold War's history.[9]

America's Containment Strategies: Evolutionary Phases

The history of American foreign policy since World War II is largely the story of how the containment doctrine was interpreted and applied to guide American initiatives toward the Soviet Union and its sometime allies. Figure 3.1 (page 60) quantitatively illustrates the pattern of conflict and cooperation the United States directed toward the Soviet Union during the Cold War and the Soviets' responses. The evidence shows at least four characteristics of Soviet-American interactions:

1. The Cold War was characterized by a high level of superpower conflict during most of its history.
2. Periods of intense conflict alternated rhythmically with periods of relative cooperation.
3. Reciprocal, action-reaction relations occurred. That is, periods when the United States directed friendly initiatives toward the Soviets were also periods when the Soviets acted with friendliness toward the United States; periods of U.S. belligerence were periods of Soviet belligerence.

Focus 3.5
MIRROR IMAGES: THE ONSET OF THE COLD WAR

• • •

The Soviet Image of the United States	The American Image of the Soviet Union
• They (the rulers) are bad. The Wall Street bankers, politicians, and militarists want a war because they fear loss of wealth and power in a communist revolution.	**• They (the rulers) are bad.** The men in the Kremlin are aggressive, power-seeking, brutal in suppressing Hungary, ruthless in dealing with their people.
They are surrounding us with military bases.	They are infiltrating the western hemisphere to attack us.
They send spies (in U-2 planes and otherwise) to destroy the workers' fatherland.	They engage in espionage and sabotage to wreck our country.
They are like the Nazis—rearming the Germans against us.	They are like the Nazis—an aggressive expansionist dictatorship.
• They are imperialistic. The capitalist nations dominate colonial areas, keep them in submission.	**• They are imperialistic.** The communists want to dominate the world.
The Latin-American regimes (except Cuba) are puppets of the USA.	They rigidly control the satellite puppet governments.
• They exploit their own people. All capitalists live in luxury by exploiting workers, who suffer insecurity, unemployment, etc.	**• They exploit their own people.** They hold down consumer goods, keep standards of living low except for communist bureaucrats.
• They are against democracy. Democratic forms are mere pretense; people can vote only for capitalist candidates.	**• They are against democracy.** Democratic forms are mere pretense; people can vote only for communist candidates.

The Soviet Image of the United States	The American Image of the Soviet Union
Rulers control organs of propaganda, education, and communication. They persecute anyone favoring communist ideas.	Rulers control organs of propaganda, education, and communication. They persecute anyone favoring western democracy.
• **They distort the truth.** They falsely accuse the USSR of desiring to impose ideology by force.	• **They distort the truth.** They pose as a friend of colonial people in order to enslave them.
• **They are immoral, materialist, selfishly individualistic.** They are only out for money.	• **They are immortal, materialistic.** They are preventing freedom of religion.
• **They (the people) are good.** The American people want peace.	• **They (the people) are good.** The Soviet people want peace.

Source: Ralph K. White, New York Times, *September 5, 1961, p., 5.*

4. Although different presidents are identified with periodic shifts in the pattern of conflict and cooperation toward the Soviet Union during the Cold War, the historical record reveals "no detectable systematic differences in the way administrations regularly [built] on their own past behavior or in the way they [responded] to the Soviet Union" (Dixon and Gaarder 1992). Instead, regardless of the party affiliation or political ideology of those in the Oval Office, continuity rather than change is the hallmark of America's Cold War behavior toward the Soviet Union.

For analytical purposes the history of the policy of containment can be divided into five chronologically ordered phases, as depicted in Figure 3.1 (for an alternative periodization, see Nincic 1989).

Cold War Confrontation, 1947–1962 A brief period of wary friendship preceded the onset of Cold War confrontation, but by 1947 all pretense of collaboration between the United States and the Soviet Union ceased, as their vital security interests collided over the issues surrounding the structure of post-World War II European politics.

In February 1946 Stalin gave a speech in which he spoke of "the inevitability of conflict with the capitalist powers. He urged the Soviet people not to be deluded that the end of the war meant that the nation could relax. Rather, intensified efforts were needed to strengthen and defend the homeland" (Lovell 1970). Shortly after this, George F. Kennan, then a U.S. diplomat in Moscow, sent to Washington his famous "long telegram" assessing the sources of Soviet conduct. Kennan's conclusions were ominous:

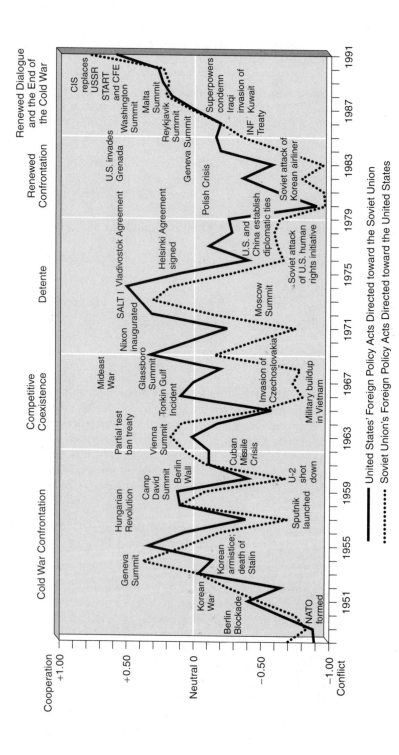

Figure 3.1 Soviet-American Relations, 1948–1991

Note: The index is the net proportion of cooperative acts and conflictual acts.

Source: Adapted from Edward E. Azar and Thomas J. Sloan, *Dimensions of Interaction* (Pittsburgh: Center for International Studies, 1973), and supplemented with data from the Conflict and Peace Data Bank. Data for 1966–1991 are from the World Event Interaction Survey, as compiled by Rodney G. Tomlinson.

"We have here a political force committed fanatically to the belief that with [the] U.S. there can be no permanent modus vivendi, that it is desirable and necessary that the internal harmony of our society be disrupted, our traditional way of life be destroyed, the international authority of our state be broken, if Soviet power is to be secure."

Kennan's ideas were circulated widely when, in 1947, the influential journal *Foreign Affairs* published his ideas in an anonymous article he signed "X." In it, Kennan argued that Soviet leaders would forever feel insecure about their political ability to maintain power against forces both within Soviet society and in the outside world. Their insecurity would lead to an activist—and perhaps aggressive—Soviet foreign policy. Yet it was within the power of the United States to increase the strain under which the Soviet leadership would have to operate, which eventually could lead to a gradual mellowing or final end of Soviet power. "In these circumstances" Kennan concluded, " it is clear that the main element of any United States policy toward the Soviet Union must be that of a long-term, patient but firm and vigilant *containment* of Russian expansive tendencies" (1947, emphasis added).

Not long after that, Harry Truman made this prescription the cornerstone of American postwar policy. Provoked in part by domestic turmoil in Turkey and Greece—which he and others believed to be communist inspired—Truman responded: "I believe that it must be the policy of the United States to support free peoples who are resisting attempted subjugation by armed minorities or by outside pressures."

Few declarations in American history were as powerful and important as this one, which eventually became known as the **Truman Doctrine**. "In a single sentence Truman had defined American policy for the next generation and beyond. Whenever and wherever an anti-Communist government was threatened, by indigenous insurgents, foreign invasion, or even diplomatic pressure . . . , the United States would supply political, economic, and, most of all, military aid" (Ambrose 1993)

Whether the policy of containment was appropriate, even at the time of its initial promulgation, remains controversial. Journalist Walter Lippmann wrote a series of articles in the New York *Herald Tribune*, later collected in a short book called *The Cold War* (1947), in which he argued that global containment would be costly for the United States, that it would militarize American foreign policy, and that eventually the United States would have to support any regime that professed anticommunism, regardless how distasteful it might be. Henry Wallace, a third-party candidate who opposed Harry Truman for the presidency, joined in Lippmann's concern when he warned of the dilemma the United States would eventually face: "Once America stands for opposition to change, we are lost. America will become the most hated nation in the world."

Lippmann's critique proved prophetic in all its details. Before the Cold War had run its course, the United States had spent trillions of dollars on national defense, had developed permanent peacetime military alliances circling the global, and had found itself supporting some of the most ruthless dictatorship in the world—in Argentina, Brazil, Cuba, the Dominican Republic, Guatemala, Greece, Haiti, Iran, Nicaragua, Paraguay, the Philippines, Portugal, South Korea, South Vietnam, Spain, and Taiwan—whose only shared characteristic was their opposition to communism. In the process America's revolutionary heritage as a beacon of liberty often was set aside as the nation found itself opposing social and political change elsewhere, choosing instead to preserve the status quo in the face of potentially disruptive revolutions.

George Kennan, too, became alarmed at the way he felt his celebrated statement was taken out of context and misinterpreted, so that "containment" became an "indestructible myth," a doctrine "which was then identified with the foreign policy of the Truman administration."

> I . . . naturally went to great lengths to disclaim the view, imputed to me by implication . . . that containment was a matter of stationing military forces around the Soviet borders and preventing any outbreak of Soviet military aggressiveness. I protested . . . against the implication that the Russians were aspiring to invade other areas and that the task of American policy was to prevent them from doing so. "The Russians don't want," I insisted, "to invade anyone. It is not in their tradition. They tried it once in Finland and got their fingers burned. They don't want war of any kind. Above all, they don't want the open responsibility that official invasion brings with it." (1967, 361)

As Kennan later lamented, "the image of a Stalinist Russia poised and yearning to attack the West, and deterred only by [America's] possession of atomic weapons, was largely a creation of the Western imagination." Cautioning against "demonizing the adversary, overestimating enemy strength and overmilitarizing the Western response" (Talbott 1990), Kennan recommended a political and economic rather than military approach to the containment of Soviet expansionism outside its existing sphere of influence. Despite that advice, the belief that defeating Soviet communism required a militantly confrontational approach became the guiding premise behind post-World War II American foreign policy.

The inability of the superpowers to maintain the sphere-of-influence posture tacitly agreed to earlier contributed to their propensity to interpret crises as the product of the other's program for global domination. When the Soviets moved into portions of eastern Europe, American leaders interpreted this as confirmation that they sought world conquest.

The Soviet Union, however, perhaps had reason to think that the Americans would readily accede to Soviet domination in eastern Europe. In 1945, for example, Secretary of State James Byrnes stated that the "Soviet Union has a right to friendly governments along its borders." Under Secretary of State Dean Acheson spoke of "a Monroe Doctrine for eastern Europe." These viewpoints and others implied in the Yalta agreements reinforced the Soviet belief that the western powers would accept the Soviets' need for a buffer zone in eastern Europe, which had been the common invasion route into Russia for more than three centuries. Hence, when the U.S. government began to challenge Soviet supremacy in eastern Germany and elsewhere in eastern Europe, the Soviet Union felt that previous understandings had been violated and that the West harbored "imperialist designs" (see also Focus 3.5).

A seemingly unending eruption of Cold War crises followed. Included were the Soviet refusal to withdraw troops from Iran in 1946, the communist coup d'état in Czechoslovakia in 1948, the Soviet blockade of West Berlin in June of that year, the communist acquisition of power on the Chinese mainland in 1949, the outbreak of the Korean War in 1950, the Chinese invasion of Tibet in 1950, and the on-again, off-again Taiwan Straits crises that followed. Hence the "war" was not simply "cold"; it became an embittered worldwide quarrel that threatened to escalate into open warfare, as the two powers positioned themselves to prevent the other from achieving preponderant power.

The United States enjoyed clear military superiority at the strategic level until 1949, for it alone possessed the ultimate "winning weapon" and the means to deliver it. This exerted a potent impact on American policy making (Herken 1982). The Soviets broke the American atomic monopoly that year, much sooner than American scientists and policymakers had anticipated. Thereafter, the Soviet quest for military equality and the superpowers' eventual relative strategic strengths influenced the entire range of their relations. As the distribution of world power became *bipolar*—with the United States and its allies comprising one pole, the Soviet Union and its allies the other—the character of superpower relations took on a different cast, sometimes more collaborative, sometimes more conflictual.

Europe, where the Cold War first erupted, was the focal point of the jockeying for influence. The principal European allies of the superpowers divided into the North Atlantic Treaty Organization (NATO) and the Warsaw Treaty Organization (WTO). These alliances became the cornerstones of the superpowers' external policies, as the European members of the Eastern and Western alliances willingly acceded to the leadership of their respective patrons.

To a lesser extent, alliance formation also enveloped states outside of Europe in the two giants' contest. The United States in particular sought to contain Soviet (and Chinese) influence on the Eurasian landmass by building a ring of pro-American allies on the very borders of the communist world. In return, the United States promised to protect its growing number of clients from external attack. Thus the Cold War extended across the entire globe.

In the rigid two-bloc system of the 1950s the superpowers talked as if war were imminent, but in deeds (especially after the Korean War) both acted cautiously. President Eisenhower and his secretary of state, John Foster Dulles, promised a "rollback" of the Iron Curtain and the "liberation" of the "captive nations" of Eastern Europe. They pledged to respond to aggression with "massive retaliation." And they criticized the allegedly "soft" and "reactive" Truman Doctrine, claiming to reject containment in favor of an ambitious "winning" strategy that would finally end the confrontation with godless communism. But communism was not rolled back in Eastern Europe, and containment was not replaced by a more assertive strategy. In 1956, for example, the United States failed to respond to Hungary's call for assistance in its revolt against Soviet control. American policymakers, despite their threatening language, promised more than they delivered. "'We can never rest,' Eisenhower swore in the 1952 presidential campaign, 'until the enslaved nations of the world have in the fullness of freedom the right to choose their own path.' But rest they did, except in their speeches" (Ambrose 1993).

Nikita Khrushchev assumed the top Soviet leadership position after Stalin's death in 1953. He claimed to accept "peaceful coexistence" with capitalism, and in 1955 the two superpowers met at the Geneva summit in a first, tentative step toward a mutual discussion of world problems. But the Soviet Union also continued, however cautiously, to exploit opportunities for advancing Soviet power wherever it perceived them to exist, as in Cuba in the early 1960s. Thus the period following Stalin's death was punctuated by a continuation of the crises and confrontations that had marked the earlier Cold War years. Now—in addition to Hungary—Cuba, Egypt, and Berlin became the flash points. In 1960 there was even a crisis resulting from the downing of an American U-2 spy plane deep over Soviet territory. Nuclear brinkmanship and massive retaliation were symptomatic of the strategies of containment through which the United States at this time hoped to balance Soviet power and perhaps force the Soviets into submission (see also Chapter 4).

Competitive Coexistence, 1962–1969 The Soviets' surreptitious placement of missiles in Cuba in 1962, the onset of the Vietnam War at about the same time, and the beginning of a seemingly unrestrained arms race cast a shadow over the possibility of superpower coexistence. The most serious test of the ability of the United States and the Soviet Union to avert catastrophe and to manage confrontation peacefully was the 1962 Cuban missile crisis—a "catalytic" event that transformed thinking about how the Cold War could be waged and expanded awareness of the suicidal consequences of a nuclear war. The superpowers stood eyeball to eyeball. Fortunately, one blinked.

At the American University commencement exercises in 1963, President Kennedy explained why tension reduction had become imperative and war could not be risked.

> Among the many traits the people of [the United States and the Soviet Union] have in common, none is stronger than our mutual abhorrence of war. Almost unique among the major world powers, we have never been at war with each other. . . .
>
> Today, should total war ever break out again—no matter how—our two countries would become the primary targets. It is an ironical but accurate fact that the two strongest powers are the two in the most danger of devastation. . . . We are both caught up in a vicious and dangerous cycle in which suspicion on one side breeds suspicion on the other and new weapons beget counterweapons.
>
> In short, both the United States and its allies, and the Soviet Union and its allies, have a mutually deep interest in a just and genuine peace and in halting the arms race. . . .
>
> So let us not be blind to our differences, but let us also direct attention to our common interests and to the means by which those differences can be resolved. And if we cannot end now our differences, at least we can help make the world safe for diversity.

Kennedy is also remembered for his clarion inaugural address two years earlier. "Let every nation know, whether it wishes us well or ill," he proclaimed, "that we shall pay any price, bear any burden, meet any hardship, support any friend, oppose any foe to assure the survival and the success of liberty." For some, the challenge was a renewal of America's Cold War challenge to the Soviet Union. For others, it was an expression of America's idealist heritage.[10] "Kennedy's eloquent peroration was the reverse of Palmerston's dictum, that Great Britain had no friends, only interests; America, in pursuit of liberty, had no interests, only friends" (Kissinger 1994a).

Kennedy's inaugural address defined an administration as resolutely anti-Soviet as its predecessors, but—especially following the crisis over missiles in Cuba—it began in both style and tone to depart from the confrontational tactics of the past. Thus competition for advantage and influence continued, but the preservation of the status quo was also tacitly accepted, as neither superpower was willing to launch a new war to secure new geostrategic gains. As the growing parity of American and Soviet military capabilities made coexistence or nonexistence the alternatives, finding ways to adjust their differences became compelling. This alleviated the danger posed by some issues and opened the door for new initiatives in other areas. For example, the Geneva (1955) and Camp David (1959) experiments in summit diplomacy set precedents for other tension-reduction activities. Installation of the "hot line," a direct communication link between the White House and the Kremlin, followed in 1963. So did the 1967 Glassboro summit and several negotiated agreements, including the 1963 Partial Test Ban Treaty, the 1967 Outer Space Treaty, and the 1968 Nuclear Nonproliferation Treaty. In addition, the United States tacitly accepted a divided Germany and Soviet hegemony in Eastern Europe (as illustrated by U.S. failure to respond forcefully to the Warsaw Pact invasion of Czechoslovakia in 1968).

Détente, 1969–1979   With the inauguration of Richard Nixon as president and the appointment of Henry Kissinger as his national security adviser, the United States tried a new approach toward containment, officially labeled *détente*. In Kissinger's words, détente sought to create "a vested interest in cooperation and restraint," "an environment in which competitors can regulate and restrain their differences and ultimately move from competition to cooperation." Several considerations prompted the new approach, including recognition that a nuclear attack would prove mutually suicidal, a growing sensitivity to the security requirements of both superpowers, and their shared concern for an increasingly powerful and assertive China.

To engineer the relaxation of superpower tensions, Nixon and Kissinger fashioned the *linkage theory*. Predicated on the expectation that the development of economic, political, and strategic ties between the United States and the Soviet Union would bind the two in a common fate, linkage would make superpower relations dependent on the continuation of mutually rewarding exchanges. In this way, linkage would lessen the superpowers' incentives for war. Linkage also made the entire range of Soviet-American relations interdependent, which made cooperation in one policy area (such as arms control) contingent on acceptable conduct in others (intervention outside traditional spheres of influence).

As both a goal of and a strategy for expanding the superpowers' mutual interest in restraint, détente symbolized an important shift in their global relationship. In diplomatic jargon, relations between the Soviets and Americans were "normalized," as the expectation of war receded. As a strategy of containment, on the other hand, the objective now was "self-containment on the part of the Russians" (Gelb 1976). "Détente did not mean global reconciliation with the Soviet Union. . . . Instead, détente implied the selective continuation of containment by economic and political inducement and at the price of accommodation through concessions that were more or less balanced" (Serfaty 1978). When in a position of superiority, the United States had practiced containment by coercion and force. From a new position of parity, containment was now practiced by seduction. Thus détente was "part of the Cold War, not an alternative to it" (Goodman, 1975).

Arms control stood at the center of the dialogue surrounding détente. The *Strategic Arms Limitation Talks (SALT)* became the test of détente's viability. Initiated in 1969, the SALT negotiations sought to restrain the threatening, expensive, and spiraling arms race. They produced two sets of agreements, the first in 1972

(SALT I) and the second in 1979 (SALT II). With their signing, each of the super-powers gained the principal objective it had sought in détente. The Soviet Union gained recognition of its status as the United States' coequal; the United States gained a commitment from the Soviet Union to moderate its quest for preeminent power in the world.

The SALT II agreement was not brought to fruition, however. It was signed but never ratified by the United States. The failure underscored the real differences that still separated the superpowers. By the end of the 1970s, détente had lost nearly all of its momentum and much of the hope it had symbolized only a few years earlier. During the SALT II treaty ratification hearings, the U.S. Senate expressed concern about an agreement with a rival that continued high levels of military spending, that sent arms to states outside its traditional sphere of influence (Algeria, Angola, Egypt, Ethiopia, Somalia, Syria, Vietnam, and elsewhere), and that stationed military forces in Cuba. These complaints all spoke to the persistence of Americans' deep-seated distrust of the Soviet Union and their understandable concern about Soviet intentions.

Renewed Confrontation, 1979–1985　The Soviet invasion of Afghanistan in 1979 ended the Senate's consideration of SALT II—and détente. "Soviet aggression in Afghanistan—unless checked—confronts all the world with the most serious strategic challenge since the Cold War began," declared President Jimmy Carter. In response the United States initiated a series of countermoves, including enunciation of the *Carter Doctrine* declaring the willingness of the United States to use military force to protect its interests in the Persian Gulf. Thus antagonism and hostility once more dominated Soviet-American relations. And once more the pursuit of power dominated the nation's strategy of containment as Eisenhower's tough talk, Kennedy's competi-tiveness, and even Truman's belligerence were rekindled. Before Afghanistan, Carter had embarked on a worldwide campaign for human rights, an initiative steeped in Wilsonian idealism that was directed as much toward the Soviet Union as others. This, too, now fell victim to the primacy of power over principle.

President Ronald Reagan and his Soviet counterparts delivered a barrage of con-frontational rhetoric reminiscent of that exchanged in the 1950s. Reagan asserted that the Soviet Union "underlies all the unrest that is going on" and, in a speech before the British parliament, implored the nations of the free world to join one another to pro-mote worldwide democracy. That clarion call not only reflected Wilsonian idealism and long-standing moralistic strains in American foreign policy. It also implied re-newal of the challenge to Soviet communism that British Prime Minister Winston Churchill launched in Fulton, Missouri, in 1946, declaring "an Iron Curtain has de-scended" across Europe, dividing East from West, and calling for the English-speak-ing nations to join together for the coming "trial of strength" with the communist world. Reagan policy adviser Richard Pipe's bold charge in 1981 that the Soviets would have to choose between "peacefully changing their Communist system . . . or going to war" punctuated the tense atmosphere.

In many respects the early 1980s were like the 1950s, as tough talk failed to be matched by aggressive action. But the first term of Reagan's administration did witness some match between words and deeds, resumption of the arms race being the most vis-ible example. The United States now placed a massive rearmament program above all other priorities, including domestic economic problems. American policymakers also spoke loosely about the "winnability" of a nuclear war through a "prevailing" military strategy which included the threat of a "first use" of nuclear weapons should a conventional war break out.

The superpowers also extended their confrontation to new territory, such as Central America, and renewed their public diplomacy (propaganda) efforts to extol the ascribed virtues of their respective systems throughout the world. A series of events punctuated the renewal of conflict.

- The Soviets destroyed Korean Airlines flight 007 in 1983.
- Shortly thereafter the United States invaded Grenada.
- Arms control talks then ruptured.
- The Soviets boycotted the 1984 Olympic Games in Los Angeles (in retaliation for the U.S. boycott of the 1980 Moscow Olympics).

The Reagan administration also embarked on a new program, the ***Reagan Doctrine***, which pledged U.S. support of anticommunist insurgents (euphemistically described as "freedom fighters") who sought to overthrow Soviet-supported governments in Afghanistan, Angola, and Nicaragua. The strategy "expressed the conviction that communism could be defeated, not merely contained." Thus "Reagan took Wilsonianism to its ultimate conclusion. America would not wait passively for free institutions to evolve, nor would it confine itself to resisting direct threats to its security. Instead, it would actively promote democracy" (Kissinger 1994a).

Understandably, relations between the United States and the Soviet Union were increasingly strained as the compound impact of these moves, countermoves, and rhetorical flourishes took their toll. The new Soviet leader, Mikhail Gorbachev, summarized the alarming state of superpower relations in the fall of 1985 by fretting that "The situation is very complex, very tense. I would even go so far as to say it is explosive."

The situation did not explode, however. Instead, the superpowers resumed their dialogue and laid the basis for a new phase in their relations.

Renewed Dialogue and the End of the Cold War, 1985–1991 Prospects for a more constructive phase improved measurably after Gorbachev assumed power in 1985. At first his goals were difficult to discern, but it soon became clear that Gorbachev felt it imperative for the Soviet Union to reconcile its differences with the capitalist West in order to have any chance of reversing the deterioration of its economy and international position. In his words, these goals dictated "the need for a fundamental break with many customary approaches to foreign policy." Shortly thereafter, he embarked on a road to domestic reform marked by political democratization and transition to a market economy. And he proclaimed the need for "new thinking" in foreign and defense policy to relax superpower tensions.

To carry out "new thinking," in 1986 Gorbachev abrogated the long-standing Soviet ideological commitment to aid national liberation movements struggling to overthrow capitalism. "It is inadmissible and futile to encourage revolution from abroad," he declared. He also for the first time embraced ***mutual security***, proclaiming that a diminution of the national security of one's adversary reduces one's own security. Soviet spokesperson Georgy Arbatov went as far as to tell the United States that "we are going to do a terrible thing to you—we are going to deprive you of an enemy."

Gorbachev acknowledged that the Soviet Union could no longer afford guns *and* butter. To reduce the financial burdens of defense and the dangers of an escalating strategic arms race, he offered unprecedented unilateral arms reductions. "We understand," Gorbachev lamented, "that the arms race . . . serves objectives whose essence is to exhaust the Soviet Union economically." Gorbachev then went even further, proclaiming his desire to end the Cold War altogether. "We realize that we are divided by profound historical, ideological, socioeconomic and cultural differences," Gorbachev noted during his first visit to the United States in 1987. "But the wisdom of politics today lies in not using those differences as a pretext for confrontation, enmity and the arms race."

The premises underlying the foreign policy strategy of containment appeared increasingly irrelevant in the context of these promising pronouncements and opportunities. As Strobe Talbott, later deputy secretary of state in the Clinton administration, put it, "Gorbachev's initiatives . . . made containment sound like such an anachronism that the need to move beyond it is self-evident" (Talbott 1990). Still, the premises of the past continued to exert a powerful grip on American foreign policy. Fears that Gorbachev's reforms might fail, that Gorbachev himself was an evil genius conning the West, or that his promises could not be trusted were uppermost in the minds of Ronald Reagan and, later, George Bush. "The Soviet Union," Bush warned in May 1989, had "promised a more cooperative relationship before—only to reverse course and return to militarism." Thus, although claiming in May 1989 its desire to move "beyond containment," the Bush administration did not abandon containment. Instead, it resurrected the linkage strategy by making U.S. cooperation contingent on continuing Soviet concessions and constructive practices.

Surprisingly, these demands were soon met. Soviet troops were withdrawn from Afghanistan in 1989. A year later the United States sought and received Soviet support for Operation Desert Shield, designed to reverse Iraqi dictator Saddam Hussein's military conquest of Kuwait. Gorbachev then announced that the Soviet Union would terminate its aid to and presence in Cuba, and he promised that it would liberalize its emigration policies and allow greater political and religious freedom.

The normalization of Soviet-American relations now moved rapidly apace.[11] The Cold War, which had begun in Europe and centered on Europe for forty-five years, ended there. All the communist governments in the Soviet "bloc" in Eastern Europe permitted democratic elections, in which Communist party candidates routinely lost. Capitalist free market principles also replaced socialism. To the surprise of nearly everyone, the Soviet Union acquiesced in these revolutionary changes. Without resistance, the Berlin Wall was dismantled, the Germanies united, and the Warsaw Pact ended. As these seismic changes shook the world, the Soviet Union itself sped its reforms to introduce democracy and a market economy, and eagerly sought cooperation with and economic assistance from the West.

The failed conservative coup against Gorbachev in August 1991 put the final nail in the coffin of Communist Party control in Moscow, the very heartland of the international communist movement. As communism was repudiated, a new age began. With communism in retreat everywhere, the face of world politics was transformed irrevocably, setting the stage for a post-containment American foreign policy.

The End of the Cold War: Competing Hypotheses

With the end of the Cold War the proposition that George Kennan advanced in his famous 1947 "X" article appeared prophetic. "The United States has it in its power," he wrote, "to increase enormously the strains under which Soviet policy must operate, to force upon the Kremlin a far greater degree of moderation and circumspection than it has had to observe in recent years, and in this way to promote tendencies which must eventually find their outlet in either the breakup of or the gradual mellowing of Soviet power." That was precisely what *did* happen—over forty years later.

Left unsettled, however, were the causes of this "victory" over communism. Did *militant* containment force the Soviet Union into submission? From this perspective nuclear weapons not only played a critical role in producing what historian John Gaddis (1986) has called "the long peace." The drive to produce them also may have helped to bankrupt the Soviet planned economy. In particular, the Reagan administration's "Star Wars" program—officially known as the Strategic Defense Initiative (SDI)—arguably convinced Gorbachev and his advisers that they could not compete with the United States (see Oberdorfer 1991). From this perspective *power* played a key role in causing the end of the Cold War (cf. Kegley 1994).

Or, instead, as Kennan maintained, did the Soviet leaders succumb to the inherent *political* weaknesses of their system, which left them unable to conduct an imperial policy abroad or retain communist control at home? What, in other words, made the Soviets more accommodating—America's intimidating military strength, or economic and political pressures?

Kennan's viewpoint is not entirely at variance with the "bankruptcy" thesis, but it does ask that we reconsider the role that ideology—*principle*—played in fomenting and perpetuating the Cold War. As we noted earlier, Soviet leaders were convinced that they were the vanguard of a socialist-communist movement that would ultimately prevail over the West. This provided the ideological framework within which the geostrategic conflict with the United States took place. Only when Soviet leaders themselves repudiated this framework—as Gorbachev did—was it possible to end the Cold War. From this perspective

> the West did not . . . win the Cold War through geopolitical containment and military deterrence. Still less was the Cold War won by the Reagan military buildup and the Reagan doctrine . . . . Instead, "victory" came when a new generation of Soviet leaders realized how badly their system at home and their policies abroad had failed. What containment did do was to preclude any temptations on the part of Moscow to advance Soviet hegemony by military means. . . . Because the Cold War rested on Marxist-Leninist assumptions of inevitable world conflict, only a Soviet leader could have ended it. And Gorbachev set out deliberately to do just that. (Garthoff 1994, 11–12; see also Porter 1992; but cf. Pipes 1995).

Just as historians have for decades debated the causes of the Cold War, explaining its demise has become a growth industry. The reasons are clear and compelling: If we can learn the causes of the Cold War's rise and demise, we will learn much about the role of power and principle, about ideals and self-interest, as the United States devises new strategies to confront the foreign policy challenges of the post-Cold War world. Clearly, however, a historical watershed had been crossed. For some this means, paradoxically, that the United States may now find that its "chief interest may lie in the survival and successful rehabilitation of the nation that was [its] principal adversary throughout [the Cold War] conflict" (Gaddis 1990). For others, however, the worry is that following resolution of the crisis produced by Russia's long-neglected domestic problems, which now demand retrenchment from foreign policy, Russia may again emerge as a superpower on the world stage. It stands at the heartland of Eurasia, a bridge between Europe and the Pacific Rim, with China and India to the south. And it remains a nuclear power. Already there are signs that the Russian Federation is flexing its muscle in its own "near abroad" (the former Soviet republics), the Balkans, and the Middle East. Thus the provocative prediction made by Alexis de Tocqueville about who will control the world's future retains its timeless intrigue.

The Goals of American Foreign Policy in the (Latest) New World Order

At the conclusion of the Gulf War with Iraq in 1991—prosecuted with Soviet acquiescence—George Bush again proclaimed that "we can see a new world coming into view. A world in which there is the very real prospect of a new world order. In the words of Winston Churchill, a world order in which 'the principles of justice and fair play protect the weak against the strong. . . . ' A world where the United Nations—freed from Cold War stalemate—is poised to fulfill the historic vision of its founders. A world in which freedom and respect for human rights find a home among all nations." The strains of Wilsonian ideals are clear.

Wilsonianism also implies American leadership in world affairs. Bush emphasized this dimension as well. "No, the United States should not seek to be the world's policeman," he declared. "But in the wake of the Cold War, in a world where we are the only remaining superpower, it is the role of the United States to marshal its moral and material resources to promote a democratic peace. It is our responsibility—it is our opportunity—to lead." Thus, as one scholar observed, the new world order Bush envisioned "contemplated American hegemony, but hegemony of a principled sort. Bush anticipated American dominance that would be both legitimate and, to some extent, welcomed by the global community" (Brilmayer 1994).

The vision of a new world order Bush offered punctuated once more the continuing appeal of Wilsonian idealism in American foreign policy. To be sure, power figured prominently in America's foreign policy during the Cold War. One advocate of realism reminds us of the Cold War reality this way:

> The liberal internationalists of the generation following [World War II], though self-styled Wilsonians for the most part, rejected Wilsonian means, as did, even more clearly, their conservative successors of the 1970s and 1980s. Among Cold War administrations, only the Carter administration made, for a time, the effort to break from the methods that otherwise prevailed in the long conflict with the Soviet Union. That effort visibly failed and was abruptly abandoned by a chastened president. (Tucker 1993–1994, 93–94)

This perspective is beyond reproach, for clearly power was the overriding element underlying the effort to contain Soviet communism in the decades following World War II—to the point that principles themselves were sometimes bastardized. Nonetheless, it is particularly telling that Henry Kissinger, himself an ardent realist, recounts in his book *Diplomacy* (1994a) how elements of the idealist paradigm punctuated the policies of presidents from Franklin Roosevelt to George Bush and informed the goals of the Clinton administration. Kissinger observed that by the end of the twentieth century, "Wilsonianism seemed triumphant. . . . For the third time in this century, America thus proclaimed its intention to build a new world order by applying its domestic values to the world at large."

Bill Clinton went to Washington on the strength of his domestic policy agenda. Often overlooked is that his foreign policy agenda was also quite ambitious—and, as Kissinger suggests, steeped in the Wilsonian tradition. Although Clinton stressed domestic issues, "there was scarcely any item on the wish-list of contemporary American internationalism—preventing aggression, stopping nuclear proliferation, vigorously promoting human rights and democracy, redressing the humanitarian disasters that normally attend civil wars—where Clinton promised a more modest U.S. role [than Bush]. On the contrary, the gravamen of the critique was that Bush had done too little, not too much" (Hendrickson 1994).

The Clinton agenda reflected the view that the end of the Cold War had not muted the challenges to America's enduring values and interests—peace and prosperity, stability and security, democracy and defense. On the contrary, the end of bipolar ideological, military, and political competition with Soviet communism opened a pandora's box of new challenges. Clinton detailed them in a September 1994 address to the United Nations:

> The dangers we face are less stark and more diffuse than those of the Cold War, but they are still formidable—the ethnic conflicts that drive millions from their homes; the despots ready to repress their own people or conquer their neighbors; the proliferation of weapons of mass destruction; the terrorists wielding their deadly arms; the criminal syndicates selling those arms or drugs or infiltrating the very institutions of a fragile democracy; a global economy that offers great promise but also deep insecurity and, in many places, declining opportunity; diseases like AIDS that threaten to decimate nations; the combined dangers of population explosion and economic decline . . . ; global and local environmental threats that demand that sustainable development becomes a part of the lives of people all around the world; and finally, within many of our nations, high rates of drug abuse and crime and family breakdown with all their terrible consequences. These are the dangers we face today.

Anthony Lake, Clinton's assistant for national security affairs, repeated and elaborated on those threats, urging *chaos* as a broader theme to the challenges now facing United States,[12] but casting it within the context of challenges to American liberty.

> In defeating fascism and prevailing over communism, we were defending an idea that comes under many names—democracy, liberty, civility, pluralism—but that has a constant face. It is the face of the tolerant society in which leaders and governments exist not to use or abuse people, but to provide them with freedom and opportunity to preserve individual human dignity. . . .

Today, those societies—from the fragile to the mature—remain under assault. Far from reaching the end of history, we are at the start of a new stage in this old struggle. This is not a clash of civilizations; rather, it is a contest that pits nations and individuals guided by openness, responsive government, and moderation against those animated by isolation, repression, and extremism.

Even as the administration positioned itself to exercise a leadership role in dealing with emerging challenges, it also defended formulas tested by years of Cold War combat. Thus James B. Steinberg, director of the State Department's policy planning staff, mixed neo-Wilsonianism and the logic of *realpolitik* in defending the strategy of deterrence as an approach to traditional security threats:

The end of the Cold War has not meant the end of leaders and states that will resort to aggression in pursuit of their interests. Consequently, while the nature of deterrence has changed, the need for it has not. While our preference always will be to integrate former adversaries into common security structures, just as we did with Germany and Japan after World War II, we also must sustain the will and capabilities to meet aggression and other threats.

Against this background of emergent challenges and persistent threats, the Clinton administration stressed three primary objectives for its foreign policy program: promoting democracy, promoting prosperity, and enhancing security.[13]

Promoting Democracy

For President Clinton and his advisers, no goal was more important than that of promoting democracy abroad. "In a new era of peril and opportunity," Clinton declared in a speech before the United Nations in September 1993, "our overriding purpose must be to expand and strengthen the world's community of market-based democracies." About the same time, Anthony Lake urged that "the successor to a doctrine of containment must be a strategy of enlargement—enlargement of the world's free community of market economies." He later defended the strategy as one "based on a belief that our most fundamental security interest lies in the expansion and consolidation of democratic and market reform."

The centrality of democratic promotion rested squarely on the belief that democracies are more peaceful than other types of political systems. This conviction is a bedrock of Wilsonian idealism which enjoys a long heritage, going back at least to Immanuel Kant's eighteenth-century treatise *Perpetual Peace*. Democracies are as willing and capable of waging war as others, but considerable scholarly inquiry demonstrates conclusively what Kant argued two centuries ago: that democracies do not engage in war with one another. Furthermore, democracies are more likely to use nonviolent forms of conflict resolution than others.[14] Thus Clinton and others in his administration would repeatedly defend the goal of democratic promotion with the observation that *democracies don't wage war on each other*. Indeed, "they . . . converted that proposition into a security policy manifesto. Given that democracies do not make war with each other, . . . the United States should seek to guarantee its security by promoting democracy abroad" (Carothers 1994a).[15]

Nowhere was the determination to promote democracy more evident than in Russia and the other *New Independent States* (former republics of the Union of Soviet Socialist Republics [USSR]). In the words of Secretary of State Warren Christopher, "Promoting democratic and market reform in Russia is the wisest and least expensive investment that we can make in America's security."

By conjoining democratic promotion with reform of former adversaries, Clinton embraced a timeworn foreign policy tradition. In each of four previous watersheds in America's response to victory in war—the Civil War, the Spanish-American War, and World Wars I and II—promotion of democracy among the vanquished became a distinctive American approach.

> When Wilson said he would "make the world safe for democracy," he was but repeating with a global perspective Abraham Lincoln's assertion in 1858 that this country could not live "half slave and half free." Roosevelt and Truman later echoed Wilson, first when they doubted that America could survive alone in a world dominated by fascism and, later, after 1945, when they attempted to promote democracy in Eastern Europe so as to block the expansionist aims of a hostile Soviet Union and . . . insisted that the democratization of Japan and Germany would be the primary aim of American occupation policy. (T. Smith, 1994c, 92–93).

Not surprisingly, the wisdom of aiding Russia in hopes of promoting democracy there did not go unchallenged. After the 1994 elections members of the new Republican-dominated Congress—already generally indisposed to foreign aid—became especially critical of continuing aid to Russia in light of the Yeltsin government's plans to sell nuclear power reactors to Iran and the Russian army's rain of destruction on the independence-minded republic of Chechnya. Moreover, as U.S.-Russian relations cooled, fear that democratic reforms in Russia would fall by the wayside further damped enthusiasm for continuing aid to Russia.

The foreign policy goal of promoting democracy raises other concerns. One is whether democracy can thrive in the absence of *economic liberalism* (that is, the existence or development of market economies). Because the correlation between democracy and economic liberalism in the United States is clear, the question is whether the former can exist without the latter (Gurr 1991).[16] If not, the latest wave of democratization (Huntington 1991) may fall victim to the more difficult task of promoting market economies where none existed previously (Huntington 1992–1993), notably in Russia and the other New Independent States but also throughout much of Eastern Europe and the Global South (the less developed world).

A second question raised by the goal of democratic promotion is whether it is consistent with other foreign policy objectives. Not all countries are equally capable of sustaining stable democracy, and not all are equally important to the United States. Therefore, a successful foreign policy strategy of democratic promotion requires selecting some countries for attention while ignoring others, including some with authoritarian regimes. Otherwise, America's resources and patience are likely to be tested, perhaps exhausted (Fukuyama 1992). Furthermore, there are instances, as in the Middle East, where the United States has no choice but to overlook the absence of democracy. There, concern for stability and security to ensure access to oil necessarily takes precedence over democratic promotion.

It is instructive at this point to return for a moment to the Cold War era, when the United States also sought to promote democracy but frequently found that it had to make trade-offs between its strategic interests—stopping communist expansion—and its idealist heritage—promoting liberty. By taking a militant, antirevolutionary position, the United States repeatedly found itself on the side of the oppressors and against the people or, in other words, against local nationalism.

President Kennedy explained this antirevolutionary instinct when he commented on the situation the United States faced in the Dominican Republic after the assassination of Dominican dictator Rafael Trujillo: "There are three possibilities in descending order of preference: a decent democratic regime, a continuation of the Trujillo regime [a dictatorship] or a Castro regime [a communist government]. We ought to aim at the first, but we really can't renounce the second until we are sure that we can avoid the third." Elsewhere that dilemma led the United States to support Fulgencio Batista and end up with Fidel Castro (Cuba); to support Ngo Dinh Diem and Nguyen Van Thieu and get Ho Chi Minh and his successors (Vietnam); and to support the Shah and be confronted with the Ayatollah Khomeini (Iran).

The United States' choices today are clearly different from those of the Cold War era, but trade-offs still have to be made. And, as ethnic conflict bubbles and spreads, choosing sides remains contentious and difficult—as the explosive situation in the Balkans so rudely reminded. The Clinton administration professed to be aware of the difficulties democratic promotion poses. Commenting on the choices faced in Russia, for example, Anthony Lake averred that "We are not starry-eyed about the prospects for spreading democracy; it will not soon take hold everywhere." Similarly, Secretary of State Christopher cautioned that "We know that Russia cannot overcome the Soviet legacy overnight. . . . We must be realistic in our expectations, steady in our support for reform, and unequivocal in our opposition to the enemies of reform." It is nonetheless clear that the choices the United States now faces as it seeks to promote democracy abroad are no less vexing and complex than those of the Cold War. Despite this, the democratic bedrock informed virtually all of the Clinton administration's foreign policy goals and the means chosen to realize them.

Promoting Prosperity

The themes of peace and prosperity derived from a focus on democracy are virtually indistinguishable from the economic agenda that motivated Clinton's drive for the White House, including domestic economic rejuvenation, enhanced competitiveness in foreign markets, and the promotion of sustainable development in the Global South (see Focus 3.6). Under Secretary of the Treasury Lawrence H. Summers highlighted the intersection of these enduring values and American foreign policy interests when he observed that "the two key pillars of any viable foreign policy are the maintenance of security and the maintenance of prosperity." Meanwhile, the Commerce Department (normally a backwater in the foreign affairs government) brimmed with activity as it sought to return the United States to an era when "the business of America is business"(Stremlau 1994–1995; see also note 7). Even the State Department shed some of its traditional aversion to commercial diplomacy. "For a long time secretaries

Focus 3.6
AMERICAN FOREIGN ECONOMIC POLICY GOALS IN THE POST-COLD WAR WORLD ORDER

• • •

In today's world . . . [t]he first priority of our foreign policy . . . is the economic security of the American people.

Our first goal is to get our own economic house in order. More than anything else, this is the most important contribution we can make to a healthy international economy and to the American people. . . .

The second major goal of our foreign economic policy is to open markets around the world, working at all three levels: global, regional, and bilateral. We intend to open up new worlds of opportunity for our businesses overseas. . . .

Our third major goal is to help build a solid economic foundation to support the world's new democracies. . . . Our goal is to help them succeed and, beyond that, to help integrate them into the world economy and the community of free nations. . . .

Our fourth goal is to promote sustainable and broad-based growth in the developing world. . . .

Our fifth goal is to improve coordination among the world's economies and modernize the 'architecture' that ties the world economy together.

—Joan E. Spero, Under Secretary of State for Economic, Business and Agricultural Affairs, September 1994

of state thought of economics as 'low policy,' while they dealt only with high science like arms control," averred Secretary of State Warren Christopher. "I make no apologies for putting economics at the top of our foreign-policy agenda."

Clinton's foreign economic agenda had several visible expressions, including: Nafta, the North American Free Trade Agreement linking the United States, Canada, and Mexico in a free trade zone; renewal of GATT, the General Agreement on Tariffs and Trade, which included provisions for a new World Trade Organization; and tough bilateral negotiating postures toward China, Japan, and the European Union on trade issues of particular salience to the United States. The common thread linking all of these initiatives was a concern for the United States' changing position in the world political economy. We will therefore give detailed attention to the goals and instruments of Clinton's foreign economic policy in Chapter 7, where we probe the opportunities and contraints the United States now faces in an interdependent world.

Enhancing Security

The disintegration of the Soviet Union and the end of Cold War competition have altered radically the security environment the United States faces. How best to adjust to those changes is now a contentious issue on the national political agenda. The Clinton administration's rhetoric revealed that it saw the challenges to the United States to be as great today as ever. Links with past patterns of American foreign policy, are clearly evident. These include a belief in the United States' special responsibility in the world, which requires both military might and interventionist means. As Clinton noted in early 1993, for example, "Our national security is . . . linked to helping prevent or resolve conflicts that can grow out of ethnic, regional, or religious tensions throughout the world." Little has changed, it seems.

But the shape of American military forces has changed. "Downsizing" and "defense conversion" have permeated national defense discussions during much of the 1990s. Hundreds of military bases at home and abroad have been closed, tens of thousands of people whose livelihood depended on military spending have lost their jobs or been forced to change them, the size of the uniformed military services has shrunk measurably, and the deadly conventional and nuclear arsenals built by the Cold War adversaries have been drastically reduced.

The Bush administration began rethinking the roles and missions of U.S. conventional and strategic (nuclear) forces in the post-Cold War world. Clinton promised to continue the reassessment with a complete review of all aspects of American military policy. That process was completed midway through his presidency. However, as we will examine in more detail in Chapter 4, neither the "bottom-up" review of conventional forces nor the "national posture review" of nuclear forces revealed marked departures from patterns already set in motion. Indeed, one (anonymous) nuclear policy official remarked at the conclusion of Clinton's review of nuclear policy in the fall of 1994 that "The clay of history is beginning to harden again."

History also dictated some of the enduring national security issues with which the Clinton administration would have to contend. The continuing challenges posed by Iran and Iraq and the sometimes related issue of nuclear proliferation were among those to which the Clinton administration assigned priority. Both are intimately tied to the enduring values and interests captured in the terms "stability" and "security."

Low-Intensity Conflict and Neo-Containment

When Anthony Lake talked of the "enemies of the tolerant society"—"extreme nationalists and tribalists, terrorists, organized criminals, coup plotters, rogue states"—he described threats that, collectively, were once encompassed under the concept *low-intensity conflict*: violence and warfare that falls short of full-scale conventional combat or nuclear confrontation. Ethnic conflict in Bosnia, tribal warfare in Rwanda and Somalia, instability in Russia's "near abroad," terrorism in Argentina and the Gaza strip, anarchy in Sierre Leone, drug trafficking in South and Central America—all are examples of the challenges and often bloody consequences of low-intensity conflict. Economic sanctions and various forms of military intervention are sometimes used to cope with such threats and to contain their contagion (see Barnet 1990). Most challenges posed by low-intensity conflict occur within rather than between nations, however, which limits the capacity of traditional foreign policy instruments to affect outcomes—and may help explain the Clinton administration's checkered record of dealing with them. Indeed, critics note that the connection between civil wars and the democratic peace is unclear, yet the pursuit of democratic promotion as security policy implies greater American involvement in conflicts where promoting democracy may not reduce violence (Carothers 1994a).

Iran and Iraq were thought to pose more traditional threats. To deal with the so-called "rogue" or "backlash states," the administration proposed a policy of "dual containment." Using language strikingly reminiscent of Kennan's famous "X" article, in which he called for containment of the Soviet Union, Lake (1994), also writing in *Foreign Affairs*, urged that "the United States has a special responsibility for developing a strategy to neutralize, contain and, through selective pressure, perhaps eventually transform these backlash states into constructive members of the international community." In apparent reference to the policies of both the Reagan and Bush administrations, which "tilted" toward Iraq in its long war with Iran, Lake described the Clinton project in the language of realism:

> Today both regimes pursue policies hostile to our interests. Building up one to counter the other is therefore rejected in favor of a policy of "dual containment." In adopting this approach, we are not oblivious to the need for a balance of power in this vital region. Rather, we seek with our regional allies to maintain a favorable balance without depending on either Iraq or Iran. . . . This is not a crusade, but a genuine and responsible effort, over time, to protect American strategic interests, stabilize the international system and enlarge the community of nations committed to democracy, free markets and peace. (Lake 1994, 48, 55)

Although dual containment built on the principles of *realpolitik*, critics worried that the policy might be self-defeating by forcing two states with a history of hostility toward each other into greater cooperation. Some also saw as seriously flawed "the unstated assumption that the regional status quo in the gulf can be maintained over the coming years, and that any changes there can be stage-managed by Washington" (Gause 1994). Dual containment nonetheless built on policies that have long guided U.S. Middle East policy, going back to the early Cold War years, if not before—namely, guaranteeing a continuing flow of oil to the world at reasonable prices and keeping other powers from supplanting American dominance in the region. The growing perception of a challenge from Islamic fundamentalism, much emanating from Southwest Asia, a fault line in what Samuel Huntington (1993a) calls a coming "clash of civilizations," adds a renewed sense of urgency to these long-standing goals. A noteworthy example is the testimony of Joseph P. Hoar, the Marine Corps general who oversaw planning and operations in the Persian Gulf region. Only a few months before the Clinton administration found it necessary to send thousands more combat troops to the Persian Gulf region in October 1994, General Hoar observed, "The likelihood remains high that the Central Command [the U.S. force responsible for rapid deployment to meet crisis situations] will be called on to respond to additional regional crises within the next decade."

Nonproliferation

No security goal figured more prominently on the Clinton agenda than stopping the spread of weapons of mass destruction—nuclear, chemical, and biological—and the ballistic missile technology that might carry them.

The United States has long been a chief advocate of the ***nuclear nonproliferation regime*** centered on the 1968 nuclear Non-Proliferation Treaty (NPT), to which nearly all nations have since subscribed. (The United States also supports controls on chemical weapons, as we note in Chapter 4.) The regime seeks to inhibit the spread of weapons technology by permitting now-nuclear states to share their knowledge of peaceful atomic energy uses with nonnuclear states at the same time that they are prevented from sharing technology related to weapons production. Export controls on the sale of existing technology to potential buyers are a crucial element of the regime. A primary objective is to permit less developed countries to have access to commercial nuclear-power plants without allowing their by-products to be funneled into bombs. The International Atomic Energy Agency (IAEA) is charged with ensuring application of the NPT regime. As a practical matter, its efforts have been devoted to ensuring that nuclear materials and their by-products, designed in the first instance for the production of electricity, are not diverted to weapons production.

Evidence suggests that North Korea—-and Iraq before it—came close to producing nuclear bombs not by diverting materials from peaceful purposes to weapons production but by building their own nuclear infrastructures, much like the United States did when it first built atomic weapons in the 1940s. The existing nonproliferation regime, with IAEA as its enforcement arm, cannot cope with this kind of proliferation, for which it was never designed. Furthermore, other states—principally Pakistan and Iraq—have proven their ability to acquire weapons technology by simply buying it on the open market. Germany and France are among those that have sold weapons-grade technology, and China has been a frequent supplier of nuclear knowledge to Iran, among others. The nonproliferation issue has acquired special urgency with the collapse of the Soviet Union and with the prospect of weapons-grade material and nuclear scientists finding their way to Global South countries eager to import them.

Today, the United States, the former Soviet Union, including Russia, Belarus, Kazakhstan, and Ukraine; Britain; and France have nuclear weapons and (with the exception of Britain) the capacity to deliver them with intercontinental missiles (see Figure 3.2). India, Israel, and Pakistan could easily assembly nuclear weapons, and several other states are plausible entrants into the once-exclusive nuclear club. Precluding their entry was a Clinton administration priority, which included a determined (and successful) effort to extend the NPT regime indefinitely when it came up for renewal in 1995.

North Korea's drive to obtain the bomb boldly challenged Clinton's priorities. In 1994 Defense Secretary Perry and others implied that nothing short of military action would blunt the forward momentum of the "rogue" state's weapons program, in violation of the nonproliferation treaty to which it is a signatory. Thus the United States positioned itself to engage in "***counterproliferation***," an ambiguous yet threatening concept with origins in the Bush administration's post-Persian Gulf thinking about the Pentagon's future mission. Counterproliferation, at least as first proffered by the Clinton administration, implied that "the United States intended to establish itself as global judge, jury, and executioner against weapons of mass destruction" (Müller and Reiss 1995; see also Pilat and Kirchner 1995).

A military crisis with North Korea was eventually averted, but at great cost to the United States. In a carefully crafted agreement, the United States, with the support of Japan and South Korea, agreed to supply North Korea with two new, proliferation-re-

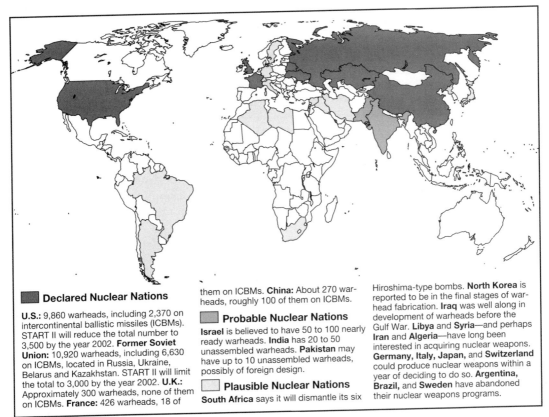

Declared Nuclear Nations

U.S.: 9,860 warheads, including 2,370 on intercontinental ballistic missiles (ICBMs). START II will reduce the total number to 3,500 by the year 2002. **Former Soviet Union:** 10,920 warheads, including 6,630 on ICBMs, located in Russia, Ukraine, Belarus and Kazakhstan. START II will limit the total to 3,000 by the year 2002. **U.K.:** Approximately 300 warheads, none of them on ICBMs. **France:** 426 warheads, 18 of

them on ICBMs. **China:** About 270 warheads, roughly 100 of them on ICBMs.

Probable Nuclear Nations

Israel is believed to have 50 to 100 nearly ready warheads. **Pakistan** may have up to 10 unassembled warheads, possibly of foreign design.

Plausible Nuclear Nations

South Africa says it will dismantle its six

Hiroshima-type bombs. **North Korea** is reported to be in the final stages of warhead fabrication. **Iraq** was well along in development of warheads before the Gulf War. **Libya** and **Syria**—and perhaps **Iran** and **Algeria**—have long been interested in acquiring nuclear weapons. **Germany, Italy, Japan,** and **Switzerland** could produce nuclear weapons within a year of deciding to do so. **Argentina, Brazil,** and **Sweden** have abandoned their nuclear weapons programs.

Figure 3.2 Proven, Possible, and Potential Entrants to the Nuclear Club
Source: Philip Morrison, Kosta Tsipis, and Jerome Wiesner, "The Future of American Defense," *Scientific American* 270 (February 1994): 40–41.

sistant nuclear reactors (plus enormous amounts of oil), in return for which North Korea would dismantle its nuclear facilities—but without guaranteed IAEA inspections for at least some time.

If the Clinton project with North Korea works, it will have fulfilled a principal foreign policy aim. Even it does succeed, however, critics argue that the NPT regime itself loses.

> Critics of the agreement say it encourages rogue states from Iraq and Iran to Pakistan to keep alive their dreams of a bomb of their own. The United States . . . agreed to reward a country for obeying a treaty it signed years ago . . . intended to contain the spread of nuclear weapons. Simply by threatening to withdraw from that treaty, [North Korea] . . . won $4 billion in reactors, billions in fuel oil and an end to the trade restrictions that . . . contributed so much to its isolation. The International Atomic Energy Agency feigned enthusiasm, but many of its officials said the concession on delaying an inspection for years would soon come back to haunt them. (Sanger 1994, E3)

Against this background, one critic asserted that "the spread of nuclear weapons and the means to deliver them has already advanced so far that the important question is no longer how to stop their proliferation, but rather how to prevent them from being used" (Cropsey 1994). Thus the elusive goal of nuclear nonproliferation increasingly appears to be beyond reach.

Multilateralism

The crisis with North Korea was ended but only with the participation and support of other nations. Similarly, dual containment was premised (but did not depend) on support from American allies. A preference for "multilateralism" was evident elsewhere as well.

Even before his inauguration, Clinton emphasized a determination to work through the United Nations and other international institutions "to resolve contentious disputes and to meet the challenges of the next century." Linking that pledge to the domestic economic considerations that had been the focus of his campaign, he declared that "America cannot and should not bear the world's burdens alone." "Assertive multilateralism," a phrase sometimes used by UN Ambassador Madeleine K. Albright, was also embraced. "There will be many occasions when we need to bring pressure to bear on the belligerents of the post-Cold War period and use our influence to prevent ethnic and other regional conflicts from erupting," Albright observed. "But usually we will not want to act alone." The implication is that the United Nations might now aggressively pursue "peace enforcement," not simply "peacekeeping," as in the past.

In May 1993, after reducing U.S. forces first placed in Somalia by the Bush administration to 5,000 troops, the Clinton administration willingly transferred control of Operation Restore Hope to the United Nations. Shortly after that, Under Secretary of State Peter Tarnoff stressed that, with rare exceptions, the U.S. would always proceed multilaterally: "We simply don't have the leverage, we don't have the influence, we don't have the inclination to use force and we certainly don't have the money to bring to bear the kind of pressure that will produce positive results any time soon." Secretary of State Christopher, among others, was quick to distance himself from the "Tarnoff Doctrine." Later he sought to parry critics of the administration's seeming reliance on collective action, correctly arguing that "multilateralism is a means, not an end. It is one of the many foreign policy tools at our disposal. And it is warranted only when it serves the central purpose of American foreign policy: to protect American interests." Thus collective action "can advance American foreign policy interests," but it "requires—and cannot replace—American leadership."

The Clinton administration's early preference for multilateralism finds a parallel in the early Truman years. The United States at that time sought to build a liberal multilateral system that would have obviated the need for a direct and continuing American political or military involvement in Europe (see Kissinger 1994a). "One world" based on the principles of collective security and economic universalism was sought (see also Chapter 7). "The system, once constituted, was envisaged to be self-regulating. Given American economic size and competitiveness, this global open door would both serve its own interests and resonate with time-honored American liberal ideas of politics and economics" (Ikenberry 1989). The objective failed as Soviet-American hostility grew and Europe failed to coalesce into a "third force" in an emerging multipolar international system (Ikenberry 1989; see also Gardner 1969). Instead, the United States made a direct military commitment to Europe (in the form of NATO), which continues even today.

Like Truman, Clinton's embrace of multilateralism was comparatively short-lived (although for different reasons). The administration did seek UN authorization in August 1994 for the use of force to oust Haiti's military leaders in an effort to restore democracy there. In doing so it arguably abandoned the Monroe Doctrine, one of the nation's most cherished proclamations, in which the United States claimed for itself the right to protect the Western Hemisphere from foreign encroachment (see also G. Smith 1994). Although the Clinton administration continued to speak of the central-ity of the United Nations in its foreign policy, in practice it moved away from its ear-lier embrace of multilateralism—particularly as it applied to collective security seem-ingly so successful in the Persian Gulf only a short time earlier (see Russett and Sutterlin 1991).[17] After a shootout in Somalia that claimed eighteen American lives, the administration devised a new policy with rules so stringent as to severely limit fu-ture American participation in UN operations. The United States now would be more selective in its support of UN peacekeeping and peace enforcement operations so as to make them "a more effective instrument of collective security."[18] In practice, the United States would exercise increasing caution about the new interventionism on be-half of humanitarian values that had become identified with collective security in the wake of the Persian Gulf War (see Chapter 4).

Clinton was tentative on the issue of NATO's future as well. Although the admin-istration's Partnership for Peace was promoted with considerable fanfare, it stopped short of extending full alliance membership to the post-Soviet states and those in Eastern Europe, as once contemplated, apparently out of fear of provoking a hostile Russian reaction. Thus efforts to transform NATO from a collective defense arrange-ment into a collective security system fell short (see also Chapter 6).

On other issues Clinton's policies looked decidedly more unilateral than multilat-eral. As the administration sought to blunt North Korea's nuclear challenge, for ex-ample, critics charged that neither the administration's preference for force nor eco-nomic pressure enjoyed the support of other Asian powers. "As always, the administration seemed caught between the embrace of an ambitious objective and the imperatives of multilateralism. It could not retreat without exposing itself to the ridicule of the hawks [who supported the use of force against North Korea if it ac-quired nuclear weapons]. It could not advance without seriously compromising its re-lations with China, Japan, and possibly South Korea" (Hendrickson 1994). Later, when an agreement was reached with North Korea that defused the crisis, Congress's new-found Republican majority saw fit to raise questions about its efficacy.

The retreat from multilateralism—a key instrumentality of Wilsonian idealism—was only one of many foreign policy setbacks suffered during Clinton's first two years in office. By January 1995, when the Republicans for the first time in forty years seized control of Congress, Clinton could claim some foreign policy successes, but the over-all record remained checkered. Were Clinton and his foreign policy team to blame? Or was it the absence of a common enemy and the dissipation of the anti-communist ideology of the Cold War era, previously used to rally domestic support for global ac-tivism? Or a rejection by the American people of the burdens of neo-Wilsonianism in the face of more compelling domestic demands? Or was the post-Cold War world indeed more complex, confusing, and dangerous—"a more lethal version of the world that existed before 1914," in the words of Clinton's first CIA director, R. James Woolsey? Compared with the slain dragon of Soviet communism, Woolsey warned, "We live now in a jungle filled with a bewildering variety of poisonous snakes, and in many ways the dragon was easier to keep track of." We will address these questions and viewpoints more fully in later chapters. Here we conclude with a brief commentary on the domestic context in which the goals of post-Cold War American foreign policy must be formulated and sustained.

Without Consensus: Charting Uncharted Waters ....

If the 1914 analogy is appropriate to the dangers now facing the United States,[19] the 1920s arguably mirror the domestic political environment in which policymakers must forge support for the goals of post-Cold War American foreign policy. Anthony Lake again, speaking before the Council on Foreign Relations in September 1994: "Today . . . we must seek to be as creative and constructive . . . as the generation of the late 1940s. . . . But we must do it in the domestic circumstances not of the 1940s but of the 1920s, when there was no single, foreign threat against which to rally public opinion and head off the destructive isolationism that followed."

As the Bush administration neared what would be its final year, Deputy Secretary of State Lawrence S. Eagleburger observed that "What is peculiar to the United States is that every generation or so we debate not only the merits of this or that policy, but the existential purpose of American foreign policy itself. Such a debate would be almost unthinkable in most other countries, where foreign policy is deemed to serve national interests, which themselves are seen as timeless and immutable." But in the United States, "we have tended to believe that our foreign policy must serve a moral purpose."

Idealists have long claimed that Wilsonianism did not fail; instead, it was simply never tried. Now, with Wilsonianism apparently triumphant, its principles finally may be put to the test. Or will they?

Today, no single moral purpose, including democratic promotion, has emerged to galvanize the American polity toward global involvement in the way anticommunism and anti-Sovietism did. As Leslie Gelb, president of the prestigious Council on Foreign Relations, has observed, "Americans will not embark on a new crusade to make the world safe for democracy and free markets. These aims are worthy. But most Americans now understand that democracy is a state of grace not readily attained and not within their power to impose. Nor are they eager to expend lives and treasure to transform sinkholes into free enterprise paradises. Americans also understand that lofty goals do not help us decide what to do in Somalia, Eastern Europe, Haiti, Bosnia, or the Persian Gulf" (Gelb 1994).

This does not mean that Americans now prefer isolationism over internationalism. As one scholar observed, "The public does not favor withdrawal from the world and in fact accepts the high degree of economic and political interdependence that has taken place over the past decades. Rather, it simply believes that the disappearance of a serious military threat requires a major reallocation of priorities. To call this isolationist is to misunderstand both its cause and extent" (Steel 1994; see also Chapter 8). As in the 1920s, then, "a relief from the burdens that international engagement brings" (Mandelbaum 1994) again animates large numbers of Americans. At the same time, however, the purpose and direction of American policy remain uncertain.

Faced with uncertainty, the past continues to shape the future. Gelb again, commenting now on the continuing hold of Cold War thinking on American foreign policy:

> Though the Soviet Union lies in ashes, we almost expect and plan for the emergence of a new Russian empire. Though Germany has evolved as one of the most stable democracies in the world, we secretly dread its reversion to authoritarianism and militarism. Though the United States has never before been as entangled in the world as it is today, we fear its return to isolationism. Most policy experts still lean on the central strategy of the Cold War: keep the Russians out, the Americans in, and the Germans down. Only, we want to execute this strategy on the cheap, at bargain basement prices. (Gelb 1994, 2; see also Mead 1994)

Although Gelb is not alone in disagreeing with such Cold War thinking, others are less certain. Zbigniew Brzezinski (1994), a political realist and national security adviser to Jimmy Carter, for example, worries about Russia's "imperial impulse" and warns that "Russia can be either an empire or a democracy, but it cannot be both." Too warm a democratic embrace of Russia without sensitivity to a "constructive geopolitical framework" could be detrimental to the United States, he argues. In a similar vein, others maintain that a Ukraine with nuclear capability would be in American interests (Mearsheimer 1993; but cf. Miller 1993) at the same time that they worry about a potential nuclear Germany (Mearsheimer 1990a). The Ukrainian case argues against an American nonproliferation policy designed to denuclearize all of the former Soviet states except Russia. The German case argues for a continued American military presence in Europe.

Thus the debate between realists and idealists, between power and principle, continues. It is as old as the republic itself, dating to the contest between Hamilton and Jefferson over which vision of national greatness would animate the nation's foreign policy in the new millennium. Debate about the strategy that best serves American national interests—internationalism or isolationism—also continues, Thus contention about the appropriate role of the United States in world affairs, which has energized American foreign policy throughout its history, again marks its entry into a new millennium.

NOTES

1. The classic statements of realism as an explicit theory can be found in Carr (1939), Kennan (1954), Morgenthau (1985), Niebuhr (1947), and Thompson (1960). Classical realism today is challenged by "neorealism," or "structural realism." This variant of realism focuses not on humankind's innate lust for power—a central construct in classical realism—but instead on states' drive for security in an anarchical world which causes them to behave in similar ways, resulting in efforts to secure power for survival. In this chapter we build primarily on classical realism as we focus on the contest of ideas about international politics as it has informed American foreign

policy. In Chapter 6 we will draw on structural (neo)realism to explain how the external environment now and in the past informs our understanding of American foreign policy. For critical discussions of both classical and structural (neo)realism, see Kegley (1994), Keohane (1986a), Mansbach and Vasquez (1981), Smith (1987), Vasquez (1983), and Waltz (1979).

2. The discussion of the Jefferson and Hamilton models for coping with the challenges the new Americans faced draws on Hunt (1987), especially pages 22–28.

3. Nearly a hundred years later the press would be credited with (held responsible for?) similarly stimulating U.S. intervention into Somalia (see Chapter 9).

4. Just as Wilson is regarded as the father of internationalism, Thomas Jefferson is regarded as one of the fathers of isolationism. Still, the two shared an important viewpoint on the morality of individuals and the state:

> Both utterly rejected in principle the traditions of European diplomacy, at the core of which was reason of state with its claim that statecraft made up an autonomous realm governed by its own rules. "We are at the beginning of an age," Wilson declared in his war message to Congress, "in which it will be insisted that the same standards of conduct and of responsibility for wrong done shall be observed among nations and their governments that are observed among the individual citizens of civilized states." (Tucker 1993–1994, 84–85)

5. "Legalism" is often treated with moral idealism as characteristic of the American world view (Kennan 1951). Its manifestations are the tendencies of American leaders to justify foreign policy actions by citing legal precedents, to assume that disputes necessarily involve legal principles, to rely on legal reasoning to define the limits of permissible behavior for states, and to seek legal remedies for conflicts. Thus, when confronted with a policy predicament, American policymakers are prone to ask not "What alternative best serves the national interest?" but instead, "What is the legal thing to do?"

6. Herman M. Schwartz (1994) argues that U.S. international economic policy in the 1920s and 1930s was deadlocked by two domestic economic groups, "nationalists," who were oriented toward the domestic market, and "internationalists," who, while also oriented toward the domestic market, were competitive in the international marketplace. The inability of either group to achieve dominance made U.S. efforts to realize a larger international role "only hesitant and erratic." After World War II the United States shifted its policy toward leadership, in part because the nationalists shifted their own calculation. Policy also shifted, Schwartz argues, because of the emergence of a third, small but influential group, "security internationalists." Fervently anticommunist and supporters of expanded military spending, the security internationalists joined other internationalists in favoring an expanded overseas presence, but like the nationalists, they feared strong labor unions at home. "This emerging third group resolved the old prewar deadlock, for now two groups could line up along a common axis of interests against the remaining group."

7. The popular aphorism (coined by Calvin Coolidge) that "the business of America is business" captures the belief that American foreign policy is often dominated by business interests and capitalistic impulses. While that view, typically ascribed to "revisionists" (see, e.g., Kolko 1969, Magdoff 1969, and Williams 1972 and 1980) was once popular, others dispute its veracity. Political scientist Ronald Steel (1994), for example, categorically asserts that "It is simply not possible to explain U.S. foreign policy in essentially economic terms. The oscillation between isolation and intervention, the persistent emphasis on morality, the obsession with freedom and democracy, the relentless proselytization cannot be stuffed into an economic straight-

jacket. American foreign policy may often be naive or hypocritical, but it cannot be confined to a balance sheet." See also Garthoff (1994).

Economic revisionism, which is referred to here, is not to be confused with other revisionist accounts that address the expansionist tendencies of the United States. Economic revisionists see the United States expanding in search of world markets for the surpluses of capitalism, whereas the diplomatic revisionist school sees the creation of an American imperium as the product of the American pursuit of national power or of its quest to impose its political system on others. For discussions of empire as a component of America's efforts to achieve political, not economic, preeminence, see Blachman and Puchala (1991), Hoffmann (1978), Liska (1978), and Lundestad (1990).

8. Realist critics warn of the dangers of a foreign policy rooted in messianic idealism, as moral absolutes rationalize the harshest punishment of international sinners, without limit or restraint, to the detriment of American interests (Kennan 1951). Arthur Schlesinger, Jr. (1977), an adviser in the Kennedy administration, observes worriedly that "All nations succumb to fantasies of innate superiority. When they act on those fantasies . . . they become international menaces."

9. The scholarly literature on the origins and evolution of the Cold War, always extensive, has grown dramatically in recent years as both the end of the Cold War and declassification of previously secret documents have yielded new information and insights. Examples include Holloway's (1994) *Stalin and the Bomb* and the essays on *The Origins of the Cold War in Europe* in Reynolds (1994). Earlier works include Gaddis (1972), Kolko (1968), Melanson (1983), Schlesinger (1986), Spanier (1988), Ulam (1985), and Yergin (1978).

10. See Bostdorff and Goldzwig (1994) for an analysis of Kennedy's often simultaneous use of idealist and pragmatic rhetoric, with special emphasis on Vietnam.

11. For a lively account of the end of the Cold War that focuses on Bush, Gorbachev, and their advisers, see Beschloss and Talbott (1993).

12. Recognizing the changing nature of international conflicts and the need for new approaches to solve them, the United States Institute for Peace in late 1994 held its tenth anniversary conference, with the theme "Managing Chaos." A summary of issues and ideas discussed at the conference may be found in the February 1995 issue of the Institute's publication, *PeaceWatch*.

13. The ideas are developed at some length in the Clinton's July 1994 report to Congress entitled *A National Security Strategy of Engagement and Enlargement*.

14. For a sampling of the burgeoning scholarly literature on the democratic peace, see Dixon (1994), Doyle (1986, 1995), Maoz and Russett (1993), Owen (1994), Raymond (1994), and Russett (1993). Smith (1993) provides a useful overview of relevant literature, and Diamond (1992) makes the case for democratic promotion from a policy viewpoint. For critical appraisals of the linkage between democracy and peace, see Carothers (1994a), Layne (1994), Mansfield and Snyder (1995), and Spiro (1994).

15. See Hendrickson (1994–1995) for an especially trenchant critique of democratic promotion and related elements of the Clinton strategy of enlargement.

16. It has long been argued that economic development is a "requisite" to democracy (Lipset 1959; also see Dahl 1989). Empirical studies that examine this proposition cross-nationally include Arat (1988), Bollen (1979), Burkhart and Lewis-Beck (1994), and Jackman (1973).

17. John Gerard Ruggie argues cogently that the meaning of multilateralism goes well beyond "three or more" and that it is a means of policy, not an end. He argues that multilateralism differs from other forms of behavior because it "coordinates behavior among three or more states

on the basis of generalized principles of conduct" (Ruggie 1992). For Americans, then, multilateralism accords well with the nation's special experiences and sense of purpose, which set it apart from others on the basis of a sense of community based on a generalized principle (Ruggie 1994b).

18. The quote is from the summary of the Presidential Decision Directive in U.S. Department of State, "The Clinton Administration's Policy on Reforming Multilateral Peace Operations," May 1994. See also Crocker (1994) and Ruggie (1994a).

19. The threat posed by nationalism and ethnic conflict is a recurring theme in Clinton administration policy pronouncements. There is a burgeoning scholarly literature on the these topics. Among recent studies that warrant mention are Gurr (1993) and Gurr and Harff (1994) on ethnicity and ethnopolitical conflict and Van Evera (1990–1991, 1994) on nationalism, hypernationalism, and war.

SUGGESTIONS FOR FURTHER READING

Ambrose, Stephen E. *Rise to Globalism: American Foreign Policy since 1938*, 7th ed. New York: Penguin, 1993.

Beschloss, Michael R., and Strobe Talbott. *At the Highest Levels: The Inside Story of the End of the Cold War*. Boston: Little, Brown, 1993.

Gaddis, John Lewis. *Strategies of Containment: A Critical Appraisal of Postwar American National Security Policy*. New York: Oxford University Press, 1982.

———. *The United States and the End of the Cold War: Implications, Reconsiderations, Provocations*. New York: Oxford University Press, 1992.

Garthoff, Raymond L. *The Great Transition: American-Soviet Relations and the End of the Cold War*. Washington, D.C.: The Brookings Institution, 1994.

Kissinger, Henry. *Diplomacy*. New York: Simon and Schuster, 1994.

Martel, Gordon, ed. *American Foreign Relations Reconsidered, 1890–1993*. London: Routledge, 1994.

Nolan, Janne E., ed. *Global Engagement: Cooperation and Security in the 21st Century*. Washington, D.C.: The Brookings Institution, 1994.

Smith, Gaddis. *The Last Years of the Monroe Doctrine, 1945–1993*. New York: Hill and Wang, 1994.

Smith, Tony. *America's Mission: The United States and the Worldwide Struggle for Democracy in the Twentieth Century*. Princeton: Princeton University Press, 1994.

Spanier, John, and Steven Hook. *American Foreign Policy since World War II*, 13th ed. Washington, D.C.: Congressional Quarterly Press, 1995.

Wittkopf, Eugene R., ed. *The Future of American Foreign Policy*, 2nd ed. New York: St. Martin's, 1994.

CHAPTER 4

. . .

THE INSTRUMENTS OF GLOBAL INFLUENCE: MILITARY MIGHT AND INTERVENTIONISM

. . .

Military power is an essential part of diplomacy.

Under Secretary of State
Lawrence S. Eagleburger, 1984

*There is no longer any need for the United States to have nuclear weapons
as an equalizer against other powers. . . . Nuclear weapons are still the big
equalizer but now the United States is not the equalizer but the equalizee.*

Representative Les Aspin, 1992

In 1949 the Soviet Union successfully tested an atomic bomb. The event had a profound impact on the Truman administration's thinking about how best to pursue the
containment of the Soviet Union. A government-wide reevaluation of American foreign policy followed.

In April 1950 the National Security Council (NSC), a top-level interagency body
that advises the president on foreign policy matters, issued its now-famous, top-secret
memorandum, *NSC 68*, which set in motion the militarization of American foreign
policy and the containment strategy that would persist for many years. A decisive sentence in NSC 68 asserted that "Without superior aggregate military strength, in being
and readily mobilizable, a policy of 'containment'—which is in effect a policy of calculated and gradual coercion—is no more than a policy of bluff." NSC 68 also called
for a nonmilitary counteroffensive against the Soviet Union, which included covert
economic, political, and psychological warfare designed to foment unrest and revolt in
Soviet bloc countries. Soon American foreign policy would become highly dependent
on the possession of powerful military, paramilitary, and related instruments through
which its fundamental goals could be pursued.

America's domestic priorities also would be shaped by its preference for military
might and interventionism, as defense spending would comprise the largest share of
discretionary (nonentitlement) federal expenditures for decades to come. Even with
the end of the Cold War defense dollars continue to account for roughly half of all discretionary federal spending. Thus NSC 68 provided the blueprint for the militarization of American foreign policy and its domestic consequences, which would continue
until the very end of the Cold War—and beyond.

. . .

With the Cold War now over, some analysts look on NSC 68 as the master plan that made victory possible. Others see it as an example of successful strategic planning that warrants emulation (Allison 1989; Blackwill 1992).[1] The reasons to engage in strategic planning for the remainder of this decade and beyond may be compelling, but the absence of clearly defined policy purposes today contrasts sharply with the early 1950s. By then the view that the Soviet Union posed a serious threat to the West was already widespread within the policy-making community, and the Truman administration already had embraced containment as the goal of American foreign policy (see Chapter 3). Thus NSC 68 could focus on the means to implement containment, not proselytize for the objective itself.

Today no overarching goal has galvanized policymakers, and the American people are more prone to shun the burdens of leadership than to embrace them. Furthermore, the threats from abroad are seemingly more diffuse, thus complicating the task of policy planning. Les Aspin, Clinton's first secretary of defense, drew attention to the contrast between the Cold War and post-Cold War worlds while still a member of Congress:

> In the old world there was only one thing that posed a threat. It was the Soviet Union. In the new world, there will be diverse threats.
>
> In the old world, the very survival of our nation was at stake. In the new world, the interests of our nation will be at risk.
>
> In the old world, we knew what threatened us. In the new world, we will have to learn what threatens us.
>
> In the old world, the policy of deterrence reduced the threat of nuclear war. In the new world, deterrence will not always stop an adversary from threatening Americans and American interests.
>
> In the old world, the two superpowers had thousands and thousands of nuclear weapons and were prepared to use them. In the new world, many nations and groups will vie to acquire nuclear weapons.

Our purpose in this chapter and the next is to examine the *instruments* of American foreign policy captured in the themes of military might and interventionism. These comprise the *means* used to achieve the political objectives of foreign policy. They include the threatened use of force, war and other forms of military intervention, propaganda, clandestine operations, military aid, the sale of arms, and economic assistance. Each has played a prominent role in American foreign policy during the past half-century—and some before that. All derive from the assumptions of *realpolitik* that informed policymakers' perceptions of the nation's security needs during the Cold War and guided their choice of the military and other interventionist approaches toward the realization of American objectives since World War II. Whether all remain appropriate to America's foreign policy future—and, if so, in what combination—is now itself a contentious political issue.

In Chapter 5 we will examine the use of intelligence operations, public diplomacy, and economic and military assistance programs as they relate to the goals of American foreign policy. Here, in Chapter 4, our primary concern is the role that the actual and threatened use of military force, conventional and nuclear, played as instruments of both compellence and deterrence designed to defend the physical security and survival

of the United States and its allies against external attack in the past and their continuing relevance to the future. Since foreign policy refers to the sum of objectives and programs whereby the government seeks to cope with its external environment, our attention is on that subset of foreign policy known as ***national security policy***—the
weapons and strategies on which the United States relies to ensure security and survival in an uncertain, dangerous, and often hostile global environment.

The Common Defense: Military Globalism and Conventional Forces

The logic of *realpolitik* encourages the practice of coercive behavior abroad. The potential dominance of military thinking on foreign policy planning is one symptom of
that instinct. The militarization of American foreign policy following World War II
occurred in part because the nation's policymakers routinely defined international political problems in terms of military solutions.[2] Not until after digesting the painful
Vietnam experience did many Americans begin to suspect that military firepower and
political influence are not synonymous.

The rhetoric of American leaders consistently has emphasized the martial outlook
derived from the assumptions of political realism. Indeed, the premise has been reiterated so often that it has become dogma (see Focus 4.1).[3]

The end of the Cold War and, with it, the unexpectedly rapid diminution of clearly
defined threats to the physical security of the United States and its allies call into question the martial spirit of American foreign policy. Adjusting the nation's military capabilities to the new world order (or disorder) is now the order of the day. Inevitably
that means we must understand how we got to where we are, as past patterns of military preparedness and interventionist practices both inform and constrain future possibilities. Thus we must understand the role played by conventional military power in
promoting and protecting the nation's security interests, the role of strategic (nuclear)
power, and the interaction between them.

Conventional Military Power during the Cold War

The network of more than four hundred overseas military bases operative at the conclusion of the Cold War and the assignment of nearly half a million soldiers and sailors
to posts and ships outside the United States are two visible manifestations of the nation's commitment to its perceived global responsibilities. A determination to contain
communism shaped those perceptions. European and Asian bases were especially important in the 1950s in enhancing the credibility of the nuclear weapons strategy of
massive retaliation (discussed below), as they provided the forward bases from which
American strategic bombers could strike at the heartland of the "communist monolith." The forward bases declined in strategic importance with the advent of the intercontinental missile, but they continued to play a role in the nation's overall national security strategy as a way of demonstrating its commitments to its allies.

Focus 4.1
THE MILITARIZATION OF AMERICAN FOREIGN POLICY: FIFTY YEARS OF POLICY PRONOUNCEMENTS

• ∗ •

"We must continue to be a military nation if we are to maintain leadership among other nations."

— Harry S Truman, 1945

"Regardless of the consequences, the nation's military security will take first priority in my calculations."

— Dwight D. Eisenhower, 1953

"Only when our arms are sufficient beyond doubt can we be certain beyond doubt that they shall never be employed."

—John F. Kennedy, 1961

"United States military strength now exceeds the combined military might of all nations in history, stronger than any adversary or combination of adversaries. . . . Against such force the combined destructive power of every battle ever fought by man is like a firecracker thrown against the sun."

— Lyndon B. Johnson, 1964

"Peace requires strength. So long as there are those who would threaten our vital interests and those of our allies with military force, we must be strong. American weakness could tempt would-be aggressors to make dangerous miscalculations."

— Richard M. Nixon, 1970

"Our military forces are capable and ready. Our military power is without equal. And I intend to keep it that way."

— Gerald R. Ford, 1976

"In the dangerous and uncertain world of today, the keystone of our national security is still military strength—strength that is clearly recognized by Americans, by our Allies, and by any potential adversary."

—Jimmy Carter, 1979

"Peace through strength is not a slogan; it's a fact of life—and we will not return to the days of hand wringing, defeatism, decline and despair."

— Ronald Reagan, 1984

> "As we seek peace, we must also remain strong. The purpose of our military might is . . . to deter war. It is to defend ourselves and our allies."
>
> — George Bush, 1989
>
> "We cannot sustain our leadership role without maintaining a defense capability strong enough to underwrite our commitments credibly."
>
> — Bill Clinton, 1994

The Atlantic Alliance and Conventional Forces in Europe

The importance of U.S. overseas troop deployments to American national security has been greater nowhere more than in Europe, where the United States has maintained thousands of troops since the 1950s as a bulwark against possible hostile encroachment against Western Europe. At one time they acted as a trip wire: In the event of an attack by Warsaw Pact forces against Western Europe, the mere presence of American troops virtually ensured that some would be killed. In this way the "wire"ensuring an American retaliation would be "tripped"—and by the other (Soviet) side—because American policymakers would have "no choice" but to respond. The trip wire was an integral element of the Eisenhower administration's national security strategy. The logic supporting the presence of American troops in Western Europe later took on various colorations, but the essential function remained the same—to avert a hostile attack against Western Europe by making credible America's commitment to its allies there.

The strategy of *flexible response* devised during the Kennedy and Johnson years and adopted as the official NATO defense posture in 1967, became the means for coping with conventional war threats. The strategy implies that the United States and its allies would now possess the capabilities (and will?) to respond to an attack by hostile forces at whatever level might be appropriate, ranging from conventional to nuclear weapons. Indeed, the NATO alliance reserved the right of "first use" of nuclear weapons if that proved necessary to repel a Soviet attack against the West. Thus conventional and nuclear military power were intimately intertwined. *Theater nuclear forces*—those directed toward regional rather than global threats—provided the link between U.S. conventional and strategic nuclear forces, thus tying American nuclear capabilities to the defense of its allies. The term itself suggested the possibility of theaterwide conflict (like World War II as prosecuted in Europe) involving *tactical nuclear weapons* (weapons designed for the direct support of combat operations) without an escalation to global conflagration involving strategic weapons.

Beyond Europe: Force Projection under Nixon, Carter, and Reagan

The strategy of flexible response envisioned increased conventional war capabilities as a substitute for reliance on massive (nuclear) retaliation. In 1962 the ability to wage "2 1/2 wars" at once was embraced as official policy. The United States would prepare to fight simultaneously a conventional war in Europe with the Soviet Union, an Asian war, and a lesser engagement (half a war?) elsewhere. (Preparation for a strategic nuclear war also continued.) With the hindsight of Vietnam—which shook the notion of American military invincibility to its very foundations—the 2 1/2 war strategy appeared excessive. At the time, however, it was not perceived that way, leading one observer to view the strategy as a "military expression of the U.S. national policy goals that reached out for Pax Americana [worldwide peace imposed by the United States] and 'world hegemony'" (Melman 1974).

Nixon changed the 2 1/2 war strategy to 1 1/2 wars. Conventional and tactical nuclear forces would now meet a major communist attack in *either* Europe *or* Asia and contend with a lesser contingency elsewhere. The reorientation of military doctrine was part of the reordering of the nation's world role envisioned in the Nixon Doctrine, which called for a lower American profile in the post-Vietnam era and for greater participation by U.S. allies in their own defense. Simultaneously, the United States adopted a "Twin Pillars" strategy toward the Middle East, a region of growing importance to the nation's vital interests as its dependence on imported oil grew. The Twin Pillars strategy sought to protect American interests by building up the political and military stature of both Iran and Saudi Arabia. The sale of billions of dollars of highly sophisticated military equipment to both figured prominently in Nixon's plans (see also Chapter 5).

The Carter administration did not alter Nixon's strategy markedly, but events in Afghanistan and the Persian Gulf in 1979 and 1980 undermined the Twin Pillars strategy. They also spurred plans already in the works to develop a Rapid Deployment Force (which later became the U.S. Central Command assigned responsibility for directing Operations Desert Shield and Desert Storm in the Persian Gulf) capable of intervening militarily in world trouble spots to defend American interests. The Carter Doctrine, enunciated in the president's 1980 State of the Union address, reaffirmed the determination of the United States to intervene in the Middle East militarily, if necessary, to safeguard American security interests.

In the European theater, the United States committed itself to deploy a new generation of *intermediate-range nuclear force (INF) weapons*. The decision was a direct response to the Soviet Union's growing medium-range nuclear capability, which was beyond the scope of the SALT negotiations on limiting strategic arms which had been underway since the late 1960s (see Chapter 3 and below). This U.S. action reflected growing concern about the credibility of the American commitment to defend Europe from a Soviet attack, captured in the concept *extended deterrence*. Was the United States, European allies worried, truly willing to risk its own destruction to defend Western Europe? The INF decision sought to guarantee that U.S. strategic forces remained "coupled" to the defense of Western Europe.

The prospect of deploying intermediate-range nuclear missiles became increasingly controversial after Ronald Reagan assumed the reigns of power and a "peace movement" emerged on both sides of the Atlantic, whose purpose was to block deployment of the INF weapons and otherwise reverse the nuclear arms race. The political potency of the emergent peace movement was fueled in part by the new administration's own hawkish rhetoric. Fear that the United States might stand aside in the event of a nuclear war in Europe was heightened when, shortly after his election,

Reagan startled European leaders with the statement that he "could see where you could have an exchange of tactical weapons against troops in the field without it bringing either one of the major powers to pushing buttons." In an environment of renewed Soviet-American hostility, the Soviet Union chose to boycott both the INF negotiations and START (Strategic Arms Reduction Talks, which replaced SALT in the early 1980s). It would be some time before productive negotiations resumed. However, the INF issue was settled in 1987 when the superpowers agreed to eliminate completely the weapons from Europe. Never before had they made an agreement to actually *disarm*.

As with the INF deployment, the Reagan administration continued some of Carter's policies, but it adopted a more assertive posture toward the nation's global aspirations. It jettisoned the belief that any conventional war with the Soviet Union would be of short duration and either be settled by negotiation or escalate to a nuclear confrontation. Instead, military planning was now predicated on the assumption that such a war would be protracted and global in scope, with fighting in numerous locations around the world, but without necessarily escalating to a nuclear catastrophe. The aggressive posture fostered the development of new defensive concepts in Europe, such as the Air-Land Battle, which anticipated close air force support of army combat maneuvers on the ground—a style of warfare vividly illustrated (via CNN!) in the Persian Gulf War.

Reagan also demonstrated a renewed willingness to intervene in trouble spots outside of Europe—as in Grenada and Lebanon—and gave greater attention to preparations for low-intensity conflicts, such as guerrilla wars and terrorist attacks. The assumption that Third World instability provided the Soviet Union "targets of opportunity," thus posing threats that might be dealt with militarily, guided that thinking.

Conventional Forces and the End of the Cold War

In a December 1988 United Nations speech, Soviet President Mikhail Gorbachev announced large-scale unilateral reductions in Soviet military forces, including force reductions in Eastern Europe and in the wider Atlantic-to-the-Urals area that went far beyond what Western military planners only a short time earlier had dreamed possible. His dramatic announcement, later followed by voluntary cuts by Eastern European nations, set the stage for new negotiations between NATO and the Warsaw Pact on Conventional Armed Forces in Europe (CFE). In 1992, after protracted negotiations whose heritage predated the CFE negotiations, a new treaty entered into force that called for eliminating from Europe thousands of tanks, artillery pieces, armored personnel carriers, infantry fighting vehicles, and heavy armament combat vehicles.

On another front, the United States and the Soviet Union in 1990 agreed to stop production and significantly reduce their stockpiles of chemical weapons. The two first engaged in bilateral chemical weapons negotiations during the Carter administration, but significant forward progress was not achieved until 1987, when the Soviet Union announced its willingness to cease production of chemical weapons, acknowledged previously undisclosed information about its chemical weapons stockpiles, and acceded to U.S. demands regarding inspections. President Bush later committed the United States to eventually destroying its existing chemical weapons stockpile. Less than two years later the two sides reached their "trailblazing agreement," as Secretary of State Baker called it.[4] Each also pledged further reductions once a multilateral agreement banning chemical weapons was reached. That goal was realized in 1992 with the Chemical Weapons Convention, to which more than 150 countries acceded. It requires parties to the treaty to destroy their chemical weapons and production facilities and to open their chemical industries to international inspection. In practice, however, the treaty is less comprehensive and more difficult to verify than its label suggests (Feith and Gaffney 1994).

Conventional Military Power beyond the Cold War

In early 1990 the Bush administration issued a new defense planning document (the recurring "Defense Policy Guidance") designed to shape the military strategy necessary to cope with the threats the nation would face in the 1992–1997 period. Despite the dramatic changes unfolding in the force postures of the NATO and Warsaw Pact alliances, the document anticipated continued Soviet-American rivalry, exposing the Bush administration to the criticism that it was blind to the opportunities now available. For example, Representative Les Aspin, then chair of the powerful Armed Services Committee in the House of Representatives, charged that "There are new realities in the world but no new thinking at home to match them" (see also Iklé 1990).

The Bush planning document did recognize that the security environment in Europe was less threatening due to the revolutionary changes that had occurred in Eastern Europe. Thus the administration sought an agreement with the Soviet Union to reduce each superpower's armed forces in the "central zone" of Europe to 195,000, but it also pledged a continued American presence in Europe to protect its own interests and those of its allies. The need for troops had always been predicated on the presence of a credible military threat to the West. Critics now argued that that threat no longer existed.

A year later, in September 1991, Bush surprised the world by announcing that the United States would remove all tactical nuclear weapons from Europe and Korea and from U.S. warships and submarines. Still, despite proclaiming that the Soviet Union was "no longer a realistic threat," he continued to insist that 1,400 aircraft-delivered bombs were needed in Europe to provide for NATO security. Gorbachev nevertheless followed Bush's lead on tactical nuclear weapons, thus further reducing the once awesome levels of conventional military and tactical nuclear power deployed in Europe.

The Persian Gulf War provided the United States with a unique opportunity to test the weapons and strategies that for decades had been designed for, but untested in, Europe. Iraq had been armed with Soviet weapons and schooled in its military thinking. The result for Iraq was disastrous—and humiliating for Soviet military strategy. "Arguably, the Iraqis were inept in exercising Soviet plans with Soviet equipment, but many Russians privately express their dismay at the mismatch and wonder how much better they might have fared" (Snow 1995).

The Bush administration moved cautiously in assimilating the lessons of the forty-two day Persian Gulf War—viewed by many as a precursor to the renewal of the U.S.

global policeman role in disrepute since Vietnam—and in adjusting to the collapse of the Soviet Union, which came less than a year after the Gulf victory. In early 1992, the *New York Times* reported on a new, working version of the Pentagon's Defense Policy Guidance, whose purpose was to "set the nation's direction for the next century." It laid out the rationale for a "Base Force" of 1.6 million active-duty troops (compared with 2.1 million at the time). The Base Force would defend against seven potential roads to a future war: defense of Lithuania and Poland from invasion by Russia, war against Iraq and North Korea following attacks on their neighbors, smaller interventions in Panama and the Philippines, and defense against an emergent, expansionist superpower.

A central thesis of the Defense Policy Guidance was that the United States should prevent the emergence of a rival superpower. The United States would maintain military dominance capable of "deterring potential competitors from even aspiring to a larger regional or global role" (cited in Gellman 1992b). The document surmised that any nation combining "modern defense, industrial and technical capacity and a sizable population base" would be capable of mounting a global threat, thus intimating that Germany and Japan might one day become military rivals of the United States.

The initial Defense Policy Guidance proved highly controversial in the United States and abroad. (Although a classified document, its contents were revealed by leaks to the press, a common mechanism used by both supporters and opponents of policy changes in Congress, the bureaucracy, and the White House.) Many of its most contentious assertions were changed or deleted by the time defense planners finalized the document a few months later. The "sole superpower" passages were among those excised. Still, the new document called for American military preeminence to sustain the nation's leadership role and to act as a catalyst to collective action. "Only a nation that is strong enough to act decisively can provide the leadership that is needed to encourage others to resist aggression," the revised document stated. "Collective action failed in the 1930s because no strong power was willing to provide the leadership behind which less powerful countries could rally against fascism. It worked in the Gulf because the United States was willing and able to provide that leadership" (cited in Gellman 1992a).

Despite criticisms directed at the Base Force proposal (see, for example, Kaufmann 1992), it became the Bush administration's military blueprint for the post-Cold War era. The United States would now prepare for more military contingencies, not fewer. Colin Powell, chairman of the Joint Chiefs of Staff, defended the new military plan. "The central idea in the [new national military] strategy is the change from a focus on global war-fighting to a focus on regional contingencies," he wrote in *Foreign Affairs*. "When we were confronted by an all-defining, single, overwhelming threat—the Soviet Union—we could focus on that threat as the yardstick in our strategy, tactics, weapons, and budget. . . . [Now] we must concentrate on the capabilities of our armed forces to meet a host of threats and not a single threat" (Powell 1992–1993).

Bill Clinton promised a rigorous, "Bottom Up Review" of the nation's defense posture and the requirements necessary to meet future needs and threats. Even before it was completed, however, his administration announced military spending cuts that constrained what the Pentagon might otherwise have projected. Regardless, the Bottom Up Review did not deviate dramatically from Bush's Base Force plan. Active military forces would be cut from 1.6 to 1.4 million under Clinton's proposal and the force levels required to meet a threat from the former Soviet areas reduced, but the Bush focus on regional conflicts remained. Under the Clinton plan, U.S. forces would be called on to fight two regional wars on the scale of the Persian Gulf War nearly simultaneously. Thus the review emphasized that highly trained and equipped forces should be retained to meet regional contingencies rapidly and without prior warning. It also anticipated that American forces would have to be able to fight in these conflicts without major support from U.S. allies.

How much would that cost? The Clinton plan originally projected defense spending by 1999 would total $1.2 trillion to support ten active army divisions, eleven active aircraft carriers and thirteen active air force fighter wings, and a three-division Marine Corps. The absence of consensus about the mlitary's role in the new world (dis)order shaped perceptions of whether the number was too high or too low. "Liberals were astonished and angry when President Clinton said that there would be no further cuts than those called for in the [Bottom Up Review]. Many military leaders, meanwhile, believed they were being asked to prepare for threats in a still-dangerous world without sufficient resources" (Graham and Harris 1994; see also Cohen 1993; Morrison, Tsipis, and Wiesner 1994; Tonelson 1993; Zakheim and Ranney 1993).

Even with the large price tag, defense spending in constant (noninflated) dollars declined markedly during the Bush and early Clinton years. (Clinton's 1995 budget proposal called for $258 billion in defense spending, compared with over $300 billion in 1990.) Following the Republican victory in the 1994 congressional elections—in which defense priorities again figured prominently—Clinton pledged to add another $25 billion to his multiyear spending projection. Still, questions about "readiness" and "effectiveness" plagued defense planning. So, too, did concern that the United States might return to the so-called "hollow forces" of the 1970s (Harrigan 1994), when, in the context of the "Vietnam syndrome," the uniformed services allegedly had too few resources to train properly.

Concepts like "readiness" and "effectiveness" are subject to different interpretations and therefore are subject to political quarrels between pro- and anti-defense advocates (a situation aggravated by Clinton's perceived vulnerability on defense issues) (Kaufmann 1994; Korb 1995). Similarly, the factors that explain the "hollow forces" of the immediate post-Vietnam period (also subject to different interpretations) do not necessarily relate to the issues that face the United States in the post-Cold War era (Ziemke 1993). What *can* be said safely is that the resource constraints now facing the United States inevitably will have an impact on the nation's future military posture. The Clinton administration chose to emphasize current readiness and troop morale at the expense of weapons modernization programs. The long-term wisdom of that choice remains to be tested (see also Romm 1992).

More trenchant as a matter of near-term strategy is the perception of external threats embodied in Clinton's Bottom Up Review. Critics doubted, for example, that two regional conflicts would: (1) occur simultaneously, (2) come without warning, and (3) be serious national security threats yet ones in which U.S. allies would choose to stand aside. They also noted that the military power of the United States, its state of readiness, and the level of its military spending far surpassed that of almost any combination of foreign foes that might be imagined. Finally, critics questioned the assumption that future conflicts would be on the order of the Persian Gulf War; instead, they predicted humanitarian intervention, counterterrorism, and other forms of military involvement arising out of enthnopolitical conflict and the proliferation of nuclear and technologically sophisticated conventional weapons[5] The underlying problem, as one analyst put it, is that "The United States is having difficulty emerging from the conceptual and institutional grip of the Cold War."

> Though we have declared the ideological confrontation ended and have tempered our political rhetoric accordingly, we have not fundamentally altered our military posture. Our defense policy no longer designates a specific enemy but nonetheless prepares for large-scale war anywhere in the world on short notice, as if we were still engaged in a strategic confrontation. We have yet to recognize that today's most urgent security problems cannot be handled by traditional methods of confrontation. (Steinbruner 1995, 5)

Military Force and Political Purposes

The discussions of conventional war planning here and of strategic doctrine later in this chapter suggest that the purpose of American military might has been primarily preventive: to deter someone else's use of military force.

In addition to prevention, American military forces have been used to *change* the behavior of others. Examples of America's reliance on this instrument of influence illustrate the modern tactic of *gunboat diplomacy*. Following the Soviet invasion of Afghanistan in 1979, the United States (with Egypt) augmented its Indian Ocean naval patrols as a signal to the Soviet Union not to extend its invasion westward. In 1983 the United States stationed a carrier task force in the Mediterranean to dissuade Libyan dictator Muammar Qaddafi from launching an attack on Sudan. In the same year the United States staged naval maneuvers on both sides of the Honduran isthmus in hopes of intimidating leftist guerrillas active in Central America and deterring Cuba, Nicaragua, and the Soviet Union from supporting them. In 1989 additional U.S. troops were sent to Panama following General Manuel Noriega's disregard of the results of the Panamanian election, a signal to Noriega that the United States might take further action. And in 1994 the United States sent thirty-five thousand troops to the Persian Gulf to deter Saddam Hussein from hostile maneuvers that might have been a prelude to the resumption of warfare over Kuwait. On these and many other occasions, the practice of gunboat diplomacy was designed for purposes other than protecting the immediate physical security of the nation or its allies. Instead, the purpose was to influence the behavior of others.

Figure 4.1 charts the frequency of these displays of force short of war—*forceful persuasion*—in the four decades from 1946 to 1984. The data show that the United States subtly but surely threatened to unleash its military might to influence the decisions of other states nearly three hundred times.[6] They also point to two peaks in post-World War II American gunboat diplomacy, one extending from 1957 to 1965, the second from 1981 to 1984. The trough between them corresponds to the Vietnam War and its aftermath, a period of restraint on the use of force encapsulated in the phrase "Vietnam syndrome."

Systematic data on the incidence of forceful persuasion attempts since 1984 are not

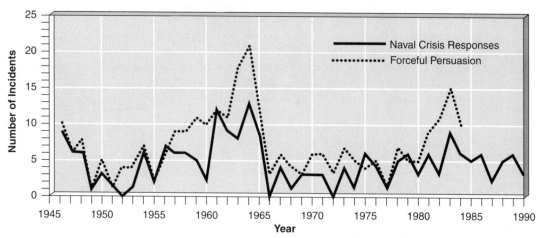

Figure 4.1 The Use of Military Force for Political Purposes, 1946–1990
Source: Adapted from Barry M. Blechman and Stephen S. Kaplan, *Force without War* (Washington, D.C.: Brookings Institution, 1978), pp. 547–53; Philip Zelikow, "The United States and the Use of Force: A Historical Summary," in George K. Osborn, Asa A. Clark IV, Daniel J. Kaufman, and Douglas E. Lute (eds.), *Democracy, Strategy, and Vietnam* (Lexington, Mass.: Lexington Books, 1987), pp. 34–36; and Adam B. Siegel, *The Use of Naval Forces in the Post-War Era: U.S. Navy and U.S. Marine Corps Crisis Response Activity, 1946–1990* (Alexandria, Va.: Center for Naval Analyses, 1991), pp. 7–11.

available, but clearly this is a recurrent theme in the U.S. exercise of global influence. Data on the use of military personnel to respond to international incidents and crises that occurred until the end of the Cold War reinforce that observation. These are charted in the second line in Figure 4.1, which traces how frequently U.S. naval and marine personnel were used to respond to crises between 1946 and 1990. The crisis data, consisting of 207 responses, are more restricted than those on the incidence of forceful persuasion, as they are confined to instances that involved the use of Navy surface ships or Marine Corps units.[7] Still, they reinforce the conclusion that policymakers frequently and consistently pursue political purposes by resort to force short of war.

Military Intervention

The maintenance of a high military profile abroad and displays of force short of war are two elements of the interventionist thrust of America's globalist foreign policy posture. A third is outright military intervention. Here, too, there has been a striking consistency in the willingness of American commanders-in-chief to intervene in the affairs of others. On eight conspicuous occasions—in Korea (1950), Lebanon (1958), Vietnam (1962 or 1965, depending on one's definition), the Dominican Republic (1965), Grenada (1983), Panama (1989), Iraq (1991), and Haiti (1994)—the United States intervened overtly with military power in another country to accomplish its foreign policy objectives. Other instances of military interventions can be found, but these—particularly the first five—account more than anything else for the label "interventionist" widely used to describe American foreign policy in the decades following World War II.

Measured in size of forces, Grenada was the smallest operation, involving only 1,900 American assault troops in an operation that met opposition from a local military force of only 1,200 troops plus roughly 700 armed Cuban construction workers. Lebanon was next in size, involving 14,000 American troops in what was essentially a bloodless intervention. Haiti ranks third, with 20,000 American personnel who were joined by other nations in a bloodless "intervasion." The Dominican intervention ranks fourth, with 22,000 troops and some combat activity on the part of American forces. Then comes Panama, with an invasion force of 24,000, who met some resistance but suffered few casualties. Korea and Vietnam were, of course, much larger. In casualties alone, the Korean War outstripped the number of troops involved in the Dominican affair by 11,000. And in the case of Vietnam—where at one point nearly 550,000 troops were engaged—the Vietnam Veterans Memorial on the Mall in the nation's capital commemorates the more than 58,000 Americans who lost their lives in an intervention that spanned two Republican and two Democratic administrations.

The intervention in the Middle East in 1990, which culminated in the Persian Gulf War, stands apart from the others in many respects. More American troops were sent there than to Vietnam (750,000 troops from the United States and elsewhere comprised the Coalition marshaled against Iraq) yet remarkably few casualties were sustained in a high-tech war that lasted only forty-three days. Moreover, it was the first overt intervention since World War II that enjoyed the acquiescence, if not outright support, of the Soviet Union. Thus is was a clear instance of *collective security*, with enforcement measures approved by the UN Security Council against an aggressor on behalf of the global community. Also, like Panama, the intervention was not rationalized in anticommunist terms.

The anticommunist impulse was evident in Korea, Lebanon, Vietnam, the Dominican Republic, and Grenada. Despite this—and the interventionist label that followed—how can we explain the far-larger number of Cold War situations in which the United States could have been expected to intervene but decided not to? These situations include, for example, the U.S. decision *not* to bail out the French in Indochina in 1954 when they faced defeat at Dienbienphu and America's *unwillingness* to use overt military force to remove the leftist Sandinista regime from power in Nicaragua in the 1980s. How can we reconcile such facts with the interventionist stigma?

The answers can be found only in the multiple sources of American foreign policy, which are outlined in Chapter 2 and examined in detail in the chapters that follow. Still, several consistent correlates governed the pattern of U.S. interventionist behavior during the Cold War. More than 150 situations invited American intervention, but the contrast between the many *potential* interventions and the *actual* number may be explained by the presence of inhibiting factors. Critical to the choice *not* to intervene were the perceived need to use nuclear weapons, the prior presence of Soviet troops, the absence of armed conflict, the absence of a specific request for intervention, or the willingness of the president to let some other component of the decision-making structure (such as Congress) veto an intervention decision (Tillema 1973). But "on those occasions when a Communist threat was thought to exist and when none of the other restraints was operative, intervention . . . followed" (Tillema 1973; see also Tillema and Van Wingen 1982; Tillema 1989). Thus anticommunism was compelling if not determinant.

Given this conclusion, the demise of communism and the Soviet challenge reasonably lead to the expectation that American interventionism is a thing of the past. That obviously is not the case. The purpose of "Operation Just Cause"—as the U.S. intervention into Panama was called—was, in the words of the U.S. ambassador to the United Nations, "to safeguard the lives of Americans, to defend democracy in Panama, to combat drug trafficking, and to protect the integrity of the Panama Canal Treaty." In short, its purpose was to defend American interests. In the Persian Gulf case, President Bush appealed to a higher purpose—to defend a weak state against the aggressive designs of a Hitler-like predator—but few doubted that concern for access to Middle Eastern oil motivated the United States and others. Again, then, defense of American interests figured prominently.

The absence of a clear challenge to the United States since communism's demise plagued the Clinton administration as it sought to explain what interests might warrant intervention abroad. Sensitive to charges by its critics that in Somalia it sought to use force without diplomacy and, in Bosnia, diplomacy without force, the administration drew a distinction following the "intervasion" of Haiti and the dispatch of troops to the Persian Gulf in 1994 between "vital" and "important" interests. By sending troops to the Middle East to stem a further Iraqi onslaught against Kuwait, the Clinton administration explained that the president was protecting a "vital" interest. In defending democracy in Haiti, on the other hand, it was an "important" interest. In cases of "important" interests, explained General John Shalikashvili, chairman of the Joint Chiefs of Staff, "we are willing to use our military power primarily for coercive purposes in support of our diplomacy." This is forceful persuasion: the use of force short of war.

The theory of political realism dictates that states act to protect their interests. Thus intervention abroad should be regarded as neither unexpected nor reprehensible. It is noteworthy that the frequency of U.S. intervention has not abated since the end of the Cold War. George Bush deployed U.S. troops abroad at least eight times during his last two years in office, and Clinton surpassed this number during his first two years. The pattern looks very much like the interventionist behavior evident during the early twentieth century, particularly during the administration of Woodrow Wilson (see Focus 3.1 p. 41), another dawn of another new era. Clearly, then, *interests* are a compelling explanation for the interventionist behavior of the United States, not only during the Cold War but also before and after it.[8]

Humanitarian Intervention

The Persian Gulf experience in collective security ignited enthusiasm for using the United Nations as an instrument of both *peacekeeping* (keeping contending parties apart) and *peace enforcement* (imposing a settlement on disputants). Three years after Operation Desert Storm ended, more than seventy thousand troops wearing blue helmets with UN insignia were participating in eighteen UN peace operations at an annual cost exceeding $3 billion. "Some of these operations and most of the troops [were] engaged in taming internal conflicts and providing humanitarian aid, situations known in U.N. parlance as 'complex political emergencies.' A few [entailed] peace enforcement, with a mandate authorizing coercive force derived from Chapter VII of the U.N.

Charter" (Crocker 1994). The United States was an eager supporter of many of these operations, whose interests they served. Eventually, however, its enthusiastic embrace of multilateralism waned. In particular, the Clinton administration's penchant toward multilateralism was blunted by the U.S. experience in Somalia as part of a multilateral force, as we discussed briefly in Chapter 3.

The Bush administration in late 1992 initiated the multilateral intervention into Somalia known as "Operation Restore Hope," hoping to bring relief from famine to thousands of starving Somalis. Earlier it had been responsible for Operation Provide Comfort, a multilateral initiative designed to protect the Kurdish people in Iraq from death and destruction at the hands of Saddam Hussein. Both efforts were distinguished from other interventions by serving *humanitarian*, not overtly political, purposes.

In July 1994 the Clinton administration launched another humanitarian intervention, Operation Support Hope, in Rwanda, where hundreds of thousands of refugees faced intolerable conditions following months of genocidal, ethnic bloodletting. Shortly thereafter former President Jimmy Carter negotiated the safe passage of Haiti's military leaders to Panama, paving the way for a U.S.-led multinational force to return Haiti's elected president, Jean-Bertrand Aristide, to power. By ridding Haiti of its military regime, Operation Restore Democracy also sought to eliminate the human rights abuses it had perpetrated on its own people.

Just as enthusiasm for multilateralism followed in the wake of the successful collective security effort in the Persian Gulf, support for humanitarian intervention grew as a way to cope with the civil and ethnic conflict that erupted throughout the world in the Cold War's wake. It also flowed naturally from the apparent "triumph" of Wilsonian liberalism at the conclusion of the Cold War which we examined in Chapter 3. As one analyst observed, "The new interventionism has its roots in long-standing tendencies of American foreign policy—missionary zeal, bewilderment when the world refuses to conform to American expectations and a belief that for every problem there is a quick and easy solution" (Stedman 1992–1993). Thus the new interventionism combined "an awareness that civil war is a legitimate issue of international security with a sentiment for crusading liberal internationalism."

Laudable as they may be, humanitarian interventions raise a host of troublesome moral, legal, and political questions. What level of human suffering is necessary before intervention is warranted? If intervention is necessary to relieve human suffering in Somalia and Rwanda, then why not in countless other places—the Sudan, Sri Lanka, Cambodia, Liberia, Tadjikistan—where poverty, starvation, ethnic violence, and the inhumanity of governments toward their own people are daily occurrences in the new world disorder? Is the restoration of law and order a legitimate reason to intervene? to protect—or promote—democracy? What obligation, and for how long, does the intervenor have to ensure that its stated goals are achieved?[9]

Sovereignty is a cardinal principle in international law and politics. It protects the territorial inviolability of the state, its freedom from interference by others, and its authority to rule its own population. The United Nations is predicated on the sovereign equality of its members, and Article 2 (7) of the charter specifically states that nothing in the charter should be construed to permit interference in matters essentially within the domestic jurisdiction of member states. Still, many legal scholars believe that "humanitarian intervention is legally permissible in instances when a government abuses its people so egregiously that the conscience of humankind is shocked." From this perspective, the humanitarian interventions in Iraq and Somalia "represented the triumph over national sovereignty of international law designed to protect the fundamental human rights of citizens in every state" (Joyner 1993; see also de Waal and Omaar 1994; Joyner 1992). Furthermore, approval of both the Kurdish and Somali interventions by the United Nations added legitimacy to the operations and the role of the United States in them.

By the time United Nations peacekeepers finally withdrew from Somalia in early 1995—literally backing their trucks and tanks toward the sea as American Marines protected their evacuation in the face of hostile warlords—it was clear that the early embrace of humanitarian intervention had been misplaced, as political considerations now loomed more important than moral or legal ones. The operation cost more then $2 billion and the lives of more than one hundred peacekeepers, including many Americans. Still, there was little visible evidence that anything had been accomplished beyond alleviating human starvation[10]—and that tragedy, too, would likely be repeated as warring factions in Somalia again used food as a weapon in their continuing internecine conflicts.[11] Meanwhile, the human toll in Bosnia continued to mount, but the international community seemed paralyzed to respond. Thus the early enthusiasm waned for humanitarian intervention as a means to cope with human suffering and to right the wrongs of a government against its own people. Long-standing disenchantment in the United States with the United Nations (Gregg 1994) reinforced the changed attitude. The now-jaundiced view was encapsulated at the time of Operation Support Hope, when a senior official responsible for Rwandan relief operations observed that "The Americans came in full of plans and promises to put everything right, and as soon as they came in, they started talking about getting out" (cited in R. Smith, 1994c).[12]

Sanctions: A Middle Ground?

Within a week after Iraq's tanks lumbered into Kuwait in August 1990, the world community—acting in a rare show of unity through the United Nations Security Council—imposed strict economic sanctions on Iraq which included a cutoff of critical Iraqi oil shipments as well as all other forms of trade. Two years later, in May 1992, the Security Council again imposed mandatory sanctions, this time against Serbia and Montenegro following the outbreak of war in Bosnia-Herzegovina. And in May 1993 the Security Council imposed an embargo on oil and weapons sales to Haiti, then still under the leadership of a military regime.

The hand of the United States was evident in each of these actions. In Iraq and the former Yugoslavia it had initiated its own unilateral sanctions before multilateral efforts were launched. It also supported (but only half-heartedly [Werleigh 1993]) the trade sanctions imposed on Haiti by the Organization of American States (OAS) in November 1991 in an effort to oust the military junta that had overthrown the first democratically elected Haitian government in twenty-nine years.

The enthusiasm for multilateral sanctions evident in the wake of the Cold War is explained in part by the search for new instruments of foreign policy influence in a domestic environment characterized by limited support for military options. *Sanctions*—

defined as "deliberate government actions to inflict economic deprivation on a target state or society, through the limitation or cessation of customary economic relations" (Leyton-Brown, 1987)—are often thought of as alternatives to military force that still permit the initiating state to express outrage at some particular action and to change the behavior of the target state. Thus sanctions occupy a middle ground between comparatively benign diplomatic action, on one hand, and coercive paramilitary or overt military intervention, on the other.

The use of sanctions is not new. The United States was a key player in two-thirds of the more than one hundred sanction attempts initiated between the end of World War I and 1990. In four out of every five of these, the United States effectively acted by itself, with only minor support from other states or international organizations (Elliott 1993, 33). What is new since the end of the Cold War is a preference for multilateralism (which, however, may prove ephemeral—at least in the United States).

The United Nations charter has always permitted the imposition of multilateral sanctions against international sinners, but this is rarely done. Sanctions applied against the white-minority regimes in Rhodesia in 1966 and South Africa in 1977 are the only UN-sponsored multilateral initiatives taken between the end of World War II and the action against Iraq in 1990 (Lopez and Cortright 1993). The difficulty in securing broad agreement for action, particularly evident during the Cold War, and the equally difficult task of maintaining discipline among the sanctioning states over a period of time help explain the paucity of broad-based multilateral initiatives. In the case of Iraq, for example, sanctions remained in place after the Gulf War to ensure its compliance with UN mandates, requiring postwar inspection of its weapons facilities and the dismemberment of its nuclear, chemical, and biological weapons programs. The United States was the principal advocate of the enforcement of those requirements, but others who were themselves hurt by the sanctions (Turkey and Jordan, for example) or who wished to resume normal commercial intercourse from which they, too, would benefit (such as France, China, and Russia) became increasingly restive.

Fortunately for United States foreign policy, Saddam Hussein deployed two divisions of his elite Republican Guards toward Kuwait in October 1994, apparently believing this calculated show of military force would cause the coalition he faced four years earlier to back down on the sanctions issue (oil exports in particular) rather than face a new crisis. The feint failed when the United States, after deploying additional U.S. forces to Kuwait and Saudi Arabia, used the occasion to garner renewed support for continuing the sanctions.

The purpose of the sanctions against Iraq varied over the years, ranging from forcing Iraq from Kuwait to creating sufficient domestic discontent for Saddam Hussein to be ousted from power (Eland 1993). That neither happened (indeed, Saddam proved not only that he remained firmly in control in Iraq but also that Iraq remained a potent military force) raises troubling questions. Are sanctions effective? Who are their victims?

Determining the effectiveness of sanctions is difficult, as "the correlation between economic pressure and changes in political or military behavior is rarely direct" (Christiansen and Powers 1993). Even in South Africa—where over the course of two decades economic pressure was applied on the white-minority regime to bring an end to the segregationist *apartheid* system and open the way for black majority rule (which has now happened)—it is difficult to determine precisely the role that economic sanctions played in the endgame. Analysts do, however, generally agree that sanctions were important if not determinative (see, e.g., Davis, 1993 Minter 1986–1987; but cf. Doxey 1990).

Cuba is a case where economic coercion failed. The United States placed sanctions on the Castro regime shortly after it assumed power in 1960. It began with a cut in the amount of sugar permitted to enter the United States under its quota system and later extended the sanctions to a full ban on all trade with Cuba. The United States then pressured other countries to follow suit. Its goals were twofold. Initially, it sought the overthrow of the Castro government. Failing that, from about 1964 onward, the aim was containing the Castro revolution and Cuban interventionism in Central and South America and Africa. The major accomplishment, however, was generally confined to "increasing the cost to Cuba of surviving and developing as a socialist country and of pursuing an international commitment" (Roca 1987).

Several factors explain Cuba's ability to withstand U.S. pressure. The support Cuba received from the Soviet Union was especially important, but the United States' inability to persuade its allies to curtail their Cuban trade and investments also figured prominently, as did Castro's charismatic leadership and popular support. Once Soviet support of Cuba ended, the United States redoubled its efforts to topple Castro through economic coercion. (This dismayed much of the rest of the world, which reproached the United States in the United Nations with a resounding repudiation of the U.S. embargo.) Still, Castro survived. And he sought to make the United States "pay" for its project by permitting large numbers of disgruntled Cubans to emigrate to Florida, where the state and federal governments would have to care for them.

As the Cuban case shows, sanctions often fail because other states will not enforce them. During the Cold War in particular, offsetting economic and military assistance provided by the Soviet Union undermined U.S. efforts. Systemic evidence on the use of sanctions since World War I indicates that the United States achieved its objective in only one of three cases (Elliott 1993, 34; see also Hufbauer, Schott, and Elliott 1990). Success was most likely when the goal was modest, the target politically unstable, the initiator and target generally friendly toward each other and conducting substantial trade, the sanctions imposed quickly and decisively, and the initiator able to avoid incurring high costs (Elliott 1993). Clearly these conditions are difficult, although not impossible, to achieve.

Who are sanctions' victims? Not Saddam Hussein, apparently. Not the military leaders in Haiti. Or the ruling elites in Serbia. Political leaders in sanctioned societies may actually benefit from external economic pressure. One reason is that the typical response to economic coercion is a heightened sense of nationalism, a *laager* mentality (circle the ox wagons to face oncoming enemies), which stimulates resistance in the target state and encourages leaders to blame all hardships on outsiders. In the case of Serbia, for example, sanctions "tended to reinforce the power of the extreme nationalists—those that they were meant to undermine. Many analysts contend that Western sanctions against Yugoslavia [were] based on the false assumption that economic pressure [would] convince Serbian President Slobodan Milošević to sue for peace when, in fact, his political life may [have depended] on a continuation of war" (Christiansen and Powers 1993; see also Woodward 1993).

Innocent civilians are often the ones who suffer most from economic coercion. Indeed, "the principal moral dilemma posed by sanctions is that the more effective they are, the more likely that they will harm those least responsible for the wrongdoing and least able to bring about change: civilians" (Christiansen and Powers 1993). Humanitarian assistance (food and medicine) are typically exempted from trade embargoes, but in authoritarian regimes political leaders are able to divert goods in short supply to serve their own needs. Thus Saddam Hussein made sure that his army was not deprived, even as the economic embargo took its toll on the Iraqi people generally. Similarly, the Haitian military regime used bribery and corruption to ensure a continual flow of goods. Meanwhile, the OAS embargo, though never applied seriously, contributed to the growing number of Haitian refugees. Ironically, concern for the influx of Haitian emigrants to the United States helped stimulate the Clinton administration's determination to abandon the embargo in favor of military intervention to rid Haiti of its military leaders and return Aristide to the Haitian presidency.

Despite their checkered record of success and the troublesome dilemma they pose by increasing the suffering of innocent victims, sanctions will continue to be used as foreign policy instruments—particularly in instances, like the former Yugoslavia, where the United States (and others) are typically unwilling to use overt military force. If nothing else, sanctions have symbolic value: They demonstrate to foreign and domestic audiences a resolve to act decisively, but short of war (Eland 1993; Lindsay 1986). As domestic and international restraints on the use of force multiply, symbols become even more valuable. Meanwhile, the growth in and diversification of international trade and financial patterns and other changes in the world political economy have reduced the number of targets vulnerable to unilateral economic coercion, thus increasing the importance of the more difficult to organize and maintain multilateral sanctions (Elliott 1993).

To Intervene or Not to Intervene?

Is there a role for American military intervention in the new world (dis)order? Does the United States still have interests that can be advanced best through intervention? Is the menu of interests broader or narrower than during the Cold War? If the United States does intervene, can it stay the course, as great powers historically have done (Luttwak 1994b)? Or do the domestic political costs of prolonged engagement outweigh the foreign policy benefits?

The range of views on these questions is wide indeed—reflecting both the absence of organizing principles for American national security policy now that the Soviet threat has disappeared and the differences of opinion within the American polity on the interests and threats at stake in the post–Cold War world. Thus, as noted in a recent study of prospective interventionist policy, "The range of views on what (if anything) should prompt intervention is immense."

- Some neoisolationists argue that there are no present or prospective external threats to our interest great enough to justify intervention.
- Others would limit our actions to steps that directly affect a narrow domestic agenda, for example, by forcing Japan to buy more American good and services.

- Still others would use intervention to create the kind of stable and prosperous world they believe offers the greatest chance for peace and prosperity at home.

- Finally, some believe that we should intervene to promote American values of democracy and human rights, as well as to relieve suffering and prevent "ethnic cleansing," even if there is no direct security impact on the United States. (Brooks and Kanter 1994, 22–23)[13]

We can confidently predict that resolving the differences of opinion inherent in these alternative postures toward the means of American foreign policy will not come easily, as they mirror the same long-standing debates about idealism and realism, power and principle, and isolationism and internationalism that animate differences about the goals of American foreign policy we saw in Chapter 3. Furthermore, because conventional military intervention constitutes only one element of American national security policy, it will not be surprising if we find similarly divergent views and pre-scriptions as they relate to the role of strategic weapons in American national security policy, to which we now turn.

Strategic Doctrine Then and Now: Nuclear Weapons as Instruments of Compellence and Deterrence ....

The clocks of Hiroshima stopped at 8:15 on the morning of August 6, 1945, when, in the blinding flash of a single weapon and the shadow of its mushroom cloud, the international arena was transformed from a balance-of-power to a balance-of-terror system. No other event marked more dramatically the change in world politics that would follow.

The United States has not used atomic weapons in anger since August 1945, but it sought throughout the Cold War to gain bargaining leverage by relying heavily on nuclear force as an instrument of strategic defense (the defense of its homeland) and as a means "to defend its interests wherever they existed" (Gaddis 1987–1988). The latter implied its willingness not only to threaten but actually to use nuclear weapons. Even today nuclear weapons continue to figure prominently in the design of American national security policy. As the Pentagon stated in its 1993 report on the roles and missions of American military forces after the Cold War, nuclear forces "truly do safeguard our way of life."

Changing perceptions of global realities have shaped American strategic doctrine over the past half-century, as the nation's leaders have struggled with the questions of what to do with nuclear weapons, what to do about them, and how to prevent others from using them. For analytic convenience, American strategy can be broken into three periods: first, the period of America's atomic monopoly (1945–1949); second, the period of American strategic superiority (1949 until roughly 1960); and, third, the transition from compellence to deterrence and from countervalue to counterforce targeting (1961–1991). A final period, one of nuclear build-down following the end of the Cold War, is also identifiable analytically and will be considered toward the end of the chapter when we examine arms control as an element of national security policy.

Strategic Doctrine during America's Atomic Monopoly

The seeds of the atomic age were planted in 1939 when the United States launched the Manhattan Project, a program at the cutting edge of science and technology designed to construct a superweapon that could be used successfully in war. J. Robert Oppenheimer, the atomic physicist who directed the Los Alamos, New Mexico, laboratory during the development of the A-bomb, observed that "We always assumed if [atomic bombs] were needed they would be used." Thus the rationale was established for a strategy based on, and backed by, the desire to possess extraordinary means of destruction with which to deal with enemies. President Truman's decision to drop the A-bomb on Hiroshima and, three days later, on Nagasaki was the culmination of that thinking. "When you have to deal with a beast you have to treat him as a beast," Truman reasoned.

Why did the United States use the bomb, which demolished two Japanese cities and took over one hundred thousand lives?[14] The official explanation is simple: The bomb was dropped "in order to end the war in the shortest possible time and to avoid the enormous losses of human life which otherwise confronted us" (Stimson and Bundy 1947). Whether the bomb was necessary to end the war remains in dispute, however—especially since Hiroshima and Nagasaki were largely civilian, not military, targets (Bernstein 1995).[15] Revisionist historians (for example, Alperovitz 1985, 1995) contend that the real motivation behind the bomb's use was preventing the expansion of the Soviet Union's postwar influence in the Far East and not a desire to save American lives. A parallel interpretation contends that the United States wanted to impress Soviet leaders with the awesome power of the weapon and America's willingness to exploit the advantages it now gave them.[16]

Regardless of its true purposes, the use of atomic means of mass destruction against Japan departed from traditional military strategy. Before the availability of atomic weapons, the instruments of war were viewed largely as means to short-range military ends. Now, however, they were also seen as instruments of diplomatic bargaining and the preservation of peace. The shift was profound: It marked the beginning of an era in which the instruments of war would be employed for the psychological purpose of molding others' behavior (including allies of the moment—in this instance, the Soviet Union).

During the period of America's atomic monopoly, the concept of *compellence* (Schelling 1966) described the new American view of nuclear weapons: They would not be used to fight but rather to get others to do what they might not otherwise do. Thus nuclear weapons were seen as synonymous with strategy itself (Summers 1989), the ultimate method of forceful persuasion known as "coercive diplomacy" (George 1992).

President Truman and Secretary of War Henry L. Stimson counted on the new weapon to elicit Soviet acceptance of American terms for settling outstanding war issues, particularly in eastern and central Europe. Truman could confidently advocate "winning through intimidation" and facing "Russia with an iron fist and strong language," because the United States alone possessed the greatest intimidator of them all—the bomb. Stimson was persuaded that the United States should "use the bomb to pry the Soviets out of Eastern Europe" (cited in LaFeber 1976). Although Stimson soon would reverse his position, his first instincts anticipated the direction American strategic thinking would take during this formative period, which NSC 68 finally crystallized. The memorandum rationalized "increasing American military and allied military capabilities across the board both in nuclear and conventional weapons [and] making it clear that whenever threats to the international balance of power manifested themselves, the United States could respond" (Gaddis 1987–1988). Should it prove necessary, the bomb was a tool that could be used.[17]

Strategic Doctrine under Conditions of Nuclear Superiority

The monopoly on atomic weapons the United States once enjoyed gave way to superiority in 1949, when, as we have noted, the Soviet Union also acquired the bomb. The assumption that America's adversaries could be made to bend to American wishes through atomic blackmail nonetheless became a cornerstone of the Eisenhower containment strategy, particularly as conceived by its chief architect, Secretary of State John Foster Dulles. Dulles sought to reshape the strategy of containment around three concepts: rollback, brinkmanship, and massive retaliation, all of which revealed the perceived utility of nuclear weapons as instruments of coercive diplomacy

Rollback identified the goal: reject passive containment of the spread of communist influence and, instead, "roll back" the Iron Curtain by liberating communist-dominated areas. Dulles pledged that the United States would practice rollback—and not merely promise it—by employing "all means necessary to secure the liberation of Eastern Europe."

The Eisenhower administration assumed that American strategic superiority would make ***brinkmanship*** practicable. In defining this concept, Dulles explained how nuclear power could be harnessed for bargaining purposes:

> You have to take chances for peace, just as you must take chances in war. Some say that we were brought to the verge of war. Of course we were brought to the verge of war. The ability to get to the verge without getting into the war is the necessary art. . . . If you try to run away from it, if you are scared to go to the brink, you are lost. We've had to look at it square in the face. . . . We walked to the brink and we looked it in the face. We took strong action. (Dulles 1952, 146)

Brinkmanship, in short, was a strategy for dealing with the Soviets by backing them into a corner with the threat of nuclear annihilation. In a confrontation, Dulles explained, atomic weapons "would come into use because, as I say, they are becoming more and more conventional and replacing what used to be called conventional weapons." In contrast to Harry Truman, then, who "viewed the atomic bomb as an instrument of terror and a weapon of last resort, Dwight Eisenhower viewed it as an integral part of American defense, and, in effect, a weapon of first resort" (Rosenberg 1983).

To convince its adversary that the United States was willing to carry out its threats, the Eisenhower administration proclaimed the doctrine of ***massive retaliation*** (labeled the "New Look" to distinguish it from Truman's strategy). This was a ***countervalue*** nuclear weapons strategy that sought to provide "the maximum deterrent at bearable cost" by threatening mass destruction of the things the Soviet leaders were perceived to value most—their population and military/industrial centers. Massive retaliation grew out of the Eisenhower administration's simultaneous impulses to save money and to challenge the perception that American foreign policy had become largely a reflexive reaction to communist initiatives. No longer would containment be restricted to retaliation to localized communist initiatives. Instead, it would target the very center of communist power and would be used to accomplish foreign policy goals.

Despite the assertiveness implied by such bold posturing, the historical record indicates that Eisenhower's administration—like Truman's—was, for the most part, cautious. As we saw in Chapter 3, few of the threats enunciated in its tough talk, such as the promise to supply military aid to those revolting against Soviet rule in Hungary in 1956, were actually carried out. The United States did sometimes threaten to use nuclear weapons (Russett 1989), but it never carried through on the threats. Nevertheless, faith in the utility of nuclear weapons as instruments of coercive diplomacy defined the 1950s, as the United States artfully pursued a compellence strategy.

Strategic Doctrine in Transition

A shift from compellence toward a strategy of *deterrence* began in the late 1950s and became readily discernible in the Kennedy and Johnson administrations. One reason for the shift was the Soviet Union's growing strategic capability. Policymakers' greater appreciation of U.S. vulnerability to nuclear attack was another. The development of intercontinental ballistic missiles (ICBMs) in particular was cause for alarm, as the United States now saw itself as being as vulnerable to Soviet attack as the Soviet Union was to an American strike. "On the day the Soviets acquired [the bomb as] an instrument and the means to deliver it," Kennedy adviser George Ball (1984) observed, "the bomb lost its military utility and became merely a means of mutual suicide . . . [for] there are no political objectives commensurate with the costs of an all-out nuclear exchange."

Kennedy himself felt it necessary to educate the world to the new strategic reality, warning of its dangers in a 1961 speech to the United Nations General Assembly:

> Today, every inhabitant of this planet must contemplate the day when this planet may no longer be habitable. Every man, woman and child lives under a nuclear sword of Damocles, hanging by the slenderest of threads, capable of being cut at any moment by accident or miscalculation or by madness. The weapons of war must be abolished before they abolish us.
>
> Men no longer debate whether armaments are a symptom or cause of tension. The mere existence of modern weapons—ten million times more powerful than any that the world has ever seen, and only minutes away from any target on earth—is a source of horror, and discord and distrust.

From Compellence to Deterrence

Deterrence means discouraging an adversary from using force by convincing the adversary that the costs of such action outweigh the potential gains. As a practical matter, strategic deterrence denotes the threat of weapons of mass destruction being used to impose unacceptably high costs directly on the homeland of an aggressive adversary.

To ensure that such costs can be imposed, a ***second-strike capability*** is necessary. This means that offensive strategic forces must be able to withstand an adversary's initial strike and retain the capacity to respond with a devastating second blow. In this way the aggressor will be assured of destruction, thus deterring the initial preemptive attack. Hence strategic deterrence implies sensitivity to the survivability of American strategic forces. In practice, the United States sought that objective through the maintenance of a ***triad of strategic weapons*** consisting of manned bombers and land- and sea-based intercontinental ballistic missiles. It continues to do so today.

The Kennedy administration's doctrine of strategic deterrence rested on the principle of ***assured destruction***—a condition realized if the country can survive an aggressor's worst possible attack with sufficient firepower to inflict unacceptable damage on the attacker in retaliation. It differed from massive retaliation in that the latter presupposed U.S. strategic superiority, which enabled the United States to choose the time and place where nuclear weapons might be used in response to an act of Soviet aggression (as defined by the United States). In contrast, the principle of assured destruction pledged that a direct attack against the United States (or perhaps its allies) would automatically result in a devastating American retaliatory nuclear strike. Hence it was concerned only with nuclear threats to American security, not the broad spectrum of threats to American interests that massive retaliation sought to prevent. During the Cold War this meant that the Soviet Union was given the initiative, under the assumption that it would not attack first if convinced that a first strike against the United States (or perhaps its NATO allies) would assure its own destruction. It is important to note that this strategy of survival through nuclear attack avoidance depended critically on the rational behavior of Soviet leaders.

American strategic doctrine also now increasingly stressed that what held for American deterrence of Soviet aggression also held for Soviet deterrence of American assertiveness. Hence mutual deterrence, based on the principle of ***mutual assured destruction (MAD),*** evolved as a description of the superpower's strategic relationship and a policy goal. The term "balance of terror" accurately described the essential military stalemate that emerged between the superpowers, inasmuch as mutual assured destruction is based on the military potential for, and psychological expectations of, widespread death and destruction for *both* combatants in the event of a nuclear exchange. In this sense nuclear deterrence "is like a gun with two barrels, of which one points ahead and the other points back at the gun's holder," writes Jonathan Schell (1984). "If a burglar should enter your house, it might make sense to threaten him with this gun, but it could never make sense to fire it." Yet preservation of a MAD world was eagerly sought: Because the price of an attack by one state on its adversary would be its own destruction, the very weapons of war—ironically—encouraged stability and war avoidance.

From Counterforce to Countervalue

The principle of assured destruction first emerged in an environment characterized by American strategic superiority. By the end of the 1960s, however, it became clear that the Soviets had an arsenal roughly equivalent to that of the United States. American policymakers now confronted gnawing questions about the utility of continually attempting to enhance the destructive capabilities of the United States. As Henry Kissinger, Nixon's national security adviser and later secretary of state, observed: "The paradox of contemporary military strength is that a gargantuan increase in power has eroded its relationship to policy. . . . The capacity to destroy is difficult to translate into a plausible threat even against countries with no capacity for retaliation. . . . [Other] nations have an unprecedented scope for autonomous action . . . [and military] power no longer translates automatically into influence."

By the time the first strategic arms limitations (SALT) agreements were signed in 1972, the orthodox view of nuclear weapons was clear: Their purpose was to prevent war, not wage it. Robert McNamara (1983), secretary of defense under Kennedy and Johnson, put it simply: "*Nuclear weapons serve no military purpose whatsoever. They are totally useless—except only to deter one's opponent from using them*" (emphasis in original). Such reasoning stimulated growing support in the mid-1980s for a "no first use" declaratory policy (Bundy et al. 1982), even though such a policy would run counter to NATO doctrine, which maintained that nuclear weapons would be used if NATO conventional forces faced defeat on the battlefield.

Although SALT I sought to restrain the superpowers' strategic competition, qualitative improvements in their weapons systems continued unabated. Inevitably this provoked new challenges to the orthodox view of the role of nuclear weapons as policy instruments. The continuing strategic debate now centered on three issues: targeting policy, warfighting strategies, and strategic defense.

Targeting and War-Fighting Like massive retaliation, the principle of assured destruction rested on the belief that deterrence could be realized by directing nuclear weapons at targets believed to be of greatest value to the adversary, namely, its population and industrial centers. The countervalue targeting doctrine joined the civilian and industrial centers of both adversaries in a mutual hostage relationship.

As early as 1962 Secretary of Defense McNamara suggested that the United States ought instead to adopt a ***counterforce*** strategy, one that targeted American destructive power on the enemy's military forces and weapons. A decade later the United States would take significant strides in this direction. Criticizing the principle of assured destruction as "insufficiently flexible and selective to allow the President to order a less than all-out nuclear attack," James Schlesinger, secretary of defense in the Ford administration, declared that the United States would pursue a counterforce capability that would enable U.S. strategic forces to attack heavily protected Soviet military targets. The "limited nuclear options" policy required the development of weapons technology providing improved accuracy in nuclear delivery systems and increased so-called ***hard-target kill*** (warhead yield) ***capacity***. (Hard-target kill capacity refers to the destructive potential of weapons directed against land-based intercontinental ballistic missile (ICBM) forces, which were vital to the second-strike capabilities of both adversaries and therefore necessary for effective deterrence.) The limited nuclear options policy also invited the addition of another lurid acronym to the arcane language of strategic planning: ***NUTs***—variously defined as "nuclear utilization target selection" or "nuclear utilization theory" (Keeny and Panofsky 1981).

President Carter extended the counterforce option in 1980s, when he signed Presidential Directive (PD) 59. Known in official circles as the "***countervailing*** or *war-fighting strategy*," the new posture sought to enhance deterrence by targeting *both* military forces and weapons *and* population and industrial centers in the Soviet Union. The change presumably was incorporated into the top-secret master plan for waging nuclear war known as the **SIOP (Single Integrated Operational Plan)**, which operationalizes strategic doctrine by selecting the military and nonmilitary targets to be attacked in the event of war (see Ball and Toth 1990).

Even as the United States modified its plans for coping with the Soviet threat, the Soviet Union continued a massive program of military spending initiated in the 1960s whose purpose was to enlarge and modernize Soviet strategic forces. Advantages in numbers of missiles, missile warheads, and missile throw-weight accrued to the Soviets, stimulating a growing chorus of alarm that moved the United States away from the accommodationist policies of the 1970s toward a decidedly more militant posture toward its Cold War adversary (see also Chapter 3). "Our ability to deter war and protect our security declined dangerously during the 1970s," scolded Ronald Reagan. Believing that the 1970s had been a "decade of neglect" for U.S. security interests, Reagan's administration embarked on the largest peacetime military buildup in the nation's history.

The Reagan administration feared in particular that Soviet technological developments had rendered the land-based leg of the strategic triad vulnerable to a devastating first strike (which would undermine second-strike capability but not eliminate it due to U.S. submarine-based forces). Further, the administration was convinced that the Soviet Union could no longer be deterred simply with the threat of assured destruction. Therefore, it pledged to develop capabilities sufficient not only to ensure the survival of U.S. strategic forces in the event of a first strike (so that a devastating second strike could be launched), but also to deter a second strike by threatening a third. Reagan officials claimed that making nuclear weapons more usable would enhance deterrence by making the nuclear threat more credible. Critics disagreed, charging that making nuclear war less unthinkable made it more likely.

Critics were especially prone to argue, based on the probability of human error or technological failure, that any outbreak of nuclear war would certainly end in nuclear catastrophe. They often pointed to the vulnerability of the nation's command, control, communications, and intelligence (C^3I) capability. A Soviet attack by comparatively few weapons would effectively "decapitate" the United States by killing its political leaders and destroying the communication links necessary to ensure a coordinated and coherent U.S. retaliation (Ball 1989; Schneider 1989). Such dangers undermined the feasibility of conducting a limited (protracted) nuclear war, they warned. Hence, critics of the Reagan administration's policies concluded that a strategy premised on the usability of nuclear weapons in war would in fact make war *more* likely, not less.

The Bush administration was not explicit about its strategic assumptions. However, while it stressed publicly that America's nuclear weapons were primarily for deterrence, it quietly continued to pursue a nuclear war-fighting capability. Bush approved changes in the SIOP that would enhance U.S. capabilities to fight and win a nuclear war by paralyzing the Soviets' war-making abilities in the opening hours of conflict. Existing strategy was redesigned to "penetrate the [Soviets'] deepest underground bunkers and 'decapitate' the entire Soviet leadership" (Toth 1989). Critics, who averred that Bush's revised SIOP took "war fighting to dangerous extremes" (Ball and Toth 1990; see also Glaser 1992; Mazarr 1990), again worried that plans to blitz Soviet leaders at the beginning of hostilities would increase rather than decrease the risk of nuclear holocaust.

Because these changes were made at the very time that the Soviet threat was diminishing, they gave testimony to the persistence of old ways of thinking about national security and strategy. Indeed, Secretary of State Baker asserted shortly before the Berlin Wall crumbled that "We are not on the verge of a perpetual peace in which war is no longer possible. We cannot disinvent nuclear weapons nor the need for continued deterrence." Hence, fears still dominated hopes, even as the Cold War waned. This led Fred Iklé (1990), who had served in the Defense Department during the Reagan administration, to conclude that "Washington's national security establishment continues to see the world in terms of the 1947 mindset."

From Offense to Defense Ronald Reagan launched perhaps the greatest challenge to the orthodox view of the utility of nuclear weapons with a dramatic call for a high-tech, "Star Wars" ***ballistic missile defense (BMD)*** system, designed to render nuclear missiles "impotent and obsolete." The ***Strategic Defense Initiative (SDI)***, as it was officially known, sought to create a "defense dominant" strategy. Believing the principle of mutual assured destruction "morally unacceptable," Reagan's program foreshadowed a distant future in which the United States would interdict offensive weapons launched toward the United States in fear or anger. The knowledge that the United States was invulnerable would also reduce the probability of war.

SDI was the object of criticism from the start, stimulating a debate that continues even today. Many experts felt that the program created expectations that technology could not fulfill until well into the next century, if ever. They also warned that if SDI were pursued the Soviets would undoubtedly increase their nuclear arsenal to ensure their ability to overwhelm U.S. defenses, while at the same time proceeding with development of their own defensive system. SDI could thus incite a rapid and extremely expensive escalation of the arms race, the outcome of which might further impair both superpowers' security (Carnesale 1985).

Still, advocates of a defense-dominant strategy maintained that "defending through active defense is preferable to defending through terrorism—the ultimate mechanism by which deterrence through threat of retaliation operates" (Congressional Research Service, 1989). Thus research on various conceptualizations of a ballistic missile defense system continued throughout the 1980s.

Bush came to office a supporter of SDI and continued to press a reluctant Congress for the funds necessary to continue research and development on the costly system. This was in spite of the diminished perception of a Soviet threat to the United States' physical security. "Even as we work to reduce arsenals and reduce tensions," Bush argued, "we understand the continuing crucial role of strategic defense." By this time, however, the notion of establishing an impenetrable shield that would render incoming missiles "impotent and obsolete" had been abandoned in favor of a less ambitious system. As the Soviet Union imploded and the Cold War ended, "scenarios of a Third World strike, a renegade Russian submarine missile attack, or an accidental or unauthorized launch became the primary justifications for the system" (Han 1992–1993).

In addition, Boris Yeltsin declared in early 1992 that Russia would be willing to cooperate on a joint defense system.

In 1991 Congress passed legislation supporting the deployment of Global Protection Against Limited Strikes (GPALS). GPALS envisioned a layered defensive system whose first line of defense would be space-based interceptors (called "brilliant pebbles") that would destroy enemy missiles in their post-boost phase by ramming into them. Ground-based interceptors, supported by orbiting and ground-based phased-array radars, would target incoming missiles that penetrated the first line of defense. The Clinton administration later scrapped most of the space-based options in favor of a largely land- and sea-based antimissile system—known by the acronym *THAAD*, for *Theater High-Altitude Area Defense* system—designed to meet current and future ballistic missile threats from the Global South (previously the Third World). The perceived success of the Patriot antimissile missile during the Persian Gulf War (but whose actual performance remains a matter of bitter controversy [Hersh 1994; Postol 1991–1992; but cf. Ranger 1993]), gave impetus to the proposed system.

Because a ballistic missile defense system may violate the 1972 Antiballistic Missile Treaty, the Clinton administration opened negotiations with Russia, hoping by focusing on the distinction between theater ballistic missiles and strategic ballistic missiles to pave the way with a "clarified" AMB treaty for deployment of a limited defensive system. Mutual assured destruction (MAD) would continue to be expected to provide defense against strategic weapons. However, the theater-based system would protect against shorter-range missiles—against which, as a practical matter, U.S. allies would be most vulnerable. The ability of such a system to protect the United States' long-run physical security and even its short-term national security interests is (not surprisingly) hotly disputed (Goldmuntz 1994; Krepon 1995).

Arms Control and National Security

The end of the Cold War witnessed a flurry of dramatic arms control and disarmament initiatives considered unimaginable less than two decades earlier. By then negotiated arms control agreements had become not only an accepted dimension of U.S. national security policy generally but also an integral element of strategic deterrence (Caldwell 1993). "The arms control process has always had as a main goal to ensure deterrence by enhancing stability and balance in the strategic relationship," explained George Shultz, Reagan's secretary of state. James Baker, Bush's secretary of state, echoed that conviction: "The main goal of arms control is to reduce the risk of war. . . . Stability requires military forces and policies such that no one can gain by striking first even in the worst crisis."

The SALT Process

The Strategic Arms Limitation Talks (SALT) negotiations were a joint effort by the Cold War adversaries to prevent the collapse of the fragile balance of terror that supported mutual assured destruction. The SALT agreements reached in 1972 (SALT I) attempted to guarantee each superpower's second-strike capability and thereby preserve the fear of retaliation on which stable deterrence presumably rested.

SALT I consisted of (1) a treaty that restricted the deployment of antiballistic missile defense (ABM) systems by the United States and the Soviet Union to equal and very low levels, and (2) a five-year interim accord on strategic offensive arms, which restricted the number of ICBM and SLBM launchers that each side was permitted to have. The ABM accord remains in force, and, as discussed above, figures prominently in discussions about designs of possible ballistic missile defense systems. The interim agreement on offensive weapons was essentially a confidence-building, stopgap measure that anticipated a comprehensive, long-term treaty limiting strategic weapons.

The SALT II treaty, signed in 1979 (but never ratified), sought that objective by substantially revising the quantitative restrictions of SALT I and by placing certain qualitative constraints on the superpowers' strategic arsenals. When SALT II was signed these limitations were expected to dampen dramatically the momentum of the superpowers' arms race. And while they may have kept the total number of strategic weapons below what otherwise would have been produced without the SALT process, the evidence (summarized in Figure 4.2) demonstrates that the spiral of weapons production—notably deliverable warheads—continued largely unabated. The destructive capacity of these weapons deserves some emphasis.

When World War II ended, there was only one atomic bomb still in existence. By 1990, the United States and the Soviet Union each had stockpiled nearly 12,000 strategic (long-range) nuclear weapons. The warheads carried aboard a single U.S. submarine contained the force equivalent to nearly 18,000 Hiroshima explosions; those on U.S. ICBMs another 27,000 Hiroshimas; and those on U.S. bombers still another 33,400. And as unimaginable as it may seem, Soviet strategic nuclear forces were capable of even greater destruction—with a megatonnage equivalent to 115,600 Hiroshima-sized explosions (Harris and Markusen 1986, 25–26). Obviously the use of these weapons, even in comparatively small numbers, would threaten the destruction not only of entire cities and countries but possibly—when radiation effects and potentially catastrophic changes in the global climate through a "nuclear winter" are considered—of the entire world population (Ehrlich et al. 1985). The threat is vividly captured in Albert Einstein's famous remark that, although he did not know what the weapons of a third world war would be, in a fourth they would be "sticks and stones."

The START Process—I

The Reagan administration followed the "dual track" of its predecessors by pursuing simultaneously arms limitation talks and a military buildup. Early in the first Reagan term there was little willingness to discuss arms limitations, but a combination of domestic and international pressure gave impetus to two sets of negotiations—the ***Strategic Arms Reduction Talks (START)***, aimed at reducing the superpowers' strategic forces, and the intermediate-range nuclear force (INF) talks, directed toward reducing theater nuclear weapons in Europe. As noted earlier, the superpowers reached a historic agreement in 1987 when they signed the INF treaty banning intermediate-range nuclear forces from Europe. Although the accord required dismantling less than 5 percent of the world's nuclear arsenals, it set the stage, as British Foreign

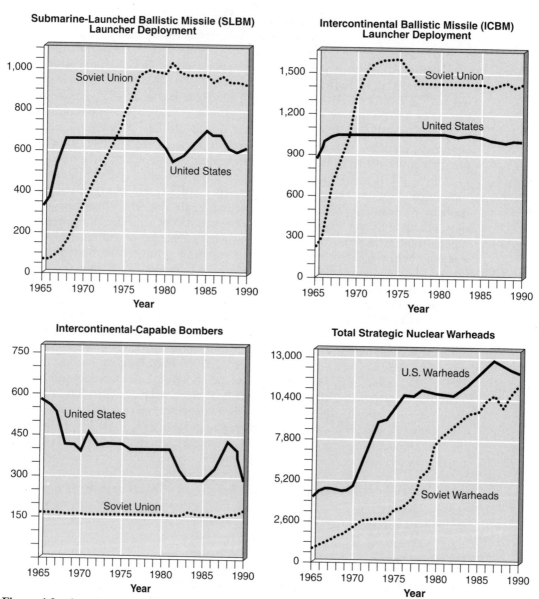

Figure 4.2 American and Soviet Strategic Delivery Vehicles and Warheads, 1965–1990
Source: Adapted from data provided by the Center for Defense Information.

Secretary Sir Geoffrey Howe put it, for "the beginning of the beginning of the whole arms control process."

On the strategic front, negotiations first stalled and then proceeded cautiously. In 1985 the superpowers finally agreed that "deep cuts" in their nuclear forces were desirable. They differed substantially in how those cuts should be accomplished, however, as their force compositions influenced their interests. As a traditional land power, the Soviet Union placed heavy reliance on land-based missiles. The United States sought to reduce the number of these, viewing them as the gravest threat to U.S. land-based forces. Conversely, the Soviets, facing an American strategic force more widely dispersed among the three legs of the strategic triad, sought cutbacks that would directly offset U.S. areas of superiority. The Soviets also expressed renewed apprehension about SDI, but the Reagan administration remained determined to forge ahead on the plan.

Both sides offered new proposals and counterproposals in the months that followed the Geneva summit. Eventually the principle of "deep cuts" became the mutually accepted goal. In 1991, after nine years of bargaining, the negotiators overcame their differences and concluded the START I treaty, committing each side to *reduce* its strategic forces by one-third. The treaty also provided a baseline for future reductions in the two sides' capabilities

Although arguably a dramatic breakthrough, START I was as significant for what it did *not* accomplish as for what it did. The six hundred page treaty only reduced the number of each side's weapons to the level in place when the START negotiations began in 1982. Moreover, a report by the Congressional Research Service (1991) at the time START I was signed made the startling observation that "The United States will be able to have a modern, more accurate, and lethal force under START than today . . . . The Soviet Union will for the most part be able to continue its modernization plans."

The START Process—II

In September 1991, responding to widespread complaints that the START I agreement barely began the kinds of arms reductions possible now that the threat of a Soviet attack had vanished, President Bush declared that the United States must seize "the historic opportunity now before us." He called long-range bombers off twenty-four-hour alert, canceled plans to deploy the long-range MX missile on rail cars, and offered to negotiate sharp reductions in the most dangerous kinds of globe-spanning missiles. Not long after that, President Boris Yeltsin declared that Russia "no longer considers the United States our potential adversary" and announced it would stop targeting American cities with nuclear missiles. Bush responded in his State of the Union Address with a series of unilateral arms cuts that would:

- Suspend production of the B-2 bomber.
- Halt development of the Midgetman mobile nuclear missile.
- Cease purchases of advanced cruise missiles.
- Cancel production of warheads used aboard Trident submarine missiles.

Within hours, Yeltsin replied to Bush's initiatives by recommending that the two powers reduce their nuclear arsenals to only 2,000 to 2,500 warheads each—far below the cuts called for in the START I agreement and almost 50 percent greater than the reductions Bush proposed. Yeltsin later announced his intention to trim Russian military spending dramatically and to reduce the size of the Russian army by half. He also proposed eliminating strategic nuclear weapons entirely by the year 2000.

Even in this hopeful climate of reciprocated reductions, Russia and the United States continued to differ on where the strategic weapons cuts should be made. Bush called for the elimination of all land-based strategic missiles with multiple warheads (MIRVs), the category in which Russia was strongest. But on submarine-launched missiles—where the United States had the advantage—Bush resisted the Russian quest for across-the-board cuts and refused to accept reductions beyond a third.

The uncertain future of Yeltsin and Russia's government complicated the arms control and disarmament process. Also troublesome was the disposition of nuclear weapons held by Ukraine, Kazakhstan, and Belarus, three former Soviet republics on whose soil nuclear weapons were deployed when the Soviet Union imploded. All signed the 1992 Lisbon protocol to the START agreement, pledging their willingness to eliminate all nuclear weapons on their territories by 1999 and to sign the Nuclear Nonproliferation Treaty (NPT) as nonnuclear states. Still, ensuring that eventuality remained uncertain. New impetus in that direction was realized in late 1993, however, when the United States, Ukraine, and Russia reached an agreement that provides for the transfer of all nuclear weapons on Ukrainian territory to Russia for their dismantlement in exchange for certain security guarantees from the United States, Russia, and Britain, and economic assistance from the United States. Belarus and Kazakhstan also followed suit, pledging either to transfer the nuclear warheads on their territories to Russia or to dismantle and destroy their strategic missile systems. These steps set the stage for the START I treaty to enter into force.

Another breakthrough occurred at the June 1992 Washington summit, when Yeltsin and Bush made the surprise announcement that Russia and the United States would make additional deep cuts in their strategic arsenals. The addendum to the START accord (which would become START II) called for a 60 percent reduction of the two powers' combined total nuclear arsenals—from about 15,000 warheads to 6,500 by the year 2003. Even more dramatically, the START II agreement, signed in early 1993, not only cut the number of warheads beyond earlier projections but also altered drastically the kinds of weapons in each country's arsenal. Under the agreement, Russia and the United States will give up all multiple warheads on their land-based ICBM missiles—a particularly dangerous, "silo-busting" capability. They also will reduce the number of submarine-launched ballistic missile warheads to no more than 1,750 (see Table 4.1).

If adhered to, START II and related unilateral initiatives could reduce the chances of war by banning the nuclear weapons that Russia and the United States would most likely use in a preemptive strike, leaving them with only weapons suited to a retaliatory strike. Bush described the hopeful future: "With this agreement [START II] the nuclear nightmare recedes more and more for ourselves, for our children, and for our grandchildren."

Strategic Defense and Arms Control beyond the Cold War

Bill Clinton promised a thorough reevaluation of the nation's strategic posture paralleling the Bottom Up Review of conventional weapons. While it was underway,

TABLE 4.1 PROJECTED IMPACT OF NUCLEAR ARMS REDUCTION
TREATIES AND INITIATIVES

United States Nuclear Arms		Type of Nuclear Weapons	Former Soviet Union Nuclear Arms	
1992	2003		1992	2003
12,000	3,500	Strategic (long-range)	10,000	3,000
8,000	5,000	Tactical (battlefield)	17,000	7,000

Source: The Defense Monitor 22 (No. 1, 1993): 3.

Clinton and Yeltsin agreed to detarget their respective strategic nuclear weapons. This meant, as Deputy Secretary of State Strobe Talbott put it, that "the pistols we have aimed at each other's heads will no longer be on hair trigger." When the strategic posture review was completed in the fall of 1994, however, it reaffirmed the Bush administration's posture but did little else. In a disappointment to those who sought further reductions in strategic nuclear weapons, no new initiatives were announced that would cut U.S. and Russian weapons below the 3,500/3,000 balance projected in the START II accord. Furthermore, the United States would continue to deploy nearly 500 nuclear weapons in Europe to deter an attack on American allies. And the long-standing doctrine of a "first use" of nuclear weapons was retained rather than adopting a no-first-use declaratory policy.[18] Finally, Clinton approved a military plan to install more accurate missiles equipped with nuclear warheads on four U.S. submarines. It was in this environment that an anonymous advocate of further reductions in offensive nuclear weapons worried that "the clay of history is beginning to harden again" (quoted in R. Smith 1994b; for a contrasting viewpoint, see Bailey 1995).

Some observers advocate further reductions in American nuclear strength based on the conviction that the capability of American conventional weapons today (a product of what has been called the Military Technical Revolution [Mazarr 1995]) is so great that American security interests would be better served *without* nuclear weapons than *with* them (see Cropsey 1994; "Does the United States Need Nuclear Weapons?" 1993). The Les Aspin quotation at the opening of this chapter encapsulates this reasoning; it bears more detailed repetition:

> Nuclear weapons were the big equalizer—the means by which the United States equalized the military advantage of its adversaries. But now the Soviet Union has collapsed. The United States is the biggest conventional power in the world. There is no longer any need for the United States to have nuclear weapons as an equalizer against other powers.
>
> If we were to get another crack at the magic wand, we'd wave it in a nanosecond. A world without nuclear weapons would not be disadvantageous to the United States. In fact, a world without nuclear weapons would actually be better. Nuclear weapons are still the big equalizer but now the United States is not the equalizer but the equalizee.

No one doubts that nuclear knowledge will remain. Advocates of continued steps toward nuclear disarmament do contend, however, that the goal of nuclear nonproliferation can never be attained as long as some states reserve to themselves the right to possess these weapons. From this perspective, a Comprehensive Test Ban treaty—embraced by the Clinton administration but previously shunned by the United States—is a first priority. "The central requirement of nonproliferation is to convince other countries that nuclear weapons are not usable and therefore not worth trying to acquire," argues one analyst. "Continued nuclear testing sends just the opposite message. By ceaselessly refining and testing these weapons, we suggest they *are* usable" (cited in Nolan 1994). Even with the dramatic cuts in nuclear weapons anticipated in START II, the number of strategic warheads will only return to the level in existence when the Nuclear Non-Proliferation Treaty (NPT) was signed in 1968. Understandably, "the [nuclear] 'have-nots' showed some resentment when the superpowers quadrupled their arsenals in the two decades *after* the signing, and that resentment persists" (Renner 1992).

What is to be done with existing weapons, granting that nuclear knowledge will remain? Separating nuclear warheads from their delivery vehicles would be an important step. Dismantling the warheads themselves and following these steps to an eventual "virtual" strategic arsenal—one in which nuclear weapons could be reassembled only in several months' time—pose visions of an eventual nuclear-free world (Mazarr 1995; see also Schell 1984).

A world without nuclear weapons, of course, remains a distant—perhaps utopian—future.[19] But is it any more unrealistic than the fall of the Berlin Wall and the end of the Cold War?[20] Meanwhile, discourse about the role of nuclear weapons in world politics and of American strategic thinking in a world in flux continues (see Daalder 1995; Miller 1994).

Power and Principle: In Pursuit of the National Interest ....

The world has changed dramatically in the past half-decade, but the means of American foreign policy—captured in the themes of military might and interventionism—remain durable patterns. Adjustments have been made, to be sure, but they have been confined largely to tactics, not fundamental reassessments of basic purposes or strategies. Thus we find that the nation's conventional military forces continue to be poised for global engagement and that nuclear weapons continue to be relied on to provide security from attack through the threat of attack. Without a new framework for policy, old ways of thinking will persist.

The outlines of a new framework remain unclear, however. Some have suggested that the choice of foreign policy means will be dictated by preferences for unilateralism, assertive multilateralism, and U.S. leadership as alternative postures toward America's future world role (Haass 1995), much as we argued in Chapter 3. Others point to the virtues of selective *dis*engagement, a posture that would "permit a drastic retrenchment of the U.S. military presence in the world. . . . From the standpoint of strict national interest, the American army could be slashed back to an expeditionary force designed to meet the modest military requirements involved in protecting

American lives abroad, combating terrorism, and maintaining a deterrent force suitable for emergency deployment" (Maynes 1990).

No resolution of these divergent viewpoints and their variants is in sight. Meanwhile, the sole-remaining-superpower syndrome will likely continue to inform the classic debate between power and principle that has long colored the nation's struggle to understand its national interests and how best to pursue them.

NOTES

1. For contrasting opinions on NSC 68, see the essays in May (1992).

2. The militarization of American foreign policy occurred not because professional military leaders assumed policy-making roles (although some, such as George Marshall, did), but because civilian leaders tended to embrace military approaches to political problems (Yarmolinsky 1970–1971, 1971). It is significant that civilian policymakers came to adopt military ways of thinking for, as Richard J. Walton (cited in Donovan 1974) astutely observed, "Civilian control versus military control is a distinction without a difference if the civilians think the same way the military does." For additional observations on this point as it applied to the decision to use the atomic bomb against Japan and to decisions during the Cold War, see Alperovitz (1985), Ambrose (1993), Feis (1966), Horowitz (1965), LaFeber (1976), and Sherwin (1973). Johnson and Metz (1995) summarize current issues in civil-military relations, which will be addressed in Chapter 11.

3. The diplomatic heritage of U.S. foreign policy is shot through with inconsistent ideas regarding America's use of military instruments and force. Americans are said to display "a peculiar ambivalence toward war. They have traditionally perceived themselves as a peaceful, non-militant people, and yet have hardly been unwarlike" (Millett and Maslowski 1984). The nation's political mythology maintains that the United States is both peace loving and unbeatable in war; that it opposes the maintenance of standing armies but concurrently keeps an effective and sizable militia; that although it enters wars only reluctantly and always for moral purposes, it then wages them enthusiastically and concludes them victoriously; that it stands opposed to the use of force to get its way internationally, but that it is prone to intervene militarily in the affairs of others "if necessary" to protect its global interests; and that it stands in awe of military power and seeks to acquire it but fears to use it.

4. Even before the agreement, however, current U.S. law required the destruction of 90 percent of the U.S. stockpile, most of which had been deemed militarily useless, by 1997.

5. See, for example, "Far Flung Frontiers of Security: The Clinton Administration's Two-War Strategy" (1995), Korb (1995), Morrison, Tsipis, and Wiesner (1994), and Steinbruner (1995).

6. Military forces can also be used to attain desired ends directly. Blechman and Kaplan's (1978) and Zelikow's (1987) inventories are concerned only with those instances where the force itself does not obtain the objective, but rather affects the perceptions of others, thereby influencing their decision(s).

7. The Korean and Vietnam Wars are excluded from the analyses, which are restricted to crises occurring in peacetime. The data also exclude humanitarian operations, intelligence and law enforcement operations, and operations routinely undertaken to support U.S. diplomacy, such as placing naval units on alert during presidential visits.

8. Anthony Lake, speaking at Harvard University in October 1994, identified seven national interests that the Clinton administration believed warranted the use of military power: "To defend against direct attacks on the United States, its citizens at home and abroad, and its allies"; "to counter aggression"; "to defend our most important economic interests"; "to preserve, promote, and defend democracy"; "to prevent the dangerous proliferation of nuclear weapons and other weapons of mass destruction, to prevent acts of terrorism, and to combat the deadly flow of drugs"; "to maintain our reliability"; and "for humanitarian purposes."

9. For discussions of these and related issues, see Carpenter (1993), de Waal and Omaar (1994), Fromkin (1994a), Hoffmann (1993), Muldoon (1995), Stedman (1992–1993), and related articles in the fall 1993 issue of *Harvard International Review* and the March 1994 issue of the *Middle East Report*.

10. Chester Crocker, assistant secretary of state for African affairs in the Reagan administration, admonishes that

> the "failure" in Somalia was not, in fact, a failure of either humanitarian intervention or muscular peacekeeping. It was a failure to apply them steadily and wisely. Much was accomplished during the U.S.-led phase (December 1992 to April 1993), but it was promptly placed at risk when the second U.N.-led operation took over amidst jolting discontinuities of leadership, tradition, military doctrine, personal chemistry, operating procedures, command and control, policy instincts and bureaucratic systems. (Crocker 1994, 23; see also Crocker 1995)

11. In July 1992, several months before the United States intervened in Somalia, the U.S. Ambassador to Kenya, Smith Hempstone, warned State Department officials in strong and sometimes racist-sounding overtones against intervention in Somalia. "I do not think Somalia is amenable to the quick fix so beloved of Americans," he said. "Leave them alone . . . to work out their own destiny, brutal as it may be. . . . Think once, twice and three times before you embrace the Somali tarbaby," he advised. He also asked, almost rhetorically, "What will we leave behind when we depart? . . . The one 'beneficial' effect a major American intrusion into Somalia is likely to have may be to reunite the Somali nation: against us, the invaders, the outsiders, the kaffirs (unbelievers) who may have fed their children but also have killed their young men. . . . In the old days, the Somalis raided for camels, women and slaves. Today they raid for camels, women, slaves and food." *U.S. New and World Report*, December 14, 1992, p. 30.

12. As the United States prepared to intervene in Haiti, analysts were quick to point out that the last time the United States had sent the Marines to that island—during the administration of Woodrow Wilson in 1915—they had stayed for nineteen years. They noted that the United States also sought then to instill democracy in Haiti, but failed.

Concern for "getting out" is one of the legacies of Vietnam, as policymakers at that time did not have a clear vision of what light at the end of what tunnel would permit them to terminate the war (Karnow 1983). Hence "quagmire" and "Vietnam" became virtually synonymous as policymakers contemplated later interventions.

13. Analyses and critiques of American interventionist policies and practices in the recent past and proposed for the future can be found in Betts (1994), Haass (1994a, 1994b), Kanter and Brooks (1994), Maynes (1995), Schraeder (1992), Shalom (1993), and T. Smith (1994b).

14. For a vivid description of the human and physical damage, see Schell (1982).

15. In retrospect, it is clear that Japan desperately wanted to surrender to the United States on acceptable terms. Tokyo was already in ruins; Japan's fate was certain. As the U.S. Strategic Bombing Survey concluded, "certainly prior to 31 December 1945 Japan would have surren-

dered even if the atomic bombs had not been dropped. . . ." The United States knew through diplomatic channels a month before actually dropping the bomb that the Japanese government wished to sue for peace (Alperovitz 1985, 1989; Miles, 1985; for rebuttals, see Alsop and Joravsky 1980, and Bundy 1988).

16. Based on now declassified documents, Bernstein writes that

> Administration leaders did not seek to avoid the use of the A-bomb. They even believed that its military use might produce a powerful bonus: the intimidation of the Soviets, rendering them, as [Secretary of State] Byrnes said, "more manageable," especially in Eastern Europe. Though that was not the dominant purpose for using the weapon, it certainly was a strong confirming one. Had Truman and his associates, like the dissenting scientists at Chicago, foreseen that the A-bombing of Japan would make the Soviets intransigent rather than tractable, perhaps American leaders would have questioned their decision. (Bernstein 1995, 150)

17. See Alperovitz and Bird (1994) for a discussion of the role of the atomic bomb in the militarization of post-World War II American foreign policy.

18. See Quester and Utgoff (1994) for a defense of the "first use" nuclear posture.

19. See Goodpaster (1993) for a reasoned blueprint of the steps required to further rein in nuclear arms.

20. See Mueller (1989) for a detailed treatment of the provocative thesis that nuclear weapons were largely irrelevant to political purposes even during the Cold War.

SUGGESTIONS FOR FURTHER READING

Alperovitz, Gar. *The Decision to Use the Atomic Bomb: And the Architecture of an American Myth.* New York: Knopf, 1995.

Cohen, Eliot A. "Constraints on America's Conduct of Small Wars." *International Security* 9 (Fall 1984): 151–81.

Freeman, Lawrence. *The Evolution of Nuclear Strategy,* 2nd ed. New York: St. Martin's, 1989.

George, Alexander L. *The Limits of Coercive Diplomacy.* Boulder, Colo.: Westview, 1994.

Haass, Richard N. *Intervention: The Use of American Military Force in the Post-Cold War World.* Washington, D.C.: Carnegie Endowment, 1994.

Jordan, Amos A., William J. Taylor, and Lawrence J. Korb. *American National Security: Policy and Process,* 4th ed. Baltimore: Johns Hopkins University Press, 1993.

Kanter, Arnold, and Linton F. Brooks, eds. *U.S. Intervention Policy for the Post-Cold War World: New Challenges and New Responses.* New York: Norton, 1994.

Kegley, Charles W., Jr., and Eugene R. Wittkopf, eds. *The Nuclear Reader: Strategy, Weapons, War,* 2nd ed. New York: St. Martin's, 1989.

Krepon, Michael. "Are Missile Defenses MAD?" *Foreign Affairs* 74 (January/February 1995): 19–24.

Schell, Jonathan. *The Abolition.* New York: Knopf, 1984.

Schraeder, Peter J., ed. *Intervention in the 1990s: U.S. Foreign Policy in the Third World,* 2nd ed. Boulder, Colo.: Lynne Rienner, 1992.

Snow, Donald M. *National Security: Defense Policy for a New International Order.* New York: St. Martin's, 1995.

CHAPTER 5

. . .

THE INSTRUMENTS OF GLOBAL INFLUENCE: COVERT ACTIVITIES, PUBLIC DIPLOMACY, AND FOREIGN AID

. . .

Intervention can be physical, spiritual, bilateral, multilateral, direct action, skills transfer, institution building; it can be so many things— a fabulous menu!

> Chester A. Crocker, Chair, Board of Directors,
> United States Institute for Peace, 1994

I don't see why we need to stand by and watch a country go Communist due to the irresponsibility of its own people.

> Special Assistant for National
> Security Affairs Henry Kissinger, 1970

On June 5, 1947, at a Harvard University commencement address, Secretary of State George C. Marshall set forth the commitment of the United States to assist in the reconstruction of war-torn Europe as a basic principle of American foreign policy. The plan was sold to a skeptical Congress and the American people on the basis of strategic arguments and as an instrument of anticommunism in the emerging Cold War struggle with the Soviet Union. Two years later, in Point Four of his inaugural address, President Truman called for "a bold new program for making the benefits of our scientific advances and industrial progress available for the improvement and growth of underdeveloped areas." Some American foreign aid programs had existed prior to this time—notably the Lend-Lease program that brought wartime assistance to American allies during World War II—but with the Marshall Plan and Point Four they became primary instruments of American foreign policy.

Congress also passed a new National Security Act in 1947. The Central Intelligence Agency (CIA), the Department of Defense, and the Joint Chiefs of Staff now became central institutions in the nation's postwar national security establishment. Each new organization sought to improve on the institutional apparatus in place prior to and during World War II. The task of the CIA, in particular, was to prevent recurrence of a catastrophe like Pearl Harbor. Evidence was available that the Japanese were about to attack the United States, but intelligence analysts and military commanders were unable to interpret the information and bring it to the attention of policymakers in a timely fashion. Thus, on December 7, 1941, Japan struck a crippling blow on the U.S. Pacific fleet, at great loss of life. In his war message to Congress, President Franklin Roosevelt would describe the day of the attack "A date which will live in infamy."

Intelligence Collection and Covert Actions

Whether better *intelligence*—information useful to policymakers about a potential enemy—would have prevented Pearl Harbor or blunted its damage remains controversial.[1] It is noteworthy that even after the CIA was formed, the United States was caught off guard in 1948 when the Soviet Union blocked allied access routes to Berlin, prompting the famous airlift of supplies to the beleaguered city. Two years later the United States was again surprised when North Korea unexpectedly invaded South Korea.

Nations have always gathered information about one another, which often means engaging in *espionage*—spying to obtain secret government information. Benjamin Franklin had engaged in European intrigue to bring the French into the Revolutionary War on the colonists' side; the British hanged Nathan Hale, an American revolutionary soldier, as a spy. According to tradition, Hale's last words were "I only regret that I have but one life to lose for my country." Today his statue adorns the entry to CIA headquarters in Langley, Virginia.

A century after Hale's execution, and even before the United States emerged from the Spanish-American War as an imperial power, the army and navy established intelligence units to collect military and naval intelligence about the capabilities of foreign powers. During World War I intercepting and decoding enemy cable and radio messages—cryptanalysis—brought the application of modern technology to intelligence work. The "Black Chamber," a small military intelligence unit responsible for this activity in the United States, continued to function after the war, only to be terminated by President Hoover's secretary of state in 1929, who found the Black Chamber's activities abhorrent to America's idealist values. Still, during the 1930s, Franklin Roosevelt and his advisers received specialized intelligence briefings about Japan and especially Germany that included radio intelligence but also a much broader array of information sources, including reports of military attachés assigned abroad (Kahn 1986).

Notably absent, however, was information from spies, as the United States did not have secret agents operating abroad. That also meant that it could not practice *counterintelligence*—"operations undertaken against foreign intelligences services . . . directed specifically against the espionage efforts of such services . . . [including] . . . efforts to penetrate them" (Holt 1995). The CIA would later become heavily involved in counterintelligence. And one of its own counterintelligence agents, Aldrich Ames, would become a spy for the enemy—the long-feared "mole" within the CIA itself. For seven years beginning in 1985, Ames sold classified information about CIA activities to the Soviet Union, resulting in the deaths of perhaps a dozen Soviet officials on the CIA payroll, widespread disruption of U.S. clandestine activities generally, and the virtual destruction of CIA operations in Moscow. In 1994 he pleaded guilty to espionage and was sentenced to life in prison for his treasonous acts.

The immediate precursor to the CIA was the Office of Strategic Services (OSS), created by President Roosevelt during World War II. Headed by General William J. "Wild Bill" Donovan, the OSS counted William J. Casey among its operatives. Casey, who four decades later would become director of the CIA, was enamored with covert intelligence operations first carried out by the OSS. These activities separated the OSS from previous U.S. intelligence operations, as the United States moved beyond merely collecting information to endeavoring to shape the outcome of events in other countries.

The United States' persistent covert involvement in the affairs of other nations (perhaps even more than its overt military involvement) contributed measurably to the interventionist label attached to post-World War II American foreign policy. NSC 68, the National Security Council document so essential to the militarization of American foreign policy, helped push the United States in that direction. As noted in Chapter 4, it called for a nonmilitary counteroffensive against the Soviet Union designed to foment unrest and revolt in Soviet bloc countries. At least some in Washington soon recognized that such broad and comprehensive undertakings could be accomplished only by the establishment of a worldwide structure for covert action (*Final Report of the Select Committee to Study Governmental Operations with Respect to Intelligence Activities*, vol. IV, 1976; hereafter cited as *Final Report*, I–VI, 1976).

In the years that followed, the CIA became infamous worldwide as the arm of the U.S. government responsible for perhaps otherwise inexplicable political events in other countries. A well-known congressional investigation of the CIA undertaken in the mid-1970s described its invasiveness this way: "The CIA has been accused of interfering in the internal political affairs of nations ranging from Iran to Chile, from Tibet to Guatemala, from Libya to Laos, from Greece to Indonesia. Assassinations, coups d'etat, vote buying, economic warfare—all have been laid at the doorstep of the CIA. Few political crises take place in the world today in which CIA involvement is not alleged" (*Final Report*, I, 1976). The accuracy of that picture may once have been disputable, but no longer: A growing volume of declassified government documents and revelations flowing from the now-defunct Soviet empire show it to be an understatement.

The Role of Intelligence and Covert Action

Covert action refers to "an activity designed to produce a result in a foreign country without the role of the United States being evident. The American role should be so well concealed that it cannot be uncovered by investigatory techniques and can be plausibly denied" (Holt 1995). Typically, then, covert actions or operations are clandestine activities undertaken abroad against foreign governments, installations, or individuals with the expressed purpose of directly influencing the outcome of political events. They are conceptually distinct from the clandestine collection of intelligence, or espionage. Espionage activities, the illegal collection of intelligence, do not attempt to influence events directly, but covert actions do.

Worries about defining a covert action did not surface until the mid-1970s, when Senate hearings, chaired by Frank Church (D-Idaho), revealed the CIA had tried to assassinate (murder for political purposes) foreign leaders. This led President Ford to issue an executive order—still in force when George Bush contemplated how to deal with Saddam Hussein—outlawing such practices. As Congress now also became increasingly involved in the oversight of intelligence activities, more refined definitions of covert actions (sometimes called "special activities") became necessary to ensure that presidents brought all proposed activities to the attention of appropriate congressional committees. In 1991, over the protest of President Bush, Congress wrote a definition of covert action into law, which read in part that covert action is "an activity or activities of the United States Government to influence political, economic, or military conditions abroad, where it is intended that the role of the United States Government will not be apparent or acknowledged publicly."

Intelligence collection itself provokes little concern or criticism. Since foreign policy decision makers are expected to protect the physical security and general welfare of the population, they require detailed information necessary for understanding the varied military, economic, political, scientific, domestic, and foreign issues and events requisite to sound policy making. Providing such information is the task of the intelligence community (described in Chapter 11). More specifically, its task is to produce *finished intelligence*, defined as "data collected from all sources—secret, official, and open—which has been carefully collated and analyzed by substantive experts specifically to meet the needs of the national leadership" (Marchetti and Marks 1974).

Much of what constitutes raw intelligence (the uncollated and unanalyzed data) is not acquired through mysterious cloak-and-dagger escapades often called *human intelligence (HUMINT)* because it comes from human, not technical sources). Rather it comes from readily available public sources, such as the reports of journalists, diplomats, and information and cultural officers, and the publications of government agencies, private businesses, and scholars. Data from such public sources are supplemented by so-called *hard intelligence*, derived from cryptanalysis and reconnaissance satellites. Thus U.S. reconnaissance satellites routinely provide invaluable information about Russian, Iranian, and Iraqi military capabilities, among others (although they failed to detect Iraq's sophisticated nuclear weapons program). And *signal intelligence (SIGINT)*—information gathered from interception and analysis of communications, electronic, and telemetry signals—routinely provides a wealth of intelligence from around the world.

Still, some clandestine intelligence activities may be necessary, particularly since access is universally denied to important information relevant to sound national security policy making. Sometimes, however, clandestine intelligence collection results in significant foreign policy ramifications. Perhaps the most celebrated case occurred in 1960, when the CIA U-2 spy plane piloted by Francis Gary Powers was shot down deep within Soviet territory on the very eve of the Paris Summit between President Eisenhower and Soviet Premier Khrushchev. The summit was never held, and American-Soviet relations became as frigid as at any point during the Cold War.

Another example occurred in 1968 when the North Koreans captured the signal intelligence spy ship *Pueblo*, operated by the navy and the National Security Agency, near the coast of North Korea. The crewmen were eventually returned, but the ship was not—which doubtless contributed to Soviet knowledge of U.S. SIGINT capabilities.

These incidents illustrate the kinds of embarrassments and complications that can arise out of an otherwise legitimate need for policy-making information. Covert actions, on the other hand, are decidedly more controversial. Among the more notorious cases exposed during the Cold War are:

- The CIA-engineered coups in Iran and Guatemala in the 1950s and Vietnam in the 1960s;
- The CIA-trained, financed, and directed armies that sought to overthrow Cuba's Castro and that conducted a "secret" war in Laos in the 1960s;
- The CIA-supported political action programs designed to prevent Marxist-oriented President Salvador Allende from winning and then exercising political power in Chile in the 1970s;
- The covert war directed against the Nicaraguan government in the 1980s.

Now that the Cold War has ended, the list grows. Recent revelations show, for example, that the CIA used clandestine operations in Poland and Romania to purchase advanced Soviet military technology. Russian officials have also acknowledged that the United States in the 1970s successfully retrieved two Soviet nuclear bombs from a sunken submarine. Those programs fit the CIA's Cold War mission, but others stretch that view to questionable proportions. For decades following the coup in Guatemala the CIA supported the Guatemalan army, channeling millions of dollars to it even in the 1980s and 1990s, at the same time that the army allegedly killed over 100,000 people and systematically engaged in human rights violations. The agency also made payments to Japan's conservative political party, the Liberal Democratic Party (LDP), which dominated Japanese politics for more than a generation. Beginning in the 1950s and continuing until the early 1970s, the CIA funded the LDP, hoping to stave off a challenge by Japanese socialists. Nevertheless, corruption—arguably fueled by CIA payments to high Japanese government officials—eventually helped topple the LDP, and in 1989 the socialists for the first time replaced the conservative LDP as Japan's governing party.

During the 1960s the United States also launched a covert action against Cheddi Jagan, prime minister of then British Guiana, believing him to be a communist. CIA activities weakened Jagan's domestic political base, after which the British granted the small South American country its independence. Thirty years later Jagan was elected president of the now-independent Guyana. Not knowing of the Kennedy administration's clandestine action against Jagan, the Clinton administration was embarrassed to learn that its nominee as ambassador to Guyana, William C. Doherty, Jr., had earlier participated in the effort to unseat Jagan as British Guiana's prime minister.

The Church committee's Senate hearings in the 1970s revealed that the CIA once tried to humiliate Fidel Castro by dusting the Cuban leader's shoes with a substance that would make his hair fall out. Less humorously, the investigation reported that Castro had survived at least eight CIA-sponsored assassination plots. Other troubling post-Cold War revelations are closer to home. The Church committee hearings also revealed that in 1959 CIA agents tested the hallucinogenic drug LSD on a houseful of unwitting people in San Francisco. More recent declassified documents reveal that many Americans were the victims of a wide variety of experiments conducted by the CIA and other government agencies.

From the end of World War II well into the 1970s, the Atomic Energy Commission, the Defense Department, the military services, the CIA and other agencies used prisoners, drug addicts, mental patients, college students, soldiers, even bar patrons, in a vast range of government-run experiments to test the effects of everything from radiation, LSD and nerve gas to intense electric shocks and prolonged "sensory deprivation." Some of the human guinea pigs knew what they were getting into; many others did not. Still others did not even know they were being experimented on. (*U.S. News & World Report*, January 24, 1994, p. 33).

Why were these "experiments" conducted? "In the life-and-death struggle with communism, America could not afford to leave any scientific avenue unexplored" (*U.S. News & World Report* January 24, 1994).

Fifty years after the end of World War II, Americans are prone to remember the horrors of the holocaust and the horrific medical experiments performed on innocent victims by the likes of Germany's Dr. Josef Mengele and Japan's General Shoro Ishii. As the pages of America's Cold War history are now also turned, it is regrettably clear that American hands, too, are tainted.

Cold War Confrontation, Competitive Coexistence, and Covert Action

If the increasingly hostile international political environment of the late 1940s and early 1950s provided the initial impetus toward covert operations and related intelligence activities (and abuses), the perceived success attributed to the CIA in carrying them out contributed to its status as a viable policy instrument. Especially important were two of its boldest and most spectacular operations—the overthrow of Premier Mohammed Mossadegh in Iran in 1953 and the coup that ousted President Jacobo Arbenz of Guatemala in 1954 (see Andrew 1995; Gasiorowski 1987; Immerman 1982; Treverton 1987). By those quick and virtually bloodless operations two allegedly pro-communist leaders were replaced with pro-Western officials. Out of such early acclaimed achievements both the agency and Washington policymakers acquired a sense of confidence in the CIA's capacity for operational success.

Allen Dulles directed the CIA throughout the 1950s. Master spy of OSS operations in Switzerland during World War II and brother of Secretary of State John Foster Dulles, Allen Dulles was personally interested in the intrigue of clandestine operations. Under his tutelage the CIA moved from being the servant of other government agencies to one that defined ways covert operations could enhance realization of specific foreign policy goals. Thus the agency achieved the enviable bureaucratic position of not only defining foreign policy programs for top-level decision makers but also providing the information on which they would base their decisions and then implementing them once they were made.

The invasion of Cuba at the Bay of Pigs in 1961 by a band of CIA-trained and financed Cuban exiles—which combined in one agency the roles of information collection, policy formulation, and program implementation—stands out as a classic case of CIA prominence in policy making. The CIA saw the Bay of Pigs operation as a way to eliminate the "problem" posed by Castro. Although engineered along the lines of the successful 1954 Guatemalan operation, the defeat suffered by the Cuban exiles tarnished the agency's reputation and cost Allen Dulles his job. Still, covert operations remained an acceptable policy option. Operation Mongoose reflected that perspective. It consisted of paramilitary, sabotage, and political propaganda activities directed against Castro's Cuba in the aftermath of the Bay of Pigs, but with much the same purpose.

Paramilitary operations were also initiated in Laos, where over 30,000 tribesmen were organized into a kind of private CIA army. As the 1960s wore on, Vietnam came to dominate the CIA, as it did other government agencies. In one CIA operation there, known as Phoenix, over twenty thousand suspected Vietcong were killed in less than four years (Lewy 1978, 281; also Marchetti and Marks 1974). (One CIA analyst would later admit that the agency "assassinated a lot of the wrong damn people" [cited in Carr 1994].)

The catalog of proven and alleged CIA involvement in the internal affairs of other nations could be broadened extensively. Not unlike policymakers' preference for military solutions to political problems, covert operations became commonplace because the assets were available to them. "To these officials, including the President, covert intervention may seem to be an easier solution to a particular problem than to allow events to follow their natural course or to seek a tortuous diplomatic settlement," write Victor Marchetti and John Marks (1974). "The temptation to interfere in another country's internal affairs can be almost irresistible, when the means are at hand." "Every administration ultimately turns to the use of covert operations" is the way a former deputy director of central intelligence put it in 1982.

We cannot understand the reliance on either covert or military forms of intervention without also recognizing how much fear of communism and the drive to contain it motivated those in charge of post–World War II American foreign policy. The war might have been cold, but it was war nonetheless. Not surprisingly, then, policymakers used the same tools as the other side, no matter how repugnant they might have been. Questions of morality and legality were irrelevant: A higher purpose—the "national security"—was being served.

Covert Actions in the 1970s and 1980s

During the 1970s domestic criticism of known intelligence abuses led both the president and Congress to impose restraints on the foreign and domestic activities of the intelligence community. By then the justification for covert operations changed sharply compared with previous decades, when their purpose had been framed in terms of opposition to international communism. Now covert actions were described simply as those secret activities designed to further American policies and programs abroad. Chile became an early target of the change.[2]

Beginning in the 1950s, the United States mounted a concerted effort in Chile to prevent the Marxist-oriented Salvador Allende from first gaining and then exercising political power. By the 1970s U.S. efforts included (1) covert activities, (2) a close working relationship between the government and giant U.S.-based multinational corporations doing business in Chile, whose corporate interests were threatened, and (3) pressure on multilateral lending institutions to do America's bidding. Anticommunist thinking contributed to the eventual overthrow of the Allende government (note Henry Kissinger's view, encapsulated in the epigraph to this chapter), but the story also illustrated U.S. willingness to use a range of instruments to oppose those willing to experiment in leftist domestic political programs. The Reagan administration's efforts to subvert the leftist Sandinista regime that came to power in Nicaragua in 1979 continued that theme.

The Reagan administration's determination to exorcise the ghost of Vietnam was nowhere more apparent than in its drive to "unleash" the CIA. Its capacity for covert actions in terms of staff and budget were greatly reenergized under William Casey, Reagan's CIA director. Casey also enjoyed wide latitude in conducting secret wars against U.S. enemies (Emerson 1988). His missions included covert support for Iranian exile groups seeking to overthrow the Ayatollah Khomeini and the provision of arms and financial assistance to military forces in Angola, Chad, Cambodia, Ethiopia, Liberia, and the Sudan.

The Reagan Doctrine underscored the intention of the United States to support anticommunist movements. "We must not break faith with those who are risking their lives on every continent from Afghanistan to Nicaragua to defy Soviet supported aggression and secure rights which have been ours from birth," Reagan declared in 1985. "Support for freedom fighters is self-defense." Reagan pledged to "support with material assistance your right not just to fight and die for freedom, but to fight and win freedom." Thus the administration, in the words of Fred C. Iklé, undersecretary of defense for policy, "tried to reduce the asymmetry, the extent to which the Soviet Union can use all means—terrorist, covert, arms shipments, what have you—to topple governments or support governments that are opposed by the people, while the United States would be left with the choice between vacating the field, abandoning the friends of democracy, or getting into an all-out conflict."

Afghanistan and Nicaragua became the most celebrated applications of the newly enunciated doctrine. Using Pakistan as a gateway, the CIA provided the anti-Marxist *mujaheddin*, (the Moslem guerrillas challenging Soviet troops and the pro-Soviet regime in Afghanistan) with guns, ammunition, and other support at a cost that by 1986 exceeded $500 million annually. The United States also decided to supply the guerrillas with U.S.-made weapons, the most important of which was a shoulder-fired anti-aircraft missile known as the Stinger (Coll 1992a, 1992b). The decision broke a cardinal rule of covert operations: Avoid sending weapons made in America so as to maintain a facade of noninvolvement. However, the weapon proved enormously successful in the hands of the insurgents and may have played a critical role in the decision of the Soviet Union to withdraw from Afghanistan.[3]

In Nicaragua the CIA supported the *contras* (so-called counterrevolutionaries who were themselves a creation of the agency) by participating in the planning and execution of naval blockades, air strikes, espionage, and propaganda operations. Its activities were of such magnitude as to spark charges that it had once more gotten out of hand. (As in Afghanistan, knowledge of U.S. support for the insurgents was an open secret.) Eventually, the U.S. role in Nicaragua figured prominently in the Iran-*contra* affair, a domestic scandal of multiple dimensions that rekindled fears of an abuse of power in the name of national security not unlike those the Watergate affair had raised a decade earlier.[4] A central issue raised by the scandal was whether funds diverted from the sale of arms to Iran in a secret arms-for-hostages deal violated a legal prohibition against continued CIA support of the *contras'* activities.

We will have more to say about the Iran-*contra* affair in later chapters. Suffice it here to note the contrasting views of secrecy and intelligence activities embraced by Oliver North, a principal figure in the Iran-*contra* affair, and Aldrich Ames, the spy-turned-traitor, summarized in Focus 5.1.

Focus 5.1
THE ZEALOT AND THE TRAITOR: CONTRASTING VIEWS ON INTELLIGENCE ACTIVITIES AND NATIONAL SECURITY

• • •

"This is a dangerous world, we live at risk and . . . this Nation is at risk in a dangerous world. . . . By their very nature covert operations or special activities are a lie. There is great deceit, deception practiced in the conduct of covert operations.

"They are at essence a lie.

"We make every effort to deceive the enemy as to our intent, our conduct, and to deny the association of the United States with those activities."

—Lt. Col. Oliver L. North, 1987

"I misled the Congress. . . . And . . . I participated in preparation of documents for the Congress that were erroneous, misleading, evasive and wrong, and I did it again here when I appeared before [the members of the House Intelligence Committee] convened in the White House Situation Room. . . . I [denied the elected representatives the facts upon which they needed to make a decision] because we have had incredible leaks from discussions with closed committees of the Congress."

—Lt. Col. Oliver L. North, 1987

"The espionage business, as carried out by the CIA and a few other American agencies, was and is a self-serving sham, carried out by careerist bureaucrats who have managed to deceive several generations of American policymakers and the public about both the necessity and the value of their work. There is and has been no rational need for thousands of case officers and tens of thousands of agents working around the world, primarily in and against friendly countries. The information our vast espionage network acquires is generally insignificant or irrelevant to our policymakers' needs. . . . Frankly, these spy wars are a sideshow which have had no real impact on our significant security interests over the years."

—Aldrich H. Ames, 1994

Ames's harsh indictment of intelligence operations and the CIA may be overdrawn, but it is not easily dismissed (see Carr 1994; Shulsky and Schmitt 1994–1995). In July 1994 *U.S. New & World Report* published a stinging indictment of the CIA—"an exclusive investigation of corruption and incompetence in America's spy service"— that revealed, among other things, the (second) collapse of the U.S. spy network in Iran, and that nearly all of the U.S. agents in East Germany were in fact double agents working for the communists (see also Pincus, 1994).

Bill Casey's emphasis on covert operations contributed to weaknesses in CIA operations. Under his tutelage the agency focused on recruiting spies (the case officers' job), resulting in poor performance on such critical matters as the impending collapse of the Soviet Union and Iraq's invasion of Kuwait. The intelligence community in 1990 did correctly predict the breakup of Yugoslavia and the ethnic bloodletting that followed (*New York Times*, November 28, 1990, p. A5). It also warned a year later of a possible coup against Mikhail Gorbachev (a warning Bush shared with Gorbachev, but which the latter chose to ignore [Andrew 1995]). And at least one CIA veteran correctly predicted that Iraq would invade Kuwait, but his forecast was similarly ignored (*New York Times*, January 24, 1991, p. A13). Bush later refuted the charge that the invasion of Kuwait reflected an intelligence failure, but clearly both the White House and the Pentagon were surprised when Iraq marched into Kuwait on August 2, 1990.

Imagery intelligence (IMINT) (computer code that must be converted into images) from U.S. satellites in July 1990 revealed a large concentration of Iraqi troops moving toward the border with Kuwait, but Bush viewed the intelligence with skepticism, in part because Hosni Mubarak of Egypt and King Hussein of Jordan both told Bush that Saddam Hussein was bluffing. Thus "the president put more faith in his own high-level Middle Eastern contacts than in the conclusions of his intelligence analysts" (Andrew 1995). Once the invasion became a reality, Bush ordered the CIA to prepare a covert action plan "to destabilize the Iraqi regime, strangle its economy, provide support for Saddam's opponents inside and outside Iraq, and identify alternative leaders" (Andrew 1995). A similar plan had been initiated a year earlier to deal with Panamanian strongman Manuel Noriega. It failed, as did the covert operation directed against Saddam Hussein. In both cases large-scale American military intervention followed.

In Search of a Rationale: Intelligence and Covert Action beyond the Cold War

Bush's authorization of covert action against Noriega and Saddam Hussein reveals a pattern consistent throughout the Cold War:

> Though presidents often underestimated the value of the intelligence they received . . ., they frequently overestimated the secret power that covert action put at their command. . . . Eisenhower's exaggerated faith in covert action led him to bequeath the disastrous Cuban operation to his inexperienced successor. Despite the fiasco at the Bay of Pigs, Kennedy, Johnson, and Nixon continued secret attempts to destabilize (if not assassinate) Castro, the only significant result of which was to lower the international reputation of the United

> States. Nixon's attempt to cover up the farcically incompetent domestic covert operations run by the White House led to his own fall from power. The fate of Nixon's successors has also, though in different ways, been powerfully affected by covert action. By pardoning Nixon, and thus appearing to condone his attempted cover-up of Watergate, Ford probably sacrificed the 1976 presidential election. The failure of the covert operation to rescue the Teheran hostages may have cost Carter a second term. Iran-Contra, which revived both the illegality and the bungling of White House covert action in the Nixon era, reduced Reagan's presidency to its lowest ebb. (Andrew 1995, 539)

Against this background and the failed efforts to predict the end of the Cold War and the onset of the Gulf War, it is not surprising that the role of intelligence, of covert action, and of the CIA itself as instruments of American foreign policy are very much in question (see also Chapter 11).

In early 1995 the Clinton administration, under pressure from Congress, launched a bipartisan review of the intelligence community that promised to address the broad range of issues related to both the structure and purpose of U.S. intelligence organizations and operations. The review followed on the heels of congressional attempts in 1992 to reform the intelligence community (see, e.g., Boren 1992, and the critique in May 1992) and especially bitter congressional criticism of Clinton's first CIA director, R. James Woolsey, whose budget proposals and vision for the future were often regarded as out of step with current realities (Prados 1993; Woolsey 1994).

Today the CIA faces an identity crisis. With the end of the Cold War and the victory over Soviet communism—the principal adversary against whom covert action was directed for more than four decades—should the agency even continue? Some analysts see the new world as an invitation for new intelligence missions, such as industrial espionage; a focus on demographic issues, like refugee flows; and environmental concerns, like global warming. Others would restrict the CIA to more traditional intelligence functions—namely, learning other governments' secrets and determining the veracity of what they say. Still others would dismantle the CIA entirely, spreading its intelligence functions among other federal agencies, like the Commerce, State, and Treasury Departments. Where covert action might fit in these alternative postures is not clear, yet the preference for clandestine operations demonstrated by every president since the onset of World War II assures that this instrument of American foreign policy will remain at the disposal of future commanders in chief.

Informal Penetration . . . .

U.S. public diplomacy and foreign aid programs are qualitatively different from the clandestine intelligence operations for which the CIA became infamous, but they form part of a nexus of informal penetrations of other societies that may have contributed to the kinds of covert and overt interventions discussed previously in this chapter and in Chapter 4. A fine line distinguishes involvement from intervention; therefore, public diplomacy and aid are also part of that interventionist strategy. With the end of the Cold War, however, the logic that once sustained these programs has dissipated. Thus their future, like the future of the CIA, is now very much in question.

Public Diplomacy

Public diplomacy is a polite term for what many would regard as straightforward propaganda (the methodical spreading of information to influence public opinion). The United States Information Agency (USIA) is in charge of American public diplomacy efforts aimed at winning support around the world for America and its foreign policy.[5] Its instruments are information and cultural activities directed overseas at both masses and elites. They serve two functions: (1) the projection, interpretation, and advocacy of current U.S. foreign policy; and (2) the portrayal of the United States as a pluralistic, tolerant, and democratic society.

The USIA carries out its tasks through a worldwide network of overseas offices using a variety of media tools, including radio, television, films, libraries, and exhibitions. Among the best known are the Voice of America, which broadcasts news, political journalism, music, and cultural programs in many different languages to various parts of the globe, and Radio Free Europe and Radio Liberty (both established by the CIA), which, during the Cold War, broadcast to Eastern Europe and the Soviet Union, respectively. The Reagan administration added Radio Marti and TV Marti, which direct their messages to Cuba, and Clinton in 1994 authorized Radio Free Asia. USIA also administers a variety of cultural exchange programs that support travel abroad by American athletes, artists, dramatists, musicians, and scholars and travel to the United States by foreign political leaders, students, and educators for study tours or other educational purposes.

Information and cultural programs are pursued in the expectation that specialized communications can be used to make the United States' image in the world more favorable. Opinion varies widely, however, regarding the propriety and effectiveness of public diplomacy as a policy instrument. Should such efforts be designed only to provide information? Should public diplomacy aggressively promote American culture and its values? Should it be linked intimately to the political contests in which the United States becomes engaged?

In practice, each role has been dominant at one time or another. The USIA strongly advocated the anticommunist containment policy during the 1950s, for example, and it later tried to justify American intervention during the Vietnam War. The Carter administration tried to shift the emphasis to cultural exchange programs, which "evoke more cooperative sentiments" when compared with information activities that have "the image of a more confrontational posture" (Adelman 1981). Reagan, however, moved sharply toward confrontation, as the USIA sought vigorously to promote U.S. policies abroad and to engage in the "war of ideas" with the nation's adversaries. Charles Z. Wick, USIA director under Reagan, proudly observed "The only war the United States has fought in the past four years has been the propaganda war." But that bold approach to "telling America's story to the world" (USIA's motto) politicized the agency's cultural and exchange programs (Weissman 1992; see also Malone 1985). Tension between these two aspects of USIA's mission—one policy-oriented, the other not—has never been resolved.

The issue of USIA's dual roles surfaced again during the Bush administration, as budgetary stringency renewed concern about how best to promote America's ideas and ideals using the broadcast media (Elliott 1989–1990). USIA's seeming inability to redirect its programming to encourage the process of democratic change sweeping Eastern Europe also raised eyebrows. USIA Director Bruce Gelb defended the agency: "Our opportunities are blossoming, not only in Eastern Europe, but around the world," he exclaimed. "But our resources are shrinking." Others saw bureaucratic inertia, including an unwillingness to abandon traditional Cold War views, as the force preventing the United States from using its public diplomacy capabilities more aggressively (Blackburn 1992; McCartney 1990).

Bureaucratic inertia, congressional restraints, and presidential disinterest cast doubt on USIA's future. In addition, the Republican Congress singled out the foreign affairs budget, which includes public diplomacy, for significant pruning. Meanwhile, the Clinton administration forced Radio Free Europe and Radio Liberty to consolidate with the Voice of America and to move from Munich, Germany, where they had been located since 1951, to Prague, where the Czech Republic will help subsidize them.

Even if it were possible to agree on the nature and role of public diplomacy, evaluating its impact is difficult. During the Polish labor turmoil of 1980, the Soviet Union criticized American broadcasts beamed at Poland as "provocative and instigatory" and as "aimed at generating among the Polish population unfriendly sentiments with regard to the Soviet Union" (cited in Adelman 1981). Did these complaints prove that such broadcasts served American interests in Poland? Or instead, were American interests—defined as preventing the deterioration of relations with the Soviet Union—damaged by them? If that situation seems ambiguous, an earlier one does not. In 1956 Hungarian freedom fighters revolting against Soviet domination received messages from Radio Free Europe implying that American assistance was on its way. It never came.

Even the exchange programs that are a part of public diplomacy seem to yield ambiguous results. Although perhaps a quarter of a million scholars and teachers have participated in the well-known Fulbright Program, some of the most vociferous foreign critics of America visited the country under the sponsorship of the United States government.

"For more than four decades, public diplomatists . . . convincingly portrayed themselves to the U.S. public as strike forces in the Cold War's 'war of ideas'" (Blackburn 1992). With the Cold War now history, what of the next four decades? Those sympathetic to the USIA see its record as one of "remarkable success" (Blackburn 1992) and thus, not surprisingly, would steer the agency to new missions in a new world. Others see continuing relevance in the old mission. Thus one sympathetic analyst responded to critics this way: "Some who disparage public diplomacy seem to believe that the advantages of the American way of life, values, and institutions are so self-evident that they do not need special promotion. They also appear to think that the future of democratic institutions is so secure that no particular effort is needed to bolster them" (Laqueur 1994). He also urged that cultural diplomacy in its widest sense, which includes high-tech competition for global audiences, has become more important compared with traditional diplomatic and military approaches to the kinds of problems and issues the United States now faces in the new world (dis)order. "There will always be room for diplomacy, but in its present form it is largely an eighteenth-century relic that badly needs rethinking and refashioning. The limits of military and economic power have become all too obvious of late. To dismantle the remaining instrument of U.S. foreign policy [public diplomacy] at this time seems more than a little foolish" (Laqueur 1994).

Economic Assistance

Since World War II the United States has provided over $280 billion in ***foreign economic aid***—loans and grants—to other countries (see Table 5.1). This is a large amount, but by no means the mammoth "giveaway" ascribed to foreign aid in the popular mind. On average, the sum is about $6 billion annually, substantially less than Americans spend each year on cigarettes and alcoholic beverages or commercial entertainment. In constant (noninflated) dollars, moreover, the amount of aid given today is dramatically less than forty years ago. In 1949 alone, the United States provided (in 1994 dollars) more than $50 billion in aid, most in the form of Marshall Plan assistance to rebuild Western Europe (*Congressional Quarterly Weekly Report*, December 17, 1994, p. 3568). And most foreign aid (miliary as well as economic) is "tied" to purchases of goods and services in the United States, helping to generate economic activity at home while also boosting trade and economic prospects in recipient countries.

Why give foreign aid at all? Realism and idealism—competing views of international politics and foreign policy explored in detail in Chapter 3—offer different answers. "For most realists, development aid [foreign aid designed to assist socioeconomic development] is a tool used by states to help maintain the status quo of the international system. . . . Rich countries provide aid because doing so improves the donors' positions in the world economy. . . . Rich states help poor states if they conform to the norms and rules of international behavior set by the rich, powerful states" (Tisch and Wallace 1994). From the perspective of political realism, then, foreign aid is an instrument of policy that fosters the donor country's foreign policy interests.

Idealists, on the other hand, "recognize the political and security concerns of donor countries but do not view these concerns as the only determinants of interstate relations." For idealists, humanitarian concerns are more important than geostrategic considerations. "Rich states provide development aid because they can afford it," accord-

TABLE 5.1 EXPENDITURES ON FOREIGN ECONOMIC AID
(LOANS AND GRANTS), 1946–1993
(BILLIONS OF DOLLARS BY FISCAL YEAR)

Postwar relief period (1946–1948)	$12.5
Marshall Plan period (1949–1952)	18.6
Mutual Security Act period (1953–1961)	24.1
Foreign Assistance Act period (1962–1992)	$232.6
Grand total	$282.3

Note: Numbers do not add to total due to different reporting concepts in the pre- and post-1955 periods.
Source: Adapted from *U.S. Overseas Loans and Grants and Assistance from International Organizations, Obligations and Loan Authorizations, July 1, 1945-September 30, 1993* (Washington, D.C.: Agency for International Development, 1994), p. 4.

ing to the idealist paradigm. "Development assistance benefits both donors and recipients because it promotes international stability and, therefore, greater opportunities for economic growth and prosperity. . . . Poor people's lives can be improved by transcending narrow state concerns, replacing them with global goals" (Tisch and Wallace 1994).

In practice, America's foreign aid programs are a mixture of the realist and idealist assumptions and motivations. Military assistance (considered later in this chapter) is an obvious manifestation of the security interests central to realist thinking, but even the economic assistance program blends these concerns with idealistic humanitarian motives.

The Agency for International Development (AID) is responsible for administering U.S. economic assistance programs. The aid it provides falls into three main categories: development assistance, economic support funds, and Food for Peace. Additional support is provided through subscriptions to multilateral lending agencies, such as the International Monetary Fund, the World Bank, and the International Development Association (IDA), the so-called "soft loan window" of the World Bank.

Economic support funds (ESF) are dollars granted or loaned to countries of special political significance to the United States.[6] The resources serve several security and political interests: "enhancing political stability, promoting economic reforms important to long-term development, promoting economic stabilization through budget and balance of payments support, and assisting countries that allow the United States to maintain military bases on their soil" (Zimmerman 1993). Economic support funds (ESF) are also used to enhance the Middle East Peace process. Egypt and Israel have been the largest recipients of economic aid since the Camp David agreement of 1978, when the United States committed itself to substantial financial rewards and security guarantees, accounting for roughly half of the total foreign economic aid pie. Nearly all of it is in the form of economic support funds. Before that, the Philippines, Thailand, and Vietnam were the largest ESF recipients (Zimmerman 1993).

Development assistance provides grants and loans to support social and economic development. Aid is typically provided through specific projects and devoted to particular functions, like health, education, agriculture, and rural development. Disaster relief assistance often falls under the rubric of development assistance. While economic support funds seek to advance short-term political objectives, development assistance is focused on the long-term development objectives of American foreign policy, but the two are often interrelated. As one analyst noted, "the sustainability of most U.S. political and security objectives, including peace, ultimately depends on the effectiveness of economic assistance as a development tool, not on a quid pro quo for political-security cooperation" (Zimmerman 1993).

Food aid is provided through the *Food for Peace* **program**, perhaps more widely known as PL (public law) 480 in reference to the Agricultural Trade Development and Assistance Act of 1954 which created it. As specified in that act, the objectives of the Food for Peace program are "to expand exports of U.S. agricultural commodities, to combat hunger and malnutrition, to encourage economic development in developing countries, and to promote the foreign policy interests of the United States" (Zimmerman 1993). The program, in which the Department of Agriculture now plays a major role, sells agricultural commodities on credit terms and makes grants for emer-

Focus 5.2
Multilateral Economic Cooperation with Russia and the Other New Independent States

• • •

Since 1990, the international community has mobilized economic assistance for Russia and the other [New Independent States] on a scale unmatched since the Marshall Plan for the reconstruction of Europe at the end of World War II. In 1993, the U.S. and other bilateral creditors rescheduled about $15 billion of Russia's debt service payments. . . .

The Group of Seven industrialized nations also has provided more than $12 billion in bilateral financing. Since then, Russia also has received $4 billion from the International Monetary Fund. . . .

The World Bank has approved more than $3 billion in lending to Russia, mainly to support sectoral reform and reconstruction (e.g., $1 billion for oil well rehabilitation. The World Bank's International Finance Corporation, which lends to private sector entities, has committed $115 million to projects in Russia.

The European Bank for Reconstruction and Development, which began operating in 1991 to assist former communist countries, has committed $980 million in loans to Russia.

On June 8, 1994, Russia signed an agreement with the Organization for Economic Cooperation and Development to provide policy guidance and technical assistance on a wide range of structural reform issues, such as competition law and policy.

Source: U.S. Department of State Dispatch 5 *(December 29, 1994): 849.*

gency relief, for promoting economic development, or for assisting voluntary relief agencies. Interestingly, PL 480 contributed to the legitimacy of the idea in Congress that commodity sales constitute a form of aid, making possible the later emphasis on military arms sales as a way of assisting other nations (Louscher 1977). The Food for Peace program totaled $52.7 billion by 1993, or about a fifth of all economic aid granted since PL 480 was passed.

Multilateral lending agencies also provide a conduit for U.S. assistance to other countries. Since the 1970s the United States has relegated large-scale infrastructure projects (basic facilities and systems like roads and regional irrigation systems) to multilateral institutions. It also has looked to them to provide much of the aid now given to Russia and the other New Independent States (see Focus 5.2). A major advantage of multilaterally directed aid is that the United States does not have to take sole responsibility for setting the tough economic criteria recipient nations must meet to qualify for multilateral support.

Aid from multilateral institutions arguably comes to recipients with fewer political strings attached than bilateral aid (although, as we will see in Chapter 7, the economic conditions are often onerous), but what to recipients is an advantage may be a disadvantage to those who supply the funds. Foreign aid has long been unpopular in Congress, and assistance to multilateral institutions is arguably the most unpopular of all because of the impression that these institutions' largesse is too readily accessible to those who oppose the United States.

This description of the principal types of foreign economic aid by itself shows that power and principle both underlie this timeworn foreign policy instrument. A brief look at how it has been used since World War II will make that even clearer.

Foreign Economic Aid: A Brief Historical Sketch

As noted earlier, the first major peacetime effort to utilize foreign aid as an instrument of foreign policy was the remarkably successful **Marshall Plan**, formally known as the European Recovery Program. Directed toward war-ravaged Western European countries, the Marshall Plan used American capital to rebuild the economic, social, and political infrastructures of European societies in the hopes of rebuilding a market for American products and enhancing Europe's ability to resist communist subversion. Later, after the outbreak of the Korean War, the emphasis shifted from recovery to containment and from Europe to Asia. The Mutual Security Act became the governing legislation for foreign aid in 1953. The title alone conveyed the overriding concern of the United States in the post-Marshall Plan period.

By the 1960s it was apparent that economic and social progress was the dominant concern of many of the newly emerging nations of the Third World (as the Global South was then called)—not the Cold War that had been the primary motivating force behind aid to that point. Castro's rise to power in Cuba demonstrated that security and economic and social progress were not incompatible concerns, but the latter gained increasing emphasis. The Foreign Assistance Act, which replaced the Mutual Security Act in 1961, created AID as the administering agency for economic assistance. Development capital and technical assistance were now given greater emphasis than defense support aid, and the Alliance for Progress was launched in an attack on incipient revolution and communism in the Western Hemisphere. The prevailing thought was not that aid would result in direct political benefits to the United States but, instead, that it would contribute to recipients' economic development. Stable democratic governments were expected to emerge in a climate of economic development, whose existence would ensure peaceful and cooperative relations among countries. This complicated reasoning is part of the intellectual heritage that informs current thinking about the democratic peace we discussed in Chapter 3 (see also Frank and Baird 1975).

Even as political development doctrines emerged to explain why foreign aid was in the United States' long-run interest, Cold War considerations—including the Vietnam War—continued to dominate the actual allocation of foreign economic aid during the 1960s. By the end of the decade 70 percent of all U.S. economic aid was directed to Asia and the Near East.

Official thinking about foreign aid took a new direction with the end of the

Vietnam War, as attention now focused on alleviating the deprivation in which hundreds of millions of people live throughout the world. Development assistance shifted from social infrastructure projects to programs designed to meet basic human needs. In part that decision was related to Congress's growing concern with linking aid allocations to the human rights practices of developing countries comprising the Third World.

The "basic needs" perspective was a critique of economic development theories that argued the benefits of economic growth would "trickle down" to the needy. That seldom happened; "dualism" is more characteristic of developing societies—with one modern, growing sector and one traditional, stagnant sector. A commitment to meeting basic human needs also enjoyed the political advantage of linking the plight of the world's poor directly to developing countries themselves. Many Third World leaders preferred to lay the blame elsewhere, asserting that their problems resulted from the inherent inequality between the world's rich and poor nations, which the international system's hierarchical structure perpetuates. In contrast, the basic human needs perspective placed blame at home.

The major foreign aid thrust returned to a sharper focus on American security interests with the election of Ronald Reagan in 1980. Basic human needs, funded with development assistance, took a back seat to the use of economic support funds for short-run political gains, notably political stability and the promotion of macroeconomic reform. Underlying the shift was the belief that the welfare orientation of the basic human needs approach "had not directly stimulated broader-based, sustainable economic growth" (Zimmerman 1993). Meanwhile, states like Guatemala, El Salvador, and Pakistan, who found themselves on the front line of the Reagan Doctrine, received large infusions of ESF aid. Pakistan was a bit troublesome, as the Symington amendment to the Foreign Assistance Act in the late 1970s prohibited further aid to that nation as long as it pursued a nuclear weapons program. The Reagan administration sidestepped the prohibition using a common practice: It "certified" there was no evidence that Pakistan was pursuing the development of nuclear weapons. Once the covert war against Russian forces in Afghanistan ended, the Bush administration dropped the certification and aid to Pakistan ended.

The Reagan administration also sought (unsuccessfully [Kegley and Hook 1991]) to link U.S. foreign aid allocations to the voting behavior of Third World nations in the United Nations (a practice the Republican-controlled House of Representatives would like to resurrect). Similarly, strategic considerations motivated its ambitious Caribbean Basin Initiative (CBI). Launched in 1984, the program of tariff reductions and tax incentives hoped to promote the growth of industry and trade in Central America and the Caribbean as a way of thwarting the economic conditions on which Marxist revolutionaries thrive.

The market-oriented approach to political problems embodied in the CBI increasingly characterized U.S. aid efforts in the 1980s and beyond. For example, "privatization" was a central goal of the Clinton administration's approach to Russia and the Ukraine. Technical assistance and training programs, support for the transition to democracy, humanitarian and food assistance, and help in dismantling weapons of mass destruction also became part of the massive aid package extended by the Bush and Clinton administrations.

Aid to America's Cold War adversary began in 1991, when a bipartisan coalition in

Congress approved $400 million to help the Soviet Union dismantle and store its chemical and nuclear weapons. A year later the Freedom Support Act authorized $425 million in assistance to the now former Soviet Union. In 1993 another $2.5 billion was authorized for Russia and the Ukraine, and in 1994 $1.25 billion more was added (Flickner 1994–1995, 13–14). Thus, in a very short time, former adversaries consumed a very large share of a shrinking foreign aid budget. In fiscal year 1994, Russia, the New Independent States, and eastern Europe consumed 19 percent of the foreign economic aid budget (*Congressional Quarterly Weekly Report*, December 17, 1994, p. 3568).

Providing aid to former adversaries is part of America's idealist heritage, which includes a recurrent history of promoting democracy in defeated enemies, as we saw in Chapter 3. Even the extraordinary task Russia and others in the former Soviet bloc faced did not deter support. "Most public officials could empathize with the new leaders of Russia and Ukraine as they faced the daunting tasks of encouraging democracy and implementing effective reform, and most preferred to risk wasting several billion dollars rather than see them fail and have the failure attributed to lack of American support" (Flickner 1994–1995). Midway through the Clinton administration, however, questions about the efficacy of the U.S. aid effort surfaced with mounting frequency, fueled in part by general dissatisfaction with foreign aid as an instrument of policy. Following the September 1994 Clinton-Yeltsin summit, attention turned increasingly toward trade and investment initiatives and incentives and away from outright grant assistance to the former Soviet Union.

As support for Russian aid experienced a slowdown, the foreign aid program as a whole faced a crossroad. Bill Clinton's national security adviser observed that AID's development programs had been "burdened with no fewer than thirty-three different goals." Still, its anticommunist underpinnings are unmistakable. Recipient nations understandably worried that the end of the Cold War would dissipate what little support remained for foreign aid. Many who depended on ESF and military aid in the past were particularly hard hit by reductions and redistributions. Some of the world's poorest countries also saw their aid receipts fall. At home, meanwhile, those who once supported foreign aid, perhaps reluctantly, now also wondered whether it still made sense. Clearly the future of this timeworn instrument of American foreign policy is shaky.

In Search of a Rationale: Foreign Economic Aid in the Post-Cold War World

Congress, as we have noted, has long been skeptical of foreign aid and its contributions both to American foreign policy and to the development of recipient countries. When the Reagan administration tried to stabilize the economies of Central American countries using foreign aid as part of a larger strategy to cope with leftist insurgencies in the region, congressional critics argued that that focus was misdirected. Instead they urged that aid be used to push for basic social and political reform to improve the lot of the least fortunate in the region as a means of stemming the appeal of leftist political forces (Sullivan 1989). The differences of opinion illustrated in this case are fundamental, as they turn on the complex nexus between economics and politics, between economic development and political development. Often these become partisan and ideological disputes, as there is little convincing evidence to demonstrate that one argument is right and the other wrong. Thus Representative Mitch McConnell (R-Kentucky)—a member of the new Republican majority in Congress determined to trim the aid program—could assert without fear of contradiction that "By any standard, the fact is most poor countries are still poor, and that is largely because of government practices and policies in the host country."

How to reform the aid program (indeed, whether to keep it) provoked a vigorous debate during the latter part of Bush's administration and the early years of Clinton's. Similar debates occurred in other donor countries as well.[7] Commonly stated goals that would give foreign military and economic aid new life included poverty reduction, human development, environmental protection, reduced military spending, enhanced economic management, development of private enterprise, enhancement of the role of women, and the promotion of democratic governance and human rights (World Bank 1993).

The Clinton administration's priorities began to emerge in late 1993 as it advanced enlargement as an alternative to containment. Speaking before the Overseas Development Council, a Washington-based private policy-planning organization, Anthony Lake noted that "the end of the Cold War forces us to look anew on the developing world. American policymakers no longer can imagine these nations as an interchangeable clump of squares on the superpower chessboard. We need a new lens and even a new vocabulary." As applied to this now "highly differentiated" group of nations, the strategy of enlargement, according to Lake, "focuses us on the goals of democracy and a form of market development that is both politically and environmentally sustainable." Announcing the administration's conclusion "that existing foreign assistance programs are incoherent and outmoded," Lake also acknowledged, "a humanitarian agenda toward the poorest nations will remain important and that conflict resolution needs to be a part of that agenda." The administration next proposed to replace the decades-old foreign assistance act with new legislation that would emphasize six goals designed to realize the administration's program of enlargement: promoting sustainable development, democracy, peace, humanitarian assistance, growth through trade and investment, and advancing diplomacy (see also Chapter 12).

Foreign aid's role in post-Cold War American foreign policy eventually became part of a larger issue: how much to spend on foreign affairs compared with domestic priorities, and why. What, in other words, were the threats that now demanded the United States' attention and resources? *Chaos* and *crisis prevention* were proposed as answers.

Secretary of State Warren Christopher, Under Secretary of State for Global Affairs Timothy Wirth, and AID Administrator Brian Atwood all spoke favorably of the new thrust. Wirth, for example, cited environmental degradation, poverty, disease, and emigration driven by civil conflict as "the primary threats to human security." Atwood identified food insecurity and population growth as twin threats to security and "major contributors to conflict and to the chaos that we worry about so much." And Christopher told Congress, "The challenge of diplomacy is to anticipate, and to prevent, crises of the future." President Clinton himself echoed these concerns as he reflected on Robert Kaplan's (1994) provocative article describing environmental decay and incipient conflict in West Africa. Prevention thus became a rationale for continued U.S. involvement in the Global South—with foreign aid a primary modality. Basing the case for prevention on diminished support for U.S. involvement abroad in the post-Cold War world, AID's Atwood argued "What I'm trying to sell is a practical program of prevention that will cost a lot less to American taxpayers than the humanitarian aid that comes in after it's too late. When you see television pictures of starving children and nations that are in conflict, it's already too late. At that point, it's very difficult and very costly to repair the damage."

Crisis prevention as an alternative to containment extends beyond the foreign aid program—for example, nuclear proliferation clearly falls here as well. Nor does the thrust depend wholly on the proposition that chaos, emanating from the Global South and elsewhere, is now the principal threat to American national security. Like other aspects of America's emerging post-Cold War foreign policy, however, the wisdom of crisis prevention and the underlying assumption of chaos are not immune to criticism. The approach reflects an idealist thrust that draws attention to transnational threats to U.S. security arguably less important than traditional (realist) state-centered challenges. A former Clinton national security council staffer articulated the concern:

> As national security doctrine, . . . chaos has a glaring problem: It has virtually nothing to say about the bulk of our national security. Nothing on the missions or structure of U.S. armed forces. Nothing on our relations with other great powers (except that we should do more to address global problems). Nothing on the democratic transformation of the former Communist states (except for the sense that most of them will be dragged into the widening gyre). . . .
>
> In fact, although many ethnic, environmental and other humanitarian problems do cross borders, it is nation states, with their armies, governments, laws and legitimacy that are—and will remain—the dominant force in world affairs. And from the Balkans to the Mideast to Asia, the greatest threat to peace remains the ambitions of nation states and leaders who are hostile to democracy and norms of international behavior. (Rosner 1994, 23)

This view is not beyond reproach, but it is not easily dismissed either. U.S. foreign military and economic aid programs were born and sustained in an environment when the perceptions of threats to American national interests were widely shared. Sharp differences of opinion marked debates about the appropriateness of foreign aid as a means to meet and parry those threats, but the goals themselves were rarely in dispute. That is no longer the case. Foreign and domestic priorities now compete with one another. Tax dollars spent to prevent crises in Asia, Africa, or Latin America are dollars Detroit, Chicago, and Los Angeles also need. Without a compelling rationale—without the sense of threat that led to the Marshall Plan in 1947 and Point Four two years later—foreign economic aid as an instrument of American foreign policy will remain under attack and its future in doubt.

Military Assistance

Foreign military aid, like its economic counterpart, is now a standard instrument of American foreign policy. In this case, however, political realism, with its focus on power and the national interest, is the dominant underlying rationale. Beginning with the Korean War, grants of military aid to other countries became an essential element of Cold War defense and security planning and a tool used to pursue several national security and foreign policy goals.[8] Sales of military equipment would later join grants, and then surpass them, as the major element of U.S. arms transfer programs.

Foreign military grants and sales plus economic support funds (discussed earlier) comprise a broad category called *security assistance*, whose purpose is related to a multitude of U.S. policy objectives. Its goals were enumerated by Assistant Secretary of State H. Allen Holmes, testifying before Congress in 1989:

- Enhancing the ability of U.S. security partners to deter and defend against aggression and instability.
- Maintaining the cohesion and strength of our alliances.
- Developing sound military-to-military relations that support our diplomatic strategy and enhance U.S. influence and prestige.
- Promoting regional stability.
- Contributing to our access to military bases and facilities abroad, thereby maintaining the strategic mobility of U.S. forces.
- Strengthening the economics of key countries that are attempting to adjust to heavy debt, depressed commodity export prices, and startling changes in the global economic environment.
- Providing support for emerging democracies while defending existing democratic institutions and values in other countries.

Two years later, as the nation basked in the afterglow of victory in both the Cold War and the Persian Gulf War, Deputy Assistant Secretary of State Sinclair Martel pronounced that operation Desert Storm had "vindicated the policy direction we have been following on security assistance for the past quarter century and longer." He explained that "the largest recipients of U.S. government foreign military sales grants—Israel, Egypt, Turkey, Greece, Portugal, and the Philippines—had directly or indirectly supported the U.S.-led war effort against Iraq by providing direct access to bases and airstrips, supplying troops, or coordinating their political and military strategy with the United States" (Hartung 1992). The not-so-subtle implication was that American arms transfer policies and programs initiated during the Cold War would continue after it.

As Table 5.2 shows, more than $400 million in U.S. military aid has been extended to other nations since the onset of the Korean War (including commercial sales approved by the government). Even that figure is likely to be on the conservative side, as it is based on unclassified information.

Historically, the Military Assistance Program (MAP) served as the principal mechanism for transferring U.S. defense articles, services, and training to other countries. The assistance took the forms of grants, requiring no repayment on the part of recipients. Since the mid-1970s the International Military Education and Training Program has governed foreign military training, whose personnel by 1994 exceeded 576,000. In early 1990 the secretary of defense described the program in his annual report to Congress as "one of the most cost-effective tools of the U.S. government. Investing in the military education and training of military personnel from friendly countries greatly enhances the capability of those countries to defend themselves, at a low cost to the American taxpayer."

TABLE 5.2 EXPENDITURES ON FOREIGN MILITARY AID
(AND SALES), 1950–1994
(BILLIONS OF DOLLARS BY FISCAL YEAR)

Military Assistance Program (MAP) and MAP merger funds	$60.6
International Military Education and Training Program	2.6
Foreign military sales (FMS) and FMS construction agreements	287.6
Commercial exports licensed under the Arms Export Control Act	66.5
Excess defense articles	6.5
Grand total	$423.8

Source: Adapted from *Foreign Military Sales, Foreign Military Construction Sales and Military Assistance Facts* (Washington, D.C.: Defense Security Assistance Agency, 1995), pp. 2ff.

Today *foreign military sales (FMS)* are the most important U.S. arms transfer program. In the decade ending in 1994, FMS accounted for $139 billion, or more than 70 percent, of U.S. military aid (including commercial sales to other countries). Even more striking is that the sales during this ten-year period *surpassed* the total sales accumulated over the more than three preceding decades. 1993 was a record year, with $32.9 billion in new agreements.

Most government-to-government sales are in cash, but the Defense Department also provided $44 billion in credits toward foreign military purchases between 1985 and 1994. Increasingly, repayment of these debts has simply been waived.

Egypt and Israel account for two-thirds of U.S. foreign military sales credits, and virtually all of their required payments have been canceled. These nations receive the lion's share of FMS credits and other forms of U.S. foreign assistance as part of the 1978 Camp David Middle East peace process, as we noted in our discussion of the foreign economic aid program.

Saudi Arabia also accounts for a large proportion of military sales. In 1993 alone Saudi Arabia entered agreements to buy $11.8 billion in new weapons, bringing its total over the life of the FMS program to more than $60 billion. In the process the desert kingdom has been transformed into a formidable military power.

Tiny Kuwait also made nearly $3 billion in purchases in 1993 as it modernized its military forces after the Persian Gulf War. In doing so, it reaffirmed that the end of the Cold War has not signaled the end of the arms trade.

Indeed, while global arms sales have declined since the 1980s (but cf. Renner, 1994), the 1990s have been an arms bonanza for the U.S. defense industry. In 1992, for example, the United States delivered more than 45 percent of all major weapons systems sold in the world and more than 60 percent of the arms transferred to the Global South (Hartung 1993, 21). The proportions were even higher in the record year of 1993. The demise of the Soviet Union, once the dominant arms sale competitor to the United States, partly explains the dramatic increase in the U.S. share of world trade. The dramatic display of new American weapons technology during the Gulf War also enhanced the attractiveness of American-made weapons to foreign buyers. Even as current market conditions change, however, the legacy of the Cold War continues to shape U.S. arms transfer policies and programs.

Foreign Military Aid: A Brief Historical Sketch

Securing allies, cementing alliances, rewarding patrons, renting overseas bases—these are among the recurring patterns that explain how the United States used military assistance in its Cold War competition with the Soviet Union and its allies.

From Korea to Vietnam   The containment policy provided a rationale for military aid to others, justified on the grounds that it augmented the capabilities of U.S. allies to resist Soviet and Soviet-backed expansionism. The NATO and SEATO (Southeast Asia Treaty Organization) alliances thus received special attention, as did those with bilateral defensive arrangements with the United States, like Taiwan. Military aid also was used for the "rental" of base rights in places like Spain and for landing rights for ships and planes elsewhere. Economic support funds were also often used for this purpose. In the Philippines, for example, sizable "side payments" were required to retain access to two large military bases, Clark Air Base and the naval facility at Subic Bay. The latter in particular increased in importance following the U.S. withdrawal from Vietnam and the loss of the port facility at Cam Ranh Bay.

Vietnam affected other calculations as well. Between 1966 and 1975 the aid program increasingly targeted not only "allies" but also "friends" (Semmel 1983), as developing nations in the then-Third World commanded greater attention and the more self-reliant Western European nations less. During the decade ending in 1975 South Vietnam, Cambodia, Laos, Pakistan, South Korea, and Taiwan—all bordering directly on the communist world and bound to the United States in defensive arrangements (see Map 5.1)—more than doubled their military aid receipts. Similar attention characterized the economic aid program, as we noted above.

The Vietnam imbroglio made policymakers and critics alike wonder how the United States had become so deeply mired in that seeming quagmire. Critics argued that U.S. foreign aid programs played a role by involving the United States in countries in which it initially had little real interest. According to this reasoning, "foreign aid is the 'slippery slope' that leads eventually to an over-extension of commitments and to a greater likelihood of military involvement" (Frank and Baird 1975).

In a related concern, critics worried that U.S. programs might have contributed to the maintenance of authoritarian regimes throughout the world. In the mid-1970s, for example, more than half of the recipients of U.S. arms were dictatorships. Were American military ties with recipient countries responsible by retarding the growth of democratic governments?

Some analysts concluded that regardless of the intentions of American military aid programs, the consequences included an increased probability of military groups in recipient countries intervening in the politics of those nations (Rowe 1974). As the flow of military aid in the form of money, equipment, and training increased, the likelihood that recipients would experience political instability in the form of military coups also increased (see also Weede 1978). Similarly, the evidence suggested that where the military was already in control, military aid increased its entrenched hold. In short, then,

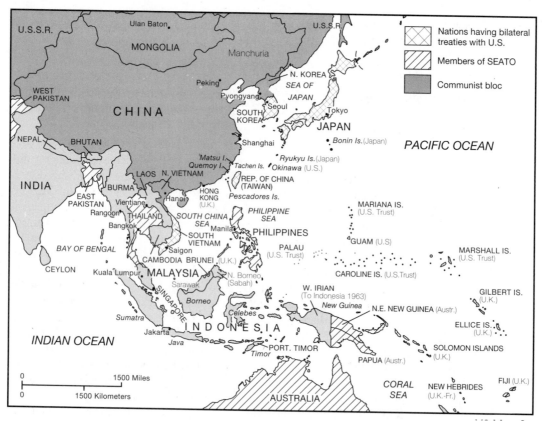

Map 5.1 The Far Eastern Front: Cold War Allies of the United States

Note: Cambodia, Laos, and South Vietnam were granted security guarantees by the SEATO alliance, although they were not formally members of it.

Source: Walter LaFeber, *The American Age: United States Foreign Policy at Home and Abroad*, 2nd ed. (New York: Norton, 1994), p. 552.

it appeared that U.S. military assistance was a "contributing factor in undermining civilian elements and increasing the incidence of praetorianism in the less developed areas of the world" (Rowe 1974).

Two decades later, the Clinton administration's determination to promote democracy abroad renewed interest in the issues raised in the aftermath of Vietnam. If at that time military aid solidified the political power of authoritarian regimes, might it now be used to encourage the growth of democracy and solidify the political power of democratic forces within recipient societies?

As noted earlier, "providing support for emerging democracies while defending existing democratic institutions and values in other countries" is among the long list of objectives U.S. security assistance hopes to realize. Thus we might expect foreign military sales under the Clinton administration to have been directed more toward emerging and established democracies than others, but this was not the case. There is virtually no relationship between the kind of political regime a country has and how much (if any) U.S. military sales aid it receives (Kegley and Blanton 1994). This may be an instance, as former Secretary of Defense James Schlesinger observes, where foreign policy objectives are "flatly in conflict." Often, he writes, "striking little attention has been paid to the relationship between means and ends. Individual tools are assumed to achieve multiple objectives—with little heed paid to their inherent limitations" (Schlesinger 1992–1993).

After Vietnam   We have already discussed the preeminence of foreign military sales in American arms transfer policies, which began in the early 1970s. The flow of arms to the Middle East achieved massive proportions during the Nixon and Ford administrations, having grown out of the persistence of the Arab-Israeli conflict combined with the sharp upsurge in world oil prices in 1973 to 1974, which gave Middle Eastern oil exporting countries substantial new financial resources. Furthermore, the arms flow was stimulated by the *Nixon Doctrine*—the pledge that the United States would provide military and economic assistance to its friends and allies but that those nations would be responsible for protecting their own security. Nixon's Twin Pillars policy, discussed in Chapter 4, built on his new doctrine. By strengthening Iran and Saudi Arabia to increase stability and prevent the spread of Soviet influence in the region, the Twin Pillars would become the building blocks of U.S. Persian Gulf policy.

The dramatic shift from grants to sales that occurred at this time also reflected a subtle shift in emphasis away from anticommunism and the benefits assumed to accrue to the United States from stable, anticommunist regimes overseas. The overriding motivation remained an overtly political one: to enhance the ability of the United States to influence others so as to realize its own foreign policy objectives. Now, however, the presumed benefits of foreign military sales also embraced economic gains, including maintenance of the domestic defense industry and a reduction in the per unit cost of defense articles, plus balance-of-trade and payments benefits. The logic provided a preview of what in the post-Cold War era would become a major consideration in the continuation of foreign military sales.

The FMS program goes back to the early days of the Kennedy administration, which began to experiment with foreign military sales as an alternative to grant assistance. Congressional opposition to outright grants, continuing adverse U.S. balance of payments, and a growing concern for the lack of an integrated logistical system among the NATO nations were among the reasons for change (Louscher 1977). The same forces then sustained it. Over time FMS became a multipurpose instrument of policy designed to symbolize American resolve, to project American credibility, and to strengthen American allies generally.

Proponents of foreign military sales argued that the United States could not curb or control other nations' desire in an intensely nationalistic world to acquire arms, and they pointed out that other Western nations—as well as the Soviet Union and its allies—were both able and willing to provide military hardware. Still, some critics worried that transfers of advanced military technology to countries and regions where conflict was frequent, as in the Middle East, would actually contribute to the likelihood of local aggression, not deter it.[9] They noted the frequency with which the United States armed both (or all) parties in Third World regional conflicts and how today's allies had a way of becoming tomorrow's enemies, as those in need of American arms to protect themselves from Soviet penetration often later became Soviet clients (in Ethiopia and Yemen in the late 1970s, for example, and in Nicaragua in the early 1980s). Finally, the Iranian revolution of 1979 demonstrated that old friends need not become Soviet allies to become new enemies. Despite pumping billions of dollars worth of arms into Iran, the United States not only failed to build the regional power that it had sought but also later faced a population bitter with resentment. As one analyst noted decades later, "Much of the bitterness felt by Iranians toward the United States is traceable to twenty-five years of massive arms shipments to the Shah, much of it for use against Iranians—clubs, tear gas, and guns, and training for the dreaded secret police in how to use them" (Barnet 1993; see also Klare 1984). Regrettably, governments' use of American-made arms against their own people was (is) not confined to Iran (Klare 1988–1989).

Like the concern once raised about supporting authoritarian regimes with military aid, critics of the continuation of military sales today cite the close correlation between U.S. arms transfers and both the capability for and incidence of violence among those armed with U.S. (and other exporters') weapons (cf. Kapstein 1994).[10] More than 20 million people have died in more than one hundred armed conflicts during the "long peace" since World War II—many with weapons supplied by outsiders. In 1990 alone, according to one estimate, thirty-one conflicts were being fought using conventional weapons (*Defense Monitor* 20, no. 4 [1991]: 3). During the 1970s and 1980s, according to U.S. government data, "Third World governments received approximately 20,000 tanks and self-propelled howitzers, 28,000 artillery pieces, 37,000 armored personnel carriers, 1,100 warships and submarines, 8,000 military aircraft (of which more than half were supersonic combat planes), 3,600 helicopters, and more than 50,000 missiles" (Renner 1994, 23; see also U.S. Arms Control and Disarmament Agency 1995; Sokolski 1994). And the numbers continue to mount. Today, in part because of the weapons reductions required by the Conventional Forces in Europe (CFE) treaty, more than thirty countries have at least 1,000 battle tanks in their arms inventories (Renner 1994, 21).

During the 1976 presidential election, and in the aftermath of Vietnam, Jimmy Carter raised concern about the consistency between massive arms sales and the nation's avowed goal of seeking world peace. Once elected, he announced a new policy of "restraint" designed to curb the explosive arms trade, but the policy was fraught with contradictions from the start and soon abandoned. Thus the only serious attempt to curb what became during the 1970s the growing trade in sophisticated American weapons of war ended in failure. George Bush would try again in the aftermath of the Persian Gulf War—but would fare no better.

The Reagan administration cast all pretense of restraint aside, declaring that "the U.S. views the transfer of conventional arms and other defense articles as an indispensable component of its foreign policy." Reagan also decided to increase the proportion of security assistance in the overall mix of U.S. foreign aid. As before, anticommunism and the perceived security threats to the nation dictated the flow of funds, with Central America now a prime target. Although the Reagan administration never received all of the aid it sought—including military and other aid for the *contras*—aid levels did grow dramatically, to the point that on a per capita basis Central American nations became among the most heavily funded of all U.S. aid recipients. Elsewhere, Pakistan received several hundreds of millions in security assistance to facilitate (and reward) its support of anti-Marxist guerrillas fighting in Afghanistan.

During Reagan's watch foreign military sales began a dramatic upward turn, resulting by the end of Bush's term, as we noted earlier, in more arms sales in one decade than in the previous three. The Middle East remained the dominant focus of attention. As war raged between Iran and Iraq during much of the 1980s, the U.S. "tilt" toward Iraq included its decision to sell high-technology goods to Saddam Hussein. France and others also supplied weapons to the Iraqis. Therefore, ironically the United States and its Coalition partners in the Persian Gulf War would face weapons they themselves had supplied. Iraq was not unique, however. As one Pentagon official described the situation in Somalia in 1992, when the Bush administration launched its humanitarian intervention there: "Between the stuff the Russians and we stuck in there during the great Cold War, there are enough arms in Somalia to fuel hostility for one hundred years" (cited in Barnet 1993).

Following the Coalition's victory over Iraq, Bush determined that the time was again ripe to seek restraints on the global arms trade, particularly in the Middle East. He invited the five permanent members of the UN Security Council (who also are the world's largest arms merchants: Britain, France, China, and Russia, and the United States) to negotiate curbs on future arms sales and to prevent the kinds of technology transfers that made Iraq's war machine possible. Even as the discussions among the so-called "P-5" proceeded, however, the sale of new arms to Middle Eastern buyers skyrocketed. Then, in 1992, as Bush faced a tough reelection bid, the president broke with past practice, seeking to capitalize politically not on his arms restraint program but on the domestic benefits of arms sales abroad.

> Foundering in the polls—and desperately searching for some semblance of an economic policy—George Bush announced an astonishing $20 billion in new arms sales during a six-week period in September and October 1992. Breaking with past political etiquette, which dictated silence on controversial arms sales in election years, the Bush team decided to turn his decisions to sell F-15s to Saudi Arabia and F-16s to Taiwan into full-scale photo opportunities, which showed that George Bush "cared" about working people. At rallies in front of cheering throngs of F-16 plant workers in Fort Worth, Texas, and F-15 production personnel in St. Louis, Missouri, Bush embraced these ill-advised arms sales as symbols of his commitment to "do everything I can to keep Americans at work." (Hartung 1993, 22)

Bill Clinton did not object to Bush's decisions, but they did provide an excuse for the Chinese to end participation in the P-5 arms restraint talks, marking the end of only the second serious effort in two decades to restrain the dangerous—if profitable—global trade in the weapons of war.

In Search of a Rationale: Foreign Military Sales in the New World

The global arms market is undergoing an number of important changes.[11] One that we have already noted is the United States' emergence as the unambiguous arms supply leader. The demise of the Soviet Union and its successor states as major arms suppliers is a major reason, but other suppliers—particularly among what had been a growing number of weapons producers in the Global South—have also diminished in number. A second change is the decline in demand as worldwide military spending shrinks—a trend which, however, may be reversed as a new generation of high-tech weapons enters the global marketplace. Third, even as demand softens for major weapons systems, it remains vigorous for light weapons—such as small guns, grenades, machine guns, and light artillery—which often find immediate use in ethnic and other civil conflicts. Fourth, a growing number of weapons are being produced by code-velopment and coproduction schemes, in which two or more countries develop new weapons systems collaboratively, thus resulting in the globalization of arms production.

The two most important trends related to the rationale of post-Cold War U.S. arms transfers are the overcapacity of global productive capacity and the commercial-ization of arms sales. The two are related and both a product of the end of the Cold War. With the United States and the Soviet Union no longer competing for Third World allies, incentives to subsidize weapons transfers have largely vanished, but many would-be buyers do not have the cash to buy armaments on their own. Furthermore, defense budgets are declining throughout the world—falling by almost one-fourth from 1986 to 1992, from nearly 4 percent of world gross domestic product to 3 per-cent (Arora and Bayoumi 1994, 24). Global productive overcapacity is the logical con-sequence, which translates in turn into fierce competition among weapons producers for remaining markets. It also translates into threats to the defense industrial bases in supplier countries and to the jobs of those who depend on them.

Like Bush before him, Bill Clinton was especially sensitive to role of jobs in the weapons export equation. Although he spoke during the 1992 presidential campaign of the need for restraint, he did not oppose the arms packages for Saudi Arabia and Taiwan Bush announced during the campaign. Furthermore, the Clinton administra-tion approved the production of a third Seawolf submarine, not because it met a mili-tary need but because it would keep the defense industrial base "warm" (Kitfield 1994). Building arms for export does the same thing. Thus the administration's long-awaited conventional arms transfer policy, issued in February 1995, stated among its goals a de-sire "to enhance the ability of the U.S. defense industrial base to meet U.S. defense re-quirements and maintain long-term military technological superiority at lower costs."

The administration also embarked on a national industrial policy by channeling de-fense dollars into the private sector for the development of dual-use (military and civil-ian) technologies (see, e.g., Fallows, 1994a). And it effectively removed many dual-use technologies from the list of previously prohibited export items by easing restrictions related to their possible military applications. So important is the defense industrial base in Pentagon thinking that it "has been called 'the fifth service' and ranked right alongside the armed services as a critical leg in America's national security posture" (Kitfield 1994).

The economics of exporting arms includes reducing the per-unit cost of defense items. But from a national, macroeconomic perspective, the arguments in favor of weapons production typically focus on jobs: Defense production produces jobs that would be lost without either continued domestic military spending or foreign military sales. Foreign military sales have the further benefit, according to proponents, of help-ing to reduce the nation's gaping trade imbalance with the rest of the world.

Critics of these justifications argue that they do not stand up well under scrutiny. Several studies indicate, for example, that the number of jobs produced for every dol-lar invested in the civilian sector is greater than in the military sector (Hartung 1994b; *The Defense Monitor* 23, no. 6 [1994]; see also Chan and Mintz, 1992). Money spent on the military is also money that cannot be spent elsewhere. "The federal government devotes only about $12 billion to help finance the more than $200 billion cost of elementary and secondary education. If this funding were doubled, 370,000 additional teaching jobs could be created" (*The Defense Monitor* 23, no. 6 (1994): 3).

The benefits of producing for the export market, furthermore, are balanced by taxpayer subsidies. Apart from government credits extended to arms purchasers (whose debts, as we have seen, are typically canceled), the Pentagon "annually spends more than $300 million for an arms export staff of 5,000 employees as well as $25 million on trade shows" (Hartung 1994b).

"Offsets," embodied in bargains arms sellers strike with buyers to secure their business, reduce the presumed balance-of-trade benefits of foreign military sales. Offsets often mean that buyers buy into licensing agreements that permit them to participate in production of the weapon system. "South Korea, in its purchase of F-16s, arranged for its own participation in the production of these aircraft and Japan's purchase of the F-16 developed into a full-fledged partnership with the United States for the development of an upgraded aircraft through the FSX [coproduction] program" (Pierre and Conway-Lanz, 1994–1995). Thus schemes designed to sweeten arms deals enable purchasers to acquire advanced weapons technology at virtually no extra cost. Furthermore, they "frequently mean taking business from American companies and giving it to foreign suppliers" (Hartung 1994b), thus drastically reducing the trade and other economic benefits to the United States.

On balance, then, the evidence supporting the positive economic benefits of producing weapons of war for sale abroad are not—at least from a national perspective—compelling. Combined with concerns about the stimulus of weapons sales to violent conflict and the absence of clear evidence that they produce positive results in, say, promoting democracy, the concerned citizen might reasonably ask, "So why do we continue to do this?" The answer, it seems, at least in a narrow context, is domestic politics: "While foreign arms sales make no large economic sense, they are lucrative for the companies and communities involved" (Hartung 1994b; see also Hartung 1994a). The rationale for foreign military sales in the post-Cold War world cannot be explained entirely by domestic politics, but more than ever, it seems, it cannot be ignored. Thus an important instrument of American foreign policy once rationalized in the *realpolitik* of balance-of-power politics and the national interest have fallen victim to the geoeconomics of the new world order.

The Elusive Quest for National Security ....

President Clinton repeatedly stressed that "We can't be strong abroad unless we're strong at home." That meant a determined effort to revitalize the domestic economy through constructive investments in civilian goods and services. Simultaneously, sensitivity to the short-term impact of defense production and arms sales on local communities and the defense industry led to decisions that diverted scarce resources into arguably less than optimal uses. Thus a domestic policy trade-off was made, but it also had important foreign policy implications. Among them was the apparent contradiction between the administration's determined effort to stem the proliferation of nuclear and other weapons of mass destruction and its active role in the spread of conventional weapons of war, viewed by many analysts as an already a serious proliferation problem.

Although the administration pointed with pride to its role in encouraging the Mid-East peace process between Israel and its Arab neighbors, its policy of "dual containment" of Iran and Iraq also encouraged continued military build-ups in the region, whose history is rife with wars and rumors of wars. Arms build-ups contribute to that volatility. Even in the post-Cold War world, the **security dilemma** retains its compelling logic: Arms acquired by one country for defensive purposes are perceived by its adversary as offensive in nature, thus causing it, too, to build up its "defenses." In the end neither is more secure than before, but the threat of destruction from violence multiplies. If the logic of *realpolitik* is correct in saying that today's friends may become tomorrow's enemies—which has happened to the United States before (in both Iran and Iraq, ironically)—the long-term security of the United States itself might be diminished by today's short-term trade-offs.

Security is typically thought of in national terms, but increasingly the problems the United States faces are transnational in character, which means they do not follow the logic of the world's borders separating political entities into nation-states. The Clinton administration, more than any other, waxed sensitive to the changing and often unfamiliar character of the security concerns facing the United States in the 1990s and beyond. As Secretary of State Warren Christopher observed during his Senate confirmation hearings, "We face a world where borders matter less and less, a world that demands we join with other nations to face challenges that range from overpopulation to AIDS, to the very destruction of our planet's life support system." The list of these challenges should also include the spread of ethnopolitical conflict, which often erupts when ethnic groups reject the borders that enclose them with neighbors whom they distrust and dislike.

The Clinton administration's emphasis on chaos and crisis prevention demonstrates sensitivity to the challenges a sometimes borderless world poses, but selling these concepts in an environment where the nation-state remains paramount is difficult. Thus long-standing instruments of policy—military might, covert action, propaganda, and foreign aid—continue to be used in pursuit of national security. Meanwhile, the French government, when confronted with the new world order, responds by kicking five CIA operatives out of France on charges they engaged in industrial espionage.

NOTES

1. In a well-known study of the Pearl Harbor attack, Wohlstetter (1962) concludes that although information of the impending attack was available, insignificant data, which she called "noise," at the time overwhelmed the important data, the true "signal." Kahn (1986) takes exception to that conclusion, arguing that "Sufficient indications of an attack simply did not exist within the mass of American intelligence data. Not one intercept, not one datum of intelligence ever said anything about an attack on Pearl Harbor or on any other possession. That there were many distractions is true but irrelevant; the most refined analysis cannot bring out what is not present." See also Carr (1994).

2. The meanings and motivations underlying some of the facts surrounding the events in Chile between 1970 and 1973 are as controversial as the actual events themselves. For relevant discussions see Fagen (1975), Farnsworth (1974), Petras and LaPorte (1972), and Sigmund (1974a, 1974b).

3. Following the Soviets' withdrawal from Afghanistan the CIA launched a covert program to buy back unused Stinger missiles. Congress reportedly provided $65 million for the program—double the cost of the roughly one thousand missiles the United States provided the *mujaheddin*. However, only a fraction of the missiles were recovered, because the CIA does not know who controls them (Moore 1994, 18).

4. Concern for domestic "dissidents" and unrest during the Vietnam War led the Nixon administration to create a special intelligence group within the White House known as "the Plumbers," whose ostensible purpose was to fix news "leaks" and "flush" dissident opinion out of the American political system. Creation of this unit was prompted by Dr. Daniel Ellsberg's release of the *Pentagon Papers*, which contained classified national security-related information. In the name of national security, the group burglarized the office of Dr. Ellsberg's psychiatrist. The Plumbers were also responsible for the surreptitious entry of Democratic National Headquarters in the Watergate Hotel complex in the summer of 1972, an action that precipitated the infamous Watergate affair and Nixon's resignation of the presidency in 1974. Nixon defended his action on grounds that national security was being served.

5. Public diplomacy is normally thought to target foreign audiences, but the Reagan administration targeted the American public in a sustained effort to build support for its Central American policies, particularly aid to the contras. The efforts were carried out by the White House Office of Public Liaison and the State Department Office of Public Diplomacy. The latter eventually came under fire from Congress, which cut off funds for its operation. See Parry and Kornbluh (1988) for a critical view of the State Department's operation, and the letters to the editor in the Winter 1988–1989 issue of *Foreign Policy* for a rejoinder.

6. The description of the types of aid that follows draws on Zimmerman (1993), who provides an extensive study of ESF aid.

7. For a sampling of the issues and ideas in the United States, see Bissell (1991), Clad and Stone (1992–1993), Graves (1991, 1993), Nelson (1992), Schaefer (1992–1993), Sewell (1991), Sewell, Storm, Lewis, Camp, Mellor, and Chen (1992), Tisch and Wallace (1994), and Zimmerman (1993).

8. The Mutual Security Act became the umbrella legislation for economic and military aid after the onset of Korea. Foreign military sales (discussed below) are now governed by the Arms Export Control Act, first passed in 1968. As of early 1995, the Foreign Assistance Act (as amended) continue to govern other military aid programs. Economic assistance is authorized by both statutes.

9. Kinsella's (1994) investigation of the impact of Soviet and American arms transfers on Middle East conflict shows they did not have parallel effects: "Soviet transfers to Egypt and Syria exacerbated conflict in the Middle East, while U.S. transfers to Israel show no such propensity. There is also some evidence that U.S. arms supplies to Iran under Shah Pahlavi may have had a dampening effect on the Iran-Iraq rivalry."

10. Critics of the Clinton administration's arms transfer policies, which they see as strikingly similar to Nixon's, worry about the consequences of Turkey's use of U.S. weapons to deal with challenges by the Kurdish people, as when it invaded Northern Iraq in early 1995. "If Turkey

persists in its misguided effort to solve the problem of Kurdish nationalism through military means, it could become Bill Clinton's Iran" (Hartung 1995).

11. For more detailed treatment of these trends, see Bitzinger (1994), Grimmett (1995), Hartung (1993), Klare (1994–1995, 1995), Pierre and Conway-Lanz (1994–1995), Spear (1994–1995), and other articles in the symposium on "A New Arms Bazaar" in the *Harvard International Review*, Winter 1994–1995.

SUGGESTIONS FOR FURTHER READING

Andrew, Christopher. *For the President's Eyes Only: Secret Intelligence and the American Presidency from Washington to Bush.* New York: HarperCollins, 1995

Berkowitz, Bruce D., and Allan E. Goodman. *Strategic Intelligence for American National Security.* Princeton, N.J.: Princeton University Press, 1991.

Bitzinger, Richard A. "The Globalization of the Arms Industry: The Next Proliferation Challenge," *International Security* 19 (Fall 1994): 170–98.

Gray, Colin S. *Weapons Don't Make War: Policy, Strategy and Military Technology.* Lawrence: University of Kansas Press, 1993.

Harkavy, Robert E., and Stephanie G. Neuman, eds. "The Arms Trade: Problems and Prospects in the Post-Cold War World," *The Annals* (535 (September 1994): 1–244.

Hartung, William D. *And Arms for All.* New York: HarperCollins, 1994.

Kessler, Ronald. *Inside the CIA: Revealing the Secrets of the World's Most Powerful Spy Agency.* New York: Pocket Books, 1992.

Klare, Michael T., and Daniel C. Thomas, eds. *World Security: Challenges for a New Century.* New York: St. Martin's, 1994.

Romm, Joseph J. *Defining National Security: The Nonmilitary Aspects.* New York: Council on Foreign Relations, 1993.

Tisch, Sarah J., and Michael B. Wallace. *Dilemmas of Development Assistance: The What, Why, and Who of Foreign Aid.* Boulder, Colo.: Westview, 1994.

Weiner, Tim, David Johnston, and Neil A. Lewis. *Betrayal: The Story of Aldrich Ames, an American Spy.* New York: Random House, 1995.

Wise, David. *Nightmover: How Aldrich Ames Sold the CIA to the KGB for $4.6 Million.* New York: HarperCollins, 1995.

Woods, Alan. *Development and the National Interest: U.S. Economic Assistance into the 21st Century.* Washington, D.C.: Agency for International Development, 1989.

Zimmerman, Robert F. *Dollars, Diplomacy, and Dependency: Dilemmas of U.S. Economic Aid.* Boulder, Colo.: Lynnne Rienner, 1993.

CHAPTER 6

. . .

THE INTERNATIONAL POLITICAL SYSTEM IN TRANSITION: POWER AND PRINCIPLE IN A NEW WORLD

. . .

Our well-being as a country depends. . . on the structural conditions of the international system that help determine whether we are fundamentally secure, whether the world economy is sound.

Secretary of State George Shultz, 1984

The multipolar world into which we are moving [is not] necessarily going to be a safer place. . . . [The democracies must] renew their commitment to a collective and cooperative approach to the major issues [and this] will require American leadership of the highest order."

Deputy Secretary of State Lawrence S. Eagleburger, 1989

Early in October 1994 U.S. intelligence sources determined that Saddam Hussein was on the move again. Reconnaissance pictures revealed that a division of Iraq's elite Republican Guard, soon followed by a second armored division, was moving toward the border with Kuwait. Within days over sixty thousand Iraqi troops and an armada of powerful weapons—a military force larger than the one used four years earlier to invade Kuwait and proclaim it Iraq's nineteenth province—again stood within striking distance of the tiny oil sheikdom.

President Clinton cautioned the American people not to "blow it [Iraq's behavior] out of proportion," but he also issued a warning: "It would be a grave mistake for Saddam Hussein to believe that for any reason the United States would have weakened its resolve on the same issues that involved us in the conflict just a few years ago." To demonstrate that, Clinton ordered additional air, naval, and ground forces to the Persian Gulf to bolster those already deployed in the region. The United States also worked closely with its allies in Europe and the Middle East to ensure their continued support of American policies.

The U.S. response to Iraq's provocation is a classic illustration of state behavior as explained by the theory of political realism. Perceiving its interests threatened by the aggressive behavior of an adversary seeking to upset the status quo, the United States moved to balance Iraq's military power with its own and that of its allies. The behavior followed the principle of "self-help" in a system characterized by the absence of central institutions capable of conflict management and conflict resolution.

. . .

To be sure, principles motivated U.S. actions, just as they did four years earlier when George Bush orchestrated global support for a collective response to Iraq's aggression. But self-interest was also clearly operative. Millions of gallons of oil flow daily from the Middle East to the United States, Europe, and Japan, where they fuel the world's most sophisticated economies. Keeping control of that vital commodity from falling into the hands of a renegade state remained as important in 1994 as it had been in 1990. Thus the politics of peace and security and the politics of material well-being intertwined to explain the Clinton and Bush administrations' resolve.

Iraq's recurring challenges in the Middle East illustrate how the external environment acts as a source of American foreign policy, providing both stimulants to action and constraints on its ability to realize its preferred goals. Changes in international conditions act as catalysts in reassessing America's national interests and the kinds of opportunities that exist for realizing its foreign policy objectives. Whether and how a change is perceived may be as important as the actual circumstances that precede the final definition of policy priorities. Hence the external environment is properly conceived as a cluster of variables shaping the international climate in which the United States competes.

We assess the impact of the international environment on American foreign policy in this chapter and the next. We begin by directing attention to three characteristics of the international system and their implications for American foreign policy:

1. The distribution of power among the world's leading political, military, and economic nation-states.
2. The emergence of the Global South on the periphery of great-power politics.
3. The proliferation of nonstate transnational actors.

In Chapter 7 we shift attention to the world political economy. There we examine the role of the United States in managing the Liberal International Economic Order and inquire into the effect of its changing power position in the world political economy on both its interests and its perceptions of its leadership role.

"Power" and "hegemony" are central concepts in our analyses in both chapters. Thus we will find it useful to draw on the tenets of political realism as we seek to understand the impact of the external environment on American foreign policy. But we also will find that the logic of *realpolitik* sometimes provides an insufficient explanation of American foreign policy in an international political and economic environment undergoing rapid change. Military power does not always translate into influence on nonmilitary issues. Furthermore, the end of the Cold War has elevated the importance of *geoeconomics* at the expense of *geopolitics* (Luttwak 1990), as the world's leading powers now compete more for market share than territorial control or common ideological bedfellows. Commercial advantage, not military might, will determine who exercises influence over whom and who feels threatened and who secure. Thus we also will draw on recent thinking about the idealist tradition in American foreign policy (now better labeled "liberal international relations theory") as we seek to understand the challenges and opportunities the external environment holds for the United States.

The Distribution of Power as a Source of
American Foreign Policy

The international political system of which the United States has been a part for over two hundred years is distinguished by two continuing attributes. The first is its *decentralized* structure. The system's principal actors—sovereign states—monopolize power in the absence of a central institution, such as a world government. No authority exists above the nation-state to enforce order. Consequently, states must rely primarily on bargaining and self-help to ensure their national security. A decentralized, competitive system places a premium on the quest for power as a means of defense and influence. In such a politically primitive system, arms races and a high incidence of violence are both recurrent and understandable.

Decentralization is related to a second basic attribute of the system—its *stratified* structure. Nations are equal in law but not in influence; power is distributed unevenly. A few political, military, and economic giants near the hierarchical apex possess a disproportionate share of influence, while many (most) others near the bottom of this metaphorical pyramid are comparatively powerless. The ascribed status of states and the distribution of resources among them are also uneven.

The theory of political realism holds that the structure of the international system, defined by the distribution of power among states, is the primary determinant of states' foreign policy behavior. Kenneth Waltz (1979)—a leading proponent of neorealist, or structural, theory—argues that only two types of systems have existed since the birth of the nation-state at the Peace of Westphalia in 1648: (1) a multipolar system, which existed until the end of World War II; and (2) a bipolar system, which characterized the distribution of power during the Cold War. In both, states protected their interests against external threats by balancing power with power.

Coalitions—alliances—were critical in the **multipolar** system. States that perceived one among them as seeking preponderant power (hegemony) joined together in a balancing coalition to preserve their own existence (national self-interest). Wars were recurrent and often determined who among existing and aspiring hegemons would dominate the post-war world. The United States itself was born in a contest between Britain and France over who would be dominant in Europe and the New World. And the historical record indicates that the architects of the new American republic were acutely aware of the perquisites and perils of power that buffeted the new nation, as we saw in Chapter 3.

The situation after World War II was quite different. Now only two powers contended for preponderance. Each still sought to balance power with power, as suggested by the strategies of containment the United States pursued to parry Soviet challenges (Gaddis 1982), but alliances were comparatively unimportant to their own survival. To be sure, the United States and the Soviet Union both sought to recruit allies to their cause: They repeatedly intervened abroad by military and in other means to counter the threat each posed to the other's clients, and the North Atlantic Treaty Organization (NATO) and the Warsaw Pact were pillars of their foreign policies. Each also mirrored the behavior of the other as both developed ever-more-sophisticated weapons of destruction. But, neorealists argue, it was the weapons themselves—nuclear weapons in particular—that balanced the antagonists' power. As long as both enjoyed a second-strike nuclear capability, neither could dominate or destroy the other. As Waltz put it, "Nuclear weapons produced an underlying stillness at the center of international politics that made the sometimes frenzied military preparations of the United States and the Soviet Union pointless, and efforts to devise scenarios for the use of their nuclear weapons bizarre" (Waltz 1993; see also Gaddis 1986; Mearsheimer 1990a, 1990b; Waltz 1964).

The neorealist argument is not beyond dispute, but it usefully orients us to an examination of American foreign policy in historical configurations of state power and the implications of possibly different configurations in the new millennium. For, as President Bush observed in 1989, "we're at the end of one era, and at the beginning of another."

Multipolarity and the Birth of the American Republic

From today's perspective it is difficult to believe that little more than two centuries ago the United States was a small, fledgling state, whose very existence was in perpetual jeopardy. With only about three million inhabitants, the thirteen colonies that proclaimed their independence from Britain were dwarfed by Europe's great powers: Britain, an island power, and France, Russia, Austria, and Prussia on the continent. Preserving the independence won at Yorktown in 1781 thus became a primary preoccupation. "It was the genius of America's first diplomats in this unemotional age that they realized the nature of their international opposition—which included all of the powers of the day, not excepting France—and adroitly maneuvered their country's case through the snares and traps of Europe's diplomatic coalitions until they irrevocably had secured national independence"(Ferrell 1988; see also Gilbert 1961).

The colonists' alliance with France was critical to the success of their rebellion against England. France supported the United States to regain a foothold on the North American continent following an earlier defeat at the hands of the British. France and England had fought a series of wars in a century-old rivalry for preponderance in Europe and control of North America. The Seven Year's War in Europe, known as the French and Indian War in America, was the most recent. With the French defeat, the 1763 Treaty of Paris assured France's virtual elimination from North America. Canada and the Ohio Valley were ceded to the British. Louisiana was relinquished to Spain, which in turn ceded the Floridas to England. England sought to consolidate control of its empire in the years that followed. The famed Boston Tea Party was brewed by its effort to squeeze more resources out of the colonies.

France reemerged as a principal security concern of the newly independent United States. Policymakers were acutely aware that French support would last only as long as it served French interests, and an undeclared war erupted between the American and French navies in 1797. Ironically, however, the French Revolution and the rise of Napoleon Bonaparte, whose ambitions centered on Europe, contributed to the continental expansion of the United States. Talleyrand (Charles Maurice de Talleyrand-Périgord), the wily French foreign minister during the Reign of Terror, hoped to regain the Louisiana territory from Spain as part of a plan to recreate France's North American empire. Napoleon later became interested in the project but, facing renewed war against England, dropped it. Focused on Europe, not on recreating an empire far from the continent, he sold to the United States the vast tract of land which doubled its size. "The 1803 sale of Louisiana to America was no mark of French friendship for the United States but the fortuitous result of a train of events that, but for the old world ambitions of Napoleon, would have drastically constricted American territorial expansion and might have extinguished American independence" (Ferrell 1988).

Napoleon's drive for European hegemony sparked more than a decade of protracted conflict and war, which finally ended in 1815 with the Congress of Vienna and the restoration of the Bourbon monarchy to the French throne. The War of 1812 was part of that systemwide conflict. The United States entered the fray against Britain, asserting its trading rights as a neutral during wartime. A century later Woodrow Wilson would use similar principles to rationalize American involvement in World War I. However, unlike its position in 1917—by which time the United States had emerged a major industrial power in the world—in 1812 the United States was still struggling to secure its independence. History records the War of 1812 as a second American victory over the English; often forgotten is that the British successfully attacked and burned Washington, D.C., forcing President James Madison to flee the capital.

In 1823 President James Monroe enunciated what would later be called the Monroe Doctrine. As we noted in Chapter 3, Monroe's statement declared that the Americas were for Americans. Although enshrined as part of the nation's isolationist heritage necessary to preserve its liberty, the United States lacked the power to make good on its implicit threat to the European powers who were its targets. Instead, Britain's power—particularly its command of the high seas—effectively "enforced" the Monroe Doctrine for nearly seventy years. Its sea power kept other European states out of the New World and permitted the United States to develop from an agrarian society into an industrial power.

The Spanish-American War, which erupted in 1898 and transformed the United States into an imperial power, had little impact on the global balance of power. In Europe, however, Germany was ascendant, challenging the French for continental hegemony in the Franco-Prussian War of 1870–1871 and posing a potential threat to England, the island power (see Kissinger 1994a). By 1914 the alliance structures of the multipolar balance-of-power system had rigidified: The guns of August that ignited World War I ended a century of great-power peace. Three years later the United States entered the war on the side of the British, French, and Russians against Germany and the Austro-Hungarian and Ottoman empires. As in the War of 1812, the legal principle of neutral rights on the high seas figured prominently in the decision for war. But political realists argue that more than principle was at stake: It was nothing less than the European balance of power, which posed potentially serious threats to American interests and security.

America entered the European war when the aggressive continental land power of Germany was about to achieve hegemony in Europe by defeating the British sea power and to acquire simultaneously the mastery of the Atlantic Ocean. The very month that war was declared by America, Britain lost 880,000 gross tons of shipping, several times more than it could possibly replace. In that same month, mutinies in the French army made France's future in the war questionable. Russia, the third member of Europe's Triple Entente, was but a few months away from its internal collapse. (Serfaty 1972, 7–8)

The United States reverted to isolationism after World War I, choosing not to become embroiled in the machinations of European power politics. But just as its balancing behavior turned the tide against German hegemonic ambitions at the turn of the century, its power proved critical in turning back the German and Japanese challenges mounted in the 1930s and 1940s. The United States, guided by Wilsonian idealism, had hoped to replace the "ugly" balance-of-power politics of the Old World with a new collective security system, embodied in the League of Nations. When that failed, it found that it had to resort to the same strategies it once deplored: joining Britain and the Soviet Union in a balancing coalition designed to prevent the Axis powers from achieving world hegemony. Once the death and destruction ceased and the ashes began to settle, the United States found that it alone emerged largely unscathed from the ravages of a world war that claimed fifty million lives.

Hegemonic Dominance: A Unipolar World

World War II transformed the American economy, which now stood preeminent in the world political economy. The gross national product (GNP) rose 72 percent between 1941 and 1944; agricultural production increased by 25 percent; and civilian consumption of goods and services rose by 20 percent (Lovell 1970, 93). In contrast, Europe lay exhausted and destroyed. Even the Soviet Union, whose armies pushed the Nazis from Stalingrad to Berlin, had suffered grievously. Its industrial, agricultural, and transportation systems had either been destroyed or severely damaged, and an estimated 6.7 million Soviet civilians perished in the war, in addition to the 11 million soldiers who were killed or missing in action. Although the United States had suffered some 405,000 killed or missing in action (Ellis 1993, 254), it had virtually no civilian casualties. Thus the ratio of Soviet to American war deaths was more than to forty to one.

The Soviet Union had, of course, secured control over much of eastern Europe following the war, and it was over this issue that Soviet-American conflict centered. On balance, however, the United States was clearly in the superior position—a true hegemonic power. In 1947 the United States alone accounted for nearly half the world's total production of goods and services. And the nation's monopoly of the atomic bomb gave it military predominance.

Only against this background can we begin to see how fundamental the shifts in the international distribution of power have been during the past five decades. The post-World War II era began with the United States possessing the capability (if not the will) to exercise greater control over world affairs than perhaps any previous nation. It alone possessed the military and economic might to defend unilaterally its security and sovereignty. Its unparalleled supremacy transformed the system during this interlude into a *unipolar* one.

So preponderant was American power that Henry Luce, editor of *Time* and *Life* magazines, already in 1941 spoke hopefully of "the American century"—of a prolonged period in which American power would enable the United States to shape the world to its interests. He based his prediction on the conviction that "only America can effectively state the aims of this war [World War II]," which included, under American leadership, "a vital international economy" and "an international moral order" (cited in LaFeber 1994).

Others worried that the United States might overextend itself. Political commentator and journalist Walter Lippmann (1943) observed in 1943 that "foreign policy consists of bringing into balance . . . the nation's commitments and the nation's power." Thus "solvency" was, for Lippmann, a critical concern as the United States embarked on its rise to globalism. He later criticized the containment foreign policy strategy, arguing among other things that the regimentation required to combat Soviet communism would hurt the economy.

Lippmann's concerns and criticisms anticipated the intense debate about the decline of American power that would occur four decades later (see also Schwenninger 1995). At the time, however, the "American century" was more compelling than concern for "solvency" and the "Lippmann gap." Still, the unipolar moment the United States enjoyed in the immediate aftermath of World War II began to change almost as soon as it was recognized. The American monopoly of the atom bomb was cracked with the successful Soviet atomic test in 1949. In 1953 the Soviet Union exploded a thermonuclear device, less than a year after the United States. And in 1957 it shocked the Western World by being the first nation to successfully test an intercontinental ballistic missile (ICBM) and to orbit a space satellite—feats that also signaled its ability to deliver a nuclear warhead far from mother Russia.

The Bipolar System

Bipolarity describes the concentration of effective world power in the hands of the United States and the Soviet Union from the late 1940s until the 1962 Cuban missile crisis (see also Wagner 1993). The less-powerful nations looked to one or the other superpower for protection, and the two world leaders energetically competed for their allegiance. NATO, which linked the United States to the defense of Western Europe, and the Warsaw Pact, which tied the Soviet Union in a formal alliance to its Eastern European satellites, were the two major products of this early competition. The division of Europe into competing blocs also provided a solution to the German question—an implicit alliance between East and West against the center. As Lord Ismay, the first Secretary General of NATO, put it, the purpose of the Atlantic Alliance was "to keep the Russians out, the Americans in, and the Germans down."

By grouping the nations of the system into two blocs, each led by a superpower with the capacity to instantaneously "veto" the existence of entire nations (Kaplan 1957), the bipolar structure bred insecurity throughout (Spanier 1990). Believing that the power balance was constantly at stake, each side perceived a gain by one as a loss for the other—a situation known in the mathematics of game theory as a "zero-sum" outcome. Recruiting new friends and allies was thus of utmost importance, while fear that an old ally might desert the fold was ever present. The bipolar structure provided little room for compromise. Every maneuver appeared to be a new initiative toward world conquest; hence every act was perceived as hostile and was to be met by a retaliatory act. Because the antagonists believed conciliation was impossible, at best only momentary pauses in the exchange of threats, tests of resolve, and challenges to the territorial status quo could be expected. Repeated great power interventions in the Third World and recurrent crises at the brink of great power war characterized bipolarity (see Brecher and Wilkenfeld 1991).

Despite endemic threats and recurring crises during the bipolar era, major war between the great powers did *not* occur. Instead, historian John Gaddis (1986) describes this as "the long peace" (see also Gaddis 1991). Paradoxically, the perpetual competition and the concentration of enormous destructive power in the hands of the contestants produced caution and stability rather than recklessness and war. Neorealists in particular, as we noted, attribute that caution and stability to nuclear weapons.[1]

The Bipolycentric System

A looser structure began to replace bipolarity in the wake of the Cuban missile crisis, as the superpowers stepped back from the nuclear precipice and eventually pursued a policy of détente. This change was evidenced in their acceptance of the view that nuclear parity was needed to preserve strategic stability (as signaled by the SALT agreements); their intermittent pledges to avert use of nuclear weapons to settle their differences; and a growing conviction that the destructiveness of modern weapons reduced the utility of defensive alliances. Catalysts of change in the system's increasingly fluid polarity structure included rapid technological advances in the superpowers' major weapons systems. ICBMs in particular decreased the need for forward bases—especially important to the United States—from which to strike the adversary.

As rigid bipolarity eroded, the emerging structure is best characterized as "bipolycentric." ***Bipolycentrism*** aptly describes the continued military superiority of the United States and the Soviet Union and the continuing reliance of the weaker alliance partners on their respective superpower patrons for security in the aftermath of the Cuban crisis. The new system also permitted measurably greater maneuverability on the part of weaker members. Hence the term ***polycentrism***, connoting the possibility of many centers of power and diverse relationships among the nations subordinate to the superpowers. In the tiered polycentric system, each superpower sought closer ties with the secondary powers formally aligned with its adversary (like those once nurtured between the United States and Romania and between France and the Soviet Union). The secondary powers in turn exploited those ties and sought to enhance their bargaining position within their own alliance by establishing relationships among themselves (for example, between Poland and West Germany). While the superpowers remained dominant militarily, greater diplomatic fluidity became evident.

The Fragmentation of the Atlantic Alliance

The diminishing gap between Soviet and American military capabilities accelerated these developments, as it reduced the credibility of the superpowers' commitment to sacrifice their own security for their allies' defense. In a system shaped fundamentally by a "balance of terror," European members of NATO in particular worried increasingly about whether the United States would sacrifice New York City for Paris or Bonn. Mounting uncertainties about the credibility of the U.S. threat of massive retaliation led France to develop its own nuclear *force de frappe* and later to withdraw from the integrated NATO command. Even the flexible response policy adopted as official NATO strategy during the Johnson administration did not restore European confidence in American promises. The policy tried to extend to Europe the principle of assured destruction of the Soviet Union should the Warsaw Pact attack Western Europe. However, for many Europeans it simply signaled the United States' reluctance to expose itself to destruction to ensure its allies' security.

These concerns accelerated the polycentric divisions already evident. Examples of the breakdown of alliance cohesion include:

- The open disapproval by many European governments of American policy in Vietnam during the 1960s.
- The refusal of landing rights to American planes resupplying Israel during the 1973 Yom Kippur War.
- The reluctance to support U.S. sanctions against the Soviet Union following its invasion of Afghanistan in 1979.
- Lukewarm support, also in 1979, of American efforts to squeeze Iran economically to force the release of American hostages there.
- Participation, over American objections, in the Yamberg pipeline project designed to transport natural gas from Siberia to Western European markets.
- Criticism of Washington's policies for dealing with domestic turmoil in Central America.

Later talk of "decoupling" Europe from American protection prompted the decision to deploy in Europe a new class of intermediate-range nuclear missiles, thus enhancing the credibility of extended deterrence. However, uneasiness persisted as peace groups on both sides of the Atlantic challenged the "Atlanticist" orientation that previously had bound the United States and Western Europe together. Western European opinion during the 1980s swung toward neutralism and pacifism at the same time that the United States undertook a massive rearmament program. The specter of Europe devastated in a "limited response" nuclear exchange—a nuclear attack confined to the European theater without escalating to general war between the superpowers—inspired the European quest of a new architecture that would prevent Europe from becoming a nuclear battleground.

Changes in the distribution of economic strength coincided with these geostrategic developments. Already by the 1960s and 1970s many of America's allies were vibrant economic entities, no longer weak dependents. The phenomenal postwar growth of the Japanese and Western European economies largely accounted for the relative decline of America's economic dominance. By 1988 the combined output of Japan and the twelve members of the European Community was more than $950 billion greater than U.S. output. Thirty years earlier, in 1960, it did not even equal U.S. output. Enhanced capabilities permitted Europe and Japan to become more assertive and accelerated the erosion of America's ability to impose its own chosen solutions on nonmilitary questions (see Chapter 7). Thus the "century" of American hegemony Henry Luce had predicted in the early 1940s proved short-lived.

The relative decline of American power increasingly constrained the nation's foreign policy options. The Nixon, Ford, and Carter administrations sought to accommodate the United States to the growing limits of American military and economic power, but the Reagan administration denied their existence. Instead, it attempted to alter perceptions and reassert American influence over external affairs through increased military spending and hawkish diplomacy. Whether the effort succeeded remains in dispute (see Nau 1990; Nye 1990), as some observers view costly commitments as counterproductive (see Kennedy 1987; Mead 1990). Regardless, the now firmly established economic strength of Japan and Europe (notably Germany) permits these actors to steer a course independent of the United States—indeed, one that often challenges the United States. Already Germany and Japan excel where arguably the real global contest of the future will be fought—on the economic battlefield.

The Splintering of the Soviet Bloc

The fragmentation of the Cold War alliances associated with rigid bipolarity was an Eastern as well as Western phenomenon. The Sino-Soviet split, dating to the 1950s, visibly illuminated the breakup of what once was seen as a communist monolith (although American policymakers were slow to see the light). Growing out of ideological differences as well as security concerns befitting two giant neighbors, the dispute was elevated in the 1960s to rivalry for leadership of the world communist movement, opening a new era of Washington-Moscow-Beijing triangular politics.

"Tripolarity" was often used in the 1960s and 1970s to describe a system comprising three nations with comparatively equal power potential vis-à-vis one another as defined by their military (especially nuclear) capabilities. Fashioned to interpret the role of China in superpower relationships and its growing independence from Moscow's control, the metaphor recognized the emergence of China as a significant regional power—one perhaps destined, as former President Nixon predicted in 1989, to become "an economic and military superpower." Nixon's own historic visit to China in February 1972 is the most celebrated symbol of triangular diplomacy of the period. "Playing the China card" thereafter became a favorite U.S. maneuver (or bluff) in its efforts to moderate Soviet behavior around the globe.

Polycentrism within the Soviet bloc extended beyond the Sino-Soviet clash. Periodic assertions of Eastern European independence, despite the shadow of the Red Army, also marked the behavior of East Germany, Poland, and Hungary during the 1950s. During the 1960s, the polycentric tendencies within the Warsaw Pact were most visible in Czechoslovakia, whose democratic experiment was abruptly terminated by Warsaw Pact military intervention in 1968. Kremlin leaders proclaimed the **Brezhnev Doctrine** (named after the Soviet Premier Leonard Brezhnev) to justify the invasion and to put other satellites tempted to experiment with domestic reform on warning about possible defection from the communist fold.

Despite that warning, East European assertions of independence from "Moscow's line" grew in the 1970s and early 1980s, presaging the far-reaching domestic and foreign policy reforms that later swept the region. In 1989, Hungary became the first socialist country in Eastern Europe to schedule free elections, Poland elected a noncommunist prime minister, East Germany's communist leadership resigned and their successors permitted destruction of the Berlin Wall, and Czechoslovakia formed a new cabinet with a noncommunist majority. Gorbachev's radical reforms under *glasnost* required new thinking in the Soviet Union's policy toward its former Eastern European satellites, as reform at home licensed reform of communist mismanagement abroad.

"Almost overnight," noted Adam Bromke (cited in Smolowe 1989), "all the rivalries and tensions in the bloc that Communist orthodoxy had papered over for decades burst into the open." Hesitant to deny Soviet allies the liberalization he must permit to save his own nation, Gorbachev repudiated the Brezhnev Doctrine in favor of the "Sinatra Doctrine," which decreed that satellite states would be permitted to "do it their way." This signaled the end of the Soviet empire in Eastern Europe. Members of the Warsaw Pact in quick succession renounced communist rule and endorsed free market democracies. With Europe now poised at the dawn of new era, Brent Scowcroft, President Bush's national security adviser, exclaimed that the surge of reform in Eastern Europe and the Soviet Union had brought about "a fundamental change in the whole international structure."

Toward Multipolarity: A Neorealist Perspective on the New Millennium

The end of the Cold War inevitably raises questions about future power configurations and the constraints and opportunities they portend. In one sense, of course, the post-Cold War system retains the bipolycentric structure of the Cold War era. The United States and Russia remain the world's preeminent military powers, as both continue to possess the nuclear second-strike capability neorealists see as critical to the stability of the Cold War power balance. But Russia is but a shadow of its predecessor internally, and even the United States now struggles from an endless list of domestic ills that have sapped its strength. "If it is true that we have emerged victorious from the Cold War," Deputy Secretary of State Lawrence S. Eagleburger observed in 1989, "then we, like the Soviets behind us, have crossed the finish line very much out of breath." Moreover, changes in the structure of the international system begin with changes in states. "We know from structural theory that states strive to maintain their positions in the system. Thus, in their twilight years great powers try to arrest or reverse their decline. . . . For a combination of internal and external reasons, Soviet leaders tried to reverse their country's precipitous fall in international standing but did not succeed" (Waltz 1993).

As bipolarity fades into history, what will replace it? *Unipolarity* already has replaced it, in the eyes of some, just as unipolarity provided a brief interlude between the multipolar system that preceded World War II and the bipolar structure that followed. The role of the United States in this reenactment of unipolarity is captured in its description as the "sole remaining superpower."

In the afterglow of the Persian Gulf War syndicated columnist Charles Krauthammer (1991) made the case not only for unipolarity as a description of system structure but also as a prescription for others' behavior. "The center of world power is the unchallenged superpower, the United States," he wrote. "There is but one first-rate power and no prospect in the immediate future of any power to rival it." Other nations will turn to the United States for leadership as they did in organizing a response to Iraqi's invasion of Kuwait and, later, in ensuring the distribution of humanitarian assistance in Somalia, he argued. "The unipolar moment means that with the close of the century's three great Northern civil wars (World War I, World War II, and the Cold War) an ideologically pacified North seeks security and order by aligning its foreign policy behind that of the United States," Krauthammer continued. "It is the shape of things to come."

Others recognize the centrality of the United States militarily but concede there are major actors ("great powers") in world politics by virtue of some combination of military and economic prowess—notably Germany and Japan, Britain and France—and that power is diffused among still other states, such as India, Brazil, and South Korea. The system is not yet multipolar, which suggests comparatively equal power among, say, five principal actors, but neither is it bipolar or unipolar, according to this viewpoint. Political scientist John Spanier (1993) describes this system as *unipolycentric*. Earlier he used the concept bipolycentrism to encapsulate changes in the interests and capabilities of Europe and Japan within the context of continuing Soviet and American military dominance. Within this new, unipolycentric configuration, he suggests, regional conflicts are more likely to erupt, as in the Persian Gulf War, because the previous Cold War antagonists no longer have incentives to restrain their clients out of fear of a local conflict escalating to a global one. The proliferation of nuclear and unconventional (chemical and biological) weapons technology is one manifestation of "the fragmentation and regionalization of power" in the post-Cold War era.[2]

The fragmentation of power underlies many challenges that states now face. A distinctive quality of many of these is that they are fundamentally *intra*national, not *inter*national. The United States arguably has some influence in the latter, but much less in the former. The reasons lie less in the structural characteristics of the international system central to realist thinking than in the challenges to structuralism mounted by issues liberal theorists see as central to the agenda of the new world order. Such issues include the disintegration caused by ethnonationalism and other internal disorders as well as the integrative forces of geoeconomics.[3]

Joseph Nye's (1992) concept of *multilevel interdependence*—a close cousin to unipolycentrism—draws attention to the integrative and disintegrative forces now operative. Nye argues that "No single hierarchy describes adequately a world politics with multiple structures. The distribution of power in world politics has become like a layer cake. The top military layer is largely unipolar, for there is no other military power comparable to the United States. The economic middle layer is tripolar and has been for two decades. The bottom layer of transnational interdependence shows a diffusion of power" Nye continues, postulating that the "layers" of world power impact directly on American foreign policy prospects:

> None of this complexity would matter if military power were as fungible as money and could determine the outcomes in all areas. In describing Europe before 1914, the British historian A. J. P. Taylor wrote that the test of a great power was the ability to prevail in war. But military prowess is a poor predictor of the outcomes in the economic and transnational layers of current world politics. The United States is better placed with a more diversified portfolio of power resources than any other country, but the new world order will not be an era of American hegemony. (Nye 1992, 88)

What is new about the emerging world order, as Henry Kissinger (1994a) observes, "is that, for the first time, the United States can neither withdraw from the world nor dominate it." Without American hegemony, the new millennium is likely to see the emergence of a new multipolar system not unlike that which existed before World War II. The United States, Japan, China, Russia, and Germany—either alone or within a united Europe—are widely regarded as the likely principal actors in the system. India is also sometimes mentioned. The multipolar prognosis builds on the assumption that economic power will increasingly rival military power, especially as the U.S.-Russian "disarmament race" gains momentum during the remainder of this decade and the salience of military threats to national security diminish.

Already these actors account for the lion's share of gross world product, as Figure 6.1 illustrates. Beyond this, however, structural theory argues that great power status and its responsibilities are not easily shunned. This is even true for Germany and Japan, whose experience in World War II (and postwar pressures from the United States) caused both to foreswear nuclear weapons. "For a country to choose not to become a great power is a structural anomaly. For that reason, the choice is a difficult one to sustain. Sooner or later, usually sooner, the international status of countries has risen in step with their material resources. . . . Japanese and German nuclear inhibitions arising from World War II will not last indefinitely; one might expect them to expire as generational memories fade" (Waltz 1993).

The United States will remain the most powerful actor, even in a multipolar system in which Germany and Japan might possess nuclear weapons (China already does). It, then, will be the power others will seek to balance—assuming realist theory is correct. The contrast with Krauthammer's prognosis is striking: America's leadership is something that would be feared, not sought. In a multipolar system, realists argue, others will seek to check the dominant power, not ally ("bandwagon") with it (Layne 1993; Walt 1990). Evidence consistent with that hypothesis is already apparent, as indicated by concern in Europe, Asia, and elsewhere about the United States' determination to pursue war against Iraq rather than let sanctions work longer (as many preferred) and to intervene militarily in Haiti, again lifting the squeeze of economic pressure prematurely.

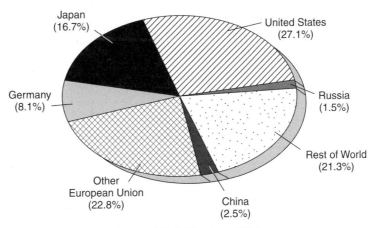

Figure 6.1 Shares of Gross World Product, 1993
Source: Adapted from *The World Bank Atlas 1995* (Washington, D.C.: The World Bank, 1994), pp. 18–19.

It is by no means clear how the United States, the "sole remaining superpower," should respond to the challenges of an emergent multipolar environment in which it, not others, may be feared. Still, it is useful to identify briefly alternative strategies the United States might pursue now and in the future. The strategies fall under the traditional rubric of unilateralism, bilateralism, and multilateralism.[4]

Unilateralism

Unilateralism can take various forms, ranging from total withdrawal from world affairs to "assertive unilateralism," which involves various forms of intervention in the affairs of other nations—whether they (and others) like it or not. The spread of American economic interests makes withdrawal an unrealistic option today, but assertive unilateralism may be feasible. Britain's nineteenth-century practice of "splendid isolationism" is a historic analogue. Britain pursued two objectives: (1) maintaining supremacy on the high seas to ensure the physical security of the homeland and to protect commercial interests abroad; and (2) preventing any one state from achieving hegemony on the European continent. To achieve the first objective, Britain maintained a naval fleet twice the size of its nearest rival. To achieve the second, it acted as the "balancer" in European conflicts by throwing its weight behind the coalition seeking to block an aspiring continental hegemon from realizing its aspirations. Continuous involvement in Europe's affairs was not necessary; instead, Britain intervened only when its security interests were threatened (see Kissinger 1994a).

As noted earlier, the United States benefited from British security policy, which enabled it to grow and prosper without European intrusions and threats to its security. The United States also acted much like the British themselves: While embracing isolationism, American leaders practiced unilateral interventionism on a recurring basis when they perceived threats to the nation's interests (see also Deibel 1992; Jonas 1966). In the two decades prior to the Japanese attack on Pearl Harbor—the high point of twentieth-century isolationism—U.S. presidents nearly twenty times dispatched troops abroad to protect America's self-defined interests. The United States also continued an intervention in Haiti from 1915 to 1934 and renewed involvement in Nicaragua only one year after ending years of previous American control.

As both the British and American examples make clear, the practice of isolationism does not mean noninvolvement but *selective* involvement. That remains true today. "Neo-isolationists want the U.S. to deal only with threats to America's physical security, political independence, and domestic liberty," notes Stanley Hoffmann (1992). He continues: "They find no such threats at present, and therefore argue that the U.S. should let other powers, and regional balances of power, take care of all the world's woes." Patrick Buchanan's (1990) "America First" posture fits this prescription. ("America First" was the slogan of pre-World War II isolationists and refers to both an organization and a movement during that period [Hamby 1992].) A contender for the Republican Party presidential nomination in 1992 and again in 1996, Buchanan urged an American foreign policy posture strikingly similar to Britain's splendid isolationism. His views, which continue to enjoy appeal within various segments of the American public, are recorded in Focus 6.1.

Buchanan also cautions that "We should look . . . with a cold eye on the interna-

Focus 6.1

AN AMERICA FIRST PRESCRIPTION FOR SPLENDID
ISOLATIONISM

• • •

- "Total withdrawal of U.S. troops from Europe [should follow Moscow's withdrawal]. . . . Once the Red Army goes home, the reason for keeping a U.S. army in Europe vanishes. . . . It is time Europe conscripted the soldiers for its own defense."

- "Still the greatest trading nation on earth, the U.S. depends for its prosperity on freedom of the seas. . . . An island-continent, America should use her economic and technological superiority to keep herself permanent mistress of the seas, first in air power, first in space."

- "This is our hemisphere; and the Monroe Doctrine should be made again the cornerstone of U.S. foreign policy."

- "We are not going to fight another land war in Asia; no vital interest justifies it; our people will not permit it. . . . If we must intervene, we can do so with air and sea power, without thousands of Army and Marine dead. It is time we began uprooting the global network of 'trip wires' planted on foreign soil to ensnare the United States in the wars of other nations, to back commitments and treaties signed before this generation of American soldiers was born."

- "We cannot forever defend wealthy nations that refuse to defend themselves; we cannot permit endless transfusions of the life blood of American capitalism into mendicant countries and economic corpses of socialism, without bleeding to death. Foreign aid is an idea whose time has passed."

Source: Patrick Buchanan, "America First—and Second, and Third," The National Interest 19 (Spring 1990): 79–81.

tionalist set, never at a loss for new ideas to divert U.S. wealth and power into crusades and causes having little or nothing to do with the true national interest of the United States." Determining the "true national interest" of the United States is, however, a contentious matter—especially in an environment where, as structural theorists argue, others will seek to balance the power of the United States. Waltz (1993) contends, for example, that "within a decade [China] will be in the great-power ranks" and that its power-projection capabilities will grow rapidly. For the United States to balance this growing power, he argues, it will have to join forces with Japan: "America, with the reduction of its forces, a Cold-War weary people, and numerous neglected problems at home, cannot hope to balance the growing economic and military might of a country of some 1.2 billion people while attending to other security interests. Unless Japan responds to the growing power of China, China will dominate its region and become increasingly influential beyond it."

Bilateralism

Like unilaterlism, bilateralism can take many forms. The U.S. security guarantees extended to several Asian nations during the Cold War and the long-standing "special relationship" between the United States and Britain are examples.

The bilateral security agreement between the United States and Japan, which dates from the 1950s and 1960s, will remain the core of U.S. security linkages to the Far East for some time. As one author noted, "The United States and Japan are loath to raise serious questions about their anachronistic bilateral defense treaty . . . out of fear of unraveling a fragile stability and thereby triggering arms races throughout the region" (Ruggie 1992; see also Johnson and Keehn, 1995). Still, the logic of structural realism leads to the conclusion, noted earlier, that Japan's dependence on the United States for security will not last.

> When every incoming American administration begins its term by proclaiming a reassessment of existing policies. . ., and when confrontation over economic issues becomes the rule rather than the exception, it is difficult to argue that American and Japanese foreign policy interests can never diverge. . . .
>
> In the immediate future, Japan, faced with an aging population and a stagnating economy, might decide to press its technological and strategic superiority before China emerges as a superpower and Russia recovers its strength. Afterward, it might have recourse to that great equalizer, nuclear technology. (Kissinger 1994a, 827–28)

The United States has courted Russia, seeking a special relationship that, in the eyes of some, depends too heavily on the survival of particular leaders and ignores U.S. interests in the other post-Soviet states. A U.S.-Russian entente may have advantages in coping with the challenges of a multipolar world (Kegley and Raymond 1994), but the survivability of Russia as a democratic, capitalist state is by no means assured. Russian democracy is fragile, its economic reforms reversible, and its domestic challenges—ranging from ethnonationalism to organized crime—formidable. Thus we are reminded that "structural change begins in a system's unit, and then unit-level and structural causes interact" to produce system change (Waltz 1993). The next change in Russia may pose a renewed security threat to the United States.

Britain and the United States have enjoyed a "special relationship" for decades. As Europe continues to integrate economically and politically, and as British leaders, often reluctantly and fitfully, conclude that their future is intimately tied to Europe's, the special relationship between Britain and its one-time North American dependents will be strained.[5] Thus the United States may find that Britain increasingly engages in balancing U.S. power rather than bandwagoning (joining) with it, as has been Britain's historical practice.

Multilateralism

Reflecting the tenets of idealism so much a part of the American heritage, multilateralism has been a central element of American foreign policy throughout the twentieth century. The United States was the principal architect of the League of Nations and the United Nations, both conceived as instruments of global peace and security. It sponsored multilateral avenues to global prosperity. It was the primary catalyst to multilateral security arrangements in Europe, Asia, the Western Hemisphere, and the South Pacific (which, it also should be noted, simultaneously served balance-of-power logic). And it was the principal enforcer of global norms in Korea and, forty years later, in Kuwait. In each case mutilateralism meant more than simply "three or more states"; collectively they suggest that ***multilateralism*** is "an institutional form which coordinates relations among three or more states on the basis of 'generalized' principles of conduct—that is, principles which specify appropriate conduct for a class of actions, without regard to the particularistic interests of the parties or the strategic exigencies that may exist in any specific occurrence" (Ruggie 1992). In the case of the League and United Nations, the principle is collective security, which means "that states respond to aggression whenever and wherever it occurs—whether or not any specific instance suits their individual likes and dislikes." In a collective security scheme, in other words, "states behave as if peace were indivisible and thereby make it so" (Ruggie 1992; see also Claude 1971).

The response of UN members to Iraq's invasion of Kuwait in 1990 is the premier example of collective security in action—indeed, it is the only one since the United Nations was created.[6] The UN Security Council authorized the use of force against Iraq, as none of its permanent members exercised their right to veto the action. This is precisely what the organization's founders had in mind—namely, that the United Nations should not take action against breaches of the peace or acts of aggression unless all of the great powers agreed (Claude 1971). The end of the Cold War made this possible, as the Soviet Union followed the U.S. lead in a situation critical to American interests. However, few analysts believe the circumstances that galvanized the world community to action in this case can be repeated elsewhere. "In fact, relying on the Gulf [War] as an example of the need for ***collective security*** demonstrates the weakness, rather than strength, of that case. It is impossible to point to another regional conflict with as potentially far-reaching implications for the United States. At most, Iraq's invasion of Kuwait called for a unique, one-time response" (Bandow 1992–1993). If the United States will not lead in the maintenance of global order and stability in the transition to a multipolar world and beyond, who will?

Collective security is of questionable utility in dealing with international threats to peace and security, especially when applied to the civil violence so prevalent in the 1990s, which plagued the Clinton administration from its start. "Restraint" eventually replaced "assertiveness" as it applied to U.S. involvement in United Nations peacekeeping and, more particularly, peace enforcement operations.[7] Moreover, the Republican Congress considered legislation that would severely limit Defense Department expenditures for UN operations, thus further sealing their future fate.

NATO long served as a multilateral bulwark against encroachments on Western Europe. As a collective defense arrangement whose very existence was predicated on there being an external enemy, however, the end of the Cold War necessarily raises questions about its continued viability. Several Eastern European countries sought membership in the alliance, but NATO ruled out immediate membership for them. Instead—and perhaps to stave off its seemingly inevitable demise—in 1991 the alliance created the North Atlantic Cooperation Council (NACC), a forum to which former communist nations were invited for purposes of promoting a dialogue with NATO members on common security matters. Building on ideas first advanced during the Bush presidency, the United States three years later promoted a "Partnership for Peace," which called for NATO military cooperation with non-NATO European states. But while the Partnership for Peace program anticipated that former Warsaw Pact states would participate with NATO in a broad range of military activities—including joint military planning and training exercises, peacekeeping activities, and crisis management—it specifically did *not* provide security guarantees to the non-NATO states or automatic membership at some future date.[8]

Sensitivity to Russian security concerns combined with fear of Russia renewing its security threat to the West animated the debate about NATO's future. The Partnership for Peace program put Russia on the same footing as other former Soviet and Warsaw Pact states who sought full membership in the alliance; Russia joined the program in June 1994 and reaffirmed its commitment a year later. Still, the process of rapprochement between NATO and its former adversaries remained incomplete. Senator Sam Nunn, chair of the influential Senate Committee on Armed Services when the Partnership for Peace program was put into place, remarked, "The day when NATO takes in Russia as a member will be the day when NATO is no longer needed as a threat-based security alliance. A stable, democratic, market-oriented Russia operating within the precepts of international law and respecting the borders of its neighbors will obviate the need for NATO as we have known it." Thus the Partnership for Peace framework is unlikely to be more than a stepping stone on the way to refashioning Europe's security framework and America's role in it, not the end point (see Kupchan 1994). Meanwhile, structural theorists hold little hope for a long-term U.S. presence in Europe.

> Europe and Russia may for a time look on NATO, and on America's presence in Western Europe, as a stabilizing force in a time of rapid change. In an interim period, the continuation of NATO makes sense. In the long run, it does not. The presence of American forces at higher than token levels will become an irritant to European states, whose security is not threatened, and a burden to America acting in a world that is becoming more competitive politically and economically as it becomes less so militarily. (Waltz 1993, 75)

Beyond partnership in NATO, how might Russia be brought into the management circle in an emergent multipolar world? Some see a new concert of powers as the mechanism of close consultation between Moscow and Washington. (Mueller 1990; Rosecrance 1994). The historical analogue is the Concert of Europe, which became a vehicle of great-power cooperation following the Congress of Vienna in 1815. After more than a decade of success in war prevention, however, the Concert was unable to prevent the outbreak of the Crimean War in 1854 and was generally ineffective in the years that followed. Eventually it broke down into polarized alliance systems. World War I resulted—a cause for concern as we contemplate the new millennium.

If rigidification is one threat to an effective concert system, antagonizing lesser powers is another. They will chafe under a system in which the great powers become defenders of the status quo and make decisions advantageous to themselves but not to others. "This would provoke not only resentment; it would also create the conditions under which disputes between the advantaged and the disadvantaged could escalate" (Kegley and Raymond 1994).

Some scholars have suggested that a **_concert-based collective security_** system might obviate the weaknesses of a concert system based solely on great-power collaboration. The great powers would continue to play leadership roles in such a system, but they would anchor their behavior in a collective security system "where small and medium powers would have a voice in pending matters if their interests were affected or if they possessed expertise in dealing with the issue in question" (Kegley and Raymond 1994; see also Kegley and Raymond 1995).

The Organization for Security and Cooperation in Europe (OSCE) arguably bears some semblance to a concert-based security system. Initiated during the era of Soviet-American détente, the Conference on Security and Cooperation in Europe, as it was then called, became the institutional framework for the 1975 Helsinki accords promoting human rights observance throughout Europe.[9] Today the OSCE and its participating states embrace a comprehensive concept of security that relates peace and prosperity directly to the promotion of democracy, the existence of market economies, and the observance of human rights. But while the OSCE boasts a permanent secretariat and a Conflict Prevention Center, it, like NATO and the European Union, has failed to keep the peace throughout Europe, notably in the former Yugoslavia. Thus its future, too, is in doubt.

Complex questions about the United States' role in the new Europe and elsewhere remain—all the more so since they take place in sea of uncharted (and perhaps unsafe) waters. As the Yugoslav experience aptly demonstrates, a multipolar future is unlikely to be a peaceful future. The reason is "rather basic. So long as there were only two great powers, like two big battleships clumsily and cautiously circling each other, confrontations—or accidents—were easier to avoid. Now, with the global lake more crowded with ships of varying sizes, fueled by different ambitions and piloted with different degrees of navigational skill, the odds of collisions become far greater" (House 1989). For some, this is cause for American retreat, not leadership. For others, the reverse is true.

The Global South in the New World Order . . . .

At the end of the World War II in 1945, fewer than sixty independent states became members of the new United Nations, named for allied coalition victorious in war the against the Axis powers. Fifty years later more than three times that number would claim seats in the world organization. Some were products of the breakup of the Soviet Union, but most grew out of the end of other empires: the British, French, Belgian, Dutch, Spanish, and Portuguese colonial territories in Africa and Asia amassed since the 1400s but especially during a particularly vicious wave of imperialism that swept the world in the late nineteenth century. That colonial experience helps to define what today are commonly called the developing countries or the Third World

The concept of a **Third World** first emerged to distinguish the growing number of newly emerging states from those identified with either the East or West in the Cold War struggle, but it soon took on largely economic connotations (Berger 1994; Wolf-Phillips 1987). The **nonaligned states** would become those determined to strike a neutral course in the Cold War contest, while the "Third World" referred to a broader group, including, for example, many Latin American nations allied with the United States. Compared with the Western industrialized nations (the **First World**), the Third World had failed to grow economically or otherwise advance toward the degree and type of economic development experienced in Western Europe and North America. The **Second World**, in this scheme, consisted of the Soviet Union, its allies, and other communist societies. For them a commitment to planned economic practices, rather than reliance on market forces to determine the supply of and demand for goods and services, was the distinguishing characteristic.

"Third World" continues to be relevant as a concept to refer to a disjuncture in the development experiences of the First World and virtually everyone else, but it also carries Cold War baggage that is difficult to discard. For example, all of Central Asia once a part of the Soviet Union—Kazakhstan, Krygyzstan, Tajikistan, Turkmenistan, and Uzbekistan—can only be described in these terms. Even Russia itself arguably shares more characteristics in common with the Third World than the First. By continuing to use the concept, however, we risk obscuring how profoundly the geoeconomic landscape has changed since the end of the Cold War. Even communist China, a leader in the nonaligned movement and with economic indicators that clearly set it apart from the First World, increasingly permits market forces to determine the shape of its economic performance. The result: China is one of the fastest growing economies in the world.

Global South is preferable as a concept to distinguish the nations of the First World—now properly thought of as the **Global North**—from the rest of the world. As always, placement of particular states within these categories is sometimes problematic. Russia is an obvious example, as are the emerging market economies in eastern Europe. Still, the confluence of particular characteristics along four dimensions distinguish the North from the South: politics, technology, wealth, and demography.

Nations comprising the Global North are democratic, technologically inventive, wealthy, and aging, as their societies tend toward zero population growth. Some in the Global South share some of these characteristics, but none all of them. Saudi Arabia is rich but not democratic; China is technologically inventive but not wealthy; India is democratic but burdened with an enormous and growing population; Singapore is both wealthy and technologically innovative, has a comparatively modest population growth rate, but is not democratic. Beyond this are many that are not democratic, technologically innovative, or wealthy, but whose demographics project a rapidly growing population that increasingly will place strain on already over-taxed social and ecological systems with too few economic resources and political capabilities to match the challenge. Many, but not all, are in Africa south of the Sahara.

Several scholars have tried to capture the differences between North and South in the new world (dis)order and, beyond that, to characterize commonalities and differences among the nations of the Global South. Focus 6.2 encapsulates some of their ideas—and displays a remarkable degree of consensus. The vision is that of a profoundly divided world which places the United States and its closest democratic friends, political allies, and economic partners on one side of a fault line separating them from most of the rest of the world. Thus the United States, the sole remaining superpower, faces challenges for which many of the foreign policy instruments of balance-of-power politics dictated by the doctrine of political realism are largely irrelevant.

Focus 6.2
FAULTLINE: THE GLOBAL NORTH VERSUS THE GLOBAL SOUTH

• • •

"There is today a vast demographic-technological faultline appearing across our planet. On one side of this line are the fast-growing, adolescent, under- resourced, undercapitalized, under-educated societies; on the other side are the rich, technologically inventive yet demographically moribund, aging populations. . . . The greatest challenge global society faces today is preventing this faultline from erupting into a world-shaking crisis."

— Paul Kennedy (1994, 4–5)

"The key to understanding the real world order is to separate the world into two parts. One part is zones of peace, wealth, and democracy. The other part is zones of turmoil, war and development. . . . Unfortunately, only 15 percent of the world's population lives in the zones of peace and democracy. Most people now live in zones of turmoil and development, where poverty, war, tyranny, and anarchy will continue to devastate lives."

— Max Singer and Aaron Wildavsky (1993, 3–7)

"Nation states will remain the most powerful actors in world affairs, but the principal conflicts of global politics will occur between nations and groups of different civilizations. The clash of civilizations will dominate global politics. The fault lines between civilizations will be the battle lines of the future. . . . The world will be shaped in large measure by the interactions among seven or eight major civilizations. These include Western, Confucian, Japanese, Islamic, Hindu, Slavic-Orthodox, Latin America and possibly African civilization"

— Samuel P. Huntington (1993a, 22–25)

"The future of the Third World is hardly all bad news. . . . But the failures. . . will greatly outweigh the successes. . . . The global dilemmas and ills capable of coalescing into a specific body of political discontent and hostility will therefore challenge the current international system and constitute the next ideological challenge. . . . 'Civilization clash' is not so much over Jesus Christ, Confucius, or the Prophet Muhammad as it is over the

Focus 6.2 *(continued)*

unequal distribution of world power, wealth, and influence, and the perceived historical lack of respect accorded to small states and peoples by larger ones."

— Graham Fuller (1995, 146–54)

"The post-Cold War . . .international system is clearly divided into two distinct groups (or tiers) of states. . . . The defining characteristics of the countries of the First Tier is their political and economic similarity: all have democratic political systems (although the form of democracy is not uniform) and they all share a commitment to market-driven capitalist economics. . . .

"The most obvious characteristic of the Second Tier is its diversity. . . . The Second Tier is marked by instability and the potential or actuality of violence that is quite absent in the First Tier. Some of this instability is a concomitant of the development process itself, as economic and political forces adjust to modernization. At the same time, . . . exclusionary nationalism . . . is tearing apart nation-states and forcing a redrawing of political maps in many places."

— Donald Snow (1995, 11–13)

Along the Demographic Divide: Population and Development

The demographic divide is central to the differences between the Global North and the Global South. Eighty percent of the world's wealth is concentrated in the North, while 80 percent of its people are in the South (see Figure 6.2). The maldistribution of wealth and people translates into sharply different living standards, crudely measured by differences in per capita gross domestic product. As illustrated in Figure 6.3, the average annual income in Japan is over sixty times greater than the average income in China, home of more than one-fifth of the world's 5.6 billion people. And the U.S. income is twenty times that of the other countries comprising the Global South.[10]

These disparities—which in many other individual cases are even more stark—in the future will widen, not narrow. Consider, for example, that in 1850 the ratio between incomes in the industrializing societies of Western Europe and the rest of the world is estimated to have been roughly two to one (Brown 1972, 42). By 1950 the gap had opened to ten to one, and by 1960 to nearly fifteen to one. Since 1950, as the developed nations nearly tripled their incomes, those at the periphery experienced virtually no change (Durning 1990, 136). Add to this the knowledge that nearly all of the world's projected population growth in the next century will occur in the Global South and it becomes clear why the gap between the world's rich and poor will continue to widen. Even if North and South were to grow economically at the same rate, say 3 percent per annum, the comparatively higher population growth rates in the South—1.9 percent versus 0.3 percent in the developed world (Lutz 1994: 4)—would erode income gains at a faster rate.

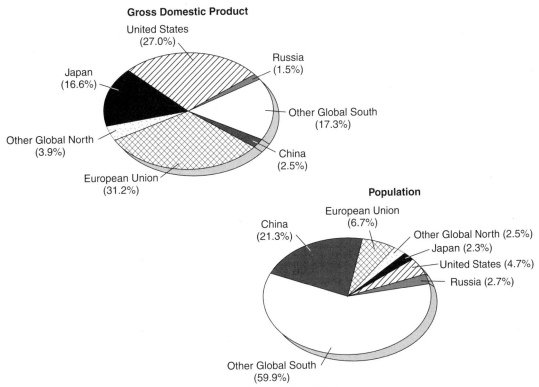

Figure 6.2 Shares of Gross World Product and Population, 1993
Source: Adapted from *The World Bank Atlas 1995* (Washington, D.C.: The World Bank, 1994), pp. 8–9, 18–19.

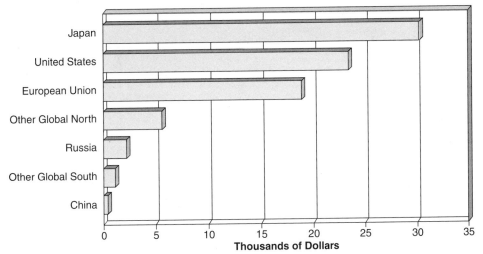

Figure 6.3 Global Variations in Per Capita Gross Domestic Product, 1993
Source: Adapted from *The World Bank Atlas 1995* (Washington, D.C.: The World Bank, 1994), pp. 8–9, 18–19.

The world's current population of 5.6 billion people is projected to grow to 6.2 billion in the year 2000 and to 8.5 billion by 2025. Such dramatic growth is simply unprecedented. It took an entire century for world population to grow from 1 billion to 2 billion, but only one decade to add its last billion. By the end of the day that you read this page, the world will have added another 250,000 people to its already burgeoning number. Furthermore, as indicated, nearly all of this growth will occur in the Global South (see Figures 6.4 and 6.5). Latin America will add 180 million people in the first

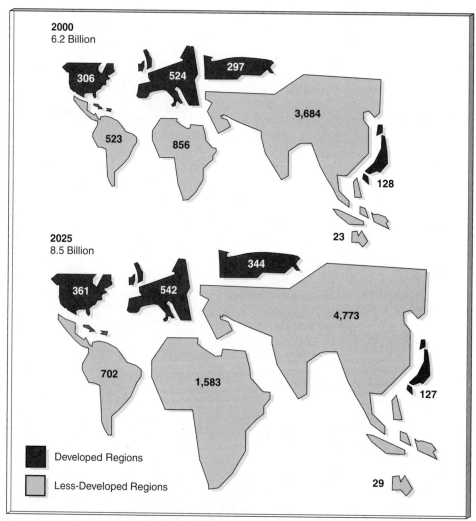

Figure 6.4 The Shape of the World's Population Future (regional figures in millions of dollars, others in billions of dollars)
Source: George D. Moffett, "Global Population Growth: 21st Century Challenges," *Headline Series* 302 (Spring 1994): 15. Based on United Nations Data.

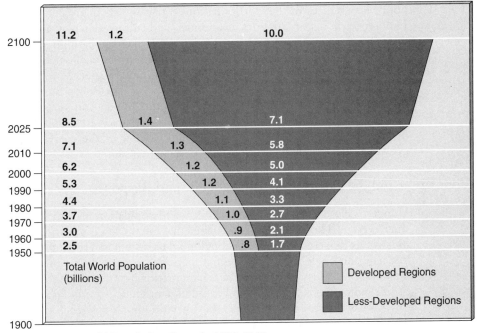

Figure 6.5 World Population Growth, 1950–2100
Source: George D. Moffett, "Global Population Growth: 21st Century Challenges," *Headline Series* 302 (Spring 1994): 19. Based on United Nations medium population projections.

quarter of the twenty-first century, Asia more than 1 billion, and Africa's population will nearly double, growing from 856 million in 2000 to 1.6 billion in 2025.

Some countries in the Global South will escape the economic stagnation associated with a rapidly rising population. Already South Korea, Taiwan, Hong Kong, and Singapore—the so-called "Asian Tigers" who belong to a somewhat larger group of Newly Industrializing Countries (NICs)—enjoy per capita incomes comparable to many Northern countries. The reason is that their economic growth rates during the decade ending in 1993 (ranging from 5.3 percent to 8.1 percent), arising out of a vigorous determination to expand global exports (of increasing concern to the United States, as we will show in Chapter 7) far surpassed their population growth rates (.7 percent to 1.2 percent).[11] The result: rising living standards.

Most in the Global South, however, will experience much different futures. The Other Global South category in Figure 6.3, for example, includes forty-five nations identified by the United Nations as the least developed of the developing countries. As a group, their annual per capita GDP stood at only $433, their 1985–1993 economic growth rates averaged less than one-tenth of 1 percent, yet their population growth rates (in 1994) exceeded 2.8 percent—far in excess of the global average of 1.6 percent. This means the population of the least developed nations in the world will double in only twenty-five years.[12] Singapore's population, on the other hand, will take nearly sixty years to double. And the population of the world's already developed nations will take more than two and a half centuries to double.

Population growth figures prominently in any explanation of the disparate economic experiences of the world's nations today and their projection into the future. Differences in history, politics, economics, and culture also play a role and are intermixed in complex and often poorly understood ways. Increasingly, however, it is clear that the momentum of global population growth poses challenges to global and national security that will affect all of the world's inhabitants. As John D. Steinbruner (1995), director of the Brookings Institution's Foreign Policy Studies program, surmised, "Both the scale and composition of this population surge will have consequences powerful enough not just to affect, but perhaps even to dominate, conceptions of international security." Here we touch on a few of the correlates of population growth as they shape the external environment as a source of American foreign policy.

Population and the Environment: Challenge and Response

Hunger is closely associated with poverty and population growth. Two centuries ago the Reverend Thomas Malthus predicted that the world's population would eventually outstrip its capacity to produce enough food to sustain its growing numbers. That has not happened, due to unprecedented increases in agricultural production—particularly since World War II. Still, achieving national and global food security remains problematic. Global food supplies are abundant globally (although the momentum of growth has slowed [Brown 1994]), but they do not always reach those most in need. Many simply cannot afford to buy food because they lack the necessary income and employment opportunities. Politics and civil conflict also impede the ability of some to acquire adequate nutrition. That reality prompted the United States to launch its humanitarian intervention into Somalia in late 1992. Insufficient food and poverty go hand in hand. Today, as many as one-fifth of earth's inhabitants live in conditions of *absolute poverty*, without access to safe water or adequate nutrition, sanitation, and health services (*Human Development Report 1994*, 1994, 134–35).

As rural poverty and joblessness spread, people migrate from the countryside to cities. Urbanization is a global phenomenon, but it is especially ubiquitous in the Global South. London, New York, and Shanghai were the only cities with populations of ten million or more in 1950. By the turn of the century some two dozen cities will be this large—all but six of them in the Global South. Lagos—the capital of Nigeria, which today claims 8 million inhabitants—illustrates "the relentless mathematics at work." "In 1950 Lagos had just 288,000 inhabitants. By century's end it will have 13.5 million. In 2010 it will have 21 million. Cities like São Paulo, Brazil, with 18 million now and swelling by half a million residents each year, do not lag far behind" (Moffett 1994, 25). As urbanization proceeds, most people will become city dwellers. "By 2025, four billion people in developing countries will be classified as urban—equivalent to the world's total population in 1975" (*World Resources 1994–95* 1994, 31). With urbanization comes increased pressures on already stretched rural agricultural systems and demands for imported food, a need for expanded social services and increased investments in social infrastructure, and, all too frequently it seems, social unrest and political turmoil, as already over-taxed municipalities are unable to respond.

People migrate to urban areas for many reasons, but jobs are uppermost. And jobs are few and hard to find, particularly where the ratio of dependent children to working-age adults is high—a natural consequence of rapidly growing populations, where the number of young people grows more rapidly than those who die. This, too, results in a heavy burden on public services, particularly the educational system, and encourages the immediate consumption of economic resources rather than their reinvestment to promote future economic growth. As the demand for new jobs, housing, and other human needs multiplies, however, the resources to meet the demand are typically scarce and inadequate.

Without jobs at home, young people in particular are encouraged to emigrate. The International Labor Organization estimates that 350 million new jobs will have to be created in the Global South during the 1990s alone (Moffett 1994, 18). Failing that, outward pressure is inevitable. Nowhere is the connection between population pressures in the South and their social and political consequences in the North more evident than in employment. The United States is especially concerned about Mexico, where illegal immigration is already a national problem. Without economic growth and the prospect of a better life in Mexico, however, the urge to go North may be irresistible. As one Mexican official put it, "The consequences of not creating (at least) 15 million jobs in the next 15 years are unthinkable. The youths who do not find them will have only three options: the United States, the streets or revolution" (cited in Moffett 1994).[13]

In addition to migration pressures, population growth multiplies global environmental stresses, whose consequences inevitably transcend national boundaries. In the extreme, population pressures and their ever-growing demands on the global habitat are a source of violent conflict (Homer-Dixon 1991; Homer-Dixon, Boutwell, and Rathjens 1993).

Increasingly many migrants (internal as well as international) can be thought of as *environmental refugees*, people forced to abandon lands no longer fit for human habitation due to environmental degradation. The number is estimated to be at least ten million, which rivals the number traditionally classified as political refugees by various national and international agencies (Jacobson 1989, 60). Some become environmental refugees due to catastrophic events, such as the explosion of the nuclear power plant at Chernobyl in the Ukraine in 1986. Others suffer the consequences of long-term environmental stress, such as excessive land use that results in *desertification* (a sustained decline in land productivity), often caused by population growth.

Deforestation often causes desertification and soil erosion, and current trends point toward rapid deforestation worldwide. The destruction of tropical rain forests to make room for farms and ranches—as in the Amazon basin of Brazil and in Indonesia—is a matter of special international concern, as it contributes markedly to global warming through the "greenhouse" effect. *Global warming* occurs when carbon dioxide (CO_2) and other gas molecules trap heat that would otherwise be remitted from earth back to the atmosphere. Carbon dioxide is routinely removed from the atmosphere by green plants during photosynthesis. When forests are cut down, the natural processes that remove greenhouse gases are destroyed, and, as the forests decay or are burned, they increase the amount of CO_2 discharged into the atmosphere. This makes deforestation doubly destructive. Destruction of tropical rains forests also destroys humankind's genetic heritage, as plant and animal species become extinct even before they are identified and classified. The world's *biodiversity* is the inevitable victim.

Although deforestation contributes heavily to the greenhouse process, the burning of fossil fuels is an even greater culprit. Here the industrial societies of the Global North—not the developing societies of the Global South—are primarily at fault, as they consume over 70 percent of the world's energy. Interestingly, however, the greatest increases in the *rate* of energy consumption are now occurring in the developing world. This means that policies and economic achievements in the Global South also will account for the greatest increases in atmospheric pollution due to fossil-fuel combustion. China alone consumes roughly 10 percent of global energy supplies—much of it by burning coal, the fossil fuel most damaging to the environment. In 1990 China alone accounted for 11 percent of global CO_2 emissions, a proportion expected to rise steeply as its energy consumption grows (*World Resources 1994–95* 1994, 65–66).

Even without economic growth, the expected doubling of the world's population over the next half-century will require tremendous increases in fossil-fuel consumption just to maintain living standards at current levels. Thus, as demographic patterns already in place unfold in the decades ahead, disruptions of the world's climate and delicate ecosystems will continue and perhaps accelerate. This makes achieving worldwide zero population growth (when births and deaths equal one another, as has already occurred in much of the Global North) a pressing global concern.

In 1992 the world community convened the United Nations Conference on the Environment and Development (UNCED) in Rio de Janeiro. The largest-ever world meeting of its kind, the so-called Earth Summit brought together more than 150 nations, fourteen hundred nongovernmental organizations, and some eight hundred journalists. UNCED addressed how environmental and developmental issues interact with one another—something not done before, as the two issues normally have been treated on separate tracks. Statements of principles relating to the management of the earth's forests, conventions on climate change and biodiversity, and a program of action—*Agenda 21*—which embodied a political commitment to the realization of a broad range of environmental and development goals (see Sitarz 1993), were among UNCED's achievements. ***Sustainable development***, a concept encapsulating the belief that the world must work toward a model of economic development that also protects the delicate environmental systems on which humanity depends for its existence, encapsulated much of UNCED's thrust.

Two years later, in 1994, the United Nations sponsored the World Population and Development Conference, thus carrying forward the theme of interrelationships on which sustainability depends. Family-planning programs designed to check excessive population growth were among the conference's contentious topics, but it also addressed measures to reduce poverty and improve educational opportunities with a view toward enhanced sustainability. An emphasis on the rights, opportunities, and economic roles of women—all proven critical in reducing population growth rate—was a distinctive feature of the conference.

American foreign policy toward population and environmental issues has fluctuated widely during the past quarter-century. During the first United Nations population conference, held in Bucharest, Romania, in 1974, North and South quarreled about the very existence of a population problem. The United States and other rich countries embraced the view that the "population explosion" (Ehrlich and Ehrlich 1990) so impeded the economic advancement of Third World countries that nothing less than a frontal attack on the causes of population growth could cure their development illnesses. Developing nations responded that the prescription was little more than another attempt by the world's rich nations to perpetuate the underdog status of the world's poor. They also pointed with anger at the consumption patterns of the North, noting that these—not population growth in the South—were the real causes of pressures on global resources.

Ten years later, at a second global population conference in Mexico City, the United States again found itself out of step with majority sentiments, but now for very different reasons. By this time the Third World had accepted the proposition that unrestrained population growth impeded progress toward economic development. They now sought more vigorous efforts by the United Nations, other multilateral agencies, and individual countries in the North to help with family planning and other programs designed to contain the "explosion." The Reagan administration, however—which at home courted the growing chorus of antiabortion sentiments—aligned itself with the Vatican and announced that population growth was not a problem. It abruptly canceled support of family-planning programs, of which the United States had long been a champion. The about-face included termination of U.S. support for the United Nations Fund for Population Activities, a prohibition that continued into the Bush administration.

By the time of the 1994 Population and Development Conference, which met in Cairo, the Democrats had seized control of the White House, placing domestic antiabortionist forces on the defensive. The United States now sought again to play a leading role in addressing global population issues. As we saw in Chapter 5, the Clinton administration viewed uncontrolled population growth as a cause of the chaos and crises that often engulf nations in the Global South. Thus the Agency for International Development prepared for a vigorous population stabilization program (see Atwood 1994), and the United States once more became a champion of the efforts by the United Nations and other governmental and nongovernmental agencies to promote family-planning programs abroad. Vice President Al Gore headed the U.S. delegation to the Cairo conference. The symbolism suggesting renewal of U.S. leadership on global population issues was not lost on the other conference participants: Gore had authored a national best-selling book on the environment, *Earth in the Balance* (Gore 1993a).

Gore also championed other changes in population and environment issues. When UNCED met in Rio de Janeiro, the United States found itself out of step with much of the world on two key issues: global warming and biodiversity. The Bush administration worked hard to water down a global Convention on Climate Change, whose purpose was to curb greenhouse gas emissions, and it refused to sign the Convention on Biodiversity. The Clinton administration reversed that decision, but midway through the Clinton presidency the Senate had not yet agreed to ratify the biodiversity agreement. Nonetheless, sustainable development became a widely used concept in the administration's foreign policy rhetoric.

The Foreign Policy Interests and Strategies of the Global South

During the Cold War the developing countries of the Third World pursued three identifiable strategies: (1) to reform the world political economy to make it more amenable to their interests; (2) to steer clear of Cold War political-military alignments; and (3) to acquire modern military capabilities to protect their sovereignty and independence. This, of course, is an oversimplification; few in the Third World pursued all of these goals simultaneously, while many others sought goals specifically tailored to their own perceptions of their unique national interests. Still, these three broad strategic categories usefully orient us to the foreign policy challenges facing the Global South as it, like the United States, adjusts to the realities of a post-Cold War World.

Reform the System

Third World nations were born into a political-economic order with rules they had no voice in devising. Beginning in the 1950s, they pursued various strategies designed to give them a greater role in shaping their own economic futures. None was more visibly or more vigorously pushed than their drive in the 1970s for a *New International Economic Order (NIEO)*, which challenged the "global liberalism" philosophy championed by the United States since World War II. The Third World's politics of resentment, challenge, and attack on the status quo were motivated in part by the gross disparities between the rich and the poor to which we have alluded. "Structural conflict" (Krasner 1985) encapsulated the contest between North and South as the NIEO turned on questions of who would govern the distribution world wealth and how they would make their choices.

The First World rebuffed the Third World's efforts at reform, and the North-South exchange gradually degenerated into a dialogue of the deaf. Still, many of the issues raised during the NIEO drive remain (see Chapter 7), even if their form is markedly different. During the 1980s—variously described as the "debt decade," the "lost decade," and the "adjustment decade"—the International Monetary Fund (IMF), with the support of the United States and others in the Global North, imposed stringent domestic reform criteria on Third World nations as a condition for help in dealing with an assortment of domestic economic ills spawned in part by excessive foreign borrowing and domestic overspending. "Privatization" became the buzzword of the 1990s, as the spread of political democracy demanded the parallel development of market economies. The common thread joining these efforts with the NIEO drive is how to integrate the developing economies into the world political economy—on terms, however, the Global South would say, still dictated by the North. Simultaneously, however, a number of countries have promoted Southern self-reliance by proposing creative regional economic schemes (Shaw 1994b).

By the 1990s whatever cohesiveness on political economy issues the Third World might once have claimed had dissipated. The Asian Tigers now challenged the United States and others in the Global North on their own economic terms, and the assertiveness of the new "cubs"—Malaysia and Thailand—portends even further provocations. Meanwhile, economic trauma in Mexico, newly tied to the United States in Nafta (the North American Free Trade Agreement) and ethnic conflict in Central and East Africa, already among the poorest of the world's poor, underscored the relentless diversity of the Global South.

Steer Clear

Diversity has always characterized the Third World. The Cold War gave it coherence, however—at least as seen through the eyes of the conflict's antagonists. Many in the Third World fed that perception through their foreign policy strategy of *nonalignment*.

Because Third World nations could not materially affect the outcome of the Cold War, they tried through nonalignment to maximize their own gains while minimizing their costs. The strategy, as preached with firebrand language at periodic summits first convened in 1961, stimulated keen efforts by each of the two superpowers to woo the uncommitted to its own side while preventing their alignment with the other. Nonalignment in effect enabled developing nations to play one side against the other in order to gain advantage for themselves. The Cold War competitors—in keeping with the sensitivity each manifested toward the other in the context of the bipolar distribution of power, perceived as a zero-sum contest—were willing players in the game.

Foreign aid was a favored foreign policy instrument the United States used to prevent defection of the nonaligned to "the other side." Between the end of the Korean War (when U.S. foreign aid efforts turned increasingly to the Third World) and 1990, the United States expended some $200 billion in foreign economic aid. Although the motivations behind these vast sums did take into account the welfare of the recipients, security concerns and an overriding emphasis on the containment of communism were the principal driving forces (see Chapter 5).

Soviet and Soviet bloc aid never rivaled that of the United States, and much of that once committed apparently never actually made it to recipient nations. The CIA reports on the allocation of $103 billion in Soviet aid to selected developing countries in selected years between 1954 and 1990 and another $9.7 billion by China between 1954 and 1989 (*Handbook of Economic Statistics, 1991*, 1991, 158–160). Eastern Europe also contributed some additional aid. The historic pattern of Soviet bloc aid, like the United States', followed the path of its strategic and geopolitical interests, with much of it concentrated in the Middle East, Southeast Asia, and the Western Hemisphere (notably Cuba and Nicaragua).

Beginning in the 1970s, members of the Organization of Petroleum Exporting Countries (OPEC) also became major contributors of foreign aid to developing nations, although their actual sums dropped measurably during the 1980s as world oil prices plummeted (*World Development Report 1994* 1994, 197). Since the 1960s, however, and even more markedly since the end of the Cold War, the United States and the other industrial societies of the Global North have been the principal sources of development aid, which Global South states receive directly from individual donor countries (bilateral aid) and also from international financial institutions (multilateral aid).

As Table 6.1 shows, a substantial volume of official development assistance flows annually from the Global North to the Global South (consisting of outright grants, loans made at concessional [less than market] rates, and contributions to multilateral institutions). Still, it has grown comparatively little in recent years. In constant (noninflated) dollars, less aid flowed from North to South in 1992 than in any of the preceding eight years (*Development Cooperation: Efforts and Politics of the Members of the Development Assistance Committee, 1993 Report* 1994, 64–65). And came at a time when the number of aid supplicants had increased, such as Russia, the New Independent States, the former Second World countries in Eastern Europe, and war-ravaged states like Afghanistan and Cambodia.

The great powers rely most heavily on foreign aid as an instrument of statecraft, as France, Germany, Japan, and the United States together provide three-fifths of the

TABLE 6.1 OFFICIAL DEVELOPMENT ASSISTANCE (ODA) FLOWING FROM THE GLOBAL
NORTH TO DEVELOPING COUNTRIES AND MULTILATERAL ORGANIZATIONS, SELECTED
YEARS, 1980–1993 (BILLIONS OF DOLLARS)

	1980	1985	1990	1991	1992	1993
Bilateral grants and loans	$16.8	$21.2	$37.2	$41.3	$41.2	$38.9
Contributions to multilateral institutions	9.2	7.6	15.8	15.4	19.6	17.0
Total ODA	26.2	28.8	53.0	56.7	60.9	56.0

Note: Individual items may not sum to totals due to rounding.
Source: Adapted from *Development Cooperation: Efforts and Policies of the Members of the Development Assistance Committee, 1994 Report* (Paris: Organisation for Economic Co-operation and Development, 1995), pp. A3–A4.

total development aid currently available. Interestingly, however, the United States no longer is the largest foreign aid donor, having been surpassed by Japan (see Figure 6.6). Furthermore, when measured against the internationally agreed on standard for what rich nations *should* extend to the poor—an amount equivalent to 1 percent of their gross national product (GNP)—no other country is less "burdened" by foreign aid than the United States (see Figure 6.7). It is also true, however, that, with the exception of Scandinavian countries, nearly all other donors likewise come up far short.

There is little prospect that this will change. Absent the Cold War, foreign aid is in search of a rationale internationally as well as within the United States (see Chapter 5). Promoting democracy and sustainable development, slowing military spending, meeting basic human needs, expanding commercial opportunities—all are among the arguments now used to perpetuate this long-standing foreign policy instrument, but none is likely to galvanize the Global North behind a concerted effort to increase development assistance flows to the Global South. The reverse, in fact, may occur, if domestic sentiments in the United States prevail there and extend elsewhere.

The end of the Cold War has not only dissipated much of the rationale that sustained foreign aid in the past, it also has removed whatever facade of strength nonalignment may once have provided the Global South. "This political device is now lost to [the states of the South]. Nonalignment died with the Cold War. More than that, the way the East-West rivalry ended, with the values and systems of the West vindicated and triumphant, undermined the very basis of the nonaligned movement, which had adopted as its foundation a moral neutrality between the two blocs" (Chubin 1993). The cogency of that conclusion is underscored by how little media attention the tenth summit of the Nonaligned Movement—its first post-Cold War summit—commanded when it convened in Jakarta, Indonesia in September 1992. That summit did, however, recognize how dramatically the contours of international politics had changed since the end of the Cold War.

Many foreign aid recipients have accepted the broader agenda of concerns that now motivate the Global North (Shaw 1994a). Still, the residue of resentment stemming from a colonial past and an underdog status in the global hierarchy persists. In a one-superpower world, the Global South is particularly sensitive to the elitist character of

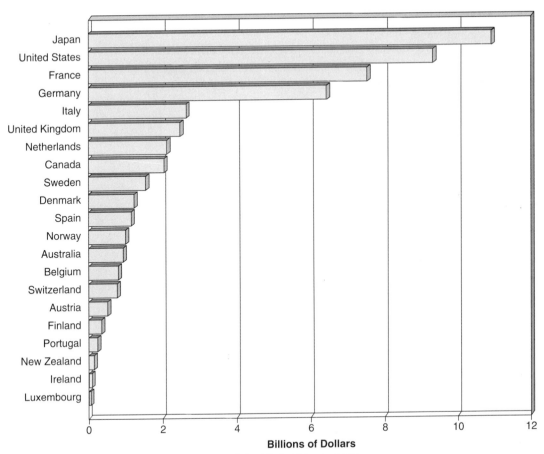

Figure 6.6 The Foreign Aid Performance of the Global North, 1993
Source: Adapted from *Development Cooperation: Efforts and Policies of the Members of the Development Assistance Committee, 1994 Report* (Paris: Organisation for Economic Co-operation and Development, 1995), p. 75.

the United Nations Security Council, and how profoundly decisions there—where the Global South has virtually no voice but in which the United States is now dominant—can affect its future (Chubin 1993; Korany 1994; see also Jonah 1993). Indeed, for the Global South, the new world order may reveal "the re-emergence of a more open and explicit form of imperialism, in which national sovereignty is more readily overridden by a hegemonic power pursuing its own self-defined national interest" (Bienefeld 1994).

Nations of the Global South have always been acutely sensitive to their independence and sovereignty. Thus the increased concern in the United Nations Security Council with humanitarian intervention to protect human rights, promote democracy, and enhance other arguably legitimate values often is perceived as a threat to the independence and integrity of those comprising the Global South. It is important to note that the benefits Third World nations may once have enjoyed as a consequence of Soviet and American efforts to win their allegiance also had their costs. More often

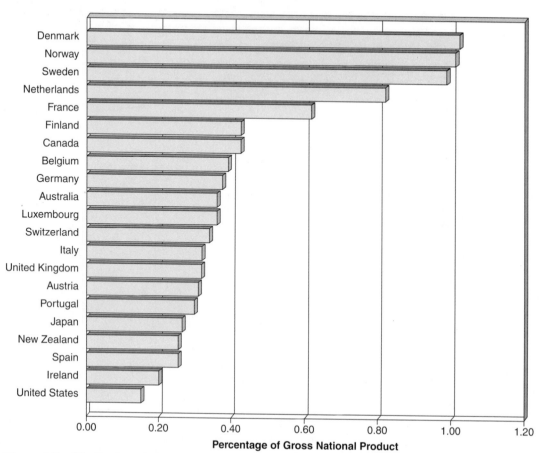

Figure 6.7   The Burden of Foreign Aid, 1993

Source: Adapted from *Development Cooperation: Efforts and Policies of the Members of the Development Assistance Committee, 1994 Report* (Paris: Organisation for Economic Co-operation and Development, 1995), p. 75.

than not, Third World nations were the battleground on which the superpowers' covert activities, paramilitary operations, and proxy wars were played out. Almost all civil wars in the Cold War era occurred in the Third World, where the number of casualties ran into the tens of millions (Singer 1991). And the pattern continues: More than 80 percent of the conflicts in the post-Cold War world have taken place in the Global South (see Focus 6.3).

Seek Military Might

Faced with seemingly endless conflict at home or abroad, it is not surprising that Third World elites would join the rest of the world in the quest to acquire modern weapons of war. Often this meant that the burden of military spending—as measured by the ratio of military expenditures to GNP—was highest among those least able to bear it.

Focus 6.3
INTRANATIONAL CONFLICT ON THE INCREASE

•   •   •

Global conflicts seem to be changing—from wars between states to wars within them. Of the 82 armed conflicts between 1989 and 1992, only three were between states. Although often cast in ethnic divisions, many also have a political or economic character.

Most conflicts are in developing countries. During 1993, 42 countries in the world had 52 major conflicts, and another 37 countries had political violence. Of these 79 countries, 65 were in the developing world.

But there have been conflicts in all regions. In Europe—Bosnia, Georgia, Turkey, and the United Kingdom. In the Middle East—Iraq, Israel, and Lebanon. In Latin America—Colombia and Guatemala. In Asia—Bangladesh, India, Indonesia, Iran, the Lao People's Democratic Republic, Myanmar, Pakistan, the Philippines, Sri Lanka, and Tajikistan. And in Africa—Angola, Chad, Ethiopia, Morocco, Somalia, South Africa, Sudan, Uganda, Zaire, and Zimbabwe.

Many of the conflicts within states are protracted. More than half the conflicts in 1993 had been under way for more than a decade, taking the lives of four to six million people. Between 1989 and 1992, more than a thousand people were dying each year in eight countries: Afghanistan, Angola, India, Peru, the Philippines, Somalia, Sri Lanka, and Sudan.

These conflicts have also caused millions of people to flee their borders to avoid repression and death. In 1983, there were nine countries from which more than 50,000 people had fled. But by 1992, there were 31. The major refugee-generating countries in the past decade: Afghanistan (4.3 million), former Yugoslavia (1.8 million), and Mozambique (1.7 million).

Since 1945, more than 20 million people have died in wars and other conflicts. Even in this era of "peace," the numbers show no signs of abating. Unless strong national and international action is taken, the death toll will continue to rise.

Source: Human Development Report 1994 *(New York: Oxford University Press, 1994), p. 47.*

Thus the societal costs of military spending—which typically exceeded expenditures on health and education—bore little relationship to the level of development.[14] Whether a state was embroiled in a war or threatened by ethnic, religious, or tribal strife at home proved more relevant.

Global expenditures on the weapons of war dropped markedly in the wake of the Cold War's demise (Arora and Bayoumi 1994; U.S. Arms Control and Disarmament Agency 1995). Military spending in the Global South also declined. With this has come a dramatic change in the relative burden of military spending. In 1993 the burden ratio for the world as a whole dropped to 3.3 percent, the lowest since 1960, and to 3.1 percent for the developing world (U.S. Arms Control and Disarmament Agency 1995, 24).

As military spending declined, so have arms purchases from foreign suppliers. The value of world arms transfers fell to $22 billion in 1993, "the lowest level since the early 1970s and . . . a 70 percent drop from the near-record peak in 1987 of $74 billion. . . . Developing country imports . . . fell from the record peak of $61 billion in 1984 to $17 billion in 1993, a 72 percent reduction" (U.S. Arms Control and Disarmament Agency 1995, 9).[15] The actual number of weapons transferred from North to South also plunged. Between 1982 and 1984, some 65,000 major weapons of various types were transferred to developing nations: tanks, artillery, armored personnel carriers, surface ships, submarines, missile attack boats, combat aircraft, helicopters, and surface-to-air missiles, among others. A decade later, from 1991 to 1993, the number fell to roughly 15,500 (U.S. Arms Control and Disarmament Agency 1995, 19).

Dramatic as this "downsizing" may be, it does not automatically mean that developing nations no longer want new weapons. Indeed, as we noted in Chapter 5, the increasing commercialization of arms exports makes it impossible for some states who might otherwise wish to buy arms to do so, for the simple reason that they do not have the cash. Thus the downward turn in arms exports may reflect less a diminution in demand than a rising inability to pay the costs of supply (Pierre and Conway-Lanz 1994–1995). That seems especially likely for Global South nations—"zones of turmoil" (Singer and Wildavsky 1993)—mired in intranational conflict.

Even as military spending and arms transfers decline generally, effective demand (the ability to pay) remains high in the Middle East and parts of Asia. And the United States, now the leading supplier of arms to others, remains heavily engaged in the arms trade (see Chapter 5). As before, persistent conflict and perpetuation of the security dilemma explain the urge to arm. Still, the human costs of preparing for war—whether intra- or international, whether for defensive or offensive purposes—remain high. The 1994 annual report of the United Nations Development Programme focuses on the costs of military spending. Focus 6.4 captures vignettes of the social trade-offs arms imports often pose.

Nonstate Actors: Transnational Agents   . . . .

Earlier we cited Joseph Nye's concept of a layer cake as a metaphor for the emergent global structure in which the United States now finds itself. "The bottom layer of transnational interdependence," he explained, "shows a diffusion of power" (Nye 1992). Of what does that bottom layer consist? It consists of a multitude of actors who know no national boundaries but who nonetheless profoundly impact the established entities that claim sovereignty in world politics (nation-states) and the people who live in them. International organizations and multinational corporations are the most ubiquitous among these nonstate actors. Transnational terrorist groups and ethnonational movements comprise other, less-benign types.

Focus 6.4
THE HUMAN DEVELOPMENT COSTS OF ARMS IMPORTS

• • •

Many countries continue to import expensive arms, even though they have a long list of more essential items. This is clear from the arms deliveries and orders in the categories covered by the UN's arms register. Some of the choices by developing countries in 1992:

- China—purchased 26 combat aircraft from Russia in a deal whose total cost could have provided safe water for one year to 140 million of the 200 million people now without safe water.

- India—ordered 20 MiG-29 fighter aircraft from Russia at a cost that could have provided basic education to all the 15 million girls out of school.

- Iran—bought two submarines from Russia at a cost that could have provided essential medicines to the whole country many times over; 13 percent of Iran's population has no access to health care.

- Republic of Korea—ordered 28 missiles from the United States for an amount that could have immunized all the 120,000 unimmunized children and provided safe water for three years to the 3.5 million people without safe water.

- Malaysia—ordered two warships from the United Kingdom at a cost that could have provided safe water for nearly a quarter-century to the five million people without safe water.

- Nigeria—purchased 80 battle tanks from the United Kingdom at a cost that could have immunized all of the 2 million unimmunized children and provided family-planning services to nearly 17 million of the more than 20 million couples who lack such services.

- Pakistan—ordered 40 Mirage 2000E fighters and three Tripartite aircraft from France at a cost that could have provided safe water for two years for all 55 million people who lack safe water, family planning services for the estimated 20 million couples in need of such services, essential medicines for the nearly 13 million people without access to health care, and basic education for the 12 million children out of primary school.

Source: Human Development Report 1994 *(New York: Oxford University Press, 1994), p. 54.*

International Organizations

The United Nations is probably the most widely known of all international organizations. It is a multipurpose organization embracing a broad array of other organizations, centers, commissions, and institutes. The distinguishing characteristic of the UN family of organizations is that governments are their members. Hence they are known as *international intergovernmental organizations (IGOs)*. There are over three hundred IGOs in existence, and their concerns embrace the entire range of political, economic, social, and cultural affairs that are the responsibilities of modern governments.

In addition to IGOs, the transnational layer of international politics also contains nearly five-thousand *international nongovernmental organizations (INGOs)*. The members of these international organizations (such as the International Federation of Red Cross and Red Crescent Societies) are individuals or societal groups, not governments. INGOs also deal with the entire panoply of transnational activities. It is useful to think of them as intersocietal organizations that help facilitate the achievement and maintenance of agreements among countries regarding elements of international public policy (Jacobson 1984). For example, making rules regarding security at international airports and the treatment of hijackers would not be possible without the cooperation of the International Federation of Air Line Pilots Associations. As a consequence, INGOs in turn have an influence on what those rules are. Their influence is arguably greatest in the Global North, where democratic institutions invite the participation of interest groups in the policy-making process. Thus INGOs help to blur the distinction between domestic and foreign policy issues.

INGOs and IGOs alike mirror the same elements of conflict and cooperation that characterize international politics generally. Accordingly, not all are appropriately conceived as agents of interdependence. NATO, for example, is a collective security arrangement. Although an international organization, historically it depended for its very existence on the presence of a credible adversary, whose hostility induced cooperation among the alliance's members.

The United States was a primary mover behind the creation of NATO, the United Nations, and a multitude of other international organizations launched in the decades following World War II. It also encouraged the economic integration of Western Europe, which in 1957 culminated in the Treaty of Rome, creating the European Economic Community comprising France, Germany, Italy, Belgium, the Netherlands, and Luxembourg. The community has since been renamed the European Union (EU) and embraces fifteen European countries.[16] Although the EU counts political and security functions among its charge, its greatest successes have come in moving Europe toward a single, integrated regional economy. Today the EU is the largest market in the world and a principal competitor as well as partner of the United States in the world political economy (see Figure 6.1).

U.S. support for an integrated Europe and other international organizations flowed naturally from the international ethos that animated America's global activism following World War II. As the nature of the international system and the United States' role within it changed, however, so did American attitudes. That is nowhere more apparent than in the response of the United States to the changing United Nations.

American idealism was a motivating force behind creation of the United Nations during the waning days of World War II. American values shaped the world organization, whose political institutions were molded after its own. Almost immediately, however, the United Nations mirrored the increasingly antagonistic Cold War competition between the United States and the Soviet Union. Thus the United States sought—with considerable success—to utilize its position as the leader of the dominant Western majority in the UN to turn the organization in the direction of its own preferred foreign policy goals. That became more difficult with the passage of time, however—especially as the decolonization process unfolded and the United States found itself on the defensive along with its European allies (most of which had been colonial powers) in the face of a hostile Third World coalition with whom the Soviet bloc typically aligned. In 1975 that coalition succeeded in passing a General Assembly resolution over vigorous U.S. protest that branded Zionism "a form of racism and racial discrimination." The vote outraged Daniel P. Moynihan, then U.S. ambassador to the United Nations, who lashed out vehemently against "the tyranny of the UN's 'new majority.'"

In the years that followed, U.S. attitudes toward the United Nations and many of its affiliated organizations ranged from circumspection to outright hostility. The Carter administration withdrew from the International Labor Organization (ILO) to protest what it regarded as the organization's anti-Western bias. The Reagan administration followed by withdrawing from the United Nations Educational, Scientific, and Cultural Organization (UNESCO). (The Clinton administration for a time considered rejoining UNESCO but then rejected the idea for budgetary reasons after the Republican victory in the 1994 congressional elections.) The Reagan administration's disenchantment with multilateralism also found expression in its indifference to and attack on the World Court and its decision to selectively withhold funds for various UN activities—a tactic the United States had long decried when the Soviet Union chose it to protest UN policies and operations it found inimical to its interests. The United States also became wary of turning to the United Nations to cope with various regional conflict situations, as it had previously done.

By the end of the Reagan administration the once-prevalent retreat from multilateralism, often accompanied by a preference for a unilateral, go-it-alone posture toward global issues, began to wane. The decision of the Soviet Union under Mikhail Gorbachev's leadership to pay its own overdue UN bills and, in the wake of its misadventure in Afghanistan, to turn (or return) to the UN Security Council to deal with conflict situations in a manner recalling the original intended purpose of the UN, helped to stimulate the reassessment of U.S. policy toward the United Nations. In response, President Reagan committed the United States to pay its own debts to the world organization, but both Bush and Clinton found Congress reluctant to make good on that pledge. By 1994 the United States had become the UN's leading debtor, with more than $730 million in unpaid bills for regular budget assessments and various peacekeeping operations (Branigin 1994, 7). The arrears in part reflected disenchantment with the budgetary procedures of the UN itself, where only fifteen countries—with the United States at the head of the list—pay 80 percent of its cost but are easily outvoted by those who pay only a tiny fraction of the bill.

The return of both the United States and the Soviet Union to the Security Council as a mechanism for dealing with global conflicts set the stage for their cooperation in responding to Iraq's invasion of Kuwait. In the years that followed, the Security Council authorized several new peacekeeping and peace enforcement operations, far outpacing any previous period in the organization's history. UN Secretary-General Boutros Boutros-Ghali championed an even broader role for the UN in the new world, proposing the creation of a volunteer force that would "enable the United Nations to deploy troops quickly to enforce a ceasefire by taking coercive action against either party, or both, if they violate it" (Boutros-Ghali 1992–1993; see also Boutros-Ghali 1992). The rapid deployment units would go into action when authorized by the Security Council and serve under the command of the secretary-general and his designees.

This and other ideas put forward by the proactive secretary-general proved controversial, however (Hall 1994; Preston 1994), as did the growing number of UN operations around the world. As their costs—both financial and political—mounted, disenchantment in the United States (long a critic of the UN's excessive bureaucracy and penchant toward mismanagement) also grew.[17] The Clinton administration, as we saw in previous chapters, now elaborated rules that would sharply constrain U.S. participation in UN military operations (see also Ruggie 1994a). And the new Republican majority in the House of Representatives, acting on the single foreign policy item in its "Contract with America" program, passed legislation that would curtail funds available for UN peacekeeping or enforcement operations and prohibit U.S. forces from serving under the command of a non-U.S. officer.

Thus the burst of enthusiasm for collective security evident during the Persian Gulf War waned, as the realities of the new world disorder—as in the former Yugoslavia and elsewhere—settled in. The Cold War that once stifled more effective use of the United Nations in conflict situations may have ended, but the difficulties continued in marshaling support in a world organization comprising nearly 200 sovereign states with widely different capabilities, interests, and willingness to pay. As in the past, the incentives to maximize individual gains rather than subordinate them to the collectivity persist.

Multinational Corporations

Since World War II multinational corporations have grown enormously in size and influence, thereby dramatically changing patterns of global investment, production, and marketing. (*Multinational corporations (mnCs)* are business enterprises organized in one society with activities abroad growing out of direct investment as opposed to portfolio investment through shareholding.) The United Nations Programme on Transnational Corporations (United Nations Programme on Transnational Corporations 1993, 99–100) estimates that in the early 1990s some thirty-seven thousand MNCs controlled assets in two or more countries and that they were responsible for marketing roughly 90 percent of Northern countries' trade. Moreover, a comparison of countries and corporations according to the size of their gross economic product shows that over 40 percent of the world's top one hundred economic entities (in 1990) are multinational corporations. Among the top fifty entities, MNCs account for only eleven, but in the next fifty they account for thirty (Kegley and Wittkopf 1995, 180–81).

Although Global South countries have spawned some multinational corporations, most are headquartered in the developed world, where the great majority of their activities originate. Using the source of foreign direct investment as a measure, the Global North accounts for 97 percent of all investment outflows and is the recipient of 25 percent of all investment inflows (Mitchell 1993, 168). The developing nations' share of direct investment did grow in the 1970s, but it plummeted during the debt crisis of the 1980s (see Chapter 7).

Historically, the United States has been the home country for the largest proportion of multinational parent companies, followed by Britain and Germany. Since the 1970s, however, the outward stocks and flows of foreign direct investment from the United States has steadily declined. During the past decade the investment world became increasingly "tripolar," with the United States, the (now) European Union, and Japan the key actors. Wholly unexpected at the beginning of the decade, tripolarity grew out of the convergence of three important interrelated trends: (1) the rapid integration of Europe, which made it possible to treat the European Community as a single investment entity; (2) the growing importance of Japan as a source of foreign direct investment; and (3) the declining role of the United States as a source of investments and its corresponding rise as a host country. By the early 1990s Europe was on a par with the United States in terms of the stock of foreign direct investment (investments in place), while Japan had surpassed the United States as a major source of foreign investment flows (transborder investments), with much of its outward investment directed to the United States itself (United Nations Centre on Transnational Corporations 1991).

Not only does the U.S.-Japan-European triad now dominate world investment patterns but the growth rate of foreign direct investments within the triad itself has outpaced the growth of investments elsewhere. The patterns emerge from a corporate strategy in which each partner to the investment triad has sought to consolidate its own market hold and to gain a foothold in the other two regions. Preferences within the triad show that the United States and the (now) European Union prefer to invest in each other over Japan and that Japan prefers to invest in the United States over Europe. The result is a serious imbalance between Japan and its other Northern partners, with the outward flow of investments much greater than the inward flow. The imbalance parallels Japan's trade surplus with other nations—notably the United States—and led for a time to serious concern within the United States about the "selling of America" (Omestad 1989). Tougher competition among the three economic blocs as well as political struggle can be expected to follow such disparities (Thurow 1992).

Although most MNCs are headquartered in the Global North, they pose little direct threat to the economies or the policy-making institutions in these large, complex societies. Not so in the case of the Global South, where the economic power and reach of multinational firms—typically American—to some extent have enabled them to become a global extension of Northern societies, serving as an engine for the transfer of investment, technology, and managerial skills across national boundaries. Although such transfers may be beneficial, in the past they have posed serious threats to the very integrity of sovereign states. Perhaps the most notorious example occurred in Chile in the early 1970s. There, International Telephone and Telegraph (ITT) sought to protect its interests in the profitable Chiltelco telephone company by seeking to prevent Marxist-oriented Salvador Allende from being elected president and subsequently by seeking his overthrow. ITT's efforts to undermine Allende included giving monetary support to his political opponents and, once Allende was elected, attempting to induce the American government to launch a program designed to disrupt the Chilean economy. Eventually Allende was killed and his government overturned.

In some instances, MNCs engage in practices that may be embarrassing to home countries—as when the West German government found that a German firm had sold mustard-gas manufacturing equipment to Libya. Or they may seem to defy their home countries—as when the French subsidiary of Dresser Industries of Dallas, Texas, exported energy technology to the Soviet Union in defiance of the Reagan administration. Ultimately behavior such as this and the ITT case raise the question of whether multinational corporations are beyond the control of governments. In practice, the question has been more salient among developing countries, and most of the efforts at control have evolved nationally rather than internationally (see Spero 1990).

Today the Global South is less fearful of the untoward effects of MNCs' involvement in their political systems than about its own ability (or inability) to attract MNC investment capital and the other perquisites that flow from it. MNCs are especially important to those who seek to emulate the economic success of the Newly Industrializing Countries (NICs), which depends on an ability to sustain growth in exports. Foreign capital is critical in this process, even though it often comes at a high price. (Broad and Cavanagh 1988)

Critics of multinationals—sometimes called "imperial corporations"—contend that they exact a cost on the Global North as well as the Global South. They note that while corporate executives often have a "broad vision and understanding of global issues," they have little appreciation of, or concern for, "the long-term social or political consequences of what their companies make or what they do" (Barnet and Cavanagh 1994; see also Barnet and Müller 1974; Kefalas 1992). These allegedly include a host of maladies, including environmental degradation, a maldistribution of global resources, and social disintegration. Beyond this, critics worry that MNCs are beyond the control of national political leaders.

> The formidable power and mobility of global corporations are undermining the effectiveness of national governments to carry out essential policies on behalf of their people. Leaders of nation-states are losing much of the control over their own territory they once had. More and more, they must conform to the demands of the outside world because the outsiders are already inside the gates. Business enterprises that routinely operate across borders are linking far-flung pieces of territory into a new world economy that bypasses all sorts of established political arrangements and conventions. (Barnet and Cavanagh 1994, 19)

The United States is not immune from these processes. "Although still the largest national economy and by far the world's greatest military power, [it] is increasingly subject to the vicissitudes of a world no nation can dominate" (Barnet and Cavanagh 1994). Meanwhile, some corporate visionaries extoll multinational corporations' transnational virtues. "There are no longer any national flag carriers," in the words of Kenichi Ohmae, a Japanese management consultant. "Corporations must serve their customers, not governments."

International Regimes

Two decades ago multinational corporations were the object of considerable animosity due to their size and "global reach" (Barnet and Müller 1974), but today "their existence has become a fact of life. They are now permanent—and influential—players in the international arena" (Spero 1990). Indeed, it is inconceivable to think how international economics might function without them, just as it is inconceivable to think that international commerce or other forms of interaction could occur in the absence of governmental rules. Thus states and nonstate actors coalesce to form international regimes that facilitate cooperative international relations.

International regimes can be thought as "sets of implicit or explicit principles, norms, rules, and decision-making procedures around which actors' expectations converge in a given issue area of international relations" (Krasner 1982). They are important in understanding the regularized patterns of collaboration in international politics. The international political system may appear anarchical (a central concept underlying the logic of political realism), but it is nonetheless an ordered anarchy. Regimes help explain that apparent anomaly.

The global monetary and trade systems created during and after World War II are clear examples of international regimes. Both evolved under the leadership of the United States—the hegemonic power in the postwar political economy—and together the two regimes helped define the Liberal International Economic Order (LIEO), embracing a combination of principles, rules, norms, and decision-making procedures that limited government intervention in the international economy and otherwise facilitated the free flow of capital and goods across national boundaries. The global system governing the mining and distribution of oil is another example. Here governments, an international organization (OPEC), and multinational corporations all play critical roles in supplying an energy-hungry world with a critical resource (see Keohane 1984).

These and other examples show that nonstate actors help to build and broaden the foreign policy agendas of national decision makers by serving as "transmission belts of policy sensitivities across national boundaries" (Keohane and Nye 1975). From that perspective, we can reasonably suggest that transnational interactions have the capacity to influence the international system by:

1. *Changing attitudes* of both elites and nonelites by altering their opinions and perceptions of reality through face-to-face contacts with citizens of different states.

2. Increasing *international pluralism* by linking national interest groups in transnational structures, usually for the purposes of transnational cooperation.

3. Increasing the constraints on states through *dependence and interdependence*— particularly in the areas of international transportation and finance.

4. Creating *new instruments of influence* enabling some governments, as a result of the unequal distribution of transnational linkages, to carry out more effectively their wishes when dealing with other governments.

5. Creating new *autonomous international actors*, capable of pursuing their interests largely outside the direct control of nation-states (Nye and Keohane 1971).

International regimes facilitate these processes. Ironically, their importance to the system as a whole may increase as the United States' dominant role in world politics wanes. The United States was instrumental in creating regimes in the postwar environment as its overriding power provided the stability and order necessary for their birth and effective functioning. In effect—and in contrast to what the logic of *realpolitik* predicts—the United States provided a collective good to other nations which enabled them as well as the hegemon to prosper. Therefore, instability might be expected as the power of the United States relative to others declines. However, the institutionalized rules put in place after World War II for the collective management of global problems in a decentralized international system persist; these rules may help to maintain order in an environment where chaos might otherwise be expected. Thus nonstate actors play a critical role in the maintenance of international equilibrium.

Transnational Terrorism and Ethnonational Movements

Transnational terrorists and ethnonational movements are exceptions. Their objective as nonstate actors is chaos, not equilibrium. Thus they pose vexing challenges to nation-states generally and to the United States in particular.

The number of international terrorist incidents has declined in recent years, as have the number attacks on American interests and personnel (see Figure 6.8)—trends not unrelated to the end of the Cold War, as the Soviet Union and the Communist states in Eastern Europe had provided both support and safe haven for terrorist groups. However, the attacks have gotten closer to home. In 1993 two CIA employees were murdered as they drove into a parking lot in Langley, Virginia. In the most dramatic event of that year, terrorists bombed the World Trade Center in New York City, killing six Americans and wounding more than a thousand—"the highest casualty total for a single terrorist attack ever recorded," according to the State Department. Several of the alleged culprits were quickly apprehended and later found guilty in U.S. courts. In early 1995, the purported ringleader of the attack was arrested in Pakistan and hustled to New York to face trial. Soon after that two U.S. consular employees in Karachi were gunned down as they car-pooled to work.

Terrorism is a tactic of the powerless directed against the powerful. Thus political or social minorities and ethnic movements often perpetrate acts of terrorism to seize the media limelight and promote their causes. Those seeking independence and sovereign statehood—like the Palestinians in the Middle East and the Basques in Spain—typify the kinds of aspirations that often animate terrorist activity. Still, many terrorist activities are supported by states, whether directly (e.g., financially) or indirectly (e.g., by providing safe havens). The United States identifies (as of 1994) seven nations as states that sponsor international terrorism: Iran, Iraq, Libya, Syria, Sudan, Cuba, and North Korea. U.S. policy calls for diplomatic, economic, and sometimes military sanctions to deal with them. The State Department described Iran as "the most dangerous sponsor and the greatest source of concern," as evidence links it to terrorist activities in France, Germany, Turkey, Switzerland, Italy, and Argentina (Atkinson 1993a; Coll and LeVine 1993; Emerson 1993). Iran especially has been closely identified with the radical Shiite Muslim group Hezbollah held responsible for terrorist acts throughout

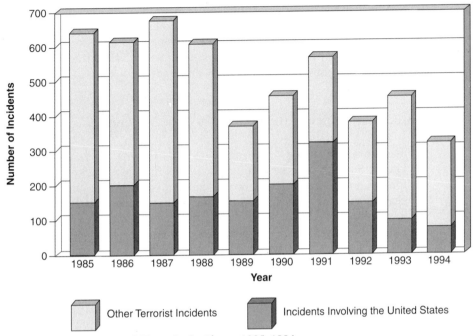

Figure 6.8 International Terrorist Incidents, 1985–1994
Source: Office of the Coordinator for Counterterrorism, U.S. Department of State, February 1995.

the world. (Saudi Arabia has supported the Sunni Muslims, with whom the Iranian-supported Shiites are often in conflict.)

Prior to the Langley murders and the Trade Center bombing, the CIA and State Department estimated that 80 percent of international terrorists incidents were "state sponsored" (Emerson 1993, C5). Now, however, there is growing concern that terrorists who embrace radical (political) Islam are increasingly "freelancers"—unattached to any particular sponsor. As one (unidentified) German official put it, "Islamic fundamentalist terrorism is unlike anything we have ever seen before, because there is not traditional hierarchy like the other secular groups" (cited in Emerson 1993). That complicates the task of intelligence agencies charged with preventing terrorism and rooting out its perpetrators.

Although radical Islamic fundamentalists are widely identified with today's international terrorist activities, a broader conception of terrorism would also incorporate government activities such as those of Serbia, which supports mass rapes and killings in Bosnia and Herzegovina. "It's a war," explained one State Department official, who added, however, that the "issue of definition is an extremely thorny and difficult one."

Thorny definitional issues aside, the spread of ethnonational movements in the wake of the Cold War encourages the weak to visit terrorism on the strong. It is increasingly evident that many people do not pledge their primary allegiance to the state and the government that rules them. Instead, they regard themselves as members of their nationality first and their own state second. That belief encourages the cultural, religious, ethnic, and linguistic communities within today's nation-states to express their own individuality. Even the United States—a "melting pot" of immigrants from around the world—today finds "multiculturalism" a growing challenge to the dominant political culture (see Chapter 8). Violence has sometimes accompanied expressions of multiculturalism within the United States. Often it invites expression abroad through terrorism, both within states and transnationally.

American Foreign Policy at the Dawn of a New Millennium   . . . .

The years immediately following World War II were fraught with opportunity for the United States as it actively embraced global responsibilities and pursued an assertive foreign policy that shaped a world compatible with the American vision. Thus the character of the international political system in the decades following World War II was largely a product of the policies and programs the United States engineered and the choices it made in responding to the challenges of the era.

The world on the horizon of the twenty-first century is still ill-defined, and the role that the United States will play in shaping it is still uncertain. As the sole remaining superpower, the United States has a greater capacity than anyone to create a new world order that once more is compatible with American interests and values. Paradoxically, however, the United States also today finds itself burdened with responsibilities. The institutions it promoted and once supported without reservation are sometimes the unwelcome symbols of a contemporary international political system that often has proven inhospitable and intractable. The emerging configuration of world power portends new challenges that arguably will prove more vexing than managing the Soviet menace. Many of those outside the circle of great powers remain skeptical of the impact of American power on their own interests and values, even as developments within those societies spill onto the larger global stage. And the relentless march of transnational interdependence poses new threats to even a superpower's ability to manage the forces that define its security and well-being.

Historically the United States has responded to external challenges either with detachment or through assertiveness. Today we live in a transitional period—one in which the old world order has passed but the shape of the new world order has yet to be determined. Whether detachment or assertiveness will characterize America's response to the challenges of the new millennium must still be decided.

NOTES

1. For critiques of the role of nuclear weapons as instruments of peace, see Kegley (1994), Mueller (1989), and Vasquez (1991).

2. Friedberg (1994) argues that "the fragmented foundation of power on which a new order will have to be built" may result not in a single, all-encompassing system, but rather in several subsystems. These might be organized regionally (Asia, Europe, America); on the basis of wealth (North vs. South); or perhaps along civilizational lines (Western, Confucian, Japanese, Hindu, Slavic-Orthodox, Islamic)." See also Huntington (1993a).

3. Not all economic forces are integrative. As Erik Peterson (1994) notes, "accelerating global economic integration is bringing national economic policies into sharper competition, especially among the advanced capitalist economies." Thus it is possible to conceive of a coming collision of the world's three preeminent capitalist centers (Europe, Japan, and the United States). Conflicts among them are explored in detail in Chapter 7.

4. See Kegley and Raymond (1994) for a thorough treatment of scenarios the United States might following in a multipolar world. The discussion that follows draws in part on this source. Khalilzad (1995) also explores alternative strategic visions and grand strategies.

5. See Warner (1989) for a discussion of the special relationship and Rasmussen and McCormick (1993) for an analysis of British sentiments toward the relationship.

6. The Korean "police action" initiated in 1950 in response to North Korea's attack on South Korea is not properly regarded as an instance of collective security for two reasons. First, the Soviet Union did not approve of the action (it was absent from the Security Council at the time in protest over the exclusion of the government of Communist China from the organization). Second, the action was taken as a recommendation under Chapter 6 of the United Nations Charter, not as a binding obligation under Chapter 7, as in the Gulf crisis.

7. Bloomfield (1994) notes that the debate about the future U.S. world role became hostage to the three "cases from hell"—Somalia, Bosnia, and Haiti. In response, he suggests that the best policy is to head off "destabilizing disorder and intolerable national behavior" before it happens. The prescription is not unlike that related to the Clinton administration's proposed crisis prevention strategy discussed in Chapter 5.

8. For a sampling of the issues related to NATO's future, see Asmus, Kugler, and Larrabee (1993), Brzezinski (1995), Duffield (1994–1995), Glaser (1993), and Harries (1993).

9. The commitment of the Soviet Union and its Eastern European allies at Helsinki to respect a wide range of fundamental human rights and to permit a greater flow of people and ideas between East and West set in motion processes that arguably encouraged political liberalization in the Soviet Union, eventually hasting the end of communist rule and, with it, the end of the Cold War.

10. Averages obscure as well as illuminate. Thus the "other Global North" and "other Global South" aggregates contain widely varying figures. Within the North, for example, Switzerland's per capita GDP in 1993 was $36,410—which surpasses even Japan's—while the figure for the Slovak Republic stood at only $1,900. And within the South, Singapore's average income stood at $19,310, compared with only $140 in Sierra Leone.

11. Data referred to in this and the previous paragraph are from the Population Reference Bureau (*1994 World Population Data Sheet*), *The World Bank Atlas 1995*, and the U.S. Arms Control and Disarmament Agency (1995). Calculations for the least developed of the less developed countries, for whom data are incomplete (and estimates at best), do not always include the same countries. Thus they should only be regarded as illustrative, not definitive. The population growth rates are rates of natural increase, which measure the excess of births over deaths.

12. Their economies, on the other hand, based on the 1985–1993 experience, will require 875 years to double in size!

13. See Eberstadt (1991), Foster (1989), and Wattenberg (1989) for discussions of the national security implications of demographic trends.

14. As in the advanced industrial societies of the North, military expenditures by Global South

countries are sometimes justified on grounds that they produce economic benefits. As the *World Development Report 1988* points out, "military spending can have positive spinoff effects, such as fostering technological innovation, training personnel who later move into civilian work, providing employment opportunities, building domestic institutions, stimulating a country's tax effort, and promoting more intensive use of existing resources. Furthermore, military industries can be a focus of industrialization activities." However, the same report observes that their positive effects often are counterbalanced by long-term costs.

15. Arms sales agreements, discussed in Chapter 5, and actual arms transfers (deliveries), discussed here, often differ widely as they measure different concepts. We can predict, however, that with the banner year in arms sales agreements concluded by the United States in 1993, actual arms transfers will increase coming years.

16. In addition to the original six, the EU includes Austria, Britain, Denmark, Finland, Greece, Ireland, Portugal, Spain, and Sweden.

17. For a sampling of the issues and some proposals for reform, see Branigin (1994); Childers with Urquhart (1994), *Defining Purpose: The U.N. and the Health of Nations* (1993), Dirks, Matthews, Rauf, Riddell-Dixon, and Sjolander (1993), Gregg (1993, 1994); Preston (1995), and Puchala (1994).

SUGGESTIONS FOR FURTHER READING

Barnet, Richard J., and John Cavanagh. *Global Dreams: Imperial Corporations and the New World Order*. New York. Simon & Schuster, 1994.

Brown, Seyom. *New Forces, Old Forces, and the Future of World Politics*. New York: HarperCollins, 1995.

Crotty, William, ed. *Post-Cold War Policy: The International Context*. Chicago: Nelson-Hall, 1995.

Gregg, Robert W. *About Face? The United States and the United Nations*. Boulder, Colo.: Lynne Rienner, 1993.

Karns, Margaret P., and Karen A. Mingst, eds. *The United States and Multilateral Institutions: Patterns of Changing Instrumentality and Influence*. Boston: Unwin Hyman, 1990.

Kegley, Charles W., Jr., and Gregory Raymond. *A Multipolar Peace: Great-Power Politics in the Twenty-First Century*. New York: St. Martin's, 1994.

Kennedy, Paul. *Preparing for the Twenty-First Century*. New York: Random House, 1993.

Keohane, Robert O., and Joseph S. Nye, Jr. *Power and Interdependence: World Politics in Transition*, 2nd ed. Glenview, Ill.: Scott, Foresman/Little, Brown, 1989.

Lincoln, Edward J. *Japan's New Global Role*. Washington, D.C.: Brookings Institution, 1993.

Moffett, George D. "Global Population Growth: 21st Challenges." *Headline Series* 302 (Spring 1994). New York: Foreign Policy Association.

Nixon, Richard. *Seize the Moment: America's Challenge in a One-Superpower World*. New York: Simon & Schuster.

Singer, Max, and Aaron Wildavsky. *The Real World Order: Zones of Peace/Zones of Turmoil*. Chatham, N.J.: Chatham House, 1993.

"The South in the New World (Dis)Order." *Third World Quarterly*, Special Issue, 15 (March 1994): 1–176.

Waltz, Kenneth N. "The Emerging Structure of International Politics," *International Security* 18 (Fall 1993): 44–79.

CHAPTER 7

• • •

THE WORLD POLITICAL ECONOMY IN TRANSITION: OPPORTUNITIES AND CONSTRAINTS IN AN INTERDEPENDENT WORLD

• • •

In today's interconnected and interdependent world, increasingly what matters are the linkages—the interactions between business and government, between politics and economics, between our domestic economy and the global economy, and between international political developments and economic change.

Under Secretary of State for Economic and Agricultural Affairs
Joan E. Spero, 1994

President Clinton and his foreign-policy advisers . . . face a situation in which diplomacy and economics must replace the militarization of the two-power world.

Former Secretary of State Henry Kissinger, 1994

"Interdependence" captures the essence of the increasingly interlocked national economies of the world and the corresponding intersection of domestic and international politics. The United States plays a leading role in this global scene. The nation's gigantic gross domestic product (GDP), which now stands in excess of $5.7 trillion, overshadows that of all other nations. American output exceeds 20 percent of the total produced in the world—more than four times its proportion of world population. The consequence of the enormous size of the U.S. economy is that little can be done in the United States without repercussions abroad. Interest rates in the United States influence interest rates abroad; domestic inflation is shared elsewhere; the general health of the U.S. economy is a worldwide concern. Once it could be said that when the United States sneezes the rest of the world catches pneumonia. That is no longer true. What remains true is that "when the United States sneezes the rest of the world catches cold" (Cooper 1988).

One reason for the worldwide importance of the American economy stems from the international position of the U.S. dollar. Dollars are a major component of the international reserves used by national monetary authorities in other countries and of the

• • •

205

"working balances" used by private banks, corporations, and individuals for international trade and capital transactions. The price of oil traded internationally is denominated in dollars, for example; dollars are also used as the capitalization basis for international lending and development institutions. And dollar is a "parallel currency," which central banks in other countries either buy or sell in currency exchange markets to maintain the value of their own currencies.

A second reason for the criticality of the American economy to global prosperity is the United States' dominant position in the global network of trade relationships. In 1994 the U.S. market—among the largest in the world—absorbed over $663 billion in imports from abroad, while the United States exported some $513 billion in products produced domestically, making it (with Germany) one of the world's two leading exporting nations.

The dominance of the United States in the world political economy was even greater in the years immediately following World War II than it is today. In 1947 the country accounted for 50 percent of the gross world product. It also was the world's preeminent manufacturing center and was unchallenged as its leading exporter. For at least the next twenty-five years the United States enjoyed a preponderance of power and influence so great as to warrant the label "hegemon." Although there is no commonly accepted definition of *hegemony*, Goldstein (1988) offers as a generic definition that "hegemony essentially consists of being able to dictate, or at least dominate, the rules and arrangements by which international relations, political and economic, are conducted."[1]

The atomic bomb symbolized the nation's awesome capabilities in the politico-military sphere, largely unchallenged until the 1962 Cuban missile crisis. In the world political economy the United States derived its hegemonic status from a preponderance of material resources, of which four sets are especially important: control over markets, raw materials, and sources of capital, and a competitive advantage in the production of highly valued goods (Keohane 1984).

The situation the United States enjoyed in the early postwar years would inevitably change as Europe and Japan recovered from the ravages of war. By 1970 its proportion of gross world product had declined to about 25 percent, roughly the level at which it has continued since. The situation would not have been especially worrisome had it not been accompanied by other developments. While the nation's proportion of gross world product stabilized, its share of both old manufactures ("sunset industries"), such as steel and automobiles, and new manufactures ("sunrise industries"), such as microelectronics and computers, continued to decline. Moreover, labor productivity was often greater in other industrial nations, where personal saving rates and levels of educational achievement also far surpassed those in the United States (Nunn and Domenici 1992). At the same time, the United States' share of international financial reserves declined precipitously and its dependence on foreign energy sources, first evident in the early 1970s, continued unabated into the 1990s. Thus in all the areas essential to hegemony—control over raw materials, capital, and markets, and competitive advantages in production—American preponderance waned.

Our purpose in this chapter is to examine the role the United States played in building and maintaining the Liberal International Economic Order that the Western industrial nations sought to create during and immediately following World War II.

We will examine the special responsibilities the United States exercises in the monetary and trade systems and how its changing power position has both affected and been affected by changes in the world political economy. The inquiry will carry us into a discussion of many of the contentious policy issues that currently rend the world political economy. Thus we will observe the interaction of politics and economics as a source of American foreign policy and also the ways in which international and domestic forces simultaneously stimulate and constrain that policy as the United States seeks to play "two-level games" (Putnam 1988)—one at the domestic level, the other at the international.

America's Hegemonic Role in the Liberal International Economic Order: An Overview ....

In 1944 the United States and its wartime allies met in the resort community of Bretton Woods, New Hampshire, to shape a new international economic structure. The lessons they drew from the interwar years—particularly the Great Depression of the 1930s—influenced their deliberations even as they continued their struggle against the Axis powers. The main lesson was that the United States could not safely isolate itself from world affairs as it had after World War I. Instead, the United States now actively led in the creation of the various rules and institutions that were to govern post-World War II economic relations. The result was the ***Liberal International Economic Order (LIEO)***, in which barriers to the free flow of trade and capital were progressively reduced, thus promoting today's interdependent world political economy.

The postwar Liberal International Economic Order rested on three political bases: "the concentration of power in a small number of states, the existence of a cluster of important interests shared by those states, and the presence of a dominant power willing and able to assume a leadership role" (Spero 1990).

Economic power was concentrated in the developed countries of Western Europe and North America. Neither Japan nor the Third World (today's Global South) posed an effective challenge to Western dominance for at least a quarter of a century, and the participation of the then-communist states of Eastern Europe and the Soviet Union in the international economy was limited. The concentration of power restricted the number of states whose agreement was necessary to make the system operate effectively.

The shared interests among these states which facilitated the operation of the system included a preference for an open economic system—one based on free trade—combined with a commitment to limited government intervention, if this proved necessary. Hence the term "liberal" economic order (see also Gilpin 1987).

The onset of the Cold War was a powerful force cementing Western cohesion on economic issues. Faced with a common external enemy, the Western nations perceived economic cooperation as necessary not only for prosperity but also for security. The perception contributed to a willingness to share economic burdens. It was also an important catalyst for the assumption of leadership by only one state—the United States—and for the acceptance of that leadership role by others (see also Ikenberry 1989).

The importance of leadership in maintaining a viable international economy was articulated by economist Charles Kindleberger (1973), who first theorized about the order and stability that preponderant powers provide as he sought to explain the Great Depression of the 1930s. Kindleberger concluded that "the international economic and monetary system needs leadership, a country which is prepared, consciously or unconsciously, . . . to set standards of conduct for other countries; and to seek to get others to follow them, to take on an undue share of the burdens of the system, and in particular to take on its support in adversity." Britain played this role from the Congress of Vienna in 1815 until the outbreak of World War I in 1914; the United States assumed the British mantle in the decades immediately following World War II. In the interwar years, however, Britain was unable to play the role of leader. And the United States, although capable of leadership, was unwilling to exercise it. The lacuna, Kindleberger concluded, was a principal cause of the national and international economic traumas of the 1930s.

Kindleberger's insights are widely regarded as a cornerstone of **hegemonic stability theory**. This theory stands in contrast to the perspective of political realism, which sees order and stability in the otherwise anarchical international political system as the product of power balances designed to thwart the aspirations of dominance-seeking states. Hegemonic stability theory, however, focuses on the role that the preponderant power of only one state—the hegemon—plays in stabilizing the system. It also captures the special roles and responsibilities of the major economic powers in a commercial order based on market forces.

From their vantage points as preponderant powers, hegemons are able to promote rules for the system as a whole that protect their own interests. Capitalist hegemons, like Britain and the United States, prefer open systems because their comparatively greater control of technology, capital, and raw materials gives them more opportunities to profit from a system free of nonmarket restraints. At the same time capitalist hegemons have special responsibilities. They must ensure that nations facing balance-of-payments deficits will find the credits necessary to finance their deficits. If the most powerful states cannot do this, they themselves are likely to move toward more closed (protected or regulated) domestic economies, which may undermine the open international system otherwise advantageous to them (Block 1977). Generally, hegemonic powers must be "willing and able to furnish an outlet for distress goods, maintain the flow of capital to would-be borrowers, serve as a lender of last resort in financial crises, maintain a structure of exchange rates, and coordinate macroeconomic policies" (Isaak 1995). In short, those most able to influence the system also have the greatest responsibility for its effective operation.

As hegemons exercise their responsibilities they confer benefits known as public or **collective goods** (benefits shared by everyone, as they cannot be excluded on a selective basis). National security is a collective good that governments provide to all of their citizens, regardless of the resources that individuals contribute through taxation. In international politics, "security, monetary stability and an open international economy, with relatively free and predictable ability to move goods, services and capital are all seen as desirable public goods. . . . More generally, international economic order is to be preferred to disorder" (Gill and Law 1988).

Those who enjoy the benefits of collective goods but pay little or nothing for them are *free riders*. Hegemons typically tolerate free riders, partly because the benefits they provide encourage other states to accept their dictates. Thus both gain something.

All states worry about their *absolute power*, but hegemonic powers typically exhibit less concern about their *relative power* position than others. That is, they are less likely than others to "worry that a decrease in their power capabilities relative to those of other nation-states will compromise their political autonomy, expose them to the influence attempts of others, or lessen their ability to prevail in political disputes with allies and adversaries" (Mastanduno 1991). And they are less likely to behave defensively on international economic policy issues compared with an aspiring hegemon or with those that feel their relative power position deteriorating—hence hegemons' greater willingness to tolerate free riders. As a hegemon's preponderance erodes, however, its behavior on trade and monetary issues can be expected to change.

> As [the hegemon's] relative economic power declines, it will feel that it is less able to afford, and thus less likely to tolerate, "free riding" by its allies that works to its relative economic disadvantage. Furthermore, as commonly perceived military threats diminish [as with the end of the Cold War], the hegemonic state will be less inclined, in economic disputes with its allies, to subordinate its national economic interests to the pursuit of political harmony or solidarity within the alliance. In short, the transformation of international economic and security structures should inspire a dominant state to act more as an "ordinary country," and strive for relative economic advantage in relations with its allies. (Mastanduno 1991, 81–82)

Why does a hegemon's power decline? Is erosion inevitable, or is it the product of lack of foresight and ill conceived policies at home and abroad? A variety of answers have been suggested. They converge on the proposition that what happens abroad and what happens at home are tightly interconnected.

Growing concern about the United States' ability to continue its leadership role in international politics received national attention with the 1987 publication of historian Paul Kennedy's treatise, *The Rise and Fall of the Great Powers*, in which he wrote:

> Although the United States is at present still in a class of its own economically and perhaps even militarily, it cannot avoid confronting the two great tests which challenge the *longevity* of every major power that occupies the "number one" position in international affairs: whether it can preserve a reasonable balance between the nation's perceived defense requirements and the means it possesses to maintain those commitments; and whether . . . it can preserve the technological and economic bases of its power from relative erosion in the face of ever-shifting patterns of global production. (Kennedy 1987, 514–15)

The danger, which he called "imperial overstretch," is similar to that faced by hegemonic powers in earlier periods—notably the Spanish at the turn of the seventeenth century and the British at the turn of the twentieth. "The United States now runs the risk," he warned, "that the sum total of [its] global interests and obligations is nowadays far larger than the country's power to defend them all simultaneously." He reiterated that theme shortly after the United States and its coalition partners attacked Iraq in January 1991: "The theory of 'imperial overstretch' . . . rests upon a truism, that a power that wants to remain number one for generation after generation requires not just military capability, not just national will, but also a flourishing and efficient economic base, strong finances and a healthy social fabric, for it is upon such foundations that the country's military strength rests in the long term" (Kennedy 1992).

Conservative critics argued "imperial overstretch" was a ruse designed to deprecate the defense-spending initiatives of the Reagan administration. However, the relationship between the health of the economy and American foreign policy was not easily dismissed, even as the Cold War waned. In the after-glow of victory in the Persian Gulf War, for example, syndicated columnist Charles Krauthammer (1991) concurred that "An American collapse to second-rank status will be not for foreign but for domestic reasons. . . . America's low savings rate, poor educational system, stagnant productivity, declining work habits, rising demand for welfare-state entitlements and new taste for ecological luxuries have nothing at all to do with engagement in Europe, Central America or the Middle East." A bipartisan report issued in 1992 by the prestigious Center for Strategic and International Studies (CSIS) reinforced that theme, concluding that "some of America's biggest trouble spots are not abroad but here at home. They are in manufacturing, capital formation, education, the federal budget, science and technology" (Nunn and Domenici 1992). Defense strategist Edward Luttwak echoed that sentiment in a controversial book, *The Endangered American Dream* (1993), in which he suggested that conservatives as well as liberals now viewed the state of the economy as critical to the ability of the United States to pursue not Cold War military conflict with the Soviet Union, but post-Cold War economic competition with Japan and Europe.

Whether the United States will be able to compete with Europe, Japan, and others is related not only to what happens at home but also to the transnational processes that erode hegemonic power. Success in maintaining an economic order based on free trade will itself eventually undermine the power of the preponderant state. "An open international economy facilitates the diffusion of the very leading-sector cluster and managerial technologies that constitute the hegemon's advantage. As its advantage erodes, the costs of maintaining collective goods that support an open economy begin to outweigh the benefits. The hegemon's commitment to free trade decays in the train" (Schwartz 1994). The growing cries for protection against foreign competition heard from domestic groups now disadvantaged by free trade reflect the waning commitment to free trade and place pressure on the lead state to close the open economic order.

This brief overview of hegemonic stability theory and how changes in the economic power position of leading states occur lays a firm foundation for understanding the responsibilities and challenges facing the United States in an interdependent world and why it increasingly seems to act as an "ordinary country." Empirical evidence to support the central tenets of the theory remains inconclusive (see Isaak 1995; Schwartz 1994), and, as we have noted, it is not without critics. Still, as our discussion of the U.S. role in the management of the international monetary and trade systems will show, hegemonic stability theory provides important insight into the dynamics of American foreign policy in a world political economy in transition.

America's Role in the Management of the
International Monetary System

As envisioned in the Bretton Woods agreements of 1944, the wartime allies sought to build a postwar international monetary system characterized by stability, predictability, and orderly growth. They created the International Monetary Fund (IMF) to assist states in dealing with such matters as maintaining stability in their financial inflows and outflows (their balance of payments) and exchange rates (the rate used by one nation to exchange its currency for another's). More generally, the IMF was intended to ensure international monetary cooperation and the expansion of trade—a role, among others, that it continues to play as one of the most influential international organizations created during and after World War II. The World Bank also was created at Bretton Woods. Its charge was to assist in postwar reconstruction and development by facilitating the transnational flow of investment capital.

In the immediate postwar years, however, the IMF and the World Bank proved unable to manage postwar economic recovery. They simply were given too little authority and too few resources to cope with the enormous economic devastation that Europe and Japan suffered during the war. The United States, now both willing and able to lead, stepped into the breach.[2]

Hegemony Unchallenged

The dollar became the key to the role that the United States assumed as manager of the international monetary system. Backed by a vigorous and healthy economy, a fixed relationship between gold and the dollar (an ounce of gold was declared to be worth $35), and a government commitment to exchange gold for dollars at any time—known as *dollar convertibility*—the dollar became "as good as gold." In fact, it was better than gold for other countries to use to manage their balance-of-payments and savings accounts. Dollars, unlike gold, earned interest, incurred no storage or insurance costs, and were in demand elsewhere, where they were needed to buy goods necessary for postwar reconstruction. Thus the postwar economic system was not simply a modified gold standard system: It was a dollar-based system.

Bretton Woods obligated each country to maintain the value of its own national currency in relation to the U.S. dollar (and through it to all others) within the confines of the mutually agreed exchange rate. Thus Bretton Woods was a *fixed exchange rate system* (in which a government sets the value of its currency at a fixed rate in relation to the currencies of other nations) whose preservation ultimately required a measure of government intervention. Because the dollar was universally accepted, it became the vehicle for system preservation, as central banks in other countries either bought or sold their own currencies using the dollar to raise or depress their value. The purpose was to stabilize and render predictable the value of the currencies needed to carry on international financial transactions.

A central problem of the immediate postwar years was how to get dollars into the hands of those who needed them most. One vehicle was the Marshall Plan, which provided Western European nations with $17 billion in assistance to buy the U.S. goods necessary to rebuild their war-torn economies. The United States also encouraged deficits in its own balance of payments as a way of providing *international liquidity* (reserve assets used to settle international accounts) in the form of dollars.

In addition to providing liquidity, the United States assumed a disproportionate share of the burden of rejuvenating Western Europe and Japan by supporting various forms of trade competitiveness and condoning discrimination against the dollar. It willingly incurred these short-run costs because the growth that they sought to stimulate in Europe and Japan was expected eventually to provide widening markets for U.S. exports.[3] The perceived political benefits of strengthening the Western World against the threat of communism helped to rationalize acceptance of these economic costs. In short, the United States willingly tolerated free riding by others.

"The system worked well. Europe and Japan recovered and then expanded. The U.S. economy prospered partly because of the dollar outflow, which led to the purchase of U.S. goods and services" (Spero, 1990). Furthermore, the dollar's top currency role facilitated the ability of the United States to pursue a globalist foreign policy. Indeed, its foreign economic and military aid programs were made possible by acceptance of the dollar as the means of paying for them. Business interests could readily expand abroad because U.S. foreign investments were often considered desirable, and American tourists could spend their dollars with few restrictions. In effect, the United States operated as the world's banker. Other countries had to balance their financial inflows and outflows. In contrast, the United States enjoyed the advantages of operating internationally without the constraints of limited finances. Through the ubiquitous dollar, the United States came to exert considerable influence on the political and economic affairs of most other nations.

By the late 1950s concern began to mount about the long-term viability of an international monetary system based on the dollar (see Triffin 1978–1979). Analysts worried about ability of such a system to provide the world with the monetary reserves necessary to ensure continuing economic growth. They also feared that the number of foreign-held dollars would eventually overwhelm the American promise to convert them into gold on demand. This would undermine the confidence others had in the soundness of the dollar and the U.S. economy. In a sense, then, the dependence of the Bretton Woods system on U.S. balance-of-payment deficits and a fixed exchange rate for the dollar meant that the system contained the seeds of it own destruction.

Hegemony under Stress

If too few dollars (lack of liquidity) was the problem in the immediate postwar years, during the 1960s the problem became one of too many dollars. The costs of extensive American military activities, including the war in Vietnam, foreign economic and military aid, and massive private investments produced increasing balance-of-payments deficits. Although encouraged earlier, the deficits were now out of control. Furthermore, U.S. gold holdings fell precipitously relative to the growing number of foreign-held dollars, undermining the ability of the United States to guarantee dollar convertibility. Given these circumstances, the possibility that the United States might devalue the dollar led to a loss of confidence by others and to their unwillingness to continue to hold dollars as reserve currency. France, under the leadership of Charles de Gaulle, went so far as to insist on exchanging dollars for gold—although arguably for reasons related as much to French nationalism as to the viability of the U.S. economy.

Along with the glut of dollars, the increasing monetary interdependence of the world's industrial economies led to massive transnational movements of capital. The internationalization of banking, the internationalization of production via multinational corporations, and the development of currency markets outside direct state control all accelerated this interconnectedness. An increasingly complex relationship between the economic policies engineered in one country and their effects on another—what we now commonly call "interdependence"—resulted. This in turn spawned a variety of comparatively formal groupings of the central bankers and finance ministers from the leading economic powers[4] who devised various ad hoc solutions (such as currency swaps) to deal with their common problems. They also decided to create Special Drawing Rights (SDRs) in the IMF—a form of reserve assets popularly known as "paper gold," whose purpose was to facilitate the growth of international liquidity by means other than increasing the outflow of dollars from the United States.

Although the United States was the chief proponent and supporter of the various management techniques devised during the 1960s, none proved sufficient to counter the "dollar crises" that surfaced in the late 1960s and early 1970s. In part this is because Bretton Woods theory and practice never quite matched. Although the Bretton Woods rules permitted states to devalue their currencies, devaluations "proved to be traumatic politically and economically. . . . [They] were taken as indications of weakness and economic failure by states and, thus, were resisted" (Walters and Blake 1992; see also Eichengreen and Kenen 1994). Thus the Bretton Woods regime never operated quite like it was intended.

Changes in the world political economy also helped to undermine Bretton Woods. By the 1960s the European and Japanese recoveries from World War II were complete, as symbolized by their currencies' return to convertibility. Recovery meant that America's monetary dominance and the dollar's privileged position were increasingly unacceptable politically, while the return to convertibility meant that alternatives to the dollar (such as the German mark and Japanese yen) as a medium of savings and exchange were now available. The United States nonetheless continued to exercise a disproportionate influence over these other states, even while it was unreceptive to their criticisms of its foreign economic and national security policies, as with the war in Vietnam.

From its position as the preponderant state, the United States came to see its own economic health and that of the world political economy as one and the same. In the case of the monetary regime in particular, American leaders treasured the dollar's status as the top currency and interpreted attacks on it as attacks on international economic stability. That view clearly reflected the interests and prerogatives of a hegemon, but it did not reflect the reality of a world political economy in transition.

The fundamental contradiction was that the United States had created an international monetary order that worked only when American political and economic dominance in the capitalist world was absolute. That absolute dominance disappeared as a result of the reconstruction of Western Europe and Japan, on the one hand, and the accumulated domestic costs of the global extension of U.S. power, on the other. With the fading of the absolute dominance, the international monetary order began to crumble. (Block 1977, 163)

The United States sought to stave off challenges to its leadership role, but its own deteriorating economic situation made that increasingly difficult. Mounting inflation—caused in part by the unwillingness of the Johnson administration to raise taxes to pay either for the Vietnam War or the Great Society at home—was particularly troublesome. As long as the value of others' currencies relative to the dollar remained fixed, the rising cost of goods produced in the United States reduced their relative competitiveness overseas. In 1971, for the first time in the twentieth century, the United States actually suffered a modest (by today's standards) trade deficit (of $2 billion), which worsened the next year. Predictably, demands grew from industrial, labor, and agricultural interests for protectionist trade measures designed to insulate them from foreign economic competition.

Policymakers laid partial blame for the trade deficit at the doorstep of major U.S. trading partners. Japan and West Germany in particular were criticized for maintaining undervalued currencies (yen and marks that did not accurately reflect the cost of goods in those countries). This made their goods attractive internationally (and to American consumers), which in turn enabled them to generate balance-of-trade surpluses by selling more overseas than they bought. Simultaneously, the relative position of the United States in international trade was deteriorating, as its share of international trade declined and Europe's and Japan's increased.

Faced with these circumstances, the United States sought aggressively to shore up its sagging position in the world political economy. In August 1971 President Nixon abruptly announced that the United States would no longer exchange dollars for gold. He also imposed a surcharge on imports into the United States as part of a strategy designed to force a realignment of others' currency exchange rates. These startling and unexpected decisions—which came as a shock to the other Western industrial nations, who had not been consulted—marked the end of the Bretton Woods regime.

The strident actions the United States took in 1971 (Nixon, as recorded on a Watergate tape: "I don't give a [bleep] about the lira") were in part a reaction to its growing interdependence with the rest of the world and its realization that it could no longer unilaterally regulate international monetary affairs. In this sense they were predictable responses of an "ordinary country" to the growing challenges it now faced in the world political economy. For the political economy as a whole, however, it was also now clear that the political bases on which the Bretton Woods system had been built lay in ruins. American leadership was no longer accepted willingly by others or exercised willingly by the United States. Power was more widely dispersed among states, and the shared interests that once bound them together had dissipated.

With the price of gold no longer fixed and dollar convertibility no longer guaranteed, the Bretton Woods system gave way to a system of *free-floating exchange rates*. Market forces rather than government intervention were now expected to determine currency values. The theory underlying the system is that a country experiencing adverse economic conditions will see the value of its currency in the marketplace decline in response to the choices of traders, bankers, and businesspeople. This will make its exports cheaper and its imports more expensive, which in turn will pull the value of its currency back toward equilibrium—all without the need for central bankers to support their currencies. In this way it was hoped that the politically humiliating devaluations of the past could be avoided. However, policymakers did not foresee that the new system would introduce an unparalleled degree of uncertainty and unpredictability into international monetary affairs.

Hegemony in Decline

According to the theory of hegemonic stability, international economic stability is a collective good that preponderant powers provide. As their power wanes—as arguably the *relative* power of the United States has done in the post-Bretton Woods era, most noticeably in the 1970s—economic instability should follow. It did: Two "oil shocks" induced by the Organization of Petroleum Exporting Nations (OPEC) and the subsequent debt crisis faced by many Third World countries and others created a new sense of apprehension and concern about the viability of the existing international economic order.

Coping with the OPEC Decade

The first oil shock came in 1973–1974, shortly after the Yom Kippur War in the Middle East, when the price of oil increased fourfold. The second occurred in 1979–1980 in the wake of the revolution in Iran and resulted in an even more dramatic jump in the world price of oil. The impact of the two oil shocks on the United States, the world's largest energy consumer, was especially pronounced—all the more so as each coincided with a decline in domestic energy production and a rise in consumption. A dramatic increase in U.S. dependence on foreign sources of energy to fuel its advanced industrial economy and a sharp rise in the overall cost of U.S. imports resulted. As dollars flowed abroad to purchase energy resources (a record $40 billion in 1977 and $74 billion in 1980), U.S. foreign indebtedness, also known as "dollar overhang," grew enormously and became "undoubtedly the biggest factor in triggering the worst global inflation in history" (Triffin 1978–1979). Others now worried about the dollar's value—which augmented its marked decline on foreign exchange markets in the late 1970s and early 1980s, as illustrated in Figure 7.1.

Global economic recession followed each oil shock. Ironically, however, inflation persisted. *Stagflation*—a termed coined to describe a stagnant economy accompanied by rising unemployment and high inflation—entered the lexicon of policy discourse. World inflation already was on the rise prior to the first oil shock and may have prompted OPEC's action, but rising oil prices accentuated inflationary pressures. Deflation would normally accompany reduced economic activity, but, in the absence of energy alternatives, the criticality of oil to the sophisticated industrial economies of the Global North inhibited such an adjustment.

The changing fortunes of the dollar in the early post-Bretton Woods monetary system reflected in part the way the leading industrial powers chose to cope with the two oil-induced recessions. In response to the first, they relied on fiscal and monetary

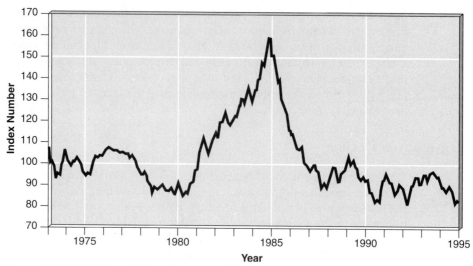

Figure 7.1 The Value of the Dollar, 1973–1995 (March 1973 = 100)

Note: The index is the weighted-average value of the U.S. dollar against the currencies of ten other major industrialized nations. The last data point is June 1995.

Source: 1973–1979: Federal Reserve System, *Annual Statistical Digest, 1970–1979* (Washington, D.C.: Federal Reserve System, 1981), p. 441; 1980–1994: *Federal Reserve Bulletin*, various issues.

adjustments to stimulate economic recovery and to avoid unemployment levels deemed politically unacceptable. In response to the second, which proved to be the longest and most severe economic downturn since the Great Depression of the 1930s, they shifted their efforts to controlling inflation through strict monetarist policies (that is, policies designed to reduce the money supply in the economy). Large fiscal deficits and sharply higher interest rates resulted. Both were particularly apparent in the United States. The other industrial nations also experienced higher levels of unemployment than they previously had been willing to tolerate.

The Debt Crisis

Many Third World countries and others by the mid-1980s owed enormous debts to Western banks and governments. Because these debts were often denominated in dollars and the interest rates charged on them tied to rates in the lending countries, rising interest rates in the United States and elsewhere caused their debt obligations to ratchet upward, with devastating results.

The accumulation of debt presents no problem "so long as the finances gained are used productively, the world economy is growing and creditor economies are open to exports of debtors. Under such conditions the borrowers will be able to repay their loans once the investments begin to produce goods. Unfortunately, none of these conditions held true during the post-OPEC price period" (Grieve 1993). The result was a debt crisis that "dominated—some would say 'consumed'—international economic discussions in the 1980s," in what effectively became the "debt decade" (Nowzad, 1990).

The specific event that triggered the debt crisis was the threat in August 1982 that Mexico would default on its loans. In addition to Mexico, others with the largest debts, including Poland, Argentina, and Brazil, required special treatment to keep them from going into default when they announced they did not have the cash needed to pay their creditors (that is, "service their debts"). Their plight was caused by heavy private and public borrowing during the 1970s, which saw private loans and investments and public loans at (nonconcessional) market rates become more important than public foreign aid for all but the poorest of countries (Burki 1983).

The first oil shock gave impetus to the "privatization" of Third World capital flows. As dollars flowed from oil consumers in the West to oil producers in the Middle East and elsewhere, the latter—unable to invest all of their newfound wealth at home—"recycled" their "petrodollars" by investing in the industrial nations, who were themselves the largest consumers of oil. In the process the funds available to private banks for lending to others increased substantially.

Many of the non-oil-exporting developing nations became the willing consumers of the private banks' investment funds. The fourfold rise in oil prices induced by the OPEC cartel hit these nations particularly hard. To pay for the sharply increased cost of oil along with their other imports, many chose to borrow from abroad to sustain their economic growth and pay for needed imports. Private banks were willing lenders, as they believed "sovereign risk"—the risk that governments might default—was virtually nonexistent, while the returns on their investments in the Third World were higher than in the industrial world.

For several reasons, however, the debtor nations found repayment of their loans increasingly difficult. Rising interest rates constituted the most important factor. In addition, some debtors made poor investment decisions, and others were victimized by "capital flight," sometimes perpetrated by corrupt officials. Many also suffered from the drop in commodity prices associated with the worldwide recession in the early 1980s, which often meant the money needed to pay off their loans simply failed to materialize. "Sovereign risk" suddenly became an ominous reality.

The IMF assumed a leadership role in securing debt relief for many Third World countries, thus keeping them from defaulting on their loans, but it did so at the cost of imposing strict conditions for domestic reform on individual debtors. Included were programs designed to curb inflation, limit imports, restrict public spending, expose protected industries, and the like. It also typically urged those it helped to increase their exports, meaning it sought an "export-led adjustment" to the debt problem.

The IMF austerity program—vigorously pushed with strong U.S. backing until 1985—could claim considerable success from a strictly financial viewpoint (see Amuzegar 1987), but its domestic burdens and political costs simply proved too overwhelming (Sachs 1989). Analysts blamed IMF conditionality for the overthrow of the Sudanese government of President Jaafar Nimeri in 1985, for example. Debt and related financial issues also inflamed domestic political conflict in many other heavily indebted nations, including Argentina, Brazil, Chile, Mexico, and Nigeria. All of this encouraged political leaders in the debtor nations to adopt a more defiant posture toward the predicament they faced (see the essays in Riley 1993b).

In this emotionally charged atmosphere the United States abandoned its earlier arm's-length policy and proposed a new plan—known as the Baker initiative after then-Secretary of the Treasury James A. Baker—to deal with the debt crisis. The Reagan administration previously had refused to perform the hegemon's classic stabilizer role due to its ideological antipathy toward intervention in the marketplace (Grieve 1993), but now it was stimulated to act by a more immediate and growing concern: the adverse impact of the debt crisis on American industries that produced for export. Thus the Baker plan sought new loans from private banks and coupled these with renewed efforts to stimulate Third World economic growth via domestic economic reforms in debtor nations. In other words, it emphasized a "market approach" to the debt problem rather than the austerity imposed through IMF conditionality. The plan failed, however, when it proved incapable of delivering the promised new resources. Brazil now announced that it would suspend interest payments on its $108 billion debt; American banks began to write off some of their loans; and riots in Venezuela over that government's austerity measures killed an estimated three hundred people in 1989, setting the stage for a new American approach to the nagging debt problem.

Announced in early 1989, the Brady initiative—named after the new secretary of the treasury—now focused on debt relief rather than debt restructuring. For the first time concern about the deteriorating situation in the debtor countries and its foreign policy implications became more important then the banks' well-being (Sachs 1989). Slowly the problems of the debtor countries receded from the headlines, spurred in part by the Brady initiative but also by lower interest rates and renewed economic growth, which in many debtor countries, by the early 1990s, sharply reduced the debt service ratio (debt as a percent of exports). Many Global South nations continued to suffer from a crushing debt burden and the discipline required by structural adjustment—often imposed from the outside—but no longer was the entire world political economy seriously threatened.[5]

The trauma and hostility caused by the debt crisis that first exploded in August 1982 is difficult to exaggerate (see Nowzad 1990). Indeed, few issues with origins in the turbulent 1970s better underscored the *mutual sensitivity* and *mutual vulnerability* that interdependence implies, or the intersection of politics and economics in the transforming world political economy. That conclusion was hammered home again in early 1995, when a sharp devaluation of the Mexican peso, caused by the inability of Mexico to make good on its short-term debts, required a U.S.-led rescue plan to ensure that the Mexican crisis would not cause deleterious waves throughout the world political economy. Some analysts asked if the United States was now committed to bailing out weak economies unable to survive on their own but on whom America's own trade and other financial fortunes depended, much as during the Cold War it had provided territorial security guarantees to those unsure about protecting themselves (Sanger 1995).

Toward Macroeconomic Policy Coordination

The 1985 Baker Plan for coping with the debt crisis coincided with other Reagan administration initiatives that marked an abrupt end to its "passive unilateralism"—commonly referred to as "benign neglect"—toward monetary and macroeconomic policy issues. Passive unilateralism now gave way to various manifestations of "pluralistic cooperation" (Bergsten 1988). The latter was especially evident in the 1985 Plaza Agreement for coping with the soaring dollar.

Passive Unilateralism, 1981–1985

The increase in U.S. interest rates which so burdened the Third World debtor nations in the early to mid-1980s also contributed to the changing fortunes of the dollar. Deficit spending by the federal government contributed to rising interest rates, as the United States itself now borrowed in capital markets to cover military and other expenditures. Beyond this, other factors that helped to restore faith in the dollar included renewed economic growth in the United States, a sharp reduction in inflation (both stimulated by a decline in oil prices caused by a global oil glut), and the perception that the United States was a safe haven for financial investments in a world otherwise marked by political instability and violence. Foreign investors therefore rushed to acquire the dollars necessary to take advantage of profitable investment opportunities in the United States. This situation contrasted sharply with the 1970s, when the huge foreign indebtedness of the United States was a principal fear.

The appreciation of the dollar was a mixed blessing for the United States. It reduced the cost of imported oil (whose price first eased and then plummeted in 1986), but it increased the cost of U.S. exports to foreign buyers, thus reducing the competitiveness of American products in overseas markets. This meant the loss of tens of thousands of jobs in industries that produced for export. It also resulted in a series of record trade deficits—$122 billion in 1985, $145 billion in 1986, and $160 billion in 1987—as imports became relatively cheaper and hence more attractive to American consumers.

The budget deficit of the federal government also reached record portions at this time, topping $200 billion annually. Simultaneously, the United States became a debtor nation for the first time in more than a half-century, as it moved in only five years from being the world's biggest creditor to being its largest debtor. The debt legacy would eventually constrain the government's policy choices in dealing with later economic downturns, as happened with the prolonged recession of 1990–1992. It also raised the prospect of a long-term decline in Americans' unusually high standard of living, as money spent tomorrow to pay today's bills would not be available to meet future problems or finance future growth. By 1991 interest payments on the national debt (the accumulation of past deficits) constituted 14 percent of all federal outlays, the third largest category of expenditures (following entitlements and defense spending); within a few years interest payments are projected to exceed defense spending (Nunn and Domenici 1992, 64–65).

In a normally functioning market, the combination of a strong dollar and severe trade imbalance would set in motion self-corrective processes that would return the dollar to its equilibrium value. Growing U.S. imports, for example—though beneficial to America's trade partners in generating jobs and thus stimulating their return to economic growth—should create upward pressure on the value of others' currencies. Conversely, a drop in American exports should ease the demand for dollars, thereby reducing the dollar's value in exchange markets. These mechanisms did not work as they should have because of the persistently high interest rates in the United States.

Pluralistic Cooperation, 1985–1989

Historically, the United States had been loath to intervene in the international marketplace to affect the value of the dollar. By 1985, however, the erosion of American trade competitiveness in overseas markets due to the overvalued dollar had become unpalatable domestically (and, as noted, helped to stimulate the Baker initiative toward the debt crisis). In response, the Group of Five (the United States, Britain, France, Japan, and West Germany) met secretly in the Plaza Hotel in New York and decided on a coordinated effort to bring down the dollar's value. The landmark agreement also committed the major economic powers to work with one another to manage exchange rates internationally and interest rates domestically. And it signaled the emergence of Japan as a full partner in international monetary management (Spero 1990).

When the Plaza agreement failed to realize its intended goals, the Group of Five reconvened in Paris at the Louvre in early 1987 to again discuss international monetary management. In the aftermath of the Louvre meeting Japan moved away from its export-led economic strategy toward one designed to stimulate domestic demand (see Balassa and Noland 1988). On the whole, however, the meeting was also a disappointment, as the important goal of macroeconomic policy coordination among the industrial nations remained unfulfilled (see Mead 1988–1989, 1989). The United States' inability to devise a politically acceptable budget-deficit reduction strategy was a critical factor in the disintegration of macroeconomic policy coordination. Eventually, however, the chronic trade and budget deficits became overwhelming, helping to precipitate the dollar's long decline from the lofty heights it had achieved by mid-decade (see Figure 7.1).

In October 1987 stock prices in markets throughout the world plummeted overnight, resulting in billions of dollars in lost equity. The market crash stimulated a partially successful effort among the industrial powers to coordinate their domestic and international efforts to stabilize the dollar, but continuing concerns about the twin U.S. deficits plagued their further efforts in this direction. The incoming Bush administration, however, showed little enthusiasm for multilateral venues for dealing with economic policy issues. Instead, it was content to permit the dollar to fall to levels believed by some experts to be below its actual purchasing power—a policy akin to the "benign neglect" of Reagan's first term.

The Failure of Pluralistic Cooperation

Maintaining a weak dollar was designed to enhance the competitiveness of U.S. exports in overseas markets, but it also attracted renewed concern about economic fundamentals in the United States.[6] Simultaneously, U.S. dependence on foreign energy sources again grew to ominous proportions, contributing not only to the trade deficit but also to the nation's vulnerability to oil-supply or price disruptions caused by some kind of crisis—which struck in August 1990 when Iraq invaded Kuwait. Ominously, perhaps, the value of the dollar in the international marketplace declined sharply in the early weeks of the Persian Gulf crisis. Normally a country viewed as a "safe haven" for investments during times of crisis will see the value of its currency appreciate; this had been the United States' typical role. In the Persian Gulf case, however, investors concluded Europe and Japan were better bets.

While the Bush administration practiced passive unilateralism toward the dollar, Germany's central bank—the Bundesbank—maintained high interest rates in an aggressive effort to contain inflationary pressures generated by the cost of unifying the former East and West Germanies. Mimicking the effects on the dollar during Reagan's first term, the mark's value soared as investors now chose to hold marks rather than dollars; this further weakened a dollar already suffering from the effects of recession at home. The dollar was dealt another blow by the Bush administration when the president proclaimed at the 1992 Republican nominating convention that the budget agreement he had worked out with Congress in 1990 in an effort to cope with the federal budget deficit was a mistake he would not repeat. Renewed fear about further growth in the already burgeoning deficit caused the dollar to plunge even further. Almost simultaneously a currency crisis in Europe—stimulated again by German monetary policy—threatened the European Community's European Monetary System, which, since its creation in 1979, sought through a semifixed exchange system to create a "zone of predictability" (Spero 1990) among Europe's currencies as a precursor to a single European currency.

As in the monetary crises of the 1960s and 1970s, existing mechanisms of macroeconomic policy coordination proved ineffective in coping with the challenges of the early 1990s. Most visible among these is the ***Group of Seven (G-7)***, which embraces the world's largest industrial democracies. Each year it holds an economic summit (which now also includes political issues) accompanied by considerable pomp and fanfare. For a time the G-7 was arguably "one of the most influential institutions of the twentieth century, bringing into a common forum the leading states of the industrial world and their most powerful personalities" (Smyser 1993), but it has since proven inadequate "as a mechanism for synchronizing economic policy to exert leadership over the world economy" (Ikenberry 1993). Its failure as a mechanism of macroeconomic policy coordination stems from "the inability of the major industrial states to make hard economic choices at home. Each government's emphasis on dealing with seemingly intractable domestic problems . . . constrains joint efforts to stimulate global economic growth or to manage monetary and trade relations, preventing G-7 governments from pursuing disciplined and synchronized fiscal and monetary policies" (Ikenberry 1993; see also Smyser 1993).

Bill Clinton went to Washington determined to be the "economic president." He quickly devised a fiscal policy that combined tax increases with spending cuts, designed to reverse the trend toward ever-increasing federal government budget deficits. And he achieved a modicum of success. When Clinton sent Congress his $1.5 trillion spending plan for 1995, he was able to boast that the budget deficit would actually get smaller for the third year in a row—something that had not happened since 1948. At the same time, however, the limitation on discretionary spending contained in the 1993 budget bill virtually eliminated the administration's ability to use fiscal policy to fine-tune the economy. This heightened the importance of monetary policy (largely the preserve of the Federal Reserve Board) to the administration's economic program. The close correlation between interest rates and the value of the dollar (lower rates should weaken the dollar and higher rates strengthen it), also arguably heightens the importance of macroeconomic policy coordination.

Although verbally committed to a greater degree of multilateral policy making than the Bush team, the Clinton administration continued the policy of benign neglect toward the sagging dollar—this time as a mechanism of righting the trade imbalance between the United States and Japan. But there was no noticeable effect on U.S. trade with Japan—indeed, the deficit persisted despite several years in which the dollar was comparatively weak. Finally, in May 1994, the administration reversed course as it coordinated a massive, sixteen-nation intervention into currency markets in an effort to prop up the dollar. Additional interventions followed.

Having abandoned its policy of benign neglect, the Clinton administration found that its efforts to prop up the sagging dollar fell short, as the dollar continued to weaken against the German mark and reached postwar lows against the Japanese yen (see Figure 7.2). Although several reasons were offered to explain this, it was especially baffling since the U.S. economy was generally sound and growing, conditions that normally would cause the dollar to rise.

Some again cited the continuing trade and government budget deficits as the causal factors. Others saw the Clinton administration's policies and performance as the primary culprit. As one senior Clinton adviser explained, "The value of the dollar on any given day is like a global referendum on all the policies of the Clinton administration combined. It is as though the world were having a huge discussion on the Internet, and the dollar's value is a snapshot of that discussion." Still others suggested that the problem lay not with the dollar but with the yen. What the Japanese called *endaka* (strong yen crisis) was, according to this reasoning, propelled by the imbalance of Japan's financial transactions with the rest of the world, leading to increased demand for the yen

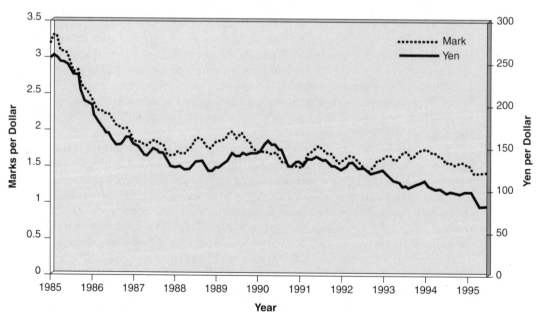

Figure 7.2   The Value of the Dollar Relative to the Mark and Yen, 1985–1995
Note: The last data points are June 1995.
Source: Federal Reserve Bulletin, various issues.

and hence its higher price (Berry 1994). It is noteworthy in this respect is that the dollar actually strengthened against some currencies at the same time as it weakened against the yen and the mark, and that other nations, seeking to stabilize their own currencies, found it prudent to tie their currencies directly to the dollar, thus reflecting confidence in its stability and value (Friedman 1994a; see also Frankel 1995).

New Forces, New Roles

Over the long-term the nation's economic health will doubtless affect the value of the dollar. The growing volume of world trade and the activities of currency speculators, who use sophisticated electronic means to carry out their transnational exchanges, now also significantly affect national currency values. Over $1 trillion in currency trading occurs each day—roughly equivalent to the total value of foreign exchange held in countries' central banks (*New York Times*, September 25, 1992, p. 1). Thus it is not surprising that Clinton administration efforts to bid up the value of the dollar failed. "The central banks were like a zookeeper trying to calm a starved gorilla by offering it a raisin for lunch" (Friedman 1994d).

As currency markets grow in size and sophistication, international sales of stocks and bonds also have mushroomed to unprecedented proportions (Schwartz 1994). These developments in the globalization of markets severely circumscribe the ability of nations—individually or collectively—to affect the value of their currencies in exchange markets. Indeed, Alan Greenspan, chairman of the Federal Reserve System, noted in testimony before the Bipartisan Commission on Entitlement and Tax Reform that the ability of the Federal Reserve System to prop up the dollar by buying it in foreign exchange markets "is extraordinarily limited and probably in a realistic sense nonexistent." The internationalization of finance and the removal of barriers to transnational capital flows also have, in Greenspan's words, "[exposed] national economies to shocks from new and unexpected sources, with little if any lag."

Like the debt crisis of the 1980s, the forces that now affect the dollar are a product of the mutual sensitivity and mutual vulnerability interdependence implies in a world in which politics and economics have become inextricably linked. Similarly, events since the two oil shocks of the 1970s have dramatically underscored the erosion of the United States' ability to play the same kind of leadership role it performed in the Bretton Woods system. The end of the Cold War has not only further diminished America's tolerance of free-riding by others, it has also further undermined the willingness of Europe and Japan to follow the lead. As one German official[7] observed near the end of the Bush administration, "The end of the Cold War has brought about a qualitative change in relations among the key players. The threat of nuclear holocaust provided a lot of glue on the economic side." The determination of the European Union to create a European-wide central bank and currency—despite the fits and starts it will inevitably encounter—is merely one manifestation of the new order in the world political economy. Thus the institutional framework of the postwar economic system which rested on the assumption of American dominance has given way to a less-certain world. Accordingly, "the U.S. economy and American economic decision making must now be adapted to an emerging global economy that no longer revolves around the United States" (Aho and Stokes 1991).

America's Role in the Management of the International Trade System ································

The volume and value of international trade have increased exponentially since World War II. Nevertheless, by posing new barriers to international trade, states increasingly pursue policies designed to meet their domestic economic goals that simultaneously threaten closure of the liberal trade regime.[8] Thus, ironically, the very success of the open, multilateral trade regime has undermined its continuation as global interdependence now often threatens sovereign prerogatives. The demise of American hegemony also encourages closure of the system, because the United States is no longer as willing or as able to bear the costs of maintaining an open regime.

An Overview of the International Trade Regime

Management responsibilities in the postwar economic system as envisaged during World War II were to be entrusted not only to the IMF and the World Bank but also to an International Trade Organization (ITO), whose purpose was to lower restrictions on trade and set rules of commerce. Policy planners hoped that these three organizations could assist in avoiding repetition of the international economic catastrophe that followed World War I. In particular, the zero-sum, ***beggar-thy-neighbor policies*** associated with the intensely competitive economic nationalism of the interwar period were widely regarded as a major cause of the economic catastrophe of the 1930s which ended in global warfare. (*Beggar-thy-neighbor policies* are efforts by one country to reduce its unemployment through currency devaluations, tariffs, quotas, export subsidies, and other strategies that enhance domestic welfare by promoting trade surpluses that can only be realized at another's expense.) Thus priority was assigned to removing barriers to trade, particularly tariffs. That was to have been ITO's charge, but it was stillborn.

The United States was the prime mover behind all three of the anticipated new agencies. ITO failed when the liberal trading system envisioned in its charter (popularly known as the Havana Charter) became so watered down by other countries' demands for exemptions from the generalized rules that Congress refused to approve it. In its place, the United States sponsored the ***General Agreement on Tariffs and Trade (GATT)***, which, although initially designed as a provisional arrangement, became the cornerstone of the liberalized trading scheme originally embodied in the ITO (see Low 1993).

Trade liberalization was to occur through the mechanism of free and unfettered international trade, of which the United States has been a strong advocate for half a century. Free trade rests on the ***most-favored-nation (MFN) principle***, which says that the tariff preferences granted to one nation must be granted to all other nations exporting the same product. The principle ensures equality in a nation's treatment of its trade partners. Thus nondiscrimination is the central norm of the trade regime.

Under the aegis of GATT and the most-favored-nation principle, a series of multilateral trade negotiations, called "rounds," aimed at reducing tariffs (and resolving related issues) have been undertaken. The eighth and most recent session, the ***Uruguay Round,*** was launched at Punta del Este in 1986 but not completed until late 1993, well beyond the original target date. The agreement included a provision for replacing GATT with a new World Trade Organization (WTO), thus resurrecting the half-century-old vision of a global trade organization "with teeth." Still, as we will note in more detail below, the excruciatingly long, often contentious Uruguay negotiations reflected increasing strain on the liberal trading regime, particularly as states move beyond the goal of tariff reduction to confront more ubiquitous and less tractable *nontariff barriers (NTBs)* to trade, which are today extensive.

NTBs cover a wide range of government regulations that have the effect of reducing or distorting international trade, including health and safety regulations, restrictions on the quality of goods that may be imported, government procurement policies, domestic subsidies, and antidumping regulations (designed to prevent foreign producers from selling their goods for less abroad than they cost domestically).

Voluntary export restrictions (VERs) are another form of protection especially popular with the United States (Low 1993). VERs are export quotas that place quantitative restrictions on certain products, such as autos, steel, textiles, and footwear. Because they are imposed by the exporting country following negotiations, VERs are "hands-off" forms of protection that require no action on the part of the importing country.

Many of these "behind-the-border" trade restraints occur outside the GATT/WTO framework and therefore technically are not transgressions of the liberal trade system it seeks to promote.[9] Still, NTBs comprise one of several *neomercantilist*[10] challenges to the principle of free trade, which have assumed prominence in American foreign economic policy as its economic preeminence relative to others has declined. Over 40 percent of the industrial world's imports are now subject to nontariff measures, a proportion that has grown sharply since the mid-1960s (*World Development Report 1991* 1991, 104–5; see also Low 1993, 74). In contrast—tariffs, at least in the area of industrial products—are now comparatively inconsequential.

Hegemony Unchallenged

The United States was the principal stimulant to all eight multilateral negotiating sessions designed to reduce trade barriers. From the end of World War II until the 1960s in particular, it also was willing to accept fewer immediate benefits than its trading partners in anticipation of the longer-term benefits of freer international trade. In effect, the United States was the locomotive of expanding world production and trade. By stimulating its own growth, the United States became an attractive market for the exports of others, and the outflow of dollars stimulated other nations' economic growth as well. Evidence supports the wisdom of this strategy: As the average duty levied on imports to the United States declined by more than half between the late 1940s and the early 1960s, world exports nearly tripled.

On the Periphery

Not all shared in the prosperity of the U.S.-backed LIEO. Many nations in the emerging Third World (now the Global South) failed to grow economically during this period or otherwise to share in the benefits of economic liberalism. Instead, their economies remained closely tied to their former colonizers. Holdovers from the imperial period of the late 1800s, time-worn trade patterns perpetuated unequal exchanges that did little to break the newly independent nations out of the yoke of their colonial past. Thus the developing nations on the periphery[11] were largely irrelevant as the new economic order emerged. They enjoyed too little power to shape effectively the rules of the game, which nonetheless seriously affected their own well-being.

The Second World

The Soviet Union and its socialist allies in Eastern Europe were also outside the decision-making circle—but largely by choice. During World War II Western planners anticipated the Soviet Union's participation in the postwar international economic system, just as they originally anticipated Soviet cooperation in maintaining the postwar political order. But enthusiasm for establishing closer economic ties between East and West began to wane once the war ended. 1947 was critical, as President Truman effectively committed the United States to an anticommunist foreign policy strategy and Secretary of State George Marshall committed the United States to aid the economic recovery of Europe. Although American policymakers considered the possibility that the Soviet Union itself might participate in the Marshall Plan, much of the Congressional debate over the plan was framed in terms of the onslaught of communism—rhetoric that certainly did not endear the recovery program to Soviet policymakers. Furthermore, Soviet leaders were determined to pursue a policy of economic autarky that would eliminate any dependence on other countries. Thus they rejected the offer of American aid. They also refused to permit Poland and Czechoslovakia—both of which had been offered Marshall Plan assistance—to accept it. Thereafter East and West developed essentially separate economic systems which excluded one another.

In sharp contrast with the liberal (market-oriented) precepts it applied to others, the United States now used trade as a Cold War weapon. In 1951, in the midst of the Korean War, Congress stripped communist countries of most-favored-nation tariff treatment. Other regulations followed designed to restrict their access to American exports, aid, and commercial credits. The United States was particularly sensitive about trade in strategic goods, items that might bolster Soviet military capabilities and thus threaten Western security. It therefore moved to embargo their sale to the Soviet Union and its allies. It also sponsored the Coordinating Committee (Cocom) as a multilateral mechanism for inducing other Western nations to join in this effort. Thus economic warfare joined political hostility as an integral element of the Cold War.

Hegemony under Stress

Domestically, four major statutes (as amended) have framed the U.S. approach to international trade issues and the multilateral negotiations that flowed from them: (1) the Reciprocal Trade Agreements Act of 1934; (2) the Trade Expansion Act of 1962; (3) the Trade Act of 1974; and (4) the Omnibus Trade and Competitiveness Act of 1988. With these laws Congress authorized the president to engage in international negotiations on trade issues, often with specific grants of authority to lower American tariff barriers if other nations would do the same. The Trade Expansion Act of 1962 and the Trade Act of 1974 set the stage for the Kennedy and Tokyo Rounds of negotiations, respectively. Another statute, the Trade Agreements Act of 1979, implemented rules agreed to during the Tokyo Round. The 1988 omnibus act was passed while the Uruguay Round was still in progress, but it contained provisions relating to the conduct of the ongoing negotiations and included "fast-track" procedures for congressional consideration of the expected agreements.[12]

The high point of the movement toward liberalized trading was reached with the Kennedy Round of negotiations in the mid-1960s, which grew out of the 1962 Trade Expansion Act. The rhetoric surrounding the act's passage cloaked trade liberalization in the mantle of national security, and the act itself was described as an essential weapon in the Cold War struggle with Soviet communism. Nonetheless, it was motivated in part by concern for maintaining American export markets in the face of growing economic competition from the European Economic Community (EEC), and it specifically granted the president broad power to negotiate tariff rates with EEC members.

Today, as during most of the past quarter century, the EEC (later called the European Community [EC] and, since 1994, the European Union [EU]) rivals Canada as the country's principal trading partner. Each accounts for roughly 20 percent of U.S. trade turnover (imports plus exports), for a total between them of nearly $460 billion in 1993 (see Figure 7.3). Similar proportions are evident in U.S. overseas investments. Of the nation's direct investment abroad in 1992, 73 percent was in industrial nations, with the European Community accounting for 57 percent of that proportion, followed by Canada with 19 percent (Scholl, Lowe, and Bargas 1993, 51).

Developments in Europe have long figured prominently in America's foreign economic policy, as well as in its national security policy. But while the United States officially has supported European efforts to create an integrated economic union, transatlantic relations have not always been smooth, as the devil is found in the details. Agricultural issues have proved especially vexing.

Progress was made during the Kennedy Round on industrial tariffs, to the point that by 1975, when the Tokyo Round began, the United States and the European Community had reduced tariff rates on industrial products to an average of about 9 percent. But little headway was made on the important question of agricultural commodities. Although agricultural trade fell beyond the purview of GATT as originally conceived, it became a matter of growing importance to the United States. The immediate challenge was posed by the EEC's Common Agricultural Policy (CAP). CAP, initiated in 1966, was a protectionist tariff wall designed to maintain politically acceptable but artificially high prices for farm products produced within the EEC. The effect was to curtail American agricultural exports to the region. The lack of progress and later disagreements on this issue began to raise doubts among American policymakers about the wisdom of promoting expansionist economic policies from which others benefited.

The president's authority to negotiate trade matters under the Trade Expansion Act expired with the end of the Kennedy Round. In the years that followed, Presidents Johnson and Nixon fought a rearguard action against increasingly strong domestic protectionist forces which demanded trade restrictions from Congress (see Low 1993).

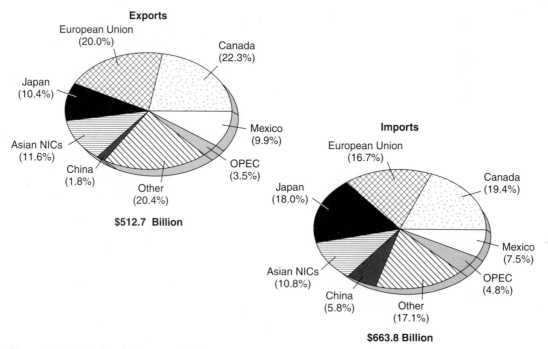

Figure 7.3 U.S. Trade Partners, 1994
Source: Adapted from U.S. Department of Commerce, *U.S. International Trade in Goods and Services*, FT-900 Supplement, December 1994: 8–12.

The strident posture assumed by the Nixon administration on international monetary issues—which terminated the Bretton Woods system—carried over into trade issues, while the collapse of the system of fixed exchange rates itself slowed progress on their resolution.

By the time the Tokyo Round commenced in 1975, trade negotiators found themselves in a radically different environment from that of the previous GATT sessions. Trade volume had grown exponentially worldwide, economic interdependence among the world's leading industrial powers had reached unprecedented levels, tariffs were no longer the principal barriers to trade, and the United States was no longer an unfaltering economic giant. In this new environment reducing barriers to the free flow of agricultural products and coping with nontariff barriers to trade received increased emphasis.

A measure of success was achieved on NTBs, as six new agreements (codes) were reached regulating government procurement, technical barriers to trade, subsidies and countervailing duties, customs valuation, import licensing, and antidumping (see Low 1993). No progress was made on agriculture, however. This shortcoming "probably more than any other single factor . . . helped to undermine the integrity and credibility of the trading system" (Low 1993; see also Graham 1979; Krasner 1979). Thus, in the years between the end of the Tokyo Round and the beginning of the Uruguay Round, GATT's rules seemed increasingly irrelevant to state practices, and protectionism in violation of the principle of nondiscrimination became increasingly rife. Growing concern about the challenge of the more economically advanced developing nations was also apparent.

Challenge from the Third World

As noted earlier, the postwar international monetary and multilateral trading systems evolved primarily under the aegis of the industrial nations of the West, whose interests and objectives they served. Developing nations on the periphery were largely outside the privileged circle, and many came to view the existing international economic structure as a cause of their underdog status. Their challenge was especially vigorous in the immediate aftermath of the first OPEC-induced oil shock.

During the 1950s developing nations began to devise a unified posture toward the superpowers and to press for consideration of their special problems and needs in the context of the global economic structure, but not until the 1960s did these efforts produce significant results. Taking advantage of their growing numbers in the United Nations, developing nations were successful in having convened, in 1964, a United Nations Conference on Trade and Development (UNCTAD). The *Group of 77 (G-77)* was formed at that time as a coalition of the world's poor to press for concessions from the world's rich. UNCTAD later became a permanent organization that often promoted the interests of the G-77, whose numbers grew to more than a hundred and whose conferences have been marked by some of the most vitriolic rhetoric of the long-standing dispute between the Global North and the Global South.

The G-77's next major victory came with the Sixth Special Session of the United Nations General Assembly, held in 1974, when it used its superior numbers to secure passage of the Declaration on the Establishment of a New International Economic Order (NIEO). Inspired in the wake of OPEC's price squeeze by the belief that "commodity power" endowed the Third World with the political strength necessary to challenge the industrial North, developing nations pressed for more rapid economic development, increased transfers of resources from industrialized to developing nations, and a more favorable distribution of global economic benefits. More fundamentally, the G-77 sought a substantial alteration of the rules and institutional structures governing the transnational flow of goods, services, capital, and technology. Simply put, the New International Economic Order sought *regime change*—a revision of the rules, norms, and procedures of the Liberal International Economic Order to serve the interests of the South rather than the North (Krasner 1985).

The Third World's drive for regime change derived from its belief that the structure of the world political economy perpetuates developing nations' underdog status. International economic institutions, such as the IMF and GATT, were (are) widely perceived as "deeply biased against developing countries in their global distribution of income and influence" (Hansen 1980). The perception was buttressed—then and now—by a legacy of colonial exploitation, the continued existence of levels of poverty and deprivation in countries of the Global South unheard of in the North, and a conviction that relief from many of the economic and associated political ills of the South can result only from changes in the policies of the North, in whose hands responsibility for prevailing conditions and the means to correct them were (are) thought to lie.

The Global North—then and now—rejected those views. Accepting them would have been tantamount to relinquishing control over key international institutions and a fundamental redistribution of global resources—two unlikely prospects. Instead, it located the cause of the Global South's economic woes in the domestic systems of developing countries themselves (see, for example, Bissell 1990). Thus proposals to alter radically existing international economic institutions, as well as the more modest elements of the program advanced during the 1970s and early 1980s, met with resistance and resentment. The United States was especially intransigent, as the Reagan administration approached the Third World primarily from the vantage point of its role in the East-West conflict, showing little interest in those aspects of Southern objectives related to transforming the Liberal International Economic Order.

As the unifying force of commodity power receded and different countries were affected in different ways by the changing economic climate of the 1980s, latent fissures within the G-77 became more evident. As a result, the Third World no longer spoke as a unified group. The differences between the more advanced of the developing nations (including a small group of fast-growing exporters of manufactured goods, known as the ***Newly Industrializing Countries [NICs]***) and the less well-off (especially the least developed of the less developed countries, sometimes called the Fourth World) became especially pronounced. Others among the more advanced developing nations, particularly in Latin America, were hardest hit by the debt crisis. These forces had the effect of dividing the G-77 into competing groups rather than uniting them behind a common cause.

The Third World's determination to replace the LIEO with a New International Economic Order is now little more than a footnote to the history of the continuing contest between the world's rich and poor nations (see Rothstein 1988). Still, many of the issues raised retain their relevance. Central among them is the role of the state in managing international economic transactions. Whereas the LIEO rests on the premise of limited government intervention, ***economic nationalists*** or ***mercantilists*** assign the state a more aggressive role in fostering national economic welfare. "In a world of competing states," political economist Robert Gilpin (1987) notes, "the nationalist considers relative gain to be more important than mutual gain. Thus nations continually try to change the rules or regimes governing international economic relations in order to benefit themselves disproportionately with respect to other economic powers." Clearly that viewpoint continues to apply to many nations in the Global South, even as "privatization" and a return to market mechanisms rather than state-run enterprises characterize recent trends domestically. Moreover, the tension between liberalism and mercantilism also applies broadly to the issues that now animate the international trade regime—including those pertinent to the U.S. foreign economic policy toward developing nations. We will treat some issues related to commodities and manufacturing here and return to related topics later, when we examine the "fair trade" challenge to free trade.

North-South Relations and the U.S. Role

Trade-related issues are at the core of the dispute between the Global North and Global South. The structure of their trade relationships evolved during the age of imperialism, when colonies existed for the presumed benefit of the colonizers. Frequently that meant that the colonies were sources of primary products—such as agricultural commodities and mineral resources—and markets for the finished manufactured goods produced in the mother country. To a striking extent, the trade patterns of the imperial past extended well beyond the formal breakup of the European colonial empires. Following the second oil shock in 1980, for example, 80 percent of the developing nations' exports were in the form of primary products and fuels; only 20 percent were manufactured products (Lewis and Kallab 1983, 248). Since then global dependence on OPEC oil has lessened, while other nations in the Global South, notably in East Asia, have become important exporters of manufactured products. But still others, particularly African nations, remain heavily dependent on primary products exports and continue to import most of their manufactured goods. OPEC nations themselves also remain heavily reliant on export revenues. Thus the terms on which the Global North and South trade with one another are especially important to developing nations.

Commodities   A central proposition in developing nations' efforts to restructure the LIEO alleged that their terms-of-trade problems stemmed from their dependence on a narrow range of primary product exports. (The *terms of trade* is a technical concept that refers to the ratio of export prices to import prices.) Many believed that the prices Third World countries received for their exports vary erratically in the short run and deteriorate steadily in the long run, whereas the prices of the manufactured goods that they import increase steadily.

The structural characteristics of the international economic order are among the alleged causes of the deteriorating terms of trade. Much of the Global South remains critically dependent on the North, not only for manufactured goods but also for technology (see Head 1989). The greater technological sophistication of the North causes natural resources to flow into markets where they can be transformed into finished goods most efficiently. In a system where those with the most money determine prices, nations in the Global South find themselves unable to determine the terms of trade for their products.

There is no question that developing nations' primary product exports are subject to sharp price fluctuations, as Figure 7.4 shows. However, whether such fluctuations result from a long-term structural deterioration of the terms of trade developing nations face or from short-term perturbations related to changes in the business cycle remains a matter of controversy among analysts. The changing resource composition of manufactured goods is also important. In 1985 and again in 1988, for example, nonfuel commodity prices turned sharply upward, but they did not regain the ground that had been lost earlier in the decade. This may reflect the industrial economies of the Global North having increasingly become uncoupled from the primary product economies of the Global South (Drucker 1994). Nevertheless, the policies political leaders pursue are influenced by perceptions as well as objective facts. Moreover, whether caused by cyclical or more deep-seated forces, swings in commodity prices have caused serious structural adjustment problems among commodity producing and exporting countries, while the secular decline in prices has exacerbated the burdens associated with their external debt.

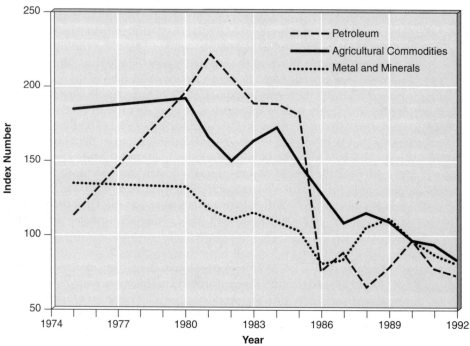

Figure 7.4 Commodity Prices, 1970–1992

Note: Real prices are annual average prices in dollars, deflated by the annual change in the manufacturing unit value (MUV) index, a measure of the price of industrial-country exports to developing countries. Prices for nonfuel primary commodities are based on a basket of thirty-three commodities.
Source: Adapted from *World Resources 1994–95* (New York: Oxford University Press for the World Bank, 1994), p. 262.

Faced with the circumstances described above, diversification of export industries, rather than continued dependence on a few primary products, became a preferred goal of many developing nations. At the same time, they sought new means of ensuring stable and remunerative prices for the commodities they already export. That was the goal of the Integrated Programme for Commodities pushed by the G-77 as a central element of its drive for a New International Economic Order (see Finlayson and Zacher 1988). As originally conceived, the program sought commodity price stabilization through a common fund supported by producing and consuming nations and administered by an international agency. A much less ambitious version was finally agreed on in 1979, but it would be another decade before the number of signatories required to bring the fund to fruition were secured. Even then, some key actors, notably the United States, were not among them. Thus what was once hailed as a revolutionary approach to a principal problem faced by many developing nations simply failed to materialize. Meanwhile, the plight of Global South nations heavily dependent on commodity exports continues.

Oil The decline of Global South commodity power is nowhere more evident than with oil. As noted previously, world oil prices plunged in the 1980s as conservation measures, economic recession, a shift to alternative sources of energy, and overproduction undermined the ability of OPEC to extract monopoly prices for its resources. The centrality of OPEC itself diminished as reduced demand for oil combined with the discovery of new oil resources in Alaska, the North Sea, and elsewhere lessened dependence on the cartel's oil. Still, much of the world remained vulnerable to interruptions in oil supplies imported from the politically volatile Persian Gulf region. The United States underscored its own sensitivity on this point when, in 1987, it made the controversial decision to escort Kuwaiti oil tankers through the perilous Strait of Hormuz, where oil tankers had become routine targets in the war between Iran and Iraq.

Even more dramatic, of course, was the "line in the sand" George Bush drew following Iraq's invasion of Kuwait in 1990. Bush did not specifically cite access to Middle Eastern oil as a reason for his militant response, but few doubted its centrality. Moreover, oil figured prominently in Saddam Hussein's thinking. If Saddam Hussein could have added Kuwait's oil reserves to Iraq's he would have wielded commanding influence over OPEC's oil production and pricing policies—and fed his insatiable drive to achieve hegemony over the Arab world.

Today the politics of oil embraces some elements of continuity with the past but also others that are dramatically different from those of two decades ago. The intersection of security and economic considerations remains, for example—although with a slightly different coloration.

> With the collapse of communism, the global security issues that were uppermost have receded. Regional security issues, however, remain. The world is now shifting back to oil dependence on the Middle East, where modernization and Islamic revivalism are in conflict. Moreover, oil's traditional relationship to other global issues continues. It is intertwined with Russia's transition to free markets and Asia's economic growth. The United States is back on the track of higher oil imports, which means that its foreign policy will remain acutely sensitive to developments in oil-exporting countries. (Stanislaw and Yergin 1993, 82)

Other elements more clearly distinguish the 1990s from the 1970s, when "oil nationalism" was at its peak. "It was the era when the world economy hung on the comments of oil ministers in the hallways of OPEC meetings and when the wrongs of colonialism were to be set right," note energy experts Joseph Stanislaw and Daniel Yergin (1993). "Today, economics is taking precedence over politics" as "many exporting countries court the international oil companies that they once shunned." Then, little could happen in the Middle East without Cold War repercussions. Now, republics of the former Soviet Union are themselves willing targets of oil exploration by the world's giant multinational oil companies. Then, achieving energy security was a primary motivation; now, reconciling energy use with environmental protection is an imperative.

Oil remains a critical commodity and thus will continue to have strategic implications in the world political economy (see Lieber 1992; Schlesinger 1990). As the world's largest oil consumer, the United States also will continue to have a major stake in the political and economic events that affect its access to this vital resource. Less clear is whether oil producers will benefit politically or economically from the emerging environment. With the passing of both oil nationalism and commodity power, oil producers may—at least for a time—be as vulnerable to untoward fluctuations in the price of their goods as other commodity producers. That situation bodes ill for developing nations' prospects of securing the equity and justice they once held out as key elements of their drive for a New International Economic Order.

Manufactures   At the same time that the North rebuffed the South's efforts at commodity price reform, it became increasingly disturbed by the growing economic challenge posed by the NICs as well as the growing importance of export markets in the Global South.

As described earlier, the rise of protectionist sentiment in the United States can be traced to the early 1970s, when domestic inflation began to erode the trade competitiveness of U.S. products abroad. Protectionism was spurred by the economic recession that followed the first oil shock and by subsequent developments at home and abroad which inhibited the process of structural adjustment to the changing world economy. Among those changes was increasing competition from the NICs, especially the four Asian Tigers (Hong Kong, Singapore, South Korea, and Taiwan), which by the mid-1980s had become among the most important U.S. trade partners. They also have consistently maintained a favorable trade balance with the United States, thereby contributing significantly to the troublesome overall U.S. trade deficit (see Figure 7.5). Their economic success and their ability to penetrate the U.S. market contributed to

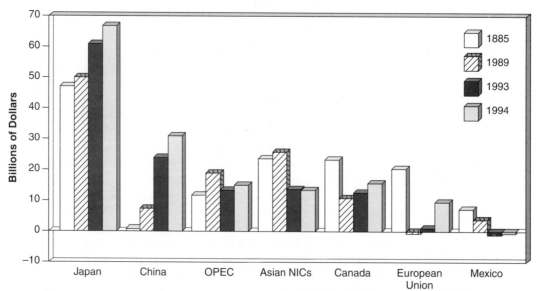

Figure 7.5   U.S. Trade Deficit with Principal Trading Partners, 1985, 1989, 1993, and 1994
Source: Adapted from U.S. Department of Commerce, "Highlights of U.S. Export and Import Trade," FT-990, December 1985: B-22-B23, C-26-C-27; U.S. Department of Commerce, "United States Foreign Trade, Summary of U.S. Export and Import Merchandise Trade, FT-900, February 1990: 5–6; U.S. Department of Commerce, *U.S. International Trade in Goods and Services*, FT-900 Supplement, December 1994: 8–17.

the view that they, like Japan, stimulated the export of American jobs and the dein-dustrialization of the U.S. economy.

Exploiting advantages in the cost of labor and access to advanced technology, the NICs achieved spectacular economic growth rates since the 1960s, compared with other Third World nations, by pursuing export-led rather than import-substitution industrialization policies. A successful export-led strategy requires access to First World markets. But the more successful it is, the more it stimulates protectionist sentiments in the importing countries. Thus early in 1989 the United States removed the Asian NICs from the list of Global South countries entitled to preferential trade treatment (described later), which placed them on a more equal footing with the industrial societies of the North.

Foreign development aid has long been an instrument used to assist economic growth and development in the Global South, but "trade, not aid" has been a persistent Southern plea, as the South feels it has systematically been denied access to markets in developed countries through tariff and nontariff barriers alike. The Multifiber Arrangement (MFA) is a classic case in point. Designed in the 1950s as a mechanism to protect U.S. textile producers from Far Eastern imports, the scheme today is an elaborate market-sharing arrangement among dozens of textile-producing countries which effectively denies access to others. Because textiles are among the simplest semi-manufactures that countries of the Global South aspiring to export-led growth might hope to ship abroad, the MFA is a blatantly discriminatory barrier to free trade. The Uruguay Round proposed to dismantle the Multifiber Arrangement, but the agreement finally reached provides instead for a gradual phase-out over a ten-year period. Only then will clothing and textiles be fully integrated into the free-trade system.

In one sense, developing nations are simply unwitting victims of the rise of protectionist sentiment in the industrial world, which is occurring at precisely the time as many in the Global South are attempting to compete in the global marketplace and in many of the goods of special interest to them. But the Global North also believes "that developing countries have invaded the trading system, numerically and in terms of demands that undermine its integrity. They have fought hard for modifications in the rules to exempt themselves from any disciplines, while at the same time expecting to benefit fully from industrial countries' obligations" (Low 1993).

Preferential (not most-favored-nation) trade treatment is an example of an exemption Third World nations sought in their drive to overcome the obstacles they face in gaining access to industrial markets. The argument is that preferential treatment would enable them to build diversified export industries capable of competing on equal terms with those in the North. In partial response to that plea, the United States established (by the Trade Act of 1974) a Generalized System of Preferences (GSP), thereby joining most other industrialized nations in maintaining a system of nonreciprocal and nondiscriminatory tariff preferences for developing nations.

Despite this apparent concession, the Tokyo Round (which approved the principle of nonreciprocity on which the GSP scheme rested) failed to grapple with the protectionist sentiments in the Global North that were often directed at products in which some developing nations already enjoyed comparative advantages, such as clothing, footwear, textiles, and steel. Following the insistence of the United States, it also included a "graduation clause," stipulating that as developing countries reached higher levels of development, they would be given less special treatment and be forced to compete on a more equal footing with Northern states. The United States used this principle to revoke the Asian NICs' preferential treatment in 1989.

The GSP is a specific example of the specialized trade treatment developing nations have sought because of their development status. The graduation concept reflects Northern sentiments that developing nations need increasingly to move toward accepting greater obligations within the trade regime. By 1982, when planning for the Uruguay Round began in earnest, the principle was established that developing nations should no longer receive separate negotiation treatment. And by the time Uruguay actually commenced, many had pursued greater liberalization on their own (Low 1993). Meanwhile, the United States has become increasingly sensitive to the concept of "reciprocity," which it sees as essential to the realization of "fair trade." That goal is now central to its trade policy.

The Second World Again

The economic isolation of East from West that began in the early Cold War continued for more than a decade. Not until the late 1960s and early 1970s did the Soviets and the Americans begin to shift significantly their views about commercial ties with "the other side." The change was especially evident once détente became official policy on both sides of the Cold War divide. Trade now became part of a series of concrete agreements across a range of issues that would contribute to what Nixon's national security adviser Henry Kissinger described as a "vested interest in mutual restraint" on the part of the superpowers. For their part, the Soviets saw expanded commercial intercourse as an opportunity to gain access to the Western credits and technology necessary to rejuvenate the sluggish Soviet economy. In addition, grain imports from the United States enabled the Soviets to supplement shortfalls in their own agricultural production. The contrast with the 1950s was striking.

The high point of détente was achieved at the 1972 Moscow summit when the two Cold War antagonists initialed the first Strategic Arms Limitation Talks (SALT) agreement. SALT was certainly the cornerstone of détente, but expanded East-West trade was part of the mortar. A joint commercial commission was established at the summit, whose purpose was to pave the way for the granting of most-favored-nation status to the Soviet Union and the extension of U.S. government-backed credits to the Soviet regime. Neither happened as envisioned. Over the objection of President Ford and Secretary of State Kissinger, Congress made MFN status contingent on the liberalization of communist policies regarding Jewish emigration. Restrictions were also placed on Soviet (and Eastern European) access to American government-backed credits. These further strained the economic ties détente once sought to nurture and contributed to a mounting Eastern debt to the West (see Stevenson and Frye 1989). Eventually Soviet leaders repudiated the 1972 trade agreement in response to what they regarded as an unwarranted intrusion into Soviet domestic affairs.

Because of congressional constraints, East-West trade stagnated in the second half of the 1970s. Furthermore, the Carter administration's commitment to a worldwide human rights campaign often led to American attacks on the Soviet Union's human rights policies. Soviet leaders' appetite for high-technology U.S. goods was seen as a source of leverage to realize American human rights objectives. As Soviet-American relations deteriorated, Carter used economic instruments to counter the Soviet Union's continued high levels of military spending; its overseas military buildup and arms transfers to the Third World; its backing of Cuban intervention in Angola, Ethiopia, and elsewhere in Africa; and its invasion of Afghanistan in late 1979. Thus the commercial ties that a decade earlier had been built to cement détente became the victim as well as the instrument of renewed Soviet-American rivalry.

Carter and his predecessors tried to use trade as an inducement to Soviet leaders to moderate their foreign policy behavior and to improve East-West relations. The Reagan administration, in contrast, saw trade as a stick that could be used to punish Soviet leaders for unwanted behavior (Spero 1990). Thus restrictions earlier placed on the export of energy technology to the Soviet Union were stiffened. The administration also pushed in Cocom for more stringent controls on the export of strategic goods to the Soviet Union. Largely in response to domestic pressures, however, it also saw fit to lift a grain embargo Carter had imposed following the invasion of Afghanistan.

As with its predecessors, the Reagan administration found that U.S. allies did not always share its views on how to deal with the Soviet Union in the economic sphere. Many Europeans saw U.S. policy as hypocritical in that it attempted to pressure its allies into not selling the Soviets energy technology at the same time as the United States sold them grain. Eventually a face-saving measure was devised that enabled the United States to back away from an unwinnable issue without conceding it had lost. The stage was now set for a more accommodative commercial policy that would parallel developments in the security sphere leading to the end of the Cold War and the eventual breakup of the Soviet Union into new states that would seek entry into the institutions comprising the Liberal International Economic Order.

Where the republics of the former Soviet Union (FSU, in the idiom of international diplomacy) and the countries of eastern Europe (emerging economies) will ultimately fit into the Liberal International Economic Order is by no means clear. Most moved rapidly toward active involvement in GATT and the IMF, the principle institutions of the LIEO, and Russia (clearly the largest economy of the lot) was granted observer status in the elite club, the Group of Seven (G-7). Cold War curbs on the sale of high-technology goods were lifted, and Cocom—the multilateral group that for decades had monitored security-sensitive exports to the communist states—was shut down.[13] Western aid—particularly from Germany—was generous by some standards, but it was clearly insufficient for the tasks that leaders of the former Soviet Union and the New Independent States face. Democratization was jolted in several eastern European countries, where former communist officials were elected to office, and privatization and the development of market economies were challenged everywhere. This was especially evident in Russia, where *mafiya* groups subverted government efforts to modernize the economic system (Handelman 1994). Thus much of the former Soviet bloc bore more resemblance to the developing nations of the Third World than to the industrial nations of the West with which they sought to become increasingly intertwined. As before, Russia and other states of the former Second World have not been a central players in the trade and monetary issues that have animated the Global North and South since the end of the Cold War.

From Free Trade to Fair Trade

Historically, the United States has espoused a laissez-faire attitude toward trade issues, believing that market forces are best able to stimulate entrepreneurial initiatives and investment choices. During the 1980s, however, it came to believe that "the playing field is tilted." This implies that American businesspeople are unable to compete on the same basis as others—notably the continental European states, Japan, and the more advanced developing countries, where governments, playing the role of economic nationalists, routinely intervene in their economies and play entrepreneurial and developmental roles directly. Senator Lloyd M. Bentsen, a long-time advocate of free trade and later Secretary of the Treasury in the Clinton administration, captured the shifting sentiment toward free trade during the debate over the 1988 omnibus trade act: "I think in theory, it's a great theory. But it's not being practiced, and for us to practice free trade in a world where there's much government-directed trade makes as much sense as unilateral disarmament with the Russians."

Not only were sentiments toward free trade shifting rapidly in the United States—at one time during the 1980s some 300 hundred bills were pending before Congress that offered protection to almost every industrial sector[14]—but signs of closure characterized the trade system itself. By the time the Uruguay Round of trade negotiations began in 1986, the system was rife with restrictive barriers, subsidies, invisible import restraints, standards for domestic products that foreign producers could not meet, and other unfair trade practices that went beyond GATT's principles (see also Anjaria 1986). To cope with the changing environment at home and abroad, the United States mounted a series of responses.

The Multilateral Venue

Other nations were not quick to accept the United States' analogy of an uneven playing field skewed to its disadvantage. As one observer put it caustically, "the more inefficient and backward an American industry is, the more likely the U.S. government will blame foreign countries for its problems" (Bovard 1991). Still, other nations were sensitive to the need to keep protectionist sentiments in the United States at bay. Because U.S. imports stimulated the economic growth of its trade partners, they conceded that new trade talks (the Uruguay Round) should not only consider traditional tariff issues and the new protectionism—particularly how to bring VERs under multilateral management—but also issues traditionally outside the GATT framework of special concern to the United States due to its comparative advantages.

The new issues included barriers to trade in services (insurance, for example), intellectual property rights (such as copyrights on computer software, music, and movies), and investments (stocks and bonds). Agriculture also remained a paramount issue to the United States, as the economic well-being of American agriculture depends more heavily on exports than do other sectors of the economy. The "Cairns group," a coalition of fourteen industrial and developing-nation agricultural exporters first organized in 1986 to press for trade liberalization in agriculture, also urged U.S. action (see Tussie 1993).

Because world trade in agriculture evolved outside of the main GATT framework, it was not subject to the same liberalizing influences as industrial products (Low 1993; Spero 1990). Agricultural trade policy is especially controversial because it is deeply enmeshed in the domestic politics of producing states, particularly those, like the United States and some members of the European Union, for which the global market is an outlet for surplus production. At the core of differences on agricultural trade are the enormous subsidies that governments of some leading producers pay farmers to keep them competitive internationally. In 1986, for example, the European Community spent over $20 billion, or more than two-thirds of its budget, on agricultural subsidies. The United States spent about $30 billion in farm support programs, more than the net income of U.S. farms (Wallis 1986, 2). Yet the perceived need for subsidies reflects fundamental structural changes in the global system of food production. New competitors have emerged among Global South producers, and markets traditionally supplied by Northern producers have shrunk as a consequence of technological innovations enabling expanded agricultural production in countries that previously experienced food deficits.

During the Uruguay Round the United States aggressively proposed to phase out all agricultural subsidies and farm trade protection programs within a decade. Its proposal gained some support but faced stiff opposition from the EC (particularly France), which viewed it as unrealistic (Low 1993). Sharp differences on the issue led to an impasse in the Uruguay Round negotiations, causing the conclusion of the talks to be delayed beyond the original 1990 target date. Three years later, when the talks finally concluded, the United States could claim a measure of success on agricultural issues, as the EC and others agreed to new (but limited) rules on export subsidies, domestic subsidies, and market access. Some domestic groups in the United States worried that increased agricultural efficiency would eventually drive small American farmers out of business. But for the industry as a whole liberalization was perceived as more beneficial to American farmers than to producers elsewhere due to the Americans' greater efficiency.

Liberalization of agricultural trade was also expected to benefit agricultural exporters in the developing world by providing them with greater access to agricultural markets in industrial world producer states. (The eventual dismantling of the Multifiber Arrangement, noted earlier, should also benefit developing-nation textile exporters.) This in turn was expected to encourage them to open their own markets to other products produced in industrial nations. Developing nations already account for nearly two-fifths of U.S. exports; more importantly, they have accounted for nearly 80 percent of U.S. export growth in recent years.

As we noted earlier, by the time of the Uruguay Round many developing nations had initiated trade liberalization on their own, thus coming to participate more fully in the GATT trade regime. In some areas, however, long-standing North-South differences continued to color issues of importance to the United States (see the essays in Tussie and Glover 1993). Trade-related intellectual property rights (TRIPs)—one of the new issues confronted at Uruguay—is among them. The United States (and other Northern nations) wanted protection of copyrights, patents, trademarks, microprocessor designs, and trade secrets, as well as prohibitions on unfair competition. Developing nations vigorously resisted these efforts along with the concept of "standardized intellectual property norms and regulations throughout the world" (Low

1993).[15] Thus little significant headway was made on TRIPs. U.S. efforts regarding trade-related investment measures (TRIMs) and services (such as banking and insurance) and the Clinton administration's efforts to abolish European restrictions on non-European produced movies and television programs (read "American") also met widespread resistance during the negotiations.

The United States had hoped during the Uruguay Round to modernize GATT itself. An agreement to replace GATT with a new *World Trade Organization (WTO)* embodied that goal. The WTO will seek to extend GATT's coverage to products, sectors, and conditions of trade not adequately covered at present. The new organization will enhance GATT's dispute settlement procedures by making the findings of its arbitration panels binding on the domestic laws of participating nations (GATT's findings are not binding) (Rabkin 1994). It also is intended to help eliminate the problem of "free-riding" by being available only to states that belong to GATT, subscribe to all of the Uruguay Round agreements, and make market access commitments. Under the GATT system, free-riding is possible when states (usually small ones) are able to benefit from trade liberalization without having to make contributions of their own (see Hufbauer and Schott 1985; Low 1993; Prestowitz 1993). Finally, the WTO embodies certain "legislative powers" that may remove the need for prolonged negotiations resulting in large "packages" embracing multiple concessions, as in previous multilateral negotiating sessions. Now it may be possible simply to amend existing rules one at a time (Rabkin 1994).

Proponents of the WTO saw it as a useful element in states' efforts to keep the instrumentalities of the liberal trade regime consonant with state practices in the increasingly complex world political economy. It was not without detractors, however. WTO's dispute settlement procedures, for example, could undermine the ability of American presidents to retaliate against unfair trade practices under section 301 of the 1974 Trade Act (discussed below) (Prestowitz 1993). More broadly, the very title of the new organization suggested potential threats to American decision-making prerogatives which sparked the ire of some critics, particularly conservatives. Witness presidential hopeful Pat Buchanan's reaction: "The glittering bribe the globalists are extending to us is this: enhanced access to global markets—in exchange for our national sovereignty" (cited in Rabkin 1994).

Environmentalists—often on the other end of the political spectrum—also worry about the WTO. They fear it will further erode their ability to protect hard-won domestic victories against the charge that environmental protection laws restrict free trade.[16] GATT's controversial rulings that a U.S. ban on the import of tuna caught by merchants who also ensnare encircling dolphins is illegal—popularly known as the "GATTzilla versus Flipper" debate—symbolizes their apprehensiveness.[17] Environmentalists worry that the World Trade Organization will perpetuate the "elitist" character of GATT (dispute panelists are appointed, not elected, and make their decisions behind closed doors), and that controls in a wide range of areas with environmental implications will be expanded and nontariff trade barriers designed purposely to protect the environment (including dolphins) disallowed. In short, they argue that the environment and sustainable development were given insufficient attention in the design of the WTO (French 1993).

Aggressive Unilateralism

At the same time that the Clinton administration pushed the Uruguay Round of multilateral negotiations to successful conclusion it pursued policies toward Europe, Japan, and others best characterized collectively as the practice of aggressive unilateralism. The approach contrasted sharply with the laissez-faire attitudes of the Bush administration, captured with the quip allegedly made by one of its economic advisers: "Potato chips, computer chips, what's the difference. They're all chips. A hundred dollars of one or a hundred dollars of the other is still a hundred dollars."

Aggressive unilateralism embraces the notion that it matters very much what an economy produces. Its elements as practiced by the Clinton administration included the following:

- Threatening the European Community with trade sanctions if it pursued a new government procurement policy alleged to discriminate against U.S. companies.
- Threatening South Korea with trade sanctions unless it permitted AT&T to compete equally with Korean firms in seeking equipment sales.
- Threatening Japan with a 100 percent increase in tariffs on luxury cars exported to the United States unless the Japanese market is opened to U.S. manufacturers.
- Accusing the European Community of unfairly subsidizing production of Airbus, rival of Boeing-built commercial jetliners.
- Intervening on behalf of Boeing to secure a $6 billion contract for the sale of commercial jetliners to Saudi Arabia.
- Redirecting Pentagon research monies to the commercial sector.
- Reinstating Super 301 provisions of the 1988 omnibus trade act to permit rapid U.S. trade retaliation following the breakdown of trade talks with Japan.
- Threatening to withdraw China's most-favored-nation trade status unless specific criteria for respecting human rights were met.

The administration's posture toward China fulfilled a campaign promise that smacked of Cold War tactics—the belief that tough economic pressure can secure explicitly political ends. Carter and Reagan had both tried this, and both failed. In the end, so did Clinton.

Clinton had tried to meet strong congressional dissatisfaction with China's human rights policies in the aftermath of the 1989 Tiananmen Square massacre of prodemocracy demonstrators by spelling out in a May 1993 executive order the conditions China would have to meet to retain its preferred trade status. As the deadline approached a year later, it was clear that little had been done to meet those conditions and that various face-saving gestures had also failed. Faced with the reality that China had now become one of the nation's most important trade partners (see Figures 7.3 and 7.5), the administration unabashedly abandoned its human rights posture and earlier campaign promise. Secretary of State Warren Christopher announced that a policy of "comprehensive engagement" would become the focus of U.S. policy, calling it "the best way to influence China's development." The purported change echoed the Bush administration's earlier emphasis on market incentives toward political liberalization—an approach Clinton viciously attacked during the 1992 presidential campaign. Meanwhile, critics charged that profits had won out over principles. Later, however, Clinton could claim victory when, after threatening to impose higher tariffs on Chinese goods, he won a commitment from the Chinese to halt their piracy of compact disks and other items in violation of intellectual property rights standards.

The administration's trade policies toward Europe, Japan, and Korea bore some resemblance to its China policies in that they rested on the premise that economic security and national security go hand in hand in the post-Cold War world. As Clinton declared early in his administration, "It is time for us to make trade a priority element of American security." "Security" and "war" would often punctuate administration rhetoric and others' interpretations of it (see Friedman 1994b), but its actions are better understood through the lens of *fair trade*, *managed trade*, and *strategic trade*. Together they infused American trade policies with a distinctly neomercantilist cast.

Fair Trade   *Fair trade* implies that American exporters should be given the same access to foreign markets as foreign producers enjoy in the United States (see also Prestowitz 1992; Stokes 1992–1993). As Clinton put it, "We will continue to welcome foreign products and services into our market, but insist that our products and services be able to enter theirs on equal terms." Fair trade is often closely associated with "reciprocity," which increasingly in recent years has meant "equal market access in terms of outcomes rather than equality of opportunities." Together the two concepts lay the basis for an interventionist trade policy (Low 1993).

Section 301 of the 1974 Trade Act embodies this interventionist thrust. It permits the United States to retaliate against others engaged in "unreasonable" or "unjustifiable" trade policies that threaten American interests. Liberalization, however—not retaliation—is the primary purpose of Section 301, and this was achieved in about one-third of the cases raised between 1975 and 1990. Retaliation occurred in about one-tenth of them (Low 1993, 88–89).

Frustrated with the tedious process of resolving disputes under Section 301, but especially with what it regarded as trade practices believed responsible for the persistent U.S. trade deficit, Congress incorporated "**Super 301**" in the 1988 Omnibus Trade and Competitiveness Act. Unlike the earlier provision, Super 301 *required* that the president identify countries engaged in unfair trade practices with a view toward negotiation to seek remedies or face U.S. retaliation on an expedited basis. Although Super 301 was "almost unanimously viewed abroad as a clear violation of the GATT" (Walters and Blake 1992), Congress's resentment of the trade policies of Japan and the four Asian NICs was glaring.

Japan is often viewed in the United States as the preeminent neomercantilist power, based on the belief that its persistent balance-of-trade and payments surpluses result from an intimate government-business alliance that tilts the playing field in its favor. The continuing trade imbalance between Japan and the United States—which runs into the tens of billions of dollars each year and climbed to a record $65.7 billion in 1994—reinforces the belief that Japan's trade policies are inherently detrimental to

American business interests (see Fallows 1994b; for a contrasting view, see Emmott 1994; also Bergsten and Noland 1993).

There is little doubt that Japan's protectionist trade policies inhibit penetration of its market by American firms. Japanese business practices, including cross-share holding patterns known as *keiretsu* which result in informal corporate bargains, also make foreign penetration difficult regardless of government policies. American consumers, however, continue to show marked preferences for Japanese products not shared by their counterparts on the other side of the Pacific Basin, where cultural traditions reinforce the view that foreign products are ill-suited to the Japanese consumer. It is a perception American producers sometimes feed—as with American automakers' practice until recently of building only cars with the steering wheel on the left rather the right, which fits the British driving pattern followed in Japan.

American exports to Japan have increased considerably in recent years, in part a product of continuing negotiations between the two countries. Among them was the Structural Impediments Initiative (SII), launched in 1989 shortly after Japan was named as one of three countries engaged in unfair trade practices under Super 301 (Brazil and India were the others). Despite a $49 billion trade deficit with Japan, the Bush administration chose not to retaliate against Japan the following year, as Super 301 permitted.

The Bush administration was clearly uncomfortable with the confrontational, unilateralist thrust of Super 301—not one case of retaliation was initiated (see Low 1993)—and thus was pleased to see it expire after 1990. Four years later the Clinton administration revived the section's provisions via executive agreement following the breakdown of the latest series of Japanese-American trade negotiations known as the "framework" talks.

Managed Trade   The framework agreement was reached at the 1993 Tokyo G-7 summit. Once the negotiations began, the United States insisted on using certain quantitative indicators to monitor whether Japan was in fact opening its markets in various sectors, including autos, telecommunications, insurance, and medical equipment. Its intransigence on the issue led to a breakdown of negotiations in early in 1994, as the government of Prime Minister Morihiro Hosokawa retorted that numerical standards would require Japan to engage in ***managed trade***[18]—in effect responding to a demand for a minimum U.S. share of the Japanese market.

Clinton would later deny that the United States ever demanded numerical import quota commitments from Japan. All the United States sought, according to U.S. Trade Representative Mickey Kantor, was an agreement on "objective criteria" to show progress in opening up Japan's markets to all foreign (not just American) goods. Japan did eventually agree that quantitative measures could be used to measure progress in opening Japanese markets in insurance, glass, and medical and telecommunications equipment, but it refused to guarantee the United States any specific market shares—thus side-stepping the contentious issue of "numerical targets." Furthermore, no agreement was reached on automobiles and auto parts. To keep pressure on the Japanese in these markets, the administration promptly set in motion the process that could lead to sanctions, although it chose to use Section 301 of the 1974 Trade Act rather than the more aggressive Super 301 provision. The administration then threatened stiff tariff increases on luxury automobiles produced by Japanese automakers for the U.S. market unless U.S. car companies and spare-parts manufactureres were guaranteed greater access to the Japanese market.

An eleventh-hour agreement was reached in the summer of 1995, in which both sides claimed victory. The United States claimed the agreement set "numerical benchmarks" that would yield measurable results in opening the Japanese market; Japanese negotiators in turn were quick to say that they had agreed to no numbers and would bear no responsibility for achieving any numerical targets. Thus, the latest round of the increasingly tense U.S.-Japanese trade dispute ended without an definitive deal—as had happened so often in the past.

Managed trade between the United States and Japan is not without precedent. In 1986 the Reagan administration made an agreement with Japan (which Bush renewed in 1991) to guarantee foreign companies 20 percent of the Japanese semiconductor market. Bush also led a trade mission to Japan that included a contingent of American auto executives, thus giving it an unabashedly neomercantilist coloration. The mission seemed to confirm the view expressed by Leon Brittan, competition commissioner of the European Community, that the Bush administration was "drifting toward a preference for managed trade" and that it sought "a certain share of the Japanese market on political rather than commercial grounds." The mission failed to accomplish much, but it left the distinct impression that the United States was just another "ordinary" power: "For the leader of the free world to travel to Tokyo with his nation's businessmen in tow was a jarring sight. This was not a leader with a vision of a New World Order; it was merely a man out to make a buck for this country" (Murray 1992–1993). Shortly thereafter the speaker of the Japanese Diet (parliament), Yoshio Sakurauchi, described the United States as "Japan's subcontractor" and American workers as lazy and illiterate. "Japan bashing" in turn became a popular American sport.

Just as the charge of "managed trade" had precedents in previous Republican administrations, the breakdown of the Clinton-Hosokawa talks led commentators to draw parallels between the Reagan administration's first-term approach to the Soviet Union on arms control and the Clinton administration's approach to Japan on trade policy (Hoagland 1994b). In both cases each partner sought a fundamental change in behavior on the part of the other. And in both cases domestic public opinion was antagonistic toward the other side, which meant that *no* agreement was better than a controversial one. Eventually, when Soviet-American relations began to warm, Reagan would repeatedly say "Trust but verify." Similarly, Mickey Kantor described his philosophy toward Japan with the phrase "Trust but quantify."

Sensitive to criticisms of the administration's tactics and objectives, Deputy Treasury Secretary Roger C. Altman defended them in *Foreign Affairs*:

> The strained relations between the Japan and the United States cannot be explained by spurious charges that the Clinton administration is pushing managed trade, capitalizing on anti-Japanese sentiment to score domestic political points or needlessly bashing Japan over economically meaningless international surpluses. Rather, the tensions arise from two fundamental and related developments: changed American priorities and the pronounced drag of Japan's huge current account surplus on global demand, economic expansion and job creation. (Altman 1994, 2; for a rejoinder, see Bhagwati 1994)

Altman also noted that "The Japanese government that berates the United States on charges of managed trade has long been in the business of targeting market outcomes itself."

Despite Altman's spirited—even hawkish—defense, other nations were suspicious of U.S. motives, fearing that the United States sought a bilateral deal with Japan that would come at their expense. European governments were especially critical of the determination of the United States to threaten unilateral sanctions in the auto-industry dispute rather than let the new World Trade Organization settle the issue. Similarly, Peter Sutherland, head of GATT, warned of the dangers of managed trade: "Governments should interfere in the conduct of trade as little as possible. Once bureaucrats become involved in managing trade flows, the potential for misguided decisions rises greatly."

Strategic Trade   Sutherland's views arguably apply even more strongly to the application of *strategic trade* to "level the playing field." Strategic trade is a form of industrial policy that seeks to create comparative advantages by targeting government subsidies toward particular industries. The strategy challenges the premises of classical trade theory and its touchstone, the principle of *comparative advantage*.

Classical international trade theory shows how international trade contributes to the welfare of trading partners. It attributes the basis for trade to underlying differences among states: Some are better suited to the production of agricultural products, such as coffee, because they have vast tracts of fertile land, for example, while others are better suited to the production of labor-intensive goods, such as consumer electronics, because they have an abundance of cheap labor.

Increasingly, however, economists now recognize that comparative advantages take on a life of their own.

> Much international trade . . . reflects national advantages that are created by historical circumstance, and that then persist or grow because of other advantages to large scale either in development or production. For example, the development effort required to launch a new passenger jet aircraft is so large that the world market will support only one or two profitable firms. Once the United States had a head start in producing aircraft, its position as the world's leading exporter became self-reinforcing. So if you want to explain why the U.S. exports aircraft, you should not look for underlying aspects of the U.S. economy; you should study the historical circumstances that gave the United States a head start in the industry. (Krugman 1990, 109)

If the contemporary pattern of international trade reflects historical circumstances, states may conclude it is in their interests to try to create advantages that will redound to the long-run benefit of their economies. Curiously, then, the logic of comparative advantage can itself be used to justify government intervention in the economy. Although the returns on strategic trade policies are often marginal (Krugman 1990), the fact that some states engage in such practices encourages others to do likewise. Indeed, the United States has become increasingly sensitive to the logic of strategic trade as the Soviet threat has ended and the U.S. power position compared with Japan and Germany, among others, has declined, thus making it more aware of the costs of free-riding by its Cold War allies and principal economic partners (Mastanduno 1991; see also Snidal 1991).

The Clinton administration's early decision to grant tax breaks and redirect government spending to high-tech industries to enhance their competitive advantages demonstrates its willingness to follow the path of others, which implies greater government involvement in and direction of particular economic sectors.[19] Clinton's attack on the EC's subsidies for the Airbus within a month of his inauguration marked in dramatic style the approach and was likely influenced by the thinking of his newly chosen chair of the Council of Economic Advisers, Laura D'Andrea Tyson. Tyson's book, *Who's Bashing Whom? Trade Conflict in High-Technology Industries* (1992)—which includes a detailed examination of the aircraft industry, among others—articulates a "cautious activist agenda" for enhancing American competitiveness along the lines strategic trade theory prescribes.

The success of government efforts to target subsidies toward particular ("strategic") industries is, as noted, mixed. While the record of Pacific Rim countries is arguably positive, it is also marked by some conspicuous failures. Notable among them is "the Japanese government's reluctance in the 1950s to support a little start-up company named Tokyo Tsushin Kogyo. The company is now known as Sony Corporation" (Blustein 1993). The key issue, then, is the ability of governments to pick "winners and losers."

In the particular case of the aircraft industry, Europeans are especially critical of the proposition that they grant subsidies while the United States does not. They correctly note that the commercial sector in the United States benefited enormously from the billions of dollars in military research and development the Pentagon spent during the Cold War, which helped to create an unequaled aerospace industry—commercial as well as military. Moreover, as the theory of strategic trade suggests, Europe's ability to compete in the industry is severely circumscribed by the advantages historical circumstances conferred on the United States. On the other hand, now that the Cold War has passed, the United States is no longer willing to permit the Europeans to "free ride" to a position that directly challenges it.

A concern for *competitiveness* ties together many of the Clinton administration's trade policy thrusts. Clinton pledged repeatedly during and after his 1992 campaign to create more "high wage, high skill" jobs for Americans. Government intervention in the economy—neomercantilism—flows naturally from that pledge. Thus in early 1994, after Clinton personally played a role in nudging Saudi Arabia toward a $6 billion commercial aircraft deal with Boeing Company and McDonnell Douglas Corporation rather than the European Airbus Industry consortium, the president would crow that this proves "that we can compete" (see also Barnes 1994).

Implicit in the Clinton administration's concern for competitiveness is the notion that trade competition from others—particularly Japan and low-wage producers on the Pacific Rim—has diminished the living standards of American workers. The policy implications are clear: Only an aggressive campaign to enhance U.S. competitiveness can reverse current trends.

Not everyone subscribes to this view of American economic woes and the policy corrective. Economist Paul Krugman, whose challenges to the assumptions of classical trade theory form much of the basis of current thinking about strategic trade, has been especially critical of what he calls the "dangerous obsession" with "competitiveness" (Krugman 1994a; see also Krugman 1994b). In particular, he is critical of the view that "the nation's real income has lagged as a result of the inability of many U.S. firms to sell in world markets" (Krugman and Lawrence 1994). He supports his controversial argument by noting that almost all of the decline in American living standards between 1973 and 1990 is explained by a decline in domestic productivity. The same is true in Europe and Japan. "In each case, the growth rate of living standards essentially equals the growth rate of domestic productivity—not productivity relative to competitors, but simply domestic productivity. Even though world trade is larger than ever before, national living standards are overwhelmingly determined by domestic factors rather than by some competition for world markets" (Krugman 1994a). "The moral," Krugman continues, "is clear":

> As a practical, empirical matter the major nations of the world are not to any significant degree in economic competition with each other. Of course, there is always a rivalry for status and power—countries that grow faster will see their political rank rise. So it is always interesting to *compare* countries. But asserting that Japanese growth diminishes U.S. status is very different from saying that it reduces the U.S. standard of living—and it is the latter that the rhetoric of competitiveness asserts. (Krugman 1994a, 35)[20]

Regionalism

In addition to multilateralism and aggressive unilateralism, a preference for building regional ecopolitical arrangements has marked the response of the United States to the changed and changing world political economy. Its manifestations include the Caribbean Basin Initiative, a program of tariff reductions and tax incentives designed to promote industry and trade in Central America and the Caribbean launched in 1984; free-trade agreements with Israel and Canada concluded in 1987 and 1989, respectively; and the North American Free Trade Agreement, signed by Canada, Mexico, and the United States in 1993.

Nafta's purpose was to intertwine Mexico and Canada with the United States as a prelude to a wider Western Hemispheric economic partnership, embodied in the Bush administration's Enterprise for the Americas Initiative. The agreement itself was an emotionally charged, high-profile issue during the 1992 presidential campaign and later, as Congress faced its approval. Third-party candidate Ross Perot made a big splash with the charge that a "giant sucking sound" would be heard as American jobs rushed to Mexico should Nafta be approved. And journalist-presidential hopeful Pat Buchanan charged that "NAFTA is not really a trade treaty at all, but the architecture of the New World Order. . . . NAFTA would supersede state laws and diminish U.S. sovereignty" (Buchanan 1993).

Nafta was directed in part (as was Buchanan's invective) against the European Union. Since the 1950s, European leaders have tried methodically to build a more united Europe, beginning especially in the economic sphere with a European-wide common market. In the mid-1980s they boldly committed themselves to create a single market by 1992—captured in the theme "Europe 1992"—and followed this with a new Treaty of Union, signed at the Dutch city of Maastricht, which anticipated the development of a single European currency and closer cooperation on foreign political and military affairs.

The latter goal was dashed by the crisis in the former Yugoslavia, which tested the EC's political resolve (see Brenner 1993). The former was postponed—perhaps quashed—by the European monetary crisis in the summer of 1992, which saw the EC's semifixed exchange rate system fail. The European Union nonetheless continues its relentless push toward a continent-wide economic union. Its latest moves included the admission of Austria, Finland, and Sweden, expanding the EU to a community of fifteen, and the conclusion of important agreements with Russia and several eastern European states that anticipate their eventual inclusion in a Europe-centered regional economy.

At present there are no visible signs that Japan wishes to build the same kinds of economic structures in the Pacific that Europe and the United States are pursuing. Indeed, Japan's imperial past continues to ignite passionate resentment and fear throughout much of Asia. The United States, meanwhile, has begun to court those nations. Shortly after the Clinton administration's Nafta victory—urged in part on the grounds that it would enhance U.S. competitiveness vis-à-vis Asia as well as Europe—Clinton hosted the Asia-Pacific Economic Cooperation (APEC) summit, where he preached the virtues of free trade and urged creation of a Pacific free-trade zone. The implication is that the administration now also wished to portray the United States as a Pacific power in the global competition for regional economic power (see also Bergsten 1994). A second summit in November 1994—which took place in Indonesia, once a fiery leader of the Third World nonaligned movement—sharpened that image, as the United States helped to stimulate an ambitious commitment by Asian and Pacific nations to develop a regional free-trade scheme by the year 2020. A month later, the United States and the thirty-three Western Hemispheric nations, meeting at the Summit of the Americas in Miami, also agreed to begin the process of building a free-trade zone, committing themselves to having a treaty in place and starting to carry it out by 2005. Preparations to bring Chile into Nafta an its next partner also moved forward.

Although Nafta and related regional initiatives were thought to be consistent with GATT's rules, analysts worried that they violated the principle of nondiscrimination underlying the liberal trade system, thus taking it one more step toward closure. In particular, many reasoned that the actions of the United States contributed to the further development of a regionally oriented political economy centered on Asia, Europe, and North America, which many analysts have long anticipated—and some have feared.[21] As the United Nations concluded in its *World Economic Survey 1991*, "Today the question is not whether these blocs will be formed, but rather how encompassing they will be and how to ensure that they will not harm the [global] trading system." The ultimate impact of the trend toward regionalization of the world political economy, both nationally and globally, remains uncertain (Kahler 1995). Pointing to the dispute settlement provisions of Nafta and the side agreements on the environment and other matters that Clinton negotiated to secure its approval by Congress, some analysts see that agreement as the progenitor of future efforts to negotiate the issues that will likely plague the world political economy in the years ahead (see, for example, Brecher 1993; Fox 1995; Hormats 1994). Moreover, bilateral and regional negotiations are likely to give the United States greater influence, as access to the American market is more important to smaller trading partners than access to their markets is to the United States.

Others are concerned with the impact that transforming economic relationships into regional centers may have on security relationships. One line of reasoning suggests that "bitter economic rivalry" is a likely outcome of a triangular world political economy because of fear that "there can be *enduring* national winners and losers from trade competition" (Borrus et al. 1992)—which is the logic underlying strategic trade theory. Strategic trade practices combined with the way technology develops and the changing relationship between civilian and military research and development will tempt states to "'grab' key technologies and markets before others can: Doing so would guarantee domestic availability of the industrial resources needed to field state-of-the-art military forces and eliminate the need to make unacceptable concessions." The result would be mercantile rivalry among the world's principal trading blocs, in which "fear of one another" may be the only force binding them together (Borrus et al. 1992).

Hegemon or Ordinary Power?

The neomercantilist challenge to the Liberal International Economic Order embodied in the rise of protectionist sentiment in the United States is in part a response to the nation's loss of control over its own economic well-being. It reflects a penchant to deal aggressively with the costs of complex interdependence—which, ironically, are products of the United States' success in promoting an open regime. The complexity of the system is itself a principal reason for the U.S. loss of control over its environment. Today there are more issues and more actors, and the weak are more assertive. The United States—still the dominant state—continues to have leverage over others. Indeed, it continues to maintain a comparatively open market for the products of others, seeks to maintain the flow of capital to would-be borrowers facing financial stress, and sometimes acts to coordinate macroeconomic policies, as would be expected of a hegemon. But its willingness to absorb the costs of leadership has waned, and its ability to affect global economic outcomes in preferred directions is simply not what it once was, as it has far less leverage over the whole system (Keohane and Nye 1989; see also Friedberg 1994). "Now," as political economist C. Fred Bergsten (1992b) has observed, "we are either in or very close to a world of three equal powers, none of which can dictate to the others or dominate the system." President Clinton confronted that uncomfortable reality at the 1994 G-7 summit, when his proposal to begin a new review of existing trade barriers was rebuffed by his European counterparts

No other country has emerged to assume the hegemonic role in the world political economy that the United States played in the decades following World War II—and none is on the horizon. The power, principles, and policies of the United States will thus continue to be pivotal. However, as geoeconomics vies with geopolitics as the defining feature of world politics, the absence of a single preponderant power and the corresponding decentralization of the world political economy will "require more complex mechanisms for negotiation and enforcement of rules." The rise of Europe and Japan also implies "a change in the assumptions about the roles of governments and firms" (Cowhey and Aronson 1992–1993).

Finally, the globalization of markets will require the development of new political institutions if states are to assert their sovereign prerogatives over transnational forces that increasingly seem to shape, rather than be shaped by, states' policies. All of these changes will challenge the United States, particularly as it plays two-level games—one focused on the world political economy in transition, the other on its own domestic economic challenges. As a consequence, the external environment is likely to provide an even more pronounced stimulus to and constraint on what the United States does abroad in the future than in the past.

NOTES

1. We confine the use of "hegemony" to America's role in the world political economy, recognizing, however, that there is a close interaction between economic and political dominance. As one analyst put it, "Hegemonic capacity has a military side as well as an economic one. In order to function, businesses need security and stability—the assurance that goods shipped will arrive, that contracts will be enforced, and that the world in general is predictable" (Schwartz 1994). For further discussions and contrasting viewpoints, see Friedberg (1989), Gilpin (1987), Huntington (1988–1989), Kennedy (1987), Rosecrance (1990), and Strange (1987). For a critique of the concept hegemony, including Goldstein's definition, see Nye (1990). For a discussion of why "primacy" may or may not matter, see Huntington (1993b) and Jervis (1993).

2. Our discussion of the international monetary and trade systems draws on Spero (1990). See also Schwartz (1994) and Walters and Blake (1992).

3. Recently declassified documents from the Truman and Eisenhower administrations clarify the role the United States played in encouraging aggressive Japanese exports to the United States. They also reveal how concern for communism in Asia stimulated choices based on political rather than economic criteria, whose consequences contributed to the ability of Japan to challenge the United States economically decades later. See Auerbach (1993) for a summary.

4. One, established in 1962 to discuss monetary issues, is known as the "Group of Ten." It comprises the finance ministers and central bank governors of the United States, Belgium, Canada, France, Great Britain, Italy, Japan, the Netherlands, Sweden, and Germany. Subgroups of the Group of Ten also now operate on a more or less continuing basis, including the Group of Three (the United States, Japan, and Germany), the Group of Five (the Group of Three plus France and Britain), and the Group of Seven (the Group of Five plus Canada and Italy).

5. Although the problems of debtor countries became less visible publicly, particularly as private investors superceded banks as the principal source of foreign capital (Gilpin 1994), large numbers of them remained severely strained. The World Bank (1995, 97) in 1995 classified fifty-one low- and middle-income countries as "severely indebted" and another thirty-three as "moderately indebted."

6. "The theology in government that a gradually declining dollar is good for U.S. competitiveness is a dangerous oversimplification," argued Jeffrey E. Garten, investment banker and author of *A Cold Peace: America, Japan and Germany and the Struggle for Supremacy*. He added that "there is no precedent in history where a major industrial power has been competitive while its currency was depreciating" (cited in Mufson, 1992). See also Givens (1995) and Kung (1995).

7. Horst Schulman, cited in Mufson (1992)—at the time director of the Institute of International Finance and a nominee to the board of the Bundesbank.

8. Although many states now subordinate international to domestic economic goals, Drucker (1994) argues that those who have done the reverse—subordinating domestic to international goals—have experienced the most robust economic growth in recent years.

9. Not all nontariff barriers are designed specifically to limit trade. Health and safety standards, for example, have come to be regarded as necessary and legitimate forms of government regulation. They have no necessary bearing on international trade, though they are sometimes used to limit external competition rather than to safeguard domestic welfare. It is often difficult, however, to distinguish legitimate nontariff barriers from regulations designed primarily to limit foreign competition and to protect domestic industries. Canada limited the import of canned beer from the United States, arguing that cans, unlike bottles, are not refillable and hence are undesirable environmentally. The United States, noting the Canadians' widespread use of cans for soft drinks, regarded the ban as a straightforward restraint on trade.

10. Neomercantilism is state intervention in economic affairs to enhance national economic fortunes. At a more technical level, it is "a trade policy whereby a state seeks to maintain a balance-of-trade surplus and to promote domestic production and employment by reducing imports, stimulating home production, and promoting exports" (Walters and Blake 1992).

11. The concept is from dependency theory, which classifies states into core (industrialized countries) and periphery (developing countries), according to their position in the international division of labor. For discussions, see Caporaso (1978), Shannon (1989), and Sklair (1991).

12. The fast-track procedures were first spelled out in the 1974 Trade Act to augment congressional implementation of agreements reached by the president. They help explain the unusual swiftness with which the Trade Agreements Act of 1979 sailed through Congress. The procedures themselves do not guarantee congressional approval, but they ensure that Congress will consider the agreements on an expedited, nonamendable basis, making it more likely that they will survive congressional scrutiny. The fast-track provisions relating to the Uruguay Round were scheduled to expire in December 1993. The Clinton administration used this and the threat that Congress might not renew the provision to its advantage in finally bringing the negotiations to conclusion. See Nivola (1990) for a discussion of Congress's role in devising trade policy.

13. The United States moved immediately to preserve the pattern of cooperation developed in Cocom, proposing that a new regime be created that would address new threats to global peace and security, such as terrorism and nuclear proliferation, and in other world regions, such as the Middle East. The membership of the new regime would be broadened and could include Russia. See "The New Trade Order: After Cocom" (1994).

14. For a detailed analysis of the congressional coalitions supporting various trade options toward the end of the Reagan administration, see Nollen and Quinn (1994). For an examination of the costs of protectionism, see Hufbauer and Elliott (1994).

15. Developing nations had earlier opposed inclusion of counterfeiting on the GATT agenda. The practice—which involves such things as Rolex watches, Apple computers, and photo-reproduced college textbooks—is widespread in much of the developing world. The United States has been especially critical of China, arguing that it engages in widespread piracy of computer software, musical compact disks, and video laser disks. Such practices are alleged to cost American companies as much as $1 billion a year (*New York Times*, July 24, 1994, p. 8).

16. The environmental consequences of free trade are subject to often vigorous dispute. For contrasting viewpoints, see Bhagwati (1993); Daly (1993); Esty (1993, 1994); and French (1993, 1994).

17. Interestingly, one of the first disputes heard by the WTO involved U.S. environmental standards for gasoline. Venezuela, a large exporter of petroleum products to the United States,

charged that U.S. requirements for cleaner-burning gasoline to reduce air pollution disadvantaged foreign producers by making gasoline produced in the United States cheaper than that produced abroad. Hence U.S. standards amounted to a restraint on trade.

18. In a free trade system, the government's role is limited to making rules governing commerce, whose direction is then determined by the behavior market forces. In a managed trade system, the government intervenes to steer trade relations in a predetermined direction as determined by the government itself.

19. The Clinton administration used a number of venues to promote its technology and industrial policy programs. Among them is the Advanced Technology Program, first authorized in 1988, which gives matching federal grants to companies developing cutting-edge technologies for the commercial sector, and the Technology Reinvestment Project, which gives matching grants for the development of dual-use (commercial and defense) technologies.

20. For a critique of Krugman's arguments and a rejoinder, see especially the essays by Clyde V. Prestowitz, Jr., Lester C. Thurow, Stephen S. Cohen, and Krugman in the July/August 1994 issue of *Foreign Affairs*. Also see Burton (1994) and Preeg (1994).

21. For a sampling, see Bergsten (1992a, 1992b); Borrus, Weber, Zysman, and Willihnganz (1992); Hormats (1994); and Mead (1990).

SUGGESTIONS FOR FURTHER READING

Bergsten, C. Fred, and Marcus Noland. *Reconcilable Differences? United States-Japan Economic Conflict*. Washington, D.C.: Institute for International Economics, 1993.

Esty, Daniel C. *Greening the GATT: Trade, Environment, and the Future*. Washington, D.C.: Institute for International Economics, 1994.

Isaak, Robert A. *Managing World Economic Change: International Political Economy*, 2nd ed. Englewood Cliffs, N.J.: Prentice-Hall, 1995.

Kenen, Peter B., ed. *Managing the World Economy: Fifty Years after Bretton Woods*. Washington, D.C.: Institute for International Economics, 1994.

Krugman, Paul. "Competitiveness: A Dangerous Obsession," *Foreign Affairs* 73 (March/April 1994): 28–44.

Low, Patrick. *Trading Free: The GATT and U.S. Trade Policy*. New York: Twentieth Century Fund Press, 1993.

Peterson, Erik R. "A Looming Collision of Capitalisms?" *Washington Quarterly* 17 (Spring 1994): 65–75.

Riley, Stephen P., ed. *The Politics of Global Debt*. New York: St. Martin's, 1993.

Sandholtz, Wayne, Michael Borrus, John Zysman, Ken Conca, Jay Stowsky, Steven Vogel, and Steve Weber. *The Highest Stakes: The Economic Foundations of the Next Security System*. New York: Oxford University Press, 1992.

Schwartz, Herman M. *States versus Markets: History, Geography, and the Development of the International Political Economy*. New York: St. Martin's, 1994.

Tussie, Diana, and David Glober, eds. *The Developing Countries in World Trade: Policies and Bargaining Strategies*. Boulder, Colo.: Lynne Rienner, 1993.

Tyson, Laura D'Andrea. *Who's Bashing Whom? Trade Conflict in High-Technology Industries*. Washington, D.C.: Institute for International Economics, 1992.

• • •

CHAPTER 8

AMERICANS' VALUES, BELIEFS, AND PREFERENCES: POLITICAL CULTURE AND PUBLIC OPINION IN AMERICAN FOREIGN POLICY

• • •

Democracies forgo certain [foreign policy] options by the nature of their societies and the whole set of ideals they represent.

Former Secretary of Defense James Schlesinger, 1985

Nobody can know what it means for a President to be sitting in that White House working late at night and to have hundreds of thousands of demonstrators charging through the streets. Not even earplugs could block the noise.

President Richard M. Nixon, 1977

Foreign policy is often seen as "above politics." Domestic interests are subservient to national interests, according to this view. When the security of the nation is at stake, Americans lay aside their partisan differences and support their government's policies. Politics, in short, stops at the water's edge.

Is this image realistic? Are foreign policy decisions made to further the nation's interests abroad without regard to domestic political consequences? Or are the foreign policy choices of political leaders influenced measurably by their anticipated effect on their popularity and power at home?

Picture for a moment the following scenario: The president's day begins in the Oval Office at 6:45 A.M. with briefings from his principal advisers. His chief domestic adviser opens with reports of growing budget deficits, sluggish economic growth, and a worsening balance-of-trade picture. The latest polls show that economic concerns and the smell of domestic political scandal have caused the president's popularity with the American people to weaken, and the president's opponents in the impending midterm congressional elections have accused him of pursuing a "wishy-washy" policy toward the nation's Middle East allies. The national security adviser is next, warning that CIA reports indicate the Middle East is about to erupt into armed conflict again and strongly urging immediate action to protect American interests and investments in the

• • •

region. A strategy session is quickly crammed into the day's agenda that includes separate consultations with representatives from the American Petroleum Institute and from groups calling themselves "Friends of Israel" and "Citizens for Arab Justice."

What factors will most influence a president confronted by such circumstances? Although we cannot get into a president's mind, we can guess what calculations are likely to shape his choices. When forced to reach a decision, it is reasonable to assume that he will ask himself, "What is the likely domestic repercussion of option *X* or *Y*? Will it enhance or erode my public standing? Will it undermine the strength of my political party? And might it convert, perhaps overnight, my political backers into antagonists?" Countless questions about the likely response of America's allies and adversaries in the region and elsewhere can also be anticipated, but the urge to give priority to the domestic consequences of foreign policy decisions may be irresistible. As one former policymaker concluded,

> [American leaders have shown a] tendency to make statements and take actions with regard not to their effect on the international scene to which they are ostensibly addressed but rather to their effect on those echelons of American opinion . . . to which the respective [leaders] are anxious to appeal. The questions, in these circumstances, [become] not: How effective is what I am doing in terms of the impact it makes on our world environment? but rather: How do I look, in the mirror of domestic American opinion, as I do it? Do I look shrewd, determined, defiantly patriotic, imbued with the necessary vigilance before the wiles of foreign governments? If so, this is what I do, even though it may prove meaningless, or even counterproductive, when applied to the realities of the external situation. (Kennan 1967, 53)

This viewpoint suggests that foreign policy decisions are likely to be guided more by a concern for the reactions they will provoke at home than abroad. Preserving one's power base and the psychological desire to be admired encourage foreign policy decisions designed to elicit favorable domestic responses. At the extreme, theater substitutes for rational policy choice; spin control becomes an overriding preoccupation.

Our purpose in this chapter and the next is to explore how American foreign policy is conditioned by the nation's internal or societal characteristics. Here we probe the impact on American foreign policy of Americans' beliefs about their political system and the way it operates, the *political culture*, and on their foreign policy attitudes and preferences, *public opinion*. Then in Chapter 9 we explore the roles that interest groups, the mass media, and presidential elections play in transmitting beliefs, attitudes, and preferences into the policy-making process. Throughout, we seek to understand how these societal forces constrain leaders' foreign policy behavior and when and how they encourage policy change.

We begin our inquiry by considering how the national attributes of and domestic conditions in the United States compare with other countries.

America in the Community of Nations: An Exceptional Case?   . . . .

The attributes that make the United States the kind of nation it is shape Americans' self-images and their perceptions of their nation's proper world role. In recent years many analysts have worried about the relative decline of the United States in the world community, making it more like an "ordinary" country (see Chapter 7). Still, the United States remains far from a typical society in the community of nations, as the data in Table 8.1, which compare its national attributes with others, make clear. It is the world's fourth-largest country in geographical size and third in population. It is endowed with vast natural resources, wealth, technology, and mobilized military power—a superpower among the democratic market economies comprising the Global North. Although the nation's economic growth, saving, investment, and energy efficiency rates are comparatively low, the nation as a whole is materially well off. Americans comprise less than 5 percent of the world's population, but in any given year they produce (and consume) a quarter or more of the world's total economic output. Personal wealth is far from equally distributed, but the "average" American is better off than his or her counterpart living almost anywhere else in the world.[1] Comparatively speaking, the American people also are highly urbanized, well educated, and have easy access to sophisticated communications systems. In short, American society and the quality of life the American people enjoy are in many respects quite unlike any other in the world.

There also is a downside evident in the United States. Violent crime is commonplace on American streets. The United States ranks Number 1 in intentional homicides in the Global North. It also ranks Number 1 in reported rapes, divorces, and percentage of the population in prison; it ranks Number 2 in drug crimes (*Human Development Report 1993*, 1993, 191–92). Such data point to a strained social fabric and a diminished quality of life.

It is tempting intuitively to assume that America's national attributes—particularly its enormous capabilities and resources—dictate its foreign policy objectives, but direct causal linkages are unwarranted. For example, simplistic, single-factor propositions such as "large, populous countries inevitably are imperialistic," "educated societies pursue peaceful foreign polices," or "militarized countries are necessarily expansionist" cannot be substantiated empirically. Too many counterexamples exist. Even the behavioral "law" that democracies do not wage war against one another requires some qualification (note the combatants in the War of 1812 and the American Civil War). Moreover, because most societal conditions remain stable over extended periods, they seldom precipitate policy change. More appropriately, national attributes such as size, resources, and economic conditions are best conceived as background factors that make some foreign policy options possible while limiting the feasibility of others.

Another way to think of the impact of societal factors is as data forming part of decision makers' perceptual maps of the world and their nation's place within it. Because images of American society may shape policymakers' thinking more strongly than some tangible conditions do (Dallek 1983), changes in American society—be they in demography, lifestyle, consumer habits, import dependence, domestic savings and investments, public and private indebtedness, or environmental quality—also may shape their views about the nation's proper international role and ultimately influence the kinds of policies and programs they propose.

The bases on which these perspectives on American society and its world rest also are rooted in policymakers' prior beliefs and experiences, as the nation's leaders are creatures of its political culture and cannot escape its influence. A closer examination of that culture is thus warranted.

TABLE 8.1 AMERICAN SOCIETY IN THE WORLD COMMUNITY:
THE COMPARATIVE U.S. RANK IN THE 1990s

National Attributes and Indicators	Date of Observation	U.S. Rank among Other Countries
Economic Status		
Gross national product (GNP)	1993	1
GNP per capita	1993	7
Average annual growth rate of gross domestic product (GDP)	1980–1990	48
Average annual growth rate of GNP per capita	1985–1993	66
Average annual rate of inflation	1985–1993	123
Share of exports in GDP	1993	141
Average annual growth rate of exports	1980–1993	42
Average annual growth rate of imports	1980–1993	19
Gross domestic savings (percent of GDP)	1991	58
Average annual growth rate of gross domestic investment	1980–1993	44
GDP output per unit of energy use	1993	66
Military Power		
Military expenditures (dollars)	1993	1
Military expenditures per capita	1993	6
Military expenditures as percentage of GNP	1993	38
Size of armed forces (active-duty personnel)	1993	3
Size of armed forces (per thousand people)	1993	49
Nuclear warheads and bombs (strategic and tactical)	1993	2
Resources		
Territorial size	1995	3
Population	1993	3
Energy consumption per capita	1993	2
Average annual growth in rate of energy production	1980–1993	77
Forest coverage as percent of land area	1990	74
Education		
Public expenditures per capita	1990	9
Public expenditures per student	1990	11
School age population per teacher	1990	12
Percent of school age population in school	1990	15
Average years of schooling	1992	1
Health		
Public expenditure per capita	1990	11
Population per physician	1990	32
Infant mortality rate	1993	21
Life expectancy at birth	1992	21
Percent of population with access to safe water	1990	1

National Attributes and Indicators	Date of Observation	U.S. Rank among Other Countries
Percent of population with access to sanitation	1990	25
Percent of infants with low birth weight	1991	17
Social		
Index of human development	1992	8
Average annual growth of population	1985–1993	140
Urban population (as percentage of total population)	1993	22
Females in labor force (percent of total)	1993	29
Radios (per thousand people)	1990	1
Televisions (per thousand people)	1990	1
Telephones (per thousand people)	1990–1992	3
Governmental		
Central government expenditures (dollars)	1993	1
Central government expenditures as percentage of GNP	1993	116

Source: U.S. Arms Control and Disarmament Agency, *World Military Expenditures and Arms Transfers 1993–1994* (Washington, D.C.: ACDA, 1995), p. 40; *The World Bank Atlas 1995* (Washington, D.C.: The World Bank, 1994), pp. 8–9ff; The World Bank, *World Development Report 1995* (New York: Oxford University Press, 1995), pp. 162–227; Ruth Leger Sivard, *World Military and Social Expenditures 1993* (Washington, D.C.: World Priorities, 1993), pp. 16, 43–47; United Nations Development Programme, *Human Development Report 1994* (New York: Oxford University Press, 1994), pp. 129–206.

Political Culture and Foreign Policy ·

The *political culture* of the United States refers to the political values, cognitions, ideas, and ideals about American society and politics held by the American people. Because these are both deep-seated and widely shared—as surely they are since most Americans have been socialized by the same cultural influences—the political culture concept taps a potentially important domestic source of American foreign policy. Indeed, it is commonplace to observe that "the nation was explicitly founded on particular sets of values, and these made the United States view itself as different from the nations of the Old World from which it originated" (McCormick 1992). Thus American foreign policy may be different from the policies of other states because the United States itself is unique.

What are the core values widely embraced in American society? Analysts' opinions on this question vary, not only because the existence of political subcultures and alienated groups makes it difficult to generalize safely about the degree to which some values are universally embraced, but also because the nation's "loosely bounded culture" (Merelman 1984) is fluid and pluralistic, allowing the individual citizen freedom to practice his or her own philosophy while still upholding a commitment to the nation. Thus the American political tradition emphasizes majoritarianism but simultaneously tolerates disagreement, parochial loyalties, and counterallegiances.

The Liberal Tradition

Despite diversity, and respect for it, certain norms dominate. There are values and principles to which most Americans respond regardless of the particular political philosophy they espouse. Although no single definition adequately captures its essence, the complementary assumptions that comprise "mainstream" American political beliefs may be labeled *liberalism*.[2] Basic to the liberal legacy is Thomas Jefferson's belief, enshrined in the Declaration of Independence, that the purpose of government is to secure for its citizens their inalienable rights to life, liberty, and the pursuit of happiness. The "social contract" among those who created the American experiment, which sought to safeguard these rights, is sacred. So, too, is the people's right to revolt against the government should it breach the contract. "Whenever any form of government becomes destructive of those ends," Jefferson concluded, "it is the right of the people to alter or abolish it."

In the liberal creed, as Jefferson affirmed, legitimate political power arises only from the consent of the governed, whose participation in decisions affecting public policy and the quality of life is guaranteed. Other principles and values embellish the liberal tradition, rooted in the seventeenth-century political philosophy of the English thinker John Locke. Included among them are individual liberty, equality of treatment and opportunity before the law ("all men are created equal"), due process, self-determination, free enterprise, inalienable (natural) rights, majority rule and minority rights, freedom of expression, federalism, the separation of powers within government, equal opportunity to participate in public affairs, and legalism ("a government of laws, not of men"). All are consistent with Locke's belief that government should be limited to the protection of the individual's life, liberty, and property through popular consent.

Together, these tenets form the basis of "popular sovereignty," which holds that "the only true source of political authority is the will of those who are ruled, in short the doctrine that all power arises from the people" (Thomas 1988). Abraham Lincoln's embrace of government of, by, and for the people affirms this fundamental principle. Because the American ethos subscribes enthusiastically to this principle, Americans think of themselves as a "free people."

American leaders—regardless of their partisan or philosophical labels—routinely reaffirm the convictions basic to the Lockean liberal tradition, as do the documents Americans celebrate on national holidays. Even those who regard themselves as political conservatives are in fact "traditional liberals who have kept faith with liberalism as it was propounded two hundred years ago" (Lipsitz and Speak 1989). Thus it is not surprising that other nations typically see few differences in the principles on which American foreign policy rests, even when political power shifts from one president to another or from one political party to the other.

Liberalism and American Foreign Policy Behavior

In a classic treatise on *The Liberal Tradition in America*, Louis Hartz (1955) argues that Lockean liberalism has become so embedded in American life that Americans may be blind to what it really is—namely, an ideology. The basis for the ideology of liberalism, so the reasoning holds, is the *exceptional American experience*. It includes the absence of pronounced class and religious strife at the time of the nation's founding, complemented by the fortuitous gift of geographic isolation from European political and military turmoil.

How have American exceptionalism and the ideology of Lockean liberalism affected American foreign policy? Strands of the linkages are evident in American diplomacy from the Monroe Doctrine to today (see Focus 8.1). To mobilize public support

Focus 8.1
AMERICAN EXCEPTIONALISM, THE LIBERAL TRADITION, AND CONTEMPORARY AMERICAN FOREIGN POLICY

• • •

"American exceptionalism expresses the conviction that the U.S. has a moral mission which flows out of its identity and which should guide its policies. Our exceptional character, which was originally used to justify disdaining alliances and quarrels of the so-called old world, has often been cited as the grounds to improve the world."

— U.S. Ambassador to the United Nations
Jeanne J. Kirkpatrick, 1984

"Our democracy encompasses many freedoms—freedom of speech, of religion, of assembly, and of so many other liberties that we often take for granted. These are rights that should be shared by all mankind."

— President Ronald Reagan, 1983

"America began free; its struggles were never to become free, but to stay free. Moreover, it never, for a single moment, lost its freedom. History, in other words, has made America naive. It has made Americans the luckiest and the least understanding people in the world. Indeed, the happy American experience with freedom may be at the root of the time-honored American inability to find its proper global place. The appeal of American isolationism and the awkwardness of American interventionism—both may be owed to the American unfamiliarity with the political oppression and social injustice that is the common experience of most of the rest of the world. Our natural consciousness of freedom has equipped us badly for the spreading of it. That may be history's bad joke on the American century."

— *The New Republic*, April 30, 1984

for U.S. actions abroad and endow policy decisions with moral value, American leaders often have cloaked their actions in the rhetoric of these ideological precepts. Principles such as self-determination and self-preservation are continually invoked to justify policy action, as "concern with wealth, power, status, moral virtue, and the freedom of mankind were successfully transformed into a single set of mutually reinforcing values by the paradigm of Lockean liberalism" (Weisband 1973).

Remaking the world in America's image is also hypothesized to have sprung from the nation's cultural traditions. The National Endowment for Democracy (NED), a controversial program launched by the Reagan administration in 1983, is a recent manifestation of a tradition with a long heritage. Its purpose is to encourage worldwide the development of autonomous political, economic, social, and cultural institutions to serve as the foundations of democracy and the guarantors of individual rights and freedoms (see Carothers 1994b).

An important synergism related to the promotion of democracy abroad is the set of beliefs that forges the premises of both classical democratic theory and capitalism into a deeply entrenched ideology of "democratic capitalism" (Greenberg 1985). While democracy and capitalism have common historical and philosophical roots, at home they have sometimes been in conflict, as capitalism in particular has led to "great inequalities of wealth and income" (McClosky and Zaller 1984). Abroad, however, the premises of democratic capitalism embedded in the American culture certainly help explain Americans' distaste for socialism and why they viewed Soviet communism as a threat to "the American way of life."

Scholars' and policymakers' ideas about how political development does (or should) occur also influenced the American foreign aid program during the Cold War. Their views illustrate the relationship between political culture and foreign policy.

Four assumptions derived from the exceptional American experience had an impact on the aid program: (1) Change and development are easy; (2) All good things go together; (3) Radicalism and revolution are bad; and (4) Distributing political power is more important than accumulating it (Packenham 1973). The first two assumptions were reflected in the economic approach of the U.S. aid program. It rested on the belief that fantastic results would flow from what in fact was a rather meager effort, and that economic development would beget political development and a host of "other good political things." The anticommunist, Cold War underpinnings of the aid program were rooted in the third assumption. And the democratic mentality that permeated the program derived from the fourth assumption, which rationalized the export of American political institutions. Together, these four assumptions, all drawn from the liberal tradition, gave coherence to otherwise disparate and inconsistent American policies.

Other illustrations can be found linking foreign policy predispositions to the influence of American values. It seems, then, that the question is not whether there is a relationship between culture and foreign policy, but how it operates. Precise answers to that question remain elusive, but one probable link can be found in the "law of anticipated reactions." The "law" posits that decision makers screen out certain alternatives because they anticipate that some options will be adversely received—an anticipation born of their intrinsic image of the American political culture which helps to define in their minds the range of permissible foreign policy goals and options. As one analyst put it, political culture's influence "lies in its power to set reasonably fixed limits to political behavior and provide subliminal direction for political action. . . . all the more effective because of [the] subtlety whereby those limited are unaware of the limitations placed on them" (Elazar 1970). Robert Kennedy's argument against using an air strike to destroy the missiles the Soviet Union surreptitiously placed in Cuba in 1962 illustrates this subtle screening process. As he himself described it:

> Whatever validity the military and political arguments were for an attack in preference to a blockade, America's traditions and history would not permit such a course of action. Whatever military reasons [former Secretary of State Dean Acheson] and others could marshal, they were nevertheless, in the last analysis, advocating a surprise attack by a very large nation against a very small one. This, I said, could not be undertaken by the U.S. if we were to maintain our moral position at home and around the globe. Our struggle against Communism throughout the world was far more than physical survival—it had as its essence our heritage and our ideals, and these we must not destroy.[3] (Kennedy 1971, 16–17)

This screening process has sometimes failed, of course—especially when principle clashes with power. Thus fear of communism helps to explain how a country committed to individual rights and liberties sometimes suppressed them in the name of national security. Similarly, the ascent of the United States to the status of a global power after World War II helps to explain how a nation committed to "limited government" nonetheless could permit the rise of an "imperial presidency," undeterred by the constitutional system of checks and balances, and justify the creation and maintenance of a gigantic peacetime military establishment (see Deudney and Ikenberry 1994).

We also must acknowledge that the ideas and ideals comprising the political culture are open to competing interpretations and are often in flux. Demographic and other developments coalesce to generate changes in otherwise durable values and beliefs (McClosky and Zaller 1984; Citrin et al. 1994). Because the political culture is not immutable, policymakers may feel less constrained by anticipated adverse reactions to their policy choices.

Political Culture in a Changing Society

Consider what happened to the 1960s' generation. Raised to believe that the United States was a splendidly virtuous country, young Americans found—through the Bay of Pigs invasion; racial discrimination in Selma, Alabama, and elsewhere; the assassinations of President Kennedy, his brother Robert, and Martin Luther King Jr.; and then Vietnam—that ideals were prostituted in practice. Outraged, large numbers of alienated Americans protested the abuses that undermined seemingly sacred assumptions. Simultaneously, the faith the American people placed in their political and other social institutions declined precipitously. American culture underwent a marked alteration as the nation wrestled with the violation of its traditional ideals, as illustrated in the book (and subsequent movie) *Born on the Fourth of July* (Kovic 1977).

With the political culture in flux, the climate of opinion encouraged policy change. A war ended ignominiously. Two American presidents were toppled: one (Lyndon Johnson) in the face of intense political pressure, the other (Richard Nixon) in disgrace. Legal barriers to racial discrimination were dismantled. New constraints were placed on the use, both overt and covert, of American force abroad; and the range of permissible action was reduced in ways that continue to shape policy thinking today. Thus it appears that changes in the political culture—whether they stem from public disillusionment, policy failure, or other causes—can affect the kinds of policies that leaders propose and the ways they are later carried out.

Today the core values comprising American society and its political culture face a new challenge: *multiculturalism*. "At the core of multiculturalism . . . is an insistence on the primacy of ethnicity over the individual's *shared and equal status as a citizen* in shaping his or her identity and, derivatively, his or her interests."

> Multiculturalism is based on the conviction that the image of America as a land of equal opportunity is not just exaggerated, but fraudulent. . . . An important purpose of multiculturalism is to justify the claims of subordinate ethnic groups to a larger share of society's goods, both tangible and intangible. From this ideological perspective, ethnicity should determine the allocation of all important benefits, such as jobs, government contracts, places in universities, legislative seats, control of the curriculum in schools and colleges, time on public television, and so forth. (Citrin et al. 1994, 9; see also Gilpin 1995)

Thus multiculturalism promotes communal rights, whereas liberalism rejects them in favor of individual rights and equal opportunity.

Multiculturalism clearly challenges the conception of the United States as a pluralistic society, one embodied in the nation's motto *e pluribus unum*—out of many, one. The motto reflects Americans' immigrant heritage which led President Reagan to describe the United States as an "island of freedom," a land placed here by "divine Providence" as a "refuge for all those people in the world who yearn to breathe free." It also reflects the conviction that diversity itself can be a source of national pride and unity, something no other nation has ever tried or claimed. This is what makes the American effort to build a multiethnic society "a bolder experiment than we sometimes remember" (Schlesinger 1992). The "melting pot" became a popular metaphor to describe the process that assimilated the newly-arrived into the dominant social and political ethos—that combination of ideas and ideals Swedish social scientist Gunnar Myrdal (1944) described over a half-century ago as "the American Creed."

Ironically, today's immigrant Americans often advocate multiculturalism and consequently challenge the European—and especially British—heritage on which the nation's civic culture rests. The 1980s saw a larger immigration into the United States than any time since the early twentieth century, and its composition was dramatically different. "In 1910 nearly 90 percent of immigrants came from Europe. In the 1980s more than 80 percent came from Asia and Latin America" (Schlesinger 1992, 120). Many of these non-Europeans "bring with them a resentment, in some cases a hatred, of Europe and the West provoked by generations of Western colonialism, racism, condescension, contempt, and cruel exploitation," observes Arthur Schlesinger, Jr. (1992). From this perspective, "the spread of Western culture is due not to any innate quality but simply to the spread of Western power. Thus the popularity of European classical music around the world—and, one supposes, of American jazz and rock, too—is evidence not of wide appeal but of 'the pattern of imperialism, in which the conquered culture adopts that of the conqueror.'"

With the American creed under stress, the nation's immigration policy also is under attack. Where migrants of European origin were once given preferential access, today the emphasis is on the skills migrants will bring with them, not their national origin. Meanwhile, many Americans have jettisoned the melting-pot metaphor. A 1993 *Newsweek* poll (August 9, 1993, p. 19) found that only 20 percent of the American people believe the United States is still a melting pot, compared with two-thirds who feel that today's immigrants "maintain their national identity more strongly." Sixty percent also expressed the view that immigration today is bad for the country, compared with a similar proportion who felt it had been good for the country in the past. These stark changes reflect, among other things, fear that immigrants threaten Americans' jobs and the widespread belief that many of them end up on states' welfare rolls. A proposal considered by the Republican-controlled House of Representatives modeled after California's Proposition 187, passed in 1994 in an attempt to exclude illegal immigrants from such publicly funded services as education and health care, is illustrative of the rising tide of resentment.

The foreign policy implications of multiculturalism are not easily assessed, largely because those in positions of power continue to subscribe to the still-dominant liberal ethos. As American society and culture change, however, leaders may find it increasingly difficult to build and maintain coalitions of support for internationalism and for particular elements of the internationalist paradigm, such as multilateral institutions or intervention on behalf of democracy. Thus multiculturalism poses yet another challenge to the maintenance of global activism in the post-Cold War world. Indeed, the end of the Cold War has actually facilitated its blossoming. The "the long war" against communism strengthened Americans' national identity, providing a "unifying dynamic [that] helped overcome ethnic and sectional differences and the ideological heritage of individualism" (Deudney and Ikenberry 1994). The end of the Cold War, in turn, encourages reemergence of ethnic and sectional differences previously muted in the anticommunist struggle. Thus, "more than in the recent past, future American foreign policy will have to be based on compromises among the advocates of rival ideologies and on shifting coalitions of supporters. While this situation may allow for flexibility in action, it also heralds a greater degree of instability and unpredictability with respect to the commitment of national energy and resources to foreign affairs" (Citrin et al. 1994; see also DeConde 1992).

As this conclusion suggests, the potential impact of changes in the dominant political culture on American foreign policy depends critically on American leaders. It depends on how those in positions of power perceive those changes and how their perceptions affect their corresponding political calculations. Thus a direct correspondence between principles and American diplomatic practice may not exist. Instead, cultural changes shape an atmosphere that makes new practices more acceptable and old ones less so. Americans' foreign policy beliefs and the opinions they express on the issues policymakers must grapple with daily help to define what is acceptable and what is not, as the changes in attitudes toward immigration that we have noted illustrate. It is appropriate, therefore, that we direct attention to the nature and impact of public opinion.

Public Opinion and Foreign Policy: An Overview . . . .

Public attitudes toward the nation's world role over the course of its history have alternated between periods of introversion and extroversion, between isolation from the world's problems and active involvement in shaping them to fit American preferences, much as American foreign policy itself has tracked these alternative postures. Public support for global activism dominated the Cold War era. The nature of internationalism has undergone fundamental changes, however, especially during and since the Vietnam War. Internationalism is now also under challenge in some quarters, as the world's "sole remaining superpower" grapples with its problems at home and its purposes abroad.

Coming to grips with the post–Cold War world will be difficult as the American people embrace sometimes competing foreign policy goals:

- They favor global activism but oppose sending economic and military aid to other nations.

- They yearn for peace through strength but are wary of international institutions.

- They fear nuclear weapons and their proliferation and support efforts to reach negotiated arms agreements with the nation's present and former adversaries.

- They oppose the use of force abroad; still, they back presidents when they choose force of arms and prefer military victory to limited war.

- They worry about the impact of free trade on their jobs, and yet many are willing to open the United States to broader involvement in the world political economy.

Little wonder that the role public opinion plays in shaping the nation's conduct is poorly understood and often suspect, and why policymakers sometimes disparage it. John F. Kennedy's view, as described by his aide, Theodore C. Sorensen (1963), is a timeless insider's view: "Public opinion is often erratic, inconsistent, arbitrary, and unreasonable—with a compulsion to make mistakes. . . . It rarely considers the needs of the next generation or the history of the last. . . . It is frequently hampered by myths and misinformation, by stereotypes and shibboleths, and by an innate resistance to innovation."

Despite this viewpoint—whether accurate or not—a vast coterie of media, political, and private groups now spend millions of dollars every year to determine what the American people think and what they are thinking about. Although modern polling ranges far beyond politics to touch virtually every aspect of Americans' private and public lives, political polling is extraordinarily pervasive (and intrusive). The seemingly axiomatic importance of political attitudes in today's world explains the compulsion to measure, manipulate, and master public opinion. As one observer put it, "Politicians court it; statesmen appeal to it; philosophers extol or condemn it; merchants cater to it; military leaders fear it; sociologists analyze it; statisticians measure it; and constitution-makers try to make it sovereign" (Childs 1965).

Foreign Policy Opinion and Its Impact ·

Democratic theory presupposes that citizens will make informed choices about the issues of the day and ultimately about who will best represent their beliefs in the councils of government. The American people in turn expect their views to be considered when political leaders contemplate new policies or revise old ones, because leaders are chosen to represent and serve the interests of their constituents. The Constitution affirms the centrality of American citizens by beginning with the words "We the people."[4]

The notion that public opinion somehow conditions public policy is appealing, but it raises troublesome questions. Do public preferences lead American foreign policy, as democratic theory would have us believe, or is the relationship more subtle and complicated? Do changes in foreign policy result from shifts in American public attitudes? Or is the relationship one of policy first and opinion second? Indeed, are the American people capable of exercising the responsibilities expected of them?

The Nature of American Public Opinion

The premise of democratic theory—that the American people will make informed policy choices—does not hold up well under scrutiny. That most Americans do not possess even the most elementary knowledge about their own political system, much less international affairs, is an inescapable fact. Moreover, people's "information" is often so inaccurate that it might better be labeled "misinformation." The following reveal the often startling levels of ignorance:

- In 1985, 28 percent of those surveyed thought that the Soviet Union and the United States fought each other in World War II; 44 percent did not know the two were allies at that time.

- In 1979, the year the SALT II treaty was signed, only 23 percent of the adult population knew the two countries involved in the SALT negotiations.

- In 1964, only 58 percent of the American public thought that the United States was a member of NATO; almost two-fifths believed the Soviet Union was a member.

- In 1983, 45 percent of the American people thought the United States supported the Sandinista government in Nicaragua, not the contras; a nearly identical number indicated they had not heard or read about the fighting between the Sandinistas and the rebels.

- In 1993, after more than year of bitter conflict in the former Yugoslavia, only 25 percent of the American people could correctly identify the ethnic group that had conquered much of Bosnia and surrounded the capital city of Sarajevo—this despite reports that half or more of them had followed events in the region.

- In 1994, 46 percent of the electorate believed that foreign aid, which accounts for less than 1 percent of the federal budget, was one of its two biggest items (welfare was the other).

- In 1985, only 63 percent of the public knew that the United States supported South Vietnam in the Vietnam War, which cost fifty-eight thousand American lives.

Evidence demonstrating the extent of political misunderstanding and ignorance about basic issues could be expanded considerably, but it would only reinforce the picture of a citizenry ill-informed about major issues of public policy and ill-equipped to evaluate government policy making. Noteworthy is that the issues about which the public is persistently ignorant are not fleeting current events but typically ones that have long figured prominently on the national or global political agendas.

The absence of basic foreign affairs knowledge does not stem from deficiencies in U.S. educational institutions. It stems from disinterest. Public ignorance is a function of public inattention, for people are knowledgeable about what is important to them. And more Americans are concerned about the outcome of major sporting events than with the shape of the political system. Again, consider some evidence:

- *Inattention to public issues:* In 1990, as tens of thousands of U.S. troops were poised for battle in Middle Eastern deserts, only 53 percent of the American public indicated they were "very interested" in following news about relations between the United States and other countries. The proportion of those closely following specific foreign policy issues or events was even lower (Rielly 1991, 9).

- *Apathy and voter turnout:* In comparison with turnout rates in other democratic countries, American voters are apathetic. The percentage of eligible voters who voted in the twelve presidential elections since World War II has ranged from 51 percent (1948) to 63 percent (1960). Ronald Reagan in 1980 and George Bush in 1988 were both elected president by only a third of the eligible electorate. For Bill Clinton the calculation is even starker: Only 55 percent of eligible voters elected to vote; of those, only 43 percent voted for him. Indeed, it is striking that "only [Lyndon] Johnson among the modern presidents won his first election by more than 55 percent of the two-party vote" (Brace and Hinckley 1993, 503).

- *Other forms of political nonparticipation:* Between 1952 and 1988 the proportion of Americans who profess to have worked for a political party or candidate during a congressional or presidential campaign never exceeded 7 percent (Conway 1991, 8). In 1994, only 5 percent of the entire population indicated they had written or spoken to a public official about a foreign affairs issue in the preceding three or four years (Gallup Poll survey for the Chicago Council on Foreign Relations).

In short, the United States purports to be a participatory system of democratic governance, but few are deeply involved in politics and most lack the interest and motivation to become involved.[5] Furthermore, most Americans are more interested in domestic affairs than in foreign policy (although concern on both counts is low). This fact led Gabriel A. Almond (1960) to conclude in his classic study, *The American People and Foreign Policy*, that public opinion toward foreign policy is appropriately thought of as "moods" that "undergo frequent alteration in response to changes in events," instead of resting on some kind of "intellectual structure." He argued that, "the characteristic response to questions of foreign policy is one of indifference. A foreign policy crisis, short of the immediate threat of war, may transform indifference to vague apprehension, to fatalism, to anger; but the reaction is still a mood, a superficial and fluctuating response."

Are Interest and Information Important?

Almond's conclusion has long been regarded as conventional wisdom, but there are important reasons to question it (Caspary 1970; Holsti 1992). Most Americans may be uninformed about and seemingly indifferent to the details of policy, but they are still able to discriminate among issues and to identify those that are salient. Foreign and national security policy issues are typically among them. When other concerns dominate, there are good reasons for it.

Consider the responses given to opinion pollsters' question, "What do you think is the most important problem facing the country today?" International issues were prominent in Americans' thinking during the height of the Cold War in the 1950s and early 1960s, typically dominating their concerns except for an occasional interruption caused by economic recessions. Not surprisingly, Vietnam emerged paramount in many of the polls taken between 1964 and 1972. Economic needs and issues headed the list of most important problems during the remainder of the 1970s. The national energy "crisis" (fundamentally a foreign policy problem) was among them. However, not until early 1980, in response to events in Iran, did an explicitly foreign policy issue emerge as the single most important concern of the American people.

Unemployment and, occasionally, other economic problems remained paramount after the Iranian hostage crisis. Then, in late 1983, the fear of war and international tensions emerged as salient. They figured prominently in the concerns of the American people as they went to the polls in November 1984 and in the months that followed. Eventually the issue dissipated, as the Reagan administration began to pursue a more conciliatory posture toward the Soviet Union. Concern for drugs emerged as the most salient issue soon after George Bush became president—doubtless a product of the new administration's own priorities, as evident in its determination to use military force to oust Panama's leader and alleged drug dealer, Manuel Noriega.[6]

The end of the Cold War understandably dampened Americans' concern for foreign and national security policy issues. The crisis over Kuwait and the war that followed rekindled interest in these issues. But with victory in hand the American people increasingly expressed concern about deficits, debts, recession, and unemployment—in short, the economy. That issue would dominate public concern during the 1992 presidential election and into the first year of the Clinton presidency. By early 1994, as economic growth was rekindled, concern for crime emerged on the agenda as the nation's most important problem as seen through the eyes of the American people.

The evidence thus supports the conclusion that the public holds firm opinions on issues it cares about and that those opinions are often stable over time, but that if conditions change, public opinion also changes. We can extend that insight even further and suggest that *the American people learn*. Again, consider some evidence.

- *Public opinion on salient questions is unwavering—the American people know what matters:* In late 1969, when the United States was still mired in Vietnam, two-fifths of the American people felt the war was morally wrong. The proportion grew to 65 percent two years later and remained at that level for more than a decade. Similarly, in 1984 only 30 percent of the American people supported U.S. military aid to the contras fighting the Nicaraguan government. The percentage was unchanged four years later, despite concerted presidential efforts to win public approval for the policy. Furthermore, large numbers of Americans attributed the causes of conflict in Central America to indigenous poverty and injustice, not, as the Reagan administration argued, to outside (Soviet and Cuban) interference.

- *Public attitudes change in response to new conditions—the American people learn:* In 1955, 27 percent of the American people believed that nuclear war between the United States and the Soviet Union would result in the complete destruction of humankind. In 1987, 83 percent believed that the United States and the Soviet Union would both be completely destroyed in an all-out nuclear war (Yankelovich and Harman 1988, 49). Between 1981 and 1990, the proportion who felt it was likely the United States would get into a nuclear war dropped from 47 to 19 percent. Between 1990 and 1994, the proportion of those who felt that defending the security of U.S. allies or protecting weaker nations from foreign aggression should be a "very important" foreign policy goal fell from 61 to 41 percent and from 57 to 24 percent, repectively (Rielly 1995, 16).

The overall record thus suggests that Americans are discerning as they contemplate the world around them. Sometimes they see foreign policy and national security issues as primary concerns, at other times they accord domestic matters priority. And they seem to engage in learning, transferring experiences in one situation or historical circumstance to another. Furthermore, their opinions about who will best handle these issues historically have been important predictors of presidential election outcomes. Strike a blow for democratic theory!

If the conclusion that the American people are indifferent to foreign policy is questionable—which it is—the relevance of their lack of knowledge is also suspect. Few people, including corporate executives, legislative aides, and political science majors and their professors would perform uniformly well on the kinds of knowledge and information questions pollsters and journalists pose to measure how well the general public is informed.

More important than interest and knowledge is whether the American people are able, in the aggregate, to hold politically relevant foreign policy beliefs. These beliefs and the corresponding attitudes that both inform and spring from them may not satisfy political analysts when they evaluate the theory and practice of American democracy. Comparatively unsophisticated foreign policy beliefs may nonetheless be both coherent and germane to the political process. Two examples, one on either side of a use-of-force issue, make the point.

- *In Central America:* Many Americans proved unable during the 1980s to identify where in Central America El Salvador and Nicaragua are or who the United States supported in the long-simmering conflicts there. But they were nonetheless unwavering in their firm conviction that young Americans should not be sent to fight in the region. From the perspective of policymakers in Washington, the latter was the important political fact.
- *In the Middle East:* Few Americans could correctly identify Kuwait or Saudi Arabia as monarchies rather than democratic political systems, but they were still willing to send American men and women to protect them and to help them win their "freedom." To policymakers in the Bush administration, the latter point was the politically relevant one.

To understand the frequent discrepancy between what Americans know, on the one hand, and how they respond to what they care about, on the other, it is useful to explore the differences between attitudes (opinions) and beliefs.

Foreign Policy Attitudes

A June 1993 *New York Times*/CBS News poll found that half of the American people felt the United States did not have a responsibility to do something about the fighting between Serbs and Bosnians in the former Yugoslavia, but a majority also indicated they would support sending U.S. ground troops to the region as part of a United Nations peacekeeping force. Two-thirds of the respondents in the same poll registered approval of President Clinton's ordering the cruise-missile attack on Iraqi's intelligence agency in retaliation for its alleged attempt to assassinate former President George Bush. Only half had heard about the proposed North American free trade zone linking the United States, Canada, and Mexico, in a free trade agreement. Of those who had, half favored the proposal and half opposed it. More than a third thought that Japan would be the world's Number 1 economic power in the next century, about half favored giving U.S. economic aid to Russia to help it reform its economy, and two out of every three Americans preferred that immigration into the United States be decreased.

These poll data capture what we normally think of as "public opinion." Often the attitudes reflected are highly volatile—and some may in fact be *nonattitudes* (the term refers to the fact that individuals often do not have opinions on matters of interest to pollsters, yet, when asked, they will offer an opinion). The character of the issue, the pace of events, new information, or a friend's opinion may provoke change. So may "herd instincts": Attitude change is stimulated by the desire to conform to what others may be thinking—especially opinion leaders and "political pundits." Indeed, it is perhaps ironic that those who are most attuned to foreign policy issues are often the most supportive of global activism and what policymakers or other opinion influentials want (Zaller 1992). Hence Americans' attitudes toward specific issues appear susceptible to quick and frequent turnabouts as they respond to cues and events in the world around them.

Public attitudes doubtless change, but even in the short run they are less erratic than often presumed. Stability rather than change is demonstrably the characteristic response of the American people to foreign and national security policy issues (Shapiro and Page 1988).[7] Furthermore, even changes observed over long stretches of time are predictable and understandable—not "formless and plastic," as Almond once described them. Two issues show that.

Americans' Defense Spending Attitudes

American opinion was comparatively stable—and silent—until the late 1960s, when a "revolt of the masses" (Russett 1972) erupted and a majority of Americans began advocating, for the first time since World War II, reductions in military spending. (The reason, of course, was dissatisfaction with the war in Vietnam.) The "revolt," however, turned out to be of short duration. By 1977 more Americans supported increases over reductions—with the level of support for more spending approaching a two-decade peak. The resurgence of support in the wake of the U.S. withdrawal from Southeast Asia was associated with the rise of conservative thinking in American domestic policies and a renewal of anti-Soviet and anticommunist sentiments (Kriesberg and Klein 1980).

By 1980, both President Carter and his challenger, Ronald Reagan, were calling for a greater defense effort. Reagan made this a centerpiece of his commitment to rebuild American defenses which, in his view, had been permitted to deteriorate dangerously during a "decade of neglect." Reagan's extreme anti-Soviet rhetoric contributed to public apprehension of Soviet behavior. For this reason, perhaps, support of greater defense spending reached levels unsurpassed since the onset of the Korean War in 1950.

Support subsided in the months and years that followed. Partly this was due to growing concern for the traditional "guns-versus-butter" trade-off, which mounting federal government deficits helped to fuel. Support also waned once the Reagan administration's rearmament program gathered speed and public fears that the U.S. military was lagging receded. By the time Reagan left office in early 1989, support for more defense spending had dissipated almost entirely. Some resurgence since then is evident, as Figure 8.1 illustrates, but expanded defense spending in the post-Cold War world does not enjoy widespread appeal. Over two decades, then, public attitudes demonstrated wide fluctuations—but quite reasonably, given the circumstances.

Americans' Internationalist Attitudes

The view that the United States ought to take an active role in world affairs enjoyed persistent public support throughout the Cold War era. Even so, measurable fluctuations are evident. During the 1960s and 1970s, in particular, support for internationalism declined. It reached a low point during the mid-1970s as a combination of worrisome concerns undermined the international ethos. The wrenching Vietnam experience challenged the assumption that military power by itself could achieve American foreign policy objectives; détente called into question the wisdom of the

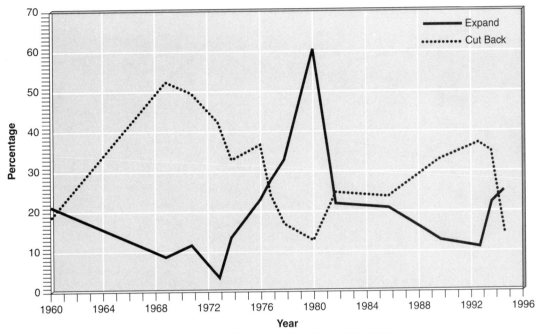

Figure 8.1 Trends in Public Opinion toward Defense Spending, 1960–1995
Source: John E. Rielly, *American Public Opinion and U.S. Foreign Policy 1991* (Chicago: Chicago Council on Foreign Relations, 1991), p. 32; John E. Rielly, *American Public Opinion and U.S. Foreign Policy 1995* (Chicago: Chicago Council on Foreign Relations, 1995), p. 12; Times Mirror Center for The People & The Press, *America's Place in the World: An Investigation of the Attitudes of American Opinion Leaders and the American Public about International Affairs*, Andrew Kohut, Director, November 1993, p. 94.

containment foreign policy strategy; and Watergate challenged the convictions that American political institutions were uniquely virtuous and that a presidency preeminent in foreign policy continued to be necessary. Despite these concerns, support for internationalism rebounded in the decade following Vietnam, with roughly 60 percent of the American people espousing internationalist attitudes in the mid-1980s, compared with only 44 percent at the time of Carter's election in 1976.

That picture remains largely unchanged in the early post-Cold War era, despite the frequent claim that the American people have turned inward as domestic challenges weigh more heavily on their thinking. Figure 8.2 reveals a slight decline in the proportion of internationalists in the early 1990s compared with the mid-1980s, but in April 1993, only 37 percent of the American people agreed with the proposition that the United States "should mind its own business and let other countries get along the best they can on their own" (Times Mirror Center for The People & The Press 1993, 31). Furthermore, various polling organizations have asked the American people since the 1940s if they "think it will be best for the future of the country if we take an active part in world affairs or if we stay out." In October 1945, 70 percent said active involvement would be best; in late 1994, 69 percent echoed that sentiment (Rielly 1995,

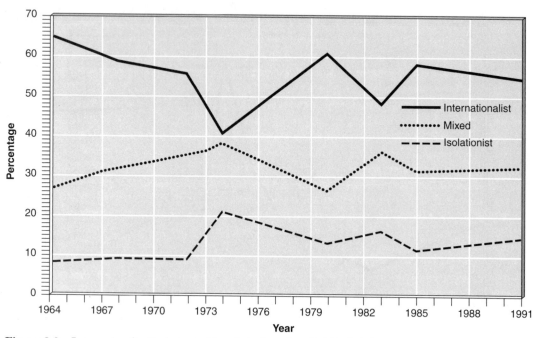

Figure 8.2 Internationalist/Isolationist Trends in American Public Opinion, 1964–1991

Note: Data for 1964 and 1968 are derived from responses to five statements concerning the general posture that the United States should assume in world affairs. The figures for later years include responses to the same five statements plus two others on possible U.S. military intervention in defense of allies. "Mixed" are respondents who cannot clearly be classified as either internationalists or isolationists.

Source: Data reprinted by permission of William Watts, president of Potomac Associates and principal investigator.

39). Support, decline, and resurgence are thus once more in evidence. And, as with defense spending, the responses are both predictable and reasonable given changes in domestic and international circumstances.

War as an instrument of national policy warrants attention as a special case of the cyclical nature of public attitudes toward foreign policy. Public approval of war appears to occur just prior to and after its inception, followed—predictably perhaps—by a gradual but steady decline in bellicose attitudes and a concomitant rise in pacific sentiments. The wars in Korea and Vietnam illustrate the patterns. During each, enthusiasm closely tracked casualty rates: As the casualty rates went up, support for the wars declined (Mueller 1971). The pattern suggests that American attitudes toward war are episodic rather than steady: In the context of actual war involvement, public attitudes range from initial acceptance to ultimate disfavor (Campbell and Cain 1965).

The swift victory of the United States and its Coalition partners in the Persian Gulf War perhaps stanched the cyclical reactions among Americans evident in other wars. Even in this case, however, many people later questioned the wisdom of the war as Iraq's Saddam Hussein—whom George Bush had likened to Hitler—remained in power after the conflict and, in October 1994, even poised forces again to threaten

Kuwait. As with defense spending and internationalism, then, the reasons underlying the American people's alternating views on war are compelling—suggesting once more that they are better able to make prudent political judgments than political pundits would sometimes have us believe (see Jentleson 1992; Kohut and Toth 1994).

Foreign Policy Beliefs

The stability of public attitudes and the learning they demonstrate are intimately related to changes that have occurred at home and abroad, thus giving rise to new foreign policy *beliefs*. Although support for active involvement in world affairs rebounded in the 1980s from its nadir in the 1970s, internationalism in the wake of the Vietnam tragedy came to wear two faces—a cooperative one and a militant one. **Cooperative** and **militant internationalism** grow out of differences among the American people, not only on the question of *whether* the United States ought to be involved in the world (a central tenet of classical internationalism) but also on *how* it should be involved (Wittkopf 1990).

The domestic consensus favoring classical internationalism captured elements of both conflict and cooperation. The United States was willing to cooperate with other nations to solve global as well as national problems; but if need be, it would also intervene in the affairs of others—using force if necessary to protect its self-defined national interests. In the years following World War II a consensus emerged in support of these forms of involvement, but in the wake of Vietnam concern about conflict and cooperation came to divide rather than unite Americans. Attitudes toward communism, the use of American troops abroad, and relations with the Soviet Union distinguished proponents and opponents of the alternative forms of internationalism.

Four identifiable belief systems flowed from these concerns, which inhered among elites as well as the mass of the American people (Holsti and Rosenau 1990; Wittkopf 1990):

1. *Internationalists* supported active American involvement in international affairs, favoring a combination of conciliatory and conflictual strategies reminiscent of the pre-Vietnam internationalist foreign policy paradigm.

2. *Isolationists*, on the other hand, opposed both types of international involvement, as the term implies.

3. *Hardliners* tended to view communism as a threat to the United States, to oppose détente with the Soviet Union, and to embrace an interventionist predisposition.

4. *Accommodationists*, in contrast, emphasized cooperative ties with other nations, particularly détente with the Soviet Union, and rejected the view that the United States could assume a unilateralist, go-it-alone posture in the world.

Although accommodationists and hardliners are appropriately described as "internationalists," it is clear their prescriptions for the United States' world role often diverged markedly. This undermined the broad-based domestic support for foreign policy initiatives that presidents in the Cold War era counted on, and made the task of coalition building that more recent presidents have faced more difficult.

Beliefs are important in understanding why public attitudes are often less fickle than might be expected. A **belief system** acts as "a set of lenses through which information concerning the physical and social environment is received. It orients the individual to his environment, defining it for him and identifying for him its salient characteristics" (Holsti 1962).

Belief systems also establish goals and order preferences. They enable people to relate systematically information about one idea to others. Importantly, this ability is not a function of information or knowledge; in fact, social cognition theory demonstrates that individuals use information short-cuts, based on their beliefs, to cope with ambiguous messages about the external environment. Paradoxically, then, ordinary citizens hold coherent attitude structures not because they possess detailed knowledge about foreign policy but because they lack it: "A paucity of information does not *impede* structure and consistency; on the contrary, it *motivates* the development and employment of structure. [Individuals attempt] to cope with an extraordinarily confusing world . . . by structuring views about specific foreign policies according to their more general and abstract beliefs" (Hurwitz and Peffley 1987).

Because of their nature, beliefs are remarkably stable. Most images concerning foreign affairs are formed during adolescence and remain more or less fixed unless somehow disturbed. Peer group influences and authority figures may exert a modifying impact on images, but only the most dramatic of international events (war, for example) have the capacity to completely alter foreign policy beliefs (Deutsch and Merritt 1965). Relevant here is philosopher Charles Sanders Pierce's instructive comment on the dynamics of image change: "Surprise is your only teacher." Thus core beliefs, formed through early learning experiences, serve as perceptual filters through which individuals orient themselves to their environment and structure how they interpret international events they encounter later in life. If beliefs do change, they are likely to be replaced by new images that continue to simplify the world, albeit in new terms (William James's adage that "most people think they are thinking when they replace one set of prejudices for another" may be appropriate here).

World War II and the events that led to it indelibly imprinted the world views of many Americans—including an entire generation of policymakers (Neustadt and May 1986). For the *Munich generation*, the message was clear: Aggressors cannot be appeased. To others, Vietnam was an equally traumatic event (Holsti and Rosenau 1984). For the *Vietnam generation*, the lesson was equally simple: There are limits to American power and the utility of military force in international politics. (A dramatically different but now popular view holds that war, once begun, should not be prosecuted "with one arm tied behind the our back.") The emergence of the distinctive beliefs associated with cooperative and militant internationalism in the wake of Vietnam thus conforms to our understanding of how beliefs change.

Has the end of the Cold War—dramatized by the crumbling of the Berlin Wall, long a symbol of the bitter East-West conflict—had a similar effect on Americans' foreign policy beliefs? Do cooperative and militant internationalism, whose Cold War roots include fear of communism and dissension over how to deal with the now moribund Soviet Union, continue to describe differences among the American people about whether and how to be involved in the world? The evidence shows they do.[8]

Individuals often ignore information that might cause them to change their beliefs or to engage in purposeful or inadvertent behavior that would otherwise reorient their perceptions to new realities.[9] Beyond this, the alternative internationalist orientations are not bound to the specific historical circumstances of the Cold War but transcend it (see Murray 1994; Russett, Hartley, and Murray 1994). The two faces of internationalism closely track idealism and realism (Holsti 1992)—competing visions of how best to deal with transnational problems, which predate the Cold War and persist as new issues compete for attention in the post-Cold War era, as we have seen in previous chapters. Thus in the mid-1990s, proponents of militant internationalism (particularly hardliners) were more likely than others to support the use of U.S. troops in places like Europe, the Middle East, and Korea, and to approve of CIA intervention abroad—including spying on friends as well as foes. Proponents of cooperative internationalism (particularly accommodationists), on the other hand, expressed greater support for such multilateral ventures as NATO's Partnership for Peace program and U.S. participation in UN peacekeeping operations—including a willingness to place U.S. troops under a non-American commander (Wittkopf 1995). The varying preferences track long-standing differences in realist and idealist prescriptions for coping with security challenges.

How do Americans' foreign policy beliefs find expression in the nation's policies? Causation is difficult to trace, but the consistency of public beliefs with the internationalist faces of American foreign policy since Vietnam is undeniable. Many of the policies pursued by the Nixon, Ford, and Carter administrations represented more accommodationist than hardline positions. President Carter's assertion in 1977 that the inordinate fear of communism had been lifted epitomized the shift to a conciliatory internationalism that tolerated diversity, and détente was its manifestation. Other elements associated with that fundamental shift included the beliefs that military power was no longer a viable instrument of policy, that the Soviet Union had become a status quo power, that the United States should assist the "forces of change" in the Third World, and that "trilateralism"—implying a deepening of cooperation—should come to characterize U.S. relations with Europe and Japan.

By the end of Carter's term in office, however, the emphasis on accommodation shifted back to a hardline posture.[10] A critical factor underlying the reversal was the Soviet Union's intervention in Afghanistan in December 1979. With that, and with Ronald Reagan's election in 1980, any remaining semblance of détente was lost. Reagan pursued a vigorous anti-Soviet and interventionist foreign policy that epitomized hardliner foreign policy beliefs. Still, he was unable to overcome the accommodationists' opposition to some of his policies. The best example is found in Central America, where despite concerted presidential efforts to win congressional and public support for a more belligerent approach to the Sandinista regime in Nicaragua, the administration came up short. The example illustrates well how public opinion sometimes constrains presidential initiatives in foreign policy, as it does the persistence of accommodationist thinking among political elites and the mass public (see Wittkopf and McCormick 1993). Moreover, during his second term in office Reagan adopted a more conciliatory posture toward the Soviet Union, reminiscent of the accommodationist orientation he earlier had so vigorously rejected. The administration also retreated from the unilateralist orientation that had led some to worry about the end of internationalism, finding solace instead in the multilateralism historically central to the internationalist ethos.

George Bush came to the White House determined to manage the Cold War competition with the Soviet Union, but as Mikhail Gorbachev pursued one conciliatory initiative after another, the president often found himself in the odd situation of having to defend himself against charges that he had done too little to stimulate the kinds of changes Soviet leaders seemed so desperately to want. Lacking what he himself called "the vision thing," Bush embarked on a policy of "status quo plus," which pleased neither his supporters nor his critics. Not until the Kuwait crisis was Bush able to seize the high ground on the national security issues for which he was uniquely prepared. As noted in previous chapters, the president spoke repeatedly in a State of the Union Address that followed shortly on the heels of the initiation of war against Iraq of the "next American century," in which the "rule of law" would reign supreme in the "new world order." Bush's vision embraced the tradition of moral idealism long evident in American foreign policy, but especially since Woodrow Wilson sought early in this century to create a "world safe for democracy." Ironically, however, even as the vision of a new world order was premised on idealism, the question of how to deal with Saddam Hussein's aggressive behavior again pitted realists (militant internationalists) and idealists (cooperative internationalists) against one another. The dichotomy was sharply displayed in the congressional debate between the proponents of force and those of sanctions, as also mirrored in public opinion polls.

Whether to use force or sanctions punctuated the debate during the Clinton administration about how best to respond to the "ethnic cleansing" perpetrated by Bosnian Serbs on their Muslim neighbors in the former Yugoslavia. As in the debate over Iraq, hardliners and accommodationists were clearly identifiable in Congress—expecially after the Republicans gained control—and elsewhere. If there was a new twist, it was that Democrats and liberals—previously among the strongest supporters of cooperative internationalism—were now supporters of intervention, while Republicans and conservatives—previously among the strongest supporters of militant internationalism—were now more cautious. The shift from Republican to Democratic control of the White House doubtless explains these changes. But they do not deny the continuing divisions within the American polity about whether and how the United States should be involved in the world. Thus internationalism continues to wear two faces: one cooperative, the other militant.

The Public "Temperament": Nationalistic and Permissive

The responsiveness of the American people—for better or worse—to events and the political information directed at them is nowhere more apparent than in the support they accord their political leaders during times of crisis and peril.

Like the citizens of other nations, Americans embrace nationalist sentiments: They value loyalty and devotion to their own nation and promotion of its culture and interests as opposed to those of other nations. Nationalism sometimes includes the ethnocentric belief that the United States is (or should be recognized as) superior to others, and should therefore serve as a model for them to emulate.

Although no one would argue that all Americans always think nationalistically on all foreign issues, generally they perceive international problems in terms of in-group loyalty and out-group competition (Rosenberg 1965). In the extreme, nationalism results in a world view that accepts the doctrine, "my country, right or wrong." Furthermore, because citizens often equate loyalty to the nation with loyalty to the current leadership, they sometimes confuse love for the representatives of the government with love for country and its symbols: my president, right or wrong.

The public's nationalistic temperament stems in part from its tendency to view "things foreign" with hostility and fear. International politics often appears esoteric, secret, complicated, and unfamiliar—a cacophony of problems better left to "experts" who allegedly "know better" (and who, in turn, are quite willing to perpetuate the notion)—rendering public attitudes in the realm of foreign policy especially vulnerable to manipulation. People who feel threatened are prone to seek strong leadership to deal with the perceived threatening agent, a tendency policymakers have long recognized. It was the Nazi Hermann Goering who expressed the idea by contending, "Voice or no voice, the people can always be brought to do the bidding of the leaders. That is easy. All you have to do is to tell them they are being attacked and denounce the pacifists for lack of patriotism." John Foster Dulles expressed the same opinion when he noted: "The easiest and quickest cure of internal dissension is to portray danger from abroad. Thus group authorities find it convenient always to keep alive among the group members a feeling that their nation is in danger from one or another of the nation-villains with which it is surrounded."

Nationalistic sentiments find expression in the way Americans respond to the foreign policy initiatives of their leaders, especially during crises or threats from abroad, where the public's response is typically "permissive" Presidents frequently realize their widest freedom of action in such circumstances, because the American people typically acquiesce in and support the decisions of their leaders.

Evidence of the permissiveness of public attitudes is found in the impact of dramatic foreign policy events and initiatives on presidential performance evaluations. Typically such events produce "rally-round-the-flag" effects that boost a president's popularity with the public. Examples abound:

- Bill Clinton's popularity with the American people spurted eleven percentage points following the June 1993 American cruise missile attack on Iraqi intelligence headquarters in Baghdad and nine points following the occupation of Haiti a year later.

- George Bush's popularity climbed by eighteen points following the initiation of military action against Iraq in January 1991.

- Ronald Reagan's approval notched upward by six points following the bombing of Libya in April 1986.

- Jimmy Carter's popularity jumped by thirteen points following the Camp David Middle East accords in September 1978.

Such changes are evident across a broad range of foreign policy events, including wars, crises, peace initiatives, and summit conferences—all of which demonstrate the nationalistic and acquiescent responses of the American people.

The American people, however, are also discriminating. Ronald Reagan's popularity plummeted by sixteen percentage points following the Iran-contra revelations in late 1986, the largest drop ever recorded by the Gallup Poll (other polls recorded even steeper declines). Contrast this with John Kennedy's experience, who found that his public approval actually rose to its peak (83 percent) following the Bay of Pigs fiasco. Both involved mistakes in judgment, but the way each president handled his mistake appears to have significantly affected public perceptions of him. (In the Iran-*contra* affair, not only did the American people disapprove of the sale of arms to Iran, they disbelieved the president's version of what happened and thought the administration was engaged in a cover-up similar to the Watergate affair [Ostrom and Simon 1989].) More typically, international crises are *approval-enhancing* events, whereas political scandals are *approval-diminishing* events (Ostrom and Simon 1989).

The Politics of Prestige

Presidents care about their popularity with the American people because it affects their ability to work their will with others involved in the policy process. Richard Neustadt (1980) explains the underlying logic: "The Washingtonians who watch a President have more to think about than his professional reputation. They also have to think about his standing with the public outside of Washington. They have to gauge his popular prestige. Because they think about it, public standing is a source of [presidential] influence." In short, the more popular a president is, the more likely he is to accomplish his political agenda. This is the essence of what Dennis M. Simon and Charles W. Ostrom (1988) call "the politics of prestige."

Presidents also care about their popularity because it affects their political latitude. Both the absolute and relative levels of presidents' popularity, evidence suggests (Ostrom and Job 1986; also James and Oneal 1991), are important in explaining America's postwar political use of force short of war: The more popular presidents are, the more they are "freed" from domestic constraints to do as they wish abroad (cf. Lian and Oneal 1993; Meernik 1994). As one member of Congress commented on Bush's popularity following the invasion of Panama, "If the President's popularity is at 80 percent, I think [he] can do whatever he wants."

"Rally-round-the-flag" events, like the invasion of Panama, significantly affect presidents' popularity. Indeed, one presidential scholar (Lowi 1985a) argues that foreign policy comprises the only arena available to presidents that permits them to improve their popularity ratings once in office. The state of the economy is the most potent (environmental) predictor of presidential popularity. It was the principal factor that undermined the Bush presidency and caused his reelection bid to fail. Still, the American people want peace as well as prosperity. Thus foreign policy sometimes figures prominently in the long-term erosion of support as well as the short-term boosts that most presidents experience. For Truman, the Korean War was the significant factor explaining the dramatic loss of public confidence in his leadership; for Johnson, the Vietnam War and riots in the cities were critical; for Nixon, it was the continuation of the Vietnam War and Watergate; and for Carter, it was his inability to secure the release of Americans held hostage in Iran.

Trends in presidential popularity are described in Figure 8.3. Presidents typically begin with a "honeymoon"—a crucial first few months after an election, in which the president is relatively free of harsh public criticism—only to find that in the long-term their popularity declines. Interestingly, the three most recent presidents have not experienced very enthusiastic honeymoons. Clinton's popularity, in fact, began to erode almost as soon as he moved into the White House, perhaps because he made the controversial issue of homosexuals in the military his first order of business. In any event, the media cut him little slack. During his first eighteen months in office, nearly two-thirds of television news evaluations of Clinton were negative, compared with the evenly balanced coverage Bush received. Press coverage was markedly less positive than Clinton's approval ratings with the mass public ("They're No Friends of Bill: TV News Coverage of the Clinton Administration" 1994).

As noted, specific events often cause erosion of presidential support, but it may also be stimulated by growing public dissatisfaction and lost patience with unfulfilled campaign promises, or perhaps by the adage that "familiarity breeds contempt."[11] With every presidential decision (or "nondecision"), opposition forms or becomes more vocal, Congress looks increasingly to its own parochial concerns, and the president's support seems to ooze away imperceptibly but steadily (see Brace and Hinckley 1992). The tendency is symptomatic of the difficulties of running a government and managing the nation's foreign policy in a manner satisfactory to a majority of Americans.

What about Ronald Reagan and George Bush? Both deserve special comment—Reagan because he was the first president since Dwight Eisenhower to serve two full terms in office, Bush because he failed in his reelection bid despite having achieved the highest approval ratings ever given a president since modern polling began more than half a century ago.

Reagan's popularity followed a predictable decline during his first term, dropping to only 35 percent approval in January 1983 largely because of the severe economic recession that marked much of this early presidency. Political analysts were prompted to predict Reagan would be a one-term president, but his fortunes changed as the economy reversed course, and little more than a year later Reagan again enjoyed the approval of a majority of Americans. Issues that affected other presidents adversely did not seem to "stick" to Reagan, leading some to describe Reagan's as a "teflon presidency," implying an immunity from the forces that eroded his predecessors' popular base. The paradox that Reagan's personal popularity outstripped public approval of many of his policies and programs—implying that his charm separated him from the problems people had with his policies—reinforced the metaphor.

Reagan's popularity continued to climb in his second term, reaching its highest point in April 1986 following the U.S. bombing of Libya. But then it fell precipitously when the Iranian arms-for-hostages deal was revealed later in the year. In the months that followed, the popularity of "the man in the teflon suit" (Ostrom and Simon 1989) again began a miraculous climb as the president's political fortunes were "born again" for the second time, but Reagan never regained the lofty popularity ratings he enjoyed before the Iran-*contra* revelations and the Watergate analogy that surrounded it. Unlike Nixon, however, he was not destroyed by the scandal's undercurrents.

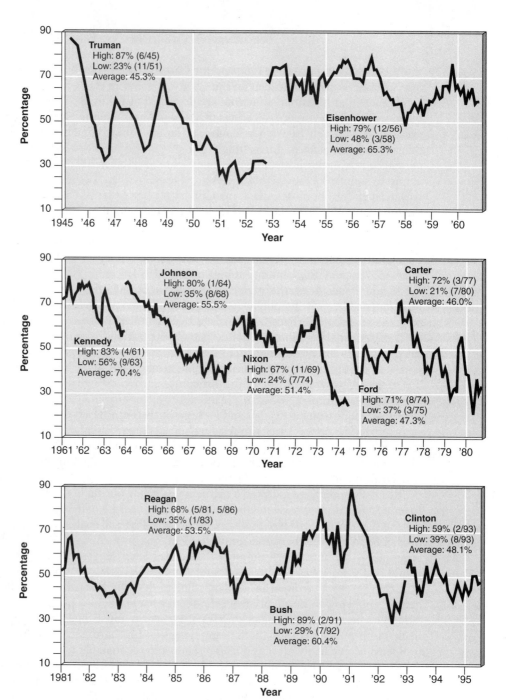

Figure 8.3 Public Approval of Presidential Performance, 1945–1995

Note: Data appear in monthly intervals beginning in June 1945 and ending in July 1995. In months with multiple polls, the last poll is used. In months where no poll was taken, the data are extrapolated using preceding and/or succeeding monthly data. The panels in the figure contain unequal numbers of monthly intervals.

Source: Adapted from *The Gallup Opinion Index*, October–November 1980; and various issues of *The Gallup Report* and *The Gallup Poll Monthly*.

So how unusual was Ronald Reagan? To some extent the public did separate its image of the president from his administration. Overall Reagan's experience was not unique, however, as the performance of the economy during his administration proved to be the decisive determinant of his popularity (Ostrom and Simon 1989). "Political drama" in the form of speechmaking, trips abroad, and approval-enhancing international events also mattered, but then so, too, did the Iran-*contra* scandal which corroded the aptness of the teflon metaphor. What distinguishes Reagan from his predecessors is that twice during his two-term presidency he was able to stem the decline of support and rebuild it. He also ended his term in office with a higher approval rating than any Cold War president, but like all of them he enjoyed less approval on leaving office than when he entered it.

George Bush's experience is similar to that of his predecessors in that the (poor) state of the economy worked against him and eventually caused his defeat by Bill Clinton in 1992. The intriguing question is why Bush could not parlay his extraordinarily high popularity levels—89 percent according to the Gallup Poll in March 1991—into political survival and longevity. The evidence suggests a couple of answers to the question.

First, Bush's popularity manifested far wider gyrations than any of his predecessors over comparable periods in office.

> Where Reagan's polls changed by more than five percentage points only twice [during his first thirty-six months in office], Bush's changed by this amount thirteen times, leading modern presidents in this kind of fluctuation. Bush's approval ratings climbed with the invasion of Panama in January 1990, fell the next month, and then fell further. They climbed again with the Gorbachev summit, plummeting the following month. They then shot up with the Persian Gulf crisis, plunged in a congressional budget fight, and skyrocketed during the Gulf War. In the wake of the Gulf victory, the polls fell again until by January 1992 Bush was lower than all presidents except Truman and Johnson entering the presidential election year. (Brace and Hinckley 1993, 501)

By this time, the state of the economy began to undermine the Bush presidency.

Second, Bush's unusually high—if wildly fluctuating—approval ratings did not sustain him, because they were "tied less to George Bush the individual and more to a remarkable clustering of events" (Brace and Hinckley 1993). Most of these were international events, including the invasion of Panama, the crisis over Kuwait and the Persian Gulf War, the fall of the Berlin Wall and the demise of communism in Eastern Europe, and the impending end of the Cold War. The White House played on each of these developments with considerable political drama, but it paid scant attention to domestic economic policy. Thus Bush's popularity appears to have been sustained almost entirely by international events, issues of comparatively low salience (Edwards, Mitchell, and Welch 1995). This made it unstable and highly susceptible to damaging negative events. "With approval maintained at an artificial high point through a series of dramatic positive events," argue political scientists Paul Brace and Barbara Hinckley (1993), "any other events and presidential activities drove the polls down." In short, Bush's approval rating with the American people was not only higher than other presidents, it was also more vulnerable to losses.

Bill Clinton's honeymoon was neither as long nor his approval rating as high as some of his predecessors—a reflection perhaps of his comparatively weak electoral base. In other ways, however, his experience during his first year in office mimicked that of his predecessors. By early summer the partisan disputes that erupted over his economic program and proposed tax increases and continuing concern about the state of the economy further eroded his approval rating, which dropped below 40 percent less than five months after his inauguration. As noted, the American people did rally around their president following the air strike against Iraq in late June 1993, but the raid had no lasting effect, as Americans' concern about jobs, unemployment, and related economic issues continued to dominate their attention in the absence of either dramatic approval-enhancing or approval-diminishing events. Some important legislative victories, particularly the passage of Nafta, buoyed Clinton's popularity in the fall. An improving economy also helped Clinton's recovery from earlier losses in popularity as he moved into the second year of his term, but the smell of domestic scandal—Whitewater—began to dog his administration. Interestingly, however, even as the economy continued to improve throughout his second year in office, Clinton did not enjoy the benefits—perhaps because, to many Americans, it seemed like "jobless growth" (Pianin 1994).[12] Then, following Republican victories in the congressional elections, much of the nation's attention seemed to turn from the president to Congress, which began to score some of the highest institutional ratings it had received in many years.

Public Opinion and Foreign Policy: An Addendum

The preceding discussion could be expanded in several ways. Here we add only a few additional observations, which relate to Americans' confidence in their political institutions, the components of the concept "public opinion," and the political and sociodemographic correlates of foreign policy attitudes and beliefs.

Confidence in Political Leaders and Institutions

The confidence that Americans place in the nation's political, economic, and social institutions is closely related to the other developments in public attitudes described above. Jimmy Carter dramatized ingredients symptomatic of the changing "public voice" when, in a 1979 nationwide speech, he spoke of "a fundamental threat to American democracy." The threat, he said, was a "crisis of confidence," reflected in "a growing disrespect for government and for churches and for schools, the news media and other institutions." Among the trends was a decline in Americans' sense of political efficacy and a general feeling of despair, alienation, and powerlessness regarding the future. An American public that once appeared to be naive, simplistic, and jingoistic (ultrapatriotic) now appeared more aware of and cynical about foreign policy issues.

Public disclosures of the half-truths regarding American involvement in Vietnam, and the revelations about what was undertaken in the name of national security by presidential staffers, military organizations, and intelligence agencies contributed to Americans' growing cynicism—especially evident during and immediately after the Vietnam War. Ronald Reagan helped to rebuild public confidence in political leaders (but not social institutions generally). However, it was dealt another blow by the revelations of the Iran-*contra* affair (Lipset and Schneider 1987; see also Craig 1993;

Sussman 1988), which once more raised concerns about the abuse of power in the name of national security. Questions about whether George Bush was completely honest about his role in the Iran-*contra* affair dogged his presidency to the very end—when he pardoned former Secretary of Defense Caspar Weinberger and other Iran-*contra* principals for any wrongdoing. The military is one institution to have enjoyed a dramatic rebound in confidence with the American people in more recent years—explained by its success in the Persian Gulf War. Congress, as noted, is another, although its "staying power" has yet to be tested.

The Public Opinion Pyramid

American society is structured like a pyramid, with a very small proportion of *policy influentials* (people who are knowledgeable about foreign affairs and who have access to decision makers) and decision makers at the top, followed by a larger component comprising the *attentive public* (those knowledgeable about foreign affairs but not necessarily with access to decision makers), with the bulk of the population making up the "mass public." The pyramid represents the three strata that make up the aggregate concept "public opinion." While estimates vary about the distribution of Americans among the three groups, most suggest that the elite comprise less than 2 percent of the population, the attentive public between 5 and 10 percent, and the mass public, by definition, the rest.

One of the sharpest distinctions in public attitudes occurs between "elites," on the one hand, and the mass public, on the other. Here the evidence is incontrovertible: Elites—decision makers, policy influentials, and opinion leaders—are markedly more supportive of active involvement in the world than is the mass public. They oppose economic protectionism and support free trade principles, basic pillars of postwar internationalism, and tend to adopt a more interventionist orientation toward world affairs than the mass of the American people.

Table 8.2 illustrates these differences between elites and masses across a range of foreign policy issues about which samples of the American public and others in leadership positions were asked in 1993 and 1994. Note in particular that leaders are markedly more supportive than the mass public of U.S. global activism, even in a "shared leadership" context; and that they are more supportive of collective security and of reduced military spending but also more willing than the mass of the American public to intervene militarily in traditional conflict situations. Similarly, they are more likely to see the success of Russia's democratic experiment as a top U.S. foreign policy priority than the mass of the American people, but they accord "getting Saddam Hussein out of Iraq" little significance. On the other hand, the mass public attaches markedly greater salience to the goal of protecting the jobs of American workers than do American leaders.

Despite these differences on particular foreign policy issues, American leaders and the mass public share much in common. In particular, elites and masses differ in similar ways on the question of *how* the United States should be involved in the world. The belief systems derived from the cooperative and militant orientations toward global activism used earlier to describe mass foreign policy attitudes apply to American leaders as well. Thus elite and mass preferences diverge on specifics, but they converge on co-

TABLE 8.2 DIFFERENCES IN THE FOREIGN POLICY PREFERENCES OF AMERICAN LEADERS AND THE MASS OF THE AMERICAN PEOPLE, 1993 (PERCENTAGES)

	Leaders	Public	Gap*
America's World Role			
The United States should assume a shared leadership role but also be the most assertive/active among the leading nations	62	27	35
Collective Security			
The United States should contribute military forces to a UN command, not keep them under U.S. officers	74	29	45
Military Spending			
Cut back defense spending	63	37	26
Dangers to World Security			
Population growth is most dangerous	21	10	11
Nationalism and ethnic hatreds are most dangerous	35	25	10
Religious fanaticism is most dangerous	12	10	2
International trade conflicts are most dangerous	5	7	-2
Use of Military Force			
Favor using troops if:			
North Korea invades South Korea	84	45	39
Iraq invades Saudi Arabia	86	58	28
Arab forces invades Israel	74	50	24
Russia invades Poland	61	39	22
Cubans attempt to overthrow Castro	19	50	-31
Long-Range Foreign Policy Goals as Top Priority			
Preventing the spread of weapons of mass destruction	84	70	14
Promoting and defending human rights abroad	28	22	6
Helping improve the living standard in developing nations	23	19	4
Promoting democracy in other nations	21	23	-2
Strengthening the United Nations	37	42	-5
Improving the global environment	45	57	-12
Protecting the jobs of American workers	37	85	-48
Specific Foreign Policy Goals as Top Priority			
Ensuring that democracy succeeds in Russia and other former Soviet states	51	24	27
Strengthening our domestic economy to improve the U.S. international position	86	73	13
Bringing about a permanent settlement between Israel and the Arabs	47	34	13
Countering the threat of North Korean militarism	24	22	2
Better managing trade and economic disputes with Japan	49	49	0
Stopping the flood of illegal immigrants into the country	29	66	-37
Getting Saddam Hussein out of Iraq	14	55	-41

* Leaders minus public. All percentages are based on those holding an opinion.

Source: Data on the use of force abroad from John E. Rielly (ed.), *American Public Opinion and U.S. Foreign Policy 1995* (Chicago: Chicago Council on Foreign Relations, 1995), p. 39. All other data adapted from the Times Mirror Center for The People & The Press, *America's Place in the World: An Investigation of the Attitudes of American Opinion Leaders and the American Public about International Affairs*, Andrew Kohut, Director, November 1993.

operative and militant internationalism as alternative orientations toward the specifics of America's foreign policy ends and means. The similarities and differences between the specifics and the general manifest themselves this way: Elites consistently subscribe to internationalist and accommodationist values in greater proportions than the mass public. The mass public, on the other hand, is more likely to hold hardline values (Holsti and Rosenau, 1990; Holsti and Rosenau, 1993; Wittkopf, 1990; Wittkopf, 1994). Thus the *structure* of elite and mass attitudes is similar, even as their specific policy preferences diverge.

Political and Sociodemographic Correlates of Foreign Policy Attitudes

Partisanship, and especially political ideology (conservative versus liberal), are important correlates of foreign policy beliefs. As noted earlier, conservatives are more likely to be hardliners while liberals tend to be accommodationists. In addition to these differences, public attitudes on specific foreign policy issues often vary by such factors as age, educational level, gender, income, occupation, racial background, religious identification, and region of the country (see, e.g., Wilcox, Ferrara, and Allsop 1993). For policymakers, knowledge about these variations is important politically, because it allows them to court some groups while ignoring others.

Income, occupation, and education are typically important in distinguishing the attentive public from the mass public. People in higher income groups, in professional occupations, and with more education are typically better informed about international affairs than their counterparts in other societal groups. As noted earlier, these are the people most likely to support what foreign policy leaders want. In May 1993, for example, the Gallup Poll found that, by a margin of 55 to 36 percent, most Americans opposed air strikes against Bosnia—a policy option then actively under consideration by the Clinton administration. Among those who followed events there "very closely," however, the balance of opinion was nearly reversed, with 53 percent of the "informed" public in favor of the action and 42 percent opposed (*The Gallup Poll Monthly* May 1993, 11). Similarly, in late 1994 only 42 percent of the mass public supported NATO's expansion into Eastern Europe—a central tenet of the Clinton administration's Partnership for Peace program—but the move was supported by 55 percent of those who closely followed news about U.S. foreign relations (based on a Gallup Poll survey for the Chicago Council on Foreign Relations).

Gender differences on foreign policy issues, particularly those related to the use of force, are among the correlates of foreign policy attitudes that have attracted attention in recent years. A "gender gap" first became evident in the 1980 election, when Ronald Reagan was found to enjoy markedly less support among female voters than among male voters. The differences, which were repeated four years later, appear to have been related to a greater fear among women of Reagan's bellicose foreign policy pronouncements and concerns about his ability to manage the risks of war (Frankovic 1982).[13]

Evidence from early in the 1988 presidential campaign indicated that Bush inherited women's distrust of Reagan, but by the time of the election in November 1988 gender differences had largely dissipated (Farah and Klein 1989; Taylor 1988; cf. Bendyna and Lake 1995). With the onset of the crisis and war in the Persian Gulf, however, wide differences between men and women on use-of-force issues were again revealed. An August 1990 media survey by the ICR Survey Research Group revealed, for example, that 79 percent of the male respondents would support sending U.S. troops to defend Saudi Arabia against a possible Iraqi attack, but only 51 percent of the females would. Five months later, as the United Nations deadline for Iraq's withdrawal from Kuwait approached, ICR asked whether the United States should go to war against Iraq if it failed to comply. Of the women 54 percent said yes, compared with 73 percent of the men. Women were also less likely than men to approve of Bush's handling of the crisis in Kuwait. Whether these differences had an effect on the 1992 presidential election is problematic, however, as exit polls revealed almost no difference in the proportion of men and women who preferred Bush over the other candidates (Bendyna and Lake 1995, 377). It is clear nonetheless that Bill Clinton was sensitive to gender-based issues as he mounted his campaign with the promise to make the composition of his administration "look like American society"; and comparatively larger numbers of women did vote for him than for Bush or Perot. (Single women, who "often believed that they had been harmed by Reagan and Bush's policies" were especially prone to vote for Clinton [Abramson, Aldrich, and Rohde 1994].) Two years later white males voted overwhelmingly for Republican congressional candidates, helping to secure the new Republican majority.

Generational changes also deserve consideration. Earlier, in commenting on the impact of Vietnam, a contrast was drawn between the Munich generation and the Vietnam generation. The electoral battle between George Bush, a World War II veteran, and Bill Clinton, a Vietnam War dissenter, epitomizes the generational changes now taking place in American policy-making circles. With it comes potentially important implications for the foreign policy thinking that the next generation of policy-makers may bring into positions of power (see Holsti and Rosenau 1980, 1984). The cyclical swings between global activism and withdrawal in American diplomatic history, Frank L. Klingberg (1983, 1990) argues, are largely generational in nature, with oscillations between each mood occurring every twenty-five to thirty years quite independently of public dissatisfaction with particular experiments (such as Vietnam or humanitarian intervention). Although detailed evidence supporting the generational thesis remains elusive, the long history of swings between introversion and extroversion identified by Klingberg and others suggests that generational effects may be especially important as the United States looks to the late 1990s and beyond.

A Public Impact on American Foreign Policy?   . . . .

The foregoing description of the attributes of American public opinion suggests a partial answer to the opinion-policy question: The proposition drawn from democratic theory that foreign policy is merely a reflection of public preferences and beliefs is too crude and simplistic. Public opinion is often described as uninformed, uninterested, acquiescent, apathetic, and manipulable, but we have also seen that it can be resistant to pressure, stable, and capable of learning. Consequently, public opinion provides neither a clear nor a consistent guide to policy making. "To be sure, the results of public opinion polls are usually sufficiently clear that public officials might *claim* that their behavior is consistent with the public will, but such a claim assumes qualities in this opinion not completely borne out empirically" (Weissberg 1976).

Rather than formulating policy by drawing on public opinion for guidance, policy-making elites are likely to base their choices on other considerations. Hence elites often define their appropriate role as one of leading rather than following. Again it is useful to quote former Kennedy adviser Theodore Sorensen (1963), who put it this way: "No president is obliged to abide by the dictates of public opinion. . . . He has a responsibility to lead public opinion as well as respect it—to shape it, to inform it, to woo it, and win it. It can be his sword as well as his compass."

The notion that policymakers see public opinion as something to be shaped, not followed, is understandable when we recall the tendency of the public to acquiesce to government decisions. The propensity to accede to leaders' choices and not to mobilize to alter them minimizes the impact on foreign policy that the public can exert. Government's responsiveness to public preferences is further reduced by the public's usual passivity. The conclusion that follows is that the American public participates (through elections, for example) without exercising power. It is involved but does not have influence.

Such a conclusion certainly requires qualification. Rather than asking if there is a direct causal connection between public opinion and the content of foreign policy, it may be more appropriate to inquire into the functions of public attitudes in the process itself.

Public Opinion as a Constraint on Foreign Policy Innovation

One of the reasons American foreign policy proved so resistant to change during the Cold War and since is that public images of international politics are themselves resistant to change. As we have already noted, fundamental beliefs regarding foreign relations are typically inflexible:

> Almost nothing in the world seems to be able to shift the images of 40 percent of the population in most countries, even within one or two decades. Combinations of events that shift the images and attitudes even of the remaining 50 or 60 percent of the population are extremely rare, and these rare occasions require the combination and mutual reinforcement of cumulative events with spectacular events and substantial governmental efforts as well as the absence of sizable cross-pressures. (Deutsch and Merritt 1965, 183)

Public opinion thus acts as a brake on policy change, not by stopping innovations but by limiting modifications because of policymakers' perceptions of the inflexibility and unpredictability of public opinion.

The constraining impact of the "Vietnam syndrome"—or what has been called a "national first commandment," namely, "there shall be no more Vietnams" (Sussman 1988)—illustrates the tendency. If decision makers *think* the public voice will not permit certain initiatives and fear that the public may become mobilized against innovations, that in itself may restrict the kinds of alternatives considered. As one pollster put it, political leaders regard public opinion "as the great gorilla in the political jungle, a beast that must be kept calm" (Sussman 1988). Their task, then, is to "keep things quiet," which means they seek "to stifle public debate on matters that people care about, or should care about." It is perhaps for these political and psychological reasons that American foreign policy is perceived by so many analysts and political leaders to be constrained by public attitudes: "Mass opinion may set general limits, themselves subject to change over time, within which government may act" because the "opinion context . . . fixes the limitations within which action may be taken" (Key 1961). "Fear of electoral punishment," even if unrealistic, serves to limit what decision makers are likely to do—if for no other reason than their (often erroneous) assumption that "the public will never stand for it" (Waltz 1971).

The inability of the Reagan administration to win support for a firmer posture toward the Sandinistas is a good example of the constraining influence of public opinion (see Sobel 1993). One analyst has gone so far as to suggest that public opinion probably prevented Reagan from launching an invasion of Nicaragua (Sussman 1988). He also argues that public opinion forced Reagan to withdraw the marines from Lebanon in 1984. These assertions are difficult to prove, but there is no doubt that large numbers of Americans feared that aid to Central America eventually would result in U.S. military involvement in the region and that support for the U.S. role in Lebanon was never widespread. Arguably apprehension about a wider U.S. role in Bosnia also explained the public's reluctance to support even limited American involvement in the Balkans during the Bush and Clinton presidencies.

Although public opinion may constrain foreign policy (by shaping the range of permissible policy options, for example), too much importance should not be ascribed to the limits it imposes. These constraints are undermined by the acquiescent attitudes of most Americans toward most foreign policy initiatives. If the public sets the outer limits of policy actions, those limits are very broad and elastic.

Indeed, a characteristic closely related to the rally-round-the-flag phenomenon is the extent to which the public is "blindly obedient" to almost any policy the government proposes. Consider the following: Before Johnson announced his Vietnam policy in 1965, only 42 percent of the public favored such an approach; after the announcement, 72 percent favored it. Only 7 percent favored an invasion of Cambodia before it occurred, but after Nixon announced the 1970 "incursion," 50 percent supported it. In May 1989, 59 percent opposed a U.S. military invasion of Panama to overthrow General Manuel Noriega after he voided Panama's election results. By October the proportion had grown to 67 percent, but following the Bush administration's action in December, 80 percent responded that the U.S. was justified in sending military forces to invade Panama to overthrow Noriega. Many more examples could be cited (Brewer 1980; Weissberg 1976; but cf. Sigelman 1979).

These data support the proposition that public opinion is inclined to approve of the decisions that leaders make. Moreover, because of the historical tendency of the public to go along with most government actions, decision makers can assume they have public support. Public passivity and acquiescence invite presidents to act first and then wait for public approval. Indeed, rather than reflecting on and responding to public opinion, policymakers most often seek to create a climate of opinion favorable to contemplated policies and then turn to public opinion to obtain support for policy actions already chosen. Theodore Roosevelt stated it bluntly: "I did not 'divine' what the people were going to think. I simply made up my mind what they ought to think and then did my best to get them to think it." Similarly, George Elsey, an adviser to President Truman confided that "The president's job is to *lead* public opinion, not to be a blind follower. You can't sit around and wait for public opinion to tell you what to do. . . . You must decide what you're going to do and do it, and attempt to educate the public to the reasons for your action."

Public Opinion as a Stimulus to Foreign Policy Innovation

Exceptions to the general rule of public apathy and powerlessness are rare, but in some instances changes in public opinion precede rather than follow changes in policy.

Consider the issue of American policy toward Mainland China's admission to the United Nations. A growing proportion of the public favored admission at the same time that influential segments of the policy-making community remained in rigid opposition to it. In 1950 less than 15 percent of the American public favored admission, but by 1969 over half supported it (Mueller 1973, 15–17), a level of support that may have made the eventual U.S. decision not to block admission possible. In much the same way, support for the recognition of China by the United States also rose dramatically in the decade before President Carter extended recognition in 1978 (Shapiro and Page 1988).[14]

Another instance where changes in public attitudes were ahead of policy shifts was the Vietnam imbroglio, where the dissatisfaction of the public with continued intervention was often deeper and more vocal than among government leaders. Similarly, public demonstrations of outrage in 1985 toward South Africa's racial policy of *apartheid* by a small group of activists appeared to rally public opinion and to be critical in bringing congressional pressure to bear on the administration to abandon its South Africa policy known as "constructive engagement." It also may have contributed to the congressional decision a year later to override a presidential veto to place sanctions on South Africa. More recently, a plurality of the general public and an even larger number of opinion leaders supported normalization of relations with Vietnam long before the Clinton administration took this initiative (Rielly 1991, 24–25; also Rielly 1995, 21). Large numbers also support entering into negotiations with Cuba and North Korea toward this end (Rielly 1995). In these cases, public preferences lay the basis for foreign policy change.

Instances like these suggest that the public occasionally may serve as a stimulus to policy change, especially when the issue is specific and the public is mobilized. But it would be incautious to suggest that changes in public attitudes *cause* policy innovation. It is probably more accurate to argue that a mobilized public can influence the course of policy only indirectly, by changing "the image of public opinion held by persons capable of affecting policy decisions" or by altering "the image of public opinion held by the public itself" (Rosenberg 1965). That is, public attitudes may serve as a source of foreign policy by affecting how policymakers think about the international environment, the choices in it, the climate of domestic opinion, and the latitude available for their decisions.

Public Opinion as a Resource in International Bargaining

There are advantages to foreign policy making that derive from quasi-democratic processes. Public attitudes may not only reduce the inclination toward risk and foreign adventure, they also may give policymakers important bargaining advantages when dealing with foreign diplomats. The more unified public opinion, and the more supportive it is of official government policy, the stronger is the leadership's bargaining power with other nations. Here public preferences are seen as a resource to be used by policymakers in the execution of foreign policy. American diplomats, for instance, may enhance their ability to get their way at the bargaining table by claiming that the American public will never tolerate a proposed concession. Such claims sometimes work because American leaders not only can describe national opinion to foreigners as they wish but also understate their capacity to manipulate public opinion. By describing themselves as victims of popular preferences, diplomatic negotiators may indeed gain considerable bargaining leverage. "The fact that this decisional process may not in reality originate in the will of the people does not diminish the significance or usefulness of symbolically casting the threshold of national tolerance in terms of public opinion" (Fagen 1960).

These observations about the functions of public opinion demonstrate the complexity of links between mass attitudes and foreign policy behavior. "A democratic myth" is what Gabriel Almond (1960) called the notion "that the people are inherently wise and just, and that they are the real rulers of the republic." That conclusion is unassailable as far as it goes, but it is also true that the relationship between opinion and policy is affected by a cluster of intervening factors, including the nature of the issue, the leadership, policymakers' perceptions, and the international and domestic circumstances prevailing at the time of decision. And when mobilized, public opinion can exert a comparatively direct and immediate impact.

Finally, we should note that over time a strong correspondence exists between public preferences and the foreign policy ends and means American leaders choose.[15] That may seem paradoxical, since much evidence supports the existence of short-run discrepancies between public attitudes and foreign policy behavior. Yet the paradox itself speaks to the indirect nexus between public opinion and foreign policy, causing us to question how "a policy making system which has mastered all the modes of resistance to outside opinion nevertheless seems, from a long-run perspective, to accommodate to it" (Cohen 1973).

We have already suggested some answers to this puzzle, particularly in the ability of policymakers to mold public opinion to fit their preferred policy choices. When they engage in such activities, however, they may later become prisoners of their own past efforts to shape public opinion to fit their policy preferences. Public opinion is thus typically a conservative force, a source of inertia that acts as a restraint on policy innovation. Or, as Alan Monroe (Monroe, 1979) concludes in a comparative study of consistency between public preferences and public policy, the policy-making system makes it "more difficult to pass publicly approved changes than to maintain the status quo."

Political Culture, Public Opinion, and American Foreign Policy   . . . .

The nature of American society and politics is conducive to strong domestic influences on its foreign policy behavior. Comparatively speaking, the United States is a ***society-dominant system*** (Friedberg 1992; Katzenstein 1977; Risse-Kappen 1991). Thus, unlike, say, France and Germany, which are state-dominated political systems, the nature of domestic structures in the United States—buttressed by a political culture that emphasizes individualism and pluralism—facilitates the expression of public opinion on foreign policy issues. It provides multiple access points to decision makers. It also demands that policymakers monitor that opinion as they maneuver to build coalitions supportive of their policies. President Bush's determined effort to build and maintain public support in Congress and elsewhere for his policies in the Persian Gulf—which were haunted by the dreaded "Vietnam syndrome"—illustrates how even in the area of national security (long believed to be "above politics"), societal forces often exert a profound impact on American foreign policy. Indeed, some lament that "foreign policy is essentially politics-driven," with greater attention often given to poll results than to policy effectiveness (Schneider 1990). The "limits" to permissible behavior may be elastic, but they cannot be ignored completely without risking policy failure. Johnson learned that in Vietnam, as did Nixon in the Watergate affair and Reagan during the Iran-*contra* scandal.

In Chapter 9 we will look more closely at the access points through which public opinion and the political culture are sometimes expressed. These include interest groups and the electoral process. We will also examine the role of the mass media, an increasingly visible "transmission belt" through which politically relevant ideas circulate in the American polity.

NOTES

1. U.S. government data show that in 1993 the top fifth of the nation's population accounted for 48.2 percent of its annual income, while the bottom fifth accounted for only 3.6 percent. It is not surprising, then, that many Americans are familiar with poverty and homelessness. According to the Bureau of the Census, 15 percent of the nation's population—nearly 40 million Americans—in 1993 lived below the poverty line as defined by the government.

2. For alternate ways of conceiving the American political culture and their implications for public policy, see Dolbeare and Edelman (1985), Elazar (1994), Morgan (1988), and Parenti (1981).

3. Although this is the orthodox interpretation of Robert Kennedy's role during the deliberations over the Cuban missiles, transcripts of taped conversations during those meetings suggest that Kennedy was actually a proponent of the invasion option, of which air strikes would obviously be a part (see "White House Tapes and Minutes of the Cuban Missile Crisis" 1985).

4. The meaning of democracy, and the democratic premise, is captured by its Greek root: demokratia = *demos* (people) + *kratia* (power).

5. Such findings invite a negative estimate of the intelligence of the American people and their importance in the political system by suggesting, as Friedrich Nietzsche concluded, that "the masses are asses." It also invites the conclusion that leaders should ignore the opinions of the masses, along the lines of Oscar Wilde's famous adage that "those who try to lead the people can only do so by following the mob." Although some may be attracted to these viewpoints, neither conclusion is warranted by the evidence, as we will demonstrate in the next section.

6. A September 1989 *New York Times*/CBS News poll found that only 1 percent of the respondents regarded war as the most important problem facing the country, but 54 percent cited drugs as important. In January 1985, by way of contrast, 23 percent answered that the most important problem was war, nuclear war, and defense, and less than 1 percent mentioned drugs. Media "agenda setting," coupled with the ability of policymakers to "frame" issues (as the Bush administration did with respect to drugs) doubtless played roles in these dramatic shifts, quite apart from "objective" changes in the external environment. Agenda setting and framing are discussed later in this chapter.

7. See also Graham (1986), Russett and Graham (1988), Wittkopf (1990) and, for a contrasting viewpoint, Holsti (1987).

8. See Hinckley (1993), Holsti (1994), Holsti and Rosenau (1994), and Wittkopf (1994, 1995).

9. The classic study of belief system rigidity is Ole R. Holsti's (1962) examination of John Foster Dulles's image of the Soviet Union. Other studies that address the factors influencing the development of political attitudes and beliefs among mass and elite publics and why they are often resistant to change include Conover and Feldman (1984), Converse (1964), Festinger (1957), Herrmann (1986), Hirshberg (1993), Hurwitz and Peffley (1987, 1990, 1992), Larson (1985), Neuman (1986), and Zaller (1992).

10. Carter's foreign policy is often thought to have been "weak" and his policies and policy-making procedures characterized by inconsistencies and incoherence. Skidmore (1993–1994) offers an alternative view that emphasizes contradictions between internal and international pressures. "International incentives, arising from the dynamics of U.S. decline, initially pulled the administration toward a strategy of adjustment to external change. Domestic constraints favoring policy rigidity, however, eventually forced Carter to abandon much of his early reformist approach in an effort to salvage his dwindling domestic popularity." See also Hoffmann (1979–1980) and Rosati (1993).

11. Much of the literature that seeks to explain fluctuations in presidential popularity focuses on the impact of economic variables. The pioneering work incorporating foreign policy was done by John Mueller (1973). Ostrom and Simon's (1985, 1989) extension of that work to the impact of political drama generally is especially illuminating.

12. After two years in office, however, Clinton's ratings compared favorabley with other presidents' rating at their two-year marks. Clinton's approval stood at 47 percent, Johnson's at 46, Ford's at 49, Carter's at 43, and Reagan's at 38. Nixon's rating was much higher (56 percent), and Bush's even more so (83 percent).

13. See also Fite, Genest, and Wilcox (1990), Shapiro and Mahajan (1986), and Smith (1984).

14. Relevant case studies on the impact of public opinion in the foreign policy domain include Gilboa (1987), Kusnitz (1984), Leigh (1976), and Levering (1976). Powlick (1991) also shows that American foreign policy officials generally accord greater weight to public opinion than is

sometimes thought, and that when opposition to a decision emerges, they try to change public opinion by "educating" it to their preferences.

15. See Monroe (1979), Page (1994), Page and Shapiro (1992), and Stimson, MacKuen, and Erikson (1994).

SUGGESTIONS FOR FURTHER READING

Almond, Gabriel A. *The American People and Foreign Policy*. New York: Praeger, 1960.

Barnet, Richard J. *The Rocket's Red Glare: When America Goes to War—The President and the People*. New York: Simon & Schuster, 1990.

Dallek, Robert. *The American Style of Foreign Policy: Cultural Politics and Foreign Affairs*. New York: Knopf, 1983.

Holsti, Ole R., and James N. Rosenau. *American Leadership in World Affairs: Vietnam and the Breakdown of Consensus*. Boston: Allen & Unwin, 1984.

Hunt, Michael H. *Ideology and U.S. Foreign Policy*. New Haven: Yale University Press, 1987.

Lind, Michael. *The Next American Nation: The New Nationalism and the Fourth American Revolution*. New York: Free Press, 1995

Mueller, John. *Policy and Opinion in the Gulf War*. Chicago: University of Chicago Press, 1994.

Page, Benjamin I., and Robert Y. Shapiro. *The Rational Public: Fifty Years of Trends in Americans' Policy Preferences*. Chicago: The University of Chicago Press, 1992.

Roberts, Sam. *Who We Are: A Portrait of America Based on the Latest U.S. Census*. New York: Times Books/Random House, 1994.

Small, Melvin. *Johnson, Nixon, and the Doves*. New Brunswick, N.J.: Rutgers University Press, 1988.

Sobel, Richard, ed. *Public Opinion and U.S. Foreign Policy: The Controversy over Contra Aid*. Lanham, Md.: Rowman & Littlefield, 1993.

Wittkopf, Eugene R. *Faces of Internationalism: Public Opinion and American Foreign Policy*. Durham, N.C.: Duke University Press, 1990.

Zaller, John R. *The Nature and Origins of Mass Opinion*. New York: Cambridge University Press, 1992.

CHAPTER 9

• • •

THE TRANSMISSION OF VALUES, BELIEFS, AND PREFERENCES: INTEREST GROUPS, THE MASS MEDIA, AND PRESIDENTIAL ELECTIONS

• • •

The government of the United States . . . is a foster child of special interests.

President Woodrow Wilson, 1913

We in the media do not focus on the national interest, but on what interests the nation. It's the policymakers who must keep the national interest clear.

Ted Koppel, *Nightline* Anchor and Managing Editor,
ABC News, 1995

According to liberal democratic theory, leaders are chosen to reflect societal values by converting public preferences into policy. By extension, American foreign policy is, in the final analysis, an expression of Americans' sentiments. As a former secretary of defense put it, "foreign policy does not rest upon a definition of the national interest. It rests on public opinion" (Schlesinger 1989).

How realistic is that viewpoint? We concluded in the last chapter that, because the United States is a society-dominant political system, public opinion is likely to play a more important role in shaping American foreign policy than in other political systems, where the power of both the state and societal groups is more centralized than in the United States (Katzenstein 1977). Still, it is not clear whose opinions are heard. Often the disjunction between elite and mass preferences is large, as we also noted in Chapter 8. Moreover, the American political system may be premised on the value that "all men are created equal," but clearly that is not the case. Some people have more access to policymakers than others, and some have more influence. Such disparities are the stuff of politics: The "outs" want to become the "ins," and they typically court the disadvantaged in their drive for power and influence. Nonetheless, disparities in power and influence within the American polity raise important questions about who really controls American foreign policy and policy making. Do elected and appointed leaders indeed devise policies that reflect general preferences? Or do they instead devise policies that cater to a privileged elite from which the leaders themselves are drawn?

Or policies that appeal to specialized interests? In short, what is the correspondence between the theory and practice of democratic liberalism in America?

We seek an answer to that question in this chapter by focusing on the access points through which public opinion and the political culture may be expressed. Specifically, we examine the social background characteristics of American leaders, the nature and influence of special interest groups on American foreign policy (including the so-called military-industrial complex), the role of the mass media in shaping and transmitting information and opinions, and finally, the impact of foreign policy attitudes and issues on presidential elections.

Democratic Liberalism in Theory and Practice

Two models compete to explain how societal preferences are translated into the political process, the elitist and pluralist models. Both provide important insights into the societal sources of American foreign policy, but each also raises troublesome questions in a political culture premised on "we the people."

Does a Power Elite Control American Foreign Policy?

The United States is undeniably a democratic society. The complication with that description is that it is also a special-interest society (as well as a bureaucratic society, an information society, a mass consumption society, a technocratic society, and so forth). In particular, when we ask whether those who make American foreign policy share the convictions and attributes of Americans in general, perplexing findings emerge.

Who Is Chosen to Lead?

In terms of numbers, not many: Only a few thousand individuals out of the 260 million Americans decide about war and peace. It is also quite clear that only certain types of people have for years been recruited into the nation's foreign policy community. Not everyone is eligible; people are selectively recruited, and those outside the mainstream are denied access and the opportunity to serve. Furthermore, because some hold advantages in the competition for positions—by virtue of family connections, income, and education—top officials are not drawn proportionately from a cross-section of American society. The result is an "elite" not only in the sense that a small minority controls policy-making power but also in the sense that America's foreign policy managers are typically drawn from an unrepresentative coterie.

The elitist character of foreign policy making becomes apparent when policymakers' backgrounds are cataloged. Remarkably similar characteristics describe America's foreign policy establishment since its rise to globalism. Consistent with what is usually meant by the term "elite," the group is comparatively small and its composition enduring, having changed little in at least half a century. Since World War II if not before, the top positions have been filled by people from the upper class who were educated at the nation's best schools. They are, as the title of a prize-winning book put it,

The Best and the Brightest (Halberstam 1972).[1] Furthermore, they have generally come from predominantly white, Anglo-Saxon, Protestant (WASP) backgrounds; a disproportionate number have been trained in law; and many have had extensive experience in big business. Indeed, most policymakers' prior careers were spent as managers or owners of major corporations and financial institutions or on the faculties of the nation's elite universities, and more often than not they served in appointed rather than elected positions while in government (Brownstein and Easton 1983; Burch 1980). The evidence from 1961 to 1988 on the career experience of executive officials in the "inner cabinet" (the secretaries of State, Defense, and Treasury and the Attorney General) shows that 81 percent previously served in the national government, 46 percent worked in private business, 62 percent were attorneys, and 27 percent had academic careers (Lowi and Ginsberg 1990, 268). The pattern continued into the Bush administration. Of its cabinet-level appointees 90 percent held previous government posts, 35 percent previous corporate posts, 40 percent had careers in law, and half were educated in the Ivy League (Dye and Zeigler 1990, 18–19). In essence, the existence of this governing elite makes popular sovereignty fictional—a myth that "served to legitimate the rule not of the people, but of a small and privileged elite" (Thomas 1988).

Bill Clinton campaigned in 1992 on the promise that he would make his administration "look like America," but the picture that later emerged is quite different. Clinton did appoint a larger number of women and minorities to top jobs in his administration than had his predecessors. He also relied more heavily on personnel who had previously held government positions (many in elected offices) and were trained in law, but he picked few with backgrounds in business or the military. In these ways the Clinton administration is distinctive. "But like all previous administrations, the friends of Bill and Hillary [were] drawn overwhelmingly from among the most-privileged, best-educated, well-connected, upper- and upper-middle-class segments of America. There is very little 'diversity' in the educational and social backgrounds of [the top 18] Clinton advisors" (Dye 1993; also see Dye 1995).

The rise of the "meritocracy" is how one observer characterized the unusually high levels of educational attainment of Clinton's appointees: "Perhaps more than any in our history, Clinton's is a government of smart people." It is also "the most networked. Friendships formed at elite colleges and law schools have been sustained through an archipelago of think tanks, foundations, councils, and associations" (Ignatius 1994).

Commonality of experience—reinforced by the short line of elites in front of the revolving door between government service and the private sector—fosters uniformity in foreign policy attitudes. The continuity of American foreign policy during the Cold War can be traced in part to the shared characteristics of the self-selecting, self-recruiting, and self-perpetuating "governing elite" in charge of that policy. Like-minded individuals "guarded" American foreign policy by instructing incumbent administrations on similar policy principles (Domhoff 1984). Often called the "Establishment" or the "Wise Men," they believed they possessed the training and experience necessary to make the right foreign policy decisions—and that public opinion would support their choices. Many names come readily to mind: Robert Lovett, John McCloy, Robert McNamara, Henry Stimson, Averell Harriman, James F. Byrnes, the Dulles brothers (Allen and John Foster), George F. Kennan, Dean Acheson, Clark Clifford, Paul Nitze, Nelson Rockefeller, Paul Warnke, the Bundy brothers (William and McGeorge), Dean Rusk, Elliot Richardson, George Ball, Richard Nixon, the Rostow brothers (Walt and Eugene), Henry Kissinger, Zbigniew Brzezinski, James Schlesinger, George Bush, Cyrus Vance, George Shultz, Alexander Haig, Dick Cheney, Caspar Weinberger, James A. Baker, Brent Scowcroft, Lawrence Eagleburger, Warren Christopher, Anthony Lake, and Joseph S. Nye.

Every postwar president—including Bush and Clinton—found himself dependent on this coterie of elites and its advice. Perhaps this is what led John F. Kennedy to respond, when urged during his 1960 campaign to hit his critics harder: "That is not a very good idea. I'll need them all to run this country."

The Council on Foreign Relations   The recruitment and advisory roles of the Council on Foreign Relations illuminate the channels through which American elites and their preferences have often been funneled into the foreign policy-making process. The council has been described as "the most influential policy-planning group in foreign affairs" (Dye 1990) and its journal, *Foreign Affairs*, as the most influential magazine in the country (by *Time* magazine). Its limited membership is drawn from among the most prestigious and best connected of the nation's financial and corporate institutions, universities, foundations, media, and government bodies. And its members (limited to fewer than twenty-five hundred), past and present, include most of those previously named as having moved through the revolving door of government service. "Every person of influence in foreign affairs" (Dye 1990) has been a member, including presidents. Among them was Jimmy Carter, who as governor of Georgia was appointed to the the Trilateral Commission, a kind of multinational wing of the council headed at the time by Columbia University political science professor Zbigniew Brzezinski. Brzezinski later became Carter's national security adviser. In all, nineteen of those who had been among the Trilateral Commission's sixty-five members were appointed to top positions or served as official advisers early in the Carter administration (*Washington Post*, January 16, 1977, pp. Al, A4)

The council's presumed influence continued into the 1980s, as most of the Reagan administration's top officials could be counted among its members. Vice President George Bush, Secretary of Defense Caspar Weinberger, Secretaries of State Alexander Haig and George Shultz, Secretary of the Treasury Donald Regan, and CIA Director William Casey were all members. Bush resigned from the council "to deflect right-wing attacks that he was part of the CFR 'conspiracy' to subvert U.S. interests to an 'international government'" (Dye 1990). However, Brent Scowcroft, who would become Bush's national security adviser, and Dick Cheney, his secretary of defense, remained. Similarly, several members of the Clinton administration's cabinet, including the president himself, are members of the prestigious organization, as is Anthony Lake, Clinton's national security adviser.

The council sees its role as building elite consensus on important foreign policy issues. "It initiates new policy directions by first commissioning scholars to undertake investigations of foreign policy questions. . . . Upon their completion, the [council] holds seminars and discussions among its members and between its members and top government officials." Furthermore, *Foreign Affairs* is "considered throughout the world to be the unofficial mouthpiece of U.S. foreign policy. Few important initiatives in U.S. policy have not been first outlined in articles in this publication" (Dye 1995).

The consistency between studies and reports initiated by the council and articles appearing in *Foreign Affairs* and actual American foreign policy since World War II has been remarkable. The council does not actively advocate particular policies, but through its initiatives, publications, and other consensus-building strategies it has played a key role in the development of such policies as containment, the NATO agreement, the Marshall Plan, the International Monetary Fund and World Bank, and diplomatic relations with China. It also effectively advocated major initiatives in American military strategy. It proposed "flexible response" as a substitute for the doctrine of "massive retaliation," for example, and it supported military involvement in Vietnam and, later, withdrawal. And its 1980s Project paved the way for a number of the Carter administration initiatives in human rights, nuclear nonproliferation, arms sales, and North-South relations.

Similarly, through the Council on Foreign Relations, the foreign policy elite called in the late 1970s for a fundamental reevaluation of Soviet-American relations in response to a perceived Soviet military buildup. Ronald Reagan followed by making a massive rearmament program a centerpiece of his foreign policy. Later, the council would urge a thaw in Soviet-American relations, and it became involved in the initiation of the Strategic Arms Reduction Talks (START) and the intermediate-range nuclear forces (INF) arms control talks with the Soviet Union. It also advocated the "no first use" principle regarding nuclear weapons—something clearly at odds with Reagan administration preferences.

Other Policy Planning Groups   The Council on Foreign Relations is the most important private policy-making entity linking the elite in American society to the government, but it is not alone. Today an array of private policy planning organizations and "think tanks" seek to exercise influence across the broad spectrum of American foreign policy, including national security and foreign economic policy. Among them are the Brookings Institution, the Carnegie Endowment for International Peace, the Cato Institute, the Center for Strategic and International Studies, the Committee for Economic Development, the Business Roundtable, the American Enterprise Institute, the Institute for International Economics, the Heritage Foundation, the Overseas Development Council, the Center for Defense Information, and the Worldwatch Institute.

The Aspen Institute, a policy discussion group, recently figured prominently in knitting together the Clinton administration's foreign policy team, successors to the generation of Wise Men. The Aspen Strategy Group, established in the early 1980s to discuss contentious arms control issues, counted nearly every senior foreign policy official among its members, including Al Gore, Les Aspin, William Perry, John Deutch, James Woolsey, Joseph Nye, Strobe Talbott, and David Gergen. The broad goal of the Aspen Strategy Group as it met through the years "was to rebuild, through regular social and intellectual exchanges, the kind of bipartisan foreign policy elite that steered the nation during the early Cold War years. It was, in that sense, a social club for smart people" (Ignatius 1994). Another goal was "to discuss issues, not resolve them. And for most of the participants, this [was] a forum for making debating points, rather than expressing deeply held convictions." Thus members of the Clinton foreign policy team may have learned how "to make clever interventions, but not how to weave a broader tapestry" (Ignatius 1994).

The cohesion and perhaps influence of the traditional foreign policy elite waned in the 1980s. It was challenged by new centers of power and wealth (Schulzinger 1985), the rise of a "counter establishment" (Blumenthal 1988) and now a strongly conservative "counterculture" (Atlas 1995), and a growing division between "the newly rich, entrepreneurial Southern and Western *cowboys* and the established, managerial Eastern *yankees*" (Dye 1990, 1995; see also Christopher 1989). It also was challenged by the ascendance of a new class of foreign policy "professionals" whose technocrat outlook differs from the traditional elitist perspective (Destler, Gelb, and Lake 1984; see also Smith 1991).

The 1990s pose still other challenges to the premises on which the Establishment's approach to American foreign policy rested for half a century. As the interlocking of American society with the world political economy proceeds, the line between foreign and domestic policy will blur even further. Pressures largely domestic will seek to shape policy in new directions (Clough 1994). Furthermore, the end of the Cold War will further accelerate the destruction of the premises on which the Establishment's influence rested.

> As long as the Cold War endured and nuclear Armageddon seemed only a missile away, the public was willing to tolerate such an undemocratic foreign policy making system. But in the eyes of most Americans the world is no longer so menacing—messy, bloody and sometimes shockingly brutal, yes, but a threat to our security and peace, no. . . . Without a clear and present danger, the public is no longer willing to trust experts to make the right decision when it comes to the lives of their sons and daughters, especially when the experts themselves are so deeply divided. (Clough 1994, 4)

Elites have long played a prominent role in foreign policy making. The social characteristics of the Clinton administration's top advisers make it clear that this will continue. But George Bush will be the last president whose foreign policy training, experience, and outlook are firmly grounded in the premises of the Establishment's Wise Men.

Elite Attitudes and Behavior

Democracy encourages the participation of different people and the expression of their often divergent preferences. Therefore, the consistency between government policy and the recommendations of a cadre of statesmen-advisers-financiers outside of government does not necessarily pose a problem for liberal democratic theory. But what if we ask the related question: Are the values and outlook of foreign policy-making elites and others with influence different from those of the American people they presumably represent? If leaders are different from those they lead, does a small minority actually control the majority?

Evidence on these questions is mixed. Elites generally have been "public regarding," perceiving themselves as "guardians of the public good"; moreover, most Americans have generally registered approval of elites' policies. (The exception, of course, was Vietnam, which destroyed much of the Wise Men's credibility and clout.) Ironically, however, the attitudes of elites and the mass public about the democratic process itself often diverge:

> Democratic values have survived because elites, not masses, govern. Elites in the United States—leaders in government, industry, education, the media, and civic affairs and the well-

educated, prestigiously employed, and politically active—give greater support to basic democratic values and "rules of the game" than do the masses. And it is because the American masses respond to the ideas of democratically minded elites that liberal values are preserved. (Dye and Zeigler 1990, 14)

But elites' commitment to liberal democratic values appears only relatively greater than that of the masses, and that commitment may turn out to be especially fragile during times of crisis. When war threatens, fearful elites tend to

respond by curtailing freedom and strengthening security. Convincing themselves that they are themselves preserving liberal democratic values, elites may cease tolerating dissent, curtail free speech, jail potential counterelites, and strengthen police and security forces in the name of "national security," or "law and order." Ironically, these steps make society less democratic rather than more so. (Dye and Zeigler 1990, 16)

Even in routine circumstances elites often frame policies to protect their advantaged positions. The result, argue Thomas R. Dye and Harmon Zeigler (1990), is that "changes and innovations in public policy come about when elites redefine their own values. However, the general conservatism of elites—that is, their interest in preserving the system—means that changes in public policy will be incremental rather than revolutionary. Public policies are often modified but seldom replaced."

Does a Military-Industrial Complex Control American Foreign Policy?

The argument that American foreign policy is democratic because the foreign policy elite represents the public at large is challenged by those who see elite opinion diverging from that of the mass public. Indeed, a "power elite" (Mills 1956) consisting of a select few allegedly governs America[2] without direction from the majority. Thus the American political system gives the public participation (elections, for example) without power and involvement without influence, while a small set of elite participants, acting both openly and behind closed doors, makes the important decisions. Even elected officials might properly be thought of more as "proximate policymakers," whose actions give official sanction "knowingly or unknowingly" to the values of the power elite, rather than as conduits through which mass preferences are translated into public policy (Dye 1990). Thus actual government authority does not reside with the people—the Lockean liberal tradition and the doctrine of popular sovereignty notwithstanding. It rests instead in the hands of a select minority who exercise substantial power over foreign policy making and public policy in general.

This discrepancy between the theory and practice of democratic governance is most visible wherever power is concentrated—allegedly a defining characteristic of the military-industrial complex.

The Theory

President Eisenhower, a highly decorated World War II general, first brought national attention to the existence of a "military-industrial complex" when he warned, in an often quoted passage from his farewell address given on January 17, 1961:

This conjunction of an immense military establishment and a large arms industry is new in the American experience. The total influence—economic, political, even spiritual—is felt in every city, every statehouse, every office of the Federal Government. We recognize the imperative need for this development. Yet we must not fail to comprehend its grave implications. Our toil, resources, and livelihood are all involved; so is the very structure of our society.

In the councils of government we must guard against the acquisition of unwarranted influence, whether sought or unsought, by the military-industrial complex. The potential for the disastrous rise of misplaced power exists and will persist.

The military-industrial complex was a threat, Eisenhower felt, because its vast power undermined the countervailing forces that would otherwise keep the abuse of power in check. "We must never let the weight of this combination endanger our liberties or democratic processes," he cautioned.

Eisenhower's warning came at about the same time as Harold D. Lasswell (1962) prophesied that a "garrison state" governed by "specialists in violence" would arise to dominate policy making and as C. Wright Mills (1956) alleged that a power elite promoted policies designed to serve its own, rather than the nation's, interests. Mills, using a somewhat different label than Eisenhower, thus described the military-industrial partnership:

> The "Washington military clique" is not composed merely of military men, and it does not prevail merely in Washington. Its members exist all over the country, and it is a coalition of generals in the roles of corporation executives, of politicians masquerading as admirals, of corporation executives acting like politicians, of civil servants who become majors, of vice-admirals who are also the assistants to a cabinet officer, who is himself, by the way, really a member of the managerial elite. (Mills 1956, 278)

According to Mills, the partnership among these interests is more a natural coalition than a conspiracy. The interests do occasionally join forces to strive for the same self-serving ends, but not necessarily by design and infrequently through coordinated activities. "The power elite," wrote Mills, "is composed of political, economic, and military [personnel], but this institutionalized elite is frequently in some tension: it comes together only on certain coinciding points and only on certain occasions of 'crisis.'" Later theorists would describe the ***military-industrial complex*** as a partnership of "(1) the professional soldiers, (2) managers and . . . owners of industries heavily engaged in military supply, (3) top government officials whose careers and interests are tied to military expenditure, and (4) legislators whose districts benefit from defense procurement" (Rosen 1973).

It is not surprising that members of this elite lack a unified voice on key issues. Nonetheless, its entrenched (if disorganized) power is believed to derive naturally from a capitalist economic system dependent on foreign involvement for economic benefit. In particular, the post-World War II arms race and the high level of U.S. military spending during the period were often attributed to the self-aggrandizing activities of the military and industrial sectors, which (so the reasoning goes) propagated policies favorable to its interests. As a "peddler of crisis" (Sanders 1983) that benefited from trouble abroad, the complex justified its existence during the Cold War by provoking fear of the Soviet menace and the need for vigilance in order "to wage a war against cutbacks and not the Soviets" (Thompson 1990). External dangers were allegedly exaggerated to rationalize unnecessary weapons programs and ensure that the military budget would continue to grow "regardless of whether there is war or peace" (Parenti 1988). In so doing, it promoted policies beneficial to itself but arguably detrimental to the nation as a whole. Even now, critics fear that money spent to continue research, development, and procurement of Cold War weapons is money that cannot be used for investments targeted at critical domestic needs.

Adherents to the thesis of a powerful military-industrial force in American society stress that its combined components outweigh other, potentially countervailing domestic forces. Thus the complex is able to predominate over other societal groups (cf. Friedberg 1992). "Each institutional component of the military-industrial complex has plausible reasons for continuing to exist and expand. Each promotes and protects its own interests and in doing so reinforces the interests of every other. That is what a 'complex' is—a set of integrated institutions that act to maximize their collective power" (Barnet 1969). As Eisenhower put it,

> The Congressman who seeks a new defense establishment in his district; the company in Los Angeles, Denver, or Baltimore that wants an order for more airplanes; the services which want them, the armies of scientists who want so terribly to test their newest views; put all of these together and you have a lobby.

In short, the military-industrial partnership is so influential because it permeates the whole of American society.

The Evidence—Part I: The Cold War Years

The belief that the interests of the military-industrial complex have been unfairly served to the possible detriment of the national interest is buttressed by considerable circumstantial evidence. Some drawn from the waning Cold War years is described below.[3]

- "In the mid-1980s, at the height of the Reagan administration's planned $2.3-trillion defense buildup, the Pentagon was spending an average of $28 million an *hour*. . . . By 1990 . . . the total defense-spending boom for the Cold War years [would] total $3.7 trillion in constant 1972 dollars—nearly enough 'to buy everything in the United States except the land: every house, factory, train, plane and refrigerator'" (Ignatius 1988, 23).
- One of every sixteen American workers relies directly on the military-industrial complex for his or her paycheck, and millions more are indirectly dependent on them as customers (Thompson 1990, 10). "More than 30 percent of mathematicians, 25 percent of physicists, 47 percent of aeronautical engineers, and 11 percent of computer programmers work in the military-industrial complex" (Lipsitz and Speak 1989, 290). "For every billion dollars that the Pentagon cuts from its arms budget, almost thirty thousand jobs will be lost by industry" (Reifenberg 1990, 22).

- The list of top fifteen companies receiving prime contract awards from the Pentagon has remained remarkably stable since World War II, especially among aerospace manufacturers (McDonnell Douglas, Lockheed, Boeing, Rockwell International, General Dynamics, General Motors, and United Technologies). "Six of the eight aerospace production lines have had a continuous contracting relationship with one military service . . . in most cases back to World War II" (Kurth 1989).

- Typically, the prime aerospace contractors receive a new contract as a current production line phases out an existing award according to the "follow-on imperative," which holds that "a large and established aerospace production line is a national resource . . . . The Defense Department would find it risky and even reckless to allow a large production line to wither and die for lack of a large production contract" (Kurth 1989).

- "The imperatives of the industrial structure are reinforced . . . by the imperatives of the political system. Four of the major production lines are located in states that loom large in the Electoral College: California (Rockwell and Lockheed-Missiles and Space), Texas (General Dynamics), and New York (Grumman). Three others are located in states that for many years had a senator who ranked high in the Senate Armed Services Committee or Appropriations Committee" (Kurth 1989).

- The Pentagon's 20,000 prime contractors and 150,000 subcontractors and vendors "labor" under a noncompetitive "funny form of capitalism," which subsidizes corporate profits and cushions contractors "from the impact of their inefficiency" by a process known as "contract nourishment" (Atkinson and Hiatt 1985). One study concluded that "virtually all large military contracts have cost overruns from 300 to 700 percent" (Parenti 1988, 88).

- Fraud, waste, bribery, and corruption have been chronic in military contracting, as attested by procurement abuses in the 1980s that included "$748 . . . for a pair of $7.61 pliers, a $7,000 coffee pot, and $600 toilet seats" (Meier 1987, 125). In the wake of such disclosures "the military . . . added seven thousand additional staffers to solve its spare-parts problems" (Reich 1985, 36).

- "In seventy-seven cases of shoddy construction work reviewed by Pentagon auditors in 1982, only once was the contractor forced to pay for his mistakes" (Atkinson and Hiatt 1985). Shoddy work encourages expansion of the Pentagon's staff and budget to manage its operations, but it continues. Even as the Cold War waned, the Pentagon pressed ahead with "a $4 billion electronic radar-jamming device that has failed crucial flight tests on fighter planes it is designed to protect" (*New York Times* October 23, 1990).

- Universities do substantial basic research for the Pentagon. Seduced into partnership, they no longer serve as a countervailing balance to the military-industrial community. "Our job," one MIT researcher noted, "is not to advance knowledge but to advance the military" (cited in Parenti 1988).

- Numerous private "consulting firms" and "nonprofit" think tanks compete for a share of military "research monies." "Few civilian analysts are to be found" in the employment of these firms, popularly known as the "beltway bandits" (because of the proximity of their offices to the interstate beltway around Washington, D.C.). Instead, they are populated with former Pentagon personnel and retired officers (Pincus 1985). "Studies that challenge higher authority, that deviate much in either tone or color from the represented service's pitch or uniform hue" are few and far between (Brewer and Bracken 1984).

- Support for Rand Corporation and other federally funded research and development centers (FFRDCs) that design and test weapon systems and devise war-fighting strategies increased by 30 percent between 1987 and 1991 (Pearlstein 1994, 31). The centers receive Pentagon contracts without competitive bidding.

- Defense spending consistently accounts for a high percentage of federal outlays. Even under conditions of massive budget deficits, federal debt, and a diminishing Soviet threat, the Bush administration in 1990 sought a $7 billion increase in military spending for 1991 and further increases each year thereafter through 1995. As a Pentagon budget official wryly noted, "Only over here do we call a $1 billion hike—we wanted a $10 billion hike—a $9 billion cut" (Thompson 1990, 6D).

These anecdotes and insights provide empirical support for the alleged existence of a complex of military-industrial interests—at least during the Cold War. But its influence on American foreign policy is easily overestimated. It may be true that pressures for increasing or continuing defense spending are brought to bear by some lobbyists and defense contractors, but it does not follow that the military-industrial partnership single-mindedly pursues this objective above all others. Indeed, the profits of many American industries that do contract work for the Pentagon do not depend heavily on it. Furthermore, war and foreign adventure, alleged by the more radical versions of the military-industrial construct to be critical to its survival, actually threaten the financial interests of corporate America and the lives (though not the prospects for promotion) of military officers. Thus the military-industrial complex undoubtedly colored much activity during the Cold War abroad and at home, particularly with respect to the structure of defense spending and the corresponding impact on the shape of the nation's military capabilities. Nevertheless, the nation's foreign policy initiatives did not derive solely from the pressures of the faceless complex; the evidence is too contradictory. Where there is interest, there is not necessarily influence.

The Evidence—Part II: The Post-Cold War Years

The end of the Cold War portends important changes in the politics of defense spending. Critics of the military industrial complex theory argue that these changes demonstrate it was "at best, inadequate and, at worst, inaccurate. The power of the military-industrial complex, if it was real, ought to have been sufficient to prevent severe budget decline, hardware cancellation, and base closings, the very events taking place in the 1990s" (Adams 1994). Certainly there is merit in this critique, but it overstates the extensiveness of the changes now taking place.

As the post-Cold War military build-down gained momentum during the Bush administration, defense advocates offered several arguments designed to slow its pace, including protecting the nation's "defense industrial base" and maintaining "excess capacity" that could be brought into production in the event of a major war. At the same time, sales of U.S. military equipment to other nations increased dramatically. Liberal Democrats in Congress, who previously opposed such arms transfers, now supported them, as concern about jobs back home and related presumed economic benefits took precedence (see Renner 1994). The sale of seventy-two advanced F-15 aircraft to Saudi Arabia in 1992 was particularly notable, as it enjoyed the support not only of congressional Democrats but also of presidential hopefuls George Bush and Bill Clinton. The Bush administration earlier had shelved the Saudi request, but Bush revived it during the campaign to keep production lines at McDonnell Douglas Corporation going and to preserve an estimated seven thousand jobs (see also Chapters 5 and 12). Clinton went a step further, supporting two weapons systems the Bush administration wanted to ax: the Seawolf submarine and the V-22 Osprey tilt-rotor aircraft. And he proposed to cut only $60 billion dollars from the $1.33 trillion five-year base-force plan already proposed by Bush. Meanwhile, the Pentagon began to pick up costs military contractors had previously paid as they sought to sell U.S. military hardware in trade shows around the world.

The Bush administration's ill-fated effort to kill the V-22 Osprey—a vertical takeoff transport plane ordered by the Marine Corps but opposed by top-level Pentagon officials as unnecessary and too expensive—illustrates how the *iron triangles* inside the defense policy process preserve weapons systems even in the face of stiff opposition. The concept refers to the bonds that link defense contractors and interest groups (the private sector), defense bureaucrats (the executive branch), and members of Congress (the legislative branch) into a single entity that is exceedingly difficult to break. In the case of the Osprey, one side of the triangle was shaky—defense bureaucrats at the top; but they faced determined opposition from the two other sides of the triangle as well as opposition from within the Pentagon.

> The interest-group side was represented by the aerospace companies (led by Boeing) and unions (led by United Auto Workers) that produced the plane. They mobilized a national network of workers and supplier companies with a toll-free hotline to Congress, and a national "Tilt Rotor Appreciation Day" capped off by a flight demonstration in Washington. Members of Congress whose districts would lose jobs and money were brought on board. Several members began weekly strategy sessions with lobbyists, and one representative hosted a cocktail party that drew two hundred lobbyists and industry officials, checkbooks at the ready. Defense PACs [political action committees] vowed to step up contributions to members of key congressional committees who had already received $2 million the year before. And the bureaucratic side of the triangle, working inside the Pentagon, was the Marine Corps, which wanted the program. (Bennett 1994a, 292)

The Osprey survived—helped in part by the support it received in the presidential campaign. Thus, by the time Bill Clinton was sworn into office, the pattern was clear:

> Politicians of all stripes seem preoccupied with keeping military spending high for economic and political reasons. The closing of military bases and weapons production lines is tenaciously fought. New justifications for military spending at home and abroad are eagerly

sought. In addition, despite the end of the Cold War and the collapse of communism, Democrats still seem fearful of being accused of being "weak on defense." ("President Clinton and the Military." *The Defense Monitor*, 22 no. 2 [1993]: 2)

Clinton affirmed that reality a year later. In his second State of the Union message he declared to loud applause that "We must not cut defense further." The pledge followed the Pentagon's "bottom-up review" which, however, seemed to have "invented" certain "requirements" "to justify the forces and structures we have rather than to cope with the world we face" (Borosage 1993–1994). Projected spending remained just below Bush's target at $1.3 trillion. This kept the budget at Cold War levels (excluding the Korean and Vietnam war years; see Figure 9.1). Moreover, despite Secretary of Defense William Perry's claim that the budget contained "no Cold War relics," many long-standing and controversial weapons systems remained (see Focus 9.1). And management of the Pentagon's massive and perennially mismanaged programs seemed to cry out for new spending before new savings could be realized. As Perry told a cost-conscious Congress during his nomination hearings, "Our financial procedures, our financial data processing systems, our financial processes are obsolete and inadequate to the task. [It will take] a substantial investment to dig us out of the hole. [I]n terms of the savings which we can accrue, which I am confident are there, we are going to have to front-end load with investments in new systems before we can have the hopes of achieving these savings."

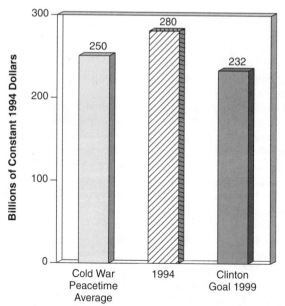

Figure 9.1 U.S. Military Spending, 1948–1999 (constant dollars)
Note: Based on Department of Defense data. 1948–1989 Cold War peacetime average excludes the Korean and Vietnam War years.
Source: "1995 Military Spending: The Real Story," *The Defense Monitor* 23 no. 5 [1994]: 3.

Focus 9.1
More Money for Cold War Weapons

• • •

	Year Weapon System Begun	1994 Funding Level (billions)	1995 Budget Request (billions)
AH-64 Apache helicopter	1991*	0.2	0.3
Ballistic missile defense	1976	2.7	3.3
C-17 Globemaster III transport plane	1981	2.4	3.0
E-8A JSTARS reconnaissance plane	1983	0.9	0.8
F-22 fighter	1982	2.1	2.5
F/A-18 Hornet fighter-bomber	1990†	1.4	1.3
JAST fighters	1994**	.03	0.2
MILSTAR communications satellite	1983	0.9	0.6
New attack submarine	1992	0.4	0.5
Nuclear aircraft carrier	1993††	1.2	2.5
RAH-66 Comanche scout helicopter	1984	0.4	0.5
Trident II nuclear missile	1979	1.1	0.7
V-22 Osprey tilt-rotor aircraft	1983	.01	0.5
Total		$13.7	$16.7

* The original Apache program was initiated in 1972.
† The original Hornet program was initiated in 1975.
** This program is a follow-on to earlier canceled aircraft programs such as MRF, AFX, and A-12.
†† The first of this class of nuclear aircraft carrier was begun in 1967.

Source: "1995 Military Spending: The Real Story," The Defense Monitor 23 no. 5 [1994]: 2.

The military-industrial complex theory does not fully explain the Clinton (and Bush) defense budget story, but it is not inconsistent with it either. In this context Mills's description of the "Washington military clique" as more a natural coalition among convergent interests than a conspiracy is revealing. The current focus of this partnership's rhetoric on "jobs" more than "profits" does not invalidate the idea. Indeed, one critic of the Clinton administration described its posture in terms

President Eisenhower would easily identify: "The political calculation that protects the military budget is simply the administration's desire not to engage in a pitched battle with the uniformed military and its industrial and congressional allies" (Borosage 1993–1994).

Do Special Interest Groups Control American Foreign Policy?

The power-elite thesis and the related theory of an influential military-industrial complex challenge the theoretical tenets of liberal democracy. If in practice an elite indeed rules, and if its behavior is supported by an all-powerful military-industrial complex and subgovernments of iron triangles, then "democratic" policy formation is a political myth. Foreign policy making under such conditions is less an expression of the values and preferences of the American people at large than a reflection of the motives and interests of a privileged few.

Juxtaposed to this conclusion is an alternative view—that individual Americans influence policy by organizing themselves into groups to petition the government on behalf of their shared interests and values. This is the basis of *pluralism* in American politics, which draws attention to the role that groups, associations, and organizations play in political life. It is also the basis of the pluralist model of public policy making, which purports to explain how liberal values and democratic institutions are preserved even while democracy in its purest form (direct participation) is precluded.

Advocates of the pluralist model acknowledge that the demands of a modern, complex government with global interests and entanglements necessarily concentrate power in the hands of a few. Citizens do not and cannot participate directly in public policy making. Nonetheless, the potential tyranny of elites is prevented and democracy preserved, because multiple interests are represented by leaders who themselves are in competition with one another. Public preferences therefore find expression through bargaining among interest-group elites who take the public into account—not because they are sincerely concerned about the public welfare (as elite theory maintains) but because the mass public exerts pressure on them through the voluntary associations they represent. From this perspective, interest groups are to be applauded, not decried. Indeed, they are a central element in the description of the United States as a society-dominated political system.

The system of checks and balances that the nation's founders devised provides citizens with multiple access points to decision makers, and interest groups provide the means of access. Thus interest groups help guard against the abuse of power by any one interest, especially the possibility that one interest would capture control of the instruments of governance, a fear uppermost in the minds of the framers of the Constitution. Competition among countervailing centers of power is the mechanism. Even iron triangles, from this perspective, are not to be deplored, as they are means of linking citizens to the various branches of government otherwise divided by the constitutional separation of powers.

Competing interest groups serve the public interest in policy making much as Adam Smith theorized that the invisible hand of the marketplace serves it in the economic sphere, with the pursuit of private interests contributing to the general welfare. The product is government for the people if not necessarily of or by them.

Types of Interest Groups

So pervasive are the organized interests in American society that the United States is often portrayed as an "interest group society." Evidence supports the description.

> In 1986 the Internal Revenue Service listed 929,415 tax-exempt organizations—an increase of nearly 43,000 in a single year. Among that throng, an observer atop the White House gatepost can count over 19,000 that, national in scope, were formed in part to press their views on the federal Executive and Legislative branches. That is *double* the number that existed in 1970; new ones form at the rate of 1,000 a year. These groups act through 11,000 Washington representatives—who are regular habitués of the White House neighborhood. (Patterson 1988, 15)

The many thousands of organizations that Americans join and support to further their causes range in size from the large, powerful groups representing comparatively heterogeneous constituencies, such as the American Association of Retired Persons (AARP, the largest interest group in the nation, with 32 million members), to smaller, more homogeneous groups organized around rather specific issues, such as the Sierra Club (650,000 members). Most are concerned primarily with economic issues and seek to promote policies that benefit the particular interests of their members. The AFL-CIO is an example in the area of organized labor, as is the American Farm Bureau in agriculture. Among the smaller proportion of *noneconomic* groups three types stand out: *public interest* groups, *single-issue* groups, and *ideological* groups (Patterson 1994).

Public interest groups differ from the economic interest groups in that they seek to represent the interests of society as a whole and to realize benefits that are often less tangible. Ralph Nader's Public Citizen is perhaps the most visible public interest group, but other prominent examples of this comparatively new breed include Common Cause and the League of Women Voters. *Single-issue groups* seek to influence policy in more narrowly defined areas, such as the environment (the Sierra Club's special concern, as witnessed in the debate over Nafta's environmental impact). The United Nations Association of America, which continually monitors and seeks to influence U.S. policy toward the United Nations, is an example in the foreign policy domain. Various ethnic interest groups with particular foreign policy concerns, which we will note in more detail later, are also properly regarded as single-issue groups. *Ideological groups*, on the other hand, are concerned with a broad array of policies but from a particular philosophical viewpoint. Americans for Democratic Action and The Conservative Caucus, for example, generally support liberal and conservative positions, respectively, in foreign and other policy arenas.

Three other types of actors should be regarded as interest groups broadly defined. First, foreign governments hire lobbyists in an effort to influence the decisions of American foreign policymakers and members of Congress on issues of importance to them. By law, nondiplomatic representatives of other nations are required to register as lobbyists; approximately one thousand registered agents represent foreign countries' interests (Schlozman and Tierney 1986, 54). Japan has been especially active in promoting its interests and protecting itself from attacks on its trade policies. In addition to hiring lobbyists, it has supported various think tanks and academic institutions. In 1988 and 1989 Japanese government agencies, corporations, and foundations spent $400 million "trying to win American 'hearts and minds,'" far more than any other foreign country (Judis 1990, 20; see also Choate 1990).

Second, departments and agencies of the U.S. government act much like interest groups. They have their own conceptions of appropriate policy and take steps to ensure their views are represented in decision-making circles. The Pentagon, for example, historically has employed (using taxpayers' dollars, of course) hundreds of "congressional liaisons" whose purpose is to secure legislation favorable to itself. As we will show in Chapter 13, the size and complexity of the American government has expanded the lobbying role of bureaucratic agencies, whose activities occur largely outside the public eye. Iron triangles are not confined to defense issues but are widely evident in other policy areas as well. Often called "issue networks" rather than iron triangles, they comprise government officials, lobbyists, and policy specialists whose shared interest and expertise in a particular "issue" bring them together.

And third, both state and local governments conduct their own foreign economic policies, and their activities (often in competition with one another), especially in the solicitation of foreign direct investment, resemble those of special interest groups (see Goldsborough 1993; Kline 1983; and Tolchin and Tolchin 1988).

Interest Groups and Foreign Policy

However reassuring to democratic theory the pluralist interpretation may be, in the foreign policy arena, where the questions at issue are often technical and remote from the daily lives of Americans, the presence of organized interests raises the specter of policy domination by narrow vested interests. Because interest-group activities are not always visible or attended by the press, interest groups are often assumed to be working secretly behind the scenes to devise policies that serve their own interests, not those of the nation. Indeed, many people firmly believe that foreign policy is determined by special interests, and their beliefs are reinforced by some dramatic evidence. For instance, the American Israel Public Affairs Committee (AIPAC)—a principal component of the so-called "Jewish" or "Israeli Lobby" with fifty-five thousand members, a staff of more than one hundred, and a budget of in excess of $12 million (Grove 1991, 8)—is often suspected of controlling America's Middle East policy (see Bard 1994, Tivnan 1987). U.S. recognition of Israel only eleven minutes after it declared its independence; congressional passage of the Jackson-Vanik amendment denying the Soviet Union promised trade benefits pending changes in its policies regarding the emigration of Soviet Jews; and the provision of $12,350 (in 1987) in U.S. military aid per Israeli soldier (*Harper's* October 1987, 15) lend credence to these perhaps exaggerated impressions. So powerful is AIPAC that its detractors claim it has made Israel "America's fifty-first state."

Ethnic interest groups—representing Americans of Jewish, Arab, Greek, Irish, and Armenian descent, and those with ancestry in the so-called Captive European Nations (the communist states in Eastern Europe), among others—have long played an active role in seeking to shape American foreign policy (understandable in a nation of immigrants). Yet one long-time Senator, Charles McC. Mathias), has worried that the effects of ethnic group lobbying may be more harmful than beneficial:

> Ethnic politics, carried as they often have been to excess, have proven harmful to the national interest. . . . They have generated both unnecessary animosities and illusions of common interest where little or none exists. There are also baneful domestic effects: fueled as they are by passion and strong feelings about justice and rectitude, debates relating to the interplay of the national interest with the specific policies favored by organized ethnic groups generate fractious controversy and bitter recrimination. (Mathias 1981, 997)

Ethnic interest groups lobby Congress and the administration on matters of immediate concern to their members. Trade is another policy arena that has evoked considerable interest group activity—again because tangible interests, such as jobs and profits, are at stake. Congress is usually the focal point of organized activities designed to affect trade policy. The economic groups involved historically have included such well-known multipurpose organizations as the Chamber of Commerce and the AFL-CIO, as well as a veritable cacophony of more specialized groups whose numbers have grown in recent years, ranging from the California Walnut Growers Association to the United Auto Workers; from the International Association of Ice Cream Manufacturers to the National Association of Stevedores; and from the Sugar Workers Council of America to the Semiconductor Industry Association (see Bauer, Pool, and Dexter 1972; Destler 1995; Destler and Odell 1987).

Despite the ubiquity of ethnic interest groups and those involved in trade policy, which to a large extent is more domestic in nature than most foreign policy matters, the interest groups involved in other foreign policy questions historically have not figured prominently in efforts to influence American foreign policy. (There are some notable exceptions, such as the China lobby, which for two decades sought to prevent U.S. diplomatic recognition of communist China.) Defense policy questions have emerged as an important exception in recent years, as did U.S. policy toward Central America during the Reagan administration. In both cases, special interest groups sought to influence policy using the tactics normally associated with domestic interest group activity, including writing letters to members of Congress, testifying at congressional hearings, meeting with members of the media, publicizing the voting records of candidates for office, working in electoral campaigns, engaging in protests and demonstrations, and the like.

During the early phases of détente, for example, a number of well-known lobbying groups (such as the Arms Control Association, the Center for Defense Information, the Council for a Liveable World, Committee for a Sane Nuclear Policy, the United Nations Association, and the Women's Strike for Peace, among others) were active proponents of U.S. efforts to relax tensions with the Soviet Union. They were opposed in their efforts by an equally prominent set of organized groups, which included the AFL-CIO, the American Legion, the American Enterprise Institute, the American Security Council, the Heritage Foundation, the National Conservative Political Action Coalition (NCPAC), the Veterans of Foreign Wars, and various ethnic interest groups (Cox 1976). Eventually, the Committee on the Present Danger emerged as an especially visible and vocal critic of détente and in particular the 1979 SALT II treaty, doubtless playing a critical role in creating a domestic political environment inhospitable to its ratification (see Caldwell 1991; Sanders 1983).

In the case of Central America, the Reagan administration confronted a broad array of organized opponents, in which various religious groups figured prominently, but it also enjoyed the support of a countercoalition of groups, which at one time numbered more than fifty (Arnson and Brenner 1993, 202). On balance, however, it appears that the opponents enjoyed the upper hand. This was especially evident in Congress where the administration's policies toward Nicaragua were never popular, as witnessed by the administration having organized its own efforts in the White House and the State Department to build public support for its policies (see Parry and Kornbluh 1988).

The Reagan administration's decision to launch its own domestic "public diplomacy" efforts on behalf of its Central American policies implies that organized interest groups do indeed have the ability to affect foreign policy. Lending further credence to that view, Reagan complained six weeks prior to leaving the presidency that an "iron triangle" in a "Washington colony," composed of the Congress, the news media, and special interest groups, was "attempting to rule the nation according to its interests and desires more than the nation's."

How Influential Are Special Interest Groups?

How effective are the lobbying efforts of interest groups, particularly in the area of foreign policy? Is it true that special-interest groups, operating both openly and behind the scenes to pressure the government for certain policy positions, in essence control public policy? Are private interests rather than the national interest being served as a result?

The following conclusions summarize the results of studies addressing the linkage between domestic interest groups and policy making with particular reference to foreign policy decisions:

- As a general rule, interest groups exert a far greater impact on domestic than on foreign policy issues, because the requirements of national security give the government elite relative immunity from domestic pressures.

- Interest group activity operates as an ever-present, if limited, constraint on policy making. But the impact *varies with the issue*; in particular, "the less the importance of the issue, the greater the likelihood of group influence" (Milbrath 1967).

- Similarly, the occasions when interest groups are most influential are rare. Interest group influences are greatest when only a small segment of the populace is affected and the issue is not in the public spotlight, attended by the mass media. "A lobby is like a night flower," AIPAC's director of foreign policy issues once noted. "It thrives in the dark and dies in the sun" (Grove 1991).

- Crises tend to stimulate interest: As the crisis level increases, the interests of more groups are likely to be at stake and groups are likely to try to exert more influence. But "as the crisis level increases further, and especially as decision time shortens, there is relatively little opportunity for group interests to be taken into account [and] the president has enormous power to shape public opinion and receives little effective challenge from interest groups" (Milbrath 1967).

- Influence between the government and interest groups is reciprocal. However, government officials are more likely to manipulate interest groups than the latter are to exercise influence over government policy.

- The ability of interest groups to mold opinion on foreign affairs is limited. Many interest groups attempt to influence public opinion rather than policy itself, but mass attitudes are seldom amenable to manipulation by interest group efforts.

- Single-interest groups have more influence than large, national, multipurpose organizations, but their influence is limited largely to their special policy interest.

- Interest groups sometimes seek inaction from government and maintenance of the status quo; such efforts are generally more successful than efforts to bring about policy change. For this reason interest groups are generally regarded as agents of policy stability.

- Interest group influences tend to expand during election years, when candidates for office are most prone to open channels of communication and to give interest groups access.

- Interest groups exercise power over policy most effectively through Congress; correspondingly, when congressional interest in a foreign policy issue mounts, interest group activity and influence increase.

- The ability of an interest group to exert influence on foreign policy increases in those situations (such as national security) where "symbols" can be created that are unlikely to be opposed by other groups with material interests in that symbol.

- Interest groups exert their greatest influence on nonsecurity issues that entail economic considerations commanding attention over a long period of time.

The foregoing characteristics of interest group efforts to shape foreign policy suggest that the mere presence of such groups, and the fact they are intended to persuade, does not guarantee their penetration of the policy-formation process. Interest groups may be effective on certain special issues. However, more often the foreign policy-making process is relatively immune to direct pressure by interest groups. An important reason is that, within the policy-making arena, interest group influences often counterbalance one another.

Interest Groups and the Politics of Policy Making

The theory of democratic pluralism postulates that the public good is served when each group in a multitude of organizations with diverse interests seeks to maximize its own interests. The ability of any one group to exert disproportionate influence is off-set by the tendency for *countervailing powers* to materialize over the disposition of any particular issue. As one group emerges and gains power, others will to spring up to balance it. When an interest group seeks vigorously to push policy in one direction, another (or a coalition of others aroused by perceived threats to their interests) will be stimulated to push policy in the opposite direction.

A historical illustration of these countervailing processes is found in the Industrial Revolution, when the threat of Big Business gaining control of American society was balanced by the emergence of Big Labor. Once Big Labor's influence threatened to become disproportionate, Big Government balanced it. Recent illustrations include the effort of the Committee on the Present Danger and its allies to defeat the SALT II treaty in response to the emergence of pro-détente lobbyists earlier in the decade; and the opposition to Nafta mounted by environmentalists and labor unions worried about the effect of the trade agreement on the environment and jobs. Similarly, the success of the Israeli lobby has led to the creation of the National Association of Arab-Americans, patterned after AIPAC, whose purpose is to take advantage of the American political process to promote a more "balanced" U.S. Middle East policy.

The presence of countervailing powers not only reduces the impact of particular interest groups; it also means that few decisions are final. No side can ever claim final victory, as each decision takes policy in one direction, only to set the stage for the next round of the contest. Often today's losers will be winners tomorrow. Consider, for example, President Carter's decision not to deploy the B-1 bomber, which he characterized as "one of the most difficult decisions that I have made since I have been in office." Opponents of the bomber included Clergy and Laity Concerned, the American Friends Service Committee, the National Taxpayers Union, the Federation of American Scientists, the Women's International League of Peace and Freedom, and Common Cause. Supporters included the weapon's prime contractor and subcontractors, their employees, and the Air Force Department (Kotz 1988; Ornstein and Elder 1978). The latter coalition lost the "battle" in 1977 but won the "war" four years later. Rockwell International kept the plane's prototype operative, and Ronald Reagan decided to deploy one hundred of the controversial and costly aircraft shortly after his election.

The presence of countervailing forces on all fronts suggests another reason for the relative impotence of interest group influence on American foreign policy: Interest groups maintain crisscrossing relationships with one another and have overlapping memberships. These relationships create *cross-pressures* within and among the multiplicity of groups operating in the domestic political setting. The number and diversity of groups striving for influence precludes the predominance of any one. Bargaining and competition prevents any one group from gaining advantage over others. Cross-pressures pull individuals in opposing directions, thereby reducing their capacity to concentrate on any single set of interests and diminishing their dedication to a single cause. Thus the fragmentation of power within a pluralistic domestic environment prevents any one organized interest from dominating the policy-making process.

The positive side of this picture is that no one interest dominates policy. That was the wish and intent of the nation's founders. The negative side is "gridlock." The term describes the seeming inability of the Republican-controlled White House and the

Democratic-controlled Congress during the Reagan and Bush administrations to cooperate with one another. But it also speaks to interest group politics. When the pursuit of one group's interests are balanced by another's, can anything be accomplished?

Political economist Mancur Olson addressed this dilemma and its consequences in two classic works, *The Logic of Collective Action* (1965) and *The Rise and Decline of Nations* (1982). His arguments draw on the theory of collective goods and the "free-rider" problem we discussed in Chapter 7. With respect to interest groups, Olson argues that small, private organizations (such as trade associations) often have an advantage over others as they seek to promote their interests, because larger groups (the American consumer) are unorganized. Individuals also have an incentive to free ride on organized interest groups, because they benefit from their activities even if they fail to share in the costs (nonunion labor, for instance, often enjoys the benefits that unionized labor has won through collective bargaining).

Building on the logic of these arguments, writer/journalist Jonathan Rauch (1994) argues that "demosclerosis" is the result: Democratic government can accomplish little that is meaningful, because each of the organized interests in American society seeks a share of the government's pie (taxes), even if this means *redistributing* wealth from one segment of society to another. "We have met the special interests and they are us," Rauch observes. "Much as mutual funds have offered ordinary people the access to almost every type of productive investment, so interest groups have offered ordinary people access to almost every kind of redistributive investment." Redistribution, then, is the key to demosclerosis: The more active government becomes, the more it stimulates the rise of interests groups whose purpose is to protect their members' benefits and seek to enlarge them. Eventually "the steady accumulation of subsidies and benefits, each defended in perpetuity by a professional interest group, calcifies government" (Rauch 1994; see also Lowi 1979). That conclusion is especially troublesome to those who would "downsize" the government and redirect power and resources from Washington to state capitals and local communities.

Policymakers routinely complain about the power of interest groups and promise to reign them in. Thus Bill Clinton echoed a long-standing theme when he declared on the night of his election that "perhaps the most important thing that we understand here in the heartland of Arkansas is the need to . . . reduce the influence of special interests and give more influence back to the . . . people." But promising change and realizing it are two vastly different things—as Clinton himself learned.

In response to various campaign financing irregularities and scandals, Congress passed election reform legislation in the 1970s to limit individuals' financial donations to candidates for political office. Inadvertently, Congress's action compounded the problem by making it easier to form *political action committees (PACs)* and enabling them to solicit voluntary contributions that could be channeled to particular candidates or to political parties. The number of PACs rose from about five hundred in 1974 to more than five thousand by the 1990s, of which more than two-fifths were associated with corporations (Patterson 1994, 392, 394). In 1988 PACs contributed more than $172 million to candidates for federal office. The largest contributor was the National Security Political Action Committee (NSPAC) whose controversial fundraising activities led the Bush campaign to disavow its support. Two years later PACs contributed about $150 million to congressional candidates, and in the first fifteen months of the 1993–1994 election cycle they contributed $70 million. PACs' campaign support is now so extensive as to warrant calling them "the new political parties" (Dye and Zeigler 1990).

PACs were particularly visible in their support of the "New Right" during the 1980s. Defense PACs supported by the nation's largest defense contractors and pro-Israel PACs are routinely among the largest contributors. By March 1994, fully eight months before the November congressional elections, for example, the contributions of only ten of the Pentagon's military contractors' PACs had contributed over $2 million to congressional campaigns. Typically the money goes to incumbent members of Congress who serve on committees with jurisdictions over the PACs' interests, such as the Armed Services committees of the House and Senate and their respective defense appropriation subcommittees. In the case of the pro-Israel PACs, who in 1984 alone spent over $4 million, "the highest concentration [of contributions in that year] was on races involving members of the Senate and House committees with Middle East jurisdictions and on opposition to five senators who supported the sale of AWACS aircraft to Saudi Arabia [in 1981]" (Uslaner 1986). Senator Charles Percy of Illinois, chair of the Senate Foreign Relations Committee, was a target of Jewish PAC efforts and lost reelection to Paul Simon, his ardent pro-Israeli rival. "All Jews in America, from coast to coast, gathered to oust Percy," claimed AIPAC's executive secretary, Tom Dine, following the election. "And American politicians . . . got the message."

PACs clearly have altered the pattern of campaign financing, and they have reinforced the view of critics of interest group politics, who argue that some groups have more leverage over the policy process than others. Still, countervailing power persists; no particular interest group dominates the entire range of foreign policy making, including national security and economics, and no particular PAC or coalition of PACs reigns supreme. Policy continues to be made through negotiated compromise among contending special interests. Foreign policy making thus resembles a taffy pull: Each group attempts to pull policy in its own direction while resisting the tugs of others. The result is that policy fails to move in any discernible direction. The struggle encourages middle-of-the-road solutions and maintenance of the status quo.

> When almost everybody is organized, society reaches a point where almost nothing can be done. Groups with limited power usually find it easier to veto someone else's proposal than to push through any positive policy of their own. When this happens, politics becomes negative, and interest groups turn into veto groups. Even where positive policies are possible, any substantial proposal has to be cleared with every relevant interest group. And the larger the number of organized groups, the more of them that must be consulted, the longer are the resulting delays, and the harder it becomes to turn any idea into action. (Deutsch 1974, 61)

Is it any wonder given these circumstances that American foreign policy manifests such continuity even in the midst of rapidly changing international circumstances? When competing interests petition the government for favors, policy resists change. Ironically, even the elitist perspective on policy making reinforces this viewpoint, as it, too, implies the prevalence of continuity over change in American foreign policy. Countervailing powers may not be operative, but the result is the same nonetheless.

Powerful military-industrial interests combined with a homogeneous policy-making elite promote the continuation of existing policy, as their interlocking interests have remained fairly constant for a half-century or more. To revise foreign policy would be to challenge entrenched and vested interests that support it. Because many influential Americans benefit from military spending, the United States steadfastly pursues military preparedness and today spends five to six times more on its military than any other nation. The imperviousness of the defense budget to sharp cuts, even in the face of budgetary stringency and the absence of a clear and present danger, attests to the influence of powerful and powerfully entrenched interests.

The elitist and pluralist models may result in essentially the same policies, but is one a better description of the impact of societal forces on the foreign policy process than the other? Although inconclusive, the balance of evidence somewhat favors the elitist model, lending credence to Richard Barnet's (1972) observation that American foreign policy is "an elite preserve . . . made for the benefit of that elite." "The flaw in the pluralist heaven," writes E. E. Schattschneider in his classic study, *The Semisovereign People* (1960), "is that the heavenly chorus sings with a strong upper-class bias." In fact, the elitist and pluralist accounts both depict a process in which the ordinary citizen matters very little in any direct sense when it comes to foreign policy making.

The Role of the Mass Media in the Opinion-Interest-Policy Process

If anyone is in a position to challenge the power of the privileged in American society, arguably it is the mass media. The communications industry—print, radio, and television—plays two pivotal roles. First, public attitudes may be influenced (created, some would say) by the information the media disseminate. Second, the behavior of policymakers themselves may be affected by the news the media report and by the images of the world they convey. From either perspective, the media are an important link in the causal chain that couples societal forces to the foreign policy process. Indeed, they seemingly are in a position to exert a potent influence on the shape of American foreign policy itself.

Many Americans are apparently taken with the notion the media shape public opinion. Indeed, some might even say that the media *are* public opinion. Government officials likewise attribute vast powers to the media. They may be right, as the evidence suggests that policymakers are able to use the mass media to mold public preferences to support their policies.

Policymakers themselves, however, are typically less than sanguine about the media. Their views have ranged from awe and fear to downright hatred, as every president has come to believe in his administration's victimization by the media. Jimmy Carter reflected that sentiment this way: "I've always been disappointed in two groups—the Iranians and the press." Carter's view and that of other presidents are perhaps best captured in Oscar Wilde's famous remark that "the President reigns for four years, but Journalism reigns forever." Thus many consider the mass media as a fourth branch of the government, sometimes called the ***fourth estate***. It is no accident, therefore, that presidents actively court the media's favor and ascribe to them the power to make or break government policy.

A broad variety of research shows that the mass media have an effect both on public opinion and on the shape of policy choices decision makers face. Still, the notion that the media are somehow able to "determine" either foreign policy or even foreign policy attitudes is questionable. The relationship between media influences and other societal sources of foreign policy behavior is more complex than this simple view suggests. A preferable hypothesis is that the mass media perform a mediating role, helping to shape both foreign policy attitudes and choices but not determining them. Let us examine this idea by looking, first, at the relationship between the mass media and the public and, second, at the relationship between the mass media and policymakers.

The Mass Media and the Public

The proposition that the mass media exercise unusual influence in shaping public attitudes is tempting if for no other reason than that they comprise the primary vehicle for the transmission of knowledge; and "knowledge is power." The institutions that provide Americans with political information are pervasive and sophisticated. Ninety-eight percent of all American households own at least one television set; and they view it an average of seven hours a day. There are over fifteen hundred daily newspapers in the United States, with total daily circulations exceeding 60 million. The three major weekly news magazines also claim nearly 10 million readers. This extraordinary establishment has the ability to determine "what the news is," to define behaviors as important actions, and thereby to make them into events.

The *agenda-setting* role of the mass media is particularly important (McCombs and Shaw 1972). Most people may be inattentive to foreign or other issues of public policy most of the time, but when they do show interest in such issues or are exposed to them, the mass media tell them what to care about. Put succinctly, "the mass media may not be successful in telling people what to think, but [they] are stunningly successful in telling their audience what to think about" (Cohen 1963). By telling us what to think *about*, however, the media also provide cues as to what to *think*, precisely because of their capacity to determine what we think about (Entman 1989). The ability of public officials to "frame" the way policy issues are presented by the media further enhances the media's capacity to shape individuals' thoughts and opinions.

The media's ability to set the agenda and to influence thinking in other ways is greatest among those who are neither interested nor involved in politics and hence lack political sophistication (Iyengar and Kinder 1987; Zaller 1992). Because most who comprise the mass public often have no prior information on which to rely in forming attitudes about new developments abroad, the media exert a potentially powerful impact on perceptions about events simply because the information they supply is new—and is often presented in a sensational way in an effort to influence "appropriate" preferences. Americans' understanding of the Soviet Union, for example, was always limited. Thus the media's portrayal of Mikhail Gorbachev and his policies of *glasnost* and *perestroika* significantly shaped perceptions of the Soviet Union and its leaders in the waning days of the Soviet empire (Hinckley 1989).

Furthermore, the attention the media give to different issues may contribute to their symbolic significance. During 1987, for example, the United States became increasingly involved in the Persian Gulf war between Iran and Iraq. However, news about its air attack on Iranian bases in the gulf region and the destruction of an Iranian domestic airliner by the *USS Vincennes* in October of that year was dwarfed by news of the dramatic Wall Street stock market crash. In "calmer times," Doris A. Graber (1993) observes, the Persian Gulf incidents "would have been the top stories."

The media not only set the agenda, they also function as **gatekeepers** by filtering the news and shaping how it is reported.[5] The gatekeeping role is especially pronounced in foreign affairs, as the menu of foreign affairs coverage offered the American people comes from remarkably few sources. Principal among them are three prestigious "newspapers of record" (the *New York Times*, *Washington Post*, and *Los Angeles Times*), two wire services (the Associated Press [AP] and United Press International [UPI]), and four national television networks (ABC, CBS, CNN, and NBC). Furthermore, newspapers such as the *New York Times* provide news to other newspapers, which typically follow their lead in the way they present news stories about foreign affairs to local audiences.

The *New York Times'* motto promises "all the news that's fit to print," but in fact there is too much news even for it. Thus, in choosing what to print, the media gatekeepers also shape the values to which Americans are exposed. Over the long run "the media tend to reinforce mainstream social values." They transmit "'normal' or legitimate issues and ideas to the public and [filter] out new, radical, or threatening perspectives" (Bennett 1980). Similarly, "pack journalism"—a troublesome phenomenon in which reporters follow the lead of one or a few others in deciding what is (or is not) news and how it should be interpreted—often leads to remarkably similar news accounts, particularly among the national print and electronic media (Graber 1993).

Clearly, as the foregoing ideas suggest, the media play a powerful role in American society. Why, then, is their impact on the public's foreign policy attitudes less direct and pervasive than might be expected?

Media Inattention to Foreign Affairs

The mass media's ability to shape foreign policy attitudes is undermined in part by the media's relative inattention to world politics and their comparatively greater concern for domestic news. Few reporters are paid to cover international affairs, and television programming is overwhelmingly oriented toward local, not national or international, news.

By some standards coverage of foreign affairs is not inconsequential. Doris Graber (1993, 361) reports that major Chicago newspapers devote about 6 percent of their space to international news and that national television networks give about 20 percent of their time to it. Still, foreign affairs certainly do not command overwhelming attention. In part this is due to the absence of a mass market for foreign policy news in the face of industry efforts to boost profits. The limited—and declining (Rosenblum 1993)—attention foreign affairs receives means that Americans remain ill-informed about the world around them at the very time that global forces are increasingly shaping their lives. One veteran AP foreign correspondent fears that American interests are being sacrificed as a result. "Had news executives used a fraction of the resources they spent on the [Persian Gulf] war to report on what was about to cause it," writes Mort Rosenblum (1993), "war might have been averted."

An exception to the comparatively scant attention other media give to foreign affairs is the coverage it receives in the national newspapers of record, sometimes called the *prestige press*. One study, for example, showed that the *New York Times* allotted over 40 percent of its total national and international coverage to foreign news (Frank 1973, 58).[6] How many people consume that coverage remains problematic, however, as the circulation of the *Times* constitutes but a fraction of the nation's newspaper subscribers.

The long-established television networks—ABC, CBS, and NBC—also devote a considerable portion of their news time to foreign affairs, as noted. Here the question is how much there is to consume: A full transcript of the typical nightly network news broadcasts, foreign and domestic, would not fill half of the front page of an average daily newspaper. Yet three-quarters of the American people routinely depend on this source for most of their foreign affairs information (Schneider 1984, 18). The proportion is even higher during times of crisis (Larson 1990).

CNN, the twenty-four hour Cable News Network, has come to occupy a place in providing world news that sets it apart from others. It maintains a global network of news-gathering offices, and its news broadcasts from around the world are seen around the world. Thus, courtesy of CNN, millions of Americans and others (including Saddam Hussein in Baghdad!) viewed at close range the dramatic aerial bombardment of Iraq at the onset of the 1991 Persian Gulf War. Two years earlier they witnessed the Chinese government's bloody suppression of prodemocracy forces on Tiananmen Square. CNN anchor Bernard Shaw captured the drama unfolding in China this way: "Unbelievably, we all came here to cover a summit, and we walked into a revolution."

Because of its continuous news coverage, CNN often reports news stories without the polish that editing normally adds to standard news broadcasts. "Reports are a mixed bag of events and interviews ranging from the trivial to the significant, with less time given to analysis and expert commentary than is typical for network television news. The emphasis is on taping whatever is readily and inexpensively available so that viewers are the first to see a breaking news event at close range" (Graber 1993). Audiences thus get a different perspective on events, as news accounts are quite different than the ninety-second predigested packages that appear on most newscasts.

Public Inattention to Foreign Affairs

Most Americans are uninterested in and ill-informed about foreign affairs, as we learned in Chapter 8. In late 1990, for example, as the Cold War was winding down and the United States was in the midst of the crisis over Kuwait, only 36 percent of the American people said they were very interested in following news about other countries and barely more than half were very interested in news of U.S. relations with other countries (Rielly 1991, 9). An earlier study found that three-quarters of the public claimed they paid attention to government and public affairs, but only about a third had above-average knowledge on these matters. Over 40 percent were poorly informed. This led the authors to conclude that, "while 76 percent of the people *say* they pay attention to politics, they clearly aren't taking notes" (Ornstein, Kohut, and McCarthy 1988, 53–54).

If the American people fail to listen to or digest news, then obviously the media are not influencing their opinions. Given a choice, Doris A. Graber observes, Americans "do not seek out foreign policy news." In December 1987, for example, as the United States and the Soviet Union prepared for a meeting designed to reduce the danger of war, NBC News broadcast an hour-long, prime-time interview with Soviet president Mikhail Gorbachev. "Only 15 percent of the national audience tuned in. Half of the viewers who at that time ordinarily watch NBC's entertainment programs switched to other networks" (Graber 1993, 361).

The Imperviousness of Beliefs

Research grounded in social psychology shows that most people do not easily change their beliefs, as we saw in Chapter 8. Popular myths notwithstanding, what they read in print and see and hear on television does not alter what they think.[7] Instead, they use information short-cuts that cause them to interpret new information in ways that reinforce, not restructure, prevailing attitudes. *Selective perception* is also a pervasive human tendency: People search for "comfortable" information that "fits" with preexisting beliefs, whereas they screen out or reject information with which they disagree. In short, we see what we want to see, we hear what we want to hear.

Selective perception is partially subconscious, stemming from the nearly universal need to maintain stable images when confronted with inconsistent and confusing information. In the parlance of psychology, everyone seeks to maintain "cognitive balance" (Festinger 1957), either by screening out information that runs counter to cherished beliefs or by suppressing information that challenges preexisting images. An individual subscribing to the simplistic belief that all revolutions and civil disturbances are communist inspired, for instance, is likely to reject or block out information that contradicts that theory, such as reports that civil conflict in South Africa stems from indigenous sources and not from outside intervention.

Selective perception is also pervasive because people are prone to avoid information with which they disagree. Most people read magazines and listen to news programs that reinforce interpretations consistent with their preconceptions. Few seek out information that challenges them. How many, for instance, routinely read magazines that reflect liberal views, such as *The Nation*, and also conservative ones, like *National Review?*

Individuals' lack of receptivity to wide-ranging ideas that challenge existing prejudices and stereotypes inhibits the mass media's ability to influence attitude change. "Selective recall" is a related tendency that reinforces attitude consistency. Even among those who are relatively sophisticated politically, long-standing ideological predispositions toward conservative or liberal perspectives shape interpretations of events communicated by the media.

Television's Inadvertent Audience

The pervasiveness of television in the homes and daily lives of millions of Americans requires that we add important caveats to the foregoing conclusions. Television has provided the mass of the American people with a huge infusion of foreign policy information that most neither like nor want. Instead, because most who watch television news see what does not interest them as well as what does—they don't "edit" the information television journalists supply by walking away from the set or turning it off—they have become an *inadvertent audience* (Ranney 1983). Even when the American people are attentive to foreign affairs, as clearly they were during the Persian Gulf War, the impact on their political knowledge of exposure to information remains slight (Bennett 1992).

What are the consequences of the intrusive force of television? First, television may explain the decline of confidence in the nation's institutional leadership witnessed during recent decades. As William Schneider (1982), a well-known political analyst, observes, "negative news makes good video. Consequently, television presents much of the news as conflict, criticism and controversy. . . . The public responds to this large volume of polarized information by becoming more cynical, more negative, and more critical of leadership and institutions." Less patience with foreign policy initiatives by individuals and institutions about which Americans are cynical and distrustful may be a related consequence of exposure to American involvement in world affairs, which television brings home but which most Americans find confusing and unnecessary. Others argue, however, that the news itself is what matters: "The confidence gap is more properly understood as a product of . . . bad news than as a reflection of the manner in which it is communicated to a gullible public by cynical, headline-seeking reporters" (Craig 1993).

Second, members of the inadvertent audience, being uninterested, are unlikely to have strong convictions about issues as do those who regularly follow foreign policy concerns. "When people with weak opinions are exposed to new information, the impact of that information is very strong. They form new opinions, and if the information they receive is negative or critical, their opinions will develop in that direction" (Schneider 1982). As Theodore Sorensen (1994) observed, members of the inadvertent audience, who watch "the screen by the hour instead of by program, . . . often find their attention unintentionally engaged by the picture unfolding before them, their interest inadvertently aroused, their opinions almost involuntarily formed, and their actions as well as reactions as voters and citizens spontaneously motivated." Still, "there is no evidence that television changes the nature of the public's concerns in the area of foreign policy," observes Schneider (1984). "These concerns remain what they always have been: peace and strength. Television simply intensifies these concerns and creates more negative and unstable public moods."

Third, television also has affected the relationship between the mass public and policymakers in important ways. Members of Congress who wish to make names for themselves (read *all*), for example, are induced to frame their foreign policy ideas in "one-liners" that will fit into the thirty-, sixty-, or ninety-second slots the evening news allocates to such issues. For the electorate it has meant that "a Presidential candidate without much prior international experience can come to office with a collection of half-minute clichés in his head masquerading as foreign policies" (Destler, Gelb, and Lake 1984). The growing importance of television in shaping electoral outcomes magnifies the impact of these "sound bites."

Because public opinion is both responsive to events and susceptible to manipulation, it is not surprising to find that policymakers energetically use television to create support for their policies, as television is now the principal means elites use to communicate to masses. A case in point occurred in 1983 when President Reagan used a masterful television speech to reverse sentiments about his policies following the death of 241 servicemen in a truck bombing of Marine headquarters in Lebanon and the invasion of Grenada which followed on its heels. Before the speech, 41 percent approved of Reagan's handling of Lebanon; after it, 52 percent approved. Before the speech, 52 percent approved of the invasion of Grenada; after it, 65 percent approved. The American people normally "rally 'round the flag"—and the president—during times of crisis and peril, as we saw in Chapter 8. The evidence in this particular case suggests the president can use the media to help define when those conditions exist.

Curiously, perhaps, the media also help to distinguish the many instances in which the president can expect to enjoy rally benefits from the fewer instances where he cannot. Political elites share similar interpretations of events in most situations that induce rally effects—or at least they choose not to voice their dissent. When recognized opposition leaders (in Congress, for example) fail to criticize a president during a crisis, "press and television accounts of the 'politics' surrounding the event will be usually full of bipartisan support for the president's actions," and the public will rally behind the president (Brody and Shapiro 1989). Sometimes, however, elites are divided. When this happens, the media understandably report it—this is "news." Faced with differences among opinion leaders about how to evaluate the situation, the public now looks to the actual events to form its own opinions. In these cases, that is, when dissent occurs, the rally phenomenon is either absent or less pervasive. The media themselves do not create dissent, but by transmitting legitimate critics' negative assessments of presidents or their performance, they become the conduits through which criticisms of presidential performance surface (Brody 1991; Brody and Shapiro 1989).

How Do Attitudes Change?

Mass foreign policy attitudes are resistant to change, but they do change. How? Television, we have suggested, plays a role, especially among those with little knowledge about or interest in foreign policy. The relationship between elites and masses also has a bearing on attitudes in the general population. When those most attuned to foreign policy adjust their beliefs to accommodate new foreign policy realities, the changes can be expected eventually to filter throughout society.

The classic explanation of the opinion-making and opinion-circulating process is known as the **two-step flow theory of communications**. As originally formulated, it says that "ideas often flow from radio and print to opinion leaders and from these to the less-active sections of the population" (Katz 1957). The dynamics of attitude change are best explained, the hypothesis holds, through the crucial channel of face-to-face contact. Members of the mass public do not actually sit down and exchange ideas with governing elites or those close to policymakers, of course. Instead, ideas become meaningful only after they have been transmitted to members of the mass public from opinion leaders such as teachers, members of the clergy, local political leaders, and others who have an above-average interest in public affairs and occupy positions allowing them to communicate frequently with others. Thus information does not flow directly from the mass media to the general population. Rather, it is transmitted first to opinion leaders (who, incidentally, inevitably distort it) and through them to the less interested or knowledgeable in mass society. Attitude change, according to this view, stems from changes in the thinking of the policy elite and those attentive to public affairs, with society at large following sometime later. Face-to-face contacts with opinion leaders are a crucial link in the diffusion process. Hence, the mass media are not the primary transmitters of ideas; nor are they the primary stimulus of mass attitude change. Instead, they are the conduits through which attitudes are first connected to the political system and then transmitted through interpersonal contact.

Television complicates this view. There are few or no apparent intermediaries between evening news anchors and the consumers of their messages. The two-step flow theory is thus clearly overly simple. A "multistep flow" theory is preferable, as it provides a more accurate description of the opinion-making and opinion-circulating process in an age of mass electronic communication.

> For one thing, the distinction between "opinion leaders" and their followers varies from issue to issue and from group to group; each of us is a leader occasionally and a follower usually. . . . In addition, the communication patterns of opinion leaders and their followers are . . . complex . . ., often with far more than two links in the chain. Opinion leaders talk to each other, crystallizing their views into a consistent stance. That stance may or may not be the media's stance; often an opinion leader will rely on the media for up-to-date information but integrate that information into long-held values, using the media more for ammunition than for guidance. . . . Finally, it turns out that nearly everyone absorbs some media content directly. We may not all pay as careful attention to a topic as opinion leaders on that topic do, but we all spend sizable portions of our lives with the media. Inadvertently, we pick up information and even values about the topic. (Sandman, Rubin, and Sachsman 1982, 4–5)

Clearly, though, even with a multistep flow of communications, the media play a crucial role in the transmission of opinions within the political system. Hence they are pivotal in the process of opinion making and opinion diffusion. Syndicated columnist William Safire has drawn particular attention to the opinion-shaping role the "Opinion Mafia"—those whom others might call "political pundits"—in his own retrospective comment on the original two-step flow theory. Arguing that in an environment when "political leaders tend to play it safe and consult polls before taking positions," more people turn to "those multimedia commentators who are ready to pound beliefs into shape while the iron of controversy and crisis is red hot" (Safire 1990).[8]

Our discussion to this point has supported the proposition that the media are able to shape public attitudes toward foreign policy, but it has also raised important questions about the pervasiveness of the media's influence. The relationship between the media and policymakers complicates our understanding of the media's role and influence as a societal source of American foreign policy.

The Mass Media and Policymakers

Ordinary Americans are often impervious to the media's influence because they tune out its messages. On the other hand, those at the top of the public opinion pyramid—policymakers, policy influentials, and the attentive public—often rely heavily on the information the communications industry disseminates. Television has a leveling effect in that even those indifferent to foreign affairs get some information about it while those making up the elite and attentive public take advantage of a broader array of information—virtually all of it from publicly available media sources. On the surface, then, it appears that the media may be most influential with those who have the most influence.

Policymakers, Policy Influentials, and the Media

To suggest that policymakers rely on the media—instead of the intelligence community, for instance—as a primary source of information may appear to be an exaggeration, but it is true. A study of roughly one hundred officials in policy positions found that nearly two-thirds reported the media were generally their most rapid source of information in crisis situations, and over four-fifths indicated the media were an important source of policy-relevant information (O'Heffernan 1991, 40).

This is the case partly because media reports about world developments are more timely and readable than official reports and are often perceived to be less biased than those of government agencies that gather data with a bureaucratic agenda in mind. Hodding Carter, a former State Department spokesperson, explained: "Most policy people, when they are not out there posturing and beating their chest in public about the effects of the media, would be happy to tell you how often they get information faster, quicker, and more accurately from the media than they get it from their official sources" (cited in O'Heffernan 1991).

Policy influentials likewise depend on media reports. Conservative writer William F. Buckley (1970)—no admirer of the news establishment of which he is a part—admitted that after hearing a radio bulletin of Egyptian President Gamal Abdel Nasser's death, "I slipped off to telephone the *New York Times* to see if the report was correct (one always telephones the *New York Times* in emergencies). The State Department called the *New York Times*, back in 1956, to ask if it was true that Russian tanks were pouring into Budapest." John Kenneth Galbraith (1969b), a former American policymaker, has also testified to the accuracy of the nation's elite newspapers: "I've said many times that I never learned from a classified document anything I couldn't get earlier or later from the *New York Times*."

Bernard Cohen, a careful student of the subject, put the special role of the prestige press this way:

> [The *New York Times*] is read by virtually everyone in the government who has an interest or responsibility in foreign affairs. . . . One frequently runs across the familiar story: "It is often said that Foreign Service Officers get to their desks early in the morning to read the *New York Times*, so they can brief their bosses on what is going on." This canard is easily buried: The "bosses" are there early, too, reading the *New York Times* for themselves. . . . The *Times* is uniformly regarded as the authoritative paper in the foreign policy field. In the words of a State Department official in the public affairs field, "You can't work in the State Department without the *New York Times*. You can get along without the overnight telegrams sooner." (Cohen 1961, 220–221)

More recent evidence suggests that policymakers now also ascribe special importance to television news accounts (see Larson 1990).

Media Vulnerability to Government Manipulation

To a considerable extent the media reflect, rather than balance, the attitudes of the government. During the 1979 Iranian hostage crisis, for example, the media rarely strayed from the government's line about what was happening (Larson 1990). Similarly, the media generally accept the government's definition of America's friends and foes. When those definitions change, the media reflect the changes. Even during the Vietnam War the media continued to the very end to give the administration's account of the conflict considerable attention.

By deferring to the government the media encourage public acceptance of the government's view of the world; basically this means the viewpoints of the president and the executive branch, who remain the primary sources of foreign policy information. Therefore, they are able most of the time to "set the agenda of coverage and frame stories to reflect official perspectives" (Graber 1993).

The crisis over Kuwait illustrates how the media and government together often shape opinion—and perhaps policy. Market research showed that the best way to frame the issue was to depict Saddam Hussein as an enemy of the American people and to use George Bush to accomplish that end. Once the issue was cast and sold in this way, some policy options became more acceptable and others less so. In particular, "the Saddam framing . . . made it possible to dismiss the leading policy alternative of economic sanctions against Iraq long before there was any empirical basis for doing so (i.e., long before it was reasonable to determine whether sanctions were working)" (Bennett 1994b).

What much of this suggests is that the media frequently operate as a conduit for the transmission of information from the governing elite to the American people rather than as a truly independent source of information about what the government is doing. Political journalist Theodore Draper describes the "game of politics and propaganda" between government officials and media representatives as one that "has become as stylized as an eighteenth-century dance."

> First the officials hand out privileged information to favored journalists ("U.S. intelligence flatly reported that . . ."). Then the journalists pass out the same information, with or without attribution, to their readers. Finally, pro-administration congressmen fill pages of the *Congressional Record* with the same articles to prove that the officials were right. (Draper 1968, 89)

The seeming collusion between media and government, whether conscious or unconscious, stems from a variety of sources, including the media's dependence on government news releases, their inability to obtain classified information, media self-censure, the government's use of "privileged" and "on background" briefings, and the fact that self-restraint is often in the media's self-interest.

Even the familiar news "leak," often used by incumbent administrations to float "trial balloons," by competing factions within the government to fight their bureaucratic battles publicly through the media, or by individuals to protect their political backsides, does not alter that conclusion. Indeed, it reinforces it. In addition to being required by their professional code of ethics to protect the confidentiality of "high government sources," reporters typically must offer such protection in order to be assured of receiving future news stories. It is clear that "high government officials" (meaning White House staffers and members of the Cabinet) are often the source of government "leaks." To cite but one example: Soon after James Baker resigned as secretary of state to take over George Bush's sagging re-election campaign "stories started suggesting that the campaign was in shambles and a loss would not be Baker's fault" (Kurtz 1993). In short, the leak is an American political institution, a practice rooted in tradition and employed routinely by officials in every branch and at every level of government.

Because of their interdependence, the media are vulnerable to government manipulation. News, in government parlance, is "manageable."[9] Because what is reported often depends on what is leaked for public consumption rather than on what has actually occurred behind closed doors, public relations and the art of governance are increasingly intertwined. Public officials themselves now engage in agenda setting and strive to place the correct "spin" on news stories that cast doubt on policymakers and their policies. In the extreme, the government effectively censors the news.

Censorship is anathema to democratic principles but occurs nonetheless, especially during periods of crisis and peril, when the nation's vital interests or security are believed to be at stake. Thus the Reagan administration denied reporters permission to observe the Grenada assault force in 1983, an intervention later revealed to be fraught with mistakes. Journalists covering the 1989 invasion of Panama also complained that the military deliberately kept them away from the action. The "pool" arrangement used during the Persian Gulf War had a similarly constraining impact. Only limited numbers of reporters were allowed to accompany military units. Their reports could only be passed on, even to journalists left behind, after having been "screened" by military authorities. Such scrutiny (censorship?) was defended as being necessary to ensure that news reports would not jeopardize U.S. forces in the region.

The control of information during the Persian Gulf War reflected the Pentagon's determination "never again to lose a public relations war." As political scientist W. Lance Bennett explains, "Many policy officials in the Defense Department and the State Department became convinced that the U.S. military defeat and eventual withdrawal from Vietnam resulted, in part, from critical media coverage of battlefield activities and sympathetic coverage of domestic opposition to government policies back home." The Gulf War gave the military a new lease on life, which they turned into "a public relations bonus" that paid huge dividends to Bush's popularity with the American people (Bennett 1994b).

Disclosures about government lies during Watergate and in areas that the government at one time routinely but liberally defined as matters of "national security" appear to have enhanced the mass media's ability to function as a check on government control. Furthermore, one of the clear lessons of the Iran-*contra* scandal is that covert foreign policy actions cannot long remain secret, despite the government's effots to hide them. Still, the fact that abuses of power seem to remain concealed for extended periods is perplexing. (For example, it was the foreign press, not the U.S. media, that first disclosed the Iranian arms-for-hostages deal.) Although Vietnam, Watergate, and the Iran-*contra* scandal stimulated a more aggressive and critical posture in parts of the fourth estate, the media and the government remain intertwined to a considerable extent in a process that invites collusion. The government's proven ability to manage the news, combined with the media's dependence on the government to get the news, perpetuates a symbiotic (incestuous?) relationship between the two institutions (see Hess 1984). Because news derived from the government itself compromises the media's capacity to scrutinize government actions in the foreign policy domain, it may be appropriate to ask not whether the media control public opinion in America but whether the government uses the media to create and manipulate public opinion (see Parenti 1986).

The Foreign Policy Agenda and "Press Politics"

Often it appears as if the media are in control, not the government. Public officials' distaste for and fear of the media seems to reflect this. They are particularly wary of television and the ability of highly visible and respected journalists, such as TV news anchors, to undermine their policies or influence. "A sixty-second verbal barrage on the evening news or a few embarrassing questions can destroy programs, politicians, and the reputations of major organizations. Political leaders fear this media power, because they often are unable to blunt it or repair the damage" (Graber 1993; see also Jordan and Page 1992).

Ironically, the media also increasingly *set the policy-making agenda*. One knowledgeable Washingtonian commented: "Ever since the breakup of the Soviet Union, it has become clear to anyone who cares to notice that in Washington the real agenda-setters for foreign policy sit not in the White House but in editorial rooms and press cubicles" (Maynes 1993–1994). Others have echoed that sentiment, arguing that a "chorus of congressional leaders, political pundits, television commentators, and print journalists" urged U.S. involvement in Somalia and elsewhere, while television images of conflict and despair have thrust the new interventionism on behalf of humanitarian values to the top of America's foreign policy agenda (Hoge 1994; Stedman 1992–1993; cf. Gowing 1994). The Cold War emphasis on Soviet expansionism and the containment of communism provided the media with "a gauge for determining the importance of events by how much they affected America's security," which tended to focus on the means but not ends of policy. Now, "in the shapeless aftermath of a clear-cut superpower rivalry the impact of media's immediacy is magnified" (Hoge 1994).

Policymakers' reliance on media information enhances the media's importance as an agent in the foreign policy process. Patrick O'Heffernan's (1991) survey of policy-making officials found that a majority rely most heavily on media information during the early stages of the policy cycle. This is a critical period, as the definition of the situation will dictate the response (see Chapter 13). By controlling the information, the media help to frame the issue.

The increasingly rapid pace of electronic news and television's global coverage also shorten the time frame for policy responses to new developments abroad. In 1961, when the Berlin Wall went up, President Kennedy took eight days to respond to the provocative action. In 1989, when the wall came down, President Bush was forced to respond overnight (Graber 1993). More broadly, by publicizing foreign events or other international developments, the media draw attention to them. Frequently that attention forces decision makers to act, rather than to ignore the situation or to hide it. As I. M. Destler, Leslie H. Gelb, and Anthony Lake (1984) suggest, the ability of policymakers to determine what is and what is not an important foreign policy issue may be adversely affected by the attention the media, especially television, accords to particular foreign policy problems. Journalist Marvin Kalb has used the term "press politics" to describe the growing "inseparability of foreign policy from its management in the news" (Bennett 1994b).

There are instances where journalists themselves or the media more generally have become agents in the diplomatic process. In 1977, for example, CBS anchor Walter Cronkite was able to secure public pledges from Egyptian and Israeli leaders that paved the way for Anwar Sadat's historic visit to Jerusalem and the Camp David accord mediated by President Carter a year later. Similarly, there is little question that CNN provided an important communications node between the United States and Iraq during the Persian Gulf War.

A recent and growing variant on this phenomenon is "role switching" between reporters and on-air commentators ("pundits") and government officials. For example, David Gergen, formerly an editor at *U.S. News & World Report* and "a baron of the punditocracy" (Grove 1993) as part of the "MacNeil/Lehrer NewsHour," held communications roles in three Republican administrations before joining Clinton's as a policy adviser. Similarly, Strobe Talbott, national security correspondent for *Time*, became Clinton's under secretary of state. Still others, like Rush Limbaugh and Pat Buchanan, have used their positions as political commentators to set and promote a particular agenda. Twice in the 1990s Buchanan has taken his project, widely disseminated via the electronic and print media, before the electorate as he campaigned for the presidency.

In summary, the relationship between the media and policymakers is both subtle and complex, with no easy conclusions about who influences whom in what circumstances. Television has quickened the pace of news and inevitably shaped the way policymakers use the media and respond to events abroad, but it by no means determines American foreign policy. It is clear nonetheless that the fourth estate is a powerful institution that affects multiple facets of American political life. Theodore White, focusing once more on the media's ability to set the agenda, usefully summarizes the media's importance:

> The power of the press in America is a primordial one. It sets the agenda of public discussion; and this sweeping political power is unrestrained by any law. It determines what people will talk and think about—an authority that in other nations is reserved for tyrants, priests, parties and mandarins. No major act of the American Congress, no foreign adventure, no act of diplomacy, no great social reform can succeed in the United States unless the press prepares the public mind. (White 1973, 327)

The Impact of Foreign Policy Attitudes and Issues on Presidential Elections

The press and public conventionally view elections as opportunities for policy change, if only for their potential to bring about new leadership. However, elections may also enable voters' preferences on foreign policy issues to be translated into policies that reflect those preferences. The important question, then, is whether voting is a viable means of expressing the public's policy preferences and thus translating them into policy.

It seems plausible that decision makers' fear of electoral punishment would lead them to propose policies designed to maintain their popularity and thus enhance their prospects for winning office. However, the "apparent immunity of the foreign policy establishment to electoral accountability" (Cohen 1973) is notable. Research on the two rival propositions has been extensive, and on the whole, the results have "not . . . been kind to democratic theory." They show "that policy voting is quite rare" and that, for a variety of reasons, citizens fail to vote for candidates on the basis of policy preferences. "In short, voters are incapable of policy rationality" (Page and Brody 1972).

The Electoral Impact of Foreign Policy Issues

Although controversial and not always consistent, evidence abounds to support the "is-sueless politics" hypothesis—that voter choice is determined neither by the nature of the issues nor candidates' positions on them (see Asher 1992). Foreign policy is no exception (cf. (Aldrich, Sullivan, and Borgida 1989). Americans clearly do hold opinions about foreign policy matters, but they are not transmitted into the policy-formation system through the electoral process. How do we account for such a failure?

One inviting explanation is that although many Americans often regard foreign policy issues as among the most important facing the nation, they still fail to arouse the depth of personal concern raised by issues closer to their daily lives. In addition, foreign policy issues are not the ones that "divide the populace into contending groups. . . . In general foreign issues, involving as they do the United States *versus* others, tend to blur or reduce differences domestically" (Nie, Verba, and Petrocik 1976).

That does not mean, however, that *party* outcomes are unaffected by foreign policy issues during presidential elections. Public views of foreign policy have been related to the partisan votes cast in each election between 1952 and 1988 (Asher 1992). Republicans benefited from those perceptions in eight of the ten elections. The 1964 election was the only one in which voter preferences on foreign policy issues clearly favored the Democrats. Although Democrats benefited from public fears of nuclear war in 1984, the Republicans benefited on the issue of war prevention.[10] By 1988, however, the Republicans could claim the high ground on both peace and prosperity. Michael Dukakis and the Democratic Party lost in a landslide—and the Republicans claimed the White House for the seventh time out of eleven Cold War presidential elections.

Four years later George Bush found himself on the defensive. Peace was in hand—indeed, after a half-century of bitter conflict, the United States had "won" the Cold War with the Soviet Union and turned the tide against Iraq's aggression—but prosperity was not. The nation's economy was in recession, concern for debts and deficits punctuated campaign rhetoric, and Bill Clinton was determined to focus attention on domestic ills, not foreign policy challenges. A sign in his Arkansas campaign headquarters proclaiming it's "The Economy, Stupid!" reflected Democratic leaders' single-mined determination to stress domestic policy. The end of the Cold War and the departure of virulent anticommunism from the domestic political agenda played to their strategy, while the partisan advantages Republicans once enjoyed on foreign policy mattered little this time (Weisberg and Kimball 1995). "Throughout the Cold War the Republican Party's reason for existence was anticommunism," observes Leon Sigal (1992–1993) in a retrospective look at what he calls "the last Cold War election" (see also Deudney and Ikenberry 1994). "Republicans could be counted on to shield America from the Red Menace, at home and abroad. . . . Now that the [Russian] bear has disappeared, what else does the G.O.P. stand for?"

As we demonstrated in Chapter 8, the state of the economy is a powerful predictor of how Americans evaluate presidential performance. It is not surprising, therefore, that George Bush attracted their ire. Clinton, on the other hand, was quick to tie the state of the economy to the United States' continuing ability to play an active role in world affairs. "America must regain its economic strength to play a proper role as leader of the world," he declared. "And we must have a president who attends to prosperity at home if our people are to sustain their support for engagement abroad." But domestic policy was Clinton's strong suit, and he played to it repeatedly.

Admittedly weak on domestic policy issues, Bush also proved vulnerable on the very issues perceived to be his long suit. The "foreign policy president" largely confined himself to "tidying up the details of the old agenda. . . . He failed by and large to assist eastern Europe and the Soviet Union in their perilous transitions, to devise a foreign policy squaring national self-determination with state sovereignty and minority rights, to stanch bloodletting in Bosnia, and to prevent the proliferation of all arms, not just weapons of mass destruction." For most Americans these were not issues of burning significance. Even the brief euphoria sparked by victory in the Persian Gulf War soon gave way to "more pressing subjects" (Omestad 1992–1993). Bush's decision to stop the war before Iraq's leader was driven from power eventually soured the views of many as they wondered whether the war had been worth the effort. In August 1992, just as Bush prepared to launch his reelection bid, a *New York Times*/CBS New poll found that 75 percent of the American people (largely regardless of party affiliation) would have continued the fighting in Iraq until Saddam Hussein was deposed. A popular bumper sticker captured the irony of Bush's situation: "SADDAM HUSSEIN STILL HAS HIS JOB. WHAT ABOUT YOU?"

Usually it is difficult to determine the separate effects of particular foreign policy questions on citizens' voting behavior. Because most elections involve a variety of often overlapping issues, some of those who vote for the winning candidate do so because of the candidate's stance on particular issues, but others do so in spite of it. Foreign policy issues thus become part of a mix of considerations, and often they are a less important ingredient than domestic political issues or judgments of past performance (Abramson, Aldrich and Rohde 1986, 1990; Fiorina 1981). As a result, voters' behavior is more likely an aggregate judgment about prior performance than a guide to future action.

Foreign Policy and Retrospective Voting

Consider President Carter's electoral fate. The public generally gave Carter high marks on personal attributes but low marks on performance. Evaluations of his foreign policy performance were especially critical. Carter's popularity surged in late 1979 in the immediate aftermath of the seizure of American embassy personnel in Teheran, but his inability to secure their release fueled public dissatisfaction with his overall performance. His challenger, Ronald Reagan, criticized the policy of détente Carter and his predecessors had promoted, called for sharply increased defense spending, and hammered away at the theme of alleged American impotence in international affairs. In this context, "the continuing crisis in Iran came to be seen as a living symbol and constant reminder of all that Reagan had been saying" (Hess and Nelson 1985).[11]

Four years later, Reagan's reputation for leadership proved a strong force motivating voters to choose the incumbent president over his challenger, Walter Mondale. Elements of Reagan's foreign policy record could easily be criticized, but four years of relative peace had put to rest fears about Reagan's recklessness. "No longer fearful that the President's policies might lead to war, the public had no compelling reason to abandon him" (Keeter 1985).

In many respects the Bush candidacy became a retrospective judgment on the Reagan years. Peace and prosperity thus redounded to Bush's benefit, as noted. Moreover, because Reagan had moved during his second term toward an accommodationist foreign policy posture and away from his "evil empire" approach to the Soviet Union, the ideological differences on foreign policy issues that bore on the electoral outcomes in 1980 and 1984 tended to disappear in 1988. Still, to the extent that voters perceived differences between the candidates on foreign policy issues, particularly their willingness to "stand up for America" (Pomper 1989), they favored Bush.

Despite the acknowledged importance of retrospective voting, history invites the conclusion that "elections are primarily a symbolic exercise that . . . offer the masses an opportunity to participate in the political system, but electoral participation does not enable them to determine public policy." "Parties do not offer clear policy alternatives," and a "candidate's election does not imply a policy choice by the electorate" (Dye and Zeigler 1990). Nevertheless, because policymakers act—evidence to the contrary—*as though* voters make choices on the basis of their policy preferences, they pay attention to the anticipated responses of voters in shaping their policy choices.

The Vietnam War in Presidential Elections

The Vietnam episode illustrates many of these conclusions about the mythology of elections as instruments of popular control. In 1964, 1968, and 1972 the American electorate had the opportunity to pass judgment on past performance in a way that might have had clear implications for future behavior on the part of their government leadership. Did they vote their preferences on the issue? What was the relationship between those preferences and policy?

Vietnam became a major foreign policy issue in 1964, when President Johnson's landslide victory was widely interpreted as a mandate for restraint in the prosecution of the growing U.S. involvement in the Southeast Asian conflict. His Republican opponent, Barry Goldwater, had campaigned on the pledge of pursuing "victory" against communism in all quarters of the globe, but especially in Vietnam by "any means necessary." Johnson's later escalation of the conflict was therefore viewed by some as a violation of his mandate, indeed, as implementation of Goldwater's program. In fact, however, as national surveys indicated:

> There was relatively little relationship between candidate and policy preference, with Johnson winning the support of both "doves" and "hawks." While 63 percent of those favoring withdrawal from Vietnam voted for the president, so did 52 percent of those who fa-

vored "a stronger stand even if it means invading North Vietnam" as did 82 per cent of those who preferred to "keep our soldiers in Vietnam, but try to end the fighting." (Pomper 1968, 251)

In fact, the results of that election as it related to Vietnam were so ambiguous as to lead one scholar to conclude: "What could the 1964 vote have told [Johnson] about popular support for various war options? In brief, it could have told him anything he cared to believe" (Boyd 1972).

By 1968 the war had reached enormous proportions by any measure. The predictable consequence, as we noted previously, was growing dissatisfaction with the war. Support declined as the length of the war increased and its casualty lists grew. Campus unrest, mass demonstrations against the war, increasingly vocal minority opposition, including challenges from within the president's own party by Eugene McCarthy and Robert Kennedy—all were indicative of the changing climate of opinion. Johnson's decision not to run for a second full presidential term was widely interpreted as a direct result of this domestic opposition. We would expect, therefore, that in 1968 the voters would have made a clear judgment on past performance and would have provided a clear mandate for the future. They didn't.

In terms of Vietnam, the 1968 vote was as "issueless" as the Eisenhower-Stevenson encounter of 1956. Although "hawks" tended to vote for Nixon in somewhat greater proportion than "doves," overall Vietnam opinions accounted for only between 1 and 2 percent of the variation in voting behavior, and "voters did not treat the 1968 election as a referendum on Vietnam policy" (Page and Brody 1972, 982). This was largely because the electorate (correctly) perceived little difference between the positions of the candidates (Nixon and Humphrey) on Vietnam policy. The voters were in fact deprived of a meaningful foreign policy choice, and the electoral mechanism thus failed as a vehicle for the expression of growing public dissatisfaction with the war.

Again in 1968, then, the electoral process failed to produce a clear foreign policy mandate for any one course of action. Nixon's later shift toward a search for "peace with honor" did not emanate from the election. Nor was the promise to end the war promptly fulfilled. An agonizingly slow process ensued. The "Vietnamization" strategy, announced phased troop withdrawals, and the beginning of peace talks in Paris all came belatedly. Not until October 1972, shortly (coincidentally?) before the next presidential election, did Secretary of State Kissinger declare to the public that "peace is at hand."

But peace was not *in* hand. So November 7, 1972, marked the first election since the Korean War election of 1952 in which foreign policy was the major issue. This time the American electorate cast their votes with the Vietnam issue uppermost in their minds (Miller et al. 1976). Less clear-cut, however, was the meaning for Vietnam policy of Nixon's landslide victory. Interpreting the victory as electoral approval for what was perceived, rightly or wrongly, as Nixon's policy of deescalation of the war may be most compelling. However, whether the voters voted as they did because they wanted a negotiated peace or because they desired a military victory nonetheless remains unanswered.

Based on our discussion in Chapter 8 of the major characteristics and functions of public opinion, the conclusion that in major electoral contests most Americans tend to support existing government actions should come as no surprise. What is surprising, perhaps—particularly in light of the public's nationalistic sentiments and the relative indifference of most Americans to foreign policy—is that a foreign policy issue became a major item on the electoral agenda at all. The explanation appears to lie in the perceived cost of the war.

When foreign policy issues begin to significantly touch the daily lives of Americans, they are likely to be looked upon much more as domestic political issues. Vietnam was precisely such an issue. Mothers and wives, fathers and sons, taxpayers and draftees—all were intimately touched by Vietnam, a fact that distinguished this war, like others, from most foreign policy questions. Yet the striking fact remains that even in the case of Vietnam, the relationship between public preferences and policy outcomes was essentially indirect, generally supporting the proposition that decision makers lead and the public follows. Little wonder that the characterization holds for the less costly and less disruptive (but infinitely more numerous) issues that comprise the bulk of U.S. foreign policy. Public preferences in general, and during elections in particular, serve as a "source" of American foreign policy, it seems, but they do so more by coloring the vocabulary of decision making than by determining the policy outcomes. Elections are not mechanisms through which the public exercises control over American foreign policy. They are instruments for the selection of personnel, not policy.[12]

Linkages between Societal Sources and American Foreign Policy · · · · · · · · · ·

The question posed at the outset of this and the preceding chapter—"In what ways do societal factors influence American foreign policy?"—has invited a series of additional questions, and, inevitably, provoked a variety of answers. It is clear, however, that the view of the United States as a society-dominated political system provides insight into the potential impact of the political culture, public opinion, elites and masses, the media, and presidential elections. The ability of citizens "to mobilize support for their demands and to organize themselves" is a characteristic feature of society-dominant systems (Risse-Kappen 1991). Similarly, elections and interest groups help to channel mass preferences and private interests into public policy in the United States, where, as we noted at the outset of this chapter, the power of both the state and societal groups is more decentralized than in many other industrial societies. Thus elites are unable to dictate completely what American foreign policy will be—which is the "top-down" view of policy making akin to the elitist model described earlier. Similarly, the mass of the American people do not determine American foreign policy from the "bottom up," a view that parallels the pluralist model. Instead, there is a constant interaction between policy makers and the public, elites and masses alike, much of it promoted through the media and the electoral system. American foreign policy emerges out of this continuing interaction. Policymakers and other elites enjoy a competitive advantage in shaping the agenda and are ultimately responsible for final decisions; important caveats and qualifications must be attached to the role that mass preferences and private interests play in shaping policy. Still, we have seen that societal factors do indeed intrude upon the policy-making process and thus serve as a source of American foreign policy.

Societal factors explain more about the *process* of formulating American policies toward the external environment than about the objectives of those actions and the particular means chosen to achieve them. Moreover, it is difficult to isolate causal connections between particular societal variables and particular actions abroad. Thus societal factors rarely if ever "determine" foreign policy actions. Instead, they exert influence primarily as part of the context within which decisions are formulated. In particular, they operate more as forces constraining foreign policy than as forces stimulating radical departures from the past.

To pinpoint better the sources of American foreign policy decisions and initiatives, we need to turn from considering factors within American society to examining the political institutions from which most foreign policy initiatives spring. As we will discover in the next three chapters, these institutions—part of the domestic structures of the American political system—are comparatively decentralized into competing power centers, thus providing multiple access points to those in the society-dominated American political system who seek to shape American foreign policy.

NOTES

1. Education and training do not guaranteed that foolish policy decisions will not be made. Indeed, one of the main points of Halberstam's book is that intelligent people are capable of making wicked and stupid decisions.

2. The term "power elite" as used in the context of foreign policy making is essentially synonymous with "the Establishment" described above, which includes those who have access to persons occupying foreign policy decision-making roles and who themselves from time to time assume positions of authority. Note, however, that the "power elite" or "the Establishment" is not necessarily synonymous with the "governing elite," a term that refers exclusively to those who occupy positions of authority in the government. Particularly at the top levels of government, of course, there is an overlap between "the Establishment" and "the governing elite"—an overlap that provides an important channel between those inside government and those on the outside.

3. Supporting data and additional information for each of these observations can be found in Atkinson and Hiatt (1985), Dolbeare and Edelman (1985), Etzioni (1984), Fossedal (1985), Goodwin (1985), Hiatt and Atkinson (1985), Parenti (1988), Pincus (1985), Proxmire (1970), and Rosen (1973).

4. When the Cold War ended, defense spending constituted about 6 percent of the gross national product. By comparison, defense spending at the end of Korean War stood at nearly 40 percent and after Vietnam at 10 percent. Even if defense spending were to decline to, say, 4 percent of GNP, its effect on the economy will arguably be less than after Korea and Vietnam.

5. The media are widely believed to be dominated by "liberals," and there is evidence to support that view (Lichter and Rothman 1981; Schneider and Lewis 1985). Interestingly, however, newspapers endorse Republican presidential candidates far more frequently than Democratic candidates. In 1988, for example, George Bush received 4 newspaper endorsements for every one received by his more liberal challenger, Michael Dukakis. An exception to the general rule was 1992, in which Bill Clinton enjoyed the endorsement of 183 daily newspapers (with a combined circulation of 17.5 million) compared with 138 for Bush (circulation 9.9 million) (*Editor & Publisher* November 7, 1992, 15). Ross Perot also picked up 4 endorsements.

A 1985 *Los Angeles Times* study found that while those who write and edit news stories are overwhelmingly liberal, barely half of those who read these same newspapers could categorize them as either liberal or conservative. It also revealed a "tendency for people to ascribe their own positions to those of their newspaper," suggesting that "readers assume that the newspaper they depend on for information shares their outlook" (Schneider and Lewis 1985). Finally, an analysis of network and wire service coverage of the 1980 presidential campaign concludes similarly: Political reporting, especially of domestic news, "reflects the canons of objectivity more often than the political opinions of the newspeople themselves" (Robinson 1983).

6. The three national news magazines, *Time, Newsweek,* and *U.S. News & World Report,* also give substantial attention to foreign affairs. Frank's data do not extend to the news magazines, but Gans (1979) usefully compares these national media to the television networks.

7. Evidence and critiques of the "minimal-effects" thesis can be found in Iyengar, Peters, and Kinder (1982) and Page, Shapiro, and Dempsey (1987).

8. See Alterman (1992) for a critical view of pundits' role, for example, in generating and sustaining support for the Bush administration's policies during the Persian Gulf crisis.

9. Tebbel and Watts (1985) provide a historical overview of the relationship between *The Press and the Presidency.* They are particularly critical of the Reagan administration's use—and abuse—of the mass media. Kern, Levering, and Levering (1984) examine the Kennedy administration, which is often credited with having been extraordinarily successful in having the news its way. Montague Kern (1984) compares Carter to Kennedy, noting that Carter's comparative lack of success with the media is explained in part because he came to office "on a wave of public and press disillusionment with the strong presidency."

10. Long-standing political lore holds that Republicans produce "peace with poverty," while Democrats bring "war with wealth." These perceptions may be changing. Gallup poll data from the mid-1970s through the early 1990s show that the Democratic Party was more often perceived as the party of peace than the Republican Party. Since 1980, on the other hand, Republicans have more often than not been perceived as better for prosperity (*The Gallup Poll Monthly,* July 1992, pp. 46–47).

11. Stories have circulated since Reagan's first inauguration day that members of his campaign staff were determined that Carter not reap any electoral benefit from the Iranian hostage crisis. Thus William Casey, Reagan campaign manager and later director of the CIA, allegedly met with Iranian officials and promised to supply Iran with military equipment in return for a promise the American hostages would not be released before the election. The hostages were finally released just minutes after Reagan was sworn in as president, and arms reportedly began to flow to Iran via Israel. For a brief account of what allegedly took place, related by a former staff member of the National Security Council responsible for Iranian affairs, see Sick (1991).

12. Ultimately, of course, elected officials do have an impact on policy. Evidence shows, for example, that the ideological dispositions of members of Congress reflect those prevalent in their districts. In turn, ideology (liberal versus conservative) often predicts policy positions on defense spending, foreign aid, protection of human rights, and other foreign and national security policy issues (Bernstein 1989; Lindsay 1990). Still, there is no *direct* causal connection between public preferences as expressed in the voting booth and the day-to-day issues that comprise American foreign policy.

SUGGESTIONS FOR FURTHER READING

Alterman, Eric. *Sound and Fury: The Washington Punditocracy and the Collapse of American Politics*. New York: HarperCollins, 1992.

Cohen, Bernard C. *The Press and Foreign Policy*. Princeton, NJ: Princeton University Press, 1963.

Friedberg, Aaron L. "Why Didn't the United States Become a Garrison State?" *International Security* 16 (Spring 1992): 109–42.

Hoge, James F., Jr. "Media Pervasiveness," *Foreign Affairs* 73 (July/August 1994): 136–44.

Jeffreys-Jones, Rhodri. *Changing Differences: Women and the Shaping of American Foreign Policy, 1917–1994*. New Brunswick, N.J.: Rutgers University Press, 1995.

Kotz, Nick. *Wild Blue Yonder: Money, Politics, and the B-1 Bomber*. Princeton: Princeton University Press, 1988.

Milbrath, Lester W. "Interest Groups and Foreign Policy," pp. 231–52 in James N. Rosenau, ed., *Domestic Sources of Foreign Policy*. New York: Free Press, 1967.

Nitze, Paul H. *Tension between Opposites: Reflections on the Practice and Theory of Politics*. New York: Scribner's, 1993.

O'Heffernan, Patrick. *Mass Media and American Foreign Policy: Insider Perspectives on Global Journalism and the Foreign Policy Process*. Norwood, N.J.: Ablex, 1991.

Patterson, Thomas E. *Out of Order*. New York: Vintage, 1994.

Skidmore, David, and Valerie M. Hudson, eds. *The Limits of State Autonomy: Societal Groups and Foreign Policy Formulation*. Boulder, Colo.: Westview, 1993.

Smith, James Allen. *The Idea Brokers: Think Tanks and the Rise of the New Policy Elite*. New York: Free Press, 1991.

Vernon, Raymond, Debora L. Spar, and Glenn Tobin. *Iron Triangles and Revolving Doors: Cases in U.S. Foreign Economic Policymaking*. New York: Praeger, 1991.

Wittkopf, Eugene R., ed. *The Domestic Sources of American Foreign Policy: Insights and Evidence*, 2nd. ed. New York: St. Martin's, 1994.

CHAPTER 10

. . .

PRESIDENTIAL PREEMINENCE IN FOREIGN POLICY MAKING

. . .

In the areas of defense and foreign affairs, the nation must speak with one voice, and only the president is capable of providing that voice.

President Ronald Reagan, 1984

The process was the author of the policy.

Under Secretary of State George W. Ball, 1962

The president of the United States is widely regarded at home and abroad as the single most powerful person in the world. The president commands the ability to unleash unprecedented destruction, directs political and economic resources unequaled in the world, and enjoys a level of legitimacy and authority at home that is the envy of political leaders around the world. Moreover, the proven ability of the presidential form of government to respond quickly and pragmatically to emergent challenges gives it advantages over other democratic forms of governance, such as the British parliamentary system (Waltz 1967).

A half-century of Cold War competition with the Soviet Union and the ideological challenge of communism contributed measurably to the rise of presidential preeminence in foreign policy making. Indeed, prior to Vietnam it was commonplace to argue that "the United States has one president, but it has two presidencies," one for domestic policy, the other for foreign and defense policy. The president's influence in the latter domain compared with the former distinguishes them. As political scientist Aaron Wildavsky (1966) argued in a classic essay, "Since World War II, presidents have had much greater success in controlling the nation's defense and foreign policies than in dominating its domestic policies. . . . The president's normal problem with domestic policy is to get congressional support for the programs he prefers. In foreign affairs, in contrast, he can almost always get support for policies that he believes will protect the nation."

Now, however, the demise of the Cold War portends perhaps dramatic changes in the nature of the modern presidency and its influence. As one columnist wrote, "The end of the Cold War has changed the stature of the president—moving him off the imperial heights of the 'most powerful man in the world' to the mundane level of a political leader struggling over incremental domestic policy questions" (Lauter 1994). Another wrote in the aftermath of the 1994 Group of Seven summit that "foreign leaders have concluded that they can safely treat him [Clinton] as offhandedly as. . . well, as he is treated at home" (Will 1994). Both observations reflect the belief that "the powers of the presidency are greatest in foreign and military policy, but without an overriding concern for such issues, the salience of the presidency will decline" (Deudney and Ikenberry 1994).

We will address this provocative thesis in the conclusion to this chapter. First, however, we must consider the forces giving rise to the power of the presidency, particularly during the past half-century, and what presidents in turn have done to ensure their control over the machinery of government responsible for making and executing the nation's foreign policy.

To guide our inquiry, we will draw on a conceptualization of the foreign policy-making process as a series of concentric circles suggested some years ago by a former policymaker, Roger Hilsman (1967). His view, depicted in Figure 10.1, reflects the theme of the United States as a society-dominant political system that we used in Chapters 8 and 9 to understand the impact of societal influences on American foreign policy. As is characteristic of such systems, political power in the American federal system is decentralized. And within the federal government, where authority and responsibility for the nation's foreign policy resides, power is fragmented, notably between the president and Congress. Reflecting these realities, Hilsman's conceptualization bends the boxes and branches of the standard government organization chart in a way that draws attention to the core, or source, of the action. Thus the innermost circle in the policy-making process consists of the president, his or her immediate personal advisers, and such important political appointees as the secretaries of state and defense, the director of the Central Intelligence Agency (CIA), and various under and assistant

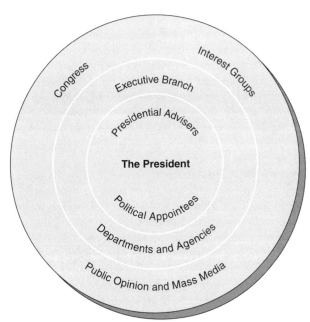

Figure 10.1   The Institutional Setting: The Concentric Circles of Policy Making
Source: Adapted from Roger Hilsman, *To Move a Nation* (New York: Doubleday, 1967), pp. 541–44.

secretaries who bear responsibility for carrying out policy decisions. All important decisions involving the fate of the nation are made (in principle) at this level.

The second circle contains the various departments and agencies of the executive branch. If we exclude from that circle the politically appointed executive heads and their immediate subordinates, already placed in the innermost circle, the second circle comprises the career professionals who provide continuity in the implementation of policy from one administration to the next, regardless of who occupies the White House. Their primary task—in theory—is to provide top-level policymakers with the information necessary to make decisions and then carry them out.

The outermost circle is what Hilsman called the "public one," consisting of Congress, interest groups, public opinion, and the mass media. Collectively, the institutions, groups, and individuals at this level are least involved in the day-to-day foreign policy process.

Building on this conceptualization, we will take three different approaches to describing the foreign affairs government in this and the next two chapters. First, in this chapter we examine the way the president and the president's immediate group of foreign affairs advisers affect American foreign policy. We direct particular attention to the National Security Council system and the role of the president's national security adviser. At issue is how presidential preferences combine with the presidential form of governance to promote what may be a distinctively American institutional approach to foreign policy making.

Second, in Chapter 11 we consider the information-gathering and policy-implementation tasks of the most important of the many government organizations involved in foreign policy. Although foreign policy making is primarily an executive function, the structural characteristics of the foreign affairs government, which define authority and divide the labor among those responsible for making and executing of foreign policy, influence presidential decisions and policy performance. The impact of this structure therefore requires examination.

Finally, in Chapter 12 we examine the governmental sources included in the third concentric circle by focusing on the role of Congress in the policy-making process. We explore in particular how the separation of powers—and the sharing of power by separate institutions—is related to the nature and conduct of American foreign policy.[1]

Foreign Affairs and the Constitution

The president's preeminent position in the foreign affairs government derives in part from the authority granted in the Constitution. It also flows from the combination of judicial interpretation, legislative acquiescence, personal assertiveness, and custom and tradition that have transformed an otherwise coequal branch of the federal government into what remains arguably the most powerful office in the world.

The Constitution specifically grants the president remarkably few powers in the foreign affairs arena. Article II provides that the president shall have the power, upon the advice and consent of the Senate, to make treaties and to appoint ambassadors and other public ministers and consuls. A later section authorizes the president to receive ambassadors and other ministers. Little else deals explicitly with matters of foreign policy. The absence of additional constitutional provi... affairs and the Constitution to observe that "it seems inc... grants support the most powerful office in the world and t... webwork of foreign activity of the most powerful nation in t...

The totality of presidential power is much greater than that... ambassadors, however. The Constitution also makes the preside... chief of the nation's armed forces,[2] and practice has transformed th... nation as the nation's chief executive officer into its leading le... Moreover, the Supreme Court ruled in a seminal case, *United States v....* *Export Corporation* (1936), that the president acts "as the sole organ of the... ernment in the field of international relations." Thus the courts, in this... cases, have repeatedly conferred on the president broad powers in foreign af...

The Constitution's provisions and interpretations have combined with prac... ensure, over time, presidential supremacy in the formulation as well as executi... American foreign policy. Thus the foreign policy of the United States is what the pr... ident says it is. And the president says what it is by concluding treaties and other agree... ments with foreign nations; by public declarations; by recognizing or not recognizing new governments; by attending international conferences; by deploying military power here or there; by encouraging or denouncing the actions of other nations, and so forth.

If the president's foreign affairs powers have grown dramatically during the nation's history, those granted Congress in the Constitution were formidable from the start. Indeed, "the specific grants of authority to the executive in foreign policy were trivial compared with the authority specifically granted to Congress" (Schlesinger 1989). The Constitution authorizes Congress to deal with the regulation of international commerce, the punishment of piracies and felonies committed on the high seas and offenses against the law of nations, and declarations of war. Congress's power to appropriate funds from the treasury and to tax and spend for the common defense and the general welfare continually imprint the conduct of foreign affairs. And the general legislative powers assigned to Congress grant it nearly limitless authority to affect the flow and form of foreign relations.

Clearly the Constitution itself—often described as an invitation to struggle between the executive and legislative branches of government—is not sufficient to explain the distribution of decision-making authority over foreign affairs shown in Figure 10.1. Authority also derived from the ability of the president to act assertively and decisively in the crisis-ridden atmosphere of the post-World War II period. The widely shared consensus that the international environment demanded an active American world role contributed to the belief that strong presidential leadership was needed. Thus the increased power of the presidency went largely unchallenged. The Vandenberg Resolution (1949), in which Congress supported a permanent American alliance with European nations (which later became NATO), and the Formosa Straits (1955), Middle East (1957), Cuban (1962), Berlin (1962), and Gulf of Tonkin (1964) resolutions, in which Congress gave the president broad power to deal with external conflict situations, fostered presidential supremacy by demonstrating a unity of purpose between the president and Congress. Together these factors eventually gave rise to what Arthur M. Schlesinger, Jr. (1973) labeled an "imperial presidency."[3]

...eeminence grew to seemingly excessive propor-
...by discontent with executive policy in Vietnam,
...of abuses by the intelligence community, chal-
...the other end of Pennsylvania Avenue. Of par-
...stion of control over American commitments
...of legislative efforts to circumscribe the exec-
...mmitments Resolution (1969), the repeal of
...e Case Act (1972), and the War Powers
...d to make it more difficult for presidents
...ise circumscribe their foreign policy lat-
...ivotal position in the foreign affairs gov-
...ear than when the Bush administration
...Hussein in late 1990. Congress even-
...Gulf, but Bush insisted to the end that
...decision. "Bush's distinctive style was to po-
...ongress as decisions were made that would eventually
...ian Gulf. For Bush and most of his key advisers. . . . Congress
...been irrelevant—except that it had to be coddled and humored because
...latent capacity to wreak political mischief" (Moore 1994). Thus power remains
concentrated in the White House.

The Supreme Court has never tried to resolve the executive-congressional war
powers dispute because it considers the issues involved as political rather than legal.
Three recent cases reaffirm a long-standing tradition.

In 1981 several members of Congress brought suit against President Reagan, arguing that he had violated the Constitution and the War Powers Resolution by sending military advisers to El Salvador.[4] The court dismissed the suit with the ruling that
a determination of whether U.S. forces in El Salvador were involved in actual or potential hostilities was a political, not a judicial, finding. The Supreme Court refused to
hear an appeal.

Six years later, as U.S. forces reflagged Kuwaiti ships with American flags to protect them in the Persian Gulf, members of Congress again asked the court to enter the
war powers fracas by declaring that the president should submit a report to Congress
under the War Powers Resolution. Again the court concluded the issue was a nonjus-
ticiable political question.[5]

The third case also involved the Persian Gulf. In late 1990 fifty-four Democratic
members of Congress sought to derail further Bush administration military deployments and action in the Persian Gulf.[6] They argued that the Constitution required that
Congress debate and authorize a declaration of war before the president could initiate
hostilities. This time the (U.S. district) court left open the door to a possible ruling
against the president's war-making power without congressional involvement—but it
also waffled: "It would be both premature and presumptuous for the court to render a
decision on the issue of whether a declaration of war is required . . . when the Congress
itself has provided no indication whether it deems such a declaration either necessary,
on the one hand, or imprudent, on the other." However, in another case involving a
National Guard reservist who protested serving in the Gulf region without congres-

sional authorization, the court followed its usual path of ruling that the issue was a political matter that went beyond the judicial realm.

The *doctrine of political questions*, a judicial construct that enables the courts to sidestep politically contentious foreign policy issues, ensures that the outcome of the inevitable presidential-congressional contest over war and related issues will be determined at any one time largely by the resources available to each branch of government. On balance, the resources available to the president are the more formidable.

The Innermost Circle: The President and His Advisers

The president's greatest resource—at least in principle—is the vast executive establishment. Most of the federal government's work force of 3.1 million civilians work in the executive branch, where collectively they bear responsibility for making and implementing the full range of America's domestic and foreign policies. What proportion of them is concerned primarily with foreign affairs is difficult to determine, but it is probably no more than 5 percent, perhaps less. Noteworthy, however, is that foreign affairs personnel are found not only in the Departments of State and Defense, where we would expect them, but also in some unusual places—the Departments of Agriculture, Education, and Transportation, for example, and in the Environmental Protection Agency, the National Aeronautics and Space Administration, and the Small Business Administration. Indeed, Office of Personnel Management data on the executive departments and agencies with employees abroad indicate that more than three-quarters of the organizations are oriented primarily toward domestic policy issues, not foreign affairs.

Executive Organization and Foreign Policy

The executive *departments* of government, and the political appointees who head them, are at the core of the policy-making process, particularly the Departments of State and Defense. The former derives its importance within the cabinet as "first among equals" (the term derives from the fact that the State Department was the first executive agency established under the Constitution in 1789). The secretary of state, in principle at least, is the president's foremost foreign policy adviser. In part this is because the State Department is the sole agency of government charged with coordinating the entire range of U.S. activities overseas. It also houses the Foreign Service, the professional diplomatic corps of the United States.

The tense international political environment of the postwar period, which directed primary emphasis toward military and defense considerations as they relate to foreign policy and national security, also made the Defense Department particularly important. The enormous size of the Pentagon, which still commands a substantial share of every annual federal budget, gives the Department of Defense clout in a policy-making environment where money and personnel mean political influence. Even with the post-Cold War military downsizing, defense spending continues at an annual clip of more than $270 billion, which constitutes more discretionary (nonentitlement) spending than all other departments and agencies combined.

The State and Defense departments are important enough to merit detailed attention; thus in Chapter 11 we will examine how they are organized to carry out their foreign affairs responsibilities. We will also examine the intelligence community, and some primarily domestic departments concerned with aspects of international economic affairs. Here we confine our attention to the president and the presidency.

The president is nominally "boss" of the employees who staff the executive departments and agencies of the foreign affairs government, but the president by no means *controls* them. That truism led Richard Neustadt (1980) to describe the president's power as the "power to persuade." The interests of executive branch organizations are not always synonymous with the interests of the president. The people who staff them commonly hold their positions long before and long after any given president's term in office, and they frequently equate organizational survival with individual survival. To them the president is often a "transient meddler in their business"—a view attributed to foreign policy professionals by an anonymous National Security Council staffer (Destler 1974), but one many others would endorse.

The Cabinet

If the president is seen as a "transient meddler" in the affairs of established organizations, departmental bureaucracies are viewed from 1600 Pennsylvania Avenue as independent, unfamiliar, unresponsive, and inaccessible.

> They are suspected again and again of placing their own, congressional, or special-interest priorities ahead of those communicated to them from the White House. Even the president's own cabinet members soon become viewed in the same light; one of the strengths of cabinet members, namely their capacity to make a compelling case for their programs, has proved to be their chief liability with presidents. (Cronin 1973, 35)

"Natural enemies" is how members of the cabinet are often described. Department chiefs become captives of the interests of the departments they administer and of the positions advanced by career professionals within them. Because chiefs are necessarily advocates for the departments they head, they are often in conflict with one another and sometimes even with the president. And because cabinet decision making is usually the casualty, the cabinet itself is a "perennial loser" (Allison and Szanton 1976).

Presidents Carter and Reagan both pledged to involve the cabinet more intimately in policy development and implementation. Neither found it particularly useful for those purposes, however (Reagan even catnapped during cabinet meetings), but Reagan did seek better communication between cabinet officials and the president's executive office through a series of cabinet councils consisting of selected cabinet heads and members of the White House staff. Two survived into Reagan's second term, the Economic Policy Council and the Domestic Policy Council. Although the cabinet council system did institutionalize the involvement of the cabinet in routine decisions, the cabinet as a group failed to penetrate "to the heart of presidential decision making" (Benze 1987). Moreover, "cabinet government" may have suited Reagan's detached management style, but it also contributed to the single most important foreign policy failure of the his administration: the Iran-*contra* scandal.

Unlike his two predecessors, George Bush did not talk about cabinet government before assuming the reins of power, but he retained Reagan's economic and domestic policy councils and willingly gave cabinet secretaries latitude within their jurisdictions. Similar to the Reagan experience, however, "the influence of cabinet secretaries individually . . . did not extend to them as a collectivity." Instead, cabinet meetings were used more as briefing sessions than for policy deliberation (Pfiffner 1990).

Bill Clinton likewise did little to infuse his cabinet with real authority. On the contrary, he undermined it. Many of his most important policy programs (health care, for example, or government reform) were managed not by department heads but by White House aides—or First Lady Hillary Rodham Clinton or Vice President Al Gore. Clinton also used task forces—"war rooms," they were called—to coordinate from the White House the activities and interests of the various individuals, departments, and agencies with a stake in particular issues. Thus Roger Altman, deputy secretary of the Treasury until his resignation over the Whitewater affair, took command of the 1993 budget bill, and William Daley, a Chicago attorney and political strategist recruited specifically for the job, guided Nafta through a reluctant Congress. The result: *adhocracy*—a system of decision making that "'minimizes reliance on regularized and systematic patterns of providing advice and instead relies heavily on the president to distribute assignments and select whom he listens to and when'" (Haass 1994a; see also Watson 1993). While there are advantages to such a system of "government by inner circle"—the system is flexible, for example, and those "in the know" tend to be few in number and loyal—there also are distinct disadvantages. Among them is the "tendency to favor people over positions" (Haass 1994a). Cabinet government inevitably is a casualty.

The erosion of cabinet policy making stems in part from "the cross cutting nature of most presidential policy issues," thus requiring "advice from a broader perspective than that of individual department heads" (Pfiffner 1990). It also grows from the disdain of bureaucrats and the permanent bureaucracy most presidents nurture. A common aspect of "adhocracy," for example, is that "it neither trusts nor respects standing bureaucracies. They are viewed as slow, unimaginative and disloyal" (Haass 1994a). In turn, every American president since World War II has relied increasingly on his personal staff and the Executive Office of the President for advice and assistance in the development of policies and programs. A *presidential subsystem* within the executive branch is the result, which often leads to differences between the presidency, on the one hand, and the established bureaucracies comprising the second concentric circle of policy making, on the other.

The Presidential Subsystem

The institutionalization of the presidency began with the Executive Reorganization Act of 1939, which authorized President Roosevelt to create the Executive Office, consisting of the White House Office and the Bureau of the Budget. The former unit was to house the president's personal assistants and their staffs. The latter, created in 1921 under the jurisdiction of the Treasury Department, was to ensure presidential control over budgetary matters and later over the president's entire legislative program.

Since 1939 the Executive Office has included a plethora of other offices and councils. The lists and labels change continually, reflecting both presidential preferences and policy priorities. In the Clinton administration they included, among others, the National Economic Council, the National Security Council, the Council of Economic Advisers, the Council on Sustainable Development, the Foreign Intelligence Advisory Board, the Office of Management and Budget, the Office of Policy Development, the Office of Science and Technology Policy, the Office of Environmental Quality, the Office of Political Affairs, the Office of the United States Trade Representative, and the Office of National Drug Control Policy.

With new offices and functions have come more people and demands for more money. By the time of Clinton's election the White House staff consisted of more than five hundred people and a budget nearing $40 million annually. Together these developments show how extensively decision-making authority over substantive and operational matters is concentrated in the White House. The institutionalized presidency is now "a powerful inner sanctum of government, isolated from traditional, constitutional checks and balances" (Cronin 1984). Moreover, an enlarged White House staff designed to increase presidential control of the executive branch becomes, in the eyes of critics, "a screen" between the executive and legislative branches that "[cuts] off the president from the government and the government from the president. The staff becomes a shock absorber around the president, shielding him from reality" (Arthur Schlesinger, in *The Wall Street Journal*, January 7, 1981).

Most presidents eventually conclude they must rely on a strong-willed chief of staff to bring order to an otherwise potentially chaotic White House staff operation. This was one of the hallmarks of the Nixon administration. Carter began his presidency with the pledge that he would never operate as Nixon had, but he, too, eventually found a strong chief of staff necessary to effective governance. Reagan and Bush began this way, and eventually, Clinton came to the same conclusion.

Clinton was renowned early in his presidency for others' easy yet time-consuming access to him, and especially for endless but inconclusive meetings ("schmooze-a-thons") involving large numbers of staff and cabinet members. Thomas "Mack the Nice" McLarty, Clinton's first chief of staff, an outgoing business person and lifelong friend, did little to minimize the free-wheeling style that contributed to the untoward effects of adhocracy. Corrective action was taken midway through the Clinton presidency with the appointment of Leon Panetta to the critical chief of staff position. A former member of Congress and director of the Office of Management and Budget, Panetta sought a more orderly White House operation which included restricting access to a president who loved to talk and hear all the options others willingly laid out. The move reflected recognition of the pressures on the president's time and the importance of managing his schedule, which can affect not only day-to-day operations but also decision-making processes and the prospects for long-range planning (Kemp 1993).

Strong chiefs of staff have proven necessary to bring order to White House decision-making processes, but they also contribute to the view that the White House staff itself distances the president from the rest of the executive branch of government. The penchant became glaring during the Nixon presidency. Roosevelt, who gave birth to the institutionalized presidency, saw his staff as a channel of communication between himself and his "line" departments and agencies. Nixon held an entirely different view. He utilized his staff less as his "eyes and ears" throughout the government and more as an independent decision-making authority between himself and the rest of the executive branch. Contrary to the intent of the Executive Reorganization Act—that presidential assistants should not have power to make decisions in their own right— Nixon's staff became the center of decision making throughout the range of domestic and foreign affairs, and assumed powers that often made them more influential than members of the cabinet. Thus Henry Kissinger, when he was special assistant for national security affairs, was more powerful than the secretaries of state or defense. And H. R. Haldeman and John Ehrlichman, who figured prominently in the Watergate affair, were more powerful than domestic department heads.

Within the Executive Office, the National Security Council (NSC) bears responsibility for foreign policy. It was as head of the NSC that Kissinger acquired greater influence than the secretaries of state or defense. Ever since, the national security adviser's role and relationship with the president have been closely scrutinized.

Kissinger's formal title was Special Assistant for National Security Affairs. The world "special" has since been dropped, and the position is sometimes referred to loosely as simply ***national security adviser***, abbreviated NSA. Others had occupied the post in previous administrations—Robert Cutler and later Gordon Gray under Eisenhower; McGeorge Bundy under Kennedy; and Bundy and Walt W. Rostow under Lyndon Johnson (see Prados 1991). None had achieved the same level of prominence and influence in the foreign affairs government as did Kissinger, however. Zbigniew Brzezinski's dominance in the Carter administration was less than Kissinger's had been under Nixon, but he, too, emerged as his boss's key foreign policy adviser. President Reagan initially sought to downgrade the role of the national security adviser—six different men held the position in Reagan's eight-year presidency— but the Iran-*contra* affair demonstrated that the national security adviser and his staff had embarked on operational activities that expanded the role of the NSC system in new and uncharted directions.[7]

Brent Scowcroft, President Bush's national security adviser, eschewed operational activities and pursued a role more akin to his pre-Reagan predecessors but without the publicity. Thus he played an active managerial role in an administration committed to lead with foreign policy as its strong suit. Anthony Lake, Clinton's NSA, assumed a low-profile role even as he reportedly worked tirelessly within the system to build support for Clinton's foreign policy and to brief reporters "on background" (not for attribution) about it. Lake earlier had served as an assistant to Henry Kissinger in the Nixon administration, resigning his post to protest the U.S. invasion of Cambodia in 1970. He later became a close adviser of Secretary of State Cyrus Vance as director of policy planning in the State Department. His deputy at the time was Samuel (Sandy) Berger, who introduced Lake to Clinton and would again join Lake as a deputy at the NSC.

Presidential preferences explain in part the variations in how different presidents draw on and interact with their in-house foreign policy advisers.[8] Still, all recent presidents, regardless of their initial predilections, have found it necessary to exert political control over foreign policy making by institutionalizing it within the White House. "The principal reason for the increasing concentration of foreign policy responsibility in the White House is our increasingly dangerous world," Theodore Sorensen (1987–1988), a White House staff member during the Kennedy administration, wrote in the wake of the Iran-*contra* scandal. "Since the days when Dean Acheson could serve as both secretary of state and Truman's personal adviser and coordinator, the overlap between national and international issues, the number and speed of thermonuclear missiles, and the foreign policy pressures from Congress, the press and public, have all mounted to a point where no president can conscientiously delegate to anyone his constitutional responsibilities in foreign affairs."

We can gain an appreciation of how presidential style and external pressures encouraged the centralization of foreign policy in the White House through a historical examination of the way different presidents have used the National Security Council and its staff and the successes and failures of this mode of "presidential governance." In the process we will gain insight into the endemic differences between the institutionalized presidency comprising the innermost circle of foreign policy making, on one hand, and the career professionals comprising the second concentric circle, on the other.

The National Security Council: Organization, Evolution, and Operation

Created by the National Security Act of 1947,[9] the purpose of the **National Security Council** is to "advise the president with respect to the integration of domestic, foreign, and military policies relating to the national security." Statutory members of the council include the president (as chair), vice president, and secretaries of state and defense. The director of central intelligence and the chairman of the joint chiefs of staff (JCS) are statutory advisers. Others also often participate, including the secretary of the treasury, the attorney general, the U.S. ambassador to the United Nations, the director of the Office of Management and Budget (OMB), heads of such organizations as the Arms Control and Disarmament Agency (ACDA), the United States Information Agency (USIA), the Agency for International Development (AID), and various presidential advisers and assistants, depending on the issues and presidential predilections.

The president is free to use the NSC as much or as little as he or she desires, and its deliberations and decisions are purely advisory. Still, it is a primary mechanism for tackling problems all presidents face: acquiring information, identifying issues, coping with crises, making decisions, coordinating actions, and ensuring agency compliance with presidential wishes. And it is the principal formal mechanism for coordinating the vast federal structure with a view toward producing a single, coherent foreign policy.

The Early Years, 1947–1961

Although created during his administration, President Truman did not use the NSC extensively, as he feared it might encroach on his constitutional prerogatives by imposing a parliamentary-type cabinet system over foreign policy decision making. Truman did not even attend NSC meetings before the outbreak of the Korean War in 1950, and the professional staff created to serve the council remained on the periphery of his relationship with his cabinet officers and departments. As a result, the council's role was largely perfunctory.

With the outbreak of the Korean War, Truman recognized the wisdom of better coordination of policy and action. He therefore directed that major national security policy recommendations come to him via the council. The famous NSC 68 memorandum is perhaps the best example of a major policy proclamation arising from Truman's NSC apparatus (see Chapter 5). By the end of his term Truman also had begun to use the NSC staff for interagency planning purposes. Both developments presaged the use to which Eisenhower put the NSC.

Coming from a professional background that emphasized the need for staff work and overall coordination, former General Eisenhower took the rudiments of the NSC structure he had inherited from Truman and transformed them into a highly formalized system which he viewed as "the central vehicle for formulating and promulgating policy" and "the primary means of imparting presidential direction and over-all coherence to the activities of the departments and agencies" (Clark and Legere 1969). A planning board and an operations coordinating board, both eventually chaired by the special assistant for national security affairs (the now-familiar position created by Eisenhower), became part of Eisenhower's NSC system. They were charged, respectively, with generating policy recommendations for consideration by the full NSC and with carrying out decisions once made.

For Truman, the National Security Council was primarily a supplementary advisory body. Eisenhower, in contrast, sought to place the NSC mechanism at the center of the policy formulation process. Still, formal council meetings were often followed by more intimate "rump" sessions, or the president would convene meetings of a small group of advisers outside the formal NSC structure to deal with urgent matters.[10] President Kennedy followed this practice extensively.

Personalizing the Staff, 1961–1969

By the time Eisenhower left office the highly institutionalized National Security Council system was being criticized as a "paper mill" which processed policies bearing little relevance to the real issues of the day. Critics also charged that the system diminished rather than expanded the range of alternatives available for presidential decision (Jackson 1965; Henderson 1988; Prados 1991). President Kennedy moved rapidly to correct these deficiencies. Shortly after his election in 1960 he appointed McGeorge Bundy as his special assistant for national security affairs and announced that the purpose of Bundy's staff would be "to assist me in obtaining advice from, and coordinating operations of, the government agencies concerned with national security." He also announced his intention to strengthen the role of the secretary of state in the area of interagency coordination.

Some observers questioned whether the new president, who had a deep personal interest in foreign affairs, actually wanted the State Department to assume a leadership role in the management of foreign affairs. In any event, insiders' accounts of the Kennedy administration indicate clearly that Kennedy was unhappy with the docile role assumed by Dean Rusk, Kennedy's choice as secretary of state, in an otherwise action-oriented administration. The State Department as an organization also proved too sluggish for White House officials. When this happened, the White House staff stepped into the perceived vacuum—not only Bundy's staff but also other members of Kennedy's personal "team," most of whom were specifically recruited for his administration rather than drawn from careerists in established bureaucracies.

Kennedy initiated the use of interagency task forces designed to serve presidential needs rather than the agencies they represented. The 1961 Bay of Pigs fiasco, from which Kennedy learned "never to rely on the experts," contributed much to his reliance on decision-making groups formulated without regard for the institutional affiliations of their members. The most celebrated was the so-called Ex Com (Executive Committee of the NSC), initially comprising some thirteen advisers on whom Kennedy relied heavily in devising a response to the surreptitious installation of Soviet offensive weapons in Cuba in October 1962. Similar but less well-known ad hoc groups dealt with crises in Berlin and Laos, paramilitary experiments being tried in Vietnam, and covert intelligence operations directed against Cuba. The NSC itself proved far less important in ensuring presidential control than these less formal groups.

Kennedy's assassination in November 1963 brought to the White House a man with little interest and less experience in foreign affairs. As the war in Vietnam escalated, however, Lyndon Johnson and his closest advisers devoted an increasing portion of their attention to Southeast Asia—to the point that by the end of Johnson's term little else seemed to command the energies of top-level decision makers.

Johnson's approach to national security matters more closely resembled Kennedy's informal style than Eisenhower's institutionalized operation. The NSC as a formal deliberative mechanism languished—a fact that, in the view of one of Johnson's critics, contributed to the Vietnam morass.

> The decisions and actions that marked our large-scale military entry into the Vietnam War in early 1965 reflected the piecemeal consideration of interrelated issues, . . . the natural consequence of a fragmented NSC and a general inattention to long-range policy planning. Consultation, even knowledge of the basic facts, was confined to a tight circle of presidential advisers, and there appears to have been little systematic debate outside that group. (Hoopes 1973b, 7)

The "Tuesday Lunch" became the institutional manifestation of the tight inner circle. Its participants included the president, the secretaries of state and defense (Rusk and Robert McNamara), the national security adviser (first McGeorge Bundy, then Walt W. Rostow, who replaced Bundy in 1966), and eventually the director of the CIA, the chairman of the joint chiefs, and the president's press secretary. Vietnam was the principal luncheon topic, while the organization itself reflected the president's approach to the war—tight personal control coupled with organizational flexibility.

The cost of Johnson's approach was the exclusion of subordinates on whom the president and his close circle of advisers depended for implementation of top-level decisions. "The top men grew to live in one world, having loyalty primarily to each other, and seeing problems in a context that their subordinates could not understand because they were outside the charmed circle." Johnson's "innate tendency to sniff treason within government walls" (Destler 1974) encouraged his tight handling of the war. Growing suspicion about subordinates having leaked government policy to the press compounded the tendency. Cut off from criticism from within, it took major policy setbacks such as the enemy's unexpected Tet Offensive at the end of January in 1968 and the poor showing of the incumbent president some six weeks later in the New Hampshire primary to force a reappraisal of Vietnam policy.

The role of Johnson's national security adviser changed with the appointment of Walt W. Rostow. Rostow continued to manage the flow of information to the president, to communicate presidential wishes to the bureaucracy, and to provide policy analysis and advice. But he did much less to encourage the free flow of ideas and alternatives to the president than had his predecessor. The result was bureaucratic distrust of Rostow's ability to present departmental viewpoints to Johnson objectively (Hoopes 1973b; cf. Mulcahy 1995).

The White House Ascendant, 1969–1981

Non-coherence describes the policy-making legacy Nixon inherited from a divided and demoralized Johnson administration in January 1969. Although the outgoing administration had not been without positive achievements in foreign policy, "its policy-making institutions, formal and informal, had little that would recommend them to its successor" (Destler 1974).

Nixon moved rapidly to restore coherence by placing the NSC at the hub of the policy-making system. When Nixon named Harvard political scientist Henry Kissinger as his special assistant for national security affairs, he directed Kissinger to establish an "Eisenhower NSC system" but "without the concurrences" (Destler 1974). The system consisted of several top-level interagency committees—nearly all directed by Kissinger—whose jurisdictions covered the entire waterfront of American foreign policy, from arms control negotiations with the Soviet Union (the Verification Panel), to crisis management (the Washington Special Actions Group), to covert operations (the 40 Committee, named for the National Security Decision Memorandum that set it up. Their task was to develop alternatives for consideration by the president and the full NSC. Because Kissinger directed nearly all of them (the Undersecretaries Committee was the exception), his role in the NSC system was pivotal (see Figure 10.2).

The system fit Richard Nixon's preferred operating style. In contrast to Eisenhower's approach (which encouraged the NSC system to focus on compromises among departments and agencies), and in contrast to the Kennedy and Johnson styles (which saw NSC meetings as forums for its members to advocate views), Nixon wanted all policy options to be laid out for his *subsequent* consideration and, above all, to maintain his flexibility.

Kissinger's influence in the system derived in part from Nixon's preference for solo

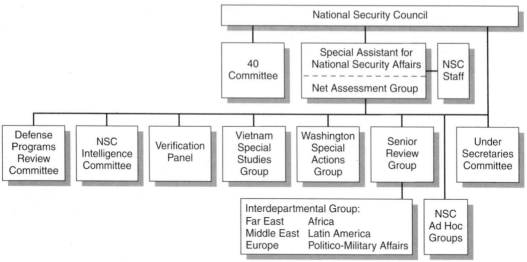

Figure 10.2 The Nixon Administration's National Security Council System

decision making. The president's trust in Kissinger further enhanced his influence. Indeed, Kissinger himself (1979) has written that "in the final analysis the influence of a Presidential Assistant derives almost exclusively from the confidence of the President, not from administrative arrangements." He also describes cogently why the influence of presidential advisers inevitably seems to grow:

> Almost all of [a president's] callers are supplicants or advocates, and most of their cases are extremely plausible—which is what got them into the Oval Office in the first place. As a result, one of the president's most difficult tasks is to choose among endless arguments that sound equally convincing. The easy decisions do not come to him; they are taken care of at lower levels. As his term in office progresses, therefore, except in extreme crisis a president comes to base his choices more and more on the confidence he has in his advisers. He grows increasingly conscious of bureaucratic and political pressures upon him; issues of substance tend to merge in his mind with the personalities embodying the conflicting considerations. (Kissinger 1979, 40)[11]

The confidence Nixon reposed in Kissinger in particular was reinforced by his spectacular diplomatic successes in China, the Soviet Union, the Middle East, and elsewhere, which came as the revelations of Watergate increasingly engulfed and paralyzed the Nixon presidency. The president's efforts to expand Kissinger's authority under such circumstances culminated in Kissinger's appointment as secretary of state, an assignment he held concurrently with his White House role which also placed him unambiguously at the pinnacle of the foreign affairs establishment as the chief architect of American foreign policy.

As Kissinger's personal influence rose, his elaborate NSC system atrophied. The decisions that led to the 1970 Cambodia incursion, for example, were a product of "catch-as-catch-can" gatherings between Nixon and his advisers outside the formal

NSC framework (Destler 1974). Other major foreign policy initiatives involving China, the Middle East, and Vietnam also evolved outside the system. The "back channel" to the Soviet leadership that Kissinger established is perhaps his most celebrated bureaucratic end-run. It led to a breakthrough in the strategic arms negotiations with the Soviets even while formal negotiations between the two sides' delegations (the "front channel") continued (see Talbott 1979).

Nothing could have made it clearer that Nixon and Kissinger now counted more than the Nixon-Kissinger NSC system.

One of Gerald Ford's first moves on the eve of his inauguration as the first non-elected president was to ask Kissinger to remain as his secretary of state and national security adviser. In his dual capacity Kissinger continued to operate what some felt was a one-man foreign policy show, one all the more apparent because the president he served was a relative novice in international affairs.

Gradually, however, Kissinger's star and the popularity of the policies he engineered waned. Much of the criticism of Kissinger came from the right wing of the president's own Republican Party—pressure that prompted Ford to drop the word "détente" from his vocabulary. Ford now saw fit to appoint Brent Scowcroft to the NSA slot. He also relented when Ronald Reagan's supporters sought to include a plank in the 1976 Republican Party platform widely interpreted as a repudiation of the Nixon-Ford-Kissinger foreign policy record.

Jimmy Carter, the Democratic presidential nominee, likewise signaled that Kissinger, his style of operation, and some of his policies would be among the first victims of a Democratic victory. Despite the campaign attacks he had launched against Kissinger's policies and operating style, President Carter's designation of Zbigniew Brzezinski as assistant for national security affairs (which came before he named his secretary of state), reaffirmed the determination of the White House to exercise foreign policy control.

Two new NSC committees were created to replace all prior ones. The Policy Review Committee was one. Chaired by a member of the cabinet chosen according to which department had the greatest stake in the issue, the Policy Review Committee assumed responsibility for long-term projects. Short-term projects (including covert intelligence operations and crisis management) fell to the Special Coordination Committee, chaired by the national security assistant, Zbigniew Brzezinski. The latter committee eventually emerged as the most influential body within the NSC structure. Brzezinski also emerged as the pivotal foreign policy adviser. Initially he was one of a "collegium" of key advisers that included Secretary of State Cyrus Vance, Secretary of Defense Harold Brown, and U.N. Ambassador Andrew Young. But Young resigned when his contacts with the Palestine Liberation Organization (in violation of established policy) were disclosed, and Vance resigned in the spring of 1980 to protest the president's abortive military rescue of American hostages in Iran.

Vance's departure marked the first time in sixty years a secretary of state resigned because of a policy dispute with the president. Although Iran was the immediate issue, conflict between the secretary and the president's national security adviser loomed in the background. Brzezinski stressed a hardline posture toward the Soviet Union and focused on the East-West conflict. Vance stressed détente and appeared more sensitive to North-South relations and global-order issues. Carter seemed unable to reconcile the often conflicting thrusts of his principal advisers. Nor did the White House–State Department rift end with Vance's departure. Carter named Senator Edmund S. Muskie as Vance's successor, but he was barely confirmed in office when Carter signed PD 59, which moved U.S. strategic doctrine in the direction of an explicit counterforce posture—and without ever consulting the new secretary of state. The move again affirmed the subsidiary role of the State Department compared with the White House staff.

The rift between Brzezinski and Vance perpetuated what by 1980 had become a recurrent concern. Should the national security adviser be primarily a manager of the decision process or primarily a personal adviser and "resident intellectual" to the president? What is the proper relationship between the national security adviser and the secretary of state?

Based on the experiences of the five presidents who occupied the Oval Office in the 1960s and 1970s, a degree of consensus emerged among practitioners and scholars about what the national security adviser should—and should not—be doing (Destler 1983b; see also "The National Security Adviser: Role and Accountability" 1980). Their activities fall along a continuum between an "inside management" role, where the adviser performs the role of facilitator, and a "leadership" role, which often places him in the potential position as a second secretary of state. The thrust of the consensus that emerged toward the end of the Carter administration is that the NSA should emphasize the "inside" role and eschew the "outside." Exemplary tasks associated with each role are listed in Focus 10.1, which also suggests that some activities midway between the "inside" and "outside" orientations may be acceptable.

The Reagan Administration: From Advocacy to Operations

Ronald Reagan arrived in Washington sensitive to the criticism of prior presidential foreign policy management systems and of the need to redress the balance between the White House and the State Department. Indeed, the new president had promised during his campaign to "restore leadership to U.S. foreign policy by organizing it in a more coherent way."

Reagan's choice of Alexander Haig as secretary of state was spotlighted as an indication of the president's desire to relocate primary control over foreign policy making in the State Department. The former NATO commander had been schooled in the ways of the White House as an assistant to Henry Kissinger and later as chief of staff during the final, embattled days of the Nixon White House. Reagan's implicit campaign pledge to downgrade the importance of the national security adviser's role was reaffirmed with the selection of Richard V. Allen for the position, whose own conception tracked the "inside management" rather than the "outside leadership" role. Furthermore, Allen was denied direct access to the Oval Office, assigned instead to report to the president through the White House counselor.

Haig played on Reagan's predilection to place the secretary of state at the forefront of the administration's foreign policy in a lengthy memorandum, submitted on inauguration day, that would have made him the administration's "foreign policy vicar" by assigning him a role in foreign affairs unprecedented since the days of John Foster

Focus 10.1
THE NATIONAL SECURITY ASSISTANT:
THE PROFESSIONALS' JOB DESCRIPTION

• • •

YES ("Inside Management")	OKAY In Moderation	NO ("Outside Leadership")
Briefing the president, handling foreign policy in-box	Discreet advice/ advocacy	Conducting particular diplomatic negotiations
Analyzing issues and choices: a. Ordering information/ intelligence b. Managing interagency studies	Encouraging advocacy by NSC staff subordinates Information and "background" communicating with press, Congress, foreign officials	Fixed operational assignments Public spokesperson Strong, visible internal advocacy (except of already established presidential priorities) Making policy decisions
Managing presidential decision processes		
Communicating presidential decisions and monitoring their implementation		
General interagency brokering, circuit-connecting, crisis management		

Source: I.M. Destler, "The Rise of the National Security Assistant," in Charles W. Kegley, Jr., and Eugene R. Wittkopf (eds.), Perspectives on American Foreign Policy: Selected Readings (New York: St. Martin's, 1983), p. 262.

Dulles. Haig was rebuffed, however, and no clearly defined organizational structure for the management of foreign policy emerged during the administration's first year, as it gave priority to domestic rather than foreign policy. Robert C. McFarlane, who became Reagan's national security adviser late in 1983, would later testify before Congress that the seeds of the Iran-*contra* scandal were sown in this environment, which was characterized by the absence of an organizational framework within which to engage in a "thorough and concerted governmentwide analysis" of critical foreign policy proposals (see McFarlane 1994). He elaborated by disclosing that people in the Reagan administration "turned to covert action because they thought they could not get Congressional support for overt activities. But they were not forced to think systematically about the fatal risks they were running." In consequence, the most distinctive characteristic of the NSC system during the Reagan administration became its involvement in operational activities well outside the boundaries established by previous presidents and national security advisers.

An assertive national security assistant might have provoked critical thinking even in the absence of an effective organizational structure designed to promote it, but Allen proved unable to mediate disputes between others in the administration or to broker the competing interests of the bureaucracies comprising the foreign affairs government. In early 1982 he was replaced by William P. Clark, a former justice on the California Supreme Court then serving as deputy secretary of state. It was the first of many personnel changes among Reagan's key foreign policy advisers in an administration plagued by personality conflicts and internecine warfare.

When Clark first became national security adviser, he hewed to the "inside" description of the job, believing that he could serve as an honest broker for others in the foreign affairs government. It took him almost a year to conclude otherwise and to learn that "Cabinet secretaries are all parochial, so you've got to decide yourself what to do." Thus he played an increasingly active role across a broad range of issues pertaining to national security policy, even asserting White House authority over arms control policy in 1983 when disputes between the State and Defense Departments became overly intense (Lord 1988; Talbott 1984). He also enhanced the policy-making role of the NSC generally and increased the number of professional staff serving the council to a level greater than at any time since Kissinger's tenure (Destler 1983a).

Clark held strongly conservative ideological convictions that led him to assume a staunchly anti-Soviet foreign policy posture. He believed, with Reagan, that the 1970s represented "a decade of neglect for the security needs of the United States." Similarly, he advocated stepped-up United States military activity in Central America and was the strongest White House voice favoring increased military spending.

By the summer of 1983, Clark was widely regarded as having become the most influential foreign policy figure in the White House. As the most conservative of the president's inner circle of advisers, he also came into conflict with other, more pragmatic White House staffers, particularly Chief of Staff James Baker. The squabbling (especially on the issue of defense spending) may have contributed to Clark's sudden and unexpected departure for the Interior Department in October 1983.

Conservative Reagan supporters, seeing the national security vacancy as an opportunity to press their policy preferences on the president, supported the candidacy of U.N. Ambassador Jeane Kirkpatrick. A committed Reaganite, Kirkpatrick had been a close ally of Clark and had occupied an unusually prominent position in the Reagan foreign policy establishment (she regularly attended NSC meetings, for example). Baker was another serious candidate. But in the end Reagan chose "Bud" McFarlane. Although McFarlane lacked the academic and intellectual credentials of a Kissinger or Brzezinski, he was an experienced foreign affairs adviser, having served as an NSC staffer under Kissinger and Scowcroft, a member of the Senate Armed Services Committee staff, and a trouble-shooter for Secretary of State Haig. McFarlane's appointment more closely resembled the "in moderation" position shown in Focus 10.1 than any of his prior counterparts.

McFarlane inherited from Clark an elaborate NSC organizational structure put into place by a National Security Decision Directive in January 1982. Patterned on a plan Johnson devised but never fully implemented because of the urgency of Vietnam, three senior interdepartmental groups (SIGs) replaced the cabinet-level Policy Review Committee instituted by the Carter administration. The SIGs were to exercise responsibility for foreign policy, military and defense policy, and intelligence. Policy considerations were to be developed for the SIGs by interdepartmental groups headed by assistant secretaries.

The Reagan NSC system never functioned as it was intended (Lord 1988). Instead, the real influence appears to have been lodged in the National Security Planning Group, a less formal network consisting of the president's closest personal advisers, which emerged as a kind of "executive committee" of the NSC not unlike Johnson's Tuesday Lunch. Moreover, the president himself was largely detached from the foreign policy-making process, preferring instead a hands-off management style.

The untoward effects of Reagan's lack of involvement and his failure to utilize the existing formal policy-making structures were emphasized by the Tower Board's postmortem on the Iran-*contra* affair. James A. Baker, chief of staff and secretary of the treasury under Reagan and secretary of state under Bush, also scored the Reagan foreign policy machine: "It was often a witches' brew of intrigue, elbows, egos, and separate agendas," he wrote in his memoirs (1995). "I can't remember any extended period of time when someone in the national security cluster wasn't at someone else's throat. The National Security Council frequently ran amok, as the Iran-*contra* scandal documented in embarrassing detail. And sometimes when the President decided a major policy issue, his subordinates would ignore his wishes and pursue their own policy schemes."

McFarlane enjoyed some successes as national security adviser, especially in breaking the long deadlock within the administration on arms control policy, but he resigned in late 1985 after becoming "overwhelmed by 'Cabinet government'" and his inability to resolve interminable squabbles among key administration officials (Cannon 1988). He was replaced by Rear Admiral John Poindexter, who would later be forced to resign because of his role in the Iran-*contra* debacle.

Early assessments of Poindexter's stewardship at the NSC were generally positive, but Poindexter raised another question when he remained on active military duty as a naval admiral. Some feared that placing a military officer in a traditionally civilian policy role might contribute unduly toward a military approach to political problems. The Iran-*contra* affair reinforced the concern, and it was raised again when Lieutenant General Colin Powell was appointed to succeed Frank C. Carlucci, who had replaced Poindexter. Interestingly, Powell's appointment came on the very day that the congressional committees investigating the Iran-*contra* affair voted to recommend that the president's national security assistant "not be an active military officer." Concern about the status of the national security adviser paralleled concern over whether the NSC staff may not also have become too dependent on professional military personnel.

The "Iran initiative," as the Tower Board called it, included an attempted strategic opening to Iran, the sale of arms to Iran via Israel and by the United States itself in an effort to secure the release of hostages held in Lebanon, and, ultimately, the diversion of profits from the arms sales to the *contras* fighting the Sandinista regime in Nicaragua. The board concluded that the initiative "ran directly counter to the Administration's own policies on terrorism, the Iran/Iraq war, and military support to Iran." It also suggested that proper use of existing structures might have averted the single most damaging foreign policy failure of the Reagan presidency.

The origins of the clandestine Iran initiative can be traced to 1984 when McFarlane launched an interagency evaluation of U.S. relations with Iran. Eventually McFarlane secretly visited Teheran armed with a cake shaped like a key and a Bible signed by the president. National security advisers had undertaken secret diplomatic initiatives in the past (technically McFarlane traveled to Iran on behalf of the president and the NSC staff, since by then he had resigned as National Security Adviser), but as the Iranian affair unfolded it took the NSC staff in a wholly new direction. The record indicates, for example, that Secretary of State Shultz and Secretary of Defense Weinberger vigorously opposed the transfer of arms to Iran,[12] that key covert action findings that authorized the arms-for-hostages swap were approved by the president without their knowledge, and that John Poindexter authorized the transfer of arms profits to the *contras* without the president's knowledge. Congress was also kept in the dark about what had become a covert operation run out of the White House in apparent contravention of the law, and it received false and misleading information from key players, notably McFarlane, Poindexter, and Poindexter's assistant, Lieutenant Colonel Oliver North (see also Chapter 12).

The Iran-*contra* affair was as much a misuse of executive power as it was a competition between the institutionalized presidency and the bureaucratic domains comprising the foreign affairs government. The NSC had become a "government within a government" spurred on by "presidential inattentiveness, ideological fervor, frustration with a Congress that seemed determined to micromanage foreign policy, and the desire of the . . . chief of central intelligence . . . to find an operational channel less vulnerable to congressional scrutiny than the CIA" (Cannon 1988). Poindexter's decision to divert funds from the sale of weapons to Iran to the *contras* without the president's explicit approval so as to protect his future deniability is particularly notable. Reactions of other NSAs to his behavior was "uniformly negative. 'This goes way beyond the borderline,' Brent Scowcroft observed. Zbigniew Brzezinski told reporters he 'could not have conceived of the situation in which I would have done that.' It was the same with Henry Kissinger. 'I was a far much more [*sic*] assertive security adviser than Poindexter,' Henry said, 'and I would never have dreamed of making a decision like that'" (Prados 1991).[13]

Perhaps the "mistakes of the Iran-Contra affair" are best viewed as merely "mistakes in judgment, and nothing more"—as the Republican minority concluded in the congressional report on its investigation of the affair. Or perhaps it was merely an "aberration"—as John Tower concluded. Nonetheless, the affair perpetuated what had become an ongoing debate about the role of the White House in the foreign policy-making process and about the characteristics and consequences of the concentration of power in the institutionalized presidency. Indeed, one analyst asserts that "it was . . . precisely the actions of such characters as Kissinger and Brzezinski that made possible the NSC staff excesses of the Reagan years" (Prados 1991). Finally, the scandal reaffirmed the truism that an effective process is critical to a sound policy. "Issues come and go," observed Colin Powell. "Process is always important."

Powell took over the national security adviser's position in December 1987 when Carlucci replaced Weinberger as secretary of defense. Under his and Carlucci's tutelage the NSC played an important and positive role in preparing for the Washington and Moscow superpower summits, and the NSA once more emerged as an effective facilitator of the foreign affairs policy process (Cannon 1988; Kirschten 1987). "We set out to restore the credibility of the institution, to restore it to its proper role as an interagency body," observed Carlucci. "That is its 'honest broker' role, and we set out to reestablish it. We took the NSC out of operations."

The Bush Administration: The "Wise Men" Take Control

Colin Powell returned to active military duty at the end of the Reagan administration and was later named chairman of the Joint Chiefs of Staff by President Bush. From that vantage point he oversaw the U.S. invasion of Panama in December 1989. Ironically, Powell as national security adviser had been involved in the Reagan administration's efforts to force Panamanian strongman Manuel Noriega from power but had then cautioned against the use of force for that purpose.

Powell was only one of many familiar faces to reappear in the Bush administration. Among them was a new troika of foreign policy officials: James Baker, Dick Cheney, and Brent Scowcroft. Baker became secretary of state. Earlier he had resigned as Reagan's secretary of the Treasury to run George Bush's election campaign, just as he had once run Gerald Ford's. Cheney became secretary of defense after Bush failed to win Senate approval of former Senator John Tower for the job. Earlier he, too, had served President Ford, as chief of staff. Scowcroft became national security adviser. He had occupied that role in the Ford administration and was, along with Tower and Edmund Muskie, a member of the Tower Board which investigated the Iran-*contra* affair.

Not only were the three seasoned practitioners of the art of governance, they were also close personal friends. Their experience in the Ford administration (in which Bush also served as CIA director), when détente was still in its heyday, gave them a common reference point in coping with the fast-paced changes in Soviet-American relations during the Bush presidency. Baker and Scowcroft also agreed at the outset that "Baker would have the lead on foreign policy, Scowcroft and the NSC would have no operational role, and Scowcroft himself would be a low-profile 'honest broker' within the administration." With this they hoped to avoid "niggling disagreements over public speeches, television interviews, ambassadorial visits, and the like" (Gergen 1989). These were the very source of past turf battles between the secretary and state and the national security adviser.

As a member of the Tower Board, Scowcroft was an outspoken critic of the NSC operations that led to the Iran-*contra* scandal. He tried therefore, apparently successfully, to involve the secretaries of state and defense in the policy process and to himself maintain close contact with the president. As one observer explained as the Bush presidency entered its last year, "The unflappable, intelligent, loyal Scowcroft has succeeded where almost every other recent national security adviser has failed: He has managed both to be a highly influential adviser to the president and to coordinate effectively the debate among the president's top foreign policy officials. Scowcroft has been able to combine these two functions because he lacks the insatiable drive toward power and fame that has crippled previous National Security Council heads" (Judis 1992).

The structure of Bush's NSC system looked quite similar to his predecessors'. A Principals Committee at the top consisted of the national security assistant (as chair), the secretaries of state and defense, the director of central intelligence, the chairman of the Joint Chiefs of Staff, and the president's chief of staff, with participation by the attorney general and Treasury secretary when issues required. The Principals Committee was charged with reviewing, coordinating, and monitoring the development and implementation of national security policy.

Positioned below the Principals Committee with participants at the rank of under secretary, the Deputies Committee acted as the senior subcabinet interagency forum for consideration of policy issues. In was served by a series of NSC policy coordinating committees that paralleled the interdepartmental groups of previous administrations in both structure and function.

As in every administration, the key question was whether the formal NSC system functioned as intended. On balance, it appears that it did not.

Although Bush was more experienced in foreign affairs than any previous president, his first move, urged by Scowcroft, was to launch a "strategic review" of foreign and national security policy; six months later, it had produced little that was new or innovative. Meanwhile, events in Eastern Europe and the Soviet Union were unfolding at a dizzying pace. Bush responded with "prudence." "Status quo plus" conceptualized American foreign policy in these turbulent days. It reflected the experience of the Bush administration's foreign policy principals two decades earlier. "The Soviet Union," Bush warned in May 1989, had "promised a more cooperative relationship before—only to reverse course and return to militarism." And Scowcroft: "You don't turn a great nation like the U.S. around quickly. We're talking about modifications in direction." Six months later, shortly after the Berlin Wall had fallen, Bush defended his reactive posture: "To those who question our prudent pace, they must understand that a time of historic change is no time for recklessness. . . . In a new Europe, the American role may change in form but not in fundamentals."

Bush's responses to Soviet initiatives, when they happened, did not evolve out of the NSC system. In the fall of 1989 when Bush agreed to meet Gorbachev at the Malta summit, for example, Secretary of Defense Cheney was not informed of the decision and no NSC meeting was held on the matter. "Similarly, no NSC meeting occurred during the October 1989 coup attempt in Panama, or the December coup attempt in the Philippines, when Bush authorized U.S. jet aircraft to prevent coup forces using air support against government troops in Manila. So far as is . . . evident, there was also no NSC meeting in connection with Bush's most ambitious foreign policy move of his first year—the Christmas 1989 invasion of Panama" (Prados 1991). These findings led the author of an NSC history to conclude that "It will not help George Bush with history that his NSC system seems organized to implement secret decisions secretly arrived at" (Prados 1991).

Secrecy was one characteristic signpost of Bush's decision-making proclivities; his preference for a tight inner circle of confidants chosen on the basis of loyalty and friendship, not institutional ties, was another. The decision process that led to the defense of Saudi Arabia in August 1990 and, later, to the war against Iraq illustrates these tendencies. Bob Woodward provides an unusual glimpse of that process as seen through the eyes of Colin Powell. His reflections are recorded in Focus 10.2.

Bush ended the war too quickly, in the eyes of some, and this, too, may have been a failure of his NSC system—or, more accurately, of his failure to use the system to its fullest. "Consensus among his advisors helped to produce a favorable military strategy, although it seemed less able to aid the president in determining U.S. objectives in the aftermath of the war. . . . Policy objectives became muddled; mixed signals were given to Iraqi dissidents; for a time, Kuwaiti revenge on Palestinians was ignored" (Wayne 1993). And Saddam Hussein remained in power.

Current History: The Clinton Administration

Midway through the Reagan presidency Anthony Lake and two of his colleagues, I. M. Destler and Leslie Gelb, wrote a provocative book on the politics of American foreign policy making that described the competition between the White House and the State Department as a contest between "courtiers" and "barons." Courtiers are those in the White House "who gain influence by responding to [presidents'] personal needs and their political priorities." Barons are senior officials "in formal charge of an important domain within the presidential realm," principally cabinet-level agencies such as the State and Defense Departments. A primary cause of the shift in power to the courtiers from the barons, they argue, "has been the triumph of politics and ideology over foreign policy. Presidents use foreign policy more frequently for political reasons. . . . This increases their distrust of the bureaucracy and drives them to pull policy control into their own White House." They also aver that the policy process has become "more personality-dependent, and thus more idiosyncratic, since staff aides are less constrained than Cabinet barons." Thus the triumph of politics and ideology has "both encouraged and enabled Presidents to seize personal control of current policy operations" (Destler, Gelb, and Lake 1984; see also Bock 1987). Lake argues in another book that a successful foreign policy results from a balance between principle and pragmatism and worried that "the balance has shifted strongly and dangerously toward the political appointees and their more ideological perspectives" (Lake 1989).

The analysis Lake and his colleagues offer is in some sense a description of their own experiences as part of the new class of "professional elites" that began to challenge the Establishment's Wise Men in the 1970s and later (see Chapter 9). Destler, for example, had served as an associate to the President's Task Force on Government Operations, Gelb was an alumnus of the Carter administration, and Lake had held positions in both the Nixon and Carter administrations—classic embodiments of the contest between courtiers and barons and the triumph of the White House over established bureaucracies. Having witnessed Kissinger and Brzezinski firsthand, Lake was determined on becoming NSA himself to avoid the foreign policy flareups and pitfalls each of them experienced. Also noteworthy is that Warren M. Christopher, Clinton's choice for secretary of state, had served as deputy secretary of state in the Carter administration (where he negotiated the release of American diplomats held

Focus 10.2

REFLECTIONS ON THE GULF WAR DECISION-
MAKING PROCESS

• • •

Powell recalled vividly the efforts he had made to present all the options in the Persian Gulf—including containment of Iraq—to the president, to make sure the full range of possibilities had been considered. It had been hard. . . .

One Friday afternoon in early October . . . Cheney and Powell had gone to the Oval Office to see Bush and Scowcroft. The sun was streaming in. For some reason the atmosphere wasn't right. There were interruptions; it was the president's office, the wrong place for this kind of discussion, Powell felt. He preferred the formality of the Situation Room, where Bush could stay focused. The mood in the Oval Office was too relaxed, too convivial—the boys sitting around shooting the shit before the weekend. . . .

Powell . . . had become increasingly disenchanted with the National Security Council procedures and meetings. Scowcroft seemed unable, or unwilling, to coordinate and make sense of all the components of the Gulf policy—military, diplomatic, public affairs, economic, the United Nations. When the principals met, Bush liked to keep everyone around the table smiling—jokes, camaraderie, the conviviality of old friends. Positions and alternatives were not completely discussed. Interruptions were common. Clear decisions rarely emerged. Often Power and Cheney returned from these gatherings and said to each other, now what did that mean? What are we supposed to do? Frequently, they had to wait to hear the answer later from Scowcroft or on television.

The operation needed a field marshal—someone of the highest rank who was the day-to-day manager, Powell felt. The president, given his other domestic and political responsibilities, couldn't be chief coordinator. It should be the national security adviser. Instead, Scowcroft had become the First Companion and all-purpose playmate to the president on golf, fishing, and weekend outings. He was regularly failing in his larger duty to ensure that policy was carefully debated and formulated. . . .

We are at a "Y" in the road," Scowcroft began. The policy could continue to be deter-and-defend, or it could switch to developing the office option.

Powell was struck once again by the informality of the rolling discussion among these . . . men who had been friends for years. There was no real organization to the proceedings as they weighted options. Ideas bounded back and forth as one thought or another occurred to one of them.

Source: Bob Woodward, The Commanders *(New York: Simon & Schuster, 1991), pp. 41, 301–2, 318.*

hostage in Iran in 1980), and that both Lake and Christopher brought with them others who had served Carter, the last Democrat to occupy the White House.[14]

Destler, Gelb, and Lake had strong advice for future assistants to the president for national security. It hued closely to the "insider management" role described in Focus 10.1.

> If the assistant is to be the director of policy formation, he should be strictly an inside operator. To avoid the massive confusion of the last decade or more, the adviser should not speak publicly, engage in diplomacy, nor undermine the secretary [of state] with Congress and the news media. A president who cannot demand that of the adviser and an adviser who cannot so forbear are simply asking for catastrophe for their administration. But while enforcing these constraints, the president much also make it clear that the assistant is the person in charge. (Destler, Gelb, and Lake 1984, 277)

This prescription is a virtual copy of Lake's behavior in the Clinton administration. He described his conception of the NSA's task shortly after his selection as making sure that Clinton "gets the wide array of alternatives, the concise information, and the broad range of advice [for decision making] that he requires." At first he played a near-invisible role as seen by the public and the media, and there is no evidence that he engaged directly in major diplomatic missions. Instead, Secretary of State Warren Christopher was the administration's chief negotiator, and he, United Nations Ambassador Madeleine Albright (a former Carter NSC aide), and sometimes Under Secretary of State Strobe Talbott and Secretary of Defense William J. Perry were its chief foreign policy spokespersons. So rarely was Lake in the spotlight that when he gave his first major foreign policy speech his colleagues teased him, saying "Garbo speaks."

At the outset of his presidency Clinton announced his intention to make foreign policy in the White House and to turn to the State Department for its implementation. Within the White House the formal National Security Council structure remained remarkably similar to Bush's (see Figure 10.3). Even many of the names remained the same. Two notable changes reflected Clinton's priorities. First, the formal responsibilities of the NSC included not only foreign, military, and intelligence aspects of American national security, as previously, but now also economic matters (in conjunction with the National Economic Council, discussed below). Second, the secretary of the treasury, the assistant to the president for economic policy, and the White House chief of staff were added as "new members." (Because the National Security Council was created by statute, the addition of these personnel as "new members" of the NSC must be considered the practice of the Clinton administration, not a formal change in its legally constituted membership.)

As with the Bush administration, the Clinton NSC system had all the trappings that would permit it to realize the president's goals: centralization of policy making in the White House, implementation by the State Department. Midway through Clinton's presidency, however, it was clear the system did not work. Following the October 1993 disaster in Somalia, which led to the death of American troops serving in the UN peacekeeping mission, Secretary of State Christopher convinced Clinton to convene weekly, hour-long foreign policy sessions with his principal foreign policy ad-

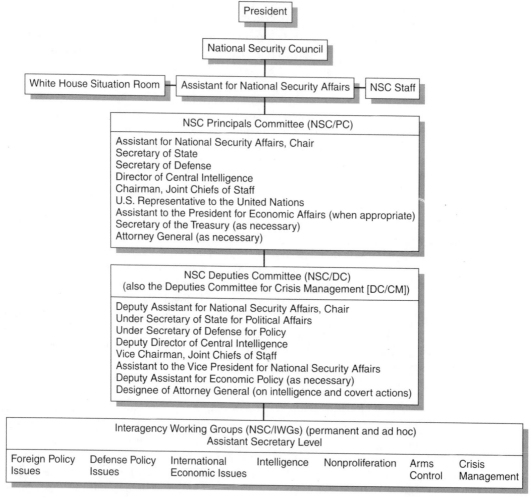

Figure 10.3   The Clinton Administration's National Security Council System
Note: The White House chief of staff later became a member of the NSC Principals Committee.
Source: Adapted from Presidential Decision Directive (PDD) 2, January 20, 1994.

visers. Other steps initiated in hopes of shoring up the administration's foreign policy performance included elevating Vice President Gore to a more visible role as foreign policy spokesperson and initiating a review of NSC procedures. (In a departure from the past, Gore's national security adviser, Leon Fuerth, was a full member of the NSC Deputies Committee.) The steps were designed to strengthen the system below the president to better anticipate crisis situations, monitor them, and communicate with the public about them (Devroy and Williams 1993).

Gore would play an increasingly visible foreign policy role in the months that followed. An activist vice president, in this and other ways he moved well beyond traditional vice presidential boundaries to become a major player in the Clinton adminis-tration (Devroy and Barr 1995; Sciolino and Purdum 1995). In other ways, however, the changes envisioned after the Somalia tragedy failed to materialize. The meetings Christopher sought did not happen, for example. Indeed, Clinton showed little inter-est in foreign policy issues and even less in the policy-making procedures outlined in Figure 10.3. Formal NSC meetings were never held to discuss his policies toward Russia—arguably among the positive achievements early in his administration. In-stead, Russian policy was discussed in less-structured settings among the administra-tion's foreign policy "principals" (Lake, Christopher, Albright, the secretary of de-fense, director of the CIA, chairman of the Joint Chiefs of Staff, and, later, White House chief of staff). Formal NSC meetings on other topics were infrequent.

Defining a new American foreign policy for the post-Cold War era will not come easily, and as we suggested in Chapter 1, may take years to emerge full-blown. Still, the public perception that the Clinton administration simply did not have its foreign pol-icy act together did little to bolster confidence in American foreign policy at home and abroad. The administration's foreign policy team being, as one writer put it, "forged mostly in the political failure of the Carter administration" (Kirschten 1993), added to the widespread belief that it was unable to respond decisively and with determination to the challenges of the post-Cold War era. The administration's propensity to "ad-hocracy" also helped little. Indeed, the "lines of authority" in the Clinton White House were likened to "a plate of spaghetti: Everyone seems to be in charge of every-one so that no one is held accountable, there is little hierarchy, and there are loops of influence and access that collide, coincide or work in blissful ignorance of one another until some fiasco looms" (Devroy 1994).

A year into the Clinton administration both Anthony Lake and his supporters won-dered whether the "inside management" role he had adopted still fit adequately the re-quirements of an effective national security adviser, particularly in an administration premised on government activism and the primacy of domestic policy. Television in particular now places a greater premium on public advocacy and defense of any ad-ministration's foreign policy than when Destler, Gelb, and Lake articulated their view of the NSA's role. Playing the insider role may now be less critical to an effective for-eign policy than once thought, and the "outside leadership" role more so (see Marcus 1994). Collegiality marked the relationship between Lake (a courtier) and other for-eign policy principals (barons). Thus the frictions of previous administrations which Lake, Christopher, and others were determined to avoid could not be blamed for the administration's shortcomings. Indeed, the development of Clinton's Haitian policies revealed not conflict but a void between Lake and Christopher, as the secretary of state largely removed himself from the policy. Jimmy Carter stepped into the void, negoti-ating the U.S. "intervasion" of the island nation over the protest of State Department officials.

It is ironic that Clinton turned to Carter not only on Haiti but also earlier to deal with a crisis over nuclear weapons proliferation in North Korea. As Clinton's foreign policy zigged one way and then zagged another, critics wondered if his foreign policy team—most with formative experience in the Carter administration—was simply not tough enough for the job. Clinton first sought to distance himself from Carter to avoid too close an association with what many saw as Carter's ineffectual ("weak") foreign policies while president, only to turn to him later to avoid the use of force (see Brock 1994). Moreover, by appearing to "contract out" foreign policy, Clinton raised anew questions about White House decision-making procedures. "Although he came into office pledging to conduct a new kind of preventive diplomacy, there [was] still a day-to-day approach to decision-making. That . . . dictated a reactive approach to solving crises and opened the door to outsiders with fresh ideas eager to fill vacuums" (Sciolino 1994).

Going beyond particular personalities and procedures, the NSC itself today bears little resemblance to its ancestry, particularly the Eisenhower years when, in some sense, its formal trappings reached their zenith. "Today most people asked about the NSC would think of the national security *adviser* and his small *staff* in the West Wing and Old Executive Office Building. In Ike's day the NSC was the president in council or, at a minimum, a reference to the NSC principals—the vice president and the secretaries of state and defense" (Prados 1991). What today is better conceived as the "National Security Council system" is nonetheless critically important. How to make both the council and the assistant for national security affairs most effective is now the issue, as neither the wisdom nor determination of presidents to exercise control over American foreign policy from the White House is any longer in question. There is no shortage of recommendations on how to realize these objectives. Ultimately, however, personal preferences, priorities, and the operating style of the president become determining variables. That conclusion will inform much of our inquiry in Chapter 14, where we will return to a consideration of presidents and their foreign policy-making approaches.

Other Executive Office Functions: Managing Economic Affairs

Before leaving the presidential subsystem, mention should be made of other units within the Executive Office which, along with the NSC, are at the immediate disposal of the president and thus contribute to presidential preeminence in foreign policy making. Principal among them are the offices and personnel responsible for economic and budgetary decision making, policy arenas that the end of the Cold War and budgetary stringency have pushed to the forefront of the presidential subsystem's agenda.

Managing the Budget

The largest, with roughly 550 staff members, is the Office of Management and Budget (OMB). OMB has responsibility for reviewing budgetary and other legislative requests coming from departments and agencies and for examining legislation passed by Congress before it is signed into law by the president. It also assists in devising plans for the organization and management of executive branch functions. Those tasks assign OMB a potentially critical voice in ensuring that agencies' plans and programs are consistent with presidential priorities.

Different presidents have employed different budgetary and management techniques to realize their objectives. In the early 1960s, Robert McNamara introduced the

Planning, Programming, and Budgeting System (PPBS) into the Defense Department as a procedure for making more-informed budgetary choices and evaluating military operations. Lyndon Johnson later ordered that PPBS be applied throughout the government. President Nixon emphasized "management by objectives." The approach entailed assigning priorities to competing objectives and choosing some programs over others.

As the 1970s wore on, concern for restraining public spending mounted. In response, Jimmy Carter implemented zero-based budgeting (ZBB). This management technique requires that each program be justified anew each year when money is requested. It did not prove effective, however, in stemming the flow of public spending.

Fueled in part by the priority the Reagan administration gave to rebuilding the nation's defensive posture, budget deficits by the mid-1980s topped $200 billion annually, and the national debt inched toward $1.5 trillion as the United States became the world's largest debtor nation. To cope with the deficit, President Reagan hoped to simultaneously cut domestic programs while preserving the administration's "supply-side"[15] economics. OMB enjoyed some successes, but when it came to trimming the largest item in the budget, which also was the most important foreign affairs item—national defense—OMB found that other players in the game led with a stronger suit. Rather than challenge a steamroller, the politically wise strategy was to trim at the margins rather than launch a frontal attack. The result, however, is that OMB was notably less effective in imposing a presidential imprimatur on the nation's foreign policy spending priorities during the 1980s than might have been expected.

By the time Bush moved into the Oval Office the government's flow of red ink was too great to ignore. Despite a "no new taxes" campaign pledge, Bush found it necessary to reach a politically contentious (and eventually costly) agreement with Congress. Designed to curb federal spending, it exposed defense and well as social programs to the budgetary ax. Bush's controversial OMB director, Richard G. Darman, often found himself in the unenviable position of the messenger people wanted to kill.

Leon E. Panetta succeeded Darman after Bush's electoral defeat. Panetta and his deputy, Alice M. Rivlin, who would succeed Panetta as OMB director in 1994 when the former congressman became Clinton's chief of staff, became leading advocates of strict budgetary discipline in an administration that promised budget reductions but found them difficult (see Woodward 1994). Meanwhile, the "management" side of OMB, already a low priority, was dealt twin blows as proposed reforms of OMB promised to merge its dual functions into one and as the administration's "reinventing government" initiative promised dramatic reductions in the size of the federal bureaucracy. "Total Quality Management" (TQM) became the core concept in this latest effort to reform management practices in the federal government (see also Chapter 13). Vice President Al Gore, architect of the management reform effort, promoted technological innovation as the key to a more responsive government. The role OMB would play in this effort seemed tangential. Not in doubt, however, is that the size of the federal budget combined with burgeoning costs of existing entitlement programs and continuing demands for new expenditures (many proposed at the expense of national security and international affairs programs) assure that OMB will remain a major player in the presidential subsystem.

Managing Economic Policy

Different presidents have devised different means to seek top-level coordination of foreign economic policy making (see Cohen 1994). President Clinton's National Economic Council (NEC), created by executive order as the economic policy counterpart to the National Security Council, is the most recent manifestation. Creation of the council symbolized Clinton's determination to show that economic policy would be at least equal in importance to national security policy during his administration (during the 1992 campaign the anticipated new body was usually referred to as an Economic Security Council). It also reflected a desire to move the "center of gravity" on economic policy away from the Treasury Department and into the White House (Safire 1993).

Twenty years earlier President Nixon had launched a Council on International Economic Policy in an unsuccessful effort to achieve dominance in foreign economic policy making similar to what his National Security Council and staff achieved in the foreign policy area. Neither Ford nor Carter emulated Nixon's efforts by creating an Executive Office unit with responsibility for international economic affairs, but both found necessary some type of top-level coordinating mechanism to promote policy coherence as America's role in the world political economy grew. Ford created an Economic Policy Board, chaired by the secretary of the treasury, whose purpose was to oversee the entire range of foreign and domestic economic policy. Carter followed with a similarly structured Economic Policy Group, but it was never as successful as Ford's initiative. Carter eventually relied on a special presidential representative to facilitate policy coordination.

During the Reagan administration the Cabinet Council on Economic Affairs was given responsibility over economic policy, and the administration's NSC apparatus eventually contained a Senior Interagency Group for International Economic Policy. The secretary of the treasury chaired both groups, which contained many of the same participants. The Bush administration adopted similar practices: An NSC policy coordinating committee chaired by an assistant secretary of the treasury exercised responsibility for international economic affairs.

The common element among the presidents from Nixon to Bush is that they perceived the need for top-level *coordination* of foreign economic policy making but eschewed the use of general-purpose, formal entities to exercise economic policy-making *control* (Porter 1983). Clinton's National Economic Council was no exception in this regard, but it was the most ambitious coordinating mechanism launched in the past two decades.

Like the National Security Council, the National Economic Council was intended to coordinate the cabinet departments and agencies with interests and responsibilities in economic policy, including international economic policy; to advise the president on economic policy decisions; and to monitor their implementation. Like National Security Adviser Anthony Lake, Robert E. Rubin, first head of the NEC and assistant to the president for economic policy, viewed his role as an "honest broker" in representing the views of executive branch departments and agencies in White House decision making. Although Rubin was given high marks in this regard, early criticisms of the council suggested that it produced more paper than policy, that the council was too big and its meetings too long. A Washington consultant hired to study the NEC for the French government concluded that "There's no structure. . . . There are lots of meetings—endless meetings and graduate seminars. Meetings without decisions and decisions without implementation. There is not a coherent philosophy" (cited in Starobin 1994).

In practice, much of the NEC's work, like that of the National Security Council, occurred below the level of "the principals" (cabinet and other members of the NEC) by their deputies and in interagency working groups dealing with particular issues. These ranged from energy economics to trade and technology policy and beyond. In much of this the NEC's role was to ensure that political considerations were aired along with economic ones. "The NEC gives me a sense of where politics are going both internally and externally," declared OMB director Leon Panetta. That is not always an easy task, however. As NEC deputy W. Bowman Cutter put it, "It is a law that the economics of an issue always run exactly counter to the politics."

The Council of Economic Advisers (CEA) is the White House unit specifically charged with focusing on the economics of economic policy making. Together with officials from OMB and the Treasury Department, the council makes economic forecasts on which the income and expenditures of the federal government are based. It has no operational responsibilities. Instead, it serves exclusively in an advisory capacity as a kind of staff arm of its "client," the president (Porter 1983). The council itself comprises three presidential appointees, usually drawn from the ranks of the most respected academic economists. The council's chairperson becomes the administration's senior economist and is responsible for establishing the positions the council takes. One of two remaining members is typically assigned international responsibilities. Laura D'Andrea Tyson, chairwoman of the CEA in the Clinton administration (before succeeding Rubin as NEC chief) was an expert in trade policy.

Created in 1946 with an eye toward short-run economic stabilization, today the CEA advises the president on the entire range of domestic and foreign economic policy issues; the value of the dollar and the U.S. trade balance are among them. The council also plays a role in managing the delicate relationship between the president and the Federal Reserve Board, an independent federal agency with broad powers over monetary policy (Feldstein 1992; Solomon 1994) . As we saw in Chapter 7, monetary policy exerts a direct impact on the dollar and trade balance. Channels of influence available to the CEA include face-to-face meetings between the president and the chair of the council, interaction with the secretary of the treasury and other senior personnel, membership on the National Economic Council, involvement of the CEA members and its staff in interagency groups, testimony before Congress, and public commentary (Feldstein 1992). The CEA also prepares the influential *Economic Report of the President*, presented annually to Congress, which is widely used inside and outside of government.

Managing Trade Policy

Clinton's National Economic Council emerged as an important player in devising his administration's trade policies. This inevitably raised the specter of turf battles with another White House agent involved in managing foreign economic policy: the Office of the United States Trade Representative.

Headed by a presidential appointee who carries the rank of ambassador as well as membership in the cabinet, the U.S. trade representative (USTR) exercises primary responsibility for developing and coordinating the implementation of international trade policy and acting as the principal trade spokesperson in the U.S. government. The office directs American participation in trade negotiations with other nations, including bilateral talks, such as the Structural Impediments Initiative and "framework" negotiations with Japan, and multilateral ventures, such as the Uruguay Round of GATT negotiations concluded in 1993.

The trade representative's roots are lodged in the Kennedy administration, then called the Special Trade Representative. The USTR achieved cabinet status during the Ford administration, when it wrested control over multilateral trade affairs from the State Department, and the office became a major player in multilateral negotiations during the Carter administration. Robert Strauss played a key role in bringing the GATT's Tokyo Round negotiations to successful conclusion. He was particularly successful not only in promoting American interests internationally but also in negotiating with American industries affected by the agreement and in placating congressional concerns. In response, a reorganization of the trade office in 1980 gave the USTR a greater voice among the many government agencies involved in determining overall American trade policy.

President Reagan pledged that his trade representative would continue to play a dominant role in orchestrating the nation's trade policies, but as the nation's once preeminent position in the global trade network began to deteriorate in the early 1980s, he proposed creation of a new cabinet-level trade department, which would combine the roles of policy development (exercised by the U.S. Trade Representative) and policy implementation (exercised by the Commerce Department). The White House never pushed the proposal vigorously, and when it failed to win congressional support the matter languished. Meanwhile, the rising value of the dollar contributed to a deterioration in the nation's trade position. Voluntary export restrictions (VERs) covering particular products were negotiated with Japan and others in an effort to ameliorate the adverse effects of the strong dollar (see Chapter 7). However, the USTR proved too weak within the administration to do anything more than negotiate these market-sharing agreements with others. Instead, benign neglect characterized the administration's general approach to trade policy as "needed coordination of monetary, trade, and industrial policy between the Treasury Department, the USTR, and the Commerce Department [was] sorely lacking" (Stokes 1992–1993).

Congress became increasingly agitated with Reagan's unwillingness to take corrective action to deal with the nation's burgeoning trade deficit. In 1986 it began consideration of a new trade bill which eventually became the Omnibus Trade and Competitiveness Act of 1988. Congress's now-assertive involvement in shaping trade policy reflected its sensitivity to the changes evident in America's position in the world political economy.

In the late 1960s, the drafting of legislation to implement the results of the Kennedy Round involved only a handful of congressional and administration trade specialists. Twenty years later, the drafting of the 1988 Omnibus Trade and Competitiveness Act included 23 committees and subcommittees in 17 subconferences and involved 199 conferees, more than a third of Congress. (Stokes 1994, 1430)

The new trade law contained no radical new departures from existing U.S. trade policy, despite many highly protectionist measures figuring prominently in the deliberations during its long gestation period. The "Super 301" provision was perhaps the exception. As noted in Chapter 7, Super 301 *required* the president to identify countries engaged in unfair trade practices and negotiate remedies with them. The USTR was charged with that responsibility, effectively solidifying the office's role as the government's principal trade policy actor in a way not previously done.

Because the Bush administration was clearly uncomfortable with the confrontational, unilateralist thrust Super 301 and did little to push it, Bush's USTR (Carla A. Hills) fared little better than Reagan's (Clayton Yeutter) in devising a governmentwide response to the trade challenges the United States increasingly faced. Both, as Bruce Stokes, a seasoned observer of trade politics and policy observed, "had less influence . . . within the executive branch and on Capitol Hill" than Robert Strauss enjoyed. "Rather than leading trade policy, a bureaucratically weak and directionless USTR . . . often [became] a victim of the political pressures around it." And that "reactive stance," he concluded, often resulted in "bad trade policy" in which "U.S. interests . . . suffered" (Stokes 1992–1993).

Stokes applauded Clinton's creation of the National Economic Council. The problem in the past, he argues, is that trade concerns were subordinated to foreign policy or strategic interests. From this perspective, the USTR's original responsibility to coordinate U.S. trade policy and to act as an honest broker between government departments and agencies implied "a judgment that trade policy is a derivative of foreign policy or farm policy, not a co-equal" (Stokes 1992–1993). "With the creation of the National Economic Council in 1993, America's international economic interests have become a major pillar of U.S. foreign policy" (Stokes 1994).

Even without the NEC, trade policy was destined to be a Clinton administration priority. Clinton named Mickey Kantor, a California attorney skilled in regulatory problems and chair of the Clinton-Gore 1992 campaign, as his trade representative. Kantor quickly assumed a high-profile role in a series of contentious trade issues involving the European Union, Nafta, the Uruguay Round, and Japan. His assertive personal style and aggressive policy postures offended some both within the United States and abroad, but he had a reputation for loyalty to the president and reflected the administration's preference for a posture of aggressive unilateralism on trade issues.

As the bureaucratic politics of White House trade policy making unfolds, the National Economic Council has a key advantage: They are the president's people. The implication is that they "are more politically attuned than the career civil servants," who increasingly have come to staff the trade representative's office and thus are less able to play the "honest broker" role once envisaged for it, and now for the NEC. "After thirty years, it is understandable that the office has developed its own bureaucratic perspective and has become a player rather than a referee," writes economics correspondent Bruce Stokes (1993). But, from the viewpoint of White House control of trade policy making, Stokes also reports a telling quip by a USTR official: "The question is not whether USTR or the NEC is making trade policy. The important thing is that the State Department or the Treasury Department is not."

The centrality of the Clinton White House in foreign economic policy making and especially the emerging prominence of the National Economic Council may be related to the administration's comparatively positive record in realizing its foreign economic objectives. "To put it bluntly," observed a prominent economic reporter, "Mr. Clinton's foreign economic policy tends to be everything that the rest of his foreign policy is not: The strategy has been fairly consistent, even if the tactics varied; his goals have been generally well articulated, the payoff for the American public clearcut, and the passions of the President obviously engaged" (Friedman 1994c).

Whether the NEC will survive the Clinton presidency is, however, problematic. Clinton's predecessors sought to control economic policy making from the White House, but all were more engaged in national security policy, where bureaucratic politics were more manageable, the payoffs greater, and the domestic political costs lower.

The prominence of Clinton's NEC was in part a function of Clinton's own preferences and priorities. Clinton lacked interest in the "high politics" of traditional peace and security issues, but "the interplay between trade, technology, educational training, economics and jobs [seemed to engage him] intellectually and animate him politically" (Friedman 1994c). The end of the Cold War reinforces these tendencies, as it arguably diminishes the importance of military security and engagement abroad while enhancing the prominence of economic security and engagement. Thus a combination of personality and historical circumstance encouraged a perhaps short-lived centralization of foreign economic policy making. As before, the reasons are found in bureaucratic politics and the political costs and benefits presidents realize. More departments and agencies with important domestic roots and often powerful congressional allies have a greater stake in international economic policy than in traditional national security policy. Without clear and consistent direction from the White House, interagency politics are likely to dominate the process and the outcome. Clinton may have been determined to give that direction, but his successors may not.

Wither Presidential Preeminence? . . . .

Continued and direct White House involvement in foreign policy is now a permanent feature of the governmental structures responsible for making and executing American foreign policy. As the United States continues to seek influence over complex external problems and as established departments and agencies continually strive to protect their own interests in coping with those problems, no other institution is fully equipped to protect the interests of the person who bears final responsibility—the president. "When things don't go well they like to blame presidents—and that's what presidents are paid for," observed John F. Kennedy. In such an environment, a personal staff, infused with the authority and prestige that only the president can claim, becomes an indispensable tool. For, as Richard Nixon noted, presidents are chosen to make things happen.

This view of the modern presidency directs attention to the role of presidential leadership in policy making. Its intellectual forefather is Alexander Hamilton. Steeped in the tradition of political realism, Hamilton urged at the Republic's founding that a strong national government was necessary to provide the national defenses the emerging nation lacked. He believed a strong executive was equally necessary for survival. "Energy in the executive is a leading character in the definition of good government," he wrote in *The Federalist* No. 70. "It is essential to the protection of the community against foreign attack."

Presidential practice has not always conformed with Hamilton's ideas. The Madisonian model, which emphasizes constitutional checks and balances, is one alternative practiced by some (William Howard Taft, for example), and the Jeffersonian model, which emphasizes party control of the machinery of government, is another with historical adherents (Woodrow Wilson and Bill Clinton). But the Hamiltonian model clearly underlies the development of presidential governance in this century, beginning especially with Franklin Roosevelt and growing to maturity with Harry Truman and the other Cold War presidents (Burns 1966; see also Hunt 1987; Neustadt, 1980). Indeed, while Hamilton argued in *The Federalist* No. 70 that "decision, activity, secrecy, and dispatch" were best achieved with a single dominant (not collective) executive, he could hardly have imagined how complete his vision would become. As James MacGregor Burns (1966) noted during the Johnson presidency, "The checks and balances were never designed to cope with the problem posed by the 'red telephone' that the president may turn to in a moment of desperation or even hysteria."

The theory and practice of presidential preeminence in policy making draws heavily on the distinction between foreign and domestic policy (Hastedt and Eksterowicz 1993). Writing about the same time as Burns, political scientist Aaron Wildavsky (1966) saw the distinction as critically important in explaining why presidents enjoy greater political success in foreign policy than in domestic, as we noted in the introduction to this chapter. The end of the Cold War challenges that notion, as we also suggested earlier, but even earlier than that presidential scholars had begun to wonder whether the "two presidencies" thesis continued to aptly describe the policy-making environment. The number of *"intermestic" policy issues*—those with both domestic and foreign content and consequences, whose growth spurted in the 1970s and 1980s as the hegemonic power of the United States in the world political economy declined—contributed to reevaluations of Wildavsky's thesis. The Vietnam War also sparked much introspection. Before Vietnam, bipartisanship was the name of the foreign policy game Congress and the president played, as politics was thought to stop at the water's edge. Vietnam changed that, as partisan and ideological cleavages now characterized foreign policy issues as routinely as domestic ones (see also Chapter 12). Wildavsky himself would later conclude that, "as ideological and partisan divisions have come to reinforce each other, . . . foreign policy has become more like domestic policy—a realm marked by serious partisan divisions in which the president cannot count on a free ride." Thus he concluded that the two presidencies thesis was "time and culture bound" (Oldfield and Wildavsky 1991; see also the essays in Shull 1991). The upshot is that presidential preeminence was no greater in the foreign policy domain than in the domestic.

The end of the Cold War mounts another, arguably more thoroughgoing, challenge to presidential government than did Vietnam. The Cold War helped "forge and modernize many vital U.S. institutions" and enabled presidents to shape the domestic agenda of domestic issues "if they could be connected, however tenuously, to national security goals." Thus the end of "the long war" is "reason to worry about the ability of parties and presidents to build coalitions for managing a modern society and economy" (Deudney and Ikenberry 1994). Specifically, the post-Cold War environment will likely offer presidents "few opportunities to act boldly and effectively, particularly with military force," whose use now promises "to frustrate presidential initiative and divide public sentiment." Accordingly, "the success of presidents in the post-Cold War era will hinge on their ability to recast public expectations about their performance in new directions, while redeploying presidential energy toward foreign opportunities linked to domestic problems" (Deudney and Ikenberry 1994).

On a more optimistic note, others see the end of the Cold War as an opportunity to develop alternative presidential leadership styles that will avert repetition of past "constitutional crises, failed presidencies, and efforts to bolster presidential popularity through foreign policy adventurism" (Hastedt and Eksterowicz 1993). In contrast with the Hamiltonian model of presidential policy making dominant during the Cold War, elements of the Madisonian and Jeffersonian models may now comport more comfortably with the intermestic issues that will command presidents' attention and congressional demands to be involved in shaping and responding to them.

So are America's two presidencies now one? The demands and expectations the Cold War placed on the president and the presidency have doubtlessly dissipated. Partisan and ideological differences about the nation's world role now also abound. But there is little in our analysis in this chapter, in prognoses other have made of the impact of the Cold War on the presidency, or in our later analysis of Congress's role in foreign policy making (Chapter 12) that undermines a central fact: The rise of presidential preeminence occurred in response to demands, foreign and domestic, to which the other branches of government, notably Congress, could not respond adequately. That was most emphatically true in the foreign policy domain—and it remains so. The reasons inhere in the nature of the international system, the central element in the theory of political realism evident in American foreign policy thinking since its founding, but especially so since World War II, during which presidential government and the imperial presidency became the operative norms (and constitutional challenges).

> The role played by the executive in foreign affairs is not due to transient factors such as the vagaries of public opinion or the momentary absence of interest group pressures. Instead, it is rooted in the requirements imposed on the nation-state by the potentially anarchic quality of the international system. . . . Policy takes precedence over politics because the international system both severely limits the sensible choices a country can make and shapes the processes by which these decisions are reached. International relations theory thus explains not only the policy choices of nations but also the existence of two presidencies. (P. Peterson 1994, 231–32)

According to this logic, the end of the Cold War may alter the agenda of American politics and priorities, but it will not alter the foremost responsibility of the president to respond to the challenges and opportunities posed by the external environment. This does not deny the idealist agenda some presidents have embraced or their prospects for its realization, but it does deny presidents' ability to ignore the character of the environment in which their preferences must be implemented. Alexander Hamilton—political realist and proponent of presidential preeminence—would be pleased.

NOTES

1. Because we discussed interest groups, the general public, and the mass media in chapters 9 and 10, attention in Chapter 12 to Hilsman's outermost concentric circle will be confined to Congress. This division follows naturally from the organizing framework for the examination of the sources of American foreign policy we use to structure this book. We recognize that Congress in particular is the target of intense "lobbying" by the nongovernmental forces elaborated in the two preceding chapters, but the governmental-nongovernmental distinction is an important one conceptually. Hence our treatment of Congress within the governmental source category.

2. Schlesinger (1989) observes that the framers of the Constitution saw designation of the president as commander in chief "as conferring a merely ministerial function not as creating an independent and additional source of executive authority." As we will see in Chapter 12, this presidential power has figured prominently in the executive-legislative dispute over war powers, especially since the Vietnam war.

3. Theodore Lowi disagrees with the view that the imperial presidency was a radically new phenomenon:

> Schlesinger chose the characterization imperial because it connotes a strong state with sovereignty and power over foreigners, as well as rank, status, privilege, and authority, and it also connotes the president's power and responsibility to do whatever he judges necessary to maintain the sovereignty of the state and its ability to keep public order, both international and domestic. The imperial presidency turns out on inspection, therefore, to be nothing more nor less than the discretionary presidency grounded in national security rather than domestic government. (Lowi 1985b, 189)

4. *Crockett v. Reagan*, 558 F. Supp. 893 (D.D.C. 1982).

5. *Lowry v. Reagan*, 676 F. Supp. 333 (D.D.C. 1987).

6. *Dellums v. Bush*, 752 F. Supp. 1141 (D.D.C. 1990).

7. John Prados (1991) argues on the basis of historical research on the National Security Council that "activities undertaken during the Reagan years are not aberrations" as they "have antecedents in the activities of previous national security staffs. Current practices have evolved from past ones, and they will recur, *unless* proper ground rules are set. To regard the Reagan excesses as merely a people problem invites repetition."

8. George (1988) identifies three different presidential management models: competitive, formalistic, and collegial. In the *competitive* model, the president purposely seeks to promote conflict and competition among his advisers, thus forcing problems to be brought to the president's attention for resolution and decision. Franklin Roosevelt is the only president to have clearly followed it.

Johnson began by emphasizing the competitive approach but gradually moved toward a *formalistic* model. This model seeks to establish clear lines of authority and to minimize the need for presidential involvement in the politicking among cabinet officials and key advisers. A "chief of staff" often provides a buffer between the president and cabinet heads. Nixon's approach to presidential management took the formalistic model to its extreme. However, Truman and Eisenhower also followed it, and Reagan began that way.

Kennedy is the best illustration of the *collegial* model, which emphasizes teamwork and group problem solving. The president operates like the hub of a wheel with spokes connecting to individual advisers and department heads, who often act as "generalists" rather than "functional specialists" concerned only with parts of particular problems. Bush and Clinton embraced styles akin to the collegial model.

9. As noted in earlier chapters, the CIA, the Department of Defense, and the Joint Chiefs of Staff were also created by the National Security Act.

10. These rump sessions may explain the apparent incongruity between Eisenhower's emphasis on the NSC system and the widespread belief that Secretary of State Dulles operated as the chief architect of American foreign policy during most of the Eisenhower years (in contrast, see Greenstein 1982, 1994). Dulles's biographer, Townsend Hoopes (1973a), also argues that the close working ties between Eisenhower and Dulles "compromised" Eisenhower's effort to use the NSC system to "orchestrate" the activities of the various foreign policy agencies into a coordinated foreign policy.

11. President Ford (1979) made a similar observation on why he eventually decided he needed a chief of staff: "Because power in Washington is measured by how much access a person has to the president, almost everyone wanted more access that I had access to give." For a study of the relationship between access and influence, see Link and Kegley (1993).

12. In testimony before Congress on the Iran-*contra* affair, Shultz described his battle with Poindexter and CIA director William Casey for control over policy making as "guerrilla warfare." He reported that at one point disputes with the White House and intelligence community caused him to submit his resignation as secretary of state.

13. Critics of Nixon-Kissinger decision-making practices regarding Vietnam, particularly the secret bombing of Cambodia, would doubtless look with jaundiced eye toward Kissinger's condemnation of Poindexter.

14. Ironically, *Newsweek*'s account of the events and processes leading to the U.S. intervention in Haiti describes Lake and Sandy Berger as "Haiti hawks" and paints them and others in less-than-flattering terms.

> Clinton's zigzag Haiti policy came to be dominated by a group of moralists who form a liberal web knotted together during the administration of President Jimmy Carter. They all speak the same language, the Carteresque "human rights first" policy of the 1980s. And they have no real feel for politics. There isn't a single former elected official among them, nor any political constituency on which they can depend. And, because Clinton eventually got the Pentagon he wanted—led by technocrats with no powerful say in policy—nobody was there to counterbalance the Haiti hawks. . . . "This is Tony's war," said one critic. . . . "He finally is able to do something he devoutly believes in." ("How Did We Get Here?" *Newsweek*, September 26, 1994, pp. 26–27)

15. Supply-side economics refers to the assumption that economic growth will be stimulated by

reducing government spending and taxation. Supply-side economists argue that by increasing incentives in the private sector, worker productivity and employment will increase and the rate of inflation will decrease. Increased government revenues will result, which will offset any tax reductions.

SUGGESTIONS FOR FURTHER READING

Barrett, David M. *Uncertain Warriors: Lyndon Johnson and His Vietnam Advisers.* Lawrence: University of Kansas Press, 1993.

Bock, Joseph G. *The White House Staff and the National Security Assistant: Friendship and Friction at the Water's Edge.* New York: Greenwood, 1987.

Destler, I. M., Leslie H. Gelb, and Anthony Lake. *Our Own Worst Enemy: The Unmaking of American Foreign Policy.* New York: Simon & Schuster, 1984.

Dryden, Steve. *Trade Warriors: USTR and the American Crusade for Free Trade.* New York: Oxford University Press, 1995.

Dumbrell, John. *The Carter Presidency: A Re-evaluation.* New York: St. Martin's, 1992.

Genovese, Michael A. *The Presidency in an Age of Limits.* Westport, Conn.: Greenwood, 1993.

George, Alexander L. *Presidential Decisionmaking in Foreign Policy: The Effective Use of Information and Advice.* Boulder, Colo.: Westview, 1980.

Koh, Harold H. *The National Security Constitution: Sharing Power after the Iran-Contra Affair.* New Haven, Conn.: Yale University Press, 1990.

Neustadt, Richard E. *Presidential Power and the Modern Presidents: The Politics of Leadership from Roosevelt to Reagan.* New York: Free Press, 1990.

Peterson, Paul E., ed. *The President, the Congress and the Making of Foreign Policy.* 1994.

Prados, John. *Keepers of the Keys: A History of the National Security Council from Truman to Bush.* New York: William Morrow, 1991.

Renshon, Stanley A., ed. *The Clinton Presidency: Campaigning, Governing, and the Psychology of Leadership.* Boulder, Colo.: Westview, 1995.

Shoemaker, Christopher C. *The NSC Staff: Counseling the Council.* Boulder, Colo: Westview, 1992.

Shull, Steven A., ed. *The Two Presidencies: A Quarter Century Assessment.* Chicago: Nelson-Hall, 1991.

CHAPTER 11

$\bullet \quad \bullet \quad \bullet$

THE ROLE OF EXECUTIVE DEPARTMENTS AND AGENCIES IN FOREIGN POLICY MAKING

$\bullet \quad \bullet \quad \bullet$

Military and ideological rivalry with the Soviet Union has been replaced by an increased focus on economic competition among the major industrialized democracies. The challenge for America is . . . in many ways a far more difficult task than our traditional alliance leadership and one that calls for energetic, creative diplomacy.

State 2000: A New Model for Managing Foreign Affairs, 1992

It's very hard to give policy advice and not somehow become identified with the policy, or at least have an intellectual stake in wanting that policy to succeed.

Director of the Central Intelligence Agency, R. James Woolsey, 1994

Global activism is a pattern of American foreign policy. Recall from Chapters 4 and 5 its manifestations: diplomatic relations with nearly every foreign government; participation in scores of international organizations; billions of dollars in economic and military assistance and sales; a capacity to strike militarily anywhere in the world; and trade and investment connections with other countries far beyond the nation's proportion of world population.

Whose activities are reflected in such involvements? Whose responsibility is it to protect the interests they represent? The president and the presidency are the easy answers; the executive departments and agencies of the federal government, and especially the State and Defense departments, are the more accurate ones.

In Chapter 10 we drew a distinction between executive branch agencies, comprising the second concentric circle of policy making, and the presidential subsystem, which makes up the innermost circle. In practice the distinction is not always clearcut, as the heads of executive departments and agencies, appointed by the president, and their immediate subordinates also make up the innermost circle of advisers. Thus the various secretaries of state, defense, and treasury who have served the nation since World War II were simultaneously members of the inner circle as well as heads of the large, complex organizations found in the second concentric circle. These organizations are critically important to those in the innermost circle. The president and his closest advisers must depend on them and on their hundreds of thousands of career professionals to manage America's day-to-day foreign relations and to implement the decisions of the president and presidential advisers. Hence the scope and magnitude of

$\bullet \quad \bullet \quad \bullet$

the responsibilities of major organizations in the second concentric circle require scrutiny.

The Department of State

As the "first among equals" in the foreign affairs government, the Department of State is the principal agent of the executive branch of government responsible for managing U.S. foreign relations. In the mid-1990s it operated a network of more than 250 diplomatic and consular posts throughout the world (principally embassies and consulates), plus delegations and missions to international organizations. In combination with representations through these field missions, the State Department's activities range from negotiating treaties and executive agreements with other nations to representing the nation in more than four dozen international organizations, from making policy recommendations to taking the steps necessary to implement choices on all aspects of America's foreign relations and interests.

The State Department is organized in the hierarchical pattern typical of most large organizations, with the secretary of state perched on top of a series of more narrowly defined offices and bureaus that divide the labor within the department. As shown in Figure 11.1, that division reflects, on one hand, the department's orientation to the major geographic regions of the world, and on the other, the necessity to cope with functional problems that transcend geographic boundaries, such as policy planning, intelligence and research, and politico-military affairs, as well as activities associated with the administration and management of any large organization. The Clinton administration's emphasis on such global issues like human rights, refugee and other population matters, and sustainable development, is reflected in its having won congressional approval for creation of a new post of under secretary of state for global affairs, whose portfolio ranges beyond traditional diplomatic tasks.

Figure 11.1 also identifies three organizations nominally attached to the State Department but beyond its immediate control:

1. The Arms Control and Disarmament Agency (ACDA), which conducts research on arms control and disarmament policy and participates in negotiations with other nations on those subjects.

2. The United States Information Agency (USIA) which is responsible for the nation's public diplomacy (cultural and informational activities directed at overseas audiences).

3. The Agency for International Development (AID)[1], which is responsible for administering its foreign economic aid programs (see also Chapter 5).

Overseas, personnel from ACDA, USIA, and AID are typically attached to the field mission, usually an embassy headed by an ambassador, over which the State Department bears primary responsibility.[2] The future of each is in doubt, however, as critics charge all three are inefficient relics of the Cold War past. Following on a Bush administration initiative, the Clinton transition team targeted ACDA for elimination,

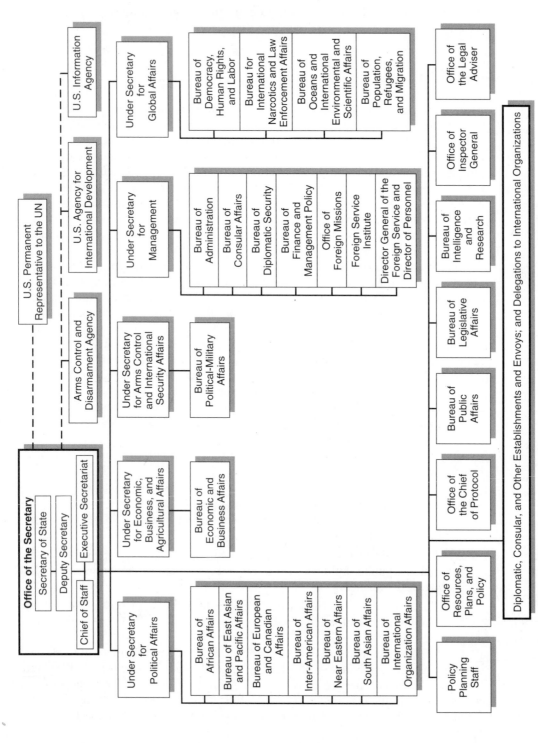

Figure 11.1 Department of State Organization Chart   *Source:* U.S. Department of State *Dispatch* 6 (May 1995): 9.

backing off only when it became convinced the agency had a unique role to play in the nuclear nonproliferation area. Later, Secretary of State Warren Christopher floated a plan to merge all three agencies into an expanded State Department, only to have Vice President Al Gore, responsible for the administration's "reinventing government" program, nix the idea. But congressional critics, now led by Senator Jesse Helms, who became chair of the Senate Foreign Relations Committee following the 1994 congressional elections, seized on the Christopher plan as part of a larger effort to launch "a fundamental and revolutionary reinvention of America's foreign policy institutions."

Decision-making responsibility within the State Department itself follows the hierarchical pattern of its organization chart. Decisions of greatest importance are made by the secretary, the deputy secretary, and the under secretaries who occupy the seventh floor of the State Department offices in the area of Washington, D.C., known as Foggy Bottom and who frequently interact with the White House. Routine decisions, important more for policy implementation than development, are made at the levels below the seventh floor, with responsibilities assigned to various regional and functional bureaus at different levels in the State Department's hierarchy. Country directors and "desk officers" within each regional bureau arguably comprise the backbone of the State Department when it comes to coordinating U.S. policy toward particular countries abroad. In practice, however, the responsibilities of the regional bureaus have been greatly diluted by the involvement of several dozen other federal agencies in the management of foreign affairs (Warwick 1975). Less than a third of the Americans stationed at U.S. missions abroad work for the State Department (Spiers 1988, 3), which means that many of the department's employees serve agencies other than their own.

The Foreign Service and Its Subculture

Within the State Department itself, the individuals who matter most are the ***Foreign Service officers (FSOs),*** who accounted (in 1994) for about ten thousand of the twenty-six thousand employees of the State Department (of which nearly ten thousand are foreign nationals working in field missions abroad). This elite corps of professional diplomats traditionally holds the most important positions within State (outside the political appointments made by the president) both at home and abroad. Lawrence Eagleberger, deputy secretary of state and then secretary of state during the waning days of the Bush administration, was himself a career foreign service professional.

The popular image of the Foreign Service, based partly on legend as well as historical fact, is that of a remarkably homogeneous diplomatic corps comprising upper-class men from the Northeast with degrees from Ivy League colleges. The Foreign Service officers corps has sought to open itself to a broader geographical, educational, ethnic, and socioeconomic spectrum. It encouraged women and African-Americans to join its ranks to rectify what Ronald Spiers, under secretary of state for management during the Reagan administration, termed a "serious" problem. Reflecting that problem, in 1989 women Foreign Service officers won a class action suit against the State Department that charged it discriminated against women by hiring more men for the Foreign Service and giving them better career assignments, performance ratings, and honors awards.[3] "Still, if the Foreign Service is no longer a smug men's club, it is more like one than any other part of the U.S. government" (Rubin 1985; see also Holmes 1994; McGlen and Sarkees 1993). Epithets that describe Foreign Service officers as "effete, snobbish, striped-pants cookie-pushers" (Rubin 1989) reflect evaluations of the composition as well as performance of the Foreign Service.

The distinctiveness of the Foreign Service is reinforced by a personnel system that is separate from the Civil Service, to which most federal employees belong. And because it is an elite corps, other groups, such as State's Civil Service employees, are, by definition, nonelite. Non-FSOs' inferior status and feeling of neglect have produced personnel problems within the State Department for decades (Warwick 1975). Thus the *State 2000* report insightfully cautioned that "We must break down the barriers that risk making us a series of fractured 'we/they' cultures, whether Foreign Service and Civil Service, women and men, or single officers and tandem couples" (U.S. Department of State 1992).

The Foreign Service embraces a distinctive subculture that promotes respect for tradition, precedent, and conformity above all else. One characteristic of the subculture is resistance to ideas from the outside. As one officer put it, "'The Foreign Service officer believes that his is an arcane craft which people on the outside cannot hope to understand.' We listen carefully and politely but seldom change our views" (*Diplomacy for the 70's* 1970). Another characteristic is timidity in delineating the State Department's jurisdiction within the foreign affairs government, which would be acceptable if other organizations were unaggressive—but they are not. Ironically, however, the norms of the Foreign Service subculture militate against a more vigorous State Department role. Especially important are three widely held beliefs:

1. The only experience that is relevant to the activities of the Department of State is experience gained in the Foreign Service.

2. The really important aspects of the foreign affairs of the United States are the political and traditional ones—negotiation, representation, and reporting. "It doesn't matter if it was a junior officer hoping for tenure, an FS-1 seeking to get into the Senior Foreign Service, or an ambassador or assistant secretary," observed one foreign service officer, "the qualities judged begin with reporting, analysis, and policy" (Bushnell 1989).

3. Overseas operations of the kind conducted by AID, USIA, the CIA, and the Department of Defense are peripheral to the main foreign policy task (Scott 1969; see also Clarke 1989).

These beliefs and the norms of the subculture may satisfy the short-term needs of the career service and the individuals within it, but they do not necessarily satisfy the long-term needs of the State Department or the requirements of American foreign policy (Scott 1970). It is significant that a recent department self-study not only used the word "parochial" to describe the State Department but also urged that "it is time to forge a new mindset. . . . We must change a culture that often breeds caution and constrains the very creativity vital to change" (U.S. Department of State 1992).

Within the Foreign Service subculture exist pressures to avoid rocking the boat: to avoid expressing controversial views that may be viewed as challenges to the wisdom of one's superiors and to avoid dress and behavior that deviate from the norms of the group. Those pressures derive partly from the assignments of the typical Foreign Service officer. Viewed as a generalist rather than a specialist, an FSO's career pattern usually involves two- or three-year tours of duty both in Washington and abroad in a variety of operating and functional positions (see Melbourne 1992). Whether one's star is allowed to shine in an assignment to political affairs in Paris rather than to budgetary affairs in Ouagadougou is thus heavily dependent on the outcome of one's evaluation by superiors.

The fiercely competitive nature of the Foreign Service has been reinforced historically by the "up-or-out" promotion system, under which a foreign service officer must advance beyond her or his present rank within a specified time or be "selected out." That principle, together with the exceptional importance of the efficiency rating, tends, as one department self-study put it, "to stifle creativity, discourage risk-taking, and reward conformity" (*Diplomacy for the 70's* 1970).

Over the years a number of developments both inside and outside the Foreign Service have disrupted the professional diplomatic corps, helping to reinforce its penchant for caution and traditionalism. Preeminent among them were the effects of McCarthyism.

"I have in my hand a list of 205 that were known to the Secretary of State as being members of the Communist party and who, nevertheless, are still working and shaping the policy in the State Department." With those words, spoken in the winter of 1950, Senator Joseph McCarthy launched an all-out attack against suspected—but never proven—"disloyalty" in the Foreign Service. The immediate thrust was directed against those charged with responsibility for the "loss" of China to communism in 1949. Eventually the entire corps of Foreign Service officers suffered the grueling humiliation of security investigations engendered by an atmosphere of hysterical anticommunism. Truman launched a loyalty program that reflected deference to McCarthyism, and, unhappily for those involved, the career-shattering and head-rolling trauma continued to plague the State Department for nearly two years following Eisenhower's election.

McCarthyism's impact on the Foreign Service was long-term and devastating:

> Talented officers resigned or were drummed out of the service. Field reports began to be couched in bland and roundabout language. Few dared to list Communist countries as career preferences, while East Asian specialization became a wasteland. Rumors and gossip were rampant in the corridors, reinforced by the spot visits of McCarthy's assistants. The virtues inculcated were caution, conformity, discretion, and prudence. (Warwick 1975, 20)

Extraordinary security consciousness and an elaborate system of horizontal clearances resulted. The latter in particular has made State's operating procedures among the most complex of all federal agencies. "Clearing" and "coordinating" with other comparably placed offices within the department and other agencies are necessary before an item can go up the chain of command. The result is "a most cautious way of doing business. It reflects an institutionalized desire to diffuse responsibility among many different offices and colleagues rather than to accept responsibility oneself" (Campbell 1971; see also U.S. Department of State 1992).

More immediately, by driving those with Asian expertise out of the diplomatic corps or into other areas within the State Department, the United States found itself woefully ill-prepared to deal with the forces underlying the determination of the Vietnamese people to carry on a war with the United States—for a hundred years, if necessary—despite America's overwhelming technological supremacy (McNamara 1995; Thomson 1972, 1994). McCarthyism effectively robbed a generation of decision makers of expertise on Asia, including China as well as Vietnam, at the very time that it needed it most.

Even as the effects of McCarthyism receded into history, the professional diplomatic corps continued to be plagued by structural problems. One such problem was a bulge at the top of the Senior Foreign Service (from which the most prized positions, including ambassadorships, are chosen), with more career officers being promoted to senior ranks than could be placed in meaningful positions (Spiers 1985). The second problem, directly related to the first, was growth in the number of political appointments to top jobs from outside the Foreign Service.[4] This exacerbated the "senior surplus" by reducing the opportunities available to career officers at the prime of their careers, when their potential to make a meaningful contribution is greatest.

Presidents have long used ambassadorial appointments to reward their political supporters, but the propensity to make political appointments also reflects their profound distrust of "careerists." "Politicians" often believe that "careerists" are not only disloyal to their policies but also actively seek to undermine them. Such suspicions derive in part from State's bureaucratic subculture and from the requirement that careerists support policy, whatever it might be, objectively and without partisanship. "Since they are representing the views of the U.S. government rather than their own," Barry Rubin (1985) observes, "FSOs are supposed to become vessels of communication, without personal views. Many of them learn to radiate blandness and to censor their own opinions. An ideal pose is to give the impression of great knowledge while revealing little of substance." Such apparent lack of conviction does not sit well with those placed in office by voters, for whom partisan loyalty and sometimes ideological purity are important yardsticks. Often, however, the demands political appointees make on those expected to serve them are contradictory.

> They want the career staff to be detached, but accuse it of being bland; they demand discipline, but can brand this as lack of imagination; they require experienced judgment, but may call this negativism. One FSO complains, "Presidents and their aides need scapegoats. They can't blame the administration so they blame the secretary of state and if they can't blame the secretary of state they criticize the department's staff." (Rubin 1985, 242)

The State Department in the Foreign Affairs Government

The subculture of the State Department combined with factors external to the organization are critical in explaining why a department that theoretically sits center-stage in the foreign affairs government is in fact ill-equipped to play a leadership role: "As long as the norms of the subculture prescribe organizational accommodation rather than combat, and caution rather than venturesomeness, and as long as the ideology assures members of the subculture that they are doing a good job, it is vain to expect bold and innovative policy" (Scott 1969). Instructively, Oliver North, the key National Security Council operative in the Iran-*contra* scandal, gave the State Department the code name "Wimp."

Two additional factors circumscribe the State Department's ability to exercise leadership in the larger foreign affairs government. One is that secretaries of state often choose—sometimes inadvertently—to remove themselves from the department rather than give it the kind of vigorous attention necessary to involve it more intimately in the policy process. The other is that the department is a bureaucratic pygmy among giants.

Secretaries of State and the State Department

Consider the secretary's role. John Foster Dulles is widely regarded as one of the most influential secretaries of state in the twentieth century, but he did little to infuse the organization with a corresponding capacity to lead. Dulles reportedly told President Eisenhower he would accept the job only if he did not have to assume responsibility for managing the department and the Foreign Service. Dean Rusk was a less dramatic secretary and, at least for a time, less visible than Dulles, but his career spanned two presidencies (Kennedy and Johnson) and thus might have been expected to leave a mark on the department. Instead, time pressures, Rusk's own personality, and his preoccupation with Vietnam prevented a more effective use of the department's expertise (*Diplomacy for the 70's* 1970).

Those who followed Dulles and Rusk—including Kissinger, Vance, Muskie, Haig, Shultz, Baker, and Christopher—did no more to build bridges between top officials and careerists in order to involve the latter more actively in policy making. Kissinger took many of his NSC staffers with him to Foggy Bottom when he left the White House, but one of the hallmarks of his stewardship was the amount of time he spent out of town. Vance was apparently more popular at State "partly due to memories of his predecessor—tales of Kissinger mistreating FSOs and ashtray-throwing tantrums [were] legion" (Rubin 1985)—but eventually Vance became enmeshed in a bureaucratic duel with the White House, which he ultimately lost. Alexander Haig, Reagan's first secretary of state, also resigned when he found himself outside the charmed circle of White House advisers in an administration otherwise known for its friction with the career staff. If there was an exception, it was George Shultz, Haig's successor, whose very survival through the end of the Reagan era suggests he was better able to satisfy the competing demands of organization person and presidential adviser. Even Shultz found himself under attack by right-wing Reaganites, however, who sought his ouster on grounds that he had become a captive of the State Department's "liberal" foreign service establishment—and hence insufficiently responsive to the president's policy preferences. (Significantly, Shultz was a vigorous critic of the Reagan administration's White House-launched initiative toward Iran which resulted in the Iran-*contra* affair, seriously damaging the Reagan presidency.)

By way of contrast, James A. Baker, Shultz's successor, reopened the chasm separating the secretary of state from the department's career professionals. Whereas Shultz "used the brightest stars of the career Foreign Service as the core of his policy-making team," Baker's style was to keep them at arm's length. "Many Foreign Service officers [complained] that Baker and his coterie of insiders . . . turned the department's seventh-floor executive suite into an inaccessible redoubt where even the most senior professional diplomats [felt] unwelcome and ignored" (Goshko 1989). "He's running a mini-NSC, not State," complained one senior diplomat. "We learn what our policy is when we read it in the newspapers."

Warren Christopher did not fare much better than Baker. Although he sometimes acted as a leading spokesperson for Clinton's foreign policy, the White House generally regarded his public performances as ineffectual, particularly on such difficult issues as Bosnia. Indeed, its willingness to "subcontract" negotiations in North Korea and Haiti to former President Jimmy Carter reflected an even deeper dissatisfaction with Christopher and his top aides at the State Department. And they won no praise from senior and mid-level Foreign Service officers either, who believed that Christopher and those around him were "nice guys" who sincerely tried to do a good job but just proved ineffective. "The indictment they [leveled] against the Clinton team [which included members of the White House staff as well as Christopher] is that its policies frequently [were] so ill-defined or so prone to sudden flip-flops that they collectively . . . became known within the bureaucracy as 'the lurch.' And, in cases where policy [was] spelled out, it often [reflected] a quasi-isolationist shrinking from leadership and activism" (Goshko 1994). Several FSOs even resigned in highly publicized protests over U.S. policy in the Balkans, and others expressed misgivings about Clinton's abandonment of the link between China's human rights policies and gaining most-favored-nation trade treatment by the United States (which they disliked from the start). Thus the chasm between professional diplomats and the political appointees in the State Department persists, contributing to the department's inability to play a more effective leadership role in the foreign affairs government.

Without Bureaucratic Muscle

A second important reason for the State Department's inability to exercise greater leadership is its relative lack of resources and bureaucratic muscle in Washington's intensely political environment. As one Foreign Service officer put it more than two decades ago, the secretary of state "is [the] most senior of cabinet members, and is charged (in theory) with responsibility for the coordination of all foreign policy activities, [but] he presides over a bureaucratic midget" (Pringle 1977–1978). Nothing has changed since. The State Department's proposed budget for 1996 was $5.6 billion compared with $257 billion for the Defense Department. Even with the expenditures of AID, ACDA, and USIA added, the total international affairs budget of the federal government comprises less than 1.5 percent of all federal expenditures. Meanwhile, the expenditures of every other department in the executive branch exceed those of the State Department—a pygmy among giants.

Centralization of foreign policy making in the White House—described by three close observers as "the triumph of politics and ideology over foreign policy" (Destler, Gelb, and Lake 1984)—grows naturally out of the State Department's lack of leadership. Ironically, however, centralization further undermines its capacity to lead, as it typically results in the "exclusion of the bureaucracy from most of the serious, presidential foreign policy business" (Destler, Gelb, and Lake 1984). And both circumstances reflect the State Department's inattentiveness to presidential needs, especially its comparative insensitivity to domestic political considerations. "Once a president comes to believe that Foggy Bottom is not attuned to politics, they are doomed to being ignored" (Gelb 1983).

Part of the reason for the belief that the State Department is insensitive to a president's political needs is that the department necessarily represents the interests of other countries, who are its "clients," in the councils of government. "From a White House perspective, efforts to accommodate the legitimate concerns of other countries are often viewed as coming at the expense of American interests, and the accommodationists are viewed as not being tough enough. Presidents usually do not have much patience with this kind of advice, find they cannot change State's penchant for it, and soon stop listening" (Gelb 1983; see also Clarke 1989). Warren Christopher proved keenly sensitive to this criticism, as he repeatedly declared that the most important "desk" in the State Department was the "American desk." That viewpoint fit well with the emphasis the Clinton White House placed on economic issues, which often bridge foreign and domestic policy issues. Despite the declared importance of the "American desk," however, the State Department found that other organizations, notably the U.S. Trade Representative and the Treasury and Commerce Departments, still played the leading roles in shaping foreign economic policy.

The determination of the White House to dominate foreign policy making stems in part from its perception that the State Department lacks responsiveness. There is "a widespread feeling" within the State Department, John Kenneth Galbraith (1969a) complained to President Kennedy, "that God ordained some individuals to make foreign policy without undue interference from presidents and politicians." More specific presidential complaints are that the State Department produces bad staff work and is slow to respond, resistant to change, reluctant to follow orders, and incapable of putting its own house in order. Although in some respects these complaints are a product of internal State Department politics, they also demonstrate that the department, like other large government organizations, often puts its own functions and programs ahead of broad policy considerations. Thus, recognizing its own penchant toward parochialism, a recent State Department self-study concluded that "There should be little wonder that the top leadership in the White House and in the Department have tended over the years to create separate, smaller mechanisms to deal with the key foreign policy agenda items—leaving [the State Department] more and more marginalized" (U.S. Department of State 1992).

The Department of Defense

The secretary of defense, together with the secretary of state and the chairman of the Joint Chiefs of Staff, bears the heaviest responsibility for advising the president on national security policy. In contrast with the State Department, however, the Defense Department is an organization so thoroughly interwoven into the fabric of American social, political, and economic life that the secretary's recommendations regarding national security greatly influence not only the foreign environment but the domestic one as well. Moreover, each of the branches of the armed forces—the army, navy, air force, and marines—has developed important and influential allies in private industry and in Congress, particularly in the armed services committees. The iron triangles linking defense contractors, defense bureaucrats, and Congress—key components of the alleged "military-industrial complex"—enable the uniformed services to fight for policies and programs (weapons systems, for example) that are sometimes at variance with the wishes of the civilian leadership. Those comprising the iron triangles—who thrive on information, access, influence, and money—sometimes exacerbate long-standing rivalries among the branches of the armed services and contribute to the defense establishment's image as a fragmented rather than unified actor (see also Chapter 13). Still, in the larger policy-making context, the military establishment's ability to draw on support from influential sectors of business and government contributes to its continuing importance in foreign policy making.

Civilian control of the military is a principle as old as the Republic itself and thoroughly interwoven into the nation's liberal political culture (Huntington 1957). Prior to World War II the issue was not a critical one, as the peacetime military establishment remained comparatively small, but since World War II the relationship between civilians, both elected and appointed, and the professional military has been an ongoing concern. The National Security Act of 1947, which laid the basis for the Department of Defense, sought a "national security establishment" that balanced civilian and military elements. The four military services were brought together in a single department headed by a civilian, the secretary of defense, but in practice the services retained considerable autonomy. Efforts to refine and reform the Department of Defense since then, such as the Defense Reorganization Act of 1958, often tried to increase civilian control by augmenting the secretary's authority over the sprawling Defense Department. The most recent reform, however—the Defense Reorganization Act of 1986—has, at least in the eyes of some critics, actually undermined civilian authority, as we will note in more detail below.

Figure 11.2 depicts the organizational structure of the Defense Department, popularly referred to simply as the "Pentagon" because of the shape of its headquarters in Arlington, Virginia. In reality the department is far more complex than the figure is able to convey (and the "Pentagon" too large for the building itself to house), but it does draw attention to the formal relationship between the secretary of defense, the military departments, each of which is headed by a civilian, and the military services that comprise them, and the Joint Chiefs of Staff, which, in the person of their chairman, is now an entity separate from the uniformed services themselves.

The Secretary of Defense and the Office of the Secretary of Defense

The secretary of defense is the president's chief adviser on defense matters, including such issues as force size and structure and weapons procurement. The secretary is assisted in carrying out his or her responsibilities by the Office of the Secretary of Defense, comprising undersecretaries and assistance secretaries responsible for more

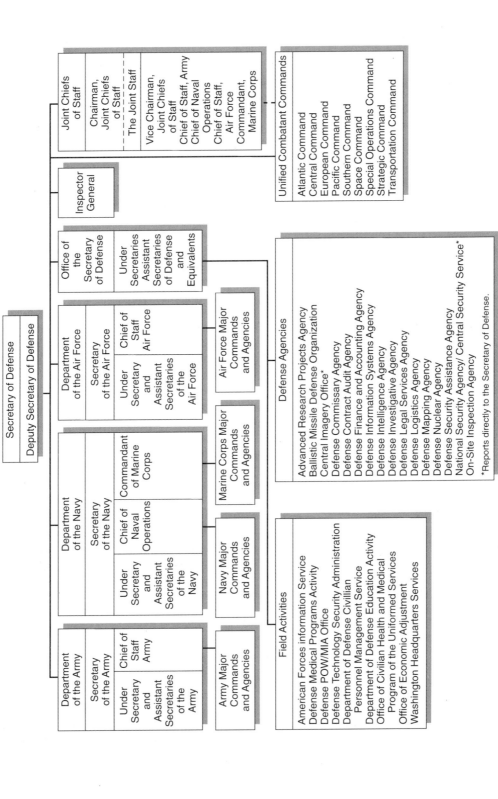

Figure 11.2 Department of Defense Organization Chart

Source: The United States Government Manual, 1994/95 (Washington, D.C.: Government Printing Office, 1994), p. 181.

discrete issues, such as acquisitions and technology, personnel and readiness, and command, control, communications, and intelligence.

The "Policy Shop"

The defense/military side of policy issues confronting both the White House and State Department also concerns the secretary and the secretary's office. Historically these units have been among the most powerful in the department. During the 1960s, for example, the Office of International Security Affairs (ISA) emerged as an influential Defense Department voice in the foreign affairs government. Contributing to its influence were Secretary of Defense Robert McNamara's ability to establish an unprecedented degree of civilian control over the sprawling military complex and the fact that Vietnam, the principal foreign policy problem of the era, was also a formidable military problem. Bureaucratic politics also mattered, as the influence of ISA proved (at least in the eyes of some) a counterweight to the sluggishness of the professional military, particularly the Joint Chiefs of Staff (described below). Paul Nitze, whose involvement in the national security establishment spans five decades, compared ISA and the joint chiefs during the Kennedy years: "It sometimes would take them [the joint chiefs] three days to blow their nose. We [ISA] would sometimes be able to get a position together within an hour. When you get into a rapidly moving situation, when the house is burning down, every president likes to see something reasonable put forward for his consideration promptly" (cited in Piller 1983).

During the Reagan and Bush presidencies the "policy shop," now divided into two units, continued to exercise a powerful voice in the Office of the Secretary of Defense. Following Clinton's election, Les Aspin, Clinton's first secretary of defense, sought an even greater role for policy, as he brought in a number of "defense intellectuals" whose tasks extended beyond traditional defense issues to encompass more novel threats to national security in the post-Cold War (dis)order. Thus the need for a distinctly "political" perspective on national security issues remains a central institutional feature within the Defense Department. Illustrative is the way Joseph S. Nye, a Harvard political scientist who served as assistant secretary of defense for international security in the Clinton administration, responded in mid-1995 to the impending conflict with Japan over tariffs on automobiles. Nye argued that "car parts and aircraft carriers"—trade and defense—not be mingled. In Nye's words: "Some have suggested that we use our security ties to twist Japan's arm on trade. . . . The tactic may work in the short term [but] after a few episodes, Japan might decide to alter its long-term strategy." The implication—perfectly reasonable from a Defense Department perspective—is that economic security and national (defense) security should be kept on separate tracks (see also Dam et al. 1993; Nye 1995).

The Military Services: Autonomy versus Centralization

Like all bureaucratic organizations, the military services within the Defense Department prize their autonomy in what historically has been the "services-dominated architecture" of the defense establishment. As one analyst noted wryly in commenting on the 1986 defense reorganization proposals, "In more than two hundred years [the Navy Department] had never met a centralization proposal that [it] liked"

(Davis 1987). Faced with this reality, different secretaries of defense have used different management strategies to bring the disparate military organizations into the service of American national security.

One strategy is "decentralization." This is the preferred strategy of the military services, because it means delegating authority to them. "When this happens, the services seek to expand their programs in competition with one another and the least restrained and the least cooperative are most rewarded" (Hammond 1994). Secretary of Defense Caspar Weinberger pursued this management strategy during the Reagan administration, which is best suited to a time of growing defense spending, as during the 1980s.

A second strategy focuses on "management of the acquisition process," including the development of new technologies and equipment. This strategy "permits the secretary of defense to have a major impact on the shape and functions of the armed services in the longer term by guiding their development and application of new technologies" (Hammond 1994). Harold Brown, defense secretary under President Carter, followed this route.

"Top-down, directive planning guidance" is a third strategy. The 1986 Defense Reorganization Act encourages this approach, and we will have more to say about it in that context later. Suffice it here to note that directive planning encourages the separate military services to integrate, not separate, their operations, and it encourages greater attention to "operational and contingency planning" and "greater weight to long-range force . . . planning" (Hammond 1994).

"Central resource management" is the final strategy and the one most notable historically. Robert McNamara practiced it during the 1960s (as did Frank Carlucci during the waning days of the Reagan administration), a period widely acknowledged as the highpoint of civilian control of the unwieldy, fractious military establishment. McNamara surrounded himself with "acerbic, even arrogant, analytically brilliant men, most of whom had made their mark in business or academic life" (Nathan and Oliver 1994). Harold Brown and Les Aspin, both of whom would later become secretaries of defense, were among McNamara's operations analysts known as the "whizz kids." Using modern management and budgetary techniques to augment its control, the Office of the Secretary of Defense (OSD) "was soon involved at virtually every level of national security management and military planning. Commanders in the Pacific and Europe were given less autonomy, and McNamara's centralized budgeting procedures led to his staff's preempting most traditional military planning" (Nathan and Oliver 1994). As power shifted from the armed serves to the OSD, McNamara "ignored or dismissed military advice, disparaged military experience and expertise, and circumvented or sacked generals and admirals who opposed him. The warfare inside the Pentagon was intense and vicious" (Kohn 1994).

Warfare in Vietnam perpetuated the warfare between civilian leaders and the armed services in Washington, as Johnson and his advisers believed they needed to control the military tightly in order to mold military operations to political objectives. Military leaders, on the other hand, "believed arrogant, uninformed, irresponsible politicians were not only preventing the winning of the war, but squandering American resources, and worse, lives" (Kohn 1994). The "lesson of Vietnam" applied by some in the Persian Gulf War—that the military cannot fight a war "with one hand tied behind its back"—had its roots here. So, too, did the "Vietnam syndrome," as the military became squeamish about interventions, fearing another Vietnam quagmire. Hawkish Reagan administration officials would later caricature the military as "wimps-in-uniform, so traumatized by their Vietnam experience that they are too timid to use force in all but the most easily won conflicts" (cited in Nathan and Oliver 1994).

Caspar Weinberger, Reagan's longtime secretary of defense, was not among the hawks. In fact, the so-called Weinberger Doctrine, enunciated during the president's first term, laid out stringent conditions for military intervention abroad to which at least the Defense Department subscribed, if not the Reagan administration as a whole. Colin Powell, chairman of the Joint Chiefs of Staff under Bush and, for a time, Clinton, subscribed to the "restrictive" view of the use of force articulated by Weinberger. Thus Powell was a reluctant warrior in the Persian Gulf, as we saw in Chapter 10. He also opposed the use of force in Bosnia, "thus appearing at odds with the Clinton administration" (Johnson and Metz 1995)—to the point that some worried about his possible insubordination (Lacayo 1993).

Weinberger also preferred decentralized management of the Pentagon, as we have noted, not the assertiveness of McNamara. Indeed, for nearly twenty years following McNamara's departure from the Pentagon, Republican administrations reversed the trend toward civilian control which McNamara symbolized, as restrictions on the military were loosed and their authority broadened.

The 1980s also witnessed a major defense reform effort, which culminated in the **Defense Reorganization Act of 1986**, the first major reorganization of the Defense Department in thirty years and the most sweeping change since its creation. The law, popularly known as the Goldwater-Nichols act after its congressional architects, sought in particular to strengthen the role of the institutions associated with the Joint Chiefs of Staff at the expense of the separate service organizations. The intent was to ameliorate the interservice rivalry that has long plagued the defense establishment by shifting power from the separate services to those responsible for coordinating them.[5]

The Joint Chiefs of Staff and the Chairman of the Joint Chiefs of Staff

The **Joint Chiefs of Staff (JCS)** consists of the senior military officer within each uniformed service and a chairman appointed by the president, who serves as the nation's chief military officer. Each service chief—the chief of staff of the Army, the chief of staff of the Air Force, the chief of naval operations, and the commandant of the Marine Corps (who heads a separate service in the Navy Department)—is responsible for advising his civilian secretary on military matters and for maintaining the efficiency and operational readiness of the military forces under his command. Until the 1986 reorganization, the joint chiefs were assisted in that task by a joint staff comprising some four hundred officers selected from each branch of the armed forces. Now, however, the joint staff explicitly serves as the chairman's staff, operating solely under his direction, authority, and control. The Goldwater-Nichols act stimulated the creation of a new "joint specialty" designed to make service on the joint staff more rewarding professionally, and it permitted civilians to serve on the joint staff, which now numbers roughly sixteen hundred. Finally, the law created a new vice chairman of the JCS, who now serves as the nation's number two military officer.

In another change, the act explicitly named the chairman of the joint chiefs as the principal military adviser to the president, the National Security Council, and the secretary of defense. Before the Goldwater-Nichols act, that task fell to the joint chiefs as a collective body, but no longer.

> The chairman had previously been merely a committee chairman—albeit with substantial prestige and opportunities for persuasion. The overall JCS was the committee, and the chairman's old role was faithfully to report and reflect the collective judgment of that body, which often amounted to an arithmetic lesson on lowest common denominators. The new law did stipulate that the chairman's advice should take into account the perspectives of the other JCS members. . . . But the law stripped away from the service chiefs the privilege of initiating access to the president, the NSC, and the secretary of defense. (Davis 1987, 188–89)

Now, in fact, the JCS chairman has "the right to give advice [to civilian policymakers] not only when asked, but also when not asked" (Perry 1989).

The law did not, however, make the chairman a member of the National Security Council, as some had proposed. Nor did it make him a commander with direct control over U.S. combat forces, a move many believed would have undermined the primacy of civilian control over the military.

Although the JCS system comprises the nation's senior military officers, they do not command combat forces in the field. Instead, they are essentially an administrative unit outside the operational chain of command. The actual command of combat forces in the field rests with nine commanders-in-chief (CINCs),[6] who receive their orders from the president as commander-in-chief through the secretary of defense. The Joint Chiefs of Staff have no independent role in this chain of command, despite its often bizarre twists and turns. The Marine Corps commandant on the scene when marine headquarters in Beirut was blown up in 1983, for example, was not responsible for security there. Instead, the Marines reported to officers offshore, who reported to "unified" commanders in London, Naples, Stuttgart, and Belgium, who in turn were responsible to Defense Secretary Caspar Weinberger and President Reagan.

The Goldwater-Nichols act moved very tentatively on this issue. As noted, it did not assign the JCS chairman command responsibilities, but it did give him authority to transmit orders from the president or the secretary of defense to the CINCs. The CINCs of unified commands in turn were given "operational command" but not complete command over forces assigned to them. The issue is a touchy one, as it bears directly on "an emotionally charged philosophical debate over how to define the relationship between the CINCs of unified commands and their subordinate forces" (*Congressional Quarterly Almanac 1986* 1987)—otherwise known as the "bureaucratic politics" so pervasive within the defense establishment.

Although the Defense Reorganization Act of 1986 did not accomplish all that its proponents had hoped, it did solidify the chairman's position as the chief military "thinker" in the government, with others assigned the primary roles as "doers." By putting him "in charge of broad new ranges of decision making in the Pentagon, with responsibilities allowing him to do more to influence and shape the overall U.S. defense establishment than any person in uniform had ever exercised before" (Davis

1987), the reorganization vastly increased the influence of the JCS chairman. Thus it arguably reduces the interservice rivalries that historically have contributed to shortcomings in the nation's military performance.

But what are its effects of the balance between civilian and military control of the defense establishment? Opponents of the more unified military system sought by the 1986 reorganization act, which included the secretaries of defense and navy, among others, argued that such a system would cut civilian policymakers off from competing viewpoints. That concern has taken on added significance, as experience with the new system has led critics to conclude that the balance between civilian and military control of the defense establishment now—to an alarming degree—tilts toward the military.

Civil-Military Relations: A New Crisis?

Critics argue that augmenting the authority and independence of the chairman of the joints chiefs under the Goldwater-Nichols act has had the unintended consequence of so dramatically enhancing the power of the armed serves that they now challenge the very principle of civilian control of the military. John Lehman, for example, who served as secretary of the navy at the time the 1986 reorganization act was passed (and was critical of it), has written that "In their understandable quest for efficiency, the military reformers have consolidated the power previously separated between the military departments, disenfranchised the civilian officials of each service, and created autocracy in the joint staff and arbitrary power in the person of the chairman" (Powell et al. 1994). Another defense strategist declared that "The Great Pentagon Reform has since shown us that the only thing worse than interservice rivalry is interservice harmony" (Luttwak 1994a).

Colin Powell in some sense encapsulated the "crisis" in civil-military relations perceived by some. The savvy general was schooled in the art of politics in part by his experience as National Security Adviser during the Reagan presidency; he became, in the words of defense specialist Richard Kohn (1994), "the most powerful military leader since George C. Marshall, the most popular since Dwight D. Eisenhower, and the most political since Douglas MacArthur." Worried that Powell had become too influential, Kohn charged that during his tenure "civilian control eroded most since the rise of the military establishment in the 1940s and 1950s."

Evidence to support the charge is found in the critical role Powell played in developing a post-Cold War military posture during the Bush administration, summarized in its Base Force plan (see Chapter 4). His role is consistent with the top-down, directive planning guidance strategy of Defense Department management that a secretary of defense might be expected to pursue. Consistent with that strategy, the Base Force proposal focused on operational, contingency, and long-range force planning as the United States prepared simultaneously to downsize its military forces and to cope with new security challenges. Powell and Secretary of Defense Dick Cheney evidently worked closely together as the plan was devised, but it is significant that Powell defended it in the pages of the prestigious journal *Foreign Affairs* (Powell 1992–1993), space normally occupied by civilian advocates of new policy departures.

So does Powell's role—and the one that future JCS chairs might now be able to pursue—portend a "crisis" is civil-military relations? While the Goldwater-Nichols act does markedly enhance the capacity of the chairman to exercise influence, it does not guarantee that the exercise of influence will be successful: "Goldwater-Nichols assures that the nation's top military officers will be *heard* by civilian policymakers, but not that they be *heeded*" (Johnson and Metz 1995). In the particular case of Colin Powell, however, his influence in shaping America's security posture for the post-Cold War world may have derived more from policymakers' own lack of imagination about the emerging new world order than from the attention they paid to his ideas. As Samuel P. Huntington, long regarded as the preeminent American thinker on civil-military relations, has written:

> Military establishments want political leaders to set forth reasonably clear goals and policies. If political leaders fail to do this, chiefs of staff have to make their own assumptions and develop their plans and programs accordingly. . . . It is to the great credit of the American military that it did not attempt to perpetuate Cold War strategies and instead took the initiative in attempting to redefine its missions and restructure its forces. It was the top political leadership which failed to adapt rapidly to the changed conditions. (Powell et al. 1994, 28)

From this perspective, then, the latest chapter in the continuing debate about civil military relations is not a crisis but, instead, a continuing search for equilibrium in a political system that itself is built on the balancing of power among institutions. If the current chapter in the continuing debate has distinctiveness, it is in the "activism of the military" in "helping define its relationship to civil authorities and to the American public" (Johnson and Metz 1995).

Having said that, we would also be remiss if we did not recall how frequently during the past half-century civilian leaders adopted military ways of thinking about political problems, as witnessed by the recurrent resort to force and other interventionist strategies the nation has long embraced. The historical record shows that civilian leaders often approach international problems in an especially "tough, macho, or militaristic spirit" that stresses the use of raw military power and lets questions of strategy dominate diplomacy (Kattenburg 1980). The roots of military machismo are lodged in the psychological reactions of individuals to the circumstances they experience in their environments and to the beliefs they maintain about those experiences (see also Chapter 14). Among the beliefs and experiences shared by civilian policymakers since World War II have been a "deep respect for military effectiveness and efficiency"; a "belief in the capacity of U.S. military forces to accomplish virtually any mission"; "fear of being perceived as weak"; "fear of losing policy control to military leaders"; and a "belief that the fame of states was a game of men" (Kattenburg 1980). The "crisis" in civil-military relations may thus reside less in the influence of the defense establishment on political leaders' thinking than on the propensity of the latter to opt for military solutions to political problems. As Adam Yarmolinsky (1971), a former Defense Department official, observed more than two decades ago, the influence that the military establishment exerts on foreign policy depends critically on "the extent to which civilians in the executive branch, in Congress, and among the public bear in mind or forget General George C. Marshall's maxim that political problems, if thought about in military terms, become military problems."

The Intelligence Community

Like the military, the intelligence community has played a prominent role in American foreign policy for nearly half a century because of the preferences of elected officials and their advisers. As Bobby Inman, a former deputy director of central intelligence, observed on his retirement from government service in 1982, "every administration ultimately turns to the use of covert operations when they become frustrated about the lack of success with diplomatic initiatives and are unwilling to use military force."

The intelligence community itself is a vast complex of operating agencies and interagency and oversight committees. The agencies involved are depicted in Figure 11.3, which also suggests that primary responsibility for managing the community rests with the director of central intelligence (DCI), who is also director of the Central Intelligence Agency. The DCI exercises his authority through the National Foreign Intelligence Board (NFIB) and the National Intelligence Council (NIC). These are bodies made up of the principals of operating agencies comprising the intelligence community (with responsibility for producing National Intelligence Estimates) and chaired by the DCI. The DCI, in turn, is responsible to the National Security Council, and through it, to the president. In practice, of course, the character of the "intelligence community" is much less orderly and harmonious than this brief description

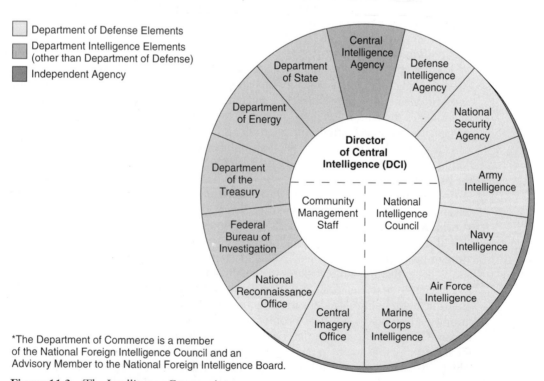

□ Department of Defense Elements

□ Department Intelligence Elements
(other than Department of Defense)

■ Independent Agency

*The Department of Commerce is a member
of the National Foreign Intelligence Council and an
Advisory Member to the National Foreign Intelligence Board.

Figure 11.3 The Intelligence Community
Source: Central Intelligence Agency, *Factbook on Intelligence* (Washington, D.C.: CIA, 1993), p. 17.

suggests. "Indeed, tribal and feudal metaphors often seem more appropriate in describing how the various collection, processing, and analytic organizations interact with one another and with policymakers" (Flanagan 1985; see also Lowenthal, 1992).

Beyond the National Security Council, oversight of the intelligence community is exercised by the President's Foreign Intelligence Advisory Board (PFIAB) and by the House and Senate Select Committees on Intelligence. Established by President Eisenhower in 1956, the PFIAB gives general counsel on the conduct of the intelligence community, including the collection and evaluation of intelligence and the execution of intelligence policy. In practice, however, it has not been a central player in the intelligence community, as presidents have viewed its utility quite differently (Holt 1995). (Carter even abolished the board, but Reagan resurrected it.)

The House and Senate Select Committees on Intelligence were created in the late 1970s following revelations of abuses committed over the previously quarter-century by intelligence agencies, including illegal activities against American citizens as well as questionable operations abroad. They authorize appropriations for the intelligence community, receive reports on intelligence analysis and production, and oversee the conduct of covert activities once the president has presented a "finding" on the need for such activities. More broadly, the president is required by law to keep Congress "fully and currently informed" of all intelligence activities, and Congress as a whole appropriates all money for the intelligence community, including money for intelligence activities secretly tucked away in the Pentagon's budget.

Despite the president's legal responsibility to keep Congress "fully and currently informed," an admonition written into law with the 1980 Intelligence Oversight Act, the system has sometimes failed. In part this is because the act also afforded the president discretion to limit prior congressional notification, and it specifically denied Congress the right to disapprove covert operations. Prior notification figured prominently in the Iran-*contra* scandal, when Congress learned that the president had failed to reveal a retroactively signed presidential finding that authorized the secret sale of arms to Iran. These and other revelations fueled Congress's ire and broke the trust that the Reagan administration had sought to build with Congress on the sensitive issue of covert operations and other intelligence activities, which had fallen into disrepute in the 1970s. As a result, questions about propriety, legality, secrecy, and control again emerged as central issues surrounding the role of intelligence in American foreign policy.

These issues still have not been settled, but during the 1990s they were joined with issues about the competence of Central Intelligence Agency and its role in a transformed world order. At issue is the kind of intelligence the United States will require in the future and what kind of intelligence apparatus can best meet those needs. Understanding the present apparatus and how it historically has related to the purposes of American foreign policy (explored in detail in Chapter 5) are necessary ingredients to answering these questions.

Intelligence Operations and the Department of Defense

The size of the intelligence community, in money and personnel, remains uncertain owing to the secrecy in which the community and its activities are shrouded. Most

how do we know if we are winning the battle?

budget estimates for the period from the 1970s through the late 1980s converge around $10–13 billion devoted to *national intelligence* (intelligence normally required for foreign policy making), formally called the National Foreign Intelligence Program [NFIP]), and personnel is estimated at 150,000–160,000. During the Bush administration the total intelligence budget (which also includes tactical intelligence on which military commanders depend, known as Tactical Intelligence and Related Activities [TIARA]) reached $30 billion. And reliable reports put the figure appropriated by Congress at $28 billion during the first two years of the Clinton presidency. Data on numbers of personnel remain sketchy (Holt 1995), however, in part because of the widespread use of various contract employees and foreign agents.

What is clear is that the Department of Defense (DOD) is the largest component of the intelligence community, consuming anywhere from two-thirds to three-fourths of the federal intelligence budget. The intelligence operations of the various branches of the armed services, the National Reconnaissance Office, the Central Imagery Office, the National Security Agency, and the Defense Intelligence Agency are the actual DOD intelligence units.

The *National Reconnaissance Office (NRO)* is the biggest spender. NRO manages the nation's satellite reconnaissance programs at an annual cost (in 1994) of $7 billion (Pincus 1994a, 34). Controlled jointly by the CIA and Defense Department, it operates under the "cover" of the Air Force, which reportedly pays the bills for the extremely costly photographic and electronic reconnaissance satellites and the rockets necessary to put them into orbit. The photographic (now "imaging") satellites for years provided enormous amounts of detailed information on military and related strategic developments in the Soviet Union and elsewhere; this proved critically important in verifying compliance with various arms control agreements. (One [anonymous] source described the NRO imaging capability by observing that the NRO "could start with a satellite picture covering all of downtown Washington and get down so close you can almost read license plates on cars" [Pincus 1994a]. Given that, the failure of high-tech reconnaissance satellites to detect Iran's nuclear program is troublesome [Shulsky and Schmitt 1994–1995].) Reconnaissance satellites also engage in electronic sensing tasks oriented toward gathering data on missile testing, on radar and the emissions of other electronic equipment, and on communications traffic.

The NRO was created in 1960 to replace the U-2 spy-plane program, but its existence was not revealed until 1973, when its name was inadvertently included in a declassified congressional document. Even so, the office remained a secret or "black" agency for nearly two decades after that, officially unacknowledged until 1992. The "secret" was not well kept either at home or abroad, however, as the Soviets were aware of the United States' ability to spy from the sky (just as the U.S. knew of similar capabilities on the Soviet side). Still, because it was useful to both superpowers to maintain the facade of secrecy, "the magic phrase 'national technical means' was invented so that the parties could talk to each other about reconnaissance satellites without using those words" (Holt 1995).

Once the Cold War ended bureaucratic inertia perpetuated the secrecy of the NRO, but Congress became increasingly restive about the resources its demanded. Arguing that the existing satellite system worked effectively, especially in an environment of reduced threat, critics began to target the NRO for closer scrutiny, a factor that contributed to the "unveiling" of the organization. New fuel was added to the controversy when, in mid-1994, the Senate Intelligence Committee complained that the NRO had concealed from Congress a $310 office building under construction near Dulles airport in Washington. Critics inside and outside the agency now charged that its continued secrecy and lavish spending reflected the inertia of Cold War thinking. "The NRO 'is a Cold War organization that still operates under a rule that puts the taxpayer last and its requirements first,' is the way one twenty year observer of the agency [put] it" (cited in Pincus 1994a).

The Central Imagery Office was created in 1993 to coordinate the processing of imaging data obtained from NRO satellites, streams of computer code that must be converted into images (Holt 1995). Data on the cost and size of this new agency are not readily available.

The **National Security Agency (NSA)**, which is responsible for signals intelligence (SIGINT), communications security, and cryptology, follows the NRO as the second most expensive DOD intelligence agency, spending (in 1994) an estimated $4 billion. Created by a classified presidential directive in 1952, NSA was not even generally acknowledged as a government organization until 1957 and, much like the NRO, did not acknowledge its own existence until 1991. Even today, references to it in government documents remain hard to find and deficient in detail, as it remains the most secretive of all intelligence agencies. Indeed, its legendary silence led people to joke that its initials stood for "No Such Agency" or "Never Say Anything."

NSA is the largest intelligence organization in terms of personnel, numbering its own employees at more than twenty thousand. However, others put the number closer to forty-five thousand (Beyers 1991, 31). One gains a sense of the magnitude of the NSA by comparing the capitol building in Washington, which houses the legislative body of the world's largest democracy and contains 718,740 square feet, with NSA's headquarters in Fort George Meade, Maryland, which encompasses 1,912,000 square feet (Pett 1984, 8-B). Moreover, its budget may be far greater than the estimated $4 billion. One report put the amount Congress appropriated in 1989 for code making and code breaking, NSA's principal tasks, at "between $10 and $15 billion," with "[NSA] and its military surrogates, the Army Intelligence and Security Command, the Naval Security Group Command, and the Air Force Electronic Security Command" the recipients (Lardner 1990b, 6; see also Bamford 1983, 109).

NSA's operations are extraordinarily technology-intensive, requiring massive supercomputers to discharge its responsibilities. The United States' ability to confidently conduct arms control negotiations with the Soviet Union during the Cold War, which required detailed knowledge of Soviet military capabilities, rested largely on NSA's sophisticated SIGINT capabilities. "Never Say Anything" is hypersecretive about what precisely those capabilities are. It supported the Iran-*contra* initiative by intercepting over a sixteen-month period ending in December 1986 scores of messages, many of which involved eavesdropping on Iranian officials' phone conversations. But this evidence was never admitted into the criminal trials of the Iran-*contra* principals because of NSA's objection that the admission of classified material relating to the agency's functions in intercepting communications would compromise national security (Lardner 1990a). It is noteworthy that while NSA operates under the authority and control of the secretary of defense, it reportedly refused to advise the secretary of the role it had played in intercepting Iranian communications on the grounds he did not need to know (Johnson 1989).

Like NSA, the *Defense Intelligence Agency (DIA)* also operates under the authority of the secretary of defense, but it is the smallest of all DOD intelligence operations, with a 1995 budget estimated at only $500 million (Holt 1995, 48). Created by Robert McNamara in 1961, the DIA was to consolidate in one agency the various intelligence units of the armed services. The latter are involved in the collection of "departmental" intelligence as opposed to "national" intelligence—that is, in collecting information germane to their tactical (battlefield) missions. In so doing, however, their intelligence product has often been skewed in the direction preferred by their parent organizations for "budgeteering" purposes.

> Thus the air force saw the development of a "bomber gap" and then a "missile gap" which never materialized. The navy was inclined to exaggerate Soviet naval power, and the army was often found estimating a number of Russian army divisions that existed only on paper. All of these activities tended to inflate budgetary requests and fundamentally to challenge the decision-making authority of the secretary of defense, particularly vis-à-vis Congress. (Ransom 1970, 103–4; see also Shulsky and Schmitt 1994–1995)

Designed to provide direct intelligence support to the secretary of defense and the Joint Chiefs of Staff (for whom the director of DIA is the principal intelligence adviser), the DIA's assignment required improved coordination and management of Defense Department intelligence resources. Moreover, policymakers assumed that the agency would take over many of the functions of the armed forces intelligence units themselves. This has never happened. DIA does represent the Defense Department on the National Foreign Intelligence Board, but the individual military departments also send observers to its meetings. Similarly, it does manage the defense attaché system, which places military representatives in U.S. field missions abroad, but the officers themselves are drawn from the armed services (Holt 1995).

Although the functions assigned the DIA appear to place it in a position superior to the army, navy, and air force, the DIA collects little information on its own, relying instead on the service intelligence agencies for its raw intelligence data. Thus the service intelligence units continue to flourish, with the result that they and DIA often duplicate efforts. These and other problems have led critics to question the need for DIA's continued existence, but as long as its enjoys the backing of the secretary of defense it will remain a formidable rival of other intelligence agencies.

Intelligence Operations and the Department of State

The *Bureau of Intelligence and Research (INR)* is the State Department's representative in the intelligence community. The department's intelligence functions arise naturally out of its general foreign affairs responsibilities, and much of what the department routinely does in the way of analyzing and interpreting information might be regarded as intelligence work. INR is the unit through which the State Department makes its input into the various interagency committees that seek to guide intelligence operations (other than covert activities), including the National Foreign Intelligence

Board. The director of INR is also the secretary of state's senior in-house intelligence adviser.

In addition to representing the State Department within the intelligence community, INR's primary objective is to introduce a "diplomatic sensitivity to intelligence reports"; and its own reports "are among the most highly regarded in the government—some say the best" (Johnson 1989). But INR does not independently collect intelligence except through normal cable traffic and reporting from overseas posts. Instead, it depends on input from other agencies, which its small staff then turns into finished intelligence reports. Within the intelligence community, therefore, the State Department has been more a consumer than a producer of intelligence. That fact combined with INR's comparatively small size lead to the suspicion that the State Department is in a relatively disadvantageous position in the highly competitive intelligence community.[7]

Intelligence Responsibilities of Other Departments and Agencies

The Treasury Department, the Energy Department, and the Federal Bureau of Investigation (FBI) are the remaining officially designated members of the intelligence community. Each plays an important role in intelligence operations, although none is concerned primarily with the collection of foreign intelligence.

Treasury's intelligence activities derive in part from the collection of foreign economic intelligence by its overseas attachés. More specific intelligence activities derive from the department's responsibilities for protecting (by the U.S. Secret Service) the president, presidential candidates, and certain foreign dignitaries; for controlling (through the Bureau of Alcohol, Tobacco, and Firearms and the U.S. Customs Service) illegal trafficking in alcohol, tobacco, firearms, and other articles entering international trade and for protecting against terrorism in international transportation facilities; and for ensuring compliance (through the Internal Revenue Service) with the Internal Revenue laws. Executing those functions has often resulted in the use of undercover personnel, paid informants, and electronic surveillance operations.

The Department of Energy maintains an Office of Intelligence responsible for the overt collection of intelligence on energy policies and developments abroad. As the department responsible for conducting nuclear weapons research, development, and production, it maintains counterintelligence capabilities regarding those weapons. It also participates with other government agencies in monitoring nonproliferation issues.

The Federal Bureau of Investigation (a Justice Department agency) is responsible for counterintelligence in the United States. The FBI's mandate is strictly domestic; therefore, it must work with the CIA, which bears responsibility for counterintelligence abroad. However, the relationship between the two agencies has long been marked by conflict (Riebling 1994), fed in part by their different perspectives and responsibilities.

To the FBI, counterintelligence means catching foreign spies, or Americans working for foreign intelligence organizations, in the United States. This devolves on the FBI because of its general responsibility for law enforcement, but spies move in and out of the United States. When they are in another country, watching them is the responsibility of the CIA.

When the FBI catches spies, it thinks in terms of putting them in jail or, if they have diplomatic immunity, of expelling them from the country. When the CIA catches spies, it thinks in terms of turning them into double agents, that is, using them to spy on the government they have been working for. (Holt 1995, 51).

Against this background, it is not surprising that recriminations over the failure for seven years to uncover Aldrich Ames's duplicity added new grist to the long-standing CIA-FBI bureaucratic feud. (For a more detailed discussion of the Ames case, see Chapter 5, especially Focus 5.1.)

Beyond its feud with the CIA, the FBI's jurisdiction over espionage, sabotage, treason, and other internal security matters has sometimes proven controversial. In 1981, for example, the FBI began investigating a coalition of organizations called the Committee in Solidarity with the People of El Salvador (CISPES), later the leading citizens' organization protesting U.S. policies in El Salvador. Although the FBI defended its surveillance, which continued for several years, by saying it was investigating alleged criminal activity, its actions were widely interpreted as an effort to intimidate the Reagan administration's political opponents and may have violated their civil rights.

Although not formally designated a member of the intelligence community, mention should be made of the Justice Department's Drug Enforcement Administration (DEA), which does carry out some intelligence activities in connection with its responsibilities as a police force, with jurisdiction over foreign and domestic aspects of narcotics production and trafficking. Thus, although its activities sometimes overlap with the CIA, the two agencies, much like the FBI and CIA, have quite different perspectives on their bureaucratic roles. "Cops think of informers as sleazeballs and stool pigeons; spies think of them as sources to be protected. Spies will back off from a prosecution that requires compromising sources; cops will not, at least not often" (Holt 1995). Regardless, DEA's role abroad has expanded in recent years, stimulated in part by the Bush administration's declaration of war on drugs and a correspondingly heightened national concern with drug trafficking.

Central Intelligence Agency

Placing the CIA last in our discussion of executive branch intelligence agencies underscores the fact that the most widely known and controversial intelligence organization is only one of many. Indeed, the CIA constitutes less than one-fifth of the intelligence community's expenditures and an even smaller percentage of its employees: Its budget (in 1994) reportedly stood at $3 billion (Holt 1995, 47), and its employees (in the early 1990s, excluding contract employees and paid informants) at twenty-two thousand (Kessler 1992, xxvii). Its attention thus derives less from its size than from its reputation for "dirty tricks" as the covert action arm of the United States government.

Created by the National Security Act of 1947 as a subsidiary of the National Security Council, the CIA was assigned responsibilities for: (1) advising the NSC on intelligence matters relating to national security; (2) making recommendations to the

NSC for coordinating the intelligence activities of the various federal executive departments and agencies; (3) correlating and evaluating intelligence and providing for its dissemination; and (4) carrying out such additional services, functions, and duties relating to national security intelligence as the NSC might direct. Those tasks reflect the interest in the concept of a central intelligence organization which evolved out of concern for the quality of intelligence analysis available to policymakers, provoked in particular by the Japanese attack on Pearl Harbor in 1941. Before long, however, the CIA's charge focused on covert psychological, political, paramilitary, and economic activities. Acquisition of the covert mission profoundly affected the agency's later activities and its relative political stature within the foreign affairs government.

We examined the CIA's covert mission and activities in detail in Chapter 5, noting how the increasingly hostile international environment of the late 1940s and early 1950s stimulated the agency's initiatives and the successes and failures that followed, as the Cold War competition evolved. Here we are concerned less with the CIA's covert activities as an instrument of American foreign policy than with their impact on the CIA itself and with the agency's role in the intelligence community and the larger foreign affairs government.

The CIA's Intelligence Responsibilities

Covert actions, clandestine intelligence collection, and counterintelligence are the responsibility of the CIA's Directorate of Operations, otherwise known as the clandestine services. The analysis division is known as the Directorate of Intelligence. Of the two, clandestine services has always been more important. Still, the early 1970s were a turning point for the agency, as divisiveness over Vietnam, public disclosures of CIA abuses of power, and the shifting distribution of international power eroded the foreign policy assumptions on which CIA clout within the policy-making community had been built. It also raised serious questions about the legality and propriety of many of the agency's actions and its role as the "central" organization in the sprawling intelligence community.

A rapid succession of directors of central intelligence (DCIs)—Richard Helms, James Schlesinger, William Colby, George Bush, Stansfield Turner, and William Casey—revealed outwardly the inner turmoil. Colby, who assumed his position during Nixon's administration and served until the end of Ford's, urged management reforms designed to enhance the CIA's communitywide role and provide improved intelligence to policymakers. His appointment was inopportune, however, as it coincided with public disclosures of CIA domestic spying—in violation of its foreign intelligence charter—including operations directed against domestic political dissidents from 1967 to 1974 and a massive mail-rifling program conducted in partial cooperation with the FBI. Clandestine operations also continued as mainstream CIA fare, as illustrated by its covert actions against the Allende government in Chile in the early 1970s. Thus an investigative report by the U.S. Senate, spearheaded by the Church Committee's probing investigation of the CIA's activities (and abuses) concluded that "The activities of the clandestine service have reflected not what the agency can do well but what the demands of American foreign policy have required at particular times. The nature of covert operations, the priority accorded them by senior policymakers, and the orientation and background of some DCIs . . . made the clandestine mission the preeminent activity within the organization" (*Final Report of the Select Committee to Study Governmental Operations with Respect to Intelligence Activities* 1976, I).

The Carter administration tried to reshape the intelligence community and to provide explicit guidance on all facets of U.S. intelligence activities, including covert operations. Congress also enhanced its oversight capabilities. And resources continued to be cut—a trend set in motion earlier, especially in the area of human intelligence (HUMINT, otherwise known as "espionage"), as the Carter administration chose to emphasize technical means of intelligence collection. Bobby Inman testified before Congress in 1982 that "the intelligence establishment" lost "40 percent of its personnel from 1964 to the mid-1970s." Later reports put the number of employees in the CIA's Directorate of Operations during the Carter administration at three thousand (Ignatius 1995, 23).[8] The CIA now faced an "identity crisis," as the agency became unsure of itself and its mission (Turner and Thibault 1982).

Following Reagan's election, many restrictions imposed during the 1970s were lifted and the intelligence community, with the CIA at the vanguard, enjoyed a resurgence not only as a servant of American foreign policy but also sometimes as a substitute for it, notably in Central America, Southwest Africa, and Southwest Asia. According to one estimate (*New York Times*, June 11, 1984, p. 1), covert operations under Reagan experienced "a fivefold increase since the last year of the Carter administration to over fifty continuing operations." By the mid-1980s previous cutbacks in budgets and personnel had been restored and probably surpassed (Taubman 1984). The number of workers in clandestine services grew to roughly seven thousand during the Reagan administration, "swollen by new recruits who were managing a global campaign of paramilitary operations against the Soviet Union" (Ignatius 1995, 23).

Meanwhile, the "numbers game"—recruiting as many foreign nationals as possible to spy for the United States—became the route to success in "The Company." Overseas agents estimated that they spent 70 to 80 percent of their time trying to recruit their "opposite number in the Kremlin's secret service," an effort widely regarded as a "misplaced expenditure of time and effort" (Hoagland 1994a, 29). Even as late as 1994 an investigative report by *U.S. News & World Report* (July 4, 1994) determined that "the pressure from DO [Directorate of Operations] managers to recruit new agents is so great that many field officers exaggerate the value of their agents, claim State Department reporting as their own, try to compromise officials of friendly governments, and even claim to have recruited nonexistent agents."

Within the clandestine services, however, the counterintelligence center (where Aldrich Ames worked) was regarded as "a place that poor performers could be sent because they could not do much harm." As described by Jeffrey H. Smith, who conducted an internal probe for CIA Director R. James Woolsey of "what went wrong," the prevailing agency attitude toward counterintelligence was "disdain bordering on contempt" (cited in R. Smith 1994a). Its roots can be traced to former CIA counterintelligence chief James Jesus Angleton, who headed the counterintelligence unit for two decades until his forced resignation in 1974. Convinced that the CIA had been penetrated by a "mole," Angleton, in ruthlessly pursuing those he suspected of spying for others, isolated other agents and sometimes destroyed their careers. His "legendary paranoia and incessant probing of valued CIA employees created 'hostility and a meanness of spirt, . . . stifled ideas, and poisoned initiative"' (Jeffrey H. Smith, cited in R. Smith 1994).

There are intriguing parallels between Angleton's CIA legacy and McCarthyism's effects on the State Department. The "witch hunts" each experienced impaired their abilities to perform their tasks effectively and seriously tarnished their image in the larger foreign affairs government, in Congress, and in the presidential subsystem. The CIA's inspector general's inquiry into the Ames defection determined that Ames had betrayed fifty-five clandestine operations, nearly twice the number originally believed. Furthermore, the inability of the agency to uncover his defection raised serious doubts not only about its ability to keep its own house in order but also, when combined with the untoward effects of the "numbers game," to respond aggressively and innovatively to the challenges of a post-Cold War world.

with masses of men, can it react quickly in modern world?

The CIA and the Management of Intelligence

The "central" in its name theoretically makes the CIA the hub of the intelligence community, as it seeks to exercise its responsibility for coordination of the intelligence community. Here, too, however, there are interesting parallels with the State Department's experience as the first among equals in the foreign affairs government. Like the State Department, in budgetary matters the CIA finds itself a comparative pygmy among giants. In the capacity of DCI, the director of the CIA exercises independent authority only over the CIA's budget. This puts the DCI at a competitive disadvantage in dealing with the other intelligence agencies, whose activities he or she is supposed to coordinate. Richard Helms, a former DCI, once estimated that the Defense Department controlled 85 percent of intelligence spending (May 1992, 66). In a similar vein, a congressional committee, noting that the DCI controlled "less than 10 percent of the combined national and tactical intelligence efforts," described the DCI's influence over the allocation of the other 90 percent as limited to that of "an interested critic" (cited in Bamford 1983).

A second coordinating mechanism at the disposal of the director of central intelligence flows from his or her responsibility to produce intelligence reports for the entire foreign affairs government. As noted earlier, the DCI chairs two units that bring together the other national intelligence agencies, the National Foreign Intelligence Board (NFIB) and the National Intelligence Council (NIC). Among their tasks is production of *National Intelligence Estimates (NIEs)*, routinely prepared on various parts of the world, and Special National Intelligence Estimates (SNIEs), prepared in response to specific requests by top-level policymakers. These reports, signed by the DCI, are supposed to be the "best judgments" of the intelligence community on their respective subjects, and large numbers are typically produced every year. Their value, however, is suspect. Described by one senator as "overly cautious, caveated, and consensus-oriented" (Boren 1992), General Norman Schwarzkopf characterized the intelligence estimates as "unhelpful mush." Others concur:

Despite the billions of dollars spent collecting and analyzing strategic intelligence, many consumers find its products lacking. "We never used the CIA stuff," recalls a former U.S. ambassador and assistant secretary of state. "It was irrelevant." A survey of intelligence consumers conducted by the Senate Select Committee on Intelligence revealed widespread disdain toward the value of the community's work. (Johnson 1992–1993, 65)

The questionable ability of the CIA to provide useful intelligence in the past raises questions about its future. Can the agency rebound as it faces the new, post-Cold War (dis)order? As we will explore in more detail in Chapter 13, bureaucratic organizations are typically resistant to change, and the CIA is no exception. Like the Foreign Service, it has developed a distinctive subculture resistant to outside forces which militates against a more assertive, communitywide intelligence role.

> Intelligence officers often compartmentalize data collected by the sensitive methods of one agency and restrict dissemination to the rest of the community. This practice is rationalized by narrowly interpreting the "need-to-know" security guidelines. But the bottom line is that the bureaucratic culture underlying the American intelligence system does not . . . guarantee that all of what is collected is subject to communitywide, objective, and rigorous analysis. (Goodman 1984–1985, 173; see also Codevilla 1992)

Another aspect of the CIA's culture that makes it look like any other bureaucracy is revealed by its tendency during the Cold War to develop a particular mindset about developments in the Soviet Union that proved fundamentally wrong: Estimates of Soviet military spending proved wrong, estimates of its economic growth proved wrong, and, ultimately, estimates of its survivability proved wrong. But all were sustained by a bureaucratic culture that viewed the Soviet Union through a Cold War prism highlighting its challenging, aggressive face.

Senator Daniel Patrick Moynihan, a long-time member of the Senate Intelligence Committee, saw much of the same evidence on which the CIA based its assessments of the Soviet Union but reached very different conclusions. Using several venues over a long period, he challenged the prognoses flowing from the (now proven) erroneous CIA assessments of the Soviet Union's prowess and prospects for survival (Moynihan 1992), but his voice went unheeded. Once proven correct, however, Moynihan became a vigorous (but still lone) advocate of a complete restructuring of the intelligence community. The centerpiece of his recommendations included moving the CIA's analytical functions to the State Department, its covert paramilitary capabilities to the Defense Department, and its counterintelligence functions to the FBI. With that, the CIA itself could be terminated.

Moynihan's proposals symbolized the views of those who would bury the CIA with the Cold War, but reform, not burial, carried the day. Burned not only by the absence of accurate intelligence about the impending implosion of the Soviet Union but also by poor intelligence prior to the Persian Gulf War, Congress launched another intelligence community reorganization effort during the Bush administration designed to shore up its continuing faults. The focus of its proposals was on centralization, not termination (see Boren 1992).

Legislation introduced in 1992 called for greater integration of the civilian and military intelligence agencies and for greater power in the hands of one person, such as the DCI, "to coordinate and set priorities for the entire intelligence community" (Boren 1992). Thus it recalled previous presidents' efforts to enhance their control of the intelligence community by enhancing the power of the DCI, who is the president's principal foreign intelligence adviser.

President Nixon, for example, first charged the DCI with making recommendations for a consolidated national foreign intelligence budget. President Ford later tried to enhance the DCI's role in the allocation of national (but not tactical) intelligence resources. Carter went even further, giving the DCI "full and exclusive authority over approval of the National Intelligence Program budget submitted to the president." To accomplish this task, the intelligence community staff, which assists the DCI (as suggested in Figure 11.3), was considerably enlarged.

Not surprisingly, the other intelligence agencies were less than enthusiastic with the efforts of Carter's DCI to expand his communitywide role. They won the day when those who joined Reagan's administration with a strong penchant toward the military were able to curb the DCI so as to preserve DOD's historic independence. A Reagan administration executive order "cast the DCI more in the role of a coordinator, rather than a manager, of community affairs." And William Casey, Reagan's director of central intelligence, "adopted a more collegial, 'board of directors' approach" to the National Foreign Intelligence Board whose members are responsible for intelligence collection and production (Flanagan 1985).

Congressional efforts to legislate intelligence reforms were shelved once Clinton became president, but Congress continued to be unhappy with both the structure and product of the intelligence community. Thus, as we noted in Chapter 5, Congress pressured a reluctant President Clinton to launch a bipartisan review of the intelligence community, which promised to address the broad range of issues related to both the structure and purpose of U.S. intelligence organizations and operations. Meanwhile, the urge to centralize in the name of greater efficiency and objectivity mirrors the same processes at work in the defense establishment, where Congress has consistently tried to strengthen the "central" institutions, notably the secretary of defense and the Joint Chiefs of Staff and its chairman, at the expense of the individual armed services (Shulsky and Schmitt 1994–1995). Not everyone agrees with the wisdom of that approach.

Intelligence Gathering and Analysis

Critics often argue that bringing the tasks of intelligence gathering, analysis, and coordination under the authority of the head of the CIA had a detrimental impact on the ultimate intelligence product.

> This consolidation exposes the entire intelligence community to the same political and cultural pressures, and reinforces the tendency of all elements to sway together with the mood of the moment. It has fostered a type of "group-think" where the pressures for unanimity override individual mental faculties—somewhat analogous to what occurs in a jury room. (Ellsworth and Adelman 1979, 158)

The CIA's inability to foresee the fall of the Shah of Iran in 1979 may have been related to the centralization of intelligence functions. As a House Intelligence Committee study noted, the CIA found itself caught in a conflict of interests: "On the one hand, the CIA had historically considered itself the Shah's booster. On the other hand, it was supposed to provide sound intelligence analysis of the Iranian political situation." The merging of intelligence gathering and analysis in the DCI did little to enable the agency to separate its estimates of the Shah's survivability from its confidence in him, since the director of the CIA was simultaneously head of the agency that collected the information and the president's chief adviser in determining what the information meant. The Iranian intelligence failure thus bore similarities to the 1961 Bay of Pigs fiasco, when the CIA first gathered the intelligence and then planned a program of action based on its own information. Ultimately its commitment to the program led it to discount intelligence that might have caused it to abandon the military option.

Iran and Cuba are only two instances of dozens of intelligence failures investigated by Congress or the media during the past several decades. Perhaps such failures are inevitable (Betts 1978), but explaining why they occur remains important.

Iran and Cuba suggest that the intelligence establishment's inability to provide policymakers with objective, timely, and accurate intelligence contributes to policy failures. Furthermore, bureaucratic culture doubtless contributes to intelligence shortcomings by favoring (and rewarding) some kinds of analyses more than others (Goodman 1984–1985). It is also true, however, that policymakers may disregard objective intelligence or otherwise seek to skew it to their purposes. During the Vietnam War, for example, CIA Director Richard Helms received an estimate only thirteen days before the American military incursion into Cambodia that an invasion would not deter continued North Vietnamese involvement in the war, but he chose not bring it to the attention of the White House. Contrariwise, the resignation of two senior CIA analysts during the first Reagan term because, they claimed, William Casey pressured them to rewrite their Central American assessments to make them more consonant with existing United States policy points to what Senate minority leader Robert Byrd described as "a shocking use of the CIA for political purposes."

Casey's role in the Reagan administration became especially controversial not only because he vigorously championed the covert option, but also because he was the first DCI to enjoy cabinet rank. This meant his roles simultaneously placed him in the position of advocating policy and providing assessments on which to base it. As in the case of the Bay of Pigs fiasco, the dual responsibilities contributed to the failure of the "initiative" toward Iran.

John Tower, chair of the commission that investigated the Iran-*contra* affair, concluded that it was little more than an "aberration." Others disagree, including Allan E. Goodman, who has held several senior staff positions in the CIA. "In this latest fiasco," he wrote in 1987, "the CIA made mistakes that are not unique to the politics and personalities involved . . . but that represent major defects in the country's system of intelligence support to foreign policy." Among them are "long-standing problems stemming from the intrusion of politics into intelligence collection and analysis" (Goodman 1987).

Robert M. Gates, deputy to CIA Director Bill Casey at the time of the Iran-*contra* affair (and later a deputy national security adviser to Bush), addressed the relationship between intelligence analysis and policy shortly after the Iran-*contra* affair became public. He wrote that "policymakers have always liked intelligence that supported what they want to do, and they often try to influence the analysis to buttress the conclusions they want to reach. They ask carefully phrased questions; they sometimes withhold information; they broaden or narrow the issue; on rare occasions they even try to intimidate. The pressures can be enormous." But, he added "there is no charge to which those in the CIA are more sensitive than that of cooking intelligence—of slanting its reports to support policy," which would "transgress the single deepest ethical and cultural principle of the CIA" (Gates 1987–1988). It is clear nonetheless that the line between intelligence and advocacy is often slender. The Tower commission found, for example, that NSC staff members were so actively involved with CIA officials in the preparation of a May 1985 Special National Intelligence Estimate (SNIE) on Iran that they may have allowed their "strong views . . . to influence the intelligence judgments" contained in it. "It is critical that the line between intelligence and advocacy of a particular policy be preserved if intelligence is to retain its integrity and perform its proper function," the commission continued. "In this instance, the CIA came close enough to the line to warrant concern."

Bill Casey often was alleged to have tailored or distorted intelligence analyses to serve the Reagan foreign policy agenda (as well as his own). Ironically, Gates, too, was charged with that transgression during confirmation hearings in 1991 leading to his appointment as Bush's CIA director. Countless questions were raised about his role in the Iran-*contra* affair, about which he professed ignorance. Scathing charges also were made that Gates slanted or suppressed intelligence during the 1980s to serve Casey's hostile, anti-Soviet views. "Gates's role . . . was to corrupt the process and ethics of intelligence," charged one former CIA division chief in the Office of Soviet Analysis. "He was Casey's filter . . . he pandered to Casey's agenda."

Gates, whose experience was in the Directorate of Intelligence—the "white" side of the agency, not in clandestine services—acknowledged the criticism that he had misjudged events in the Soviet Union. He also shot back at his critics, describing the CIA's army of analysts as "close-minded, smug, arrogant," and prone to "flabby, complacent thinking and questionable assumptions." Gates won confirmation in the end, but the glimpse the American people were given of the bitter, internal fighting in an agency once regarded to be among the nation's elite foreign policy institutions did little to build confidence in its ability to deal imaginatively and aggressively with the emerging post-Cold War agenda.[9]

Management and Oversight of Covert Actions

A related thread running throughout the many inquiries into intelligence operations is how to exercise control over covert operations. At the level of the presidential subsystem this is the responsibility of the National Security Council. Through its specialized committees—variously called the "208 Committee," the "40 Committee," or simply the Special Coordination or Principals Committee—the NSC apparatus is ultimately responsible for approving covert actions and seeing that they meet applicable legal regulations (such as the prohibition against assassination of foreign political leaders).

Since the 1970s, Congress has been determined to pinpoint more precisely responsibility for the initiation and monitoring of covert operations. The Hughes-Ryan Amendment to the 1974 Foreign Assistance Act (repealed by the 1980 Intelligence Oversight Act) required that the president certify to Congress (that is, "find") that an executive-approved covert action is "important to the national interests of the United

States." The law required that the DCI inform Congress of the ***presidential finding*** in a "timely manner." In practice, the requirement meant informing the House and Senate committees on intelligence, armed services, appropriations, and foreign affairs and relations. Theoretically this meant that anywhere from roughly forty-five to two hundred members of Congress and their staffs could be knowledgeable about impending covert actions. The 1980 Intelligence Oversight Act cut the number of committees to only two. A widespread belief that Congress cannot keep a secret underlay the determination to cut the number.

The process of informing Congress did not have to be completed prior to implementating the covert action, however (within twenty-four hours became the understanding). The concept of ***plausible denial*** stimulated the requirement. Plausible denial means that the president is not apprised of current or pending covert actions in order to save him or her from the possible embarrassment of a "blown" operation. Secretary of State Kissinger testified before Congress that from 1972 to 1974 President Nixon personally and directly approved all covert operations, and that he believed with "almost certain knowledge" that the same had been true previously (House Select Committee on Intelligence, cited in *Final Report of the Select Committee to Study Governmental Operations with Respect to Intelligence Activities* 1976, I). Other testimony before Congress, however, indicated that "one means of protecting the president from embarrassment was not to tell him about certain covert operations, at least formally. . . . The concept of 'plausible denial' was taken in an almost literal sense: 'The government was authorized to do certain things that the president was not advised of'" (*Final Report of the Select Committee to Study Governmental Operations with Respect to Intelligence Activities* 1976, I).

Plausible denial surfaced again during the Iran-*contra* affair, as hearings before Congress demonstrated that some of those involved, notably National Security Adviser John Poindexter, undertook actions in the president's name without his explicit knowledge. "Although convinced the president would approve the use of proceeds from the Iranian arms sales for the *contras* as an 'implementation' of his policy, Poindexter 'made a very deliberate decision not to ask the president' so that he could 'insulate [him] from the decision and provide some future deniability'" (Treverton 1990, citing testimony before Congress).

Available evidence suggests other ways in which top-level management of covert operations by the nation's elected officials has been lax. The Senate's extensive inquiry in the mid-1970s into the intelligence community found, for example, that verbal checks by telephone rather than extensive face-to-face discussions were used to approve proposals. When formal meetings and extended discussions did occur, they were directed primarily at new innovations rather than thorough examinations of ongoing projects. During 1975, for example, the 40 Committee met nine times to discuss Angola (compared with one National Security Council meeting on the subject), and an Interagency Working Group on Angola met twenty-four times between August 1975 and January 1976 (*Final Report of the Select Committee to Study Governmental Operations with Respect to Intelligence Activities* 1976, I, 55).

And the tendency continued, despite the Senate's intensive probe and blistering final report on the absence of meaningful controls on intelligence actions (and abuses). As one analyst observed in commenting on the Carter administration, "A tendency reportedly has grown within the CIA to forward only a few broad covert action categories to the president and make in-house decisions on all the supposedly routine ones. Although these routine operations are allegedly offsprings of earlier presidential findings, this permits the agency to by-pass the White House and Congress" (Johnson 1980, 148). In all, the number of specific covert operations subjected to top-level interagency scrutiny appears to have been small (see also Johnson 1989; Treverton 1987).

The scope of the presidential finding that certifies covert actions to Congress, as required by the 1980 Intelligence Oversight Act, can have an important impact on their control. In particular, whether findings are conceived in broad or narrow terms is a matter of concern to both Congress and the executive branch. Stansfield Turner, DCI during the Carter administration, explains:

> Under a broad finding, an operation can be expanded considerably; with a narrow one, the CIA has to go back to the president to obtain a revised finding if there is any change of scope. The Congress is wary of broad findings; they can easily be abused. The CIA is afraid of narrow findings; they can be a nuisance. What has evolved is a working understanding that whenever the activity being carried out under a finding is widened past the original description to the Congress, the CIA will advise the committee. (Turner 1985, 169; see also Holt 1995)

Even in this respect, however, there is room for interpretation and possible abuse. Take the issue of the CIA's mining of Nicaragua's harbors in 1984.

> On January 31, 1984, DCI William Casey met with the House Intelligence committee and mentioned the mining, though the meeting was primarily about releasing funds for the overall *contra* project. The House committee apparently did not share its information with its Senate colleagues. . . .
> Casey first met with the full Senate Intelligence committee on March 8, for over an hour, but this meeting too dealt primarily with authorizing the release of funds, over which the Intelligence committee was fighting a jurisdictional battle with appropriations. Only one sentence dealt with the mining, and it, like the rest of the briefing, was delivered in Casey's inimitable mumble. Many on the committee did not learn of the mining until a month later, and then almost by accident. (Treverton 1990, 83)

Technically Casey nodded to the letter of the law with his reference to what became a politically explosive covert operation, but the episode angered even Republican members of Congress, such as Senator Barry Goldwater (see also Chapter 12), who had supported the administration's desire to return covert actions into more vigorous service of the nation's foreign policy. This was because Casey's attitude seemed to flaunt the very idea that covert actions are subject to democratic governance by the nation's election officials, however difficult that may sometimes be.

The Iran-*contra* revelations reinforced Congress's uneasiness about its oversight responsibilities with respect to covert actions. It now insisted that all presidential findings approving covert actions and all significant changes in them be made in writing. And it pushed to be notified of such operations within specified time periods, thus closing the loophole the Reagan administration had used to ignore Congress as it pursued its Iranian initiative and support of the *contras*. Only by closing the loophole could Congress "have some input in the final decision instead of being informed of a fait accompli" (Holt 1995), but the Bush administration thwarted the drive. How best to control clandestine operations thus remains a troublesome and contentious issue.

An inherent tension exists between the principle of democratic governance, which depends on access to information so that citizens can make informed decisions, and the secrecy that surrounds the collection of intelligence and covert intelligence operations. Clearly policymakers must demand the best available information about the present and future status, capabilities, and intentions of foreign powers if they are to protect the nation's security and welfare, as their constitutional obligations require. During the Cold War, however, this often meant trimming at the edges of citizens' political and civil rights, and it certainly urged the secrecy anathema to the democratic responsibility of the nation's citizens. Critics asked at the time what policy making behind closed doors portended for the democratic control of foreign policy making. Their question remains: Can a democratic society long absolve itself from responsibility for the conduct of its government officials without also running the risk of losing sight of who is serving whom, for what purpose, and in pursuit of what ideals? The question goes to the heart of a fundamental and persistent democratic dilemma.

Economic Agencies: Agents of Political Economy

The State and Defense Departments are the preeminent executive departments concerned with foreign policy and national security. In a complex and economically interdependent world, however, their jurisdiction, particularly the former's, impinges upon and is infringed upon by other executive departments whose policy responsibilities spill over into the international arena. A brief look at four essentially domestically oriented departments that are also concerned with foreign economic affairs provides additional evidence about the complexities of the foreign affairs government and its role in making and implementing American foreign policy.

Department of the Treasury

Concern for the position of the U.S. dollar in the international monetary system gives Treasury a keen interest in international affairs. Its responsibilities include tax policy, tariffs, the balance of trade and payments, exchange rate adjustments, and the public debt. Thus Treasury is the principal department in which domestic and international financial and fiscal policy recommendations are formulated. Stephen D. Cohen (1994) describes the ascendancy of the Treasury Department to a position of power in the area of international economic policy making as "the outstanding organizational feature of U.S. international economic policy since the end of World War II." He attributes Treasury's "ascendency to power" to three overarching factors: "the relative international decline of U.S. economic strength, as measured in the deterioration of the U.S. balance of payments and recurring dollar weaknesses; the increased impact of the external sector on domestic economic policy management; and the increased interest of the government in achieving a broad range of economic policy goals."

The importance of the Treasury Department has often brought the secretary of the treasury, who serves as the chief financial officer of the United States, into the most intimate circle of presidential advisers, where he has been able to influence foreign as well as domestic policy making. The roster of influentials would begin with Alexander Hamilton, the nation's first treasury secretary. In the past half-century it would George M. Humphrey, Douglas Dillon, John Connally, William Simon, Michael Blumenthal, G. William Miller, James A. Baker, Nicholas F. Brady, and Lloyd Bentsen, among others.

The Treasury Department's importance manifests itself in various ways. The secretary has often been proposed as a statutory member of the National Security Council, for example, where he typically participates. He also was a member of the Clinton adminstration's National Economic Council and chaired major White House economic policy-coordinating bodies in previous administrations. Other key roles include the secretary's duties as the U.S. governor of the International Monetary Fund, the World Bank, and the Inter-American, Asian, and African development banks. Those assignments give the Treasury secretary and Department a major voice in the often contentious decisions regarding United States participation in, and the level of contributions to, multilateral lending institutions, and in the complex issues involved in maintaining and operating of the international monetary system.

The office of the assistant secretary for international affairs is the main unit within Treasury that carries out the department's international responsibilities. During the Clinton administration it also was more actively engaged in shaping trade policy than during the Reagan and Bush presidencies. It is organized into subunits responsible for monetary affairs, developing nations, trade and investment policy, and Arabian Peninsula affairs. Through these units the office assists the secretary of the treasury and the under secretary for international affairs in the formulation and execution of international financial, monetary, commercial, energy, and trade policies and programs. The office also "backstops" the secretary's roles as cochair of the U.S.-Saudi Arabian Joint Commission on Economic Cooperation, the U.S.-Israel Joint Committee for Investment and Trade, the U.S.-China Joint Economic Committee, and chair of the National Advisory Council on International Monetary and Financial Policies.

Other units within the Treasury Department include the Bureau of Alcohol, Tobacco, and Firearms, the United States Customs Service, and the United States Secret Service. Each performs limited intelligence activities relevant to foreign affairs, as noted earlier.

Department of Commerce

The Commerce Department is specially concerned with foreign economic policy issues that relate to the expansion and protection of American commerce abroad. Unlike the secretary of the treasury, however, the secretary of commerce and the Commerce Department as a whole historically have not been principal actors in foreign economic policy making. Instead, as indicated in Chapter 10, the United States Trade Representative plays the lead role in the *development* of trade policy. Since 1980, however, when the government's trade-related responsibilities were reorganized, the Commerce Department has been the principal agency with *operating* responsibilities in the trade area (other than agricultural trade).

Specific trade responsibilities of the Commerce Department include administration of countervailing duty and antidumping statutes,[10] foreign commercial representation and export promotion, trade policy analysis, and foreign compliance with trade agreements. Those duties are discharged by the International Trade Administration, headed by the under secretary for international trade, whose charge relates to issues of import administration, international policy and programs, and trade development. A second under secretary discharges responsibilities relating to export administration, including licensing of high-technology exports and nuclear nonproliferation issues.

As we saw in detail in Chapter 7 and noted again earlier in this chapter, the Clinton adminstration more than any of its predecessors was determined to fuse domestic and international economic policy into a single venue. Clinton's Commerce Secretary, Ronald H. Brown, a former chair of the National Democratic Committee, was an especially vigorous—and successful—advocate of using the Commerce Department to expand America's influence around the world, particularly among the "Big Emerging Markets," most of which are in Asia (Stremlau 1994–1995). Presidential support is necessary for the success of Commerce's assertive strategy, but it is facilitated by the fact that (since 1980) the Commerce Department, not the State Department, is responsible for U.S. commercial representation abroad. The ***U.S. and Foreign Commercial Service*** seeks to enhance the competitiveness of American businesses abroad through a network of nearly four dozen district offices in the United States and posts located in more than sixty countries throughout the world. This brings together in one organization those seeking to encourage American firms to sell abroad and those who deal with the potential buyers of American products.

Although the Clinton administration enhanced the role of the Commerce Department in trade policy implementation, historically it has been a comparatively weak actor in the development of foreign economic policy. In part this reflects an aversion to close ties between the manufacturing sector and government bureaucrats. Thus, as former Commerce Secretary Malcolm Baldrige (1983), observed, "trade is the only major cabinet function where policy is made in one department (the United States trade representative) and carried out in another (Department of Commerce)." As a result, "trade policy has to be 'brokered' among the other cabinet departments, instead of being advocated." The Reagan administration proposed to bridge the anomaly by creating a new Department of International Trade and Industry (the acronym for the proposed department, DITI, bore striking resemblance to Japan's Ministry of International Trade and Industry, MITI, after which the new agency was presumably modeled), but it failed to gain congressional support during Reagan's first term and anything more than lip service in his second. Instead, Congress moved to enhance the role of the U.S. Trade Representative in the development of trade policy, which remains the case. Thus, even an activist Commerce Department remains more an implementor than designer of new directions in U.S. trade policy.

Department of Agriculture

In 1994 the United States exported $45 billion of domestically produced agricultural products, making it one of the largest producers for the world marketplace. Exports of particular products, such as grain and soybeans, also account for a substantial share of total world exports. Ensuring continued access to overseas markets was a priority goal of American negotiators during the Uruguay Round of GATT trade talks, as we saw in Chapter 7, in part because of the criticality of the export market to the welfare of American farmers. Necessarily, therefore, the Department of Agriculture has a major stake in the administration of foreign economic policy.

Particular departmental interests include promoting the sale of agricultural commodities abroad, including the sale or distribution of surplus commodities owned by the government under Public Law 480 and the Food for Peace Program, allocating import quotas for certain agricultural commodities, and participating in international negotiations relating to world trade in agricultural products.

The *Foreign Agricultural Service (FAS)*, operating under the authority of the under secretary for international affairs and commodity programs, is the principal subdivision of the department concerned with international affairs. Its primary purpose is promoting sales of American agricultural commodities overseas. Toward that end, it maintains agricultural counselors and attachés in more than seventy-five American embassies abroad and a parallel group of international trade specialists in Washington. The FAS is responsible for formulating, administering, and coordinating Agriculture Department policies and programs as they relate to multilateral conventions and organizations, such as the World Trade Organization (WTO) and the Food and Agriculture Organization (FAO) of the United Nations, and for providing support for U.S. agricultural representatives during international negotiations. Its overseas attachés also act as a worldwide agricultural intelligence and reporting system on supply, demand, and commercial trade conditions relating to agricultural products.

FAS also manages (in cooperation with the Agency for International Development) agricultural functions under Public Law 480, the Food for Peace program, designed to meet immediate needs in countries of the Global South and improve their economies in the long run (while also enhancing market opportunities for American exporters). Included under PL 480 are long-term credit sales for American dollars, whereby the government dispenses commodity surpluses it purchases to support the American farmer. Humanitarian donations to foreign governments, voluntary relief agencies, and international institutions, such as the World Food Program of the United Nations, are included.

Department of Labor

Gathering information, proffering advice, administering selected programs, and participating in international negotiations (especially in the International Labor Organization [ILO], the World Trade Organization, and the Organization for Economic Cooperation and Development)—those, too, are the international affairs functions of the Labor Department, but with a view toward their importance for the American wage earner rather than the agricultural, business, or financial communities. They are carried out by the Bureau of International Labor Affairs headed by the deputy under secretary for international affairs. Among other things, the department's authority traditionally has carried with it a special concern for immigrant labor and for assessing the impact of trade agreements, such as Nafta, on American workers. It also has involved Labor with the State Department in the provision of labor attachés for assignment abroad and with the Agency for International Development in the execution of technical assistance activities overseas. The department also bears responsibility for the administration of the trade adjustment assistance programs for workers under the Trade Act of 1974, which provides restitution to those adversely affected by foreign trade competition.

Administrative Structures and the Politics of Policy Making   . . . .

The executive agencies that comprise the foreign affairs government are so numerous and multifaceted that no brief description could adequately capture either the breadth of their interests or the depth of their involvement in matters of foreign policy. As a way of explicating governmental sources of American policy, however, the description provided here demonstrates a distinguishing characteristic of American foreign policy making—decision making by and within a disparate set of exceedingly large and complex organizational structures. Effecting control over them and dealing with the consequences of their behavior are important presidential concerns for political, legal, and other reasons. Still, presidents depend on the organizations and agencies comprising the foreign affairs government, without which it would be impossible to accomplish their foreign policy agendas.

The organizations comprising the second concentric circle of policy making also often have their own agendas, as we have seen in this chapter. And they have the capacity to derail presidential preferences, an idea we will explore in more detail in Chapter 13. Part of that derives from the comparative political resources of each. During the Cold War these placed the Defense Department in a preeminent position, in part because of its size but also more immediately because its tentacles reach deep into the American economy, society, and politics. The State Department, on the other hand, suffers from a lack of identity within the American polity and a corresponding domestic constituency to support its foreign affairs role. Legally it is preeminent; politically it is not. It represents a broad and diffuse constituency—"the American people"—while other departments (Defense, Commerce, Treasury, Labor, and Agriculture) draw support from clearly identifiable domestic groups. Little wonder that "the first among equals" often finds itself out of sync when critical issues that go beyond traditional diplomacy shape the choices presidents and their advisers make.

The CIA does not fit neatly into the picture, as it enjoys no identifiable domestic support but clearly has exercised a critical foreign policy role during the course of its history. In this case the urgency of the Cold War competition clearly explains its prominent role in the foreign affairs government. The obsolescence of that role, as we have seen, now also raises important questions about its continued utility.

Congress frequently is an intimate part of the complex interagency politicking in which government agencies often become engaged and has the capacity to affect their relative political influence within the executive branch. The convenient partnership between certain bureaucracies and their congressional allies helps explain, for example, the political functions of bureaucratic "leaks" to the press. They become mechanisms for cuing others within the political system, such as Congress, of impending changes in policies or programs which they can then attack or defend. In the political struggle between Congress and the president, however, the president is generally in the more commanding position when it comes to foreign policy. Exploring why that is so is the subject of the next chapter.

NOTES

1. Technically, AID is a subsidiary unit of the International Development Cooperation Agency (IDCA), the government's coordinating unit for U.S. economic relations with developing nations. The Overseas Private Investment Corporation (OPIC) is the other component of the IDCA. Its seeks to promote economic development in the Global South by encouraging private U.S. investments and assisting U.S. firms who wish to invest there.

2. The legal mandate that the ambassador supervise the activities of other agencies attached to U.S. field missions has been described as a "polite fiction" (Pringle 1977–1978). Even within the State Department the power of ambassadors has declined as modern telecommunications and travel have increased Washington's capacity to handle a broad range of foreign affairs details. As one Foreign Service officer commented wryly upon resigning his post in the Moscow embassy in 1980, "We don't need an ambassador in Moscow . . . because he has nothing to do" (cited in Rubin 1985). On the other hand, both law and executive orders "give ambassadors (who report to the secretary of state) authority over American government personnel abroad. If the secretary of state objects to a particular intelligence activity, only the president can override him. Secretaries of state have objected and have made it stick" (Holt 1995).

3. Female case workers in the CIA launched a similar complaint against their agency in the early 1990s.

4. The 1980 Foreign Service Act specified that ambassadorial appointments will "normally" go to career officers, but the law has had little practical effect. Since the 1960s the number of political (noncareer) appointments has averaged about 30 percent. Carter had fewer than any other president (an average of 24 percent during his presidency), and Kennedy and Reagan the most (33 percent). Midway through the Clinton presidency the proportion stood at 31 percent (data provided by the Presidential Appointments Staff, U.S. Department of State).

5. Several factors converged to give impetus to the defense reform movement, which Congress spearheaded. A principal issue was the quality of advice that the joint chiefs provided civilian leaders (which Harold Brown once described as "worse than nothing") and, more broadly, their capacity to command the separate and powerful military services. General David C. Jones, chairman of the Joint Chiefs of Staff from 1978 to 1982, became a catalyst to the reform movement when, in his final testimony before Congress, he charged that "the fundamental balance of influence within the defense establishment is oriented too much toward the individual services," and concluded that "fundamental defense deficiencies cannot be solved with dollars alone." A year later, General Edward C. Meyer, chief of staff of the army, sounded a similar theme: "If we were trying to convince an enemy that we were able to go to war with a system that works like this, he would laugh." Robert W. Komer, under secretary of defense for policy in the Carter administration, predicted that "a system which is so inadequate in peacetime will perform even worse in crisis or war." A 1985 study by the staff of the Senate Armed Services Committee confirmed that prognosis when it blamed poor interservice coordination for the failure of the 1980 Iranian hostage rescue mission and for shortcomings in the 1983 invasion of Grenada. These events, plus the truck bombing of marine headquarters in Beirut in 1983, were the principal forces behind Congress's determination to take the lead in defense reform.

6. There are five geographically oriented unified commands, the Atlantic, Central, European, Pacific, and Southern, and four others organized by function, the Space, Special Operations, Strategic, and Transportation commands.

7. Paralleling the earlier discussion of the State Department's bureaucratic subculture, Rubin (1985) observes that "Because INR is seen as a specialized and research-oriented bureau outside the policy-making chain of command, many FSOs consider an INR assignment detrimental to their careers."

8. The contraction of intelligence support became a matter of public controversy when President Reagan in 1984 asserted that "the near destruction of our intelligence capability" was partly responsible for the car bombing of the U.S. embassy in Beirut in that year. He later explained to Jimmy Carter, who demanded an apology for the comment, that he had not meant to suggest that "you or your administration was responsible for the decline in intelligence-gathering capability" or for the Beirut bombing. A White House spokesman later suggested that Reagan had been talking about "a decade-long trend and climate in Congress." Senator Moynihan took umbrage, responding that the comment "undermines—I am prepared to say betrays—almost a decade of sustained bipartisan efforts in Congress to reconstruct an intelligence community whose budgets had run down steadily through the first half of the 1970s and began to rise sharply in the second" (see also Pickett 1985).

9. Once he became director, Gates launched an internal study of the "politicization" of intelligence, which he defined as "deliberately distorting analysis or judgments to favor a preferred line of thinking irrespective of evidence." The task force found a "disturbing" degree of politicization within the agency but also concluded it was less pervasive than many critics alleged.

10. Countervailing duties are import taxes that offset the special advantages that imports have due to subsidies provided by the exporting nation; they are designed to place subsidized imports on the same price footing as other imports and domestic products. Dumping means selling exports for prices below those in the exporter's own domestic market. Antidumping regulations are designed to make up the difference between the exporter's price and the foreign market value when the selling price is less than the fair value.

SUGGESTIONS FOR FURTHER READING

Bamford, James. *The Puzzle Palace.* New York: Penguin, 1983.

Cohen, Stephen D. *The Making of United States International Economic Policy: Principles, Problems, and Proposals for Reform,* 4th ed. Westport, Conn.: Praeger, 1994.

Feaver, Peter Douglas. *Guarding the Guardians: Civilian Control of Nuclear Weapons in the United States.* Ithaca, N.Y.: Cornell University Press, 1992.

Gates, Robert M. "The CIA and American Foreign Policy," *Foreign Affairs* 66 (Winter 1987–1988): 215–30.

Hendrickson, David C. *Reforming Defense: The State of American Civil-Military Relations.* Baltimore: Johns Hopkins University Press, 1988.

Holt, Pat M. *Secret Intelligence and Public Policy: A Dilemma of Democracy.* Washington, D.C.: CQ Press, 1995.

Ikenberry, G. John, David A. Lake, and Michael Mastanduno, eds. *The State and American Foreign Economic Policy.* Ithaca, N.Y.: Cornell University Press, 1988.

Johnson, Loch H. *America's Secret Power: The CIA in a Democratic Society*. New York: Oxford University Press, 1989.

Kohn, Richard. "Out of Control: The Crisis in Civil-Military Relations," *The National Interest* 35 (Spring 1994): 3–17.

McGlen, Nancy E., and Meredith Reid Sarkees. *Women in Foreign Policy: The Insiders*. New York: Routledge, 1993.

Melbourne, Roy M. *Conflict and Crisis: A Foreign Service Story*. Lanham, Md.: University Press of America, 1992.

Rubin, Barry. *Secrets of State: The State Department and the Struggle over U.S. Foreign Policy*. New York: Oxford University Press, 1985.

Yarmolinsky, Adam. *The Military Establishment: Its Impact on American Society*. New York: Harper & Row, 1971.

CHAPTER 12

• • •

THE ROLE OF CONGRESS IN FOREIGN POLICY MAKING

• • •

To me bipartisan foreign policy means a mutual effort . . . to unite our official voice at the water's edge so that America speaks with maximum authority against those who would divide and conquer us and the free world.

President Bill Clinton, 1994

The preferred stance is to let the president make the decisions and, if it goes well, praise him, and if it doesn't, criticize him.

House Foreign Affairs Committee Chair Lee Hamilton, 1994

"The president proposes, Congress disposes." That simple aphorism has long described Congress's role in foreign policy making. Representative Lee Hamilton's description of Congress's "preferred stance" reflects that viewpoint. Thus many analysts see Congress's role as primarily a negative one—to function as a public critic of the president and otherwise place limits on presidential behavior.

In the decade following U.S. withdrawal from Vietnam, however, Congress also sought actively to shape various policies and policy making procedures, as illustrated by the following:

- In 1970 Congress "repealed" the Gulf of Tonkin Resolution that gave President Johnson, as he interpreted it, a "blank check" for prosecuting undeclared war in Southeast Asia.

- In 1973 Congress overrode President Nixon's veto to write the War Powers Resolution into law, thus requiring the president to consult Congress before dispatching troops abroad.

- In 1974 Congress embargoed arms sales to Turkey in retaliation for its invasion of Cyprus, despite the objectives of the Ford administration.

- In 1974 Congress refused to permit the president to extend most favored nation (MFN) trade treatment to the Soviet Union by linking MFN to the emigration of Soviet Jews.

- In 1975 Congress ensured American withdrawal from Vietnam by denying the president authority to provide the South Vietnamese government emergency military aid to forestall its imminent collapse in the face of communist forces.

- In 1976 Congress prohibited continued CIA expenditures to bolster anti-Marxist forces fighting in Angola.

- In 1978 the Senate adopted a reservation to the Panama Canal neutrality treaty permitting the United States to use military force to reopen the canal if it were closed for any reason.

- In 1980 Congress passed legislation asserting its right to receive prior executive branch notice of impending covert intelligence activities.

- In 1982 Congress denied the Defense Department and the CIA funds for the purpose of overthrowing Nicaragua's government.

- In 1983 Congress invoked provisions of the War Powers Resolution to limit the time military forces could remain in Lebanon.

- In 1985 Congress cut from two hundred to fifty the number of land-based MX missiles to be deployed in fixed silos.

- In 1986 Congress overrode a presidential veto to place economic sanctions on South Africa.

These examples of congressional assertiveness in response to the so-called "imperial presidency" of the Vietnam era reflect Congress's effort to ensure itself a greater voice in foreign policy making. By writing certain conditions into legislation and otherwise placing a distinctively legislative stamp on American foreign policy, a sometimes submissive Congress raised its voice in shaping the nation's foreign affairs, often at the expense of the president. As Under Secretary of State William D. Rogers lamented in 1979, "foreign policy has become almost synonymous with lawmaking. The result is to place a straitjacket of legislation around the manifold complexity of our relations with other nations." Ronald Reagan echoed that sentiment in 1985, exclaiming, "We have got to get to the point where we can run a foreign policy without a committee of 535 telling us what we can do." Indeed, by this time critics charged that Congress, not the president, was acting in an "imperial" fashion (Jones and Marini 1988; see also Califano 1994).

The Reagan administration challenged a broad array of reforms put into place by the "imperial Congress" to assert its own foreign policy prerogatives (Warburg 1989). The trend continued into the early 1990s, as the Bush administration adopted an almost defiant posture toward Congress's foreign policy role. Bush "wielded the threat of a veto effectively, and even when signing important foreign policy legislation, made claims of executive power which implied that Congress did not have the same legislative authority in foreign policy as in other fields and that seemed to ignore the role of Congress in foreign policy granted by the Constitution" (*Congress and Foreign Policy 1991* 1992). The high point occurred in 1991: In signing the authorization to use force against Iraq passed by Congress, Bush denied that it in any way altered the president's prerogatives to use force when and how he alone saw fit. Two years later, in December 1992, Bush sent U.S. ground troops to Somalia without an explicit congressional authorization.

The pendulum began to swing back following the Persian Gulf War. Congress passed legislation broadening the agenda for negotiation of a North American Free

Trade Agreement to include such matters as environmental protection. It adopted conditions for continuing China's most favored nation (MFN) trade status (twice vetoed by Bush). It held hearings on U.S. policy toward Iraq prior to the Persian Gulf War that seemed to vindicate Congress's position that sanctions should have been imposed on Iraq long before Bush applied them. It proposed to initiate sanctions against those who would assist Iran or Iraq in developing weapons of mass destruction or advanced conventional weapons. It took steps to curtail the new interventionism on behalf of humanitarian values, notably in Somalia. It recommended lifting the trade embargo against Vietnam. It terminated funding for the enforcement of a United Nations embargo on the sale of arms to Bosnia and later demanded that the arms embargo be lifted. And it launched a determined effort to hamstring American participation in future UN peacekeeping operations.

In this chapter we examine Congress's role in American foreign policy making. We begin with a brief look at the record of executive-legislative foreign policy interactions since World War II and continue by examining the institutional characteristics of Congress that favor its more passive role vis-à-vis the executive. We then examine legislative prerogatives and practices in three areas in which the Constitution assigns Congress especially formidable foreign policy powers—treaties, war, and money. Implicit throughout is whether the timeworn aphorism that "the president proposes, Congress disposes" retains its pertinence in the post-Cold War world or whether it requires rethinking.

Congress and the President: The Historical Record . . . .

Although Congress seeks to assert its foreign policy authority in various ways, it has always been wary of restricting presidential flexibility in foreign policy making. As Senator Richard Lugar remarked when Congress considered its response to the Clinton administration's dispatch of troops to Haiti in 1994, "Any resolution that we can adopt won't really bind the administration. There'll always be an escape hatch." Congress's reluctance to bind the president contributes to the applicability of the "proposes-disposes" characterization of the overall relationship between the president and Congress. Still, the precise nature of the relationship is more complex than this simple description suggests. Often the president receives political credit for ideas born on Capitol Hill when they are brought to fruition. Moreover, presidential dominance was more evident before the Vietnam buildup in 1965 than since. In fact, extending the chronology suggested by Frans R. Bax (1977), six comparatively distinct phases characterize executive-legislative relations during the past half-century.

Phases in the Relationship between Congress and the President

Accommodation describes the pattern of relations from roughly 1943 to 1951. The nation's goals of globalism, anticommunism, and containment of perceived Soviet expansionism were forged during that time through a variety of specific foreign policy initiatives and programs in which Congress willingly participated. Bipartisanship (discussed more fully below) captures the essence of the accommodative atmosphere of the period.

Accommodation was followed by *antagonism*, a phase that lasted from 1951 to 1955. McCarthyism fell within this period. So, too, did congressional recriminations over who "lost" China, disenchantment with "limited" war in Korea and the firing of a general (Douglas MacArthur) who independently sought to expand that war, and growing concern over the cost of foreign aid and Truman's commitment of troops to Europe. Efforts by the Senate to curb presidential treaty-making powers symbolized the antagonisms of the period.

A period of congressional foreign policy *acquiescence* followed during the decade ending in 1965. In was during this period that Congress passed the "area resolutions" granting presidents broad authority to deal with conflict in the Middle East, Berlin, Cuba, the China straits, and Vietnam as they alone saw fit. A bipartisan spirit was again dominant as Congress agreed with most of the specific foreign policy decisions made by the three presidents who held office during the period. Any lingering doubts Congress may have had about some of them were "simply swallowed," as Congress preferred "not to share the responsibility of decision with the president" (Bax 1977). By backing presidential decisions in a manner that legitimated them to the public, Congress helped to build a broad-based, anticommunist foreign policy consensus.

Presidents, for their part, encouraged the acquiescent congressional mood, since a passive role made consultation with or deference to "mere legislators" unnecessary. Following the massive Vietnam buildup in 1965, however, congressional docility began to dissipate. Highly publicized Senate Foreign Relations Committee hearings, chaired by J. William Fulbright, fed the growing perception that the war in Vietnam was a major mistake. Still, Congress refused to exercise the constitutional prerogatives at its disposal to constrain presidential behavior. Congress was in a state of *ambiguity*.

Richard Nixon's decision to expand the Vietnam War into Cambodia in the spring of 1970 transformed ambiguity into *acrimony*. During the next three years the Senate passed a variety of measures to curtail the president's ability to keep or use American troops in Indochina, but the House typically refused to support them. However, in 1971 both chambers adopted language that proscribed the use of funds authorized or appropriated by Congress "to finance the introduction of United States ground combat troops into Cambodia, or to provide United States advisors to or for Cambodian military forces in Cambodia." Significantly, the bill was passed only *after* the spring offensive of 1970 had been completed. Other efforts to restrict expenditures were also largely symbolic. Nevertheless, Congress had begun to participate in the termination of America's role in the tragic Indochina conflict.

The high point of congressional acrimony occurred in 1973, when Congress passed the War Powers Resolution over President Nixon's veto. As noted earlier, for a least a decade after this, congressional *assertiveness*—though subject to ebbs and flows—best describes how Congress sought to be heard and treated as a coequal in foreign policy making. Disenchantment with Vietnam and, later, Watergate gave rise to the changed and changing congressional mood. Revelations a decade later of executive abuses in Central America rekindled the embers of disenchantment.

The shape of executive-congressional foreign policy contention since Vietnam is arguably different from that of earlier historical periods. As one long-time Capitol Hill staff member concluded, "In no previous era of congressional ascendancy has the

United States borne the burdens of world leadership. And in no previous era of presidential counterreformation has the White House confronted such a formidable array of procedural weapons at the legislature's disposal" (Warburg 1989). Nonetheless, the impact of Vietnam and subsequent events in moving Congress from acquiescence toward assertiveness deserves emphasis. Acquiescence is possible only when a broad national consensus exists on the general purposes of policy and when the specific means the president chooses to pursue them are generally successful (Bax 1977). Those conditions crumbled in the wake of Vietnam. The experience borne of that war thus affirms an earlier historical pattern: An assertive congressional mood typically has coincided with and followed each major American war. The post-Civil War Reconstruction era, the post-World War I "return to normalcy" period, and the years following the Korean War provide striking parallels. Concerted congressional efforts to preempt presidential foreign policy prerogatives followed each of them.

The rekindling of congressional foreign policy activity following the Persian Gulf War fits this well-established pattern. More broadly, the end of the Cold War invites greater participation by Congress in shaping an American foreign policy for the new world order. "As perceptions of external threat have receded," political scientist James M. Lindsay (1994a) observes, "the American public is now more likely to tolerate legislative dissent on foreign affairs. Faced with fewer electoral costs in opposing the president, members of Congress are more likely to deal the president public rebuffs."

Bipartisanship

The proposition that "politics stops at the water's edge"—long a part of the nation's cherished political mythology—was a sure victim of the changed and changing nature of executive-legislative relations in the post-Vietnam Cold War era. If Lindsay is correct, it will continue to be a casualty in the post-Cold War era.

Bipartisanship is the practical application of the "water's edge" consensual ideal. As noted, it is often used to describe the cordial and cooperative relationship between Congress and the executive during much of the Roosevelt, Truman, and Eisenhower presidencies—the period when the United States rejected isolationism, embraced internationalism, and developed the postwar strategy for containment of the Soviet Union. Congress and the president often acted as partners in these efforts, especially on matters involving Europe. The famous conversion of Arthur Vandenberg, Republican senator from Michigan who coined the "water's edge" aphorism, symbolized the emergent bipartisan spirit. Once a staunch isolationist, Vandenberg used his position as chair of the powerful Senate Foreign Relations Committee after World War II to engineer congressional support for NATO and the Marshall Plan.

To be sure, partisan and ideological differences between the president and Congress and within the latter were never absent during the heyday of bipartisanship. Republican Senator Robert A. Taft, for example, personified many of the elements of congressional antagonism between 1951 and 1955. He opposed NATO, criticized Truman for failing to declare war in Korea and concentrating too much power in the White House, and worried that containment would result in continuing U.S. involvement in world affairs, which he opposed. His neoisolationist sentiment and its associated criticisms were a minority voice, however—one that the anticommunist consensus muted as Congress moved from a posture of antagonism toward the president in the early 1950s to acquiescence in the latter half of the decade. Not until the Vietnam War challenged the premises of the anticommunist consensus were the premises of bipartisanship itself also questioned. Now foreign policy increasingly became the object of factional and partisan dispute. No longer did politics stop at the water's edge.

Numerous policy issues illustrate the increasingly antagonistic congressional attitude that emerged in the wake of Vietnam and Watergate. Prominent among them are Congress's embargo of arms sales to Turkey and its denial of funds to affect political outcomes in Angola during the Ford administration; the many reservations Congress attached to the two Panama Canal treaties when they came up for ratification during the Carter administration; and the prohibition against sending foreign aid to countries that refused to abide by congressionally mandated international nuclear nonproliferation safeguards during the Reagan administration.

Presidents invariably appeal to bipartisanship to win political support for their programs. Often they use bipartisan commissions as a vehicle to that end. The commissions President Reagan appointed to seek alternative policies for Central America, strategic defense, and military base closings, are prominent examples, as is the bipartisan study of the CIA's future which the Clinton administration launched in 1995 (at Congress's insistence). George Bush also underscored the importance he attached to bipartisanship when he called in his inaugural address for "a new engagement . . . between the executive and the Congress." "There's grown a certain divisiveness," he lamented. "And our great parties have too often been far apart and untrusting of each other. It's been this way since Vietnam. That war cleaves us still." He continued, saying "A new breeze is blowing—and the old bipartisanship must be made new again." As we have noted, however, Bush was openly antagonistic toward Congress's foreign policy role. Thus "gridlock" applied to foreign as well as domestic policy during his presidency.

The urge to restore bipartisanship to foreign policy making stems from a desire to restore the halcyon mood of the early post-World War II era. Beyond this, advocates of bipartisanship see it as a vehicle promoting the policy coherence and consistency necessary to an effective foreign policy (Kissinger and Vance 1988; Winik 1989). Such a view assumes a broad-based agreement within American society about the appropriate American role in world affairs, similar to that once provided by deeply held anticommunist values. Critics, on the other hand, argue that bipartisanship is a tool used to stifle the expression of divergent viewpoints which is the heart of democratic governance (Falk 1983; Nathan and Oliver 1994). Too often, they say, its appeal is motivated by the goal of blurring the separation of powers which assigns different foreign policy roles and responsibilities to Congress and the president. As one member of Congress put it, "calls for bipartisanship usually seek to have Congress follow the president, never the opposite" (Hamilton 1988). Yet, as Justice Louis Brandeis wrote (in *Myers v. United States* 1926), the purpose of the separation-of-powers doctrine is "not to avoid friction but . . . to save the people from autocracy."

Because the bipartisan concept itself is often used for partisan purposes, its precise meaning is unclear.[1] One simple, yet useful measure is how often a majority of Republicans and Democrats agree with the president's position on foreign policy issues that come before Congress. Figure 12.1 uses this measure to trace bipartisan be-

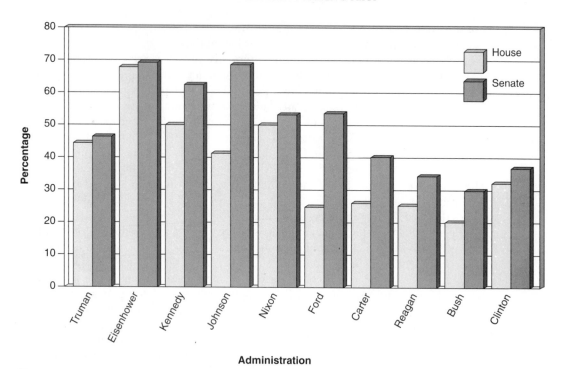

Figure 12.1 Congressional Support of Presidential Policy from Truman to Clinton
Note: Each bar represents the percentage of foreign policy votes on which a majority of both parties supported the president's position. Data for Clinton are for the 103rd Congress (1993–1994) only.
Source: Data through 1988 from James M. McCormick and Eugene R. Wittkopf, "Bipartisanship, Partisanship, and Ideology in Congressional-Executive Foreign Policy Relations, 1947–1988," *Journal of Politics* 52 (November 1990): 1085; data for the Bush and Clinton administrations compiled by McCormick and Wittkopf from various issues of the *Congressional Quarterly Weekly Report*.

havior in each house of Congress from Truman to Clinton. It shows a gradual decline in bipartisanship following the Eisenhower presidency and an especially sharp decline in the House beginning with Ford. Clearly bipartisanship is in retreat, especially since Vietnam.

Shifts in the partisan and ideological support accorded different presidents underlie these changes. During the Cold War, Democratic presidents consistently enjoyed their greatest foreign policy support not only from their own partisans but also from liberals, regardless of party. Eisenhower, a Republican president, also enjoyed support from liberal Democrats as well as from members of his own party. Since Eisenhower, however, Republican presidents have received their greatest support from conservatives and comparatively little from liberals. The changing patterns of foreign policy voting in Congress suggest that partisan attachments and ideological predispositions now reinforce one another. Before Vietnam partisanship and ideology cross-cut one another, muting differences between Congress and the president; now they magnify them. Republicans have become the party of conservative internationalism and

Democrats the party of liberal internationalism, thus bringing both parties into alignment with their postures on domestic policy.

The end of the Cold War might have been expected to moderate the partisan and ideological disputes characteristic of congressional-executive relations since Vietnam, as many of them played out in differing perceptions about how best to deal with the perceived Soviet threat. As perceptions of external threat receded, however, members of Congress also found incentives to distance themselves from presidential initiatives (Lindsay 1994a; see also McCormick and Wittkopf 1990b). Two key congressional votes in the early post-Cold War environment—one during Bush's administration, the other during Clinton's—support the latter view, thus suggesting that partisan and ideological disputes will persist, not dissipate.

The first vote came in early 1991, when the Bush administration asked Congress to support its determination to use force to evict Saddam Hussein from Kuwait. The United Nations Security Council had earlier authorized the use of force against Iraq under the collective security provisions of the UN charter. Thus Bush did not ask for a declaration of war, only to replace sanctions with force as the policy instrument. After days of often eloquent debate, on January 12 Congress gave Bush what he wanted: By a vote margin of 250 to 183 in the House and 52 to 47 in the Senate, Congress authorized the use of force against Iraq—a victory for Bush, albeit a slim one, particularly in the Senate. Indeed, it was the closest use-of-force vote since the War of 1812 against Britain. And the vote totals reveal why: Nearly all of Bush's support in the Senate came from Republicans, as only ten Senate Democrats supported the president, seven of them from the South (i.e., conservatives). On the House side, 87 percent of the president's support came from Republicans and southern Democrats. Northern Democrats opposed the president overwhelmingly. Thus the response of Congress to what was widely heralded as the first post-Cold War crisis and a "defining moment" in the emerging new world order proved to be remarkably reminiscent of the post-Vietnam past.

Clinton's victory on Nafta was clearly bipartisan and thus outwardly different from the Persian Gulf vote. Now it was the Republicans who provided the Democratic president with his greatest support, and Democratic members of Congress the least. Still, the partisan and ideological coalitions widely in evidence on previous foreign policy issues remained largely intact, as southern Democrats joined Republicans in opposition to northern Democrats (a pattern evident on several national security issues voted on later). Clinton rightly savored victory as he broke the "gridlock" that had characterized policy making during the period of divided government from 1981 to 1993, when one party controlled of the White House and the other Congress. Whether Nafta signaled a new era in congressional-executive relations remained problematic, however, as many congressional votes on other key foreign policy issues continued to fall along predictable cleavages, which the Republican victory in the 1994 congressional elections—and the return to divided government—magnified.

Congress's Foreign Policy Role: Illustrative Cases

Case studies of particular policy issues illustrate Congress's role in American foreign policy making. Here we use two such cases to show (1) how Congress uses procedure to assert its prerogatives, (2) how the perceived need to protect presidential flexibility in promoting America's world position constrains congressional assertiveness, and (3) how partisan and ideological concerns color both. The first case examines U.S. arms sales policy since the mid-1970s, the second the Reagan administration's policy toward Nicaragua and its efforts to provide aid to the *contras*.

Congress and Arms Sales Policy

The Nixon administration stimulated congressional involvement in arms sales policy. As the value of foreign military sales skyrocketed during the Nixon presidency, Congress became concerned about the potentially untoward consequences of the Nixon Doctrine, which rationalized providing sophisticated equipment to Third World countries (particularly Iran, and the Arab countries opposed to Israel). In 1975 Congress passed a law, later incorporated into the Arms Export and Control Act, requiring the executive to inform Congress of prospective major arms sales and enabling Congress to veto them within a specified time.[2] Significantly, that law stipulated that congressional disapproval need only be expressed in a concurrent resolution of the two houses of Congress, thus avoiding the threat of a presidential veto. The procedure, whose origins date to the early 1930s, is known as a ***legislative veto*** (see Fisher 1993).

In 1983 the Supreme Court ruled in the *Chadha* case that the legislative veto based on concurrent resolutions was unconstitutional.[3] Congress responded in 1986, when it decided that the enactment of a joint resolution, rather than a concurrent resolution, could block an arms sale. Since a joint resolution is subject to presidential veto, this effectively means that Congress is now able to stop a major arms sale only if a two-thirds majority in both houses votes to block it. The change substantially altered the procedural balance of power in favor of the president, who now needs only to find a third-plus-one minority in either the House or the Senate to move an arms sale forward—or the president can simply veto Congress's action. Still, Congress never exercised its powers to veto major arms sales prior to the *Chadha* ruling, nor has it successfully done so since. The possibility of congressional disapproval nonetheless has encouraged presidents to make significant alterations in controversial arms sales proposals.

Jimmy Carter pledged during the 1976 presidential campaign to restrain the excessive trade in arms in which the United States had become involved. But once in the White House, he quickly concluded that the nation's interests and commitments required continued foreign military sales. Early in his administration he exempted from his own arms restraint policies an Iranian request to purchase advanced-technology airborne warning and control system aircraft (AWACS). Congress approved the deal only after the administration agreed to strict conditions governing delivery and use of the sophisticated technology. A year later, in 1978, in what was considered a major political achievement, the administration again won congressional support for a massive arms package involving Israel, Egypt, and Saudi Arabia—but this time only after agreeing to increase the number of warplanes destined for Israel.

The Carter arms package included the sale to Saudi Arabia of F-15 aircraft, the most sophisticated jet fighters in the American arsenal; but, to secure congressional approval in the face of strong opposition by the pro-Israeli lobby, the planes were not equipped with bomb racks or air-to-air missiles. The Saudis chafed under the restrictions and repeatedly sought the additional equipment. Upon assuming office, the

Reagan administration determined that the Saudis should have the equipment, and, in addition, sought to sell them AWACS. The administration thus pitted itself against the powerful Israeli lobby and its congressional supporters, who generally concur with the view of the Israeli lobby that "arms sales to the Arabs endanger Israel, threaten the stability of the Middle East, and perpetuate the arms race" (Bard 1994; see also Crabb and Holt 1992; Tivnan 1987).

As expected, the Democratic-controlled House voted against the proposed sale. To win approval in the Senate, the White House launched an intensive campaign that targeted a handful of Senators considered maneuverable. Seven Republican senators who earlier opposed the AWACS deal now decided to switch. In a dramatic forty-eight to fifty-two vote, the Senate rejected a resolution to disapprove the arms deal. Thus Reagan won his first major foreign policy test with Congress—but the victory required the expenditure of an extraordinary amount of political capital and was secured only after the president elevated the issue to a test of the credibility of a presidential commitment. Members of Congress also learned the costs of taking on the powerful Israeli lobby, as many of the senators who supported the arms sale lost their reelection bids.

Three years later, in 1984, Reagan again faced formidable opposition to a proposed sale of portable Stinger antiaircraft missiles to Jordan and Saudi Arabia. This time, to the surprise of many, Reagan chose not to fight. Reagan's retreat "was the first time in the sixteen-year history of direct congressional involvement in arms sales that a president had withdrawn an arms sales proposal without stating that he would resubmit it to Congress at a future date" (*Congressional Quarterly Almanac 1984* 1985). Interestingly, the administration would shortly send Stingers to Saudi Arabia under the president's emergency power, thus bypassing Congress altogether. It was only the second time a president chose to circumvent Congress's role with this unusual procedure.

Reagan did fight on a third important Mideast arms package, however. Saudi Arabia was again the intended arms recipient, and again intensive White House lobbying proved necessary to save the weapons deal. In this case the effort sought to sustain a presidential veto of a measure that would have blocked a $258 million sale. The president prevailed by a single vote, when in June 1986, thirty-four members of the Senate gave Reagan the minimum number he needed to reverse an earlier decision and to allow the sale to go forward. Some who switched their votes indicated they had done so because of the president's argument that his ability to manage foreign policy was at stake. Others suggested that by deleting certain weapons from the arms package (notably Stinger missiles), their earlier objections no longer mattered. Significantly, however, the case was the first time that both houses of Congress moved to block a major arms sale, thus requiring a sustained presidential veto in order to proceed with it.

Late in 1986 press reports from the Middle East revealed that even while the administration was seeking congressional approval for the arms sale to Saudi Arabia, it also was engaged in a secret arms deal with Iran that again circumvented Congress altogether. This transaction set in motion what eventually became known as the Iran-*contra* affair. As details came to light, Congress's attention riveted on possible violations of congressional rules prohibiting covert actions against the Sandinista regime and on whether the president had violated the constitutional provision granting Congress the power to appropriate funds. Initially, however, the question was whether the president had violated the Arms Control and Export Act, which required congressional assent to major arms sales. Congress eventually concluded that he had.

The Iran-*contra* affair clouded consideration of the administration's proposals in 1987 to sell Saudi Arabia Maverick air-to-ground missiles and other weapons, including advanced F-15 fighters. Timeworn arguments about threats to Israeli security again figured in the congressional-executive dialogue, as did an Iraqi missile attack on the *USS Stark* in the Persian Gulf which killed thirty-seven U.S. sailors. Congressional opposition was so widespread that the administration withdrew both proposals. The administration did eventually score a victory when Congress approved a compromise proposal to sell the fighter aircraft (but not the missiles) to the Saudis. Ironically, the Iran-*contra* affair actually may have helped secure the presidential victory, as the compromise worked out with Congress "was a spirit born of shared burnout" over the "seemingly unending" scandal, and "reflected a recognition by pro-Israeli legislators and AIPAC strategists that it was not a good time to pile on a staggering Reagan administration" (Warburg 1989).

Despite this victory and others in 1988, both Congress and the president were by now dissatisfied with the state of arms sales procedures. Expecting opposition, the president kept impending sales secret as long as possible and otherwise approached Congress in a confrontational manner. Proposals were sent to Congress without giving the additional twenty-day grace period before a formal notification was filed, as had become customary; and members of Congress routinely introduced resolutions of disapproval as soon as the administration announced them. Prior consultation between the president and Congress rarely occurred. Thus, by the time Ronald Reagan departed the White House "there was consensus throughout Washington that the process was 'broke'" (Warburg 1989).

The Bush administration did little to alleviate the conflict between Congress and the president. On the contrary, its pre- and post-Persian Gulf War policies toward Iraq continued to fuel it. Congressional Democrats, for example, were quick to seize on prewar exports of high-technology goods to Iraq, designed to moderate Iraqi behavior, as a contributing cause of the subsequent war. (Friedman's *Spider's Web* [1993] is an especially critical account of "Iraqgate," and Juster's "The Myth of Iraqgate" [1994] a useful counterweight.) And after the war Democrats and many Republicans expressed concern that the continuation of major arms sales to the Middle East undermined the credibility of an earlier administration initiative purportedly directed toward curbing the flow of deadly weapons to the volatile region.

The differences between Congress and the president came to a head in September 1992, when shortly before Congress adjourned, the Bush administration announced its intention to sell more F-15 fighter aircraft to Saudi Arabia. Despite objections, Congress failed to stop the proposed sale. Among the many reasons is that presidential candidate Bill Clinton endorsed the proposal. Another is that congressional Democrats, once resistant to selling arms to the Arabs, supported the sale to protect jobs now threatened by the post-Cold War downsizing of the military (see also Chapter 9). Thus a well-established pattern continues: The president continues to propose arms sales to other countries, and Congress continues to dispose of them— but in ways that typically give the presidents most of what they want.

Congress and the Reagan Administration's Nicaraguan Policy

The Reagan administration's advocacy of *contra* aid, unlike its arm sales experiences, often was thwarted by Congress; and by the end of his second term, Reagan had largely abandoned efforts to win congressional approval of his preferred policies. The Nicaragua situation also differed in that congressional resistance centered in the House rather than the Senate. The Reagan administration usually forwent efforts to win support for arms sales to Arab countries in the Democratic-controlled House, preferring instead to concentrate on the Senate where it had a greater chance of avoiding outright defeat. In the *contra* aid case, on the other hand, every major battle from mid-1983 onward was determined in the House, where nearly all of the Republicans typically supported the president and a (narrow) majority of Democrats opposed him. The president's only significant victory in the House came in 1986.

The *contra* aid story began in 1979 when the dictatorial regime of Anastasio Somoza, long supported by the United States, collapsed. An anti-Somoza coalition known as the Sandinista National Liberation Front (FSLN) succeeded it. The Reagan administration, alarmed by what it believed to be growing Cuban and Soviet influence in Nicaragua (and in Central America generally), authorized U.S. support for Nicaraguan exiles in Honduras, known as *contras* (counterrevolutionaires), already fighting the allegedly Marxist Sandinistas. With U.S. support, the *contras* grew in numbers and their actions became bolder. In 1984, with the help of the CIA, they mined Nicaraguan ports, leading the Sandinistas to bring suit against the United States in the World Court on a charge of violating international law.

Congress grew apprehensive about America's efforts to overthrow an internationally recognized and established government. The CIA's covert actions were rationalized as a method of protecting Nicaragua's neighbors from the leftist regime, but it became increasingly clear that the *contras* themselves sought nothing less than the overthrow of the Sandinistas.

Congress moved against that objective. Reagan administration officials denied that U.S. policy sought the overthrow of the Nicaraguan government. Instead, they argued, its purpose was the interdiction of Soviet- and Cuban-supplied arms to leftist insurgents in El Salvador. House Democrats nonetheless succeeded in December 1982 in passing the so-called Boland amendment, which prohibited the use of CIA and Defense Department funds for operations specifically aimed at overthrowing the Nicaraguan government.[4] In 1984, following the mining episode, the Senate joined the House in refusing to approve additional funds to undermine the Sandinista regime. The Senate's action, which reversed its earlier posture of checking the more aggressive House in its fight with the president, was animated less by a change of heart than by the belief that the CIA had shirked its legal responsibility to keep Congress "fully and currently informed" about covert operations. Republican Senator Barry Goldwater, chair of the Senate Intelligence Committee, expressed the resentful congressional mood in a pithy "Dear Bill" letter to CIA Director William Casey:

> I've been trying to figure out how I can most easily tell you my feelings about the discovery of the president having approved mining some of the harbors in Central America.
>
> It gets down to one, little, simple phrase: I am pissed off.

> Bill, this is no way to run a railroad and I find myself in a hell of a quandary. . . . The president has asked us to back his foreign policy. Bill, how can we back his foreign policy when we don't know what the hell he is doing? (*Congressional Quarterly Weekly Report* April 14, 1984, 833)

Later refusals to resume U.S. aid to the *contras* reflected public sentiments on the issue, as poll after poll showed that a majority of the American people sided with Congress, not the president (Sobel 1989; Wittkopf and McCormick 1993).

The Reagan administration mounted an intensive lobbying campaign to reverse congressional opposition to its policies, which continued to be especially pronounced in the House. Eventually, it succeeded. In June 1986 the House narrowly approved a $100 million humanitarian and military aid package for the *contras*. The president thus prevailed over the Democratic leadership in the House, which, drawing an analogy with Vietnam, opposed military aid out of fear that it would be the first step toward direct U.S. military involvement. As House Speaker Thomas P. "Tip" O'Neill argued, "I see us becoming engaged step-by-step in a military situation that brings our boys directly into fighting."

The administration's victory in the House required the investment of considerable presidential capital. Reagan appealed his case directly to the American people by going over the heads of Congress in nationally televised appeals. The "Great Communicator" referred to the *contras* as "freedom fighters" and "our brothers," while those opposing aid to the insurgents were labeled "new isolationists." "They are courting disaster," Reagan warned, "and history will hold them accountable." The administration described the "strategic threat" in dire terms: "another Cuba"; "a privileged sanctuary for terrorists and subversives just two days' driving time from Harlingen, Texas"; and "a permanent staging ground for terrorism, a home away from home for Khadafy, and the Ayatollah, just three hours by air from the U.S. border." In March 1986 the president asserted that "Those who would compromise must not compromise the freedom fighters' lives nor their immediate defensive needs. They must not compromise freedom."

No new military aid was approved in 1987, but Congress did provide additional humanitarian aid. At the same time that the Reagan administration remained adamant in its determination not to abandon the *contras*, however, Congress increasingly emphasized the imperative of a political settlement. Costa Rican President Oscar Arias Sanches formulated a peace proposal, endorsed by the other Central American governments, whose objective was a negotiated political settlement (which later won Arias the Nobel Peace Prize). Congress generally supported that process while the Reagan administration remained skeptical, but its support of the *contras* waned as the Arias proposals became the focus of determined diplomatic efforts.

In March 1988 the Sandinistas and *contras* agreed to a cease-fire and the eventual inclusion of the *contras* in Nicaraguan political life. As the fall congressional and presidential elections approached, placing blame for the possible future "loss" of Nicaragua to communism colored the debate over Nicaraguan policy. However, neither party capitalized on the theme as both were weary of the long *contra* aid battle from which neither benefited politically.

George Bush recognized as much. Shortly after his election he struck a bipartisan accord with Congress to assist the *contras* until February 1990, by which time the Sandinista government promised to hold free elections. With that agreement, Congress and the president joined hands in moving U.S. policy toward Nicaragua from the battlefield to the negotiating table. Surprisingly, Nicaraguan President Daniel Ortega, the Sandinista candidate, lost in the February elections. With that, a new chapter in American foreign policy toward Central America opened. The one it closed continues to warrant attention, however, as it demonstrates American leaders' reluctance to become involved in conflict situations that might require commiting U.S. troops. Both Congress and the executive resorted to procedural gimmickry to keep a politically unpopular program alive, but in the end Congress abandoned the program whose objectives were vague and chances of success remote (Warburg 1989).

Obstacles to Congressional Foreign Policy Making   ·

Although Congress at times plays an assertive foreign policy role (notably following war) and at others an acquiescent one, neither description overrides the fact that Congress as an institution is poorly equipped to compete effectively with the president when it comes to directing the nation's foreign relations. Three interrelated factors explain this: parochialism, organizational weaknesses, and lack of expertise.

Parochialism

Congress is more oriented toward domestic than foreign affairs. All 435 members of the House are up for reelection every two years, as is a third of the Senate. Continual preoccupation with reelection creates pressure to attend more to domestic than to international concerns. The pressure is especially acute on the House side, and perhaps explains why the ten provisions of the House Republicans' "Contract with America" during the 1994 election included only one foreign policy item. While the president has a national constituency, all 535 members of Congress have much more-narrowly construed electoral bases and correspondingly restricted constituency interests. The end of the Cold War arguably exacerbates these tendencies, as it encourages the expression of preferences toward particular ethnic groups (Shain 1994–1995). Thus, in the words of former Under Secretary of State William D. Rogers (1979), "With the fate of the entire House and a third of the Senate in the hands of the voters every 730 days, Congress is beholden to every short-term swing of popular opinion. The temptation to pander to prejudice and emotion is overwhelming."

Because senators and representatives depend for their survival on satisfying their constituents' rather limited interests, "being national-minded can be a positive hazard to a legislative career" (Sundquist 1976). Thus a foreign policy problem may be viewed from a representative's Polish, Israeli, or Irish constituent viewpoint. Similarly, military needs may be weighed by the benefits of industries located within a senator's state or representative's district. "Asked one day whether it was true that the navy yard in his district was too small to accommodate the latest battleships," Henry Stimson (chair of the House Naval Affairs Committee early in the century) replied, 'That is true, and that is the reason I have always been in favor of small ships'" (cited in Sundquist 1976).

The president's vantage point is much different. Having a nationwide constituency, the president's outlook on foreign policy problems is broader. The president can usually afford to alienate some local or narrow interests (by refusing to support a protective trade restriction, for example) without fear of electoral retribution. And while the president is rewarded for thinking in long-run terms rather than for the moment, a senator or representative is not. "With their excessively parochial orientation," former Senator J. William Fulbright explains, members of Congress "are acutely sensitive to the influence of private pressure and to the excesses and inadequacies of a public opinion that is all too often ignorant of the needs, the dangers, and the opportunities in our foreign relations." (Fulbright and two of his successors as chairs of the Senate Foreign Relations Committee, Frank Church of Idaho and Charles Percy of Illinois, lost reelection bids in part because they assumed leadership roles in foreign rather than domestic affairs.)

Interest in and attention to foreign policy issues by members of Congress is typically short-lived and strongly influenced by their newsworthiness (Crabb and Holt 1992). According to Republican Senator Daniel J. Evans of Washington, the legislative process has degenerated into "reading yesterday's headlines so that we can write today's amendments so that we can garner tomorrow's headlines." Often amendments are passed with little expectation of becoming law. As one Senate aide observed, "It has come to be an accepted part of the game that amendments are passed and press releases claiming credit are issued, with the understanding that most of these items will be tossed in the wastebasket when the bill goes to conference with the House." The "hundred barons phenomenon"—all senators want to be seen as directing the nation's foreign policy—explains the seemingly pointless behavior (Oberdorfer and Dewar 1987).

The congressional committee system, where the institution's real work is done, reinforces parochialism. Members of Congress serve on committees to enhance their prospects for reelection, expand their influence within chambers, devise good public policy, and position themselves for new careers (Fenno 1973; see also Burgin 1993; Smith and Deering 1990). Although distinguished performance in congressional committees may further each of those goals, reelection depends primarily on constituent service. Such concerns deflect congressional attention from substantive policy issues. *Newsweek* expressed the sentiment this way in January 1991: "Forget . . . the Persian Gulf: The secret obsession of all 435 members of the U.S. House of Representatives is reapportionment and redistricting."

Gaining a committee assignment germane to the interests of people back home is critical to the effective performance of constituent service. Congressional committees reflect these preferences, which in turn help to shape the legislative process.

Farm state members want to deal with agriculture while city people do not, so the agriculture committees are rural and proagriculture in their composition. The military affairs committees are dominated by partisans of the military, urban affairs committees by members from the cities, interior committees by proreclamation westerners, and so on. By custom, the judiciary committees are made up exclusively of lawyers. Within each committee, there is further specialization of subcommittees and of individual members. The decisions of the specialists have to be accepted by their colleagues most of the time without more than a cursory examination; a fresh and exhaustive review of every question by every member is obviously impossible. And through logrolling, the advocates of various local interests form coalitions of mutual support. (Sundquist 1976, 600)

Given these incentives and the behaviors they encourage, congressional attention to foreign affairs is often fleeting and shallow. Indeed, "sacrificing overall consistency and coherence of national policy for narrow interests and short-term objectives . . . is the natural consequence of the political calculus that inevitably dominates congressional decision making" (Blechman 1990).

Organizational Weaknesses

Power and responsibility within Congress are fragmented. President Truman's famous quip, "The buck stops here!" has no counterpart in Congress. Over half of the standing committees in both the House and Senate have broadly defined jurisdictions that give them some foreign affairs responsibility (see Table 12.1). Unlike the executive branch, where policy debates take place in private with a single individual, the president, often making the final choice, congressional debates are perforce public, with final choices made by counting yeas and nays, and with decision making diffuse. Under these conditions, policy consistency and coordination are most unlikely.

During the 1970s Congress undertook several procedural reforms that decentralized power from the committee to the subcommittee level, encouraged challenges to the seniority system, and reduced the importance of leadership positions.[5] As a consequence it became more difficult than ever to locate power and authority in Congress. "There are 165 different people in the House and Senate who can answer to the proud title 'Mr. Chairman,' having been given committees or subcommittees of their own" (Broder 1986, 9). Accordingly, the congressional leadership cannot speak for the institution as a whole, and Congress rarely speaks with a single voice. Newt Gingrich determined to reverse the trend toward fragmented leadership when he became speaker of the House, but his success, particularly in the foreign policy domain, remained to be seriously tested.

The rise of single-issue politics—which subjects members of Congress to evaluation not on the basis of their entire record but only their performance on particular issues—exacerbates the problems associated with the diffusion of power. Noting that the 385 committees and subcommittees of Congress are scouted by more than thirteen hundred registered lobbyists, one former official lamented that instead of a two-party system Capitol Hill resembles "a 385-party system" (cited in Crabb and Holt 1992, 275).

The fragmentation of power and responsibility in Congress frustrates executive-legislative consultation and coordination and makes Congress appear irresponsible. When facing a skeptical electorate, for example, these conditions enable individual senators and representatives to deflect criticism with the defense, "I didn't do it; it was everyone else." Individual accountability is reduced further by the congressional penchant for dealing with issues in procedural terms rather than confronting them directly. A striking illustration occurred with the Senate's consideration of two contro-

TABLE 12.1   FOREIGN AFFAIRS RESPONSIBILITIES OF COMMITTEES IN THE HOUSE AND SENATE

Senate Committee	Foreign Affairs Responsibility	House Committee
Agriculture, Nutrition, and Forestry	Foreign agricultural policy and assistance	Agriculture
Appropriations	Appropriation of revenues, rescission of appropriations	Appropriations
Armed Services	Defense, national security, national security aspects of nuclear energy	National Security
Banking, Housing, and Urban Affairs	Defense production, international economic policy, export and foreign trade promotion	Banking and Financial Services; Commerce; International Relations
Budget	Budgetary matters, concurrent budget resolution	Budget
Commerce, Science, and Transportation	Merchant marine, marine fisheries, oceans, coastal zone management, nonmilitary space sciences and aeronautics	Commerce; Resources; Science
Energy and Natural Resources	Energy policy, nonmilitary development of nuclear energy	Commerce; Science
Environment and Public Works	Environmental policy, regulation of nuclear energy, ocean dumping, environmental aspects of outer continental shelf lands	Science
Finance	Revenue measures, customs, foreign trade agreements, tariffs, import quotas	Ways and Means
Foreign Relations	Relations with foreign nations, treaties, executive agreements, international organizations, foreign assistance, intervention abroad, declarations of war, terrorism, international environmental and scientific affairs	International Relations
Governmental Affairs	Organization and reorganization of the executive branch, organization and management of nuclear export policy	Government Reforms and Oversight
Intelligence	Intelligence activties, covert operations	Intelligence
Judiciary	Immigration and refugees, espionage	Judiciary
Labor and Human Resources	Regulation of foreign labors	Economic and Educational Opportunities

Note: Descriptions of the foreign affairs responsibilities are derived from the jurisdictions of the Senate committees in the 104th Congress, with the corresponding jurisdictions of House committees matched to those as closely as possible. All are standing committees of the respective houses of Congress except the Intelligence committees, both of which are select committees.

versial treaties to cede American control of the Panama Canal to Panama. Senators took record votes on over fifty amendments, nearly twenty reservations, a dozen understandings, and several conditions—nearly ninety proposals for change of one kind or another.

The temptation to deal with matters procedurally is often irresistible. In the Panama Canal case, for example, many of the proposed changes were commonly billed as "improvements," which made it easier to vote for a politically unpopular document. Thus procedure becomes a useful tool for coping with single-issue politics, allowing members of Congress to conceal their true positions, thus deflecting potential electoral criticism. (In the case of the Panama Canal, however, it is noteworthy that over half of the thirty-eight senators who supported the treaties lost in their next campaign for reelection.) They also can avoid direct confrontation with the president by couching their opposition in procedural arguments to which the executive branch has no retort:

> If done directly, a Congressional decision—for example, to disapprove money for a new aircraft carrier—would require that more than half of all Congressmen conclude that the Navy can do with fewer carriers. . . . This would involve a stark confrontation with expertise that would be very uncomfortable for a Congressman. If a showdown is reached on the carrier issue, the vote is almost certain to be cloaked in procedures (motions to table, etc.) that would allow the Congressman to justify his vote, if he needed to, on a procedural question rather than on the merits of the case. (Aspin 1976, 165).

Using procedure to avoid direct responsibility does not mean that members of Congress are incapable of performing their jobs. On the contrary, masking their votes' real effects in procedural gobbledygook allows them more readily to take the road of conscience instead of the road of convenience. A different sort of Congress's seeming irresponsibility arises out of the very sluggishness of the legislative process. Slow, deliberative procedures may be inherent in a body charged with reconciling disparate views, but delays are prolonged by the dispersion of power and responsibility between two houses, their further fragmentation within a complex structure of committees and subcommittees (which slows the legislative process on major issues to "near paralysis" [Burgin 1993]), and the near absence of party discipline. The Senate's cloture rule, requiring an extraordinary majority for terminating debate, is another restraint on initiative. "The result is that any piece of legislation must surmount an obstacle course of unparalleled difficulty. . . . Few things happen quickly. Policies eventually adopted are often approved too late. . . . And in the process of overcoming the countless legislative hurdles, policies may be compromised to the point of ineffectiveness" (Sundquist 1976). Contrast that picture with the president's proven ability to act quickly and decisively, as rapidly moving international developments frequently require. "Presidents can procrastinate too," James L. Sundquist (1976) observes, "but unlike Congress they are not compelled to by any institutional structure."

A final form of irresponsibility is found in the frequent tendency of members of Congress to "leak" information. A glaring example of the recurrent problem took place in 1987, when the Senate Intelligence Committee voted not to make public a report on its closed-door hearings on the Iran-*contra* affair, only to have NBC News acquire the first half of it three days later. Within two weeks the other half appeared in the *New York Times*. Senator Patrick J. Leahy later resigned as vice chair of the committee when it was learned he had leaked the unclassified committee report—and at precisely the time the committee was trying to demonstrate that Reagan administration officials, not members of Congress, were most often responsible for leaking classified government information. An even more flagrant violation occurred in 1995, when Representative Robert C. Torricelli, a Democrat from New Jersey, revealed classified information allegedly implicating the CIA in a pair of murders in Guatemala—despite his oath "not [to] disclose any classified information received in the course of my service with the House of Representatives."

Congressional leaks arise from the independence that senators and representatives prize and from the benefits they can realize by placing issues in the mass media's spotlight. (Torricelli cited "moral obligation" in defending his behavior.) One of the consequences is that the president often uses "executive privilege" to conceal information—particularly classified information—thus preventing congressional involvement in policy making. In the extreme, the president may also purposely bypass Congress altogether, as Reagan did in his clandestine arms-for-hostages operation orchestrated by Robert McFarlane, his national security adviser. Oliver North, the NSC staffer primarily responsible for managing the Iran-*contra* deal, argued in defense of the initiative that secrecy was necessary because of Congress's penchant to leak information.

Lack of Expertise

The third organizational weakness contributing to Congress's "respondent" relationship with the president derives from the White House's comparatively greater command of technical expertise and from its ability to control the flow of information. We have already observed this in our discussion of the departments and agencies comprising the policy-making system's second concentric circle, all of which are *executive* branch organizations. Although they sometimes resist presidential orders, as we will see in Chapter 13, these organizations contribute enormously to presidential supremacy over Congress, which must depend on the executive branch for the information critical to sound policy recommendations (see West and Cooper 1990).

Congress has tried to overcome its lack of expertise in several ways. It has expanded the overseer role of the General Accounting Office periodically, and it created the Office of Technology Assessment to evaluate scientific and technical proposals and the Congressional Budget Office to assist in analyzing budget options and preparing the annual budget resolution. More important, perhaps, it dramatically increased the size of the professional staff serving congressional committees and individual members of Congress. Growth exploded during the 1970s but continued throughout the 1980s, bringing the total number of personal and committee staff employees to more than fifteen thousand by 1991 (Mann and Ornstein 1993, 69). Added staff resources give Congress a greater capacity to assert an independent congressional position and the means to become involved in policy questions where congressional interest and expertise previously may have been lacking (Crabb and Holt 1992). Furthermore, in an atmosphere where knowledge is power, congressional staffs exercise greater influence over the direction of policy. The technical experts filling staff roles, and the networks of communications and coalitions that have developed among them, enable them to steer policy, operating as an "invisible force in American lawmaking" (Fox and Hammond 1977). Interestingly, however the growth of legislative staff is one trend the Republican majority sharply reversed after it assumed the reigns of congressional power in January 1995. It also targeted the Office of Technology Assessment for possible elimination.

Individual members of Congress often develop considerable policy expertise. The committee system and the penchant to allocate positions of authority according to the rules of seniority mean that some senators and representatives often spend their entire legislative careers specializing in their committees' areas of jurisdiction. Because incumbents are returned to office more often than not (at least they were before the 1994 electoral earthquake), it is not uncommon to find congressional careers that span a quarter-century or more—much longer than any postwar president is even allowed by the Constitution to remain in office.

Historically, specialization by entrenched members of Congress has been especially prominent in the Senate and House Armed Services committees (the latter now called the Committee on National Security), where southern Democrats in particular have claimed considerable expertise on national security issues. Members of these committees now also receive large amounts of intelligence from the CIA, contributing to their ability to arrive at policy judgments independent of the president. Congress's committee and seniority systems also facilitate the patron-client relationships between Congress and the foreign policy bureaucracy described in the previous chapter. Such relationships sometimes subvert presidential interests, but they also provide Congress power vis-à-vis the executive.

Still, all members of Congress cannot be experts on all matters of policy, but the president can be—and is. When expertise is lacking, people look to the experts—that is, the executive. This tendency is especially pronounced in matters of foreign policy and national security. Moreover, members of Congress are especially ill-equipped to acquire the kinds of information that would enable them to better monitor, and hence influence, decision making in times of crisis. Following the Ford administration's use of marines to rescue the ship *Mayaguez* from its Cambodian captors in May 1975, for example, a survey revealed that the press was the principal source of information for many members of Congress. This was even true for a majority of those serving on congressional committees directly concerned with foreign and national security policy. Little wonder that one (anonymous) member of Congress cynically observed, "the actions of the United States are not secret to other nations, only to Congress and the American people" (*Congressional Quarterly Weekly Report* November 13, 1976). Little wonder also that Congress's role is largely negative, functioning primarily as a public critic of what the executive has already done.

The Powers of Congress and Foreign Policy Making

The Constitution gives Congress farther-reaching foreign policy powers than it gives the president. Its authority over treaties, war, and money in particular place it in a commanding position, enabling it to set overall policy much like a board of directors does in private enterprise. At least that is how it seems, but the reality is quite different.

Treaties

Treaty-making powers rest in the Senate, whose advice and consent by a two-thirds vote is necessary before the president can consummate (with the exchange of instruments of ratification) a treaty with another country. (This effectively gives control to only thirty-four of the 535 members of Congress.) The Senate Foreign Relations Committee bears primary responsibility for conducting the hearings and investigations on which senatorial advice and consent are based. These and related foreign affairs responsibilities once made Foreign Relations Committee the most prestigious of all Senate committees. In recent years, however, ideological divisions have prevented it from speaking with a single voice. More importantly, perhaps, it does not serve senators' other interests. As one member of the committee put it: "Well, you know, it is fun to hobnob with foreign leaders and discuss world affairs, but it doesn't get me any place with my Senate colleagues. . . . Foreign Relations doesn't have much legislative jurisdiction that's important to other senators—it's nothing like Finance or Appropriations" (cited in Smith and Deering 1990; see also McCormick 1993). The committee nonetheless remains a primary forum for the discharge of Congress's foreign policy responsibilities.

Despite the importance of the Constitution's treaty clause, the precise mechanism through which the Senate proffers advice and consent to the president is ambiguous. The provision has been controversial from the very beginning of the Republic. In barest form the process consists of the president, in the capacity of the nation's chief diplomat, negotiating through representatives a treaty with another nation, and the Senate then merely voting up or down. More frequently, advice is given in written communications between the executive and the legislature or by including members of Congress on the treaty-negotiation team. The latter practice has been widespread ever since the Senate rejected the Versailles Treaty ending World War I, which was negotiated without senatorial representation on the Peace Commission headed by Woodrow Wilson.

Consent to treaties is still established by a two-thirds vote, but the Senate also often attaches reservations to treaties. These may take the form of amendments that require the executive to renegotiate the terms of the treaty with other signatories—a potentially inhibiting obstacle, particularly with the increase in the number of multilateral treaties. Alternatively, reservations or "conditions" may simply incorporate the Senate's interpretation of the treaty without any binding effect on the parties to it. Other variants are reservations that apply only to the United States. The most celebrated example is the so-called Connally Amendment to the Statute of the International Court of Justice. According to this reservation, the United States reserves the right to determine whether matters falling under the court's compulsory jurisdiction clause are essentially within the domestic jurisdiction of the United States, and hence beyond the Court's purview.

The Senate's role in the treaty-making process became the subject of a sharp dispute in 1987 between the Reagan administration and Congress over the administration's announced reinterpretation of the 1972 Anti-Ballistic Missile (ABM) treaty. The reinterpretation would have permitted the administration to test technology as part of its Strategic Defense Initiative (SDI), previously thought to be prohibited by the ABM treaty. SDI was the immediate issue, of course, but broad constitutional questions were also at stake. Although treaty interpretation is understood to be an executive function, conformity to senatorial understanding is also expected. A reinterpretation that would significantly revise a prior understanding could constitute an amendment of sufficient gravity to require again the Senate's advice and consent. Without the ability to obtain from the executive branch reliable information about treaty negotiations, the Senate's constitutional prerogatives in the treaty-making process would be severely impaired.

The State Department's legal adviser contended that nothing in the original ratification record precluded a broad interpretation of what was permitted under the ABM treaty (Sofaer 1987). Nearly all of those who had participated in the actual negotiation of the treaty disputed that, however, as did Senator Sam Nunn, chair of the powerful Armed Services Committee. Concluding that the document submitted by the Nixon administration fifteen years earlier permitted only a narrow interpretation (Nunn 1987), Nunn spearheaded an effort to block the broad interpretation. The Senate placed restrictions on SDI tests and funds that had the effect of enforcing a narrow interpretation, and it attached a reservation to the ratification resolution for the INF treaty that reflected its sense of the Senate's role in any future reinterpretation of that treaty. Reagan questioned the reservation's constitutionality but proceeded with the ratification process nonetheless. Thus the Senate protected its treaty-making powers and warned future presidents against unilateral treaty reinterpretations. Significantly, the Clinton administration announced early that it supported the narrow or traditional interpretation of the ABM treaty—although it later found that its efforts to develop a theater-based missile defense system also raised questions about the system's consistency with the treaty (see Chapter 4). It also worried that the efforts of the newly-elected Republican Congress to revive the Star Wars SDI effort would rekindle old issues with the Russians.

The ABM confrontation aside, the Senate's treaty ratification record has on the whole been quite positive. The most famous treaty failure occurred in 1920, when the Versailles Treaty came up short of the two-thirds majority that would have opened the way for U.S. membership in the League of Nations. Since then, however, the Senate has rejected only three treaties, while two others that failed to receive a two-thirds majority were subject to reconsideration (Committee on Foreign Relations, United States Senate 1993, xv). This record attests simultaneously to congressional deference to presidential initiatives and to general agreement between the president and Congress on most foreign policy issues. What the historical record fails to show is also noteworthy, namely, those occasions when treaties were not presented for a vote due to known legislative opposition. The Carter administration's decisions not to proceed with a comprehensive test ban treaty and to shelve the Threshold Test Ban Treaty and the Peaceful Nuclear Explosives Treaty are examples (Warburg 1989).

Executive agreements are the usual method presidents use to make international agreements that avoid altogether the necessity of securing the advice and consent of the Senate. The Supreme Court has ruled that these government-to-government agreements have the same legal force as treaties, and thus become part of the "supreme law of the land," but they may be concluded without legislative scrutiny. Early examples include the agreements governing the Lend Lease Act of 1941, which enabled the United States to provide war materials to its World War II allies, and Truman's aid to

Greece and Turkey in the late 1940s. Others include the Paris peace agreement on Ending the War and Restoring Peace in Vietnam (1973); the SALT I accord on offensive weapons (1972); and various bilateral agreements covering American military base rights in Spain, the Azores, Diego Garcia, Bahrain, and Iceland.

These illustrations show that executive agreements often cover critically important aspects of America's foreign relations. And their quantity indicates they are a preferred mechanism for reaching international accords. Of the nearly eight thousand international agreements concluded between 1946 and 1992, 95 percent have been executive agreements (Committee on Foreign Relations, United States Senate 1993, 14) and hence not subject to the formal approval procedures of the Senate. Many of these are based on statutory directives, and others are entered into pursuant to treaty provisions, both of which require legislative input. Still, the vast number affirm the president's wide latitude to negotiate international agreements unrestrained by constitutional checks and balances.

Evidence that executive agreements pose a potential challenge to congressional oversight is seen in Congress's periodic attempts to block such maneuvers. One of the most sustained efforts occurred in 1953–1954, when Republican Senator John Bricker of Ohio proposed a constitutional amendment that would have greatly restricted the president's treaty-making powers and ability to manage the day-to-day conduct of foreign affairs. The proposal fell only one vote short of the two-thirds majority necessary for Senate approval (a necessary condition in the long process of constitutional revision).

Two decades later, while the nation was still deeply mired in the Vietnam War, the congressional assault on executive prerogatives led to a statute (known as the Case Act after its sponsor, Republican Senator Clifford Case of New Jersey) that required the president to submit to Congress all international agreements within sixty days of their execution. The enactment culminated a process begun in the late 1960s, when the Senate unearthed the breadth and depth of overseas commitments the executive had entered into without Congress's knowledge. Not only did the Senate discover secret agreements and de facto understandings, but it also gained knowledge about covert activities and paramilitary operations the president had authorized with neither the knowledge nor approval of Congress. The essence of Congress's findings was that the president had repeatedly made commitments to foreign governments in secret talks while downplaying their importance at home.

Although the Case Act augmented Congress's capacity to be informed of international agreements made by the executive (including agencies other than the State Department), it did little to redress the imbalance between presidential and congressional authority over treaty making in general or executive agreements in particular (cf. Collier 1988; Johnson 1984; McCormick 1992). The president remains the initiator of agreements with other nations, determining which are to be treaties and which executive agreements; and the president still is not required to obtain congressional advice or consent before doing either. Moreover, the law protects the secrecy of executive agreements by providing that they need be forwarded only to the relevant Senate and House committees, under an injunction of secrecy, if the president determines that public disclosure would endanger national security. Thus the statute may have complicated presidents' lives, but it has not substantially restricted their freedom.

War

The Constitution is clear on where war-making powers lie. It st
Section 8 that "the Congress shall have power . . . to declare war." Elsew
(Article II, Section 2), the Constitution also specifies that "the Preside
Commander-in-Chief of the Army and Navy of the United States." Of the tw
sions, the latter has proven the more important, as the president has used that p
sion to justify stationing troops all over the world. Presidents have also used it to ju
tify American military intervention in Korea (1950–1953), Lebanon (1958), the
Dominican Republic (1965–1966), Vietnam (1965–1973), Grenada (1983), Panama
(1989), the Persian Gulf (1990–1991 and 1994), and Somalia (1992–1994). Yet in none
of those cases was military action accompanied by a formal declaration of war. In the
Persian Gulf case, Congress did authorize the president to use military force to remove
Iraqi forces from Kuwait once he certified to Congress that all peaceful means to resolve the dispute had been exhausted. But it did not declare war.

Protracted American involvement in Vietnam prompted congressional efforts to
redress the war-making balance. At issue was whether President Johnson exceeded his
constitutional powers by repeatedly escalating the nation's involvement without a corresponding congressional mandate. Johnson argued that his authority rested on the
Gulf of Tonkin Resolution, passed by Congress in August 1964. The joint resolution
gave the president approval "to take all necessary measures to repel any armed attack
against the forces of the United States and to prevent further aggression."

As the quagmire of Vietnam deepened, the meaning of the Gulf of Tonkin
Resolution became the source of intense debate. With hindsight, it is now recognized
that Congress was duped by a president who controlled the information and hence the
policy. On four previous occasions Congress had authorized the president to use
armed forces to defend certain geographical areas (in the 1955 Formosa Straits
Resolution, the 1957 Eisenhower Middle East Doctrine Resolution, the 1962 Cuban
Resolution, and the 1962 Berlin Resolution). The magnitude and duration of
America's military involvement in Vietnam and the Johnson administration's insistence that the resolution was the "functional equivalent" of a declaration of war is what
made this situation different. Congress repudiated Johnson's interpretation when it repealed the Gulf of Tonkin Resolution in 1970. It then took concrete steps to limit future presidential war-making prerogatives, embodying them in the *War Powers
Resolution*, passed in 1973 over President Nixon's veto.

The War Powers Resolution: Constitutional and Legal Issues

Several provisions in the act try to ensure congressional consent in decisions to deploy
American troops abroad. First, the resolution stipulates that the president should inform Congress when he or she introduces forces "into hostilities or into situations
where imminent involvement in hostilities is clearly indicated by the circumstances."
This first provision triggers a second, which prohibits troop commitments from extending beyond sixty days without specific congressional authorization (although this
period can be extended up to ninety days if the safety of American troops is at stake).
Third, any time American forces become engaged in hostilities without a declaration

POLICY MAKING

443

tes in Article I,
here, however
nt shall be
o provi-
rovi-

...nal authorization, the law enables Congress to direct the ... troops by a concurrent resolution of the two houses of ...easure would not require the president's signature to take ...tive veto and may no longer be constitutional because of ...a ruling in 1983. Presumably that provision of the War ...ull and void. The sixty-day limit and various consulting and ...wever, remain intact.

...aged the constitutionality of the War Powers Resolution in ...zed its practical consequences. He argued that the sixty-day ...esolution provisions "purport to take away, by a mere leg-...hich the president has properly exercised under the Con-...undred years." They are unconstitutional, he asserted, be-...ich the constitutional powers of a branch of government can be alte... ; the Constitution—and any attempt to make such alterations by legislation alone is clearly without force." He also claimed the resolution would "seriously undermine the nation's ability to act decisively and convincingly in times of international crisis" and that it would "give every future Congress the ability to handcuff every future president."

The courts' typical resort to the "doctrine of political questions" makes it unlikely that the constitutionality of the War Powers Resolution will ever be judicially tested. Meanwhile, even though the resolution remains a monument to Congress's assertive reaction to the so-called imperial presidency, it has not effectively restrained the president's use of force abroad without congressional involvement (and is widely regarded as having failed in that attempt). The United States has used its armed forces abroad more than four dozen times since the resolution was passed. In thirty-one of these instances (as of February 15, 1994) the president submitted reports to Congress under the resolution, but seldom has Section 4(a)(1), which would set the sixty-day clock in motion, been cited or reference been made to actual or imminent hostilities. For its part, Congress has invoked the provisions of the act only once, in 1983, when in connection with the deployment of U.S. marines to Lebanon, it declared that Section 4(a)(1) had become operative—but it went on to authorize the marines to stay in Lebanon for eighteen months. In the case of the Persian Gulf War, Congress stated that its authorization to use force against Iraq "constituted specific statutory authorization within the meaning of the War Powers Resolution" (Collier 1994a).

Nearly every president since Nixon has claimed the War Powers Resolution is unconstitutional. Thus, when President Bush ordered military forces into Panama in December 1989, he submitted a report about the intervention to Congress "consistent with the War Powers Resolution" but neither cited the provision of the act that would limit the duration of force deployments nor recognized the legitimacy of the act itself. (However, he did announce that U.S. troops were expected to be home in less than two months [60 days].) "I have an obligation as president to conduct the foreign policy of this country as I see fit," he exclaimed.

Bush adopted a similar posture during the crisis over Kuwait leading to the Persian Gulf War. A week after the invasion of Kuwait he submitted a report "consistent with the War Powers Resolution" indicating that he had deployed U.S. forces to the region to deter further Iraqi aggression. He did not cite section 4(a)(1) of the resolution,

which would have started the sixty-day clock, and spe
involvement in hostilities is imminent." He reaffirm
lowing the dispatch of an additional 150,000 troop
"The deployment will ensure that the coalition h
tion should that be necessary."

On November 29, 1990, the UN Security
essary means" to evict Saddam Hussein from K
mandates by January 15, 1991. The Bush administrati
dent did not need any additional congressional authorizatio
1994b; see also Moore 1994). In the end, of course, the Congress
of force, but the Bush administration sought Congress's support for po
reasons. It insisted to the very end that the president had a legal right to
against Iraq "regardless of any action that Congress might or might not take" (M
1994).

What Are Consultations?

Beyond constitutional and related legal questions, never clearly answered, the War
Powers Resolution points to two other interrelated issues that have plagued its applicability from the beginning: What constitutes "consultation," and what constitutes "imminent hostilities"?

The War Powers Resolution seeks to ensure greater congressional participation in
decisions authorizing the use of force by requiring consultation between the executive
and legislative branches "in every possible instance" prior to committing U.S. forces
to hostilities or to situations likely to result in such. Presidents generally claim to have
met this requirement, but rarely has serious and meaningful debate between the two
branches occurred prior to a presidential decision on the use of force. As we have
noted, Congress, too, seldom has sought to limit the use of force once set in motion.
Several cases illustrate these points.

The prior consultation issue surfaced during Ford's and Carter's administrations
and repeatedly during Reagan's. In 1986, after a surprise nighttime attack on Tripoli
and Benghazi to punish Libyan leader Muammar Qaddafi's alleged support of international terrorism, Republican House leader Robert H. Michel, one of the dozen or
so lawmakers briefed by the Reagan White House just before the Libyan raid, expressed the sentiment that "we really ought to have some sort of vehicle for getting
Congress into the mix, so we're not left out in the cold." A proposal followed to establish a special consultative group within Congress to which the president could turn
in future situations. The idea, although not acted on at the time, remained alive and
became a point of contention during the Persian Gulf crisis. Congressional leaders appointed a bipartisan consultative group comprising the Congress's leaders and key
committee chairs in an effort to facilitate consultation on developments in the Persian
Gulf region. Bush had met with group occasionally, but he ignored it when he made
the critical decision to send many thousands more troops to the region (Collier 1994b),
which unequivocally moved the United States toward an offensive capability.

Still no agreed-on mechanism exists to ensure that the president will weigh congressional views before making a decision to use force. The Clinton administration's

ecision to launch a cruise missile attack against Iraq's intelligence center in June 1993 is illustrative: The administration reportedly notified congressional leaders shortly before the attack but did not consult them on specific courses of action. As Dennis DeConcini, then chair of the Senate Intelligence Committee put it, "They've got their minds made up, and they don't want to dare really consult."

All of these cases illustrate an important fact: Once the decision to use force is put into action, Congress's power is severely circumscribed. One example makes the point. President Bush informed members of Congress at 6:00 P.M. on December 19, 1989, after making the decision but before implementing it, of his intention to invade Panama. The actual invasion began seven hours later, at 1:00 A.M., December 20. There is little that Congress could have done at this point. Thus Congress cannot effectively make war against a president's war-making powers.

What Are Imminent Hostilities?

The Reagan administration's policies in Central America, the Middle East, and elsewhere provoked repeated concerns in the Democratic-controlled Congress about the latter's role in the use of force abroad. In two cases, Lebanon and the Persian Gulf, the question of whether U.S. forces were placed in danger of "imminent hostilities" as envisaged by the War Powers Resolution figured prominently in the congressional-executive contest. Both also illustrate why Congress finds it difficult to terminate a military operation already in place.

American marines were first sent to Lebanon in 1982 (under the president's authority as commander in chief) with the expectation that their presence there would be brief. A year later they were still in Lebanon. As conditions worsened some members of Congress began to ask whether the U.S. troops were subject to imminent hostilities, which would trigger the sixty-day War Powers clock. In August 1983 the marines suffered two fatalities and several casualties, prompting Reagan to secure congressional authorization for the marine presence in Beirut. In the weeks that followed, U.S. forces were drawn more actively into the Lebanese civil conflict. Meanwhile, negotiations between Congress and the president resulted in a compromise authorizing the marines to stay in Lebanon for eighteen months. Although the Lebanon resolution was passed by both houses and signed by Reagan in mid-October, the president still did not concede the applicability of the War Powers Resolution: "I do not and cannot cede any of the authority vested in me under the Constitution as president and as commander in chief of the United States armed forces. Nor should my signing be viewed as any acknowledgment that the president's constitutional authority can be impermissibly infringed by statute."

The controversy escalated when terrorists truck-bombed marine headquarters in Beirut, killing 241 marines and navy personnel. In the months following the tragedy, Reagan defended his policies, accusing his congressional critics of wanting to "cut and run." Then, in a dramatic about-face, he announced in February 1984 that the marines would be stationed on ships offshore. Shortly thereafter, a complete evacuation from Lebanon was ordered.

Reagan and his secretary of state, George Shultz, both alleged that the debate over the applicability of the War Powers Resolution and other congressional misgivings about the American presence in Lebanon contributed to the terrorism there. Shultz was especially critical of the War Powers Resolution, arguing—much as President Nixon had when he vetoed the measure—that the provisions that U.S. troops must be withdrawn from conflict situations unless Congress authorizes their continued presence "practically invite an adversary to wait us out."

The controversy over Lebanon had barely subsided when the administration's Persian Gulf policies came under attack. In May 1987 an Iraqi warplane fired two Exocet missiles at the *USS Stark*, mistakenly believing it to be an Iranian ship, and killing thirty-seven U.S. sailors. The *Stark* was part of a large and growing naval presence in the Persian Gulf whose mission included protection of Kuwaiti oil tankers (re-registered to fly American flags) from attacks in the protracted Iran-Iraq war. The decision to reflag and protect the Kuwaiti tankers sought to prevent Iranian expansionism from threatening other U.S. friends in the region and to keep the Soviet Union from expanding its influence in the Gulf area. Members of Congress, however, were concerned that they had not been consulted on the reflagging operation, and in the months following the *Stark* incident they continued to press for a greater voice in Persian Gulf policies.

The *Stark* incident prompted a vigorous debate in Congress about the applicability of the War Powers Resolution. The Reagan administration never conceded the point, but it did begin in the fall of 1987 to submit reports to Congress on developments in the Persian Gulf consistent with the resolution. One addressed the destruction of an Iranian civilian airliner by the *USS Vincennes* which was mistakenly believed to have been a hostile Iranian military plane. Then, in August 1988, a cease-fire in the Iran-Iraq war removed the circumstances causing the executive-legislative dispute, as U.S. military forces were gradually withdrawn from the Gulf region.

The prolonged clash over Persian Gulf policy set the stage for efforts in 1988 to amend the War Powers Resolution itself. Of particular concern were criteria for determining when hostilities were imminent enough to require invoking its procedures. Little was accomplished then, however, just as little had been accomplished by the issues raised during and after the Persian Gulf War. In part this is because Congress itself remains divided about the wisdom of the resolution. Some members feel the resolution is an ill-advised, unnecessary intrusion on the president's authority. Others believe that the law has worked in the sense that it has facilitated communication between the president and Congress and has given the latter some policy leverage that it otherwise lacked. Still others believe that it needs to be reshaped to better address the problem of consultation and to constrain the president's ability to put U.S. troops into harm's way. Underlying these differing viewpoints are partisan and ideological differences over the wisdom of particular policies, which in turn affect perceptions of the procedural issues over which Congress and the president differ. As one expert concluded, "Decisions to invoke the War Powers Resolution are likely to be based on broad political judgments about the role of Congress in U.S. foreign and security policy or about the particular situation under consideration, rather than measurable facts on whether forces are in hostilities or imminent hostilities" (Collier 1987).

Jacob K. Javits, architect of the War Powers Act, wrote shortly before his death that the resolution "did not, and does not, guarantee the end of presidential war, but it does present Congress with the means by which it can stop presidential war if it has the will to act" (Javits 1985). In most instances it appears that Congress lacks the will—in part because short, decisive military actions by the president (like the interventions in Grenada, Panama, and the Persian Gulf, and the attack on Libya) tend to be politically popular at home. When they are unpopular, as came to be the case with the humanitarian intervention in Somalia, Congress shows more backbone.

War Powers, Collective Security, and Peacekeeping[6]

The Persian Gulf War and later interventions in Somalia, the Balkans, and Haiti have added new elements to the War Powers debate, as they invite questions about Congress's role in authorizing U.S. participation in United Nations military or peacekeeping operations. The issue was left unresolved at the United Nations' creation in 1945, when it was anticipated that member states would conclude agreements placing military forces at the disposal of the new organization. The UN Participation Act, the implementing legislation for U.S. participation in the United Nations, makes it clear that congressional approval is required for any agreement designating U.S. military forces for United Nations use, but that further congressional approval would not be necessary before they could be made available to the UN Security Council for enforcement action.

The Cold War prevented conclusion of any agreements with provisions for placing U.S. forces at the UN's disposal. Absent that, what role should Congress play? When President Clinton announced that U.S. warships would enforce restoration of sanctions against Haiti once an agreement to restore civilian rule there broke down, should Congress have been consulted, as many members thought? And should it have been consulted before Clinton pledged U.S. participation in a NATO enforcement of a UN-authorized "no-fly" zone over Bosnia-Hercegovina? or before he dispatched roughly three hundred-fifty U.S. troops to Macedonia to join a Security Council-authorized UN mission intended to prevent widening of the war in Bosnia?[7] And did the War Powers Resolution apply to Somalia, where what began in December 1992 as a U.S. humanitarian relief mission authorized by the UN Security Council became by May 1993 a UN operation in which U.S. forces found themselves engaged in occasional deadly military confrontations?

Congress made sporadic attempts to play a larger role in defining the U.S. purpose and mission in Somalia, leading eventually, as we have noted, to the Clinton administration's pledge to remove U.S. forces from the African nation by March 31, 1994. Despite this, the House of Representatives passed a resolution that used the legislative veto section of the War Powers Resolution—presumed to have been a dead letter since the Supreme Court's *Chadha* ruling—to direct the president to remove U.S. troops from Somalia. The Senate did not act on the House proposal, but Congress as a whole did cut off funds for further operations in Somalia (unless Congress later authorized more). Unanswered, however, was the larger question of how Congress should integrate and exercise its constitutional powers with respect to war making, the requirements of the War Powers Resolution, and the responsibilities of the UN Security Council, a creature of a multilateral treaty to which the United States is a signatory.

Like Bush, Clinton looked increasingly to the United Nations Security Council for his authority to use force, not to Congress (or the Constitution?). As he honed the military option to unseat Haiti's military regime, for example, he said he "welcomed" congressional support for the contemplated action, but added: "Like my predecessors of both parties, I have not agreed that I was constitutionally mandated to get it." Shortly after that, "he told the American public that he was prepared to use military force to invade Haiti, referring to a UN Security Council [resolution] as authority and his willingness to lead a multilateral force 'to carry out the will of the United Nations'" (Fisher 1994–1995). Such a justification continues the trend toward the expansive use of presidential power especially evident since War World II, arguably well beyond what the framers of the Constitution had in mind when they created the system of check and balances.

The Republican Congress, which came into power in January 1995, determined to reign in U.S. participation in United Nations operations. Legislation considered in both the House and Senate would bar the president from placing U.S. forces under foreign command as part of a UN peacekeeping operation—a move opposed by Clinton officials as an affront to the president's powers—and would reduce U.S. contributions to UN operations by the amount the Defense Department spent supporting past peacekeeping activities. Republican presidential contender Robert Dole also introduced legislation in the Senate that would repeal the War Powers Resolution (similar legislation was introduced and later defeated in the House). "It makes sense to untie the president's hands in the use of force to defend U.S. interests," he told the Senate Foreign Relations Committee, "but we need to rein in the blank check for U.N. peacekeeping."[8] While the Clinton administration welcomed the idea of scrapping the War Powers Resolution, as its predecessors also surely would have, it viewed the new restrictions on the president's authority to dispatch troops for UN operations as too high a price to pay.

And so the debate continues. As it does, the historical record demonstrates that the War Powers Resolution has failed in its intention to redress the balance between Congress and the president because, quite simply, the president has not conceded he is bound by its provisions and because Congress cannot ensure enforcement. "What *should* Congress do when the president fails to consult them before committing the nation to battle?" asked one observer rhetorically. "How *should* Congress respond when the president fails to comply with the provisions of the law of the land?" (Warburg 1989).[9] Furthermore, the growing post-Cold War reliance of multilateral military operations authorized by the United Nations has added a novel new challenge to Congress's constitutional war-making responsibilities. Meanwhile, the president remains preeminent in determining when and how to use American military force abroad.

Money

What about the power of the purse? Since Congress has the exclusive power to appropriate funds for foreign as well as domestic programs, we should expect that here, more than in any other area, Congress would assert its authority over foreign affairs. And, in some respects at least, that has been the case.

Managing Foreign Aid Expenditures

The perennially unpopular foreign aid program is a case in point. Because it depends directly on Congress's appropriation of money, the program enables Congress to scrutinize the executive's conduct of foreign policy and thereby place a legislative stamp on certain aspects of U.S. behavior overseas. "Here is where a host of foreign spending projects on a State Department or Pentagon wish list can be pared. Here is where legislators can attempt to steer foreign procurement contracts toward local firms. Here is where the specter of '535 secretaries of state' is inevitably raised by critics of an aggressive congressional role" (Warburg 1989).

Congress frequently exercises its power of the purse by dramatically cutting the president's foreign aid requests. Part of the reason for this penchant is that foreign aid cuts, unlike many other areas of the budget, are unlikely to adversely affect local constituents' interests. Moreover, Congress characteristically "earmarks" foreign aid funds for particular countries. Special-interest groups and ethnic lobbies are important in determining who gets how much, with the result that flexibility in the president's use of this long-standing policy instrument is severely impaired.

In addition to earmarking, "conditionality"—directives, provisos, and restrictions that Congress writes into the annual foreign aid bill—has become a centerpiece of congressional-presidential struggles over foreign aid funding.

Congressionally imposed conditions take many different forms (see Turner 1988). Bans on aid to countries taking certain actions—such as human rights violations, seizing U.S. fishing vessels, granting sanctuary to terrorists, and the like—are commonplace. Aid also has been made conditional on recipients meeting certain standards, such as cooperating with the United States in the interdiction of drug trafficking, holding free elections, or voting in agreement with the United States on UN resolutions. In the case of the Freedom Support Act of 1992, which authorized U.S. foreign assistance for the republics of the former Soviet Union, Congress linked the flow of aid to the removal of Russian troops from the Baltic states. The list goes on. In fact, Congress reportedly directs where half of all development loan funds and over 90 percent of all U.S. security assistance is to go (Kondracke 1990, 20). In recent years the aid bill often became so encumbered with conditions that it simply failed to be approved. The regular annual foreign aid authorization bill passed only twice during Reagan's eight-year presidency and never during Bush's. Only stopgap measures kept the aid program alive, with congressional appropriations committees effectively exercising sole jurisdiction over it.

Congress also resorts to reporting requirements to ensure executive compliance with legislative restrictions built into the foreign assistance act and other foreign policy legislation. The Freedom Support Act, for example, requires annual reports on the effectiveness of U.S. assistance to the former Soviet Union. The pervasiveness of reporting today is indicated by the explosion in the number of reporting requirements, from two hundred in 1973 to more than eight hundred in 1988 (Collier 1989, 37).

From Congress's point of view, reporting requirements serve several purposes. They provide Congress with information (now tacitly the practice with the reporting requirements in the War Powers Resolution); promote consultation (the Refugee Assistance Act of 1980, for example, defines particular means of executive-legislative consultation); focus attention on a problem (as occurs with the annual required publication of human rights practices in other countries); provide a means of control (the Fishery Conservation Management Act of 1976 requires that fisheries agreements be submitted to Congress within a specified time period); and oversee implementation (as with provisions in the Anti-Apartheid Act of 1986 passed over Reagan's veto) (Collier 1988).

Although reporting requirements are useful to Congress, their number is now so great that "Congress has difficulty keeping track of them, the executive branch agencies fulfilling them, and members and staff reading the submitted reports" (Collier 1988). Moreover, from the president's point of view, the required reports and certifications create inappropriate congressional *micromanagement*—excessive legislative interference in the conduct of America's foreign relations. Congress imposed nearly three hundred individual reporting requirements on the Agency for International Development, for example, leading AID employees in Global South countries to "complain that they spend so much time filling out reports to Congress that they have only an afternoon a week to help the poor" (Kondracke 1990). (Republicans were especially critical of the Democrat-controlled Congress's propensity to micromanage during the Bush administration, but once in control of Congress they behaved similarly. Lamenting Republicans' close scrutiny of the foreign affairs budget following their electoral victory, Democratic Senator Joseph R. Biden caustically observed that "When the Republicans were in the White House, they kept on saying, 'Don't micromanage foreign policy.' But they have turned out to be the biggest micromanaging, tinkering fools around." [See Focus 12.1.])

Congressionally imposed conditions often force the president to balance priorities in such a way that American policy sometimes seems contorted, if not outright contradictory. The Anti-Drug Abuse Act, for example, required the Reagan administration to certify that Panama under the leadership of Manuel Noriega was cooperating in drug-traffic control when, in fact, it was known to be the center of massive drug-trafficking and money-laundering operations (see Kempe 1990). "Yet the president was reluctant to let fly the guillotine on aid to Panama—in part because of concern about the security of the Panama Canal, and in part because of fears that Noriega would embarrass the United States with revelations about his former long-standing relationship with the CIA and the *contras*" (Warburg 1989).

Often presidents are able to avoid such situations by taking advantage of loopholes Congress typically provides. The most general permits the president to ignore restrictions that he or she believes to compromise the United States' security interests. Loopholes fit Congress's tendency to afford the president some flexibility at the same time that it seeks to influence the overall direction of policy—but while also escaping responsibility and criticism for its management. For example, the Freedom Support Act's requirement that tied U.S. aid to the withdrawal of Russian troops from the Baltic states is one that the president could waive. Concern for possible adverse effects on the nation's interests and security underlies such seemingly contradictory impulses.

The Bush administration twice sought unsuccessfully to overhaul the U.S. foreign aid program by sweeping away congressional restrictions. The Clinton administration renewed that effort in early 1994, opening discussions with Congress on a new plan designed to appropriate aid not for specific countries or programs but in pursuit of broad

Focus 12.1
PRESIDENT CLINTON RESPONDS TO THE REPUBLICAN
CONGRESS, MAY 1995

• • •

Legislation that Congress is considering . . . would place new restrictions on how America conducts its foreign policy and slash our budget in foreign affairs. I believe these bills threaten our ability to preserve America's global leadership and to safeguard the security and prosperity of the American people in the post-Cold War world.

The world is still full of dangers but more full of opportunies, and the United States must be able to act aggressively to combat foreign threats and to make commitments and then to keep those commitments. These bills would deprive us of both those capabilities.

Supporters of the bills call them "necessary costcutting measures." But in reality, they are the most isolationist proposals to come before the United States Congress in the last 50 years. They are the product of those who argue passionately that America must be strong, and then turn around and refuse to pay the price of that strength or to give the presidency the means to assert that strength.

The price of conducting our foreign policy is, after all, not very high. Today slightly more than 1 percent of the budget. . . . That 1 percent, which includes contributions to the multilateral development banks, helps to dismantle nuclear weapons, saves lives by preventing famine, immunizing children, and combating terrorists and drug-traffickers.

Bills in both the House and the Senate place new restrictions on our ability to respond to these dangers, as well as to take advantage of all the opportunities that are out there for the United States. . . .

. . . These constraints represent nothing less than a frontal assault on the authority of the president to conduct the foreign policy of the United States and on our nations' ability to respond rapidly and effectively to threats to our security.

Repeatedly, I have said there are right ways and wrong ways to cut the deficit. This legislation is the wrong way. We did not win the Cold War to walk away and blow the opportunites of the peace on shortsighted, scatter-shotted budget cuts and attempts to micromange the United States' foreign policy.

foreign policy goals. Six goals were cited, all in keeping with other elements of the administration's foreign policy program: promoting sustainable development, democracy, peace, humanitarian assistance, growth through trade and investment, and advancing diplomacy. Earmarks would be eliminated, as would traditional budgetary distinctions between military and economic assistance. Although Congress voiced support for revamping a program no longer guided by a compelling rationale, as during the Cold War, it quickly became clear that Congress would not willingly relinquish its right to place a legislative imprimatur on American foreign policy. "We will not give to an unelected bureaucracy . . . authority to spend dollars any way they want, so long as they call it 'pursuit of democracy' or 'expanding economic development,'" asserted David R. Obey of the House Appropriations Subcommittee on Foreign Operations. "There will be no blank checks." That warning became even clearer as the Republicans took the reigns of congressional leadership from the Democrats following the 1994 elections, as they targeted foreign aid for sharp budget cuts—and possible total elimination as an instrument of American foreign policy.

Managing Military Expenditures

Military spending is another budgetary area in which Congress can and does play a major role. During the 1950s and 1960s, Congress often voiced its views on the defense budget by appropriating *more* for defense than was asked for by the president. But as executive-congressional relations moved from acquiescence to ambiguity and then to acrimony, Congress began cutting administration requests substantially, much as it did with foreign aid. Moreover, its micromanagement of the Pentagon increased steadily. A Bush administration White Paper complained that "some thirty committees and seventy-seven subcommittees claim some degree of oversight . . . and more than fifteen hundred congressional staffers devote nearly all of their time to defense issues" (*Wall Street Journal* December 18, 1989: A10). The administration also complained that "the Pentagon alone spent $50 million and five hundred 'man-years' in fiscal 1989 writing reports to satisfy Congress" (cited in Burgin 1993, 342). Meanwhile, Congress makes an increasing number of changes in the president's defense budget requests. In 1970 Congress made 830 program changes during the annual budgetary cycle; by 1988 the number had grown to nearly 2,800 (Blechman 1990, 41).

The motivation to micromanage is tied directly to the factors that differentiate the perspective of members of Congress on foreign and national security policy issues from that of the president. Political grandstanding for electoral purposes is a powerful incentive. For example Congress debated (and voted on) virtually all of the important strategic and many conventional weapons systems requiring production decisions during the Reagan administration's military build-up in the 1980s, when the incentives to micromanage were especially strong. The decisions Congress faced included the MX missile, the Strategic Defense Initiative (SDI), the Stealth bomber program, antisatellite systems, chemical weapons, the Trident II submarine, the B-1 bomber, cruise missiles, nuclear-powered aircraft carriers, and anti-aircraft guns and tactical aircraft. Administration preferences, which are "the greatest single influence on congressional choices" (Blechman 1990), framed the debates on these systems. Before Reagan, decisions on them typically would have been made in congressional committees; now, however, they became the object of much activity on the floor of the respective chambers of Congress, where members debated them to enhance their visibility. As Senator Gaylord Nelson noted wryly, "the floor is being used as an instrument of political campaigning far more than it ever was before." Electoral incentives in the form of financial contributions and constituency support also multiplied as the guns-instead-of-butter spending priorities of the Reagan administration helped to politicize defense policy (Lindsay 1987).[10]

The same parochialism that motivates members of Congress to serve on committees fuels Congress's micromanagement of the defense budget, as members are alert to the impact of defense spending on their constituencies.[11] Neglect of long-term policy is a natural consequence. As a former staff member of the (then) House Armed Services Committee observed, "there is a natural constituency for concentration on weapons systems in the here and now. It is difficult for members to focus on the big issues because of the lack of time, because of the need to get reelected, and because of the fact that constituency service, not policy oversight, is what is necessary today to stay in office" (cited in Art 1985; see also Blechman 1990).

The question is how to get Congress to focus on policy, not programs. In Pentagon jargon, "policy oversight" is captured in issues of "force structure" or "force design." The consensus is that on these issues, Congress does not do well (Art 1985). As a former House Armed Services Committee staff member observed, "Members of Armed Services get into policy but only obliquely. For example, on the Lehman power projection or sea control issue [during the Reagan presidency]. . . we made a decision in favor of the former by authorizing a six-hundred-ship navy, but we did it this way: We justified a carrier by stating the policy behind it rather than the reverse. We did not debate which policy we needed and then determine the best weapons systems to achieve it. The members of the committee thus back into policy" (cited in Art 1985).

Neglecting policy oversight may undermine Congress's capacity to exercise the power of the purse effectively, but for individual members such avoidance is politically astute. "The only thing worse than taking on an issue that will not make a legislator look good is taking on one that will make him look bad. The political incentives as they are structured on Capitol Hill . . . put the bias on the short term, the specific, the details, the programs that can be grabbed, manipulated, changed, and sold" (Art 1985).

How will the end of the Cold War affect Congress's role in defense policy making? Is Congress more likely to focus on policy rather than programs now that the United States no longer faces a powerful military foe? Or is congressional parochialism, borne of the demands of the electoral cycle, likely to continue to dominate the process? The early post-Cold War world provides conflicting signals—but the balance of both theory and evidence points toward a perpetuation of past patterns of behavior.

As the Cold War came to an end following Bush's election, the administration moved haltingly at best in responding to the emergent challenges. Secretary of Defense Dick Cheney in particular seemed determined to keep the Cold War cold (Schumacher 1990), as he testified before Congress that this is "the worst possible time to contemplate changes in defense strategy." That posture provoked a sharp reaction on Capitol Hill. Sam Nunn, chair of the Senate Armed Services Committee, and Les Aspin, chair of the House Armed Services Committee, moved to fill the "policy vacuum" created by the administration's unwillingness to respond to the end of the Cold

War. "Nunn attacked [Cheney's] position as incomprehensible, and argued that the administration's defense policy was riddled with 'big blanks.' Aspin reached a similar conclusion, arguing that 'there are new realities in the world, but no new thinking at home to match them'" (Stockton 1993). Nunn and Aspin acted on their convictions when the Senate and House Armed Services Committees drafted their own defense budgets, setting out markedly different priorities from the Bush administration's budget requests.

Nunn's and Aspin's response to broad policy issues as the Cold War waned is not easily explained by the imperative of reelection or the demands of constituent service. A sense of "duty" and a belief that addressing policy issues is "part of their job" are perhaps better explanations (Stockton 1993). Still, the opportunity to score political points is not easily dismissed. Public opinion polls repeatedly showed that the American people favored slashing the defense budget after the fall of the Berlin Wall. "President Bush's [defense budget request for fiscal year 1991] ran counter to this opinion surge and created a juicy political opportunity for congressional Republicans and Democrats to propose much deeper military cuts" (Stockton 1993). Indeed, Congress's desire to spend the "peace dividend" to meet domestic—read "constituency"—needs followed a well-established pattern.

In some ways the end of the Cold War has added incentives to "strategize" as well as to micromanage: "While voters may have had little interest in such topics in the past, the demise of the Soviet threat allows legislators to link proposals on strategy to more immediate voter concerns" (Stockton 1995). Still, the policy vacuum into which Congress stepped in 1990–1991 is unlikely to be repeated. In fact, the Defense Reorganization Act of 1986 (the Goldwater-Nichols Act) virtually assures that the president will continue to dominate the shape of defense policy, as it requires that each annual budget request to Congress be accompanied by a comprehensive report on overall national security strategy. Congress's incentive, then, is to use its power of the purse not to shape overall policy but rather its implementation. And immediate constituency interests promise to figure prominently in the calculations. As one defense expert observed caustically, "Politicians of both parties see the [defense] budget as a jobs program. No longer does the defense debate take place between hawks and doves, but between those who have defense facilities and those who don't" (Korb 1995a).

Constraints on the Power of the Purse

Congressional actions on the foreign aid and defense budgets demonstrate Congress's willingness to exercise its power of the purse, although its instruments for doing so are not finely honed and its motives sometimes circumspect. Elsewhere, however, the frequency with which Congress has used its fiscal powers to cope with a dominant executive has been remarkably irregular. There are examples, of course: In 1976 the Clark amendment barred the use of funds for any activities involving Angola; in the early 1980s the Boland amendment sought to prevent covert activities in Central America; in the early 1990s when Congress invoked the Pressler amendment to bar economic and military aid to Pakistan because of its nuclear weapons program; and in the mid-1990s Congress cut off funds to enforce the arms embargo against Bosnia. Historically, however, such actions are the exception rather than the rule. Indeed, these four stories are as notable for their uniqueness as for their illustration of Congress exercising the power of the purse.

More characteristic of presidential-congressional relations is the fate of the much-publicized Cooper-Church amendment, which sought to cut off funds for U.S. war efforts in Cambodia following Nixon's "incursion" into the country in 1970. The amendment failed. In fact, Congress cut off Cambodian war funds only after (then known) U.S. military activity had ceased, and Congress never failed to appropriate the funds for the war that the Johnson and Nixon administrations sought. Two decades later Congress again cut off funds for a U.S. operation, this one in Somalia. Again, however, the target date (March 31, 1994) was the one the administration had already announced for terminating the U.S. role.

The largely symbolic Cooper-Church amendment illustrates the difficulty inherent in getting even a majority of 535 independent-minded lawmakers to agree on a specific proposal—a prospect made all the more difficult when the proposal challenges the president. Thus, as we noted earlier, Senator Lugar advised in regard to Clinton's Haiti policies that "Any resolution that we can adopt won't really bind the administration. There'll always be an escape hatch." More generally, however, the extent to which money can be used to affect the nation's foreign policy is limited. Simply put, it is difficult to legislate foreign policy or to equate lawmaking with foreign policy making. Programs, but not necessarily policies, require appropriations. Hence, some of the most important aspects of America's foreign relations do not require specific and direct appropriations of money.

Substantive legislation—lawmaking—is Congress's primary vehicle for affecting foreign policy making. Like the president, however, Congress also has other instruments of influence at its disposal (Lindsay 1994a, 1994b). It can frame the terms of debate on particular issues using congressional hearings, committee reports, and speeches, for example. Similarly, it can shape the contestants in the policy process by implementing structural changes. In 1986, for example, Congress created a new under secretary of defense for acquisition, whose task was to reduce waste, fraud, and abuse in the defense acquisition process. The "effort proceeded from a simple assumption about bureaucratic life: If you want a policy to succeed, make sure some agency in the bureaucracy will champion it" (Lindsay 1994a).

Despite these and other avenues of influence outside the realm of substantive legislation, Congress is limited in the effective use of its powers by the division of congressional responsibility among many different committees, the breakdown of party unity, and the erosion of congressional leadership. This fact is nowhere more evident than in the funding process, where, within each house of Congress, the substantive committees having jurisdiction over particular programs authorize expenditures, but another committee makes the actual appropriations.

In 1974 Congress passed the Budget and Impoundment Control Act in an attempt to consolidate some control over the purse. The law created the Congressional Budget Office and the budget committees in the two houses of Congress. It also required that Congress specify overall spending targets in an annual budget resolution. In principle, Congress is now required to face squarely the unwelcome political task of weighing federal spending against federal income. In practice, Congress continues to postpone the tough choices. Since passage of the Budget Act federal deficits have mushroomed;

appropriations bills are passed later than ever, if at all, and deadlines imposed by the act have routinely been ignored. Moreover, "budgets submitted by presidents and budget resolutions passed by Congress have been chronically unreliable and deceptive. They regularly underestimate spending and overestimate revenues, producing deficits far beyond presidential and congressional projections" (Fisher 1993).

To cope with inadequacies in the budgetary process, Congress passed deficit reduction acts in 1985 and again in 1987, but neither proved effective in stemming the flow of red ink. To deal with the situation, a new tack was tried with the Budget Enforcement Act of 1990. Rather than promising deficit reduction, attention now focused on spending limits. Spending caps were specified for three program categories: defense, international, and domestic. "Fire walls" were erected between the categories to prevent Congress from taking money from defense (the "peace dividend") to pay for domestic programs. Some members of Congress chafed under the restriction, arguing that the end of the Cold War called for a shift in priorities from security to domestic needs. Once the fire walls expired, however, defense advocates urged their replacement to prevent what they saw as a process that could cripple the nation's security requirements.

The Budget Enforcement Act is the fourth reform of the budget process in less than two decades. As with other procedural legislation passed by Congress, it is based on "the belief that changing *how* decisions are made will in turn affect *which* decisions are made" (Lindsay 1994a). Almost before the ink was dry, however, critics began to wonder about its effects (Thurber and Durst 1993).

Even if the 1990 reform law fails to achieve its lofty goals, analysts generally agree that it enhances the president's budgetary power at the expense of Congress. Existing devices already give the president discretion to spend as he or she pleases, irrespective of congressional wishes and oversight, thus providing substantial fiscal independence. *Impoundment*, which is a presidential refusal to spend money appropriated by Congress, is one mechanism. Others include discretionary funds and reprogramming decisions. Each enables the executive to undertake activities that may differ from congressional wishes and intent.

Discretionary funds, for example, are monies provided the president to deal with situations unforeseen at the time of the annual budget process, but they often have been used for nonemergencies. For example, Johnson used $1.5 billion in contingency funds embedded in the Defense Department budget to finance military operations in Southeast Asia during 1965 and 1966 (Nathan and Oliver 1976, 495–96). Similarly, the Reagan administration used $10 million in CIA discretionary funds to finance the *contras* during its first term (Copson 1988, 4). It also used its discretionary authority and "reprogrammed" funds to finance activities in El Salvador at the same time that Congress sought to curtail military assistance to the country (Burgin 1993).

Reprogramming is a nonstatutory control mechanism devised by Congress and the executive to deal with contingencies that neither branch has anticipated. The device, which permits funds within an appropriation category to be moved from one purpose to another (for example, from shipbuilding to submarine construction), is widely used by the Defense Department. The sums involved are often quite large, which opens the mechanism to charges that it can be used by the president to undermine Congress's constitutional power of the purse. An example Congress found "particularly objectionable" was "the Pentagon's practice of requesting funds for a program, being turned down by Congress, and then spending other appropriated funds for the rejected program" (Fisher 1993). Not surprisingly, therefore, Congress has progressively increased its scrutiny of reprogrammings to prevent abuses of a system advantageous to both ends of Pennsylvania Avenue.

Constraining the executive's flexibility in using funds appropriated by Congress was a principal purpose of the Budget and Impoundment Control Act. It specified that the president had two avenues, both subject to congressional review, by which to impound funds: Temporary spending delays, which can extend up to twelve months, are known as *deferrals;* permanent efforts to cancel budget authority are known as *rescissions*. Court rulings in the aftermath of the *Chadha* decision on the legislative veto restricted the comprehensiveness of Congress's role in these matters compared with the intent of the 1974 budget law (Fisher 1991, 1993). This clouds an assessment of the act's effects in constraining the president's budgetary latitude, but the overall record suggests that it has not been severely limited.

Intelligence community financing is one area in which Congress has been especially reluctant to fix leaks from the fiscal faucet. Indeed, financial support for intelligence remains the best-known example of Congress giving dollars to the president that remain outside the direct control of Congress as a whole.

The House and Senate Intelligence Committees are now empowered to authorize expenditures by the intelligence community (most of which is embedded in the Defense Department's budget), but periodic efforts to have the actual costs of intelligence operations released publicly have routinely failed. The pattern persists even in the aftermath of the Cold War and the pledge of both Congress and the president to be forthcoming on intelligence and related security matters. Thus in late 1993 Congress passed an intelligence bill widely reported to contain $28 billion to support the nation's intelligence agencies, but it still refused to disclose the amount. Reflecting the preferences of the Clinton administration (which reversed an earlier promise to "take seriously" suggestions that it disclose the magnitude of intelligence spending), John W. Warner, vice chair of the Senate Intelligence Committee, reflected long-standing sentiments about the nation's interests and security when he stated that "Not a single major nation in this world discloses the top line of their [intelligence] budget. I don't know what we have to gain as a nation—standing alone—on this."

It could not be anticipated from the practice of intelligence appropriations that the executive branch would engage in covert intelligence activities by bypassing the congressional funding process altogether; yet this is exactly what happened during the Iran-*contra* affair. Between $3 and $4 million in profits from the sale of arms to Iran in early 1986 was diverted to the *contras* at precisely the time the Boland amendment banned U.S. government support for the guerrillas. Staff members of the president's National Security Council also solicited millions of dollars in funds from private contributors in the United States and from foreign governments to keep the *contras* afloat—despite the Congress's having in effect determined that the United States should distance itself from the anti-Sandinista cause.

Lieutenant Colonel Oliver North testified before Congress that, in his opinion, the withholding of appropriations by Congress did not prevent the president from pursuing his foreign policy objectives using private or foreign-donated funds. Admiral John

Poindexter, North's boss at the NSC, concurred, arguing that the executive branch could circumvent Congress by using nonappropriated funds. Furthermore, he defended the withholding of information from Congress on grounds that the NSC was using private and third-country funds, not money appropriated by Congress. The congressional inquiry into the Iran-*contra* affair also revealed that William Casey, director of central intelligence during the Reagan administration until his death in 1987, had expressed interest in creating an off-the-shelf, stand-alone, self-financed intelligence organization capable of conducting covert activities without ever being held accountable to Congress or anyone else.

The Constitution of the United States places the power of the purse directly in the hands of Congress. The North/Poindexter/Casey logic would undermine the system of checks and balances between the executive and legislative branches of government which is the essence of the American political system. By "placing in the same branch the ability to make war and fund it," Louis Fisher (1988), an expert on the powers of Congress and the president, has written, "executive use of funds obtained outside the appropriations process would create a government the framers feared the most: union of sword and purse." As James Madison wrote, "Those who are to *conduct a war* cannot in the nature of things, be proper or safe judges, whether a war ought to be *commenced, continued*, or *concluded*. They are barred from the latter functions by a great principle in free government, analogous to that which separates the sword from the purse, or the power of executing from the power of enacting laws" (cited in Fisher 1988).

"To preserve the system of checks and balances," concludes Fisher, "foreign policy must be carried out with funds appropriated by Congress. Allowing foreign policy to be conducted with funds supplied by private parties and foreign governments . . . would fundamentally subvert the Constitution and undermine the powers of Congress as a coequal branch." Ronald Reagan's secretary of state, George Shultz, a vigorous critic of the Iran-*contra* connection, agreed: "You cannot spend funds that the Congress doesn't either authorize you to obtain or appropriate. That is what the Constitution says, and we have to stick to it. . . . We have this very difficult task of having a separation of powers that means we have to share power. Sharing power is harder, . . . but that's the only way" (cited in Henderson 1988).

Is Congress Either Able or Willing?

The election of Bill Clinton in 1992 ended twelve uninterrupted years of divided government—but only briefly, as it unexpectedly turned out. "Gridlock" popularly described the conflict and inaction that accompanied the partisan divisions between Congress and the president across a broad array of both foreign and domestic policy issues. The Iran-*contra* affair during the Reagan administration and the seemingly endless series of vetoes and veto threats during the Bush presidency are testimony to the often bitter conflicts between the Republican presidents and the Democratic-controlled Congress evident for more than a decade. Some hoped the end of divided government would enhance the prospects for effective governance in the post-Cold War era. Others were less than sanguine, believing that the sources of conflict between Congress and the executive and the reasons for the government's seeming ineptitude go beyond partisan divisions along Pennsylvania Avenue (Mann and Ornstein 1993; Sundquist 1993). How foreign policy will fare in the contest between Congress and the president in the post-Cold War era thus remains uncertain—a conclusion all the more stark with the seizure of congressional control by the Republican Party for the first time in forty years.

Having said that, it is also clear that the president will remain the leading partner— if not always the senior partner—in devising responses to the challenges and opportunities the nation now faces. Foreign and defense policy issues are sometime described as falling into three categories: crisis policy, structural policy, and strategic policy (Ripley and Franklin 1991). Congress has virtually no role in crisis decision making, but it is a central component of the exceedingly complex institutional labyrinth in which structural and strategic policy is made.[12] Still, the resources available to the White House in the process whereby policy emanates from this maze are clearly more formidable than those available to Congress. In the areas of treaties, war, and money, the Constitution would appear to make Congress, not the president, preeminent; but the reverse has in fact been true. Congress has made some strides toward coping with its structural inadequacies, but power remains diffused, the ability to assume and discharge responsibility remains fragmented, and the incentives to favor parochial needs rather than the broader picture continue. Hence, there is little that warrants a revision of the initiator-respondent view of executive-legislative relations, even in the post-Cold War environment which sometimes portrays the president as just an "ordinary" player in policy game. Even now Congress remains comparatively far removed from the center of foreign policy power; it has authority, but it follows more than it leads. Thus the president proposes, Congress disposes.

That view should not obscure the positive contributions Congress can make. As former Representative Les Aspin (1976) observes, Congress "is a conservative organization—cautious and reluctant to initiate change," but it still functions reasonably well as an avenue for expressing constituent and other views and interests, as an overseer of government policies and resource allocations, and as a "guardian" of the processes of government. Even former Senator J. William Fulbright (1979), once an outspoken critic of presidential dominance in foreign policy making, concluded that Congress is most effective "in the authorization of military and major political commitments, and in advising broad policy directions, while leaving to the executive the necessary flexibility to conduct policy within the broad parameters approved by the legislature."

NOTES

1. One definition associates bipartisanship with "unity in foreign affairs" as reflected in "policy supported by majorities within each political party"; another depicts it as a set of "practices and procedures designed to bring about the desired unity" (Crabb 1957). For a review of the idea and practice of bipartisanship, see Collier (1989).

2. Eventually the law set the period for congressional consideration at thirty days. According to the Arms Export Control Act, any sale exceeding $14 million in major defense equipment or $50 million in defense articles or services is subject to congressional review. By mutual agreement, presidents are expected to give Congress twenty days' advance notice before submitting a

formal proposal for approval to allow the two branches to reach compromises on politically sensitive issues.

3. *Immigration and Naturalization Service v. Chadha*, 103 S. Ct. 2764 (1983). The court's ruling applied to cases in which Congress had expressly granted administrative power to the executive. Since not all legislation fit the conditions addressed by the court, the import of the *Chadha* case is more restricted than once thought. Applicability to the legislative veto provisions of the War Powers Resolution remains unresolved.
Although the legislative veto had come to be viewed as a necessary instrument to protect Congress from the executive's usurpation of legislative prerogatives, the record shows that the president willingly accepted legislative veto provisions in exchange for the flexibility Congress granted the president (Fisher 1993). Noteworthy in this regard is that more than two hundred new legislative vetoes were enacted into law between 1983 and 1991 (Fisher 1993, 83). Most of these are committee and subcommittee vetoes. Thus the evidence indicates that the device continues to be useful to both the legislative and executive branches.

4. The Boland amendment, named after its sponsor, Edward P. Boland, Democratic representative from Massachusetts and chair of the House Intelligence Committee until 1984, figured prominently in the Iran-*contra* affair, in which a central question was whether the restrictions contained in the amendment applied to the president and the National Security Council. Although Reagan signed the Boland amendment into law, he maintained "it so happens that it does not apply to me."
Actually there were several Boland amendments that reflected changes in congressional concern about providing military aid to the *contras*. Critics of Congress charge that "In effect, the congressional majority foreordained something like the Iran-*contra* 'scandal' by attempting to hogtie the president with the Boland Amendment" (Jeffrey 1988).

5. See Cavanagh (1982–1983), Pfiffner (1992), and Smith and Deering (1990) for examinations of changes in Congress since the 1960s, and Drischler (1985) and Lindsay (1987, 1988) for insight into their importance for the enactment of foreign affairs legislation.

6. This section draws heavily on Collier (1993, 1994b).

7. The Clinton administration reported that the troops were dispatched to Macedonia in accordance with the UN Participation Act, as amended in 1949, which permits up to one thousand personnel to be assigned to the United Nations for noncombatant activities.

8. Interestingly, Bob Dole, then a freshman senator, co-sponsored the War Powers Resolution with Senator Jacob Javits.

9. Theodore Lowi (1985b) has argued that the War Powers Resolution does not give Congress new power to participate in war-making decisions, but that it does in effect give the president "blanket power to use military force for sixty days, without legislative authorization," which "legitimizes a war-making power that heretofore had been based on customary practice and precedent."

10. Defense procurement is typically regarded as a pork-barrel issue which members of Congress use to cultivate constituency support. During the debate on the B-1 bomber, for example, the Air Force and its industrial allies lobbied Congress with the argument that they would profit from the project with increased jobs and dollars in their states and congressional districts (Kotz 1988; Ornstein and Elder 1978). Interestingly, however, congressional votes on strategic-weapons issues are best explained not by constituency interests (as the military-industrial complex thesis would argue) but instead on the basis of Congress members' political ideology

(Lindsay 1990). Although foreign and national security policy often are thought to be above politics, evidence abounds to shows that they are as frequently characterized by partisan and ideological disputes as are domestic issues. See Bernstein (1989), Bernstein and Anthony (1974), Fleisher (1985), McCormick (1985), McCormick and Black (1983), McCormick and Wittkopf (1990a, 1990b), Moyer (1973), Taylor and Rourke (1995), and Wayman (1985).

11. See Bartels (1991) for a evidence that Congress responded to constituency preferences in supporting increased defense spending during Reagan's first term.

12. The difference between structural and strategic policy is not clear cut. Ripley and Franklin (1991) suggest that "structural policies and programs aim primarily at procuring, deploying, and organizing military personnel and materiel, presumably within the confines of previously determined strategic decisions." What they call "subgovernments"—typically "composed of members of the House and Senate, members of congressional staffs, bureaucrats, and representatives of [interested] private groups and organizations"—are principal actors in the structural policy arena. Strategic policies, on the other hand, "assert and implement the basic military and foreign policy stance of the United States toward other nations. Policy planning and proposals resulting from that planning stem primarily from executive branch activities. . . . Although congressional influence can be important, that influence is often used to respond supportively to executive branch agencies."

SUGGESTIONS FOR FURTHER READING

Bax, Frans R. "The Legislative-Executive Relationship in Foreign Policy: New Partnership or New Competition?" *Orbis* 20 (Winter 1977): 881–904.

Blechman, Barry M. *The Politics of National Security: Congress and U.S. Defense Policy.* New York: Oxford University Press, 1990.

Collier, Ellen S. "Bipartisan Foreign Policy and Policymaking since World War II," *CRS Report for Congress.* Washington, D.C.: Congressional Research Service, 1989.

Crabb, Cecil V., Jr., and Pat M. Holt. *Invitation to Struggle: Congress, the President and Foreign Policy,* 4th ed. Washington D.C.: Congressional Quarterly Press, 1992.

Fisher, Louis. *Presidential War Power.* Lawrence: University of Kansas Press, 1995.

Franck, Thomas M., and Edward Weisband. *Foreign Policy by Congress.* New York: Oxford University Press, 1979.

Jones, Gordon S., and John A. Marini, eds. *The Imperial Congress: Crisis in the Separation of Powers.* New York: Pharos Books, 1988.

Lindsay, James M. *Congress and the Politics of U.S. Foreign Policy.* Baltimore: Johns Hopkins University Press, 1994.

Mann, Thomas E., ed. *A Question of Balance: The President, the Congress, and Foreign Policy.* Washington, D.C.: The Brookings Institution, 1990.

Ripley, Randall B., and James M. Lindsay, eds. *Congress Resurgent: Foreign and Defense Policy on Capitol Hill.* Ann Arbor: University of Michigan Press, 1993.

Warburg, Gerald Felix. *Conflict and Consensus: The Struggle between Congress and the President over Foreign Policymaking.* New York: Harper & Row, 1989.

West, William F., and Joseph Cooper. "Legislative Influence v. Presidential Dominance: Competing Models of Bureaucratic Control," *Political Science Quarterly* 104 (Winter 1990): 581–606.

CHAPTER 13

THE PROCESS OF DECISION MAKING: ROLES, RATIONALITY, AND THE IMPACT OF BUREAUCRATIC ORGANIZATION

• • •

As modern bureaucracy has grown, the understanding of change and the formulation of new purposes have become more difficult. Like men, governments find old ways hard to change and new paths difficult to discover.

President Richard M. Nixon, 1970

In so many of the ex post facto *investigations, [outsiders] take individual documents and assume that people sat around the table in a seminar-type discussion, having all the facts. . . . But that is rarely the case. Usually decisions are made in a very brief time with enormous pressure and uncertain knowledge.*

Former Secretary of State Henry Kissinger, 1977

Many different people, widely dispersed throughout the government, make American foreign policy. We have examined the offices and their overall organization—the governmental superstructures. We now consider the decision-making *process*—how the roles or formal positions within the superstructure policymakers occupy influence their foreign policy decisions, especially in an environment demanding innovation and adaptation to new realities.

Our inquiry in previous chapters gives a glimpse of what we can expect to find. First, the very size of the government—the incredibly complex organizational structures into which the millions of federal employees fit and the maze of channels through which innovative ideas must pass before they become new policies—is likely to work against the understanding of change and the formulation of new purposes, much as President Nixon lamented more than two decades ago. Apart from cabinet-level departments, the federal roster includes over sixty different departments and agencies and over 1,250 advisory boards and commissions. Add Congress—which, as we have seen, often acts more like 535 separate interests than one unified body—and we can begin to appreciate how the very size of government inhibits policy change in response to new realities.

Second, the politics of policy making within this maze of multiple and often overlapping institutions is more conducive to the status quo than to change. Money and personnel mean political power. Once acquired, institutions protect them. They oppose changes that threaten to erode their sources of influence. Incremental changes at the edge are acceptable, but fundamental reorientations that would require massive budgetary and personnel cuts must be resisted.

The reasons why individuals in the foreign affairs government protect their "fiefdoms" is best explained by the roles they occupy and the patterns of demands and expectations that define those roles. As we will see in this chapter, role requirements exert a powerful impact on individual behavior and thus the pattern and process of American foreign policy.

Roles as a Source of Foreign Policy ....

Role theory posits that the positions and the processes, rather than the characteristics of the people who decide, influence the behavior and choices of those responsible for making and executing the nation's foreign policy. Furthermore, changes in policy presumably result from changes in role conceptions rather than from changes in the individuals who occupy the roles. Individuals are not unimportant, from this perspective, but the institutional roles that individuals occupy mold their behavior and constrain their decision-making latitude.

Role theory recognizes that a person's behavior can be distinguished from the role he or she occupies. Nonetheless, each role (or position) carries with it social and psychological demands and expectations that shape perceptions of how it should be performed. These pressures, which include personal and peer pressures as well as those of "the boss," affect both attitudes and actions. And they influence *anyone* filling a particular role, regardless of personal preferences. Thus every individual behaves similarly to others who have occupied the same role.

To suggest that roles influence thoughts and behavior should not be disturbing. Everyone plays many roles in life. Unless we are hermits, we sometimes find ourselves in social situations with which we have had no prior experience. We typically respond to such new circumstances by behaving according to our image of appropriate conduct. Witness the changes observable when people shift from the role of student to employee, or to new parent, or politician. Most act subconsciously in the manner they believe is expected. Their vocabulary and ideas undergo subtle change, as does their outlook. The various roles each of us play in life explain and predict our attitudes and behavior in important ways.

Policymakers are not immune from this phenomenon. Each policy-making role carries with it certain expectations, obligations, and images of appropriate behavior—pressures that push the new occupant of an office to think and act like his or her predecessor. The newcomer's style and mannerisms may be markedly different from the predecessor's, but orientations toward crucial issues will be similar.[1] "It's an old story in Washington that where you stand depends on where you sit. That's a practical acknowledgment of the fact that people's views change as they change responsibilities," political journalist David Broder observed. An example: while campaigning, Jimmy Carter criticized Henry Kissinger's "personal diplomacy" and advocated less emphasis on private talks with foreign leaders. Yet in the first seven months in office, Carter played host to no fewer than eighteen foreign heads of state. (Years later Bill Clinton would opt to trade his jogging shorts and stops at the local McDonald's for more formal business attire befitting the dignity of the presidency, despite his preferred populist image as a "man of the people.")

There are limits to role theory's ability to explain policy-making behavior, of course. A forceful personality may actually redefine the role to extend the boundaries of permissible behavior, as Franklin Roosevelt did when he expanded the scope and authority of the presidency. Ronald Reagan's habit of taking many naps and frequent vacations—a propensity that reflected his relaxed style in an office that heretofore demanded sleepless attention to the duties of governance—also transcended customary role requirements, although in another direction.

Furthermore, particular roles permit more than one interpretation, and some have boundaries so wide and elastic that the behavior of individuals within them is almost unpredictable. Although high positions allow several interpretations—as evidenced, for example, by the contrast between Eisenhower's and Kennedy's concept of the presidency or between Bush's and Clinton's conception of the role of government in political life—each interpretation is, in effect, a specific role.[2] Still, variations in individual behavior will continue to depend on the interpretation a new occupant of her or his role adopts. And it should be noted that certain types of people *become* their roles more easily than others, as they are prone to embrace whatever they inherit (Snyder 1980).

The ability to frame alternative definitions of the same policy-making roles attests to one of the ways the individual source category (elaborated in Chapter 14) affects the foreign policy process. Recall from Chapter 10, for example, how different presidents have chosen to organize their White House foreign policy staff to accomplish the same fundamental goal (promoting and protecting American national interests). The differences are sometimes profound. Johnson's approach to the Vietnam War and Nixon's insulation from the larger foreign affairs government, for example, proved to have lasting consequences for the policy problems each faced. Even leaders who may sometimes be given considerable leeway to act as they wish usually acquiesce to the prevailing norms associated with their position. Behavioral conformity is especially evident in the formal roles government positions embody, where norms governing performance are backed by legal obligations and sanctions and not merely social pressures. Watergate is a case in point: Richard Nixon discovered the system's intolerance for illegal conduct even by the president.

This line of reasoning has substantial implications for American foreign policy. Role theory's premise—that people's conduct conforms to their roles—means that to understand the nature of American foreign policy we must examine the behavior most often associated with foreign policy-making roles in addition to examining individuals themselves. That focus also enables us to understand a potentially potent source of foreign policy change. Because roles shape goals, policy innovations may derive from changes in major policy-making roles or individuals' conceptions of them. If the decision-making system with its existing roles and their prevailing interpretations changes, then policy redirections may follow.

In this chapter we investigate two interpretations of American decision-making procedures that embrace rival images of role-induced behavior—the *rational decision-making model* and the *bureaucratic politics model*. The two offer sometimes competing, sometimes complementary views of roles as sources of American foreign policy.

Foreign Policy Making as a Rational Process　. . . . .

President Carter's campaign strategists attempted to portray a particular image of their candidate when he was running for reelection in 1980. In an often-televised commercial, Carter was photographed in the Oval Office, working industriously late into the night, poring over documents. He was pictured as a deep thinker, intellectually absorbed in the tasks of the office, —making the decisions that only he could make—formidable choices on which the nation's destiny would depend. Viewers were asked to compare his qualifications—his intelligence, experience, dedication, energy, and diligence—with those of his opponent.

The footage did more than attempt to sell the candidate, though. It also reinforced a popular view of the policy-making process at the nation's nerve center on Pennsylvania Avenue: that fateful decisions are made by *rational* actors engaged in orderly, contemplative processes. In this ***rational decision-making model,*** American foreign policy results from a deliberate intellectual process in which the central figures carefully choose what is best for the country and select tactics appropriately designed to promote its national interests.

Thus the question "Is foreign policy making rational?" is a curious one. We tend, almost instinctively, to think, "How could it be otherwise?" Indeed, it is disconcerting to picture something as important as foreign policy choice, where the stakes are the lives of millions of people and perhaps the survival of the nation itself, as governed by incoherence, emotions, or irrational impulses. The notion of rational policy making is much more comforting. Political leaders also try to cultivate public images of themselves as decisive, unfettered by subconscious psychological drives, able to manage the stress and burden of their position, endowed with boundless energy, and prepared to guide the country safely through crises while pursuing the nation's best interests. Their efforts are frequently successful because we prefer to think of our leaders' decisions as the product of rational deliberations.

What constitutes rationality as it applies to foreign policy decision making? Although "rationality" is loosely used in a variety of ways, it generally refers to "actions chosen by the nation . . . that will maximize strategic goals and objectives" (Allison 1971). This implies purposeful, goal-directed behavior that occurs when "the individual responding to an international event . . . uses the best information available and chooses from the universe of possible responses that alternative most likely to maximize his goals" (Verba 1969; see also Levi 1990; Moser 1990; Zagare 1990).

Rationality is often the standard used to evaluate policy-formulation processes, because a counter model, premised on nonrational behavior (in which action is driven by emotional predispositions, subconscious impulses, and nonintellectual forces) is not very useful.

The Rational Actor Model

The rational actor model treats the nation-state as a ***unitary-actor***, a single, homogeneous entity, and presumes that all policymakers go through the same rational thought processes to make value-maximizing choices defining national interests and options.

[The assumption] allows one to consider all decision makers to be alike. If they follow the [decision] rules, we need know nothing more about them. In essence, if the decision maker behaves rationally, the observer, knowing the rules of rationality, can rehearse the decisional process in his own mind and, if he knows the decision maker's goals, can both predict the decision and understand why that particular decision was made. (Verba 1969, 225)

Scholars who study decision making and advise policymakers on ways to improve their policy-formulation skills describe the perfect rationality role model as a sequence of decision-making activities involving the following intellectual steps:

1. *Problem recognition and definition.* The necessity for choice begins when policymakers perceive an external problem with which they must deal and attempt to define objectively its distinguishing characteristics. Objectivity requires full information about the actions, motivations, and capabilities of other actors as well as the state of the international environment and trends within it. The search for information must be exhaustive, and all the facts relevant to the problem must be gathered.

2. *Goal selection.* Next, those responsible for making foreign policy choices must determine what they want to accomplish. This disarmingly simple requirement is often difficult. It requires the identification and ranking of *all* values (such as security, democracy, freedom, and economic well-being) in a hierarchy from most- to least-preferred.

3. *Identification of alternatives.* Rationality also requires the compilation of an exhaustive list of *all* available policy options and an estimation of the costs associated with each alternative course of action as it relates to the goals and values decision makers hope to realize.

4. *Choice.* Finally, rationality requires selecting from competing options the single alternative with the best chance of achieving the desired goal(s). For this purpose, policymakers must conduct a rigorous means-ends, cost-benefit analysis, one guided by an accurate prediction of the probable success of each option.

Clearly, the requirements of perfect rationality are stringent. Nonetheless, policymakers often describe their own decision-making procedures as rational. A former Kennedy adviser, for example, described an eight-step process for policy making that the Kennedy administration sought to follow which is consistent with the rational model we have described: (1) agreeing on the facts; (2) agreeing on the overall policy objective; (3) precisely defining of the problem; (4) canvassing all possible solutions; (5) listing the possible consequences flowing from each solution; (6) recommending one option; (7) communicating the option selected; and (8) providing for its execution (Sorensen 1963).

Elements of this idealized version of decision making have in fact been exhibited, or at least approximated, in past situations. The 1962 Cuban missile crisis—described by Dean Rusk as "the most dangerous crisis the world has ever seen"—illustrates several ways the deliberations of the key American policymakers conformed to a rational process (Allison 1971; for re-assessments by U.S. and Soviet participants, see Blight, Nye, and Welch 1987; Blight and Welch 1989). Once Washington discovered the presence of Soviet missiles in Cuba, President Kennedy charged the crisis decision-making group he formed to "set aside all other tasks to make a prompt and intensive survey of the dangers and all possible courses of action." Six options were ultimately identified: Do nothing; exert diplomatic pressure; make a secret approach to Cuban leader Fidel Castro; invade Cuba; launch a surgical air strike against the missiles; and blockade Cuba. Goals had to be prioritized before a choice could be made among these six. Was removing the Soviet missiles, retaliating against Castro, or maintaining the balance of power the objective? Or did the missiles pose little threat to vital U.S. interests? "Do nothing" could not be eliminated as an option until the missiles were determined to pose a serious threat to national security.

The Bush administration's decision to send ground troops to Somalia in late 1992—described in Focus 13.1—also illustrates the approximation of rationality that often describes decision-making processes. This is not the whole story of that decision process, of course, but we do have a clear sense that it was punctuated by value priorities, efforts to relate means to ends, and preferred courses of action to cope with the situation in Somalia—all central canons of rational choice.

Rationality and Reality: The Limits to Rational Choice

Despite the apparent application of rationality in these (and other) cases, the rational role model is more an idealized standard used to evaluate behavior than an actual description of real-world behavior. One participant in the Cuban missile deliberations, Theodore Sorensen, suggested why rational procedures are difficult to follow:

> Each step cannot be taken in order. The facts may be in doubt or dispute. Several policies, all good, may conflict. Several means, all bad, may be all that are open. Value judgments may differ. Stated goals may be imprecise. There may be many interpretations of what is right, what is possible, and what is in the national interest. (Sorensen 1963, 19–20)

Despite the virtues promised by rational choice, then, the impediments to its realization are substantial. Some are human. They derive from deficiencies in the intelligence, capability, and psychological needs and aspirations of those who make foreign policy decisions under conditions of uncertainty. Others are organizational. Individuals meeting in groups make most policy decisions. As a result, most decisions require group agreement about the national interest and the wisest course of action to pursue. Reaching agreement is not easy, however, as reasonable people with different human characteristics and values understandably disagree about goals or preferences and the probable results of alternative options. Thus the impediments to sound (rational) policy making are substantial. Let us examine them in greater detail.

Tardy Problem Recognition

Decision makers often neglect evidence of an impending problem until it confronts them directly or reaches crisis proportions, as people seldom foresee improbable

Focus 13.1

THE ROAD TO SOMALIA: THE BUSH ADMINISTRATION'S DECISION TO SEND U.S. GROUND TROOPS

• • •

The Somali crisis was touched off by the ouster of the country's longtime dictator, President Mohamed Siad Barre, in January 1991. By early [1992], the collapse of all governmental authority combined with drought, the continuation of traditional clan warfare and growing chaos had led to mass starvation, and made Somalia [in the words of one AID official] "the most acute humanitarian tragedy in the world. . . ."

U.S. foreign policy making had gone into low gear during the presidential campaign, but after the election, pressure grew on several fronts for more dramatic action in Somalia [beyond the emergency food airlift Bush had ordered in August].

On November 12, Assistant Secretary of State Robert L. Gallucci, the department's chief of political-military affairs, recommended that the United States lead a coalition to save Somalia from starvation under a UN Security Council authorization to use "all necessary means," including armed forces. [Acting Secretary of Lawrence S. Eagleburger], convinced by Gallucci's arguments, became an advocate of more forceful U.S. action.

On November 16, senior representatives of U.S. relief organizations working in Somalia met with UN officials and appealed for more protection. About the same time a Senate delegation headed by Democratic Senator Paul Simon of Illinois and a House delegation under Democratic Representative John Lewis of George were calling for more security after visits to Somalia.

The first of four NSC Deputies Committee [a National Security Council panel just below the cabinet level] meetings leading to Bush's decision to send ground troops convened at the White House on Friday, November 20. . . . Such meetings are normally secret, but news of this one was revealed the day before in the *New York Times* op-ed page and on the MacNeil-Lehrer News Hour. Both reports favorably cited recommendations for U.S. military action by Frederick C. Cuny, a relief expert who was an AID consultant in Somalia as he had been in the U.S. military relief for the Kurds in northern Iraq. Cuny advocated using twenty-five hundred U.S. troops with air and naval support to open supply lines. At the time, this was considered a bold proposal.

In the first day of interagency discussion, Under Secretary of Defense Paul Wolfowitz hinted at the possibility of using U.S. ground troops, but the general representing the joint chiefs, the uniformed military, said little. . . .

Focus 13.1 *(continued)*

On November 21, the second day of discussions, [Admiral David Jeremiah, the vice chairman of the Joint Chiefs of Staff], who coordinates with [JCS Chairman General Colin L. Powell] daily, startled the groups by saying that "if you think U.S. forces are needed" on land in Somalia, "we can do the job." . . . Jeremiah's statement transformed the use of U.S. ground troops—an option that previously had been considered "fantasy land" by nonmilitary policy makers—into a leading possibility.

What brought the shift in Pentagon thinking is a matter of speculation. . . . [One] official familiar with the thinking of Powell and Defense Secretary Richard B. Cheney says they were willing to "do more than put a Band-Aid on the problem" because the situation in Somalia is so stark and "what we do can make a big difference."

Presidential National Security Adviser Brent Scowcroft, who held several discussions with Bush, was among those in the administration receptive to a major U.S. military initiative. . . .

Two more Deputies Committee meetings were held at the White House on November 23 and 24. Meanwhile, Cheney and Powell were thinking harder about the dangers of U.S. military intervention, especially after a briefing . . . by Brigadier General Frank Libutti, commander of the U.S. airlift operations into Somalia. If the United States were not careful, he said, its troops would be in Somalia for ten or fifteen years.

When Bush met his senior advisers in the National Security Council on November 25, he began by declaring that "we want to do something about Somalia." He had three options before him: increased support for existing U.N. efforts, a U.S.-organized coalition effort without the participation of American ground troops, or a major U.S. effort to lead a multinational force in which U.S. ground troops took the leading role.

Powell . . . took no position on what should be done, but expressed concern about the use of ground troops and questioned whether conditions in Somalia would permit the smooth handoff of military responsibilities to a U.N. peacekeeping force.

After what one participant called "a broad discussion," Bush decided that if the UN Security Council agreed, and other nations would join the effort, U.S. combat troops would lead an international force to Somalia. . . .

Source: Don Oberdorfer, "The Road to Somalia," Washington Post National Weekly Edition, December 14–20, 1992: 6–7.

events (Boffey 1983). The reason is that people are prone psychologically to deny the existence of troublesome problems (even when they might be partially responsible for them), and often avoid facing information suggesting the necessity for difficult choices.

Inadequate Information

Henry Kissinger once observed that "when the scope for action is greatest, the knowledge on which to base such action . . . is at a minimum." The information required to define a problem is often incomplete, outdated, or unavailable, and critical variables such as others' intentions are not open to scrutiny. In addition, "information overload"—the availability of too much information—may also undermine rationality. Discrepant and contradictory information makes distinguishing the significant from the irrelevant difficult.

Inaccurate Information

The information on which decision makers' choices are based is screened, sorted, and rearranged by their advisers. Distortion is compounded by the tendency of advisers to tell their superiors what they want to hear rather than supplying them with the cold, hard facts, and by policymakers' all-too-human tendency to reject unfamiliar or disturbing information.

Deficient Information Gathering

Policymakers rarely search for *all* pertinent information. Instead, they base decisions on partial information.[3] Rationality is compromised, because if an exhaustive search had generated additional information, conceivably a different set of policy choices would have been considered. Moreover, rather than admit error, leaders are prone to cling to bad decisions and to search energetically for new information that justifies their previous mistaken choices (Wilensky 1967).

Ambiguous National Interests

When facing a policy problem it is not sufficient to insist that the national interest be served. That merely begs the question. The more difficult intellectual task requires "prioritizing" *all* possible goals according to their ability to promote the nation's welfare.

Rationally identifying what is best is difficult because every goal has associated costs as well as possible unanticipated long-run consequences. "Rational" goal selection, therefore, frequently means choosing the lesser of two evils. For instance, if a leader's goals include (1) the economic development of fledgling democracies in eastern Europe and the former Soviet Union and (2) the reduction of the federal budget deficit, one national interest may be achieved only at the expense of the other. Or consider the goals of (1) promoting democracy in other countries and (2) supporting the principle of national self-determination. The former may undermine the latter by rationalizing suppression of minority ethnic groups.

The Constraint of Time Pressure

Because policymakers work constantly with overloaded agendas and short deadlines, time is rarely available for careful identification of possible courses of action and for a cool-headed assessment of their consequences. "There is little time for leaders to reflect. They are locked in an endless battle in which the urgent constantly gains on the important. The public life of every political figure is a continual struggle to rescue an element of choice from the pressure of circumstance" (Kissinger 1979).

Options that are not identified cannot be considered, for, as Thomas Schelling asks, "How do you make a list of things you would never have thought of?" (cited in Bloomfield 1974). In fact, instead of identifying options on their own, presidents usually are presented with an abbreviated list of "feasible" options by their advisers and by bureaucratic agencies. During a crisis in particular, the pressure to shorten the search for options is intense, which limits the range of alternatives considered to the first ones that come to mind (usually those derived from prior analogous situations).

"Satisficing"

Rational decision making is compromised most by the way foreign policy choices are actually reached. Policymakers do not choose the option or set of options that has the maximum chance of realizing desired goals (Lindblom 1959; March and Simon 1958). Instead, they typically terminate their evaluation as soon as an alternative surfaces that appears superior to those already considered. Herbert Simon (1957) describes this as *satisficing* behavior. Rather than seeking optimal alternatives, decision makers are routinely content to select the choice that meets minimally acceptable standards. For this reason they frequently face "unresolvable" choices that preclude satisfaction across competing preferences; instead of "optimal" choices, often only "admissible" ones are available (see Levi 1990; Slovic, Fischhoff, and Lichtenstein 1977). Had they acted rationally by engaging in maximizing behavior, they would choose the one choice "best" able to produce preferred results.

The difficulties of ascertaining correctly the payoffs attached to available options reduce the prospects for rational choice (and promote satisficing instead). Even in the best of circumstances—even if policymakers could obtain full information and were able to identify all the options available to realize the preferred goal—"guesstimates" about the relative utility and efficacy of each alternative still often guide the choice.

Because determining the best (rational) choice is difficult, "muddling through" better describes how choices perceived to be feasible and pragmatic often win out. And this may, in fact, be reasonable. "A wise policy-maker," Charles Lindblom (1959) summarizes, "expects that his policies will achieve only part of what he hopes and at the same time will produce unanticipated consequences he would have preferred to avoid. If he proceeds through a succession of incremental changes, he avoids serious lasting mistakes." Some past leaders have been known to advocate this less-than-comprehensive, trial-and-error method for making difficult decisions. "It is common sense," noted Franklin D. Roosevelt "to take a method and try it; if it fails, admit it frankly and try another."

Psychological Restraints

Foreign policy is made not by states but by human beings acting on behalf of states. Hence, decision-making processes cannot be separated from psychodynamics (Simon 1985), and decisions therefore may be rooted less in logic than in the subconscious needs and drives of decision makers (see Chapter 14). The need to be liked, the desire to be popular, and the temptation to look decisive, even heroic, may interfere with rational judgment and ultimately sacrifice the nation's welfare. Decision makers also tend to be overconfident about their judgments and analytical skills and to overestimate their abilities and wisdom so as to maintain their "illusion of control" (Langer 1975).

Personal emotional needs and passions also may lead decision makers to confuse their own goals with those of the nation. If they come to see themselves as indispensable to the nation's welfare, they may equate what is good for them with what is good for the country. When this happens, policy initiatives may be undertaken to maintain or strengthen the leader's power and popularity, possibly at the expense of the nation's interests.

The confusion of national and personal needs is sometimes used to show how irrefutably irrational many foreign policy choices have been. The classic example is Adolf Hitler, whose determination to seek military conquest of the entire European continent proved disastrous for Germany. A more recent example is Saddam Hussein's determination to fight the technologically (if not numerically) superior United States and its coalition of allies, facing sure defeat, rather than to withdraw from Kuwait. In both cases we can explain the apparent discrepancy between what is (may be) good for the nation and what is (may be) good for the nation's leaders by distinguishing between *procedural rationality* and *instrumental rationality* (Zagare 1990).

Procedural rationality is what we have described to this point. It is the kind of rationality that relates to the decision-making dynamics of small groups and large-scale bureaucratic organizations. It is the definition of rationality that underlies the theory of political realism, which sees all states as acting in fundamentally similarly ways. Like the rational actor model we have described, realism, too, sees nation-states as single, unitary-actors whose (rational) decision processes result in choices that seek to maximize benefits to national interests and minimize costs. **Instrumental rationality**, on the other hand, is a more limited view of rationality. It says simply that individuals have preferences, and that when faced with two (or more) alternatives, they will chose the one that yields the preferred outcome—and this is rational behavior. Although we might dispute some individuals' preferences, we cannot dismiss them as "crazy" or their choices as "irrational" because they result in negative consequences for the nation as a whole or for the individuals themselves.

Our review of how policymakers actually make decisions warrants the conclusion that the ideal requirements of rational problem solving are seldom met in real life (see Focus 13.2). Preconceived notions pass for facts. Decisions are made to satisfy immediate, not long-term needs. Decision makers avoid the task of formulating a coherent strategy. They have a natural reluctance to reach decisions and a strong temptation to pass the buck. They usually weigh only a few alternatives and ponder only a small number of consequences. Decision makers rarely achieved full knowledge, even though the

Focus 13.2
Foreign Policy Decision Making in Theory and Practice

• • •

The Ideal Process	Actual Performance
Accurate, comprehensive information	Distorted, incomplete information
Clear definition of national goals	National goals biased by personal motivations and organizational interests
Exhaustive analysis of all options	Limited number of options considered, none thoroughly analyzed
Selection of optimal course of action most capable of producing desired results	Selection of course of action by political bargaining and compromise
Effective statement of decision and its rationale to mobilize domestic support	Confusing and contradictory statements of decision, designed primarily for media
Instantaneous evaluation of consequences followed by correction of errors	Superficial policy evaluation, uncertain responsibility, poor follow-through, and delayed correction

volume of information may be staggering. Instead, they scan only the information they regard as most relevant to the decision. Often they reach a decision first and find reasons (information) to support it only later. The result is not rationality, with each step leading logically to a value-maximizing choice, but something quite different—a haphazard, trial-and-error, seat-of-the-pants process conducted in a rush based on "gut-it-out," best-guess calculations strongly influenced by social pressures (Anderson 1987). Thus the process looks decidedly indecisive and improvisational, and the degree of rationality in foreign policy decision making typically "bears little relationship to the world in which officials conduct their deliberations" (Rosenau 1980).

What are the implications of such a conclusion? If the nation's behavior is not the product of public officials laden with exceptional skills and cognitive powers, untiringly collecting accurate information and logically deriving conclusions to maximize the country's national interests, is the rational role model completely irrelevant to the "real world"? And should we reject it out-of-hand in our quest to understand how American foreign policy is made?

In some respects the model of rational choice is little more a caricature, a straw man easily destroyed by even superficial knowledge about how people and organizations make choices on a daily basis, as they must. Still, even if we know that rationality is more ideal than real, the rational role model is useful in understanding how decision making occurs, all the more so because policymakers aspire to rational decision-making behavior, and on occasion may even approximate it.

> Officials have some notion, conscious or unconscious, of a priority of values; . . . they possess some conceptions, elegant or crude, of the means available and their potential effectiveness; . . . they engage in some effort, extensive or brief, to relate means to ends; and . . . therefore, at some point they select some alternative, clear-cut or confused, as the course of action that seems most likely to cope with the immediate situation. (Rosenau 1980, 304–305)

The practical relevance of the rational model finds special expression in administrative theory, which seeks to explain how bureaucratic organizations should be designed to serve the best interests of the state and its citizens. The theory is obviously relevant in any modern organization, public or private, and nowhere more so than in American foreign policy making: Given America's incredibly varied global interests, large-scale bureaucracy is necessary. Neither sufficient time nor resources are available to manage foreign relations without the support of large organizations, which facilitate rational decision making in ways that would otherwise be impossible (Goodsell 1985). Before we reject the rational role model completely, then, we must first consider a subsidiary hypothesis: that the U.S. foreign policy-making machinery enhances the prospects for rational decision making, even if the ideal is not always realized.

Administrative Theory and Foreign Policy Rationality

The idea that modern bureaucracy—by virtue of the roles it creates—enhances the prospects for rational decision making stems from the German scholar Max Weber's (1864–1920) seminal theories. Large-scale bureaucracies contribute to efficient administration and rationality, Weber reasoned, by how they are organized and operate:

- Structured on the principle of division of labor, bureaucracies make each person in the machinery of government a specialist, even an expert, at her or his job; functional divisions among agencies as well as within them (as, for example, in the separation of diplomatic and defense responsibilities between the State and Defense departments) assigns different tasks to different people qualified in different ways.

- Dividing authority among competing organizations enhances the probability that all policy options will be considered before decisions are reached. "Multiple advocacy" (George 1972) results from interagency bargaining, because the process requires defending positions and negotiation prevents any one agent from unilaterally making a critical policy decision.

- Authority is distributed hierarchically, and a clear chain of command delineates who is responsible for what and to whom. It is easier to get things done when everyone has a clear idea of who is subordinate to whom, who has authority over what, and what role each cog in the machinery should perform. Precious time does not have to be devoted to deciding who has the power to decide.

- Rules specify how each major function or task is to be performed and prescribe standard operating procedures for each task. Hence, rather than deliberating about the best method for handling a problem, the professional bureaucrat can concentrate on mastering those methods.

- Bureaucracies rely on a system of records, written documents systematically gathered and stored to facilitate intelligence retrieval, provide a data bank of past decisions, and increase the information available for making future decisions.

- In principle, bureaucracies recruit "the best and brightest" personnel on the basis of achievement and aptitude rather than on the basis of ascriptive criteria such as ethnicity, gender, wealth, or family background.

- Similarly, personnel are compensated and promoted on the basis of their achievements, thus placing decision-making responsibility in the hands of those deemed most competent. "Merit" determines who is "selected up" and who is "selected out," rather than criteria such as seniority, personal characteristics, ingratiation, or favors to superiors.

- Administrative norms allow some specialists the luxury of engaging in "forward planning." Unlike the president, whose role requires that attention be focused on the crisis of the moment, bureaucracies can consider long-term needs.

This portrayal of the bureaucratic policy process outlines the theoretical basis for the view that bureaucracies contribute to the rational decision-making procedures described above. Before we jump to the conclusion that bureaucratic decision making is a modern panacea, however, we should emphasize that these propositions tell us how bureaucratic decision making *should* occur but not how it *does* occur. Bureaucratic practice and the foreign policy outcomes it produces suggest that bureaucracies *cause* problems as well as *solve* them.

The Case against Bureaucratic Foreign Policy Making . . . .

Bureaucracies exist, at least in principle, to help the president carry out presidential policies. In practice, the president is dependent on those in the foreign affairs government to get things done. Thus, as Henry Kissinger advised, "to understand what the government is likely to do, one has to understand the bureaucratics of the problems."

What are some of the consequences of presidential dependency on bureaucracies? Does it limit the president's power over American foreign policy? Are bureaucracies "ruling servants," in control of policy by virtue of their power to impede? Indeed, does the bureaucracy rule while the president merely reigns?

Those troublesome questions have been raised by past presidents' recurrent complaints that they were unable to persuade, even coerce, their own bureaucracy to support their policy decisions. Subordinates have often appeared insubordinate; rather than helping to get things done, they have opposed presidential directives. "You know," Ronald Reagan once said, "one of the hardest things in a government this size is to know that down there, underneath, is that permanent structure that's resisting everything you're doing." Indeed, political scientist and former presidential adviser Richard E. Neustadt observed that, "to a degree, the needs of bureaucrats and president are incompatible. The better one is served, the worse will be the other."

Although it is an exaggeration to speak of the "bureaucratic captivity" of presidents, they are heavily dependent on the bureaucracy for information, for identifying problems, for advocating solutions and, most importantly, for implementing presidential orders. Correspondingly, presidents' leeway is markedly constrained by the government they are elected to run.

The very enormity of the federal bureaucracy is a constraint. The federal civilian workforce (excluding postal workers) totaled 2.2 million in 1993. Almost 2 million more were on active military duty in the uniformed military services. The employees were ensconced in roughly two thousand separate but overlapping government agencies. Presidents come and go, but these millions of bureaucrats remain. Only about thirty-three hundred officials are "policymakers"—individuals appointed by and subject to being fired by the president. The rest are career civil servants, whose independence and job security are protected by an elaborate system of rules and regulations. As a result, foreign policy decisions necessarily are made by many individuals within a massive but fragmented governmental structure, most of whom are beyond the immediate reach of elected public officials. As Woodrow Wilson put it in a timeless description, "Nobody stands responsible for the policy of government . . . a dozen men originate it; a dozen compromises twist and alter it; a dozen offices put it into execution."

Bureaucratic Behavior: Interorganizational Attributes

How do large bureaucratic organizations relate to one another? How do individuals behave within complex organizational settings? Does administrative theory hold in practice? Or is it like the model of rational choice, more an ideal than an accurate description of reality?[4]

At least eight characteristics of administrative decision making are important to an understanding of bureaucratic behavior and its impact on foreign policy. These characteristics, defined in the following sections, summarize the *bureaucratic politics model* of foreign policy decision making.[5] Roughly speaking, they can be divided into attributes that describe how bureaucratic organizations relate to one another, on one hand, and how they shape the roles occupied by people within them, on the other.

Parochialism

Bureaucracies are driven to protect their jurisdictions. They define issues and take stands on them to promote their self-interests. Indeed, "since a public bureaucracy is concerned with special and limited aspects of public policy, to a degree it resembles the ordinary private pressure group" (Freeman 1965). As James M. Fallows, President Carter's chief speechwriter, observed, "The chief force motivating most top bureaucrats, cabinet secretaries, and even some White House aides is job security—you can predict a bureaucrat's reaction to almost any issue by the way it will affect their job or fiefdom. That's what comes first."

Individuals who occupy bureaucratic roles are not immune to the parochialism that often places organizational interests ahead of national interests. A candid list of the criteria by which career bureaucrats judge their success would have to include a handsome salary, how many people are under their authority, measurable opportunities for advancement, and a large office near the parking garage. Consider the following description from an investigative report on the CIA by *U.S. News & World Report*:

> Current and retired members of the clandestine service say the CIA's darkest secret is the fact that the agency's sanctum sanctorum resembles the Department of Agriculture more than James Bond's MI6 or Jack Ryan's CIA. Too many operations officers, these critics charge, are more interested in chasing promotions than prying loose other nations' secrets. Says Richard Kerr, a former deputy director of central intelligence . . . : "What they're doing today is good for the DO [clandestine services]—not for the country." (July 4, 1994, p. 43)

White House efforts to centralize control over foreign policy making are partially a response to the problems parochialism poses.

Competitiveness

Far from impartial, neutral administrators that obediently carry out presidential orders, the departments and agencies comprising the foreign affairs government frequently compete with one another for influence. As a staff member of the Clinton administration's National Security Council once noted, organizations take stands on issues that advance their interests and maneuver to protect them against other organizations and senior officials, including the president (Halperin, 1971). Although not intentionally malicious, many agency heads nonetheless confuse their organization's welfare with the nation's:

> National security managers have a personal investment in the health and aggrandizement of their own bureaucratic organizations. They equate the national interest and their organization's interest as a matter of course. They will fight to maintain an obsolete air base, build redundant weapons systems, proliferate arms around the world by certifying that the nation's "vital interests" are at stake when it is merely their own budgets. (Barnet 1972, 122; see also Baritz 1985)

Heads of bureaucratic organizations are not insensitive to the nation's interests. Indeed, in the struggle among bureaucracies that characterizes policy-making debate, what is best for the country dominates the bargaining dialogue. For several years prior to the Persian Gulf War, for example, the United States authorized the sale of advanced-technology goods to Iraq (which, ironically, may have enhanced Iraq's ability to wage war against the United States). The Commerce Department, following its mandate to promote international trade, became a vigorous proponent of technology sales to Iraq. Commerce usually prevailed in the interorganizational policy process because it was able to build a "'winning coalition' in favor of liberal export controls" with the State Department, whose arguments extended beyond economics to an array of diplomatic concerns. Together Commerce and State blocked the Defense Department's objections. Thus, "each agency's separate organizational mission and essence caused it to have a different perception of national security and, therefore, different reasons for supporting either trade promotion or trade control" (Jones 1994).

Still, the incidence with which agency officials propose policies that blatantly benefit their own organizations attests to the parochial outlook and selfish concerns that typically dominate bureaucratic thinking. Consider the following example. After the collapse of the Soviet Union, the CIA's clandestine services, officially known as the Directorate of Operations, shut down its operations there, believing that Russia no longer posed much of a threat. Less than two years later the decision was reversed by the CIA official responsible for operations in the former Soviet Union and Eastern Europe. Why? Because "a decision to stop targeting Russia would cost the agency five hundred overseas jobs for case officers [those whose job is to recruit and oversee individuals who conduct espionage and provide information to the agency]" (*U.S. News & World Report*, July 4, 1994).

The reasons for competitive intergovernmental politics are numerous. Kissinger (1969) suggests one: "The decision maker will always be aware of the morale of his staff. . . . [He] cannot overrule it too frequently without impairing its efficiency. . . . Placating the staff then becomes a major preoccupation of the executive." Another reason is that most agency heads are not only tied *to* their own organization but also *by* it: "A secretary of a federal department almost invariably becomes more the agent of the permanent bureaucracy under his command than a free agent, mainly because he must rely upon the permanent officials for expert information and analysis" (MacMahon 1951). Thus, caught in the middle between higher-level elected officials and their advisers on one side, and the career professionals in an organization on the other, the typical agency head must try to satisfy both. The pressures encourage competition with other organizations for scarce resources and power. Policy success in such an atmosphere tends to be defined more in terms of organizational interests than of the national interest.

"Red tape" is what most Americans associate with bureaucracy. John D. Dingell (D-Michigan), while chair of the House Energy and Commerce Committee, held widely publicized congressional hearings that exposed governmental abuses ranging from Pentagon subcontracting to contaminated blood. Based on that experience, he took issue with the argument that rules and regulations alone explain government inefficiency: "The problem in government lies not in the number of rules but the fact that the rules are not properly done and people enforcing them aren't competent and managers are indifferent to the public interest all the way up to the White House."

Imperialistic Task Expansion

Driven to protect their own interests and promote their own influence, bureaucratic agencies invariably seek to enlarge their budgets and staffs, both absolutely and in relation to other agencies. Bureaucratic agencies also typically seek to increase their prerogatives and functional powers. Thus the Defense Department (among others) sought aggressively to capture part of the CIA's $3 billion share of the intelligence budget at a time when the agency searched for a new post-Cold War mission in the face of intense scrutiny by Congress and others. The reasons are clear. Size is a sign of security, expansion an indicator of importance, and, to some extent, prestige and influence can be conferred only by growth. Other things being equal, larger bureaucracies have greater access, greater credibility, greater resources, greater durability—and greater influence. (Such organizations usually have more enemies as well!) Thus, most organizations strive to maintain and enhance their budget and personnel.

The raison d'être of administrative organization is efficiency through the performance of discrete tasks by independent units; a division of labor that clearly differentiates functions permits experts to specialize. This rationale led in 1947 to creation of a separate Central Intelligence Agency, whose ostensible purpose was to coordinate the gathering of foreign intelligence, and in 1961 to creation of the Agency for International Development (AID) to specialize in the administration of foreign aid and technical assistance.

Practice, however, frequently fails to conform to theory. Imperialistic bureaucracies seek to perform the tasks for which other agencies have been assigned responsibility. That inclination explains why the Council on International Economic Policy created by President Nixon did not become an effective coordinator of economic policy making: It became merely another competitor jockeying for a piece of the policy action among those preexisting units needing coordination. The Clinton administration's National Economic Council may have fared better, although the jury is still out.

Bureaucratic imperialism also explains why so many different agencies are independently involved in gathering roughly the same intelligence information (for example, the State Department, the Defense Department, and the CIA, among others), and why the three military services have found it "absolutely essential" that each develop its own capabilities in areas where the other services specialize (as evidenced by the fact that the army at one time had more support aircraft than the air force). The result: Instead of a bureaucratic division of labor, functions are often duplicated.

The bureaucratic imperatives of the uniformed military services, which include not only imperialism but also competitiveness and endurance, are well illustrated by the meaning that each branch attached to the Persian Gulf War as each positioned itself for the oncoming debate about the military's role in the post-Cold War world. Focus 13.3 provides a glimpse of how the war stimulated "new thinking" in the Pentagon and among its congressional and interest-group supporters shortly after its victorious conclusion.

Endurance

Bureaucracies are survival-oriented. Both the number and size of administrative units responsible for promoting and protecting America's activist foreign policy interests have increased enormously. More new units have been created or expanded than phased out or cut back. Once in place, they usually persist and grow, even in the face of great adversity (see Kaufman 1976). The Agency for International Development, for example, whose primary purpose during the Cold War was to aid poor countries as a way of fighting communism, today finds that America's own inner cities are environments ripe for sharing expertise first gained working abroad—which coincidentally helps to justify the agency's continued existence (*New York Times*, June 26, 1994).

Focus 13.3

BUREAUCRATIC COMPETITIVENESS AND TASK EXPANSION: MILITARY RIVALRY IN THE AFTERMATH OF VICTORY IN THE PERSIAN GULF

• • •

As the Defense Department begins its most dramatic restructuring of the armed forces in decades, the services are in tough competition for declining dollars. Although such budget rivalries are hardly new, the Persian Gulf War is being used to reshape the debates on the future roles and missions of the military. . . .

Senior U.S. military officials say they were most concerned during the initial days of the gulf crisis about the vulnerability of Saudi Arabia. . . . The only ground-based American forces aligned against Iraqi troops in late August were an airborne infantry division and marine units ill-equipped to battle heavy armor, plus an air force fighter wing with no more weapons than it could carry under its wings.

This experience has spurred the air force to create two special combat wings that, for the first time, would include a mix of fighter, bomber and attack planes that could be dispatched in crises. Until now, air force tactical wings have been composed of a single type of aircraft.

The army, with its thousands of tons of heavy armor and hundreds of thousands of combat troops, was hit hardest by the military's limited sealift and airlift capacity. Once content to let the navy and air force worry about such capacity, army officials now say they will press the other services to increase resources for sealift and airlift operations.

The army wants the navy, for instance, to be able to transport at least two divisions simultaneously within thirty days of call-up—not just one division, as the navy had planned. Navy officials readily agree that more of the Pentagon budget needs to be invested in transport ships. . . .

The Marine Corps, which has spent billions of dollars on amphibious landing operations, conducted no amphibious assaults against Iraq, but argues that this kind of war-fighting capability should not be abandoned because the fear of an amphibious attack kept several Iraqi divisions diverted toward the sea during the war.

All the services have appeared equally eager to use the Gulf War in sales pitches for more purchases of the kinds of weapons that proved most successful. The air force and navy, for instance, are using memories of the pinpoint strikes by "stealth" F-117A fighter-bombers to push for continuation of the stealth B-2 bomber and development of a stealth carrier-based plane for the navy.

Focus 13.3 *(continued)*

At the same time, the services are pointing to the deficiencies that were evident in the war in arguing for improved and expanded new systems. The navy, for example, which dropped primarily "dumb bombs" and had only a limited number of high- technology, precision-guided missiles, is now using the success of the air force's "smart" weapons in lobbying to expand its own arsenal....

The navy, annoyed that it received so little credit for its aerial bombing attacks, discovered what officials believe is one of the reasons. "We didn't realize," says one naval official, "how lousy the video recorders were on our aircraft until we saw them side by side with the air force's. We had junk. The air force guys had nice clean pictures." Better recorders are sure to be on the navy's new shopping list.

Source: Molly Moore, "The Armed Services and the Nibbling Rivalries," Washington Post National Weekly Edition, *June 17–23, 1991, p. 31.*

Bureaucratic growth is arguably a response to new challenges and changing circumstances. With the end of the Cold War, for example, the State Department opened fourteen new embassies in the former Soviet Union and expected to increase its number of diplomats there by nearly half. The Commerce Department also quadrupled the number of trade promotion officials assigned to the region, the Treasury Department increased its economic analysts from three to eleven, and AID, traditionally oriented exclusively toward the Global South, created a twenty-five person team to speed delivery of technical and humanitarian assistance to the former Soviet Union (Priest 1992, 33). Historically, however, organizational "reforms" designed to streamline government have often created *new* organizations to coordinate and regulate the activities of existing ones. The result is not enhanced efficiency, but rather the addition of new layers to a burgeoning bureaucracy. As Secretary of the Navy John Lehman complained in 1985, "It would be impossible for me or anyone to accurately describe to you the system with which, and within which, we must operate. There are thousands upon thousands of offices and entities and bureaus that have been created over the years to deal episodically with aspects of defense."

Bureaucratic Behavior: Intraorganizational Attributes

The interorganizational side of bureaucratic behavior just described is easily summarized: All bureaucratic organizations pursue their own purposes, promote their own power, enhance their own position in the governmental hierarchy, and strive to endure. Successful pursuit of those objectives flows in part from and in turn reinforces internal standard operating procedures and the way bureaucratic organizations mold the behavior of their role occupants.

Secrecy and Exclusiveness

Bureaucratic agencies seek to minimize interference in and regulation of their operations. To the extent possible, they keep their proceedings secret from potential enemies—including the president—who might use such knowledge to attack their operations publicly, and they conceal activities that can injure their public image. "There are no secrets in Washington," President Kennedy observed, "except the things I need to know." Conversely, bureaucratic secrets are "leaked" selectively for propaganda purposes when their release is politically advantageous.

Attitudinal Conformity

Every bureaucracy eventually develops a shared "mind set" or dominant way of looking at reality, which few challenge. The process of recruitment and self-selection brings together individuals who already share many basic attitudes. The Foreign Service, for instance, has sought for employees "young people they consider most like the successful officers already in the system" (Harr 1969). Free thinkers or people who might "rock the boat" or "make waves" are not welcomed; instead, those subscribing to the agency's dominant values are preferred.[6]

Attitudinal conformity is reinforced in small-group decision-making situations, where social pressures that reinforce group norms sometimes produce *groupthink*, a cohesiveness and solidarity of outlook that may lead to dysfunctional policy choices as the group's search for unanimity overrides the realistic appraisal of alternative policy choices (Janis 1982). President Johnson's habit of addressing Bill Moyers, his resident "dove" on Vietnam, as "Mr. Stop-the-Bombing" illustrates the pressures toward conformity small decision-making groups often generate. The Kennedy administration's disastrous Bay of Pigs decision in 1961 contained numerous elements of groupthink (Janis 1982), as did the Reagan administration's policy revisions regarding Iran and the Lebanese hostage crisis in 1985–1986 that led to the Iran-*contra* affair ('t Hart 1990). Even decision processes that lead to success, as in the Bush administration's decisions that brought about victory in the Gulf War, are susceptible to concurrence-seeking behavior and pressures toward attitudinal conformity. For example, even some in the "inner circle" of decision making, such as Secretary of State James A. Baker and JCS Chairman Colin Powell, were unwilling to challenge the dominant views articulated by Bush and his national security adviser, Brent Scowcroft. To do so "would have meant undermining one's own political standing at the White House" (Hybel 1993).

Once an individual enters a bureaucratic organization, socialization to its "mission" and its "essence" (Allison and Halperin 1972) reinforces conformity to the organization's central norms. Recruits are quickly educated into their role and the acceptable attitudes that go with it. Nonconformity can result in loss of influence or, in the extreme, one's job. On the other hand, those who conform to peer-group attitudes, who are perceived as team players, are rewarded. "Promotions are awards given to bureaucrats for accepting organizational myths" cynically describes this phenomenon.

Shared convictions about an organization's role and mission are important in maintaining organizational morale, but the line is not always clear between a healthy commitment to an organization's welfare and what is detrimental to larger purposes. Institutional mind sets discourage creativity, dissent, and independent thinking, undermining rational policy making. The Department of State, for instance, has found in numerous self-studies that pressures producing uniformity of thought and stifling creativity have been persistent problems.

Deference to Tradition

Because decision making in complex organizations is conducted according to *rules*, bureaucrats are prone to defer to tradition and standard operating procedures rather than invent a new way to deal with a new problem. "A man comes to an assignment," Charles Frankel (1969) observed, "and he is told what policy is. He must find a way to navigate through the storms, to resist the pressures of people and events, and to turn over the policy to his successor in the same condition in which it was when he received it from his predecessor." A former staff member of the National Security Council dubbed this respect for ritual and precedent the "curator mentality" (Thomson 1994).

Reliance on Historical Analogies

When a decision point is reached, policymakers are prone to search history impressionistically for parallels that suggest options for dealing with the emergent problem. That tendency—which often results in a misreading of historical lessons (Neustadt and May 1986)—helps account for continuity in American foreign policy. The "Munich" analogy, for example, was drawn on by a generation of policymakers as evidence that it is impossible to appease aggressors. As noted in Chapter 3, the analogy refers to the 1938 British and French agreement that permitted Nazi Germany to annex a large part of Czechoslovakia in return for what British Prime Minister Neville Chamberlain called "peace in our time." Instead, war broke out in Europe a year later, with the apparent lesson that an aggressor cannot be stopped short of fighting it.[7]

George Bush drew on the Munich analogy directly as he prepared the nation for war against Saddam Hussein, whom he described as a modern-day Hitler. Indeed, so strong was his commitment to the analogy that it "acted as a barrier to the search for information that could have jeopardized its validity" (Hybel 1993). Heavy reliance on analogical thinking before and after Iraq's invasion of Kuwait limited the administration's ability to follow the canons of *procedural rationality*, thus calling into question the *instrumental rationality* of its decisions, particularly the choice of war over containment through the sustained application of sanctions. By no means does this detract from the administration's success in bringing Iraq to its knees, but it does establish that "success does not prove rationality" (Hybel 1993).

Other attributes of bureaucratic behavior as it relates to foreign policy making could be added to this discussion, but they would not change the conclusion drawn from it: that the decision-making system profoundly influences the behavior of those who occupy institutionally defined decision-making roles. Given this, we now shift attention to some of the major policy consequences of those attributes.

Policy Consequences of Organizational Decision Making . . . .

Because American foreign policy is a product of organizational decision-making processes, it is useful to consider how bureaucratic behavior shapes both policy and policy making. Some conspicuous repercussions of bureaucratic processes follow.

Bureaucratic Resistance to Change

In the realm of broad foreign policy conceptions and goals, the president and the executive bureaucracies may be natural enemies. Because many upper-echelon career officials have retained their positions for years, sometimes even decades, their long-held assumptions about American foreign policy may be as deeply entrenched as the bureaucracies for which they work. Fundamental assumptions—about Soviet motives during the Cold War and Russian imperialism since, about the continuing wisdom of globalism and the utility of force, and about other themes that have defined American foreign policy for five decades—have been bureaucratic conventional wisdom, unworthy of further reexamination. Presidents intermittently come to power with fresh ideas about foreign policy essentials, eager to implement new approaches, only to find that old ways of thinking are firmly entrenched. The Carter administration found, for example, that many in the State Department were unresponsive to some of its early foreign policy initiatives on human rights and arms sales. "Some of the older generation of diplomats openly didn't . . . believe in the efficacy or wisdom of such notions as campaigns for human rights or restraint in arms sales abroad," observed one department insider. "They fully expected that most of the new initiatives would soon be dropped, and they did everything they could to see that the day of abandonment came sooner rather than later" (Carter 1981). The experience suggests that failures to change foreign policy can be attributed in part to a bureaucracy's refusal to support a new administration's new ideas.

The end of the Cold War now demands a fresh appraisal of old ways of thinking, but participants in the bureaucratics of Cold War policy making are likely to view the future through the prism of the past. "The ghost in the Pentagon" (Iklé 1990) is the way a former under secretary of defense described the "enduring mind-set" of military planners as they contemplated the first evidence that the Cold War was indeed passing. This recognition is perhaps what prompted George Bush to pledge at the 1989 Malta summit that he would "kick our bureaucracy and push it as fast as I possibly can" to achieve a new arms control agreement with the Gorbachev regime.

Even if new realities are recognized, however, reorienting standard operating procedures and reallocating existing resources to new problems is not easy. Nowhere is that more apparent than in the Pentagon, where decisions on weapons systems and what they are designed to do often take decades to come to fruition. Thus when Clinton's first secretary of defense, Les Aspin, undertook a "bottom-up" review of the U.S. military, he confronted a simple yet enduring fact: "The military machine cannot turn around on a dime" (Sweetman 1994). The task, then, was to rethink the purpose and utility of Cold War weapons in a post–Cold War world while simultaneously reducing defense spending to the levels sought by the White House without threatening either the nation's security or its ability, as anticipated by Aspin, to fight and win two simultaneous regional conflicts. The order was too tall, as Aspin fell short in the ability to manage a complex organization in transition. He resigned less than a year after assuming an office for which he had arguably spent a lifetime preparing.

Bureaucratic Competition and Foreign Policy Inertia

Bureaucratic competition encourages its own inertia as well as inertia in policy. The overwhelming complexity of the foreign affairs machinery, with its entrenched and competing bureaucracies, limits what leaders can do and casts doubt on Washington's capacity to act expeditiously. Even now, reaching consensus and taking decisive action is inhibited because policy is formulated and implemented by many individuals situated in a complex institutional arrangement. Bureaucrats in charge of the different agencies usually disagree: They want different policies and define situations differently because of their differing vantage points. The result is policy formulation that often comes down to a tug of war among competing agencies, a high-stakes political game in which differences are settled at the lowest common denominator. Henry Kissinger described the process this way:

> Each of the contending factions within the bureaucracy has a maximum incentive to state its case in its most extreme form because the ultimate outcome depends, to a considerable extent, on a *bargaining process.* The premium placed on advocacy turns decision making into a *series of adjustments among special interests*—a process more suited to domestic than to foreign policy. This procedure neglects the long-range because the future has no administrative constituency and is, therefore, without representation in the adversary proceedings. Problems tend to be slighted until some agency or department is made responsible for them. . . . The outcome usually depends more on the pressures or the persuasiveness of the contending advocates than on a concept of over-all purpose. (Kissinger 1969, 268; emphasis added)

In addition, fundamental or far-reaching choices are discouraged by the conservative nature of organizational policy making. The inclination among career officials to "go along in order to get along" encourages acceptance of prevailing policies and the status quo. Furthermore, bureaucracies typically administer programs created by prior decisions. Most bureaucrats therefore see themselves as loyal, even unquestioning, implementors of past policies rather than the creators of their own. The greater the loyalty to specific administrative tasks, the greater the commitment to the policy being implemented. "To try and believe in what one is doing, . . . to see broader problems in narrow terms derived from one's own specific activities," is a natural part of a bureaucrat's role, but the result is that "the information and judgments bureaucrats provide for use in the making of policies tend to be strongly biased in favor of the continuation, rather than the modification, much less the reversal, of existing policies. . . . Thus a bureaucracy inevitably comes down heavily on the side of established policies and strongly resists change" (Reischauer 1968).

Bureaucratic Sabotage of Presidential Foreign Policy Initiatives

The popular impression that American foreign policy is little more than what the president says it is can be misleading. The president alone does not make foreign policy. Policy must not only be pronounced but also carried out, and for that task the chief executive must rely on the bureaucracies comprising the executive branch. Hence, what the government's departments and agencies choose to implement becomes American foreign policy: Policy is what is done, not just what is said.

Because bureaucracies are by nature exclusive, parochial, and interested primarily in protecting their own power and authority, we should not be surprised that few agencies cheerfully carry out presidential directives they perceive as harmful to their organizations. When threatened, bureaucrats are inclined to put themselves first and to defend their own welfare. Therefore, the often intractable foreign affairs machinery is capable of disloyalty to the president it ostensibly serves. And since change, or the prospect of change, is often threatening (because policy change almost invariably entails some redistribution of influence in the government hierarchy), bureaucratic agencies frequently resist top-level executive policy proposals.

Nearly every president has complained at one time or another that the federal bureaucracy ostensibly designed to serve him undercut his policy by refusing to carry out orders expeditiously. Witness President Truman's prediction prior to General Eisenhower's succession to the White House: "He'll sit here and he'll say, 'Do this! Do that!' *And nothing will happen.* Poor Ike—it won't be a bit like the army. He'll find it very frustrating." Or reflect on President Kennedy's observation that giving the State Department an instruction was like dropping it in the dead-letter box. As Dick Cheney, Bush's secretary of defense, put it when he was President Ford's chief of staff, "There is a tendency before you get to the White House or when you're just observing it from the outside to say, 'Gee, that's a powerful position that person has.' The fact of the matter is that while you're here trying to do things, you are far more aware of the constraints than you are of the power. You spend most of your time trying to overcome obstacles to getting what the president wants done."

Most often, bureaucratic inaction and lack of responsiveness manifest themselves as lethargy. The government machinery grinds slowly, and sometimes appears motionless. (To quote the tongue-in-cheek characterization of James H. Boren, founder of the International Association of Professional Bureaucrats, "One must always remember that freedom from action and freedom from purpose constitute the philosophical basis of creative bureaucracy.") Procrastination appears endemic and is easily interpreted as intentional when in fact it is often inadvertent. It simply takes time to move people, paper, and processes along, and completing even the simplest requests routinely involves delay. An impatient president can easily mistake the crawling pace for insubordination, even sedition (because the effect—braking or abrogating policy decisions—is the same). But everyday bureaucratic inaction should not be confused with planned foot dragging; the differences between slothful protraction and disobedient noncompliance are real.

Still, willful bureaucratic sabotage is not a mere figment of leaders' imaginations. It can take several forms. Bureaucracies can withhold or slant vital information. They can provide advice showing reasons why recommended policy changes will not work, and they can circulate that advice to those in a position to challenge the policy change. They can leak information to Congress or discreetly contact interest groups capable of mobilizing opposition to a directive the bureaucrats find intolerable. Or they can delay policy implementation by demanding time to study the problem thoroughly (to death, that is)—a tactic known as "paralysis by analysis"—or by complexifying it into incomprehensibility (violating the KISS principle: "Keep It Simple, Stupid!"). And bureaucracies can buck a presidential directive by interpreting it in such a way that it is administered differently than proposed or with a change in emphasis. The result, of course, is no results. It has been said in this context that bureaucracies never change the course of the ship of state—they just adjust the compass.

Sometimes bureaucratic sabotage can be direct and immediate, as President Kennedy discovered in the midst of the 1962 Cuban missile crisis. While Kennedy sought to orchestrate U.S. action and bargaining, his bureaucracy in general and the navy in particular were in fact controlling events by doing as they wished.

> [The bureaucracy chose] to obey the orders it liked and ignore or stretch others. Thus, after a tense argument with the navy, Kennedy ordered the blockade line moved closer to Cuba so that the Russians might have more time to draw back. Having lost the argument with the president, the navy simply ignored his order. Unbeknownst to Kennedy, the navy was also at work forcing Soviet submarines to surface long before Kennedy authorized any contact with Soviet ships. And despite the president's order to halt all provocative intelligence, an American U-2 plane entered Soviet airspace at the height of the crisis. When Kennedy began to realize that he was not in full control, he asked his secretary of defense to see if he could find out just what the navy was doing. McNamara then made his first visit to the navy command post in the Pentagon. In a heated exchange, the chief of naval operations suggested that McNamara return to his office and let the navy run the blockade. (Gelb and Halperin 1973, 256)[8]

Another example of bureaucratic disobedience occurred during the tense period *preceding* the Cuban missile crisis in 1962. Kennedy had concluded in March 1961 that Jupiter missiles in Turkey should be removed. He felt they were obsolete and exacerbated Soviet fears of encirclement and possible American attack from just beyond the Soviet border. The president therefore instructed the State Department to negotiate withdrawal of the American missiles. Turkish officials disapproved, however, so the State Department reasoned that the diplomatic thing to do was to comply with the Turkish request that the missiles stay. Convinced that the benefits of removing the missiles far outweighed the costs, however, Kennedy reiterated his command. He then "dismissed the matter from his mind," Robert Kennedy (1971) reports, because "the president believed he was president and that, his wishes having been made clear, they would be followed and the missiles removed." But to his amazement Kennedy discovered during the Cuban missile crisis months later that the State Department had ignored his instructions—the missiles were still in Turkey. Because the crisis centered in part on the issue of weapons on the adversary's periphery, the president was, needless to say, angry about the complications this blatant disregard of his orders now caused.[9]

President Clinton also experienced a form of bureaucratic sabotage of his policy toward Haiti. At the same time that he sought to return Jean-Bertrand Aristide to power, replacing Haiti's military regime with the nation's last popularly elected president, the CIA repeatedly told Congress that, according to its psychological profile of Aristide, he was mentally unfit to rule. As the Clinton administration began to consider options for deposing Haiti's military leader, it shunned covert action, as officials in both the White House and State Department did not trust the CIA to carry out its mission.

They believed the CIA was anti-Aristide, partly because of his leftist political platform (Devroy and Smith 1993).

The conflict between the administration and the CIA was particularly embarrassing to the president, whose policies toward Haiti were already widely under attack from various quarters, but it was a classic illustration of the different purposes and perspectives policymakers and intelligence analysts bring to policy problems. Indeed, intelligence consumers and producers rarely speak the same language. Instead, they characteristically appear like "two closely related tribes that believe, mistakenly, that they speak the same language and work in the same manner for agreed outcomes. . . . Indeed, one is often reminded of George Bernard Shaw's quip about Britons and Americans being divided by a common tongue" (Lowenthal 1992).

These incidents illustrate how bureaucracies sometimes perceive themselves as autonomous agents, or at least act that way. Untethered, they contribute to the appearance of the United States as a rudderless ship of state.

Managing Bureaucratic Intransigence

The "bureaucratic captivity" of American foreign policy is easily exaggerated. Although bureaucracies have a grip on presidential policies, presidents are not powerless to respond. They can employ a variety of methods to handle recalcitrant agencies and obstructionist officials.

Consider the strategy of Franklin D. Roosevelt, the "master" of managing federal bureaucracies. An astute politician, Roosevelt overcame policy-implementation obstacles through a divide-and-rule strategy. "Planned disorganization and confusion" aptly describes it.

> [He] deliberately organized—or disorganized—his system of command to insure that important decisions were passed on to the top. His favorite technique was to keep grants of authority incomplete, jurisdictions uncertain, charters overlapping. The result of this competitive theory of administration was often confusion and exasperation on the operating level; but no other method could so reliably insure that in a large bureaucracy, filled with ambitious men eager for power, the decisions, and the power to make them, would remain with the president. . . . Franklin allowed no one to discover the governing principle. (Schlesinger 1958, 527; see also George 1980)

In short, Roosevelt sought to control policy by denying control to those around him.

The "Kissinger solution" represents a second, rather blunt but highly effective strategy: Punish the disobedient agency by excluding it from future decision making or circumvent it by creating a smaller, substitute unit. Removing a bureaucracy from influence—especially on issues that vitally concern it—can have considerable therapeutic value, making a hostile agency less intent on opposing presidential policy every time its own parochial interests are at stake.

President Kennedy employed a third tactic: causing disturbance *within* a recalcitrant agency by skipping the normal chain of command and dealing directly with lower-echelon officials. By upsetting standard operating procedures and going through unusual channels of communication, Kennedy obtained needed information and avoided bureaucratic bottlenecks. A related Kennedy tactic was to encourage a re-calcitrant official's voluntary resignation by hinting that he or she was no longer in favor. Kennedy "would plant newspaper reports that the official was planning to resign. After reading a sufficient number of these reports, the official would grasp what was happening and turn in his resignation" (Berkley 1978).

Richard Nixon practiced yet a fourth strategy, described best by his words to George Shultz when the latter was director of the Office of Management and Budget (OMB):

> You've got to get us some discipline, George. You've got to get it, and the only way you get it, is when a bureaucrat thumbs his nose, we're going to get him. . . . They've got to know that if they do it, something's going to happen to them, where anything can happen. I know the Civil Service pressure. But you can do a lot there. There are many unpleasant places where Civil Service people can be sent.

This punitive approach requires a stomach for vindictiveness, because dismissals, forced resignations, and demotions risk adverse publicity and are time-consuming. Not only are grievance proceedings protracted and embarrassing, but even identifying the individual responsible for the insubordination among the faceless bureaucracy can be a challenge. (John Roche, a Johnson policy adviser, once recommended that the chief executive "fire the s.o.b." who had sabotaged one of the president's pet programs. "Fire him!" screamed Johnson. "I can't even find him!") These obstacles may explain why politeness is often preferred to punishment; the common approach is to remove an obstructionist employee by giving him or her a promotion or special assignment to a prestigious-sounding but meaningless position. To "squeeze" an intransigent bureaucrat from a position, the victim is "layered over" by assigning others to perform his or her duties.

The belief that changing people can solve disloyalty problems and get the bureaucracy moving lies behind the impulse to punish obdurate staff. "Let me control personnel," George Kennan once said, "and I will ultimately control policy. For the part of the machine that recruits and hires and fires and promotes people can soon control the entire shape of the institution." In practice, however, those presidents who have carefully picked their "own" people and instructed them to get their agencies to obey executive orders often have discovered that instead "their" people have, in Nixon aide John Ehrlichman's words, "married the natives." Typically, cabinet officers come to define themselves as spokespersons for the departments they run instead of servants of the presidents who appointed them. The problem is not simply that obstructionist individuals are at fault. The roles within the policy-making process create incentives for disobedience to the president and loyalty to the organization and its people and programs.

President Carter practiced a fifth method by attacking causes instead of symptoms: He proposed to regain control of government by reorganizing it. "We must give top priority to a drastic and thorough revision and reorganizing of the federal bureaucracy."

Reorganization attempts have been frequent and were implemented not only by Carter but also Truman, Johnson, Nixon, Reagan, and, most recently, Clinton.

Symptomatic of the magnitude of the problem—and indicative of why solutions are so intractable—is the fact that reorganization seldom demolishes existing organizations. As noted earlier, most entrenched bureaucracies have perfected survival tactics: In the words of former Secretary of State James F. Byrnes, the "nearest thing to immortality on Earth is a government bureau." Evidently reorganization (or even what Secretary of the Navy John Lehman termed "deorganization" (not greater centralization and unification of authority, but decentralization and greater accountability) is not a final solution.

Carter also sought revision of the regulations governing civil servants' employment with the Civil Service Reform Act, which put some seven thousand top bureaucrats into a Senior Executive Service, entitling them to earn bonuses for outstanding job performance but separating them from job tenure (a virtual guarantee of permanent employment). The reform permitted the chief executive and cabinet officers to reassign upper-middle management personnel and, where deemed necessary, to replace those not moving quickly enough or in the right direction. Similar reforms followed in the Foreign Service with the creation of Senior Foreign Service. These innovations augmented the president's managerial capabilities, but they did not guarantee agency responsiveness to presidential orders.

Like his predecessors, Ronald Reagan sought to exercise greater control over the federal bureaucracy. He campaigned for office by openly opposing the government he sought to run, berating its size and promising to reduce, reorganize, and streamline it. "Government is not the solution, it is the problem," Reagan declared in his first inaugural speech.

Vice President Al Gore, point man of the Clinton administration's "reinventing government" initiative launched in 1993, echoed some of Reagan's earlier sentiments. "Our problems don't come from bad workers," he noted. "Rather we have good people trapped in bad systems." The Clinton administration thus proposed energizing the government by cutting red tape, making it more consumer-oriented, eliminating unnecessary programs and consolidating others, and making government workers more productive. The administration's goal, as described by Gore (1993b), was not to "dismantle and abandon large chunks of government," as sought by the Reagan administration, but to focus "on how well [the government] performs." ***Total Quality Management (TQM)*** became the buzzword. Drawing on the ideas of management consultant W. Edwards Deming, the core idea was to make the government operate more like a business.[10] At the same time, the Clinton plan called for the elimination of some 250,000 federal jobs, a work force reduction of about 12 percent. "We are sympathetic to the idea of more effective but smaller government," Gore declared. "We know that we need a government appropriate for this age of shrunken resources."

The Clinton plan won high praise for its objectives, but many, particularly in Congress, were skeptical of the administration's ability to achieve its lofty goals. Reagan's failure to live up to his promises may have colored their assessments. During his presidency big government got bigger, as federal spending went up, not down, and budget outlays as a percentage of the GNP rose to peacetime records. Moreover, while reductions in some agencies' personnel were implemented, overall the number of federal civilian and military employees grew by 7 percent between 1980 and 1987, from to 4.9 million to 5.3 million. Even if Clinton succeeded where Reagan failed—and midway through the Clinton presidency the number of federal employees had in fact dropped—some feared that unless bureaucratic red tape were also cut, the end result would be the worst of all possible worlds, perpetuating what some management analysts have dubbed "hollow government" (Carney 1994).

Clinton eschewed another Reagan strategy designed to control the bureaucracy: infiltrating it with political operatives. To gain a top government post candidates were required to pass an "ideological censorship" test (Barber 1985). The number of political appointees increased by a third, from roughly twenty-two hundred to more than thirty-three hundred (Struck 1985, 31). The program was predicated on the belief that patronage would purchase loyalty from those whose jobs depended on the president— for they are the only employees who can easily be relieved of their duties. The goal was driven by the perceived need, in the words of Navy Secretary Lehman, "to roll back the accretion of layers of centralized bureaucracy and restore a crisper accountability."

In contrast with Reagan's "ideological litmus test," Clinton sought to appoint people whose symbolism as reflected in their race, gender, and ethnicity fit his campaign pledge to make his administration "look like America." Because management skills and executive competency often were accorded secondary priority, many important foreign policy posts remained unfilled well into Clinton's second year in office while some of his initial appointees either were fired or voluntarily moved on.

Thus the goal of making the federal bureaucracy responsive to presidential priorities and political preferences remains as elusive as ever. Indeed, whether the federal bureaucracy can be made measurably more tractable is questionable. A key problem is that most presidents serve for only four years, a few eight at most. It is impossible to reform a complex and recalcitrant bureaucracy so quickly. Whether the foreign affairs government's responsiveness and willingness to take direction can be increased thus also remains doubtful. "Those who think we're powerless to do anything about the greenhouse effect," George Bush warned in 1988, "are forgetting about the White House effect. As president, I intend to do something about it." But well into his presidency, Bush learned the power of the "bureaucratic effect" as his "Commerce and Interior departments waged constant guerrilla warfare against any effort to make good on the president's prior commitments" (Talbott 1989).

Les Aspin's fate is an illustration of how those who would change the face of government can be victimized by the power bureaucratic organizations wield. Aspin had enormous insight into defense policy issues as a result of many years of experience on Capitol Hill, including his chairmanship of the powerful House Armed Services Committee. But he was not seasoned in the ways of the Pentagon. From the beginning, then, there was a distance between the uniformed military services, who had grown accustomed to relative autonomy during the previous twelve years, and Aspin and his "faculty club" of outsiders who came determined to trim defense spending and to reassert civilian control over the vast military establishment. Aspin and his aides in turn divided "the admirals and generals into two camps—'new thinkers' and 'old guard'— and . . . suggested that they [found] too many of the latter" (Gellman 1993).

Aspin repeatedly stated that his "bottom-up" review of future defense requirements was a "collegial" process that fully involved the professional military. Nonetheless, friction between the military and civilian elements in the Pentagon was an open secret. It was fueled further by disagreements about how best to handle the

U.S. role in Haiti and in Somalia, where in October 1993, eighteen American personnel were killed. Shortly thereafter, the army mounted a vigorous campaign against further defense budget cuts, arguing that the Clinton administration's plans would leave the army "substantially weakened" and ultimately pose a threat to the nation's security. "The outcome of these reductions may be a future force which does not possess the technological superiority required to prevail over all potential conflicts arising from the changing world order" (cited in Lancaster 1993). Caught between the military's demands for more resources and OMB's pressure to live with less, Aspin announced his resignation. Ironically, Clinton also announced in his 1994 State of the Union Address that "We must not cut defense further."

There exists a long history of failed efforts to control bureaucratic growth and reform the federal bureaucracy even in the face of determined presidential challenges. Arguably this is explained in part by Congress's unwillingness during much of the past half-century to trim federal programs and the agencies that administer them. The Republican Party promised to reverse that posture when it won majority control of Congress in 1994. Time will tell whether its promise bears fruit.

Compartmentalized Policy Making and Foreign Policy Inconsistency

Because each foreign affairs department and agency has its *own* definition of proper goals, the U.S. government sometimes pursues incompatible foreign policies. An incident from the Shah's final days in Iran which set the stage for the taking of the American embassy and American diplomatic personnel illustrates the point.

The U.S. response to the unfolding drama was clouded by a quarrel between the National Security Council staff in Washington and the State Department's representatives in both Teheran and Washington regarding how different the "facts" looked to those in the White House compared with those in the field. The divergent views, and the bickering and struggle that followed, led to a tragic outcome. William Sullivan, the U.S. Ambassador to Iran, concluded that the difference in views held by the NSC and the State Department bureaucracy in Washington extended to the "instructions that were sent to the embassy or, more often, to the absence of any instructions whatsoever. . . . By November 1978 [national security adviser] Brzezinski began to make his own policy and established his own 'embassy' in Iran." Not longer after that, Sullivan writes, "it became apparent that my views were no longer welcome at the White House" (Sullivan 1980).

Sullivan (1980) contends that the White House ignored his recommendation that, upon the Shah's fall from power, the U.S. should not cast its fate with the Bakhtiar government because, in his view, it "was a chimera the Shah had created to permit a dignified departure, that Bakhtiar himself was quixotic and would be swept aside by the arrival of Khomeini and his supporters in Teheran." As history records, the ambassador's dire predictions proved correct even while Brzezinski's policy prevailed. Iran fell into revolution, and American personnel became its victims.

Another example of the untoward effects of bureaucratic struggle occurred in response to the Laotian situation in 1960, when the State Department and the CIA gave aid to opposing armies. A former official gives a disturbing recollection of policy inconsistency that bureaucratic competition produced:

The Agency [CIA] supported Indonesian rebels against Sukarno while State was trying to work with Sukarno. It supplied and emboldened the anticommunist Chinese guerrillas in Burma over the protests of the Burmese government and the repeated protestations of the State Department in Washington and our ambassador in Burma that we were doing no such thing. . . .

[The CIA] meddled elsewhere, to the consternation of the State Department and friendly governments. In the mid-1950s, its agents intruded awkwardly in Costa Rica, the most stable and democratic country in Latin America. While the agency was trying to oust José Figueres, the moderate socialist who became the Costa Rican president in a fair election in 1953, the State Department was working with him and our ambassador was urging President Eisenhower to invite him to the United States to enhance his prestige. So it went the world around. (Simpson 1967, 103)

Turf battles and the pursuit of incompatible objectives seem to be endemic. The differences early in the Bush administration about what to do with, for, and about Mikhail Gorbachev illustrate their recurrence. While President Bush and Secretary of State Baker spent their time attempting to convince the Soviets (and the American public) that they truly wished Gorbachev's domestic reforms and foreign policy redirection to succeed, Secretary of Defense Cheney and Vice President Quayle publicly proclaimed their reservations about Gorbachev's prospects and peaceful intentions, and a secret team was established in the White House to discredit Gorbachev's credibility. Because the professed goal of "ending the Cold War" was not endorsed by all of the administration's factions, initiatives to end that conflict appeared timid, tardy, and inconsistent (see Beschloss and Talbott 1993).

Bureaucratic Pluralism and Foreign Policy Compromise

Bureaucratic pressures diminish presidents' ability to assert control and lead. Rather than selecting policies from alternative recommendations and turning to the bureaucracy to implement them, presidents often choose among agreed-on bureaucratic solutions and then seek to mobilize their action on the decisions reached.

That image does not conform to the popular view of presidents determining policy goals through rational processes. However, most if not all presidential decisions are affected by the options that bureaucracies offer. Hence, policy determination is more realistically pictured as a product of bargaining through an accommodative political process that reconciles conflicting recommendations, with presidents necessarily acting as "power brokers" to resolve their competing agencies' conflicting demands. Policy results from compromise, not the president's priorities.

Seen in this way, the chief executive is an arbitrator of interagency disputes, and policy making entails settling jurisdictional struggles. Presidential decisions must reconcile divergent claims in order to maintain a modicum of harmony within the government. In many ways the captive president's role is primarily to govern by managing his or her own bureaucracy. "The president is beset with too many often conflicting opinions," James Baker observed in 1987 as Reagan's chief of staff, "and he spends an inordinate time resolving differences among his advisers who are there because their existence has been legislated." How to get bureau chiefs, assistant secretaries, and agency heads to do what is needed and prevent their rebellion dominates presidents' attention. "Somehow a president must try to make a ministry out of what is at best a coalition" (Lowi 1967).

When viewed from the perspective of the role any president must play, the reasons for compromise, incrementalism, and caution in policy making become apparent. The president is surrounded on a daily basis by advisers, including members of the cabinet, who so interpret their jobs as to make maximum claims on their agencies' behalf. Having heard from one supplicant the extreme of one side of a policy dispute, and then the other extreme from another, the president must forge the terms of settlement.

But look at the setting in which the president must make a choice, having "to operate in a world populated with countervailing organizations which believe his every move is of concern to them, and must therefore be cleared with them" (Cleveland 1959). Advocates of competing viewpoints must be allowed to struggle regularly, and all contestants must attempt to remain friends. The politicized situation encourages the participants to make maximum claims as bargaining points, but all expect a compromise settlement, in part because the president must give everyone something in order to elicit their future cooperation. Thus the president is driven to satisfy most advocates partially rather than a few agencies fully; to keep future options open by appearing neutral and hedging rather than allowing the opposition to become adamant or allied; and to deal in increments and adjustments, inching toward fundamental goals step by step, gaining only a little but never losing a lot.

Permitting foes to save face is also an important part of this game. Because policy making involves constant struggle, with much give and take, "the profusion of so many centers of power makes building the kind of consensus necessary for positive action a formidable task" (Hilsman 1990). Ironically, then, American foreign policy's resistance to adaptive change may flow not from the concentration of power but from its diffusion. The jumble of policy-making centers and increases in their number decrease presidents' capacity to take visionary initiatives. Because policy directions are set through long-established intra- and interagency bargains that reflect an established distribution of influence, policy disruptions are unlikely unless the distribution of influence itself is changed. Perhaps it was this kind of environment that stimulated Dean Acheson's memorable remark that a secretary of state's most essential quality is "the killer instinct."

Other Effects of Bureaucratic Decision Making

The preceding discussion has identified some of the basic characteristics and consequences of bureaucratic policy-making behavior, but still others are discernible.

Among them is *ad hoc decision making*. Preoccupied with each day's immediate crisis, leaders rarely think long-term. Often, they confront only issues that have reached crisis proportions. Critics of the Bush administration directed attention to its penchant for ad hoc decision making, complaining that American policy appeared to react passively to others' decisions or issues as they arose, even at a time when vision seemed most necessary. Bush was not alone, however. As one State Department official described the Carter administration's decision making: "Adhocracy gone mad seemed too often to be the order of the day, with policy careening from crisis to crisis with no more certain guide than the decisions of the moment" (Carter 1981). The unattractive picture suggests policy by improvisation instead of planning. Rather than choices being made in light of carefully considered national goals, trial-and-error responses to policy problems as they surface are more characteristic.

A related consequence of bureaucratic behavior is *decision avoidance*. Most of us think of presidents as decisive—an image presidents willingly cultivate. Harry Truman (1966) put it this way: "The greatest part of the president's job is to make decisions—big ones and small ones . . . The president—whoever he is—has to decide. He can't pass the buck to anybody. No one else can do the deciding for him. That's his job."

Unfortunately, comparatively few presidents adhere to Truman's advice. Many, quite proficient at passing the buck, manage not to decide. "Presidents are, in the eyes of bureaucrats, notorious for putting off decisions or changing their minds. They have enough decisions to make without looking for additional ones. In many cases, all the options look bad and they prefer to wait" (Gelb and Halperin 1973).

The psychological incentives for ignoring problems or postponing their confrontation are enormous. Not taking direct action or letting the force of momentum determine policy outcomes avoids criticism and opposition. Particularly in the foreign policy realm, where the wrong decision can mean the difference between life and death for millions,[11] it is tempting to seek refuge from decision-making burdens by simply denying that a problem exists.

A third potential effect of bureaucratic decision making is the so-called *risky-shift phenomenon*. People deciding in groups are reluctant to appear overly cautious or, worse, fearful. Hence they act differently together than they would alone. For psychological reasons they reach shift-to-risk decisions under peer-group pressure. Thus groups, it has been argued, are usually dominated by their most reckless (and neurotic) member. People will sacrifice themselves for and take chances on behalf of others that they would not normally take when acting for themselves alone. When decision responsibilities are shared, risky alternatives are more likely because no member of the group making the risky decision can be held personally responsible for proposing a policy that produces failure. Bureaucracy generally encourages caution and restraint, as we have noted. However, when policy making becomes concentrated in the hands of a few, as it is prone to do when the nation faces an external threat, the penchant for caution may be overcome and even reversed. "Madness," Friedrich Nietzsche argued, "is the exception in individuals but the rule in groups."

Yet another product of decision making in large, complex organizations is the increased likelihood of *unmanaged policy initiatives*. Some individuals occasionally have the opportunity to take unilateral initiatives. If policy making is really determined at the implementation stage and not at the declaratory stage (when the president or his staff proclaims the policy), then what bureaucrats actually do defines the real policy. In a sense, then, every bureaucrat has the opportunity to be a policymaker. "In the intricate sticky webs of paperwork, the principle of accountability flutters and expires. Responsibility gets diffused; finally it disappears. Everyone is responsible; therefore no one is responsible. It is 'the system'" (Kilpatrick 1985).

A revealing illustration occurred during the Vietnam War. After President Nixon finally declared a cessation of the bombing over North Vietnam in 1972 in the hope of encouraging bargaining concessions from the North Vietnamese, General John D.

Lavelle of the air force took it on himself to order hundreds of pilots to attack North Vietnamese territory. Over a three-month period he continued to order dropping the bombs in clear violation of the president's official policy. To the North Vietnamese, not surprisingly, the president's policy proclamation mattered little: American policy had *not* changed.

The covert actions of Lt. Colonel Oliver North in the Iran-*contra* affair fit this mold. A gung-ho underling intoxicated with the desire to pursue Cold War confrontation by any means necessary, North "seized upon the 'neat idea'" of using profits from clandestine arms sales to what Secretary of State George Shultz had termed a terrorist regime (the anti-American government of Iran) to support the *contras*, opponents of the leftist Sandinista government in Nicaragua. Moving "under cover," North set up an illegal plan to divert secret funds from the arms sales in order to provide the *contras* clandestine military support. His operation established a "secret government" or "government within a government" to conduct a "secret war." This "junta" felt it had been forced to manipulate the real U.S. government to get what it wanted because it could not secure public approval or congressional authorization for its action (Draper 1990). In the end the carefully crafted plan backfired at the same time that it jeopardized basic democratic principles. "There was a concern," Lyndon Johnson's former adviser Clark Clifford put it, "that our nation not resort to the tactics of our enemies in order to resist them." Convicted of lying to Congress (even though he claimed to have received the tacit approval of President Reagan), North was given a light sentence by presiding Judge Gesell, who, in pronouncing the sentence "reiterated the jurors' view that North was not a leader but a 'low-ranking subordinate' who presumably was not entirely responsible for what he did" (Fitzgerald 1989). His conviction was later set aside by a U.S. Appeals Court.

Some allege that the cruelest and most inhumane features of American conduct abroad are caused not by evil men and women, but by the institutions in which evil behavior is sometimes bred. Bureaucratic decision making, in other words, not deficiencies of those who work in those settings, accounts for past immoral decisions and the ***dehumanization of foreign policy***.

Here observers note that specialization discourages the humanitarian's role in the policy-making process. An army of technocrats—individuals who only know how to perform certain tasks and who feel no responsibility for anything beyond the narrow confines of their job—carry out decisions. More often than not they give unquestioning loyalty to their agency without doubting its motives. Bureaucratic policy making conceals the overall content of the policy, and bureaucrats who evaluate the ethics of their assigned mission find that their judgment and loyalty are questioned. Even the managers, the agency heads, are isolated from the policy product; a manager's true product is management.

Because the foreign affairs government spreads decision responsibility, assigning credit—or blame—for what the United States does abroad becomes a hopeless task. Without clear-cut responsibility for policy initiatives, managers and those they manage are shielded from their role in producing foreign policy actions that, on a personal level, they might regard as morally repugnant or socially harmful. The anonymity of the policy-making process, critics note, produced Vietnam: A reading of *The Pentagon*

Papers (1971) gives the impression that no one was to blame for the way the war was ruthlessly prosecuted (see also McNamara 1995). It was the faceless bureaucratic system, and not people, that produced the product.

The untoward consequences of vast yet faceless governmental structures manifest themselves in wartime in "bureaucratic homicide," a term coined during the Vietnam War but not confined to it.

> In general, those who plan do not kill and those who kill do not plan. . . . The bureaucratization of homicide is responsible for the routine character of modern war, the absence of passion, and the efficiency of mass-produced death. . . . At every level of government the classic defense of the bureaucratic killer is available: "I was just doing my job!" The essence of bureaucratic government is emotional coolness, orderliness, implacable momentum, and a dedication to abstract principle. Each cog in the bureaucratic machine does what it is supposed to do. The . . . military establishment . . . kills cleanly, and usually at a distance. America's highly developed technology makes it possible to increase the distance between killer and victim and hence to preserve the crucial psychological fiction that the objects of America's lethal attention are less than human. (Barnet 1972, 13–14)

Cutting as these remarks are, they continue to ring true in today's technologically sophisticated conflict environment, as illustrated during the Persian Gulf War, where massive air strikes against Iraq caused thousands of civilian casualties even as U.S. and allied forces remained unengaged in ground combat.

Those responsible for the war against Iraq were not without compassion, apparently. The decision to end the ground war after only one hundred hours was made in part because it seemed to be turning into a massacre. General Colin L. Powell, chairman of the Joint Chiefs of Staff, was particularly concerned about unnecessary carnage once U.S. military objectives were achieved: "'There's almost a psychic cost to be borne if we ask our troops to continue military operations when it's clear we've won,' he warned. Bludgeoning a defeated foe was not only distasteful but also 'not American,' Powell believed. 'There is . . . chivalry in war'" (Atkinson 1993). Ironically, however, critics—including large numbers of average Americans—now believe that the failure to "eliminate" Saddam Hussein deprived the United States of political victory even as it decisively won the military battle (Hilsman 1992).

Roles and the Process of Decision Making: Credits and Debits . . . .

The impact of role-induced bureaucratic behavior on foreign policy making is seriously at odds with the rational role model. Although the texts we are likely to read in a high-school civics course make historical policy decisions sound reasonable, the memoirs of past participants in the decision-making process—including presidents— and an objective treatment of the diplomatic record leave quite a different impression. To contemporary eyewitnesses and to others who have later probed the record of events, those happenings often did not look orderly or rational. At times they appear more like scenes from the theater of the absurd. To some, the American foreign policy-making process contributes to its recurrent failures (Etheredge 1985); to others, it makes the United States its "own worst enemy" (Destler, Gelb, and Lake 1984).

How valid are the villain image of foreign policy-making procedures and the corollary hypothesis that the decision-making process within large-scale organizations is characterized by malaise? The symptoms are numerous and need not be recounted here, except, perhaps, to note that "bureaucrat" and "bureaucracy" are concepts that seldom command respect; to many they demand derision.

Still, we must be careful not to overstate or misrepresent the impact of large-scale organizations on American foreign policy making. "Bureaucrat" need not be a dirty word. (If a bureaucrat is anyone who works for a publicly funded organization at the federal, state, or local level, their numbers are very large indeed!) The negative side of the ledger must be balanced by the clear advantages of modern bureaucracy. In fact, the conduct of American foreign policy would not be possible without a modern bureaucracy and the kind of organizational support career professionals alone can provide. Though deficient in many respects, bureaucratic government is nonetheless indispensable to a great power's practices.

It is not the enormous size of the government that alone makes officials appear to be continually tripping over each other (although that is part of the problem). Nor is the propensity for the policy-making system to stumble and blunder due merely to self-serving people (although they contribute to the problem as well). The formidable challenges posed by today's complex world make bureaucratic government necessary even as they make it look unresponsive to a changing environment. "Inveighing against big government," observes syndicated columnist George Will, "ignores the fact that government, though big, is often too weak." The solution, therefore, is not to do away with bureaucratic government, but to run it efficiently and shape its power to national purposes. For that, vigorous leadership is required.

In the final analysis, then, bringing out the best that the foreign affairs bureaucracy has to offer—and preventing the worst that it can produce—rests with the president and his or her principal advisers. But can they make a difference? Or was the eminent sociologist Max Weber correct when he argued, "In a modern state the actual ruler is necessarily and unavoidably the bureaucracy"? To address that question, we must examine the fifth and final source of American foreign policy: individual leaders.

NOTES

1. It has been shown, for example, that people promoted in the armed services develop more favorable attitudes toward the army than those who are not promoted, and that commissioned officers are more pro-army than enlistees (Stouffer et al. 1949); that length of service in the U.S. House of Representatives affects members' attitudes toward foreign aid (Rieselbach 1964); and that the role requirements (that is, committee experience) of U.S. senators shapes their attitudes toward the secretary of state (Rosenau 1980). See also Lieberman (1965) and Singer (1965).

2. George Bush confessed in November 1989 at a White House reception honoring Ronald Reagan that he had difficulty adjusting to his new role as president after serving as Reagan's vice president: "When the announcer said 'Mr. President,' well, I fell back to where I comfortably was for eight years. It seemed most appropriate."

3. This may not be entirely illogical. Anthony Downs (1957) suggests that the rational voter cannot afford to gather all the information available about all candidates prior to deciding for

whom to vote: The costs involved are too high for the resultant payoff. Instead, voters base decisions on partial information such as the candidate's party label. Similar logic about the costs of acquiring information apply to a wide array of decision situations.

4. Achen (1989) argues that rational decision making by a unitary actor and bureaucratic politics are not competing models. Instead, drawing on rational choice theory, he argues that bureaucratic politics "will ordinarily produce" rationality: "Collective decisions are representable by a cardinal utility function that is a weighted average of the preferences of the actors involved, with the weights proportional to actors' power to influence the focal actor." The argument requires limitations based on technicalities, but generally the conclusion is that "a state that makes decisions in this fashion is representable as a unitary rational actor."

5. For further discussions of the bureaucratic political model, see Allison (1971), Allison and Halperin (1972), Hilsman (1990), Kissinger (1969), and Townsend (1982). For critiques, see Art (1973), Bendor and Hammond (1992), Caldwell (1977), and Krasner (1972).

6. Some organization theorists note that *new* units within administrative agencies (for example, the State Department's Bureau of Human Rights in the Carter administration) recruit ideologues and risk takers, whereas old ones recruit cautious, security-conscious personnel who are more likely to protect their stakes in the status quo than to express their policy preferences and push reforms.

7. The lessons of the 1930s also led policymakers to conclusions about the appropriateness of interventionist and noninterventionist trade policy regarding manufactured and agricultural goods (Goldstein 1989). The result, as we noted in Chapter 7, is that international trade in the industrial and agricultural sectors developed quite differently.

8. Although this anecdote illustrates graphically the potential ability of bureaucratic agencies to defy political leaders, its historical accuracy has been questioned. For an examination of the events surrounding the account, see Caldwell (1978).

9. The Turkish missiles have long figured prominently in the Cuban missile story. Kennedy was believed to have been intransigent on the issue of trading U.S. missiles in Turkey for Soviet missiles in Cuba, but a transcript of a crucial meeting of the ExCom declassified twenty-five years after the event reveals that Kennedy was more willing to compromise on withdrawal of the U.S. missiles than previously thought. He apparently worried about how he could justify going to nuclear war over missiles his own advisers considered obsolete (Bundy and Blight 1987–1988).

10. Deming's is "the philosophy of nonhierarchical management style, employee 'empowerment,' and customer satisfaction. . . . The problem with this 'entrepreneurial' model of government, its critics say, is that government is not and should not function like a business. Businesses respond to the bottom line; government is supposed to respond to laws written in the public interest" (Carney 1994). The effort to make government behave more like the private sector actually began during the Bush administration. Richard G. Darman, Bush's director of OMB, was a primary catalyst behind the 1990 Chief Financial Officers Act, designed to improve government agencies' financial management. For a critical review of TQM as applied to government, see Wieseltier (1993).

11. For an analysis of how policy may evolve from the inertia of previous decisions and a *fait accompli* from the depths of the bureaucracy, see Warner Schilling (1973), "The H-Bomb Decision: How to Decide without Actually Choosing."

SUGGESTIONS FOR FURTHER READING

Allison, Graham T. *Essence of Decision: Explaining the Cuban Missile Crisis.* Boston: Little, Brown, 1971.

Anderson, Paul A. "What Do Decision Makers Do When They Make a Foreign Policy Decision?" pp. 285–308 in Charles F. Hermann, Charles W. Kegley, Jr., and James N. Rosenau, (eds.), *New Directions in the Study of Foreign Policy.* Boston: Allen and Unwin, 1987.

Hilsman, Roger. *The Politics of Policy Making in Defense and Foreign Affairs: Conceptual Models and Bureaucratic Politics,* 2nd ed. Englewood Cliffs, N.J.: Prentice-Hall, 1990.

Hybel, Alex Roberto. *Power over Rationality: The Bush Administration and the Gulf Crisis.* Albany: State University of New York Press, 1993.

Janis, Irving L. *Groupthink: Psychological Studies of Policy Decisions and Fiascoes,* 2nd ed. Boston: Houghton Mifflin, 1982.

Jones, Christopher M. "American Prewar Technology Sales to Iraq: A Bureaucratic Politics Explanation," pp. 279–96 in Eugene R. Wittkopf (ed.), *The Domestic Sources of American Foreign Policy: Insights and Evidence.* New York: St. Martin's, 1994.

Khong, Yuen Foong. *Analogies at War: Korea, Munich, Dien Bien Phu and the Vietnam Decisions of 1965.* Princeton: Princeton University Press, 1992.

Nathan, James A., ed. *The Cuban Missile Crisis Revisited.* New York: St. Martin's, 1992.

Smith, Steve. "Policy Preferences and Bureaucratic Position: The Case of the American Hostage Rescue Mission," *International Affairs* 61 (Winter 1984–1985): 9–25.

Snyder, Richard C., H. W. Bruck, and Burton Sapin, eds. *Foreign Policy Decision-Making: An Approach to the Study of International Politics.* New York: Free Press, 1962.

't Hart, Paul. *Groupthink in Government: A Study of Small Groups and Policy Failure.* Baltimore: Johns Hopkins University Press, 1990.

Walker, Stephen G. "Role Theory and the Origins of Foreign Policy," pp. 269–84 in Charles F. Hermann, Charles W. Kegley, Jr., and James N. Rosenau, eds., *New Directions in the Study of Foreign Policy.* Boston: Allen and Unwin, 1987.

Wilson, Heather. "Missed Opportunities: Washington Politics and Nuclear Proliferation," *The National Interest* 34 (Winter 1993–1994): 26–36.

• • •

CHAPTER 14

LEADER CHARACTERISTICS AND FOREIGN POLICY PERFORMANCE

• • •

If I have learned anything in a lifetime in politics and government, it is the truth of the famous phrase, "History is biography"— that decisions are made by people, and they make them based on what they know of the world and how they understand it.

Vice President George Bush, 1987

One of the most unsettling things for foreigners is the impression that our foreign policy can be changed by any new president on the basis of the president's personal preference.

Former Secretary of State Henry Kissinger, 1979

Picture a president sitting alone in the Oval Office, wrestling with a crisis that threatens the lives of thousands of Americans living abroad and tens of thousands of others, possessing the power to unleash massive military might against the assailants. Assume that this particular president is impulsively competitive, is prone to act brashly to attract attention, is inclined to take risks to exploit opportunities, views the world as a jungle in which one must perpetually claw and scratch for power, is distrustful of others, is contemptuous of his adversaries, and has a quick temper. Assume also that the president is driven by a fear of failure stemming from low self-esteem, a fear overcome in the past by dramatic and successful actions that restored his self-confidence. How is such a president likely to respond to the crisis he faces? Will he confine himself to the canons of rational choice, in which nothing but the interests of the United States are permitted to color his decision-making behavior? Or will his response be affected significantly by his unique characteristics—his background, his beliefs, and his personality traits?

Properly speaking, nation-states are incapable of acting or thinking. They are inanimate symbols for collectivities—the people within their borders. In reality, foreign policy decisions are made by a remarkably few people acting on behalf of states, most conspicuously the president and the president's inner circle of advisers. "The management of foreign affairs," Thomas Jefferson maintained, is "executive altogether." Harry Truman concurred, exclaiming "I make American foreign policy." For these reasons, the personal characteristics of those empowered to make decisions on behalf of the nation are crucial.

In this chapter we examine the hypothesis that individuals are an important source of American foreign policy. We look at the leaders themselves, the people who occupy the decision-making roles at the highest echelons of government, particularly presidents, and explore whether and how their personal aspirations, anxieties, convictions, memories, and experiences influence American foreign policy.

Individuals as a Source of Foreign Policy

Because of the president's power and preeminence, it is tempting to think of foreign policy as determined exclusively by presidential preferences and to personalize government by identifying a policy with its proponents. Ralph Waldo Emerson's aphorism, "There is properly no history, only biography," dramatizes the popular impression that individual leaders are the makers and movers of history. This **_hero-in-history_** model of foreign policy making finds expression in the practice of attaching the names of presidents to the policies they promulgate (for example, the Truman Doctrine, the Kennedy Round), as if the individuals were synonymous with the nation itself, and of routinely attributing foreign affairs successes and failures to the administration in which they occurred. New leaders are assumed to make a difference.

The conviction that the individual who holds office makes a difference is one of the major premises underlying the democratic electoral system. Thus each new administration seeks to distinguish itself from its predecessor and to highlight policy departures as it seeks to convey the message that it has engineered a new (and better) order. The media's tendency to label presidential actions "new" abets those efforts. Hence leadership and policy are portrayed as synonymous, and changes in policy and policy direction are often perceived as results of the predispositions of the leadership.

A consideration of the idiosyncratic characteristics of individuals draws attention to the psychological foundations of human conduct. Perceptions, personal needs, and drives are all important determinants of the way people act. Correspondingly, decision makers' inner traits influence how they respond to various situations. The cognitions and responses of decision makers are determined not by "the 'objective' facts of the situation . . . but [by] their 'image' of the situation;" that is, they "act according to the way the world appears . . . not necessarily according to the way it 'is'" (Boulding 1959). That principle correctly suggests that images shape foreign policy behavior.

Perceptions are not simple reflections of what is passively observed. Instead, they are influenced by the memories, values, needs, and beliefs the observer brings to the situation (see Falkowski 1979; Jönsson 1982). Everyone's perceptions are biased by personality predispositions and inner drives, as well as by prior experiences and future expectations. What occurs in decision makers' heads is therefore important.

As we shift attention from the way issues are debated to the debaters themselves, we must ask if contrasts among decision makers make a difference in policy—in content as well as in style. Does the type of person elected to or selected for policy-making positions affect the nation's international conduct? Do the particular personal qualities of the people holding policy positions determine the course a nation charts for itself in foreign affairs? Or would others holding those positions during the same period have acted similarly? Do changes in leadership stimulate changes in foreign policy? If so, in what ways, and under what conditions? We now turn to these intriguing questions.

Individuals and Foreign Policy Performance ·····························

No two individuals are identical; each person differs in some way from every other. This personal diversity is exhibited by the major figures in post-World War II American foreign policy. Compare "give 'em hell" Harry Truman, soft-spoken Ike Eisenhower, charismatic Jack Kennedy, "Tricky Dick" Nixon, "down-home" Jimmy Carter, Hollywood "Dutch" Reagan, "preppie" George Bush, and "Slick Willie" Clinton. Apparent differences in policy elites' personalities may nevertheless mask important similarities. The relevant question, therefore, is not how different are the individuals who make American foreign policy, but, instead, what impact do leaders' peculiar traits have on their decision-making behavior.

Although it is difficult to generalize, it is easy to demonstrate that policymakers' personal characteristics influence their behavior, as in-depth case studies of particular decision makers abound.[1] Many probe the life history of policymakers to describe their psychological makeup and world view. These psychobiographies invariably assume that leaders' personalities are determined by their early childhood experiences, their relationships with parents and peers, their self-concept, and the like. These background factors are presumed to mold the leaders' personalities and beliefs and their later decision-making styles and policy-making behavior.

Psychobiography: Personal Characteristics and Foreign Policy Behavior

Consider the psychological consequences of President Woodrow Wilson's stern and often punitive childhood. Wilson's inability to please his rigid father as a child is hypothesized to have created an all-consuming need in later life to attain self-esteem, which accounts for Wilson's approach to the realization of his idealistic policy programs. As president, Wilson compulsively strove to perform great deeds to compensate for his fear of rejection. Most notable was his intense battle to create the League of Nations, a passion explained by Wilson's overriding need to attain a puritanic "state of grace" (George and George 1964).

The first American secretary of defense, James Forrestal, is the object of another illustrative psychobiography (Rogow 1963). Driven and worrisome, Forrestal became obsessed by paranoiac fantasies. He not only feared foreigners but distrusted his own friends and coworkers. His career ended tragically in suicide.

The possible relationship between a leader's psychological profile and his policy behavior is suggested by investigations of the ways President Kennedy's personality may have been instrumental in the decisions he made during the Cuban missile crisis. According to one (controversial) interpretation (Mongar 1974), Kennedy suffered most of his life from a neurotic conflict between an overpowering fear of failure, on one hand, and an overwhelming need for assistance, on the other. The first stemmed from his inability to compete successfully with his older brother (Joe, Jr.), a son given unfair advantage in a contrived competitive family environment. Joe, Jr., was introduced by his father to friends as a future president of the United States, and his mother held him up as a model for the other children, especially Jack, and gave him a free hand in disciplining them. In that atmosphere it became impossible for Jack to attain an equal portion of attention, recognition, and affection from his parents, which undermined the younger Kennedy's self-assurance. A succession of childhood illnesses permitted him to avoid fruitless competition, and he resorted to "the manipulation of fantasy to protect his [preferred self-] image of greatness." Thus self-deception served as a defense mechanism to protect him from his fears of weakness.

Maturity helped young Jack Kennedy strengthen his self-image. As his personality took shape, Kennedy still needed to prove his personal worth. His search for adventure, and his restlessness, intellectualism, and acceptance of difficult tasks reflected this abiding compulsion. To protect his preferred self-image, he habitually disarmed criticism "by modestly calling attention to minor shortcomings. This witty self-derision, which reflected a merciless introspection, undermined criticism early and simultaneously elicited reassurance and support from other people."

Kennedy's words and actions as president during the Cuban missile crisis, Thomas Mongar avers, can be traced to his unresolved inner conflicts. That crisis became a "game," an opportunity to recover self-esteem; Kennedy's actions were made for psychotherapeutic rather than for strategic reasons (such as preventing a change in the nuclear balance of power). The risks were not trivial. When asked about the probability of nuclear war and the destruction of civilization resulting from risky U.S. actions, Kennedy coolly replied "between one in three and even." Kennedy's major decisions, Mongar argues, were shaped by his personal motives.

Is Kennedy's situation unique, or do emotional and personality needs strongly influence other policymakers' responses to foreign policy situations? Consider the case of Henry Kissinger, a decision maker whose extraordinary childhood deviated markedly from the typical route to power. He escaped from Nazi persecution in his native Germany; studied in high school at night while working all day; was drafted into the army; attended college at Harvard; and then became a college professor and served as presidential foreign policy adviser, culminating in his appointment as the first Jewish secretary of state.

Kissinger arguably relied on ideas developed during his early experiences to deal with analogous personal and national problems later in life (Isaak 1975). Personally insecure, yet egocentric, Kissinger felt that uncertainty was the very essence of international politics. He consistently acted as a policymaker on his beliefs, first, that people are limited in what they can do, and second, that because of the complexity of life, many imponderables make history move. Ironically, however, the principle of uncertainty that supported his pessimistic world view may also have been the source of his successes, for Kissinger's achievements may be attributed in part to his ability to use ambiguity, negotiated compromise, and secrecy—as well as public relations strategies ingeniously devised to enhance his image—in his conduct of diplomacy.[2]

Kissinger's embrace of political realism as a theory of international politics also was shaped by his unusual past. *Realpolitik* stresses the expectation of conflict between states, not collaboration, the need to increase power relative to one's adversaries, the inadequacy of moral precepts as a guide to foreign affairs, and distrust of others' motives. Each of these finds a counterpart in the "lessons" Kissinger derived from his personal experiences during the crucial formative period of his political awakening. It seems, then, that Kissinger's disdain of moralism and his corresponding preference to ask not "What is right, and what is wrong?" but "Who is strong, and who is weak?" was rooted in his uncertain, insecure youth.

These brief synopses of Wilson, Forestall, Kennedy, and Kissinger illustrate the varied personalities of those who have risen to positions of power in the American foreign policy establishment and the impact of their needs, background, and prior experiences on their later outlook and policy-making behavior. We can explore these ideas further by looking specifically at the relationship between presidential character and presidential performance. Here James David Barber's analysis of presidents' personal traits and leadership styles is particularly informative.

Presidential Character: Types and Consequences

According to Barber, presidents can be understood best by observing their "style" (habitual ways of performing political roles), "world view" (politically relevant beliefs), and especially "character"—"the way the President orients himself toward life—not for the moment, but enduringly" (Barber 1992).

Two dimensions of *presidential character* are critical: the energy presidents put into the job (active or passive) and their personal satisfaction with their presidential duties (negative or positive). The first captures presidents' image of their job description. Active presidents are movers and shakers, energetically engaged in the challenge of leading, eagerly attentive to the responsibilities of office, and willing to accept the task of policy formulation and management. Conversely, passive presidents prefer to steer an even course, maintaining existing arrangements and avoiding the conflict that invariably accompanies changes in policy.

The second dimension reflects presidents' level of contentment with their job. This varies because some presidents have not enjoyed the position they achieved and have looked with disfavor on the burden of awesome responsibility. Such negative types, Barber notes, tend to have had childhood experiences that make them dutifully accept but not enjoy the demands that go with holding power.

The bidimensional character of each president permits his or her classification into one of four categories: passive-negative, passive-positive, active-negative, and active-positive. Barber distinguishes among the four this way: "Active-positive presidents want most to achieve results. Active-negatives aim to get and keep power. Passive-positives are after love. Passive-negatives emphasize their civic virtue. The relation of activity to enjoyment in a president thus tends to outline a cluster of characteristics, to set apart the adapted from the compulsive, compliant, and withdrawn types."

Not surprisingly, Barber contends that presidents with active-positive characters are best equipped to direct the nation's foreign policy and to meet its challenges and crises. Active-positives are self-respecting and happy, open to new ideas, and able to learn from their mistakes. Their energies are no longer consumed with conquering the

	Positive	Negative
Active	Franklin Roosevelt Harry Truman John Kennedy Gerald Ford Jimmy Carter George Bush Bill Clinton	Woodrow Wilson Herbert Hoover Lyndon Johnson Richard Nixon
Passive	William Taft Warren Harding Ronald Reagan	Calvin Coolidge Dwight Eisenhower

Figure 14.1 Barber's Classification of Twentieth-Century Presidents by Their Character Type

developmental traumas associated with youth but instead are directed outward toward achievement. As policymakers, therefore, active-positives have a greater capacity for growth and flexibility. Figure 14.1 identifies active-positive presidents as well as the other types comprising Barber's typology.

Barber's research shows that the behavior of leaders with similar skills and values can be quite different, depending on their character. A leader's inner self, and especially his or her degree of self-confidence and self-esteem, critically affect performance. Thus personality traits and emotional needs developed during childhood influence all decision makers' careers and conduct. Let us consider some vignettes from Barber's work[3] and then, emulating his methodology, extrapolate from it to assess the character of the nation's forty-second president, Bill Clinton.

Woodrow Wilson

An active-negative president, Woodrow Wilson proved incapable of compromising with Senate irreconcilables and others disposed against the League of Nations. "'Accept or reject'—that was the way Wilson posed the question." In the end his "narrow insistence on a failing course of action" cost him what he cherished so deeply.

Warren G. Harding

A passive-positive, Harding longed to be America's "best loved" president, but history remembers him as perhaps "'the worst President,' the zero point for all scales of 'presidential greatness.'" He came to power at the end of the first epic struggle of the twentieth century and set aside the national debate on the League of Nations in favor of a "return to normalcy" (read "isolationism") and then initiated the Washington Conference on Naval Disarmament and related agreements designed to secure peace in the Pacific. But "his early success was based on illusions—illusions that helped to produce the debacle of the 1930s" (Wolfowitz 1994).

Harry S Truman

An active-positive president, Harry Truman took "massive initiatives at a time when such initiatives seemed unlikely, given the circumstances of his accession to office, his own qualifications, and the condition of the country." Why? Many of Truman's bold foreign policy actions—the Truman Doctrine, the Marshall Plan, NATO, and the Korean intervention—arguably stemmed from Truman's decisive personality.

Dwight D. Eisenhower

Although Barber submits that Eisenhower is difficult to categorize, he concludes Ike was a passive-negative. Eisenhower "did not feel a duty to save the world or become a great hero, but simply to contribute what he could the best he was able." This was the passive side of his character. The negative side, observes Barber, was reflected in his feelings that he was imposed on by an unnecessarily heavy schedule. Indeed, Eisenhower claimed his heart attack in September 1955 was triggered "when he was repeatedly interrupted on the golf links by unnecessary phone calls from the State Department."

John F. Kennedy

Like Truman, Barber maintains that John Kennedy's active-positive character contributed to his crisis-management capabilities (Mongar's analysis notwithstanding). He was able to learn from his prior mistakes and disastrous experience in the Bay of Pigs fiasco of April 1961. By October 1962, "In command, in the assessment of information, in the technique of consultation, and in the empathy with his opponent, clearly John Kennedy had grown. He was, at that point, a professional president."

Lyndon B. Johnson

Barber concludes that Johnson was, like Wilson, an active-negative president. The "fantastic pace of action in his presidency," motivated by humanitarian concerns and a commitment to the pursuit of happiness and creating a better world, revealed the activism in Johnson's character. The "tough, hard, militaristic" posture he assumed toward his enemies evinced his negativism. A 1952 statement while a member of the Senate, in which he declared that he was "prepared to reduce Moscow to rubble to stop communist aggression anywhere," revealed that side of his character.

Richard M. Nixon

An active-negative president, Richard Nixon is a revealing contrast with Truman and Kennedy. "The danger in his presidency," Barber wrote while Nixon was still in the White House, "is the same as the danger Wilson, Hoover, and Johnson succumbed to: rigid adherence to a failing line of policy." Nixon's decision to widen the Vietnam War by invading Cambodia in the spring of 1970 was symptomatic: "To see in President Nixon the character of Richard Nixon—the character formed and set early in his life— one need only read over his speech on the Cambodian invasion, with its themes of power and control, its declaration of independence, its self-concern, its damning of doubters, and its coupling of humiliation with defeat" (Barber 1977). Nixon reached this critical decision without urging from his advisers, and the manner in which the president announced his decision "flabbergasted" his defense secretary, Melvin Laird. Indeed, to many in Washington

> the process by which the president had decided and acted was . . . as scary as the invasion itself. As the story of the crisis decision making came out—the fact that senior State Department officials had been suddenly cut off from key cablegrams, that military orders were issuing directly from the White House, and especially the nearly complete isolation of the president from congressional opinions as he stepped out beyond his most sanguine military advisors—the president's judgment as a professional came into question. (Barber 1977, 439)

Extreme personal isolation ultimately destroyed the Nixon presidency.

Gerald R. Ford

Entering office in the wake of the Watergate scandal and Nixon's resignation, Barber notes that Ford exceeded the low expectations many held for his presidency and showed a capacity to grow and learn. Although "a step-by-step thinker," Ford approached the task of policy making with the positive attitude and activism characteristic of active-positives: "Just as all the props were collapsing in Vietnam, he unrealistically called for hundreds of millions more in military aid. He turned foreign policy over to a wizard of dramatic negotiation [Henry Kissinger] whose ad hoc successes obscured deepening world chaos. And he stood as firm and fast as he could against all sorts of 'wild' schemes to spend the country out of recession, countering them with some tame schemes of his own."

Jimmy Carter

Noting that Carter came to Washington full of high expectations at a time of low hopes, Barber predicted that the energetic, "up and at 'em" active-positive Carter would enjoy life in the Oval Office and would find that it could be fun. Barber also warned, however, that Carter's troubles would spring "from an excess of an active-positive virtue: the thirst for results." His prediction proved accurate. Carter's character eventually led him impatiently to pursue too many goals simultaneously—a penchant that lent credibility to the frequent charges that he was inconsistent and indecisive, that he lacked a clear sense of priorities, and that he abandoned policy objectives almost as soon as they were announced in favor of still newer objectives, which then also were shelved.

Ronald Reagan

Reagan's personality and ideology reveal inconsistent traits. "What makes it difficult to sort out Reagan's operative world view," observed Barber (1981) on the day of Reagan's first inauguration, "is his peculiar way with rhetoric. Obviously, it dominates his political style." Reagan's way with words, which led to the appellation "Great

Communicator," concealed his true feelings, but his "take-it-easy" style and optimism made Reagan a passive-positive, "the receptive, compliant, other-directed character whose life is a search for affection as a reward for being agreeable and cooperative rather than personally assertive." Reagan's aides described him even during crisis situations "as 'uninvolved in the planning process,' 'secluded,' and 'disconcertedly disengaged'" (McElvaine 1984). Reagan's heavy dependence on his advisers, his willingness to delegate, and his detachment from the policy process were all evident in the Iran-*contra* scandal, clearly the low point of the Reagan presidency.

Reagan's passive-positive character also embraaced sentimentality, and romantic infatuation, and the lack of a coherent ideology. Although widely regarded as the most ideological of Cold War presidents, Barber notes that Reagan "was never in any serious or thoughtful way an ideologue," his conservatism was "circumstantial, not visceral." Indeed, Reagan adhered to a simple "black and white" outlook and was uninterested in facts and unaffected by them (see Dallek 1984; Glad 1983).

Reagan's life had been spent playing roles, an experience that may have colored his conception of the presidency. Thirty years of show business, following scripts written and directed by others, instilled a theatrical style in his performance. As he once revealingly commented: "Politics is just like show business. You have a hell of an opening, coast for a while, and then have a hell of a close."

George Bush

George Herbert Walker Bush was an active-positive president. Noting that "Mr. Bush wants a mission . . . [and] sees himself as enlivened and inspired," Barber asked at the time of his inauguration: "Could he move out into the real world and take on the challenge of forging peace and justice . . . in a new and different way? Given Mr. Bush's past, that is conceivable. He is not stuck with consistency" (Barber 1989).

Barber also worried, however, that "The basic question about Bush . . . is not character, but world view. What is his vision?" Many others asked the same question.

Several distinguished signposts marked Bush's career as a public servant—member of Congress, chair of the Republican National Committee, director of the CIA, envoy to China, ambassador to the United Nations, and vice president—but it lacked creativity, curiosity, and ingenuity. His near invisibility as vice president is affirmed by the absence of a clear-cut record of where Bush stood—if anywhere—in the events leading to the Iran-*contra* scandal. Thus Bush could be described as "comforting in the ease with which he seems to undertake his awesome tasks, but disconcerting because he has left few footprints where he has been and offers a still fainter road map of where he would go" (Gerstenzang and Meyer 1990).

Bush himself disparaged "the vision thing," but it dogged his entire presidency. His preference for prudence and pragmatism led to a cautious—indeed, timid—response to the dramatic developments in Europe and the Soviet Union leading to the end of the Cold War. Thus he exercised little control over events, instead reacting to others' initiatives that shaped the future. Even the early stages of the crisis over Kuwait, in which Bush mounted a determined diplomatic and military counterpoise to Saddam Hussein, evoked criticism. Columnist David S. Broder observed:

For the first eight years of the decade, we had, in Ronald Reagan, an actor-president. What we now have, in George Bush, is a reactor-president: The more he proves himself highly competent with the comeback, the more maddening is his reluctance to move first. . . .

Over time, a reactive president will increasingly be constrained by circumstances not of his making. His leadership will inevitably come to be questioned. (Broder 1990, 4)[4]

The Persian Gulf crisis and resultant war illustrated other facets of Bush's character and style. Drawing on his extensive contacts with and courtship of world leaders, Bush personally engineered the Coalition that fought the war against Iraq, reflecting a long-standing preference for personal politics (Mullins and Wildavsky 1992). At home his preference for a small, inner circle of advisers chosen on the basis of personal ties and loyalty rather than expertise or independent thinking promoted secrecy that helped to conceal the president's thinking from Congress and the public and thus to preserve the administration's flexibility, as we saw in previous chapters. But Bush made the final decisions. His furtive, "I'm in charge" style was anticipated in his response to earlier criticisms of his decision to send secret missions to China shortly after the 1989 Tiananmen Square massacre and again following the invasion of Panama at the end of the year: "I have an obligation to conduct the foreign policy of this country in the way I see fit."

In the end, however, even Bush's handling of the Persian Gulf War, the high point of his White House years, was tainted by "the vision thing" and by questions about his ability to learn, as Barber had predicted:

All of us in his generation were taught the same lesson: get dangerous dictators early. Knowing what he should do, Bush did it well. But the lesson did not include when to end the war or whether to leave the dictator in office. . . . It is unwise to speak ill of an opponent personally as President Bush did repeatedly in regard to Saddam Hussein. Having done so, however, anyone with experience should know that such personal disparagement signals a determination to remove that person from office. For the president to claim that he did not intend his actions to be so interpreted is worse than misleading. It verges on amateurishness. (Mullins and Wildavsky 1992, 55)

Bill Clinton

"Like President Thomas Jefferson, [President] William Jefferson Clinton is politically active-positive, has strong political skills, and keeps working for what he believes is best." This is how Barber described Clinton on his inauguration (*The News & Observer*, Raleigh, N.C., January 17, 1993, p. 10).

In many ways Clinton is an ideal illustration of the active-positive character. His interest in politics and policy is unique among modern presidents, he is energetic, enthusiastic, intelligent, confident, articulate, and pragmatic. Like Jimmy Carter, however, these characteristics also led him to "to take on large numbers of personal responsibilities, so much so that it is difficult for his administration to move on more than one track at a time" (Greenstein 1993–1994). Clinton also suffered from an inability to communicate his record and program to the public. In this way "he is the antithesis of Ronald Reagan, who was notoriously innocent of policy specifics but gifted at evoking larger themes." Thus the early Clinton presidency stumbled more than once—several times, in fact, in the foreign policy arena.

Clinton's energy is one sign of his active-positive mode, and his philosophy of government shaped the style of his administration as well as his agenda. After more than a decade of Republican rule in which government was viewed as the problem, not the solution, Clinton's agenda was rooted in the principle of government activism. "The biggest single thing is that there is a belief within this [administration] that government should be used to try to solve social problems," observed White House counselor David R. Gergen on the anniversary of Clinton's inauguration. "As someone who worked in the White House in the 1980s [when Republicans occupied it], that is a major change, to believe in government as a catalyst to solve problems." Still, Clinton's frenetic pace did not always produce its desired results. In the words of a frustrated Democratic member of Congress, who first went to Capitol Hill during the Eisenhower administration: "I think he may be trying too hard. I'm reluctantly coming to the conclusion that he has the dreaded Carter disease—no focus, no continuity, confusing motion with accomplishment."

"Doing good" is a theme that runs throughout Clinton's populist political career, and he realized significant achievements both as governor and as president. Still, Clinton often failed to get credit for his accomplishments while sometimes evoking genuine loathing among his detractors. Criticism of any chief executive goes with the territory, but in Clinton's case it goes deeper—to his character.

> It is an assessment of the man as a whole, of what is bred in the bone, one of those national gut decisions that happens in politics, something that solidifies after the accumulation of evidence passes some unseen tipping point: Lincoln is honest, Carter is weak, Reagan is decent but doddering, Bush is a wimp. Only Richard Nixon and now Bill Clinton have been tagged with nicknames that reflected a popular suspicion that the president of the United States could not be fully trusted: Tricky Dick and Slick Willie. (Kelly 1994, 23)

The William Jefferson in Clinton's name comes from his father, who was killed in an auto accident three months before he was born. He was raised by his mother, Virginia, and stepfather, Roger Clinton, whom his mother married in 1950 and who came from an Arkansas political family. Virginia instilled in him the optimism that goes with his active-positive character. "Clinton also may owe to [her] the character trait that was perhaps the essential determinant of his political success—an unusually large need for adulation, a hunger for affirmation from others so intense that approval is seen almost as an entitlement" (Kelly 1994). His high school principal, who recognized his political talents, pushed him to run for class office. He won, but classmates argued that the rules made it easier for band members to win than football players or cheerleaders (Maraniss 1992). Clinton was in the band.

In 1963 Clinton met John F. Kennedy in the White House rose garden while participating in Boy's Nation leadership camp. The handshake set the young Clinton on a path that would return him to the White House thirty years later as the nation's forty-second president.

Educated at Georgetown, Oxford, and Yale Universities, Clinton returned to

Arkansas, where he lost a bid for Congress in 1974 but won the attorney general's office two years later. Five terms as governor followed. Along the way he would pick up the support of influential Arkansans, including chicken mogul Don Tyson, and many others outside the small, southern state who would later be called "f.o.b.s"—friends of Bill. His character and reputation also began to mold into one. "Clinton began to garner a reputation in Arkansas that now besets him nationally, a reputation for slipperiness and waffling in excess of even the norm of politics. . . . Jokes about Clinton's honesty, about his predilection for saying whatever his listener of the moment wanted to hear, about his willingness to reverse himself, were common midway through his second term and grew steadily through his five terms as Governor" (Kelly 1994).

Clinton promised Arkansans he would serve out his fifth term as governor and not run for the presidency while still in office—but he didn't and did. His indefatigable determination to be president explained the decision but also added another target for critics of his character. "After all this time, there is no longer any difference between the inner Bill Clinton and the political Bill Clinton," lamented a long-time Little Rock political analyst. "His whole life is one long reelection campaign aimed at the presidency. Everything he does has been shaped by that" (cited in Maraniss 1992).

Clinton's continuing reelection campaign manifests itself in his infectious rapport with others—which, however, also is not beyond reproach.

> Clinton can take a group of people—people who may disagree with each other vehemently—and convince them that their differences are minor, peripheral. . . . He will shave, wheedle, compromise, and cajole until he finds—or creates—common ground. He is notorious for leading people to believe that he agrees with them entirely. . . without ever quite committing himself to their position. This is a gift given only to the best politicians. It is how difficult things get done. It is also easily abused, especially when the practitioner has an imprecise, or relative, sense of moral principle.
>
> And so, Bill Clinton's greatest strength may be inseparable from his most disheartening weakness. The president truly likes people—his personal affection, and attention, [are] authentic—but he likes them indiscriminately. He has trouble drawing lines, disagreeing, disappointing them. (Klein 1994, 18)

Compromise, as Clinton sees it, is not a character flaw but an essential element in the political process and his drive to do good. The line between compromise and indecision is fine, however. Even Clinton adviser George Stefanopoulos, the frequent target of Clinton's legendary temper, complained that "the worst thing about him is that he never makes a decision" (cited in Woodward 1994). That attribute plagued his foreign policy performance almost from the beginning. In Bosnia, Somalia, Haiti, China, and elsewhere, promises were made and pledges taken, only to be revised, reversed, or remain unfulfilled. "A sense of confusion about defining and pursuing centrally important national interests" plagued the administration (Wolfowitz 1994). It soon became "the conventional diplomatic wisdom" that "the pledges of the president of the United States are to be regarded more as well-meaning sentiments than actual commitments" (Kelly 1994).

The roots of presidential character, argues Barber, are in the past. And the past haunted Clinton's presidency, as "no one is surprised any more when the president reverses himself on a matter of policy, or breaks a promise, or axes an old friend," wrote one analyst two years into the Clinton presidency.

> What makes this sad, even tragic, rather than merely sordid, is that Bill Clinton's predicament owes itself directly to Bill Clinton's promise. The president's problems did not come about because he was a cheap political hack. They came about because he was not. For what happened to Clinton happened because he wanted, more than anything in life, to get to where he is today, and because he wanted this, at least in part, in order to do good—and because the great goal of doing good gave him license to indulge in the everyday acts of minor corruption and compromise and falsity that the business of politics demands. Bill Clinton was perceptive enough to master politics—but not perceptive enough to see what politics was doing to him. (Kelly 1994, 24)

Leadership and the Impact of Leadership Styles

Leaders' personalities impact foreign policy performance in many ways, ranging from grand designs to their choice of advisers and way they organize their advisory systems. Alexander George (1988), for example, describes three different approaches presidents have evolved for managing the tasks they all face of mobilizing available information, expertise, and analytical resources for effective policy making: the *formalistic*, *competitive*, and *collegial models*. In a formalistic model, clear lines of authority minimize the need for presidential involvement in the inevitable politicking among cabinet officers and presidential advisers; in the competitive model, the president purposely seeks to promote conflict and competition among presidential advisers; and in the collegial model, teamwork and group problem solving are sought, with the president acting like the hub of a wheel with spokes connecting to individual advisers and agency heads. What approach a president chooses and how it operates in practice will be shaped by the president's personality: by his or her cognitive style (analogous to world view), sense of efficacy and competence, and general orientation to political conflict.

Building on these and related ideas, Margaret G. Hermann and Thomas Preston (1994) refer to the types of authority patterns presidents use in dealing with their advisers (formal versus informal) and the way they seek to coordinate them (building concurrence and a sense of community versus accomplishing a task) to devise a typology of presidential leadership: the Chief Executive Officer, the Director/Ideologue, the Team Builder and Player, and the Analyst/Innovator (see Figure 14.2).

Chief Executive Officers "want their preferences to prevail and to have a formal chain of command—to sit on top of a well-defined hierarchy." Director/Ideologues also want their preferences to prevail, but presidents of this type have "a cause [they are] promoting or a problem [they need] to see solved that focuses [their] attention and energies." Team Builders and Players, "like the captain of a football team," depend on others "to work with [them] to make things happen." Presidents of this type are "interested in arriving at decisions through consensus and [see themselves] at the center of the information-gathering process." Finally, Analyst/Innovators, like Director/Ideologues, have a cause that focuses their attention, but presidents of this type are interested in gathering information on all aspects of the problem and in getting a diverse range of perspectives and opinions on possible solutions. . . to insure

Focus of Policy Coordination	Authority Pattern	
	Formal	Informal
Focus on Political Process	Chief Executive Officer (Truman and Nixon)	Team Builder and Player (Johnson, Ford, and Carter)
Focus on Substance of Problem	Director/Ideologue (Reagan)	Analyst/Innovator (Franklin Roosevelt)

Figure 14.2 Typology of Presidential Leadership Based on Advisory Systems' Patterns of Authority and Policy Coordination
Source: Margaret G. Hermann and Thomas Preston, "Presidents and Their Advisers: Leadership Style, Advisory Systems, and Foreign Policymaking," in Eugene R. Wittkopf (ed.), *The Domestic Sources of American Foreign Policy: Insight and Evidence*, 2nd ed. (New York: St. Martin's, 1994), p. 346.

[they are] making the best as well as the most 'doable' decision" (Hermann and Preston 1994).

Figure 14.2 includes presidents who illustrate each of the types just described. Figure 14.3 in turn summarizes characteristics of the advisers likely to be selected by presidents comprising the leadership types and the patterns of relations likely to characterize the advisory systems themselves.

Some presidents, of course, fit one leadership type at one time, and another type at other times. Each calls for different advisers and evokes variant leader-adviser relationships. Bush, for example, used the team approach for many of his foreign policy decisions. "Advisers were seen as a source of emotional support with Bush desirous of keeping his advisers laughing and in a good mood. . . . Group cohesion and minimization of open disagreements were the order of the day. At issue was making decisions that would play well with Congress, the media, and public opinion" (Hermann and Preston 1994). When backed into a corner, however, as at times with his policies toward Panama, Kuwait, and China, Bush shifted his focus and demeanor to the Director/Ideologue type.

> He became a man with a mission wanting advisers who would act as advocates and implementers of *his* policy decisions. . . . Only advisers who shared in Bush's vision became part of the inner circle. . . . Disagreements when they appeared were tolerated on means but not ends. . . . Motivation changed from the need for approval and support to promoting a cause, and coordination, in turn, switched from concurrence among relevant advisers to accomplishing a task. (Hermann and Preston 1994, 352; see also Woodward 1991)

Clinton, too, showed signs of different leadership characteristics and different tendencies toward his advisors depending on the issues and circumstances.

> When he is wrestling with what a particular policy should be, Clinton is the analyst and innovator, wanting to be at the center of what is going on and wanting to have policies argued and debated in front of him. At these times he seeks out expert opinion and encourages pre-

Focus of Policy Coordination	Authority Pattern	
	Formal	Informal
Focus on Political Process	• Loyalty Important • Advisers Used as Sounding Board • Interested in Focusing on Important Decisions • Interested in Evaluating Rather Than Generating Options • Leader-Dominated Group-Think Possible • Procedures Well-Defined and Highly Structured	• Advisers Seen as Part of Team • Sharing of Accountability • Group Cohesion Is Valued • Advisers Provide Psychological Support • Options Sought that Minimize Conflict and Disagreement
Focus on Substance of Problem	• Select Advisers Who Share Cause/Concern/ Ideology • Advisers Seen as Implementors and Advocates • Advisers Tailor Information to Fit Biases • One or Two Advisers Play Gatekeeper Roles for Information and Access • Decisions Shaped by Shared Vision • Disagreements Center on Means Rather Than Ends	• Wants Experts as Advisers • Advisers Seen as Providing Information and Guidance • Open to Using Bureaucracy to Get Information • Time Spent on Generating Options and Considering Consequences • Seeks "Doable" Solution to Problem • Disagreement Is Valued

Figure 14.3 The Influence of Presidential Leadership Style on Advisory Selection and Organization
Source: Margaret G. Hermann and Thomas Preston, "Presidents and Their Advisers: Leadership Style, Advisory Systems, and Foreign Policymaking," in Eugene R. Wittkopf (ed.), *The Domestic Sources of American Foreign Policy: Insight and Evidence*, 2nd ed. (New York: St. Martin's, 1994), p. 349.

sentation of a range of possible options. . . . When, on the other hand, Clinton becomes convinced of a particular option, he wants a chain of command that is loyal and skilled in massaging the political process. He becomes the CEO [Chief Executive Officer] interested in having his advisers facilitate getting others on board. (Hermann and Preston 1994, 354; see also Woodward 1994)

Presidential advisers are chosen to serve the president, but they are also among the many different people presidents must court if they are to realize their goals. Presidents' other constituents—their followers—include the departments and agencies that make up the foreign affairs government, Congress, other world leaders, and, of course, the electorate. Successful leadership is determined by how presidents respond to the demands and expectations of each of these constituencies.

Why are some leaders successful and others not? Historian Garry Wills (1994a, 1994b; see also Hermann 1986) argues that followers are essential to leaders (their "first and all-encompassing need") and suggests that leaders and followers must share a common goal. "Followers do not submit to the person of the leader. They join him [or her] in pursuit of the goal" (Wills, 1994b). The effective leader, then, "is one who mobilizes others toward a goal shared by leader and followers." In a democracy, Wills argues, this often means an effective leader must defer to the demands of public opinion and abandon principle for the sake of compromise—actions typically held in low regard but perhaps necessary to sustain followership, without which leaders cannot exist and leadership be sustained.

Others, however, are seemingly uncomfortable with this viewpoint, particularly when it comes to foreign policy and interactions with other nations, friend and foe. Henry Kissinger (1994a), a distinguished political historian as well as former policymaker, urges in his book *Diplomacy* that power, principle, and analytical thinking are the bedrock of successful foreign policy leadership throughout history. He specifically disparages modern political leaders "who measure their success by the reaction of the television evening news," which makes them prisoners of "the purely tactical, focusing on short-term objectives and immediate results." The historical analogue is Napoleon III, France's leader in the second half of the nineteenth century, who "sought to impress his public by magnifying the pressures he had set out to create. In the process, he confused foreign policy with the moves of a conjurer. For in the end, it is reality, not publicity, that determines whether a leader has made a difference."

Personality Traits and Foreign Policy Orientations: An Alternative Approach

Another way to assess the impact of individuals' idiosyncratic characteristics on their foreign policy behavior is to investigate foreign policy beliefs associated with different personality traits.

The number of available personality-trait classifications is large. Most, unfortunately, are based almost exclusively on samples of the entire U.S. population instead of elites. Still, we can identify ten personality types, representing clusters of traits, that are especially important in shaping foreign policy attitudes, beliefs, and behavior.[5]

- *The Nationalist.* **Nationalism** is a state of mind that gives primary loyalty to one nation-state to the exclusion of other possible objects of affection (such as other countries, family, or extranational entities like the European Union or a religion). Nationalists glorify their own nation and exaggerate its virtues while denigrating others. Because nationalists develop an ego involvement with their state, they tend to defend its right to superiority (Stagner 1971).

- *The Militarist.* **Militarism** defines the individual's attitude toward aggression. The militarist views hostility as unexceptional and accepts the use of force as a legitimate means to achieve national goals. Research offers little support for the often popular impression that aggressiveness is rooted in human nature (Maslow 1966). On the contrary, an individual's predisposition toward aggression is a learned trait.

- *The Conservative.* As a psychological concept, **conservativism** denotes a cluster of interrelated personality characteristics rather than a political philosophy. It refers to hostility and suspicion, rigidity and compulsiveness, intolerance, and perceptual and judgmental inflexibility. It incorporates an inclination to condemn others' weakness and imperfection and to blame the disadvantaged for their misfortunes. Lacking compassion, the conservative has a need to discern hierarchy and rank and to resolve self-doubts by exaggerating others' inferiorities ("I'm okay—you're so-so"). The conservative greets new ideas not with curiosity but with fear. Conservative dispositions are found most often among the uninformed, the poorly educated, the less intelligent, and among those who are socially isolated yet conforming, submissive, and lacking in self-confidence (McClosky 1958).

- *The Pragmatist.* Expediency, intellectualism, impatience, eagerness, ambition, detachment, experimentalism, and tough-minded bravado are characteristic of a temperamental ***pragmatism***. "Pragmatists are interested in what works; their prime criterion of value is success. It is the very definition of pragmatism to turn away from a belief in fixed principles toward the truth of concrete results" (Miroff 1976). Pragmatists' need for control overcomes their fear of power; indeed, they are drawn to it, tempted by it, and eager to exercise it to get things done without regard for ideals and morality. Indeed, as John Kennedy arguably illustrates (Miroff 1976) pragmatists' dispassionate pursuit of rational solutions and promising results may violate moral principles and rationalize the violation with the classic excuse that "the ends justify the means."[6]

- *The Paranoid.* ***Paranoia*** is a psychoneurotic disorder characterized by excessive suspicion, fear, and distrust of others. Paranoids believe that people are out to "get" them, and their expectation becomes the driving force behind their behavior. Normally we do not expect politicians to manifest such symptoms, but under stressful conditions they may be prone to display some characteristics of the disorder, whose effects can impair their performance. The first secretary of defense, James Forrestal, is an example (Rogow 1963). A dogmatic sense of certainty, superiority, and self-confidence are aspects of the paranoid temperament that coexist alongside mistrust and fear of deception (as psychobiographies of classic paranoids, Adolf Hitler and Joseph Stalin, reveal). The tendency of some Americans holding positions of power to think conspiratorially has provoked inquiry into *The Paranoid Style in American Politics* (Hofstadter 1965), as one classic work on the subject is titled. Paranoids fear citizens of their own country as well as foreigners.

- *The Machiavellian.* Deriving its name from the philosopher/adviser to the prince of Florence in Renaissance Italy, ***Machiavellianism*** is a personality syndrome emphasizing strategy and manipulation over principle and sentiment. A compulsion to acquire power and exercise it effectively dominates the Machiavellian's attention above all other values. Conventional morality, love for and empathy toward others, and ideological goals may all be sacrificed if they interfere with controlling others—for the cold exploitation of others gives the Machiavellian his or her greatest satisfaction. Politicians who display the syndrome are motivated most by the desire to win and the fear of losing; they seek to exercise influence for the satisfaction, prestige, and arousal of emotions in others it provokes, not for the sake of demeaning opponents or carrying out a policy program. Because taking advantage of others is their primary motive, Machiavellians provoke competition and take risks to create opportunities for gaining concessions (Christie and Geis 1970). The trait is strongly associated with the psychological need for power (McClelland 1975).

- *The True Believer.* "Fanatic," "ideologue," "terrorist," and "crusader" are words often associated with **true believers**. They are the joiners of mass religious, political, or ideological movements. Whether militant Christians, Islamic fundamentalists, ultranationalists, ideological terrorists, communists, or fascists, true believers share with other like-minded individuals the need to join a cause and to sacrifice themselves for its advancement. Their willingness is not animated by the power of ideas, as true believers will join any movement that fulfills their need for something to worship and perhaps for which to die. The need to join a cause—any cause—is rooted in personal frustration, low self-esteem, a sense of humiliation, a craving for status, and a search for control of one's life. Adherents seek to lose themselves in a glorified mass movement and to regain a sense of personal worth by identifying totally with the doctrine or group, whose status and power confers status and power on its adherents. Because true believers need to believe in the absolute truth and virtue of their chosen movement, they are motivated to coerce people to their way of thinking and to compete with all other movements. Fanatical patriots who place their country above everything else (including themselves), for instance, are intolerant of foreigners and strive to spread their nation's way of life beyond its borders. Eric Hoffer's *The True Believer* (1951) remains the definitive exploration of this mentality.

- *The Authoritarian.* **Authoritarianism** is a constellation of predispositions that includes adherence to conventional values and condemnation of those who reject them. Authoritarians crave authority, obeying leaders submissively and uncritically while abusing the rights of subordinates. Authoritarians think in stereotypes; they see themselves as victims, are cynical about other people's motives, and value force and order (Adorno et al. 1950).

- *The Antiauthoritarian.* **Antiauthoritarianism** refers to a partially integrated attitude syndrome exhibited by introspective people uncomfortable with order and power. Antiauthoritarians impulsively embrace left-wing political views emphasizing idealism, optimism, and a preference for change (Kreml 1977).

- *The Dogmatist.* The personality trait of **dogmatism** is characterized by a closed mind. Dogmatists—prisoners of past attitudes—form opinions and refuse to modify them despite contrary evidence. Unreceptive to forming new images, they are intolerant of ambiguity and inconsistent information. Perceptual inflexibility is particularly endemic, as is passionate attachment to authority figures. Established doctrines are important to the dogmatist; hence, dogmatism is equated with rigidity (Rokeach 1960).

These ten types are examples of categories of personality traits that may have relevance to foreign policy. The types are neither exhaustive nor mutually exclusive, as some are associated with others. Additional constructs pertinent to policy making are also identifiable. For example, Harold Lasswell (1930) examined politicians' attitudes and dispositions and deduced the existence of three basic types of figures: the agitator, the administrator, and the theorist. Similarly, Jeane Kirkpatrick (1974), Reagan's first ambassador to the United Nations, has differentiated four types of female politicians: the leader, the personalizer, the moralizer, and the problem solver.

Distinguishing among personality traits is important because the categories provide tools for explaining leaders' behavior and for making predictions. Predictions are possible (though not always accurate) because a leader's traits influence his or her response to international events (Pruitt 1965). Personality traits also operate as prime determinants of foreign policy attitudes, as the illustrations that follow show.

Nationalism and Foreign Aggressiveness

Generally speaking, the more nationalistic the policymaker, the more warlike and aggressive will be his or her foreign policy attitudes. Leaders maintaining strong attachments to their nation are prone to emit hostility, loathing, and toughness toward foreigners. They frequently perceive international conflict and competition as inevitable and therefore appropriate. Nationalists oppose transcendent policies that compromise national sovereignty and privilege. They also oppose foreign aid when given for others' benefit and promote policies that accentuate differences between their country and others. Advancing national self-interest is the nationalist's supreme foreign policy principle.

Authoritarianism and Policy Consistency

Authoritarians form and maintain attitudes in conformity with the groups to which they belong. They reject new information running counter to prior images and search for information that reinforces existing beliefs. Such individuals base actions on opinions and affections rather than facts and inquiry. Once committed to a position, they are reluctant to change it. The foreign policy goals of a state ruled by an authoritarian (Germany under Hitler, for example) are unlikely to show significant change, because authoritarians' behavior is governed by the psychological need for consistent images. Their emphasis on protocol and rule-based procedures reinforces policy consistency. States run by authoritarian personalities are thus not inclined toward foreign policy innovation. Authoritarianism also correlates with isolationist foreign policy attitudes, Cold War thinking, and resistance to international conciliation (Levinson 1957; Rosenberg 1967).

Conservatism and Isolationism

The conservative personality holds a pessimistic view of both human nature and the human prospect, and accordingly sees inequality between nations as an inevitable, if not desirable, feature of international affairs. Foreigners are seen as threatening outsiders. The best way to deal with other nations, the conservative personality believes, is to avoid them. Both isolationists and conservatives are reluctant to become involved with others or to assume responsibility for them. They oppose the rear-ranging of institutions for the purpose of correcting imbalances or promoting social and economic equality. They resist legislation that might interfere with a man's (or a nations's) autonomy and the disposition of his property, and they are, for the most part, inhospitable to social change. There is in both conservatism and most forms of isolationism the . . . same implicit belief that one's own good fortune—and, by extension, the nation's good fortune—is part of the natural order of things. (McClosky 1967, 84)

Isolationism is also closely correlated with "aversive" (tending to avoid, shut out, deny) dispositions rather than "appetitive" (tending to embrace, reach out, accept) temperaments. The mass public embraces isolationist policies more enthusiastically than do American leaders, and isolationist attitudes are most prevalent among the less educated segments of society (McClosky 1967; Wittkopf 1990).

These illustrations barely scratch the surface in describing the potential correlation between personality traits and foreign policy beliefs. The danger with such suggestive correlations is that they tempt one to assume that they can be used safely to predict the behavior of each individual. The correlations describe relationships based on collec-tivities that may not hold for each individual within them. Still, if we want to anticipate a particular leader's foreign policy orientation, we can classify the leader by observing his or her traits and then predict the expected foreign policy orientation, provided we recognize the limitations of this approach (see also Hermann 1983; Winter et al. 1991). To illustrate how a leader's personality traits may influence his or her policy prefer-ences, let us consider a well-known example.

John Foster Dulles and the Soviet Union

According to an authoritative interpretation (Holsti 1962), former Secretary of State John Foster Dulles's behavior toward the Soviet Union was driven by his prior beliefs rather than by Soviet conduct. "Built on the trinity of atheism, totalitarianism, and communism, capped by a deep belief that no enduring social order could be erected upon such foundations," his belief system was predicated on three strong convictions: (1) the Russian people were basically good, but Soviet leaders were irredeemably bad; (2) Soviet national interest, which sought to preserve the state, was good, in contrast with the implacably bad, atheistic international communism; and (3) the Soviet state was good but the Communist Party was bad.

What were the sources of Dulles's beliefs? His perceptions were shaped in part by his childhood experiences, his relationship with his parents and his peer groups, and his psychological needs and personal predispositions—his basic personality. Dulles came from a celebrated, well-connected elite background that boasted two previous secretaries of state. He presumably inherited his moralistic, evangelic attitude toward most issues from his father, a stern Presbyterian minister. John Foster Dulles was per-haps the most unabashed moralist ever to sit in the office of the secretary of state (Barnet 1972); for him the purpose of policy was the pursuit of morality. He believed that the Cold War was essentially a moral rather than a political conflict. In his mind, the "insincere," "immoral," and "brutal" Soviet leadership was hateful because its creed was "godless." Two universal faiths competed, one good and the other evil.

Symbolically, Dulles routinely carried a copy of the New Testament in one coat pocket and a copy of Marx's *Communist Manifesto* in the other (Hoopes 1973a). No compromise could be made with a philosophy opposed to religion.

Other aspects of Dulles's background also may have affected his later outlook. For instance, his early training and practice in business law may have inculcated an aggressive "can do" attitude, "an inspired ability to calculate risks and gamble on them," and a habit of mind that "carried over into his diplomacy, where countries 'were all instinctively rivals and opponents of his own client, America'" (Barnet 1972). Moreover, his personal views may have been a product of his "Establishment" and elitist background. As Dulles's biographer Richard S. M. Goold-Adams observers, Dulles "was never in touch with people who knew hunger, poverty, or personal failure. Believing in addition that everyone must make the most of themselves in life and that those who do not have something wrong with them, he never seriously tried to understand the people whose misfortune it is to get left on the bottom rungs of the ladder" (cited in Barnet 1972).

A self-described conservative with a strong authoritarian bent, John Foster Dulles's conduct exhibited the traits associated with those personality types. His attitude toward the weak and poor was indicative of his conservative mind: adversity and poverty are the fault and character weaknesses of individuals and serve as a measure of their worth. His authoritarianism as secretary of state was legendary: Back your superior, buck your subordinates. Dulles "demanded what he called 'positive loyalty' from all employees of the State Department, but he felt none himself toward subordinates who were unjustly attacked by McCarthy" for their alleged but unverified communist sympathies (Barnet 1972).

As secretary of state, Dulles's rigid, doctrinaire beliefs and personality traits predetermined his reactions to the Soviets and led him to distort information so as to reduce any discrepancies between his knowledge and his perceptions (Holsti 1962). Dulles's psychological need for image maintenance led him to reject all information that conflicted with his preexisting belief that the Soviet Union could not be trusted. Friendly Soviet initiatives were seen as deception rather than true efforts to reduce tension. For example, Soviet military demobilizations were attributed to necessity (particularly economic weakness) and bad faith (the released men would be put to work on more lethal weapons). Similarly, the Austrian State Treaty[7] was explained as Soviet frustration (the failure of its European policy) and weakness (their system was "on the point of collapse") (Holsti 1962). Thus, in Dulles's image, the Soviets could do only harm and no good. If they acted cooperatively, it was either because they were dealing from a position of weakness or because they were trying to deceive the United States into a position of unpreparedness. When they did anything bad, it supported Dulles's prior image that the Soviets were incapable of virtuous behavior. The Cold War policies of John Foster Dulles, we may reasonably conclude, were derived from his entrenched negative beliefs—what Henry Kissinger (1962) termed an "inherent bad faith" model of the Soviet leadership.

Dulles's inflexible image and unwillingness to accept any uncomfortable information was reinforced by his extreme faith in his own judgment and lack of respect for that of others, whom he regarded as his inferiors. Dulles felt "he was uniquely qualified to assess the meaning of Soviet policy. This sense of indispensability carried over into the day-to-day operations of policy formulation, and during his tenure as secretary of state he showed a marked lack of receptivity to advice" (Holsti 1962).

Other Examples

The Dulles example makes a convincing case for the influence of individual variables on policy behavior, for it seems clear that Dulles's foreign policy behavior was firmly rooted in his belief system and personality traits. Other examples also reinforce that conclusion.[8]

Consider Henry Kissinger's need for personal acceptance, his reputed distrust of democratic foreign policy, and his intolerance of dissent, and note in turn his insistence on secrecy, his "taste for solo performances," and his substitution of private for public diplomacy (Starr 1984). Similarly, LBJ's intense need to be loved and feel in control of his fate fed his penchant during the Vietnam War to surround himself with advisers who provided him information he wanted to hear—that his popularity with the American people was enduring and that the war was going well (Kearns 1976). Johnson's immense ego involvement with affairs of state also led him to "personify" his policies and to think of himself as the embodiment of the nation itself, as illustrated by his statements regarding his Vietnam policies: "By 1965, Johnson was speaking of 'my Security Council,' 'my State Department,' 'my troops.' It was *his* war, *his* struggle; when the Vietcong attacked, they attacked *him*. On one occasion, a young soldier, escorting him to an army helicopter, said: 'This is your helicopter, sir.' 'They are *all* my helicopters, son,' Johnson replied" (Stoessinger 1985). "The White House machinery became the president's psyche writ large" (Kearns 1976).

Consider as well Harry Truman, a president who "was prone to back up his subordinates to an extent that was indiscriminate" (DeRivera 1968). A decisive person, Truman expected loyalty and was intolerant of disrespect. Hence when he was confronted with blatant insubordination from General Douglas MacArthur (an authoritarian who wanted to call the shots and expand the war with the communists in Asia), the president dealt with the insubordination decisively: "You're fired!" Able to give loyalty himself, Truman expected it from others.

President Eisenhower illustrates the difficulties of evaluating the psychological bases of diplomatic conduct, because his low-key approach produced results that were not at the time recognized as a part of his design. Historians have reevaluated his presidency and now see strength and command where previously they perceived inattention and indifference to the duties of office (see Ambrose 1990). Eisenhower's personality contributed to his "hidden hand" managerial approach and its quiet effectiveness (Greenstein 1982).

And the perplexing case of Richard Nixon lingers. Some of Nixon's conduct, both in and out of office, appears explicable only in light of his private conflicts and emotional problems. Consider David Abrahamsen's (1977) psychoanalytic probing, which diagnoses Nixon as a disturbed personality, at war with himself since the traumatic events and parental disputes of his unhappy childhood. Those conflicts were never resolved, making Nixon unstable, indecisive, and, above all, self-consciously unsure of himself. They account for Nixon's obvious discomfort in the White House, his inability to maintain warm personal relationships, his paranoid distrust of those around him, his self-absorption, and his competitive, adversarial approach toward his political opponents. By conquering and destroying to become the "victor," Nixon during crises could temporarily remove his self-doubts and submerge his private conflicts. Still, those personal problems may have subconsciously attracted Nixon to failure, because inwardly he felt inadequate and suspected that he did not deserve success. Decisions motivated by such personal factors may have contributed to the tragedies of Vietnam and Watergate.

These examples certainly suggest that the content and conduct of American foreign policy may in some instances be profoundly influenced by policymakers' personal characteristics. Still, both the occasions for the exercise of that influence and its extent are likely to be constrained by a variety of factors, to which we now turn.

Limits on the Explanatory Power of Individual Factors . . . .

Can continuities and change in post-World War II American foreign policy be traced to leaders' personal attributes? As intuitively inviting as that interpretation might be, it ignores the fact that individuals are only one of several sources of American foreign policy, any of which can limit severely the impact that leaders exert on the direction of foreign policy. The question, then, is under what conditions are leaders' individual characteristics likely to be influential?

When Are Individual Factors Influential?

In general, the influence of personal characteristics on policy-making conduct *increases* in direct proportion to the following factors:

- *The individual's level of advancement in the decision-making structure.* The higher one climbs in the hierarchy of the foreign affairs government, the more the occupant's personality will affect policy.

- *The ambiguity and complexity of the decision-making situation.* Because people respond to bewildering and uncertain situations emotionally rather than rationally and calmly, perceptions of circumstances are important. At least four types of foreign policy situations bring psychological (nonlogical) drives into play because of their notable ambiguity: (1) new situations, where the individual has had little previous experience and few familiar cues to assist in the definition of the situation; (2) complex situations, involving a large number of different factors; (3) contradictory situations, which encompass many inconsistencies and incompatibilities; and (4) situations devoid of social sanctions, which permit freedom of choice because societal definitions of appropriate options are unclear (DiRenzo 1974).

- *The level of self-confidence and ego in the individual.* Decision makers' subjective faith in their own ability to control events—their self-esteem, self-confidence, and belief in themselves—strongly determines the extent to which they will dare to allow their own preferences to set policy directions (DeRivera 1968). Conversely, in the absence of such assurance (or narcissistic ego inflation), self-doubt will inhibit risk taking and leadership.

- *The level of the individual's personal involvement in the situation.* When people believe their own interests and welfare are at stake, their response is governed primarily by their private psychological needs. They cease to appear cool and rational and begin to act emotionally. Compare student behavior when mechanically taking class notes during a lecture with behavior when called upon to recite or when negotiating with a professor over an exam grade. Likewise, when policymakers assume personal responsibility for policy management (and become ego-involved in outcomes), their reactions frequently display heightened emotion and their personalities are revealed. Contrast President Johnson's behavior with respect to Vietnam in 1963 (cautious) with his behavior in 1968 (excited, compulsive), by which time the war had become "his war."

- *A scarcity of available information.* When facing a decision in which pertinent information is unavailable, gut likes or dislikes tend to dictate policy choices. Conversely, "the more information an individual has about international affairs, the less likely is it that his [or her] behavior will be based upon nonlogical influences" (Verba 1969). Other things being equal, ample information reduces the probability that decisions will be based on psychological drives and personal needs.

- *Power having been assumed recently or under dramatic circumstances* . When an individual first enters office, the formal requirements of the role are least likely to circumscribe what he or she can do. That holds true especially for newly elected presidents, who routinely enjoy a "honeymoon" period during which they are relatively free of criticism and extraordinary pressure. So, too, cabinet members and other top-level officials usually experience a brief period during which their personal freedom is great and their decisions encounter little resistance. Moreover, when a leader comes to office following a dramatic event (a landslide election or the assassination of a predecessor), "the new high-level political leader can institute his [or her] policies almost with a free hand. Constituency criticism is held in abeyance during this time" (Hermann 1976).

Crisis conditions often bring together circumstances that enhance individuals' potential impact on the policy process. Because crises upset "business as usual," they typically upset the influences that otherwise affect how foreign policy is made, thus permitting individual factors to play a larger-than-usual role in affecting foreign policy decisions. It is not coincidental that the great leaders of history have customarily arisen during periods of extreme challenge. The moment may make the person rather than the person the moment, in the sense that crisis can liberate a gifted leader from the constraints that normally would inhibit his or her capacity to engineer change.

A foreign policy crisis is "a situation that (1) threatens high-priority goals of the decision-making unit [for example, foreign policymakers], (2) restricts the amount of time available for response before the decision is transformed, and (3) surprises the members of the decision-making unit by its occurrence" (Hermann 1972). When such a situation arises, several things typically happen (Hermann 1969, 416–17):

- The highest level of government officials will make the decision(s) (because of the perceived threat to national goals or interests).

- Bureaucratic procedures usually involved in foreign policy making will be side-stepped (because high-ranking officials can commit the government to action without the normal deference to bureaucracies).

- Information about the situation is at a premium (because time limits decision makers' ability to acquire new information).

- Selection among options is often based on something other than information about the immediate situation (for example, because of the short time, analogies with prior situations may be inaccessible).

- Personal antagonisms and disagreements among policymakers will remain subdued (because of the urgent need for consensus).

- Extreme responses are encouraged (because of limited information and the enhanced importance of the policymakers' personalities).

Especially noteworthy for our purposes is that crises encourage formation of ad hoc decision-making groups which are given broad authority (Hermann and Hermann, 1989). In crises, then, decision making elites truly govern. Bureaucratic procedures are short-circuited and decision responsibility is redistributed from the usual centers of government power. Hence, one of the greatest role-induced constraints on individual decision makers is circumvented.

Moreover, a "crisis alters organizational plans and objectives by disrupting the regular schedule of activities." As a result, "personnel assignments are reallocated and top-level decision makers focus their attention exclusively on the crisis, postponing action on other matters that may originally have had a higher priority on their scale of values" (Robinson 1972). During the Cuban missile crisis, for example, some of the members of the ad hoc crisis-management team were "relieved" of their organizational affiliations. Assigned the role of "skeptical generalists," "they were charged with examining the policy problem as a whole, rather than approaching the issues in the traditional bureaucratic way whereby each man confines his remarks to the special aspects in which he considers himself to be an expert and avoids arguing about issues on which others present are supposedly more expert than he" (Janis 1982).

Finally, evidence from case studies indicates that the domestic political implications of policy options are not given their usual intense consideration in crisis situations (Paige 1972; cf. Hampson 1988).[9] This further liberates individuals from their typical constraints, thus encouraging the expression of individual values and increasing the likelihood that decision makers' personal characteristics will imprint policy. Indeed, the individual leader's personality now may be determinative, as the usual institutional and societal barriers to decisive action are suspended. In a situation that simultaneously challenges a nation's will and the president's self-esteem, governmental decision processes can easily become fused with the chief executive's psychodynamic processes. Furthermore, the resolution of a policy crisis under such circumstances could depend ultimately on the outcome of a personal, emotional crisis (DiRenzo 1974). It is instructive to note in this context that the influence of personality on the decisions of American foreign policymakers has been especially strong when the use of force has been involved (Etheredge 1978)—and force is often the option chosen in crisis situations.

Although crises are endemic to international politics, they capture only a fraction of the countless decisions made on a continuing basis by members of the foreign affairs government, including the nation's highest leaders. Thus, innate drives and personal predispositions are not all-powerful determinants of foreign policy behavior in all contexts. Rather, they vary with the nature of the decision problem, the decision maker's psychological disposition toward the situation, and his or her subjective definition of its importance.

Are there other situations that elevate the potency of leaders' personal characteristics as policy determinants? One such situation may be when a decision centers on broad, abstract conceptions of the nation's basic policy goals. Unlike occasions when policymakers are asked to find a pragmatic solution to a specific problem, in this case attention focuses on doctrinal and ideological issues, thus making leaders' value preferences, fundamental beliefs, and inner needs especially influential.

Consider the divergent postures assumed by past presidents on the issue of containing communism. In the specific context of Indochina, where five different presidents were confronted with the necessity of deciding if and how a "war" with communism should be waged, personality became a visible influence on how each reacted. A former policy planner illustrates the phenomenon:

> Truman was obdurate, tough, and determined to demonstrate these traits in his policies . . . . [H]e felt challenged by the rise of communism in Southeast Asia and became determined to arrest it. Eisenhower, far more at ease in the office, accustomed to high command, and not in need of establishing his credentials as a tough leader with the Congress, was relatively relaxed and more aloof. He alone among the five presidents involved was able to absorb a defeat to communism in Indochina [that of the French] and to provide such a defeat with a domestic appearance of success by way of gradually increasing U.S. responsibility in Southeast Asia. . . . Kennedy was sophisticated, eager, and daring to the point of adventurousness. He accordingly did not shy away from undertaking new commitments. . . . Johnson suffered from the combination of an enormous inferiority complex in regard to handling affairs of state, and an enormous feeling of superiority, experience, and self-confidence in handling and manipulating the movers, shakers, and sleepers in American politics. His inferiority complex . . . put him in wholly unwarranted awe of the national security and foreign affairs expert advisers he inherited from Kennedy [and] the intellectuals who surrounded him. . . . Accordingly, Johnson accepted the ill-conceived scenarios of the graduated escalation school of thought in regard to Vietnam. . . . Finally, Nixon's negative manipulative traits of a highly insecure (proto-paranoid) but extremely ambitious power-seeker . . . led him to deceive the public into believing he was withdrawing from Vietnam when in fact he was not only continuing but intensifying the war. . . . [H]e managed also to convince the public that he was turning defeat in Vietnam into standoff . . . by changing the most fundamental premise of American foreign policy, namely, the coequation in the U.S. public's mind of American security with the defeat of communism everywhere. (Kattenburg 1980, 227)

Knowing that different presidents responded differently to similar situations, another intriguing question follows: How different are the personalities of those comprising the decision-making elite?

Do Policy-Making Elites and Politicians Have Similar Personality Profiles?

In terms of background and experience, a remarkably homogeneous collection of people have made up America's postwar foreign policy establishment. Recall from Chapter 9 the similarities of those who have managed American foreign policy since 1945. To be sure, the nation's postwar presidents, their advisers, and other opinion elites have displayed different personality predispositions and espoused different beliefs (Holsti and Rosenau 1984; Wittkopf 1990; see also McGlen and Sarkees 1993), but these differences do not override important similarities. Several considerations support that observation.

It is commonly assumed that positions of power and prestige command respect and honor and therefore are naturally desired by nearly everyone. ("In America, anyone can grow up to be president.") But are they? It may be more realistic to recognize that only a small proportion of the American public even desires the power of public office. Moreover, those who actually become involved or active politically constitute an even smaller portion of the citizenry.

When we carefully examine America's postwar foreign policymakers, we discover that they share a distinctive set of personal characteristics that set them apart from the average person. Participation in politics and political aspiration may be functions of personality, with the consequence that those who seek top positions share psychological traits that make them more like one another and less like "average" Americans.

Those attracted to political careers conventionally are thought to possess an instinct for power. Political leaders are power seekers. What motivates their choice? The classic psychological interpretation sees "the political animal" attempting to overcome a poor self-image: "The power seeker . . . pursues power as a means of compensation against deprivation. *Power is expected to overcome low estimates of the self*, by either changing the traits of the self or of the environment in which it functions" (Lasswell 1974). Accordingly, politicians seek positions of power that confer attention and command deference, respect, and status to overcome their personal sense of inadequacy. Erich Fromm has argued in a similar vein that "the lust for power is rooted in weakness and not in strength, and that fundamentally this motive is a desperate attempt to gain secondary strength where genuine strength is lacking" (cited in DiRenzo 1974).

The disturbing suggestion here is that policymakers are power-hungry. Though they may claim they enter politics to do good and serve the public, in fact they subconsciously seek leadership to compensate for their personal insecurities and to bolster their own self-esteem by holding power over others. Bruce Buchanan describes this now conventional view of presidential aspirants' motives:

Recent national experience—and common sense—tell us that those who make the final presidential sweepstakes are [persons] of near fanatical personal ambition who show themselves willing to sacrifice health, family, peace of mind, and principle in order to win the prize. To the question, "What price success?" presidential candidates are near-unanimous in responding: "Any price." (Buchanan 1978, 154)

This image of leaders' psychological motives can easily be exaggerated, as clear differences in motivation and belief are also evident. Generalizations about the *response* of people to the acquisition of power are less risky, perhaps. For if the motives that drive individuals to seek positions of authority are mixed, their reactions to the privileges and ascribed importance of the office are relatively patterned. Those with power, whether conferred by election or appointment to high office, become personally absorbed in the roles they play, let their egos and identity become involved with it, and become intoxicated with the sense of power, purpose, and importance they derive from the experience. After all, they find themselves making history, attended by press and public. Even the most self-assured individuals can easily confuse personal identity with the role played and mistake the power conferred by the position for personal power. The next step is to inflate one's own importance in the overall scheme of things: to think that one has made things happen when in fact things have happened only because of the power one controls, or to assume that, being powerful, one is indispensable. Individuals playing roles often become, in their own minds, the masks they wear. As a former U.S. ambassador to India, John Kenneth Galbraith, observes (in the gender-exclusive language of the time), bureaucrats and officials

> enjoy power not by personal right but from association. An official of the Pentagon or the State Department is dispensing authority that derives not from his personal qualities but from the majesty and power of the United States. There is interesting proof of the point in the life style of . . . an American ambassador to a country of more than marginal consequence [who] is accorded considerable deference by most people, including himself, until the day he retires. Then he disappears. . . . It was the United States . . . that made the man important and not, unhappily, any quality of the man himself. This fact, not surprisingly, quite a few organization men fail to grasp. In consequence, they parade the power under the impression it is their own. The contrast between the biggest authority and the smallest man is an unpleasant thing to see. (Galbraith 1973, 315)

Galbraith's point is important in understanding the hypothesized influence of individuals on the nation's destiny: The office can make the person as much as the person can make the office. People become elite only because they occupy elite positions and not because, as they sometimes assume, they are inherently special. In that respect the impact of the office on the officeholder makes those in the foreign policy elite more alike than different.

Do Individuals Make a Difference?
Psychological Limits on Policy Change

> In a sense, I had known that "power" might feel like this, just as I had known, before I ever had a drink, that whiskey goes to the head. The taste of power, or whatever it was that I tasted that first day, went to my head too, but not quite as I had been warned it would. I had come into the office with projects and plans. And I was caught in an irresistible movement

of paper, meetings, ceremonies, crises, trivialities. There were uncleared paragraphs and cleared ones, and people waiting for me to tell them what my plans were, and people doing things that had nothing to do with my plans. I had moved into the middle of a flow of business that I hadn't started and wouldn't be able to stop. There were people in place to handle this flow, and established machinery in operation to help me deal with it. The entire system was at my disposal. In a word, I had power. And power had me. (Frankel 1969, 5–6)

This recollection by a new policymaker of his first day in office illuminates the connection between policymaker and policy position. The policy-making system influences the behavior of those who work within it.[10] Although we cannot speak precisely about what makes a politician a politician, our discussion in the previous chapter documented the similarity of outlook among those who occupy roles within the foreign affairs government—regardless, by implication, of the idiosyncratic variations among the individuals themselves and their projects and plans. As individuals enter new groups, they experience enormous pressure to conform to the prevailing and preexisting views of that group. They find that they must "go along to get along." Rewarded for accepting the views of their superiors and predecessors, and punished or ostracized for questioning them, few resist. Authority and tradition are seldom challenged.

The psychological tendency to accept the views of those with whom we interact frequently is sobering. It suggests that certain types of situations elicit certain uniform behaviors regardless of the different personalities involved. Because people behave differently when in different groups and when engaged in different activities, it is uncommon for all but those with unusually strong personalities to resist group pressures and role demands. All people are inclined to adapt themselves and sometimes their personalities to their roles or positions (see Lieberman 1965), each of which has certain expected ways of behaving and attitudes associated with it. Often these are governed by preexisting decision norms embedded in and reinforced by social processes within an institutional structure. All role occupants tend to conform to the rituals, vocabulary, and beliefs defined by these preexisting norms. As one review of research on this phenomenon concludes:

> If there has been one important lesson coming from all the research in social and personality psychology . . . it is that situations control behavior to an unprecedented degree. It is no longer meaningful, as it once was, to talk in terms of personality "types," of persons "low in ego strength," or of "authoritarians"—at least it is not meaningful if we wish to account for any substantial portion of an individual's behavior. . . . Rather, we must look to the situation in which the behavior was elicited and is maintained if we hope ever to find satisfactory explanations for it. The causes of behavior we have learned are more likely to reside in the nature of the environment than inside the person. And although the operation of situational forces can be subtle and complex in the control of behavior, it can also be extremely powerful. . . . Research . . . seems to indicate that . . . [in] "real life" we are often faced with a situation or role which demands behavior of a certain kind and, over a period of time, our beliefs are likely to change in a way consistent with this situation or role behavior. (Haney and Zimbardo 1973, 40–42); for a contrasting view, see Gallagher 1994)

This conclusion applies to the presidency as well, where the formal and informal norms of the office—the demands of the job, its constitutional obligations, and its public pressures—arguably permit less freedom of individual expression than many others. "Both its prominence and its symbolic functions make the presidential office a more important molder of its incumbents than any other in the nation" (Truman 1951). Indeed, "The historical consistency of the president's responsibilities produces a like consistency in the kinds of exposures he will encounter as he goes about the business of performing his functions" (Buchanan 1978). "The higher a man stands in the social scale," Leo Tolstoy observed, "the more manifest is the predetermination and inevitability of his every act."

These pressures provide a potent explanation for the persistence and continuity characteristic of American foreign policy during the Cold War and why even now adjustments to new realities seem so difficult: For nearly five decades the individuals comprising the policy-making establishment accepted the prevailing image of the world and bent their behavior, and ultimately their beliefs, to that of their predecessors. As James Rosenau (1980) concluded, "Even the president must function within narrowly prescribed limits, so much so that it would be easier to predict the behavior of any president from prior knowledge of the prevailing state of that role than from data pertaining to his past accomplishments, orientations, and experiences." There are definite limits to the amount of change individual leaders can engineer. The external environment, societal factors, governmental characteristics, and role-induced constraints restrict the range of permissible policy choices. Durable policy prescriptions were advanced for decades, despite changing international circumstances. The names of the actors may have changed as the Cold War was played out, but the script remained the same. Changing it now may be imperative, as the external world is radically different with the passing of the Cold War. But many of the individuals remain the same and, as we have seen, people are slow to adjust their thinking to new realities. Even those of the successor political generation, like Bill Clinton, remain prisoners not only of their own political ambitions but also of the domestic and international forces that continue to mold the behavior of individuals once they rise to positions of prominence. In Clinton's own words: "At least on the international front, I would say the problems are more difficult than I imagined them to be [as a candidate]."

Additional Restraints on Individual Initiative and Policy Innovation

In addition to the constraints discussed above, other considerations properly falling within the individual source category also narrow the range of alternatives available to leaders. Among them are the following:

- The tendency of policymakers, like the general public, to maintain preexisting images and to view and interpret new information so as to preserve rather than change their perceptual models of reality.

- The propensity of policymakers to avoid decision-making responsibilities altogether by relying on reassuring illusions and rationalizations (Janis 1989).

- The impact of "organizational norms, routines, and standard operating procedures [which] may . . . constrain the manner in which issues are defined, the range of options that may be considered, and the manner in which executive decisions are implemented by subordinates" (Holsti 1976).

- The legacy of past policies—in the form of treaties signed with other countries, previous budgetary decisions, prior commitments, and the like—which may reduce considerably the range of available choice and limit changes in existing policy to only incremental revisions.

- The tendency of decision makers to feel subjective, if subconscious, loyalties toward pet programs (and the people associated with them), often resulting in a reluctance to withdraw support from them despite their diminishing utility.

- The tendency for acquiescent personalities (people who are "team players") to make it to positions of power and for "rugged individualists" and reformers to be systematically selected out.

- The preference of individuals for incremental change, which is encouraged by the tendency of most to focus attention on familiar experiences and to shy away from the unfamiliar.

- The desire of policymakers to be loved and respected, together with their concern for earning a "place in history," which instill the preference to do what is popular even if it is unwise.

- The reliance of policymakers on established rules and procedures for decision making.

- The stagnating effect promoted by length in public service. As President Nixon said in 1972, "It is inevitable [that] when an individual has been in a cabinet position or, for that matter, holds any position in government, after a certain length of time he becomes an advocate of the status quo; rather than running the bureaucracy, the bureaucracy runs him."

When these psychological and circumstantial restraints on policy initiatives are added to the many domestic and external factors discussed in the preceding chapters, we can appreciate why policy "change, as it occurs, does so in acts of renewing, repairing, or improving existing relationships or commencing new ones that correspond to familiar patterns [and why] diplomacy . . . normally resembles more the act of gardening than of bulldozing" (Seabury 1973).

The Questionable Utility of the "Hero-in-History" Thesis

The interpretation at the beginning of this chapter articulated a potentially powerful source of change in American foreign policy: Since so much authority is concentrated in the hands of so few, it is logical to assume that the decision-making elite in charge of foreign policy can, with relative ease, choose to revise—indeed, revolutionize—America's foreign policy. Change the people in charge, it is assumed, and the policy itself will often change in turn. In short, change the leadership, and then look for a change in American foreign policy.

The theory and evidence summarized in this chapter force us to question the utility of this "hero-in-history" model of American foreign policy making.[11] At the very least, the thesis is much too simple. By attributing policy variation to a single source, it tries to explain everything and succeeds in explaining little.

Why? To recapitulate, we find that the people who make American foreign policy are not that different from one another after all. Only certain types of people seek positions of power, and top leaders are recruited from similar backgrounds and rise to the top in similar ways. Consequently, they share many attitudes and personality characteristics. Moreover, once in office, their behaviors are shaped by the positions they occupy; they typically see their options differently from within the system than they did outside it. Often they conform their beliefs to the beliefs of their peers and predecessors. The pressures imposed by the office and decision-making setting elicit similar policy responses from diverse personalities. The result: Different individuals often pursue their predecessors' policies and respond to international events consistently. American policymakers thus routinely display a propensity for incremental change, perpetuation of established routines of thought and action, and preservation of established policies.

This reasoning invites the conclusion that, even though the president and his or her immediate circle of advisers constitute one of the most powerful institutions in the world, and even though, in principle, they have the resources to bring about prompt and immediate change by the decisions they make, those powers are in fact seldom exercised. In today's complex world, it is difficult for great leaders to "emerge," and momentous decisions are rare. Personal characteristics influence the style with which decisions are reached, but the overall thrust of American foreign policy remains highly patterned and fixated on the past. As Ole Holsti (1973) puts it, "Names and faces may change, interests and policies do not." Thus Henry Kissinger's comment in 1976, as the nation prepared to elect a new president, remains a timeless and telling observation: "The essential outlines of U.S. policy will remain the same no matter who wins the U.S. presidential election."

NOTES

1. The studies by Barber (1992), Donovan (1985), and Stoessinger (1985) provide insights to the personalities and beliefs of the postwar presidents that are particularly relevant to foreign policy formulation.

2. Woodward and Bernstein (1979) provide a less-than-flattering glimpse of this man who otherwise was successful as a diplomat. Hersh (1983) offers another critical appraisal. For overviews of Kissinger's world view and "operational code" and an assessment of their impact on his policy performance, see Caldwell (1983) and Walker (1977).

3. Unless otherwise noted, all quotations from Barber in this section are from the fourth (1992) edition of his book.

4. See also Hermann (1989); Mullins and Wildavsky (1992); and Schneider (1990).

5. Useful elaborations of the personality types discussed below can be found in Hermann with Milburn (1977), Hopple (1982), Kreml (1977), Levinson (1957), McClosky (1958), Rokeach (1960), and Stagner (1971).

6. Stoessinger (1985) argues that American foreign policymakers can be characterized as either *pragmatists* or *crusaders*.

The crusader tends to make decisions based on a preconceived idea rather than on the basis of experience. Even though there are alternatives, he usually does not see them. If the facts do not square with his philosophy, it is too bad for the facts. Thus, the crusader tends toward rigidity and finds it difficult, if not impossible, to extricate himself from a losing posture. He does not welcome dissent and advisers will tend to tell him what he wants to hear. He sets out to improve the world but all too often manages to leave it in worse shape than it was before. (Stoessinger 1985, xiii)

Pragmatists, on the other hand, come closer to fitting the "perfectly rational" decision maker described in Chapter 13. A pragmatist seeks facts, according to Stoessinger, welcomes advice, accepts criticism, considers alternatives, and cherishes the flexibility that permits adjusting policy to new realities and changing its course where necessary.

7. The Austrian State Treaty, initiated by the Soviet Union, called for the peaceful withdrawal of Soviet and American occupation forces from Austria in return for the promise that the Austrians would maintain a policy of neutrality in the East-West dispute.

8. Psychological profiling of foreign leaders was at one time extensively used by intelligence agencies, but its practice has diminished since the end of the Cold War, in part due to personnel changes and budget cuts (Omestad 1994). An interesting example is the profile of Saddam Hussein drawn by Jerrold M. Post (1993), who for many years headed the CIA's political psychology operations.

9. Kennedy's perception of the 1962 Cuban situation as a crisis was influenced by his feeling that Soviet Premier Nikita Khrushchev had reneged on a promise not to complicate the president's delicate domestic political situation at the time of the forthcoming congressional elections, in which the president's Republican opponents were calling for sterner measures against Castro's Cuba.

10. Zbigniew Brzezinski, President Carter's national security adviser, describes these influences thus:

When the pressure is high, it's essential to be very low-key and to cool everybody's moods rather than contribute to a heightened sense of anxiety and tension. . . .

It's important not only to have control over your emotions but also over your schedule and work habits. That means discriminating about what you want to do and, once you have made that decision, acting expeditiously. Never let your desk be cluttered or your briefcase overflow.

Beyond that, it's crucial to come into government with a larger perspective of what you wish to accomplish, with clear priorities because, once in office, you tend to be so overwhelmed by events that it is very easy to lose perspective and get absorbed in specifics. You can become increasingly responsive to situations rather than using your power to shape situations and to define outcomes. (*U.S. News & World Report*, May 20, 1985: 65)

11. The terminology is borrowed from the timeless "great man" versus "Zeitgeist" debate. At the core of the controversy is the perhaps unanswerable question of whether the times must be conducive to the emergence of great leaders, or whether, instead, great people would have become famous leaders regardless of when and where they lived. For a discussion, see Greenstein (1969).

SUGGESTIONS FOR FURTHER READING

Ambrose, Stephen E. *Eisenhower: Soldier and President.* New York: Simon & Schuster, 1990.

Barber, James David. *The Presidential Character: Predicting Performance in the White House*, 4th ed. Englewood Cliffs, N.J.: Prentice-Hall, 1992.

Buchanan, Bruce. *The Presidential Experience: What the Office Does to the Man.* Englewood Cliffs, N.J.: Prentice-Hall, 1978.

DeRivera, Joseph H. *The Psychological Dimension of Foreign Policy.* Columbus, Oh.: Charles E. Merrill, 1968.

Etheredge, Lloyd S. *A World of Men: The Private Sources of American Foreign Policy.* Cambridge, Mass.: MIT Press, 1978.

Greenstein, Fred I., ed. *Leadership in the Modern Presidency.* Cambridge, Mass.: Harvard University Press, 1989.

Hermann, Charles F., ed. *International Crises: Insights from Behavioral Research.* New York: Free Press, 1972.

Janis, Irving L. *Crucial Decisions: Leadership in Policymaking and Crisis Management.* New York: Free Press, 1989.

Jones, Charles O. *The Trusteeship Presidency: Jimmy Carter and the United States Congress.* Baton Rouge: Louisiana State University Press, 1988.

Kelman, Herbert C., ed. *International Behavior* New York: Holt, Rinehart & Winston, 1965.

Maraniss, David. *First in His Class: A Biography of Bill Clinton.* New York: Simon & Schuster, 1995.

McCullough, David G. *Truman.* New York: Simon & Schuster, 1992.

Mullins, Kerry, and Aaron Wildavsky. "The Procedural Presidency of George Bush," *Political Science Quarterly* 107 (Spring 1992): 31–62.

Roberts, Jonathan M. *Decision-Making during International Crises.* New York: St. Martin's Press, 1988.

Wills, Garry. *Certain Trumpets: The Call of Leaders.* New York: Simon & Schuster, 1994.

CHAPTER 15

• • •

AT THE DAWN OF A NEW MILLENNIUM: THE FUTURE OF AMERICAN FOREIGN POLICY

• • •

I know of no change in policy, only of circumstances.

Secretary of State John Quincy Adams, 1823

What is new about the emerging world order is that, for the first time, the United States can neither withdraw form the world nor dominate it.

Former Secretary of State Henry Kissinger, 1994

"As we stand at the threshold of a new century, America faces a challenge that recalls the opportunities and dangers that we confronted at the end of the First and the Second World Wars," Secretary of State Warren Christopher wrote in early 1995. "Then, as now, two paths lay before us: to claim victory and withdraw, or with U.S. leadership to build a more peaceful, free, and prosperous world for America and people everywhere" (Christopher 1995). Which path will the United States follow in the aftermath of the Cold War, the third global conflict of the twentieth century?

The situation the United States faces today is different from that which framed its choices following World War I. In that new world order, Britain, France, and the vast oceans separating the United States from Europe could be expected to protect American national security. The circumstances today are even more dramatically different from those American policymakers faced following World War II, the second twentieth-century new world order. Then a battle-tested and militarily powerful Stalinist Soviet Union embracing an alien ideology was poised in the very center of Europe, and neither Britain and France nor the Atlantic Ocean could any longer guarantee American national security. Now the security challenges are less immediate, but the perceived options for someone or something other than the United States to protect them are also less obvious than before. Thus the United States is at a crossroad at the dawn of a new millennium, but the choices it must make are not easy ones.

In today's chaotic, complex world, where no clear and present danger simplifies assessments, what comprises the national interest is (as always) ambiguous. Without consensus at home about the challenges of the post-Cold War world, setting priorities for the uses of American power abroad understandably provokes controversy. Accordingly, the clarity of vision and consistency of purpose so crucial to a successful foreign policy have yet to crystallize. Still, the symptomatic delay, indecision, and ambivalence now evident cannot persist without ultimately harming America's core values and interests: peace and prosperity, stability and security, democracy and defense. As the State Department's Management Task Force (U.S. Department of State 1992) warned shortly before Clinton's inauguration, "If we are not clear about where we want to go and about our options for getting there, we will not fare well in the post-Cold War era."

The question the United States now confronts is whether it has the ability to chart new foreign policy directions as the world evolves from an all-encompassing global conflict to more diffuse challenges. What are the prospects for a consistent yet visionary American foreign policy in the world now unfolding? Presidents George Bush and Bill Clinton stood astride this transitional period, as the turbulent waters unleashed by the end of the Cold War demanded the articulation of American foreign policy principles to be followed in an uncharted future. The foreign policy successes and failures of Bush's and Clinton's successors will be shaped by the combination of continuing international and domestic political influences that both stimulate and constrain American foreign policy and its ability to adapt innovatively to changed and changing circumstances.

Given the prevailing disagreement in the mid-1990s about policy priorities, predicting the likely future direction of American foreign policy is a hazardous undertaking. Only the foolish would claim to foresee what will unfold, as "we are entering a new world . . . and many well-established generalizations about world politics may no longer hold" (Jervis 1991–1992). We do, however, possess intellectual resources that provide clues about the future. As a well-known dictum notes, the best qualification of a prophet is to have a good memory. Past patterns of American diplomacy and historical experience, many traceable to the very beginning of the republic, enable us to sketch reasonable scenarios and to forecast some alternative directions.

New Challenges, Recurring Debates

As we have argued throughout *American Foreign Policy: Pattern and Process*, the past informs the future. Armed with a long-term perspective, we see that alongside momentous changes in the world over the past two hundred years, the debate about the future of American foreign policy in previous epochs, as in our own, has consistently revolved around the costs and advantages of three sometimes overlapping, sometimes incompatible impulses. The first is the choice between isolationism and internationalism; the second is between realism and idealism; the third between intervention and noninterference. As in previous periods of transition, today's policy debates center on these perennial controversies, which reflect different world views or conceptual lenses, each contending for acceptance. Political scientist Stanley Hoffmann provides a glimpse of the on-going debate:

> Neo-isolationists want the U.S. to deal only with threats to America's physical security, political independence, and domestic liberty. They find no such threats at present, and therefore argue that the U.S. should let other powers, and regional balances of power, take care of all the world's woes. Realists . . . want the U.S. to continue to be the holder of the world

balance of power, the arbiter of the main regional power groups, and the watchdog against all potential imperialistic trouble-makers. Internationalists want a greater role for multilateral institutions and more emphasis on human needs and rights, the environment, and democracy. (Hoffmann 1992, 59; see also Hoffmann 1995; Haass 1995)

Future American leaders will bear the burden of reconciling these divergent viewpoints. How will they strike a balance? What forces and factors in the peculiarly American process of formulating foreign policy will influence their capacity to respond adaptively? To guide thinking about the probable answers, we should look more closely at the issues dividing adherents to these contending perspectives.

Isolationism versus Internationalism

American foreign policy since the nation's founding evinces identifiable cyclical swings between isolationism and internationalism. Because American policymakers historically have been unable to reconcile the advantages of withdrawing from the world with the benefits of reforming it, the nation's global posture has alternated between periods of global involvement and retrenchment. The relative value of each view has never been conclusively determined, as one conception has dominated at one time only to be replaced later by the other. We saw these themes played out in Chapter 3 and in many of the more specific issues in American foreign policy patterns and processes discussed in later chapters.

After World War II the United States embarked on a global foreign policy, which committed it to involvement in every corner of the world, however remote. Global activism reached its zenith in the Vietnam War, which in turn stimulated an inward turn and a growing neo-isolationist mood. Still, global activism continued to dominate the thinking of elites, most of whom never abandoned the international ethos, despite growing differences among them about the means of American foreign policy. With the end of the Cold War, however, the timeless debate about the wisdom of global activism compared with the advantages of a retreat from its burdens has resurfaced and arguably now animates elites as well as the mass of the American people. Thus the ends of American foreign policy, not just its means, are increasingly at issue.

Bill Clinton and others in his administration remained committed advocates of American activism. "[We must] fulfill our responsibility as the world's sole superpower," Clinton repeatedly urged. Others, however, believe that the United States, having won the Cold War, should eschew global responsibilities. Alan Tonelson of the Economic Strategic Institute, a vocal and articulate advocate of retrenchment, is among those who urges this alternative course. In his words, "U.S. policy should focus on equipping America to flourish in this world, not on transforming or even stabilizing it" (*Christian Science Monitor*, March 14, 1995, p. 18; see also Tonelson 1994). A "minimalist" posture like this "is the favored view of those who see only modest U.S. interests in the world (and only weak threats to them) and who take a narrow view of U.S. responsibility and obligation to meet other challenges" (Haass 1995). That view arguably animated many of the Republicans in Congress who, following their electoral victory in 1994, called for severe cuts in foreign aid, restricted participation in UN peacekeeping operations, and dismemberment of such long-standing symbols of

American global activism as the Agency for International Development, the Arms Control and Disarmament Agency, and the U.S. Information Agency.

Even the Clinton administration itself evinced a kind of neo-isolationism, as it endorsed the thesis that domestic problems require priority not only at home but also abroad. Thus it emphasized free trade, open markets, and the need to promote American "competitiveness" in overseas markets. Although many of these actions are consistent with the international ethos, "the main Clinton objective has not been free trade per se, but a return to growth, hence to fuller employment at home. The president is more interested in the liberal vision at home than the liberal vision abroad. Or rather, the latter serves the former" (Hoffmann 1995).

Thus, as the United States looks toward the new millennium, the issue it faces is in some sense timeless: Should the United States be a global power, or should it instead assume a less ambitious posture? Controversy over the answer is unlikely to cease, as reasonable people will assess differently the benefits and costs of intrusive globalism.

Idealism versus Realism

The history of American diplomacy also may be written in terms of the influence of two divergent schools of thought about international politics: realism and idealism. When Secretary of State Henry Kissinger defined America's major foreign policy problem as avoiding "oscillations between [an] excessive concern with power and the total rejection of power," he underscored the pronounced impact these incompatible outlooks periodically have exerted on American policy making and, less directly, how they also have colored the separate consideration of the costs and benefits of isolationist and internationalist stratagies.

As a world view and theory, realism has been most popular when international events seemed to confirm its pessimistic assumptions. In threatening eras—as during the Cold War, when the balance of terror, arms races, and coercive diplomacy appeared to define world politics—policymakers typically found realism a comfortable world view and concluded that the United States should pursue its self-interest with policies based on power calculations. The American preoccupation with geopolitical spheres of influence and military balances, and the equation of national power with military might, derived from the assumptions of *realpolitik*. Correspondingly, debates about military preparedness, the utility of alliances, and related issues were routinely cloaked in the language of realism. The prescription that the United States "act realistically" by seeking power and maintaining international order through military strength and reasoned strategy attracted a large following.

The intellectual tradition of political realism rejects moralism in foreign policy and assumes instead that survival is the nation's only acceptable ethical obligation. National power is the best route to its realization. Curiously, however, even when international circumstances lent credence to this counsel (as during the Cold War), the precepts of idealism remained alive.

Idealism tends to stress threats to global rather than national security. Such contemporary issues as environmental degradation, poverty, and sustainable development fall under the idealists' umbrella. Even during the Cold War they sought to universalize the humanitarian ideals and moral principles to which the United States traditionally aspired, prescribing support for international organizations, international law, arms control and disarmament, human rights, and, above all, perhaps, democratic governance. Embracing these goals and institutional means, idealists believed in the possibility of creating a more secure, prosperous, and just world order, one compatible with American values.

Realism and idealism are continuing traditions in American diplomacy. They compete with each other to define the nation's foreign policy objectives, and yet they also coexist with one another in sometimes uncomfortable ways. While one tradition may predominate in certain periods—as idealism did after 1915 and realism after 1945—neither has ever dispelled the influence of the other. Thus, as we found in Chapter 3, the American foreign policy tradition encompasses both prudent realism and moral idealism. The competing traditions vie continuously because each responds to two indispensable needs: to protect the nation from external threats in a hostile world and to stand for ideals worthy of emulation. The duality they engender accounts historically for the United States' willingness to pursue seemingly contradictory foreign policy goals and for its difficulty in defining a doctrine to govern the circumstances in which various policy instruments, including covert intervention into the affairs of others and resort to military force, should be employed.

Today's climate of opinion continues to reflect both the realist and idealist traditions. Particularly pronounced is the reassertion of America's ideals in an effort to enlarge the community of democratic states. The mission draws its inspiration from many sources, including James Madison, who wrote on February 2, 1792, in "Universal Peace," that "in the advent of republican governments [will be found] not only the prospect of a radical decline in the role played by war but the prospect as well of a virtual revolution in the conduct of diplomacy." That thesis underpinned American foreign policy during Woodrow Wilson's presidency, and it has continued. "Wilson not only responded to the wellsprings of American motivation, but took it to a new and higher level. All his successors have been Wilsonian to some degree, and subsequent American foreign policy has been shaped by his maxims" (Kissinger 1994a).

Liberal internationalists build their enthusiasm for democratic promotion on Wilson's thinking. Interestingly, today many committed realists, not just Wilsonian idealists, embrace the goal of enlarging the circle of democratic states. Henry Kissinger, for example, long a leading spokesperson for the doctrine of realism, sounded more like a reconstructed idealist when he advocated that "America must try to forge the widest possible moral consensus around a global commitment to democracy" (Kissinger 1994a). Similarly, Richard Nixon averred on the eve of his death in 1994 that "What we need today is a mission beyond peace. . . . After containing communism for forty-five years, . . . our goal now should be to enlarge free-market democracy."

Thus realists, long antagonistic to the proposition that domestic politics have any positive bearing on foreign policy behavior, seem to have joined idealists in treating participatory democracy as a value on which American policy can now profitably be centered and whose expansion serves the nation's security interests. The Clinton administration enthusiastically embraced that connection, as expressed, for example, in the president's 1994 State of the Union Address: "Democracies don't attack each other," the president declared. "Ultimately the best strategy to ensure our security and to build a durable peace is to support the advance of democracy elsewhere." The fact that liberal democracies are mature "civil societies" (Gellner 1994) that seek to treat their own citizens fairly is an additional incentive. In short, then, an intellectual revolution may be unfolding, as American policymakers and policy influentials of both realist and idealist persuasions share an increasingly common conviction about the virtues of democratization.

Bill Clinton also helped to nudge idealism and realism closer to each other. Terming his prospective policy "democratic realism," Clinton promised during his 1992 presidential campaign to strengthen America's power and position by pushing for worldwide acceptance of the democratic values that underpin America's liberal political culture. He also played to the public mood favoring a continued strong defense, one consistent with realist thinking. Like Clinton, then, and to some extent his predecessors including Ronald Reagan and George Bush, the next U.S. president will likely ground American foreign policy in some combination of both realism and idealism. As *The Economist* (April 1, 1995, p. 17) editorialized, "If democracies are really the best bulwark against war, many seemingly hard choices between idealism and *realpolitik* can be simplified abruptly. All good things can be made to go together." The relative emphasis will depend on emerging circumstances, but, regardless, concern for power and principle will remain intermingled.

Today, then, the issue is not whether idealism *or* realism will guide thinking about the nation's world role, as both patently continue to shape contemporary thinking. The real issue is *how* the United States should promote its power and principles in the world. Here a major division exists between the advocates of multilateralism and the proponents of unilateralism.

Recall that the Clinton administration's initial foreign policy plunge placed it squarely in the multilateral camp. In November 1992 Clinton argued that "multilateral action holds promise as never before" and that there exists an opportunity "to reinvent the institutions of collective security." Such faith in organized responses to global challenges reflects the Wilsonian belief that concerted action through international institutions can foster peace. Midway through the Clinton presidency Secretary of State Warren Christopher (1995) emphasized that American leadership required the United States to "galvanize the support of allies, friends, and international institutions in achieving common objectives."

"Assertive multilateralism," often embraced in the early Clinton presidency, is a liberal internationalist approach that seeks to preserve American involvement abroad at reduced cost by working through alliances and international organizations, which enable a sharing of the burdens (Haass 1995). In contrast, unilateralists counsel that the United States should go it alone on the world stage. They resist what they regard as "irresponsible" involvement in remote places like Somalia, Rwanda, and even Haiti, where pressing humanitarian needs are obvious but where challenges to U.S. interests are not. Defining American interests more narrowly than multilateralists, unilateralists insist that overseas engagements be restricted to those that enhance U.S. security and prosperity, regardless of whether other members of the international community support the choice. Clinton leveled a broadside at such thinking in a major foreign policy address in 1995, describing unilateralists as "isolationists" who "would eliminate any meaningful role for the United Nations, . . . deny resources to our peacekeepers and even to our troops, and . . . refuse aid to the fledgling democracies and to all those fighting poverty and environmental problems that can literally destroy hopes for a more democratic, more prosperous, more safe world."

Multilateralism and unilateralism exist in constant tension. Like internationalism and isolationism, each has benefits and each liabilities—which is why presidents typically rely on some combination of the competing policy approaches to realize their policy preferences. Both will shape the nation's thinking about its preferred response to the external circumstances that will dominate the international scene during the remainder of this century and into the next. Because the proper balance defies easy definition disagreement about their appropriate mix also undoubtedly will persist.

Challenges to unilateralism in the new world order are especially stark. They include the absence of a foreign policy consensus in the United States and persistent questions about the material and nonmaterial costs of leadership. Thus Henry Kissinger asked, almost rhetorically, whether the United States can "act internationally only as a result of multilateral consensus" (*Christian Science Monitor*, March 14, 1995, p. 18). Building that consensus is also difficult, however, as opinions among the nation's Cold War allies about the challenges they face now differ widely. Furthermore, in today's world political economy, the nation's politico-military allies are also its principal commercial competitors and hence are understandably reluctant to accede to American leadership. Hegemony requires not just a willingness to lead but also a willingness to follow. The deference other great powers previously exhibited will not persist without a common external threat to cement their cooperation.

Intervention versus Noninterference

American foreign policy today draws from both the realist and the idealist legacies, which point to divergent conclusions about what the United States should do to realize its foreign goals. These alternative postures also are evident in a third issue of American foreign policy: the use of American military might and other interventionist means to promote (or force) changes in other countries' policies and internal practices.

The diplomatic history of the United States is rife with examples of intervention in the affairs of others, ranging from its wrath against Native Americans in the nineteenth century to its "dollar diplomacy" in the Western Hemisphere early in this century, from covert involvement in European and Japanese domestic politics following World War II to the use of force against Iraq in the name of collective security in the aftermath of the Cold War. Figure 15.1 gives some sense of the persistence of interventionist behavior throughout American history. It summarizes the number of times presidents saw fit to dispatch American troops abroad. The provocations were widely dissimilar and thus required vastly different levels of American commitment. Still, the figure conveys some sense of how deeply interventionism is entrenched in the American experience.

Though entrenched, there is also a pronounced tension between intervention and noninterference throughout the American experience in world affairs. "No society has more firmly insisted on the inadmissibility of intervention in the domestic affairs of

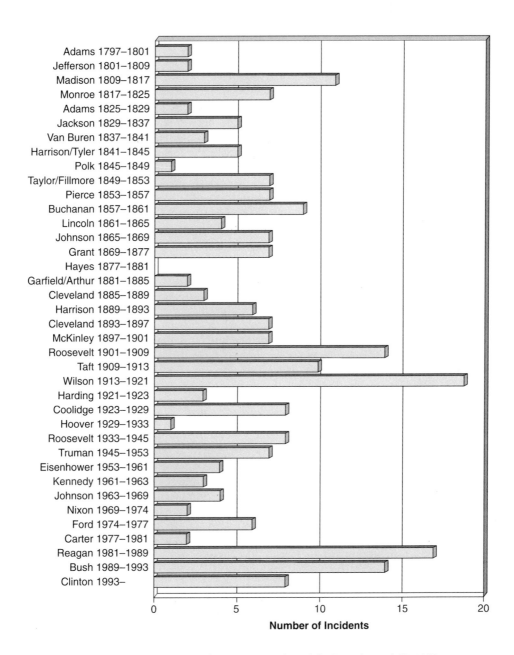

Figure 15.1   Initiation of the Use of U.S. Forces Abroad, by President, 1797–1993

Source: Adapted from Ellen C. Collier, "Instances of Use of United States Armed Forces Abroad, 1778–1993," *CRS Report for Congress*, October 7, 1993.

other states, or more passionately asserted that its own values were universally applicable," Kissinger (1994a) observed. But "no country has been more reluctant to engage itself abroad even while undertaking alliances and commitments of unprecedented reach and scope."

The post-Cold War world has witnessed a continuation of America's propensity to intervene, concomitant with its hesitation to do so. Many analysts had thought that in the absence of the East-West conflict, the United States would shed its interventionist garb. They had hoped America's foreign policy would revert to its nineteenth-century heritage, adamantly insisting that no state has a right to intervene in the internal affairs of another (cf. Schwarz 1995). In the formative years of the American experience "American diplomatic utterances [were] filled with denunciations of [interventions]," it has been argued. Now, however, the United States has reversed its traditional posture and taken the position that democracy is an "entitlement" (Roth 1995) and that, accordingly, "warlike measures against nondemocratic states for the crime of being nondemocratic" are now permissible (Hendrickson 1994).

Democratic promotion is in some sense a prescription for intervention. Nixon (1994) recognized this even as he urged that the United States strive to enlarge free-market democracy: "At times it will be necessary to use American power and influence to defend and extend freedom in places thousands of miles away if we are to preserve it at home." Similarly, Morton Halperin (1993), a member of Clinton's National Security Council staff, urged that "when a people attempts to hold free elections and establish a constitutional democracy, the United States and the international community should not only assist but should 'guarantee' the result." The Clinton administration's 1994 national security report to Congress, titled the *National Security Strategy of Engagement and Enlargement*, embraced Halperin's prescription.

If the urge to promote democracy should turn into a crusade to spread its virtues, as the intervention in Haiti ("Operation Restore Democracy") suggested it might, the United States will continue its interventionist propensities, sometimes under multilateral auspices, sometimes unilaterally. Furthermore, there is evidence that the transition from nascent to mature democracy is often conflict-prone (Mansfield and Snyder 1995), perhaps predicting more rather than fewer U.S. interventions in the future.

The Pentagon's 1994 annual planning document, *Planning Guidance for Fiscal 1996–2001*, concluded (as had preceding ones) that "the reemergence of a global threat during this planning period is neither likely nor plausible . . . . A military resurgence of significant magnitude to threaten current U.S. allies directly with conventional forces is unlikely to occur until the middle of the next decade, at the earliest." This posture statement deviates markedly from actual practice, however, which witnessed a continued compulsion to prepare for foreign military engagements. The impulse to enlarge the democratic community, predicated on the belief that the types of governments in power elsewhere affect U.S. security, rationalized continuing support for American capabilities to intervene throughout the world.

Rhetoric and action underscored the importance the Clinton administration attached to the use of force as a means of exerting American influence internationally. Building on Clinton's announcement in December 1994 that he would increase military spending over the next six years, the administration's budget called for $1,302 billion in defense spending between 1995 and 1999, keeping it near Cold War levels.

With resources of such magnitude devoted to military capability, the United States "for the foreseeable future will exceed by a huge margin the capability of any other nation in the world" and will remain "the only country in the world spending to fight two major wars at the same time without the help of allies" (*The Defense Monitor 23* no. 5 [1994]: 1). The administration's preference for continued military preparedness (and its aggressive export of U.S. arms) demonstrate the continuing appeal of the realist belief that the preservation of peace depends on preparations for war.

In addition to concern for military preparedness, Clinton renewed support for enhanced counterterrorist capabilities and for rapidly deployable forces to carry out peace-making, peace-keeping, and peace-building operations. The Pentagon's 1995 *National Military Strategy* statement added "peace engagement" for the purpose of preventive diplomacy to the principal missions of the U.S. armed forces and expressed concern for their ability to cope with "a broad range of potential challenges" (see Stedman 1995 for a critique). Expanded intelligence-gathering capabilities and increases for security-supporting assistance to the Global South were also sought.

Interestingly, however, the criteria for the United States to use force abroad have been defined in increasingly restrictive ways (Haas 1994b; Maynes 1995). Concern about America's credibility and its willingness to undertake risks may well result, breeding suspicion that the United States will only participate in overseas operations guaranteed to succeed without the loss of American lives. If so, liberal internationalism, dedicated to the promotion of democracy and human rights, could be "in crisis" (Hoffmann 1995), as the United States moves away from interventionism on behalf of Wilsonian ideals.

Our future forecasts again contain mixed messages: A propensity to intervene on behalf of American values and interests is evident, as are continued preparations to do so. However, this willingness is combined with a reluctance to bear interventionism's costs in blood, and sometimes in treasure as well. Here, then, history is clearly our guide. Although the United States is perhaps a reluctant giant as the world's sole remaining superpower, past patterns dictate that it will more often opt for intervention than noninterference to secure its enduring interests and values: peace and prosperity, stability and security, democracy and defense. The only unfinished post-Cold War task is defining when and how military intervention, coercive diplomacy, and other forms of intervention should be employed in pursuit of America's interests and values—but then this has always been an ongoing task.

Geopolitics or Geo-Economics?

There is a potential new wrinkle to America's interventionist impulse, a possibility suggested by the Clinton administration's conclusion "that we have arrived at a juncture where economic concerns need to be paramount." That viewpoint deviates from the logic embraced by political realists, who argue that military security is primary and economics secondary in the overall scheme of things.

Responding to the increasingly interdependent global marketplace and the dependence of American prosperity on it, the Clinton administration made the expansion of U.S. commercial exports a primary goal. Because opening markets and creating jobs are critical, Clinton proposed in 1993 an "Open Markets 2000" trade initiative, arguing that "Just as our security cannot rest on a hollow army, neither can it rest upon a hollow economy." At about the same time, the Department of State Management Task Force (U.S. Department of State 1992) described the twofold challenge to which the United States hoped to respond: "to compete successfully in commercial terms and to organize the competition to serve the interests of an expanding world economy." The report added that "We must be clear that international economic policy *is* foreign policy."

Secretary of State Warren Christopher, more than any of his predecessors, vigorously argued that the role of his department was to advocate American interests in the policy process. He viewed building bridges across the barriers, intellectual and political, that had long separated national security and foreign economic policy as an indispensable step in that process. "It used to be said that balance-of-power diplomacy and arms control were 'high politics,' and economics 'low politics.' President Clinton and I reject that distinction," he declared. "We are convinced that political and economic diplomacy are indivisible" (Christopher 1995). He added that "history will judge this priority [promoting open markets and sustainable economic growth] to be a distinctive imprint—and a lasting legacy—of this administration's foreign policy." Because political and economic diplomacy are indivisible, "America can only flourish in a world where trade is rising and barriers are falling. America's economic strengths at home and abroad are mutually reinforcing. At bottom, U.S. security depends on a strong economy. And in today's global economy, America's economic well-being increasingly depends on our ability to open foreign markets and promote free trade and investment."

Geo-economic imperatives make a return to protectionism and the high tariff walls of the 1930s, thus helping to deepen a devastating global depression, an unlikely long-term prospect. The lesson that free trade cannot be abandoned has probably been learned, but determining what constitutes "fair trade" remains a contentious issue. Furthermore, the Clinton administration's hardline approach toward Japan, which included retaliatory tariff threats, suggests that intervention in the marketplace may be necessary to rebalance the playing field long regarded—rightly or wrongly—as tilted against American businesses. Clinton's posturing, if not always his actions, presages that the government will continue actively to help American businesses expand their presence in foreign markets and that this potentially neomercantilist effort to enlarge the U.S. share of global trade will involve the government itself—sometimes in obtrusive, interventionist ways—in the promotion of U.S. business interests overseas.

Popular as neomercantilism may be, the penchant to use foreign economic policy for largely domestic purposes runs counter to a central idealist proposition: that free trade can promote prosperity and peace. Wilson argued that "the removal . . . of all economic barriers and the establishment of an equality of trade conditions" would facilitate international security and the spread of liberty. Like the democratic peace proposition, then, idealists see expanded commercial intercourse as a route to lasting peace. Ironically, however, expanded trade and commerce now also pose a remarkable challenge to the very ability of policymakers to control their own national fates outside the military/security sphere: "The global economy is literally out of control, not subject to the rules of accountability and principles of legitimacy that apply to relations between individuals and the state. States hesitate to impose their own rules unilaterally, out of fear of inefficiency and self-damage. Thus liberalism [read "idealism"], successful in reducing the state's power, has created a formidable anonymous new power" (Hoffmann 1995).

Continuity or Change? The Sources of American Foreign Policy · · · · · · · · · · ·

The intrusion of domestic politics into foreign policy making in democratic polities is a disadvantage that—at least in the eyes of some observers—undermines their ability to deal effectively with foreign policy crises and other external challenges. As the French political sociologist Alexis de Tocqueville (1969 [1835]) argued more than a century ago, democracies are "decidedly inferior" to centralized governments in the management of foreign relations because they are prone to "impulse rather than prudence." Democracies, so this reasoning goes, are slow to respond to external dangers, but once they are aroused, overreact to them. George Kennan, intellectual father of the Cold War foreign policy strategy of containment and a strong proponent of realist thinking, reflected on democratic foreign policy performance this way:

> I sometimes wonder whether a democracy is not uncomfortably similar to one of those prehistoric monsters with a body as long as this room and a brain the size of a pin: he lies there in his comfortable primeval mud and pays little attention to his environment; he is slow to wrath—in fact, you practically have to whack his tail off to make him aware that his interests are being disturbed; but, once he grasps this, he lays about him with such blind determination that he not only destroys his adversary but largely wrecks his native habitat. You wonder whether it would not have been wiser for him to have taken a little more interest in what was going on at an earlier date and to have seen whether he could not have prevented some of these situations from arising instead of proceeding from an undiscriminating indifference to a holy wrath equally undiscriminating. (Kennan 1951, 59)

Fear that the nature of the American polity reduces its capacity to adjust to changing conditions and new challenges lies at the center of concerns about its ability to adapt to the latest new world order—or disorder. Can America adjust to a world undergoing profound change? Or will it fail to adapt, muddling through with a combination of "little attention to [the] environment" and "blind determination" to have its way once it notices what it happening?

The balance sheet on forces now at work at home and abroad yields no firm conclusions. Yet our understanding of the sources of American foreign policy—the external environment, conditions within American society, the structural characteristics of the government, the roles occupied by decision makers, and the characteristics of decision makers themselves—leads us to conclude that only here, in the confluence of these forces, can we find the clues that will reveal the nation's response to the events unfolding at the dawn of a new millennium.

Individuals as Sources of American Foreign Policy

Any administration's foreign policy reflects the character of the person sitting in the innermost sanctuary of power, the Oval Office. A president's *individual* or idiosyncratic qualities influence policy style, but many restraints reduce the impact of personality on policy itself. All recent presidents have found it necessary to bend strong convictions to the force of competing political pressures, because successful presidential performance requires a willingness to satisfy political constituents at home and abroad. That is the art of politics. Sometimes, however, the art of politics leads contemporary critics and later historians to portray presidents as chameleons whose capacity to lead is compromised by their desire to please the plethora of diverse groups on whom their popularity and power depend.

Bill Clinton's experience is illustrative. His "active-positive" character predisposed him to assert governmental prerogatives in foreign and especially domestic policy. Clinton sought to prove that government is part of the solution, not just the problem. Thus he energetically pursued an ambitious agenda directed at the simultaneous realization of multiple goals, but his ability to achieve them was compromised time and again— most dramatically by the outcome of the 1994 congressional elections. Clinton now faced a resurgent and reassertive Republican Congress which, unlike the president, embraced a philosophy that less government is better. The change arguably reflected a shift in the climate of domestic opinion toward conservative political values and away from the liberal values Clinton himself embraced.

While George Bush suffered from "the vision thing"—the absence of a world view to guide the pragmatic, adaptive president through the dramatic changes that accompanied the end of the Cold War—Clinton proved unable to *communicate* his vision, a shortcoming that contributed to the suspicion that he, too, lacked focus. Furthermore, the combination of Clinton's presidential character and personality predispositions drove him to take strong positions, only to back away from confrontation when popular and elite approval failed to materialize. An extreme pragmatic, committed to reconciling differences among contending factions, Clinton, like Franklin D. Roosevelt, experimented with piecemeal solutions to vexing problems in a quest to discover what would work. In the process, his instinctive urge to engineer reforms eventually gave way to temporizing. Prone to back off in the face of opposition and generally displaying fecklessness and mood swings (Drew 1994), Bill Clinton fell short of the many major policy changes he originally envisioned, in foreign as well as domestic policy (Michalak 1995). Like his/their predecessors, then, both Bill Clinton and his supporters inside and outside of government experienced the limits to change that even an energetic, dynamic president can accomplish.

Roles and Foreign Policy Making

A president is not the personification of the state. Clinton, like all of his predecessors, discovered that his ability to move in new directions is restricted by his predecessors' prior commitments and policies, the actions and preferences of the individuals already in position to implement policy, and his own conception of how he was expected to perform the *role* of president.

The constraints of the past were nowhere more evident during the Clinton presidency than in the Middle East. Even though Clinton wanted to focus on domestic, not foreign policy, he repeatedly found that ongoing conflicts in the region and prospects for alleviating them—including the seemingly timeless feud between Israel and its Arab neighbors and between the United States, on the one hand, and Iran and Iraq, on the other—demanded his attention. Thus, despite his preferences, the role require-ments of the presidency demanded that Clinton direct attention abroad, not just at home. Bush, on the other hand, experienced the reverse pressures. Determined to fo-cus attention on foreign policy as one of the few remaining Wise Men of the Munich generation, the Bush presidency itself fell victim to demands to balance challenges at home with problems abroad, especially as the end of the Cold War diminished the threat that for so long had riveted the attention of the nation and its policymakers on foreign policy issues. In each case, then, the man behind the desk in the Oval Office found that he alone could not determine what was expected of him.

The backgrounds of those appointed to fill foreign policy-making roles invariably shape the decisions that are made. It is noteworthy that many of Clinton's advisers were veterans appointed by previous administrations, carrying with them well-worn conceptual baggage. These foreign policy managers were insiders, which helps to ex-plain why Cold War precepts and related experiences often shaped their perspectives. Such scripts are difficult to discard.

Beyond the immediate entourage, however, Clinton more than any other president sought to shape a federal establishment that reflected "America." Thus more women and minorities were appointed to the cabinet and other policy-making roles—the three thousand or so politically appointed positions in the federal government identified in the so-called "plum book" (because of the color of its cover)—than in any previous ad-ministration. At the next echelon, however, where millions of public employees are charged with the day-to-day management and implementation of the nation's public policy, domestic as well as foreign, the administration could do little to transform the face of bureaucracy. At the top tier of the "permanent government"—those "who run the country no matter who is president"—90 percent of the posts continued to be held by white males, making it "look more like the United States Senate" than America (Weiner 1994, 4).

Here in the "permanent government" the role requirements that constrain indi-vidual latitude are particularly acute. "Bureaucratic politics" is the phrase we used to explain the how and why of individuals' behavior in the multitude of large-scale orga-nizations that comprise the foreign affairs government. "Bureaucrat" is the way many Americans otherwise choose to disparage them.

It is now popular sport for presidential candidates to "run against Washington." Typically this means reducing the size of government, defined as reducing the num-ber of "bureaucrats" who comprise it. Widespread public ire is seldom directed at gov-ernment employees themselves (witness the outpouring of sympathy for those victim-ized in the 1995 terrorist bombing of the federal office building in Oklahoma City). Instead, the roles bureaucrats occupy and the regulations and presumed waste that bu-reaucracy generate are what typically stimulate anger. Increasingly, however, it also seems that many Americans believe the government itself to be a threat to their con-stitutionally guaranteed rights and liberties.

Clinton's "Reinventing Government" initiative did more than most administra-tions to reduce both the size of government and the regulations typically associated with it. (Administration critics argue that it also encouraged excessive government in-trusiveness.) With that, however, comes a shift in the comparative distribution of po-litical and professional managers of the federal establishment. As one seasoned observer put it in commenting on the balance of presidential-congressional war-making power: "Increased numbers of political appointees pose serious risks: a layer of inexperienced policy makers subject to frequent turnover, the exclusion of many career professionals from agency deliberations, and greater administrative instability and incompetence. . . . This climate will tempt short-term political appointees to augment presidential power and ignore congressional controls" (Fisher 1994–1995). Are the nation's enduring interests and values—peace and prosperity, stability and security, democracy and defense—better served by career politicians or career professionals?

Governmental Sources of American Foreign Policy

Adaptations in America's foreign policy as it faces the new millennium also will be shaped by the structure of the nation's presidential system of government, in which separate institutions, the president and Congress, share foreign policy responsibility. In the past, the president has been preeminent, but as domestic and international forces increasingly challenge the president's once dominant position—"the most powerful person in the world"—moving American foreign policy in new directions may prove even more difficult than in the past.

The overlapping organizations that comprise the foreign affairs government, while nominally at the president's command, are not easily moved, as the role requirements of career professionals reward caution, not innovation. Furthermore, new presidents—often viewed, as we saw Chapter 10, as "transient meddlers" in the business of the people who staff the foreign affairs government—frequently find that their preferences are not top priorities in an environment that equates organizational survival with individual survival. Thus Bill Clinton, who went to Washington committed to "change," lamented after his first year in office that "There really is a Washington culture here that, on the one hand, needs to be changed, but on the other, has to be dealt with if you want to get anything done."

Presidents continue to concentrate their foreign policy authority in the White House in part because the bureaucracy is so resistant to change. Still, the resistance displayed reveals the considerable extent to which the governmental machinery is beyond direct presidential control:

> Presidents operate on the brink of failure and in ignorance of when, where, and how failure will come. They do not and cannot possibly know about even a small proportion of government activity that bears on their failure. They can only put out fires and smile above the ashes. They don't know what's going on—yet they are responsible for it. And they feed that responsibility every time they take credit for good news not of their own making. (Lowi 1985b, 190)

Taking into account an independent-minded Congress, in addition to bureaucratic resistance, we can easily understand how the structure of the American government acts as a brake on policy innovation. Bipartisanship has sometimes muted the Constitution's invitation for struggle between Congress and the president. However, without consensus about the nation's appropriate world role, Congress, tempted by destructive partisanship, has assumed imperial dimensions of its own (Lindsay 1994b).

Polarizing forces within Congress greatly reduce the president's capacity to win and preserve goodwill on Capitol Hill. Likewise, persistent divided government—with the White House controlled by one party and Congress the other—exacerbates the inability of either branch, but especially the president, who bears primary responsibility for U.S. foreign relations, to be a force for policy change. Prior to Clinton's election, the White House had been under Republican control for all but four of the previous twenty-four years. And prior to the election of the Republican 104th Congress in 1994, Congress had been under continuous Democratic control since 1954, having briefly slipped into the majority in the House and Senate on the force of Eisenhower's electoral coattails in 1952.

Coming on the heels of victory in the Persian Gulf and the end of the Cold War, the Republicans' 1994 win bears striking resemblance to their electoral successes in 1918 and 1946, when, following the other two global conflicts of the twentieth century, they also wrested control of Congress from the Democrats, even as a Democrat occupied the White House. There are other parallels among the three elections, which arguably frame the choices Republicans will again have to make at the dawn of the new millennium. One writer put it this way shortly after the Republican victories:

> In each case, the country was in transition from war, the incumbent was vulnerable, the political agenda in flux. Bill Clinton looks weak and vulnerable, as Woodrow Wilson looked old and ill in 1919 and Harry Truman seemed not-quite-presidential in 1947. The end of the Cold War, like the end of World Wars I and II, has generated controversies over isolationism vs. internationalism, immigration and downsizing a war-expanded military. Now as then, the economy is puzzling experts with deflationary and inflationary crosstides, issues of tax cuts vs. budget restraint and the uncertainties of the business cycle and stock market, all potentially aggravated by the lack of coordination between the Republican legislative and Democratic executive branches. (Phillips 1995, 22)

Following World War I, the Republican Congress turned away from Wilsonian internationalism, shunning the Versailles Treaty and thus ensuring that the United States would not join the League of Nations. Without U.S. membership, the League was destined to fail. After World War II, however, the Republican Congress joined Truman in shaping America's response to the challenge of Soviet communism and thus the prolonged period of global activism that characterized the Cold War. Which path will the Republicans now choose? After World War I they became the dominant party for a decade, but after World War II it was the Democrats. Did their divergent foreign policy choices determine their different domestic policy positions (Phillips 1995)?

Republicans have typically been less prone to restrict the president's foreign policy powers, as in his ability to make war, for example, than Democrats. But they also have inclined more toward unilateralism than multilateralism. Thus the "early snapshots" from the Republican 104th Congress painted "an uneven landscape . . . with remarkable similarity to the kind of thinking that dominated the Cold War. Republicans [seemed] to want to maintain or increase defense spending, boost American leadership, and emphasize traditional security interests" (Sciolino 1995). The agenda differed sharply from Clinton's, thus portending the conflicts with the White House that followed. If the balance of power between the executive and Congress remains in flux, more of the same can be expected. If, however, the 1994 congressional election turns out to be a realigning election that breaks the New Deal coalition which has largely dominated congressional politics since the 1930s, thus bringing it more into accord with presidential politics, such thinking may become the wave of the future, not just the past.

Societal Sources of American Foreign Policy

Because the United States is a society-dominant political system, the ability of the president to work his will in Congress ultimately will be influenced by the support his policies enjoy among the American people. Indeed, the potential influence of societal forces in a globally interdependent world is especially potent, as foreign policy is often little more than an extension of domestic policy. Thus the Clinton administration repeatedly urged that foreign policy *is* domestic policy. Politics does not stop at the water's edge.

The American public's definition of national priorities is likely to be driven increasingly by concerns about the economic foundations of national security. Although it is commonplace to argue that the American people are turning inward, there is little evidence to suggest that this is an isolationist plunge like that which characterized the period between the two world wars. Instead, the American people want their leaders to prioritize issues and be selective, with greater attention now given to domestic over global concerns. In part this focus doubtless reflects public apathy and misinformation about American foreign policy: The American public is rarely knowledgeable about its presidents' stance on international issues, and recent polls indicate that the average American is indifferent to most of the president's foreign policy decisions. These facts negate the democratic proposition that an informed citizenry will dictate American leaders' policy choices. Lack of concern and consensus curtail the potential impact of public opinion, as does the entrenched public perception that all presidents are defenders of the Washington status quo, despite most recent chief executives' claims to the contrary. Still, presidents cannot ignore—without inviting political peril—the post-Cold War priorities that the American people now attach to the home front.

Even as the American people look inward rather than outward, pressures from powerful interests in the United States continue to dictate large expenditures on national defense. Defense spending declined each year in the decade ending in 1995, but it continues to command enormous resources. "Of every federal dollar subject to annual review and appropriation, forty-eight cents will go to the Pentagon" (Stevenson 1995, 18). A concern for jobs and an urge to keep the defense industrial base "warm" are potent domestic sources behind the urge to spend on the military.

The Clinton administration's inability to use the defense budget to control the growth of the federal debt and dramatically reduce the annual budget deficit speaks to the inherent trade-offs between competing goals and the inertia that flow from domestic pressures. Many analysts worry, however, that American power will wane if the federal budget deficit is not corrected. Debt and deficit reductions will require painful adjustments in prevailing policy priorities. "Balancing the budget" has become a political hot button, but it remains to be seen how many politicians have the stomach to sustain a commitment to the difficult domestic choices necessary to support the required foreign and domestic policy adjustments.

As House Republicans savored their 1994 electoral triumph, they could claim their victory was a "mandate" for their Contract with America. Survey data show, however, that few Americans understood what the contract implied, and fewer still were knowledgeable of its particulars. This is typical of the electoral process, which rarely clarifies the range of public support for specific policies. Voter preferences, then, are a breeding ground for policy evolution, not revolution. Meanwhile, interest groups and political action committees continue to press their special causes, leading policy makers to navigate a middle course among the shoals of America's political pluralism.

The electronic media seemingly play an increasingly prominent role in shaping political agendas and causing policymakers to pander to public preferences. The ***perpetual election***—constant polling to determine presidents' standing with the American people—arguably forces presidents to choose the path of convenience, not conscience, when faced with tough choices. Foreign policy challenges and crises often boost presidents' popularity at home, but the state of the economy typically exerts a more enduring impact. Even here, however, the challenges facing the United States in a rapidly changing world political economy have caused skittishness in the public mood, as witnessed by Clinton's inability to reap the political gains normally associated with a healthy and growing economy.

Fear of "jobless growth" in the U.S. economy helps explain the apparent anomaly of Clinton's experience. It also underlies much growing sentiment against immigrants, whose urge to migrate to "the land of the free" intensifies as population growth and ethnic conflict abroad push millions from their homelands. Multiculturalism is an expression of new immigrant groups' rejection of the "melting pot" metaphor long used to describe the process that assimilated new Americans into the established social system. Meanwhile, growing dissatisfaction with affirmative action principles put into place decades ago to ensure equal employment opportunities for all Americans promises to rend society as it faces the new millennium. Thus emergent challenges in American society itself will continue to focus attention on domestic challenges, undermining its ability to reach consensus on an appropriate world role for the new era.

The Cold War stimulated the cohesiveness that bound the American nation together for so long. As we noted in Chapter 8, the "the long war" against communism strengthened Americans' national identity, providing a "unifying dynamic [that] helped overcome ethnic and sectional differences and the ideological heritage of individualism" (Deudney and Ikenberry 1994). It also contributed immensely to the emergence of presidential preeminence in foreign policy. Paradoxically, then, the end of the Cold War has eroded a principal pillar on which the legitimacy of presidential power has rested for a half-century at precisely the time when strong leadership at home may be required.

External Sources of American Foreign Policy

As the world's sole remaining superpower, the United States has a greater opportunity now than ever to shape a world consonant with its longstanding interests and values:

peace and prosperity, stability and security, democracy and defense. But just as the persistent federal government budget deficit—to which we can now add soaring trade deficits with other countries—strained the ability of policymakers to take corrective action, they undermined the willingness of others to accede to American leadership. Instead of conceding these concerns and downplaying America's own vulnerabilities, however, Clinton followed the path blazed by Bush and Reagan. While putting a humanistic face on intervention on behalf of democracy, the timeworn goal of preserving American hegemonic status arguably motivated him (Chomsky 1994). Clinton underscored his dedication to preserving American leadership, cautioning in 1994, "We can't just cut and run. It would send the wrong signal. Our leadership in world affairs would be undermined at the very time when people are looking to America to promote peace and freedom in the post-Cold War world."

The United States does maintain unmatched military strength and doubtless continues to exercise disproportionate political influence over international affairs. Some would argue that these assets assure that America is not in decline and therefore not predestined to retreat. But such a conclusion ignores the decline of the U.S. resource base relative to that of other nations, however measured. Compared with its competitors, U.S. economic performance no longer enables the nation to exercise political leverage at will, and America, although a giant, is like Gulliver, increasingly tied to others by many strings. The United States can neither act alone in an interdependent world nor expect to regain the power it possessed immediately after World War II, when it was not just stronger than anyone but stronger than everyone.

Instead, present trends point to the emergence of a new multipolar international system. As we noted in Chapter 6, the United States will continue to be first among equals at the top of the great-power hierarchy, but it will face growing competition from economic powerhouses that now challenge the U.S. leadership position in the world political economy—and that also may come to challenge it militarily. Already China, Japan, and the European Union are poised to join the United States at the apex of world power. The Pentagon's objective as first outlined in the 1992 *Defense Policy Guidance*—namely, to prevent the emergence of a rival superpower—proved highly unrealistic, which is why it was later abandoned. Thus, like the American century, the "unipolar moment" will pass.

Already America's Cold War allies often differ from the United States in their assessment of global priorities and how to respond to the challenges of the post-Cold War world. That is nowhere more evident than in Europe's and America's inability to devise coordinated strategies to deal with ethnonationalism, tribal conflict, and Islamic fundamentalism, a force especially salient to the United States. Meanwhile, economic competition among the world's current and emergent capitalist economies is rising at the same time that the United States' ability and willingness to manage the world economy are diminishing. Faced with these new realities, the United States may learn to view the world less through an idealist lens and more through a realist one, as conflict rather than cooperation among rival capitalisms predictably increases (Hart 1992; E. Peterson 1994). The shift of the Clinton administration from its early, enthusiastic embrace of assertive multilateralism to a more restrained and self-reliant unilateral approach is perhaps indicative of how the future will resemble past periods in America's diplomatic history.

Although some historical patterns in international politics will undoubtedly find counterparts in the new millennium, new patterns will also unfold. Their force is already evident at the transnational layer of international politics, where the ongoing revolution in information technology has opened a window onto a world that truly knows no borders. Even now, for example, the world political economy "is literally out of control, not subject to the rules of accountability and principles of legitimacy that apply to relations between individuals and the state" (Hoffmann 1995), as we noted earlier in this chapter. The inability of the United States and others in the Global North to prop up the value of the dollar during the Bush and Clinton presidencies—despite repeated, coordinated interventions of their central banks involving billions of dollars—is but one visible glimpse of the challenges the information age will pose.

A glimpse of the second challenge is provided by the violent conflict, environmental degradation, and incentives to emigrate that the concentration of world population growth in the Global South portends. We simply have no experience in coping with the domestic and international challenges of a world of six, eight, or ten billion people. But that is the world on the horizon at the dawn of a new millennium, one that the Global North and Global South may both wish to avoid but that will be thrust on them nonetheless. It is also a world in which the precepts of action implied in the recurring debates in the United States between isolationism and internationalism, idealism and realism, and intervention and noninterference may be found wanting.

The Problematic Future

Clearly, many of the challenges of the twenty-first century will not fit well with a foreign policy designed for the circumstances of the past half-century. A new vision for a new world is an idea whose time has come. The Bush and Clinton administrations have served in the watershed between the Cold War that has ended and the dawn of a new world still dimly perceived. Will the United States and the presidents who cross the threshold of the new century pragmatically adjust the United States to the new millennium, protecting and promoting its enduring values and interests?

Former Secretary of State Dean Acheson once noted that "there are fashions in everything, even in horrors . . . and just as there are fashions in fears, there are fashions in remedies." Insofar as that telling aphorism is true, global trends may eventually distance American foreign policy from the power approach it relentlessly pursued for nearly five decades during the Cold War and move it toward a broadened conception of national security. But resistance to acceptance of new fashions is evident.

As before, the issue today is whether the conventional assumptions that guided American foreign policy for a half-century remain warranted. Today's world necessitates many hard choices. "There are periods of history," Stanley Hoffmann (1989) observes, "when profound changes occur all of a sudden. . . . We are now in one of those periods, which obliges the United States to rethink its role in the world, just as it was forced to do by the cataclysmic changes that followed the end of the Second World War." "What is in order," Irving Kristol (1990) urges, "is some new, imaginative thinking about America's role in the world, and not a mere projection of yesterday's role and policy."

Whether changes will occur depends in part on the capacity of the American democracy to recruit into office farsighted, courageous leaders able to offer a positive vision of the future and a program to reach it. Trend is *not* destiny. The world that emerges in the new millennium will be influenced by the assumptions today's and tomorrow's policymakers make about global realities and by their capacity to act decisively and wisely in responding to emerging challenges.

The person empowered to make the fundamental choices, the president, is only one element in the equation that will define the outcome. Other factors will join presidential influence to drive collectively the policy process ultimately shaping the policy direction that eventually emerges. Indeed, the process—more than the individuals involved in it—will parent the policy, for the policy-making process and the conditions that influence it will not only stimulate efforts to cope with external challenges but also constrain a president's ability to implement the design chosen. "All of [the nation's past presidents], from the most venturesome to the most reticent, have shared one disconcerting experience: the discovery of the limits and restraints—decreed by law, by history, and by circumstances—that sometimes can blur their clearest designs or dull their sharpest purposes," noted Emmet John Hughes (1972). "I have not controlled events, events have controlled me" President Lincoln lamented.

Most of the assumptions made by American policymakers in the immediate aftermath of World War II proved to be remarkably resilient for more than five decades, and they arguably served the nation well. Now, however, the structure of the world system on which those assumptions were based no longer exists, and old solutions may not fit new situations. Although past policy has the force of momentum behind it, and that force is awesome, the question is whether American leaders have the will to chart new foreign policy directions. Will the parameters of American foreign policy be redrawn, and can accommodative adjustments to the new realities be expected? Realization of the enduring values and interests of the United States in the new millennium may depend on the answers.

SUGGESTIONS FOR FURTHER READING

Bernstein, Michael, and David E. Adler, eds. *Understanding American Economic Decline.* Cambridge: Cambridge University Press, 1994.

Brilmayer, Lea. *American Hegemony: Political Morality in a One-Superpower World.* New Haven, Conn.: Yale University Press, 1994.

Campbell, Colin, and Bert A. Rockman, eds. *The Clinton Presidency: First Appraisals.* Chatham, N.J.: Chatham House, 1996.

Fromkin, David. *In the Time of the Americans: FDR, Truman, Eisenhower, Marshall, MacArthur— The Generation That Changed America's Role in the World.* New York: Knopf, 1995.

Gardner, Hall. *Surviving the Millennium: American Global Strategy, the Collapse of the Soviet Empire, and the Question of Peace.* Westport, Conn.: Praeger, 1994.

Garten, Jeffrey E. *A Cold Peace: America, Japan, Germany, and the Struggle for Supremacy.* New York: Times Books, 1993.

Goldstein, Judith, and Robert O. Keohane, eds. *Ideas and Foreign Policy: Beliefs, Institutions, and Political Change.* Ithaca, N.Y.: Cornell University Press, 1993.

Holt, Richard. *The Reluctant Superpower: A History of America's Economic Global Reach*. New York: Kodansha, 1995.

Joffe, Josef. "'Bismarck' or 'Britain'? Toward an American Grand Strategy after Bipolarity," *International Security* 19 (Spring 1995): 94–117.

Johnson, Robert H. *Improbable Dangers: U.S. Conceptions of Threat in the Cold War and After*. New York: St. Martin's, 1994.

Petras, James, and Morris Morley. *Empire or Republic? American Global Power and Domestic Decay*. New York: Routledge, 1995.

Steel, Ronald. *Temptations of a Superpower*. Cambridge, Mass.: Harvard University Press, 1995.

Toffler, Alvin, and Toffler, Heidi. *Creating a New Civilization: The Politics of the Third Wave*. Atlanta: Turner Publications, 1995.

Tucker, Robert W., and David C. Hendrickson. *The Imperial Temptation: The New World Order and America's Purpose*. New York: Council on Foreign Relations Press, 1992.

Wittkopf, Eugene R., ed. *The Future of American Foreign Policy*. New York: St. Martin's, 1994.

APPENDIX

· · ·

A Chronology of Selected Foreign Policy Events, January 1945 through September 1995

· · ·

Roosevelt Administration

1945

United States rejects Soviet request for $6 billion reconstruction loan

Churchill, Roosevelt, and Stalin sign Yalta agreement

United States recognizes Soviet control of Outer Mongolia

United States approves transfer of Kurile Islands to Soviet Union

Romanian government turns pro-Soviet

Arab League Pact signed in Cairo

Last German V-2 rocket falls on Britain

Roosevelt dies; Vice President Truman succeeds to the presidency

Truman Administration

1945

V-E Day (German surrender to Allied forces in Europe), May 8

Truman cancels Lend-Lease allocations and shipments to the Allies

Truman sends Harry Hopkins to Moscow to discuss postwar settlement

Allied Control Council for Germany establishes four-power occupation of Berlin and right to determine Germany's boundaries

San Francisco Conference approves United Nations (UN) Charter

Western nations recognize Polish government

Truman informs Stalin that American scientists have successfully detonated world's first atomic bomb

Churchill, Stalin, and Truman attend Potsdam Conference

United States drops atomic bomb on Hiroshima, August 6

Soviet Union declares war on Japan and sends troops into Manchuria

United States drops atomic bomb on Nagasaki, August 9

Chiang-Kai-shek and Molotov sign Sino-Soviet friendship treaty

Soviet-Polish treaty recognizes Oder-Neisse line as Poland's western border

Ho Chi Minh declares independent Vietnam Republic

V-J Day (Japan surrenders to Allied forces), August 14

Council of Foreign Ministers meets in London

Iranian rebellion, supported by Soviet arms, erupts; civil war continues in China

Nuremberg War Crimes Tribunal convenes in Germany

Big Three meet at Moscow Conference; Secretary of State James F. Byrnes agrees to recognize Romanian and Bulgarian satellite governments

Yugoslavia is declared a Federated People's Republic

1946

People's Republic of Albania proclaimed

Soviet Union protests British role in Greek civil war

George C. Marshall mediates armistice in Chinese civil war

Mao Tse-tung's communists and Chiang Kai-shek's Nationalists resume Chinese civil war

United States protests the continued presence of Soviet troops in Iran

United States leads UN involvement in Iranian crisis over Soviet protest

· · ·

Churchill delivers militantly anti-Soviet Iron Curtain speech in Fulton, Missouri

Soviets withdraw troops from Iran

Council of Foreign Ministers convene Paris Peace Conference

General Lucius Clay stops reparations to Soviet zone of Germany

Soviets reject Baruch Plan to destroy atomic weapons and place control of nuclear energy in international hands

United States grants independence to the Philippines

United States joins the United Nations Educational, Scientific, and Cultural Organization (UNESCO)

Truman tells Congress China received $600 million since V-J Day, and aid will continue

United States protests Soviet economic exploitation of Hungary

Secretary of State Byrnes outlines U.S. policy for German war recovery in Stuttgart speech

United States backs anti-Soviet faction in Turkish Straits crisis

Nuremberg Tribunal sentences ten Nazis to death and others to life imprisonment

Japan's wartime leaders imprisoned or hanged following Tokyo trials

United States signs treaty of friendship and commerce with China

United States begins first peacetime atomic tests in Bikini Atoll

Iran crushes independence movement in Azerbaijan with U.S. aid

Yugoslavia shoots down U.S. aircraft

Soviets agree to troop exit from Trieste and arms inspection

Treaties at New York Foreign Ministers Conference confirm U.S. recognition of Soviet control in southeastern Europe

United States and Britain begin joint administration of their occupation zones in Germany

Bulgaria is declared a People's Republic

War breaks out in Vietnam

1947

United States charges violation of Yalta agreement following communist electoral victory in Poland

Britain and France sign a fifty-year Treaty of Alliance and Mutual Assistance at Dunkirk

United States abandons efforts to mediate between Chinese Nationalists and communists

Truman Doctrine pledges aid to Greece, Turkey, and others resisting communism

Big Four Foreign Ministers Conference in Moscow concludes without agreement

Communists smash Hungarian ruling party

United Nations makes the United States trustee for Pacific islands

Secretary of State George C. Marshall announces European Recovery Program (Marshall Plan)

Under Soviet pressure, Poland and Hungary decline Marshall Plan assistance

George F. Kennan's "X" article proposing U.S. containment of Soviet communism, based on 1946 telegram sent from Moscow, published in *Foreign Affairs*

National Security Act creates Defense Department, National Security Council (NSC), and Central Intelligence Agency (CIA)

United States proposes Japanese peace treaty to make Japan a stronghold against communism in the Far East

Soviet Union charges that the United States threatens war

India proclaimed independent and partitioned into India and Pakistan

Marshall refers Korean independence question to UN General Assembly

Crisis erupts in Kashmir (which is claimed by both India and Pakistan)

General Agreement on Tariffs and Trade (GATT) treaty signed by twenty-three countries

Rio Pact for collective defense of Western Hemisphere commits the United States and Latin American republics to mutual assistance against aggression

Comintern revived by Soviet Union and greatly expanded as Cominform

Romania becomes a People's Republic following the abdication of King Michael

1948

United States announces European reconstruction will occur without Soviet collaboration

Mohandas Gandhi assassinated in India

Communist coup occurs in Czechoslovakia

Juan Perón retains Argentinean presidency over U.S. complaints

Brussels Treaty calls for cooperation among Belgium, France, Luxembourg, the Netherlands, and the United Kingdom

Soviet Union refuses to meet in Allied Control Council because of Western obstruction in Germany

Organization of European Economic Cooperation (OEEC) established to disburse Marshall Plan funds

Organization of American States (OAS) created to replace the Pan American Union

Israel declares independence, receives immediate U.S. recognition

War erupts between Israel and the Arab League

United States provides military aid to Chinese Nationalists

Vandenberg Resolution pledges U.S. support for Brussels Treaty and defense agreements in Europe

Soviet Union stops road and rail traffic between Berlin and the West; airlift begins

Yugoslavia's Marshall Tito breaks with Cominform and proclaims neutrality in East-West dispute

Rebellion in Malaya begins

Separate North and South Korean governments established

Brussels Treaty powers, Canada, and the United States meet in Washington to create North Atlantic defense treaty

UN General Assembly adopts Universal Declaration of Human Rights

1949

"Point Four" of Truman's inaugural address promises aid to developing countries

Council for Mutual Economic Assistance (Comecon) is initiated for Soviet assistance in Europe

Huk rebels lead Philippine insurgency

United States guided missile launched to record height of 250 miles

Israel admitted to the United Nations

Negotiating powers invite Denmark, Iceland, Italy, Norway, and Portugal to adhere to the North Atlantic Treaty

Soviet Union protests that prospective North Atlantic Treaty Organization (NATO) is contrary to UN Charter

NATO (first permanent U.S. alliance concluded in peacetime) formed with signing of North Atlantic Treaty

London Ten-Power Agreement creates the Council of Europe

Berlin blockade lifted; separate East and West German governments established

French install Bao Dai as head of Vietnamese puppet government

United States withdraws occupation forces from South Korea

Vietnamese state established with capital at Saigon

Soviet Union acquires atomic bomb

Nationalists flee mainland China to island of Formosa Taiwan

Joint Chiefs of Staff advise against U.S. occupation of Formosa

State Department issues China White Paper placing blame for communist takeover on Nationalists' corruption

Mao Tse-tung unifies mainland China and proclaims People's Republic of China

Soviet Union and its European satellites recognize People's Republic of China

Greek civil war ends in communist defeat

Mutual Defense Assistance Act pledges U.S. aid to countries vulnerable to communist pressure

Truman and Shah of Iran declare U.S.-Iranian solidarity

India recognizes Communist China

1950

Britain recognizes Communist China

Truman announces the United States will take no military measures to protect Formosa

Secretary of State Dean Acheson reaffirms "hands-off" policy for Formosa

United States announces intention to build hydrogen bomb

Soviet Union begins eight-month boycott of UN Security Council

Senator Joseph McCarthy claims State Department is riddled with communists and communist sympathizers

Far Eastern Economic Assistance bill assures continued aid to Formosa

Soviet Union and Communist China sign thirty-year Mutual Aid Pact

National Security Council issues Memorandum No. 68

United States, Britain, and France issue Tripartite Declaration promising protection of Israel's boundary lines

United States gives France military assistance to fight Vietnamese rebels

North Korean forces invade South Korea and capture Seoul; U.S. troops enter Korea with orders to defend Formosa and prevent Chiang's forces from attacking mainland China

Chiang Kai-shek and General Douglas MacArthur meet on Formosa

McCarren Act, calling for severe domestic restrictions of communists, passed by Congress over presidential veto

United States invades North Korea; South Korean troops cross thirty-eighth parallel

Greece and Turkey accept North Atlantic Council invitation to participate in Mediterranean defense planning

General Eisenhower named Supreme Allied Commander of Europe by North Atlantic Council

East German-Polish treaty ends dispute over border

Communist Chinese forces occupy Tibet

Tibet appeals to United Nations but China rejects UN appeal for cease-fire

Communist China enters Korean War

UN General Assembly passes the Uniting for Peace Resolution

1951

UN General Assembly accuses China of aggression in Korea

U.S. troops stationed in NATO countries

House Minority Leader Joseph W. Martin discloses MacArthur letter endorsing use of Chiang's troops to open second front on Chinese mainland

Truman recalls General MacArthur, who sought U.S. invasion of mainland China

Secretary of State Marshall tells Senate that Chinese Nationalists were beaten by communists due to lack of public support and "the character of government"

Treaty establishing European Coal and Steel Community (ECSC) signed

Mohammed Mossadegh appointed Prime Minister of Iran, nationalizes Anglo-Iranian Oil Company

United States and Philippines sign mutual security pact

McCarren's Internal Security subcommittee begins hearings on "subversive" influences on U.S. foreign policy

Truman proposes $307 million aid program to Nationalist China

ANZUS Pact signed by Australia, New Zealand, and the United States

Mutual Security Act pledges U.S. military assistance throughout the world

Korean truce line (thirty-eighth parallel) accepted at United Nations

1952

Franco-German crisis erupts over administration of Saar region

Soviet Union creates three-mile buffer zone on East German border

Greece and Turkey join NATO

United States doubles size of Military Assistance Advisory Group on Formosa

European Defense Community (EDC) treaty signed by Belgium, France, Italy, Luxembourg, the Netherlands, and West Germany

Cyprus begins fight for independence

Gamal Abdel Nasser emerges as leader following ouster of Egyptian monarchy

Britain successfully completes first atomic test

United States explodes first hydrogen bomb at Eniwetok Atoll

National Security Agency created by a classified presidential directive

Truman considers using atomic bomb on Moscow and Leningrad to prompt a Soviet agreement on Korea

Fulgencio Batista seizes power in Cuba

Eisenhower Administration

1953

Eisenhower announces end of Formosa's neutralization, thereby unleashing Chiang Kai-shek to attack Chinese mainland

Secretary of State John Foster Dulles pledges to "roll back" the Iron Curtain and liberate Eastern Europe

Chinese Nationalists attack Communist Chinese mainland

Greece, Turkey, and Yugoslavia sign treaty of friendship

Stalin dies; power struggle erupts involving Malenkov, Molotov, and Khrushchev

Eisenhower administration proposes nuclear weapons to redress personnel gaps in European rearmament

Vietnamese rebels attack Laos

Soviet Union extends diplomatic recognition to East Germany

Soviet tanks crush riots in East Berlin

Korean armistice signed at Panmunjom

Congressional resolution supports "liberation" of Eastern Europe

Dulles threatens resumption of Korean War

Soviet Union announces possession of hydrogen bomb

Shah of Iran returns from abroad to claim throne after CIA-designed coup overthrows government of Prime Minister Mohammed Mossadegh

Pact of Madrid approves U.S. naval bases in Spain

United States and South Korea sign mutual defense treaty

Eisenhower proposes "atoms for peace" plan at United Nations

1954

Dulles proclaims policy of deterrence through massive retaliation

Big Four foreign ministers meet in Berlin; Soviets reject German unification

Inter-American Conference in Caracas passes anticommunist declaration

Soviet Union accelerates Third World aid program to gain influence

United States and Japan sign mutual defense agreement

U.S. creates Food for Peace Program

Dulles proposes Anglo-American military intervention in Vietnam

Geneva Conference on Korea and Indochina opens

Nasser becomes prime minister of Egypt

Dien Bien Phu falls to Vietnamese communists

France, Britain, and the United States reject Soviet bid to join NATO

CIA helps conservative military officers overthrow a reform-minded Guatemalan government

Geneva Accords partition Vietnam and with U.S. support terminate French rule in Indochina

French National Assembly refuses to ratify treaty establishing the European Defense Community

Senator Joseph McCarthy attempts to prove communist infiltration of the U.S. Army in nationally televised hearings; Senate censures McCarthy

Algerian war for independence from France begins

Southeast Asia Treaty Organization (SEATO) created

Quemoy-Matsu crisis erupts; Dulles declares the United States is prepared to use atomic bomb on mainland China

Britain, Italy, Yugoslavia, and the United States sign a Memorandum of Understanding ending the Trieste dispute

Paris agreements signed; West Germany invited to join NATO and rearm

United States signs a mutual defense treaty with Nationalist Chinese on Formosa

1955

Soviet Union ends the state of war with Germany

Baghdad Pact between Iraq and Turkey signed

Eisenhower pledges U.S. forces will remain in Europe as long as necessary

Bandung Conference convenes the nonaligned countries of Asia and Africa

West Germany joins NATO

Soviet Union signs a treaty with the Pankow regime of the Soviet occupied zone of Germany, granting it the prerogatives of a state

Iran, Pakistan, and the United Kingdom join Baghdad Pact

Soviet Union, Albania, Bulgaria, Czechoslovakia, East Germany, Hungary, Poland, and Romania form the Warsaw Pact

Soviet Union evacuates occupation forces from Austria and signs Austrian State Treaty requiring Austrian neutrality

United States and Communist China hold ambassadorial-level talks in Geneva

Taiwan Straits crisis develops; Eisenhower pledges defense of Formosa and the Pescadores Islands

First conference on the peaceful uses of atomic
energy convenes in Geneva
Ngo Dinh Diem announces suspension of elections
in South Vietnam
U.S. military advisers sent to South Vietnam

1956

Soviet Premier Khrushchev consolidates power;
attacks Stalin's policies at the Twentieth
Communist Party Congress
Pravda announces the dissolution of Cominform
United States offers aid to rebellious East European
countries
United States withdraws offer of assistance in
Aswan Dam project, accuses Nasser of playing
the Soviet Union against the West
Seventy nations, including the United States and
the Soviet Union, create International Atomic
Energy Agency
Nasser nationalizes Suez Canal
Israeli military attacks Egyptian troops in Sinai
Peninsula
Britain and France intervene in Egypt by occupying
Suez Canal area
Soviet forces suppress Hungarian revolution
Japan admitted to United Nations
Britain, France, and Israel agree to cease-fire and
withdrawal from Suez

1957

Eisenhower Doctrine pledges U.S. aid to Middle
Eastern countries resisting communist takeovers
United States agrees to supply Britain with guided
missiles
Treaties of Rome establishing the European
Economic Community (EEC) and European
Atomic Energy Community (Euratom) signed
United States resumes military support of Saudi
Arabia in exchange for lease of Dhahran airfield
U.S. military aid supplied to Jordan's King Hussein
United States accedes to Baghdad Pact as an
associate member
Britain tests hydrogen bomb
Syria expels U.S. embassy officials for allegedly
plotting coup; United States expels Syrian
ambassador in retaliation
Soviet Union develops intercontinental ballistic
missile (ICBM) capability

United States builds Defense Early Warning
System (DEW line) in Canada
UN General Assembly condemns Soviet
intervention in Hungary
Soviet Union launches Sputnik I and II, first earth
satellites

1958

United States launches its first space satellite,
Explorer I
Mao Tse-tung announces "Great Leap Forward" to
promote Chinese industrialization and
agricultural production
Egypt and Syria form United Arab Republic with
Nasser as president
United Nations convenes Law of the Sea
Conference
Last U.S. ground troops leave Japan
Soviet Union announces a unilateral suspension of
all nuclear arms tests
Vice President Nixon confronts hostile protesters
on South American tour
European Parliamentary Assembly meets for the
first time in Strasbourg
Khrushchev visits Beijing
Iraq's army takes power in bloody coup, allies with
United Arab Republic
U.S. Marines land in Lebanon; Soviet Union
protests intervention
U.S. nuclear submarine *Nautilus* navigates beneath
the North Pole to link the Atlantic and Pacific
oceans for first time
China bombards Quemoy; United States pledges
defense of the island
Khrushchev refuses to back China in Formosan
crisis
Soviet Union protests U.S. violation of its air space
Soviet Union offers United Arab Republic
assistance to build Aswan Dam
Soviet Union announces desire to terminate the
four-power agreement on the status of Berlin
Charles de Gaulle elected president of the French
Republic
Batista overthrown in Cuba; Fidel Castro assumes
power

1959

Anglo-Greek-Turkish agreement pledges
independence for Cyprus

Dalai Lama flees Tibet during revolt

Iraq withdraws from Baghdad Pact

OAS members reiterate principle of nonintervention at Santiago Conference

Vice President Nixon and Soviet Premier Khrushchev hold "kitchen debate" in Moscow about the relative merits of their countries' systems

United States denounces Soviet activity in widening civil war in Laos

Central Treaty Organization (CENTO) formed to replace Baghdad Pact for Middle East defense

Khrushchev visits the United States for Camp David meetings

Khrushchev proposes total world disarmament to UN General Assembly

Members of European Free Trade Association ("The Seven") ratify treaty

Inter-American Development Bank formed

Antarctic Treaty prohibits any military use of the region

1960

United States and Japan sign Treaty of Mutual Cooperation and Security

France explodes nuclear device, becomes fourth nuclear power

Soviet Deputy Premier Anastas Mikoyan visits Cuba

Ten-nation UN Disarmament Committee begins negotiations in Geneva

U-2 spy plane piloted by Francis Gary Powers shot down over Soviet territory; Khrushchev cancels U.S. tour in response

Military coup in Turkey

Communist states withdraw from the UN disarmament negotiations in Geneva

China resumes shelling of Quemoy

United States denounces Soviet presence in Cuba

UN Peacekeeping forces intervene to manage Congo crisis

U.S. Navy sent to Nicaragua and Guatemala to guard against Cuban threat

Soviet Union calls for ouster of UN secretary general and substitution of "troika" system

Khrushchev disrupts twenty-fifth United Nations anniversary session by pounding his shoe on table

United States develops submarine-launched ballistic missile (SLBM)

Organization of Petroleum Exporting Countries (OPEC) formed

United States and Canada join members of the OEEC to form the Organization for Economic Cooperation and Development (OECD)

1961

United States breaks relations with Cuba

Kennedy Administration

Kennedy proposes Alliance for Progress

Patrice Lumumba is killed; Soviets threaten unilateral action in the Congo

Union of South Africa leaves British Commonwealth

United States calls SEATO to action in Laos

Soviet Union agrees to Laotian cease-fire and peace talks

Soviet Union launches first person, Major Yuri Gagarin, into space

UN General Assembly condemns *apartheid* in South Africa

Invasion of Cuba at the Bay of Pigs by CIA-trained exiles fails

First American astronaut, Alan Shepard, launched into space

Dominican Republic dictator, Rafael Trujillo, assassinated; CIA involvement alleged

Kennedy and Khrushchev confer at Vienna summit conference

Syria secedes from the United Arab Republic

East Germany builds Berlin Wall with Soviet help to separate East and West Berlin

United States mobilizes for second Berlin airlift

Congress passes Foreign Assistance Act

Peace Corps made permanent U.S. agency

United States and Soviet Union resume nuclear weapons testing

United States sends additional military advisers to Vietnam

Cuba is declared a socialist republic based on Marxist-Leninist principles

Albania and Soviet Union break diplomatic relations

India seizes Portuguese Goa

1962

Kennedy signs Trade Expansion Act
U.S. military presence in Vietnam expanded
OAS votes to expel Cuba
Indonesian insurgency erupts against Dutch rule
Soviet Union releases U-2 pilot Francis Gary Powers
United States sends 5,000 troops to Thailand
during Laotian crisis
Laos agreement signed in Geneva
John Glenn becomes the first American to orbit the
earth
Seventeen-nation disarmament conference
convenes in Geneva
United States breaks diplomatic relations, suspends
aid to Peru following coup
France recognizes Algerian independence
U-2 photographs reveal Soviet missile sites in Cuba
Pro-Nasser revolutionaries overthrow monarchy in
Yemen
Sino-Indian border clash erupts
U.S. Navy blockades Cuba to prevent missile
installation by Soviets
Kennedy and Khrushchev end war threat with
Cuban missile agreement

1963

French President de Gaulle vetoes Britain's
admission to the Common Market
United States thwarts effort to let Beijing replace
Chinese Nationalist delegation at the United
Nations
Ten thousand additional U.S. military personnel
sent to Vietnam
Egypt, Syria, and Iraq discuss unity but fail to reach
agreement
Organization of African Unity (OAU) Charter
adopted in Addis Ababa
"Hot Line" agreement establishes direct
communication link between White House and
Kremlin
Kennedy speech at the American University urges
end to Cold War
First Yaoundé Convention (between the European
Economic Community and seventeen African
countries) signed
Limited Nuclear Test Ban Treaty signed
prohibiting nuclear tests in atmosphere, in outer
space, and under water

China lays claim to Soviet-occupied territory
De Gaulle announces France will not sign Limited
Test Ban Treaty
CIA backs assassination of South Vietnamese
President Ngo Dinh Diem
Operation Big Lift airlifts 14,500 U.S. troops to
Germany to demonstrate U.S. capability to
reinforce NATO forces rapidly
Kennedy assassinated; Vice President Johnson
succeeds to presidency

Johnson Administration

Military leaders oust Dominican Republic
President Juan Bosch; rebellion erupts
Greek-Turkish armed conflict erupts in Cyprus
Kennedy Round of Multilateral Trade Negotiations
begins

1964

France recognizes People's Republic of China
Panamanians riot over U.S. occupation of Canal
Zone; United States and Panama break
diplomatic relations
Soviet-Romanian rift develops
UN peacekeeping force (UNFICYP) enters Cyprus
Group of 77 formalized to pursue the objectives of
Third World countries
OAS members impose trade sanctions on Cuba
Gulf of Tonkin Resolution gives Johnson
congressional support to expand war in Vietnam
United Nations Conference on Trade and
Development (UNCTAD) convenes in Geneva
Brezhnev replaces Khrushchev as Soviet leader
U.S. warplanes bomb Ho Chi Minh Trail in Laos
China explodes its first nuclear device
Insurgencies against Portuguese rule erupt in
Angola and Mozambique

1965

United States escalates war by bombing North
Vietnam and sending 125,000 additional combat
troops to South Vietnam
United States launches world's first commercial
telecommunications satellite, *Early Bird*
Kashmir crisis culminates in war between India and
Pakistan

Soviet and East German authorities block land access to Berlin when West German Parliament holds session in West Berlin

United States intervenes in the Dominican Republic

Indonesian army crushes attempted coup, slaughters 500,000 people

Rhodesia issues unilateral declaration of independence; Britain imposes oil embargo on Rhodesia

1966

Indira Gandhi, Jawaharlal Nehru's daughter, becomes prime minister of India

Coups occur in Ghana, Nigeria, and Syria

France removes its armed forces from NATO military command

Civil war erupts in Uganda

International days of protest held against U.S. policy in Vietnam

United States begins bombing Hanoi-Haiphong area of North Vietnam

Johnson links U.S. action in Vietnam to Truman Doctrine

Chou En-lai visits Romania

European Economic Community establishes Common Agricultural Policy (CAP)

China tests its first guided missile

United States pledges at Manila Conference to continue Vietnam War until "just peace" reached

Unpiloted Surveyor I makes successful lunar landing

Chinese "Cultural Revolution" attempts to purge society of bourgeois elements

1967

United States and Soviet Union among over sixty nations that sign UN treaty governing exploration and use of outer space

United States deploys multiple warhead missiles (Soviet Union follows in 1968)

United States and Soviet Union increase commercial and cultural exchanges

Johnson and Vice President Nguyen Cao Ky of Vietnam confer at Guam

United States lends Bolivia military support against Cuban insurgency led by Ché Guevara

Arab-Israeli Six-Day War erupts

Suez Canal closed (until June 1975)

Treaty establishing a single executive for the European Community (EC) by replacing with one Commission and one Council the ECSC High Authority and the EEC and Euratom Commission enters into force

Association of South-East Asian Nations (ASEAN) created

Johnson and Soviet Premier Aleksey Kosygin meet for Glassboro summit

Biafra rebels against Nigerian rule, leading to bitter civil war

De Gaulle makes "Free Quebec" speech supporting French Canadian separatist movement during state visit to Canada

People's Republic of South Yemen proclaimed

King Hussein of Jordan visits Soviet Union

Ché Guevara killed in Bolivian ambush

1968

North Korea seizes U.S. intelligence ship *Pueblo* within or near its territorial waters

North Vietnamese and Vietcong forces launch Tet Offensive against U.S. and South Vietnamese troops; regarded a major setback for the United States

U.S. troops massacre Vietnamese civilians at My Lai

Johnson asks for peace settlement in Vietnam; announces he will not seek reelection

Martin Luther King, Jr., civil rights leader and winner of 1964 Nobel Peace Prize, assassinated

Vietnam peace talks begin in Paris

Communist Party leaders in Czechoslovakia endorse policy of resisting Soviet pressure

Haiti charges the United States with bombing its capital

Nuclear non-Proliferation Treaty signed at the United Nations

Warsaw Pact troops invade Czechoslovakia to quell "Prague Spring"

U.S. ambassador to Guatemala killed by terrorists

Treaty prohibiting nuclear weapons in Latin America enters into force

Violent antiwar demonstrations occur during Democratic National Convention in Chicago

Albania withdraws from Warsaw Pact

Peru nationalizes U.S. oil interests

Nixon elected president; promises "secret" plan to end Vietnam War

NATO denounces Soviet intervention in Czechoslovakia

Crew of *Pueblo* released by North Korea

Nixon Administration

1969

Nixon supports strategic arms talks; recommends deployment of antiballistic missiles (ABMs) to enhance U.S. bargaining position

Secret U.S. bombing of Cambodia begins

National Security Council study recommends U.S. support for white African regimes

Sino-Soviet border clashes erupt along Ussuri River and on Damansly Island

Nixon calls for "Vietnamization" of Southeast Asian war, announces troop reductions

French President de Gaulle resigns and is replaced by Georges Pompidou

El Salvador and Honduras engage in military clash

First phase (75,000 soldiers) of U.S. troop withdrawal from Vietnam begins

Nixon signals new line toward Beijing by allowing American tourists to bring home $100 worth of Chinese-made goods

Neil Armstrong becomes the first person to set foot on the moon

Second Yaoundé Convention signed

North Korea shoots down U.S. reconnaissance plane over Sea of Japan

Nixon Doctrine reduces U.S. commitment overseas and asks allies to share in the defense burden

North Vietnamese President Ho Chi Minh dies

Violence escalates between Protestants and Catholics in Northern Ireland

Nixon suspends Seventh Fleet's nineteen-year-long patrol of Taiwan Straits

First round of Strategic Arms Limitations Talks (SALT) talks held in Helsinki, Finland

Congress bars involvement of U.S. ground troops in Laos and Thailand

1970

Albania and People's Republic of China conclude trade agreement

First NATO communications satellite launched from Cape Kennedy

United States invades Cambodia

Student protests against Vietnam War result in four deaths by National Guard at Kent State University; 448 American universities close or go on strike

Senate repeals Gulf of Tonkin Resolution

United States offers cease-fire plan to end Arab-Israeli fighting

Soviet Union and West Germany sign friendship treaty affirming European borders as permanent

Nasser dies; Anwar Sadat becomes president of Egypt

Salvador Allende, a socialist, elected president of Chile

U.S. forces in Vietnam reduced to below 400,000

Treaty normalizing relations between Poland and West Germany signed in Warsaw

1971

Seabed Arms Control Treaty signed

Canada and People's Republic of China exchange diplomatic envoys

U.S.-China relations warm as China hosts U.S. table-tennis team

India-Pakistan war erupts following crisis in Bengal

Bengal, renamed Bangladesh, gains independence

The *New York Times* begins publication of the *Pentagon Papers*

National Security Advisor Henry Kissinger secretly visits China to arrange Nixon visit

Nixon inaugurates New Economic Policy (NEP), effectively suspending the 1944 Bretton Woods Agreement and convertibility of the U.S. dollar

United States and Soviet Union reach "accidents measures" agreement designed to reduce risk of nuclear war

People's Republic of China takes China's seat in the United Nations

Fighting in Indochina spreads to Laos and Cambodia

Four-Power Agreement on Berlin signed by World War II allies

United States conducts large-scale bombing of North Vietnam and Vietcong supply routes in Cambodia

1972

Britain, Denmark, and Ireland agree to join European Community by 1973

Nixon visits China, pledges normalization of relations in Shanghai Communiqué

Lon Nol takes control of Cambodian government

Britain assumes direct control of Northern Ireland

United States and Soviet Union sign Biological Weapons Convention

Nixon orders Haiphong Harbor mined and widens air war against Vietnam

United States returns Okinawa to Japan

Nixon becomes first American postwar president to visit Soviet Union

United States and Soviet Union sign interim SALT agreement and ABM Treaty

Watergate affair begins as burglars of Democratic National Headquarters in the Watergate complex are arrested

United States and North Vietnam resume Paris peace talks

Soviet Union purchases massive amounts of U.S. grain

Sadat expels all Soviet advisers and technicians from Egypt

Japan recognizes People's Republic of China and begins trade relations

Palestinian terrorists kill Israeli athletes and others in Munich Olympic Village

Philippine President Ferdinand Marcos declares martial law in response to alleged "communist rebellion"

SALT II talks begin in Geneva

"Basic Treaty" signed by East and West Germany

Paris peace talks break down; United States resumes heavy bombing of North Vietnam on Christmas day

1973

Vietnam cease-fire signed in Paris provides for withdrawal of U.S. troops from Vietnam within sixty days

United States and China open liaison offices in each other's capitals

United States and Soviet Union sign agreement to prevent nuclear war

Conference on Security and Cooperation in Europe (CSCE) begins

Chile's socialist President Allende killed in military coup; CIA complicity alleged

Algiers summit of nonaligned nations begins

Juan Perón returns from exile, elected president of Argentina

East and West Germany establish diplomatic relations

Yom Kippur War erupts between Israel and its Arab adversaries

Arab members of OPEC impose oil embargo on Western supporters of Israel

Founding session of the Trilateral Commission is held in Tokyo

Talks on Mutual and Balanced Force Reductions (MBFR) in Europe begin

Congress passes War Powers Resolution over Nixon's veto

UN Conference on the Law of the Sea convenes with 157 participants

Tokyo Round of GATT trade negotiations begins

OPEC's six Persian Gulf members double the price of crude oil

1974

Military coup in Ethiopia places Marxist regime in power

Cuba sends troops to Yemen

Organization of Arab Petroleum Exporting Countries (OAPEC) lifts oil embargo

Military coup in Lisbon ends Portuguese rule in Guinea-Bissau and Mozambique

India explodes its first nuclear device

Group of 77 passes the Declaration on the Establishment of a New International Economic Order (NIEO)

Secretary of State Kissinger mediates Golan Heights cease-fire between Syria and Israel

United States and Soviet Union sign ABM Protocol Treaty on limitation of antiballistic systems and Threshold Test Ban Treaty limiting underground nuclear tests

Turkish-Greek conflict erupts when Turkey invades Cyprus following coup

Military regime in Greece resigns

Nixon resigns as Congress prepares impeachment; Vice President Ford becomes president

Ford Administration

Greece withdraws from NATO integrated command in protest over Turkish involvement in Cyprus

Ford pardons Nixon for any criminal offenses committed while in office; widespread domestic protest ensues

Hughes-Ryan amendment requires CIA to report covert operations to Congress

Jackson-Vanik amendment to U.S. Trade Act places restrictions on provisions for most-favored-nation status for the Soviet Union and other communist nations

Ford-Brezhnev meeting in Vladivostok results in agreement on principles to govern arms control

Arab League endorses Palestine Liberation Organization (PLO) as sole legitimate representative of the Palestinian people

United States suspends all military aid to Turkey following Turkish invasion of Cyprus

1975

U.S.-Soviet trade agreement nullified

Vietnam launches a full-scale invasion of Cambodia, its former ally

European Community and forty-six African, Caribbean, and Pacific (ACP) countries sign first Lomé Convention

United States lifts embargo on arms sales to Pakistan and India

Senate publishes report of CIA plots to assassinate foreign leaders

Civil war widens in Lebanon

Lon Nol regime in Cambodia falls to insurgents led by Pol Pot

Last U.S. troops leave Vietnam as Saigon falls to communist forces

Mayaguez seized by Cambodia; U.S. Marines killed in rescue operation

Civil war intensifies in Angola

U.S. and Soviet spacecrafts achieve linkup

Final act of the Conference on Security and Cooperation in Europe signed in Helsinki

UN General Assembly brands Zionism "racial discrimination" over strong U.S. and Israeli protests

Biological Weapons Convention enters into force

United States condemns Cuban intervention in Angola and elsewhere in Africa

Ford visits China, but Taiwan remains obstacle to improved relations

Egypt and Israel reach agreement providing for Israeli withdrawal from Sinai and creation of UN buffer zone

1976

Insurgents supported by Cuba win control in Angola

Group of 77 proposes an integrated Programme for Commodities and "Common Fund" at UNCTAD IV meetings in Nairobi

Isabel Perón ousted from power in Argentina and placed under arrest

Kissinger tours Africa; Rhodesian compromise introduced

U.S.-Soviet Underground Nuclear Test agreement signed

Syria sends 30,000 peacekeeping troops into Lebanon under auspices of Arab League

U.S. ambassador to Lebanon slain

Israeli commando raid at Entebbe Airport in Uganda rescues 103 hijacked passengers

Mao Tse-tung dies

Carter Administration

1977

Carter grants limited amnesty to Vietnam War draft evaders and military deserters

Carter pledges phased withdrawal of U.S. troops from South Korea

Argentina, Brazil, El Salvador, and Guatemala reject U.S. aid in reaction to attacks on their human rights practices

Angola invades Zaire

Soviet Union charges U.S. human rights stance constitutes interference in its internal affairs

Israeli prime minister Menachem Begin pledges never to negotiate over "liberated" territory

Spain holds first elections in thirty-eight years and legalizes Communist Party

Carter cancels B-1 bomber, proposes development of cruise missile

U.S. resumes diplomatic representation in Cuba

Carter and Panamanian president sign Panama Canal treaties

Vietnam is admitted to the United Nations

United States and Soviet Union agree to adhere to existing SALT pact while SALT II negotiations continue

United States withdraws from International Labor Organization (ILO)

UN Security Council unanimously votes arms embargo against South Africa

Somalia breaks relations with Cuba, expels all Soviet advisers, and renounces 1974 friendship treaty with Moscow

Egyptian President Sadat visits Israel, other Arab states break relations with Egypt in protest

1978

Kampuchea (Cambodia) breaks relations with Vietnam after border clash

Ethiopian army, aided by Soviets and Cubans, captures Somali stronghold of Jijiga

Israeli armed forces invade southern Lebanon

Carter postpones production of neutron bomb

President Mohammed Daud of Afghanistan overthrown by procommunist forces

Sino-Japanese peace treaty signed

Camp David summit reaches framework for peace between Egypt and Israel

Vietnam withdraws request for U.S. war reparations; United States announces intention to establish diplomatic relations with Vietnam

United States and Soviet Union sign convention prohibiting hostile uses of environmental modification techniques

Karol Cardinal Wojtyla of Poland becomes Pope John Paul II, furthers communications between Catholic Church and Eastern European leaders

China breaks negotiations with Vietnam

Shah of Iran orders military takeover to control protests against his regime

United States ends three-year Turkish arms embargo

Soviet Union announces testing of neutron bomb as well as decision not to put it into production

Carter administration establishes diplomatic relations with Beijing and renounces mutual defense treaty with Taiwan

1979

Deng Xiaoping becomes first top-ranking Chinese Communist leader to visit the United States

Kampuchea National United Front takes Phnom Penh and six other provinces with help of 100,000 Vietnamese troops

Shah leaves Iran; Ayatollah Khomeini returns triumphant from exile

Soviets deploy 10,000 troops in disputed islands north of Japan

China invades Vietnam in retaliation for its intervention in Kampuchea

Israeli Prime Minister Begin and Egyptian President Sadat sign a formal peace treaty in Washington

China allows 1950 Soviet friendship treaty to expire

United States cuts aid to Pakistan to deter Pakistan's acquisition of nuclear weapons

Tanzanian forces end Idi Amin's eight-year rule in Uganda

European Community launches European Monetary System

Europeans vote in first direct election of 410-member European Parliament

Carter and Soviet President Brezhnev sign SALT II agreement in Vienna

Vietnam joins Comecon

Nicaraguan dictator Antonio Somoza resigns and Sandinista rebels come to power

Central Treaty Organization dissolved

Treaty on exploitation of moon's riches agreed to by UN Committee on Peaceful Uses of Outer Space

Brezhnev offers unilateral withdrawal of 20,000 troops and 1,000 tanks from East Germany

Carter announces decision to deploy MX missile system

Iranian students seize hostages in U.S. embassy in Teheran

United States freezes Iranian assets

NATO agrees to deploy 572 U.S. cruise and medium-range missiles in Western Europe

Second Lomé Convention between the European Community and ACP countries signed

Soviet troops enter Afghanistan, install Babrak Karmal as prime minister

Islamic fundamentalists seize Grand Mosque in Mecca

Panama Canal Act returns Canal Zone to
Panamanian jurisdiction, leaving canal under
U.S. administration through 1999

1980

Carter imposes economic sanctions on the Soviet
Union for its invasion of Afghanistan

United States announces sale of $280 million in
defensive arms to Taiwan

United States and China complete process of
normalizing relations

Senate tables SALT II treaty in light of Soviet
invasion of Afghanistan

Carter Doctrine pledges U.S. defense of Persian
Gulf oil fields

United States obtains access to military facilities in
Oman, Kenya, and Somalia

UN Security Council Resolution 465 censures Israel

Rhodesia becomes independent, renamed Zimbabwe

Carter breaks diplomatic relations with Iran

U.S. military operation to rescue hostages in Iran
aborted; Secretary of State Cyrus Vance resigns
in protest

Marshal Tito of Yugoslavia dies

European Community foreign ministers agree to
sanctions against Iran

United States leads boycott of Moscow Olympics
over Soviet presence in Afghanistan

Israel annexes East Jerusalem

Presidential Directive 59 gives Soviet military targets
priority over cities in U.S. strategic warplan

Polish Solidarity workers' strike wins right to form
independent unions

Soviet Union threatens military intervention to end
Polish liberalization

Iraq invades Iran in controversy over Shatt al Arab
waterway

Boatlift brings 125,000 Cuban refugees to the
United States

"Gang of Four" trial opens in China as criticisms of
Mao Tse-tung mount

United States rejects Brezhnev proposal for
nonintervention in Persian Gulf

1981

Greece becomes the tenth member of the European
Community

The European currency unit (ECU) replaces the
European unit of account (EUA)

Reagan Administration

Fifty-two American hostages released by Iran after
444 days in captivity

United States announces international terrorism
will replace human rights as foreign policy
priority

United States halts aid to Nicaragua

Reagan wounded in assassination attempt

Nonaligned nations call for withdrawal of Soviet
troops from Kampuchea and Afghanistan

Zimbabwe announces diplomatic ties with Soviets

Rightist coup fails in Spain

United States sends military advisers to El Salvador

United States lifts Soviet grain embargo

Socialist candidate François Mitterand becomes
president of France

Pope John Paul II wounded in assassination attempt

United States casts sole vote against a World
Health Organization (WHO) proposal to limit
sale of infant formula in Third World

Israeli jets destroy Iraq's nearly completed nuclear
reactor

United States and China announce joint
monitoring of Soviet missile development from
China

Saudi Arabia proposes peace plan that names East
Jerusalem as capital of independent Palestinian
state

U.S. Navy jets shoot down two Libyan fighters over
Mediterranean Sea

At UN, Secretary of State Alexander Haig berates
Soviet's international behavior

China makes peace overture to Taiwan, is rebuffed

Egyptian President Sadat assassinated

Commonwealth nations decry the superpowers'
slide from détente to confrontation

Twenty-two-nation Cancún summit on North-
South relations convenes

Ninety-three nonaligned nations issue a report
describing the United States as the only threat
to world peace and prosperity

Reagan's remark that nuclear war could be limited
to Europe unleashes storm of protests

Congress approves sale of airborne warning and
control systems (AWACs) to Saudi Arabia

Polish government imposes martial law; United States retaliates with economic sanctions against Poland and the Soviet Union

1982

United States offers "zero-option" arms control proposal

Reagan announces United States will resume development of chemical weapons

Caribbean Basin Initiative announced

UN approves Law of the Sea Treaty; United States announces it will not sign

British Falkland Islands are captured by Argentine forces; Reagan pledges U.S. support for Great Britain

British land troops on the Falkland Islands, Argentine forces surrender

Nicaragua signs $166 million aid agreement with the Soviet Union

United States condemns alleged Soviet and Cuban-backed military buildup in Nicaragua

Brezhnev announces temporary freeze on deployment of Soviet SS-20 missiles

United States accuses Soviet Union of widespread use of chemical warfare agents

Morocco agrees to U.S. use of Moroccan air bases during emergencies in the Middle East

Spain becomes sixteenth member of NATO

Israel invades Lebanon and surrounds the PLO by laying seige to West Beirut

United States suspends comprehensive test ban negotiations

Japan announces plans to increase military spending

United States embargoes sale of equipment for natural gas pipeline between Siberia and Western Europe; European Community protests U.S. ban

Marines land in Lebanon as part of multinational peacekeeping force

United States assists Mexico with a multibillion-dollar debt relief plan

Defense Department papers advocating a "winnable" nuclear war strategy cause outrage in Europe

Lebanese President Bashir Gemayel assassinated

Lebanese Christian forces massacre hundreds in Palestinian refugee camps

Polish government bans the Solidarity union;

United States suspends Poland's most-favored-nation trade status in retaliation

Soviet President Leonid Brezhnev dies; Yuri Andropov becomes Communist Party general secretary

Indira Gandhi asks the Soviet Union for assistance in building several nuclear power stations

1983

United States and Honduras hold joint war games in Central America

Reagan's Strategic Defense Initiative (SDI—"Star Wars") proposal seeks to render nuclear weapons "impotent and obsolete"

International Monetary Fund (IMF) lending capability increased substantially

Soviet Union proposes a nuclear free zone in Central Europe

Pope John Paul II meets with General Jaruzelski and Solidarity union leader Lech Walesa in Poland

Reagan endorses Central American peace efforts of the Contadora Group (Mexico, Colombia, Panama, and Venezuela)

United States and France assist Chad and the Sudan following Libyan attack on Chad

Philippine opposition leader Benigno Aquino assassinated on return to Manila from the United States

Soviet Union shoots down a Korean passenger plane after it strays into Soviet airspace

Truck-bomb attack in Beirut kills 241 U.S. military personnel

United States invades Grenada

Raul Alfonsin elected president of Argentina, ending eight years of military rule

PLO forces are evacuated from Lebanon to several Middle Eastern nations

Syria downs two U.S. jets during a U.S. raid on Syrian positions

West Germany deploys U.S. Pershing II missiles

1984

Rev. Jesse Jackson secures release of Navy pilot downed by Syria

Terrorists assassinate president of American University of Beirut

Pakistani scientist claims Pakistan can produce nuclear weapons

William Buckley, CIA station chief in Beirut, is kidnapped

U.S. Marines in Beirut withdraw to offshore ships

Soviet leader Andropov dies; Chernenko assumes power

CIA assists *contras* in mining the main Nicaraguan port

Reagan meets with Deng Xiaoping in China, signs agreements on economic and technological relations

Seven major industrialized countries issue a declaration on East-West relations and arms control at London summit

Soviet Union and several Soviet allies refuse to participate in the summer Olympic games in Los Angeles

Indian army attacks Sikh holy shrine, killing Sikh leader Jarnail Bhindranwale and hundreds of others

Britain and China reach agreement on the future of Hong Kong

International banks agree to reschedule Mexico's debt obligations

Congress bans direct or indirect military aid to the *contras*

Prime Minister Indira Gandhi of India assassinated by Sikh bodyguards

1985

United States launches first space shuttle for exclusively military purposes

PLO Leader Yasser Arafat and Jordan's King Hussein agree on framework for peace

Soviet leader Chernenko dies; Gorbachev becomes Communist Party general secretary

United States and Soviet Union begin comprehensive arms control negotiations

Eighty Asian and African countries convene in Bandung

Israel withdraws from Lebanon

Terry A. Anderson of the Associated Press is kidnapped in Beirut

Reagan visits Bitburg cemetery where Nazi soldiers are buried, provoking protests by Jewish leaders and others

Reagan announces the United States will continue to honor the unratified SALT II treaty

Gorbachev proposes a ban on nuclear weapons by 2000

Radio Marti begins broadcasts to Cuba; Castro breaks a U.S.-Cuba immigration pact and threatens to end his cooperation on hijackings in protest

Shi'ite Muslims hijack TWA airliner

South African President P. W. Botha declares state of emergency

Reagan approves shipment of arms to Iran

United States and China sign a nuclear cooperation agreement

Reagan and Gorbachev meet in Geneva to discuss arms control and the future of U.S.-Soviet relations

Palestinians hijack Italian cruise liner *Achille Lauro*

U.S. Navy fighter planes force Egyptian airliner carrying four fleeing Palestinian hijackers to land in Sicily

Yasser Arafat renounces terrorist acts outside Israeli-occupied territories

Reagan authorizes covert CIA assistance to *contras*

Ireland and Britain sign treaty giving Ireland role in Northern Ireland

Terrorists attack holiday travelers on the Israeli airline El Al at Rome and Vienna airports

1986

United States withdraws from UNESCO

Reagan authorizes arms shipments to Iran in an effort to win release of American hostages

U.S. space shuttle *Challenger* explodes seventy-four seconds after liftoff

President-for-life Haitian Jean-Claude Duvalier abdicates and flees

Philippine President Marcos flees to Hawaii, Corazon Aquino becomes new president

Senate approves treaty outlawing genocide thirty-seven years after Truman sent it to the Senate

United States orders Soviet Union to cut its UN staff in New York by a third

Reagan orders a military attack against Libya in retaliation for its alleged sponsorship of state terrorism

United States sends five hundred TOW precision-guided antitank missiles to Israel for shipment to Iran

OPEC nations condemn U.S. bombing of Libya but reject new oil embargo

Soviet nuclear reactor at Chernobyl explodes, emitting radiation over Europe

Kurt Waldheim, former UN secretary-general, accused of complicity in World War II atrocities as Nazi officer

New Zealand withdraws from ANZUS defense pact

World Court rules against United States in Nicaraguan case; United States ignores decision

U.S. military joins Bolivia in war on international drug trafficking

Reagan administration reaffirms South African policy of "constructive engagement"; Bishop Desmond Tutu condemns the United States

East-West security pact grants signatories right to observe troop maneuvers in any European state

Summit of nonaligned nations held in Zimbabwe

GATT nations meet in Uruguay to plan new round of global trade negotiations

Reagan administration leaks "disinformation" about Libya to journalists; Assistant Secretary of State Bernard Kalb resigns in protest

Plane carrying arms to the *contras* as part of National Security Council supply operation shot down over Nicaragua; Eugene Hasenfus captured

Reagan and Gorbachev meet in Reykjavik, Iceland; discuss strategic and intermediate-range nuclear weapons and possible elimination of all nuclear forces

General Motors and IBM announce suspension of operations in South Africa

Northern Mariana Islands become U.S. commonwealth, ending status as UN trust territories administered by the United States

Saboteurs sink Icelandic whaling ship to protest Iceland's violation of international ban on whaling

Attorney General Edwin Meese reveals diversion of money from Iranian arms sales to the *contras*

United States exceeds SALT II treaty limits with deployment of B-52 bomber equipped to carry cruise missiles

Demonstrations by Chinese students calling for democratic reforms spread

Soviet Union ends internal exile of Soviet dissident and Nobel Peace Prize winner Andrei D. Sakharov

United States increases import duties on some European Community products in response to high Spanish tariffs on U.S. feed grains; EC pledges to retaliate

1987

United States lifts ban on export of oil drilling equipment to Soviet Union

Reagan administration announces intention to sell $2.2 billion in military equipment to Egypt, Saudi Arabia, and Bahrain

Soviet Union resumes nuclear testing because of U.S. refusal to join its moratorium begun in August 1985

United States, Canada, Japan, and European Space Agency announce intention to operate jointly a space station in the mid-1990s

Brazil suspends interest payments on its foreign debt

Finance ministers of the leading industrial powers meeting at the Louvre in Paris agree to stabilize the U.S. dollar

Mexico signs agreement with its creditor banks for massive loan

United States offers naval protection to Kuwaiti oil tankers

United States and Soviet Union agree to establish centers for information exchange on missile tests and military activities

United States reveals illegal exports to the Soviet Union by Japanese and Norwegian firm enabled the Soviet Union to develop quieter submarines

United States launches massive Central American military exercise with Honduras

USS Stark struck by missiles fired by an Iraqi fighter in the Persian Gulf

New Zealand parliament bans nuclear-armed and nuclear-powered ships from New Zealand's ports

Afghan rebels reportedly down a Soviet transport plane with U.S. supplied Stinger missile

Reagan administration announces it will cut off all aid to Panama as opposition to government of Panamanian military ruler General Manuel Noriega grows

President Jayewardene of Sri Lanka and Prime Minister Rajiv Gandhi of India sign agreement to end rebellion of Sri Lankan Tamil minority

Reagan offers peace proposal to Nicaragua in cooperation with House Speaker Jim Wright

Western nations send minesweepers to Persian Gulf

Soviet Union confirms deployment of SS-24 missile, first to be launched from railroad cars

Defense Department approves testing of ground-based, space-based, and ground-launched components of SDI system

Costa Rican President Oscar Arias Sanchez awarded Nobel Peace Prize for his Central American peace efforts

Soviet Union agrees to repay all of its $245 million debt to the United Nations

U.S. stock market crashes; markets plummet worldwide

United States delays sale of high-technology equipment to China in retaliation for sale of Chinese Silkworm missiles to Iran

United States supplies Chad with Stinger missiles for its war with Libya

Spain announces it will not renew its bilateral defense agreement with the United States

UN Security Council condemns South African entry into Angola to combat Angolan and Cuban troops

Reagan and Gorbachev sign intermediate-range nuclear forces (INF) treaty during Washington summit

UN passes resolution "strongly deploring" Israel's reaction to Palestinian violence in the West Bank and Gaza Strip

1988

United States and Canada sign free-trade agreement

Noriega indicted by federal grand juries in Florida on racketeering and drug trafficking charges

Nicaraguan President Daniel Ortega agrees to negotiate with the Nicaraguan resistance

United States announces intention to end special trade privileges granted Hong Kong, Singapore, South Korea, and Taiwan

Gorbachev announces Soviet Union will withdraw its troops from Afghanistan

United States announces Romania's loss of most-favored-nation trade status

United States sends 3,200 troops to Honduras amid charges of border crossings by Nicaraguan soldiers

Finance ministers of the Group of Seven pledge to support the U.S. dollar

The right-wing National Republican Alliance (ARENA) gains control of the legislative assembly in El Salvador

Reagan criticizes Soviet human rights practices during Moscow summit

Worldwide conference of acquired immune deficiency syndrome (AIDS) researchers held in Stockholm

Thirty-nine nations sign agreement to permit commercial mining of Antarctica; strict environmental guidelines included

U.S. cruiser *Vincennes* shoots down an Iranian commercial jetliner over the Persian Gulf; all 290 aboard are killed

Saudi Arabia agrees to buy between $12 and $30 billion worth of military equipment from Britain

Iran and Iraq accept UN peace terms calling for a cease-fire

Soviet and American scientists meet at Nevada test site for first joint nuclear test

North and South Korea open talks in Panmunjom in anticipation of joint session of their parliaments

Turkey opens its borders to thousands of Kurds fleeing Iraqi advance against Kurdish rebels amid claims Iraq used poisonous gas

United States releases funds to pay UN dues; authorizes payment of back debt

World Bank agrees to lend Argentina $1.25 billion without agreement between Argentina and the IMF for domestic restructuring program

Generals Augusto Pinochet in Chile and Alfredo Stoessner in Paraguay fall from power

Gorbachev becomes new Soviet president, confirms hold on power

United States and the Philippines agree to extend U.S. access to military facilities at Subic Bay and Clark Air Force Base

United States denies visa to PLO leader Yasser Arafat seeking to address UN on Palestine; General Assembly deplores U.S. action and moves Palestine debate to Geneva

Soviet parliament approves sweeping constitutional changes

Gorbachev addresses UN, announces plan to sharply reduce Soviet military forces in Europe

Angola, Cuba, and South Africa sign agreement providing for Namibian independence and withdrawal of Cuban troops from Angola

International Court of Justice agrees to hear Nicaraguan suit against Honduras for harboring *contras*

India and Pakistan agree not to attack each other's nuclear power installations

1989

European Community bans some cattle imports; U.S. retaliates

U.S. fighters down two Libyan jets over Mediterranean Sea

Bush Administration

Bush attends funeral of Japanese Emperor Hirohito

International conference on the ozone layer convenes in London; European Community agrees to ban production of chlorofluorocarbons

U.S. Treasury Secretary Nicholas F. Brady announces Third World debt reduction plan

Iranian Ayatollah Khomeini calls on Muslims to execute Salman Rushdie, author of *The Satanic Verses*

Gorbachev, on visit to Cuba, rejects "exporting revolution"

Israeli Prime Minister Yitzhak Shamir reveals plans for elections in occupied territories as part of peace proposal

United States and Japan reach agreement on coproduction of FSX fighter plane

Kenya calls for worldwide ban on ivory trade to save the elephant from extinction

Gorbachev visits China in first Sino-Soviet summit in thirty years

United States opens way for retaliation by charging Brazil, India, and Japan engage in unfair trade practices

Bush presents plan for conventional-force reductions in Europe at fortieth anniversary NATO Summit in Brussels

Chinese troops massacre hundreds in assault on Tiananmen Square prodemocracy demonstrators; United States announces sanctions against China

Agreement reached on reducing Mexican debt under Brady Plan

Cuba and South Africa withdraw forces from Angola

Solidarity assumes power in Poland, first noncommunist government in Eastern Europe

Hungary's Communist Party becomes Socialist Party; hardline party chief Karoly Grosz ousted

Soviet Foreign Minister Eduard Shevardnadze concedes Soviet radar installation at Krasnoyarsk violates 1972 ABM Treaty

Gorbachev declares Brezhnev Doctrine "dead," pledges not to interfere in Eastern European upheaval

East Germany opens its borders to the West; thousands cross Berlin Wall unopposed

Iran-Iraq War ends

Bulgarian leader Todor Zhivkov ousted after thirty-five years in power

Elections held in Namibia; South West African People's Organization (SWAPO) captures majority in constituent assembly

Philippine rebels attempt coup; U.S. supports Aquino government with military show of force

Bush and Gorbachev meet at Malta to discuss trade and arms reductions

U.S. National Security Adviser Brent Scowcroft arrives in Beijing in surprise visit

Cuban President Fidel Castro pledges to uphold socialism, fight global domination by U.S. of new world order

First noncommunist government in forty-one years assumes power in Czechoslovakia

Tibet's Dalai Lama accepts Nobel Peace Prize; remains committed to nonviolence in seeking end to China's forty-year occupation of Tibet

Central American presidents meet in regional peace summit, seek end to U.S. aid to *contras* and demobilization of rebels in El Salvador

Noriega named chief of government; Panamanian assembly declares "state of war" exists with United States

United States invades Panama

Romanian dictator Ceausescu overthrown, tried, and executed

OAS, by a vote of twenty to one, "deeply deplores" U.S. invasion of Panama

Soviet Congress of People's Deputies condemns 1939 Nazi-Soviet nonaggression pact and secret protocols dividing Europe into spheres of influence

1990

South African government frees Nelson Mandela after twenty-seven-year imprisonment

Bush meets in Cartagena, Colombia, with Latin American presidents to deal with drug trade

Violeta Barrios de Chamorro defeats Sandinista President Ortega, ends decade of leftist rule in Nicaragua; United States promises to lift sanctions

Israel accepts U.S. proposal for involving Palestinians in preliminary peace talks with Israel

Lithuania declares independence; Gorbachev warns Lithuania to end revolt

East Germany holds first free elections; coalition favoring quick unification victorious

Namibia, Africa's last colony, becomes independent; ends seventy-five years of South African rule

Hungarians hold first free elections after forty-three years of Communist rule

American hostage Robert Polhill released by Shiite Moslem militants in Beirut after 1,182 days in captivity

European Community adopts plan for political union by 1993

President F. W. de Klerk and African National Congress leader Nelson Mandela begin talks on ending white-minority rule in South Africa

Communist rebels in the Philippines warn United States to "go home" as negotiations on future of U.S. bases begin

Romanians vote in nation's first free elections in more than fifty years

United States renews most-favored-nation trade status for China

Bush and Gorbachev sign chemical weapons accord during Washington summit

Gorbachev agrees to permit a reunited Germany to remain in NATO, pledges to remove 380,000 Soviet troops from East Germany

Berlin Wall "Checkpoint Charlie" removed

Iraq threatens Kuwait with military attack to force compliance with OPEC oil production quotas

Liberian rebels overrun most of Monrovia; U.S. military attaché expelled

Iraq invades Kuwait, overthrows Kuwaiti government

UN Security Council orders worldwide embargo on trade with Iraq

U.S. troops dispatched to Persian Gulf region

Soviet Union joins United States in backing UN Security Council resolution calling for enforcement of Iraq embargo

Cambodian factions agree to peace plan, UN supervision

World War II victors sign treaty giving sanction to German reunification

Israel blasts unanimous UN Security Council resolution blaming it for Palestinians' deaths

Treaty on Conventional Forces in Europe eliminates thousands of non-nuclear weapons

British Prime Minister Margaret Thatcher resigns, ends tenure as Europe's longest-serving prime minister in twentieth century

Bush promises to seek U.S.-Mexican free-trade agreement

UN Security Council authorizes use of force against Iraq

Iraq fires surface-to-surface missile in first test since invasion of Kuwait

Kohl's Christian Democrat and Christian Social Union coalition wins first free all-German elections since 1932

Bush visits Chile during Latin American trip in first U.S. presidential visit in thirty years

Uruguay Round of GATT trade negotiations collapses

1991

President Bush announces collective military action against Iraq

Council of Europe votes to accept Czechoslovakia as a member

Canada announces intention to enter U.S.-Mexico talks on NAFTA

United States and Colombia agree to improve trade and fight drug trafficking in Colombia

Persian Gulf War ends

Bush pledges United States will destroy its stockpile of chemical weapons

Serbian and Croatian Presidents Milosevic and Tudjman agree to cooperate to avert a breakup of Yugoslavia

United States withdraws last of its medium-range nuclear missiles from Europe

UN Security Council condemns Iraqi repression of Kurds; United States air-drops supplies for Kurds in northern Iraq

Bush announces proposals on arms limitations in the Middle East

France announces intention to sign 1968 nuclear Nonproliferation Treaty

Soviet troops withdraw completely from Hungary, Czechoslovakia

Serb-dominated Yugoslav army begins repression in Slovenia and Croatia

South African government announces willingness to sign nuclear Nonproliferation Treaty

Warsaw Pact formally disbands

Bush and Gorbachev sign Strategic Arms Reduction Treaty (START)

China announces it will sign nuclear Nonproliferation Treaty

Soviet President Gorbachev resigns as secretary general of Soviet Communist Party

Ukrainian Parliament declares independence from Soviet Union; Byelorussia, Moldavia, Azerbaijan, Crimea, Tadzikistan follow

Argentina, Brazil, and Chile renounce chemical weapons

Croatia and Slovenia secede from Yugoslavia, Macedonia declares independence

UN General Assembly votes to admit North and South Korea, the Marshall Islands, Micronesia, Estonia, Latvia, and Lithuania

Haitian President Aristide overthrown in a military coup

1959 Antarctic Treaty banning military activity and limiting scientific research expanded to halt mining and oil exploration activities, set guidelines for waste disposal

UN Security Council subjects Iraq to a permanent ban on nuclear, chemical, and biological weapons

NATO defense ministers agree on reduction in tactical nuclear bombs stockpiled in Europe

European Community and the European Free Trade Area agree to establish a European free-trade area

United States orders ban on trade with Haiti

Russia, Ukraine, and Byelorussia declare end to Soviet Union, proclaim a new "Commonwealth of Independent States" (CIS) open to all Soviet

Republics; leaders agree to joint control of former Soviet nuclear weapons

UN General Assembly endorses conventional arms register to record information on weapons imports and exports

North and South Korea sign agreement pledging a peaceful coexistence

Russia, Kazakhstan, Byelorussia, and Ukraine promise to carry out all cuts in nuclear weapons agreed to by Bush and Gorbachev

Bosnia and Herzogovina ask the United Nations to send peacekeeping forces

Gorbachev resigns as the president of the Soviet Union

1992

Peace treaty ends twelve-year civil war in El Salvador

European Community formally recognizes independence of Croatia and Slovenia

China and India establish diplomatic relations with Israel

Pakistan reveals nuclear weapon capability, promises restraint in interest of nonproliferation

United States moves to end production of chemicals detrimental to the ozone layer

Bush administration lifts curbs on high-tech exports to China

UN Security Council resolves to send peacekeeping troops to Croatia

United States and Mexico release "Integrated Border Plan" addressing pollution problems along U.S.-Mexico border

U.S. Congress ties renewal of China's most-favored-nation trade status to human rights reforms

Iraq refuses to allow UN team to dismantle Scud missile production plants as mandated by Gulf War cease-fire

United Nations admits Armenia, Azerbaijan, Kazakhstan, Kyrgyzstan, Moldova, Tajikistan, Turkmenistan, Uzbekistan, and San Marino

UN Human Rights Commission votes to condemn Cuba for human rights violations

North and South Korea agree to mutual inspection of suspected nuclear weapons sites

Iranian planes bomb rebel bases in first major Iranian attack on Iraqi targets since 1988 cease-fire

European Community and United States recognize Bosnia-Herzegovina

France suspends nuclear weapons testing

UN commission demarcating Iran-Iraq border awards Kuwait part of Iraq's only operating seaport and part of an oil field along the countries' borders

Afghanistan's collapsed government relinquishes power to Mujaheddin rebels

China conducts its largest nuclear test

France and Germany agree to a joint military force outside auspices of NATO

United States and four CIS nuclear members agree to comply with START

World's leading arms suppliers agree to stop spread of nuclear, chemical, and biological weapons technology

Danish voters reject Maastricht treaty on European Union

UN Conference on Environment and Development (UNCED) opens in Rio de Janeiro

UNCED delegates approve treaty to reduce greenhouse gas emissions; United States refuses to support biodiversity convention

Bush and Yeltsin agree to reduce nuclear arsenals to half of levels mandated by START

NATO announces removal of all U.S. ground-based tactical nuclear weapons from Europe

U.S. Senate calls for immediate moratorium and eventual ban on nuclear testing

UN Security Council authorizes use of force to ensure delivery of humanitarian aid to Bosnia-Herzegovina

South Korea and China establish diplomatic relations; Taiwan breaks diplomatic relations with South Korea

Tenth summit of the Nonaligned Movement convenes in Jakarta, Indonesia

Vietnam agrees to return personal effects of U.S. personnel left from Vietnam War

Cuba and Russia sign trade accord, agree to maintain Cuban intelligence-gathering station

UN Security Council imposes naval blockade against Yugoslavia

UN Security Council authorizes U.S.-led military forces to "use all necessary means" to help deliver food and humanitarian assistance to Somalia

NATO announces willingness to enforce a no-fly zone over Bosnia

1993

European Community launches open internal economic market

Czechoslovakia splits into the Czech Republic and Slovakia

Over 120 nations sign landmark treaty outlawing chemical weapons

Israeli Knesset overturns law prohibiting Israelis' contact with PLO members

Clinton Administration

Terrorist bomb explodes in parking garage below World Trade Center in New York City

NATO members fail to agree on U.S. proposal to send peacekeeping troops to Bosnia

UN Security Council approves resolution to send UN peacekeeping force to Somalia

Bosnian Serbs reject UN-sponsored peace plan; tougher sanctions against Yugoslavia follow

Denmark ratifies Maastricht treaty, reversing 1992 defeat

United States and allied forces carry out attacks against Somali warlord Mohammed Farah Aidid

UN Security Council votes to impose oil, arms, and financial embargo on Haiti

Clinton orders missile attack on Iraq's intelligence headquarters after alleged plot to assassinate former President Bush

United States deploys 350 troops to Macedonia to participate in UN Protection Force

Russia extends moratorium on nuclear testing; United States reciprocates by extending its own moratorium

United States accuses China of violating the Missile Technology Control Regime, imposes sanctions on China and Pakistan

United States and Russia agree to build joint international space station by end of decade

Israeli Prime Minister Rabin and PLO Chairman Arafat sign preliminary accord, shake hands

China conducts underground nuclear weapon test, effectively breaks global moratorium

NATO agrees to offer former Warsaw Pact states

and others "partnerships for peace" as first step toward full alliance membership

North Korea blocks thorough UN inspection of nuclear weapons sites

U.S. Congress, Canadian parliament approve Nafta

Uruguay Round of GATT negotiations brought to successful conclusion

Britain and Ireland agree on framework for peace in Northern Ireland

United States withdraws combat troops from Somalia

Ukraine announces it will deactivate its nuclear arsenal

1994

United States and North Korea reach agreement on international inspection of North Korea's nuclear sites

United States ends nineteen-year trade embargo against Vietnam

United States agrees to increase aid to Kazakhstan after President Nazarbayev agrees to adhere to nuclear Nonproliferation Treaty

U.S. CIA counterintelligence officer Aldrich Ames and wife Rosario arrested on espionage charges

NATO fighters shoot down Bosnian Serb planes in first-ever combat action

Members of Organization for Economic Cooperation and Development, except United States, agree to ban hazardous-waste exports to Global South countries

Brazil and bank creditors agree to restructure Brazilian debt, ending decade-long global "debt crisis"

Thousands of refugees flee Rwanda to escape massacre

Israeli Prime Minister Rabin and PLO Chairman Arafat sign accord to implement Palestinian self-rule in Gaza Strip and Jericho

Clinton extends China's most favored-nation-status, human rights connection abandoned

UN War Crimes Commission set up to investigate war crimes in Bosnia

Presidents of Mexico, Colombia, and Venezuela agree to create common market

Russia formally enrolls in NATO's "Partnership for Peace" program

South Africa readmitted to UN General Assembly after twenty-year suspension

G-7 leaders meet in twentieth annual economic summit of industrial powers

United States signs the UN Convention on the Law of the Sea

UN Security Council authorizes U.S.-led multinational invasion force to oust Haitian military regime

United States stops sale of fighter aircraft to Pakistan when Pakistan fails to halt its nuclear weapons program

Russian officials deny that weapons-grade uranium seized in Germany was smuggled out of former Soviet Union

Japan agrees to spend $100 million to atone for its occupying forces' brutal behavior during World War II

Third UN Conference on Population and Development adopts sweeping program to stabilize world population growth

Former President Carter negotiates peaceful removal of Haitian military leaders; U.S. troops arrive in Haiti

Iraq deploys troops near Kuwait border; United States sends troops to Persian Gulf area

President Aristide returns to power in Haiti

Israel and Jordan sign peace treaty

Iraq recognizes Kuwait border in attempt to persuade United Nations to lift some sanctions

United States secretly transfers to the United States from Kazakhstan over 1,300 pounds of poorly protected weapons-grade uranium

Norwegian voters reject entry into European Union

United States hosts first summit of Western Hemisphere nations in three decades; nations agree to create free-trade zone

Yeltsin says Russia will use "all measures available" to disarm rival forces in breakaway Chechnya

U.S., Canada, and Mexico agree to eventually admit Chile to Nafta

Former President Carter flies to Sarajevo in attempt to resolve civil war; Bosnian Serbs agree to four-month ceasefire

1995

Clinton offers $20 billion to Mexico for peso rescue; action sidesteps Congress

First regional summit involving Israel backs peace talks

United States imposes punitive trade sanctions on China, largest in U.S. history

UN tribunal in first-ever move charges Serbian General Zeljko Meakic with genocide

Iraq allegedly sells oil in secret plan that skirts UN ban

U.S. dollar plunges on international markets despite coordinated, central bank market interventions

Nerve gas attack on Tokyo subways kills twelve, sickens thousands

Clinton visits Haiti to mark withdrawal of U.S. forces, assumption of police role by multinational forces

United States ends thirty-five year Cuban policy, negotiates with Cuba to return future boat people to Cuba

United States cuts off all trade with Iran; move enjoys little international support

Europe commemorates fiftieth anniversary of World War II victory (V-E Day)

Russia modifies Iranian nuclear reactor sale plan during U.S.-Russian summit in Moscow

UN conference agrees to indefinite extension of the nuclear Nonproliferation Treaty

Bosnian Serbs kill UN peacekeepers, hold others hostage to avert NATO air strikes

First meeting of the Conference of Parties under the Framework Convention on Climate Change convenes in Berlin

United States and Japan reach trade deal on automobiles, avert threatened U.S. punitive tariffs

Clinton administration grants Taiwan's president visa for unofficial visit to United States

U.S. space shuttle *Atlantis* docks with Russian space station *Mir*

China arrests Chinese-born American human rights activist for illegally obtaining China's state secrets

Bosnian Serbs overrun UN-designated "safe area"; later attack other safe areas

United States announces it will normalize relations with communist Vietnam

Congress votes to block additional U.S. loans to Mexico

Secret U.S. diplomatic efforts to help restore democracy to Nigeria disclosed

Croatia launches attack on Croatian Serbs, threatening renewed and wider war

U.S. Congress repudiates Clinton policy by voting to lift arms embargo against Bosnia; Clinton vetoes measure

Hiroshima marks 50th anniversary of destruction by first atomic bomb used in war

Clinton becomes first U.S. president to call for a ban on all nuclear tests worldwide

China conducts fourth underground nuclear test in 14 months

China initiates military exercises, fires guided missiles into sea near Taiwan

India and China hold talks aimed at reducing forces along disputed Himalayan border

Coordinated effort by United States, Japan, and Germany drives the value of the dollar to its highest levels in six months

U.S. Senate stalls ratification of Chemical Weapons Convention; treaty's future in doubt

NATO warplanes attack Bosnian Serb targets in response to bombing of Sarajevo; begin biggest military campaign in NATO's history

Zaire announces it will force Rwandan refugees to leave country

United Nations convenes Fourth World Conference on Women in Beijing; Hillary Rodham Clinton attends as honorary chair of U.S. delegation

France begins series of nuclear tests in South Pacific, abandoning its three-year moratorium

Bosnia's warring sides agree to framework for peace; United States continues aggressive diplomatic effort in former Yugoslavia

Pro-democracy candidates win last election in Hong Kong before British colony is taken over by China in 1997

Israel and the Palestine Liberation Organization agree to pact ending Israel's military occupation of West Bank cities; Prime Minister Rabin and PLO chief Arafat sign agreement in Washington

French police kill suspect in string of terrorist bombings believed supported by Algerian extremists

REFERENCES

• • •

ABRAHAMSEN, DAVID. (1977) *Nixon vs. Nixon: An Emotional Tragedy*. New York: Farrar, Straus and Giroux.

ABRAMSON, PAUL R., JOHN H. ALDRICH, AND DAVID W. ROHDE. (1994) *Change and Continuity in the 1992 Elections*. Washington, D.C.: CQ Press.

———. (1990) *Change and Continuity in the 1988 Elections*. Washington, D.C.: CQ Press.

———. (1986) *Change and Continuity in the 1984 Elections*. Washington, D.C.: CQ Press.

ACHEN, CHRISTOPHER H. (1989) "When Is a State with Bureaucratic Politics Representable as a Unitary Rational Actor?" Paper presented at the annual meeting of the International Studies Association, London, March 29–April 1.

ACHESON, DEAN. (1969) *Present at the Creation*. New York: Norton.

ADAMS, GORDON. (1994) "The New Politics of the Defense Budget," pp. 106–19 in Eugene R. Wittkopf (ed.), *The Domestic Sources of American Foreign Policy: Insights and Evidence*, 2nd ed. New York: St. Martin's Press.

———. (1988) "The Iron Triangle: Inside the Defense Policy Process," pp. 70–78 in Charles W. Kegley, Jr., and Eugene R. Wittkopf (eds.), *The Domestic Sources of American Foreign Policy: Insights and Evidence*. New York: St. Martin's.

ADELMAN, KENNETH L. (1981) "Speaking of America: Public Diplomacy in Our Time," *Foreign Affairs* 59 (Spring): 913–36.

ADORNO, THEODORE W., ELSE FRENKEL-BRUNSWIK, DANIEL J. LEVINSON, AND R. NEVITT SANFORD. (1950) *The Authoritarian Personality*. New York: Harper.

AHO, C. MICHAEL, AND BRUCE STOKES. (1991) "The Year the World Economy Turned," *Foreign Affairs* 70 (no. 1): 160–78.

ALDRICH, JOHN H., JOHN L. SULLIVAN, AND EUGENE BORGIDA. (1989) "Foreign Affairs and Issue Voting: Do Presidential Candidates 'Waltz before a Blind Audience?'" *American Political Science Review* 83 (March): 123–41.

ALLISON, GRAHAM T. (1989) "National Security Strategy for the 1990s," pp. 198–241 in Edward K. Hamilton (ed.), *America's Global Interests: A New Agenda*. New York: Norton.

———. (1971) *Essence of Decision: Explaining the Cuban Missile Crisis*. Boston: Little, Brown.

ALLISON, GRAHAM T., AND MORTON H. HALPERIN. (1972) "Bureaucratic Politics: A Paradigm and Some Policy Implications," *World Politics* 24 (Spring Supplement): 40–80.

ALLISON, GRAHAM T., AND PETER SZANTON. (1976) "Organizing for the Decade Ahead," pp. 227–70 in Henry Owen and Charles L. Schultze (eds.), *Setting National Priorities: The Next Ten Years*. Washington, D.C.: Brookings Institution.

ALMOND, GABRIEL A. (1960) *The American People and Foreign Policy*. New York: Praeger.

———. (1954) *The Appeals of Communism*. Princeton: Princeton University Press.

———. (1989) "Do Nuclear Weapons Matter?" *New York Review of Books* 36 (April): 57–58.

ALPEROVITZ, GAR. (1995) "Hiroshima: Historians Reassess," *Foreign Policy* 99 (Summer): 15–34.

———. (1985) *Atomic Diplomacy: Hiroshima and Potsdam*, rev. ed. New York: Penguin.

ALPEROVITZ, GAR, AND KAI BIRD. (1994) "The Centrality of the Bomb," *Foreign Policy* 94 (Spring): 3–20.

ALSOP, JOSEPH, AND DAVID JORAVSKY. (1980) "Was the Hiroshima Bomb Necessary? An Exchange," *New York Review of Books*, October 23, pp. 37–42.

ALTERMAN, ERIC. (1992) "Operation Pundit Storm," *World Policy Journal* 9 (Fall/Winter): 599–616.

ALTMAN, ROGER C. (1994) "Why Pressure Tokyo?" *Foreign Affairs* 73 (May/June): 2–6.

AMBROSE, STEPHEN E. (1993) *Rise to Globalism: American Foreign Policy since 1938*, 7th rev. ed. New York: Penguin.

———. (1990) *Eisenhower: Soldier and President*. New York: Simon & Schuster.

AMUZEGAR, JAHANGIR. (1987) "Dealing with Debt," *Foreign Policy* 68 (Fall): 140–58.

ANDERSON, PAUL A. (1987) "What Do Decision Makers

Do When They Make a Foreign Policy Decision?" pp. 285–308 in Charles F Hermann, Charles W. Kegley, Jr., and James N. Rosenau (eds.), *New Directions in the Study of Foreign Policy*. Boston: Allen and Unwin.

ANDREW, CHRISTOPHER. (1995) *For the President's Eyes Only: Secret Intelligence and the American Presidency from Washington to Bush*. New York: HarperCollins.

ANJARIA, S. J. (1986) "A New Round of Global Trade Negotiations," *Finance & Development* 23 (June): 2–6.

ARAT, ZEHRA. (1988) "Democracy and Economic Development: Modernization Theory Revisited," *Comparative Politics* 21 (October): 21–36.

ARNSON, CYNTHIA J., AND PHILIP BRENNER. (1993) "The Limits of Lobbying: Interest Groups, Congress, and Aid to the Contras," pp. 191–219 in Richard Sobel (ed.), *Public Opinion in U.S. Foreign Policy: The Controversy over Contra Aid*. Lanham, Md.: Rowman & Littlefield.

ARORA, VIVEK B., AND TAMIM A. BAYOUMI. (1994) "Reductions in World Military Expenditure: Who Stands to Gain?" *Finance & Development* 31 (March): 24–27.

ART, ROBERT J. (1985) "Congress and the Defense Budget: Enhancing Policy Oversight," *Political Science Quarterly* 100 (Summer): 227–48.

———. (1973) "Bureaucratic Politics and American Foreign Policy: A Critique," *Policy Sciences* 4 (December): 467–90.

ASHER, HERBERT B. (1992) *Presidential Elections and American Politics*, 5th ed. Pacific Grove, Calif.: Brooks/Cole.

ASMUS, RONALD D., RICHARD L. KUGLER, AND F. STEPHEN LARRABEE. (1993) "Building a New NATO," *Foreign Affairs* 72 (September/October): 28–40.

ASPIN, LES. (1976) "The Defense Budget and Foreign Policy: The Role of Congress," pp. 115–74 in Franklin A. Long and George W. Rathjens (eds.), *Arms, Defense Policy, and Arms Control*. New York: Norton.

ATKINSON, RICK. (1993) "A Trail of Death across Europe Leads to Iran," *Washington Post National Weekly Edition*, November 29–December 5, pp. 14–15.

ATKINSON, RICK, AND FRED HIATT. (1985) "Oh, That Golden Safety Net: The Pentagon Never Met a Defense Contractor It Wouldn't Bail Out," *Washington Post National Weekly Edition*, April 22, pp. 6–8.

ATLAS, JAMES. (1995) "The Counterculture," *New York Times Magazine*, February 12, pp. 32–38ff.

ATWOOD, J. BRIAN. (1994) "More than Words: USAID's Approach to the Population Problem," *Harvard International Review* 16 (Fall): 28–29, 77–78.

AUERBACH, STUART. (1993) "How the U.S. Built Japan Inc.," *Washington Post National Weekly Edition*, July 26–August 1, p. 21.

BAILEY, KATHLEEN. (1995) "Why We Have to Keep the Bomb," *Bulletin of the Atomic Scientists* 51 (January/February): 30–37.

BAKER, JAMES A., III (1995) *The Politics of Diplomacy: Revolution, War and Peace*. New York: Putman,

BALASSA, BELA, AND MARCUS NOLAND. (1988) *Japan in the World Economy*. Washington, D.C.: Institute for International Economics.

BALDRIGE, MALCOLM. (1983) "At Last, Hope for Coherent Policy," *New York Times*, June 19, p. F2.

BALL, DESMOND. (1989) "Can Nuclear War Be Controlled?" pp. 284–90 in Charles W. Kegley, Jr., and Eugene R. Wittkopf (eds.), *The Nuclear Reader: Strategy, Weapons, War*. New York: St. Martin's.

BALL, DESMOND, AND ROBERT C. TOTH. (1990) "Revising the SIOP: Taking War-Fighting to Dangerous Extremes," *International Security* 14 (Spring): 65–92.

BALL, GEORGE. (1984) "White House Roulette," *New York Review of Books* 31 (November 8): 5–11.

———. (1976) *Diplomacy for a Crowded World: An American Foreign Policy*. Boston: Atlantic-Little, Brown.

BAMFORD, JAMES. (1983) *The Puzzle Palace*. New York: Penguin.

BANDOW, DOUG. (1992–1993) "Avoiding War," *Foreign Policy* 89 (Winter): 156–74.

BARBER, JAMES DAVID. (1992) *The Presidential Character: Predicting Performance in the White House*, 4th ed. Englewood Cliffs, N.J.: Prentice-Hall.

———. (1989) "George Bush: In Search of a Mission," *New York Times*, January 19, p. A31.

———. (1985) *The Presidential Character*, 3rd ed. Englewood Cliffs, N.J.: Prentice-Hall.

———. (1981) "Reagan's Sheer Personal Likability Faces Its Sternest Test," *Washington Post*, January 20, p. 8.

———. (1977) *The Presidential Character*, 2nd ed. Englewood Cliffs, N.J.: Prentice-Hall.

BARD, MITCHELL. (1994) "The Influence of Ethnic Interest Groups on American Middle East Policy," pp. 79–94 in Eugene R. Wittkopf (ed.), *The Domestic Sources of American Foreign Policy: Insights and Evidence*, 2nd ed. New York: St. Martin's.

BARITZ, LOREN. (1985) *Backfire: A History of How American Culture Led Us into Vietnam and Made Us Fight the Way We Did*. New York: Morrow.

BARNES, FRED. (1994) "Saudi Doody," *New Republic*, March 14, pp. 10–11.

BARNET, RICHARD J. (1993) "Still Putting Arms First," *Harper's* 286 (February): 59–65.

———. (1990) "U.S. Intervention: Low-Intensity Thinking," *Bulletin of the Atomic Scientists* 46 (May): 34–37.

———. (1972) *Roots of War: The Men and Institutions behind U.S. Foreign Policy*. Baltimore: Penguin.

———. (1969) *The Economy of Death*. New York: Atheneum.

BARNET, RICHARD J., AND JOHN CAVANAGH. (1994) *Global Dreams: Imperial Corporations and the New World Order*. New York: Simon & Schuster.

BARNET, RICHARD J., AND RONALD E. MÜLLER. (1974) *Global Reach: The Power of the Multinational Corporations*. New York: Simon & Schuster.

BARTELS, LARRY M. (1991) "Constituency Opinion and Congressional Policy Making: The Reagan Defense Buildup," *American Political Science Review* 85 (June): 457–74.

BAUER, RAYMOND A., ITHIEL DE SOLA POOL, AND LEWIS ANTHONY DEXTER. (1972) *American Business and Public Policy*, 2nd ed. Chicago: Aldine-Atherton.

BAX, FRANS R. (1977) "The Legislative-Executive Relationship in Foreign Policy: New Partnership or New Competition?" *Orbis* 20 (Winter): 881–904.

BENDOR, JONATHAN, AND THOMAS H. HAMMOND. (1992) "Rethinking Allison's Models," *American Political Science Review* 86 (June): 301–22.

BENDYNA, MARY E., AND CELINDA C. LAKE. (1995) "Gender and Voting in the 1992 Presidential Election," pp. 372–82 in Karen O'Connor (ed.), *American Government: Readings and Cases*. Boston: Allyn & Bacon.

BENNETT, STEPHEN EARL. (1992) "The Persian Gulf War's Impact on Americans' Political Information." Revised version of a paper presented at the American National Election Studies' Conference on "The Political Consequences of War," Washington, D.C., February 28.

BENNETT, W. LANCE. (1994a) *Inside the System: Culture, Institutions, and Power in American Politics*. New York: Harcourt Brace Jovanovich.

———. (1994b) "The Media and the Foreign Policy Process," pp. 168–88 in David A. Deese (ed.), *The New Politics of American Foreign Policy*. New York: St. Martin's.

———. (1980) *Public Opinion in American Politics*. New York: Harcourt Brace Jovanovich.

BENZE, JAMES G., JR. (1987) *Presidential Power and Management Techniques: The Carter and Reagan Administrations in Historical Perspective*. New York: Greenwood.

BERGER, MARK T. (1994) "The End of the Third World?" *Third World Quarterly* 15 (June): 257–75.

BERGSTEN, C. FRED. (1994) "APEC and World Trade," *Foreign Affairs* 73 (May/June): 20–26.

———. (1992a) "The Primacy of Economics," *Foreign Policy* 87 (Summer): 3–24.

———. (1992b) "The World Economy after the Cold War," *California Management Review* 34 (Winter): 51–65.

———. (1988) *America in the World Economy: A Strategy for the 1990s*. Washington, D.C.: Institute for International Economics.

BERGSTEN, C. FRED, AND MARCUS NOLAND. (1993) *Reconcilable Differences? United States-Japan Economic Conflict*. Washington, D.C.: Institute for International Economics.

BERKLEY, GEORGE E. (1978) *The Craft of Public Administration*. Boston: Allyn & Bacon.

BERNSTEIN, BARTON J. (1995) "The Atomic Bombings Reconsidered," *Foreign Affairs* 74 (January/February): 135–52.

BERNSTEIN, ROBERT A. (1989) *Elections, Representation, and Congressional Voting Behavior: The Myth of Constituency Control*. Englewood Cliffs, N.J.: Prentice-Hall.

BERNSTEIN, ROBERT A., AND WILLIAM ANTHONY. (1974) "The ABM Issue in the Senate, 1968–1970: The Importance of Ideology," *American Political Science Review* 68 (September): 1198–1206.

BERRY, JOHN M. (1994) "Dollar's Continuing Slide Really Reflects Japan's Problems, Analysts Say," *Washington Post*, June 30, p. A25.

BESCHLOSS, MICHAEL R., AND STROBE TALBOTT. (1993) *At the Highest Levels: The Inside Story of the End of the Cold War*. Boston: Little, Brown.

BETTS, RICHARD K. (1994) "The Delusion of Impartial Intervention," *Foreign Affairs* 73 (November/December): 20–33.

———. (1978) "Analysis, War and Decision: Why Intelligence Failures Are Inevitable," *World Politics* 31 (October): 61–89.

BEYERS, DAN. (1991) "The National Security Agency Exists—Pass It On," *Washington Post National Weekly Edition*, September 2–8, p. 31.

BHAGWATI, JAGDISH. (1994) "Samurais No More," *Foreign Affairs* 73 (May/June): 7–12.

———. (1993) "The Case for Free Trade," *Scientific American* 269 (November): 41–49.

BIENEFELD, MANFRED. (1994) "The New World Order: Echoes of a New Imperialism," *Third World Quarterly* 15 (March): 31–48.

BISSELL, RICHARD E. (1991) "After Foreign Aid—What?" *Washington Quarterly* 14 (Summer): 23–33.

———. (1990) "Who Killed the Third World?" *Washington Quarterly* 13 (Autumn): 23–32.

BITZINGER, RICHARD A. (1994) "The Globalization of the Arms Industry: The Next Proliferation Challenge," *International Security* 19 (Fall): 170–98.

BLACHMAN, MORRIS J., AND DONALD J. PUCHALA. (1991) "When Empires Meet: The 'Long Peace' in Long-Term Perspective," pp. 177–201 in Charles W. Kegley, Jr. (ed.), *The Long Postwar Peace:*

Contending Explanations and Projections. New York: HarperCollins.

BLACKBURN, PAUL P. (1992) "The Post-Cold War Public Diplomacy of the United States," *Washington Quarterly* 15 (Winter): 75–86.

BLACKWILL, ROBERT D. (1992) "Blackwill's Commentary," pp. 121–24 in Ernest R. May (ed.), *American Cold War Strategy: Interpreting NSC 68.* Boston: Bedford Books.

BLAKE, DAVID H., AND ROBERT S. WALTERS. (1987) *The Politics of Global Economic Relations*, 3rd ed. Englewood Cliffs, N.J.: Prentice-Hall.

BLECHBURN, BARRY M. (1990) *The Politics of National Security: Congress and U.S. Defense Policy.* New York: Oxford University Press.

BLECHMAN, BARRY M., AND STEPHEN S. KAPLAN. (1978) *Force without War.* Washington, D.C.: Brookings Institution.

BLIGHT, JAMES G., JOSEPH S. NYE, JR., AND DAVID A. WELCH. (1987) "The Cuban Missile Crisis Revisited," *Foreign Affairs* 66 (Fall): 170–88.

BLIGHT, JAMES G., AND DAVID A. WELCH. (1989) *On the Brink: Americans and Soviets Re-examine the Cuban Missile Crisis.* New York: Hill and Wang.

BLOCK, FRED L. (1977) *The Origins of International Economic Disorder.* Berkeley and Los Angeles: University of California Press.

BLOOMFIELD, LINCOLN P. (1994) "The Premature Burial of Global Law and Order: Looking beyond the Three Cases from Hell," *Washington Quarterly* 17 (Summer): 145–61.

———. (1974) *The Foreign Policy Process: Making Theory Relevant.* Beverly Hills, Calif.: Sage.

BLUMENTHAL, SIDNEY. (1988) *The Rise of the Counter Establishment.* New York: Harper & Row.

BLUSTEIN, PAUL. (1993) "East Asia's Economic Lesson for America," *Washington Post National Weekly Edition*, March 15–21, p. 20.

BOCK, JOSEPH G. (1987) *The White House Staff and the National Security Assistant: Friendship and Friction at the Water's Edge.* New York: Greenwood.

BOFFEY, PHILIP M. (1983) "'Rational' Decisions Prove Not to Be," *New York Times*, December 6, pp. C1, C17.

BOLLEN, KENNETH A. (1979) "Political Democracy and the Timing of Development," *American Sociological Review* 44 (August): 572–87.

BOREN, DAVID L. (1992) "The Intelligence Community: How Crucial?" *Foreign Affairs* 71 (Summer): 52–62.

BOROSAGE, ROBERT L. (1993–1994) "Inventing the Threat: Clinton's Defense Budget," *World Policy Journal* 10 (Winter): 7–14.

BORRUS, MICHAEL, STEVE WEBER, JOHN ZYSMAN, AND JOSEPH WILLIHNGANZ. (1992) "Mercantilism and

Global Security," *The National Interest* 29 (Fall): 21–29.

BOSTDORFF, DENISE M., AND STEVEN R. GOLDZWIG. (1994) "Idealism and Pragmatism in American Foreign Policy Rhetoric: The Case of John F. Kennedy and Vietnam," *Presidential Studies Quarterly* 24 (Summer): 515–30.

BOULDING, KENNETH E. (1959) "National Images and International Systems," *Journal of Conflict Resolution* 3 (June): 120–31.

BOUTROS-GHALI, BOUTROS. (1992–1993) "Empowering the United Nations," *Foreign Affairs* 72 (Winter): 89–102.

———. (1992) *An Agenda for Peace: Preventive Diplomacy, Peacemaking, and Peace-Keeping.* New York: United Nations.

BOVARD, JAMES. (1991) "Fair Trade Is Unfair," *Newsweek*, December 9, p. 13.

BOYD, RICHARD W. (1972) "Popular Control of Public Policy: A Normal Vote Analysis of the 1968 Election," *American Political Science Review* 66 (June): 429–49.

BRACE, PAUL, AND BARBARA HINCKLEY. (1993) "George Bush and the Costs of High Popularity: A General Model with a Current Application," *PS: Political Science & Politics* 26 (September): 501–6.

———. (1992) *Follow the Leader: Opinion Polls and the Modern Presidents.* New York: Basic Books.

BRANIGIN, WILLIAM. (1994) "Boutros-Ghali Rushes In," *Washington Post National Weekly Edition*, November 30–December 6, pp. 6–7.

BRECHER, JEREMY. (1993) "Global Village or Global Pillage?" *The Nation* 257 (December 6): 685–88.

BRECHER, MICHAEL, AND JONATHAN WILKENFELD. (1991) "International Crises and Global Instability: The Myth of the 'Long Peace,'" pp. 85–104 in Charles W. Kegley, Jr. (ed.), *The Long Postwar Peace: Contending Explanations and Projections.* New York: HarperCollins.

BRENNER, MICHAEL J. (1993) "EC: Confidence Lost," *Foreign Policy* 91 (Summer): 24–43.

BREWER, GARRY D., AND PAUL BRACKEN. (1984) "Who's Thinking about National Security?" *Worldview* 27 (February): 21–13.

BREWER, THOMAS L. (1980) *American Foreign Policy.* Englewood Cliffs, N.J.: Prentice-Hall.

BRILMAYER, LEA. (1994) *American Hegemony: Political Morality in a One-Superpower World.* New Haven, Conn.: Yale University Press.

BROCK, DAVID. (1994) "Jimmy Carter's Return," *American Spectator* 27 (December): 26–38.

BRODER, DAVID S. (1990) "The Reactor President," *Washington Post National Weekly*, August 27–September 2, p. 4.

———. (1986) "Who Took the Fun Out of Congress?"

Washington Post National Weekly Edition, February 17, pp. 9–10.

BRODY, RICHARD A. (1991) *Assessing the President: The Media, Elite Opinion, and Public Support*. Stanford, Calif.: Stanford University Press.

BRODY, RICHARD A., AND CATHERINE R. SHAPIRO. (1989) "A Reconsideration of the Rally Phenomenon in Public Opinion," pp. 77–102 in Samuel Long (ed.), *Political Behavior Annual*, vol. 2. Boulder, Colo.: Westview.

BRONFENBRENNER, URIE. (1961) "The Mirror Image in Soviet-American Relations," *Journal of Social Issues* 17 (no. 3): 45–56.

BROOKS, LINTON F., AND ARNOLD KANTER. (1994) "Introduction" in *U.S. Intervention Policy for the Post-Cold War World: New Challenges and New Responses*. New York: Norton.

BROWN, LESTER R. (1994) "Facing Food Insecurity," pp. 132–52 in Lester R. Brown, Alan Thein Durning, Christopher Flavin, Hilary F. French, Nicholas Lenssen, Marcia D. Lowe, Ann Misch, Sandra Postel, Michael Renner, Peter Weber, and John E. Young, *State of the World 1994*. New York: Norton.

———. (1972) *World without Borders*. New York: Vintage Books.

BROWNSTEIN, RONALD, AND NINA EASTON. (1983) *Reagan's Ruling Class*. New York: Pantheon.

BRZEZINSKI, ZBIGNIEW. (1995) "A Plan for Europe," *Foreign Affairs* 74 (January/February): 26–42.

———. (1994) "The Premature Partnership," *Foreign Affairs* 73 (March/April): 67–82.

BUCHANAN, BRUCE. (1978) *The Presidential Experience: What the Office Does to the Man*. Englewood Cliffs, N.J.: Prentice-Hall.

BUCHANAN, PATRICK J. (1993) "America First—NAFTA Never," *Washington Post National Weekly Edition*, November 15–21, p. 25.

———. (1990) "America First—and Second, and Third," *The National Interest* 19 (Spring): 77–82.

BUCKLEY, WILLIAM F. (1970) "On The Right," *National Review*, October 24, pp. 1124–25.

BUNDY, MCGEORGE. (1988) *Danger and Survival*. New York: Random House.

BUNDY, MCGEORGE, AND JAMES G. BLIGHT. (1987–1988) "October 27, 1962: Transcripts of the Meetings of the ExCom," *International Security* 12 (Winter): 30–92.

BUNDY, MCGEORGE, GEORGE F. KENNAN, ROBERT S. MCNAMARA, AND GERALD SMITH. (1982) "Nuclear Weapons and the Atlantic Alliance," *Foreign Affairs* 60 (Spring): 753–68.

BURCH, PHILIP H., JR. (1980) *Elites in American History: The New Deal to the Carter Administration*. New York: Holmes and Meier.

BURGIN, EILEEN. (1993) "Congress and Foreign Policy: The Misperceptions," pp. 333–63 in Lawrence C.

Dodd and Bruce I. Oppenheimer (eds.), *Congress Reconsidered*, 5th ed. Washington, D.C.: CQ Press.

BURKHART, ROSS E., AND MICHAEL S. LEWIS-BECK. (1994) "Comparative Democracy: The Economic Development Thesis," *American Political Science Review* 88 (December): 903–10.

BURKI, SHAHID JAVED. (1983) "UNCTAD VI: For Better or for Worse?" *Finance & Development* 20 (December): 16–19.

BURNS, JAMES MACGREGOR. (1966) *Presidential Government: The Crucible of Leadership*. Boston: Houghton Mifflin.

BURTON, DANIEL F., JR. (1994) "Competitiveness: Here to Stay," *Washington Quarterly* 17 (Autumn): 111–22.

BUSHNELL, PRUDENCE. (1989) "Leadership at State: The Neglected Dimension," *Foreign Service Journal* 66 (September): 30–31.

CALDWELL, DAN. (1993) "From SALT to START: Limiting Strategic Nuclear Weapons," pp. 895–913 in Richard Dean Burns (ed.), *Encyclopedia of Arms Control and Disarmament*, vol. 2. New York: Scribner's.

———. (1991) *The Dynamics of Domestic Politics and Arms Control: The SALT II Treaty Ratification Debate*. Columbia: University of South Carolina Press.

——— (ed.). (1983) *Henry Kissinger: His Personality and Policies*. Durham, N.C.: Duke University Press.

———. (1978) "A Research Note on the Quarantine of Cuba, October 1962," *International Studies Quarterly* 22 (December): 625–33.

———. (1977) "Bureaucratic Foreign Policy Making," *American Behavioral Scientist* 21 (September–October): 87–110.

CALIFANO, JOSEPH A., JR. (1994) "Imperial Congress," *New York Times Magazine*, January 23, pp. 40–41.

———. (1975) *A Presidential Nation*. New York: Norton.

CAMPBELL, ANGUS, PHILIP E. CONVERSE, WARREN E. MILLER, AND DONALD E. STOKES. (1960) *The American Voter*. New York: Wiley.

CAMPBELL, JOEL, AND LEILA CAIN. (1965) "Public Opinion and the Outbreak of War," *Journal of Conflict Resolution* 9 (September): 318–29.

CAMPBELL, JOHN FRANKLIN. (1971) *The Foreign Affairs Fudge Factory*. New York: Basic Books.

CANNON, LOU. (1988) "An 'Honest Broker' at the NSC," *Washington Post National Weekly Edition*, August 22–28, pp. 6–8.

CAPORASO, JAMES A. (ed.). (1978), "Dependence and Dependency in the Global System;" Special issue. *International Organization* 32 (Winter): 1–300.

CARNESALE, ALBERT. (1985) "Special Supplement: The Strategic Defense Initiative," pp. 187–205 in George E. Hudson and Joseph Kruzel (eds.), *American Defense Annual 1985–1986*. Lexington, Mass.: Heath.

CARNEY, ELIZA NEWLIN. (1994) "Still Tying to Reinvent Government," *National Journal*, June 18, pp. 1442–43.

CAROTHERS, THOMAS. (1994a) "The Democracy Nostrum," *World Policy Journal* 11 (Fall): 47–53.

———. (1994b) "The NED at 10," *Foreign Policy* 95 (Summer): 123–38.

CARPENTER, TED GALEN. (1993) "Foreign Policy Peril: Somalia Set a Dangerous Precedent," *USA Today* 121 (May): 10–13.

CARR, CALEB. (1994) "Aldrich Ames and the Conduct of American Intelligence," *World Policy Journal* 11 (Fall): 19–28.

CARR, E. H. (1939) *The Twenty-Years' Crisis 1919–1939: An Introduction to the Study of International Relations.* London: Macmillan.

CARTER, HODDING III. (1981) "Life Inside the Carter State Department," *Playboy* 28 (February): 96ff.

CASPARY, WILLIAM R. (1970) "The 'Mood Theory': A Study of Public Opinion," *American Political Science Review* 64 (June): 536–47.

CAVANAGH, THOMAS E. (1982–1983) "The Dispersion of Authority in the House of Representatives," *Political Science Quarterly* 97 (Winter): 623–37.

CHAN, STEVE, AND ALEX MINTZ (eds.). (1992) *Defense, Welfare, and Growth.* London: Routledge.

CHILDERS, ERSKINE, WITH BRIAN URQUHART. (1994) "Renewing the United Nations Systems," *Development Dialogue*, no. 1. Upsala, Sweden: Dag Hammarskjold Foundation.

CHILDS, HAROLD L. (1965) *Public Opinion: Nature, Formation, and Role.* Princeton, N.J.: Van Nostrand.

CHOATE, PAT. (1990) *Agents of Influence.* New York: Knopf.

CHOMSKY, NOAM. (1994) *World Orders Old and New.* New York: Columbia University Press.

CHRISTIANSEN, DREW, AND GERARD F. POWERS. (1993) "Unintended Consequences," *Bulletin of the Atomic Scientists* 49 (November): 41–45.

CHRISTIE, RICHARD, AND FLORENCE L. GEIS. (1970) *Studies in Machiavellianism.* New York: Academic Press.

CHRISTOPHER, ROBERT C. (1989) *Crashing the Gates: The De-WASPing of America's Power Elite.* New York: Simon & Schuster.

CHRISTOPHER, WARREN. (1995) "America's Leadership, America's Opportunity," *Foreign Policy* 98 (Spring): 6–27.

CHUBIN, SHAHRAM. (1993) "The South and the New World Order," *Washington Quarterly* 16 (Autumn): 87–107.

CITRIN, JACK, ERNST B. HAAS, CHRISTOPHER MUSTE, AND BETH REINGOLD. (1994) "Is American Nationalism Changing: Implications for Foreign Policy," *International Studies Quarterly* 38 (March): 1–31.

CLAD, JAMES C., AND ROGER D. STONE. (1992–1993) "New Mission for Foreign Aid," *Foreign Affairs* 72 (no. 1): 196–205.

CLARK, KEITH C., AND LAURENCE J. LEGERE (eds). (1969) *The President and the Management of National Security: A Report by the Institute for Defense Analyses.* New York: Praeger.

CLARKE, DUNCAN L. (1989) *American Defense and Foreign Policy Institutions: Toward a Sound Foundation.* New York: Harper & Row.

CLARKE, JONATHAN. (1993) "The Conceptual Poverty of U.S. Foreign Policy," *Atlantic Monthly* 272 (September): 54–66.

CLAUDE, INIS L., JR. (1971) *Swords into Plowshares*, 4th ed. New York: Random House.

CLEVELAND, HARLAN. (1959) "Dinosaurs and Personal Freedom," *Saturday Review* 42 (February 28): 12–14ff.

CLOUGH, MICHAEL. (1994) "Grass-Roots Policymaking: Say Good-Bye to the 'Wise Men,'" *Foreign Affairs* 73 (January/February): 2–7.

CODEVILLA, ANGELO. (1992) "The CIA's Identify Crisis: How Central Is Central Intelligence?" *The American Enterprise* 3 (January/February): 29–37.

COHEN, BERNARD C. (1973) *The Public's Impact on Foreign Policy.* Boston: Little, Brown.

———. (1963) *The Press and Foreign Policy.* Princeton, N.J.: Princeton University Press.

———. (1961) "Foreign Policy Makers and the Press," pp. 220–28 in James N. Rosenau (ed.), *International Politics and Foreign Policy.* New York: Free Press.

COHEN, ELIOT A. (1993) "Beyond 'Bottom Up,'" *National Review*, November 15, pp. 40–43.

COHEN, STEPHEN D. (1994) *The Making of United States International Economic Policy: Principles, Problems, and Proposals for Reform*, 4th ed. Westport Conn.: Praeger.

COLL, STEVE. (1992a) "The CIA's Covert Afghan War," *Washington Post National Weekly Edition*, August 24–30, pp. 11–13.

———. (1992b) "The Other Battle for Afghanistan," *Washington Post National Weekly Edition*, August 31–September 6, pp. 10–11.

COLL, STEVE, AND STEVE LEVINE. (1993) "A Global Militant Network," *Washington Post National Weekly Edition*, August 16–22, pp. 6–7.

COLLIER, ELLEN C. (1994a) "War Powers Resolution: Presidential Compliance," *CRS Issue Brief 81050*, February 15. Washington, D.C.: Congressional Research Service.

———. (1994b) "The War Powers Resolution: Twenty Years of Experience," *CRS Report for Congress*, January 11. Washington, D.C.: Congressional Research Service.

———. (1993) "War Powers and U.N. Military Actions:

A Brief Background of the Legislative Framework," *CRS Report for Congress*, December 21. Washington, D.C.: Congressional Research Service.

———. (1989) "Bipartisan Foreign Policy and Policymaking since World War II," *CRS Report for Congress*, November 9. Washington, D.C.: Congressional Research Service.

———. (1988) "Foreign Policy by Reporting Requirement," *Washington Quarterly* 11 (Winter): 75–84.

———. (1987) "War Powers and the Persian Gulf," *Congressional Research Service Review*, November/December, pp. 23–24.

COMMAGER, HENRY STEELE. (1983) "Misconceptions Governing American Foreign Policy," pp. 510–17 in Charles W. Kegley, Jr., and Eugene R. Wittkopf (eds.), *Perspectives on American Foreign Policy*. New York: St. Martin's.

———. (1965) "A Historian Looks at Our Political Morality," *Saturday Review* 48 (July 10): 16–18.

Committe on Foreign Relations, United States Senate. (1993) *Treaties and Other International Agreements: The Role of the United States Senate*. Washington, D.C.: Government Printing Office.

Congress and Foreign Policy 1991, U.S. House of Representatives, 102nd Congress. (1992) Washington, D.C.: Government Printing Office.

Congressional Quarterly Almanac 1986. (1987). Washington, D.C.: Congressional Quarterly, Inc.

Congressional Quarterly Almanac 1984. (1985). Washington, D.C.: Congressional Quarterly, Inc.

CONGRESSIONAL RESEARCH SERVICE. (1991) *Soviet–U.S. Relations*. Washington, D.C.: Congressional Research Service.

———. (1989) "Soviet–U.S. Relations: A Briefing Book," *CRS Report for Congress*. Washington, D.C.: Congressional Research Service.

CONOVER, PAMELA J., AND STANLEY FELDMAN. (1984) "How People Organize the Political World: A Schematic Model," *American Journal of Political Science* 28 (February): 95–126.

CONVERSE, PHILIP E. (1964) "The Nature of Belief Systems in Mass Publics," pp. 206–61 in David E. Apter (ed.), *Ideology and Discontent*. New York: Free Press.

CONWAY, M. MARGARET. (1991) *Political Participation in the United States*, 2nd ed. Washington, D.C.: CQ Press.

COOPER, RICHARD N. (1988) "International Economic Cooperation: Is It Desirable? Is It Likely?" *Washington Quarterly* 11 (Spring): 89–101.

COPSON, RAYMOND W. (1988) "The Reagan Doctrine: U.S. Assistance to Anti-Marxist Guerrillas," *CRS Issue Brief*, March 11. Washington, D.C.: Congressional Research Service.

COWHEY, PETER F., AND JONATHAN D. ARONSON.

(1992–1993) "A New Trade Order," *Foreign Affairs* 72 (no. 1): 183–95.

COX, ARTHUR MACY. (1976) *The Dynamics of Détente*. New York: Norton.

CRABB, CECIL V., JR. (1986) *Policy-Makers and Critics: Conflicting Theories of American Foreign Policy*, 2nd ed. New York: Praeger.

———. (1957) *Bipartisan Foreign Policy: Myth or Reality*. Evanston, Ill.: Row, Peterson and Company.

CRABB, CECIL V., JR., AND PAT M. HOLT. (1992) *Invitation to Struggle: Congress, the President and Foreign Policy*, 4th ed. Washington, D.C.: CQ Press.

CRAIG, STEPHEN C. (1993) *The Malevolent Leaders: Popular Discontent in America*. Boulder, Colo.: Westview.

CROCKER, CHESTER. (1995) "The Lessons of Somalia," *Foreign Affairs* 74 (May/June): 2–8.

———. (1994) "The Rules of Engagement in a New World," *Washington Post National Weekly Edition*, May 16–22, pp. 23–24.

CRONIN, THOMAS E. (1984) "The Swelling of the Presidency: Can Anyone Reverse the Tide?" pp. 345–59 in Peter Woll (ed.), *American Government: Readings and Cases*. Boston: Little, Brown.

———. (1973) "The Swelling of the Presidency," *Saturday Review of the Society* 1 (February): 30–36.

CROPSEY, SETH. (1994) "The Only Credible Deterrent," *Foreign Affairs* 73 (March/April): 14–20.

DAALDER, IVO H. (1995) "What Vision for the Nuclear Future?" *Washington Quarterly* 18 (Spring): 127–42.

DAHL, ROBERT. (1989) *Democracy and Its Critics*. New Haven, Conn.: Yale University Press.

DALLEK, ROBERT. (1984) *Ronald Reagan: The Politics of Symbolism*. Cambridge, Mass.: Harvard University Press.

———. (1983) *The American Style of Foreign Policy: Cultural Politics and Foreign Affairs*. New York: Knopf.

DALY, HERMAN E. (1993) "The Perils of Free Trade," *Scientific American* 269 (November): 50–57.

DAM, KENNETH, JOHN DEUTCH, JOSEPH S. NYE, JR., AND DAVID M. ROWE. (1993) "Harnessing Japan: A U.S. Strategy for Managing Japan's Rise as a Global Power," *Washington Quarterly* 16 (Spring): 29–42.

DAVIS, JENNIFER. (1993) "Squeezing Apartheid," *Bulletin of the Atomic Scientists* 49 (November): 16–19.

DAVIS, VINCENT. (1987) "Organization and Management," pp. 171–99 in Joseph Kruzel (ed.), *American Defense Annual 1987–1988*. Lexington, Mass.: Lexington.

DE TOCQUEVILLE, ALEXIS. (1969 [1835]) *Democracy in America*. New York: Doubleday.

DE WAAL, ALEX, AND RAKIYA OMAAR. (1994) "Can Military Intervention Be 'Humanitarian?'" *Middle East Report* 24 (March–June): 3–8.

DeConde, Alexander. (1992) *Ethnicity, Race, and American Foreign Policy*. Boston: Northeastern University Press.

Defining Purpose: The U.N. and the Health of Nations. (1993). Washington, D.C.: United States Commission on Improving the Effectiveness of the United Nations.

Deibel, Terry L. (1992) "Strategies before Containment: Patterns for the Future," *International Security* 16 (Spring): 79–108.

DeRivera, Joseph H. (1968) *The Psychological Dimension of Foreign Policy*. Columbus, Oh.: Merrill.

Destler, I.M. (1995) *American Trade Politics: System Under Stress*, 3rd ed. Washington, D.C.: Institute for International Economics.

———. (1983a) "The Evolution of Reagan Foreign Policy," pp. 117–58 in Fred I. Greenstein (ed.), *The Reagan Presidency*. Baltimore: The Johns Hopkins University Press.

———. (1983b) "The Rise of the National Security Assistant," pp. 260–81 in Charles W. Kegley, Jr., and Eugene R. Wittkopf (eds.), *Perspectives on American Foreign Policy*. New York: St. Martin's.

———. (1974) *Presidents, Bureaucrats, and Foreign Policy: The Politics of Organizational Reform*. Princeton, N.J.: Princeton University Press.

Destler, I. M., Leslie H. Gelb, and Anthony Lake. (1984) *Our Own Worst Enemy: The Unmaking of American Foreign Policy*. New York: Simon & Schuster.

Destler, I.M., and John S. Odell. (1987) *Anti-Protection: Changing Forces in United States Trade Politics*. Washington, D.C.: Institute for International Economics.

Deudney, Daniel, and G. John Ikenberry. (1994) "After the Long War," *Foreign Policy* 94 (Spring): 21–35.

Deutsch, Karl W. (1974) *Politics and Government*. Boston: Houghton Mifflin.

Deutsch, Karl W., and Richard L. Merritt. (1965) "Effects of Events on National and International Images," pp. 132–87 in Herbert C. Kelman (ed.), *International Behavior*. New York: Holt, Rinehart & Winston.

Development Cooperation: Efforts and Politics of the Members of the Development Assistance Committee, 1993 Report. (1994). Paris: Organisation for Economic Co-operation and Development.

Devroy, Ann. (1994) "The Shakedown Cruise: Year Two," *Washington Post National Weekly Edition*, April 11–17, p. 11.

Devroy, Ann, and Stephen Barr. (1995) "Reinventing the Vice Presidency," *Washington Post National Weekly Edition*, February 27–March 5, pp. 6–7.

Devroy, Ann, and R. Jeffrey Smith. (1993) "Oceans Apart over Intervention," *Washington Post National Weekly Edition*, October 3–9, pp. 8–9.

Devroy, Ann, and Daniel Williams. (1993) "Vice President in Charge of the World," *Washington Post National Weekly Edition*, December 13–19, pp. 11–12.

Diamond, Larry. (1992) "Promoting Democracy," *Foreign Policy*, 87 (Summer): 25-46.

Diplomacy for the 70's: A Program of Management Reform for the Department of State. (1970). Washington, D.C.: Department of State.

DiRenzo, Gordon J. (ed.). (1974) *Personality and Politics*. Garden City, N.Y.: Doubleday-Anchor.

Dirks, Gerald, Robert O. Matthews, Tariq Rauf, Elizabeth Riddell-Dixon, and Claire Turenne Sjolander. (1993) "The State of the United Nations, 1993: North-South Perspectives," *ACUNS Reports and Papers*, no. 5. Providence, R.I.: Academic Council on the United Nations, Brown University.

Dixon, William J. (1994) "Democracy and the Peaceful Settlement of International Conflict," *American Political Science Review* 88 (March): 14–32.

Dixon, William J., and Stephen M. Gaarder. (1992) "Presidential Succession and the Cold War: An Analysis of Soviet–American Relations, 1948–1988," *Journal of Politics* 54 (February): 156–75.

"Does the United States Need Nuclear Weapons?" (1993) *The Defense Monitor* 22 (no. 10).

Dolbeare, Kenneth M., and Murray J. Edelman. (1985) *American Politics*, 5th ed. Lexington, Mass.: Heath.

Domhoff, G. William. (1984) *Who Rules America Now?* Englewood Cliffs, N.J.: Prentice-Hall.

Donovan, Hedley. (1985) *Roosevelt to Reagan*. New York: Harper & Row.

Donovan, John C. (1974) *The Cold Warriors: A Policy-Making Elite*. Lexington, Mass.: Heath.

Downs, Anthony. (1957) *An Economic Theory of Democracy*. New York: Harper & Row.

Doxey, Margaret. (1990) "International Sanctions," pp. 242–61 in David G. Haglund and Michael K. Hawes (eds.), *World Politics: Power, Interdependence, and Dependence*. Toronto: Harcourt Brace Jovanovich.

Doyle, Michael W. (1995) "Liberalism and World Politics Revisited," pp. 83–106 in Charles W. Kegley, Jr. (ed.), *Controversies in International Relations Theory: Realism and the Neoliberal Challenge*. New York: St. Martin's.

———. (1986) "Liberalism and World Politics," *American Political Science Review* 80 (December): 1151–69.

Draper, Theodore. (1990) *A Present of Things Past*. New York: Hill and Wang.

———. (1968) *The Dominican Revolt*. New York: Commentary.

DREW, ELIZABETH. (1994) *On the Edge: The Clinton Presidency*. New York: Simon & Schuster.

DRISCHLER, ALVIN PAUL. (1985) "Foreign Policy Making on the Hill," *Washington Quarterly* 8 (Summer): 165–75.

DRUCKER, PETER F. (1994) "Trade Lessons from the World Economy," *Foreign Affairs* 73 (January/February): 99–108.

———. (1986) "The Changed World Economy," *Foreign Affairs* 64 (Spring): 768–91.

DUFFIELD, JOHN S. (1994–1995) "NATO's Functions After the Cold War," *Political Science Quarterly* 109 (Winter): 763–87.

DULLES, JOHN FOSTER. (1952) "A Policy of Liberation," *Life*, May 19, p. 19ff.

DURNING, ALAN. (1990) "Ending Poverty," pp. 135–53 in Lester R. Brown, Christopher Flavin, Sandra Postel, Linda Starke, Alan Durning, Jodi Jacobson, Michael Renner, Hilary F. French, Marcia Lowe, and John E. Young, *State of the World 1990*. New York: Norton.

DYE, THOMAS R. (1995) *Who's Running America?: The Clinton Years*, 6th ed. Englewood Cliffs, N.J.: Prentice-Hall.

———. (1993) "The Friends of Bill and Hillary," *PS: Political Science & Politics* 26 (December): 693–95.

———. (1990) *Who's Running America?: The Bush Era*, 5th ed. Englewood Cliffs, N.J.: Prentice-Hall.

DYE, THOMAS R., AND HARMON ZEIGLER. (1990) *The Irony of Democracy*, 8th ed. Pacific Grove, Calif.: Brooks/Cole.

EBERSTADT, NICHOLAS. (1991) "Population Change and National Security," *Foreign Affairs* 70 (Summer): 115–31.

EDWARDS, GEORGE C., III, WILLIAM MITCHELL, AND REED WELCH. (1995) "Explaining Presidential Approval: The Significance of Issue Salience," *American Journal of Political Science* 39 (February): 108–34.

EHRLICH, PAUL R., AND ANNE H. EHRLICH. (1990) *The Population Explosion*. New York: Simon & Schuster.

EHRLICH, PAUL R., CARL SAGAN, DONALD KENNEDY, AND WALTER ORR ROBERTS. (1985) *The Cold and the Dark: The World after Nuclear War*. New York: Norton.

EICHENGREEN, BARRY, AND PETER B. KENEN. (1994) "Managing the World Economy under the Bretton Woods System: An Overview," pp. 3–57 in Peter B. Kenen (ed.), *Managing the World Economy: Fifty Years after Bretton Woods*. Washington, D.C.: Institute for International Economics.

ELAND, IVAN. (1993) "Think Small," *Bulletin of the Atomic Scientists* 49 (November): 36–40.

ELAZAR, DANIEL J. (1994) *The American Mosaic: The Impact of Space, Time, and Culture on American Politics*. Boulder, Colo.: Westview.

———. (1970) *Cities of the Prairie*. New York: Basic Books.

ELLIOTT, KIM ANDREW. (1989–1990) "Too Many Voices of America," *Foreign Policy* 77 (Winter): 113–31.

ELLIOTT, KIMBERLY ANN. (1993) "A Look at the Record," *Bulletin of the Atomic Scientists* 49 (November): 32–35.

ELLIS, JOHN. (1993) *The World War II Databook*. London: Aurum Press.

ELLSWORTH, ROBERT F., AND KENNETH L. ADELMAN. (1979) "Foolish Intelligence," *Foreign Policy* 36 (Fall): 147–59.

EMERSON, STEVEN. (1993) "The Accidental Terrorist," *Washington Post*, June 13, p. C5.

———. (1988) *Secret Warriors: Inside the Covert Military Operations of the Reagan Era*. New York: G. Putnam's Sons.

EMMOTT, BILL. (1994) *Japanophobia: The Myth of the Invincible Japanese*. New York: Times Books.

ENTMAN, ROBERT M. (1989) "How the Media Affect What People Think: An Information Processing Approach," *Journal of Politics* 51 (May): 347–70.

ESTY, DANIEL. (1994) *Greening the GATT: Trade, Environment, and the Future*. Washington, D.C.: Institute for International Economics.

———. (1993) "GATTing the Greens: Not Just Greening the GATT," *Foreign Affairs* 72 (November/December): 32–36.

ETHEREDGE, LLOYD S. (1985) *Can Governments Learn? American Foreign Policy and Central American Revolutions*. New York: Pergamon.

———. (1978) *A World of Men: The Private Sources of American Foreign Policy*. Cambridge, Mass.: MIT Press.

ETZIONI, AMITAI. (1984) "Military Industry's Threat to National Security," *New York Times*, April 6, p. A35.

FAGEN, RICHARD R. (1975) "The United States and Chile: Roots and Branches," *Foreign Affairs* 53 (January): 297–313.

———. (1960) "Some Assessments and Uses of Public Opinion in Diplomacy," *Public Opinion Quarterly* 24 (Fall): 448–57.

FALK, RICHARD. (1983) "Lifting the Curse of Bipartisanship," *World Policy Journal* 1 (Fall): 127–57.

FALKOWSKI, LAWRENCE S. (ed.). (1979) *Psychological Models in International Politics*. Boulder, Colo.: Westview.

FALLOWS, JAMES. (1994a) "Flat Growth," *Atlantic Monthly* 274 (November): 134–39.

———. (1994b) *Looking at the Sun*. New York: Pantheon.

"Far Flung Frontiers of Security: The Clinton Administration's Two-War Strategy." (1995) *The Defense Monitor* 23 (no. 1).

FARAH, BARBARA G., AND ETHEL KLEIN. (1989) "Public Opinion Trends," pp. 103–28 in Gerald M. Pomper, Ross K. Baker, Walter Dean Burnham, Barbara G.

Farah, Marjorie Randon Hershey, Ethel Klein and Wilson Carey McWilliams, *The Elections of 1988: Reports and Interpretations*. Chatham, N.J.: Chatham House.

FARNSWORTH, ELIZABETH. (1974) "Chile: What Was the U.S. Role? More than Admitted," *Foreign Policy* 16 (Fall): 127–41.

FEIS, HERBERT. (1966) *The Atomic Bomb and the End of World War II*. Princeton, N.J.: Princeton University Press.

FEITH, DOUGLAS J., AND FRANK GAFFNEY, JR. (1994) "Toxic Treaty," *New Republic*, September 5, pp. 21–22.

FELDSTEIN, MARTIN. (1992) "The Council of Economic Advisers and Economic Advising in the United States," *Economic Journal* 102 (September): 1223-34.

FENNO, RICHARD F., JR. (1973) *Congressmen in Committees*. Boston: Little, Brown.

FERRELL, ROBERT H. (1988) *American Diplomacy: The Twentieth Century*. New York: Norton.

FESTINGER, LEON. (1957) *A Theory of Cognitive Dissonance*. Evanston, Ill.: Row, Peterson.

Final Report of the Select Committee to Study Governmental Operations with Respect to Intelligence Activities, U.S. Senate, 94th Congress, 2nd Session. (1976). Washington, D.C.: Government Printing Office.

FINLAYSON, JOCK A., AND MARK W. ZACHER. (1988) *Managing International Markets: Developing Countries and the Commodity Trade Regime*. New York: Columbia University Press.

FIORINA, MORRIS P. (1981) *Retrospective Voting in American National Elections*. New Haven, Conn.: Yale University Press.

FISHER, LOUIS. (1994–1995) "Congressional Checks on Military Initiatives," *Political Science Quarterly* 109 (Winter): 739–62.

———. (1993) *The Politics of Shared Power: Congress and the Executive*, 3rd ed. Washington, D.C.: CQ Press.

———. (1991) *Constitutional Conflicts between Congress and the President*, 3rd ed. Lawrence: University of Kansas Press.

———. (1988) "Foreign Policy Powers of the President and Congress," *The Annals* 449 (September): 148–59.

FITE, DAVID, MARC GENEST, AND CLYDE WILCOX. (1990) "Gender Differences in Foreign Policy Attitudes: A Longitudinal Analysis," *American Politics Quarterly* 18 (October): 492–512.

FITZGERALD, FRANCIS. (1989) "Annals of Justice: Iran-Contra," *The New Yorker*, October 16, pp. 51–84.

FLANAGAN, STEPHEN J. (1985) "Managing the Intelligence Community," *International Security* 10 (Summer): 58–95.

FLEISHER, RICHARD. (1985) "Economic Benefit, Ideology, and Senate Voting on the B-1 Bomber," *American Politics Quarterly* 13 (April): 200–211.

FLICKNER, CHARLES. (1994–1995) "The Russian Aid Mess," *The National Interest* 38 (Winter): 13–18.

FORD, GERALD R. (1979) *A Time to Heal*. New York: Harper & Row.

FOSSEDAL, GREGORY A. (1985) "The Military-Congressional Complex," *Wall Street Journal*, August 8, p. 22.

FOSTER, GREGORY D. (1989) "Global Demographic Trends to the Year 2010: Implications for U.S. Security," *Washington Quarterly* 12 (Spring): 5–24.

FOX, ANNETTE BAKER. (1995) "Environment and Trade: The NAFTA Case," *Political Science Quarterly* 110 (Spring): 49–68.

FOX, HARRISON W., JR., AND SUSAN WEBB HAMMOND. (1977) *Congressional Staffs: The Invisible Force in American Lawmaking*. New York: Free Press.

FRANK, CHARLES R., JR., AND MARY BAIRD. (1975) "Foreign Aid: Its Speckled Past and Future Prospects," *International Organization* 29 (Winter): 133–67.

FRANK, ROBERT S. (1973) *Message Dimensions of Television News*. Lexington, Mass.: Lexington Books.

FRANKEL, CHARLES. (1969) *High on Foggy Bottom*. New York: Harper & Row.

FRANKEL, JEFFREY A. (1995) "Still the Lingua Franca: The Exaggerated Death of the Dollar," *Foreign Affairs* 74 (July/August): 9–16.

FRANKOVIC, KATHLEEN A. (1982) "Sex and Politics—New Alignments, Old Issues," *PS* 15 (Summer): 439–48.

FREEMAN, J. LEIPER. (1965) "The Bureaucracy in Pressure Politics," pp. 23–35 in Francis E. Ranke (ed.), *Bureaucratic Power in National Politics*. Boston: Little, Brown.

FRENCH, HILARY F. (1994) "Can the Environment Survive Industrial Demands?" *USA Today* 122 (January): 66–69.

———. (1993) "The GATT: Menace or Ally," *World Watch* 6 (September-October): 12–19.

FRIEDBERG, AARON L. (1994) "The Future of American Power," *Political Science Quarterly* 109 (Spring): 1–22.

———. (1992) "Why Didn't the United States Become a Garrison State?" *International Security* 16 (Spring): 109–42.

———. (1989) "The Strategic Implications of Relative Economic Decline," *Political Science Quarterly* 104 (Fall): 401–31.

FRIEDMAN, ALAN. (1993) *Spider's Web: The Secret History of How the White House Illegally Armed Iraq*. New York: Bantam.

FRIEDMAN, THOMAS L. (1994a) "Never Mind Yen. Greenbacks Are the New Gold Standard," *New York Times*, July 3, p. E5.

———. (1994b) "Trade War Isn't So Swell Either," *New York Times*, March 6, p. E4.

———. (1994c) "What Big Stick? Just Sell," *New York Times*, October 2, p. E3.

———. (1994d) "When Money Talks, Governments Listen," *New York Times*, July 24, p. E5.

FROMKIN, DAVID. (1994a) "Don't Send in the Marines," *New York Times Magazine*, February 27, pp. 36–37.

———. (1994b) "What Is Wilsonianism?" *World Policy Journal* 11 (Spring): 100–111.

FUKUYAMA, FRANCIS. (1992) "The Beginning of Foreign Policy," *New Republic*, August 17 and 24, pp. 24–32.

FULBRIGHT, J. WILLIAM. (1979) "The Legislator as Educator," *Foreign Affairs* 57 (Spring): 719–32.

FULLER, GRAHAM. (1995) "The Next Ideology," *Foreign Policy* 98 (Spring): 145–58.

GADDIS, JOHN LEWIS. (1992) *The United States and the End of the Cold War: Implications, Reconsiderations, Provocations.* New York: Oxford University Press.

———. (1991) "Great Illusions, the Long Peace, and the Future of the International System," pp. 25–55 in Charles W. Kegley, Jr. (ed.), *The Long Postwar Peace: Contending Explanations and Projections.* New York: HarperCollins.

———. (1990) "Coping with Victory," *Atlantic Monthly* 265 (Winter): 49–60.

———. (1987–1988) "Containment and the Logic of Strategy," *The National Interest* 10 (Winter): 27–38.

———. (1986) "The Long Peace: Elements of Stability in the Postwar International Sys[chtem," *International Security* 10 (Spring): 99–142.

———. (1983) "Containment: Its Past and Future," pp. 16–31 in Charles W. Kegley, Jr., and Eugene R. Wittkopf (eds.), *Perspectives on American Foreign Policy.* New York: St. Martin's.

———. (1982) *Strategies of Containment: A Critical Appraisal of Postwar American National Security Policy.* New York: Oxford University Press.

———. (1972) *The United States and the Origins of the Cold War.* New York: Columbia University Press.

GALBRAITH, JOHN KENNETH. (1973) "The Decline of American Power," pp. 311–50 in Lloyd C. Gardner (ed.), *The Great Nixon Turnaround.* New York: New Viewpoints.

———. (1970–1971) "The Plain Lessons of a Bad Decade," *Foreign Policy* 1 (Winter): 31–45.

———. (1969a) *Ambassador's Journal.* Boston: Houghton Mifflin.

———. (1969b) "The Power of the Pentagon," *The Progressive* 33 (June): 29.

GALLAGHER, WINIFRED. (1994) "How We Become What We Are," *Atlantic Monthly* 274 (September): 38–55.

GANS, HERBERT J. (1979) *Deciding What's News.* New York: Vintage Books.

GARDNER, RICHARD N. (1990) "The Comeback of Liberal Internationalism," *Washington Quarterly* 13 (Summer): 23–39.

———. (1969) *Sterling-Dollar Diplomacy: The Origins and the Prospects of Our International Economic Order.* New York: McGraw-Hill.

GARTHOFF, RAYMOND L. (1994) "Looking Back: The Cold War in Retrospect," *Brookings Review* 12 (Summer): 10–13.

GASIOROWSKI, MARK J. (1987) "The 1953 Coup D'Etat in Iran," *International Journal of Middle East Studies* 19 (August): 261–86.

GATES, ROBERT M. (1987–1988) "The CIA and American Foreign Policy," *Foreign Affairs* 66 (Winter): 215–30.

GAUSE, F. GREGORY, III. (1994) "The Illogic of Dual Containment," *Foreign Affairs* 73 (March/April): 56–66.

GELB, LESLIE H. (1994) "Quelling the Teacup Wars: The New World's Constant Challenge," *Foreign Affairs* 73 (November/December): 2–6.

———. (1983) "Why Not the State Department?" pp. 282–98 in Charles W. Kegley, Jr., and Eugene R. Wittkopf (eds.), *Perspectives on American Foreign Policy.* New York: St. Martin's.

———. (1976) "What Exactly Is Kissinger's Legacy?" *New York Times Magazine*, October 31, pp. 13–15 passim.

GELB, LESLIE H., AND MORTON H. HALPERIN. (1973) "The Ten Commandments of the Foreign Affairs Bureaucracy," pp. 250–59 in Steven L. Spiegel (ed.), *At Issue: Politics in the World Arena.* New York: St. Martin's.

GELLMAN, BARTON. (1993) "Pin Stripes Clash with Stars and Bars," *Washington Post National Weekly Edition*, June 28-July 3, pp. 31–32.

———. (1992a) "On Second Thought, We Don't Want to Rule the World," *Washington Post National Weekly Edition*, June 1–7, p. 31.

———. (1992b) "The U.S. Aims to Remain First among Nonequals," *Washington Post National Weekly Edition*, March 16–22, p. 19.

GELLNER, ERNEST. (1994) *Conditions of Liberty: Civil Society and Its Rivals.* London: Penguin.

GEORGE, ALEXANDER L. (1992) *Forceful Persuasion: Coercive Diplomacy as an Alternative to War.* Washington, D.C.: United States Institute for Peace.

———. (1988) "Presidential Management Styles and Models," pp. 107–26 in Charles W. Kegley, Jr., and Eugene R. Wittkopf (eds.), *The Domestic Sources of American Foreign Policy: Insights and Evidence.* New York: St. Martin's.

———. (1980) *Presidential Decisionmaking in Foreign Policy: The Effective Use of Information and Advice.* Boulder, Colo.: Westview.

———. (1972) "The Case for Multiple Advocacy in Making Foreign Policy," *American Political Science Review* 66 (September): 751–85.

GEORGE, ALEXANDER L., AND JULIETTE L. GEORGE.

(1964) *Woodrow Wilson and Colonel House: A Personality Study*. New York: Dover.

GERGEN, DAVID. (1989) "The Bush Administration's Three Musketeers," *Washington Post National Weekly Edition*, April 17–23, pp. 23–24.

GERSTENZANG, JAMES, AND RICHARD MEYER. (1990) "Growing Gulf Crisis Has Turned a Quiet Bush into an Angry Man," *Morning Advocate*, November 27, p. 7A.

GILBERT, FELIX. (1961) *The Beginnings of American Foreign Policy: To the Farewell Address*. New York: Harper Torchbooks.

GILBOA, EYTAN. (1987) *American Public Opinion toward Israel and the Arab-Israel Conflict*. Lexington, Mass.: Lexington.

GILL, STEPHEN, AND DAVID LAW. (1988) *The Global Political Economy: Perspectives, Problems, and Policies*. Baltimore: Johns Hopkins University Press.

GILPIN, KENNETH N. (1994) "New Third World Fear: Investors Could Walk Away," *New York Times*, April 24, p. F4.

GILPIN, ROBERT. (1987) "The Political Economy of International Relations." Princeton, N.J. Princeton University Press.

GILPIN, TODD. (1995) "After the Failed Faiths: Beyond Individualism, Marxism, and Multiculturalism," *World Policy Journal* 12 (Spring): 61–68.

GIVENS, W. L. (1995) "Economic Cocaine: America's Exchange Rate Addition," *Foreign Affairs* 74 (July/August): 17–21.

GLAD, BETTY. (1983) "Black-and-White Thinking: Ronald Reagan's Approach to Foreign Policy," *Political Psychology* 4 (March): 33–76.

GLASER, CHARLES L. (1993) "Why NATO Is Still Best: Future Security Arrangements for Europe," *International Security* 18 (Summer): 5–50.

———. (1992) "Nuclear Policy without an Adversary: U.S. Planning for the Post-Soviet Era," *International Security* 16 (Spring): 34–78.

GLYNN, PATRICK. (1992) "The Storm after the Storm: What's Our Defense Now?" *The American Enterprise* 3 (September/October): 33–43.

GOLDMUNTZ, LAWRENCE. (1994) "On The Right," *National Review*, August 15, pp. 32–36.

GOLDSBOROUGH, JAMES O. (1993) "California's Foreign Policy," *Foreign Affairs* 72 (Spring): 88–96.

GOLDSTEIN, JOSHUA S. (1988) *Long Cycles: Prosperity and War in the Modern Age*. New Haven, Conn.: Yale University Press.

GOLDSTEIN, JUDITH. (1989) "The Impact of Ideas on Trade Policy: The Origins of U.S. Agricultural and Manufacturing Policies," *International Organization* 43 (Winter): 31–71.

GOODMAN, ALLAN E. (1987) "Reforming U.S. Intelligence," *Foreign Policy* 67 (Summer): 121–36.

———. (1984–1985) "Dateline Langley: Fixing the Intelligence Mess," *Foreign Policy* 57 (Winter): 160–79.

———. (1975) "The Causes and Consequences of Détente, 1949–1973." Paper presented at the National Security Education Seminar, Colorado Springs, Colo., July.

GOODPASTER, ANDREW J. (1993) *Further Reins on Nuclear Arms: Next Step for the Major Nuclear Powers*. Washington, D.C.: The Atlantic Council.

GOODSELL, CHARLES T. (1985) *The Case for Bureaucracy*, 2nd ed. Chatham, N.J.: Chatham House.

GOODWIN, JACOB. (1985) *Brotherhood of Arms: General Dynamics and the Business of Defending America*. New York: Times Books.

GORE, AL. (1993a) *Earth in the Balance: Ecology and the Human Spirit*. New York: Plume.

———. (1993b) "This Time We Mean Business," *Washington Post National Weekly Edition*, September 20–26, p. 25.

GOSHKO, JOHN M. (1994) "Undiplomatic Doubts at Foggy Bottom," *Washington Post National Weekly Edition*, June 27–July 3, p. 31.

———. (1989) "Foreign Policy in Turmoil—or Transition?" *Washington Post National Weekly Edition*, March 13–19, p. 7.

GOWING, NIK. (1994) "Discounting the 'CNN Factor,'" *Washington Post National Weekly Edition*, August 8–14, p. 23.

GRABER, DORIS A. (1993) *Mass Media and American Politics*, 4th ed. Washington, D.C.: CQ Press.

GRAHAM, BRADLEY, AND JOHN F. HARRIS. (1994) "The Pentagon's Costly Goals," *Washington Post National Weekly Edition*, August 15–21, pp. 10–11.

GRAHAM, THOMAS R. (1979) "Revolution in Trade Politics," *Foreign Policy* 26 (Fall): 49–63.

GRAHAM, THOMAS W. (1986) "Public Attitudes towards Active Defense: ABM and Star Wars, 1945–1985." Cambridge, Mass.: Center for International Studies, Massachusetts Institute of Technology.

GRAVES, ERNEST. (1993) "Restructuring Foreign Assistance," *Washington Quarterly* 16 (Summer): 189–98.

———. (1991) "The Future of U.S. Security Assistance and Arms Sales," *Washington Quarterly* 14 (Summer): 47–56.

GRAY, COLIN S., AND KEITH PAYNE. (1980) "Victory Is Possible," *Foreign Policy* 39 (Summer): 14–27.

GREENBERG, EDWARD S. (1985) *Capitalism and the American Political Ideal*. Armonk, N.Y.: Sharpe.

GREENSTEIN, FRED I. (1994) "The Hidden-Hand Presidency: Eisenhower as Leader, a 1994 Perspective," *Presidential Studies Quarterly* 24 (Spring): 233–241.

———. (1993–1994) "The Presidential Leadership Style

of Bill Clinton: An Early Appraisal," *Political Science Quarterly* 108 (Winter): 589–601.

———. (1982) *The Hidden Hand Presidency: Eisenhower as Leader*. New York: Basic Books.

———. (1969) *Personality and Politics*. Princeton, N.J.: Princeton University Press.

GREGG, ROBERT W. (1994) "The U.S.—UN Relationship: Troubled Past, Uncertain Future," pp. 257–273 in Eugene R. Wittkopf (ed.). *The Future of American Foreign Policy*, 2nd ed. New York: St. Martin's.

———. (1993) *About Face? The United States and the United Nations*. Boulder, Colo.: Lynne Rienner.

GRIEVE, MALCOLM J. (1993) "Debt and Imperialism: Perspectives on the Debt Crisis," pp. 51–68 in Stephen P. Riley (ed.), *The Politics of Global Debt*. New York: St. Martin's.

GRIMMETT, RICHARD F. (1995) "Conventional Arms Transfers to Developing Nations, 1987–1994," *CRS Report for Congress*, August 4. Washington, D.C.: Congressional Research Service.

GROVE, LLOYD. (1993) "David Gergen, a True Team Player," *Washington Post National Weekly Edition*, July 26-August 1, pp. 12–13.

———. (1991) "Israel's Force in Washington," *Washington Post National Weekly Edition*, June 24–30, pp. 8–9.

GURR, TED ROBERT. (1993) *Minorities at Risk: A Global View of Ethnopolitical Conflict*. Washington, D.C.: United States Institute for Peace.

———. (1991) "America as a Model for the World? A Skeptical View," *PS: Political Science & Politics* 24 (December): 664–67.

GURR, TED ROBERT, AND BARBARA HARFF. (1994) *Ethnic Conflict in World Politics*. Boulder, Colo.: Westview.

HAASS, RICHARD N. (1995) "Paradigm Lost," *Foreign Affairs* 74 (January/February): 43–58.

———. (1994a) "Bill Clinton's Adhocracy," *New York Times Magazine*, May 29, pp. 40–41.

———. (1994b) *Intervention: The Use of American Military Force in the Post-Cold War World*. Washington, D.C.: Carnegie Endowment.

———. (1994c) "Military Force: A User's Guide," *Foreign Policy* 96 (Fall): 21–37.

HALBERSTAM, DAVID. (1972) *The Best and the Brightest*. New York: Random House.

HALL, BRIAN. (1994) "Blue Helmets, Empty Guns," *New York Times Magazine*, January 2, pp. 20–25ff.

HALPERIN, MORTON H. (1993) "Guaranteeing Democracy," *Foreign Policy* 91 (Summer): 105–22.

———. (1971) "Why Bureaucrats Play Games," *Foreign Policy* 2 (Spring): 70–90.

HAMBY, ALONZO L. (1992) "America First—Revisited," *The American Enterprise* 3 (March/April): 76–77.

HAMILTON, LEE H. (1988) "Congress and the Presidency in American Foreign Policy," *Presidential Studies Quarterly* 18 (Summer): 507–11.

HAMMOND, PAUL Y. (1994) "Central Organization in the Transition from Bush to Clinton," pp. 163–81 in Charles F. Hermann (ed.), *American Defense Annual 1994*. New York: Lexington.

HAMPSON, FEN OSLER. (1988) "The Divided Decision-Maker," pp. 227–47 in Charles W. Kegley, Jr., and Eugene R. Wittkopf (eds.), *The Domestic Sources of American Foreign Policy: Insights and Evidence*. New York: St. Martin's.

HAN, ALBERT. (1992–1993) "No Defense for Strategic Defense," *Harvard International Review* 156 (Winter): 54–57.

Handbook of Economic Statistics, 1991. (1991). Washington, D.C.: Central Intelligence Agency.

Handbook of Economic Statistics, 1989. (1989). Washington, D.C.: Central Intelligence Agency.

HANDELMAN, STEPHEN. (1994) "The Russian 'Mafiya,'" *Foreign Affairs* 73 (March/April): 83–96.

HANEY, CRAIG, AND PHILIP ZIMBARDO. (1973) "Social Roles, Role-Playing, and Education," *Behavioral and Social Science Teacher* 1 (no. 1): 24–45.

HANSEN, ROGER D. (1980) "North-South Policy—What's the Problem?" *Foreign Affairs* 58 (Summer): 1104–28.

HARR, JOHN ENSOR. (1969) *The Professional Diplomat*. Princeton, N.J.: Princeton University Press.

HARRIES, OWEN. (1993) "The Collapse of 'The West,'" *Foreign Affairs* 72 (September/October): 41–53.

HARRIGAN, ANTHONY. (1994) "Hollowing Out America's Defenses," *National Review*, July 11, pp. 40–44.

HARRIS, JOHN B., AND ERIC MARKUSEN. (1986) "Nuclear Weapons and Their Effects," pp. 24–26 in John B. Harris and Eric Markusen (eds.), *Nuclear Weapons and the Threat of Nuclear War*. San Diego: Harcourt Brace Jovanovich.

HART, JEFFREY A. (1992) *Rival Capitalists: International Competitiveness in the United States, Japan, and Western Europe*. Ithaca, N.Y.: Cornell University Press.

HARTUNG, WILLIAM D. (1995) "Nixon's Children: Bill Clinton and the Permanent Arms Bazaar," *World Policy Journal* 12 (Summer): 25–35.

———. (1994a) *And Arms for All*. New York: HarperCollins.

———. (1994b) "The Phantom Profits of the War Trade," *New York Times*, March 6, p. 13.

———. (1993) "Welcome to the U.S. Arms Superstore," *Bulletin of the Atomic Scientists* 49 (September): 20–26.

———. (1992) "Curbing the Arms Trade: From Rhetoric to Restraint," *World Policy Journal* 9 (Spring): 219–47.

HARTZ, LOUIS. (1955) *The Liberal Tradition in America*. New York: Harcourt Brace and World.

HASTEDT, GLENN P., AND ANTHONY J. EKSTEROWICZ. (1993) "Presidential Leadership in the Post Cold War Era," *Presidential Studies Quarterly* 23 (Summer): 445-58.

HEAD, IVAN L. (1989) "South-North Dangers," *Foreign Affairs* 68 (Summer): 71–86.

HENDERSON, PHILLIP G. (1988) *Managing the Presidency: The Eisenhower Legacy—From Kennedy to Reagan.* Boulder, Colo.: Westview.

HENDRICKSON, DAVID C. (1994–1995) "The Democratist Crusade: Intervention, Economic Sanctions, and Engagement," *World Policy Journal* 11 (Winter): 26–43.

———. (1994) "The Recovery of Internationalism," *Foreign Affairs* 73 (September/October): 26–43.

HENKIN, LOUIS. (1972) *Foreign Affairs and the Constitution.* Mineola, N.Y.: Foundation Press.

HERKEN, GREGG. (1982) *The Winning Weapon: The Atomic Bomb in the Cold War, 1945–1950.* New York: Vintage.

HERMANN, CHARLES F. (1972) "Some Issues in the Study of International Crisis," pp. 3–17 in Charles F. Hermann (ed.), *International Crises: Insights from Behavioral Research.* New York: Free Press.

———. (1969) "International Crisis as a Situational Variable," pp. 409–21 in James N. Rosenau (ed.), *International Politics and Foreign Policy.* New York: Free Press.

HERMANN, MARGARET G. (1989) "Defining the Bush Presidential Style," *Mershon Memo,* Spring, p. 1.

———. (1986) "Ingredients of Leadership," pp. 167–92 in Margaret G. Hermann (ed.), *Political Psychology.* San Francisco: Jossey-Bass.

———. (1983) "Assessing Personality at a Distance: A Profile of Ronald Reagan," *Mershon Center Quarterly Report* 7 (Spring): 1–8.

———. (1976) "When Leader Personality Will Affect Foreign Policy: Some Propositions," pp. 326–33 in James N. Rosenau (ed.), *In Search of Global Patterns.* New York: Free Press.

HERMANN, MARGARET G., AND CHARLES F. HERMANN. (1989) "Who Makes Foreign Policy Choices and How: An Empirical Inquiry," *International Studies Quarterly* 33 (December): 361–87.

HERMANN, MARGARET G., WITH THOMAS W. MILBURN (eds). (1977) *A Psychological Examination of Political Leaders.* New York: Free Press.

HERMANN, MARGARET G., AND THOMAS PRESTON. (1994) "Presidents and Their Advisers: Leadership Style, Advisory Systems, and Foreign Policymaking," pp. 340–56 in Eugene R. Wittkopf (ed.), *The Domestic Sources of American Foreign Policy: Insights and Evidence,* 2nd ed. New York: St. Martin's.

HERRMANN, RICHARD K. (1986) "The Power of Perceptions in Foreign-Policy Decision Making: Do Views of the Soviet Union Determine the Policy Choices of American Leaders?" *American Journal of Political Science* 30 (November): 841–75.

HERSH, SEYMOUR M. (1994) "Missile Wars," *The New Yorker,* September 26, pp. 86–99.

———. (1983) *The Price of Power: Kissinger in the Nixon White House.* New York: Summit Books.

HESS, STEPHEN. (1984) *The Government/Press Connection.* Washington, D.C.: Brookings Institution.

HESS, STEPHEN, AND MICHAEL NELSON. (1985) "Foreign Policy: Dominance and Decisiveness in Presidential Elections," pp. 129–54 in Michael Nelson (ed.), *The Elections of 1984.* Washington, D.C.: CQ Press.

HIATT, FRED, AND RICK ATKINSON. (1985) "The Defense Boom: Uncle Sam Is a Cream of a Customer," *Washington Post National Weekly Edition,* April 29, pp. 19-22.

HILSMAN, ROGER. (1992) *George Bush vs. Saddam Hussein: Military Success! Political Failure?* Novato, Calif.: Lyford Books.

———. (1990) *The Politics of Policy Making in Defense and Foreign Affairs,* 2nd ed. Englewood Cliffs, N.J.: Prentice-Hall.

———. (1967) *To Move a Nation.* New York: Doubleday.

HINCKLEY, RONALD H. (1993) "Neo-Isolationism: A Threat or a Myth?" *The Wirthlin Report* 3 (January): 1–3.

———. (1989) "American Opinion toward the Soviet Union," *International Journal of Public Opinion Research* 1 (no. 3): 242–57.

HIRSHBERG, MATTHEW S. (1993) *Perpetuating Patriotic Perceptions: The Cognitive Function of the Cold War.* Westport, Conn.: Praeger.

HOAGLAND, JIM. (1994a) "Old Boys at the CIA," *Washington Post National Weekly Edition,* March 14–20, p. 29.

———. (1994b) "Pushing Japan to the Brink," *Washington Post National Weekly Edition,* February 28-March 6, p. 29.

HOFFER, ERIC. (1951) *The True Believer.* New York: Harper and Brothers.

HOFFMANN, STANLEY. (1995) "The Crisis of Liberal Internationalism," *Foreign Policy* 98 (Spring): 159–77.

———. (1993) "Out of the Cold: Humanitarian Intervention in the 1990s," *Harvard International Review* 16 (Fall): 8–9, 62.

———. (1992) "Bush Abroad," *New York Review of Books* 39 (November 5): 54–59.

———. (1989) "What Should We Do in the World?" *Atlantic Monthly* 264 (October): 84–96.

———. (1979–1980) "Muscle and Brains," *Foreign Policy* 37 (Winter): 3–27.

———. (1978) *Primacy or World Order: American Foreign Policy Since the Cold War.* New York: McGraw-Hill.

HOFSTADTER, RICHARD. (1965) *The Paranoid Style in American Politics and Other Essays*. New York: Knopf.

HOGE, JAMES F., JR. (1994) "Media Pervasiveness," *Foreign Affairs* 73 (July/August): 136–44.

HOLLOWAY, DAVID. (1994) *Stalin and the Bomb: The Soviet Union and Atomic Energy 1939–1956*. New Haven, Conn.: Yale University Press.

HOLMES, GENTA HAWKINS. (1994) "Diversity in the Department of State and the Foreign Service," *State Magazine* 375 (March): 18–25.

HOLSTI, OLE R. (1995) "Theories of International Politics and Foreign Policy: Realism and Its Challengers," pp. 35–65 in Charles W. Kegley, Jr. (ed.), *Controversies in International Relations Theory: Realism and the Neoliberal Challenge*. New York: St. Martin's.

———. (1994) "Public Opinion and Foreign Policy: Attitude Structures of Opinion Leaders after the Cold War," pp. 36–56 in Eugene R. Wittkopf (ed.), *The Domestic Sources of American Foreign Policy Insights and Evidence*, 2nd ed. New York: St. Martin's.

———. (1992) "Public Opinion and Foreign Policy: Challenges to the Almond-Lippmann Consensus," *International Studies Quarterly* 36 (December): 439–66.

———. (1987) "Public Opinion and Containment," pp. 20–58 in Terry L. Deibel and John Lewis Gaddis (eds.), *Containing the Soviet Union*. Washington, D.C.: Pergamon-Brassey's.

———. (1976) "Foreign Policy Formation Viewed Cognitively," pp. 18–54 in Robert Axelrod (ed.), *Structure of Decision: The Cognitive Maps of Political Elites*. Princeton, N.J.: Princeton University Press.

———. (1973) "Foreign Policy Decision-Makers Viewed Psychologically." Paper presented at the Conference on the Successes and Failures of Scientific International Relations Research, Ojai, Calif., June 25–28.

———. (1962) "The Belief System and National Images: A Case Study," *Journal of Conflict Resolution* 6 (September): 244–52.

HOLSTI, OLE R., AND JAMES N. ROSENAU. (1994) "The Foreign Policy Beliefs of American Leaders after the Cold War: Persistence or Abatement of Partisan Cleavages?" pp. 127–47 in Eugene R. Wittkopf (ed.), *The Future of American Foreign Policy*, 2nd ed. New York: St. Martin's.

———. (1993) "The Structure of Foreign Policy Beliefs among American Opinion Leaders—After the Cold War," *Millennium: Journal of International Studies* 22 (Summer): 235–78.

———. (1990) "The Structure of Foreign Policy Attitudes: American Leaders, 1976–1984," *Journal of Politics* 52 (February): 94–125.

———. (1984) *American Leadership in World Affairs: Vietnam and the Breakdown of Consensus*. Boston: Allen & Unwin.

———. (1980) "Does Where You Stand Depend on When You Were Born? The Impact of Generation on Post-Vietnam Foreign Policy Beliefs," *Public Opinion Quarterly* 44 (Spring): 1–22.

HOLT, PAT M. (1995) *Secret Intelligence and Public Policy: A Dilemma of Democracy*. Washington, D.C.: CQ Press.

HOMER-DIXON, THOMAS F. (1991) "On the Threshold: Environmental Changes as Causes of Acute Conflict," *International Security* 16 (Fall): 76–116.

HOMER-DIXON, THOMAS F., JEFFREY H. BOUTWELL, AND GEORGE W. RATHJENS. (1993) "Environmental Change and Violent Conflict," *Scientific American* 268 (February): 38–45.

HOOPES, TOWNSEND. (1973a) *The Devil and John Foster Dulles: The Diplomacy of the Eisenhower Era*. Boston: Little, Brown.

———. (1973b) *The Limits of Intervention*. New York: McKay.

HOPPLE, GERALD. (1982) *Biopolitics, Political Psychology and International Politics*. New York: St. Martin's.

HORMATS, ROBERT D. (1994) "Making Regionalism Safe," *Foreign Affairs* 73 (March/April): 97–108.

HOROWITZ, DAVID. (1965) *The Free World Colossus*. New York: Hill and Wang.

HOUSE, KAREN ELIOT. (1989) "As Power Is Dispersed among Nations, Need for Leadership Grows," *Wall Street Journal*, February 21, pp. A1, A10.

HUFBAUER, GARY CLYDE, AND KIMBERLY ANN ELLIOTT. (1994) *Measuring the Costs of Protection in the United States*. Washington, D.C.: Institute for International Economics.

HUFBAUER, GARY CLYDE, AND JEFFREY J. SCHOTT. (1985) *Trading for Growth: The Next Round of Trade Negotiations*. Washington, D.C.: Institute for International Economics.

HUFBAUER, GARY CLYDE, JEFFREY J. SCHOTT, AND KIMBERLY ANN ELLIOTT. (1990) *Economic Sanctions Reconsidered: History and Current Policy*, 2nd ed. Washington, D.C.: Institute for International Economics.

HUGHES, EMMET JOHN. (1972) *The Living Presidency*. New York: Coward, McCann and Geoghegan.

Human Development Report 1994. (1994). New York: Oxford University Press.

Human Development Report 1993. (1993). New York: Oxford University Press.

HUNT, MICHAEL H. (1987) *Ideology and U.S. Foreign Policy*. New Haven, Conn.: Yale University Press.

HUNTINGTON, SAMUEL P. (1993a) "The Clash of Civilizations?" *Foreign Affairs* 72 (Summer): 22–49.

———. (1993b) "Why International Primacy Matters," *International Security* 17 (Spring): 68–83.

———. (1992–1993) "What Cost Freedom? Democracy

and/or Economic Reform," *Harvard International Review* 15 (Winter): 8–13.

———. (1991) *The Third Wave: Democratization in the Late Twentieth Century*. Norman: University of Oklahoma Press.

———. (1988–1989) "The U.S.—Decline or Renewal?" *Foreign Affairs* 67 (Winter): 76–96.

———. (1957) *The Soldier and the State: The Theory and Politics of Civil-Military Relations*. Cambridge, Mass.: Belknap.

HURWITZ, JON, AND MARK PEFFLEY. (1992) "International Events and Foreign Policy Beliefs: Public Response to Changing Soviet-U.S. Relations," *American Journal of Political Science* 36 (May): 431–61.

———. (1990) "Public Images of the Soviet Union: The Impact of Foreign Policy Attitudes," *Journal of Politics* 52 (February): 3–28.

———. (1987) "How Are Foreign Policy Attitudes Structured? A Hierarchical Model," *American Political Science Review* 81 (December): 1099–1120.

HYBEL, ALEX ROBERTO. (1993) *Power over Rationality: The Bush Administration and the Gulf Crisis*. Albany: State University of New York Press.

IGNATIUS, DAVID. (1995) "Is the CIA's New Mission Impossible?" *Washington Post National Weekly Edition*, March 13–19, pp. 23–24.

———. (1994) "The Best and the Brightest, 1990s Style," *Washington Post National Weekly Edition*, March 14–20, pp. 24–25.

———. (1988) "Is This Any Way for a Country to Buy Weapons?" *Washington Post National Weekly Edition*, July 4–10, p. 23.

IKENBERRY, G. JOHN. (1993) "Salvaging the G-7," *Foreign Affairs* 72 (Spring): 132–39.

———. (1989) "Rethinking the Origins of American Hegemony," *Political Science Quarterly* 104 (Fall): 375–400.

IKLÉ, FRED CHARLES. (1990) "The Ghost in the Pentagon," *The National Interest* 19 (Spring): 13–20.

IMMERMAN, RICHARD H. (1982) *The CIA in Guatemala: The Foreign Policy of Intervention*. Austin: University of Texas Press.

ISAAK, ROBERT A. (1995) *International Political Economy: Managing World Economic Change*, 2nd ed. Englewood Cliffs, N.J.: Prentice Hall.

———. (1977) *American Democracy and World Power*. New York: St. Martin's.

———. (1975) *Individuals and World Politics*. North Scituate, Mass.: Duxbury Press.

IYENGAR, SHANTO, AND DONALD R. KINDER. (1987) *News That Matters: Television and American Opinion*. Chicago: University of Chicago Press.

IYENGAR, SHANTO, MARK D. PETERS, AND DONALD R. KINDER. (1982) "Experimental Demonstrations of the 'Not-So-Minimal' Consequences of Television News Programs," *American Political Science Review* 76 (December): 848–58.

JACKMAN, ROBERT W. (1973) "On the Relationship of Economic Development to Political Performance," *American Journal of Political Science* 17 (August): 611–21.

JACKSON, HENRY M. (1965) *The National Security Council: Jackson Subcommittee Papers on Policy-Making at the Presidential Level*. New York: Praeger.

JACOBSON, HAROLD K. (1984) *Networks of Interdependence: International Organizations and the Global Political System*. New York: Knopf.

JACOBSON, JODI. (1989) "Abandoning Homelands," pp. 59–76 in Lester R. Brown, Christopher Flavin, Sandra Postel, Linda Starke, Alan Durning, Lori Heise, Jodi Jacobson, Michael Renner, and Cynthia Pollack Shea, *State of the World 1989*. New York: Norton.

JAMES, PATRICK, AND JOHN R. ONEAL. (1991) "The Influence of Domestic and International Politics on the President's Use of Force," *Journal of Conflict Resolution* 35 (June): 307–32.

JANIS, IRVING L. (1989) *Crucial Decisions: Leadership in Policymaking and Crisis Management*. New York: Free Press.

———. (1982) *Groupthink: Psychological Studies of Policy Decisions and Fiascoes*, 2nd ed. Boston: Houghton Mifflin.

JAVITS, JACOB K. (1985) "War Powers Reconsidered," *Foreign Affairs* 64 (Fall): 130–40.

JEFFREY, DOUGLAS A. (1988) "Executive Authority under the Separation of Powers," pp. 41–67 in Gordon S. Jones and John A. Marini (eds.), *The Imperial Congress: Crisis in the Separation of Powers*. New York: Pharos Books.

JENTLESON, BRUCE W. (1992) "The Pretty Prudent Public: Post Post-Vietnam American Opinion on the Use of Military Force," *International Studies Quarterly* 36 (March): 49–74.

JERVIS, ROBERT. (1993) "International Primacy: Is the Game Worth the Candle?" *International Security* 17 (Spring): 52–67.

———. (1991–1992) "The Future of World Politics: Will It Resemble the Past?" *International Security* 16 (Winter): 39–73.

———. (1991) "Will the New World Be Better?" pp. 7–19 in Robert Jervis and Seweryn Bialer (eds.), *Soviet-American Relations after the Cold War*. Durham, N.C.: Duke University Press.

JOHNSON, CHALMERS, AND E. B. KEEHN. (1995) "The Pentagon's Ossified Strategy," *Foreign Affairs* 74 (July/August): 103–114.

JOHNSON, DOUGLAS, AND STEVEN METZ. (1995) "Civil-Military Relations in the United States: The State of the Debate," *Washington Quarterly* 18 (Winter): 197–213.

JOHNSON, LOCH K. (1992–1993) "Smart Intelligence," *Foreign Policy* 89 (Winter): 53–69.

———. (1989) *America's Secret Power: The CIA in a Democratic Society*. New York: Oxford University Press.

———. (1984) *The Making of International Agreements*. New York: New York University Press.

———. (1980) "Controlling the Quiet Option," *Foreign Policy* 39 (Summer): 143–53.

JONAH, JAMES O. C. (1993) "Differing State Perspectives on the United Natinos in the Post-Cold War World," *ACUNS Reports and Papers*, No. 4. Providence, R.I.: Academic Council on the United Nations, Brown University.

JONAS, MANFRED. (1966) *Isolationism in America 1935–1941*. Ithaca, N.Y.: Cornell University Press.

JONES, CHRISTOPHER M. (1994) "American Prewar Technology Sales to Iraq: A Bureaucratic Politics Explanation," pp. 279–96 in Eugene R. Wittkopf (ed.), *The Domestic Sources of American Foreign Policy: Insights and Evidence*, 2nd ed. New York: St. Martin's.

JONES, GORDON S., AND JOHN A. MARINI (eds). (1988) *The Imperial Congress: Crisis in the Separation of Powers*. New York: Pharos Books.

JÖNSSON, CHRISTER. (1982) *Cognitive Dynamics and International Politics*. New York: St. Martin's.

JORDAN, DONALD L., AND BENJAMIN I. PAGE. (1992) "Shaping Foreign Policy News: The Role of TV News," *Journal of Conflict Resolution* 36 (June): 227–41.

JOYNER, CHRISTOPHER C. (1993) "When Human Suffering Warrants Military Action," *Chronicle of Higher Education*, January 27, p. A52.

———. (1992) "International Law" pp. 229–44 in Peter J. Schraeder (ed.), *Intervention into the 1990s: U.S. Foreign Policy in the Third World*, 2nd ed. Boulder, Colo.: Lynne Rienner.

JUDIS, JOHN B. (1992) "Statecraft and Scowcroft," *New Republic*, February 24, pp. 18–21.

———. (1990) "The Japanese Megaphone," *New Republic*, January 22, pp. 20–25.

JUSTER, KENNETH I. (1994) "The Myth of Iraqgate," *Foreign Policy* 94 (Spring): 105-19.

KAHLER, MILES. (1995) "A World of Blocs: Facts and Factoids," *World Policy Journal* 12 (Spring): 19–27.

KAHN, DAVID. (1986) "The United States Views Germany and Japan in 1941," in Ernest R. May (ed.), *Knowing One's Enemies: Intelligence Assessment Before the Two World Wars*. Princeton, N.J.: Princeton University Press.

KANTER, ARNOLD, AND LINTON F. BROOKS (eds). (1994) *U.S. Intervention Policy for the Post-Cold War World: New Challenges and New Responses*. New York: Norton.

KAPLAN, MORTON A. (1957) *System and Process in International Politics*. New York: Wiley.

KAPLAN, ROBERT. (1994) "The Coming Anarchy," *Atlantic Monthly* 273 (February): 44–76.

KAPSTEIN, ETHAN B. (1994) "America's Arms-Trade Monopoly," *Foreign Affairs* 73 (May/June): 13–19.

KARNOW, STANLEY. (1983) *Vietnam: A History*. New York: Viking.

KATTENBURG, PAUL. (1980) *The Vietnam Trauma in America Foreign Policy, 1945–75*. New Brunswick, N.J.: Transaction Books.

KATZ, ELIHU. (1957) "The Two-Step Flow of Communications," *Public Opinion Quarterly* 21 (Spring): 61–78.

KATZENSTEIN, PETER J. (1977) "Introduction: Domestic and International Forces of Foreign Economic Policy," *International Organization* 31 (Spring): 587–606.

KAUFMAN, HERBERT. (1976) *Are Government Organizations Immortal?* Washington, D.C.: Brookings Institution.

KAUFMANN, WILLIAM W. (1994) "Hollow Forces? Current Issues of U.S. Military Readiness," *Brookings Review* 12 (Fall): 24–29.

———. (1992) *Assessing the Base Force: How Much Is Too Much?* Washington, D.C.: Brookings Institution.

KEARNS, DORIS. (1976) *Lyndon Johnson and the American Dream*. New York: Harper & Row.

KEENY, SPURGEON M., JR. (1993) "Arms Control during the Transition to the Post-Soviet World," pp. 175–97 in Joseph Kruzel (ed.), *American Defense Annual 1993*. New York: Lexington.

KEENY, SPURGEON M., JR., AND WOLFGANG K. H. PANOFSKY. (1981) "MAD vs. NUTS: Can Doctrine or Weaponry Remedy the Mutual Hostage Relationship of the Superpowers?" *Foreign Affairs* 60 (Winter): 287–304.

KEETER, SCOTT. (1985) "Public Opinion in 1984," pp. 91–111 in Gerald M. Pomper, Ross K. Baker, Charles E. Jacob, Scott Keeter, Wilson Carey McWilliams, and Henry A. Plotkin, *The Election of 1984: Reports and Interpretations*. Chatham, N.J.: Chatham House.

KEFALAS, A.G. (1992) "The Global Corporation: Its Role in the New World Order," *National Forum* 72 (Fall): 26–30.

KEGLEY, CHARLES W., JR. (1994) "How Did the Cold War Die? Principles for an Autopsy," *Mershon International Studies Review* 38 (April): 11–41.

KEGLEY, CHARLES W., JR., AND SHANNON L. BLANTON. (1994) "America's Policy Conundrum: The Promotion of Democratic Nation Building and US Arms Exports," *Brown Journal of World Affairs* 2 (Winter): 65–75.

KEGLEY, CHARLES W., JR., AND STEVEN W. HOOK. (1991) "U.S. Foreign Aid and U.N. Voting: Did Reagan's Linkage Strategy Buy Deference or Defiance?" *International Studies Quarterly* 35 (September): 295–312.

KEGLEY, CHARLES W., JR., AND GREGORY A. RAYMOND.

(1995) "Great Power Relations: Paths to Peace in the Twenty-First Century," pp. 154–165 in Charles W. Kegley, Jr. and Eugene R. Wittkopf (eds.), *The Global Agenda: Issues and Perspectives*, 4th ed. New York: McGraw-Hill.

———. (1994) *A Multipolar Peace? Great-Power Politics in the Twenty-first Century*. New York: St. Martin's.

KEGLEY, CHARLES W., JR., AND EUGENE R. WITTKOPF. (1995) *World Politics: Trend and Transformation*, 5th ed. New York: St. Martin's.

KELLY, MICHAEL. (1994) "The President's Past," *New York Times Magazine*, July 31, pp. 20–29ff.

KEMP, GEOFFREY. (1993) "Presidential Management of the Executive Bureaucracy," pp. 32–48 in Robert J. Art and Seyom Brown (eds.), *U.S. Foreign Policy: The Search for a New Role*. New York: Macmillan.

KEMPE, FREDERICK. (1990) *Divorcing the Dictator: America's Bungled Affair with Noriega*. New York: G.P. Putnam's.

KENNAN, GEORGE F. (1995) "On American Principles," *Foreign Affairs* 74 (March/April): 116–26.

———. (1976) "The United States and the Soviet Union, 1917–1976," *Foreign Affairs* 54 (July): 670–90.

———. (1967) *Memoirs*. Boston: Little, Brown.

———. (1954) *Realities of American Foreign Policy*. Princeton, N.J.: Princeton University Press.

———. (1951) *American Diplomacy, 1900–1950*. New York: New American Library.

[KENNAN, GEORGE F.] "X." (1947) "The Sources of Soviet Conduct," *Foreign Affairs* 25 (July): 566–82.

KENNEDY, PAUL. (1994) "Overpopulation Tilts the Planet," *New Perspectives Quarterly* 11 (Fall): 4–6.

———. (1992) "A Declining Empire Goes to War," pp. 344–46 in Charles W. Kegley, Jr., and Eugene R. Wittkopf (eds.), *The Future of American Foreign Policy*. New York: St. Martin's.

———. (1987) *The Rise and Fall of the Great Powers*. New York: Random House.

KENNEDY, ROBERT F. (1971) *Thirteen Days*. New York: Norton.

KEOHANE, ROBERT O. (ed.). (1986a) *Neorealism and Its Critics*. New York: Columbia University Press.

———. (1986b) "Realism, Neorealism and the Study of World Politics," pp. 1–26 in Robert O. Keohane (ed.), *Neorealism and Its Critics*. New York: Columbia University Press.

———. (1984) *After Hegemony: Cooperation and Discord in the World Political Economy*. Princeton, N.J.: Princeton University Press.

KEOHANE, ROBERT O., AND JOSEPH S. NYE, JR. (1989) *Power and Interdependence: World Politics in Transition*, 2nd ed. Glenview, Ill.: Scott, Foresman/Little, Brown.

———. (1975) "International Interdependence and Integration," pp. 363–414 in Fred I. Greenstein and Nelson W. Polsby (eds.), *International Politics. Handbook of Political Science*, vol. 8. Reading, Mass.: Addison-Wesley.

KERN, MONTAGUE. (1984) "The Press, the Presidency, and International Conflicts: Lessons from Two Administrations," *Political Psychology* 5 (March): 53–68.

KERN, MONTAGUE, PATRICIA W. LEVERING, AND RALPH B. LEVERING. (1984) *The Kennedy Crises*. Chapel Hill: University of North Carolina Press.

KESSLER, RONALD. (1992) *Inside the CIA: Revealing the Secrets of the World's Most Powerful Spy Agency*. New York: Pocket Books.

KEY, V. O. (1961) *Public Opinion and American Democracy*. New York: Knopf.

KHALILZAD, ZALMAY. (1995) "Losing the Moment? The United States and the World After the Cold War," *Washington Quarterly* 18 (Spring): 87–107.

KILPATRICK, JAMES J. (1985) "An Overstuffed Bureaucracy," *The State*, April 23, p. 8A.

KINDER, DONALD R. (1986) "Presidential Character Revisited," pp. 233–55 in Richard R. Lau and David O. Sears (eds.), *Political Cognition*. Hillsdale, N.J.: Lawrence Erlbaum Associates.

KINDER, DONALD R., AND SUSAN T. FISKE. (1986) "Presidents in the Public Mind," pp. 193–218 in Margaret G. Hermann (ed.), *Political Psychology*. San Francisco: Jossey-Bass.

KINDLEBERGER, CHARLES P. (1973) *The World in Depression, 1929–1939*. Berkeley: University of California Press.

KINSELLA, DAVID. (1994) "Conflict in Context: Arms Transfers and Third World Rivalries during the Cold War," *American Journal of Political Science* 38 (August): 557–81.

KIRKPATRICK, JEANE J. (1974) *Political Women*. New York: Basic Books.

KIRSCHTEN, DICK. (1993) "Muscled UP?" *National Journal*, February 20, pp. 454-58.

———. (1987) "Competent Manager," *National Journal*, February 28, pp. 468–69 ff.

KISSINGER, HENRY. (1994a) *Diplomacy*. New York: Simon & Schuster.

———. (1994b) "Reflections on Containment," *Foreign Affairs* 73 (May/June): 113–30.

———. (1979) *White House Years*. Boston: Little, Brown.

———. (1969) "Domestic Structure and Foreign Policy," pp. 261–75 in James N. Rosenau (ed.), *International Politics and Foreign Policy*. New York: Free Press.

———. (1962) *The Necessity of Choice*. Garden City, N.Y.: Doubleday.

KISSINGER, HENRY, AND CYRUS VANCE. (1988) "Bipartisan Objectives for American Foreign Policy," *Foreign Affairs* 66 (Summer): 899–921.

KITFIELD, JAMES. (1994) "The New Partnership," *National Journal*, August 6, pp. 1840–44.

KLARE, MICHAEL T. (1995) "Controlling the Global Trade in Arms," pp. 85–94 in Charles W. Kegley, Jr., and Eugene R. Wittkopf (eds.), *The Global Agenda: Issues and Perspectives*, 4th ed. New York: McGraw-Hill.

———. (1994–1995) "Awash in Armaments: Implications of the Trade in Light Weapons," *Harvard International Review* 17 (Winter): 24–26 75–76.

———. (1988–1989) "Deadly Convergence: The Perils of the Arms Trade," *World Policy Journal* 6 (Winter): 141–68.

———. (1984) *American Arms Supermarket*. Austin: University of Texas Press.

KLEIN, JOE. (1994) "The Politics of Promiscuity," *Newsweek*, May 9.

KLINE, JOHN. (1983) *State Government Influence in U.S. International Economic Policy*. Lexington, Mass.: Lexington Books.

KLINGBERG, FRANK L. (1990) "Cyclical Trends in Foreign Policy Revisited in 1990," *International Studies Notes* 15 (Spring): 54–58.

———. (1983) *Cyclical Trends in American Foreign Policy Moods: The Unfolding of America's World Role*. Lanham, Md.: University Press of America.

KNUDSEN, BAARD B. (1987) "The Paramount Importance of Cultural Sources: American Foreign Policy and Comparative Foreign Policy Research Reconsidered," *Cooperation and Conflict* 22 (no. 2): 81–113.

KOHN, RICHARD H. (1994) "Out of Control: The Crisis in Civil-Military Relations," *The National Interest* 35 (Spring): 3–17.

KOHUT, ANDREW, AND ROBERT C. TOTH. (1994) "Arms and the People," *Foreign Affairs* 73 (November/December): 47–61.

KOLKO, GABRIEL. (1969) *The Roots of American Foreign Policy*. Boston: Beacon Press.

———. (1968) *The Politics of War*. New York: Random House.

KONDRACKE, MORTON. (1990) "How to Aid A.I.D.," *New Republic*, February 26, pp. 20–23.

KORANY, BAHGAT. (1994) "End of History, or Its Continuation? The Global South and the 'New Transformation' Literature," *Third World Quarterly* 15 (March): 7–15.

KORB, LAWRENCE J. (1995a) "The Indefensible Defense Budget," *Washington Post National Weekly Edition*, July 17–23 1995, p. 19.

———. (1995b) "The Readiness Gap. What Gap?" *New York Times Magazine*, February 26, pp. 40–41.

———. (1994) "The United States," pp. 19–56 in Douglas J. Murray and Paul R. Viotti (eds.), *The Defense Policies of Nations: A Comparative Study*, 3rd ed. Baltimore: Johns Hopkins University Press.

KOTZ, NICK. (1988) *Wild Blue Yonder: Money, Politics, and the B-1 Bomber*. Princeton: Princeton University Press.

KOVIC, RON. (1977) *Born on the Fourth of July*. New York: Pocket Books.

KRASNER, STEPHEN D. (1985) *Structural Conflict: The Third World against Global Liberalism*. Berkeley: University of California Press.

———. (1982) "Structural Causes and Regime Consequences," *International Organization* 36 (Spring): 185–206.

———. (1979) "The Tokyo Round: Particularistic Interests and Prospects for Stability in the Global Trading System," *International Studies Quarterly* 23 (December): 491–531.

———. (1972) "Are Bureaucracies Important? (or Allison Wonderland)," *Foreign Policy* 7 (Summer): 159–79.

KRAUTHAMMER, CHARLES. (1991) "The Unipolar Moment," *Foreign Affairs* 70 (no. 1): 23–33.

KREML, WILLIAM P. (1977) *The Anti-Authoritarian Personality*. Oxford, Eng.: Pergamon Press.

KREPON, MICHAEL. (1995) "Are Missile Defenses MAD?" *Foreign Affairs* 74 (January/February): 19–24.

KRIESBERG, LOUIS, AND ROSS A. KLEIN. (1980) "Changes in Public Support for U.S. Military Spending," *Journal of Conflict Resolution* 24 (March): 79–110.

KRISTOL, IRVING. (1990) "The Map of the World Has Changed," *Wall Street Journal*, January 3, p. A6.

KRUGMAN, PAUL. (1994a) "Competitiveness: A Dangerous Obsession," *Foreign Affairs* 73 (March/April): 28–44.

———. (1994b) *Peddling Prosperity: Economic Sense and Nonsense in the Age of Diminished Expectations*. New York: Norton.

———. (1990) *The Age of Diminished Expectations: U.S. Economic Policy in the 1990s*. Cambridge, Mass.: MIT Press.

KRUGMAN, PAUL R., AND ROBERT Z. LAWRENCE. (1994) "Trade, Jobs and Wages," *Scientific American* 270 (April): 44–49.

KUNZ, DIANE B. (1995) "The Fall of the Dollar Order: The World the United States is Losing," *Foreign Affairs* 74 (July/August): 22–26.

KUPCHAN, CHARLES A. (1994) "Strategic Visions," *World Policy Journal* 11 (Fall): 112–22.

KURTH, JAMES R. (1989) "The Military-Industrial Complex Revisited," pp. 196–215 in Joseph Kruzel (ed.), *American Defense Annual 1989–1990*. Lexington, Mass.: Lexington.

KURTZ, HOWARD. (1993) "How Sources and Reporters Play the Game of Leaks," *Washington Post National Weekly Edition*, March 15–21, p. 12.

KUSNITZ, LEONARD A. (1984) *Public Opinion and Foreign Policy: America's China Policy, 1949–1979*. Westport, Conn.: Greenwood.

LACAYO, RICHARD. (1993) "The Rebellious Solder," *Time*, February 15, p. 32.

LaFeber, Walter. (1994) *The American Age: United States Foreign Policy at Home and Abroad*, 2nd ed. New York: Norton.

———. (1976) *America, Russia, and the Cold War 1945–1975*. New York: Wiley.

Lake, Anthony. (1994) "Confronting Backlash States," *Foreign Affairs* 73 (March/April): 45–55.

———. (1989) *Somoza Falling*. Boston: Houghton Mifflin.

Lancaster, John. (1993) "Ammunition against Budget Cuts," *Washington Post National Weekly Edition*, November 22–28, p. 32.

Langer, E. J. (1975) "The Illusion of Control," *Journal of Personality and Social Psychology* 32 (no. 6): 311–28.

Langer, William L., and S. Everett Gleason. (1952) *The Challenge to Isolation, 1937–1940*. New York: Harper.

Laqueur, Walter. (1994) "Save Public Diplomacy," *Foreign Affairs* 73 (September/October): 19–24.

Lardner, George, Jr. (1990a) "Dragging the NSA into the Glare of the Court," *Washington Post National Weekly Edition*, March 26-April 1, pp. 7–8.

———. (1990b) "No Such Agency," *Washington Post National Weekly Edition*, March 26-April 1, pp. 6–7.

Larson, Deborah Welch. (1985) *Origins of Containment: A Psychological Explanation*. Princeton, N.J.: Princeton University Press.

Larson, James F. (1990) "Television and U.S. Foreign Policy: The Case of the Iran Hostage Crisis," pp. 301–12 in Doris A. Graber (ed.), *Media Power in Politics*, 2nd ed. Washington, D.C.: CQ Press.

Laski, Harold J. (1947) "America—1947," *The Nation* 165 (December): 641–44.

Lasswell, Harold D. (1974) "The Political Personality," pp. 38–54 in Gordon J. DiRenzo (ed.), *Personality and Politics*. Garden City, N.Y.: Doubleday-Anchor.

———. (1962) "The Garrison State Hypothesis Today," pp. 51–70 in Samuel P. Huntington (ed.), *Changing Patterns of Military Politics*. New York: Free Press.

———. (1930) *Psychopathology and Politics*. Chicago: University of Chicago Press.

Lauter, David. (1994) "Anti-Politician Hate Becoming Institutional Phenomenon," *Sunday Advocate*, July 10, p. 4E.

Layne, Christopher. (1994) "Kant or Cant: The Myth of the Democratic Peace," *International Security* 19 (Fall): 5–49.

———. (1993) "The Unipolar Illusion: Why New Great Powers Will Rise," *International Security* 17 (Spring): 5–51.

Leigh, Michael. (1976) *Mobilizing Consent: Public Opinion and American Foreign Policy, 1937–1947*. Westport, Conn.: Greenwood.

Levering, Ralph B. (1976) *American Opinion and the Russian Alliance, 1939–1945*. Chapel Hill: University of North Carolina Press.

Levi, Isaac. (1990) *Hard Choices: Decision Making under Unresolved Conflict*. New York: Cambridge University Press.

Levinson, Daniel J. (1957) "Authoritarian Personality and Foreign Policy," *Journal of Conflict Resolution* 1 (March): 37–47.

Lewis, John P., and Valeriana Kallab (eds). (1983) *U.S. Foreign Policy and the Third World: Agenda 1983*. New York: Praeger.

Lewy, Guenter. (1978) *America in Vietnam*. New York: Oxford University Press.

Leyton-Brown, David. (1987) "Introduction," pp. 1–4 in David Leyton-Brown (ed.), *The Utility of International Economic Sanctions*. New York: St. Martin's.

Lian, Bradley, and John R. Oneal. (1993) "Presidents, the Use of Military Force, and Public Opinion," *Journal of Conflict Resolution* 37 (June): 277–300.

Lichter, S. Robert, and Stanley Rothman. (1981) "Media and Business Elites," *Public Opinion* 4 (October/November): 42–46, 59–60.

Lieber, Robert J. (1992) "Oil and Power after the Gulf War," *International Security* 17 (Summer): 155–76.

Lieberman, Seymour. (1965) "The Effects of Changes in Roles on the Attitudes of Role Occupants," pp. 155–68 in J. David Singer (ed.), *Human Behavior and International Politics*. Chicago: Rand McNally.

Lindblom, Charles E. (1959) "The Science of Muddling Through," *Public Administration Review* 19 (Spring): 79–88.

Lindsay, James M. (1994a) "Congress and Foreign Policy: Avenues of Influence," pp. 191–207 in Eugene R. Wittkopf (ed.), *The Domestic Sources of American Foreign Policy: Insights and Evidence*, 2nd ed. New York: St. Martin's.

———. (1994b) *Congress and the Politics of U.S. Foreign Policy*. Baltimore: Johns Hopkins University Press.

———. (1990) "Parochialism, Policy, and Constituency Constraints: Congressional Voting on Strategic Weapons Systems," *American Journal of Political Science* 34 (November): 936–60.

———. (1988) "Congress and the Defense Budget," *Washington Quarterly* 11 (Winter): 57–74.

———. (1987) "Congress and Defense Policy: 1961 to 1986," *Armed Forces and Society* 13 (Spring): 371–401.

———. (1986) "Trade Sanctions as Policy Instruments: A Re-examination," *International Studies Quarterly* 30 (June): 153–73.

Link, Michael W., and Charles W. Kegley, Jr. (1993) "Is Access Influence? Measuring Adviser-Presidential Interactions in Light of the Iranian Hostage Crisis," *International Interactions* 18 (no. 4): 343–64.

LIPPMANN WALTER. (1947) *The Cold War: A Study in U.S. Foreign Policy*. New York: Harper.

———. (1943) *U.S. Foreign Policy: Shield of the Republic*. Boston: Little, Brown.

LIPSET, SEYMOUR M. (1959) "Some Social Requisites of Democarcy," *American Political Science Review* 53 (March): 69–105.

LIPSET, SEYMOUR MARTIN, AND WILLIAM SCHNEIDER. (1987) "The Confidence Gap During the Reagan Years, 1981–1987," *Political Science Quarterly* 102 (Spring): 1–23.

LIPSITZ, LEWIS, AND DAVID M. SPEAK. (1989) *American Democracy*. New York: St. Martin's.

LISKA, GEORGE. (1978) *Career of Empire: America and Imperial Expansion over Land and Sea*. Baltimore: Johns Hopkins University Press.

LOPEZ, GEORGE A., AND DAVID CORTRIGHT. (1993) "Sanctions: Do They Work?" *Bulletin of the Atomic Scientists* 49 (November): 14–15.

LORD, CARNES. (1988) *The Presidency and the Management of National Security*. New York: Free Press.

LOUSCHER, DAVID J. (1977) "The Rise of Military Sales as a U.S. Foreign Assistance Instrument," *Orbis* 20 (Winter): 933–64.

LOVELL, JOHN P. (1970) *Foreign Policy in Perspective*. New York: Holt, Rinehart & Winston.

LOW, PATRICK. (1993) *Trading Free: The GATT and U.S. Trade Policy*. New York: Twentieth Century Fund Press.

LOWENTHAL, MARK M. (1992) "Tribal Tongues: Intelligence Consumers, Intelligence Producers," *Washington Quarterly* 15 (Winter): 157–68.

LOWI, THEODORE J. (1985a) *The Personal President*. Ithaca, N.Y.: Cornell University Press.

———. (1985b) "Presidential Power: Restoring the Balance," *Political Science Quarterly* 100 (Summer): 185–213.

———. (1979) *The End of Liberalism*. New York: Norton.

———. (1967) "Making Democracy Safe for the World," pp. 295–331 in James N. Rosenau (ed.), *Domestic Sources of Foreign Policy*. New York: Free Press.

LOWI, THEODORE J., AND BENJAMIN GINSBERG. (1990) *American Government*. New York: Norton.

LUNDESTAD, GEIR. (1990) *The American "Empire."* London: Oxford University Press.

LUTTWAK, EDWARD N. (1994a) "Washington's Biggest Scandal," *Commentary*, May, pp. 29–33.

———. (1994b) "Where Are the Great Powers?" *Foreign Affairs* 73 (July/August): 23–28.

———. (1993) *The Endangered American Dream: How to Stop the United States from Becoming a Third World Country and How to Win the Geo-Economic Struggle for Economic Supremacy*. New York: Simon & Schuster.

———. (1990) "From Geo-Politics to Geoeconomics," *The National Interest* 20 (Summer): 17–23.

LUTZ, WOLFGANG. (1994) "The Future of World Population," *Population Bulletin* 49 (June): 1–47. Washington, D.C.: Population Reference Bureau.

MACMAHON, ARTHUR W. (1951) "The Administration of Foreign Affairs," *American Political Science Review* 45 (September): 836–66.

MAGDOFF, HARRY. (1969) *The Age of Imperialism*. New York: Monthly Review Press.

MALONE, GIFFORD D. (1985) "Managing Public Diplomacy," *Washington Quarterly* 8 (Summer): 199–213.

MANDELBAUM, MICHAEL. (1994) "A Struggle between Two Pasts," *World Policy Journal* 11 (Fall): 95–103.

MANN, THOMAS E., AND NORMAN J. ORNSTEIN. (1993) *Renewing Congress: A Second Report*. Washington, D.C.: American Enterprise Institute for Public Policy and the Brookings Institution.

MANSBACH, RICHARD W., AND JOHN A. VASQUEZ. (1981) *In Search of Theory: A New Paradigm for Global Politics*. New York: Columbia University Press.

MANSFIELD, EDWARD D., AND JACK SNYDER. (1995) "Democratization and War," *Foreign Affairs* 74 (May/June): 79–97.

MAOZ, ZEEV, AND BRUCE M. RUSSETT. (1993) "Normative and Structural Causes of Democratic Peace, 1946–1986," *American Political Science Review* 87 (September): 624–38.

MARANISS, DAVID. (1992) "Bill Clinton, Born to Run," *Washington Post National Weekly Edition*, July 20–26, pp. 6–10.

MARCH, JAMES G., AND HERBERT M. SIMON. (1958) *Organizations*. New York: Wiley.

MARCHETTI, VICTOR, AND JOHN D. MARKS. (1974) *The CIA and the Cult of Intelligence*. New York: Knopf.

MARCUS, RUTH. (1994) "Clinton's Very Private Adviser," *Washington Post National Weekly Edition*, December 27-January 2, pp. 10–11.

MASLOW, ABRAHAM H. (1966) "A Comparative Approach to the Problem of Destructiveness," pp. 156–59 in Janusz K. Zawodney (ed.), *Man and International Relations: Contributions of the Social Sciences to the Study of Conflict and Integration*, vol. I. San Francisco: Chandler.

MASTANDUNO, MICHAEL. (1991) "Do Relative Gains Matter? America's Response to Japanese Industrial Policy," *International Security* 16 (Summer): 73–113.

MATHIAS, CHARLES MCC., JR. (1981) "Ethnic Groups and Foreign Policy," *Foreign Affairs* 59 (Summer): 975–98.

MAY, ERNEST R. (1992) "Intelligence: Backing into the Future," *Foreign Affairs* 71 (Summer): 63–72.

———. (1984) "The Cold War," pp. 209–30 in Joseph S. Nye, Jr. (ed.), *The Making of America's Soviet Policy*. New Haven, Conn.: Yale University Press.

MAYNES, CHARLES WILLIAM. (1995) "Relearning Intervention," *Foreign Policy* 98 (Spring): 96–113.

———. (1993–1994) "A Workable Clinton Doctrine," *Foreign Policy* 93 (Winter): 3–20.

———. (1990) "America without the Cold War," *Foreign Policy* 78 (Spring): 3–25.

MAZARR, MICHAEL. (1995) "U.S. Nuclear Policy for a Transformed World." Paper presented at the annual meeting of the International Studies Association, Chicago, February 1995.

———. (1990) "Beyond Counterforce," *Comparative Strategy* 9 (no. 2): 147–62.

McCARTNEY, JAMES. (1990) "Washington May Let European Reform Fizzle," *The State*, March 11, pp. D1, D5.

McCLELLAND, DAVID C. (1975) *Power: The Inner Experience*. New York: Irvington.

McCLOSKY, HERBERT. (1967) "Personality and Attitude Correlates of Foreign Policy Orientation," pp. 51–109 in James N. Rosenau (ed.), *Domestic Sources of Foreign Policy*. New York: Free Press.

———. (1958) "Conservatism and Personality," *American Political Science Review* 52 (March): 27–45.

McCLOSKY, HERBERT, AND JOHN ZALLER. (1984) *The American Ethos: Public Attitudes Toward Capitalism and Democracy*. Cambridge, Mass.: Harvard University Press.

McCOMBS, MAXWELL E., AND DONALD L. SHAW. (1972) "The Agenda-Setting Function of Mass Media," *Public Opinion Quarterly* 36 (Summer): 176–85.

McCORMICK, JAMES M. (1993) "Decision Making in the Foreign Affairs and Foreign Relations Committees," pp. 115–53 in Randall B Ripley and James M. Lindsay (eds.), *Congress Resurgent: Foreign and Defense Policy on Capitol Hill*. Ann Arbor: University of Michigan Press.

———. (1992) *American Foreign Policy and Process*. Itasca, Ill.: Peacock.

———. (1985) "Congressional Voting on the Nuclear Freeze Resolutions," *American Politics Quarterly* 13 (January): 122–36.

McCORMICK, JAMES M., AND MICHAEL BLACK. (1983) "Ideology and Voting on the Panama Canal Treaties," *Legislative Studies Quarterly* 8 (February): 45–63.

McCORMICK, JAMES M., AND EUGENE R. WITTKOPF. (1990a) "Bipartisanship, Partisanship, and Ideology in Congressional-Executive Foreign Policy Relations, 1947–1988," *Journal of Politics* 52 (November): 1077–1100.

———. (1990b) "Bush and Bipartisanship: The Past as Prologue?" *Washington Quarterly* 13 (Winter): 5–16.

McCORMICK, THOMAS J. (1989) *America's Half-Century: United States Foreign Policy in the Cold War*. Baltimore: Johns Hopkins University Press.

McELVAINE, ROBERT S. (1984) "Do We Really Want an 'Active President'?," *Washington Post National Weekly Edition*, July 2, p. 28.

McFARLANE, ROBERT C. (1994) *Special Trust*. New York: Cadell & Davies.

McGLEN, NANCY E., AND MEREDITH REID SARKEES. (1993) *Women in Foreign Policy: The Insiders*. New York: Routledge.

McGOWAN, PATRICK J. (1975) "Meaningful Comparisons in the Study of Foreign Policy," pp. 52–58 in Charles W. Kegley, Jr., Gregory A. Raymond, Robert M. Rood, and Richard A. Skinner (eds.), *International Events and the Comparative Analysis of Foreign Policy*. Columbia: University of South Carolina Press.

McNAMARA, ROBERT S. (1995) *The Tragedy and Lessons of Vietnam*. New York: Times Books.

———. (1983) "The Military Role of Nuclear Weapons: Perceptions and Misperceptions," *Foreign Affairs* 62 (Fall): 59–80.

MEAD, WALTER RUSSELL. (1994) "No Cold War Two: The United States and the Russian Federation," *World Policy Journal* 11 (Summer): 1–17.

———. (1990) "On the Road to Ruin," *Harper's* 280 (March): 59-64.

———. (1989) "American Economic Policy in the Antemillennial Era," *World Policy Journal* 6 (Summer): 385–468.

———. (1988–1989) "The United States and the World Economy," *World Policy Journal* 6 (Winter): 1–45.

MEARSHEIMER, JOHN J. (1993) "The Case for a Ukrainian Nuclear Deterrent," *Foreign Affairs* 72 (Summer): 50–66.

———. (1990a) "Back to the Future: Instability in Europe after the Cold War," *International Security* 14 (Summer): 5–56.

———. (1990b) "Why We Will Soon Miss the Cold War," *Atlantic Monthly* 266 (August): 35–50.

MEERNIK, JAMES. (1994) "Presidential Decision Making and the Political Use of Military Force," *International Studies Quarterly* 38 (March): 121–38.

MEIER, KENNETH J. (1987) *Politics and the Bureaucracy*, 2nd ed. Monterey, Calif.: Brooks/Cole.

MELANSON, RICHARD A. (1983) *Writing History and Making Policy: The Cold War, Vietnam, and Revisionism*. Lanham, Md.: University Press of America.

MELBOURNE, ROY M. (1992) *Conflict and Crisis: A Foreign Service Story*. Lanham, Md.: University Press of America.

MELMAN, SEYMOUR. (1974) *The Permanent War Economy*. New York: Simon & Schuster.

MERELMAN, RICHARD M. (1984) *Making Something of Ourselves: On Culture and Politics in the United States*. Berkeley: University of California Press.

MICHALAK, STANLEY. (1995) "Bill Clinton's Adventures in the Jungle of Foreign Policy," *USA Today* 123 (March): 10–14.

MILBRATH, LESTER W. (1967) "Interest Groups and Foreign Policy," pp. 231–52 in James N. Rosenau (ed.), *Domestic Sources of Foreign Policy*. New York: Free Press.

MILES, RUFUS E., JR. (1985) "Hiroshima: The Strange Myth of Half a Million American Lives Saved," *International Security* 19 (Fall): 121–40.

MILLER, ARTHUR H., WARREN E. MILLER, ALDEN S. RAINE, AND THAD A. BROWN. (1976) "A Majority Party in Disarray: Policy Polarization in the 1972 Election," *American Political Science Review* 70 (September): 753–78.

MILLER, STEVEN E. (1994) "Dismantling the Edifice: Strategic Nuclear Forces in the Post-Soviet Era," pp. 65–83 in Charles W. Hermann (ed.), *American Defense Annual* 1994, New York: Lexington Books.

———. (1993) "The Case Against a Ukrainian Nuclear Deterrent," *Foreign Affairs* 72 (Summer): 67–80.

MILLETT, ALLAN R., AND PETER MASLOWSKI. (1984) *For the Common Defense*. New York: Free Press.

MILLS, C. WRIGHT. (1956) *The Power Elite*. New York: Oxford University Press.

MINTER, WILLIAM. (1986–1987) "South Africa: Straight Talk on Sanctions," *Foreign Policy* 65 (Winter): 43–63.

MIROFF, BRUCE. (1976) *Pragmatic Illusions: The Presidential Politics of John F. Kennedy*. New York: McKay.

MITCHELL, GEORGE H., JR. (1993) "Economics and Development," pp. 145–69 in John Tessitore and Susan Woolfson (eds.), *A Global Agenda: Issues before the 48th General Assembly of the United Nations*. Lanham, Md.: University Press of America.

MOFFETT, GEORGE D. (1994) "Global Population Growth: 21st Century Challenges," *Headline Series* 302 (Spring). New York: Foreign Policy Association.

MONGAR, THOMAS M. (1974) "Personality and Decision-Making: John F. Kennedy in Four Crisis Decisions," pp. 334–72 in Gordon J. DiRenzo (ed.), *Personality and Politics*. Garden City, N.Y.: Doubleday-Anchor.

MONROE, ALAN D. (1979) "Consistency between Public Preferences and National Policy Decisions," *American Politics Quarterly* 7 (January): 3–19.

MOORE, MIKE. (1994) "How George Bush Won His Spurs: The President and the Power to Make War," pp. 181–90 in Eugene R. Wittkopf (ed.), *The Domestic Sources of American Foreign Policy: Insights and Evidence*, 2nd ed. New York: St. Martin's.

MORGAN, EDMUND S. (1988) *Inventing the People: The Rise of Popular Sovereignty in England and America*. New York: Norton.

MORGENTHAU, HANS J. (1985) *Politics among Nations*, revised by Kenneth W. Thompson. New York: Knopf.

———. (1969) "Historical Justice and the Cold War," *New York Review of Books* 13 (July 10): 10–17.

MORRISON, PHILIP, KOSTA TSIPIS, AND JEROME WIESNER.

(1994) "The Future of American Defense," *Scientific American* 270 (February): 38–45.

MOSER, PAUL K. (ed.). (1990) *Rationality in Action: Contemporary Approaches*. New York: Cambridge University Press.

MOYER, WAYNE. (1973) "House Voting on Defense: An Ideological Explanation," pp. 106–42 in Bruce Russett and Alfred Stepan (eds.), *Military Force and American Society*. New York: Harper & Row.

MOYNIHAN, DANIEL PATRICK. (1992) "End the 'Torment of Secrecy,'" *The National Interest* 27 (Spring).

MUELLER, JOHN. (1990) "A New Concert of Europe," *Foreign Policy* 77 (Winter): 3-16.

———. (1989) *Retreat from Doomsday: On the Obsolescence of Major War*. New York: Basic Books.

———. (1973) *War, Presidents and Public Opinion*. New York: Wiley.

———. (1971) "Trends in Popular Support for the Wars in Korea and Vietnam," *American Political Science Review* 65 (June): 358–75.

MUFSON, STEVEN. (1992) "Superpower or Sri Lanka?" *Washington Post National Weekly Edition*, September 7–13, pp. 6–7.

MULCAHAY, KEVIN V. (1995) "Rethinking Groupthink: Walt Rostow and the National Security Advisory Process in the Johnson Administration," *Presidential Studies Quarterly* 25 (Spring): 237–50.

MULDOON, JAMES P. (1995) "What Happened to Humanitarian Intervention?" *Bulletin of the Atomic Scientists* 51 (March/April): 60–61.

MÜLLER, HARALD, AND MITCHELL REISS. (1995) "Counterproliferation: Putting New Wine in Old Bottles," *Washington Quarterly* 18 (Spring): 143–54.

MULLINS, KERRY, AND AARON WILDAVSKY. (1992) "The Procedural Presidency of George Bush," *Political Science Quarterly* 107 (Spring): 31–62.

MURRAY, ALAN. (1992–1993) "The Global Economy Bungled," *Foreign Affairs* 72 (no. 1): 158–66.

MURRAY, SHOON KATHLEEN. (1994) "Change and Continuity in American Elites' Foreign Policy Beliefs: A 1988–1992 Panel Study." Paper presented at the annual meeting of the International Studies Association, Washington, D.C., March 29-April 1.

MYRDAL, GUNNAR. (1944) *An American Dilemma: The Negro Problem in Modern Democracy*. New York: Harper.

NATHAN, JAMES A., AND JAMES K. OLIVER. (1994) *Foreign Policy Making and the American Political System*, 3rd ed. Baltimore: Johns Hopkins University Press.

———. (1976) *United States Foreign Policy and World Order*. Boston: Little, Brown.

"The National Security Adviser: Role and Accountability." (1980) *Hearings Before the Committee on Foreign Relations, United States Senate*. Washington,

D.C.: Government Printing Office (96th Congress, 2nd Session).

NAU, HENRY R. (1990) *The Myth of America's Decline: Leading the World Economy in the 1990s*. New York: Oxford University Press.

NELSON, JOAN M. (1992) "Beyond Conditionality: Foreign Aid and the Changing Global Agenda," *Harvard International Review* 15 (Fall): 4–7, 61.

NEUMAN, W. RUSSELL. (1986) *The Paradox of Mass Politics: Knowledge and Opinion in the American Electorate*. Cambridge, Mass.: Harvard University Press.

NEUSTADT, RICHARD E. (1980) *Presidential Power*. New York: Wiley.

NEUSTADT, RICHARD E., AND ERNEST R. MAY. (1986) *Thinking in Time: The Uses of History for Decision Makers*. New York: Free Press.

"The New Trade Order: After COCOM." (1994), *Atlantic Council Bulletin* 5 (August 17).

NIE, NORMAN H., SIDNEY VERBA, AND JOHN R. PETROCIK. (1976) *The Changing American Voter*. Cambridge, Mass.: Harvard University Press.

NIEBUHR, REINHOLD. (1947) *Moral Man and Immoral Society*. New York: Scribner's.

NINCIC, MIROSLAV. (1989) *Anatomy of Hostility: The U.S.-Soviet Rivalry in Perspective*. Chicago: Harcourt Brace Jovanovich.

NIVOLA, PIETRO S. (1990) "Trade Policy: Refereeing the Playing Field," pp. 201–53 in Thomas E. Mann (ed.), *A Question of Balance: The President, the Congress, and Foreign Policy*. Washington, D.C.: Brookings Institution.

NIXON, RICHARD. (1994) *Beyond Peace*. New York: Random House.

NOLAN, JANNE E. (1994) "The U.S. Nuclear Arsenal," *Brookings Review* 12 (Spring): 30–33.

NOLLEN, STANLEY D., AND DENNIS P. QUINN. (1994) "Free Trade, Fair Trade, Strategic Trade, and Protectionism in the U.S. Congress, 1987–88," *International Organization* 48 (Summer): 491–525.

NOWZAD, BAHRAM. (1990) "Lessons of the Debt Decade," *Finance & Development* 27 (March): 9–13.

NUNN, SAM. (1987) "The ABM Reinterpretation Issue," *Washington Quarterly* 10 (Autumn): 45–57.

NUNN, SAM, AND PETE DOMENICI. (1992) *The CSIS Strengthening of America Commission*. Washington, D.C.: Center for Strategic and International Studies.

NYE, JOSEPH S., JR. (1995) "The Case for Deep Engagement," *Foreign Affairs* 74 (July/August): 90–102.

———. (1992) "What New World Order?" *Foreign Affairs* 71 (Spring): 83–96.

———. (1990) *Bound to Lead: The Changing Nature of American Power*. New York: Basic Books.

NYE, JOSEPH S., JR., AND ROBERT O. KEOHANE. (1971) "Transnational Relations and World Politics: An Introduction," *International Organization* 25 (Summer): 329–49.

OBERDORFER, DON. (1991) *The Turn: From the Cold War to a New Era*. New York: Poseidon Press.

OBERDORFER, DON, AND HELEN DEWAR. (1987) "The Capitol Hill Broth Is Being Seasoned by a Lot of Cooks," *Washington Post National Weekly Edition*, October 26, p. 12.

O'HEFFERNAN, PATRICK. (1991) *Mass Media and American Foreign Policy: Insider Perspectives on Global Journalism and the Foreign Policy Process*. Norwood, N.J.: Ablex.

OLDFIELD, DUANE M., AND AARON WILDAVSKY. (1991) "Reconsidering the Two Presidencies," pp. 181–90 in Steven A. Shull (ed.), *The Two Presidencies: A Quarter Century Assessment*. Chicago: Nelson-Hall.

OLSON, MANCUR. (1982) *The Rise and Decline of Nations*. New Haven, Conn.: Yale University Press.

———. (1965) *The Logic of Collective Action*. Cambridge, Mass.: Harvard University Press.

OMESTAD, THOMAS. (1994) "Psychology and the CIA: Leaders on the Couch," *Foreign Policy* 95 (Summer): 105–22.

———. (1992–1993) "Why Bush Lost," *Foreign Policy* 89 (Winter): 70-81.

———. (1989) "Selling Off America," *Foreign Policy* 76 (Winter): 119-40.

ORNSTEIN, NORMAN J., AND SHIRLEY ELDER. (1978) *Interest Groups, Lobbying and Policymaking*. Washington, D.C.: CQ Press.

ORNSTEIN, NORMAN J., ANDREW KOHUT, AND LARRY MCCARTHY. (1988) *The People, the Press, and Politics*. Reading, Mass.: Addison-Wesley.

OSGOOD, ROBERT E. (1953) *Ideals and Self Interest in America's Foreign Relations*. Chicago: University of Chicago Press.

OSTROM, CHARLES W., JR., AND BRIAN L. JOB. (1986) "The President and the Political Use of Force," *American Political Science Review* 80 (June): 541–66.

OSTROM, CHARLES W., JR., AND DENNIS M. SIMON. (1989) "The Man in the Teflon Suit: The Environmental Connection, Political Drama, and Popular Support in the Reagan Presidency," *Public Opinion Quarterly* 53 (Fall): 353–87.

———. (1985) "Promise and Performance: A Dynamic Model of Presidential Popularity," *American Political Science Review* 79 (June): 334–58.

OWEN, JOHN M. (1994) "How Liberalism Produces Democratic Peace," *International Security* 19 (Fall): 87–125.

PACKENHAM, ROBERT A. (1973) *Liberal America and the Third World*. Princeton, N.J.: Princeton University Press.

PAGE, BENJAMIN I. (1994) "Democratic Responsiveness?

Untangling the Links between Public Opinion and Policy," *PS: Political Science & Politics* 27 (March): 25–29.

PAGE, BENJAMIN I., AND RICHARD A. BRODY. (1972) "Policy Voting and the Electoral Process: The Vietnam War Issue," *American Political Science Review* 66 (September): 979–95.

PAGE, BENJAMIN I, AND ROBERT Y. SHAPIRO. (1992) *The Rational Public: Fifty Years of Trends in America's Public Policy Preferences*. Chicago: University of Chicago Press.

PAGE, BENJAMIN I., ROBERT SHAPIRO, AND GLENN R. DEMPSEY. (1987) "What Moves Public Opinion?" *American Political Science Review* 81 (March): 23–43.

PAIGE, GLENN D. (1972) "Comparative Case Analysis of Crises Decisions: Korea and Cuba," pp. 41–55 in Charles F. Hermann (ed.), *International Crises: Insights from Behavioral Research*. New York: Free Press.

PARENTI, MICHAEL. (1988) *Democracy for the Few*, 5th ed. New York: St. Martin's.

———. (1986) *Inventing Reality*. New York: St. Martin's.

———. (1981) "We Hold These Myths to Be Self-Evident," *The Nation* 232 (April 11): 425–29.

———. (1969) *The Anti-Communist Impulse*. New York: Random House.

PARKINSON, C. NORTHCOTE. (1972–1973) "The Five Other Rules," *Foreign Policy* 9 (Winter): 108–16.

PARRY, ROBERT, AND PETER KORNBLUH. (1988) "Iran-Contra's Untold Story," *Foreign Policy* 72 (Fall): 3–30.

PATERSON, THOMAS G. (1979) *On Every Front: The Making of the Cold War*. New York: Norton.

PATTERSON, BRADLEY H., JR. (1988) *The Ring of Power*. New York: Basic Books.

PATTERSON, THOMAS E. (1994) *The American Democracy*, 2nd ed. New York: McGraw-Hill.

PEARLSTEIN, STEVEN. (1994) "The Hill Shines a Light on the Shadow Pentagon," *Washington Post National Weekly Edition*, August 5–11, p. 31.

The Pentagon Papers as Published by The New York Times. (1971). Toronto: Bantam Books.

PERRY, MARK. (1989) *Four Stars: The Joint Chiefs of Staff in the Post-War Era*. Boston: Houghton Mifflin.

PETERSON, ERIK. (1994) "Looming Collision of Capitalisms?" *Washington Quarterly* 17 (Spring): 65–75.

PETERSON, PAUL E. (1994) "The President's Dominance in Foreign Policy Making," *Political Science Quarterly* 109 (Summer): 215–34.

PETRAS, JAMES F., AND ROBERT JR. LaPORTE. (1972) "Can We Do Business with Radical Nationalists? Chile: No," *Foreign Policy* 7 (Summer): 132–58.

PETT, SAUL. (1984) "Spy vs. Spy," *The State*, April 22, pp. B1, B8.

PFIFFNER, JAMES P. (1992) "The President and the

Postreform Congress," pp. 211-32 in Roger H. Davidson (ed.), *The Postreform Congress*. New York: St. Martin's.

———. (1990) "Establishing the Bush Presidency," *Public Administration Review* 50 (January/February): 64–73.

PHILLIPS, KEVIN. (1995) "Some Unnerving Precedents," *Washington Post National Weekly Edition*, January 16–22, pp. 22–23.

PIANIN, ERIC. (1994) "What Does He Have to Do?" *Washington Post National Weekly Edition*, October 24–30, p. 6.

PICKETT, GEORGE. (1985) "Congress, the Budget, and Intelligence," pp. 157–79 in Alfred C. Maurer, Marion D. Tunstall, and James M. Keagle (eds.), *Intelligence: Policy and Process*. Boulder, Colo.: Westview.

PIERRE, ANDREW, AND SAHR CONWAY-LANZ. (1994–1995) "Desperate Measures: Arms Producers in a Buyer's Market," *Harvard International Review* 17 (Winter): 12–15, 70–72.

PILAT, JOSEPH F., AND WALTER F. KIRCHNER. (1995) "The Technological Promise of Counter-proliferation," *Washington Quarterly* 18 (Winter): 153–66.

PILLER, GEOFFREY. (1983) "DOD's Office of International Security Affairs: The Brief Ascendancy of an Advisory System," *Political Science Quarterly* 98 (Spring): 59–78.

PINCUS, WALTER. (1994a) "A Highflier, but Still Mired in the Cold War," *Washington Post National Weekly Edition*, August 15–21.

———. (1994b) "Mission Improbable: Is It Time to Reconsider the CIA's Role?" *Washington Post National Weekly Edition*, May 30–June 5, pp. 6–7.

———. (1985a) "The Military's New, Improved 'Revolving Door,'" *Washington Post National Weekly Edition*, March 18, p. 33.

PIPES, RICHARD. (1995) "Misinterpreting the Cold War," *Foreign Affairs* 74 (January/February): 154–60.

POMPER, GERALD M. (1989) "The Presidential Election," pp. 129–52 in Gerald M. Pomper, Ross K. Baker, Walter Dean Burnham, Barbara G. Farah, Marjorie Randon Hershey, Ethel Klein, and Wilson Carey McWilliams, *The Election of 1988: Reports and Interpretations*. Chatham, N.J.: Chatham House.

———. (1968) *Elections in America: Control and Influence in Democratic Politics*. New York: Dodd, Mead.

PORTER, BRUCE D. (1992) "A Country Instead of a Cause: Russian Foreign Policy in the Post-Soviet Era," *Washington Quarterly* 15 (Summer): 41–56.

PORTER, ROGER B. (1983) "Economic Advice to the President: From Eisenhower to Reagan," *Political Science Quarterly* 98 (Fall): 403–26.

POST, JERROLD M. (1993) "The Defining Moment of Saddam's Life: A Political Psychology Perspective on the Leadership and Decision Making of Saddam Hussein during the Gulf Crisis," pp. 49–66 in Stanley A. Renshon (ed.), *The Political Psychology of the Gulf War: Leaders, Publics, and the Process of Conflict*. Pittsburgh: University of Pittsburgh Press.

POSTOL, THEODORE A. (1991–1992) "Lessons of the Gulf Experience with Patriot," *International Security* 16 (Winter): 119–71.

POWELL, COLIN L. (1992–1993) "U.S. Forces: Challenges Ahead," *Foreign Affairs* 71 (Winter): 32–45.

POWELL, COLIN L., JOHN LEHMAN, WILLIAM ODOM, SAMUEL HUNTINGTON, AND RICHARD KOHN. (1994) "An Exchange on Civil-Military Relations," *The National Interest* 36 (Summer): 23–31.

POWLICK, PHILIP J. (1991) "The Attitudinal Bases for Responsiveness to Public Opinion among American Foreign Policy Officials," *Journal of Conflict Resolution* 35 (December): 611–41.

PRADOS, JOHN. (1993) "Woolsey and the CIA," *Bulletin of the Atomic Scientists* 49 (July/August): 33–38.

———. (1991) *Keepers of the Keys: A History of the National Security Council from Truman to Bush*. New York: William Morrow.

PREEG, ERNEST H. (1994) "Krugmanian Competitiveness: A Dangerous Obfuscation," *Washington Quarterly* 17 (Autumn): 111–22.

PRESTON, JULIA. (1995) "A Bloated World Body," *Washington Post National Weekly Edition*, January 30–February 5, pp. 6–7.

———. (1994) "Boutros-Ghali Rushes In," *Washington Post National Weekly Edition*, January 10–16, pp. 10–11.

PRESTOWITZ, CLYDE V., JR. (1993) "Letting the GATT Out of the Bag," *Washington Post National Weekly Edition*, December 6–12, p. 25.

———. (1992) "Beyond Laissez Faire," *Foreign Policy* 87 (Summer): 67–87.

PRIEST, DANA. (1992) "Showing Up Where You'd Least Expect," *Washington Post National Weekly Edition*, April 27–May 3, p. 33.

PRINGLE, ROBERT. (1977–1978) "Creeping Irrelevance at Foggy Bottom," *Foreign Policy* 29 (Winter): 128–39.

PROXMIRE, WILLIAM. (1970) *Report from Wasteland*. New York: Praeger.

PRUITT, DEAN G. (1965) "Definition of the Situation as a Determinant of International Action," pp. 393–432 in Herbert C. Kelman (ed.), *International Behavior*. New York: Holt, Rinehart & Winston.

PUCHALA, DONALD J. (1994) "Outsiders, Insiders, and UN Reform," *Washington Quarterly* 17 (Autumn): 161–73.

PUTNAM, ROBERT. (1988) "Diplomacy and Domestic Politics: The Logic of Two-Level Games," *International Organization* 42 (Summer): 427–60.

QUESTER, GEORGE H., AND VICTOR A. UTGOFF. (1994)

"No-First-Use and Nonproliferation: Redefining Extended Deterrence," *Washington Quarterly* 17 (Spring): 103–14.

RABKIN, JEREMY. (1994) "Trading In Our Sovereignty?" *National Review* 46 (June 13): 34–36, 73.

RANGER, ROBIN. (1993) "Theater Missile Defenses: Lessons from British Experiences with Air and Missile Defenses," *Comparative Strategy* 12 (no. 4): 399–413.

RANNEY, AUSTIN. (1983) *Channels of Power*. New York: Basic Books.

RANSOM, HARRY HOWE. (1970) *The Intelligence Establishment*. Cambridge, Mass.: Harvard University Press.

RASMUSSEN, JORGEN, AND JAMES M. MCCORMICK. (1993) "British Mass Perceptions of the Anglo-American Special Relationship," *Political Science Quarterly* 108 (Fall): 515–41.

RAUCH, JONATHAN. (1994) *Demosclerosis: The Silent Killer of American Government*. New York: Times Books.

RAYMOND, GREGORY A. (1994) "Democracies, Disputes, and Third Party Intermediaries," *Journal of Conflict Resolution* 38 (March): 24–42.

REICH, ROBERT B. (1985) "How Much Is Enough?" *New Republic*, August 12 and 19, pp. 33–37.

REIFENBERG, JAN. (1990) "Economies Built on Arms," *World Press Review* 37 (January): 22–23.

REISCHAUER, EDWIN O. (1968) "Redefining the National Interest: The Vietnam Case." Paper presented at the annual meeting of the American Political Science Association, Washington, D.C. September 2–7.

RENNER, MICHAEL. (1994) "Monitoring Arms Trade," *World Watch* 7 (May–June): 21–26.

———. (1992) "Finishing the Job," *World Watch* 5 (November–December): 10–17.

Report of the President's Special Review Board. (1987). Washington, D.C.: Government Printing Office.

REYNOLDS, DAVID (ed.). (1994) *The Origins of the Cold War in Europe: International Perspectives*. New Haven, Conn.: Yale University Press.

RIEBLING, MARK. (1994) *Wedge: The Secret War between the FBI and CIA*. New York: Knopf.

RIELLY, JOHN E. (ed.). (1995) *American Public Opinion and U.S. Foreign Policy 1995*. Chicago: Chicago Council on Foreign Relations.

———. (ed.). (1991) *American Public Opinion and U.S. Foreign Policy 1991*. Chicago: Chicago Council on Foreign Relations.

———. (ed.). (1979) *American Public Opinion and U.S. Foreign Policy 1979*. Chicago: Chicago Council on Foreign Relations.

RIESELBACH, LEROY N. (1964) "The Demography of the Congressional Vote on Foreign Aid, 1939–1958," *American Political Science Review* 58 (September): 577–88.

RILEY, STEPHEN P. (ed.). (1993a) "Conclusions," pp. 189–96 in Stephen P. Riley (ed.), *The Politics of Global Debt*. New York: St. Martin's. *The Politics of Global Debt*. New York: St. Martin's.

———. (1993b) *The Politics of Global Debt*. New York: St. Martin's.

RIPLEY, RANDALL B., AND GRACE A. FRANKLIN. (1991) *Congress, the Bureaucracy, and Public Policy*, 5th ed. Pacific Grove, Calif.: Brooks/Cole.

RISSE-KAPPEN, THOMAS. (1991) "Public Opinion, Domestic Structure, and Foreign Policy in Liberal Democracies," *World Politics* 43 (July): 479–512.

ROBINSON, JAMES A. (1972) "Crisis: An Appraisal of Concepts and Theories," pp. 20–35 in Charles F. Hermann (ed.), *International Crises: Insights from Behavioral Research*. New York: Free Press.

ROBINSON, MICHAEL JAY. (1983) "Just How Liberal Is the News? 1980 Revisited," *Public Opinion* 6 (February/March): 55–60.

ROCA, SERGIO. (1987) "Economic Sanctions against Cuba," pp. 87–104 in David Leyton-Brown (ed.), *The Utility of International Economic Sanctions*. New York: St. Martin's.

RODMAN, PETER W. (1993) "Bill's World," *National Review* 45 (November 15): 3–18.

ROGERS, WILLIAM D. (1979) "Who's in Charge of Foreign Policy?" *New York Times Magazine*, September 9, pp. 44–50.

ROGOW, ARNOLD A. (1963) *James Forrestal: A Study in Personality, Politics, and Policy*. New York: Macmillan.

ROKEACH, MILTON. (1960) *The Open and Closed Mind: Investigations into the Nature of Belief Systems and Personality Systems*. New York: Basic Books.

ROMM, JOSEPH J. (1992) "Laid Waste by Weapons Lust," *Bulletin of the Atomic Scientists* 48 (October): 15–23.

ROSATI, JEREL A. (1993) "Jimmy Carter, a Man before His Time? The Emergence and Collapse of the First Post-Cold War Presidency," *Presidential Studies Quarterly* 23 (Summer): 459–76.

ROSECRANCE, RICHARD. (1994) "A New Concert of Powers and U.S. Foreign Policy," pp. 61–75 in Eugene R. Wittkopf (ed.), *The Future of American Foreign Policy*, 2nd ed. New York: St. Martin's.

———. (1990) *America's Economic Resurgence: A Bold New Strategy*. New York: Harper & Row.

ROSEN, STEVEN J. (ed.). (1973) *Testing the Theory of the Military-Industrial Complex*. Lexington, Mass.: Heath.

ROSENAU, JAMES N. (1980) *The Scientific Study of Foreign Policy*. New York: Nichols.

———. (1966) "Pre-Theories and Theories of Foreign Policy," pp. 27–92 in R. Barry Farrell (ed.), *Approaches to Comparative and International Politics*. Evanston, Ill.: Northwestern University Press.

ROSENBERG, DAVID ALAN. (1983) "The Origins of Overkill: Nuclear Weapons and American Strategy, 1945–1960," *International Security* 7 (Spring): 3–71.

ROSENBERG, MILTON J. (1967) "Attitude Change and Foreign Policy in the Cold-War Era," pp. 278–334 in James N. Rosenau (ed.), *Domestic Sources of Foreign Policy*. New York: Free Press.

———. (1965) "Images in Relation to the Policy Process: American Public Opinion on Cold War Issues," pp. 277–36 in Herbert C. Kelman (ed.), *International Behavior*. New York: Holt, Rinehart & Winston.

ROSENBLUM, MORT. (1993) *Who Stole the News? Why We Can't Keep Up with What Happens in the World and What We Can Do about It*. New York: Wiley.

ROSNER, JEREMY D. (1994) "Is 'Chaos' a Threat to National Security?" *Washington Post National Weekly Edition*, August 22–28, p. 23.

ROSTOW, EUGENE V. (1993) *Toward Managed Peace: The National Security Interests of the United States, 1759 to the Present*. New Haven, Conn.: Yale University Press.

ROTH, BRAD R. (1995) "Evaluating Democratic Progress: A Normative Perspective," *Ethics & International Affairs* 9: 55–77.

ROTHSTEIN, ROBERT L. (1988) "Epitaph for a Monument to a Failed Protest? A North-South Retrospective," *International Organization* 42 (Autumn): 725–48.

ROWE, EDWARD T. (1974) "Aid and Coups d'Etat: Aspects of the Impact of American Military Assistance Programs in the Less Developed Countries," *International Studies Quarterly* 18 (June): 239–55.

RUBIN, BARRY. (1989) "Legacy of State," *Foreign Service Journal* 66 (September): 32–34.

———. (1985) *Secrets of State: The State Department and the Struggle Over U.S. Foreign Policy*. New York: Oxford University Press.

RUGGIE, JOHN GERARD. (1994a) "Peacekeeping and U.S. Interests," *Washington Quarterly* 17 (Autumn): 175–84.

———. (1994b) "Third Try at World Order? America and Multilateralism after the Cold War," *Political Science Quarterly* 109 (Fall): 552–70.

———. (1992) "Multilateralism: The Anatomy of an Institution," *International Organization* 46 (Summer): 561–98.

RUSSETT, BRUCE. (1993) *Grasping the Democratic Peace: Principles for a Post-Cold War World*. Princeton: Princeton University Press.

———. (1989) "The Real Decline in Nuclear Hegemony," pp. 177–93 in Ernst-Otto Czempiel and James N. Rosenau (eds.), *Global Changes and Theoretical Challenges*. Lexington, Mass.: Lexington Books.

———. (1972) "The Revolt of the Masses: Public Opinion on Military Expenditures," pp. 299–319 in Bruce M. Russett (ed.), *Peace, War, and Numbers*. Beverly Hills, Calif.: Sage.

Russett, Bruce, and Thomas W. Graham. (1988) "Public Opinion and National Security Policy Relationships and Impact," pp. 239–57 in Manus Midlarsky (ed.), *Handbook of War Studies*. London: Allen & Unwin.

Russett, Bruce, Thomas Hartley, and Shoon Murray. (1994) "The End of the Cold War, Attitude Change, and the Politics of Defense Spending," *PS: Political Science & Politics* 27 (March): 17–21.

Russett, Bruce, and James S. Sutterlin. (1991) "The U.N. in a New World Order," *Foreign Affairs* 70 (Spring): 69–83.

Sachs, Jeffrey. (1989) "Making the Brady Plan Work," *Foreign Affairs* 68 (Summer): 87–104.

Safire, William. (1993) "Who's Got Clout," *New York Times Magazine*, June 20, pp. 25–28ff.

———. (1990) "Forming Public Opinion," *New York Times*, December 10, p. A15.

Sanders, Jerry W. (1983) *Peddlers of Crisis: The Committee on the Present Danger and the Politics of Containment*. Boston: South End Press.

Sandman, Peter M., David M. Rubin, and David B. Sachsman. (1982) *Media*, 3rd ed. Englewood Cliffs, N.J.: Prentice-Hall.

Sanger, David E. (1995) "A Struggle to Deal with a $20 Billion Precedent," *New York Times*, February 23, pp. C1, C3.

———. (1994) "Who Won in the Korea Deal," *New York Times*, October 23, p. E3.

Schaefer, Peter Faesch. (1992–1993) "Foreign Policy: Repairing the Damage, Rethinking the Mandate, Rewriting the Law," *The American Enterprise* 3 (November/December): 65–69.

Schattschneider, E. E. (1960) *The Semisovereign People*. New York: Holt, Rinehart & Winston.

Schell, Jonathan. (1984) *The Abolition*. New York: Knopf.

———. (1982) *The Fate of the Earth*. New York: Avon Books.

Schelling, Thomas C. (1966) *Arms and Influence*. New Haven, Conn.: Yale University Press.

Schilling, Warner R. (1973) "The H-Bomb Decision: How to Decide without Actually Choosing," pp. 240–60 in Morton H. Halperin and Arnold Kanter (eds.), *Readings in American Foreign Policy*. Boston: Little, Brown.

Schlesinger, Arthur M., Jr. (1992) *The Disuniting of America: Reflections on a Multicultural Society*. New York: Norton.

———. (1989a) "The Legislative-Executive Balance in International Affairs: The Intentions of the Framers," *Washington Quarterly* 12 (Winter): 99–107.

———. (1986) *The Cycles of American History*. Boston: Houghton Mifflin.

———. (1984) "In the National Interest," *Worldview* 27 (December): 5–8.

———. (1977) "America: Experiment or Destiny?" *American Historical Review* 82 (June): 505–22.

———. (1973) *The Imperial Presidency*. Boston: Houghton Mifflin.

———. (1967) "Origins of the Cold War," *Foreign Affairs* 46 (October): 22–52.

———. (1958) *The Coming of the New Deal*. Boston: Houghton Mifflin.

Schlesinger, James. (1992–1993) "Quest for a Post-Cold War Foreign Policy," *Foreign Affairs* 72 (no. 1): 17–28.

———. (1990) "Oil and Power in the Nineties," *The National Interest* 19 (Spring): 111–15.

———. (1989) *America at Century's End*. New York: Columbia University Press.

Schlozman, Kay Lehman, and John T. Tierney. (1986) *Organized Interests and American Democracy*. New York: Harper & Row.

Schneider, Barry R. (1989) "Invitation to a Nuclear Beheading," pp. 291–301 in Charles W. Kegley, Jr., and Eugene R. Wittkopf (eds.), *The Nuclear Reader: Strategy, Weapons, War*, 2nd ed. New York: St. Martin's.

Schneider, William. (1990) "The In-Box President," *Atlantic Monthly* 265 (January): 34–43.

———. (1984) "Public Opinion," pp. 11–35 in Joseph S. Nye, Jr. (ed.), *The Making of America's Soviet Policy*. New Haven, Conn.: Yale University Press.

———. (1982) "Bang-Bang Television: The New Superpower," *Public Opinion* 5 (April/May): 13–15.

Schneider, William, and L. A. Lewis. (1985) "Views on the News," *Public Opinion* 8 (August/September): 6–11, 58–59.

Scholl, Russell B. (1989) "The International Investment Position of the United States in 1988," *Survey of Current Business* 69 (June): 41–49.

Scholl, Russell B., Jeffrey H. Lowe, and Sylvia E. Bargas. (1993) "The International Investment Position of the United States in 1992," *Survey of Current Business* 73 (June): 42–55.

Schraeder, Peter J. (ed.). (1992) *Intervention into the 1990s: U.S. Foreign Policy in the Third World*. Boulder, Colo.: Rienner.

Schulzinger, Robert D. (1985) *The Wise Men of Foreign Affairs: The History of the Council on Foreign Relations*. New York: Columbia University Press.

Schumacher, Mary. (1990) Washington, D.C.: Georgetown University.

Schwartz, Herman M. (1994) *States versus Markets: History, Geography, and the Development of the International Political Economy*. New York: St. Martin's.

Schwarz, Benjamin. (1995) "The Diversity Myth:

America's Leading Export," *Atlantic Monthly* 275 (September): 57–67.

SCHWENNINGER, SHERLE R. (1995) "America's New Solvency Crisis," *World Policy Journal* 12 (Summer): 1–24.

SCIOLINO, ELAINE. (1995) "Global Concerns? Not in Congress," *New York Times*, January 17, pp. E1, 4.

———. (1994) "Diplomatic Subcontracting's Fine if You Get Good Help," *New York Times*, September 25, p. E6.

SCIOLINO, ELAINE, AND TODD S. PURDUM. (1995) "Gore Is No Typical Vice President in the Shadows," *New York Times*, February 19, pp. 1, 16.

SCOTT, ANDREW M. (1970) "Environmental Change and Organizational Adaptation: The Problem of the State Department," *International Studies Quarterly* 14 (March): 85–94.

———. (1969) "The Department of State: Formal Organization and Informal Culture," *International Studies Quarterly* 13 (March): 1–18.

SEABURY, PAUL. (1973) *The United States in World Affairs.* New York: McGraw-Hill.

SEMMEL, ANDREW K. (1983) "Evolving Patterns of U.S. Security Assistance 1950–1980," pp. 79–95 in Charles W. Kegley, Jr., and Eugene R. Wittkopf (eds.), *Perspectives on American Foreign Policy.* New York: St. Martin's.

SERFATY, SIMON. (1978) "Brzezinski: Play It Again, Zbig," *Foreign Policy* 32 (Fall): 3–21.

———. (1972) *The Elusive Enemy: American Foreign Policy Since World War II.* Boston: Little, Brown.

SEWELL, JOHN W. (1991) "Foreign Aid for a New World Order," *Washington Quarterly* 14 (Summer): 35–45.

SEWELL, JOHN W., PETER M. STORM, JOHN P. LEWIS, SHARON L. CAMP, JOHN W. MELLOR, AND LINCOLN C. CHEN. (1992) "Challenges and Priorities in the 1990s: An Alternative U.S. International Affairs Budget, FY 1993." Washington, D.C.: Overseas Development Council.

SHAIN, YOSSI. (1994–1995) "Ethnic Diasporas and U.S. Foreign Policy," *Political Science Quarterly* 109 (Winter): 811–41.

SHALOM, STEPHEN ROSSKAMM (ed.). (1993) *Imperial Alibis: Rationalizing U.S. Intervention after the Cold War.* Boston: South End Press.

SHANNON, THOMAS RICHARD. (1989) *An Introduction to the World-System Perspective.* Boulder, Colo.: Westview.

SHAPIRO, ROBERT Y., AND HARPREET MAHAJAN. (1986) "Gender Differences in Policy Preferences: A Summary of Trends from the 1960s to the 1980s," *Public Opinion Quarterly* 50 (Spring): 42–61.

SHAPIRO, ROBERT Y., AND BENJAMIN I. PAGE. (1988) "Foreign Policy and the Rational Public," *Journal of Conflict Resolution* 32 (June): 211–47.

SHAW, TIMOTHY M. (1994a) "Beyond Any New World Order: The South in the 21st Century," *Third World Quarterly* 15 (March): 139–46.

———. (1994b) "The South in the 'New World (Dis)Order': Towards a Political Economy of Third World Foreign Policy in the 1990s," *Third World Quarterly* 15 (March): 17–30.

SHERWIN, MARTIN J. (1973) "The Atomic Bomb and the Origins of the Cold War," *American Historical Review* 78 (October): 945–68.

SHULL, STEVEN A. (ed.). (1991) *The Two Presidencies: A Quarter Century Assessment.* Chicago: Nelson-Hall.

SHULSKY, ABRAM N., AND GARY J. SCHMITT. (1994–1995) "The Future of Intelligence," *The National Interest* 38 (Winter): 63–72.

SICK, GARY. (1991) "The Election Story of the Decade," *New York Times*, April 15, p. A15.

SIGAL, LEON V. (1992–1993) "The Last Cold War Election," *Foreign Affairs* 71 (Winter): 1–15.

SIGELMAN, LEE. (1979) "Rallying to the President's Support: A Reappraisal of Evidence," *Polity* 11 (Summer): 542–61.

SIGMUND, PAUL E. (1974a) "Chile: What Was the U.S. Role? Less than Charged," *Foreign Policy* 16 (Fall): 142–56.

———. (1974b) "The 'Invisible Blockade' and the Overthrow of Allende," *Foreign Affairs* 52 (January): 322–40.

SIMON, DENNIS M., AND CHARLES W. OSTROM, JR. (1988) "The Politics of Prestige: Popular Support and the Modern Presidency," *Presidential Studies Quarterly* 18 (Fall): 741–58.

SIMON, HERBERT A. (1985) "Human Nature in Politics: The Dialogue of Psychology with Political Science," *American Political Science Review* 79 (June): 293–304.

———. (1957) *Administrative Behavior.* New York: Macmillan.

SIMPSON, SMITH. (1967) *Anatomy of the State Department.* Boston: Houghton Mifflin.

SINGER, J. DAVID. (1991) "Peace in the Global System: Displacement, Interregnum, or Transformation?" pp. 56–84 in Charles W. Kegley, Jr. (ed.), *The Long Postwar Peace: Contending Explanations and Projections.* New York: HarperCollins.

———. (ed.). (1965) *Human Behavior and International Politics.* Chicago: Rand McNally.

SINGER, MAX, AND AARON WILDAVSKY. (1993) *The Real World Order: Zones of Peace/Zones of Turmoil.* Chatham, N.J.: Chatham House.

SITARZ, DANIEL (ed.). (1993) *Agenda 21: The Earth Summit Strategy to Save Our Planet.* Boulder, Colo.: Earthpress.

SIVARD, RUTH LEGER. (1989) *World Military and Social Expenditures.* Washington, D.C.: World Priorities.

SKIDMORE, DAVID. (1993–1994) "Carter and the Failure of Foreign Policy Reform," *Political Science Quarterly* 108 (Winter): 699–729.

SKLAIR, LESLIE. (1991) *Sociology of the Global System.* Baltimore: Johns Hopkins University Press.

SLOVIC, PAUL, BARUCH FISCHHOFF, AND SARAH LICHTENSTEIN. (1977) "Behavioral Decision Theory," *Annual Review of Psychology*, vol. 28: pp. 1–39.

SMITH, GADDIS. (1994) *The Last Years of the Monroe Doctrine, 1945–1993.* New York: Hill and Wang.

SMITH, JAMES ALLEN. (1991) *The Idea Brokers: Think Tanks and the Rise of the New Policy Elite.* New York: Free Press.

SMITH, MICHAEL JOSEPH. (1987) *Realist Thought from Weber to Kissinger.* Baton Rouge: Louisiana State University Press.

SMITH, R. JEFFREY. (1994a) "The CIA's Ill-Advised Dumping Ground," *Washington Post National Weekly Edition*, August 1–7, p. 32.

———. (1994b) "Clinton Goes for the Bush Nuclear Plan," *Washington Post National Weekly Edition*, September 26–October 2, pp. 16–17.

———. (1994c) "Spooked by the Shadow of Somalia," *Washington Post National Weekly Edition*, September 12–18, p. 16.

SMITH, STEVEN S., AND CHRISTOPHER J. DEERING. (1990) *Committees in Congress*, 2nd ed. Washington, D.C.: CQ Press.

SMITH, TOM W. (1984) "The Polls: Gender and Attitudes toward Violence," *Public Opinion Quarterly* 48 (Spring): 384–96.

SMITH, TONY. (1994a) *America's Mission: The United States and the Worldwide Struggle for Democracy in the Twentieth Century.* Princeton, N.J.: Princeton University Press.

———. (1994b) "In Defense of Intervention," *Foreign Affairs* 73 (November/December): 34–46.

———. (1994c) "Winning the Peace: Postwar Thinking and the Defeated Confederacy," *World Policy Journal* 11 (Summer): 92–102.

———. (1993) "Making the World Safe for Democracy," *Washington Quarterly* 16 (Autumn): 197–214.

SMOLLER, FRED. (1986) "The Six O'Clock Presidency: Patterns of Network News Coverage of the President," *Presidential Studies Quarterly* 16 (Winter): 31-49.

SMOLOWE, JILL. (1989) "There Goes the Bloc," *Time*, November 6, pp. 48–51.

SMYSER, W.R. (1993) "Goodbye, G-7," *Washington Quarterly* 16 (Winter): 15–28.

SNIDAL, DUNCAN. (1991) "Relative Gains and the Pattern of International Cooperation," *American Political Science Review* 85 (September): 701–26.

SNOW, DONALD M. (1995) *National Security: Defense Policy for a New International Order*, 5th ed. New York: St. Martin's.

SNYDER, MARK. (1980) "The Many Me's of the Self-Monitor," *Psychology Today* 13 (March): 32–40ff.

SOBEL, RICHARD (ed.). (1993) *Public Opinion and U.S. Foreign Policy: The Controversy over Contra Aid.* Lanham, Md.: Rowman & Littlefield.

———. (1989) "The Polls—A Report: Public Opinion about United States Intervention in El Salvador and Nicaragua," *Public Opinion Quarterly* 53 (Spring): 114–28.

SOFAER, ABRAHAM D. (1987) "The ABM Treaty: Legal Analysis in the Political Cauldron," *Washington Quarterly* 10 (Autumn): 59–75.

SOKOLSKI, HENRY D. (1994) "Nonapocalyptic Proliferation: A New Strategic Threat?" *Washington Quarterly* 17 (Spring): 115–27.

SOLOMON, BURT. (1994) "Though Clinton's Got the Willies . . . the Fed May Be Doing Him a Favor," *National Journal*, May 7, pp. 1086–87.

SORENSEN, THEODORE C. (1994) "Foreign Policy in a Presidential Democracy," *Political Science Quarterly* 109 (no. 3): 515–28.

———. (1987–1988) "The President and the Secretary of State," *Foreign Affairs* 66 (Winter): 231–48.

———. (1963) *Decision Making in the White House: The Olive Branch or the Arrows.* New York: Columbia University Press.

SPANIER, JOHN. (1993) *Games Nations Play*, 8th ed. Washington, D.C.: CQ Press.

———. (1990) *Games Nations Play*, 7th ed. Washington, D.C.: CQ Press.

———. (1988) *American Foreign Policy Since World War II*, 11th ed. Washington, D.C.: CQ Press.

SPEAR, JOANNA. (1994–1995) "Beyond the Cold War: Changes in the International Arms Trade," *Harvard International Review* 17 (Winter): 8–11, 70.

SPERO, JOAN EDELMAN. (1990) *The Politics of International Economic Relations*, 4th. ed. New York: St. Martin's Press.

SPIERS, RONALD I. (1988) "The 'Budget Crunch' and The Foreign Service," Address during Foreign Service Day at the Department of State, May 6, U.S. Department of State, *Current Policy*, no. 1073.

———. (1985a) "Managing the State Department," Address before the Carnegie Endowment for International Peace and the American Foreign Service Association, September 26, U.S. Department of State, *Current Policy*, no. 747.

SPIRO, DAVID E. (1994) "The Insignificance of the Liberal Peace," *International Security* 19 (Fall): 50–86.

STAGNER, ROSS. (1971) "Personality Dynamics and Social Conflict," pp. 98–109 in Clagett G. Smith (ed.), *Conflict*

Resolution: Contributions of the Behavioral Sciences. Notre Dame, Ind.: University of Notre Dame Press.

STANISLAW, JOSEPH, AND DANIEL YERGIN. (1993) "Oil: Reopening the Door," *Foreign Affairs* 72 (September/October): 81–93.

STAROBIN, PAUL. (1994) "The Broker," *National Journal,* April 16, pp. 878–83.

STARR, HARVEY. (1984) *Henry Kissinger: Perceptions of International Politics.* Lexington: University Press of Kentucky.

STEDMAN, STEPHEN JOHN. (1995) "Alchemy for a New World Order," *Foreign Affairs* 74 (May/June): 14–20.

———. (1992–1993) "The New Interventionists," *Foreign Affairs* 72 (no. 1): 1–16.

STEEL, RONALD. (1994) "The Lure of Detachment," *World Policy Journal* 11 (Fall): 61–69.

STEINBRUNER, JOHN D. (1995) "Reluctant Strategic Alignment: The Need for a New View of National Security," *Brookings Review* 13 (Winter): 5–9.

STEPHANSON, ANDERS. (1994) "The United States," pp. 23–52 in David Reynolds (ed.), *The Origins of the Cold War in Europe: International Perspectives.* New Haven, Conn.: Yale University Press.

STEVENSON, ADLAI E., AND ALTON FRYE. (1989) "Trading with the Communists," *Foreign Affairs* 68 (Spring): 53–71.

STEVENSON, CHARLES W. (1995) "How Much for Defense? It Depends. . . .," *Christian Science Monitor,* March 3, p. 18.

STIMSON, HENRY L., AND MCGEORGE BUNDY. (1947) *On Active Service in Peace and War.* New York: Harper & Row.

STIMSON, JAMES A., MICHAEL B. MACKUEN, AND ROBERT S. ERIKSON. (1994) "Opinion and Policy: A Global View," *PS: Political Science & Politics* 27 (March): 29–35.

STOCKTON, PAUL N. (1995) "Beyond Micromanagement: Congressional Budgeting for a Post-Cold War Military," *Political Science Quarterly* 110 (Summer): 233–59.

———. (1993) Congress and Defense Policy-Making in the Post-Cold War Era," pp. 235–59 in Randall B. Ripley and James M. Lindsay (eds.), *Congress Resurgent: Foreign and Defense Policy on Capitol Hill.* Ann Arbor: University of Michigan Press.

STOESSINGER, JOHN G. (1985) *Crusaders and Pragmatists: Movers of Modern American Foreign Policy.* New York: Norton.

STOKES, BRUCE. (1994) "The American Marketplace Has Gone Global," *National Journal,* June 18, pp. 1426–30.

———. (1993) "In Your Face," *National Journal,* August 21, pp. 2068-2072.

———. (1992–1993) "Organizing to Trade," *Foreign Policy,* 89 (Winter): 36-52.

STOLER, MARK A. (1987) "The Mission Concept and the Role of Ideology in American Foreign Policy: A Historical Assessment," *Jerusalem Journal of International Relations* 9 (March): 45–67.

STOUFFER, SAMUEL A., EDWARD A. SUCHMAN, LELAND C. DEVINNEY, SHIRLEY A. STAR, AND ROBIN M. WILLIAMS, JR. (1949) *The American Soldier.* Princeton, N.J.: Princeton University Press.

STRANGE, SUSAN. (1987) "The Persistent Myth of Lost Hegemony," *International Organization* 41 (Autumn): 551–74.

STREMLAU, JOHN. (1994–1995) "Clinton's Dollar Diplomacy," *Foreign Policy* 97 (Winter): 18–35.

STRUCK, MYRON. (1985) "A Bumper Crop of Plums: Political Appointments Are Proliferators," *Washington Post National Weekly Edition,* May 20, p. 31.

SULLIVAN, MARK P. (1989) "Central American and U.S. Foreign Assistance: Issues for Congress," *CRS Issue Brief.* Washington, D.C.: Congressional Research Service.

SULLIVAN, WILLIAM H. (1980) "Dateline Iran: The Road Not Taken," *Foreign Policy* 40 (Fall): 175–86.

SUMMERS, HARRY G., JR. (1989) "A Bankrupt Military Strategy," *Atlantic Monthly* 263 (June): 34–40.

SUNDQUIST, JAMES L. (ed.). (1993) *Beyond Gridlock? Prospects for Governance in the Clinton Years—and After.* Washington, D.C.: Brookings.

———. (1976) "Congress and the President: Enemies or Partners?" pp. 583–618 in Henry Owen and Charles L. Schultze (eds.), *Setting National Priorities: The Next Ten Years.* Washington, D.C.: Brookings Institution.

SUSSMAN, BARRY. (1988) *What Americans Really Think: And Why Our Politicians Pay No Attention.* New York: Pantheon.

SWEETMAN, BILL. (1994) "Aspin's Review Didn't Go Deep Enough," *Washington Post National Weekly Edition,* December 27–January 2, pp. 8–9.

TALBOTT, STROBE. (1990) "Rethinking the Red Menace," *Time,* January 1, pp. 66-72.

———. (1989) "Why Bush Should Sweat," *Time,* November 6, p. 59.

———. (1984) *Deadly Gambits.* New York: Knopf.

———. (1979) *Endgame.* New York: Harper & Row.

TAUBMAN, PHILIP. (1984) "Secret Budgets Become a Public Issue," *Gainesville Sun,* September 30, p. B5.

TAYLOR, ANDREW J., AND JOHN T. ROURKE. (1995) "Historical Analogies in the Congressional Foreign Policy Process," *Journal of Politics* 57 (May): 460–68.

TAYLOR, PAUL. (1988) "The GOP Has a Woman Problem," *Washington Post National Weekly Edition,* July 4–10, p. 9.

TEBBEL, JOHN, AND SARAH MILES WATTS. (1985) *The Press and the Presidency.* New York: Oxford University Press.

'T HART, PAUL. (1990) *Groupthink in Government: A Study of Small Groups and Policy Failure.* Baltimore: Johns Hopkins University Press.

"They're No Friends of Bill: TV News Coverage of the Clinton Administration." (1994), *Media Monitor* 8 (July/August).

THOMAS, KEITH. (1988) "Just Say Yes," *New York Review of Books* 35 (November 24): 43–45.

THOMPSON, KENNETH W. (1960) *Political Realism and the Crisis of World Politics.* Princeton, N.J.: Princeton University Press.

THOMPSON, RANDAL JOY. (1990) "Mandates for AID Reform," *Foreign Service Journal* 67 (January): 34–36.

THOMSON, JAMES C., JR. (1994) "How Could Vietnam Happen? An Autopsy," pp. 255–64 in Eugene R. Wittkopf (ed.), *The Domestic Sources of American Foreign Policy: Insights and Evidence,* 2nd ed. New York: St. Martin's.

———. (1972) "On the Making of U.S. China Policy, 1961–69: A Study in Bureaucratic Politics," *The China Quarterly* 50 (April/June): 220–43.

THURBER, JAMES A., AND SAMANTHA L. DURST. (1993) "The 1990 Budget Enforcement Act: The Decline of Congressional Accountability," pp. 375–97 in Lawrence C. Dodd and Bruce I. Oppenheimer (eds.), *Congress Reconsidered,* 5th ed. Washington, D.C.: CQ Press.

THUROW, LESTER. (1992) *Head to Head: Coming Economic Battles among Japan, Europe, and America.* New York: William Morrow.

TILLEMA, HERBERT K. (1989) "Foreign Overt Military Intervention in the Nuclear Age," *Journal of Peace Research* 26 (May): 179–95.

———. (1973) *Appeal to Force: American Military Intervention in the Era of Containment.* New York: Crowell.

TILLEMA, HERBERT K., AND JOHN R. VAN WINGEN. (1982) "Law and Power in Military Intervention: Major States After World War II," *International Studies Quarterly* 26 (June): 220–50.

TIMES MIRROR CENTER FOR THE PEOPLE & THE PRESS. (1993) *America's Place in the World: An Investigation of the Attitudes of American Opinion Leaders and the American Public About International Affairs.* Washington, D.C.: Times Mirror Center.

TISCH, SARAH J., AND MICHAEL B. WALLACE. (1994) *Dilemmas of Development Assistance: The What, Why, and Who of Foreign Aid.* Boulder, Colo.: Westview.

TIVNAN, EDWARD. (1987) *The Lobby: Jewish Political Power and American Foreign Policy.* New York: Simon & Schuster.

TOLCHIN, MARTIN, AND SUSAN TOLCHIN. (1988) *Buying into America: How Foreign Money Is Changing the Face of Our Nation.* New York: Times Books.

TONELSON, ALAN. (1994) "Clinton's World: The Realities of America's Post–Cold War Foreign Policy," pp. 44–49 in Eugene R. Wittkopf (ed.), *The Future of American Foreign Policy,* 2nd ed. New York: St. Martin's.

———. (1993) "Superpower without a Sword," *Foreign Affairs* 72 (Summer): 166–80.

TOTH, ROBERT C. (1989) "U.S. Shifts Nuclear Response Strategy," *Los Angeles Times,* July 23, p. A1.

TOWNSEND, JOYCE CAROL. (1982) *Bureaucratic Politics in American Decision Making.* Washington, D.C.: University Press of America.

TREVERTON, GREGORY F. (1990) "Intelligence: Welcome to the American Government," pp. 70–108 in Thomas E. Mann (ed.), *A Question of Balance: The President, the Congress, and Foreign Policy.* Washington, D.C.: Brookings Institution.

———. (1987) *Covert Action: The Limits of Intervention in the Postwar World.* New York: Basic Books.

TRIFFIN, ROBERT. (1978–1979) "The International Role and Fate of the Dollar," *Foreign Affairs* 57 (Winter): 269–86.

TRUMAN, DAVID B. (1951) *The Governmental Process.* New York: Knopf.

TRUMAN, HARRY S. (1966) *Public Papers of the Presidents of the United States, Harry S. Truman, 1952–53.* Washington, D.C.: Government Printing Office.

TUCKER, ROBERT W. (1993–1994) "The Triumph of Wilsonianism?" *World Policy Journal* 10 (Winter): 83–99.

———. (1990) "1989 and All That," *Foreign Affairs* 69 (Fall): 93–114.

TUGWELL, REXFORD GUY. (1971) *Off Course: From Truman to Nixon.* New York: Praeger.

TURNER, ROBERT F. (1988) "The Power of the Purse: Controlling National Security by Conditional Appropriations," *Atlantic Community Quarterly* 26 (Spring): 79–96.

TURNER, STANSFIELD. (1985) *Secrecy and Democracy: The CIA in Transition.* Boston: Houghton Mifflin.

TURNER, STANSFIELD, AND GEORGE THIBAULT. (1982) "Intelligence: The Right Rules," *Foreign Policy* 48 (Fall): 122–38.

TUSSIE, DIANA. (1993) "Holding the Balance: The Cairns Groups in the Uruguay Round," pp. 181–203 in Diana Tussie and David Glover (eds.), *The Developing Countries in World Trade: Policies and Bargaining Strategies.* Boulder, Colo.: Lynne Rienner.

TUSSIE, DIANA, AND DAVID GLOVER (eds.). (1993) *The Developing Countries in World Trade: Policies and Bargaining Strategies.* Boulder, Colo.: Lynne Rienner.

TYSON, LAURA D'ANDREA. (1992) *Who's Bashing Whom? Trade Conflict in High-Technology Industries.* Washington, D.C.: Institute for International Economics.

ULAM, ADAM B. (1985) "Forty Years of Troubled Coexistence," *Foreign Affairs* 64 (Fall): 12–32.

UNITED NATIONS. (1991) *World Economic Survey 1991.* New York: United Nations.

UNITED NATIONS CENTRE ON TRANSNATIONAL CORPORATIONS. (1991) *World Investment Report 1991: The Triad in Foreign Direct Investment.* New York: United Nations.

UNITED NATIONS PROGRAMME ON TRANSNATIONAL CORPORATIONS. (1993) "World Investment Report 1993," *Transnational Corporations* 2 (August): 99–123.

U.S. ARMS CONTROL AND DISARMAMENT AGENCY. (1995) *World Military Expenditures and Arms Transfers 1993–1994.* Washington, D.C.: Government Printing Office.

U.S. DEPARTMENT OF STATE. (1992) *State 2000: A New Model for Managing Foreign Affairs.* Washington, D.C.: Department of State.

USLANER, ERIC M. (1986) "One Nation, Many Voices: Interest Groups in Foreign Policy Making," pp. 236–57 in Allan J. Cigler and Burdett A. Loomis (eds.), *Interest Group Politics*, 2nd ed. Washington, D.C.: CQ Press.

VAN DEN HAAG, ERNEST. (1985) "The Busyness of American Foreign Policy," *Foreign Affairs* 64 (Fall): 113–29.

VAN EVERA, STEPHEN. (1994) "Hypotheses on Nationalism and War," *International Security* 18 (Winter): 5–39.

———. (1990–1991) "Primed for Peace: Europe after the Cold War," *International Security* 15 (Winter): 7–57.

VASQUEZ, JOHN A. (1991) "The Deterrence Myth: Nuclear Weapons and the Prevention of Nuclear War," pp. 205–23 in Charles W. Kegley, Jr. (ed.), *The Long Postwar Peace: Contending Explanations and Projections.* New York: HarperCollins.

———. (1983) *The Power of Power Politics.* New Brunswick, N.J.: Rutgers University Press.

VERBA, SIDNEY. (1969) "Assumptions of Rationality and Non-Rationality in Models of the International System," pp. 217–31 in James N. Rosenau (ed.), *International Politics and Foreign Policy.* New York: Free Press.

WAGNER, R. HARRISON. (1993) "What Is Bipolarity?" *International Organization* 47 (Winter): 77–106.

WALKER, MARTIN. (1990) "The U.S. and the Persian Gulf Crisis," *World Policy Journal* 7 (Fall): 791–99.

WALKER, STEPHEN G. (1977) "The Interface between Beliefs and Behavior: Henry Kissinger's Operational Code and the Vietnam War," *Journal of Conflict Resolution* 21 (March): 129–68.

WALLERSTEIN, IMMANUEL. (1974) "The Rise and Future Demise of the World Capitalist System: Concepts for Comparative Analysis," *Comparative Studies in Society and History* 16 (September): 387–415.

WALLIS, ALLEN. (1986) "U.S.-EC Relations and the International Trading System," Address before the Luxembourg Society for International Affairs, October 8, U.S. Department of State, *Current Policy*, no. 889.

WALT, STEPHEN M. (1990) *The Origins of Alliances.* Ithaca, N.Y.: Cornell University Press.

WALTERS, ROBERT S., AND DAVID H. BLAKE. (1992) *The Politics of Global Economic Relations*, 4th ed. Englewood Cliffs, N.J.: Prentice-Hall.

WALTZ, KENNETH N. (1993) "The Emerging Structure of International Politics," *International Security* 18 (Fall): 44–79.

———. (1979) *Theory of International Politics.* Reading, Mass.: Addison-Wesley.

———. (1971) "Opinions and Crisis in American Foreign Policy," pp. 47–55 in Douglas M. Fox (ed.), *The Politics of U.S. Foreign Policy Making.* Pacific Palisades, Calif.: Goodyear.

———. (1967) *Foreign Policy and Democratic Politics.* Boston: Little, Brown.

———. (1964) "The Stability of a Bipolar World," *Daedalus* 93 (Summer): 881–909.

WARBURG, GERALD FELIX. (1989) *Conflict and Consensus: The Struggle between Congress and the President over Foreign Policymaking.* New York: Harper & Row.

WARNER, GEOFFREY. (1989) "The Anglo-American Special Relationship," *Diplomatic History* 13 (Fall): 479–99.

WARWICK, DONALD P. (1975) *A Theory of Public Bureaucracy: Politics, Personality, and Organization in the State Department.* Cambridge, Mass.: Harvard University Press.

WATSON, JACK H., JR. (1993) "The Clinton White House," *Presidential Studies Quarterly* 23 (Summer): 429–35.

WATTENBERG BEN J. (1989) *The Birth Dearth.* New York: Pharos Books.

WAYMAN, FRANK WHELON. (1985) "Arms Control and Strategic Arms Voting in the U.S. Senate," *Journal of Conflict Resolution* 29 (June): 225–51.

WAYNE, STEPHEN J. (1993) "President Bush Goes to War: A Psychological Interpretation from a Distance," pp. 29–48 in Stanley A. Renshon (ed.), *The Political Psychology of the Gulf War: Leaders, Publics, and the Process of Conflict.* Pittsburgh: University of Pittsburgh Press.

WEEDE, ERICH. (1978) "U.S. Support for Foreign Governments, or Domestic Disorder and Imperial Intervention, 1958–1965," *Comparative Political Studies* 10 (January): 497–527.

WEINER, TIM. (1994) "The Men in the Gray Federal Bureaucracy," *New York Times*, April 210, p. E4.

WEISBAND, EDWARD. (1973) *The Ideology of American Foreign Policy: A Paradigm of Lockian Liberalism.* Beverly Hills, Calif.: Sage.

WEISBERG, HERBERT F., AND DAVID C. KIMBALL. (1995) "Attitudinal Correlates of the 1992 Presidential Vote: Party Identification and Beyond," pp. 72–111 in Herbert F. Weisberg (ed.), *Democracy's Feast: Elections in America.* Chatham, N.J.: Chatham House.

WEISSBERG, ROBERT. (1976) *Public Opinion and Popular Government.* Englewood Cliffs, N.J.: Prentice-Hall.

WEISSMAN, WILLIAM J. (1992) "Should U.S. Cultural Relations Be a Tool of 'Public Diplomacy?'" *International Studies Notes* 17 (Fall): 1–7.

WERLEIGH, CLAUDETTE ANTOINE. (1993) "Haiti and the Halfhearted," *Bulletin of the Atomic Scientists* 49 (November): 20–23.

WEST, WILLIAM F., AND JOSEPH COOPER. (1990) "Legislative Influence vs. Presidential Dominance: Competing Models of Bureaucratic Control," *Political Science Quarterly* 104 (Winter): 581–606.

"White House Tapes and the Minutes of the Cuban Missile Crisis." (1985), *International Security* 10 (Summer): 164–203.

WHITE, RALPH K. (1984) *Fearful Warriors: A Psychological Profile of U.S.-Soviet Relations.* New York: Free Press.

WHITE, THEODORE H. (1973) *The Making of the President, 1972.* New York: Atheneum.

WIESELTIER, LEON. (1993) "Total Quality Meaning," *New Republic,* July 19 and 26, pp. 16–18ff.

WILCOX, CLYDE, JOSEPH FERRARA, AND DEE ALLSOP. (1993) "Group Differences in Early Support for Military Action in the Gulf: The Effects of Gender, Generation, and Ethnicity," *American Politics Quarterly* 21 (July): 343–59.

WILDAVSKY, AARON. (1966) "The Two Presidencies," *Trans-Action* 4 (December): 7-14.

WILENSKY, HAROLD L. (1967) *Organizational Intelligence: Knowledge and Policy in Government and Industry.* New York: Basic Books.

WILL, GEORGE F. (1994) "The Porcelain Presidency," *Newsweek,* July 25, p. 62.

WILLIAMS, WILLIAM APPLEMAN. (1980) *Empire as a Way of Life.* New York: Oxford University Press.

———. (1972) *The Tragedy of American Diplomacy,* 2nd ed. New York: Delta.

WILLS, GARRY. (1994a) "Certain Trumpets: The Call of Leaders." New York: Simon & Schuster.

———. (1994b) "What Makes a Good Leader?" *Atlantic Monthly* 273 (April): 63–80.

WINIK, JAY. (1989) "Restoring Bipartisanship," *Washington Quarterly* 12 (Winter): 109–22.

WINTER, DAVID G., MARGARET G. HERMANN, WALTER WEINTRAUB, AND STEPHEN G. WALKER. (1991) "The Personalities of Bush and Gorbachev Measured at a Distance: Procedures, Portraits, and Policy," *Political Psychology,* 12 (no. 2): 215–245.

WITTKOPF, EUGENE R. (1995) "Faces of Internationalism Revisited." Paper presented at the annual meeting of the American Political Science Association, Chicago, August 31–September 3.

———. (1994) "Faces of Internationalism in a Transitional Environment," *Journal of Conflict Resolution* 38 (September): 376–401.

———. (1990) *Faces of Internationalism: Public Opinion and American Foreign Policy.* Durham, N.C.: Duke University Press.

WITTKOPF, EUGENE R., AND JAMES M. MCCORMICK. (1993) "The Domestic Politics of Contra Aid: Public Opinion, Congress, and the President," pp. 73–103 in Richard Sobel (ed.), *Public Opinion in U.S. Foreign Policy: The Controversy over Contra Aid.* Lanham, Md.: Rowman & Littlefield.

WOHLSTETTER, ROBERTA. (1962) *Pearl Harbor: Warning and Decision.* Stanford, Calif.: Stanford University Press.

WOLF-PHILLIPS, LESLIE. (1987) "Why 'Third World?': Origin, Definitions and Usage," *Third World Quarterly* 9 (October): 1311–27.

WOLFERS, ARNOLD. (1962) *Discord and Collaboration.* Baltimore: Johns Hopkins University Press.

WOLFOWITZ, PAUL D. (1994) "Clinton's First Year," *Foreign Affairs* 73 (January/February): 28–43.

WOODWARD, BOB. (1994) *The Agenda: Inside the Clinton White House.* New York: Simon & Schuster.

———. (1991) *The Commanders.* New York: Simon & Schuster.

WOODWARD, BOB, AND RICK ATKINSON. (1990) "Launching Operation Desert Shield," *Washington Post National Weekly Edition,* September 3–9, pp. 8–9.

WOODWARD, BOB, AND CARL BERNSTEIN. (1979) *The Final Days.* New York: Simon & Schuster.

WOODWARD, SUSAN L. (1993) "Yugoslavia: Divide and Fall," *Bulletin of the Atomic Scientists* 49 (November): 24–27.

WOOLSEY, R. JAMES. (1994) "Intelligence Quotient: The Mission of the CIA in a New World," *Harvard International Review* 16 (Fall): 34–37, 80.

WORLD BANK. (1995) *Global Economic Prospects and the Developing Countries, 1995.* Washington, D.C.: World Bank.

WORLD BANK. (1993) *Global Economic Prospects and the Developing Countries, 1993.* Washington, D.C.: World Bank.

World Development Report 1994. (1994). New York: Oxford University Press.

World Development Report 1991. (1991). New York: Oxford University Press.

World Development Report 1988. (1988). New York: Oxford University Press.

World Resources 1994–95. (1994). New York: Oxford University Press.

YANKELOVICH, DANIEL, AND SIDNEY HARMAN. (1988) *Starting with the People.* Boston: Houghton Mifflin.

YARMOLINSKY, ADAM. (1971) *The Military Establishment: Its Impact on American Society.* New York: Harper & Row.

———. (1970–1971) "The Military Establishment (or How Political Problems Become Military Problems)," *Foreign Policy* 1 (Winter): 78–97.

YERGIN, DANIEL. (1978) *Shattered Peace: The Origins of the Cold War and the National Security State.* Boston: Houghton Mifflin.

ZAGARE, FRANK C. (1990) "Rationality and Deterrence," *World Politics* 42 (January): 238–60.

ZAKHEIM, DOV S., AND JEFFREY M. RANNEY. (1993) "Matching Defense Strategies to Resources: Challenges for the Clinton Administration," *International Security* 18 (Summer): 51–78.

ZALLER, JOHN R. (1992) *The Nature and Origins of Mass Opinion.* New York: Cambridge University Press.

ZELIKOW, PHILLIP D. (1987) "The United States and the Use of Force: A Historical Summary," pp. 31–81 in George Osborn, Asa A. Clark IV, Daniel J. Kaufman, and Douglas E. Lute (eds.), *Democracy, Strategy, and Vietnam.* Lexington, Mass.: Lexington Books.

ZIEMKE, CAROLINE F. (1993) "Rethinking the Mistakes of the Past: History's Message to the Clinton Defense Department," *Washington Quarterly* 16 (Spring): 47–60.

ZIMMERMAN, ROBERT F. (1993) *Dollars, Diplomacy, and Dependence: Dilemmas of U.S. Economic Aid.* Boulder, Colo.: Lynne Rienner.

GLOSSARY

• • •

absolute poverty A condition of life characterized by no access to safe water or adequate nutrition, sanitation, or health services that currently describes as many as one-fifth of the earth's inhabitants.

accommodationists Those who, in the wake of the Vietnam War, emphasized cooperative ties with other nations, particularly détente with the Soviet Union, and rejected the view that the United States could assume a unilateralist posture in the world; proponents of multilateralism in the post-Cold War world.

ad hoc decision making A behavior in which decisions are made in reaction to others' decisions or issues as they arise, focusing on each day's immediate crisis and avoiding long-term thinking.

adhocracy A system of decision making that allows the president flexibility to devise advisory committees and make assignments to address a specific situation or need without relying on the usual, established patterns of providing advice through cabinet officials or bureaucratic organizations.

agenda setting The role that the mass media play in telling the public which issues to think about.

antiauthoritarianism An attitude syndrome exhibited by introspective people uncomfortable with order and power.

assured destruction The capacity to survive an aggressor's worst possible attack with sufficient firepower to inflict unacceptable damage on the attacker in retaliation; a key feature of the Kennedy and Johnson administrations' doctrine of strategic deterrence.

attentive public People who are attentive to and knowledgeable about foreign affairs but who do not necessarily have access to decision makers.

authoritarianism A constellation of predispositions that includes adherence to conventional values and condemnation of those who reject them; authoritarians crave authority and obediently submit to leaders.

ballistic missile defense (BMD) A means of defending against attacks from intercontinental ballistic missiles.

beggar-thy-neighbor policies Efforts to enhance domestic welfare by means of currency devaluations, tariffs, quotas, export subsidies, and other strategies that promote trade surpluses at other nations' expense.

belief system Conceptual lens through which individuals receive and process information that orients them to their physical and social environment, helping them to establish goals, order preferences, and relate ideas systematically to one another.

biodiversity The natural abundance of plant and animal species, humankind's genetic heritage, which is threatened by rapidly increasing extinctions due to deforestation and other environmental damage.

bipartisanship The practical application of the proposition that "politics stops at the water's edge"; used to describe the cooperative relationship between Congress and the executive branch during much of the Roosevelt, Truman, and Eisenhower presidencies.

bipolar (bipolarity) A global structure in which power is concentrated in two centers or poles; effective world power was so distributed from the late 1940s until the 1962 Cuban missile crisis, with the United States and its allies comprising one pole and the Soviet Union and its allies the other.

• • •

617

bipolycentrism A global power structure somewhat looser and more fluid than a bipolar one, in which the alliance partners of the primary powers form relationships among themselves while continuing to rely on their great power patrons for security.

Brezhnev Doctrine A Soviet doctrine, named after Premier Leonid Brezhnev, intended to justify the 1968 invasion of Czechoslovakia and to put other communist states on warning about the dangers of defection from the socialist fold.

brinkmanship A willingness during the Eisenhower administration to go to the brink of nuclear war as a means of bargaining with the Soviet Union.

Bureau of Intelligence and Research The State Department's representative in the intelligence community, which is charged with introducing a diplomatic sensitivity to intelligence reports.

bureaucratic politics model A perspective that stresses the policy-making effects of interaction and competition among bureaucratic organizations and the competing roles of people within them.

Carter Doctrine President Jimmy Carter's declaration that the United States was willing to use military force to protect its interests in the Persian Gulf.

collective goods (public goods) Benefits shared by everyone, from which no one can be excluded on a selective basis (e.g., national security).

collective security A system embodied in international organizations, such as the United Nations, in which member states pledge to join together to oppose aggression by any state, whenever and wherever it occurs.

collegial model An executive decision-making approach that emphasizes teamwork and group problem solving, in which the president is likened to the hub of a wheel, with spokes connecting to individual advisers and agency heads.

comparative advantage A key principle in classical international trade theory which states that all states will benefit if each specializes in those goods it produces comparatively cheaply and acquires, through trade, goods that it can only produce at a comparatively higher cost.

compellence The view of nuclear weapons as the means by which one nation can coerce other nations to conform to its will.

competitive model An approach to executive decision making in which the president purposely seeks to promote conflict and competition among presidential advisers.

concert-based collective security An international political system in which the great powers play leadership roles but anchor their behavior in a collective security system to ensure small and medium powers a voice in matters affecting them.

conservatism A psychological concept denoting a cluster of interrelated personality characteristics including hostility and suspicion, rigidity and compulsiveness, intolerance, inflexibility, and lack of compassion.

containment A foreign policy strategy, initiated by President Truman, designed to inhibit the expansion of the Soviet Union's power and influence in world affairs.

cooperative internationalism Support for active involvement in world affairs that stresses the United States' willingness to cooperate with other nations to solve global as well as national problems.

counterforce A nuclear weapons strategy that seeks deterrence by targeting an adversary's weapons and military forces.

counterintelligence Operations directed specifically against the espionage efforts of foreign intelligence services, including efforts to penetrate them.

counterproliferation A concept that implies the United States itself will act as the sole global arbiter and destroyer of weapons of mass destruction.

countervailing powers A description of interest-group activity in which disproportionate political influence possessed by one group will cause one or more opposing groups to balance it by pushing policy in the opposite direction.

countervailing (war-fighting) strategy A plan, embodied in President Carter's Presidential Directive (PD) 59, to enhance deterrence by targeting not only the Soviet Union's population and industrial centers but also its military forces and weapons.

countervalue A nuclear weapons strategy that seeks deterrence by threatening destruction of the things an adversary is believed to value most—its population and military-industrial centers.

covert action A clandestine activity typically undertaken abroad against foreign governments, installations, or individuals with the expressed purpose of directly influencing the outcome of political events.

cross-pressures Forces that arise within and among special interest groups by virtue of their overlapping memberships and crisscrossing relationships, which reduce the groups' effectiveness by pulling members in opposite directions.

decision avoidance Bureaucratic behavior in which policymakers delay decision making or delegate it by "passing the buck."

Defense Intelligence Agency (DIA) The Defense Department agency responsible for collecting national (rather than tactical) intelligence; the principal intelligence adviser to the secretary of defense and the Joint Chiefs of Staff.

Defense Reorganization Act of 1986 (Goldwater-Nichols act) A law that sought to shift power from the separate branches of the armed services to the institutions associated with the Joint Chiefs of Staff in an effort to ameliorate interservice rivalry.

deferrals Temporary spending delays by which the president, subject to congressional review, can impound funds for up to twelve months.

dehumanization of foreign policy A potential effect of bureaucratic decision making that allows specialization to obscure or displace ethical and humanitarian concerns in the policy-making process.

democracy A political system characterized by free elections and universal suffrage.

dependent variable That which an investigator seeks to explain; in the foreign policy context, a nation's foreign policy behavior is the dependent variable.

desertification A sustained decline in land productivity resulting from long-term environmental stress, often caused by population growth.

détente A strategy of containment initiated in 1969 that emphasized the need for superpower cooperation and restraint and sought to create a movement away from competition and toward cooperation.

deterrence A strategy intended to discourage an adversary from using force by convincing it that the costs of such action outweigh the potential gains.

development assistance Grants and loans provided for social and economic development, typically for health, education, agriculture, rural development, or disaster relief; designed to serve American long-term foreign policy objectives.

discretionary funds Monies Congress provides the president to deal with situations unforeseen at the time of the annual budget process.

doctrine of political questions A judicial construct that enables the courts to sidestep contentious foreign policy issues separating Congress and the president, such as war powers, by holding the issues are political rather than legal.

dogmatism A personality trait exhibited by closed-minded people, who form opinions and refuse to modify them despite contrary evidence.

dollar convertibility A U.S. government commitment during the Bretton Woods regime to exchange gold for dollars at any time on demand. Convertibility is an arrangement in which a government permits its currency to be freely exchanged for the currencies of other nations.

dollar diplomacy U.S. policy from 1900 to 1913, intended to protect rapidly growing business interests in the Caribbean and Central America and characterized by President Taft as "substituting dollars for bullets."

domino theory A popular metaphor in the 1960s which asserted that one country's fall to communism would stimulate the fall of those adjacent to it.

economic liberalism The existence or development of market economies.

economic nationalists (mercantilists) Those who assign the state an aggressive role in fostering national economic welfare, stressing their own national interests in international economic transactions rather than the mutual benefit of all trading partners.

economic support funds (ESF) Dollars granted or loaned to countries of special political significance to the United States to advance short-term political objectives.

environmental refugees People forced to abandon lands no longer fit for human habitation due to environmental degradation; currently describes at least ten million people.

espionage The illegal collection of intelligence; spying to obtain secret government information.

exceptional American experience The absence of pronounced class and religious strife at the time of America's founding complemented by its geographic isolation from European political turmoil.

executive agreements International agreements that do not require the advice and consent of the Senate; have the same legal force as treaties, which require Senate approval.

extended deterrence A strategy that seeks to deter an adversary from attacking one's allies; describes the U.S. commitment to defend Western Europe from a Soviet or Warsaw Pact attack during the Cold War.

external source category The attributes of the international system and the characteristics and behaviors of the state and nonstate actors comprising it; includes the global environment and any actions occurring abroad that influence a nation's foreign policy decisions.

fair trade A precept stating that a nation's exporters should be given the same access to foreign markets as foreign producers enjoy in that nation.

finished intelligence Data obtained from all sources—secret as well as public—that have been expertly assembled and analyzed specifically to meet the nation's foreign policy needs.

First World A term used during the Cold War era to designate industrialized nations with democratic governments and market economies, chiefly in Western Europe and North America.

fixed exchange rate system A monetary system in which a government sets the value of its currency at a fixed rate in relation to the currencies of other nations.

flexible response A U.S. and NATO defense posture that implied the United States and its allies were willing and able to respond to a hostile attack at whatever level was appropriate—either conventional or nuclear.

Food for Peace program A program created by the Agricultural Trade Development and Assistance Act of 1954 (PL 480) that sells agricultural commodities on credit and makes grants to provide emergency relief, promote economic development, and assist voluntary relief agencies.

forceful persuasion Displays of military force short of war intended to influence the decisions of other states.

Foreign Agricultural Service (FAS) The principal subdivision of the Agriculture Department concerned with international affairs, which is designed to promote sales of American agricultural commodities overseas.

foreign economic aid Monetary loans and grants to other countries, often tied to purchases of goods and services in the United States.

foreign military sales (FMS) A foreign military assistance and arms transfer program designed as an alternative to grant assistance that has made the United States the world's leading arms supplier.

foreign policy The goals that a nation's officials seek to attain abroad, the values that give rise to those objectives, and the means or instruments used to pursue them.

Foreign Service officers (FSOs) Members of an elite corps of professional diplomats traditionally holding the most important positions with the State Department, both at home and abroad.

formalistic model An approach to executive decision making in which clear lines of authority minimize the need for presidential involvement in the inevitable politicking among cabinet officers and presidential advisers.

fourth estate The mass media, regarded by some as so powerful as to be considered a fourth branch of the U.S. government.

free-floating exchange rates Currency values that are determined by market forces rather than government intervention.

free riders Those who enjoy the benefits of collective (public) goods but pay little or nothing for them.

gatekeepers The function of the mass media in filtering the news and shaping how it is reported, particularly noticeable in foreign affairs.

General Agreement on Tariffs and Trade (GATT) An international organization created after World War II to promote and protect the most-favored-nation (MFN) principle as the basis for free international trade.

Global North A term used in the post-Cold War system to denote the nations formerly thought of as the First World. Defining characteristics are democracy, sophisticated technology, wealth, and near zero population growth.

Global South A term useful in the post-Cold War system to denote the countries previously comprising the Third World. Global South nations may possess some but not all of the defining characteristics of the Global North (democracy, sophisticated technology, wealth, and steady-state populations).

global warming A change in the earth's climate patterns that occurs when carbon dioxide and other gas molecules trap heat that would otherwise be remitted from earth back into the atmosphere.

governmental source category Those aspects of a government's structure that limit or enhance decision makers' foreign policy choices. Examples in the United States include the constitutional separation of powers and the bureaucratization of policy making in the executive branch.

Group of 7 (G-7) An ad hoc group of the world's largest industrial democracies that seeks macroeconomic policy coordination; the G-7 holds a much-publicized annual economic summit.

Group of 77 (G-77) A coalition of the world's poor (the Global South) allied to press for concessions from the world's rich (the Global North). Formed in 1964, the G-77 now comprises over one hundred developing nations.

groupthink Social pressures that reinforce group norms in small decision-making groups; a cohesiveness and solidarity of outlook that may lead to dysfunctional policy choices.

hard intelligence Information that policymakers receive from cryptanalysis and reconnaissance satellites.

hard-target kill capacity The destructive potential of weapons (warhead yield) directed against land-based intercontinental ballistic missiles (ICBMs).

hardliners Those who, in the wake of Vietnam, viewed communism as a threat to the United States, opposed détente with the Soviet Union, and embraced an interventionist position; proponents of unilateralism in the post-Cold War world.

hegemonic stability theory A perspective that focuses on the role of the preponderant power in stabilizing the international economic system; defines the special roles and responsibilities of the major economic power (hegemon) in a commercial order based on market forces.

hegemony A preponderance of power and influence so great as to enable a nation to dictate or shape the rules governing the conduct of international relations, both political and economic.

hero-in-history model The view that individual leaders are the makers and movers of history; in foreign policy making, it finds expression in the practice of attaching presidents' names to the policies they promulgate.

human intelligence (HUMINT) The fruits of espionage that come from human, not technical, sources of intelligence.

idealism A body of thought that believes fundamental reforms of the system of international relations are possible. The idealist agenda includes open diplomacy, freedom of the seas, removal of trade barriers, self-determination, general disarmament, and collective security.

ideological groups Interest-group organizations that address a wide array of policies but from a particular philosophical viewpoint (e.g., Americans for Democratic Action).

imagery intelligence (IMINT) Information gathered from satellites in computer code, which must be converted into images.

impoundment A presidential refusal to spend money appropriated by Congress.

inadvertent audience People who are exposed to

foreign affairs information transmitted by television that most neither like nor want.

independent variables Factors that exert a causal impact on a dependent variable. In the foreign policy context, a nation's foreign policy behavior is the dependent variable and the source categories and factors contained within them are the independent variables, or inputs.

individual source category A decision maker's personal traits—including values, talents, and prior experiences—that influence his or her foreign policy choices and thus potentially impact a nation's foreign policy.

instrumental rationality A conceptualization of rationality that stresses individual preferences; it predicts that decision makers, when faced with multiple alternatives, will choose the one believed to yield their preferred outcome.

intelligence Information useful to policymakers about a potential enemy.

intermediate-range nuclear force (INF) weapons U.S. nuclear weapons systems deployed in Europe in the 1980s in response to the Soviet Union's growing medium-range nuclear capability; eliminated from Europe with the 1987 INF disarmament treaty.

intermestic policy issues Issues with both domestic and foreign content and consequences.

international intergovernmental organizations (IGOs) International organizations whose members are governments (e.g., the United Nations).

international liquidity A government's's retention of reserve assets to be used to settle international accounts.

international nongovernmental organizations (INGOs) International organizations whose members are individuals or societal groups (e.g., the International Federation of Red Cross and Red Crescent Societies).

international regimes Coalitions of state and nonstate actors observing common principles, norms, rules, and decision-making procedures to facilitate cooperative efforts in a given issue area of international relations.

internationalists Supporters of active American involvement in international affairs, favoring a combination of conciliatory and conflictual strategies to solve global and national problems.

intervening variable A factor that links an

independent variable to a dependent variable. In the foreign policy context, the foreign policy-making process is the intervening variable that links inputs (the source categories) to outputs (foreign policy behavior).

iron triangles Interrelated interests that link defense contractors and interest groups (the private sector), defense bureaucrats (the executive branch), and members of Congress (the legislative branch) into a single entity whose bonds are exceedingly difficult to break.

isolationism A policy of aloofness or political detachment from international affairs; Thomas Jefferson advocated isolationism as the best way to preserve and develop the United States as a free people.

isolationists Those who oppose the United States actively involving itself in international affairs, whether by conciliatory or conflictual means.

Joint Chiefs of Staff (JCS) A body consisting of the senior military officer within each uniformed service and a chairman appointed by the president, who serves as the nation's chief military officer.

Kellogg-Briand Pact A 1928 agreement, also known as the Pact of Paris, that renounced war as an instrument of national policy.

legislative veto The ability of Congress to express disapproval of a presidential initiative, such as a major arms sale, by a concurrent or joint resolution of both houses.

Lend-Lease Act A law enacted in 1941 that permitted the United States to assist other nations deemed vital to U.S. security, thus committing the United States to the Allied cause against the Axis powers.

Liberal International Economic Order (LIEO) A system of rules and institutions that have governed post-World War II economic relations, in which barriers to the free flow of trade and capital have been progressively reduced. Limited government intervention in economic affairs is a key principle of the system.

liberal internationalism A political tradition based on global activism and a belief that liberal democracies must lead in creating a peaceful world order through multilateral cooperation and effective international organizations.

liberalism A tradition based on the political philosophy of John Locke and codified by Thomas Jefferson in the Declaration of Independence; it is based on the advocacy of liberty and the belief that legitimate political power arises only from the consent of the governed, whose participation in decisions affecting public policy and the quality of life is guaranteed.

liberty Individual freedom.

linkage theory A strategy of containment fashioned by Richard Nixon and Henry Kissinger that stressed economic, political, and strategic ties designed to bind the United States and the Soviet Union in a common fate that would lessen the incentives for war.

low-intensity conflict Violence or warfare that falls short of full-scale conventional combat or nuclear confrontation.

Machiavellianism A personality syndrome emphasizing strategy and manipulation over principle and sentiment, characterized especially by the compulsion to acquire and exercise power.

managed trade A system in which a government intervenes to steer trade relations in a direction that the government itself has predetermined.

Manifest Destiny The belief, common in the nineteenth century, that the United States was destined to spread across the North American continent, and eventually beyond it.

Marshall Plan A program that used American capital to rebuild Western Europe's economic, social, and political infrastructures after World War II in order to ensure a market for American products and to enhance Europe's ability to resist communist subversion.

massive retaliation A doctrine proclaimed by the Eisenhower administration designed to deter attack and accomplish foreign policy goals by threatening mass destruction of Soviet population and military-industrial centers.

micromanagement Legislative involvement in the conduct of America's foreign relations often regarded by presidents as excessive interference in executive responsibilities.

militant internationalism Support for active involvement in world affairs, stressing the United States' willingness to protect its self-defined national interests with the use of force if necessary.

militarism A state of mind in which hostility is viewed as unexceptional and force is accepted as a legitimate means of achieving national goals.

military-industrial complex A partnership of military professionals, leaders of industries dependent on military contracts, high government officials whose political interests are linked to military expenditure, and legislators whose constituents benefit from defense spending.

Monroe Doctrine A policy articulated by President James Monroe stating that the New World would not be subject to the same forces of colonization that the Europeans had perpetrated on others.

most-favored-nation (MFN) principle The cornerstone of free trade, which states that the tariff preferences granted to one nation must be granted to all other nations exporting the same product, thus ensuring equality in a nation's treatment of its trade partners.

multiculturalism An emphasis on the importance of ethnicity in shaping individuals' identities and interests, thus promoting communal rights over individual rights and universal opportunity.

multilateralism A means to foreign policy ends that coordinates relations among three or more states on the basis of generalized principles of conduct (e.g., collective security).

multilevel interdependence A global power structure similar to unipolycentrism, illustrated by the metaphor of a layer cake. The top layer, military might, is unipolar; the middle layer, economics, is tripolar; and the bottom layer, transnational interdependence, shows a diffusion of power.

multinational corporations (MNCs) Business enterprises organized in one society with activities abroad growing out of direct investment, as opposed to portfolio investment through share holding.

multipolar (multipolarity) A global structure in which power is spread among four or more major powers; describes the European-centered international system prior to World War I and perhaps the emerging post-Cold War system in which the United States, Japan, China, Russia, and Germany (alone or within a united Europe) may be the major powers.

Munich Conference A 1938 meeting among Britain, France, and Germany leading to a failed agreement that ceded much of Czechoslovakia to Nazi Germany in exchange for what the British prime minister called "peace in our time." Source of the widespread conviction that aggressors cannot be appeased.

mutual assured destruction (MAD) A "balance of terror" in which combatants' essentially equal capability to cause widespread death and destruction in a nuclear exchange encourages stability and the avoidance of war; a description and U.S. and Soviet nuclear strategy during much of the Cold War.

mutual security The belief that a diminution of the national security of one's adversary reduces one's own security.

national intelligence Intelligence normally required for foreign policy making.

National Intelligence Estimates (NIEs) Reports prepared on various parts of the world intended to be the "best judgments" of the intelligence community on their respective subjects.

National Reconnaissance Office (NRO) The agency responsible for managing the nation's satellite reconnaissance programs; controlled jointly by the CIA and Defense Department and operated under the "cover" of the Air Force.

national security adviser (NSA) The head of the National Security Council staff and the president's principal foreign policy adviser within the presidential subsystem.

National Security Agency (NSA) The Defense Department agency responsible for signals intelligence (SIGINT), communications security, and cryptology.

National Security Council (NSC) A unit within the presidential subsystem created by the National Security Act of 1947 to "advise the president with respect to the integration of domestic, foreign, and military policies relating to the national security."

national security policy The weapons and strategies on which the United States relies to ensure security and survival in an uncertain, dangerous, and often hostile global environment.

nationalism A state of mind that gives primary loyalty to one nation-state to the exclusion of other possible objects of affection.

neomercantilism State intervention in economic affairs designed to strengthen the nation's economy by maintaining a balance-of-trade surplus by stimulating domestic production, reducing imports, and promoting exports.

New Independent States (NIS) The former republics of the Union of Soviet Socialist Republics (USSR).

New International Economic Order (NIEO) A movement among the Third World nations in the 1970s seeking to gain a greater role in shaping their own economic futures and determining who would govern the distribution of world wealth and how they would make their choices.

Newly Industrializing Countries (NICs) Among the more advanced of the developing nations, a small group of fast-growing exporters of manufactured goods. Principal among them are the "Asian Tigers": Hong Kong, Singapore, South Korea, and Taiwan.

Nixon Doctrine President Richard Nixon's pledge in 1970 that the United States would provide military and economic assistance to its friends and allies but would hold those nations responsible for protecting their own security.

nomological mode of explanation A type of explanation that uses lawlike statements, relating cause to effect, to explain an event or class of events.

nonaligned states Newly emerging states determined to strike a neutral course in the Cold War.

nontariff barriers (NTBs) Government regulations that reduce or distort international trade (e.g., health and safety regulations and restrictions on the quality of goods that may be imported).

NSC 68 A top-secret memorandum issued by the National Security Council in 1950 which called for increased military spending and a nonmilitary counteroffensive against the Soviet

Union that included covert economic, political, and psychological warfare designed to foment unrest and revolt in Soviet bloc countries.

nuclear non-proliferation regime A system centered on the 1968 nuclear Nonproliferation Treaty (NPT), which seeks to halt the spread of nuclear weapons by permitting nuclear states to share their knowledge of peaceful atomic energy uses with nonnuclear states while prohibiting them from sharing weapon-producing technology.

NUTS/NUT An acronym(s) for the counterforce strategic-planning concept of nuclear utilization target selection or nuclear utilization theory.

Open Door The U.S. policy toward China initiated by Secretary of State John Hay in 1899, which supported free competition for trade with China and opposed dividing China into spheres of influence.

paranoia A psychoneurotic disorder characterized by excessive suspicion, fear, and distrust of others.

peace enforcement The use of a United Nations military force to impose a settlement on the parties in a political or military conflict.

peacekeeping The use of a United Nations military force to keep disputants in a conflict apart to prevent fighting.

perpetual election Constant polling to determine presidents' standing with the American people.

plausible denial A tenet by which the president is not apprised of current or pending covert actions in order to save him or her from the possible embarrassment of a "blown" operation.

pluralism A model of public policy making in which individual citizens organize themselves into groups to petition the government on behalf of their shared interests and values, and whose competition explains political decisions.

policy influentials People who are knowledgeable about foreign affairs and who have access to decision makers.

policy pattern A way of generalizing about and describing the overall thrust and direction of foreign policy.

political action committees (PACs) Branches of business and interest groups that raise money to provide campaign funds for political parties or individual candidates for office.

political culture The political values, cognitions, ideas, and ideals about a nation's society that the people of that society hold in common.

political realism A school of thought in international relations which holds that the structure of the international system, defined by the distribution of power among states, is the primary determinant of states' foreign policy behavior. Political realism views conflict as a natural state of affairs and urges nation-states to seek power to protect their interests.

polycentrism A concept suggesting many centers of power in the international system, in which secondary powers are able to form diverse relationships among themselves both within their own alliance and with the secondary powers formally aligned with their adversary.

pragmatism A psychological temperament characterized by the dispassionate pursuit of rational solutions and promising results, sometimes at the expense of moral or ethical principles.

presidential character The way a president orients himself or herself to life, especially the level of energy that goes into the job and the level of satisfaction derived from presidential duties.

presidential finding The president's certification to Congress that an executive approved covert action is "important to the national interests of the United States."

presidential subsystem A division within the executive branch that has arisen as presidents rely increasingly on their personal staffs and on the Executive Office of the President for advice and assistance in developing policies and programs, often leading to differences between the presidency and the established bureaucracy.

procedural rationality A conceptualization of rationality that is based on perfect information and a careful weighing of all possible courses of action; it underlies the theory of political realism, which views all states as acting in fundamentally similar ways as they make value-maximizing choices to enhance their national security.

public diplomacy The methodical spreading of information to influence public opinion; a polite term for propaganda.

public interest groups Organizations that seek to represent the interests of society as a whole and to realize benefits that may be intangible (e.g., Ralph Nader's Public Citizen).

rational decision-making model A perspective that hypothesizes that foreign policy results from a deliberate intellectual process in which the central figures carefully choose what is best for the country and select tactics appropriately designed to promote the national interest.

Reagan Doctrine President Ronald Reagan's pledge of U.S. support for anticommunist insurgents who sought to overturn Soviet-supported Marxist regimes.

realists Those who argue that the distribution of power in the international system, more than anything else, influences how its nation-members act. Realists stress the importance of the external source category in foreign policy making.

recissions A mechanism by which the president, subject to congressional review, can impound funds by permanently canceling budget authority.

reprogramming A nonstatutory control mechanism devised by Congress and the executive to deal with unanticipated contingencies by permitting funds within an appropriation category to be moved from one purpose to another.

risky-shift phenomenon A potential effect of bureaucratic decision making in which members of decision-making groups, reluctant to appear fearful, act more recklessly together than they would individually.

role source category This category includes the socially prescribed behaviors and legally sanctioned norms attached to policy-making positions; It takes into account the impact of an office on the behavior of the officeholder.

role theory A perspective which says that the positions decision makers occupy rather than their individual characteristics influence their behavior and choices in making and executing foreign policy.

Roosevelt Corollary President Theodore Roosevelt's extension of the Monroe Doctrine that justified the use of American power, including military force, to oppose Latin American revolutions and to bring hemispheric economic affairs under U.S. control.

sanctions Governmental actions designed to inflict economic deprivation on a target state or society by limiting or cutting off customary economic relations; often used as alternatives to military force.

satisficing The behavior by which decision makers are content to select an alternative that meets minimally acceptable standards rather than continuing to seek an optimal solution.

second-strike capability The ability of offensive strategic forces to withstand an aggressor's initial strike and retain the capacity to respond with a devastating second blow.

Second World A term used during the Cold War to designate the Soviet Union, its allies, and other communist societies, distinguished by a commitment to planned economic practices rather than reliance on market forces to determine supply and demand.

security assistance A program of foreign military grants and sales plus economic support funds intended to serve a wide range of U.S. policy objectives.

security dilemma A vicious-circle situation in which the defensive weapons a country acquires are perceived by its adversary to be offensive, thus causing it, too, to build up its "defenses."

selective perception A pervasive human tendency to search for "comfortable" information that "fits" with one's preexisting beliefs and to screen out or reject information with which one disagrees.

signal intelligence (SIGINT) Information gathered from interception and analysis of communications, electronic, and telemetry signals.

Single Integrated Operational Plan (SIOP) A top-secret master plan for waging nuclear war that operationalizes strategic doctrine by selecting the military and nonmilitary targets to be attacked in the event of war.

single-issue groups Interest-group organizations that seek to influence policy in narrowly defined areas (e.g., the Sierra Club).

societal source category Those nongovernmental

characteristics of a nation's society that influence its relations with other nations; examples include major value orientations, degree of national unity, and extent of industrialization.

society-dominated system A political system characterized by strong domestic influences on foreign policy behavior (e.g., the United States). Such a system focuses policymakers' attention on societal sources of foreign policy.

source categories Five forces that influence a nation's foreign policy: (1) the external (global) environment; (2) the societal environment; (3) the governmental setting in which policy is made; (4) the roles policymakers occupy; and (5) policymakers' individual characteristics.

sovereignty A cardinal principle in international law and politics which affirms that no authority is above the states; it protects the territorial inviolability of the state, its freedom from interference by others, and its authority to rule its own population.

stagflation A stagnant economy accompanied by rising unemployment and high inflation.

Strategic Arms Limitation Talks (SALT) Negotiations initiated in 1969 that sought to restrain the Soviet-American arms race by limiting offensive strategic weapons. They produced two sets of agreements: the 1972 SALT I agreement limiting strategic offensive weapons and the Antiballistic Missile (ABM) treaty, and the 1979 SALT II treaty.

Strategic Arms Reduction Talks (START) Negotiations aimed at reducing the strategic forces of the United States and the Soviet Union and its successors. Agreements reached in 1991 and 1993 commit the nuclear powers (including the nuclear heirs of the former Soviet Union) to eliminate or reduce significantly the number of strategic weapons in their arsenals.

Strategic Defense Initiative (SDI) A futuristic, "defense dominant" ballistic missile defense strategy initiated during the Reagan administration. Also known as "Star Wars," SDI sought to use space-based technology to interdict offensive weapons launched toward the United States.

strategic trade A form of industrial policy that seeks to create comparative advantages in international trade by targeting government subsidies toward particular industries.

Super 301 A provision of the 1988 Omnibus Trade and Competitiveness Act that required the president to identify countries engaged in unfair trade practices, with a view toward negotiation to seek remedies or face U.S. retaliation.

sustainable development A concept encapsulating the belief that the world must work toward a model of economic development that also protects the delicate environmental systems on which humanity depends for its existence.

tactical nuclear weapons Nuclear weapons designed for the direct support of combat operations.

terms of trade The ratio of export prices to import prices.

Theater High-Altitude Area Defense (THAAD) A projected land- and sea-based ballistic missile defense system designed to meet threats from the Global South.

theater nuclear forces Nuclear forces directed toward regional rather than global threats.

Third World A term used during the Cold War era to designate states that had failed to grow economically or otherwise advance toward the degree and type of economic development experienced in Western Europe and North America; included most countries in Asia, Africa, and Latin America.

Total Quality Management (TQM) The philosophy of nonhierarchical management advocated by management consultant W. Edwards Deming that, applied to government, strives to make the government operate more like a business.

triad of strategic weapons A force consisting of piloted bombers and land- and sea-based intercontinental ballistic missiles that the United States maintains as a means of strategic deterrence.

true believers Adherents to mass religious, political, or ideological movements who share with other like-minded individuals the need to join a cause and sacrifice themselves for its advancement.

Truman Doctrine President Harry S Truman's dictum that "it must be the policy of the United

States to support free peoples who are resisting attempted subjugation by armed minorities or by outside pressures."

two-step flow theory of communications A hypothesis stating that ideas do not flow directly from the mass media to the general population; rather they are transmitted first to opinion leaders and through them to the less interested, less knowledgeable members of society.

unilateralism Conducting foreign affairs individually rather than acting in concert with others.

unipolar (unipolarity) A global power structure in which one nation enjoys unparalleled supremacy, possessing the military and economic might to defend unilaterally its security and sovereignty (e.g., the United States' status as the "sole remaining superpower" in the post-Cold War world).

unipolycentrism A global system in which, although one nation is militarily central, other states wield political power by virtue of some combination of military and economic prowess.

unitary actor The nation-state viewed as a single, homogeneous decision-making entity; the concept presumes that all policymakers go through the same rational processes to make value-maximizing choices defining national interests and choices.

unmanaged policy initiatives A potential effect of decision making in complex organizations, in which policy is effectively determined at the implementation stage, occasionally affording individual bureaucrats the opportunity to take unilateral initiatives.

Uruguay Round The eighth in a series of multilateral trade negotiations aimed at reducing tariffs and resolving related issues under the aegis of GATT and the most-favored-nation principle. Launched in 1986 but not completed until late 1993, it included a provision replacing GATT with a new World Trade Organization (WTO).

U.S. and Foreign Commercial Service A branch of the Commerce Department that seeks to enhance the competitiveness of American businesses abroad by bringing together those who encourage U.S. firms to export and those who deal with potential buyers of American products.

voluntary export restrictions (VERs) Export quotas imposed by the exporting country following negotiations, which place quantitative restrictions on specified products and require no action by the importing country.

War Powers Resolution Legislation passed in 1973 to limit presidential war-making prerogatives.

World Trade Organization (WTO) An international organization created by the Uruguay Round to replace GATT; the WTO will seek to extend GATT's coverage of products, sectors, and conditions of trade and will have broader authority over trade disputes.

zero-sum A situation in which when one side wins, the other necessarily loses.

Christopher H. Achen, quote from "When Is a State with Bureaucratic Politics Representable as a Unitary Rational Actor?" Paper presented at the annual meeting of the International Studies Association, London, March 29–April 1, 1989. Reprinted with the permission of the author.

Roger C. Altman, excerpts from "Why Pressure Tokyo?," *Foreign Affairs* 73 (May/June 1994): 2–6. Copyright © 1994 by the Council on Foreign Relations, Inc. Reprinted with the permission of *Foreign Affairs*.

Robert J. Art, quote from "Congress and the Defense Budget: Enhancing Policy Oversight," *Political Science Quarterly* 100 (Summer 1985): 227–248. Copyright © 1985. Reprinted with the permission of the Academy of Political Science.

J. Brian Atwood, excerpts from "More Than Words: USAID's Approach to the Population Problem," *Harvard International Review* 16 (Fall): 28–29, 77–78. Reprinted with the permission of *Harvard International Review*.

Figure 3.1: "Soviet-American Relations, 1948–1991" adapted from Edward E. Azar and Thomas J. Sloan *Dimensions of Interaction* (Pittsburgh: Center for International Studies, 1973), and supplemented with data from the Conflict and Peace Bank. Data for 1966–1991 are from the World Event Interaction Survey as compiled by Rodney G. Tomlinson. Reprinted by permission.

Doug Bandow, quote from "Avoiding War," *Foreign Policy* 89 (Winter 1992–1993): 156–174. Copyright © 1992 by Carnegie Endowment for International Peace. Reprinted with the permission of *Foreign Policy*.

Figure 14.1: "Barber's Classification of Twentieth-Century Presidents by Their Character Type" adapted from David Barber, *The Presidential Character: Predicting Performance in the White House*, 4th ed. Copyright © 1992. Reprinted with the permission of Prentice-Hall, Inc.

James David Barber, excerpts from "George Bush: In Search of a Mission," *New York Times* (January 19, 1989): A31. Copyright © 1989 by The New York Times Company. Reprinted with the permission of *The New York Times*.

Mitchell Bard, quote from "The Influence of Ethnic Interest Groups on American Middle East Policy," pp. 79–94 in Eugene R. Wittkopf (ed.), *The Domestic Sources of American Foreign Policy: Insights and Evidence*, 2nd ed. Copyright © 1994 by St. Martin's Press, Inc. Reprinted with the permission of the publisher.

Richard J. Barnet, excerpts from *Roots of War: The Men and Institutions Behind U.S. Foreign Policy*. Copyright © 1972 by Richard J. Barnet. Reprinted with the permission of Simon & Schuster, Inc.

Barton J. Bernstein, quote from "The Atomic Bombings Reconsidered," *Foreign Affairs* 74 (January/February 1995): 135–152. Copyright © 1995 by the Council on Foreign Relations, Inc. Reprinted with the permission of *Foreign Affairs*.

Michael Borrus, Steve Weber, John Zysman, and Joseph Willihnganz, excerpts from "Mercantilism and Global Security," *The National Interest* 29 (Fall 1992): 21–29. Copyright © 1992 by The National Interest. Reprinted with the permission of National Affairs, Inc.

Paul Brace and Barbara Hinckley, excerpts from "George Bush and the Costs of High Popularity: A General Model with a Current Application," *PS: Political Science & Politics* 26 (September 1993): 501–505. Copyright © 1993 by American Political Science Association. Reprinted with the permission of the publisher.

David S. Broder, quote from "The Reactor President," *Washington Post National Weekly*, (August 27–September 2, 1990): 4. Copyright © 1990 by The Washington Post Writers Group. Reprinted with permission.

Focus 6.1: "An America First Prescription for Splendid Isolationism" from Patrick Buchanan, "America First- and Second, and Third," *The National Interest* 19 (Spring 1990): 79, 80, 81. Copyright © 1990 by The National Interest. Reprinted with the permission of National Affairs, Inc.

Eliza Newlin Carney, quote from "Still Trying to Reinvent Government," *National Journal* (June 18, 1994): 1442–1443. Copyright © 1994. Reprinted with the permission of *National Journal*.

Shahram Chubin, quote from "The South and the New World Order," *Washington Quarterly* 16 (Autumn 1993): 87–105. Copyright © 1993 by Center for Strategic and International Studies, Georgetown University. Reprinted with the permission of MIT Press.

Jack Citrin, Ernst B. Haas, Christopher Muste, and Beth Reingold, excerpts from "Is American Nationalism Changing: Implications for Foreign Policy," *International Studies Quarterly* 38 (March 1994): 1–31. Copyright © 1994. Reprinted with the permission of Basil Blackwell, Ltd.

Michael Clough, quote from "Grass-Roots Policymaking: Say Good-Bye to the 'Wise Men,'" *Foreign Affairs* 73 (January/February 1994): 2–7. Copyright © 1994 by the Council on Foreign Relations, Inc. Reprinted with the permission of *Foreign Affairs*.

Ellen C. Collier, excerpts from "War Powers Resolution: Presidential Compliance," in *CRS Issue Brief 81050* (February 15, 1994). Washington, D.C.: Congressional Research Service. Reprinted by permission.

Focus 3.1: "Dawn of a New Millennium: The Use of American Forces Abroad Initiated during the Roosevelt, Taft, and Wilson Administrations, 1901–1921" adapted from Ellen C. Collier, "Instances of United States Armed Forces Abroad, 1778–1993," *CRS Report for Congress* (October 7, 1993). Reprinted by permission.

Chester A. Crocker, excerpts "The Rules of Engagement in a New World," *Washington Post National Weekly Edition* (May 16–22, 1994): 23–24. Reprinted with the permission of the author.

Table of nuclear capabilities, U.S. and USSR, from *The Defense Monitor* 22, no. 1 (1993): 3. Copyright © 1993 by the Center for Defense Information. Reprinted with the permission of the publisher.

Figure 9.1: "U.S. Military Spending, 1948–1999 (constant dollars)" from "1995 Military Spending: The Real Story," *The Defense Monitor* 23, no. 5 (1994): 3. Based on Department of Defense data. Copyright © 1994 by the Center for Defense Information. Reprinted with the permission of the publisher.

Focus 9.1: "More Money for Cold War Weapons," and quotes from "1995 Military Spending: The Real Story," *The Defense Monitor* 23, no. 5 (1994): 2. Copyright © 1994 by the Center for Defense Information. Reprinted with the permission of the publisher.

Focus 10.1: "The National Security Assistant: The Professionals' Job Description" from I. M. Destler, "The Rise of the National Security Assistant" from *Perspectives on American Foreign Policy: Selected Readings*, edited by Charles W. Kegley, Jr. and Eugene R. Wittkopf (New York: St. Martin's Press, 1983), page 262. Reprinted by permission.

I. M. Deudney and G. John Ikenberry, excerpts from "After the Long War," *Foreign Policy* 94 (Spring 1994): 21–35. Copyright © 1994 by the Carnegie Endowment for International Peace. Reprinted with the permission of *Foreign Policy*.

John Foster Dulles, excerpts from "A Policy of Liberation," *Life* (May 19, 1952): 19 ff. Copyright © 1952. Reprinted with the permission of *Life*.

Robert F. Ellsworth and Kenneth L. Adelman, quote from "Foolish Intelligence," *Foreign Policy* 36 (Fall 1979): 147–159. Copyright © 1979 by the Carnegie Endowment for International Peace. Reprinted with the permission of *Foreign Policy*.

Louis Fisher, excerpts from "Congressional Checks on Military Initiatives," *Political Science Quarterly* 109 (Winter 1994–1995): 739–762. Copyright © 1994. Reprinted with the permission of the Academy of Political Science.

Louis Fisher, excerpts from "Foreign Policy Powers of the President and Congress," *The Annals* 449 (September 1988): 148–159. Reprinted with the permission of the author.

Charles Flicknew, quote from "The Russian Aid Mess," *The National Interest* 38 (Winter 1994–1995): 13–18. Copyright © 1994 by The National Interest. Reprinted with the permission of National Affairs, Inc.

Aaron L. Friedberg, excerpts from "Why Didn't the United States Become a Garrison State?" *International Security* 16 (Spring 1992): 109–142. Copyright © 1992 by the President and Fellows of Harvard College & Massachusetts Institute of Technology. Reprinted with the permission of MIT Press.

Thomas L. Friedman, excerpts from "What Big Stick? Just Sell," *New York Times* (October 2, 1994): E3. Copyright © 1994 by The New York Times Company. Reprinted with the permission of *The New York Times*.

Graham Fuller, quote from "The Next Ideology," *Foreign Policy* 98 (Spring 1995): 145–158. Copyright © 1995 by Carnegie Endowment for International Peace. Reprinted with the permission of *Foreign Policy*.

Figure 8.3: "Public Approval of Presidential Performance, 1945–1995" adapted from *The Gallup Poll Index* (October–November 1980) and various issues of *The Gallup Report* and *The Gallup Poll Monthly*. Reprinted with the permission of The Gallup Organization.

Raymond L. Garthoff, excerpts from "Looking Back: The Cold War in Retrospect," *Brookings Review* 12 (Summer 1994): 10–13. Copyright © 1994. Reprinted with the permission of Brookings Institution.

Robert M. Gates, excerpts from "The CIA and American Foreign Policy," *Foreign Affairs* 66 (Winter 1987–1988): 215–230. Copyright © 1987 by the Council on Foreign Relations, Inc. Reprinted with the permission of *Foreign Affairs*.

Leslie H. Gelb, excerpts from "Quelling the Teacup Wars: The New World's Constant Challenge," *Foreign Affairs* 73 (November/December 1994): 2–6. Copyright © 1994 by the Council on Foreign Relations, Inc. Reprinted with the permission of *Foreign Affairs*.

Allan E. Goodman, quote from "Dateline Langley: Fixing the Intelligence Mess," *Foreign Policy* 57 (Winter 1984–1985): 160–179, Copyright © 1984 by the Carnegie Endowment for International Peace. Reprinted with the permission of *Foreign Policy*.

John M. Goshko, excerpts from "Foreign Policy in Turmoil—or Transition?" *Washington Post National Weekly Edition* (March 13–19, 1989): 7. Copyright © 1994 by The Washington Post Writers Group. Reprinted with the permission of *The Washington Post*.

Richard N. Haass, excerpts from "Bill Clinton's Adhocracy," *New York Times Magazine* (May 29, 1994) 40–41. Copyright © 1994 by The New York Times Company. Reprinted with the permission of *The New York Times*.

Craig Haney and Philip Zimbardo, quote from "Social Roles, Role-Playing, and Education," *Behavioral and Social Science Teacher* 1, no. 1 (1973): 24–45. Copyright © 1973. Reprinted by permission.

William D. Hartung, quote from "Welcome to the U.S. Arms Superstore," *Bulletin of the Atomic Scientists* 49 (September 1993): 20–26. Copyright © 1993 by the Educational Foundation for Nuclear Science. Reprinted with the permission of *Bulletin of the Atomic Scientists*.

David C. Hendrickson, excerpts from "The Recovery of Internationalism," *Foreign Affairs* 73 (September/October 1994): 26–43. Copyright © 1994 by the Council on Foreign Relations, Inc. Reprinted with the permission of *Foreign Affairs*.

Margaret G. Hermann and Thomas Preston, excerpts from "Presidents and Their Advisers: Leadership Style, Advisory Systems, and Foreign Policymaking," pp. 340–356 in Eugene R. Wittkopf (ed.), *The Domestic Sources of American Foreign Policy: Insights and Evidence*, 2nd ed. Copyright © 1994 by St. Martin's Press, Inc. Reprinted with the permission of the publisher.

Figure 14.2: "Typology of Presidential Leadership Types Based on Advisory Systems' Patterns of Authority and Policy Coordination" from Margaret G. Hermann, and Thomas Preston "Presidents and Their Advisers: Leadership Style, Advisory Systems, and Foreign Policymaking" in Eugene R. Wittkopf (ed.), *The Domestic Sources of American Foreign Policy: Insights and Evidence*, 2nd ed., page 346. Reprinted by permission.

Figure 14.3: "The Influence of Presidential Leadership Style on Advisory Selection and Organization" from Margaret G. Hermann, and Thomas Preston "Presidents and Their Advisers: Leadership Style, Advisory Systems, and Foreign Policymaking" in Eugene R. Wittkopf (ed.), *The Domestic Sources of American Foreign Policy: Insights and Evidence*, 2nd ed., page 349. Reprinted by permission.

Figure 10.1: "The Institutional Setting: The Concentric Circles of Policy Making" adapted from Roger Hilsman, *To Move a Nation* (New York: Doubleday, 1967), pp. 541–544. Copyright © 1967 by Roger Hilsman. Reprinted with the permission of the author and Doubleday, a division of Bantam Doubleday Dell Publishing Group, Inc.

Stanley Hoffmann, excerpts from "The Crisis of Liberal Internationalism," *Foreign Policy* 98 (Spring 1995): 159–177. Copyright © 1995 by the Carnegie Endowment for International Peace. Reprinted with the permission of *Foreign Policy*.

Stanley Hoffmann, excerpts from "Bush Abroad," *New York Review of Books* 39 (November 5, 1992); 54–59. Copyright © 1992 by Nyrev, Inc. Reprinted with the permission of *The New York Review of Books*.

Stanley Hoffmann, quote from "What Should We Do in the World?" *Atlantic Monthly* 264 (October 1989): 84–96. Copyright © 1989. Reprinted by permission.

Ole R. Holsti, quote from "Public Opinion and Foreign Policy: Challenges to the Almond-Lippmann Consensus," *International Studies Quarterly* 36 (December 1992): 439–466. Copyright © 1992 by International Studies Association. Reprinted with the permission of Blackwell Publishers.

Ole R. Holsti, excerpts from "The Belief System and National Images: A Case Study," *Journal of Conflict Resolution* 6 (September 1962): 244–252. Copyright © 1962 by Sage Publications, Inc. Reprinted with the permission of the publisher.

Karen Eliot House, quote from "As Power Is Dispersed among Nations, Need for Leadership Grows," *Wall Street Journal* (February 21, 1989): A1, A10. Copyright © 1989 by Dow Jones & Company. Reprinted with the permission of *The Wall Street Journal*.

Focus 6.3: "Intranational Conflict on the Increase" from *Human Development Report 1994* (New York: Oxford University Press, 1994), page 47. Copyright © 1994. Reprinted by permission.

Focus 6.4: "The Human Development Costs of Arms Imports" from *Human Development Report 1994* (New York: Oxford University Press, 1994), page 54. Copyright © 1994. Reprinted by permission.

Samuel P. Huntington, excerpts from "The Clash of Civilizations?" *Foreign Affairs* 72 (Summer 1993): 22–49. Copyright © 1993 by the Council on Foreign Relations, Inc. Reprinted with the permission of *Foreign Affairs*.

Jon Hurwitz and Mark Peffley, quote from "How Are Foreign Policy Attitudes Structures? A Hierarchical Model," *American Political Science Review* 81 (December 1987): 1099–1120. Copyright © 1987 by American Political Science Association. Reprinted with the permission of the publisher.

David Ignatius, excerpts from "The Best and the Brightest, 1990s Style," *Washington Post National Weekly Edition* (March 14–20, 1994): 24–5. Copyright © 1994 by The Washington Post Writers Group. Reprinted with the permission of *The Washington Post*.

David Ignatius, excerpts from "Is This Any Way for a Country to Buy Weapons?" *Washington Post National Weekly Edition* (July 4–10, 1988): 23. Copyright © 1988 by The Washington Post Writers Group. Reprinted with the permission of *The Washington Post.*

G. John Ikenberry, excerpts from "Salvaging the G-7," *Foreign Affairs* 72 (Spring 1993): 132–139. Copyright © 1993 by the Council on Foreign Relations, Inc. Reprinted with the permission of *Foreign Affairs.*

Loch K. Johnson, quote from "Controlling the Quiet Option," *Foreign Policy* 39 (Summer 1980): 143–153. Copyright © 1980 by the Carnegie Endowment for International Peace. Reprinted with the permission of *Foreign Policy.*

John B. Judis, quote from "Statecraft and Scowcroft," *New Republic* (January 22, 1992): 20–25. Copyright © 1992 by The New Republic, Inc. Reprinted with the permission of *New Republic.*

Michael Kelly, excerpts from "The President's Past," *New York Times Magazine* (July 31, 1994): 20–29ff. Copyright © 1994 by The New York Times Company. Reprinted with the permission of *The New York Times.*

George F. Kennan ("X") excerpts from "The Sources of Soviet Conduct," *Foreign Affairs* 25 (July 1947): 566–582. Copyright 1947 by the Council on Foreign Relations, Inc. Reprinted with the permission of *Foreign Affairs.*

Paul Kennedy, excerpts from "Overpopulation Tilts the Planet," *New Perspectives Quarterly* 11 (Fall 1994): 4–6. Copyright © 1994 by Center for the Study of Democratic Institutions. Reprinted with the permission of the publisher.

Henry Kissinger, excerpts from *Diplomacy.* Copyright © 1994 by Henry A. Kissinger. Reprinted by permission.

Henry Kissinger, excerpts from "Domestic Structure and Foreign Policy" from *American Foreign Policy: Three Essays.* Originally published in *Daedalus* 95, no. 2 (Spring 1966): 503–529, issue titled "Conditions of World Order." Copyright © 1966 by the American Academy of Arts and Sciences. Copyright © 1969 by Henry A. Kissinger. Reprinted with the permission of W. W. Norton & Company, Inc.

Joe Klein, quote from "The Politics of Promiscuity," *Newsweek* (May 9, 1994). Copyright © 1994. Reprinted by permission.

Richard H. Kohn, excerpts from "Out of Control: The Crisis in Civil-Military Relations," *The National Interest* 35 (Spring, 1994): 3–17. Copyright © 1994 by The National Interest. Reprinted with the permission of National Affairs, Inc.

Charles Krauthammer, excerpts from "The Unipolar Moment," *Foreign Affairs* 70, no. 1 (1991): 23–33 Copyright © 1991 by the Council on Foreign Relations, Inc. Reprinted with the permission of *Foreign Affairs.*

Paul Krugman, excerpts from "Competitiveness: A Dangerous Obsession," *Foreign Affairs* 73 (March/April 1994): 28–44. Copyright © 1994 by the Council on Foreign Relations, Inc. Reprinted with the permission of *Foreign Affairs.*

Walter LaFeber, excerpts and maps from *The American Age: United States Foreign Policy at Home and Abroad,* 2nd ed. Copyright © 1994 by W. W. Norton & Company, Inc. Reprinted with the permission of the publisher.

Anthony Lake, excerpts from "Confronting Backlash States," *Foreign Affairs* 73 (March/April 1994): 45–55. Copyright © 1994 by the Council on Foreign Relations, Inc. Reprinted with the permission of *Foreign Affairs.*

Walter Laqueur, quote from "Save Public Diplomacy," *Foreign Affairs* 73 (September/October 1994): 19–24. Copyright © 1994 by the Council on Foreign Relations, Inc. Reprinted with the permission of *Foreign Affairs.*

Harold J. Laski, quote from "America—1947," *The Nation* 165 (December 1947): 641–644. Reprinted by permission.

James M. Lindsay, excerpts from "Congress and Foreign Policy: Avenues of Influence" pp. 191–207 in Eugene R. Wittkopf (ed.), *The Domestic Sources of American Foreign Policy: Insights and Evidence,* 2nd ed. Copyright © 1994 by St. Martin's Press, Inc. Reprinted with the permission of the publisher.

Theodore J. Lowi, excerpts from "Presidential Power: Restoring the Balance," *Political Science Quarterly* 100 (Summer 1985): 185–213. Copyright © 1985. Reprinted with the permission of the Academy of Political Science.

Michael Mastanduno, excerpts from "Do Relative Gains Matter? America's Response to Japanese Industrial Policy," *International Security* 16 (Summer 1991): 73–113. Copyright © 1991 by the President and Fellows of Harvard College & Massachusetts Institute of Technology. Reprinted with the permission of MIT Press.

Charles McC. Mathias, Jr., quote from "Ethnic Groups and Foreign Policy," *Foreign Affairs* 59 (Summer 1981): 975–998. Copyright © 1981 by Council on Foreign Relations, Inc. Reprinted with the permission of *Foreign Affairs.*

George D. Moffett, quote from "Global Population Growth: 21st Century Challenges," *Headline Series* 302 (Spring 1994). Copyright © 1994 by Foreign Policy Association, Inc. Reprinted with the permission of the Foreign Policy Association.

Figure 6.4: "The Shape of World Population" and Figure 6.5: "World Population Growth, 1950–2100" from George D. Moffett, "Global Population Growth: 21st Century Challenges," *Headline Series* 302 (Spring 1994). Copyright © 1994 by Foreign Policy Association, Inc. Reprinted with the permission of the Foreign Policy Association.

Mike Moore, quote from "How George Bush Won His Spurs: The President and the Power to Make War," pp. 181–190 in Eugene R. Wittkopf (ed.), *The Domestic Sources of American Foreign Policy: Insights and Evidence*, 2nd ed. Copyright © 1994 by St. Martin's Press, Inc. Reprinted with the permission of the publisher.

Focus 13.3: "Bureaucratic Competitiveness and Task Expansion: Military Rivalry in the Aftermath of Victory in the Persian Gulf" from Molly Moore, "The Armed Services and the Nibbling Rivalries," *Washington Post National Weekly Edition* (June 17–23, 1991): 31. Copyright © 1991 by The Washington Post Writers Group. Reprinted with the permission of *The Washington Post*.

Figure 3.2: "Proven, Possible, and Potential Entrants to the Nuclear Club" from Philip Morrison, Kosta Tsipis, and Jerome Wiesner, "The Future of American Defense," *Scientific American* 279 (February 1994): 40–41. Copyright © 1994. Reprinted with the permission of *Scientific American*.

Kerry Mullins and Aaron Wildavsky, quote from "The Procedural Presidency of George Bush," *Political Science Quarterly* 107 (Spring 1992): 31–62. Copyright © 1992. Reprinted with the permission of the Academy of Political Science.

Excerpts from *New Republic* (April 30, 1984). Copyright © 1984 by The New Republic, Inc. Reprinted with the permission of *New Republic*.

Excerpts from "How Did We Get Here?" *Newsweek* (September 26, 1994): 26–27. Copyright © 1994 by Newsweek, Inc. Reprinted with the permission of *Newsweek*.

Bahram Nowzad, excerpts from "Lessons of the Debt Decade," *Finance & Development* 27 (March 1990): 9–13. Reprinted with the permission of the International Monetary Fund.

Joseph S. Nye, Jr., excerpts from "What New World Order?" *Foreign Affairs* 71 (Spring 1992): 83–96. Copyright © 1992 by the Council on Foreign Relations, Inc. Reprinted with the permission of *Foreign Affairs*.

Focus 13.1: "The Road to Somalia: The Bush Administration's Decision to Send U.S. Ground Troops" from Don Oberdorfer, "The Road to Somalia," *Washington Post National Weekly Edition* (December 14–20, 1992): 6–7. Copyright © 1992 by Washington Post Writers Group. Reprinted with the permission of *The Washington Post*.

Table 6.1: "Official Development Assistance (ODA) Flowing from the Global North to Developing Countries and Multilateral Organizations, Selected Years, 1971–1992 (billions of dollars)" adapted from *Development Cooperation: Efforts and Policies of the Members of the Development Assistance Committee, 1993 Report* (Paris: Organization for Economic Cooperation and Development, 1994), pp. 156–157. Reprinted with the permission of the OECD.

Figure 6.6: "The Foreign Aid Performance of the Global North, 1993" and Figure 6.7: "The Burden of Foreign Aid, 1993" adapted from *Development Cooperation: Efforts and Policies of the Members of the Development Assistance Committee, 1993 Report* (Paris: Organization for Economic Cooperation and Development, 1994), p. 81. Reprinted with the permission of OECD.

Erik Peterson, excerpts from "Looming Collision of Capitalisms?" *Washington Quarterly* 17 (Spring 1994): 65–75. Copyright © 1994 by the Center for Strategic and International Studies, Georgetown University. Reprinted with the permission of MIT Press.

Kevin Phillips, quote from "Some Unnerving Precedents," *Washington Post National Weekly Edition* (January 16–22, 1995): 22–23. Copyright © 1995. Reprinted with the permission of the author.

Colin L. Powell, excerpts from "U.S. Forces: Challenges Ahead," *Foreign Affairs* 71 (Winter 1992–1993): 32–45. Copyright © 1992 by Council on Foreign Relations, Inc. Reprinted with the permission of *Foreign Affairs*.

Colin L. Powell, John Lehman, William Odom, Samuel Huntington, and Richard Kohn, excerpts from "An Exchange on Civil-Military Relations," *The National Interest* 36 (Summer 1994): 23–31. Copyright © 1994 by The National Interest. Reprinted with the permission of National Affairs, Inc.

William B. Quandt, quote from "The Middle East in 1990," *Foreign Affairs* 70, no. 1 (1991): 49–69. Copyright © 1991 by Council on Foreign Relations, Inc. Reprinted with the permission of *Foreign Affairs*.

Edwin O. Reischauer, excerpts from "Redefining the National Interest: The Vietnam Case," Paper presented at the annual meeting of the American Political Science Association, Washington, D.C. September 2–7, 1968. Reprinted with the permission of American Political Science Association.

Table 8.2: "Differences in the Foreign Policy Preferences of American Leaders and the Mass of the American People, 1993 (percentages)." Data on the use of force abroad from *American Public Opinion and U.S. Foreign Policy 1995*, edited by John E. Rielly (Chicago: Chicago Council on Foreign Relations, 1995), page 39. All other data adapted from the Times Mirror Center for the People and the Press, *America's Place in the World: An Investigation of the Attitudes of American Opinion Leaders and the American Public about International Affairs*, Andrew Kohut, Director, November 1993. Reprinted by permission.

James N. Rosenau, excerpts from *The Scientific Study of Foreign Policy* (New York: Nichols, 1980). Copyright © 1980. Reprinted by permission.

Jeremy D. Rosner, quote from "Is 'Chaos' a Threat to National Security?," *Washington Post National Weekly Edition* (August 22–28, 1994): 23. Copyright © 1994 by The Washington Post Writers Group. Reprinted with the permission of *The Washington Post*.

John Gerard Ruggie, excerpts from "Multilateralism: The Anatomy of an Institution," *International Organization* 46 (Summer 1992): 561–598. Copyright © 1992 by the Board of Regents of the University of Wisconsin System. Reprinted with the permission of MIT Press.

David E. Sanger, quote from "Who Won in the Korean Deal," *New York Times* (October 23, 1994): E3. Copyright © 1994 by The New York Times Company. Reprinted with the permission of *The New York Times*.

William Schneider, excerpts from "Bang-Bang Television: The New Superpower," *Public Opinion* 5 (April/May 1982): 13–15. Copyright © 1982 by the American Institute for Public Policy Research. Reprinted with the permission of the publisher.

Tony Smith, quote from "Winning the Peace: Postwar Thinking and the Defeated Confederacy," *World Policy Journal* 11, no. 2 (Summer 1994): 92–102. Copyright © 1994 by World Policy Institute. Reprinted with the permission of World Policy Institute.

Theodore C. Sorensen, excerpts from "The President and the Secretary of State," *Foreign Affairs* 66 (Winter 1987–1988): 231–248. Copyright © 1987 by the Council on Foreign Relations, Inc. Reprinted with the permission of *Foreign Affairs*.

Joseph Stanislaw and Daniel Yergin, excerpts from "Oil: Reopening the Door," *Foreign Affairs* 72 (September/October 1993): 81–93. Copyright © 1993 by the Council on Foreign Relations, Inc. Reprinted with the permission of *Foreign Affairs*.

Stephen John Stedman, excerpts from "The New Interventionists," *Foreign Affairs* 72, no. 1 (Winter 1992–1993): 1–16. Copyright © 1992 by Council on Foreign Relations, Inc. Reprinted with the permission of *Foreign Affairs*.

Ronald Steel, excerpts from "The Lure of Detachment," *World Policy Journal* 11, no. 3 (Fall 1994): 61–69. Copyright © 1994 by World Policy Institute. Reprinted with the permission of World Policy Institute.

John D. Steinbruner, excerpts from "Reluctant Strategic Alignment: The Need for a New View of National Security," *Brookings Review* 13 (Winter 1995): 5–9. Copyright © 1995. Reprinted with the permission of Brookings Institution.

Bruce Stokes, excerpts from "The American Marketplace Has Gone Global," *National Journal* (June 18, 1994): 1426–1430. Copyright © 1994. Reprinted with the permission of *National Journal*.

Bruce Stokes, excerpts from "Organizing to Trade," *Foreign Policy* (Winter 1992–1993): 36–52. Copyright © 1992 by Carnegie Endowment for International Peace. Reprinted with the permission of *Foreign Policy*.

William H. Sullivan, excerpts from "Dateline Iran: The Road Not Taken," *Foreign Policy* 40 (Fall 1980): 175–186. Copyright © 1980 by Carnegie Endowment for International Peace. Reprinted with the permission of *Foreign Policy*.

James L. Sundquist, excerpts from "Congress and the President: Enemies or Partners?" from Henry Owen and Charles L. Schultze, editors, *Setting National Priorities: The Next Ten Years*, pp. 583–618. Copyright © 1976. Reprinted with the permission of the Brookings Institution.

Robert W. Tucker, excerpts from "The Triumph of Wilsonianism?" *World Policy Journal* 10, no. 4 (Winter 1993–1994): 83–99. Copyright © 1993 by World Policy Institute. Reprinted with the permission of the publisher.

Robert W. Tucker, quote from "1989 and All That," *Foreign Affairs* 69 (Fall 1990): 93–114. Copyright © 1990 by the Council on Foreign Relations, Inc. Reprinted with the permission of *Foreign Affairs*.

Excerpts from *U.S. News and World Report* (July 4, 1994): 43. Copyright © 1994. Reprinted with the permission of *U.S. News & World Report*.

Excerpts from *U.S. News and World Report* (January 24, 1994): 33. Copyright © 1994. Reprinted with the permission of *U.S. News & World Report*.

Excerpts from *U.S. News and World Report* (May 20, 1985): 65. Copyright © 1985. Reprinted with the permission of *U.S. News and World Report*.

Sidney Verba, excerpts from "Assumptions of Rationality and Non-Rationality in Models of the International System" from *The International Systems*, edited by Klaus Knorr and Sidney Verba, pp. 93–117. Reprinted with the permission of Princeton University Press.

Kenneth N. Waltz, excerpts from "The Emerging Structure of International Politics," *International Security* 18 (Fall 1993): 44–79. Copyright © 1993 by the President and Fellows of Harvard College & Massachusetts Institute of Technology. Reprinted with the permission of MIT Press.

Figure 8.2: "Internationalist/Isolationist Trends in American Public Opinion, 1964–1991." Data reprinted by permission of William Watts, president of Potomac Associates and principle investigator.

Focus 3.5: "Mirror Images: The Onset of the Cold War" from Ralph K. White, *New York Times* (September 5, 1961): 5. Copyright © 1961 by The New York Times Company. Reprinted with the permission of *The New York Times.*

Focus 10.2: "Reflections on the Gulf War Decision-Making Process" from Bob Woodward, *The Commanders*, pp. 41, 301–302, 318. Copyright © 1991. Reprinted by permission.

Figure 6.1: "Shares of Gross World Product, 1993," Figure 6.2: "Shares of Gross World Product and Population, 1993." and Figure 6.3: "Global Variations in Per Capita Gross Domestic Product, 1993" adapted from *The World Bank Atlas 1995* (Washington, DC: The World Bank, 1994), pp. 8–9, and 18–19. Reprinted by permission.

Figure 7.4: "Commodity Prices, 1970–1992" adapted from *World Resources 1994–95* (New York: Oxford University Press for the World Bank, 1994), page 262. Copyright © 1994. Reprinted by permission.

INDEX

• • •

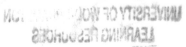